GARDENS
OF ENGLAND & WALES

1995

A GUIDE TO NEARLY 3,500 GARDENS THE MAJORITY OF WHICH ARE NOT NORMALLY OPEN TO THE PUBLIC

THE NATIONAL GARDENS SCHEME CHARITABLE TRUST
HATCHLANDS PARK, EAST CLANDON, GUILDFORD, SURREY GU4 7RT
TEL 01483 211535 FAX 01483 211537
Reg Charity No: 279284

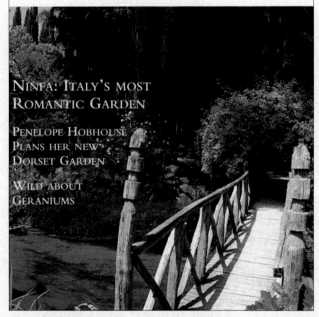

Contents

Published by the National Gardens Scheme, Hatchlands Park, East Clandon, Guildford, Surrey GU4 7RT

Editor: The Director, National Gardens Scheme

Cover illustration of Hawarden Castle, Clwyd by Val Biro

A catalogue record for this book is available from the British Library.

Typeset in Linotron Bell Centennial by Land & Unwin (Data Sciences) Limited, Bugbrooke.

Text printed and bound by Wm Clowes Ltd, Beccles.
Cover colour section printed by George Over Limited, Rugby.
Colour illustrations printed by MN Productions, Northampton
ISBN 0-900558-27-X ISSN 0141-2361

The National Gardens Scheme Charitable Trust

'The Gardens Scheme' was started at the suggestion of Miss Elsie Wagg, a member of the council of the Queen's Nursing Institute, as part of a national memorial to Queen Alexandra whose deep and sympathetic interest in district nursing was well known.

Although this country was renowned for its gardens, few people had the opportunity to see them, so that when 600 were opened in 1927 the response was such that the experiment became a national institution. The Scheme, now called the **National Gardens Scheme Charitable Trust**, has continued and expanded ever since, in 1994 raising more than £1,600,000 from nearly 3,500 gardens.

The National Gardens Scheme helps many deserving causes, the first call on its funds being in support of its original beneficiary, the **Queen's Nursing Institute** and, with them, the **Nurses Welfare Service** for the relief of district and other nurses in need – be this caused by old age, difficulties through illness or the stress and pressure of their work.

Since 1949 a contribution has been made to the **Gardens Fund of The National Trust** to help maintain gardens of special historic or horticultural interest. In 1984 the increasing popularity of the Scheme made it possible to extend further its charitable work by assisting the **Cancer Relief Macmillan Fund** with funds for training **Macmillan Nurses** in the continuing care of those suffering from cancer and their families. In 1986 the Scheme took on the charitable work previously organised by Gardeners' Sunday in aid of the **Gardeners' Royal Benevolent Society** and the **Royal Gardeners' Orphan Fund**.

Many other national and local charities also benefit from the Scheme, since garden owners may, if they so wish, allocate an agreed proportion of the proceeds of an opening for the National Gardens Scheme to another charity. The names of these additional charities are published in the descriptive entries for the gardens.

We wish to emphasise that the majority of the gardens listed are privately owned and are only opened on the dates shown in the text through the generosity of the owners wishing to support this charity. These gardens are **NOT OPEN** to the public on other dates except by prior agreement.

The Chairman and Council wish to express their deep gratitude to all those whose generous support of the National Gardens Scheme makes it possible to help these most worthwhile charities. We hope that you will enjoy visiting many of these gardens.

Thank you for your support.

Chairman

THE BRITISH ANTIQUE DEALERS' ASSOCIATION

Patron, President and Council of The National Gardens Scheme Charitable Trust

Headquarters Hatchlands Park, East Clandon, Guildford, Surrey, GU4 7RT. Tel. 01483 211535 Facsimile 01483 211537

Auditor Gilbert Allen & Co., Church Down, Bordyke, Tonbridge TN9 1NR

Solicitor Crossman Block, 199 Strand, London WC2R 1DR

Bankers Royal Bank of Scotland PLC
10 North St, Guildford, Surrey GU1 4AF

Registered Charity Number 279284

* Executive Committee Member
ø County Team

Relevant organisations and publications

The National Trust

Certain gardens opened by The National Trust are opened in aid of the National Gardens Scheme on the dates shown in this book. Information about the regular opening of these gardens is given in the 1995 *Handbook for Members and Visitors* (issued free to members), published by The National Trust (Enterprises) Ltd (£4.50 plus 70p for postage; subject to alteration) and obtainable from 36 Queen Anne's Gate, London SW1H 9AS or from any National Trust Property. The National Trust Gardens Handbook (£3.95) provides more detailed information on the Trust's gardens and is sold in bookshops and National Trust shops.

Scotland's Gardens Scheme

Raises funds through the opening of gardens for the Queen's Nursing Institute (Scotland), the Gardens Fund of The National Trust for Scotland and over 160 other charities nominated by the garden owners. Handbook with all details of openings published mid-February. Tours: one six-day coach tour. Free brochure available. Handbook (£3.00 inc. p & p) from Scotland's Gardens Scheme, 31 Castle Terrace, Edinburgh EH1 2EL Telephone 0131-229 1870, Fax 0131-229 0443

The National Trust for Scotland

Established in 1931. In its care are over 100 properties. As well as castles, cottages, mountains, islands and historic sites, the Trust has in its care 25 major Scottish gardens. The National Trust for Scotland, 5 Charlotte Square, Edinburgh EH2 4DU Telephone 0131-226 5922 Fax 0131 243 9302

The Ulster Gardens Scheme

A list of the private gardens open to the public under the Ulster Gardens Scheme can be obtained from: The Public Affairs Manager, The National Trust, Rowallane, Saintfield, Co. Down, BT24 7LH. Telephone Saintfield (01238) 510721

The Automobile Association Guide to Britain

Days out in Britain gives details of more than 2,000 places of interest in England, Wales, Scotland, Channel Islands and Northern Ireland together with location maps and 1995 calendar of events. Available from AA bookshops and all good booksellers. Price £7.99.

The Historic Houses Association

Represents over 1,300 private owners of historic houses and outstanding gardens. It runs the HHA/Christie's Garden of the Year Award; helps administer a scheme for training gardeners and organises periodic seminars. A quarterly magazine is available to members and friends of the Historic Houses Association and on subscription. HHA, 2 Chester Street, London SW1X 7BB. Telephone 0171-259 5688.

Irish Heritage Properties (HITHA)

Publishes annually an illustrated booklet with information on over 60 properties. Available from Irish Heritage Properties, Hillsbrook, Dangle Valley, Bray, Co Wicklow. Tel/Fax 353-1-2862777

The Automobile Association

The AA has kindly arranged for information on gardens open for the Scheme to be available from their local offices.

The Royal Automobile Club

The RAC has kindly arranged that their RAC Touring Information Department (0181-686 0088) can provide details of locations of gardens open for the Scheme.

The Garden History Society

This international society campaigns to protect our garden heritage. Members receive the Society's acclaimed Journal and Newsletter. The Garden History Society, 5 The Knoll, Hereford HR1 1RU.

Royal Gardens

SANDRINGHAM HOUSE AND GROUNDS Norfolk

By gracious permission of Her Majesty The Queen, the House and grounds at Sandringham will be open on the following days:

From 13th April to 2nd October inclusive daily.

Please note that the **house only** will be **closed** to the public from 18 July to 3rd August inclusive and that the house and grounds will be closed from 23rd July to 2nd August inclusive. Coach drivers and visitors are advised to confirm these closing and opening dates nearer the time.

Hours

Sandringham House: 11 to 4.45; Sandringham museum and grounds: 10.30 to 5.

Admission Charges

House, grounds and museum: adults £4.00, OAPs £3.00, children £2.00. Grounds and museum only: adults £3.00, OAPs £2.50; children £1.50.

Advance party bookings will be accepted. There are reductions in admission fees for pre-paid parties. Picnicking is not permitted inside the grounds. Dogs are not permitted inside the grounds. Free car and coach parking.

Sandringham Church

This will be open as follows, subject to weddings, funerals and special services: when the grounds are open as stated above, hours 11-5 April to September, 1-5 during October. At other times of the year the church is open by appointment only.

Enquiries

The Public Access Manager, Estate office, Sandringham or by telephone 9-1, 2-4.30 Monday to Friday inclusive on King's Lynn 772675.

Sandringham Flower Show

This will be held on Wednesday 26th July.

FROGMORE GARDENS Berkshire

By gracious permission of Her Majesty The Queen, the Frogmore Gardens, Windsor Castle, will be open from 10.30-7 on the following days:

Wednesday May 3 and Thursday May 4.

Coaches by appointment only: apply to the National Gardens Scheme, Hatchlands Park, East Clandon, Guildford, Surrey, GU4 7RT (Telephone 01483 211535) stating whether May 3 or 4, and whether morning or afternoon. Admission £1.50 accompanied children free. Dogs not allowed. Royal mausoleum also open, free of charge, both days. Entrance to gardens and mausoleum through Long Walk gate. Visitors are requested kindly to refrain from entering the grounds of the Home Park. Light refreshments will be available at the free car park (near the outer gate to the gardens).

FROGMORE HOUSE Berkshire

Also open but not for NGS. Entrance only from Frogmore Gardens. Admission Adults £2.50, over 60's £2, under 17 £1, children under age of 8 not admitted.

General Information

‡ following a garden name in the Dates of Opening list indicates that those gardens sharing the same symbol are nearby and open on the same day. ‡‡ indicates a second series of nearby gardens open on the same day.

- ¶ Opening for the first time.
- ❀ Plants/produce for sale if available.
- ♿ Gardens with at least the main features accessible by wheelchair.
- ✗ No dogs except guide dogs but otherwise dogs are usually admitted, provided they are kept on a lead. Dogs are not admitted to houses.
- ● Gardens marked thus, which open throughout the season, give a guaranteed contribution from their takings to the National Gardens Scheme.
- ▲ Where this sign appears alongside dates in the *descriptive* entry for a garden it denotes that this garden is *also open* regularly to the public on days other than those for the NGS. Details of National Trust gardens can also be found in the *National Trust Gardens Handbook;* see page 9.

Children All children must be accompanied by an adult.

Additional Charities Nominated by Owner (ACNO) Where the owners of 'private' gardens (not normally open to the public) have nominated some other cause to receive an agreed share from the admission money, the name of the other cause is included in the descriptive entry as (Share to ....) with an ® or © to indicate whether it is a Registered Charity or a Charitable Cause.

Tea When this is available at a garden the information is given in capitals, e.g. TEAS (usually with home-made cakes) or TEA (usually with biscuits). There is, of course, an extra charge for any refreshments available at a garden. Any other information given about tea is a guide only to assist visitors in finding somewhere in the area for tea. TEAS in aid of ... is used where part or all the proceeds go to another organisation.

Distances and sizes In all cases these are approximate.

Open by appointment Please do not be put off by this notation. The owner may consider his garden too small to accommodate the numbers associated with a normal opening or, more often, there may be a lack of car parking space. It is often more rewarding than a normal opening as the owner will usually give a guided tour of the garden. The minimum size of party is either stated in the garden description or can be found out when making the appointment; usually 2. If the garden has normal open days, the entrance fee is as stated in the garden description.

Coach parties Please, by appointment only unless stated otherwise.

Houses Not open unless this is specifically stated; where the house or part-house is shown an additional charge is usually made.

Buses Continuance of many bus services is a matter of considerable uncertainty, especially on Sundays. It is strongly recommended that any details given in this guide be checked in advance.

National Trust Members are requested to note that where a National Trust property has allocated an opening day to the National Gardens Scheme which is one of its normal opening days, members can still gain entry on production of their National Trust membership card (although donations to the Scheme will be welcome). Where, however, the day allocated is one on which the property would *not* normally be open, then the payment of the National Gardens Scheme admission fee will be required.

Professional photographers Photographs taken in a garden may not be used for sale or reproduction without the prior permission of the garden owner.

Lavatories Private gardens do not normally have outside lavatories. Regretably, for security reasons, owners have been advised not to admit visitors into their houses to use inside toilets.

ENGLAND

Avon

Hon County Organiser: Mrs Mary Bailey, Quakers, Lower Hazel, Rudgeway, Bristol BS12 2QP Tel 01454 413205

Assistant Hon County Organisers: Dr Margaret Lush, Hazel Cottage, Lower Hazel, Rudgeway, Bristol BS12 2QP Tel 01454 412112
Mrs Amanda Osmond, Church Farm House, Hawkesbury, nr Badminton, Avon GL9 1BN Tel 01454 238533
Mrs Ann Pockney, Chester House, Blackmoor, Lower Langford, Bristol BS18 7HJ Tel 01934 863190

Avon Leaflet: Mrs Jean Damey, 2 Hawburn Close, Bristol BS4 2PB Tel 0117 9775587

Hon County Treasurer: J K Dutson Esq., The Firs, Rockhampton, Nr Berkeley, Glos GL13 9DY Tel 01454 413210

DATES OF OPENING

By appointment

For telephone numbers and other details see garden descriptions. Private visits welcomed

Algars Manor, Iron Acton
Bourne House, Burrington
Church Farm, Lower Failand
Coombe Dingle Gardens, Bristol
15 Darlington Place, Bathwick
Highview, Portishead
Hill House, Wickwar
Jasmine Cottage, Clevedon
10 Linden Rd, Clevedon
Madron, Ostlings Lane, Bathford
The Manor House, Walton-in-Gordano
Petty France Hotel, Dunkirk
Portland Lodge, Lower Almondsbury
Sherborne Garden, Litton
The Urn Cottage, Charfield
Vine House, Henbury

Parties only

Brewery House, Southstoke
Old Down House, Tockington
West Tyning, Beach

Regular openings

For details see garden descriptions

Crowe Hall, Widcombe
10 Linden Road, Clevedon. Every 4th Sunday April to October
Madron, Ostlings Lane, Bathford. Thurs June 8 to Aug 3
The Manor House, Walton-in-Gordano. Wed & Thurs April 19 to Sept 14
Pearl's Garden. Every Sun in May and June
Stanton Prior Gardens, nr Bath. Every Wed May 3 to Aug 30
University of Bristol Botanic Garden

February 13 Monday
The Urn Cottage, Charfield

March 5 Sunday
Rock House, Elberton

March 11 Saturday
Langford Court, Langford

March 12 Sunday
Langford Court, Langford

March 26 Sunday
Jasmine Cottage, Clevedon

March 27 Monday
The Urn Cottage, Charfield

April 1 Saturday
Old Down House, Tockington

April 2 Sunday
Sherborne Garden, Litton
Old Down House, Tockington

April 9 Sunday
Failand Court, Lower Failand
The Manor House, Walton-in-Gordano

April 13 Thursday
Jasmine Cottage, Clevedon

April 16 Sunday
Algars Manor & Algars Mill, Iron Acton

April 17 Monday
Algars Manor & Algars Mill, Iron Acton

April 20 Thursday
Jasmine Cottage, Clevedon

April 22 Saturday
Brackenwood Garden Centre, Portishead ‡
Clevedon Court, Clevedon ‡

April 23 Sunday
Brackenwood Garden Centre, Portishead
Coley Court & The Little Manor, Coley & Farrington Gurney
Crowe Hall, Widcombe

April 24 Monday
Brackenwood Garden Centre, Portishead
The Urn Cottage, Charfield

April 25 Tuesday
Brackenwood Garden Centre, Portishead

April 26 Wednesday
Brackenwood Garden Centre, Portishead

April 27 Thursday
Jasmine Cottage, Clevedon

April 30 Sunday
Jasmine Cottage, Clevedon
Petty France Hotel, Dunkirk
Severn View, Thornbury

May 4 Thursday
Jasmine Cottage, Clevedon

May 7 Sunday
Coombe Dingle Gardens, Bristol
Sherborne Garden, Litton

May 8 Monday
Coombe Dingle Gardens, Bristol

May 10 Wednesday
Windmill Cottage, Backwell
May 11 Thursday
Jasmine Cottage, Clevedon
May 14 Sunday
Barrow Court, Barrow Gurney
Severn View, Thornbury
May 17 Wednesday
Highview, Portishead
May 18 Thursday
Jasmine Cottage, Clevedon
May 20 Saturday
Church Farm, Lower Failand
Parsonage Farm, Publow
May 21 Sunday
Church Farm, Lower Failand
Goblin Combe, Cleeve
Hill House, Wickwar
Parsonage Farm, Publow
Severn View, Thornbury
May 25 Thursday
Jasmine Cottage, Clevedon
May 28 Sunday
Algars Manor & Algars Mill, Iron Acton
Jasmine Cottage, Clevedon
Pearl's Garden, Coalpit Heath
Severn View, Thornbury
May 29 Monday
Algars Manor & Algars Mill, Iron Acton
The Manor House, Walton-in-Gordano
Pearl's Garden, Coalpit Heath
The Urn Cottage, Charfield
June 1 Thursday
Jasmine Cottage, Clevedon
June 4 Sunday
Churchill Court, Churchill
Clifton Gardens, Bristol
Sherborne Garden, Litton
June 8 Thursday
Jasmine Cottage, Clevedon
June 11 Sunday
Goblin Combe, Cleeve
Harptree Court, East Harptree
Severn View, Thornbury
Tranby House, Whitchurch
The Urn Cottage, Charfield
June 14 Wednesday
Windmill Cottage, Backwell
June 15 Thursday
Jasmine Cottage, Clevedon
June 17 Saturday
Gatcombe Court, Flax Bourton
Highview, Portishead
June 18 Sunday
Crowe Hall, Widcombe
Gatcombe Court, Flax Bourton
Hazel Cottage, Lower Hazel
The Manor House, Walton-in-Gordano
Stonewell House, Churchill Green
June 21 Wednesday
Stanton Prior Gardens, nr Bath
June 22 Thursday
Jasmine Cottage, Clevedon
June 25 Sunday
Badminton House, Badminton
Brooklands, Burnett
Doynton House, Doynton
Jasmine Cottage, Clevedon
Stanton Drew Gardens
June 28 Wednesday
Brooklands, Burnett
2 Old Tarnwell, Upper Stanton Drew
Windmill Cottage, Backwell
June 29 Thursday
Jasmine Cottage, Clevedon
July 1 Saturday
Bellevue, Publow
West Tyning, Beach
July 2 Sunday
Bellevue, Publow
Brewery House, Southstoke
University of Bristol Botanic Garden
West Tyning, Beach
July 6 Thursday
Jasmine Cottage, Clevedon
July 9 Sunday
Failand Court, Lower Failand
July 12 Wednesday
Windmill Cottage, Backwell
July 13 Thursday
Jasmine Cottage, Clevedon
2 Old Tarnwell, Upper Stanton Drew
July 15 Saturday
Bryncrug, Mangotsfield
July 16 Sunday
Bryncrug, Mangotsfield
The Manor House, Walton-in Gordano
July 18 Tuesday
2 Old Tarnwell, Upper Stanton Drew
July 19 Wednesday
Highview, Portishead
July 20 Thursday
Jasmine Cottage, Clevedon
July 22 Saturday
Tranby House, Whitchurch
July 23 Sunday
Lady Farm, Chelwood
Tranby House, Whitchurch
July 26 Wednesday
Windmill Cottage, Backwell
July 27 Thursday
Jasmine Cottage, Clevedon
July 30 Sunday
Jasmine Cottage, Clevedon
Stanton Prior Gardens, nr Bath
August 3 Thursday
Jasmine Cottage, Clevedon
August 6 Sunday
Dyrham Park
August 9 Wednesday
Windmill Cottage, Backwell
August 10 Thursday
Jasmine Cottage, Clevedon
August 13 Sunday
Highfield House, Chew Magna
August 17 Thursday
Jasmine Cottage, Clevedon
August 19 Saturday
Highview, Portishead
August 20 Sunday
The Manor House, Walton-in-Gordano
Tranby House, Whitchurch
August 24 Thursday
Jasmine Cottage, Clevedon
August 27 Sunday
Jasmine Cottage, Clevedon
August 31 Thursday
Jasmine Cottage, Clevedon
September 3 Sunday
Bellevue, Publow
University of Bristol Botanic Garden
September 13 Wednesday
Windmill Cottage, Backwell
September 16 Saturday
Old Down House, Tockington
September 17 Sunday
Bourne House, Burrington
Old Down House, Tockington
September 20 Wednesday
Highview, Portishead
September 25 Monday
The Urn Cottage, Charfield
October 1 Sunday
Sherborne Garden, Litton
October 16 Monday
The Urn Cottage, Charfield

DESCRIPTIONS OF GARDENS

Algars Manor & Algars Mill ❀ Iron Acton 9m N of Bristol. 3m W of Yate/Chipping Sodbury. Turn S off Iron Acton bypass B4059, past village green, 200yds, then over level Xing (Station Rd). TEAS **Algars Manor**. *Combined adm £1.50 Chd 20p. Easter Sun, Mon April 16, 17, May 28, 29 (2-6)*

Algars Manor ❀ (Dr & Mrs J M Naish) 3-acre woodland garden beside R Frome; mill-stream; native plants mixed with azaleas, rhododendrons, camellias, magnolias, eucalyptus. Picnic areas. Early Jacobean house (not open) and old barn. Featured in NGS video 3. *Private visits also welcome* **Tel 01454 228372**

Algars Mill (Mr & Mrs J Wright) entrance via Algars Manor. 2-acre woodland garden beside R Frome; spring bulbs, shrubs; early spring feature of wild Newent daffodils. 300-400 yr old mill house (not open) through which mill-race still runs

Badminton ♿❀ (The Duke & Duchess of Beaufort) 5m E of Chipping Sodbury. Large garden designed 10 years ago. Still in the process of being created. Mixed and herbaceous borders; many old-fashioned and climbing roses; conservatories and orangery; walled kitchen garden recreated in Victorian style ¼m from house with a new glasshouse. TEAS. *Adm £1.50 OAPs/Chd £1 under 10 free (Share to The Garden History Society®). Sun June 25 (2-6)*

Barrow Court ❀ Barrow Gurney 5m SW Bristol. From Bristol take A370 and turn E onto B3130 towards Barrow Gurney; immediate right, Barrow Court Lane, then ½m, turn R through Lodge archway. 2 acres of formal gardens, designed by Inigo Thomas in 1890. Architectural garden, with sculpture and pavilions; arboretum; on going renovations to paths; stonework, replanted yew hedging and parterres. C17 E-shaped house (not open). Parking limited. TEAS. *Adm £1 Chd 50p. Sun May 14 (2-6)*

Bellevue ♿✲❀ (Mr & Mrs J A Heaford) Publow. 7m S of Bristol, A37 Bristol-Wells to Pensford Bridge. Turn L off A37 and L again into Publow Lane and ½m on to Publow Church. Mature 1¼-acre garden in lovely setting opp historic Publow Church. Wide variety of plants with much thought given to colour and foliage. Brook with some streamside planting. Trees, shrubs, vegetables, pergola and gravel garden. Many drought tolerant plants to cope with sandy soil and gently sloping site. Extensively replanted by present owners since 1980. TEAS at the Old Vicarage in aid of All Saints, Publow July 1, 2; St Peters Hospice Sept 3. *Adm £1 Chd free. Sat, Sun July 1, 2 (2-5) Sun Sept 3 (2-6)*

Bourne House ♿✲❀ (Mr & Mrs Christopher Thomas) 12m S Bristol. N of Burrington. Turning off A38 signposted Blagdon-Burrington; 2nd turning L. 4 acres, and 2 paddocks. Stream with waterfalls & lily pond; new pergola; mature trees, and shrubs. New mixed borders; roses; bulbs; large area of cyclamen 'neapolitanum'. TEAS. *Adm £1.50 Chd free. Sun Sept 17 (2-6). Private visits of 4 and over welcome, please* **Tel 01761 462494**

Regular Openers. See head of county section.

Brackenwood Garden Centre Woodland Garden ✲❀ (Mr & Mrs John Maycock) 131 Nore Rd, Portishead. From Bristol A369 (10m). M5 Junc 19. Walk lies behind Brackenwood Garden Centre, open daily 9-5. **Tel 01275 843484**, 1m from Portishead on coast rd to Clevedon. 8-acre woodland garden featured on the cover of 'Beautiful Gardens of Britain' Calendar 1994. Rhododendrons, camellias, Japanese maples and pieris; secluded woodland pools with waterfowl; many rare trees and shrubs; abundant wild flowers, birds and mammals. Magnificent views of the Bristol Channel to Wales and the Severn Bridge. New Restaurant/Tea-Room, lunches and refreshments all day. *Adm £1.30 Chd 60p. Sat, Sun, Mon, Tues, Wed April 22, 23, 24, 25, 26 (10-5)*

Brewery House ❀ (John and Ursula Brooke) 2½m S of Bath off A367, L onto B3110, take 2nd R to Southstoke or bus to Cross Keys. House is ¼m down Southstoke Lane. Please park where signed and walk down. ⅔-acre garden on 2 levels. Fine views; top garden walled. Many unusual plants. Water garden. All organic. Partly suitable for wheelchairs. Plants for sale. Cream TEAS in aid of Village Hall. *Adm £1 Chd free. Sun July 2 (2-6). Private visits welcome, please* **Tel 01225 833153**

Brooklands ♿✲❀ (Mr & Mrs Patrick Stevens) Burnett. 2m S Keynsham on B3116. Turn R into Burnett Village. 1½-acre garden; mature trees and variety of ornamental shrubs; rose garden; herbaceous border; extensive planting of shrub roses and clematis; fine views of distant Mendip Hills. Ploughman lunches and TEAS in aid of St Michael's Church, Burnett. *Adm £1 Chd free. Sun June 25 (10-6), Wed June 28 (2-7)*

Bryncrug ✲❀ (Mrs Margaret Jones) 23 Charnhill Ridge Mangotsfield. ½m from Staplehill on the Mangotsfield Rd B4465 and at the bottom of the hill turn R into Charnhill Drive and in 30yds turn L to Charnhill Ridge. Small town garden, densely planted with interesting trees and shrubs, many in dry shade; pond; conservatory and unusual front garden. Featured in Nov 93 Practical Gardening. TEAS in aid P.D.S.A. *Adm £1 Chd 20p. Sat, Sun July 15, 16 (1-5)*

Church Farm ♿❀ (Mr & Mrs N Slade) Lower Failand, 6m SW Bristol. Take B3128 out of Bristol to Clevedon Rd via Clerk-Combe Hill, turn R down Oxhouse Lane opp garage; or turn off M5 at junction 19 towards Bristol. 1st R through Portbury, turn L into Failand Lane. L past Church then R into private rd. House is 1st R. Parking adj to Church. 3-acre garden started in 1974; run on organic principles; large collection clematis, unusual plants and trees. Cream TEAS Sat, Sun May 20, 21 only. *Adm £1 Chd 25p (Share to ARC®). Sat, Sun May 20, 21 (2-5). Private visits welcome Weds April 1 to end of Sept, please* **Tel 01275 373033**

By Appointment Gardens. These owners do not have a fixed opening day usually because they do not like crowds or have insufficient parking space. Owner will often give guided tour.

Churchill Court ♿✂❀ (Mr & Mrs J Murray) Church Lane, Churchill. 15m SW of Bristol on A38. Churchill Court lies between the comprehensive school and St John's Church in Church Lane. 1m from Churchill traffic lights. 2 acres of garden around an historically interesting house set against a backdrop of a Norman Church. Mixed herbaceous and shrub borders, rock garden, range of unusual trees and shrubs, interesting mature specimen trees and an organic kitchen garden feature in this beautiful setting. TEAS in aid of The Royal British Legion Women's Section. *Adm £1.50 Chd free. Sun June 4 (2-6)*

¶Clevedon Court ✂ (The National Trust) Clevedon. 1½m E of Clevedon, on Bristol rd (B3130), signposted from exit 20 M5. C18 terraced garden developed by the Elton family with high walled terraces, sheltered and backed by a bank of trees overlooking the Moors. Many tender species of shrubs and perennials flourish together with splendid magnolias and an old Mulberry tree. TEAS. *Adm £1.50 Chd free. Sat April 22 (2-5)*

Clifton Gardens ✂ Bristol. Close to Clifton Suspension Bridge. *Combined adm £1.50 Chd 25p. Sun June 4 (2-6)*

9 Sion Hill ❀ (Mr & Mrs R C Begg) Entrance from Sion Lane. Small walled town garden, densely planted; climbing & herbaceous plants; herb garden; old roses

16 Sion Hill ♿ (Drs Cameron and Ros Kennedy) Entrance via green door in Sion Lane, at side of No 16. Small pretty town garden with pond, several interesting shrubs and trees

17 Sion Hill ♿❀ (Mr & Mrs Philip Gray) Entrance from Sion Lane. Town garden with trees and shrubs. TEAS

Coley Court & The Little Manor ✂❀ Teas at **Manor Farm**. *Combined adm £1.50 Chd free. Sun April 23 (2-6)*

Coley Court (Mrs M J Hill) East Harptree, 8m N of Wells. Take B3114 through East Harptree turn L signed Coley and Hinton Blewitt. From A39 at Chewton Mendip take B3114 2m, sign on R, Coley, Hinton Blewitt, follow lane 400yds to white house on L before bridge. 1-acre garden, open lawn, stone walls, spring bulbs; 1-acre old Somerset orchard. Early Jacobean house (not open)

The Little Manor (Mrs K P P Goldschmidt) Farrington Gurney on A39. Turn E in village on to A362 towards Radstock-600yds turn L. ¾-acre spring garden; many varieties of bulbs, flowering trees, many rare shrubs; rose garden. Early C17 house with attractive courtyard

Coombe Dingle Gardens ♿❀ 4m NW of Bristol centre. From Portway down Sylvan Way, turn left into the Dingle and Grove Rd. From Westbury-on-Trym, Canford Lane sharp right at beginning of Westbury Lane. From Bristol over Downs, Parrys Lane, Coombe Lane; turn left and sharp right into the Dingle and Grove Rd. TEAS **Hillside**. *Combined adm £1.50 Chd free. Sun, Mon May 7, 8 (2-6). Private visits and parties by appt Jan-June* **Tel 01179 681979** *or* **01179 681287**

Hillside ♿ (Mrs C M Luke) 42 Grove Rd. 2 acres late Georgian lay-out. Victorian rose garden; fine trees, shrubs. Walled kitchen garden

Pennywell ❀ (Mr & Mrs D H Baker) Grove Rd. 2 acres; varied collection trees and shrubs incl 50ft span flowering cherry; rockery, organic kitchen garden. Views over adjoining Blaise Castle Estate, Kingsweston Down and the Trym Valley. Exhibition of sculpture by Mary Donington. Plant stall (in aid of Friends of Blaise)

Crowe Hall ❀ (John Barratt Esq) Widcombe. 1m SE of Bath. L up Widcombe Hill, off A36, leaving White Hart on R. Large varied garden; fine trees, lawns, spring bulbs, series of enclosed gardens cascading down steep hillside. Italianate terracing and Gothick Victorian grotto contrast with park- like upper garden. Dramatic setting, with spectacular views of Bath. Featured in NGS gardens video 2. TEAS. *Adm £1.50 Chd 30p. Suns March 26; May 14, 28; July 16, for NGS Suns April 23, June 18 (2-6). Also private visits welcome, please* **Tel 01225 310322**

¶15 Darlington Place ✂❀ (Miss Lewis White) Bathwick. Take 2nd turning on R as you ascend Bathwick Hill which is the rd leading from the town to the University. A peaceful little garden near the centre of Bath with a wonderful view of the City. Mostly herbaceous plants, many of them unusual, grown for yr-round scent and colour. Donations. *Private visits welcome by appt, please* **Tel 01225 462460**

Doynton House ♿❀ (Mrs C E Pitman) Doynton. 8m E of Bristol, ¾m NE of A420 at E end of Wick. Mature, old-fashioned 2-acre garden with herbaceous borders, shrubs and lawns. TEAS by W.I. *Adm £1 Chd 20p. Sun June 25 (2-6)*

Dyrham Park ♿✂❀ (The National Trust) 8m N of Bath. 12m E of Bristol. Approached from Bath-Stroud Road (A46), 2m S of Tormarton interchange with M4, exit 18. Situated on W side of late C17 house. Herbaceous borders, yews clipped as buttresses, ponds and cascade, parish church set on terrace. Niches and carved urns. Long lawn to old west entrance. Deer Park. TEAS. *Adm incl Deer Park £2.60 Chd £1.30. Sun Aug 6 (12-5)*

Failand Court ♿❀ (Mr & Mrs B Nathan) Lower Failand, 6m SW of Bristol. Take B3128 out of Bristol to Clevedon Rd. Via Clerk-Combe Hill, turn R down Oxhouse Lane opp garage; or turn off M5 Junc 19 towards Bristol. 1st R through Portbury, turn L into Failand Lane. 1m along Oxhouse Lane. Park in Oxhouse Lane and at church. 1¼-acre mature garden originally landscaped by Sir Edward Fry. Further developed by Miss Agnes Fry. Interesting trees, shrubs and vegetable garden. TEAS. *Adm £1 Chd 25p. Suns April 9, July 9 (2-5)*

Gatcombe Court ✂❀ (Mr & Mrs Charles Clarke) Flax Bourton. 5m as the crow flies W of Bristol. Take A370 towards Weston-super-Mare, at B3130 intersection go N towards Nailsea for 200yds, turn R (E) and after 100yds follow small lane L down through the trees. Approx 2 acres of ornamental garden, terraced with stone walls on which climbing roses grow, with lawns, borders, herb garden and old yew hedges, set on a wooded hillside. TEAS. *Adm £1 Chd 50p (Share to Flax Bourton Church®). Sat, Sun June 17, 18 (2-6)*

¶Goblin Combe ✲❀ (Mrs H R Burn) Cleeve. 10m S of Bristol on A370, turn L onto Cleeve Hill Rd just before Lord Nelson Inn. After 300 yds turn L onto Plunder St, first drive on R. Car parking near the bottom of the drive just beyond the Plunder St turning. 2 acre terraced garden with interesting collection of trees, shrubs and borders, surrounded by orchards, fields and woodlands. Magnificent views. TEAS. *Adm £1 Chd 25p (Share to The Music Space Trust®). Suns May 21, June 11 (2-6)*

Harptree Court ♿❀ (Mr & Mrs Richard Hill) East Harptree, 8m N of Wells via A39 Bristol Rd to Chewton Mendip; then B3114 to East Harptree, gates on L. From Bath via A368 Weston-super-Mare Rd to West Harptree. Large garden; fine old trees in lovely setting; woodland walks; handsome stone bridge; subterranean passage, Doric temple, lily pond and paved garden. TEAS. *Adm £1 Chd free. Sun June 11 (2-6)*

Hazel Cottage ❀ (Dr & Mrs Brandon Lush) Lower Hazel 700yds W of Rudgeway from A38; 10m N of Bristol. ½-acre cottage garden in rural setting with wide variety of plants and shrubs incl alpines and some unusual varieties. TEAS. *Adm £1 Chd free (Share to BRACE®). Sun June 18 (2-6)*

Highfield House ♿✲❀ (Mr & Mrs R A Webb) Chew Magna. 7m S Bristol. A37 Bristol-Wells rd; at top of Pensford Hill take B3130 to Chew Magna and proceed to top of High St. Large C19 garden extensively re-planted during the last 4yrs by the present owners. Mixed shrub and herbaceous borders; open lawns containing some unusual specimens. Fine stone-walled vegetable and flower garden; other interest - small flock of pedigree Hampshire Downs. TEAS. *Adm £1 Chd free. Sun Aug 13 (2-6)*

¶Highview ✲❀ (Mike & Mary Clavey) Portishead. From Bristol take the A369 (10m) M5 Junction 19, 1½m from Portishead on Coast Rd to Clevedon, take L turn into Hillcrest Rd. Property found at end of a private drive bottom of steep hill. Please park in Hillcrest Rd. 1-acre garden made from scratch by owners since 1987. Large collection of heathers, variety of plants in mixed borders. Herbaceous and rockery plants, miniature rose bed, water features. Alpine bed. Lovely channel views. Garden slightly on slope. TEAS. *Adm £1 Chd free. Weds May 17, July 19, Sept 20; Sats June 17, Aug 19 (2-5.30). Also private visits welcome for parties of 6 or over, please* **Tel 01275 849873**

Hill House ♿✲❀ (Dr & Mrs Richard Adlam) 4m N of Chipping Sodbury on B4060. Through Wickwar, L by wall signed to M5; then 200yds on L. 7 acres of land, of which 4 acres of gardens originally designed and planted by Sally, Duchess of Westminster. Gold/silver plantings in gravel; pleached lime walk; wild flowers and bulbs; owls and pheasant aviaries, peacocks, flock of Southdown sheep. TEAS. *Adm £1.50 Chd 50p. Sun May 21 (2-6)*

Iford Manor see Wiltshire

By Appointment Gardens. See head of county section

Jasmine Cottage ✲❀ (Mr & Mrs Michael Redgrave) 26 Channel Rd, Clevedon. 12m W of Bristol (junction 20 off M5). Follow signs to seafront and Pier, continue N on B3124, past Walton Park Hotel, turn R at St Mary's Church. Medium-sized garden created by owners from a wooded shelter belt for interest in all seasons. Old-fashioned roses; clematis, pergola; mixed shrub borders; island beds; gravel beds, pond and potager. Many unusual herbaceous, tender perennials and climbers. Plants propagated from the garden available in adjoining nursery. New toilet facilities. Pre-booked Teas only on Thurs in April and May. TEAS Thurs in June to Aug and Suns. Parties to pre-book. *Adm £1 Chd free. Suns March 26, April 30, May 28, June 25, July 30, Aug 27, (2-6). Every Thurs April 13 to Aug 31 (2.30-5.30). Private visits welcome all the year, please* **Tel Clevedon (01275) 871850**

¶Lady Farm ✲❀ (Mr & Mrs M Pearce) Chelwood. On the A368 ½m E of Chelwood Bridge X-rds (A37 & A368) 9m S of Bristol and 9m W of Bath. The existing garden, started 10 yrs ago, covers an area of 1 acre, but a further 6 acres are currently being developed. Surrounding the farmhouse and courtyard are shrub and herbaceous borders, climbers, roses and a terrace overlooking a recently created, spring fed watercourse which flows into a lake in the valley with adjacent rock features. Extensive shelter belts have, and are, being planted, and woodland and lakeside walks are in the early stages of development. This garden is NOT recommended for children under 14. TEAS. *Adm £1 Chd 50p. Sun July 23 (2-6)*

Langford Court ♿✲❀ (Sir John & Lady Wills) Langford. 11m S of Bristol on A38, drive gates off Langford Lane, signed Burrington. To the N of the A38. Large garden in lovely setting; fine old trees; topiary; orangery; shrubs; daffodils and crocuses. TEAS in aid of St John's Ambulance. *Adm £1 Chd free. Sat, Sun March 11, 12 (2-5)*

¶10 Linden Road ✲❀ (Ruth & William Salisbury) Clevedon. Coming from the seafront, head up Alexandra Rd opp the Pier, cross the roundabout. Linden Rd is between the Midland and Barclays Banks. No 10 is 150yds on the R. A very small but richly planted seaside town garden. Over 400 different species of trees, shrubs and plants grow in 3 areas, the largest being 35′ × 40′. A garden developed with children in mind and having shape, form and colour throughout the year. TEAS *Adm £1 Chd free. Private visits (max 5) welcome Sun March 19, 4th Sun in the month April to Oct, please* **Tel 01275 874694**

Madron ✲❀ (Mr & Mrs Martin Carr) Ostlings Lane, Bathford. Approx 3½m, E of Bath close to A4. At Batheaston roundabout take A363 Bradford-upon-Avon Rd; then 1st turning L, Ostlings Lane is immediataly on R alongside Crown Inn. At top of short rise 100yds stone pillars on L are entrance to Madron - 2nd house on L along drive. 1¼-acre garden created over 11 yrs on site overlooking the Avon valley and surrounding hills. Borders and banks with shrubs, hardy and tender perennials, with particular emphasis on plant and colour associations and water garden, all set amidst fine lawns with conifer and deciduous trees. Featured in Practical Gardening, April 1992. TEAS. *Adm £1 Chd free. Thurs June 8 to Aug 3 by prior appt only (2.30-5) other times by arrangement, please* **Tel 01225 859792**

The Manor House ♿✻❀ (Mr & Mrs Simon Wills) Walton-in-Gordano, 2m NE of Clevedon. Entrance on N side of B3124, Clevedon to Portishead Rd, just by houses on roadside nearest Clevedon. Clevedon-Portishead buses stop in Village. 4-acres; plantsman's garden featured in 'Country Life' 1989, trees, shrubs, herbaceous and bulbs mostly labelled. Coaches by appt only. TEAS (Suns, Mons only) in aid of St Peters Hospice Bristol. *Adm £1.50, Acc chd under 14 free (Share to St Peter's Hospice, Bristol®). Sun April 9, Mon May 29, Suns June 18, July 16, Aug 20 (2-6) Weds and Thurs April 19 to Sept 14 (10-4). Private visits welcome all year, please* **Tel 01275 872067**

Old Down House ♿❀ (Mr & Mrs Robert Bernays) Tockington, 10m N of Bristol. Follow brown Tourist Board signs to Old Down from A38 at Alveston. 5 acres divided into small formal and informal gardens by hedges and walls; topiary, shrubs; azaleas, rhododendrons, camellias; extensive lawns; rock garden; fine trees (weeping beeches, etc). Herbaceous borders, semi-wild areas; fine views to Severn and Welsh hills. TEAS. *Adm £1 Chd free (Share to Bristol Age Care ®). Sat, Sun April 1, 2, Sept 16, 17 (2-6). Private parties welcome, please* **Tel 01454 413605**

¶2 Old Tarnwell ✻❀ (Ken & Mary Payne) Upper Stanton Drew. Lies 6m S of Bristol between the B3130 and A368 just W of Pensford. Further detailed directions will be given when an appt. is made. A quart of good plants poured into a quarter pint sized plot featuring various colour themed borders, ornamental grasses, ferns, clematis and a well stocked "puddle"! Possibly the smallest, most intensively planted garden in the Yellow Book with the greatest range of plants for its size (total 0.02 acres). Plenty of ideas for small gardeners! Regret not suitable for children. *Adm £1. Only by appt. Wed June 28, Thurs July 13, Tues July 18 (10-9), please* **Tel 01275 333146**

Parsonage Farm ✻❀ (Andrew Reid Esq) Publow. 9m S of Bristol. A37 Bristol-Wells; at top of Pensford Hill, almost opp B3130 to Chew Magna, take lane which runs down side of row of houses; 250yds on R. 3½-acre woodland garden with large collection of trees and shrubs incl rhododendrons, azaleas and conifers; tuffa-stone rockery and heather garden. Partly suitable for wheelchairs. TEAS in aid of All Saints, Publow. *Adm £1 Chd free. Sat, Sun May 20, 21 (2-5)*

Pearl's Garden ♿✻❀ (Mr & Mrs D Watts) Coalpit Heath. NE Bristol. Take Downend (Westerleigh Rd) to Tomarton Rd past "Folly" public house over motorway and garden is 500yds on L. From junction 18 on M4, turn N on the A46 and almost immed L signposted Pucklechurch. After 5½m the garden is on R shortly before bridge over the motorway. 2 acres developed since 1966; mixed trees, flowering shrubs with 100 varieties of hollies; herb and water gardens; peafowl. Good views over Bristol from outside stairs. TEAS. *Adm £1.50 Chd free. Each Sun in May and June. For NGS Sun, Mon May 28, 29 (2-6). Also private visits welcome May and June, please* **Tel 01179 562953**

Portland Lodge ✻ (Mr & Mrs F S Jennett) 8 Knole Close. About 1m from Almondsbury interchange. Turn off A38 to Lower Almondsbury on Over Lane, R at War Memorial, L into Pound Lane and L again into Knole Close. Small, windswept hillside garden with panoramic view over R Severn. Designed by owner since 1979 to create a sheltered haven. Garden has 3 levels; circular lawns and densely planted mixed borders of small trees, shrubs and perennials. Gravel used to improve drainage on heavy clay soil. *Adm £1 Chd free. Open by appt. only April-October (except Suns) Private parties also welcome for parties of 4 or over, please* **Tel 01454 615175**

¶Petty France Hotel ♿❀ (W J Fraser Esq) Badminton. On A46 5m N exit 18 M4. Edge of Badminton Estate. Chipping Sodbury 5m. 2 acres of mature shrubs and trees incl specimen cedar, 200-yr-old yew hedge, medlar and tulip tree. Vegetable garden and herbs. Many spring flowers and shrubs. TEAS. *Adm £1 Chd free. Sun April 30 (2-6) Private parties also welcome please* **Tel 01454 238361**

¶Rock House ✻❀ (Mr & Mrs John Gunnery) Elberton. B4461 Severn Bridge to Alveston. From bridge, in Elberton, take 1st turning L to Littleton-on-Severn and turn immed R. 1-acre walled garden undergoing restoration. Pond and old yew tree. Good collection spring plants incl several species snowdrops, primroses, hellebores. *Adm £1 Chd free (Share to St John's Church, Elberton). Sun March 5 (2-6)*

Severn View ✻❀ (Mr & Mrs Eric Hilton) Thornbury, 1½m E of Thornbury. On A38 Bristol side of Wye Vale Nurseries. (Grovesend is postal address, but ignore signpost to it) 1-acre; notable for large rock garden with wide range of alpine plants, many rare, grown in screes, raised beds, troughs, rock walls, peat beds etc. Also shrubs, herbaceous borders; 3 alpine houses and many frames. Fine views of Severn Valley. *Adm £1 Acc chd free. Suns April 30, May 14, 21, 28, June 11 (2-5)*

Sherborne Garden ♿❀ (Mr & Mrs John Southwell) Litton. 15m S of Bristol, 7m N of Wells. On B3114 Litton to Harptree, ½m past Ye Olde Kings Arms. 4 acre landscaped garden developed from fields since 1964 offering wide variety of shrubs, trees and herbaceous plants, incl. many unusual items. Collections of hollies, ferns, hostas, species roses, grasses, daylilies; ponds, pinetum. Picnic area. Featured on 'Gardeners World' and 'Garden Club'. *Adm £1.50 Chd free. Suns & Mons June through Sept. For NGS: Suns April 2, May 7, June 4, Oct 1 (11-6). Home-made TEAS June 4. At other times tea and biscuits. Private visits and parties welcome throughout year, please* **Tel 01761 241220**

Stanton Drew Gardens ♿✻❀ 7m S Bristol A37 Bristol-Wells; at top of Pensford Hill take B3130 to Chew Magna. After 1m turn towards Stanton Drew at thatched round house. Cautiously negotiate humpbacked bridge and the gardens are just after the bridge. Parking is supervised. Refreshments in aid of Village Funds. *Combined adm £1.50 Chd free. Sun June 25 (12-6)*

¶Hall Cottage (Mr & Mrs I Watkins) This small garden is typically cottage, with a strong emphasis on vegetables neatly set in plots surrounded by grass paths, with colour from herbaceous and bedding borders, pond and fruit areas. 2 greenhouses provide the facilities for raising all the stock and many more interesting plants are available for sale

Rectory Farm House (Dr & Mrs J P Telling) ½-acre garden surrounding C15 Church House later used as a farmhouse. Garden completely redesigned and replanted over the past 2yrs. Trees, shrubs, mixed borders, pond and new rock garden

Stanton Court (Dr R J Price & Partners) A new garden established from 1986 to complement the recreational needs of a Nursing Home. Ideal for disabled visitors. Access for elderly persons a priority. Our aim is minimal maintenance with maximum variety. The wide range of plants have been largely donated by the locality. Pond; terrace garden; patio; large sweeping borders; cut flower beds and fruits in season. Mature copper beech and cedars

Stanton Prior Gardens ♿✿❀ 6m from Bath on A39 Wells Rd; at Marksbury turn L to Stanton Prior; gardens either side of Church set in beautiful countryside in unspoilt village. Ploughmans lunch & cream TEAS. *Combined adm £2 Chd free. Every Wed May 3 to Aug 30 (12-5). For NGS Wed June 21, Sun July 30 (11-5); private visits welcome all year, parties by appt, please* **Tel 01761 471942**

Church Farm (Mr & Mrs L Hardwick) Herbaceous borders, rock garden, scree garden; shrub roses, many unusual plants, wild area with ¼-acre pond; ducks and geese

The Old Rectory (Lt Col & Mrs Patrick Mesquita) 1-acre garden incl medieval pond. Landscaped and replanted since 1983, with unusual shrubs and plants, apple and pear arches and pergola with white roses and clematis; a newly-created knot garden

¶Stonewell House ♿✿❀ (Mr & Mrs J Dornton) Churchill Green. 14m S of Bristol, off A368 to Weston-super-Mare. Through village of Churchill, past Comp School, Sports Centre. Follow parking signs. Garden of approx 1¼ acres designed and laid out 10 yrs ago; features over 200 roses, many old-fashioned & species. Interesting layout, incorporating trees and shrubs, against setting of The Mendips. TEAS. *Adm £1.50 Chd free. Sun June 18 (2-6)*

Tranby House ✿❀ (Paul & Jan Barkworth) Norton Lane, Whitchurch. ½m S of Whitchurch Village. Leave Bristol on A37 Wells Rd, through Whitchurch Village 1st turning on R, signposted Norton Malreward. 1¼-acre informal garden, designed and planted to encourage wildlife. Wide variety of trees, shrubs, and flowers; ponds and new wild flower meadow; plants and pressed flower pictures for sale in aid of The Wildlife Trust. Partly suitable for wheelchairs. TEA. *Adm £1.50 Chd free. Sun June 11; Sat July 22, Suns July 23, Aug 20 (2-5.30)*

University of Bristol Botanic Garden ♿✿❀ Bracken Hill, North Rd, Leigh Woods, 1m W of Bristol via Clifton. Cross suspension bridge, North Rd is 1st R. As featured on Gardeners World 1993 and 1994, Superintendent Nicholas Wray, (presenter). 5-acre garden supporting approx 4,500 species; special collections incl cistus, hebe, ferns, salvia and sempervivum, plus many native plants. Range of glasshouses and large Pulhams rock garden. TEAS. *Adm £1 Chd 50p (Share to Friends of Bristol University Botanic Garden®). Private visits welcome all year, please* **Tel 01179 733682**. *For NGS Suns July 2, Sept 3 (11-5)*

The Urn Cottage ✿❀ (Mr A C & Dr L A Rosser) 19 Station Road, Charfield. 3m W of Wotton-under-Edge and 3m E of M5 exit 14. In Charfield turn off main road at the The Railway Tavern, then 400 yds on L: short walk from parking. ¾-acre cottage garden made from scratch by owners since 1982 and still developing. Natural materials used throughout to complement stone built cottage and country setting. Wide variety and profusion of plants in mixed borders of differing character, incl, small streamside gardens. TEAS. *Adm £1 Chd 10p. Mons Feb 13, March 27, April 24, May 29, Sept 25, Oct 16, (2-4) Sun June 11 (2-6) Disabled please telephone first. Parties by appt all year* **Tel 01453 843156**

Vine House ♿ (Mrs T F Hewer) Henbury Rd, Henbury, 4m N of Bristol. Bus stop: Salutation, Henbury, 50yds. 2-acres; trees, shrubs, water garden, bulbs, naturalised garden landscaped and planted by present owner since 1946. TEAS. *Adm £1 OAPs/Chd 50p (Share to Friends of Blaise®). Private visits welcome all year, please* **Tel 01179 503573**

West Tyning ♿✿❀ (Mr & Mrs G S Alexander) Beach. From Bath (6m) or Bristol (7m) on A431. From Bitton village turn N up Golden Valley, signposted Beach. Continue up lane for 2m to Wick–Upton Cheyney Xrds, turn R up Wick Lane for 200 yards. Parking in adjacent field. 1¼-acre garden, much altered through the years. Since 1986 aiming for a more informal woodsey look, easy plants. New shrubs, trees, roses, geraniums and other ground cover. Rock garden, curved mixed borders, woodland garden with stone paths and circular beds, planting continuing in newly cleared copse. TEAS with home-made cakes. *Adm £1 Chd free. Sat, Sun July 1, 2 (2-6). Private visits welcome for 10 or more. Please* **Tel 01179 322294**

Windmill Cottage ✿❀ (Alan & Pam Harwood) Hillside Rd, Backwell. 8m SW of Bristol. Take A370 out of Bristol to Backwell, ½m past Xrds/traffic lights, turn L into Hillside Rd. Parking available in Backwell recreation area, on R hand side of main rd (10 min walk). Hillside Rd is single track lane with no parking (unless by prior arrangement or special reasons). Parking also at New Inn. Into a 2-acre plot put a plentiful variety of plants, add to this a pinch of knowledge and a sprinkling of wildflowers, together with a reasonable amount of ground cover; blend in some colour and a generous dash of fragrance. Bind the whole thing together with a large collection of clematis, balanced with a proportion of vegetables. A good supply of enthusiasm to be added at regular intervals, allow to develop over a period of 8 to 10 yrs, adjusting quantities as the ingredients mature and set into a rocky outcrop. TEAS. *Adm £1 Chd 50p. Weds May 10, June 14, July 12; Aug 9, Sept 13 (2-5.30); June 28, July 26 (5-8). Groups welcome by appt, please* **Tel 01275 463492**

Regular Openers. Too many days to include in diary. Usually there is a wide range of plants giving year-round interest. See head of county section for the name and garden description for times etc.

Bedfordshire

Hon County Organiser: Mr & Mrs C Izzard, Broadfields, Keysoe Row East, Bedford MK44 2JD

DATES OF OPENING

By appointment
For telephone numbers and other details see garden descriptions. Private visits welcomed

Broadfields, Keysoe Row East
88 Castlehill Road, Middle End, Totternhoe
Kings Arms Path Garden, Ampthill
Seal Point, Luton

Parties only
Bendish Lodge, Kings Walden
Grove Lodge, 6 Deepdale, Potton
Toddington Manor, Toddington

Regular opening
For details see garden descriptions

Luton Hoo Gardens, Luton
Toddington Manor, Toddington. Easter Sat to Oct 1, (Closed Mon except Bank Hol Mon)

March 18 Saturday
Swiss Garden, Biggleswade

April 2 Sunday
Broadfields, Keysoe Row East

April 9 Sunday
Broadfields, Keysoe Row East

April 15 Saturday
Woburn Abbey, Woburn

April 16 Sunday
Bendish Lodge, Kings Walden
Kings Arms Path Garden, Ampthill

April 19 Wednesday
Bendish Lodge, Kings Walden

April 30 Sunday
Howard's House, Cardington

May 7 Sunday
The Old Stables, Hockliffe

May 14 Sunday
Luton Hoo Gardens, Luton
Odell Castle, nr Bedford

May 21 Sunday
Aspley Guise Gardens, Bletchley, Bucks

May 28 Sunday
88 Castlehill Road, Middle End, Totternhoe
Milton House, nr Bedford

May 30 Tuesday
Seal Point, Luton

June 4 Sunday
Bendish Lodge, Kings Walden
The Old Stables, Hockliffe
Southill Park, nr Biggleswade
Yielden Gardens

June 7 Wednesday
Bendish Lodge, Kings Walden

June 11 Sunday
Woodleys Farm House, Melchbourne

June 25 Sunday
Grove Lodge, 6 Deepdale, Potton
Howard's House, Cardington
Woburn Abbey, Woburn

June 27 Tuesday
Seal Point, Luton

June 28 Sunday
Swineshead Gardens

July 2 Sunday
Toddington Manor, Toddington

July 9 Sunday
88 Castlehill Road, Middle End, Totternhoe
47 Hexton Road, Barton-le-Clay ‡
The Old Stables, Hockliffe
The Rectory, Barton-le-Clay ‡

July 16 Sunday
Odell Castle, nr Bedford

July 22 Saturday
Broadfields, Keysoe Row East

July 23 Sunday
Broadfields, Keysoe Row East

July 25 Tuesday
Seal Point, Luton

August 6 Sunday
The Old Stables, Hockliffe

August 22 Tuesday
Seal Point, Luton

September 24 Saturday
Swiss Garden, Biggleswade

DESCRIPTIONS OF GARDENS

Aspley Guise Gardens 2m SW of M1 (Exit 13) towards Woburn Sands. Entrance from Church Rd. *Combined adm £2 Chd £1. Sun May 21 (2-6)*

Aspley House ✲ (Mr & Mrs C I Skipper) House on E side of village. 5 acres; shrubs and lawns. William and Mary house (not open). TEAS

The Rookery ✲ (C R Randall Esq) 5 acres; rhododendrons and woodland. Woburn Sands Band and local childrens orchestra in attendance

¶**Bendish Lodge** ✲❀ (Vicki & David De La'Mare) Kings Walden. Leaving M1 junction 10 follow signs to Luton Airport and Breachwood Green, heading towards Whitwell. Leaving A1(M) junction 6 follow signs to Codicote and Whitwell, 2m W. A charming small country garden surrounded by rolling fields. Old oak and walnut trees, early spring flowers, herbaceous plants enhancing mixed borders of colour and interest throughout the year. Old stables, delightful dovecote with doves, also farmhouse chickens. TEAS. *Adm £2.50 Chd free. Suns, Weds April 16, 19, June 4, 7 (2-5). Private visits welcome for parties of 10 and over, please* **Tel 01438 871742**

Broadfields ♿ (Mr & Mrs Chris Izzard) Keysoe Row East. Leave Bedford on Kimbolton Rd B660 approx 8½m. Turn R at Keysoe Xrds by White Horse public house ½m on R. 3 acres; herbaceous borders; spring bulbs, summer bedding, fuchsias; mature trees; shrubs; vegetable and fruit gardens. TEAS. *Adm £1.50 Chd 50p. Suns April 2, 9 (2-6) Sat July 22 (2-6) Sun July 23 (10-2). Private visits welcome, please* **Tel 01234 376326**

88 Castlehill Road ✲❀ (Chris & Carole Jell) Middle End, Totternhoe. 2m W of Dunstable, R turn off B489 Aston-Clinton Rd. Fronting main rd approx ½m through village. Elevated position with fine views across Aylesbury Vale and Chilterns. Adjoining Totternhoe Knolls Nature Reserve. ½-acre, S sloping on limestone and clay, entirely created by owners. Plantsman garden for all seasons; designed as small gardens within a garden since 1986; shrubs; climbers and herbaceous. TEAS. *Adm £1 Chd free. Suns May 28, July 9 (2-6). Also private visits welcome, please* **Tel 01525 220780**

Grove Lodge ✻❀ (Peter Wareing & Jean Venning) 6 Deepdale, Potton. 2m E of Sandy on 1042 towards Potton, past RSPB Reserve, downhill to Xrds. L at 'Locomotive' - lane to TV mast; first house on R. 1½-acre sandy hillside garden; conifers; heathers, shrubs, incl rhododendrons, climbing roses, herbaceous border, orchard with wild flowers, rockery banks with pond. **Deepdale Lodge** (Richard & Deanna Brawn) opposite; displays of hanging baskets; containers with colourful displays & new conservatory. TEAS in aid of R.A.T.S. *Combined adm £1.50 OAP £1 Chd 50p. Sun June 25 (2-6). Private visits welcome for parties of 12 and over, please* **Tel 01767 261298**

47 Hexton Road ♿❀ (Mrs S H Horsler) Barton-le-Clay. 6m N of Luton on the B655 Barton-le-Clay to Hitchin Rd (Hitchin 5m). Set in ¼ acre cottage garden with mixed borders. *Adm £1 Chd 50p. Sun July 9 (2-6)*

Howard's House ♿ (Humphrey Whitbread Esq) Cardington. 2m SE of Bedford. Large walled flower and vegetable gardens; flowering cherries and clematis, mature trees. Tea Bedford. *Adm £1.50 Chd 50p. Suns April 30, June 25 (2-6)*

Kings Arms Path Garden ♿✻❀ Ampthill Town Council (Mrs N W Hudson) Ampthill. Free parking in town centre. Entrance opp. old Market Place, Ampthill, down Kings Arms Yard. Small woodland garden of about 1½ acres created by plantsman the late William Nourish. Trees, shrubs, bulbs and many interesting collections. Maintained since 1987 by 'The Friends of the Garden.' Teas at adjacent Bowling Club or nearby tea shops. *Adm 50p Chd 25p. Suns Feb 12, (2-4). May 28, June 18, Aug 27, Oct 15 (2.30-5). For NGS Sun April 16 (2.30-5). Private group visits welcome, please* **Tel 01525 402030**

Luton Hoo Gardens ♿✻❀ Luton; junction 10 M1. Entrance at Park St gates. The mansion house where you can view the Wernher Collection is set in a Capability Brown landscape with formal gardens and a secluded rock garden. TEAS. *Adm gardens only £2.50 OAPs £2.25 Chd £1. Easter to Oct 15, Fris, Sats, Suns (12-5). For NGS Sun May 14 (12-5)*

Milton House ♿✻ (Mr & Mrs Clifton Ibbett) nr Bedford. N of Bedford on the A6. The drive to the house is on the R, S of the village of Milton Ernest. Formal, terrace and sunken gardens set in large grounds with lakes and waterfall. TEAS in aid of All Saints Parish Church, Milton Ernest. *Adm £2 Chd 50p. Sun May 28 (2-6)*

Odell Castle (The Rt Hon Lord Luke) Odell. NW of Bedford. From A6 turn W through Sharnbrook; from A428, N through Lavendon and Harrold. Station: Bedford 10m. Terrace and lower garden down to R. Ouse. House built 1962 on old site, using original stone. TEA. *Adm £1 Chd free. Suns May 14, July 16 (2-6)*

The Old Stables ✻❀ (Mr & Mrs D X Victor) 3m N of Dunstable. From A5 in Hockliffe, W on A4012. Turn R after ¼m (signposted Church End), then L at Church. Follow lane for ½m and take field track on R. 2 acres incl walled garden. Alpines, mixed herbaceous and shrub borders. Wide range of plants incl hardy geraniums, erodiums, dianthus, saxifrages, euphorbias, deutzias and clematis. National collections of alpine dianthus and oxalis. *Adm £1.50 Chd 50p. Suns May 7, June 4, July 9, Aug 6 (12-6)*

The Rectory ♿ (Canon Peter Whittaker) Barton-Le-Clay. Barton-Le-Clay is 6m N of Luton. From A6 turn E on to B655 then to Church Rd. Bus Bedford to Luton. 2 acres with background of Chilterns; moat, herbaceous border, mature trees, lawns; overlooked by C12 church. TEAS. *Adm £1.50 Chd 50p. Sun July 9 (2-6)*

Seal Point ✻❀ (Mrs Danae Johnston) 7 Wendover Way. In NE Luton, turning N off Stockingstone Rd into Felstead Way. A small sloping most exciting town garden with many unusual herbaceous plants, climbers and trees; water features, topiary cats and bonsai; beds with oriental flavour representing yin and yang; original ornaments, grasses, ferns, architectural plants and much more. TEA by arrangement. *Adm £1.50 Chd under 14 free. Tues May 30, June 27, July 25, Aug 22 (2-6). Private visits welcome, also small groups, please* **Tel 01582 661567**

Southill Park ♿❀ (Mr & Mrs S C Whitbread) 5m SW of Biggleswade. Large garden, rhododendrons, renovated conservatory. *Adm £2 Chd 50p. Sun June 4 (2-5.30)*

¶Swineshead Gardens ♿✻ 3m from Kimbolton between A6 and B660. TEAS. *Combined adm £2 Chd 50p (Share to St Nicholas Church Restoration®, Village Hall Fabric Fund®). Sun June 28 (2-6)*

¶Chapel Close Cottage (Mrs J Smith) High Street. Tiny cottage garden. Limited space has been filled with traditional, old-fashioned shrubs and perennials. Small but impressive collection of tub grown fuchsias

¶Manor Farm ❀ (Michael & Diana Marlow) High Street. 3-acre garden designed and created by present owners over 16yrs and still evolving. The yard of this C16 farm has been converted into a courtyard garden with brick paths winding between raised beds, the old well and lawns. A landscaped area with young yew hedging and lawns provides views of planted bank and stream flowing into large pond. Extensive kitchen garden, soft fruit garden and new orchard with old varieties of top fruit. Paddock, woodland park with wildlife pond. Rare breed poultry and geese

¶Stables House ❀ (Dawn & Peter Wells) High Street. A very new garden designed and created by the owners. The former stableyard is defined by a curved wall, pergola and trellis work, within which raised beds for shrubs, herbs and an ornamental pond have been built. The sloping rear paddock is planted to frame views of open fields and create a flow of colour with small trees, shrubs and herbaceous plants. A rockery accommodates changing levels

¶Manor House (Mr & Mrs W R F Chamberlain) Green Lane. An old, gracious garden with sweeping lawns, rose beds and herbaceous borders, screened by evergreens, conifers and mixed woodland. Kitchen garden

¶Sale Cottage (Mrs K Hinde) Sandy Lane. A small enclosed garden. Significant feature is the wide variety of container grown plants in tubs, sinks, troughs and hanging baskets

¶Swiss Garden ♿✂ (Bedfordshire County Council) Old Warden, Biggleswade. Signposted from A1 and A600. 2m W Biggleswade, next door to the Shuttleworth Collection. 9 acres of landscaped gardens set out in 1830s alongside a further 10 acres native woodland with lakeside picnic area. Garden includes many tiny buildings, footbridges, ironwork features and intertwining ponds. Romantic landscape design highlighted by daffodils, rhododendrons and old rambling roses in season. *Adm £2 Concessions £1 Chd 75p Family £4 (Share to Friends of the Swiss Garden©). Sats March 18, Sept 24 (10-6 last admission 5.15)*

Toddington Manor ♿❀ (Sir Neville & Lady Bowman-Shaw) Exit 12 M1. Signs in village. House and gardens restored by present owners. Walled garden with greenhouses and herb garden; beautiful roses and shrubs; lakeside walks in the woods. Rare Breeds Centre and Vintage Tractor collection. Cricket on pitch in front of house at weekends. Best months June and July. Gift Shop, home made TEAS. *Adm £3 OAP's £2 Chd £1.50. Special rates for parties. Open Easter Sat to Oct 1 (11-6). (Closed Mon except Bank Hol). Daily (11-6) For NGS Sun July 2 (11-6)*

Woburn Abbey ✂ (The Marquess of Tavistock) Woburn. Woburn Abbey is situated 1½m from Woburn Village, which is on the A4012 almost midway from junctions 12 and 13 of the M1 motorway. 22 acres of private garden originally designed by Wyattville, with recent restoration of the The Duchess' rose garden. Unique hornbeam maze with C18 temple by Chambers. TEAS. *Adm £1 Chd free. Sat April 15, Sun June 25 (11-5)*

Woodleys Farm House ♿✂❀ (Hon Mrs Hugh Lawson Johnston) Melchbourne. Leave A6 10m N of Bedford, or 4m S of Rushden. House reached by lime avenue before reaching village of Melchbourne. Small garden 1½ acres, with roses, lawns, shrubs and herbaceous plants. TEAS in aid of Church Restoration Fund. *Adm £1 Chd free. Sun June 11 (3-6)*

¶Yielden Gardens ✂❀ Beds, Northants border 14m N of Bedford, 4m S of Rushden. Adjacent to A6 and A45. Cream teas and plants available at the Old Post Office in aid of St Mary's Church. *Combined adm £2.50 Chd free. Sun June 4 (2-6)*

The Manor (Mr & Mrs E Woolf) 2.5 acres. Formal rose garden surrounding fish pond. Shrubberies leading to tennis court. Herbaceous borders, ornamental garden, greenhouses

¶The Old Rectory (Mr & Mrs P Rushton) 2.5 acres of established gardens. Many fine trees, ornamental pond, herb garden, shrubberies

¶Rifle Range Farm (Mr & Mrs R Paynter) 1-acre garden, established 20yrs. Mixed shrubberies and herbaceous borders, many wildlife features

By Appointment Gardens. See head of county section

Berkshire

Hon County Organiser: Bob Avery Esq, 'Jingles', Derek Rd., Maidenhead, SL6 8NT Tel 01628 27580

Asst Hon County Organisers: (Central) Mrs J Granville, Holly Copse, Goring Heath, Nr Reading Tel 01491 680303
The Hon Mrs J A Willoughby, Buckhold Farm, Pangbourne Tel 01734 744468
(NW) Mrs C M J Povey, Bussock Mayne, Snelsmore Common, Newbury Tel 01635 248347
(SW) Mrs P P A Meigh, Fishponds, West Woodhay, Nr Newbury Tel 01488 668269
Mrs M A Henderson, 'Ridings', Kentons Lane, Wargrave, RG10 8PB Tel 01734 402523
(Publicity & Brochures) Mrs J Bewsher, Arcturus, Church Road, Bray, Berks SL6 1UR Tel 01628 22824

Hon County Treasurer: Bob Avery Esq

DATES OF OPENING

By appointment

For telephone numbers and other details see garden descriptions. Private visits welcomed

Blencathra, Finchampstead
Fairing, Littlewick Green
Jasmine House, nr Windsor
Simms Farm House, Mortimer, nr Reading
Whiteknights, The Ridges, Finchampstead

Parties only

Englemere, Kings Pride, Ascot
Little Bowden, Pangbourne
Scotlands, Cockpole Green, nr Wargrave
Silwood Park, Ascot
Swallowfield Park, nr Reading
Wasing Place, Aldermaston

Regular openings

For details see garden description

Englefield House, Theale. Tues, Weds, Thurs April to June incl and every Mon all year

Meadow House, nr Newbury. See text for details
The Old Rectory, Burghfield. See text for details.
Waltham Place, White Waltham. Weds April to Sept

March 26 Sunday
Foxgrove, Enborne, nr Newbury
April 2 Sunday
Welford Park, nr Newbury
April 9 Sunday
Blencathra, Finchampstead
Kirby House, Inkpen ‡
West Woodhay House, Inkpen ‡
April 17 Monday
Swallowfield Park, nr Reading
April 23 Sunday
Folly Farm, nr Reading
Odney Club, Cookham
Old Rectory Cottage, nr Pangbourne
The Old Rectory Farnborough, Wantage
Scotlands, Cockpole Green, nr Wargrave
April 30 Sunday
Foxgrove, Enborne, nr Newbury
Simms Farm House, Mortimer, nr Reading
May 3 Wednesday
Frogmore Gardens, Windsor
May 4 Thursday
Frogmore Gardens, Windsor
May 7 Sunday
Bussock Wood, Snelsmore Common, nr Newbury
May 14 Sunday
Beenham House, Beenham ‡
Englefield House, Englefield, nr Theale ‡
Fox Hill, Inkpen
Hurst Gardens, nr Reading
Jasmine House, nr Windsor
The Old Rectory, Farnborough, Wantage
Padworth Common Gardens
Silwood Park, Ascot
Whiteknights, The Ridges, Finchampstead
May 21 Sunday
Aldermaston Park, Aldermaston ‡
Alderwood House, Greenham Common
Blencathra, Finchampstead
Old Rectory Cottage, nr Pangbourne
Silwood Park, Ascot ‡‡
Sunningdale Park, Ascot ‡‡
Wasing Place, Aldermaston ‡
May 28 Sunday
Bowdown House, Greenham Common
Englemere, Kings Ride, Ascot
Little Bowden, Pangbourne
Stone House, Brimpton
Waltham Place, White Waltham
May 29 Monday
Folly Farm, nr Reading
June 4 Sunday
Mariners, Bradfield
Trunkwell Park, Beech Hill
June 7 Wednesday
Swallowfield Park, nr Reading
June 11 Sunday
Foxgrove, Enborne, nr Newbury
Meadow House, nr Newbury
Padworth Common Gardens
June 17 Saturday
Eton College Gardens, Windsor
June 18 Sunday
Alderwood House, Greenham Common
Basildon Park, Lower Basildon
Old Rectory Cottage, nr Pangbourne
Peasemore Gardens
Summerfield House, Crazies Hill, nr Wargrave
Wasing Place, Aldermaston
June 25 Sunday
Folly Farm, nr Reading
Kirby House, Inkpen ‡
The Old Rectory, Farnborough, Wantage ‡‡
West Woodhay House, Inkpen ‡
Woolley Park, nr Wantage ‡‡
June 28 Wednesday
Rooksnest, Lambourn Woodlands
July 2 Sunday
Combe Manor, Combe
Stone House, Brimpton
July 9 Sunday
Chieveley Manor, nr Newbury
The Harris Garden, Whiteknights, Reading
Little Bowden, Pangbourne ‡
Old Rectory Cottage, nr Pangbourne ‡
Stanford Dingley Village Gardens
July 16 Sunday
Ockwells Manor, Maidenhead
July 23 Sunday
Bussock Mayne, Snelsmore Common
The Old Mill, Aldermaston
July 30 Sunday
Waltham Place, White Waltham
August 6 Sunday
Bloomsbury, Padworth Common Gardens
August 20 Sunday
Hurst Gardens, nr Reading
Scotlands, Cockpole Green, nr Wargrave
September 3 Sunday
Trunkwell Park, Beech Hill
October 8 Sunday
Silwood Park, Ascot

DESCRIPTIONS OF GARDENS

Aldermaston Park ♿❀ (Blue Circle Industries plc) Newbury 10m W; Reading 10m E; Basingstoke 8m off A340 S. 137-acres, surrounding Victorian Mansion (1849) with modern offices making interesting contrast of architecture. Fine trees; specimen rhododendrons and shrubs; large lawns; 11-acre lake with lakeside walk. TEA. *Adm £2 Chd free. Sun May 21 (10-4)*

Alderwood House ✿❀ (Mr & Mrs P B Trier) Greenham Common. S of Newbury take A 339 towards Basingstoke for approx 3m. Turn L towards the Main Gates of RAF Greenham Common. Turn R immediately before gate along track to house. Interesting 2½-acre garden started in 1904. On many levels with a number of rare trees and shrubs. Old roses, herbaceous border, conservatory and fine vegetable garden. TEAS. *Adm £1 Chd 50p. Suns May 21, June 18 (2-6)*

Basildon Park ♿ (Lord & Lady Iliffe; The National Trust) Lower Basildon, Reading. Between Pangbourne and Streatley, 7m NW of Reading on W of A329. Private garden designed and planted by Lady Iliffe with help of Lanning Roper. Open once a year for this occasion. Mainly old roses but other interesting plants constantly being added by owner. TEAS in NT house. *Adm 50p Chd free. ▲For NGS Sun June 18 (2-6)*

Beenham House ❀ (Prof & Mrs Gerald Benney) Beenham. ½-way between Reading and Newbury, 1m N of A4; entrance off Webbs Lane. 21 acres of grounds and garden; old Lebanon cedars, oaks, hornbeams; recent plantings. Good views of park and Kennett Valley. Regency house (not open). Coach parties by appt. TEAS. *Adm £1.50 Chd free (Share to St Mary's Church, Beenham®). Sun May 14 (2-6)*

Blencathra ♿❀ (Dr & Mrs F W Gifford) Finchampstead. Entrance from private drive at the NW end of Finchampstead Ridges on B3348 between Finchampstead War Memorial and Crowthorne Station. Parking on joint private drive or The Ridges. Disabled passengers may alight near the house. 11-acre garden which present owners started in 1964, laid out and maintained with minimum of help. In 'Good Gardens Guide' since 1993. Many varied mature trees; lawns; heathers; rhododendrons; azaleas; wide range of conifers; three small lakes and stream; bog areas and spring bulbs. Interesting throughout year. TEAS. *Adm £1.80 Chd free. Suns April 9, May 21 (2-6); also private visits welcome - parties welcome, please* **Tel 01734 734563**

Bowdown House ♿ (Mr & Mrs M Dormer) Newbury. 3m Newbury, Greenham Common N. On Bury's Bank Rd 2m past Greenham Golf Club. Lutyen's parterre gardens in style of Gertrude Jekyll; fine trees and rare shrubs. 50 acres of ancient woodland, now a nature reserve in care of BBONT. House by Sir Oswald Partridge Miln. TEA. *Adm £1.50 Chd free (Share to BBONT®). Sun May 28 (2-5.30)*

Bussock Mayne ♿✾❀ (Mr & Mrs C Povey) Snelsmore Common. 3m N of Newbury on B4494. A variety of specimen trees, herbaceous beds, shrubs, fine rock and water garden. Use of swimming pool and tennis court. Set in 5 acres. TEAS. *Adm £1.50 Chd free. Sun 23 July (2-6)*

Bussock Wood ❀ (Mr & Mrs W A Palmer) Snelsmore Common. 3m N of Newbury. On B4494 Newbury-Wantage Rd. Bluebells, fine trees and views; sunken garden with lily pond. Early Briton Camp. TEAS. *Adm £1 Chd 10p (Share to Winterbourne Parish Church®). Sun May 7 (2-6)*

Chieveley Manor ♿✾❀ (Mr & Mrs C J Spence) 5m N Newbury. Take A34 N pass under M4, then L to Chieveley. After ½m L up Manor Lane. Large garden with fine view over stud farm. Walled garden containing borders, shrubs and rose garden. Listed House (not open). TEAS. *Adm £1 Chd free (Share to St Mary's Church Chieveley®). Sun July 9 (2-6)*

Combe Manor ❀ (Lady Mary Russell) Combe. Approx 10m from Newbury or from Andover. From M4 in Hungerford, turn L after passing under railway bridge; over cattle grid onto Hungerford Common; turn R 400yds later and follow signs to Inkpen; pass The Swan on L, bear R at junction and then almost immediately L to Combe Gibbet and Combe. The Manor stands ½m from the village beside the church. 2 acres of lawns, borders, roses, shrubs and fruit trees. Walled garden with C17 gazebo, C11 church adjoining will be open. TEAS. *Adm £1.50 Chd free. Sun July 2 (2-6)*

Englefield House ✾❀ (Sir William and Lady Benyon) nr Theale. Entrance on A340. 7 acres of woodland garden with interesting variety of trees; shrubs; stream and water garden; formal terrace with fountain and borders. Commercial garden centre in village. Deer park. Part of garden suitable for wheelchairs. Home made TEAS Long Gallery NGS days only. *Open every Mon all yr and Mons, Tues, Weds, Thurs from April 1 to June incl (10-dusk). Adm £2 Chd free (Share to St Mark's Church®). ▲For NGS Sun May 14 (2-6). Private parties welcome, please* **Tel 01734 302504**

¶Englemere ❀ (The Chartered Institute of Building) Englemere. From M3 leave at junction 3 follow the A332 signposted Ascot. Englemere is located on the R. From M4 leave at junction 6 signposted Windsor travel on A355 then A332 through Windsor Great Park signposted Ascot. At the Racecourse roundabout continue on A335 signposted Bagshot. Englemere is a few 100yds from the roundabout on the L. 14-acre garden featuring pleasant lawns surrounded by mature trees providing walks in shady undergrowth. The garden is particularly noted for its variety of azaleas and rhododendrons. The grounds surround the historical mansion which is a former home of Field Marshall Lord Roberts of Kandahar and the estate was declared a royal residence by King George VI. Picnics welcomed or visitors may wish to take a cream tea in the house and see some of the tributes to Lord Roberts. Englemere is the HQ of The Chartered Institute of Building who have cared for the ground since 1972. TEAS. *Adm £1.50 Chd free. Sun May 28 (2-6). Parties welcome, please* **Tel 01344 23355**

Eton College Gardens ♿✾ (Provost & Fellows). Stations: Windsor ¾m Eton ½m. Bus: Green Line 704 & 705 London-Windsor 1m. Luxmoore's Garden is an island garden created by a housemaster about 1880; reached by beautiful new bridge; views of college and river. Provost's and Fellows' Gardens adjoin the ancient buildings on N and E sides. Parking off B3022 Slough to Eton rd, signposted. TEAS in aid of Datchet PCC. *Combined adm £1 Chd 20p. Sat June 17 (2-6)*

Fairing ♿✾❀ (Mr & Mrs M P Maine) Littlewick Green. Turn S into Littlewick Green off A4. 3m W of Maidenhead. 1-acre plant lover's garden developed since 1990. Colour-schemed borders give yr-round interest with large variety of hardy plants. Ornamental herb garden. TEA. *Adm £1 Chd free. Private visits welcome April to Sept, please* **Tel 01628 822008**

Folly Farm ♿✾❀ (The Hon Hugh & Mrs Astor) Sulhamstead, 7m SW of Reading. A4 between Reading/Newbury (2m W of M4 exit 12); take rd marked Sulhamstead at Mulligans Restaurant 1m after Theale roundabout; entrance 1m on right, through BROWN gate marked 'Folly Farm Gardens'. One of the few remaining gardens where the Lutyens architecture remains intact. Garden, laid out by Gertrude Jekyll, has been planted to owners' taste, bearing in mind Jekyll and Lutyens original design. Raised white garden, sunken rose garden; spring bulbs; herbaceous borders; ilex walk; avenues of limes, yew hedges, landscaped lawn areas, formal pools. Some recent simplifications and new planting. House (not open). TEAS. *Adm £1.50 Chd free (Share to West Berkshire Marriage Guidance Trust®). Sun April 23, Mon May 29, Sun June 25 (2-6)*

Foxgrove ♿✾❀ (Miss Audrey Vockins) Enborne, 2½m SW of Newbury. From A343 turn R at 'The Gun' 2m from town centre. Bus: AV 126, 127, 128; alight Villiers Way PO 1m. Small family garden with adjoining nursery (Foxgrove Plants); interesting foliage plants, troughs, raised beds, spring bulbs, naturalised in orchard; double primroses, snowdrop species and varieties; peat bed. TEAS. *Adm £1 Chd free. Suns March 26, April 30, June 11 (2-6)*

Fox Hill ♿❀ (Mrs Martin McLaren) Inkpen. Between Hungerford and Newbury, turn off A4 at sign saying Kintbury and Inkpen. Drive into Kintbury. Turn L by shop onto Inkpen Rd. After approx 1m, turn R at Xrds. After passing village signpost saying Inkpen, turn 1st L down bridleroad. Garden 2nd on L. Car park in field. 3-acre garden, blossom, bulbs, many interesting shrubs. Newly planted. Small formal garden and duck pond. TEAS. *Adm £1 Chd free. Sun May 14 (2-6)*

Frogmore Gardens ♿✗ (by gracious permission of Her Majesty The Queen) Windsor Castle; entrance via Park St gate into Long Walk (follow AA signs). Visitors are requested kindly to keep on the route to the garden and not stray into the Home Park. Station and bus stop; Windsor (20 mins walk from gardens); Green Line bus no 701, from London. Limited parking for cars only (free). 30 acres of landscaped gardens rich in history and beauty. Large lake, fine trees, lawns, flowers and flowering shrubs. The Royal Mausoleum, within the grounds, will also be open free of charge. Refreshment tent in car park on Long Walk (from where there is a 5 min walk to the gardens). **Coaches by appointment only** (apply to NGS, Hatchlands Park, East Clandon, Guildford, Surrey GU4 7RT enc. s.a.e. or **Tel 01483 211535** stating whether May 3 or 4; am or pm). *Adm £1.50 Chd free. Wed May 3, & Thurs May 4 (10.30-7; last adm 6.30)*

The Harris Garden & Experimental Grounds ♿✗❀ (University of Reading, School of Plant Sciences) Whiteknights, Reading RG6 2AS. Turn R just inside Pepper Lane entrance to University campus. 12-acre research and teaching garden extensively redeveloped since 1989. Rose gardens; shrub rose, herbaceous and annual borders, winter garden, bog garden, herb garden, walled garden etc. Gertrude Jekyll border new in 1993. Extensive glasshouses. Most plants labelled. TEAS. *Adm £1 Chd free. Sun July 9 (2-6)*

Highclere Castle, nr Newbury see Hampshire

¶Hurst Gardens ♿✗❀ In the village of Hurst which is on the A321 between Twyford and Wokingham. For the first time the owners of these 2 gardens, which offer an interesting contrast in size and approach, are opening jointly. TEAS at Hurst Lodge. *Combined adm £2 Chd free. Suns May 14, Aug 20 (2-5.30)*

Hurst Lodge (Mr & Mrs Alan Peck). Large 5 acre old garden which has been cared for by members of the same family for over 75 yrs. It features lawns and mature trees, a recently created rockery, pond and bog garden, a formal parterre, a walled garden with herbaceous borders, a large kitchen garden as well as camellias azaleas, rhododendrons, magnolias, flowering cherries, a variety of Japanese maples and bulbs

Reynolds Farm (Mr & Mrs Christopher Wells) was started by the present owners from scratch. This has allowed a considerable range of hard to come by trees, shrubs and plants to be grown. The owners freely admit to a lack of classical design, but like Topsy the garden just grew. Best described as an example of greed and indigestion; greed an inability to refuse a new plant, indigestion an inability to find somewhere to plant it

Jasmine House ✗ (Mr & Mrs E C B Knight) Hatch Bridge, 2m W of Windsor. Off A308 Windsor-Maidenhead opp Windsor Marina; follow signs from new roundabout by Jardinerie Garden Centre. ⅓-acre garden designed for all-yr interest with conifers (over 150 different), dwarf rhododendrons, hostas; sink gardens; trees notable for decorative bark; ornamental pools; collection of Bonsai. Garden featured in RHS Journal (March 1979); 'The Gardens of Britain' & 'Mon Jardin et Ma Maison' (Feb 82). Teas Country Gardens Garden Centre (1m). *Adm £1 Chd free. Sun May 14 (2-6). Private visits welcome May to August, please* **Tel 01753 841595**

Kirby House ✗ (Richard Astor Esq) Turn S off A4 to Kintbury; L at Xrds in Kintbury towards Combe. 2m out of Kintbury. Turn L immediately beyond Crown & Garter. House and garden at bottom of hill. 6 acres in beautiful setting. Formal rose borders, replanted herbaceous border in kitchen garden, newly planted colour theme border between yew buttress hedges. C18 Queen Anne house (not open). TEAS at **West Woodhay House.** *Combined adm with* **West Woodhay House** *£2 Chd 25p (Share to St Swithins Church®). Suns April 9, June 25 (2-6)*

Little Bowden ♿❀ (Geoffrey Verey Esq) 1½m W of Pangbourne on Pangbourne-Yattendon Rd. Large garden with fine views; woodland walk, azaleas, rhododendrons, bluebells. Heated swimming pool 50p extra. TEAS. *Adm £2 Chd free. Suns May 28, July 9 (2.30-6). Parties welcome, please* **Tel 01734 843441**

Mariners ♿✗❀ (Mr & Mrs W N Ritchie) 7m W of Reading. From Theale (M4 exit 12 take A340) towards Pangbourne 1st L to Bradfield. Pass through wood and turn L by farm. 1st R after War Memorial into Mariners Lane. 1-acre charming well-designed garden, owner maintained; made from heavy clay field, now matured; large variety of plants; herbaceous and shrub border; rose, clematis; silver leaved plants. TEAS & ice cream. *Adm £1 Chd 20p. Sun June 4 (2-6)*

Meadow House ♿✗❀ (Mr & Mrs G A Jones) Ashford Hill is on the B3051 8m SE of Newbury. Take turning at SW end of village signposted Wolverton Common and Wheathold. Meadow House on R approx 300yds along lane. Approx 1½-acre plantsman's garden. Pond with waterside planting; mixed shrub and herbaceous borders. Many unusual plants. TEAS. *Adm £2 Chd free (Share to Newbury Victim Support®). ▲For NGS Sun June 11 (2-6).* **Tel 01734 816005**

North Ecchinswell Farm, nr Newbury see Hampshire

Ockwells Manor ♿✗❀ (Mr & Mrs B P Stein) Maidenhead. Exit 8/9 off M4. A404M towards Henley. 1st slip rd to L to Cox Green and White Waltham. R at 1st roundabout. L at 2nd roundabout. Follow rd to end and turn R. 3½ acres of formal garden around mediaeval Manor House. Listed grade 1 (not open); walled garden; clipped yews; small maze; lime avenue; swimming pool; peacocks, ornamental ducks and geese; farm animals; woodland walk. TEAS. *Adm £1.50 Chd free. Sun July 16 (2-6)*

Regular Openers. See head of county section.

Odney Club ♿❀ (John Lewis Partnership) Cookham. Car park in grounds. 120 acres; lawns, garden and meadows on R. Thames; specimen trees. Cream TEAS River Room. *Adm £1.50 Chd free (Share to Sue Ryder Foundation®). Sun April 23 (2-6)*

The Old House, Silchester see Hampshire

The Old Mill ♿ (Mrs E M Arlott) Aldermaston. On A4 between Reading and Newbury, take A340 then follow signs. 7 acres; lawns; walks; flower beds; shrubs; R Kennet flows through with sluices and hatches. Fine Old Mill House (not open). TEAS. *Adm £1 Chd free. Sun July 23 (2-6)*

Old Rectory Cottage ✂❀ (Mr & Mrs A W A Baker) Tidmarsh, ½m S of Pangbourne, midway between Pangbourne and Tidmarsh turn E down narrow lane; L at T-junction. 2-acre cottage garden and wild garden with small lake bordered by R Pang. Unusual plants, spring bulbs, roses climbing into old apple trees, ferns, hellebores and lilies. White doves and golden pheasants. Featured on TV and in many gardening books. *Adm £1 Chd free (Share to BBONT®). Suns April 23, May 21, June 18, July 9 (2-6)*

The Old Rectory, Burghfield ♿✂❀ (Mr & Mrs R R Merton), 5m SW of Reading. Turn S off A4 to Burghfield village; R after Hatch Gate Inn; entrance on R. Medium-sized garden; herbaceous and shrub borders; roses, hellebores, lilies, many rare and unusual plants collected by owners from Japan and China; old-fashioned cottage plants; autumn colour. Georgian house (not open). TEA. *Adm £1 Chd 50p (Share to Save the Children® & NCCPG Local Group®). The last Weds of every month except Nov-Dec & Jan (11-4)*

The Old Rectory, Farnborough ✂❀ (Mrs Michael Todhunter) 4m SE of Wantage. From B4494 Wantage-Newbury Rd, 4m from Wantage turn E at sign for Farnborough. Outstanding garden with unusual plants: fine view; old-fashioned roses; collection of small flowered clematis; herbaceous borders. Beautiful house (not open) built c.1749. Teas in village. *Adm £1.50 Chd free (Share to All Saints, Farnborough®). Suns April 23, May 14, June 25 (2-6)*

Padworth Common Gardens ♿✂❀ Rectory Rd, Padworth Common. ½-way between Reading and Newbury. 1½m S of A4 take Padworth Lane at Padworth Court Hotel. TEAS. *Combined adm £1.50 Chd free. Suns May 14, June 11 (2-6)*

Bloomsbury (Mr & Mrs M J Oakley) Upper Lodge Farm. Medium-sized, with white garden; orchard garden with woodland planting and old shrub roses; courtyard garden with pots; large polytunnel with specimen conservatory plants; unusual trees and shrubs; nursery. Field walk to C11 church. *Also open Sun Aug 6 (2-6)*

Honeyhanger (Mrs Jenny Martin) Rectory Rd. Medium-sized with unusual trees, shrubs. Courtyard with pots. Woodland, some mature and some new plantings. Tropical house, aviary, pond

Peasemore Gardens 7m N of Newbury on A34 to M4 junction 13. N towards Oxford then immed L signed Chievely. Through Chievely and onto Peasemore approx 3½m. TEAS. *Combined adm £1.50 Chd free. Sun June 18 (2-6)*

The Old Rectory, Peasemore ♿❀ (Mr & Mrs I D Cameron) Georgian house with fine trees in lovely setting. Shrub roses, peonies, large rose border and herbaceous border

Paxmere House ♿❀ (The Hon Mrs John Astor) Opp The Old Rectory. 2-acre cottage garden. Roses, shrubs, etc

Peasemore House ♿ (Mr & Mrs Richard W Brown) Past 3 thatched cottages on R entering Peasemore. Garden on R behind flint and brick wall. 2½ acres traditional garden with lovely trees, shrubs and roses with extensive views over arable downland

Rooksnest ✂❀ (Dr & Mrs M D Sackler) Earls Court Farm, Lambourn Woodlands. Situated approx 3m from the A338 (Wantage) Rd along the B4000. Nearest village, Lambourn. Rooksnest signposted on the B400 in both directions, ie whether approaching from Lambourn or from the A338. Approx 10-acre exceptionally fine traditional English garden. Recently restored with help from Arabella Lennox-Boyd. Includes terraces; rose garden; lilies; herbaceous borders; herb garden; many specimen trees and fine shrubs. TEAS. *Adm £1.50 Chd 50p. Wed June 28 (2-5)*

Scotlands ♿❀ (Mr Michael & The Hon Mrs Payne) In centre of triangle formed by A4130 (was A423) E of Henley-on-Thames, the A321 to Wargrave A4 at Knowl Hill - midway between Warren Row Village and Cockpole Green. 4 acres; clipped yews; shrub borders; grass paths through trees to woodland and pond-gardens with Repton design rustic summer house. Rocks with waterfall and new gazebo. Featured in Good Garden Guide. TEAS. *Adm £2 Chd free. Suns April 23, Aug 20 (2-6). Private parties welcome, please* **Tel 01628 822648**

Silwood Park ♿ (Imperial College) Ascot. 1½m E of Ascot in the junction of A329 and the B383. Access from the B383 200 metres N of the Cannon Inn. 240 acres of parklands and natural habitats, surrounding fine C19 house by Waterhouse, architect of the Natural History Museum. Japanese garden under restoration; pinetum, young arboretum specialising in oaks and birches. Two nature walks (1m & 2m) through oak and beech woodland to lake. TEAS. *Adm £1 Chd 50p. Suns May 14, 21; Oct 8 (2-6). Parties by appt, please* **Tel 01344 23911**

Simms Farm House ♿✂❀ (H H Judge Lea & Mrs Lea) Mortimer, 6m SW of Reading. At T-junction on edge of village, from Grazeley, turn R uphill; L by church into West End Rd; at next Xrd L down Drury Lane; R at T-junction. 1-acre garden with mixed shrub borders, small rockery; Bog garden; formal pond; unusual plants. Lovely view. TEA. *Adm £1 Chd 50p. Sun April 30 (2-6); Private visits welcome, please* **Tel 01734 332360**

Stanford Dingley Village Gardens ✂❀ Between Reading and Newbury. Pretty village with ancient Church and bridge over R Pang. Parking in field. TEAS. *Combined adm £1.50 Chd 50p. Sun July 9 (2-6) including:*

Bradfield Farm (Mr & Mrs Newton) ½-acre. Wide variety of plants. Further 5-acres mixed broadleaf planting in 1990

Bridge Cottage (Mr & Mrs M Ranwell) Pretty ½-acre cottage garden. Deep mixed borders. Interesting terrace and tub planting

The Manor House ❀ (Mr & Mrs Park) Close to church, 3-acre garden planted informally; water gardens. TEAS

Stone House ♿❀ (Mr & Mrs Nigel Bingham) Brimpton, 6m E of Newbury. Turn S off A4 at junction by Coach & Horses, signed Brimpton and Aldermaston. ½m W of T-junction by War Memorial signed Newbury. Medium-sized garden in attractive park; naturalised bulbs; rhododendrons; water garden; extensive collection plants and shrubs; walled kitchen garden; picnic area. TEA. *Adm £1 Chd free (Share to Brimpton Church®). Suns May 28, July 2 (2-6)*

Summerfield House ❀ (Mr & Mrs R J S Palmer) Crazies Hill. Midway between Henley-on-Thames and Wargrave. 2m E of Henley on A423, take turn at top of hill signed Cockpole Green, then turn R at Green. Garden opp village hall. 7 acres, herbaceous and shrub borders, many recently planted rare trees, large working greenhouse, 1½-acre lake plus 20 acres parkland. House (not open) formerly Henley Town Hall, originally constructed in 1760 in centre of Henley and moved at end of C19. TEAS. *Adm £1.50 Chd under 12 free. Sun June 18 (2-6)*

Sunningdale Park ❀ (Civil Service College) Ascot. 1½m E of Ascot off A329 at Cannon Inn or take Broomhall Lane off A30 at Sunningdale. Over 20 acres of beautifully landscaped gardens reputedly laid out by Capability Brown. Terrace garden and victorian rockery designed by Pulham incl cave and water features. Lake area with paved walks; extensive lawns with specimen trees and flower beds; impressive massed rhododendrons. Beautiful 1m woodland walk. Cream TEAS. *Adm £1.80 Chd free. Sun May 21 (2-5)*

Swallowfield House ♿❀ (Country Houses Association) 5m S of Reading off B3349, entrance nr village hall. Level grounds of 25 acres which incl a large walled garden and herbaceous borders, rose beds, vegetable gardens, massed rhododendrons and many specimen trees. There are wide lawns and gravel paths, with a small lake and a wooded walk to the R Loddon. Visit dogs' graves. The distinguished house (open) was built in 1689 for Lord Clarendon. Home-made TEAS. *Adm £2.50 Chd free. (Share to Country Houses Association®). Mon April 17, Wed June 7 (2-5). Parties welcome, please* **Tel 0171 836 1624**

Trunkwell Park ♿❀ (Trunkwell Project) Beech Hill. From Reading: M4 junction 11 follow Basingstoke sign approx. ¼m at roundabout turn L and follow Three Mile Cross-Spencers Wood. Centre of Spencers Wood look for Beech Hill Rd on R and follow into Beech Hill Village (centre) and follow signs. From Basingstoke follow A33 to Wellington roundabout turn L following Beech Hill signs. At village turn R. Located in grounds of Trunkwell House Hotel. Parking and toilets. Conducted tours. This 3-acre site with large Victorian walled garden is run by the Charity Horticultural Therapy as a teaching and therapeutic centre where people with special needs are encouraged to participate in a wide range of horticultural activities designed to improve skills and to gain confidence. Located on Berkshire/Hants border in very attractive surroundings, Trunkwell caters to an increasing number of clients daily, so why not come and witness that disability is no handicap to rewarding and successful gardening. Part of garden dedicated to Wildlife Conservation. Plants for sale, bedding in June. TEAS. *Adm £1 Chd free. Suns June 4, Sept 3 (2-6)*

Waltham Place ♿❀ White Waltham. 3½m S of Maidenhead. Exit 8/9 on M4, then A423(M) or M40 exit 4 then A404 to A4 Maidenhead exit and follow signs to White Waltham. 40 acres of gardens incorporating woodland, lake. Magnificent trees particularly a splendid weeping beech, kitchen gardens; glasshouses, wonderful walled garden with spectacular red border, Japanese herb, butterfly gardens. Many interesting and unusual plants. Both farm and garden are an enclosed organic system. Home-made cream TEAS, plants and dried flowers (May 18 & July 30 only). *Adm £2 Chd 50p (Share to Thames Valley Adventure Playground®). Suns May 28, July 30 (2-7), Wednesdays during April to September (2-5)*

Wasing Place ♿❀ (Lady Mount) Aldermaston, SE of Newbury. Turn S off A4 at Woolhampton; or 3m E take A340 to Aldermaston. ½m drive. Large garden; unusual shrubs and plants, rhododendrons; azaleas; lawns, walled and kitchen garden; greenhouses, herbaceous borders. C12 church. TEAS in aid of St Nicholas Church, Wasing. *Adm £1.50 Chd free. Suns May 21, June 18 (2-6). Private visits for 20 or over welcome, please* **Tel 0173521 3398**

Welford Park ♿❀ (Mrs J L Puxley) 6m NW of Newbury on Lambourn Valley Rd. Entrance on Newbury/Lambourn Rd (fine gates with boot on top). Spacious grounds; spring flowers; walk by R. Lambourn. Queen Anne house (not open). TEAS. *Adm £1 Chd free (Share to Welford Church©). Sun April 2 (2-4.30)*

West Silchester Hall, nr Reading see Hampshire

West Woodhay House ♿✲ (H Henderson Esq) 6m SW of Newbury. From Newbury take A343. At foot of hill turn R for East Woodhay and Ball Hill. 3½m turn L for West Woodhay. Go over Xrds in village, next fork R past Church. Gate on L. Parkland; large garden with bulbs, roses, shrubs, lake, woodland garden. Large walled kitchen garden, greenhouses. TEAS. *Combined adm £2 Chd 25p (Share to West Woodhay Church®) with* **Kirby House**. *Suns April 9, June 25 (2-6)*

Whiteknights ✲❀ (Mr & Mrs P Bradly) Finchampstead. Midway along Finchampstead Ridges on B3348 between Finchampstead War Memorial and Crowthorne Station. 2½ acres, lawns, Japanese water garden, dwarf conifers, interesting plantings, fruit and vegetable garden. Tudor Life in Miniature Exhibition. Cream TEAS in aid of Guide Dogs for the Blind. *Adm £1.50 Chd 50p. Sun May 14 (2-5.30). Private visits and parties welcome, please* **Tel 01734 733274**

Woolley Park ♿✗ (Mr & Mrs Philip Wroughton) 5m S of Wantage on A338 turn L at sign to Woolley. Large park, fine trees and views. Two linked walled gardens beautifully planted. Teas close to Old Rectory, Farnborough. *Adm £1. Sun June 25 (2-6)*

By Appointment Gardens. These owners do not have a fixed opening day usually because they do not like crowds or have insufficient parking space. Owner will often give guided tour.

Buckinghamshire

Hon County Organiser: Mrs H Beric Wright, Brudenell House, Quainton, nr Aylesbury, Bucks HP22 4AW Tel 01296 655250

Assistant Hon County Organisers: Mrs D W Fraser, The Old Butcher's Arms, Dark Lane, Oving, Aylesbury HP22 4HP Tel 01296 641026

Mrs C S Sanderson, Wellfield House, Cuddington, Aylesbury HP18 0BB Tel 01844 291626

Hon County Treasurer: Dr H Beric Wright

DATES OF OPENING

By appointment

For telephone numbers and other details see garden descriptions. Private visits welcomed

Blossoms, nr Great Missenden
Chalfont St Giles Gardens
Charlton, Dorney Reach, nr Maidenhead
Chasea, Cheddington Gardens, Leighton Buzzard
Dorneywood Garden, Burnham
Gracefield, Lacey Green, Princes Risborough
Great Barfield, High Wycombe
Hall Barn, Beaconsfield
Harewood, Chalfont St Giles
The Manor Farm, Little Horwood, nr Winslow
The Manor House, Bledlow, nr Princes Risborough
The Manor House, Princes Risborough
Old Farm, Brill Gardens
Old Manor Farm, Cublington
6 Oldfield Close, Little Chalfont
Pasture Farm, Longwick, nr Princes Risborough
Peppers, Great Missenden
Rose Cottage, Cheddington Gardens, Leighton Buzzard
Spindrift, Jordans, Beaconsfield
22 Spring Gardens, Newport Pagnell
Springlea, Seymour Plain, Marlow
Tramway Farm, Brill, nr Thame
Turn End, Haddenham
Walmerdene, Buckingham
The Wheatsheaf Inn, Weedon
Whitewalls, Marlow
Wichert, Ford, nr Aylesbury
56 Windmill St, Brill Gardens

Parties only

Campden Cottage, Chesham Bois
Ketchmere Close, Long Crendon Gardens
Overstroud Cottage, Great Missenden

Regular Openings

For details see garden description

Turn End, Haddenham. Every Wed April to June

February 19 Sunday
Great Barfield, High Wycombe

March 12 Sunday
Campden Cottage, Chesham Bois
Springlea, Seymour Plain, Marlow

March 19 Sunday
Oving Gardens, nr Aylesbury

April 9 Sunday
Campden Cottage, Chesham Bois ‡
The Old Vicarage, Padbury
6 Oldfield Close, Little Chalfont ‡
Quoitings, Marlow
Springlea, Seymour Plain, Marlow
Walmerdene, Buckingham

April 16 Sunday
Overstroud Cottage, Great Missenden

April 23 Sunday
Great Barfield, High Wycombe
Leap Hill, Brill Gardens, nr Thame ‡
Long Crendon Gardens, nr Thame ‡

April 30 Sunday
Nether Winchendon House, nr Aylesbury
Whitewalls, Marlow

May 7 Sunday
Cliveden, Taplow
The Manor House, Bledlow, nr Princes Risborough ‡
Overstroud Cottage, Great Missenden
Pasture Farm, Longwick, nr Princes Risborough ‡
Springlea, Seymour Plain, Marlow
Winslow Hall, nr Buckingham

May 8 Monday
Spindrift, Jordans, Beaconsfield

May 14 Sunday
Ascott, nr Leighton Buzzard
Chalfont St Giles Gardens ‡
Peppers, Great Missenden ‡
Quainton Gardens, nr Aylesbury
The White House, Denham Village

May 16 Tuesday
Stowe Landscape Gardens, Buckingham

May 21 Sunday
Campden Cottage, Chesham Bois
The Edge, Chalfont St Giles ‡
Favershams Meadow, Gerrards Cross ‡

May 28 Sunday
Brill Gardens, nr Thame
The Manor House, Princes Risborough ‡
Sheredon, Longwick, nr Princes Risborough ‡

June 4 Sunday
Chartridge Centre, Chesham ‡
6 Oldfield Close, Little Chalfont ‡
Pollards, Whiteleaf, nr Princes Risborough
Springlea, Seymour Plain, Marlow
Whitchurch Gardens, nr Aylesbury

June 11 Sunday
Campden Cottage, Chesham Bois
The Claydons, nr Winslow
Cublington Gardens, nr Aylesbury
Hall Farm, Little Linford, nr Newport Pagnell
Overstroud Cottage, Great Missenden
Turn End, Haddenham

June 17 Saturday
The Old Vicarage, Padbury

June 18 Sunday
Askett Gardens nr Princes Risborough ‡
Barn's Piece, Nether Winchendon, nr Thame ‡‡
Chalfont St Giles Gardens ‡‡‡
Cuddington Gardens, nr Thame ‡‡
Fevershams Meadow, Gerrards Cross ‡‡‡
59 The Gables, Haddenham ‡‡‡‡
Gipsy House, Great Missenden
Hillesden House, nr Buckingham ‡‡‡‡‡
The Manor House, Bledlow, nr Princes Risborough ‡
The Old Vicarage, Padbury ‡‡‡‡‡
Pasture Farm, Longwick, nr Princes Risborough ‡
Turn End, Haddenham ‡‡‡‡
Walmerdene, Buckingham ‡‡‡‡‡
Weir Lodge, Chesham

June 19 Monday
Walmerdene, Buckingham

June 21 Wednesday
59 The Gables, Haddenham

June 25 Sunday
Cheddington Gardens, nr Leighton Buzzard
Dinton Gardens, nr Aylesbury
Gracefield, Lacey Green, Princes Risborough
Long Crendon Gardens, nr Thame ‡
Loughton Gardens, nr Milton Keynes
The Manor House, Hambledon, nr Henley-on-Thames
Old Farm, Brill Gardens, nr Thame ‡
Quainton Gardens, nr Aylesbury
Westcott House, Gawcott, nr Buckingham

June 26 Monday
Westcott House, Gawcott, nr Buckingham

June 28 Wednesday
Cublington Gardens, nr Aylesbury

July 2 Sunday
The Edge, Chalfont St Giles
Flint House, Penn Street Village, nr Amersham ‡
Great Barfield, High Wycombe
Overstroud Cottage, Great Missenden
Springlea, Seymour Plain, Marlow
Watercroft, Penn ‡

July 5 Wednesday
Dorneywood Garden, Burnham **by written appointment only**

July 9 Sunday
Chearsley Gardens, nr Thame
The Manor House, Princes Risborough
Prestwood Gardens, nr Great Missenden
Watercroft, Penn
The White House, Denham Village

July 12 Wednesday
Chearsley Gardens, nr Thame

July 15 Saturday
Bucksbridge House, Wendover

July 16 Sunday
Bucksbridge House, Wendover
Campden Cottage, Chesham Bois
Chicheley Hall, Newport Pagnell
The Manor Farm, Little Horwood, nr Winslow
Sheredon, Longwick, nr Princes Risborough

July 19 Wednesday
Dorneywood Garden, Burnham **by written appointment only**

July 23 Sunday
Hughendon Manor, High Wycombe
Nether Winchendon House, nr Aylesbury
Whitewalls, Marlow

July 30 Sunday
Springlea, Seymour Plain, Marlow

August 5 Saturday
Dorneywood Garden, Burnham **by written appointment only**

August 6 Sunday
Campden Cottage, Chesham Bois

August 12 Saturday
Dorneywood Garden, Burnham **by written appointment only**

August 20 Sunday
Ascott, nr Leighton Buzzard
Chartridge Centre, Chesham

August 27 Sunday
Peppers, Great Missenden

August 28 Monday
Spindrift, Jordans, Beaconsfield

September 3 Sunday
Campden Cottage, Chesham Bois
Overstroud Cottage, Great Missenden
Quoitings, Marlow
Springlea, Seymour Plain, Marlow
West Wycombe Park, West Wycombe

September 10 Sunday
59 The Gables, Haddenham
Pasture Farm, Longwick, nr Princes Risborough

September 13 Wednesday
59 The Gables, Haddenham

September 17 Sunday
Cliveden, Taplow
Great Barfield, High Wycombe
Turn End, Haddenham

October 1 Sunday
Campden Cottage, Chesham Bois

February 18 Sunday 1996
Great Barfield, High Wycombe

DESCRIPTIONS OF GARDENS

Ascott ♿✿ (Sir Evelyn and Lady de Rothschild; The National Trust) Wing, 2m SW of Leighton Buzzard, 8m NE of Aylesbury via A418. Bus: United Counties 141 Aylesbury-Leighton Buzzard. Beautiful surroundings and layout. Garden part formal, part natural; many specimen trees, shrubs, naturalised bulbs, sunken garden; lily pond. *Adm £3 Chd £1.50 Under 5 free.* ▲*For NGS Suns May 14, Aug 20 (2-6). Last adm 5pm*

¶**Askett Gardens** ❀ 1m from Princes Risborough on A4010 to Aylesbury. At Black Horse roundabout, turn into Askett village. Parking off Letter Box Lane 1st turning L. TEAS. Plant stall in car park. *Combined adm £2 Chd free (Share to Hodgkinson's Disease Association®). Sun June 18 (2-6)*

¶**The Bell House** (Mr & Mrs J R Hughes) Approx ⅓ acre. Charming old-fashioned country cottage garden with stream and herbaceous border, informally planted

¶**The Bell House Barn** ♿ (Mrs Christine Ramsay) Approx ⅔-acre. Large romantic cottage garden with hardy perennials, shrubs and roses, (formerly part of Bell House garden). Backcloth of mature trees in parkland setting

¶**Meadow View** ✿ (Dr & Mrs R K Clarke) ⅓-acre garden with mixture of herbaceous borders, summer bedding, roses, shrubs and small pool

¶**Mulberry House** ♿✲ (Mr & Mrs M D Ashby) 1-acre garden with large variety of shrubs, herbaceous borders, rockery and pond. Several specimen trees incl mulberry

¶**Old Rose Cottage** ♿✲ (Mr & Mrs G A Davies) 1-acre garden with long N facing walled border mainly herbaceous and shrubs, specimen trees of whitebeam, spruce, beech and maple. Collection of hardy geraniums, old roses and holly. Herb garden, island heather and conifer bed. TEAS

¶**The Old Wick** ♿❀ (Mr & Mrs P Dewe) A larger village garden planted for all-yr interest with fine spruce and conifer trees, small stream and pond

¶**Three Ways Cottage** ♿ (Dr & Mrs P N J Appleton) 1-acre garden in what had been the orchard behind 3 cottages. Informal garden with mixed beds of herbaceous plants and shrubs, some self seeded annual poppies. Small kitchen garden of fruit trees, herbs and vegetables. TEAS

¶**Barn's Piece** ✲ (Mr & Mrs N Cox) Nether Winchendon. 5m SW of Aylesbury , 5m from Thame, (1½m from Cuddington) house lies half-way up Barrack Hill. Limited parking so please follow directions in village. ¾-acre garden with wide range of interesting and unusual plants and trees. Mixed borders, roses, terraces with troughs and pots, recently restored pond area; small brick-paved vegetable garden. Wonderful views. Teas and plants at **Cuddington**. *Adm £1 Chd free. Sun June 18 (2-6)*

Blossoms ♿✲❀ (Dr & Mrs Frank Hytten) Cobblers Hill, 2½m NW of Great Missenden by Rignall Road (signed to Butlers Cross) to King's Lane (1½m) then to top of Cobblers Hill, R at yellow stone marker and in 50yds R at stone marked Blossoms. [Map ref SP874034]. 4-acre garden begun as hill-top fields in 1923, plus 1-acre beechwood. Lawns, trees, old apple orchard, small lake, water gardens, woodland, troughs, scree garden and several patios. Large areas of bluebells, wild daffodils, fritillaria and other spring bulbs. Flowering cherries and many interesting trees incl small collections of acer, eucalyptus and salix; foliage effects throughout the year. TEAS. *Adm £1.50. Private visits only, please* **Tel 01494 863140**

Brill Gardens 7m N of Thame. Turn off B4011, (Thame to Bicester), or turn off the A41 at Kingswood, both signed to Brill. C17 windmill open Suns 2.30-5.30

Sun April 23 (2-6)

Leap Hill ♿✲❀ (Mr & Mrs R Morris-Adams) Thame Rd. Garden approx 1m from Brill centre. 2 acres, roses, shrubs, herbaceous and spring bulbs; pond, new bog area and rockery, vegetable garden and new woodland area. Extensive views towards Chilterns. Sculptures by Fred Close. Teas at **Long Crendon Gardens**. *Adm £1 Chd free*

Sun May 28 (2-6)

TEAS in village hall in aid of WI. *Combined adm £1.80 Chd free*

Old Farm ✲ (Dr & Mrs Raymond Brown) South Hills, off Windmill St. Parking by windmill. ½-acre established garden around 3 terraces of old shrub roses; secluded position with high open views over Otmoor; kitchen garden, soft fruit, mature and younger trees, interesting shrubs, small pond; conservatory added to C17 stone and brick cottage (not open). Garden featured in 'Homes & Gardens' Aug 94. *Private visits welcome, please* **Tel 01844 238232**

The Old Vicarage ♿✲❀ (Mr & Mrs P Toynbee) The Square. ¾-acre, partly-walled garden with areas of interest in sun and shade. Arches and ornamental features. Ideas to interest children, as seen on 'Gardeners World'

56 Windmill Street ✲ (Mr & Mrs C D Elliott) Pocket-handkerchief, walled clay garden featuring imaginative use of space, colour-schemed borders in raised beds incl interesting foliage, uncommon plants, pergola, patio, many containers. Featured in 'Gardeners World' book. *Private visits welcome, please* **Tel 01844 237407**

Sun June 25 (2-6)

Old Farm (Dr & Mrs Raymond Brown) For description see above. Teas available at The Pheasant. *Adm £1 Chd free*

Bucksbridge House ♿✲❀ (Mr & Mrs J Nicholson) Heron Path, Wendover. ½m S of Wendover. Chapel Lane is 2nd turn on L off A413 towards Amersham. House is on L at bottom of lane. Georgian house with established 2-acre garden; large herbaceous border, unusual shrubs, roses, laburnum arches, an ornamental vegetable garden and 2 well stocked greenhouses. Also available pots and sculptures by Frances Levy. TEAS in aid of St Mary's Church. *Adm £1.50 Chd free. Sat, Sun July 15, 16 (2-6)*

Campden Cottage ✲❀ (Mrs P Liechti) 51 Clifton Rd, Chesham Bois, N of Amersham. From Amersham-on-the-Hill take A416; after 1m turn R (E) at Catholic Church. From Chesham take A416; and first turning L after beech woods. ½-acre derelict garden restored by owner since 1971; plantsman's garden of yr-round interest; fine collection of unusual and rare plants. Hellebores in March. Featured on TV 'Gardeners World' and in 'The New Englishwoman's Garden' 1987 and the 'Good Gardens Guide 1995'. Please use car park signed on main rd. Teas Old Amersham. No push chairs. *Adm £1.50 Chd free. Suns March 12, April 9, May 21, June 11, July 16, Aug 6, Sept 3, Oct 1, (2-6). Also by appt for parties with TEAS. No coaches. Please* **Tel 01494 726818**

Chalfont St Giles Gardens Off A413. TEAS in aid of Iain Rennie Hospice. *Combined adm £2 for 3 gardens or £1 per garden Chd free. Suns May 14, June 18 (2-6)*

Concordia ✲ (Mr & Mrs D E Cobb) 76 Deanway. Parking in Deanway. A small challenging garden on a difficult sloping site. Herbaceous and shrub borders; rock garden; fruit trees; collection of unusual orchids. *Private visits also welcome, please* **Tel 01494 873671**

Halfpenny Furze ♿✲❀ (Mr & Mrs R Sadler) Mill Lane. From London take A413 signed Amersham. Mill Lane is ¼m past mini roundabouts at Chalfont St Giles. Limited parking in Mill Lane, 1-acre plantsman's garden on clay: part woodland (rhododendrons, azaleas, acers, magnolias, cercis, cercidiphyllum) part formal (catalpa, cornus, clerodendrum, unusual shrubs, roses and mixed borders). Plants for sale if available. TEAS. *Private visits also welcome, please* **Tel 01494 872509**

North Down ✼ (Mr & Mrs J Saunders) From Halfpenny Furze, short uphill walk L into Dodds Lane. Garden is 250yds on R. Limited parking in Dodds Lane. Approx ¾-acre garden on N facing slope; stony, free-draining soil on gravel and flint. Interest throughout yr, some unusual plants, vistas. Mixed beds, shrubs, with rhododendrons, azaleas, acers; spring bulbs. Small bog garden; climbers; collection of sempervivums; patio with water feature. *Private visits also welcome, please* **Tel 01494 872928**

¶Chartridge Centre ✼ (Chartridge Conference Centre Ltd) 2½ miles from Chesham. At large roundabout in Chesham leaving large duck pond on L, take exit L signposted Chartridge. Continue 2½m passing Chartridge Park Golf Club and The Bell House. Chartridge Conference Centre on the R. The drive is just before the sign. Ample free car parking. Approx 26-acre mature gardens and woodland, general layout as originally designed in 1920s. Fine specimen trees including oak and sequoia redwoods. Outstanding rhododendrons and azaleas. Lime tree avenue and woodland walks. Paths through sweeping lawns to small ponds. TEA. *Adm £1.50 Chd 50p. Suns June 4, Aug 20 (2-5)*

Charlton ❀ (Mrs L Rutterford) 5 Harcourt Rd, Dorney Reach, nr Maidenhead. Turn S off A4 approx 3m E of Maidenhead into Marsh Lane (signposted Dorney Reach) continue 1m; Harcourt Road is 2nd on R over motorway bridge. Approx ¾-acre garden on light free draining soil organically cultivated and designed to provide interest throughout the yr. Mixed borders with variety of shrubs, hardy perennials, climbers and annuals; small pond, vegetables, fruit. (Suitable for wheelchairs if dry). TEA. *Adm £1. Private visits only, welcome all year, please* **Tel 01628 24325**

Chearsley Gardens 4m NE Thame turn E off B4011 at Long Crendon, or 7m SW of Aylesbury turn W off A418. Gardens and parking are signposted in village. TEAS in Village Hall. *Combined adm £2 Chd free. Sun July 9, Wed July 12 (2-6)*

¶5 Bernards Close ♿✼ (Mrs Mary Fowler) Pleasing small garden planted for colourful yr-round appeal. Trees, interesting mixture of shrubs, incl many fuchsias; conifers and heathers

The Cottage ✼❀ (Mr & Mrs Tony Hall) Very small organic cottage garden kept in order with use of railway sleepers; unusual vegetables; wildlife pond; small but interesting herbaceous beds and alpines, hanging baskets and pots

Manor Farm ♿✼ (Mr & Mrs Michael Heybrook) 1¼-acre walled garden adjoining old farmhouse and fruit farm. Unusual plants in mixed shrub and herbaceous borders; old roses, clematis and other climbers. Tranquil pond area, mature trees

4 Old Plough Close ✼ (Mr & Mrs John Hillier) ¼-acre garden designed and planted by owners on 45 degrees slope. Terraced beds, rockeries and small pond; unusual conifers and ferns to create all yr interest. Small collection of bonsai

Cheddington Gardens 11m E of Aylesbury; turn off B489 at Pitstone. 7m S of Leighton Buzzard; turn off B488 at Cheddington Station. Gardening books stall. TEAS on the green. *Combined adm £2 Chd free (Share to Methodist Chapel and St Giles Church, Cheddington®). Sun June 25 (2-6)*

Chasea (Mr & Mrs A G Seabrook) Medium-sized garden on clay; assorted tubs and baskets round pool on patio; shrubs and conifers; perennials and bedding. *Private visits welcome, July only, please* **Tel 01296 668923**

Cheddington Manor ✼ (Mr & Mrs H Hart) 3½-acres; small lake and moat in informal setting, roses, herbaceous border, and interesting mature trees

34 Gooseacre (Mrs Barbara Smith) A well-designed partly paved small garden with magnificent views over the Chilterns. Delightful water feature, patio, mixed shrubs and climbers for all yr interest

The Old Reading Room ♿❀ (Mr & Mrs W P Connolley) ⅓-acre cottage garden; shrubs, perennials, bedding and small fern collection; trees incl ginkgo biloba

Rose Cottage ✼❀ (Mr & Mrs D G Jones) ¼-acre cottage garden planted for all yr interest with accent on colour; old roses; small scree area with unusual plants and conservatory. Partly suitable for wheelchairs. *Private visits welcome, please* **Tel 01296 668693**

21 Station Road ♿ (Mr & Mrs P Jay) ½-acre informal garden with wildflower conservation area; herbaceous and shrub borders; herbs and kitchen garden

Woodstock Cottage ✼ (Mr & Mrs D Bradford) 42 High Street. Delightful cottage garden with rear courtyard and patio

Chicheley Hall ♿✼ (The Trustees of the Hon Nicholas Beatty & Mrs John Nutting) Chicheley, on A422 between Bedford and Newport Pagnell; E of Newport Pagnell and 3m from junction 14 of M1. Georgian House (open) set in spacious lawns, herbaceous borders, roses on mellowed brick walls; woodland planted with bulbs; formal lake attributed to London & Wise 1709 after Hampton Court. TEAS. *Adm £1.50 Chd 50p. ▲For NGS Sun July 16 (2.30-5)*

The Claydons ✼ 2½m SW of Winslow. Follow signs to Claydons. Mediaeval church, car parking. TEAS in village hall in aid of WI. *Combined adm £2 Chd 20p. Sun June 11 (2-6)*

Ashton ♿ (Mr & Mrs G Wylie) Botyl Rd, Botolph Claydon. ⅓-acre plot on clay with superb views on site of former barnyard. Mixed beds of shrubs and herbaceous plants

Beech House ♿❀ (Mr & Mrs D Dow) Church Way, E Claydon. ¼-acre walled garden, derelict in 1977; mixed borders, shrubs, flowers; paved features, small alpine beds

1 Emerald Close (Mr & Mrs L B Woodhouse) E Claydon. Small garden with collection of deciduous and coniferous Bonsai

Littleworth Farm (Mr & Mrs M O'Halloran) Main feature of the 1½ acres is a walled herbaceous garden with stone terracing designed by David Stevens and planted 6yrs ago to give all yr colour; also roses and formal kitchen garden

Pond Cottage ♿ (Mr & Mrs Brian Kay) Botolph Claydon. ¼-acre garden framed by C17 cottage and C19 barn, developed on clay since 1975. Bulbs, shrubs, foliage and fruit trees; mixed borders, peat bed, troughs

The Pump House ♿ (Mr & Mrs P M Piddington) St. Mary's Rd, E Claydon. ¾-acre, trees, shrubs, borders, vegetable and herb garden, fish pools

Cliveden ♿✱ (The National Trust) 2m N of Taplow. A number of separate gardens within extensive grounds, first laid out in the C18 incl water garden, rose garden; herbaceous borders; woodland walks and views of the Thames. Suitable for wheelchairs only in part. TEAS. *Adm grounds only £4. Parties £3.50 Chd £2. ▲For NGS Suns May 7, Sept 17 (11-6)*

Cublington Gardens from Aylesbury take Buckingham Rd (A413). At Whitchurch (4m) turn R to Cublington. TEAS. *Combined adm £2.50 Chd free. Sun June 11, Wed June 28 (2-5)*

Old Manor Farm ♿✱❀ (Mr & Mrs N R Wilson) Reads Lane. Large garden in process of being redesigned; rose and 'yellow' gardens, herbaceous borders; swimming pool with collection of planted tubs; ha ha and walled vegetable garden. **Private visits by written appt**

The Old Rectory ♿✱❀ (Mr & Mrs J Naylor) 2-acre country garden with herbaceous border, rosebeds, shrubs and mature trees; vegetables; ponds, climbing plants

Cuddington Gardens ❀ 3½m NE Thame or 5m SW Aylesbury off A418. Winners of Best Kept Village competition 1994. TEAS in aid of Darby & Joan and Village Hall Restoration Fund. Parking at The Old Rectory (1m from Barn's Piece). *Combined adm £1.50 Acc chd free. Sun June 18 (2-6)*

The Old Post ♿ (Mr & Mrs Robert Fleming) ½-acre family garden planted for yr-round interest. Wisteria colonnade, wychert wall, shrub, herbaceous and mixed borders; shady beds and vegetables

The Old Rectory ✱ (Mr & Mrs R J Frost) Former Victorian rectory with stunning views over Winchendon valley. 2-acre garden bounded by mature trees, laid out with beds of mixed shrubs, rockery, herbaceous island bed, paved rose garden with fish pond; pavilion. Variety of planted containers incl mangers around courtyard

Tyringham Hall ♿ (Mr & Mrs Ray Scott) Water and bog garden, patios and lawns surround mediaeval house. Dell with well and waterfall

Wellfield House ♿ (Mr & Mrs C S Sanderson) ½-acre garden surrounding Victorian house. Mixed borders for all-yr interest; roses, shaded areas. Newly constructed terrace with rockery and small water feature

Dinton Gardens 4m SW Aylesbury or 4m NE Thame. Gardens signed in village. **TEAS** in Village Hall in aid of Dubrovnik Appeal for Children. Parking at Perryfield and Haddenham Low House. *Combined adm £2 Acc chd free. Sun June 25 (2-6)*

Appletree Cottage ✱ (Mr & Mrs J K Mitchell) High St. A village centre garden begun from scratch in 1985. A blend of trees, shrubs, conifers and flowers on several levels designed to give privacy on an exposed site and good foliage colour whilst complementing neighbouring gardens

Haddenham Low House ♿✱❀ (Dr & Mrs P J Edwards) on Oxford Rd A418 between Haddenham and Dinton turnings. This ½-acre garden has been created from field and farmyard since 1989. Many trees planted to exclude noise from increased traffic. 2 formal herbaceous beds; special interest, medicinal plants

Hermits Cottage ♿✱ (Mr & Mrs M Usherwood) Westlington. ¾-acre surrounding old thatched cottage at Westlington end of village. Front open with shrubs and trees; rear partially wychert-walled incl kitchen garden; mixed borders with open and shaded areas at rear adjacent to water features

¶**Honeysuckle Cottage** ♿ (Shaun Lee) ½-acre garden developed from meadow in last 3 yrs. Designed, planted and maintained by young man with special needs. Mixed borders planted mainly with perennials for colour all summer. Vegetable garden, fruit trees and soft fruit

Orchard Cottage ✱ (Mr & Mrs H C Bingham) High St. 10-yr-old garden of ⅓-acre designed for minimum maintenance and all yr colour, variety and interest; sculpted lawns, hidden vistas, pergola and patios; shrubberies, ornamental and fruit trees, roses, mixed borders, plants for perfume and to attract butterflies

Perryfield ♿✱ (Mr & Mrs J Gray) New Rd. ⅓-acre with mature trees and planted for colour contrast; small water garden; island beds, mainly herbaceous and shrubs; some bedding. Footpath from car park to Hermits Cottage

¶**Westlington House** ♿✱ (Mr & Mrs J Archer) Large manor house garden approx 3 acres incorporating walled gardens, orchard, vegetable gardens, greenhouses. Many specimen trees set in 20 acres of parkland

Dorneywood Garden ♿✱❀ (The National Trust) Dorneywood Rd, Burnham. From Burnham village take Dropmore Rd, and at end of 30mph limit take R fork into Dorneywood Rd. Dorneywood is 1m on R. From M40 junction 2, take A355 to Slough then 1st R to Burnham, 2m then 2nd L after Jolly Woodman signed Dorneywood Rd. Dorneywood is about 1m on L. 6-acre country garden with shrubs, rose garden, mixed borders and dell. TEAS. *Adm £2.50 Chd under 15 free. Garden open* **by written appt only** *on Weds July 5, 19, Sats Aug 5, 12 (2-5.30). Apply to the Secretary, Dorneywood Trust, Dorneywood, Burnham, Bucks SL1 8PY*

The Edge ✱❀ (Mr & Mrs D Glen) London Rd, Chalfont St Giles. Garden is ¼m towards Chalfont St Peter from The Pheasant Xrds on A413 nr Kings Rd. Georgian cottage with landscaped garden of ¾ acre, created by owners. Partially enclosed with walls and yew hedges, interesting shrubs incl magnolias, wisterias, climbing and shrub roses. TEAS. *Adm £1 Chd free. Suns May 21, July 2 (2-6)*

Favershams Meadow ♿✱ (Mr & Mrs H W Try) 1½m W of Gerrards Cross on A40. Turn N into Mumfords Lane opp lay-by with BT box. Garden ¼m on R. 1½-acre garden. Mixed herbaceous, knot, parterre and separate blue and white garden. Beautiful roses on house and in David Austin rose garden. Attractive brick paved vegetable garden. Garden maintained to a very high standard, always being improved. TEAS in aid of the Red Cross and The Wexham Gastrointestinal Trust. *Adm £1.50 Chd free. Suns May 21, June 18 (2-6)*

Flint House ♿✂ (Mr & Mrs David White) Penn Street Village, 2m SW of Amersham. Turn S off A 404 into village. Opp church (open). Parking in church car park. 1½-acre garden surrounding C19 flint vicarage; herbaceous borders, shrubs and climbing roses, raised alpine bed, herb garden; urns and rose 'hoops' beside tennis court. Geraniums in garden room. TEA. *Adm £1.50 Chd 20p. Sun July 2 (2-6)*

59 The Gables ♿❀ (Mrs A M Johnstone) Haddenham. Off A418 6m W of Aylesbury, 3m E of Thame. Travelling S along Churchway, The Gables is 2nd turning L after Miles' Garage. This small garden (60′ × 35′) has undergone some changes since last opening; herbaceous border widened; new mini pond. Planted for all season interest. Bonsai, ferns, ivies. *Adm £1 Chd under 10 free. Suns June 18, Sept 10; Weds June 21, Sept 13 (2-6)*

Gipsy House ♿✂❀ (Mrs F Dahl) Gt Missenden. A413 to Gt Missenden. From High St turn into Whitefield Lane, continue under railway bridge. Large Georgian house on R with family additions. York stone terrace, pleached lime walk to writing hut; shrubs, roses, herbs, small walled vegetable garden, orchard and gipsy caravan and maze for children. Limited access for wheelchairs. Teas locally. *Adm £1.20 Chd 30p (Share to Roald Dahl Foundation®). Sun June 18 (2-5.30)*

Gracefield ♿❀ (Mr & Mrs B Wicks) Lacey Green. Take A4010 High Wycombe to Aylesbury Rd. Turn R by Red Lion at Bradenham, up hill to Walters Ash; L at T-junction for Lacey Green. Brick and flint house on main rd beyond church facing Kiln Lane. 1½-acre mature garden; many unusual plants, trees, mostly labelled; orchard, soft fruit, shrub borders, rockery; plants for shade, sink gardens. Two ponds. Ploughman's lunches, TEAS and plants in aid of local Macmillan Nurses Group. *Adm £1.50 Chd free. Sun June 25 (11.30-5). Parties welcome by* **written appt** *May to Sept*

Great Barfield ♿✂❀ (Richard Nutt Esq) Bradenham, A4010 4m NW of High Wycombe 4m S of Princes Risborough. At Red Lion turn into village and turn R. Park on green. Walk down No Through Road. 1½-acre garden, designed for views, lay out, contrast and colour, as background for unusual plants. Michael Gibson in 'The Rose Gardens of England' says that it is a plantsman's garden in the best possible sense of the term and not to be missed to see how all plants should be grown to the best advantage. Feb now not only famous for snowdrops and hellebores but willows and a variety of bulbs; drifts of crocus; May unique collections of Pulmonarias and Bergenias; also red Trilliums now naturalised. July old-fashioned and climbing roses, Lilies including naturalised L. martagon. Sept considerable collection of colchicum, autumn colour and Sorbus berries. NCCPG national collection of leucojum (spring & late April); celandine (April); iris unguicularis. Sales of unusual plants. TEAS. *Adm £1 Chd under 16 free (Share to Berks, Bucks and Oxon Group of NCCPG®). Suns Feb 19 (2-5), April 23 (2-5.30), July 2 (2-6), Sept 17 (2-5). Private visits and parties welcome, please* **Tel 01494 563741**. *First opening in 1996 Sun Feb 18 (2-5), subject to unforeseen events*

Hall Barn (The Dowager Lady Burnham) Lodge gate 300yds S of Beaconsfield Church in town centre. One of the original gardens opening in 1927 under the National Gardens Scheme, still owned by the Burnham family. A unique landscaped garden of great historical interest, laid out in the 1680's. Vast 300-yr-old curving yew hedge. Extensive replanting in progress after severe gale damage. Formal lake. Long avenues through the Grove, each terminating in a temple, classical ornament or statue. Obelisk with fine carvings in memory of Edmund Waller's grandson who completed the garden about 1730. *Garden open* **by written appointment only**. *Applications to The Dowager Lady Burnham, Hall Barn, Beaconsfield, Buckinghamshire HP9 2SG*

Hall Farm, Little Linford ♿✂❀ (Hon Richard & Mrs Godber) 2m N of Newport Pagnell between Gayhurst & Haversham overlooking Great Ouse valley. 3-acre hilltop farmhouse garden created over last 15 yrs. Mixed borders; trees and shrubs. Walled garden with converted barn and conservatory; secluded swimming pool with sun loving plants. Also kitchen garden, herbs; orchard and water garden. Flower display in beautiful C13/14 village church. Plants and cream TEAS in aid of Little Linford Church. *Adm £1.30 Chd free. Sun June 11 (2-6)*

Harewood ♿✂❀ (Mr & Mrs John Heywood) Harewood Rd, Chalfont St Giles. Chalfont and Latimer Met Line tube station ¾m. From A404 Amersham-Rickmansworth Rd, at mini roundabout in Little Chalfont Village turn S down Cokes Lane. Harewood Rd is 200yds on L. 1 acre; fine yew and box hedges; established conifers; wide variety unusual shrubs and hardy plants; many climbers incl roses, clematis, wisterias; pool, sink gardens; planted for yr-round interest. Emphasis on foliage and colour contrast. Cream TEAS. *Adm £1.50 Chd free (Share to Arthritis & Rheumatism Council®). Private visits welcome, please* **Tel 01494 763553**

Hillesden House ♿✂❀ (Mr & Mrs R M Faccenda) Hillesden, 3m S of Buckingham via Gawcott. Follow Hillesden signs after Gawcott on Calvert Rd. 6 acres developed since 1978 from virgin land on site of C16 Manor House by superb Perpendicular Church 'Cathedral in the Fields'; large lawns, shrubberies; rose, alpine and foliage gardens; interesting clipped hedges; conservatory; large lakes and deer park; commanding views over countryside. TEAS in aid of Hillesden Church. *Adm £1.50 Chd under 12 free. Sun June 18 (2-6)*

Hughenden Manor ♿✂❀ (The National Trust) 1½m N of High Wycombe on W side of Great Missenden Rd A4128; [Grid ref: SU866955 on OS sheet 165]. 5 acres with lawns, terraced garden, herbaceous border, formal annual bedding, orchard and woodland walks. The Trust has undertaken restoration work in accordance with photographs taken at the time of Disraeli's death. Teas available. *Adm House & Garden £3.60 Chd £1.80 Family £9.* ▲*For NGS Sun July 23 (12-6). Last adm 5.30*

Regular Openers. Too many days to include in diary. Usually there is a wide range of plants giving year-round interest. See head of county section for the name and garden description for times etc.

Long Crendon Gardens 2m N of Thame B4011 to Bicester. TEAS. *Combined adm £2 Chd free*

Sun April 23 (2-6)

Manor House ♿✻❀ (Sir William & Lady Shelton) turn R by church; house through wrought iron gates. 6 acres; lawns sweep down to 2 ornamental lakes, each with small island; walk along lower lake with over 20 varieties of willow; fine views towards Chilterns. House (not open) 1675. TEAS

The Old Crown ❀ (Mr & Mrs R H Bradbury) 100yds past Chandos Inn. 1 acre on steep SW slope. Old-fashioned and other roses and climbers. Flowering shrubs, herbaceous plants. Spring bulbs, assorted colourful containers in summer; 2 vegetable patches

Old Post House ♿❀ (Mr & Mrs Nigel Viney) In the picturesque High St at corner of Burts Lane. Attractive cottage garden. Interesting spring & summer shrubs, and planting. Small produce stall

Springfield Cottage ♿❀ (Mrs Elizabeth Dorling) 6 Burts Lane. ¼-acre very secluded, mature garden. Foliage predominating all yr with primroses, bluebells, herbaceous borders, flowering shrubs and many clematis

Sun June 25 (2-6) NT Centenary year **The Old Courthouse**. Flower festival at St Mary's Church

Croft House ♿ (Cdr & Mrs Peter Everett) Thame Rd. In square, white wrought iron railings. ½-acre walled garden; plants and shrubs of botanical interest especially to flower arrangers. TEAS

8 Ketchmere Close ♿❀ (Mr & Mrs A Heley) 1991, 1992 & 1993 award winner incl Booker Garden Centre Competition for the best kept garden under 100ft in Buckinghamshire. Colourful split level garden with extensive views. Wide range of shrubs, conifers, rockery and water feature. *Parties welcome, please* **Tel 01844 201422**

Manor House ♿✻❀ (Sir William & Lady Shelton) Description with April opening

The Old Crown ❀ (Mr & Mrs R H Bradbury) Description with April opening

Windacre ♿❀ (Mr & Mrs K Urch) 62 Chilton Rd, next to Primary School. 1-acre; roses, interesting shrubs, herbaceous plants, orchard, main features sunken lawns, conifers and trees. Cream TEAS

Loughton Village Gardens 1m W of Milton Keynes City Centre. 3m S of Stony Stratford and 3m N of Bletchley off Watling St; or Junction 14 of M1 or A5 to Portway Roundabout on H5 Portway and follow signs. TEAS and plant sales in aid of Parish Church and the Apert's Syndrome Support Group. *Combined adm £2 Chd free. Sun June 25 (1.30-6)*

Cell Farm Cottage ♿✻❀ (Mr & Mrs D J Oakley) 1 The Green. C16 cottage. Project started in 1990; site shared with livery stables. Shrubs, perennials, climbing roses, containers. Garden dominated by horse chestnut tree

Fullers Barn ♿✻❀ (Mr & Mrs John Walker) The Green. ⅓ acre bordered by stream and surrounded by parkland. Planted 6yrs ago on old farmyard. Borders, pond, shrubs, raised beds and vegetables, fruit trees and greenhouse

2 The Green ✻ (Mr & Mrs A Cirigliano) 150ft x 20ft colourful village garden. Pool, borders, containers and productive vegetable garden; limited space fully used

¶**The Old Bakehouse** ✻ (Miss Gail Kingswell) 2, School Lane. ¼ acre. Project begun in summer 1994. Small cottage garden at front. Formal parterre in rear courtyard; informal garden beyond. Surrounds Grade 11 listed house, barns and stables

The Old School ♿✻❀ (Mr & Mrs George Button) School Lane. 3½ acre garden developed over 12yrs. Ornamental pond, orchard, wild area, shrubs interestingly planted. Boundary formed by Loughton Brook

The Manor Farm ♿✻❀ (Mr & Mrs Peter Thorogood) Little Horwood signposted 2m NE Winslow off A413. 5m E Buckingham and 5m W Bletchley turning S off A421. Hilltop farmhouse garden on acid clay, laid out and replanted 1986. Wide range of alpines and plantsman's plants for yr-round interest in colour, form and foliage; good roses, pergola, 100′ hosta border, herbaceous, wild flower meadow, damp garden, lovely views. Cream TEAS in aid of Gt. Horwood W.I. and stalls. *Adm £1.50 Chd free (Share to Andy Birt Trust and Stoke Mandeville Hospital Spinal Injuries Unit®). Sun July 16 (2- 6). Private visits welcome April to Sept, please* **Tel 01296 714758**

The Manor House, Bledlow ✻❀ (The Lord & Lady Carrington) ½m off B4009 in middle of Bledlow village. Station: Princes Risborough, 2½m. Paved garden, parterres, shrub borders, old roses and walled kitchen garden. House (not open) C17 & C18. Water and species garden with paths, bridges and walkways, fed by 14 chalk springs. Also a new 2-acre garden with sculptures and landscaped planting. Partly suitable wheelchairs. TEA May, TEAS June. *Adm £2 Chd free (Share to Garden History Society® June only). Suns May 7, June 18 (2-6); also private visits welcome May to Sept (2-4.30), please* **Tel 01844 343499**

The Manor House, Hambleden ✻ (Maria Carmela, Viscountess Hambleden) Hambleden. NE of Henley-on-Thames, 1m N of A4155. Conservatory; shrubs and old-fashioned rose garden. TEA at Hambleden Church. *Adm £1.50 Chd 20p. Sun June 25 (2-6)*

The Manor House, Princes Risborough ♿✻❀ (Mr & Mrs J Vellacott) From High Wycombe take A4010 to Princes Risborough. Turn L down High St. L at Market Square and bear R. The house is R of church, public car park beyond. From Aylesbury-Thame follow signs to town centre and turn R at Market Square. 2 acres surrounding C17 house (not open), large walled garden designed by NT in 1972 with pond, box balls and mixed borders, orchard with blue and white borders leading to gazebo. Informal rose garden bordered by nut walk and woodland. TEAS in aid of St Marys Church. *Adm £2 Chd under 15 free. Suns May 28, July 9 (2-5). Private visits welcome, please* **Tel 01844 343168**

Nether Winchendon House ♿✻ (Mr & Mrs R Spencer Bernard) Nether Winchendon, 5m SW of Aylesbury; 7m from Thame. Picturesque village, beautiful church. 5 acres; fine trees, variety of hedges; naturalised spring bulbs; shrubs; herbaceous borders. Tudor manor house (not open) home of Sir Francis Bernard, last British Governor of Massachusetts. TEA weather permitting. *Adm £1.30 Chd under 15 free. ▲For NGS Suns April 30, July 23 (2-5.30)*

The Old Vicarage, Padbury ♿✻❀ (Mr & Mrs H Morley-Fletcher) Padbury 2m S of Buckingham on A413 follow signs in village. 2½ acres on 3 levels; flowering shrubs and trees; rose garden, parterre. Display collection of hebes; pond and sunken garden, new conservatory and terrace. Fine views. TEAS in aid of League of Friends of Buckingham Hospital. *Adm £1.50 Chd free. Sun April 9 (2-5), Sat, Sun June 17, 18 (2-6)*

6 Oldfield Close ✻❀ (Mr & Mrs Jolyon Lea) Little Chalfont. 3m E of Amersham. Take A404 E through Little Chalfont, turn 1st R after railway bridge, then R again into Oakington Ave. From M25 junction 18 take A404 to Amersham. In 2m turn L at Xrds (Lodge Lane & Church Grove) then bear R into Oakington Ave. Plantsman's ⅙-acre garden of borders, peat beds, rock plants, troughs and small alpine house. Over 2,000 species and varieties of rare and unusual plants incl cassiopes, daphnes, fritillaries, alpines and bulbs. Plant stall in aid of Bethany Village Leprosy Society, in India. *Adm £1 Chd free. Suns April 9, June 4 (2-5). Private visits welcome all yr, please* **Tel 01494 762384**

Overstroud Cottage ✻❀ (Mr & Mrs J Brooke) The Dell, Frith Hill. Amersham 6m Aylesbury 10m. Turn E off A413 at Gt Missenden onto B485 Frith Hill to Chesham. White Gothic cottage set back in layby 100yds up hill on L. Parking on R at Parish Church. Cottage originally C16 hospital for Missenden Abbey. Garden with ideas for yr-round interest; on two levels carved from chalk quarry. Borders of artistic planting schemes; flowering shrubs. Step-over apples; lily pond; herb and sink gardens; collection of hellebores; bulbs, primulas, pulmonarias, hardy geraniums, species roses, clematis and traditional cottage plants. Not suitable for children or push chairs. TEAS at Parish Church. *Adm £1 Chd 50p (Share to The Ralph Sutcliffe Fund for Meningitis Research®). Suns April 16, May 7, June 11, July 2, Sept 3 (2-6). Parties welcome by appt, please* **Tel 01494 862701**

Oving Gardens 5m NW of Aylesbury signposted off A413 at Whitchurch. Also signposted 1m E of Waddesdon off A41. Hot drinks and snacks. *Combined adm £1 Chd free. Sun March 19 (12-4)*

Manor Close ✻ (Mr & Mrs R J Hawkins) Manor Rd. Mature, established garden of 1½ acres herbaceous borders; brick pathways, many spring bulbs, spectacular views over countryside

The Old Butchers Arms ✻❀ (Mr & Mrs Denys Fraser) ¼-acre sloping chalk garden featured in 'Gardeners World' magazine. Hellebores, clematis, old roses, shrubs and herbaceous plants flank wide grass paths, paved, tiled and wood-chip areas. Ornamental brick and gravel rope-swagged walkways, all maturing over past 10 yrs

Pasture Farm ♿✻❀ (Mr & Mrs R Belgrove) Thame Rd. Longwick, nr Princes Risborough. 1m W of Longwick on the Thame Rd. A4129. 4m E of Thame. Farm entrance 50yds from layby. Garden at top of farm track. ½-acre labelled plantswoman's garden. Herbaceous border, rockery. White garden with shrubs, perennials, bulbs and annuals. Integral nursery with perennials incl unusual white varieties. TEAS. *Adm £1 Chd free (Share to Aston Sandford Church Appeal®). Suns May 7, June 18, Sept 10 (2-6). Also private visits welcome, please* **Tel 01844 343651**

Peppers ♿✻❀ (Mr & Mrs J Ledger) 4 Sylvia Close, Gt Missenden. A413 Amersham to Aylesbury Rd. At Great Missenden by-pass turn at sign Great & Little Kingshill (Chiltern Hospital). After 400yds turn L, Nags Head Lane. After 300yds turn R under railway bridge. Sylvia Close 50yds on R. Park in cricket field. Approx 1 acre. Wide variety of plants, shrubs, trees, incl uncommon conifers, collection of acers, unusual containers, spring and autumn colour. TEAS. Donation from plant sale and teas to local charities (Workaid). *Adm £1 Chd free. Suns May 14, Aug 27 (10-5). Private visits welcome, please* **Tel 01494 864419**

Pollards ♿✻❀ (Mr & Mrs George Baker) Upper Icknield Way. ¾m NE of Princes Risborough via A4010; turn up Peters Lane at Monks Risborough. 1½-acre garden on chalk; formal and informal beds; orchard, vegetables and herbs. *Adm £1 Chd free. Sun June 4 (2-6)*

Prestwood Gardens ✻ From Amersham or Aylesbury turn off A413 at Gt Missenden. Take A4128 to High Wycombe through Prestwood. At end of High St as rd bears L go straight on. Anchor Cottage is adjoining Pinecroft on RH-side in Honor End Lane. Parking in public car park in High St, 300yds. TEAS at Anchor Cottage. *Combined adm £1 Chd free (Share to Save the Children Fund®). Sun July 9 (2-6)*

Anchor Cottage (Group Captain & Mrs D L Edwards) ¼-acre garden with colour for all seasons. Pergola, pond, roses, shrubs and shade loving plants. TEAS

Pinecroft (Mrs B Checkley & Mr & Mrs P Smith) An enthusiast's very small and wide garden. Good use made of difficult shaped area with features

Quainton Gardens 7m NW of Aylesbury. Nr Waddesdon turn N off A41

Sun May 14 *(2-6) Combined adm £1.50 Chd free (Windmill open for National Windmill Day)*

Brudenell House ♿❀ (Dr & Mrs H Beric Wright) Opp. Church. 2-acre garden surrounding old rectory. Specimen trees planted about 1830. 80' herbaceous border backed by rose hedge. Wide range of flowering shrubs and perennials. Pond, bulbs, wooden sculptures, and room to wander. TEAS in aid of Quainton Sports Club

Capricorner ♿✻ (Mr & Mrs A Davis) Small garden created in former stable yard, planted for yr-round interest with many scented plants; semi-wild area with trees

Thorngumbald ♿ (Mr & Mrs J Lydall) Cottage garden heavily planted with wide selection of old-fashioned plants, organically grown; small pond, conservatory; attempts to encourage wild life

Sun June 25 *(2-6) Combined adm £2 Chd free*

Brudenell House (description with May opening). TEAS

Capricorner (description with May opening)

Cross Farmhouse ✻ (Mr & Mrs E Viney) 1-acre garden flanking hill with old farm pond. Mixed shrub and herbaceous planting emphasising shape, texture and colour of foliage, and use of ground cover

Grange Leys ♿ (Mr & Mrs G Rodwell) House at far end of North End Rd, parking adjacent. 1-acre informal, romantic garden with many mature trees. Herbaceous shrubs, roses and pond area

Hatherways ♿❀ (Mr & Mrs D Moreton) A cottage garden which has gradually emerged from near wilderness. Bog garden, interesting shrubs, herbaceous plants and bulbs. Plant stall in aid of NSPCC

¶35 Lower Street ♿ (Mr D Burn) 3yr-old small, S-facing rear garden with mixture of curved herbaceous and shrub borders. Raised vegetable and flower beds

Thorngumbald (description with May opening)

Quoitings ♿✄❀ (Kenneth Balfour Esq) Oxford Rd, Marlow, 7m E of Henley, 3m S of High Wycombe; at Quoiting Sq, in Marlow turn N out of West St (A4155); garden 350yds up Oxford Rd on L. 2½-acres secluded garden with wide range of conifers and magnificent trees incl tulip, lime and pomegranate. Grand display of self propagated tulips and polyanthus followed by colourful mixed flower and dahlia beds; lawns; ha-ha; vistas. C17/18 house (not open) formerly home of Historiographer Royal to William IV and Queen Victoria. Brass Band. TEAS. *Adm £2 Chd free. Suns April 9 (1-5), Sept 3 (1-6)*

Sheredon ♿❀ (Mr & Mrs G Legg) Thame Rd, Longwick. Between Princes Risborough and Thame on A4129 next to Longwick PO. Winner of 'Booker' best large garden in Bucks 1993. Also featured in Ltd Edition Magazine Sept 94. ⅓-acre colourful garden, large pond with bog plants, many roses and unusual plants. Natural wood arches leading to attractive smaller gardens. Organic vegetable garden with melon house. Large collection of fruits and berries with mixed fruit tree orchard and grapes. Chickens and aviary. Many garden and water plants for sale. Cream TEAS on Sun July 16 only. *Adm £1 Chd 25p. Suns May 28 (2-6), July 16 (11-6)*

Spindrift ❀ (Mr & Mrs Eric Desmond) Jordans, 3m NE of Beaconsfield. From A40, midway between Gerrards Cross and Beaconsfield turn N into Potkiln Lane; after 1m turn L into Jordans village; at far side of green turn R. Park in school playground. Garden for all seasons on different levels full of surprises. Herbaceous border, variety of unusual hardy plants, fine hedges and specimen trees; hosta and hardy geranium collection; dell with pond; acid-loving shrubs. Model terraced vegetable and fruit garden with greenhouses and vines. Inspired by Monet, nasturtium arches surrounded by iris, poppies and peonies. Partly suitable for wheelchairs. Member of Horticultural Research Assoc. Cream TEAS. *Adm £1.50 Chd under 12 20p. Mons May 8, Aug 28 (2-5). Private visits welcome, please* **Tel 01494 873172**

¶22 Spring Gardens ✄❀ (Sue Gill) Newport Pagnell. From Milton Keynes on A5 take A422 towards Bedford. Ignore sign Newport Pagnell West. At next roundabout turn L to Newport Pagnell. Take 1st R (Willen Rd). Spring Gardens is 2nd R. Narrow brick path winds through plantswoman's tiny (3m × 20m) sheltered town garden crammed with many rare, interesting and tender plants. Pond, collection of unusual ivies and scented leaved geraniums. TEAS. *Adm £1. Small groups welcome by appt (March to Oct), please* **Tel 01908 614459**

Springlea ♿✄❀ (Mr & Mrs M Dean) Seymour Plain. 1m from Marlow, 2½m from Lane End off B482. From Lane End pass Booker airfield on L then in 1m pass Seymour Court, L at pillar-box on grass triangle. ⅓-acre secluded garden backed by beechwoods. Flower arrangers' garden for colour, foliage and all yr interest. Spring bulbs, azaleas, rhododendrons, unusual trees, shrubs. Rockery, pond, waterfall, bog garden, hostas. Arched walkway with labelled clematis collection. 60′ herbaceous border against high brick wall with many climbers, racing pigeon loft. Award winner of large garden 1991 and 1992 in Buckinghamshire. Great selection of unusual plants. TEAS by WI (not March or April). *Adm £1.50 Chd free. Suns March 12 (1-5), April 9, May 7, June 4, July 2, 30, Sept 3 (2-6). Private visits and groups welcome March to October, please* **Tel 01628 473366**

Stowe Landscape Gardens ❀ (The National Trust) 3m NW of Buckingham via Stowe Ave. Follow brown NT signs. One of the supreme creations of the Georgian era; the first, formal layout was adorned with many buildings by Vanbrugh, Kent and Gibbs; in the 1730s Kent designed the Elysian Fields in a more naturalistic style, one of the earliest examples of the reaction against formality leading to the evolution of the landscape garden; miraculously, this beautiful garden survives; its sheer scale must make it Britain's largest work of art. TEAS. *Adm £3.80 Chd £1.40. ▲For NGS Tues May 16 (10-5). Last adm 4pm*

Tramway Farm ✄❀ (Mr & Mrs K Richardson) Ludgershall Rd. 7m N of Thame, turn off B 4011, Thame-Bicester or turn off A41 at Kingswood; both signed. 1-acre clay garden in hidden valley along the banks of a stream with wildlife pond; herbaceous borders with long season of interest, vegetable plot and mature spinney with spring bulbs. *Adm £1. Private visits welcome April - Sept, please* **Tel 01844 238249**

Turn End ✄❀ (Mr & Mrs Peter Aldington) Townside, Haddenham. From A418 turn to Haddenham between Thame (3m) and Aylesbury (6m). Turn at Rising Sun into Townside. BR Hadd and Thame Parkway. This acre seems much more. Through archways and round corners are several secret gardens. A sweeping lawn bounded by herbaceous beds and a wooded glade with snowdrops, narcissi and bluebells. Old roses, iris and climbers abound. A sunny gravel garden has raised beds, alpine troughs and sempervivum pans. The house designed and built by the owners encloses a courtyard and fish pool. Featured in 'Country Life', 'The Garden', 'Practical Gardening'. Home-made TEAS. *Adm £1.50 Chd 50p (Share to HDA Haddenham Helpline®). ▲For NGS Suns June 11, 18; Sept 17 (2-6). Also open Weds April to June (2-5). Collecting box, no Teas. Groups by appt at other times, please* **Tel 01844 291383**

By Appointment Gardens. These owners do not have a fixed opening day usually because they do not like crowds or have insufficient parking space. Owner will often give guided tour.

Walmerdene ♿✗❀ (Mr & Mrs M T Hall) 20 London Rd Buckingham. From Town Centre take A413 (London Rd). At top of hill turn R. Park in Brookfield Lane. Cream House on corner. Small town garden, unusual plants mostly labelled; species and hybrid hellebores; bulbs; herbaceous; euphorbias; climbing shrub and species roses; geraniums; clematis. Sink garden, rill garden, 2 ponds, white and yellow border; 2 greenhouses, small conservatory and grapehouse. TEAS. *Adm £1 Chd free. Sun April 9 (2-5) Sun, Mon, June 18, 19 (2-6). Private visits and parties welcome, May, June, July, please* **Tel 01280 817466**

Watercroft ♿❀ (Mr & Mrs P Hunnings) Penn 3m N of Beaconsfield on B474, 600yds past Penn Church. Medium-sized garden on clay; white flowers, new herb garden planted 1993, rose walk, weeping ash; kitchen garden; pond, wild flower meadow. New planting in meadow, plants and honey for sale. C18 house, C19 brewhouse (not open). TEAS in aid of Holy Trinity Church, Penn. *Adm £1.50 Chd 30p. Suns July 2, 9 (2-6)*

Weir Lodge ♿✗❀ (Mr & Mrs Mungo Aldridge) Latimer Rd Chesham. Approx 1m SE of Chesham. Turn L from A416 along Waterside at junction of Red Lion St and Amersham Rd. From A404 Rickmansworth-Amersham Rd turn R at signpost for Chenies and Latimer and go for 4m. Parking at Weir House Mill (McMinns) dangerous turning. ¾-acre garden on bank of R. Chess. Recovered from dereliction in 1983 by owners. Stream and ponds with planted banks. Gravelled terrace with sun loving plants. Assorted containers; shrub and mixed beds; wild flowers. Mature trees incl fine beeches in adjoining paddock. TEAS in aid of Chesham Society. *Adm £1 Chd free. Sun June 18 (2-6)*

Westcott House ✗❀ (Mr & Mrs H S Hodding) Gawcott 2m S of Buckingham off A421 Buckingham to Oxford Rd. House on corner of Radclive Rd. ½-acre cottage garden; shrubs, herbaceous plants, alpines; small collection of bonsais; two peat beds. *Adm £1 Chd free (Share to Holy Trinity Church, Gawcott Restoration Fund®). Sun, Mon, June 25, 26 (2-5)*

West Wycombe Park ✗ (Sir Francis Dashwood; The National Trust). West Wycombe. 3m W of High Wycombe on A40. Bus: from High Wycombe and Victoria. Landscape garden; numerous C18 temples and follies incl Temple of the Winds, Temple of Venus, Temple of Music. Swan-shaped lake, with flint bridges and cascade. *Adm (grounds only) £2.50 Chd £1.25. ▲For NGS Sun Sept 3 (2-5)*

The Wheatsheaf Inn ♿✗❀ (Mrs W Witzmann) Weedon. 2m N of Aylesbury off A413 Buckingham-Aylesbury rd. Black and White thatched Tudor Inn opp 15′ brick wall of 'Lilies'. Parking in courtyard and village. Since 1985 3 acres of field turned into a formal, flower and wild garden; with pond, roses, shrubs, perennials, spring bulbs, heather, conifers. Badminton and croquet lawn. Yr-round interest and fine views. Front has a preservation 400-yr-old walnut probably planted when the Old Wheatsheaf Coaching Inn was built. Many other old trees incl hazel grove for thatching. New paved area developed for shade-loving plants. Recommended by Gardening 'Which' magazine. *Adm £1 Chd free. Private visits welcome, please* **Tel 01296 641581**

Whitchurch Gardens 4m N of Aylesbury on A413. TEAS. *Combined adm £2 Chd free. Sun June 4 (2-6)*

¶7 High Street ♿ (Mrs J M Ryder Richardson) A family garden with croquet lawn bordered by roses and shrubs with far-reaching views to Waddesdon Manor, A secret garden lies in the most westerly corner

Kempsons Farm ♿❀ (Mr G Band & Miss S Wells) Church Headland Lane. Converted barn set in 1-acre garden established in 1993. Set high on outskirts of the village behind the church, surrounded by paddocks and far-reaching views towards Cresslow Manor, the garden features a large natural looking pond stocked with assorted fish incl Koi carp, cascading waterfall and Japanese bridge; young shrubs and continuing planting, with patio and stable courtyard

Mullions ✗ (Dr & Mrs L I Holmes-Smith) ⅓-acre picturesque cottage garden behind C17 cottage. 2 ponds and garden on 3 terraces

¶The Old Cottage ♿✗ (Mr Roger Gwynne-Jones) ¾-acre cottage garden with herbaceous border, herb garden and wild area. Sloping lawn with grand views over Vale of Aylesbury

¶The Old Granary ✗ (Mr & Mrs P V Betts) Formerly part of a farmyard, now entering its 3rd season, the garden is being developed as mixed borders, retaining walls of local stone. Gravel paths lead past the old farm granary to a paddock with views of open countryside

Priory Court ♿❀ (Mr & Mrs H Bloomer) 52 High St. ⅔-acre partly walled former C17 rectory garden. Herbaceous and mixed borders, roses and herbs. Wild shady areas, vegetables and fruit. TEAS in aid of church

¶Yew Tree Cottage ♿✗ (Mr & Mrs B S Foulger) 3 tier garden with fish pond, patios and small wooded area, the whole offering sanctuary for wildlife. Panoramic views over the Vale of Aylesbury

The White House ♿❀ (Mr & Mrs P G Courtenay-Luck) Denham Village. Approx 3m NW of Uxbridge, off A40 between Uxbridge and Gerrards Cross. Denham Village is signposted from A40 or A412; nearest main line station Denham Green. Underground Uxbridge. Parking in village rd. The White House is opp the Norman church in centre of village. 17 acres comprising 6 acres formal garden and an 11-acre paddock. Old flagstone terrace surrounds 2 sides of C18/19 house, leading to new yorkstone terrace; garden being restored to former glory; rejuvenation of old yew hedges, reclamation of lawns and shrubberies. R Misbourne meanders through lawns containing shrubberies, flower beds, orchard and developing rose garden. Large walled vegetable garden and restored Victorian greenhouses. Cream TEAS. *Adm £2 Acc chd free (Share to St Mary's Church, Denham Village®). Suns May 14, July 9 (2-5)*

¶Whitewalls ♿✗ (Mr W H Williams) Marlow. From Marlow town centre cross over bridge. 1st L white garden wall, 3rd house on L. Thames-side garden approx ½-acre with spectacular view of weir. Large lily pond, interesting planting of trees, shrubs and herbaceous perennials. Many colourful containers. Sight of large conservatory with exotic plants. Teas available in Marlow. *Adm £1.50 Chd free. Suns April 30, July 23 (2-6). Private visits and parties welcome, please* **Tel 01628 482573**

¶**Wichert** ♿✗ (Mr & Mrs R Clarke) Ford. 5m SW of Aylesbury, 5m ENE of Thame. From Aylesbury A418 towards Thame. L at Bugle Horn into Portway. After 3m L into Ford. Approx 100yds beyond Xrds L into drive immed after Old Bakehouse. Approx 1½ acres developed into separate gardens since 1990. Silver and Pearl, shade, fern, kitchen and pavement gardens; maze, pond and wild garden with indigenous British trees. *Adm £1 Chd free. Private visits only, please* **Tel 01296 748431**

Winslow Hall ♿ (Sir Edward & Lady Tomkins) Winslow. On A413 10m N of Aylesbury, 6m S of Buckingham. Free public car park. Winslow Hall (also open), built in 1700, designed by Christopher Wren, stands in a beautiful garden with distant perspectives, planted with many interesting trees and shrubs. In spring, blossom, daffodils and the contrasting foliage of trees combine to make the garden particularly attractive. TEA. *Adm house & garden £3 garden only £1.50 Chd free. Sun May 7 (2-6)*

Cambridgeshire

Hon County Organisers:

South: Lady Nourse, Dullingham House, Dullingham, Newmarket, Suffolk CB8 9UP Tel 01638 508186

North: Mrs M Thompson, Stibbington House, Wansford, Peterborough PE8 6JS Tel 01780 782043

Assistant Hon County Organisers:

South: John Drake Esq., Hardwicke House, Highditch Road, Fen Ditton Tel 01223 292246

Timothy Clark Esq, Nether Hall Manor, Soham, Ely CB7 5AB Tel 01353 720269

Hon County Treasurer (North Cambridgeshire): Michael Thompson Esq.

DATES OF OPENING

By appointment

For telephone numbers and other details see garden descriptions. Private visits welcomed

90 Bannold Rd, Waterbeach
Chippenham Park, nr Newmarket
Greystones, Swaynes Lane, Comberton
Hardwick House, Fen Ditton Gardens
83 High Street, Harlton
15 Latham Rd, Cambridge
Melbourn Bury, Royston
Mill House, North End, Bassingbourn
Netherhall Manor, Soham
Nuns Manor, Shepreth
Padlock Croft, West Wratting
Scarlett's Farm, West Wratting
31 Smith Street, Elsworth
Tetworth Hall, nr Sandy
Weaver's Cottage, West Wickham

Parties only

Clare College, Fellows Garden, Cambridge
Emmanuel College & Fellows' Garden
Hardwicke Farm, Great Gransden
Peckover House, Wisbech
Robinson College, Grange Road, Cambridge
Unwins Seeds Ltd, Histon

Regular opening

For details see garden descriptions

The Crossing House, Shepreth
Docwra's Manor, Shepreth. Every Mon, Wed, Fri and selected Suns. Also Bank Hol Mons

March 11 Saturday
Monksilver Nursery, Cottenham

March 26 Sunday
Barton Gardens, Cambridge

April 2 Sunday
Downing College, Cambridge

April 8 Saturday
Monksilver Nursery, Cottenham

April 9 Sunday
Chippenham Park, nr Newmarket
King's College Fellows Garden, Cambridge
Trinity College Fellows' Garden, Cambridge

April 16 Sunday
Netherhall Manor, Soham

April 17 Monday
Weaver's Cottage, West Wickham

April 29 Saturday
Padlock Croft, West Wratting
Scarlett's Farm, West Wratting
Weaver's Cottage, West Wickham

May 8 Sunday
Ely Gardens
Scarlett's Farm, West Wratting

May 13 Saturday
Monksilver Nursery, Cottenham

May 14 Sunday
Docwra's Manor, Shepreth
Netherhall Manor, Soham

May 21 Sunday
Tetworth Hall, nr Sandy

May 27 Saturday
Island Hall, Godmanchester
Padlock Croft, West Wratting
Scarlett's Farm, West Wratting
Weaver's Cottage, West Wickham

May 28 Sunday
Fen Ditton Gardens
Tetworth Hall, nr Sandy

May 29 Monday
Padlock Croft, West Wratting
Scarlett's Farm, West Wratting
Weaver's Cottage, West Wickham

June 4 Sunday
Leckhampton, Cambridge
Thorpe Hall, (Sue Ryder Foundation), Peterborough
Willingham Gardens

June 9 Friday
Wimpole Hall, Royston

June 10 Saturday
Monksilver Nursery, Cottenham

June 11 Sunday
Ely Gardens
Madingley Hall, Cambridge

June 17 Saturday
Farm Cottage, Barton Gardens, Cambridge

Padlock Croft, West Wratting
Scarlett's Farm, West Wratting
Weaver's Cottage, West Wickham

June 18 Sunday
Alwalton Gardens
Bainton House, Stamford
Chippenham Park, nr Newmarket
Farm Hall, Godmanchester
Greystones, Swaynes Lane, Comberton
Horningsea Gardens, Cambridge
Inglethorpe Manor, nr Wisbech
The Manor, Hemingford Grey
Melbourn Bury, Royston
Melbourn Lodge, Royston
31 Smith Street, Elsworth
Sutton Gardens, nr Ely
Whittlesford Gardens

June 22 Thursday
Peckover House, Wisbech

June 25 Sunday
Abbots Ripton Hall, nr Huntingdon
Bourn Lodge, Bourn
Grantchester Gardens
Hardwicke Farm, Great Gransden
Stibbington House, Wansford
West Wratting Park, West Wratting

July 2 Sunday
Downing College, Cambridge
Elton Hall, Elton, nr Peterborough
83 High Street, Harlton
Mill House, North End, Bassingbourn
Nuns Manor, Shepreth
Upton Gardens, nr Peterborough

July 8 Saturday
Emmanuel College & Fellows' Garden
Monksilver Nursery, Cottenham

July 9 Sunday
Clare College, Fellows Garden, Cambridge

July 16 Sunday
Anglesey Abbey, Cambridge
Whittlesford Gardens
Willingham Gardens

July 22 Saturday
Padlock Croft, West Wratting
Scarlett's Farm, West Wratting
Weaver's Cottage, West Wickham

July 23 Sunday
King's College Fellows Garden, Cambridge
Pamisford Gardens, nr Cambridge
Robinson College, Grange Road, Cambridge

July 30 Sunday
Farm Cottage, Barton Gardens, Cambridge
Stibbington Gardens, nr Peterborough
Wytchwood, Great Stukeley

August 6 Sunday
Netherhall Manor, Soham

August 10 Thursday
Peckover House, Wisbech

August 12 Saturday
Monksilver Nursery, Cottenham
Unwins Seeds Ltd, Histon

August 13 Sunday
Anglesey Abbey, Cambridge
Netherhall Manor, Soham

August 27 Sunday
15 Latham Road

September 3 Sunday
Docwra's Manor, Shepreth

September 9 Saturday
Monksilver Nursery, Cottenham

October 8 Sunday
Chippenham Park, nr Newmarket

October 14 Saturday
Monksilver Nursery, Cottenham

DESCRIPTIONS OF GARDENS

Abbots Ripton Hall ✤ (Lord & Lady De Ramsey) Abbots Ripton. Past Huntingdon on A1 signposted Abbots Ripton. In village turn L on B1090, 500yds turn L into Hall Lane. 7½-acre garden containing many fine old trees; shrubs, rose circle and grey border designed by Humphrey Waterfield. Oldest rose in garden is called rosa shailers white; osmarea burkwoodii hedge; arboretum with very rare trees planted by Humphrey Waterfield; large rosa chinensis mutablilis. Although most of the plants in the garden are named, the Head Gardener is available to answer your questions. TEAS. *Adm £2 Chd £1. Sun June 25 (2-6)*

Alwalton Gardens ✤ Alwalton. 4m W of Peterborough, next to E of England showground. Parking at Village Hall. TEAS. *Combined adm £2 Chd free. Sun June 18 (2-6)*

The Forge ♿ (Mr & Mrs M Watson) Large cottage garden. Deep bed vegetables

Manor House ❀ (Mr & Mrs M Holmes) 1½-acre garden, walled formal garden, topiary. Views over R Nene

Oak Cottage ♿ (Mr & Mrs J Wilson) Small enclosed garden with roses and lilies

The Old Rectory ♿ (Mr & Mrs J Gooding) Walled garden with mature trees, lawns, borders

9 Oundle Road ♿ (Mr & Mrs C Leary) Medium-sized garden, mixed borders, pond, shrubs, rose arbour

Anglesey Abbey ♿✤❀ (The National Trust) 6m NE of Cambridge. From A14 turn N on to B1102 through Stow-cum-Quy. 100 acres surrounding an Elizabethan manor created from the remains of an abbey founded in reign of Henry I. Garden created during last 50 years; avenues of beautiful trees; groups of statuary; hedges enclosing small intimate gardens; daffodils and 4,400 white and blue hyacinths (April); magnificent herbaceous borders (June). Lunches & TEAS. *Adm garden only £3.50 Chd £1.75. Suns July 16, Aug 13 (11-5.30)*

Bainton House ♿ (Major W & Hon Mrs Birkbeck) Stamford. 4m E of Stamford on B1443 in Bainton Village. Turn N at Bainton Church. Entrance 400yds on the L. Approx 3 acres mature garden, shrubs, mixed borders, wild flowers and woodland. TEAS in aid of Macmillan Nurses. *Adm £1.50 Chd free. Sun June 18 (2-5.30)*

90 Bannold Rd ✤❀ (Mr & Mrs R L Guy) Waterbeach. 7m N of Cambridge on E of A10. Feature front winter garden. Coloured barks and many small bulbs. Best time in early spring. *Collection Box. Also open* **92 Bannold Rd.** *Private visits welcome from Feb to end April, please* **Tel 01223 863661**

Barton Gardens 3½m SW of Cambridge. Take A603, in village turn R for Comberton Rd. Teas in village hall. *Combined adm £1.25 Chd 25p (Share to GRBS®). Sun March 26 (2-5)*

Farm Cottage ✤ (Dr R Belbin), 18 High St. Cottage garden with water feature. Courtyard garden. *Also open Sat June 17, Sun July 30*

The Gables ♿ (P L Harris Esq) 11 Comberton Rd. 2-acre old garden, mature trees, ha-ha, spring flowers

14 Haslingfield Road ♿ (J M Nairn Esq) Orchard, lawns, mixed domestic

¶**Kings Tythe** (Maj C H Thorne) Comberton Road. Small domestic garden; good through way to larger gardens of **Town's End** and **The Gables**

31 New Road ♿ (Dr D Macdonald) Cottage garden
Orchard Cottage, 22 Haslingfield Road ♿ (Mr J Blackhurst) Interesting mixed domestic. ½-acre garden with raised vegetable beds
The Seven Houses ♿❀ (GRBS) Small bungalow estate on L of Comberton Rd. 1½-acre spring garden; bulbs naturalised in orchard. Gift stall
Town's End ♿ (B R Overton Esq) 15a Comberton Rd. 1-acre; lawns, trees, pond; extensive views

¶**Bourn Lodge** ♿❀ (Mr Lawson) Bourn. 10m W of Cambridge off old A45 (now A428) as you approach Bourn Airfield which runs parallel to A428. Turn off main rd to Bourn, about 2m further. As you approach village take 1st R to Caxton. 200yds further, orange traffic mirror and Bourn Lodge sign; drive to house opp. Natural garden of approx 1½ acres; herbaceous and shrub borders; shrub roses; 2 man-made ponds; planted up with wild flowers and native trees. *Adm £1.50p. Sun June 25 (11-5)*

Chippenham Park ♿❀ (Mr & Mrs Eustace Crawley) Chippenham. 5m NE of Newmarket 1m off A11. Walled parkland with mature and newly planted rare trees, large lake with 3 islands. 7 acres of garden and woods containing roses, mixed borders of some rare shrubs, perennials and unusual trees. The spring gardens around the lake are dramatically beautiful and becoming more so after extensive replantings. The summer gardens have been greatly extended and replanted in recent years, and the Autumn colours are superb. Specialist plant stall. TEAS. *Adm £1.50 Chd free (Share to St Margaret's Church, Chippenham®). Suns April 9, June 18, Oct 8 (11-5). Also private visits welcome for parties of 4 and over, please* **Tel 01638 720221**

Christ's College ♿ (Fellows) Cambridge. Large college garden near city centre; some form of garden since C16; present design from mid C19; 'Milton's Mulberry Tree'; large herbaceous borders and mature trees. *Adm £1 Chd free. Sat July 9 (2-6)*

Clare College, Fellows' Garden (Master & Fellows) Cambridge. The Master and Fellows are owners of the Fellows' Garden which is open; the Master's garden (nearby) is not open to the public. Approach from Queen's Rd or from city centre via Senate House Passage, Old Court and Clare Bridge. 2 acres; one of the most famous gardens on the Cambridge Backs. TEAS. *Adm £1 Chd under 13 free. Sun July 9 (2-6). Private visits welcome, please* **Tel 01223 333 222**

The Crossing House ♿ (Mr & Mrs Douglas Fuller and Mr John Marlar) Meldreth Rd, Shepreth, 8m SW of Cambridge. ½m W of A10. King's Cross-Cambridge railway runs alongside garden. Small cottage garden with many old-fashioned plants grown in mixed beds in company with modern varieties; shrubs, bulbs, etc, many alpines in rock beds and alpine house. *Collecting box. Open daily, any reasonable time. Parties by appt, please* **Tel 01763 261071**

Docwra's Manor ♿❀ (Mrs John Raven) Shepreth, 8m SW of Cambridge. ½m W of A10. Cambridge-Royston bus stops at gate opposite the War Memorial in Shepreth. 2½-acres of choice plants in series of enclosed gardens. Small nursery. TEA May 14, Sept 3 only, in aid of Shepreth Church Funds. *Adm £1.50 Chd free. All year Mon, Wed, Fri (10- 4), Suns April 2, May 7, June 4, July 2, Aug 6, Oct 1 (2-5), also Bank Hol Mons (10-4). Proceeds for garden upkeep. Also private visits welcome, please* **Tel 01763 261473, 261557, 260235.** *For NGS Suns May 14, Sept 3 (2-6)*

¶**Downing College** ♿ (The Master & Fellows of Downing College) Regent Street. Centre of Cambridge opp the University Arms Hotel to the S of Parkers's Piece. Parking within the College. Approach from Regent St only. Fine example of 16-acre garden in a classical setting. Wilkins' Greek revival buildings, frame wide lawns and paddock. Mature and newly planted rare trees. Unusual view of the Roman Catholic Church. Master's garden. Fellow's garden and walled rose garden with period roses. TEAS. *Adm £1.50 Chd 50p. Suns April 2, July 2 (2-6)*

Elton Hall (Mr & Mrs William Proby) Elton. 8m W of Peterborough, 5m N of Oundle off A605. 8 acres of garden surrounding large house dating from late C15. Formal gardens front the Gothic C18 side of house. Magnificent rose garden replanted with help of Peter Beales and contains many old-fashioned varieties; many other borders. Sunken garden with lily pond developed by owners with Rupert Golby. Ancient knot garden; arboretum planted in 1983. Bressingham Plant Centre in walled garden. TEAS. *Adm garden only £2 Chd £1.* ▲*Sun July 2 (2-5)*

Ely Gardens ♿❀ 16m N of Cambridge on A10. *Share to Old Palace Sue Ryder Home®*
Mon May 8 (2-5) *Combined adm £1 Chd 50p*
Old Bishops Palace 1½ acres with small lake, iris walk and herbaceous border wonderfully restored by two expert voluneers to its original C17. Famous for its plane tree - oldest and largest in country
The Old Fire Engine House Restaurant and Gallery (Mr & Mrs R Jarman) Delightful walled country garden with mixed herbaceous borders and wild flowers. Situated just W of the Cathedral. TEAS
Sun June 11 (2.30-5.30) *Combined adm £3 Chd 50p single garden £1*
58 Barton Road (Mrs R Sadler) Small wildlife garden with pond and many interesting plants to attract bees, birds and butterflies
Belmont House, 43 Prickwillow Rd (Mr & Mrs P J Stanning) Designed ½-acre garden with interesting and unusual plants
Rosewell House 60 Prickwillow Road. (Mr & Mrs A Bullivant). Well stocked garden with emphasis on perennial planting and splendid view of cathedral and surrounding fen-land
The Bishops House To R of main Cathedral entrance. Walled garden, former cloisters of monastery. Mixed herbaceous, box hedge, rose and kitchen garden
31 Egremont St (Mr & Mrs J N Friend-Smith) A10 Lynn Rd out of Ely. 2nd L. Approx 1 acre. Lovely views of cathedral, mixed borders, cottage garden. Ginkgo tree, tulip tree and many other fine trees
Old Bishops Palace Description with May opening. TEAS

Emmanuel College Garden & Fellows' Garden ♿✗ in centre of Cambridge. Car parks at Parker's Piece and Lion Yard, within 5 mins walk. One of the most beautiful gardens in Cambridge; buildings of C17 to C20 surrounding 3 large gardens with pools; also herb garden; herbaceous borders, fine trees inc Metasequoia glyptostroboides. On this date access allowed to Fellows' Garden with magnificent Oriental plane and more herbaceous borders. Teashops in Cambridge. *Adm £1 Chd under 16 free. Sat July 8 (2.30-5.30). Private visits welcome, please* **Tel 01223 65411**

¶**Farm Hall** ✗ (Prof & Mrs Marcial Echenique) Godmanchester. Fronting West St (Offord/St Neots rd B1043) 2m S of Huntingdon, 15m NW of Cambridge (A14). Early C18 country house (not open) on edge of Godmanchester. Set in 24 acres of parkland with mature trees. Formal layout on its main axis: in front a rectangular pond or canal flanked by an avenue of poplars ending at the R Ouse; behind a long avenue of limes more than 200yrs old. Charming walled garden with formal box hedges, herbaceous borders and fruit trees. Rose garden with lily pond surrounded by yew hedge; statuary; wooded walk with wild flowers. TEAS in aid of church. *Adm £2 Chd 50p. Sun June 18 (2-5)*

Fen Ditton Gardens ✗❀ 3½m NE of Cambridge. From A14 Cambridge-Newmarket rd turn N by Borough Cemetery into Ditton Lane; or follow Airport sign from bypass. Teas in church hall. *Combined adm £1.50 Chd 50p (Share to Sue Ryder Foundation®). Sun May 28 (2-5.30)*

Hardwicke House ✗❀ (Mr J Drake) 2 acres designed to provide shelter for plants on exposed site; divided by variety of hedges; species roses; rare herbaceous plants; home of national collection of aquilegias, collection of plants grown in this country prior to 1650. Please park in road opposite. Large sale of plants in aid of NGS; rare aquilegias from National Collection; foliage plants and rare herbaceous plants. **Exceptional rare plant sale for NGS.** *Also private visits welcome, please* **Tel 01223 29 2246**

The Old Stables (Mr & Mrs Zavros) Large informal garden; old trees, shrubs and roses; many interesting plants, herbs and shrubs have been introduced. House (not open) converted by owners in 1973 from C17 stables

The Rectory (Revd & Mrs L Marsh) New garden being laid out around new rectory. Visitors invited to inspect progress over next few years as owners wish to continue their support for the NGS

Grantchester Gardens ❀ 2m SW of Cambridge. AI0 from S, L at Trumpington (Junction 11, M11). M11 from N, L at Junction 12. Palestrina Singers will be performing at the Old Vicarage. Craft Fair at Manor Farm, quality handmade goods; wooden toys; pottery, stained glass; glass blowing demonstration; honey and demonstrations of beekeeping. TEAS. *(Share to Grantchester Church®). Sun June 25 (2-6)*

43 Broadway ♿✗ (Mr & Mrs R Hill) 2 separate footpaths from Broadway. 1-acre lawns and formal garden with trees and alpine sink gardens; rest paddock backing onto farm meadows

Home Grove ♿ (Dr & Mrs C B Goodhart) 1-acre mature, orchard-type garden with shrub roses. Specimen trees and lawns and carefully planned kitchen garden

North End House ♿ (Mr & Mrs A Frost) 1 acre, shrub and herbaceous borders; old-fashioned roses; water garden and rockery. Small conservatory

The Old Mill ♿ (Jeremy Pemberton Esq) ½-acre on both sides of Mill Race in attractive rural setting. The Old Mill, mentioned in Rupert Brooke's poem 'Grantchester', was burnt down in 1928

The Old Vicarage ♿✗❀ (Lord & Dr Archer) 2½ acres; house dating from C17; informal garden laid out in mid C19 with C20 conservatory; lawn with fountain; ancient mulberry tree; many other interesting trees incl cut-leaf beech; beyond garden is wilderness leading to river bank bordered by large old chestnut trees immortalised by Rupert Brooke, who lodged in the house 1910–1912

Greystones, Swaynes Lane ♿✗❀ (Dr & Mrs Lyndon Davies) Comberton. 5m W of Cambridge. From M11 take exit 12 and turn away from Cambridge on A603. Take first R B1046 through Barton to Comberton; follow signs from Xrds. Garden of approx ½ acre attractively planted with wide range of flowering plants framed by foliage and shrubs. Gravel bed and troughs give contrast; vegetable garden. TEAS. *Adm £1 Chd 50p (Share to Herbal Research®). Sun June 18 (2-5.30). Private visits welcome, please* **Tel 01223 264159**

Hardwicke Farm ♿✗ (Mr & Mrs N H M Chancellor) Gt Gransden. Situated mid way between the villages of Gt Gransden and Caxton (A1198) 12m W of Cambridge, 8m S of Huntingdon, 12m N of Royston. House on R travelling towards Gt Gransden. 4-acre garden, herbaceous border, shrubs and recently planted courtyard incorporating 1830 red brick barn. Decorative pond and conservatory. TEAS in aid of WI. *Adm £1.50 Chd 50p. Sun July 2 (2-6). Parties by appt, please* **Tel 01954 719483**

Hardwicke House see Fen Ditton Gardens

83 High Street, Harlton ♿✗❀ (Dr Ruth Chippindale) 7m SW of Cambridge. A603 (toward Sandy); after 6m turn L (S) for Harlton. ⅓-acre interesting design which includes many different features, colours and a wide diversity of plants. TEAS. *Adm £1 Chd free (Share to Harlton Church Restoration Fund®). Sun July 2 (2-6); also by appointment* **Tel 01223 262170**

¶**Horningsea Gardens** ❀ TEAS. *Combined adm £1.50 Chd 50p (Share to Village Church® & Arthur Rank Hospice®). Sun June 18 (2-5.30)*

¶**15 Abbots Way** (Mr & Mrs D Edwards) Horningsea. 4m NE of Cambridge from A1307 Cambridge-Newmarket Rd. Turn N at borough cemetery to Horningsea or take B1047 N from A14. 1-acre developing plantswoman's garden on old flood bank of R Cam; overlooking river and water meadows. Spring and natural pond. Clematis and solomon's seal amongst fine collection of rare and unusual plants, shrubs and trees. Entrance to car park and garden signposted nr village hall; no access to garden via Abbots Way

By Appointment Gardens. Avoid the crowds. Good chance of a tour by owner. See garden description for telephone number.

The Lodge ✿ (N M Buchdal) Clayhithe Road, Horningsea. 5m NE of Cambridge to Newmarket Rd. 1½m of A14 on Clayhithe Rd (B1047), ¾m out of Horningsea on L towards R Cam. 3 acres of well landscaped garden framed by mature willows and old native trees; many shrubs and old roses; large water garden and many wide herbaceous borders. Unusual plants for sale from specialist nursery on site. Car park

Inglethorpe Manor ✿❀ (Mr & Mrs Roger Hartley) Emneth, near Wisbech. 2m S of Wisbech on A1101. 200yds on L beyond 40mph derestriction sign. Entrance opp Ken Rowe's Garage. Large garden with interesting mature trees incl giant wellingtonia, lawns, mixed and herbaceous borders, shrub roses, rose walk and lakeside walk. Victorian house (not open). Plants for sale and TEAS in aid of NSPCC. *Adm £1.50 Chd free. Sun June 18 (2-6)*

Island Hall ♿✿❀ (Mr Christopher & The Hon Mrs Vane Percy) Godmanchester. In centre of Godmanchester next to car park, 1m S of Huntingdon (A1) 15m NW of Cambridge (A604). Station: Huntingdon (1m). 3-acre grounds, of important mid C18 mansion. Tranquil riverside setting with replica of original Chinese bridge over millstream to island. The garden has been restored during last 10 yrs. New shrubberies have been planted, vistas created. There are new formal borders and blue and white borders. Wild flowers have been encouraged on the island. Plants and TEAS in aid of Godmanchester Church Fabric Fund. *Adm £1.50 Chd free. Sat May 27 (2-5)*

King's College Fellows' Garden ♿✿ Cambridge. Fine example of a Victorian garden with rare specimen trees. Colour booklet available £1.50, free leaflet describing numbered trees. TEAS. *Adm £1 Chd free. Suns April 9, July 23 (2-6)*

15 Latham Road ♿✿❀ (Dr J F Procope) Cambridge. Latham Rd lies between Cambridge and Trumpington, running W off the Trumpington Rd 200yds S of the Botanical Gardens. The entry marked by a pink cottage on the N side with a panda crossing over the Trumpington Rd to the S. 'Whitsunden', 15 Latham Rd is at the far end on L. Enclosed Edwardian suburban garden, 1¼ acres approx, restored. Laid out in compartments around central octagonal lawn. Sunken garden. *Adm £1.50 Chd 50p. Sun Aug 27 (2-6). Private visits welcome, please* **Tel 01223 352948**

Leckhampton ♿✿ (Corpus Christi College) 37 Grange Rd, Cambridge. Grange Rd is on W side of Cambridge and runs N to S between Madingley Rd (A1303) and A603; drive entrance opp Selwyn College. 10 acres; originally laid out by William Robinson as garden of Leckhampton House (built 1880); George Thomson building added 1964 (Civic Trust Award); formal lawns, rose garden, small herbaceous beds; extensive wild garden with bulbs, cowslips, prunus and fine specimen trees. TEAS. *Adm £1 Chd free. Sun June 4 (2-6)*

Madingley Hall Cambridge ✿ (University of Cambridge) 4m W, 1m from M11 Exit 13. C16 Hall set in 7½ acres of attractive grounds. Features include landscaped walled garden with hazel walk, borders in individual colours and rose pergola. Meadow, topiary and mature trees. TEAS. *Adm £1.50 Chd free (Share to Madingley Church Restoration Fund®). Sun June 11 (2.30-5.30)*

¶**The Manor** ♿❀ (Mr & Mrs P S Boston) Hemingford Grey. 4m E of Huntingdon off A14. Entrance to garden by small gate off river towpath. No parking at house except disabled by arrangement with owners. Park in village or alongside playing fields. Garden designed and planted by the author Lucy Boston, surrounds the C12 manor house on which her Green Knowe Books were based. 4 acres divided into different areas with topiary; one of the best collections of old shrub roses in Cambridgeshire, and herbaceous borders with mainly scented plants. Enclosed by river, moat and wilderness. TEAS. *Adm £1.50 Chd 50p. Sun June 18 (2-5.30)*

Melbourn Bury ♿✿❀ (Mr & Mrs Anthony Hopkinson) 2¼m N of Royston; 8m S of Cambridge; off the A10 on edge of village, Royston side. 5 acres; small ornamental lake and river with wildfowl; large herbaceous border; fine mature trees with wide lawns and rose garden. TEAS. *Combined adm with* **Melbourn Lodge** *£2 Chd free. Sun June 18 (2- 6). Private visits welcome for parties of 4 and over, please* **Tel 01763 261151**

Melbourn Lodge ♿✿❀ (J R M Keatley Esq) Melbourn 3m N of Royston, 8m S of Cambridge. House in middle of Melbourn village. 2-acre garden maintained on 9 hrs work per week in season. C19 grade II listed house (not open). TEAS at Melbourn Bury. *Combined adm with* **Melbourn Bury** *£2 Chd free. Sun June 18 (2-6)*

Mill House ♿✿❀ (Anthony & Valerie Jackson) North End. On the NW outskirts of Bassingbourn 1m from Church, on the rd to Shingay. Take North End at the war memorial in the centre of Bassingbourn which is just W of the A1198, 2m N of Royston. Garden created out of open countryside by garden designer owners. Clever use of walls, pergolas, water and varying land levels provide a backdrop for many very fascinating plants notably viticella clematis, giving interest and colour throughout the year. Rare plants for sale. *Adm £1.50 Chd free. Sun July 2 (2-5.30). Private visits welcome in July, please* **Tel 01763 243491**

Monksilver Nursery ✿❀ (J L Sharman) Cottenham. 6m N of Cambridge. Take A45 or M11 onto A604, take 1st turn to Oakington, Cambridge and Dry Drayton, go over flyover, through Oakington and Westwick. Monksilver Nursery is then 1m from Westwick on RH-side. 1 acre of formal garden in process of development. Herbaceous borders and yew hedges, rare trees, shrubs. National collections (NCCPG) of galeobdolon, lamium and vinca. Large collections of helianthus, chrysanthemum, aster, echinops, veronica, sedum, monarda, lathyrus, potentilla, pulmonaria and centaurea. *Donations. Sats March 11, April 8, May 13, June 10, July 8, Aug 12, Sept 9, Oct 14 (10-4)*

Netherhall Manor ✿ (Timothy Clark) Soham. Enter Soham from Newmarket, Tanners Lane is 1st R 80yds after Webbs Store. Enter Soham from Ely, Tanners Lane is 2nd L after War Memorial. 1-acre walled garden incl courtyard featured on Geoffrey Smiths 'World of Flowers' and 'Gardeners World'. April-Crown Imperials, Victorian hyacinths and old primroses. May-florists ranunculus (picotee and bizarre), and tulips (rose, bizarre, byblomen). Also during Aug formal beds of Victorian pelargonium, calceolaria, lobelia and heliotrope a seasonal kitchen garden. *Adm £1 Chd 50p Suns April 16, May 14, Aug 6, 13 (2-5). Private visits welcome, please* **Tel 01353 720269**

Nuns Manor ♿✂❀ (Mr & Mrs J R L Brashaw) Frog End Shepreth. 8m SW of Cambridge 200yds from A10 Melbourn-Shepreth Xrds. C16 farmhouse surrounded by owner-maintained 2-acre garden (extended 1987); interesting plants, large pond, woodland walk, kitchen garden. Mixed and herbaceous borders. TEA weather permitting. *Adm £1 Chd free. Sun July 2 (2-6); also private visits welcome April to July, please* **Tel 01763 260313**

Padlock Croft ♿✂❀ (Mr & Mrs P E Lewis) West Wratting. From dual carriageway on A604 between Linton and Horseheath take turning N (Balsham W Wratting); Padlock Road is at entry to village. Plantsman's organic garden of ⅔-acre, home of the National Campanula Collection; mixed borders, troughs, alpine house etc inc rare plants; rock and scree gardens; potager with raised beds; bantams and ducks. *Combined adm £1.50 Chd 50p with* **Scarletts Farm** *and* **Weavers Cottage.** *Sats April 29, May 27; Mon May 29; Sats June 17, July 22 (2-6). Private visits also welcome, weekdays, please* **Tel 01223 290383**

Pampisford Gardens ♿✂❀ 8m S of Cambridge on A505. TEAS at the Old Vicarage in aid of RDA. *Combined adm £2 Chd free. Sun July 23 (2-5.30)*

Beech Corner (Dr & Mrs B E Bridgland) 22 Church Lane. Rear garden has been planned as a small paved courtyard leading round into mini woodland

The Dower House (Dr & Mrs O M Edwards) 7 High Street. Medieval house surrounded by well designed and interesting garden

Glebe Crescent A group of pensioners houses with very colourful small gardens

No **3** (Mr & Mrs Rutter)

No **4** (Mr & Mrs Duller)

No **5** (Mr & Mrs Frosdick) Won the 1st prize for best kept small garden in S Cambs

No **6** (Mr & Mrs Freestone)

The Old Vicarage (Mr & Mrs Nixon) Next to Church in village. 2½-acres; mature trees; shrub and herbaceous borders with good ground cover plants; small Victorian style conservatory planted with rare species

Peckover House ♿✂❀ (The National Trust) Wisbech. In centre of Wisbech town, on N bank of R Nene (B1441). Garden only open. 2-acre Victorian garden; rare trees, inc maidenhair (Ginkgo), tulip trees etc. Many old-fashioned roses and colourful borders. Orange trees growing in well-stocked greenhouse. TEAS. *Adm £1 Chd 50p. ▲Thurs June 22, Aug 10 (2-5)*

Robinson College ♿✂❀ (Warden & Fellows) Cambridge. Gardens surround college and are enclosed by Grange Rd, Adams Rd, Sylvester Rd and Hershel Rd, ½m W of the centre of Cambridge. Access is by Porter's Lodge on Grange Rd and Thorneycreek Gate, Herschel Rd, (off Grange Rd). Ample parking in surrounding rds. From M11 turn E at Junction 12 (A603); turn L into Grange Rd after ½m. 8-acre garden created in 1979 by landscaping several Edwardian gardens. The site is bisected by the Bin Brook, with a pool at its centre. Programme of planting since 1982. Wide range of trees, snake bark maples (acer spp), parrotia persica, sequoiadendron giganteum pendulum and celtis australis; numerous shrubs; cistus sp. ceanothus impressus, southmead and blue mound and other plants from the Mediterranean and New Zealand. Wide range of shade of shade-tolerant species. TEA. *Adm £1 Chd free. Sun July 23 (2-6). Private visits welcome for parties of 10 and over, please* **Tel 01223 311431**

Scarlett's Farm ♿✂❀ (Mr & Mrs M Hicks) Padlock Rd, West Wratting. From dual carriageway on A604 between Linton and Horseheath taking turning N (W Wratting 3½); Padlock Road is at entry to village. Scarlett's Farm at end of Padlock Road. ⅓-acre mixed country garden, planted for long season of interest; small nursery attached. TEAS. *Combined adm £1.50 Chd 50p with* **Padlock Croft** *and* **Weavers Cottage.** *(Except May 8) £1 garden on its own. Sats April 29, May 27, June 17, July 22, Mons May 8, 29 (2-6). Private visits welcome, please* **Tel 01223 290812**

31 Smith Street ♿✂❀ (Drs J D & J M Twibell) Elsworth. Approx 9m from Cambridge, Huntingdon, St Ives and St Neots. From A45 (St Neots) enter village and turn L at T-junction at "Poacher" public house. 2nd house on L. 2nd house on R on entering village from Hilton end. ¾-acre cottage garden. Herbs, scented, insectivorous and other unusual plants. National collections of artemisia (featured Channel 4 Garden Club Sept 1992) and nerium oleander. TEA. *Adm £1 Chd 50p. Sun June 18 (2-6). Private visits welcome, please* **Tel 0954 267 414**

Stibbington Gardens 8m W of Peterborough off the A1. 107 Elton Rd is W of A1 on B671 Elton Rd S of Wansford. Old Castle Farmhouse is in Stibbington Village E of A1. Signed Stibbington from A1. TEAS at Old Castle Farmhouse. *Combined adm £1 Chd free. Sun July 30 (2-6)*

107 Elton Road ✂ (Mr & Mrs J Ferris) 1 acre, comprising lawns with many roses; mainly annuals and dahlias; enclosed with mature trees

Old Castle Farmhouse ♿❀ (Mr & Mrs J M Peake) Cul-de-sac S of church. Mainly lawn and shrubs with pond, garden borders a small backwater of R Nene and covers approx 2 acres

Stibbington House (Mr & Mrs Michael Thompson) Wansford. 8m W of Peterborough W of A1 on B671 Elton Rd S of Wansford. Approx 3 acres of trees, shrubs, mixed borders, lawns running down to mill stream (R Nene). Site of old paper mill. River walks. Picnic in field by river. TEAS. *Adm £1.50 Chd free. Sun June 25 (12-5)*

Sutton Gardens ♿✂❀ 6m W of Ely on A142, turn L at roundabout into village. TEAS. *Combined adm £2 Chd free. Sun June 18 (2-6)*

1 Church Lane ♿❀ (Miss B M & Miss B I Ambrose) Small garden near church, filled with an unusual range of shrubs, climbers (clematis), perennials and alpines; silver and gold plants. Raised beds, troughs, greenhouse. Teas at 5 Church Lane in aid of Sutton WI

¶51 High Street (Mr A Wilkinson) Medium-sized garden on sloping site, herbaceous borders, terrace, conservatory with vine. Tender perennials include salvias, daturas, gloriosa lilies and summer flowering bulbs

¶7 Lawn Lane ♿❀ (Mr & Mrs R Kybird) Small garden with many hanging baskets and containers; fuchsias, penstemons, hardy geraniums, roses, hostas, clematis and shrubs incl photima

¶8 Lawn Lane ❀ (Mr & Mrs H J Fortin) Small garden closely planted and colourful, with rockery, formal pool, terrace and curved lawns on 2 levels. Secluded vegetable corner. Meticulously cared for by plantaholic

91 The Row ♿❀ (Mr & Mrs M Cooper) Recently created organic garden bordering open fenland. Traditional English hedgerow and pond to encourage wildlife. (Great crested newts in pond). Collection of herbs; secluded scented garden. TEAS in aid of Sutton Scout Group

Tetworth Hall ❀ (Lady Crossman) 4m NE of Sandy; 6m SE of St Neots off Everton-Waresley Rd. Large woodland and bog garden; rhododendrons; azaleas, unusual shrubs and plants; fine trees. Queen Anne house (not open). TEA in aid of Waresley Church. *Adm £1.50 Chd free. Suns May 21, 28 (2-6.30). Private visits welcome April 15 to June 15, please* **Tel 01767 50212**

Thorpe Hall ♿✲ (Sue Ryder Foundation) Thorpe Rd, Longthorpe, Peterborough. 1m W of Peterborough city centre. Thorpe Hall 1665 Grade I house in Grade II listed garden with original walls; gate piers; urns and niches. Unique garden in course of replanting. Victorian stone parterre; iris collection; rose garden and 1650 herbaceous borders. TEAS. *Adm Garden only £1 Chd 50p (Share to Sue Ryder Foundation®). Sun June 4 (2-5.30)*

Trinity College, Fellows' Garden ♿✲ Queen's Road, Cambridge. Garden of 8 acres, originally laid out in the 1870s by W.B. Thomas; lawns with mixed borders, shrubs, specimen trees. Drifts of spring bulbs. *Adm £1 Chd free. Sun April 9 (2-6)*

¶Unwins Seeds Ltd ✲ (Mr & Mrs David Unwin) Impington Lane, Histon. 3m N of Cambridge, 1m off A14 on B1049. Follow signs for Histon and Cotterham. At traffic lights nr Rose & Crown in centre of Histon, turn R into Impington Lane. Trial gardens of approx 6 acres where 4,500 varieties of annuals, biennials, perennials and vegetables from seed are assessed. Many new and experimental strains are on show. The company uses the gardens to determine the garden worth of new varieties and monitor the trueness to type of strains it already lists. *Adm £1.50 Chd under 14 free. Sat Aug 12 (12-5)*

¶Upton Gardens ✲❀ 5m W of Peterborough. Turn off A47 between Castor and Wansford at roundabout signed Upton. Plants and TEAS in aid of St John The Baptist Church. *Combined adm £1.50 Chd free. Sun July 2 (2-5)*

¶43 Church Walk (Mr & Mrs M Bell) Approx ¼-acre garden with lots of interest, large pond, many shrubs and colourful patio tubs. Vegetable patch and soft fruit. Orchard

¶Primrose Cottage (Mr & Mrs D Burton) Cottage garden with shrubs and herbaceous plants. Wildlife pond; lots of interest especially some unusual plants

Rose Cottage ✲ (Mr & Mrs K W Goodacre) 36 Church Walk, Upton. Small cottage garden; pond; herbs; octagonal greenhouse; many varieties of colourful plants and shrubs

Weaver's Cottage ♿✲❀ (Miss Sylvia Norton) Streetly End, West Wickham. From dual carriageway on A604 between Linton and Horseheath take turning N (Balsham, West Wratting) then 1st turning R (Streetly End 1¼m). Keep L at triangle. Weaver's Cottage is 5th on the R. ½-acre garden planted for fragrance with bulbs; shrubs; herbs; perennials; honeysuckle; old shrub and climbing roses. National Lathyrus Collection. TEA. *Combined adm £1.50 Chd 50p with* **Padlock Croft** *and* **Scarletts Farm.** *Sats April 29, May 27, June 17, July 22, Mon May 29 (Mons April 17 garden open on its own) (2-6). Visitors welcome any time by appt* **Tel 01223 892399**

West Wratting Park ♿✲❀ (Mr & Mrs Henry d'Abo) 8m S of Newmarket. From A11, between Worsted Lodge and Six Mile Bottom, turn E to Balsham; then N along B1052 to West Wratting; Park is at E end of village. Georgian house (orangery shown), beautifully situated in rolling country, with fine trees; rose and herbaceous gardens; walled kitchen garden, now a tree nursery. TEA. *Adm £1 Chd free. Sun June 25 (2-7)*

¶Whittlesford Gardens ✲❀ 7m S of Cambridge. 1m NE of Junction 10 of the M11 and A505. TEAS. *Combined adm £2 Chd 50p (Share to Village Church®). Suns June 18, July 16 (2-6)*

¶The Guildhall (Dr P & Dr M Spufford) North Road. Small knot garden next to medieval half-timbered building (not open). *June 18 only*

¶7 Duxford Road (Mr & Mrs J Eastwood) Organic low maintenance garden, planted to encourage wildlife. Fishpond and small bog garden, lots of pretty places to sit and enjoy

¶58 Duxford Road (Mr & Mrs J Bryant) Large garden with mature fruit trees, lawns, mixed borders, pond and summerhouse. *June 18 only*

¶15 West End (Mr & Mrs A Watson) Small garden with ornamental pond and mixed borders

¶26 West End (Mrs & Mrs W Wight) 2 acres of casual wild garden consisting of paths, shrubs, trees and other items, populated with chickens, pheasants and assorted pigeons

¶5 Parsonage Court ♿ (Mr & Mrs L Button) Medium-sized garden with wide range of trees, shrubs and annual plants, large pond and attractive terrace with pergola. Please park on main rd

¶Brook Cottage (R Marshall Esq & Ms J Lewis) Newton Road. Small untidy cottage garden with good variety of plants bordered by stream. Peaceful setting

¶Moonrakers (Mr & Mrs K Price) Royston Road. 1½ acres wildlife garden, with old espalier apple trees in kitchen garden surrounded by hedgerows, trees, shrubs and pond. *June 18 only*

¶Scotts Garden (Mr & Mrs M Walker) Shady walled garden, mixed herbaceous borders with many foliage plants. Small formal pond. *July 16 only*

¶12 Swallow Croft (Miss J Woodley) Small garden with hanging baskets. *July 16 only*

Regular Openers. Too many days to include in diary. Usually there is a wide range of plants giving year-round interest. See head of county section for the name and garden description for times etc.

Willingham Gardens ✿❀ 10m N of Cambridge on B1050 off new A14. TEAS. *Combined adm £1.50 Chd 50p. Sun June 4 (2-6)*

66 Balland Field (Mr & Mrs G Burton) Interesting garden in new housing estate with unusual plant containers holding annuals among shrubs and hardy plants; pond. Runner-up in BBC Look East Gorgeous Gardens Competition 1994. Please park along Berrycroft

60a Church Street (Mrs Y Rutherford & Dr M Spratling) Small intimate garden with unexpected detail and numerous scented plants, Pergola, pools, parterre and conservatory; raised beds

15a High Street (Mr & Mrs A Robinson) ½-acre informal garden with herbaceous perennials, shrubs, unusual trees, fruit and vegetables

40 Over Road (Mr & Mrs F Burdett) Small cottage-style plantsman's garden with herbaceous borders, alpine troughs, unusual plants and a small pond to encourage wildlife

4 Rampton End (Mr & Mrs R Curtis) 1-acre plantsman's garden with a shrub and hardy plant collection distributed through a series of garden rooms, 140yds long. Holly, carousel and vegetable gardens. Mediterranean garden developing. Work area for chrysanthemums and propagation; greenhouses. Featured on C4's 'Gardening Club'

Sun July 16 (2-6) *Combined adm £1 Chd 30p*

66 Balland Road (Mr & Mrs G Burton) Description above

43a Church Street (Mr & Mrs S Dyson) 100yd long ¾-acre garden with vegetables, fruit, greenhouses and numerous hanging baskets

45a Church Street (Mr & Mrs K Ellwood) 100yd long ⅓-acre garden with lawn, flower borders, mixed containers, large vegetable garden with greenhouse and fruit

Wimpole Hall ♿✿❀ (National Trust) Arrington. 5m N of Royston signed off A603 to Sandy 7m from Cambridge or off A1198. Part of 350-acre park. First sight of reinstatement of Victorian Parterres on N lawns. Rose garden and fine trees, marked walks in park. Guided tours available 11.00, 15.00 hrs given by Head Gardener. Lunches & TEA. *Adm £1 Chd free (Guided Tours) £2. ▲Fri June 9 (10.30-5)*

Wytchwood ✿❀ (Mr & Mrs David Cox) Gt Stukeley. 2m N of Huntingdon. Turn off B1043 into Owl End by Great Stukeley village hall. Parking at village hall and in Owl End. 1 acre yr-round interest. Lawns, shrubs, perennial plants, trees, pond, roses, area of wild plants and grasses. Vegetables and rare poultry. In 1992 this garden finished in the top ten of Gardener Of The Year competition. Sponsored by Garden News and Thompson and Morgan Seeds. TEAS. *Adm £1 Chd 50p. Sun July 30 (2-5.30)*

Cheshire & Wirral

Hon County Organiser: Nicholas Payne Esq, The Mount, Whirley, Macclesfield, Cheshire SK11 9PB Tel 01625 426730

Assistant Hon County Organisers: Mrs T R Hill, Salterswell House, Tarporley, Cheshire CW6 OED
Mrs N Whitbread, Lower Huxley Hall, Hargrave, Chester CH3 7RJ

DATES OF OPENING

By Appointment

For telephone numbers and other details see garden descriptions. Private visits welcomed

Ashton Hayes, Chester
37 Bakewell Road, Hazel Grove
Bluebell Cottage, Dutton
The Old Hall, Willaston
Orchard Villa, Alsager
The Quinta, Swettenham
Rosewood, Puddington
2 Stanley Road, Heaton Moor
The Well House, Tilston
Willow Cottage, Prestbury
Woodsetton, Alsager

Parties only

Cherry Hill, Malpas
Manley Knoll, Manley
The Mount, Whirley
Penn, Alderley Edge
5 Pine Hey, Neston
85 Warmingham Road, Crewe
Wood End Cottage, Whitegate

Regular openings

For details see garden descriptions

Arley Hall & Gardens, Northwich. Every Tues to Sun inc & Bank Hols April to Sept
Capesthorne, Macclesfield. See text for dates
Cholmondeley Castle Gardens, Malpas. For dates see text
Dunge Farm Gardens, Kettleshulme. Daily April 1 to Aug 31
Norton Priory, Runcorn. See text for dates
Peover Hall, Knutsford. Mons, Fris May to Oct
The Quinta, Swettenham. Open daily
Stonyford Cottage Nursery, Northwich. Tues to Suns & Bank Hols, April to Oct

April 9 Sunday

Poulton Hall, Bebington, Wirral
The Well House, Tilston

April 14 Friday

Penn, Alderley Edge

April 16 Sunday

The Old Hall, Willaston
Penn, Alderley Edge

April 17 Monday
Penn, Alderley Edge
April 23 Sunday
Woodsetton, Alsager
April 30 Sunday
Penn, Alderley Edge
85 Warmingham Road, nr Crewe
May 1 Monday
Penn, Alderley Edge
May 7 Sunday
Beeston House, Bunbury
Tushingham Hall, Whitchurch
Willaston Grange, South Wirral
May 8 Monday
Orchard Villa, Alsager
May 14 Sunday
Haughton Hall, Tarporley
Lyme Park, Disley
The Quinta, Swettenham
Rode Hall, Scholar Green
May 16 Tuesday
Orchard Villa, Alsager
May 20 Saturday
Peover Hall, Knutsford
May 21 Sunday
Dorfold Hall, Nantwich
Hare Hill Gardens, Over Alderley
Peover Hall, Knutsford
Rosewood, Puddington
May 23 Tuesday
Orchard Villa, Alsager
May 24 Wednesday
The Quinta, Swettenham
Reaseheath, nr Nantwich
May 28 Sunday
Bolesworth Castle, Tattenhall
Henbury Hall, nr Macclesfield
Manley Knoll, Manley
Penn, Alderley Edge
May 29 Monday
Ashton Hayes, Chester
Penn, Alderley Edge
May 30 Tuesday
Orchard Villa, Alsager
May 31 Wednesday
Reaseheath, nr Nantwich
June 3 Saturday
Arley Hall & Gardens, Northwich
June 4 Sunday
Little Moreton Hall, Congleton
The Old Hall, Willaston
June 6 Tuesday
Orchard Villa, Alsager
June 7 Wednesday
Cholmondeley Castle Gardens, Malpas
Reaseheath, nr Nantwich
June 10 Saturday
The Old Parsonage, Arley Green
June 11 Sunday
Cherry Hill, Malpas
Norton Priory, Runcorn
The Old Parsonage Arley Green
Poulton Hall, Bebington, Wirral ‡
The Stray, Neston ‡
June 13 Tuesday
Orchard Villa, Alsager
June 14 Wednesday
Reaseheath, nr Nantwich
June 17 Saturday
Briarfields, Aston
Ness Gardens, Ness
June 18 Sunday
Briarfields, Aston
The Old Hough, Warmingham
The Well House, Tilston
June 20 Tuesday
Orchard Villa, Alsager
June 21 Wednesday
Reaseheath, nr Nantwich
June 25 Sunday
Burton Village Gardens, Burton
85 Warmingham Road, nr Crewe
June 26 Monday
Tatton Park, Knutsford
June 27 Tuesday
Orchard Villa, Alsager
June 28 Wednesday
35 Heyes Lane, Timperley
Reaseheath, nr Nantwich
July 2 Sunday
Free Green Farm, Lower Peover
35 Heyes Lane, Timperley
5 Pine Hey, Neston
Wood End Cottage, Whitegate
July 5 Wednesday
Reaseheath, nr Nantwich
July 8 Saturday
Broxton Old Hall, nr Malpas
July 9 Sunday
The Mount, Whirley ‡
Stonyford Cottage Nursery, Northwich
Whirley Hall, Macclesfield ‡
July 12 Wednesday
Reaseheath, nr Nantwich
July 15 Saturday
Bridgemere Garden World, Bridgemere
July 16 Sunday
85 Warmingham Road, nr Crewe
July 19 Wednesday
Reaseheath, nr Nantwich
July 23 Sunday
Mill House,Great Barrow
July 26 Wednesday
Reaseheath, nr Nantwich
August 2 Wednesday
Capesthorne, Macclesfield
Ness Gardens, Ness
August 6 Sunday
Bluebell Cottage, Dutton
August 20 Sunday
Dunham Massey, Altrincham
August 27 Sunday
Lyme Park, Disley
August 28 Monday
Thornton Manor, Wirral

DESCRIPTIONS OF GARDENS

Arley Hall & Gardens ♿❀ (Hon M L W Flower), 6m W of Knutsford. 5m from M6 junctions 19 & 20 & M56 junctions 9 & 10. 12 acres; gardens have belonged to 1 family over 500 yrs; great variety of style and design; outstanding twin herbaceous borders (one of earliest in England); unusual avenue of clipped Ilex trees, walled gardens; yew hedges; shrub roses; azaleas, rhododendrons; herb garden; scented garden; woodland garden and walk. Arley Hall and Private Chapel also open. Lunches and light refreshments (in C16 converted barn adjacent to earlier 'Cruck' barn). Gift shop. Specialist plant nursery. *Adm Gardens & Grounds only £2.80, Chd under 16 £1.40. Hall £1.80 extra; Chd 90p under 5 free (Share to Great Budworth Church Restoration Fund®). April to Sept (hall opening times vary during April & Sept) every Tues to Sun incl & Bank Hols (12-5) last adm to gardens 4.30. For NGS Sat June 3 (12-5).* **Tel 01565 777353**

Ashton Hayes (Michael Grime Esq) Chester. Midway between Tarvin and Kelsall on A54 Chester-Sandiway rd; take B5393 N to Ashton and Mouldsworth. Approach to Ashton Hayes can be seen halfway between Ashton and Mouldsworth. The ¾m drive is beside former lodge. About 12 acres, incl arboretum and ponds. Predominantly a valley garden of mature trees and flowering shrubs. Great variety of azaleas and rhododendrons; notable embothrium. TEAS. *Adm £1.50 OAPs £1 Chd 50p (Share to Church of St John the Evangelist, Ashton Hayes®). Mon May 29 (2-6). Private visits welcome, please* **Tel 01829 51209**

37 Bakewell Road ✿ (Mr & Mrs H Williams) Hazel Grove. From Manchester on A6 following signs to Buxton, bear R at Rising Sun Public House, Hazel Grove. Taking the Macclesfield Rd (A523) take 1st R (Haddon Rd) then 1st L into Bakewell Rd. Small suburban garden 17yds × 6½yds heavily planted with azaleas, rhododendrons (several rare and unusual varieties), hydrangeas; pool and waterfall. Excellent example of how much can be planted in a small area. *Adm £1.50 Chd free. Private visits welcome for parties of 6 and over, May & June, please contact Mr Cofield* **Tel 0161 491 4952**

Beeston House ♿✿❀ (Mr & Mrs B S Jenkins) Bunbury. Off A49 3m S of Tarporley, 10m N of Whitchurch. Turn W at Bunbury Xrds lge brown sign for Beeston Castle 100yds from A49. 3 acres of traditional English country garden, rhododendrons, azaleas, flowering shrubs, foliage plants and herbaceous borders all designed to create all the year round interest. TEAS. *Adm £2 Chd 50p (Share to Tarporley War Memorial Hospital®). Sun May 7 (2-6)*

¶Bluebell Cottage ♿✿❀ (R L & D Casey) Lodge Lane, Dutton. Midway between Runcorn & Northwich off A533. From M56 (junction 10) take A49 Whitchurch Rd for 3m, turn R on A533 towards Runcorn at traffic lights. Lodge Lane is the 1st turning L approx 1.3m. Gardens are immed beyond canal bridge. 1½-acre garden in attractive setting adjacent to canal. The colourful gardens have been developed in a series of 'rooms' to grow a wide variety of plants in a cottage garden theme. There is an herbaceous border planted in the Gertrude Jekyll colour style. A yellow garden, a small bog area, herb garden and many other interesting features incl a variety of containers. The garden is surrounded by natural hedging to attract wild life and an adjacent area is being developed to create a wild flower meadow. TEA. *Adm £1.50 Chd 50p. Sun Aug 6 (1-5.30). Private visits welcome between May and Sept, please* **Tel 01928 713718**

Bolesworth Castle ♿✿❀ (Mr & Mrs A G Barbour) Tattenhall. Enter by lodge on A41 8m S of Chester or 1m N of Broxton roundabout. Landscape with rhododendrons, shrubs and borders. Woodland walk replanted 1993/4. TEAS. *Adm £2 Chd free (Share to Harthill & Burwardsley Churches®). Sun May 28 (2-5.30)*

¶Briarfields ♿✿❀ (Tony & Liz Gentil) 5m S of Nantwich or 6m N of Whitchurch on A530. Grid Ref SJ611460. A garden in the making on a 10-acre site. Designed on sound ecological lines it includes an orchard of old and interesting varieties, bee and butterfly garden, 5-acre wildflower meadow, wildlife pond and woodland. TEAS in aid of The Children's Society. *Adm £2. Sat, Sun June 17, 18 (12-5)*

Bridgemere Garden World ♿✿❀ On A51 7m S of Nantwich, 1m N of Woore. Follow brown tourist signs from Nantwich. The Garden Kingdom over 22 enjoyable and peaceful gardens showing many different styles of plant grouping. It includes the recreated Bridgemere Garden World prize winning exhibition gardens from Garden Festivals, Chelsea Flower Show Gold Medal gardens and the garden where the Gardeners' Diary television programme is filmed. *Adm £1.50 OAPs and Chd over 8yrs £1. Sat July 15 (10-5)*

Broxton Old Hall ✿ (Mr & Mrs Malcolm Walker) Nr Malpas. 1m E of Broxton roundabout on A534. Turn R after Frog Manor Hotel, ½m to entrance on R. Large garden imaginatively designed and planned in the last 6yrs and of great interest and beauty. Rhododendrons, formal gardens with box and yew hedges, herbaceous borders, rose and walled gardens, terraced lawns with far reaching views, lake, yew avenue, follies and woodland walks. TEAS. *Adm £2.50 Chd £1. Sat July 8 (2-5)*

Burton Village Gardens ✿❀ 9m NW of Chester. Turn off A540 at Willaston-Burton Xrds (traffic lights) and follow rd for 1m to Burton. Ample free parking. TEAS at Rake House. *Combined adm £2 Chd free (Share to St Johns Hospice®). Sun June 25 (2-6)*

Bank Cottage (Mr & Mrs J R Beecroft) Small, very colourful, mixed cottage garden with old roses backing on to village cricket ground

Rake House (Mr & Mrs R I Cowan) Enclosed sandstone courtyard, relaid with original cobbles and York stone, with pond; old orchard and potagered vegetable garden. TEAS in aid of St John's Hospice

Briarfield ❀ (Mr & Mrs P Carter) About an acre of rare trees and shrubs together with fruit and vegetable garden in woodland setting. Short woodland trail to and from **Lynwood**

Lynwood ❀ (Mr & Mrs P M Wright) On the fringe of the village on the Neston Road. ⅓-acre garden with shrub borders; rockery, pond with waterfall, pergola, arbour with climbers, heathers and alpines

Capesthorne ♿ (Mr & Mrs W A Bromley-Davenport) 5m W of Macclesfield. 7m S of Wilmslow on A34. Bus stop: Capesthorne (Congleton to Manchester route). Medium-sized garden; daffodil lawn; azaleas, rhododendrons; flowering shrubs; herbaceous border; lake, pool and arboretum. Georgian chapel built 1722 on view. Hall open from 1.30-3.30 (extra charge). Illustrated book on garden/woodland walks available at £1. Historic parks and gardens. TEAS and LUNCHES. Free car park. *Adm garden £2.25 OAPs £2 Chd £1; Hall extra £2.50 Chd £1. Combined tickets £4, £3.50, £1.50. Suns April to Sept incl; Weds May to Sept incl; Tues & Thurs June to July; also Good Fri & Bank hols. For NGS Wed Aug 2 (12-6).* **Tel 01625 861221**

Cherry Hill ♿❀ (Mr & Mrs Miles Clarke) Malpas. 2m W of Malpas signed from B5069 to Chorlton. Massed bulbs in spring; walks through pine woods and rhododendrons to trout lake; walled garden, herbaceous borders, shrub roses. Ornamental vegetable garden. TEAS in attractive house overlooking Welsh mountains. Cricket ground. *Adm £2 Chd 50p. Sun June 11 (2-6). Private visits welcome for parties of 8 & over, please* **Tel 01948 860355**

By Appointment Gardens. These owners do not have a fixed opening day usually because they do not like crowds or have insufficient parking space. Owner will often give guided tour.

Regular Openers. Too many days to include in diary. Usually there is a wide range of plants giving year-round interest. See head of county section for the name and garden description for times etc.

Cholmondeley Castle Gardens ♿❀ (The Marchioness of Cholmondeley) Malpas. Situated off A41 Chester/Whitchurch rd and A49 Whitchurch/Tarporley rd. Romantically landscaped gardens full of variety. Azaleas, rhododendrons, flowering shrubs; rare trees; herbaceous borders and water garden. Lakeside picnic area; rare breeds of farm animals, incl llamas, gift shops. Ancient private Chapel in the park. Tearoom offering light lunches etc. TEAS. *Adm gardens only £2.60 OAPs £1.80 Chd 75p. April Suns & Bank Hol Mons (12-5.30); May to October, Weds, Thurs (12-5); Suns & Bank Hol Mons (12-5.30). Reduced rate for coach parties. For NGS Wed June 7 (12-5).* **Tel 01829 720383** *or* **720203**

Dorfold Hall ✂❀ (Mr & Mrs Richard Roundell) Nantwich. 1m W of Nantwich on A534 between Nantwich and Acton. 18-acre garden surrounding C17 house with formal approach; lawns and recently planted herbaceous borders; spectacular spring woodland garden with rhododendrons, azaleas, magnolias and bulbs. TEAS in aid of Acton Parish Church. *Adm £2 Chd 75p. Sun May 21 (2-5.30)*

● **Dunge Farm Gardens** ✂❀ (Mr & Mrs David Ketley) Kettleshulme. Take B5470 rd from Macclesfield. Kettleshulme is 8m from Macclesfield. Turn R in village signed Dunge Farm Gardens and Goyt Valley and in ½m at Xrds, turn R down lane to Dunge Farm. Surrounded by romantic hills and set in 5½ acres, at 1000ft, this is the highest garden in Cheshire; mature trees, woodland, stream with waterfall, bog gardens, herbaceous borders, species rhododendrons, magnolias, acers and meconopsis plus roses. Yr-round interest, an oasis in the Pennine foothills. TEAS. *Adm £2 weekdays £2.50 Sat, Sun, Bank Hols Chd free (Share to NGS®). Open daily April 1 to Aug 31 (10.30-6).* **Tel 01663 733787**

Dunham Massey ♿✂❀ (The National Trust) Altrincham. 3m SW of Altrincham off A56. Well signed. Garden over 20 acres, on ancient site with moat lake, mount and orangery. Mature trees and fine lawns with extensive range of shrubs and herbaceous perennials suited to acid sand, many planted at waterside. Set in 350 acres of deer park. TEA. *Adm £2 Chd £1 (car entry £2). ▲For NGS Sun Aug 20 (12-5)*

Free Green Farm ♿✂ (Sir Philip & Lady Haworth) Lower Peover. Free Green Lane connects the A50 with the B5081. From Holmes Chapel take the A50 past the Drovers Arms. L into Free Green Lane, the farm is on the R. From Knutsford take the A50, turn R into Middlewich Lane (B5081), turn L into Broom Lane, turn L into Free Green Lane, the farm is on the L. 2-acre garden with pleached limes; herbaceous borders; ponds and new parterre. Parking in field behind house (sign posted) not on lane. Natural British woodland for conservation. TEAS in aid of Cancer Research Campaign. *Adm £2 Chd 50p. Sun July 2 (2-6)*

Hare Hill Gardens ✂ (The National Trust) Over Alderley. Between Alderley Edge and Prestbury, turn off N at B5087 at Greyhound Rd [118:SJ85765]. Bus: Cheshire E17 Macclesfield–Wilmslow (passing BR Wilmslow and Prestbury) to within ¾m. Stations: Alderley Edge 2½m, Prestbury 2½m. Attractive spring garden featuring a fine display of rhododendrons and azaleas. A good collection of hollies and other specimen trees and shrubs. The 10-acre garden includes a walled garden which hosts many wall shrubs including clematis and vines. The borders are planted with agapanthus (African lily) and geraniums. Partially suitable for wheelchairs. *Adm £2.50 Chd £1.25. ▲For NGS Sun May 21 (10-5.30)*

Haughton Hall ❀ (Mr & Mrs R J Posnett) Tarporley. 5m NW of Nantwich, 6m SE of Tarporley via Beeston Castle; N of A534 Nantwich, Wrexham Rd. Medium-sized garden; species of rhododendron, azaleas, shrubs, rock garden; lake with temple; waterfall. Collection of ornamental trees. Home-made TEAS. *Adm £2 Chd 50p. Sun May 14 (2-6)*

Henbury Hall ♿✂ (Mr & Mrs Sebastian de Ferranti) nr Macclesfield. 2m W of Macclesfield on A537 rd. Turn down School Lane, Henbury at Blacksmiths Arms: East Lodge on R. Large garden with lake, beautifully landscaped and full of variety. Azaleas, rhododendrons, flowering shrubs, rare trees, herbaceous borders. TEAS in aid of East Cheshire Hospice. *Adm £2 Chd 50p. Sun May 28 (2-5)*

35 Heyes Lane ✂❀ (Mr & Mrs David Eastwood) Timperley. Heyes Lane is a turning off Park Rd (B5165) 1m from the junction with the A56 Altrincham-Manchester rd 1½m N of Altrincham. Or from A560 turn W in Timperley Village for ¼m. Newsagents shop on corner. A small suburban garden 30′ × 90′ on sandy soil maintained by a keen plantswoman member of the Organic Movement (HDRA). An all yr round garden; trees; small pond; greenhouses; fruit and vegetables with a good collection of interesting and unusual plants. TEA. *Adm £1 Chd free (Share to Parrswood Centre for Rural Education, Didsbury®). Wed June 28, Sun July 2 (2-5)*

Little Moreton Hall ♿✂❀ (The National Trust) Congleton. On A34, 4m S of Congleton. 1½-acre garden surrounded by a moat and bordered by yew hedges, next to finest example of timber-framed architecture in England. Herb and historic vegetable garden, orchard and borders. Knot garden based on design in 'The English Gardener' published by Leonard Meager in 1670, though probably Elizabethan in origin. Adm includes entry to the Hall with optional free guided tours. Wheelchairs and electric mobility vehicle available. Disabled toilet. Picnic lawns. Shop and restaurant serving coffee, lunches and afternoon teas. TEAS. *Adm £3.50 Chd 1.80. ▲For NGS Sun June 4 (12-5.30 last admission 5)*

Lyme Park ✂ (The National Trust) Disley. 6m SE of Stockport just W of Disley on A6 rd. 17-acre garden retaining many original features from Tudor and Jacobean times; high Victorian style bedding; a Dutch garden; a Gertrude Jekyll style herbaceous border; an Edwardian rose garden, a Wyatt orangery and many other features. Also rare trees, a wild flower area and lake. Donations to NGS. *Adm £3 per car to estate £1 to gardens, pedestrians free. ▲For NGS Suns May 14, Aug 27 (11-5)*

Manley Knoll ♿ (Mrs D G Fildes) Manley, NE of Chester. Nr Mouldsworth. B5393. Quarry garden; azaleas and rhododendrons. TEAS. *Adm £1 Chd 25p. Sun May 28 (2-6). Private visits welcome for parties 20 to 30, please* **Tel 01928 740226**

¶Mill House ✂❀ (Mr & Mrs Julian Aaron) Great Barrow. Great Barrow (Barrow on modern maps) is on the B5132 between the A56 and the A51 5½m E of Chester. Mill House is at the end of Mill Lane a cul de sac. Mill Lane starts at the village pump 50yds N of the White Horse Inn. [Map Ref 475684 OS sheet 117]. The site of a Mill recorded in the Doomsday Book, Mill House and its garden of something short of an acre is surrounded by fields and woodland attached to the village of Great Barrow. The charm of this garden is its blend of water and fine trees in a pastoral setting. It includes the Mill rush & well and an organic kitchen garden featuring uncommon vegetables in raised beds. The visits can include a field walk (suitable for dogs) to a new ½-acre wood planted in 1986. TEAS. *Adm £1.50 Chd 75p (Share to The Friends of Barrowmore Village Settlement©). Sun July 23 (2-5)*

The Mount ♿✂❀ (Mr & Mrs Nicholas Payne) Whirley. The Mount is situated about 2m due W of Macclesfield along A537 rd. Opp Blacksmiths Arms at Henbury, go up Pepper St, turn L into Church Lane which becomes Anderton Lane in 100yds. The Mount is about 200yds up Anderton Lane on L. Adequate parking. The garden is approx 1½ acres and is of architectural character with hedges, terraces and walls. About ¼-acre of rhododendrons, azaleas, roses, herbaceous and some bedding plants; and also interesting trees including eucryphia nymansensis, fern leaved beech and sciadopitys. The garden is very much compartmentalized with lawns; shrubberies; herbaceous border; swimming pool and short vista of Irish Yews. TEAS. *Adm £2 Chd 50p. Sun July 9 (2-5.30). Parties welcome, please* **Tel 01625 426730**

Ness Gardens ♿✂❀ (University of Liverpool) Neston. Between Neston and Burton, 10m NW of Chester; 4m from end of M56; signed A540 and A550. 45 acres of landscaped gardens. Notable collection of rhododendrons, azaleas, camellias, magnolias, cherries, rowans, birches, conifers, roses, primulas, lilies, etc. Large rock and alpine garden; terrace gardens; herbaceous borders; plants for autumn and winter colour; conservatory and greenhouses; woodland and water gardens; laburnum arch. Tree and nature trails; Chinese plants collected by George Forrest. Children's play and picnic area (no ball games). Parts of the gardens suitable for wheelchairs. No dogs. Free parking for over 1000 cars. Licensed refreshment rooms, gift shop. TEAS. *Adm £3.50 Chd (10-18)/OAP £2.50, Family £8. For NGS Sat June 17, Wed Aug 2 (9.30-5).* **Tel 0151 3368733**

Norton Priory ♿✂❀ (Norton Priory Museum Trust Ltd) Tudor Road, Manor Park, Runcorn. Runcorn New Town 1m, Warrington 5m. From M56 Junction 11 turn for Warrington and follow signs. From Warrington take A56 for Runcorn and follow signs. 16 acres well established woodland gardens; Georgian summerhouses; rock garden and stream glade; 3-acre walled garden of similar date (1760s) recently restored. Georgian and modern garden designs; fruit training; rosewalk; colour borders; herb garden, cottage garden and exhibition. New projects underway: restoration of ancient pear orchard; cydonia (tree quince) collection. Plants for sale from the Walled Garden collection. Priory remains of museum also open. *Combined adm £2.50 Concessions £1.30. Daily April to October (12-5) weekends and bank hols (12-6) Nov to March (12-4) (Walled garden closed Nov-Feb). For NGS Sun June 11 (12-6). Horticultural Show Sept 17.* **Tel 01928 569895**

The Old Hall ♿✂❀ (Dr & Mrs M W W Wood) Hadlow Rd, Willaston S Wirral, 8m NW of Chester on village green. ¾-acre; mixed border; interesting plants; daffodils; winter flowering shrubs and colour. C17 house. TEAS. *Adm £1.50 Chd free (Share to Muscular Dystrophy Group®). Suns April 16, June 4 (2-6); also private visits welcome, please* **Tel 0151 327 4779**

The Old Hough ♿✂ (Mr & Mrs D S Varey) Warmingham. [OS sheet 118. Grid Ref: 699624]. 5m from either junction 17 or 18 on M6. From Middlewich take A50 to Nantwich, after approx 2m turn L to Warmingham. At T-junction turn L garden is ½m on R. From Sandbach take A533 to Middlewich, just after Elworth Village turn L to Warmingham. At T-junction turn R, garden is approx 2½m on L. Young garden in old setting. 2½ acres surrounding listed C16 to C19 house with large courtyard. Extensive use of stone and brick for paths, walls and ornaments. Enclosed formal gardens to S with quiet lawns; varied climbers; mixed borders with interesting shrubs, bulbs, roses, ferns and ivies. Central goldfish pond fed by planted rill: young yew hedges to make future divisions. Informal gardens to N & W with wildlife pond, mature oak wood, herbaceous borders, young trees with interesting bark. Garden to relax in. Ample parking and toilet facilities. TEAS in aid of Warmingham Church. *Adm £2 Chd 50p (Share to St Leonard's Church, Warmingham®). Sun June 18 (2-6)*

The Old Parsonage ♿❀ (The Hon Michael & Mrs Flower) Arley Green; 5m NNE of Northwich and 3m Great Budworth; 6m W Knutsford; 5m from M6 junctions 19, 20 and M56 junction 10. Follow signposts to Arley Hall and Gardens and at central crossroad follow notices to The Old Parsonage. The Old Parsonage lies across park at Arley Green, a cluster of old buildings in a very attractive rural setting beside a lake. 2-acre garden has old established yew hedges sheltering herbaceous and mixed borders, shrub roses and climbers, a newly planted woodland garden and pond, with some unusual young trees and foliage shrubs. Waterplants, rhododendrons, azaleas, meconopsis. Plant stall. TEAS. *Adm £2 Chd £1 (Share to Save the Children®). Visitors will be admitted to* **Arley Hall Gardens** *(teas, plants, shop available) at concessionary rate (£2 Chd under 17 £1) on production of their Old Parsonage ticket. Sat, Sun June 10, 11 (2-6)*

Orchard Villa ♿✂❀ (Mr & Mrs J Trinder) 72 Audley Rd, Alsager. At traffic lights in Alsager town centre turn S towards Audley, house is 300yds on R beyond level Xing. Long and narrow, this ⅓-acre has been designed to grow a wide range of herbaceous plants, iris and alpines ferns and grasses in scree, peat, raised, light and shade beds. TEAS. *Adm £1.50 Chd Free. Bank Hol Mon May 8;* TEA *Tues May 16, 23, 30; June 6, 13, 20, 27 (1.30-5); also private visits welcome for parties of 2 and over, please* **Tel 01270 874833**

Penn ✂❀ (R W Baldwin Esq) Macclesfield Rd, Alderley Edge. ¾m E of Alderley Edge village, on B5087, Alderley Edge-Macclesfield rd. Turn L into Woodbrook Rd for car parking. 2½ acres. This garden, which has been built up by the present owner and his late wife for 45 years, contains an exceptional collection of flowering shrubs and trees, on a hillside looking over the Cheshire plain. The many hundreds of rhododendron species and cultivars include some Himalayans (Macabeanum, rex, eximium, montroseanum, etc, now small forest trees), yellow & blue species (wardii, augustinii etc.), many famous cultivars such as Loderi, Cornish Cross, Penjerrick, Mariloo, Naomi, Prelude, Laura Aberconway), masses of azaleas plus a wide range of camellias & magnolias including superb varieties from Cornwall, and many fairly rare trees including gingko, davidia (handerchief tree), golden elm, embothriums, plus for added interest 2 sequoia sempervirens (now 30ft high struck in 1965 from a block of wood bought in the Muir woods across the Golden Gate in San Francisco). TEAS. *Adm £2 OAPs £1.50 Chd 50p. Fri April 14, Suns April 16, 30, May 28, Mons April 17, May 1, 29 (2-5). Parties welcome by written appt*

Peover Hall ✂ (Randle Brooks Esq) Over Peover. 3m S of Knutsford on A50, Lodge gates off Blackden Lane. 15-acres. 5 walled gardens: lily pond, rose, herb, white and pink gardens; C18 landscaped park, moat, C19 dell, rhododendron walks, large walled kitchen garden, Church walk, purple border, blue and white border, pleached lime avenues, fine topiary work. Dogs in park only. TEAS. *Adm £1.50 Chd £1. Mons & Thurs (2-5) May to Oct. NOT Bank Hols. Other days by appt for parties. For NGS Sat, Sun May 20, 21 (2-6)*

5 Pine Hey ♿✂❀ (Mr & Mrs S J Clayton) Neston. A540 Chester to Hoylake Rd. Turn off at the Shrewsbury Arms (Roast Inn) traffic lights towards Neston. Turn R at T-junction drive through Neston past cross on the L, then fork L at traffic lights and continue along Leighton Rd, past the old Windmill and Earl Drive on the L. Pine Hey is the next on L. The garden covers approx ¾ acre and is laid out informally with different areas, including a copse, new water garden, stream and lawns each with its own character. The main objective is to make it an all-yr garden, and there is an element of surprise when first entering. TEAS in aid of Wirral Methodist Housing Association. *Adm £1.50 Chd free (Share to Wirral Methodist Housing Association). Sun July 2 (2-5). Private parties welcome, please* **Tel 0151 3363006**

Poulton Hall ♿ (The Lancelyn Green Family) Poulton Lancelyn, 2m from Bebington. From M53, exit 4 towards Bebington; at traffic lights (½m) R along Poulton Rd; house 1m on R. 2½ acres; lawns, ha-ha, wild flower meadow, shrubbery, walled gardens with literary associations. Cream TEAS. *Adm £1.50 Chd 20p. Suns April 9, June 11 (2-6)*

The Quinta ♿✂ (Sir Bernard Lovell) Swettenham. Turn E off A535 at Twemlow (Yellow Broom Cafe) and follow signs to Swettenham. 15-acre collection of rare trees and shrubs leading to woodland walks overlooking the Dane Valley and to the thirty-nine step descent to Swettenham Brook. A site of special biological importance. TEA NGS days, Bank Hols & parties by arrangement. *Adm £2 Acc chd free (Share to St Peter's Church, Swettenham®). Open daily until sunset. For NGS Sun May 14, Wed May 24 (10-sunset). Parties welcome, please* **Tel 01477 571254**

Reaseheath ♿✂❀ (Reaseheath College) nr Nantwich. 1½m N of Nantwich on the A51. The Gardens, covering 12 acres, are based on a Victorian Garden surrounding Reaseheath Hall and contain many mature trees of horticultural interest. The gardens are used as a teaching resource. There are specialised features of particular interest including, glasshouses; model fruit garden; rose garden; woodland garden; lakeside bog garden and extensive shrub borders, lawns and sports facilities. TEA. *Adm £2. Weds May 24, 31, June 7, 14, 21, 28, July 5, 12, 19, 26 (2-4.30). Parties welcome, please* **Tel 01270 625131**

Rode Hall ❀ (Sir Richard & Lady Baker Wilbraham) Scholar Green [National Grid reference SJ8157] 5m SW of Congleton between A34 and A50. Nesfield's terrace and rose garden with view over Humphrey Repton's landscape is a feature of Rode gardens, as is the Victorian wild flower garden with a grotto and the walk to the lake past the old Stew pond. Other attractions include a restored ice house and working walled kitchen garden. TEAS. *Adm £2 Chd free (House extra £2) (Share to All Saints Odd Rode Parish Church®). Sun May 14 (2-5.30)*

¶Rosewood ✂❀ (Mr & Mrs C E J Brabin) Puddington. 6m N of Chester turn L (W) off Chester to Hoylake A540 to Puddington. Bear L at village green and follow NGS signs. 1-acre garden incl small wood, pond well planted with bogside species, mixed herbaceous, shrub beds with new plantings of rhododendron, azalea species and hybrids; many unusual trees. Most of the new plantings are grown from seed by owner. TEAS. *Adm £1.50 Chd free (Share to St Nicholas' Church, Burton®). Sun May 21 (2-6)*

2 Stanley Road ✂❀ (Mr G Leatherbarrow) Heaton Moor. Approx 1½m N of Stockport. Follow Heaton Moor Rd off A6. Stanley Rd on L. 1st house on R. Tiny town garden with all year interest, packed with interesting plants, creating a secret cottage garden atmosphere. Old species and English roses, clematis, hardy geraniums, ivies, varied evergreens, daphnes, hellebores, delphiniums, mixed herbaceous; ponds. Max no. of visitors 2 – no room for more. Not suitable for less agile. TEA. *Adm £2 Chd 75p. Private visits welcome April to Sept, please* **Tel 0161 442 3828**

¶Stonyford Cottage Nursery & Garden ♿✂❀ (Mr & Mrs Anthony Overland) Cuddington. 6m W of Northwich. Turn R off A556 (Northwich to Chester). At Xrds ¾m past A49 junction (signpost Norley-Kingsley). Entrance in ½m on L. A 2-acre garden developed around Stonyford Brook and pool displaying an increasing range of herbaceous perennials, shade and moisture loving plants. 2 bridges linked by a wooded island lead into the main area with terrace, rock garden, pergola and pool side features. The adjacent nursery has a wide variety of herbaceous perennials and less common plants for sale. TEAS (NGS day only). *Adm £1.50 Chd free (Share to Francis House Children's Hospice®). April to Oct Tues to Sun & Bank Hols (10- 5.30). For NGS Sun July 9 (2-6)*

The Stray ♿✽❀ (Mr & Mrs Anthony Hannay) Neston. Approx 10m NW of Chester. ½m NW of Shrewsbury Arms (traffic lights). Turn off A540 into Upper Raby Rd. After 3⁄10m turn R into unmade lane and The Stray is immediately on the L. 1½ acres of new shrubs, herbaceous border and espalier fruit set in an old garden. Replanting commenced in 1991. A chance to see a new garden maturing. TEAS in aid of RNLI. *Adm £1.50 Chd free. Sun June 11 (2-6)*

Tatton Park ♿✽❀ (Cheshire County Council: The National Trust) Knutsford. Well sign-posted on M56 junction 7 and from M6 junction 19. 2½m N of Knutsford. Gardens contain many unusual features and rare species of plants, shrubs and trees. Considered to be the very finest and most important of all gardens within The National Trust they rank among England's 'Top Ten'. Features include orangery by Wyatt, fernery by Paxton, Japanese, Italian and rose gardens. Greek monument and African hut. Hybrid azaleas and rhododendrons, swamp cypresses, tree ferns, tall redwoods, bamboos and pines. An exotic garden offering a new and delightful surprise round every corner, a palimpsest of 200 years development by the Egerton family. The Tatton Garden Society part of the garden will also be open. TEAS. *Adm £2.50 Group £2 Chd £1.70 Group £1.40.* ▲*For NGS Mon June 26 (10.30-5)*

Thornton Manor ❀ (The Viscount Leverhulme) Thornton Hough, Wirral. From Chester A540 to Fiveway Garage; turn R on to B5136 to Thornton Hough village. From Birkenhead B5151 then on to B5136. From M53, exit 4 to Heswall; turn L after 1m. Bus: Woodside-Parkgate; alight Thornton Hough village. Large garden of yr-round interest. TEAS. *Free car park. Adm £2 OAPs £1 Chd 50p. Bank Hol Mon Aug 28 (12-7)*

Tushingham Hall (Mr & Mrs P Moore Dutton) 3m N of Whitchurch. Signed off A41 Chester-Whitchurch Rd; Medium-sized garden in beautiful surroundings; bluebell wood alongside pool; ancient oak, girth 26ft. TEAS. *Adm £1.50 Chd 30p (Share to St Chad's Church, Tushingham®). Sun May 7 (2-6.30)*

85 Warmingham Road ✽❀ (Mr & Mrs A Mann) Approx 3m N of Crewe town centre on the road between Leighton Hospital and Warmingham Village. Close by White Lion Inn, Coppenhall. ⅓-acre plantsman's garden, with shrubs, perennial borders, raised beds, troughs, rock garden, peat garden, pond and greenhouse with cacti and succulents. Speciality alpines. TEA. *Adm £1 Chd free. Suns April 30, June 25, July 16 (1-5). Private visits welcome for parties of 12 and over May to Sept, please* **Tel 01270 582030**

The Well House ✽❀ (Mrs S H French-Greenslade) Tilston, nr Malpas. 12m S of Chester, follow signs to Tilston from A41 S of Broxton roundabout, taking Malpas Rd through Tilston. House and antique shop on dangerous bend. Parking if possible in a field or on roadside. Approx ¾-acre small cottage garden, divided by a natural stream. Land over the stream, only acquired autumn 1990, is reached by a bridge; all plantings still very young. Attractive summerhouse, tiny pond and pumped waterfall. Winding paths through variety of small areas; herbs; shrubs and secret garden. At its best when the many bulbs are out in the spring. TEAS. *Adm £2 Chd 25p (Share to Cystic Fibrosis®). Suns April 9, June 18 (2-5.30). Private visits also welcome for parties of 4 and over March - July, please* **Tel 01829 250332**

Whirley Hall ♿✽ (Sir William & Lady Mather) Macclesfield. [OS sheet 118 map ref 875746]. The Hall is N of Knutsford Rd (A537) to Macclesfield going E, take the 2nd turning L after Monks Heath traffic lights up Whirley Lane. The Hall is 1m on L. Going W out of Macclesfield, 70yds after Broken Cross fork R along Whirley Rd, the Hall is 1¼m on R. 1½ acres of lawns, shrubs, borders, flagged terraces and kitchen garden. *Adm £2 Chd 50p (Share to St Catherine's Church, Birtles®). Sun July 9 (2.30-6)*

Willaston Grange ♿ (Sir Derek and Lady Bibby) Willaston. A540 Chester to West Kirby until opposite the new Elf Garage. Proceed down B5151 Hadlow Rd, towards Willaston. Borders, rock garden, vegetable garden, orchard, about 3 acres. Special feature - woodland walk. TEAS. *Adm £1.50 OAPs £1 Chd free. Sun May 7 (2-6)*

¶**Willow Cottage** ✽ (Mr & Mrs Martin Tolson) Straight behind the Admiral Rodney Public House in Prestbury. An intensively planted small cottage garden of less than 1⁄10-acre. *Adm £1 Chd 50p. Private visits (max of 10) welcome May to July (2.30-5), please* **Tel 01625 828697**

Wood End Cottage ✽❀ (Mr & Mrs M R Everett) Grange Lane, Whitegate. Turn S off A556 (Northwich/Chester) to Whitegate village, opp school follow Grange Lane for 300 yds. ½-acre sloping to a natural stream; developed as a plantsman's garden. Mature trees; herbaceous; clematis; raised beds. TEAS. Large plant stall. *Adm £1.50 Chd 50p (Share to British Epilepsy Assoc®). Sun July 2 (2-6); also private parties welcome in May, June, July, please* **Tel 01606 888236**

Woodsetton ✽❀ (Mr & Mrs Eric Barber) Alsager. At town centre follow B5078, take 3rd turning L into Pikemere Road and then 2nd turning on R. Approx 1-acre, interesting plants; trees; shrubs; rhododendrons; large natural wildlife pool, scree and alpines. TEAS. *Adm £1.50 Chd free (Share to St. Lukes Hospice 'Grosvenor House', Winsford, Cheshire®). Sun April 23 (1.30-5) also private visits welcome May, June, July, please* **Tel 01270 877623**

Clwyd

See separate Welsh section beginning on page 314

Cornwall

Hon County Organiser: G J Holborow Esq, Ladock House, Ladock, Truro, Cornwall TR2 4PL Tel 01726 882274

Assistant Hon County Organisers: Mrs D Morison, Boskenna, St Martin, Manaccan, Helston TR12 6BS Tel 01326 231 210

Mrs Richard Jerram, Trehane, Trevanson, Wadebridge PL27 7HP Tel 01208 812523

Mrs Michael Latham, Trebartha Lodge, North Hill, Launceston PL15 7PD Tel 01566 82373

Leaflet/Yellow Books Tony Shaw Esq, Rope House, Cliff Street, Mevagissey, nr St Austell, Cornwall PL26 6QL Tel 01726 842819

Hon County Treasurer: Mrs Cynthia Bassett, 5 Athelstan Park, Bodmin, PL31 1DS Tel 01208 73247

DATES OF OPENING

By appointment

For telephone numbers and other details see garden descriptions. Private visits welcomed

Chyverton, Zelah
Trelean, St Martin-in-Meneage
Trevegean, Manor Way, Heamoor
Woodland Garden & Nursery, Garras

Regular openings

For details see garden descriptions

Bosvigo House, Truro. Wed to Sat, March to Sept
Carwinion, Mawnan Smith. Open daily
Catchfrench Manor, St Germans. March 1 to Oct 31
Heligan Manor Gardens, Mevagissey. Open daily
Ken Caro, Bicton, nr Liskeard. Sun, Mon, Tues, & Wed April 15 to June 28, Tues, Wed July & Aug
Lanterns, Restronguet, nr Mylor. Open daily
Pencarrow, Bodmin. Open daily
Peterdale, Millbrook. Sun, Mon, Tues, Wed April 9 to June 29, Sun, Mon July 2 to Aug 29
Prideaux Place, Padstow. Easter Sun to Sept 28
Trebah, Mawnan Smith. Open daily
Tregrehan, Par. Daily mid March to end of June
Trewithen, Probus, nr Truro. Mon to Sat March 1 to 30 Sept
Treworder Mill, Truro. Every Wed 17 May to June 28
Woodland Garden & Nursery, Garras. Sats April 15 to 30 Sept

March 26 Sunday
Trengwainton, Penzance

April 2 Sunday
Tremeer, St Tudy

April 8 Saturday
Bosloe, Mawnan Smith ‡
Glendurgan, Mawnan Smith ‡

April 9 Sunday
Trelissick, Feock

April 23 Sunday
Oak Lodge Woodland Garden, Nanstallon, nr Bodmin
St Michael's Mount, Marazion

April 30 Sunday
Boconnoc, nr Lostwithiel
Estray Parc, Budock
High Noon, Ladock ‡
Ladock House, Ladock, Truro ‡
Penwarne, nr Falmouth
Polgwynne, Feock

May 3 Wednesday
Antony, Torpoint

May 7 Sunday
Cotehele House, St Dominick, Saltash
Pinetum, Harewood
Tregrehan, Par

May 14 Sunday
Creed House, Creed ‡
The Hollies, Grampound, nr Truro ‡
Nansawsan House, Ladock
Trenance, Launceston

May 17 Wednesday
Treworder Mill, Truro

May 18 Thursday
Headland, Polruan

May 21 Sunday
Carclew Gardens, Perran-ar-Worthal
Lanhydrock, Bodmin
Paradise Park, Hayle
Pinetum, Harewood

May 24 Wednesday
Treworder Mill, Truro

May 25 Thursday
Headland, Polruan

May 28 Sunday
Loveny, Tremaddock Bridge, St Neot

May 31 Wednesday
Treworder Mill, Truro

June 4 Sunday
Jimmers, St Neot ‡
Northwood Farm, St Neot ‡
The Old Barn, St Neot ‡

June 7 Wednesday
Treworder Mill, Truro

June 11 Sunday
Lamorran House, Upper Castle Rd, St Mawes
Oak Lodge Woodland Garden, Nanstallon, nr Bodmin
Trerice, nr Newquay

June 14 Wednesday
Ince Castle Gardens, Saltash
Treworder Mill, Truro

June 18 Sunday
Mary Newman's Cottage, Saltash
Scawn Mill, nr St Pinnock
Tregilliowe Farm, Ludgvan

June 21 Wednesday
Treworder Mill, Truro

June 25 Sunday
Ferny Park, Bossiney, Tintagel
Pine Lodge Gardens, Cuddra, St Austell
Roseland House, Chacewater
Water Meadow, Luxulyan

June 28 Wednesday
Treworder Mill, Truro

July 1 Saturday
Berriow Bridge & Middlewood Gardens, nr Launceston

July 2 Sunday
Berriow Bridge & Middlewood Gardens, nr Launceston

July 9 Sunday
Long Cross Victorian Gardens, Trelights
Roseland House, Chacewater
Treviades Gardens, Constantine

July 16 Sunday
Tregilliowe Farm, Ludgvan

Trenance, Launceston

July 30 Sunday
The Old Rectory, Marazion

August 2 Wednesday
The Old Rectory, Marazion

August 6 Sunday
Bosvigo House, Truro
Pinetum, Harewood

August 20 Sunday
Ferny Park, Bossiney, Tintagel

September 24 Sunday
Trebartha, nr Launceston

DESCRIPTIONS OF GARDENS

Antony ✂ (National Trust: Trustees of the Carew Pole Trust) 5m W of Plymouth via Torpoint car ferry; 2m NW of Torpoint, N of A374; 16m SE of Liskeard; 15m E of Looe. In a Repton landscape with fine vistas to the R Lynher. Features a formal courtyard, terraces, ornamental Japanese pond and knot garden. National collection of hemerocallis (500 varieties) **Antony Woodland Garden and Woods**: an established woodland garden and natural woods extending to 100 acres. Designed as one of natural beauty and scientific interest. Over 300 types of camellias. TEAS. *Adm £2.50 Chd £1.25. ▲For NGS Wed May 3 (1.30-5.30)*

Berrow Bridge & Middlewood Gardens ✂❀ Hillbrooke. [OS map ref: SX 273752] Situated where B3254 crosses R Lynher between Launceston & Liskeard. Park at Berriow Bridge where tickets & map available. In a lovely valley below Bodmin Moor, several gardens show a variety of landscape styles from small cottages with secret & surprising gardens, roses, unusual plants, streams & natural stone, to a larger riverside garden with sculptures and woodland walk. (Featured on TV). TEAS in aid of North Hill Village Hall. *Combined adm £2 Chd free. Sat, Sun July 1,2 (2-6)*

Boconnoc ♿❀ (Mr & Mrs J D G Fortescue) 2m S of A390. On main rd between middle Taphouse and Downend garage, follow signs. Privately owned gardens covering some 20 acres, surrounded by parkland and woods. Magnificent old trees, flowering shrubs and views. TEAS. *Adm £1.50 Chd free (Share to Boconnoc Church Window Fund®). Sun April 30 (2-6)*

Bosloe ♿✂ (The National Trust) Mawnan Smith, 5m S of Falmouth. In Mawnan Smith, take Helford Rd and turn off for Durgan. Medium-sized garden; fine view of R Helford. *Adm £1 Chd free. ▲For NGS Sat April 8 (2-5)*

Bosvigo House ♿✂❀ (Mr & Mrs M Perry) Bosvigo Lane. ¾m from Truro centre. At Highertown, near Sainsbury roundabout, turn R beside Shell garage, down Dobbs Lane. After 500yds entrance to house is on L, after nasty L-hand bend. 3-acre garden still being developed surrounding Georgian house (not open) and Victorian conservatory. Series of enclosed and walled gardens with mainly herbaceous plants for colour and foliage effect. Woodland walk. Many rare and unusual plants. Partly suitable for wheelchairs. Featured in NGS video 3. TEAS, served in servants' hall on charity Suns only. *Adm £1.50 Chd 50p. Open Weds to Sats, March to end Sept (11-6). For NGS Sun Aug 6 (2-5)*

Carclew Gardens ✂ (Mrs Chope) Perran-ar-Worthal, nr Truro. From A39 turn E at Perran-ar-Worthal. Bus: alight Perran-ar-Worthal 1m. Large garden, rhododendron species; terraces; ornamental water. TEAS. *Adm £1.50 Chd 50p (Share to Barristers Benevolent Fund®). Sun May 21 (2-5.30)*

●**Carwinion** ❀ (Mr H A E Rogers) Mawnan Smith via Carwinion Rd. An unmanicured or permissive valley garden of some 10 acres with many camellias, rhododendrons and azaleas flowering in the spring. Apart from an abundance of wild flowers, grasses, ferns etc, the garden holds the premier collection of temperate bamboos in the UK. TEAS April to Oct (2-5.30). *Adm £2 Chd free. Open daily throughout the year (2-5.30). Private visits welcome, please* **Tel 01326 250258**

●¶**Catchfrench Manor** ✂❀ (Mr & Mrs J R Wilks) St Germans. To south of A38 5 miles E of Liskeard signposted Catchfrench. Recently purchased by the present owners who have restored the semi-derelict Manor House and are now starting to restore the 25-acre historic Repton landscaped garden to *Red Book* design. A fine spring garden with magnolias, rhododenrons and camellias now being restored. TEAS. *Adm £2 Chd £1. Mon to Sat March 1 to Oct 31 (10.30-4.30)*

Chyverton (Mr N T Holman) Zelah, N of Truro. Entrance ¾m SW of Zelah on A30. Georgian landscaped garden with lake and bridge (1770); large shrub garden of great beauty; outstanding collection magnolias, acers, camellias, rhododendrons, primulas, rare and exotic trees and shrubs. Visitors personally conducted by owners. Featured in NGS video 3. *Adm £3 (parties over 20 persons by arrangement) Chd under 16 free. Private visits welcome weekdays March to June by appt, please* **Tel 01872 540324**

Cotehele House ✂❀ (The National Trust) 2m E of St Dominick, 4m from Gunnislake (turn at St Ann's Chapel); 8m SW of Tavistock; 14m from Plymouth via Tamar Bridge. Terrace garden falling to sheltered valley with ponds, stream and unusual shrubs. Fine medieval house (one of the least altered in the country); armour, tapestries, furniture. Dogs in wood only and on lead. Lunches and TEAS. *Adm house, garden & mill £5 Chd £2.50; garden, grounds & mill £2.50 Chd £1.50. Sun May 7 (11-5.30)*

Creed House ♿❀ (Mr & Mrs W R Croggon) Creed. From the centre of Grampound on A390 (halfway between Truro & St Austell). Take rd signposted to Creed. After 1m turn L opp Creed Church and the garden is on L. Parking in lane. 5-acre landscaped Georgian Rectory garden. Tree collection; rhododendrons; sunken alpine and formal walled herbaceous gardens. Trickle stream to ponds and bog. Natural woodland walk. Restoration began 1974 – continues & incl recent planting. TEAS. *Adm £1.50 Chd free. ▲Sun May 14 (2-5.30).* **Tel 01872 530372**

Estray Parc (Mr & Mrs J M Williams) Penjerrick. Leave Penjerrick main entrance on R follow the rd towards Mawnan Smith until entrance to The Home Hotel on L. Directly opp turn R and follow the signs. In 1983 most of this 3-acre garden was a bramble thistle-infested field. A considerable variety of plants have been introduced and continuous grass cutting has produced passable sloping lawns interspersed by a large collection of trees and shrubs. *Adm £1.50 OAP £1 Chd 50p. Sun April 30 (2-6)*

Ferny Park ✲❀ (Mrs Mendoza) Bossiney. B3263 1½m N of Tintagel 3m S of Boscastle. ½-acre garden with natural stream creating water feature. Park in rd opp or at bottom of hill. Plant sale. TEAS. *Adm £1 Chd free. Suns June 25, Aug 20 (2-5)*

Glendurgan ✲❀ (The National Trust) Mawnan Smith, take rd to Helford Passage, 5m SW of Falmouth. Follow NT signposts. Walled garden, laurel maze, giants stride, valley with specimen trees, bluebells and primulas running down to Durgan fishing village on R Helford. Large car park. *Adm £2.80 Chd £1.40. ▲For NGS Sat April 8 (10.30-5.30)*

Headland ✲ (Jean & John Hill) Battery Lane, Polruan. On E of Fowey estuary; leave car in public park; walk down St Saviour's Hill, turn L at Coast Guard office. 1¼-acre cliff garden with sea on 3 sides; mainly plants which withstand salty gales but incl sub-tropical. Spectacular views of Coast; cove for swimming. Cream TEAS. *Adm £1 Chd 50p. Open every Thurs June, July, Aug, Sept. For NGS Thurs May 18, 25 (2-8)*

●**Heligan Manor Gardens** ♿❀ (Mr Tim Smit) Pentewan. From St Austell take B3273 signposted Mevagissey, follow signs. Heligan Manor Gardens is the scene of the largest garden restoration project undertaken since the war. Of special interest in this romantic Victorian garden are; the fern ravine, 4 walled gardens with peach houses, vineries, melon grounds, a splendid collection of Beeboles, crystal grotto, Italian garden with a pool, an Elizabethan beacon 'Mount' and a large tropical Japanese valley garden. All are connected by an intricate web of over 2½m of ornamental footpaths, most unseen for more than half a century. TEAS and light refreshments. *Adm £2.80 OAP £2.40 Chd £1.60. Open every day (10-4.30). Groups welcome,* **Tel 01726 844157**

High Noon ❀ (R E Sturdy) Ladock. 7m E of Truro on A39. 3½ acres ornamental trees, rhododendrons, camellias, and magnolias, 10yrs old; rose garden; daffodils; lawns; formal pool; S-facing slope with good views. *Combined adm with* **Ladock House** *£2 Chd free. Sun April 30 (2-5.30)*

The Hollies ♿❀ (Mr J & Mrs N B Croggon) Grampound, nr Truro. In centre of village on Truro-St Austell rd. 2-acre garden of unusual design; unusual mixed planting of trees, shrubs and alpines. TEAS. *Adm £1 Chd free. Sun May 14 (2-5.30).* **Tel 01726 882474**

By Appointment Gardens. See head of county section

Ince Castle Gardens & Grounds ♿❀ (Viscount & Patricia, Viscountess Boyd of Morton) 5m SW of Saltash. From A38 at Stoketon Cross take turn signed Trematon, Elmgate. 5 acres with lawns and ornamental woods; shell house and dovecote. TEA. *Adm £1.50 Chd free. Wed June 14 (2-6)*

Jimmers, St Neot ✲❀ (Mr & Mrs P Kent) On L up Bush Hill. ¾-acre garden laid out in rooms with surprises and changes in atmosphere; varied planting; interesting trees; shrubs incl small collection of hollies, perennials, two ponds, patio, lawns and views; tranquil setting. *Combined adm with* **The Old Barn** and **Northwood Farm** *£3 Chd free. Sun June 4 (2-5.30)*

● **Ken Caro** ✲❀ (Mr & Mrs K R Willcock) Bicton, Pensilva, 5m NE of Liskeard. From A390 to Callington turn off N at Butchers Arms, St Ive; take Pensilva Rd; at next Xrds take rd signed Bicton. 2 acres mostly planted in 1970, with a further 2-acre extension in 1993; well-designed and labelled plantsman's garden; rhododendrons, flowering shrubs, conifers and other trees; herbaceous borders. Panoramic views. Collection of waterfowl and aviary birds. Featured in NGS video 2. *Adm £2 Chd 50p. April 15 to June 28 every Sun, Mon, Tues, Wed; Tues & Weds only July & Aug (2-6).* **Tel 01579 62446**

Ladock House ♿ (Mr G J & Lady Mary Holborow) Ladock. 7m E of Truro on A39. Car park and entrance by church. Georgian old rectory with 4 acres of lawns, rhododendrons, camellias and azaleas with woodland garden. All planted during last 15yrs. TEAS in aid of Ladock Church. *Combined adm with* **High Noon** *£2 Chd free. Sun April 30 (2-5.30)*

Lamorran House ✲❀ (Mr & Mrs Dudley-Cooke) Upper Castle Rd, St Mawes. First turning R after garage; sign posted to St Mawes Castle. House ½m on L. Parking in rd. 4-acre sub-tropical hillside garden with beautiful views to St Anthonys Head. Extensive water gardens in Mediterranean and Japanese settings. Large collection of rhododendrons, azaleas, palm trees, cycads, agaves and many S hemisphere plants and trees. TEAS. *Adm £2 Chd free. Sun June 11 (10-5).* **Tel 01326 270800**

Lanhydrock ♿✲❀ (The National Trust) Bodmin, 2½m on B3268. Station: Bodmin Parkway 1¾m. Large-sized garden; formal garden laid out 1857; shrub garden with good specimens of rhododendrons and magnolias and fine views. Lunches and TEAS. Closed Mondays. *Adm house, garden and grounds £5.40 Chd £2.90; garden only £2.50 Chd £1.25. Family ticket (2 adults and 2 Chd) £14.50. Sun May 21 (11-5.30; last adm to house 5)*

●**Lanterns** ❀ (Mrs I Chapman) Mylor. 1m NE of Mylor. From Mylor follow the Restronguet Passage/Pandora Inn rd signs, Lanterns is on the RH-side before reaching the waterfront. ½-acre mature garden in natural setting planted by owners. Wide variety of shrubs, bulbs, herbaceous perennials, climbers, conservatory/greenhouse plants. Interesting in any season; small streams and dry areas; waterside walks. Owner always pleased to advise on plants and planting. *Collecting box. Open every day throughout the year (11am-dusk)*

Long Cross Victorian Gardens ♿❀ (Mr & Mrs Crawford) Trelights, St Endellion. 7m N of Wadebridge on B3314. Charm of this garden is mazelike effect due to protecting hedges against sea winds; views of countryside and sea scapes (Port Isaac and Port Quinn Bays) Garden specially designed to cope with environment of Cornwall's N Coast. Cream TEAS, coffee, evening meal. *Adm £1 Chd free. Sun July 9 (10.30-5.30). Private visits welcome for parties of 25 and over, please* **Tel 01208 880243**

Loveny (Mr & Mrs J G Thompson) Tremaddock Bridge, St Neot. Take rd L of the London Inn. Up steep hill. L past school. Follow NGS posters. Park in lane. Riverside gdn with mature trees and shrubs; TEAS in aid of Cancer Relief. *Adm £1 Chd free. Sun May 28 (2-6)*

Mary Newman's Cottage ✤❀ (Tamar Protection Society) Culver Rd, ¼m from Saltash town centre; park on waterfront. Cottage garden with herbaceous, annuals and herbs. Overlooks R Tamar and Bridges. Recently restored C15 cottage, former home of Sir Francis Drake's first wife. TEAS. *Adm £1 Chd free (Share to Tamar Protection Society©). Sun June 18 (2-5).* **Tel 01752 822211**

¶Nansawsan House ✤❀ (Mr & Mrs Michael Cole) Ladock. 7m E of Truro on A39. Parking at Falmouth Arms or Parish Hall. Car parks. 1½ acres, part of a once larger Victorian garden. Rhododendrons, camellias, shrubs, trees and borders. CREAM TEAS in aid of Ladock Church. *Adm £1.50 Chd 50p. May 14 (2-5)*

Northwood Farm, St Neot ✤ (Mr & Mrs P K Cooper) take rd out of village to Wenmouth Cross. L and first R. Follow very narrow rd and NGS posters to Farm on R. House & garden on site of a China Clay Dri used 150 yrs ago. House rebuilt from barn and garden from old sunken pits still being developed. Discovery of several natural springs led to creation of ponds now with collection of water birds. *Combined adm with* **The Old Barn** *and* **Jimmers** *£3 Chd free. Sun June 4 (2-5.30)*

¶Oak Lodge ♿✤❀ (Mr & Mrs Miller) Nanstallon, Nr. Bodmin. From Bodmin, take A30 SW following signs for Redruth, for approx 2m. Turn R at top of hill and follow signs to Nanstallon. Proceed through village and take 2nd turning R on a L bend. Oak Lodge is approx 1.3m along this road on the R. Set at the edge of woodland, the 7-acre property is gradually being developed around the original trees into informal gardens, natural woodland walks carpeted with bluebells and other wild flowers in springtime, and an arboretum. TEA in aid of Diabetic Assoc. *Adm £1.50 Chd free. ▲For NGS Suns April 23, June 11 (2-6)*

The Old Barn, St Neot ♿❀ (Mrs H S Lloyd) nr Liskeard. Turn R by garage, down lane to Holy Well. Cross field. 1st on L. Park in field. Riverside garden, mature trees, shrubs; mixed perennials, roses, clematis, pelargoniums, lawns, pond with water lilies. TEAS. *Combined adm with* **Northwood Farm** *and* **Jimmers** *£3 Chd free. Sun June 4 (2-5.30)*

The Old Rectory ♿❀ (Dr & Mrs Senior) Marazion. 3½m E of Penzance on hillside W end of Marazion. Marazion to Penzance coast rd end of town bear R edge of marsh. Keep R up hillside, garden 800yds on R; limited parking in narrow lane. Large car parks W Marazion. ½-acre garden started 1964, overplanted by optimistic owners fantasizing Mediterranean climate. A plantsman's garden. TEAS in aid of West Cornwall Hospital, Penzance, League of Friends. *Adm £2 Chd free. Sun, Wed July 30, Aug 2 (2-6)*

Paradise Park ♿✤❀ (Mr Michael Reynolds) Hayle. Follow the A30 to Hayle, go to St Ives/St Erth roundabout then follow official brown and white signs to Paradise Park. The 2-acre walled garden is part of the 14 acres of Paradise Park. The park opened in 1973 as 'The rare and endangered birds breeding centre'. In recent yrs much effort has been expended to make the gardens a suitable setting for what has become a bird breeding collection of international importance. The World Parrot Trust is based here. In the walled garden and elsewhere are pergolas, trellis and gazebos; climbing roses, clematis, lilies and passiflora are featured. *Open throughout the yr from 10am to 5pm.* Cafe in Park. *Adm £4.95 (£1 reduction for members of any garden society) Chd £2.95. Sun May 21 (10-5)*

●Pencarrow ♿❀ (Molesworth-St Aubyn Family) 4 miles N.W. Bodmin, signed off the A389. 50 acres of formal and woodland gardens laid out in the 1840's by Sir William Molesworth Bt. Marked walks past the Victorian Rockery, Italian and American Gardens, Lake and Ice House. Over 650 different varieties of rhododendrons, also an Internationally known specimen conifer collection. *House, Tearooms and Craft Centre open Easter Sun - October 15. Adm £1.50 Chd free. Sun-Thur incl (1.30-5)*

Penwarne (Dr & Mrs H Beister) 3¼m SW of Falmouth. 1½m N of Mawnan. Garden with many varieties of flowering shrubs, rhododendrons, magnolias, New Zealand shrubs, formal and informal garden; walled garden. Ornamental ducks. *Adm £1 Chd 50p. Sun April 30 (2-5)*

Peterdale ✤❀ (Mrs Ann Mountfield) St John's Road, Millbrook. Take new rd to Southdown. 1st L at new roundabout, straight ahead up St Johns Rd. Peterdale last bungalow on L. Small garden started 1980 from field; designed and created by owner on different levels; interesting collection of shrubs, trees, herbaceous plants combined with many old roses, recent waterfall and pond area. Truly a plantsperson's garden. TEA. *Adm £1.50 Chd free. Sun, Mon, Tues, Wed, April 9 to June 29, Sun, Mon July 2 to Aug 29 (2-6).* **Tel 01752 823364**

Pine Lodge Gardens ♿✤❀ (Mr & Mrs R H J Clemo) Cuddra. On A390 E of St Austell between Holmbush and Tregrehan. Follow signs. 6-acre garden set in 30 acres woodland and parkland with lake, pinetum, arboreturm. Wide range well-labelled rare plants, shrubs in herbaceous borders using original designs and colour combinations. Rhododenderons, camellias, specimen trees. Many interesting features, incl bog garden, fish pond. TEAS. *Adm £2 Chd free. Sun June 25 (1-5).* **Tel 01726 73500**

Pinetum ♿✂❀ (Mr & Mrs G R Craw) Harewood. 6m SW of Tavistock. From A390 Tavistock-Callington Rd proceed towards Calstock. After 1m follow sign to Harewood Parish Church. At church continue straight on. 3rd house on R. Walkways meander through 2-acre pinetum full of maturing, uncommon, specimen trees of botanical and ornamental intrigue interspersed with shrubs, plants and garden features for yr-round colour and interest. TEAS. *Adm £1.50 Chd free. Suns May 7, 21; Aug 6 (2-5.30)*

Polgwynne ♿✂❀ (Mrs P Davey) Feock. 5m S of Truro via A39 (Truro-Falmouth rd) and then B3289 to 1st Xrds: straight on ½m short of Feock village. 3½-acre garden and grounds. Fruit and vegetable garden, woodlands extending to shore of Carrick Roads; magnificent Ginkgo Biloba (female, 12′ girth) probably the largest female ginkgo in Britain; other beautiful trees; many rare and unusual shrubs. Lovely setting and view of Carrick Roads. TEAS. *Adm £1.50 Chd free. Sun April 30 (2-5.30).* **Tel 01872 862612**

●**Prideaux Place** ♿ (Mr & Mrs Prideaux-Brune) Padstow. On the edge of Padstow follow brown signs for Prideaux Place, from ring rd (A389). Surrounding Elizabethan house the present main grounds were laid out in the early C18 by Edmund Prideaux. Ancient deer park with stunning views over Camel estuary; victorian woodland walks currently under restoration. Newly restored sunken formal garden. A garden of vistas. Cream TEAS. *Adm £1.50 Chd free. Easter Sunday to Sept 28 (1.30-5); Bank Hols (11-5)*

Roseland House ❀ (Mr & Mrs Pridham) Chacewater, nr Truro. Situated in Chacewater 4m W of Truro, at Truro end of main st. Parking in village car park (100yds) or surrounding rds. 1-acre garden, with a large range of plants, some unusual, many scented, most plants in the garden propagated for sale. Garden is divided into several different areas, with pond, old orchard and Victorian conservatory (open). TEAS. *Adm £1.50 Chd free. Suns June 25, July 9 (2-5).* **Tel 01872 560451**

St Michael's Mount ✂❀ (The Rt Hon Lord St Levan; The National Trust) Marazion. ½m from shore at Marazion by Causeway; otherwise by ferry. Flowering shrubs; rock plants, castle walls; fine sea views. TEAS. *Adm Castle & gardens £3.50, Chd £1.75 (under 16). ▲For NGS Sun April 23 (10.30-4.45)*

¶**Scawn Mill** ✂❀ (Mrs A Ball & Dr Julian Ball) St Keyne. From the A38 at the E end of Dobwalls take the R sign posted to Duloe, Herodsfoot and Looe for 1½ m. Turn R at sign for Scawn and continue for 1m down to the river. Water lily lake lying beside the West Looe River terraced with azaleas, black pines and Japanese Maples. Walks beside primulas, herbaceous border and Japanese garden. Public footpath following West Looe River through woodland to Herodsfoot. TEAS. *Adm £1.50 Chd free. Sun June 18 (2-5.30)*

● **Trebah** ❀ (Trebah Garden Trust) 4m from Falmouth. Follow tourism signs from Hillhead Roundabout on A39 approach to Falmouth. Excellent parking (free) and access for coaches. 25-acre S facing breathtaking ravine garden, planted in 1850's by Charles Fox. The extensive collection of rare and mature trees and shrubs incl glades of huge tree ferns over 100 years old and sub-tropical exotics. Hydrangea collection covers 2½ acres. Water garden with waterfalls and rock pool stocked with mature Koi Carp. A magical garden of unique beauty for the plantsman, the artist and the family. Play area and trail for children. Use of private beach. Tea/Coffee and light refreshments. *Adm £2.80 OAPs £2.40 Chd and disabled £1. Open every day throughout year (10.30-5 last admission).* **Tel 01326 250448**

Trebartha (The Latham Family) North Hill, SW of Launceston. Nr junction of B3254 & B3257. Wooded area with lake surrounded by walks of flowering shrubs; woodland trail through fine woods with cascades and waterfalls; American glade with fine trees. TEAS. *Adm £1.50 Chd 50p (Share to North Hill Parish Church Roof Fund®). Sun Sept 24 (2-5.30)*

Tregilliowe Farm ♿❀ (Mr & Mrs J Richards) Penzance-Hayle A30 Rd from Penzance turn R at Crowlas Xrds. After approx 1m turn sharp L on to St Erth Rd. 2nd farm lane on R. 2-acre garden still developing. Herbaceous beds with wide range of perennials and grasses. Raised Mediterranean bed. TEAS June in aid of Save The Children. July in aid of St Julias Hospice. *Adm £1.50 Chd free. Suns June 18, July 16 (2-6).* **Tel 01736 740654**

Tregrehan ♿✂❀ (T Hudson Esq) Tregrehan. Entrance on A390 opp Britannia Inn 1m W of St Blazey. Access for cars and coaches. Garden largely created since early C19. Woodland of 20 acres containing fine trees, award winning camellias raised by late owner and many interesting plants from warm temperate climes. Show greenhouses a feature containing softer species. TEA. *Adm £2 Chd 50p. Mid March to end June daily. Not open Easter Sunday. For NGS Sun May 7 (10.30-5)*

Trelean ❀ (Sqn-Ldr G T Witherwick) St Martin-in-Meneage. 8m E of Helston. From Helston take St Keverne rd B3293; after 4m turn L for Mawgan and St Martin then follow Mudgeon sign. A garden of 3 acres contained within an area of naural beauty of 20 acres set by the Helford Riverside. The garden has a comprehensive collection of trees, conifers, shrubs and herbacious plants, full of colour and horticultural interest from May to August, autumn colour a speciality in September and Ocober. The garden has featured in the national press and RHS Journals. A natural, informal garden. No open days but groups and individuals welcome by appt from May to Oct. If convenient, tour by owner creator. *Adm £1.50 Chd free. By appt only* **Tel 01326 231255**

Trelissick ♿✂❀ (The National Trust; Mr & Mrs Spencer Copeland) Feock, 4m S of Truro, nr King Harry Ferry. On B3289. Planted with tender shrubs; magnolias, camellias and rhododendrons with many named species characteristic of Cornish gardens. Fine woodlands encircle the gardens through which a varied circular walk can be enjoyed. Superb view over Falmouth harbour. Georgian house (not open). TEAS. *Adm £3.40 Chd £1.90. ▲For NGS Sun April 9 (1-5.30)*

Tremeer Gardens St Tudy, 8m N of Bodmin; W of B3266, all rds signed. 7-acre garden famous for camellias and rhododendrons with water; many rare shrubs. *Adm £1 Chd 50p. Sun April 2 (2-5).* **Tel 01208 850313**

¶**Trengwainton** (The National Trust) 2m N W of Penzance, ½ mile West of Heamoor on Penzance-Morvah rd (B3312), ½m off St Just rd (A3071) The garden of mainland Britain perhaps most favoured for the cultivation of exotic shrubs and trees. Plantsman's delight. TEAS. *Adm £2.60 Chd £1.30. ▲For NGS Sun March 26 (10.30-5.30)*

¶**Trenance** (Mr & Mrs J Dingle) Launceston. Follow signs for Leisure Centre along Dunheved Rd. At College end of rd take sharp L bend and immediately after this take another L turning into Windmill Hill. Trenance is approx 200yds on L. A 1¾-acre garden for all seasons designed in the 1920's and restored and replanted by the present owners during the last 20 yrs. A wide variety of trees and shrubs incl rhododendrons, camellias, azaleas, acers and magnolias; heathers and conifers, primulas, herbaceous borders, roses and clematis with several smaller gardens within the main garden. TEA. *Adm £1.50 Chd 50p. Suns May 14, July 16 (2-6)*

Trerice (The National Trust) Newlyn East 3m SE of Newquay. From Newquay via A392 and A3058; turn R at Kestle Mill (NT sign-posts). Small manor house, rebuilt in 1571, containing fine plaster ceilings and fireplaces; oak and walnut furniture and tapestries. The summer-flowering garden is unusual in content and layout and there is an orchard planted with old varieties of fruit trees. A small museum traces the history of the lawn mower. Lunches & TEAS. *Adm house & garden £3.60 Chd £1.80. ▲For NGS Sun June 11 (11-5.30). Guided garden tour 2.30*

Trevegean (Mr & Mrs E C Cousins) 9 Manor Way. Take Penzance by-pass; take first L off roundabout towards Treneere and Heamoor. Sharp R turn for Manor way. ⅓-acre divided into series of enclosed areas; planting some formal, informal, topiary garden, shrubs and perennials; connected by brick and slab paths some edged with box. TEAS. *Adm £1 Chd free (Share to St Julias Hospice Hayle®). Private visits welcome for parties of 30 and over April 1 to end of June (2-5), please* **Tel 01736 67407**

Treviades Gardens Off the Falmouth to Constantine R at High Cross - 1m on the Falmouth side of Constantine and N of Port Navas. At High Cross, turn to Port Navas. The gardens are on the L going down the hill. Travelling from the Truro area follow the A39. Use the Penryn by-pass. At Hillhead Roundabout, follow the signs to Constantine. *Combined adm £2.50 Chd free (Share to CRMF®). Sun July 9 (2-5.30)*

Treviades Barton (Mr & Mrs M J Ford) Series of walled gardens, each one with own character (i.e. roses in one); vegetable garden and small arboretum
Treviades Wollas (Mrs Watson) S facing med sized garden in two parts - leading down to small water garden fed by two springs

● **Trewithen** (A M J Galsworthy Esq) Truro. ½m E Probus. Entrance on A390 Truro-St Austell Rd. Sign posted. Large car park. Internationally renowned garden of 30 acres laid out by Maj G Johnson between 1912 & 1960 with much of original seed and plant material collected by Ward and Forrest. Original C18 walled garden famed for towering magnolias and rhododendrons; wide range of own hybrids. Flatish ground amidst original woodland park. Featured in NGS video 2. TEAS. *Adm £2.50 Chd £1.50 Group £2.20. Mon to Sat March 1 to Sept 30 (10-4.30). Special arrangements for coaches. Mrs Norman* **Tel 01726 882763**

Treworder Mill (Derek & Pearl Rutter) Kenwyn. 2½m W of Truro. A390 Truro to Redruth. Turn at Treliske Hospital roundabout. Pass Duchy Hospital. Turn L at T junction. Car parking at bottom of hill. R Kenwyn Valley Garden. 2¾ acres with streams and a wide range of moisture-loving plants including Candelabra primulas and hostas in a woodland setting. Interesting natural pond area. *Adm £1.50 Chd free. May 17 to June 28 every Weds 10-12 noon and 2-5.* **Tel 01872 73314** *evenings*

¶**Water Meadow** (Philip & Rose Lamb) Luxulyan 5m NW of St Austell, 6m S of Bodmin. [Map ref SX 052582.] Park in village street between church and school. Turn by church, garden 200yds downhill on L. 1½-acre garden on sloping site with Grade II listed grotto. Large pond with waterside planting and bog garden with extensive primula, astilbe, gunnera, arum lilies etc. Gravel garden surrounded by shrub roses & herbaceous planting. Specimen trees and shrubs with recently established mixed borders. TEAS in aid of WI. *Adm £1.50 Chd free. Sun June 25 (2-5)*

●**Woodland Garden** (Mr & Mrs N Froggatt) On Helston/St Keverne Rd B3293, turn R ¼m past Garras village at Woodland Garden sign. Entrance on R after ½m. Informal 2½-acre garden in wooded valley, planted in the last 14 years with camellias, rhododendrons, magnolias, trees and shrubs, primulas and many unusual plants. Planting and development continue. Lovely spring succession of wild daffodils, primroses and then bluebells. Small pond and stream. ¼-mile walk to 9 acres on Goonhilly Downs, an impressive area of heathers (especially the Erica Vagans, best July-Sept). Dogs allowed only on Downs. *Adm £1 Chd free. Sats April 15 to Sept 30 (2-5).* **Tel 01326 221295**

Cumbria

Hon County Organiser: (South) Mrs R E Tongue, Paddock Barn, Winster, Windermere LA23 3NW
Assistant Hon County Organiser: (North) Mrs E C Hicks, Scarthwaite, Grange-in-Borrowdale, Keswick CA12 5UQ

DATES OF OPENING

By appointment

For telephone numbers and other details see garden descriptions. Private visits welcomed

The Beeches, Houghton nr Carlisle
Copt Howe, Chapel Stile, Ambleside
38 English Street, Longtown
Galesyke, Wasdale
Greystones, Embleton
High Beckside Farm, Cartmel
High Hesket School, Carlisle
Palace How, Brackenthwaite
Rydal Mount, Eskdale Green, nr Gosforth
Scarthwaite, Grange-in-Borrowdale

Parties only

Askham Hall, Penrith
Fellside, Millbeck, nr Keswick
Green Bank, Grasmere
Greencroft House, Great Strickland
Halecat, Witherslack
Higham Hall College, Bassenthwaite Lake
Lindeth Fell Country House, Bowness-on-Windermere
St Annes, Great Langdale
Wood Hall, Cockermouth

Regular openings

For details see garden descriptions

Brockhole, Windermere. Daily March 24 to Nov 2
Higham Hall College, Bassenthwaite Lake. Daily all year
Holehird, Windermere. For details see text
Holker Hall & Gardens. Suns to Fris April 2 to Oct 31
Hutton-the-Forest, Penrith. For details see text
Levens Hall, Kendal. Daily except Fris and Sats April 2 to Sept 28
Lingholm, Portinscale, Keswick. Daily April 1 to Oct 31
Matthew How, Troutbeck. Every day May 14 to June 3
Muncaster Castle, Ravenglass. Daily

April 14 Friday
Copt Howe, Chapel Stile, Ambleside

April 15 Saturday
Copt Howe, Chapel Stile, Ambleside

April 16 Sunday
Copt Howe, Chapel Stile, Ambleside

April 17 Monday
Copt Howe, Chapel Stile, Ambleside

April 19 Wednesday
Green Bank, Grasmere

April 24 Monday
Levens Hall, Kendal

April 29 Saturday
Copt Howe, Chapel Stile, Ambleside

April 30 Sunday
Copt Howe, Chapel Stile, Ambleside
Dallam Tower, Milnthorpe

May 1 Monday
Copt Howe, Chapel Stile, Ambleside

May 3 Wednesday
Lingholm, Portinscale, Keswick

May 6 Saturday
Copt Howe, Chapel Stile, Ambleside

May 7 Sunday
Copt Howe, Chapel Stile, Ambleside
Green Bank, Grasmere ‡
The Nook, Helton, nr Penrith
Rydal Mount, Eskdale Green, nr Gosforth
Stagshaw, Rothay Road, Ambleside ‡

May 8 Monday
Copt Howe, Chapel Stile, Ambleside

May 10 Wednesday
Rydal Mount, Eskdale Green, nr Gosforth

May 11 Thursday
Muncaster Castle, Ravenglass

May 13 Saturday
Acorn Bank, Temple Sowerby, nr Penrith
Copt Howe, Chapel Stile, Ambleside

May 14 Sunday
Browfoot, Skelwith Bridge, Ambleside ‡
Copt Howe, Chapel Stile, Ambleside ‡
Fell Yeat, Kirkby Lonsdale
Green Bank, Grasmere ‡
Lindeth Fell Country House, Bowness-on-Windemere ‡‡
Matson Ground Settlement, Windermere ‡‡

May 17 Wednesday
Brockhole, Windermere

May 20 Saturday
Copt Howe, Chapel Stile, Ambleside
Galesyke, Wasdale

May 21 Sunday
Browfoot, Skelwith Bridge, Ambleside ‡
Copt Howe, Chapel Stile, Ambleside ‡
Galesyke, Wasdale
Halecat, Witherslack ‡‡
High Beckside Farm, Cartmel ‡‡
Palace How, Brackenthwaite
St Annes, Great Langdale ‡

May 24 Wednesday
Brackenburn, Manesty, nr Keswick
Brockhole, Windermere

May 27 Saturday
Copt Howe, Chapel Stile, Ambleside

May 28 Sunday
Browfoot, Skelwith Bridge, Ambleside ‡
Copt Howe, Chapel Stile, Ambleside ‡
Fellside, Millbeck, nr Keswick
Holehird, Windermere

May 29 Monday
Copt Howe, Chapel Stile, Ambleside

June 4 Sunday
Blakeholme Wray, Newby Bridge ‡
Hazelmount, Thwaites, Millom
Stagshaw, Rothay Road, Ambleside
Station House, Lamplugh, nr Workington
Yews, Middle Entrance Drive, Bowness-on-Windermere

June 10 Saturday
Acorn Bank, Temple Sowerby, nr Penrith

June 11 Sunday
Greystones, Embleton
Hutton-the-Forest, Penrith

June 17 Saturday
Rannerdale Cottage, Buttermere
June 18 Sunday
Dallam Tower, Milnthorpe
Fell Yeat, Kirkby Lonsdale
Rannerdale Cottage, Buttermere
July 2 Sunday
Askham Hall, Penrith ‡
The Mill House, Sebergham
Whitbysteads, Askham ‡
July 8 Saturday
Sizergh Castle, nr Kendal
July 9 Sunday
Beckfoot Gardens, Duddon Bridge
High Hesket School, Carlisle
Weston House, Crosby Ravensworth
July 16 Sunday
Dallam Tower, Milnthorpe ‡
Halecat, Witherslack ‡
High Cleabarrow, Windermere ‡‡
Holehird, Windermere ‡‡
July 22 Saturdaay
Acorn Bank, Temple Sowerby, nr Penrith
July 23 Sunday
38 English Street, Longtown
July 30 Sunday
Hutton-the-Forest, Penrith ‡
Marton House, Long Marton, Appleby ‡
August 2 Wednesday
Lingholm, Portinscale, Keswick
August 27 Sunday
Rydal Mount, Eskdale Green, nr Gosforth
August 30 Wednesday
Rydal Mount, Eskdale Green, nr Gosforth
September 9 Sunday
Matson Ground Settlement, Windermere
September 25 Monday
Levens Hall, Kendal

DESCRIPTIONS OF GARDENS

Acorn Bank ♿✂❀ (The National Trust) Temple Sowerby. 6m E of Penrith on A66; ½m N of Temple Sowerby. Bus: Penrith-Appleby or Carlisle-Darlington; alight Culgaith Rd end. Medium-sized walled garden; fine herb garden; orchard and mixed borders; wild garden with woodland/riverside walk. Dogs on leads only woodland walk. *Adm £1.60 Chd 80p. April 1 to Oct 31 daily (10-5). For NGS Sats May 13, June 10, July 22 (10-5)*

Askham Hall ✂❀ (The Earl & Countess of Lonsdale) 5m S of Penrith. Turn off A6 for Lowther and Askham. Askham Hall is a pele tower, incorporating C14, C16 and early C18 elements in courtyard plan. Formal outlines of garden with terraces of herbaceous borders and original topiary, probably from late C17. Shrub roses and recently created herb garden. Kitchen garden. TEA. *Adm £1 Chd free (Share to Askham & Lowther Churches®). Sun July 2 (2-5.30). Private parties welcome, please* **Tel 01931 712208**

¶Beckfoot Gardens ✂ (Mr & Mrs J Atkinson) Duddon Bridge, Broughton-in-Furness. ⅔-acre woodland garden recently created in dell with beck flowing through into R Duddon. Choice plantings of shrubs and perennials on steep banks. Surrounds converted mill; use made of disused mill machinery. Paths steep in places. TEAS. *Adm £1.50 Chd 50p. Sun July 9 (2-5)*

The Beeches ✂❀ (Mr & Mrs J B McKay Black) 42 The Green, Houghton. 2m NE of Carlisle. Leave M6 at junction 44. Take A6264 (Hexham & Carlisle Airport). After 1m turn R over M6 into village. Parking in lay-by on R at end of village green. The Beeches is 10 yards further. Plantsman's garden approx ¾-acre. Herbaceous, mixed borders, raised beds of alpines, peat garden, troughs and pool. Many dwarf bulbs in Spring, dwarf bulbs in pots and bulb frame. Good collections of hostas and dwarf rhododendrons. *Adm £1.50 Chd free. Private visits Feb to July incl, please* **Tel 01228 22670**

¶Blakeholme Wray ✂ (Mr & Mrs W T Rooney) Newby Bridge. [Grid Ref GR 384 895] Blakeholme Wray is 2m N of Newby Bridge on A592. 4 acres garden, 22 acres woodland. An outstanding position with lawns sweeping down to the shore of Windermere. Informal planting is ongoing under present owners: massed rhododendrons and azaleas, damson orchard, wild orchids, bluebell carpets, ancient woodland walk, abundant wildlife. Partially suitable for wheelchairs. *Adm £1.50. Sun June 4 (12-5)*

Brackenburn (Prof & Mrs D C Ellwood) Manesty. Take rd signed Portinscale and Grange off A66. Follow all signs for Grange. Garden is 1½ acres on the mountainside on RH-side of rd 3½m from A66. The Garden has wonderful views of Lake Derwent Water. There are several water features planted for damp acid conditions with many rhododendrons, azaleas, ferns and primulas. Brackenburn is the former home of author Sir Hugh Walpole. *Adm £1.50 Acc chd free (Share to Scottish terrier emergency care scheme®). Wed May 24 (2-5)*

Brockhole ♿ (Lake District National Park) Windermere. 2m NW of Windermere on A591 between Windermere and Ambleside. 10 acres formal gardens, designed by Thomas Mawson. Acid soils and mild aspect, many unusual or slightly tender plants, shrub roses, herbaceous borders, scented garden. 20 acres informal grounds, wide variety of trees and shrubs. Picnic area, adventure playground, boat trips on Lake Windermere. Garden walks. Restaurant and tea rooms. *Adm free (Pay & display car parking £2.20 per car, season ticket for car park £14). Daily March 24 to Nov 2; for NGS Wed May 17, 24 (10-5).* **Tel 015394 46601**

Browfoot ❀ (Mr Trevor Woodburn) Skelwith Bridge 2½m SW of Ambleside on A593. Turn down lane at Skelwith Bridge. Woodland garden developed by owner; rhododendrons; azaleas; species trees and natural rock garden. Approx 2 acres. Parking & TEAS provided by and in aid of the Community Centre, only on May 14. *Adm £1.30 Chd 40p. Suns May 14, 21, 28 (11-5)*

Regular Openers. Too many days to include in diary. Usually there is a wide range of plants giving year-round interest. See head of county section for the name and garden description for times etc.

Copt Howe ❀ (Professor R N Haszeldine) Chapel Stile. Great Langdale ¼m W of Chapel Stile on B5343. 2-acre plantsman's garden, newly extended. Scenic views Langdale Pikes. Extensive collections of acers (especially Japanese), camellias, azaleas, rhododendrons, quercus, fagus, rare shrubs and trees, unusual perennials; herbaceous and bulbous species; alpines and trough gardens; rare dwarf and large conifers; Expedition plants from Far East. Featured by the media, gardening magazines. *Adm £2; OAP £1.50; Chd free. April 14, 15, 16, 17, 29, 30; May 1, 6, 7, 8 (1.30-5) May 13, 14, 20, 21, 27, 28, 29 (10-5.30). Cream TEAS and plants May 14, 21. Plants on many other days (Share to Langdales Society© May 14, Friends of the Lake District® other days). Private visits welcome April to end Sept, please* **Tel 015394 37685**

Dallam Tower ♿ (Brigadier & Mrs C E Tryon-Wilson) Milnthorpe, 7m S of Kendal. 7m N of Carnforth, nr junction of A6 and B5282. Station: Arnside, 4m; Lancaster, 15m. Bus: Ribble 553, 554 Milnthorpe-Lancaster via Arnside, alight at Lodge Gates. Medium-sized garden; natural rock garden, waterfalls, rambler and polyanthus roses; wood walks, lawns, shrubs. *Adm £1 Chd free. Suns April 30, June 18, July 16 (2-5)*

38 English Street ✲❀ (Mr & Mrs C Thomson) Longtown, Carlisle. M6 junction 44, A7 for 6m into Longtown. 300yds on L next door to Annes Hairdressers. Entrance through open archway. Terraced house garden. Red sandstone and water features; containers and troughs, pergola and herbaceous. TEA. *Adm £1 Acc chd free (Share to Cat Protection League®). Sun July 23 (2-5). Private visits and parties welcome, please* **Tel 01228 791364**

Fell Yeat ♿✲❀ (Mr & Mrs O S Benson) Casterton, nr Kirkby Lonsdale. Approx 1m E of Casterton Village on the rd to Bull Pot. Leave A65 at Devils Bridge, follow A683 for a mile, take the R fork to High Casterton at the golf course, straight across at two sets of Xrds, the house is immediately on the L about ¼m from no through rd sign. 1-acre informal country garden with mixed borders, herbaceous, old roses, small fernery, herb garden and small pond. Extensive views of the Lune Valley from a still developing garden. Holds and is building up the National Collection of Ligularias. TEAS (in aid of S Lakeland Cot Death Group®). *Adm £1 Chd 20p. Suns May 14, June 18 (1.30-5)*

Fellside ✲ (Mr & Mrs C D Collins) Millbeck, 2m N of Keswick. Turn off A591 Keswick-Bassenthwaite rd opp sign to Millbeck (2m from Keswick); at T-junc in Millbeck village turn right; garden 300yds on left. 1-acre, informal, shrub garden; 300 varieties of rhododendrons, camellias, azaleas, on steep terraced site. Pretty glen with beck; magnificent views of Derwent Water and Bassenthwaite. Tea John Gregg, The Cottage, Millbeck or The Old Mill (Nat Trust) Mirehouse. *Adm 60p Chd 30p. Sun May 28 (2-5). Parties welcome, please* **Tel 01687 72547**

Galesyke ✲ (Christine & Mike McKinley) Wasdale. From the N enter Gosforth and follow signposts to Nether Wasdale. Pass through Nether Wasdale, following signs to the Lake and Wasdale Head. After approx ¾m, entrance on R. From the S head towards Santon Bridge turn off A595 at Holmrook or app from Eskdale. Turn R at Santon Bridge following signs to Wasdale Head. Approx 3m to entrance. Secluded landscaped riverside garden on the banks of the R Irt with magnificent views of the Screes and Wasdale Fells. Approx 1½ acres the garden contains a variety of mature trees and flowering shrubs. There is access to a riverside meadows walk and to the far bank with its secluded woodland walks. TEA. *Adm £1.20 Chd under 12 free. Sat, Sun May 20, 21 (11.30-5). Private visits for parties of 6 and over please* **Tel 019467 26267**

Green Bank ✲ (Mr & Mrs Reg Gifford) Grasmere. 4m from Ambleside off the A591 Keswick Rd. Turn R between Swan Hotel and its car park. 5-acre steep hillside garden with woodland walks and mountain stream under a 5yr renovation plan. Features a unique collection of rare trees, rhododendrons, camellias and azaleas brought to England by the late Michael Black from Bhutan, Chile, Nepal, etc. Great interest to plant enthusiasts. Teas in adjacent hotels or cafes in Grasmere. *Adm £2 Chd/OAPs £1. Wed April 19, Suns May 7, 14 (10.30-5).* **Tel 015394 35496**

Greencroft House ♿✲ ❀ (Mr & Mrs W Irving) Gt Strickland, 7m S of Penrith. Off A6 at Hackthorpe, signed to Gt Strickland ¾m. Approx 1-acre of a series of small gardens of different character: herbs; alpines; shrubs; water and herbaceous plants. *Adm £1. Private visits welcome June and July for parties of 12, please* **Tel 01931 712236**

Greystones ✲❀ (Mr & Mrs D Cook) Embleton. Just off A66, 4m E of Cockermouth, 2m W of Bassenthwaite Lake. Take turning marked 'Wythop Mill' with watermill sign. Lane 200yds on R. 1 acre of mostly new garden being developed on various levels around mature trees, with shrubs, herbaceous beds and borders, woodland garden, ponds, scree, spring bulbs. Organic fruit and vegetable beds. Teas at Wythop Mill ½m. *Adm £1 Chd free. Sun June 11 (2-5). Private visits welcome, (mid/late April usually good) please* **Tel 017687 76375**

Halecat ♿❀ (Mrs Michael Stanley) Witherslack, 10m SW of Kendal. From A590 turn into Witherslack following the Halecat brown signs. L in township at another brown sign and L again, signpost 'Cartmel Fell'; gates on L [map ref. 434834]. Medium-sized garden; mixed shrub and herbaceous borders, terrace, sunken garden; gazebo; daffodils and cherries in Spring, over 70 different varieties of hydrangea; beautiful view over Kent estuary to Arnside. Nursery garden attached. TEA. *Adm £1 Chd free (Share to Leukaemia Campaign®). Suns May 21, July 16 (2-5). Also private parties welcome, please* **Tel 0144 852229**

Hazelmount ♿✲❀ (Mrs J Barratt) Thwaites, Millom, 2m from Broughton-in-Furness off A595 up hill after crossing Duddon River Bridge. 5-acre woodland garden, small lake with stream; spring display of species rhododendrons, azaleas and flowering shrubs. Mature trees and exceptional views of Duddon Estuary and sea. TEAS. *Adm £1 Chd free. Sun June 4 (2-5.30)*

High Beckside Farm ✿ (Mr & Mrs P J McCabe) Cartmel. 1¼m N of Cartmel. Take the Haverthwaite Rd, from the PO in the village. A newly created conservation area, a wild garden with ponds, waterfalls, waterfowl; flowering bushes and a number of rare trees. An arboretum in the very early stages of formation. 11 acres of wild flowers on a hillside with fine views. A small house garden. Approx ¼m from house to conservation area. Stout shoes. TEA. *Adm £1.25 Chd free. Sun May 21 (1-5). Private visits welcome, please* **Tel 015395 36528**

High Cleabarrow ♿✿❀ (Mr & Mrs R T Brown) 3m SE of Windermere off B5284 Crook to Kendal Rd (nr Windermere Golf Course). 1½-acre newly designed and planted garden comprising wide variety of herbaceous, old-fashioned roses, shrubs, unusual plants on different levels; woodland area. TEAS. *Adm £1.20 Chd 50p. Sun July 16 (1.30-5.30)*

¶Higham Hall College ♿✿ (Alasdair Galbraith) Bassenthwaite Lake. 7m N of Keswick 4m SE of Cockermouth. Take rd signed Castle Inn off A66 at N end of Bassenthwaite Lake. Higham Hall is signed after ½m. 4 acres of informal Victorian gardens incl pond, woodland walk, specimen trees, lawns, sunken rose garden. Rhododendrons. Parkland views towards Skiddaw. *Donations. Open all year, every day (9-dusk).* **Tel 017687 76276**

High Hesket School ♿✿❀ (Mr P Howard) Nr Carlisle. The school is just off the A6 halfway between Penrith and Carlisle. Backs onto the A6 but visitors must turn off to High Hesket and will find the school at the top of the hill. Wildlife Garden featuring a variety of habitats – pond, bog, meadows, hedge and tree plantings. Cultivated Garden for flowers and vegetables, specially designed Maths and Science Area with waterfall, sundial, sand pit etc. The development was started in 1990 and occupies ½ acre of the school's playing field. It won the 1991 Cumbria County Council Environment Award for best project by a school, college or youth group. TEA. *Adm £1 Chd free (Share to High Hesketh School Association©). Sun July 9 (1-5). Private visits welcome, please* **Tel 016974 73386**

Holehird (Lakeland Horticultural Society) ✿ Patterdale Road, Windermere. ½m N of Windermere town on A591. Turn R onto A592 to Patterdale. Garden signposted on R ¾m on A592. Car park along private drive. The garden of nearly 5 acres is set on a hillside with some of the best views in Lakeland, with a great diversity of plants that grow well in this area, incl alpine and heather beds and a collection of rhododendrons and azaleas. The walled garden is mostly herbaceous. National collections of astilbes, polystichum ferns and hydrangeas. Partially suitable wheelchairs. *Garden always open. Entrance by donation £1 Chd free. Warden available throughout summer (10-5). Coach parties by appointment, volunteer guides available* **Tel 015394 46008**. *For NGS Suns May 28, July 16 (10-5)*

●Holker Hall & Gardens ♿✿ (Lord & Lady Cavendish) Cark-in-Cartmel. 4m W of Grange-over-Sands. 12m W of M6 (junction 36). Magnificent formal and woodland gardens developed by the Cavendish family over two centuries. Woodland walks amongst exotic trees and shrubs with ancient oak, sycamore and beech. Carpets of bulbs accompany rhododendrons, azaleas and magnolias in spring. In summer unusual trees and shrubs in flower, incl eucryphias and many members of the styracaceae (the National Trust collection is being established). Formal areas incl the elliptical and summer gardens near the house. An extensive cascade in woodland garden, and a wildflower meadow in high summer. Winners of Christies - H.H.A. Garden of the Year Award (1991). C19 Wing of Holker Hall, Lakeland Motor Museum, deer park. Exhibitions, Adventure Playground, Deer Park, Shop & Cafeteria. *Garden tours by arrangement. Discounted Adm & catering to groups 20+ by prior arrangement, group organiser free. Great Garden and Countryside festival June 2, 3 and 4. Adm prices not available at time of going to press. Sun to Fris April 2 to Oct 31 (10-6 last entry 4.30)*

Hutton-in-the-Forest (Lord Inglewood) 5m NW of Penrith. 3m from exit 41 of M6. Magnificent grounds with C18 walled flower garden, terraces and lake. C19 Low garden, specimen trees and topiary; woodland walk and dovecote. Mediaeval House with C17, C18 and C19 additions. TEAS. *Adm £2 gardens, grounds, £3.50 house, gardens & grounds Chd free gardens, grounds £1.50 house & garden & grounds. Gardens and grounds open daily all year except Sats (11-5). House and tea room open (1-4) Easter Sun, Mon April 16, 17 and Thurs, Fris, Suns and Bank Hol Mons from April 30 to Oct 1. Also Weds in Aug. For NGS Suns June 11, July 30 (11-5)*

Levens Hall ♿✿❀ (C H Bagot Esq) 5m S of Kendal on Milnthorpe Rd (A6); Exit 36 from M6. 10 acres incl famous topiary garden and 1st ha-ha laid out by M Beaumont in 1694. Magnificent beech circle; formal bedding; herbaceous borders. Elizabethan mansion, added to C13 pele tower, contains superb panelling, plasterwork and furniture. Steam collection illustrating history of steam 1830-1920. Only gardens suitable for wheelchairs. *Adm House & Garden £4.20 OAPs £3.80 Chd £2.50. Garden only £2.90 OAPs £2.70 Chd £1.80. Reduction for groups. April 2 to Sept 28. House and garden, gift shop, tearoom. children's play area, picnic area. Sun, Mon, Tues, Wed, Thurs house (11-4.30), grounds (10-5), steam collection (2-5). Closed Fri & Sat. For NGS Mons April 24, Sept 25 (10-5)*

Lindeth Fell Country House Hotel ♿ (Air Commodore & Mrs P A Kennedy) 1m S of Bowness on A5074. 6-acres of lawns and landscaped grounds on the hills above Lake Windermere, probably designed by one of the Mawson school around 1907; majestic conifers and specimen trees best in spring and early summer with a colourful display of rhododendrons, azaleas and Japanese maples; grounds offer splendid views to Coniston mountains; rose garden and herbaceous border newly developed. Top terrace suitable for wheelchairs. TEAS in hotel 50p. *Adm £1 Chd free. Sun May 14 (2-5). Also private parties welcome, please* **Tel 01539 443 286**

By Appointment Gardens. These owners do not have a fixed opening day usually because they do not like crowds or have insufficient parking space. Owner will often give guided tour.

Lingholm ♿✂❀ (The Viscount Rochdale) Keswick. On W shore of Derwentwater; Portinscale 1m; Keswick 3m. Turn off A66 at Portinscale; drive entrance 1m on left. Ferry: Keswick to Nicol End, 10 mins walk. Bus: Keswick to Portinscale, 1m. Formal and woodland gardens; garden walk 1m; rhododendrons, azaleas, herbaceous borders etc. Spring daffodils, autumn colours. Plant centre. Free car park. TEAS. *Adm £2.70 (incl leaflet) Chd free. April 1 to Oct 31 daily. For NGS Weds May 3, Aug 2 (10-5)*

Marton House ✂❀ (Mr & Mrs M S Hardy-Bishop) Long Marton, Turn off A66 2m W of Appleby signposted Long Marton. Follow rd through village under bridge. House/Car park on R. A 4½ acre walled garden nestling in the foothills of the Pennines. Magnificent Cedar of lebanan, herbaceous borders, new Italian garden leading to small lake, ducks, woodland walk, views. Ongoing landscaping and refurbishment. Cream TEAS. *Adm £1.50 Chd 25p. Sun July 30 (1-5.30)*

Matson Ground ♿✂❀ (Matson Ground Settlement) Windermere. From Kendal turn R off B5284 signposted Heathwaite, 100yds after Windermere Golf Club entrance. Lane joins another in ¼m. Continue straight on. Garden is on L after ¼m. From Bowness turn L onto B5284 from A5074. After ¾m turn L at Xrds follow sign to Heathwaite. Garden on L ¾m along lane. A watercourse flows through the ornamental garden ending at a large pond in the wild garden of meadow grassland with spring bulbs and later wild flowers. Azaleas and rhododendrons, large mixed shrub/herbaceous borders and some very imaginative topiary work. Landscape designer John Brookes has been behind much of the recent changes in the garden. There is also a ½-acre walled kitchen garden being run on organic methods with greenhouses and a dovecote. Adjacent to the ornamental garden is a 2-acre amenity woodland. TEAS. *Adm £1 Chd 50p. Suns May 14, Sept 9 (1-5)*

Matthew How ✂ (Mr & Mrs John Griffiths) Troutbeck. 2½m equidistant from Windermere & Ambleside. From Windermere after Lakes School turn R up Bridge Lane off A591. From Ambleside L up Holbeck Lane between Townend (NT) and Post office. 1-acre cottage terraced garden on steep fell site. Surrounding C17 (Yeoman Farmers House). Lovely views overlooking Troutbeck Valley. Spring bulbs; rhododendrons, camellias, azaleas, box hedges, topiary and troughs. Rich wild bird life incl. nut hatches and pied fly catchers, woodpeckers and warblers etc. TEA when possible. *Adm £1 Chd free (Share to Troutbeck Village Hall®). Open daily Sun May 14 until Sun June 3 (12-5). Also private visits welcome anytime please* **Tel 01539 433276**

¶The Mill House ✂❀ (Kay I Jefferson) Sebergham. Take junction 41 off M6 A5305 Penrith to Wigton Rd into Sebergham turning to L into an easily missed lane just before bridge over river Caldew. 200 yds up lane, after bungalow take L fork in drive. ½-acre garden set in secluded valley around the water mill; features millstream and pond, a large herbaceous border and a gravel garden; fruit and vegetable garden. TEA. *Adm £1 Chd free. Sun July 2 (1.30-4.30)*

Muncaster Castle ♿❀ (Mrs P R Gordon-Duff-Pennington) 1m E of Ravenglass, 17m SW of Whitehaven on A595. 77 acres; famous large collection of species rhododendrons, azaleas and camellias, some unique in UK; arboretum; historic and scenic site at foot of Eskdale. Owl centre. Giftshops. Also extensive plant centre. Coach parties and schools by appt. Special arrangements for disabled at front gate. CAFE. *Castle, Garden and Owl Centre 1995 Adm price on application* **Tel 01229 717614**. *Gardens and Owl Centre open all year. Castle open daily from Mar 26 to Oct 29 except Mons (also open all Bank Hol Mons). Castle (1-4) garden and Owl Centre (11-5). For NGS Thurs May 11 (11-5)*

The Nook ♿❀ (Mr & Mrs P Freedman) Helton. Penrith N 5m from B5320, take signs to Askham-Haweswater. Turn R into Helton. ½-acre terraced rock garden, beds and tubs, alpines, ornamental pool, goldfish, bog plants, fruit and herb garden; magnificent views over R Lowther and parkland. Homemade provisions for sale. TEAS. *Adm £1 Chd free. Sun May 7 (11-4)*

Palace How ♿✂❀ (Mr & Mrs A & K Johnson) Brackenthwaite, Loweswater, 6m SE of Cockermouth on B5292 and B5289 or from Keswick 10m over Whinlatter Pass, through Lorton village, follow signs for Loweswater. Established 11-yr-old damp garden set in lovely situation amongst mountains. Acid soil supporting unusual trees and shrubs, especially rhododendrons and acers. Pond with bog plants; iris; candelabra primulas; Himalayan poppies and hostas, roses and alpines. Teas at Loweswater Village Hall in aid of W Cumbria Hospice at Home. *Adm £1.40 Chd free. Sun May 21 (11-5). Private visits and parties welcome, please* **Tel 01900 85648**

Rannerdale Cottage ❀ (The McElney Family) Buttermere. 8m S of Cockermouth, 10m W of Keswick. ½-acre cottage garden with beck and woodland walk overlooking Crummock Water, splendid mountain views. Herbaceous, shrubs, roses, perennial geraniums, tree peonies, pond with fish. TEAS. *Adm £1 Chd free. Sat, Sun June 17, 18 (11-5)*

Rydal Mount ❀ (Don & Toni Richards) Eskdale Green, Holmrook. Turn off A595 where signed 6m to Eskdale Green. Turn sharp R opp Eskdale Stores. 2nd house on R. 1½-acre garden on natural rock facing SW. Heathers and tree heaths with shrubs and small trees favouring acid soil; eucalyptus and American blueberrys; water garden. Blueberry TEAS. *Adm 75p Chd free (Share to West Cumbria Hospice at Home®). Suns, Weds May 7, 10; Aug 27, 30 (2-5). Also private visits welcome, please* **Tel 019467 23267**

St Annes ❀ (Mr & Mrs R D Furness) Great Langdale. 5m from Ambleside on B5343. Follow signs for Langdale/Old Dungeon Ghyll. At Skelwith Bridge take R hand fork and at Elterwater take R hand. Through Chapel Stile, ¾m on L hand side travelling W. 3-acre partial woodland with established variety of conifers and trees, azaleas and rhododendrons. Natural rock faces with alpines, streams and rocky paths. Magnificent views Langdales. Partially suitable for wheelchairs. TEAS. *Adm £1 Chd free. Sun May 21 (10.30-5). Open for groups by appt, please* **Tel 015394 37271**

Scarthwaite ✿❀ (Mr & Mrs E C Hicks) Grange-in-Borrowdale. From Keswick take B5289 to Grange; cross on road bridge, suitable for mini buses, house ¼m on L. ¼m walk from far side of bridge for coach parties. Ferns, cottage garden plants and many others closely packed into ⅓ acre. *Adm £1.50 Acc chd free. Private visits and parties welcome, please* **Tel 01768 777 233**

Sizergh Castle ♿✿ (The National Trust) nr Kendal. Close to and W of the main A6 trunk road, 3m S of Kendal. An approach road leaves A6 close to and S of A6/A591 interchange. ⅔-acre Limestone Rock Garden is the largest owned by the National Trust; it has a large collection of Japanese maples, dwarf conifers, hardy ferns, primulas, gentians and many other perennials and bulbs; water garden with bog and aquatic plants; on walls around main lawn are shrubs and climbers, many half-hardy; rose garden contains specimen roses along with shrubs, climbers, ground cover and lilies; also wild flower banks, herbaceous border, crab apple orchard with spring bulbs and 'Dutch' garden. *Castle & gdn adm £3.30 Chd £1.70; Gdn adm £1.70 Chd 90p (Share to Cheshire Home at Holehird®). For NGS Sat July 8 (12.30-5.30)*

Stagshaw ✿ (The National Trust) ½m S of Ambleside. Turn E off A 591, Ambleside to Windermere rd. Bus 555 Kendal-Keswick alight Waterhead. Woodland gdn incl fine collection of rhododendrons and azaleas. Ericaceous trees & shrubs incl magnolias, camellias, embothriums. Views over Windermere. *Adm £1 Chd 50p. For NGS Suns May 7, June 4 (10-5.30)*

Station House ♿❀ (Mr & Mrs G H Simons) Wright Green. Lamplugh approx 6m from Workington, Whitehaven and Cockermouth signposted off A5086 Lilyhall-Workington from Cockermouth-Egremont Rd ½m under disused railway line from Workington-Whitehaven A595 at Leyland roundabout take rd signposted Branthwaite-Loweswater. 2-acre garden created over site of disused railway line and station. Features shrubs and trees; vegetable and fruit garden. Morning coffee/TEAS. *Adm 50p Chd 25p. Sun June 4 (10.30-4.30)*

¶Weston House ♿✿❀ (Mrs L Parker) Crosby, Ravensworth. From Kendal take A6 in Shap Turn R by bakers. 3m in village T-junction L - ½ m at church. From Penrith on A6 turn L in Shap. 1½-acres surrounded by stream and river Livennet, tributary of Eden. Old Vicarage garden under reclamation. New shrub and rose borders, shady walks, herbaceous. TEAS. *Adm £1 Chd free. Sun July 9 (2-5)*

Whitbysteads ❀ (The Hon Mrs Anthony Lowther) Askham nr Penrith 8m from Penrith. Turn R at Eamont Bridge off the A6. Turn L at Y fork after Railway Bridge signed Askham. Through village, turn R at Queen's Head. 1-acre garden on several levels surrounding farmhouse on edge of fells, featuring wide variety shrub roses, unusual herbaceous plants and geraniums. Pergola; fountain. Magnificent views over Eden Valley. TEAS. *Adm £1 Chd free (Share to St Michael & All Angels Church, Lowther®). Sun July 2 (2-5)*

¶Wood Hall ✿❀ (Mr & Mrs W Jackson) Cockermouth. Entrance to drive in large lay-by ¼m N (towards Carlisle) off the A595/A594 roundabout nr Cockermouth. A 5½-acre Thomas Mawson garden, with terraces, walls, small feature gardens, lawns, woods and paths. Venerable trees and newer planting. Alpines, shrubs and herbaceous plants. *Adm £1 Acc chd free. Private visits welcome, please* **Tel 01900 823585**

Yews ✿❀ (Sir Oliver & Lady Scott) Bowness-on-Windermere. Middle Entrance Drive, 50yds. Medium-sized formal Edwardian garden; fine trees, ha-ha, herbaceous borders. TEAS. *Adm £1 Chd free (Share to Marie Curie Cancer Care®). Sun June 4 (2-5.30)*

Derbyshire

Hon County Organiser: Mr & Mrs R Brown, 210 Nottingham Rd, Woodlinkin, Langley Mill, Nottingham NG16 4HG Tel 01773 714903

Hon County Treasurer: Mrs G Nutland, 4 Sadler Close, Adel, Leeds LS16 8NN

DATES OF OPENING

By appointment

For telephone numbers and other details see garden descriptions. Private visits welcomed

Birchfield, Ashford in the Water
Bluebell Arboretum, Smisby
Cashel, Kirk Ireton
Cherry Tree Cottage, Hilton
Dam Farm House, Yeldersley Lane
Darley House, nr Matlock
Dove Cottage, Clifton, Ashbourne
Gamesley Fold, Glossop
Green Farm Cottage, Offcote
159 Longfield Lane, Ilkeston
23 Mill Lane, Codnor
Oaks Lane Farm, Brockhurst
The Old Slaughterhouse, Shipley Gate
The Riddings, Kirk Ireton
Valezina Hillside, Heage

Parties only

Field House Farm, Rosliston, nr Burton-on-Trent
32 Heanor Road, Codnor
The Limes, Apperknowle
57 Portland Close, Mickleover
Thatched Farm, Radbourne
Tissington Hall, nr Ashbourne

Regular openings

For details see garden descriptions

Dam Farm House, Yettersley Lane. Suns April 23, May 28, June 11, 25, Aug 13
Lea Gardens, nr Matlock. Daily March 20 to July 16

Renishaw Hall, nr Sheffield. Fri, Sat, Sun June, July, Aug to Sept 17

April 9 Sunday
Meynell Langley, Kirk Langley
Radburne Hall, nr Derby
Shottle Hall Guest House, Belper
April 16 Sunday
32 Heanor Road, Codnor
57 Portland Close, Mickleover
April 17 Monday
Renishaw Hall, nr Sheffield
April 19 Wednesday
57 Portland Close, Mickleover
April 23 Sunday
Field House Farm, Rosliston, nr Burton-on-Trent
Fir Croft, Calver, nr Bakewell
April 26 Wednesday
Field House Farm, Rosliston, nr Burton-on-Trent
April 30 Sunday
The Riddings, Kirk Ireton
May 3 Wednesday
The Old Slaughterhouse, Shipley Gate
May 6 Saturday
Sudbury HM Prison, Sudbury
May 7 Sunday
Cherry Tree Cottage, Hilton
The Limes, Apperknowle
May 8 Monday
Cherry Tree Cottage, Hilton
Renishaw Hall, nr Sheffield
May 14 Sunday
Broomfield College, Morley
Dam Farm House, Yeldersley Lane ‡
Dove Cottage, Clifton, Ashbourne ‡
Fir Croft, Calver, nr Bakewell
32 Heanor Road, Codnor
The Limes, Apperknowle
Thatched Farm, Radbourne
May 21 Sunday
Field House Farm, Rosliston, nr Burton-on-Trent
The Limes, Apperknowle
57 Portland Close, Mickleover
May 24 Wednesday
Field House Farm, Rosliston, nr Burton-on-Trent
The Old Slaughterhouse, Shipley Gate
57 Portland Close, Mickleover
May 28 Sunday
Darley House, nr Matlock
Dove Cottage, Clifton, Ashbourne
The Limes, Apperknowle
May 29 Monday
Renishaw Hall, nr Sheffield
June 1 Thursday
Kedleston Hall, Derby
June 4 Sunday
Fir Croft, Calver, nr Bakewell
Thatched Farm, Radbourne
June 11 Sunday
Cherry Tree Cottage, Hilton
Darley House, nr Matlock
The Old Slaughterhouse, Shipley Gate
June 14 Wednesday
Cherry Tree Cottage, Hilton
The Old Slaughterhouse, Shipley Gate
June 18 Sunday
Field House Farm, Rosliston, nr Burton-on-Trent
Fir Croft, Calver, nr Bakewell
The Poplars, Derby
June 21 Wednesday
Field House Farm, Rosliston, nr Burton-on-Trent
The Poplars, Derby
June 22 Thursday
Oaks Lane Farm, Brockhurst
June 24 Saturday
Mount Cottage, Ticknall
Sudbury HM Prison, Sudbury
June 25 Sunday
Cashel, Kirk Ireton
Darley House, nr Matlock
Dove Cottage, Clifton, Ashbourne
Mount Cottage, Ticknall
210 Nottingham Road, Woodlinkin
The Poplars, Derby
Prospect House, Swanwick
Tudor House Farm, Kirk Langley
July 1 Saturday
Stainsborough Hall, Hopton, nr Wirksworth
July 2 Sunday
Cherry Tree Cottage, Hilton
32 Heanor Road, Codnor
Lea Hurst, nr Matlock
The Limes, Apperknowle
Locko Park, Spondon
23 Mill Lane, Codnor
July 9 Sunday
Daisy Hill Cottage, Longford
Darley House, nr Matlock
Oaks Lane Farm, Brockhurst
July 16 Sunday
Bluebell Arboretum, Smisby
Dam Farm House, Yeldersley Lane
Fanshawe Gate Hall, Holmesfield
Field House Farm, Rosliston, nr Burton-on-Trent
Hardwick Hall, Doe Lea
The Limes, Apperknowle
159 Longfield Lane, Ilkeston
July 19 Wednesday
Fanshawe Gate Hall, Holmesfield
Field House Farm, Rosliston, nr Burton-on-Trent
July 22 Saturday
Tissington Hall, nr Ashbourne
July 23 Sunday
Dove Cottage, Clifton, Ashbourne
Shottle Hall Guest House, Belper
July 26 Wednesday
Calke Abbey, Ticknall
July 29 Saturday
Sudbury HM Prison, Sudbury
August 6 Sunday
Daisy Hill Cottage, Longford
32 Heanor Road, Codnor ‡
23 Mill Lane, Codnor ‡
August 13 Sunday
Davlyn 31 The Crescent, Braston
Dove Cottage, Clifton, Ashbourne
August 27 Sunday
Dove Cottage, Clifton, Ashbourne
August 28 Monday
Renishaw Hall, nr Sheffield
Tissington Hall, nr Ashbourne
September 2 Sunday
Broomfield College, Morley
September 17 Sunday
Bluebell Arboretum, Smisby
October 15 Sunday
Bluebell Arboretum, Smisby

DESCRIPTIONS OF GARDENS

Birchfield ♿✕ (Brian Parker) Dukes Drive, Ashford in the Water. 2m NW of Bakewell on A6 to Buxton. Beautifully situated terraced garden of approx ¾ acre mostly constructed within last 8 yrs. Designed for all-yr-round colour, it contains a wide variety of shrubs and perennials, bulbs, roses, water and scree gardens. Areas of copse with wild flowers are being developed in adjacent field. TEA. *Adm £1 Chd free (Share to John Thornhill Memorial Trust, Great Longstone®). Private visits welcome April to Sept, please* **Tel 01629 813800**

¶Bluebell Nursery ✲❀ (Robert & Suzette Vernon) Blackfordby. From the A50 Burton on Trent to Ashby-de-la-Zouch Rd, turn for Smisby by the Mother Hubbard public house, 1m NW of Ashby. Arboretum is on L after ½m down Annwell Lane. 5-acre embryo Arboretum planted in the last 3 yrs incl many young specimens of rare trees and shrubs. Wide range of interesting plants for sale. Bring wellingtons in wet weather. *Adm £1 Chd 50p (Share to MENCAP®). Suns July 16, Sept 17, Oct 15 (2-5). Private visits welcome, please* **Tel 01283 222091**

Broomfield College ♿✲❀ Morley on A608, 4m N of Derby and 6m S of Heanor. Landscaped garden of 10 ha; shrubs, trees, rose collection, herbaceous borders; glasshouses; walled garden under restoration; garden tours and advice; demonstrations. Light lunches and cream TEAS. *Adm £1 Chd 20p. Sun May 14 (12-4.30); Sun Sept 2 (10.30-4.30 incl chrysanthemum show)*

Calke Abbey ✲ (The National Trust) Ticknall. 9m S of Derby on A514 between Swadlincote and Melbourne. Extensive walled gardens constructed in 1773. Divided into flower garden, kitchen garden and physic garden. Restoration commenced in 1987. Surrounding the walled garden the pleasure ground has been re-fenced and replanting is underway. Ruined orangery is subject to recent fundraising appeal. Lunches and TEAS. *Adm £2 Chd £1. Wed July 26 (11-5)*

¶Cashel ❀ (Anita & Jeremy Butt) Kirk Ireton. Turn off B5023 (Duffield-Wirksworth rd). 2m S of Wirksworth. Follow rd to Kirk Ireton take sharp R turn at church corner. Follow lane for 200 metres. Garden on R, car parking at top of garden, 100 metres beyond the house. 2½ acres of gradually developing garden situated on a sloping site on the edge of Kirk Ireton Village with views of the Ecclesbourne Valley. Many interesting trees, plants and shrubs. TEAS in aid of local church. *Adm £1 Chd free. Sun June 25 (2-5). Private visits welcome, please* **Tel 01335 370495**

Cherry Tree Cottage ✲❀ (Mr & Mrs R Hamblin) Hilton. 7m W of Derby, turn off the A516 opp The Old Talbot Inn in village centre. Parking - small public car park in Main St. Additional parking Hilton Village Hall, Eggington Rd. A plant lover's C18 cottage garden, about ⅓-acre with herbaceous borders; large herb garden; small pool and scree garden. Many unusual and interesting plants; collections of snowdrops, specie aquilegias, old dianthus and hellebores. Featured in 'Small Gardens', 'Garden Answers' and 'Gardeners World' 1991. Also in Good Garden Guide. *Adm £1 Chd free. Suns May 7, June 11, July 2, Mon May 8, Wed June 14 (2-5). Visitors and groups welcome by appt. weekdays April, May, June and July only. Visitors also welcome to see the snowdrops and hellebores, weather permitting, please* **Tel 01283 733778**

Daisy Hill Cottage ♿❀ (Peter and Joy Beales) On the edge of Longford, approx 9m due W of Derby. Cottage is situated on the lane from Longford to Sutton-on-the-Hill. ⅓-acre simple cottage garden with perennial and dried flower beds; vegetable garden; herb garden. TEAS if fine weather. *Adm £1 Chd free (Share to Ashbourne Animal Rescue®). Suns July 9, Aug 6 (2-5)*

Dam Farm House ♿✲❀ (Mrs J M Player) Yeldersley Lane, Ednaston, 5m SE of Ashbourne on A52, opp Ednaston Village turn, gate on right 500yds. 2-acre garden beautifully situated contains mixed borders, scree. Unusual plants have been collected many are propagated for sale. TEAS (some Suns). *Adm £2 Chd free. Suns April 23, May 28, June 11, 25, Aug 13 (1.30-4). For NGS Suns May 14, July 16 (1.30-4). Private visits and groups welcome April 1 to Oct 31, please* **Tel 01335 360291**

Darley House ♿✲❀ (Mr & Mrs G H Briscoe) Darley Dale, 2m N of Matlock. On A6 to Bakewell. 1½ acres; originally set out by Sir Joseph Paxton in 1845; being restored by present owners; many rare plants, trees; balustrade and steps separating upper and lower garden, a replica of Haddon Hall. As featured on BBC 'Gardeners World'. Picture Gallery. Plants and extensive range of seeds available. TEA. *Adm £1.50 Chd free. Suns May 28, June 11, 25, July 9 (2-5). Private visits and groups welcome Tues and Thurs May 2 to Sept 28, please* **Tel 01629 733341**. *Private parties welcome anytime by appt, please* **Tel 01629 650403**

Davlyn 31 The Crescent ✲❀ (Dave & Lynda Melbourne) Breaston. Directly on A6005 between Long Eaton and Draycott. 2m from M1 exit no 25. ⅓-acre cottage garden. A surprise round every corner of this delightful garden with herbaceous borders; hosta beds, pergolas, arbours, two ponds, bog garden. Japanese garden surrounded by red trellis containing bridge and Buddha, vegetable plot, 3 greenhouses, window boxes, hanging baskets, stone trough. The garden is an extension of their home. Opening for the last time. TEA. *Adm £1 Chd free. Sun Aug 13 (10-4)*

Dove Cottage ✲❀ (Anne and Stephen Liverman) Clifton. 1½m SW of Ashbourne. ¾-acre garden by R Dove extensively replanted and developed since 1979. Emphasis on establishing collections of hardy plants and shrubs incl alchemillas, alliums, berberis, geraniums, euphorbias, hostas, lilies, variegated and silver foliage plants inc astrantias. Plantsmans garden featured on Channel 4 'Garden Club', 'Good Garden Guide' and 'Gardeners World Cottage Garden 1995'. TEA. *Adm £1.50 Chd free (Share to British Heart Foundation®). Suns May 14, 28, June 25, July 23, Aug 13, 27 (1.30-5). Private visits welcome, please* **Tel 01335 343545**

¶Fanshawe Gate Hall ✲❀ (Mr & Mrs John Ramsden) Holmesfield. Situated on the edge of the Peak National Park. 1m E of Holmesfield Village. Follow B6054 towards Owler Bar. 1st R turn after Robin Hood Inn. Marked Old Hall on OS map. C13 seat of the Fanshawe family. Old-fashioned cottage-style garden approx 2 acres. Many stone features, fine C16 dovecote. Upper walled garden with mixed borders, shrubs, climbers, herb plantings, water features, rose beds, terracing and lawns. Rose-lined drive planted in combination of gold and blue. Lower courtyard enhanced by small formal knot garden and herb border. The garden continues to develop with particular emphasis on plantings of old-fashioned unusual varieties with interest in variegated subjects. TEAS. *Adm £1 Chd free. Sun, Wed July 16, 19 (11-5)*

¶**Field House Farm** ♿✂❀ (Keith & Judy Thompson) Rosliston. From junction 11 (M42) take A444 NW to Castle Gresley. Turn L to Linton and Rosliston. From A38 turn E at Barton Turns fly-over on to Walton-on-Trent Rd (width restriction). From Walton follow signs to Rosliston. Farm is signposted up drive between Rosliston and Coton-in-the-Elms. An artistic plant collector's ¾-acre farmhouse garden with some unusual features. 2 ponds, mature shrubs, spring bulbs, 'dry' bog garden, secret garden, stone garden, wildlife garden and herbaceous borders. Incl many hardy geraniums, hostas and penstemons. TEAS. *Adm £1 Chd free. Suns, Weds, April 23, 26, May 21, 24, June 18, 21, July 16, 19 (2-6). Private visits of 10 & over welcome, please* **Tel 01283 761472**

Fir Croft ✂❀ (Dr & Mrs S B Furness) Froggatt Rd, Calver, Via Sheffield. 4m N of Bakewell; between Q8 filling station and junction of B6001 with B6054. Plantsman's garden; rockeries; water garden and nursery; extensive collection (over 2000 varieties) of alpines, conifers. New tufa and scree beds. *Collection box. Nursery opens every Sat, Sun, Mon (1-6) March to Dec. Adjacent garden for NGS Suns April 23, May 14, June 4, 18 (2-6)*

Gamesley Fold Cottage ✂❀ (Mr & Mrs G Carr) Glossop. Off Glossop-Marple Rd nr Charlesworth, turn down the lane directly opp St Margaret's School, Gamesley. White cottage at the bottom. Old-fashioned cottage garden down a country lane with lovely views of surrounding countryside. A spring garden planted with herbaceous borders, wild flowers and herbs in profusion to attract butterflies and wildlife. Featured in Good Housekeeping. TEAS. *Adm £1 Chd free. Private visits and parties May 1 to Sept 30 welcome, please* **Tel 014578 67856**

Green Farm Cottage ✂❀ (Mr & Mrs Peter Bussell) Offcote. 1½m NE of Ashbourne on T-junction Bradley-Kniveton-Ashbourne. Take Wirksworth Rd out of Ashbourne (B5035) and follow Offcote signposted (approx 1¼m). ⅓-acre garden designed, constructed and maintained from a wilderness in 1978 by the present owners. Terraces, lawns, a good show of spring flowering bulbs, wide variety of perennials incl several varieties of geraniums and hellebores, shrubs and trees; greenhouse, vegetable plot and small orchard area. *Adm £1 Acc chd free. Private visits (max 20) welcome April to Sept, please* **Tel 01335 343803**

Hardwick Hall ♿✂❀ (The National Trust) Doe Lea, 8m SE of Chesterfield. S of A617. Grass walks between yew and hornbeam hedges; cedar trees; herb garden; herbaceous borders. Finest example of Elizabethan house in the country; very fine collection of Elizabethan needlework, tapestry. Restaurant in Old Kitchens. TEAS on days the Hall is open. *Adm hall and garden £5.50 Chd £2.70 garden only £2 Chd £1. Sun July 16 (12-5.30 last entry 4.30)*

32 Heanor Road ♿✂❀ (Mr & Mrs Eyre) 300yds from Codnor Market Place on A6007 towards Heanor. Down lane at side of Hunt's shop, last bungalow on L. Parking on main rd. 1-acre garden with lawns, variety of trees, shrubs, herbaceous borders, rockery, scree; 2 ponds, pergola, spring and summer bedding. Highly commended 1994 Amber Valley 'Best Kept Garden' competition. TEA. *Adm **£1 Chd** free (Share to Multiple Sclerosis Research®). Suns **April** 16, May 14, July 2, Aug 6 (2-6). Coach parties welcome Wed afternoon (picnic) June to Aug, please* **Tel 01773 746626**

Kedleston Hall ♿✂ (The National Trust) 3m NW of Derby. Signposted from junction of A38/A52. 12-acre garden. A broad open lawn, bounded by a ha-ha, marks the C18 informal garden. A formal layout to the W was introduced early this century when the summerhouse and orangery, both designed by George Richardson late C18, were moved to their present position. The gardens are seen at their best during May and June when the azaleas and rhododendrons are one mass of colour. The Long Walk, a woodland walk of some 3m, is bright with spring flowers. Guided walk of gardens and Long Walk at 2pm. TEA. *Adm £1.50 Chd 75p. Thurs June 1 (11-5)*

● **Lea Gardens** ♿❀ (Mr & Mrs Tye) Lea, 5m SE of Matlock off A6. A rare collection of rhododendrons, azaleas, kalmias, alpines and conifers in a delightful woodland setting. Light lunches, TEAS, home-baking. Coaches by appt. *Adm £2.50 Chd 50p daily, season ticket £3.50. Daily March 20 to July 16 (10-7)*

Lea Hurst (Residential Home) ✂❀ (Royal Surgical Aid Society) Holloway. 6m SE of Matlock off A6, nr Yew Tree Inn, Holloway. Former home (not open) of Florence Nightingale. Large garden consisting of rose beds, herbaceous borders, new shrubbery incl varieties, ornamental pond, all set in beautiful countryside. New wildlife garden 1994. TEAS in aid of RSAS. *Adm £1 Chd free. Sun July 2 (2-5)*

The Limes ♿❀ (Mr & Mrs W Belton) Crow Lane, Apperknowle, 6m N of Chesterfield; from A6l at Unstone turn E for 1m to Apperknowle; 1st house past Unstone Grange. Bus: Chesterfield or Sheffield to Apperknowle. 2½ acres with herbaceous borders, lily ponds, roses and flowering shrubs, scree beds & rockeries; hundreds of naturalised daffodils and formal bedding with massed bedding of pansies in the spring, geraniums and bedding plants in summer. Putting green and large natural pond with ducks and geese. Nature trail over 5 acres. Home-made TEAS. *Adm £1 Chd 25p. Suns May 7, 14, 21, 28; July 2, 16 (2-6). Coach, private parties and evening visits of 10 and over, welcome, please* **Tel 01246 412338**

Locko Park ✂❀ Spondon, 6m NE of Derby. From A52 Borrowash bypass, 2m N via B6001, turn to Spondon. Large garden; pleasure gardens; rose gardens. House by Smith of Warwick with Victorian additions. Chapel, Charles II, with original ceiling. TEA. *Adm £1 Chd 30p. Sun July 2 (2-5)*

159 Longfield Lane ♿✂❀ (David & Diane Bennett) Ilkeston (Stanton side) off Quarry Hill, opp Hallam Fields Junior School. A house in a garden, a large, informal over-flowing garden that works for its owners with fruit, vegetables, shrubs, flowers, two small fish ponds and a conservatory. A strong emphasis on texture, colour and lots of unexpected corners. Home-made TEAS. *Adm £1 Chd free. Sun July 16 (2-5.30). Private visits of 6 and over welcome, May to July, please* **Tel 01159 325238**

Meynell Langley ♿❀ (Godfrey Meynell Esq) Between Mackworth and Kirk Langley on A52 Derby-Ashbourne rd. Turn in at green iron gate by grey stone lodge on N side of road. Trees, lawns, daffodils, lake, views. TEAS in Regency country house. *Adm £1.50 Chd 50p. Sun April 9 (2-6)*

23 Mill Lane ♿✂❀ (Mrs S Jackson) Codnor. 12m NW of Nottingham. A610 Ripley 10m N of Derby, A38 Ripley. 2 car parks nearby. Lawns, herbaceous borders, small pond, waterfall; fruit trees; clematis. Amber Valley 'Best Kept Garden' competition 2nd 1994. TEA. *Adm £1 Chd free. Suns July 2, Aug 6 (11-6). Private visits also welcome June to Sept, please* **Tel 01773 745707**

Mount Cottage ♿✂❀ (Mr & Mrs J T Oliver) 52 Main Street, Ticknall, 9m S Derby, adjacent entrance Calke Abbey NT and Wheel Public House. Medium-sized cottage garden, herbaceous borders, shrubs, lawns, small pool area, numerous roses, surrounding C18 cottage. TEAS outdoors weather permitting. *Adm £1 Chd free. Sat, Sun June 24, 25 (11-5)*

210 Nottingham Rd (Mr & Mrs R Brown) Woodlinkin, nr Codnor; A610. ½-acre; collections of old, modern shrub and climbing roses; geraniums; shrubs; trees. TEA. *Adm £1 Chd free. Sun June 25 (2-5)*

Oaks Lane Farm ✂❀ (Mr & Mrs J R Hunter) Brockhurst, Ashover nr Chesterfield. At Kelstedge 4m from Matlock on A632 Chesterfield Rd, just above Kelstedge Inn, turn L up narrow rd, then turn R ½m, garden is 150yds on R. Partly suitable for wheelchairs. ¾-acre informal plantsman's garden in beautiful situation with herbaceous borders, natural streams and pond. Newly constructed small water garden. Many varieties of hostas, euphorbia and old-fashioned roses. Partially suitable for wheelchairs. TEA. *Adm £1 Chd free. Thurs June 22 (11-5), Sun July 9 (1-5). Also private visits welcome May to Sept, please* **Tel 01246 590324**

The Old Slaughterhouse ✂❀ (Robert & Joyce Peck) Shipley Gate. 1m S of Eastwood, take Church St from Sun Inn traffic lights, and over A610, L to narrow rd to Shipley Boat Inn; parking near Shipley Lock (Erewash Canal) and Inn. ¾-acre long, narrow garden, restored from overgrown ash tip since 1984; 200-yrs-old stone aqueduct over river; over 400 trees planted; hard and soft surfaces; division into 'rooms'; wide variety of planting; hidden pond; pleasant extra walks in Erewash Valley (canal and river sides). TEAS. *Adm £1 Chd free (Share to Eastwood Volunteer Bureau© June 11). Weds May 3, 24, June 14; Sun June 11 (2-6). Private visits welcome, please* **Tel 01773 768625**

The Poplars ♿✂❀ (The Clemson Family) Duffield Rd, Derby. Off A6 N of Derby. (200yds S of The Broadway Inn and opp N end of Belper Rd) ½m N of cathedral. ¼-acre garden; design dates from 1882; many original features. Variety of herbaceous plants, shrubs, herbs, fruit. *Adm £1 Chd free. Suns June 18, 25; Wed June 21 (2-5)*

Regular Openers. See head of county section.

57 Portland Close ✂❀ (Mr & Mrs A L Ritchie) Mickleover. Approx 3m W of Derby, turn R off B5020 Cavendish Way then 2nd L into Portland Close. Small plantsman's garden, wide variety of unusual bulbs, alpines and herbaceous plants. Special interest in sink gardens, hostas, named varieties of primulas (single and double); auriculas (show, border, alpine and doubles), violas and hardy geraniums. Featured in 'Good Garden Guide'. *Adm 75p Chd free under 16. Suns, Weds April 16, 19, May 21, 24 (2-5.30). Private visits also welcome of 10 and over, please* **Tel 01332 515450**

Prospect House ♿✂❀ (Mr & Mrs J W Bowyer) 18 Pentrich Rd, Swanwick; turn at traffic lights A61 to B6016 Pentrich. Park main rd. ¾-acre; conifers, shrubs, herbaceous plants, cordyline palms, carpet bedding with sedums, sempervivums, echeverias; collection cacti; succulents, shrub and leaf begonia, abutilons various; rock plants; geraniums; pelargoniums, hostas. Greenhouses; kitchen garden. TEA. *Adm £1 Chd 10p. Sun June 25 (1.30-6)*

Radburne Hall ✂ (Mrs J W Chandos-Pole) Radburne, Kirk Langley, 5m W of Derby. W of A52 Derby-Ashbourne rd; off Radburne Lane. Large landscape garden; large display of daffodils; shrubs; formal rose terraces; fine trees and view. Hall (not open) is 7-bay Palladian mansion built c1734 by Smith of Warwick. Ice-house in garden. *Adm £1 Chd 50p. Sun April 9 (2.30-6)*

Renishaw Hall ♿❀ (Sir Reresby & Lady Sitwell) Renishaw. Renishaw Hall is situated equidistant 6m from both Sheffield and Old Chesterfield on A616 2m from its junction with M1 at exit 30. Italian style garden with terraces, old ponds, yew hedges and pyramids laid out by Sir George Sitwell c1900. Interesting collection of herbaceous plants and shrubs; nature trail; museum; lakeside walk. Shop provides wine, souvenirs, antiques. TEAS. *Adm £3 OAPs £2 Chd £1. Every Fri, Sat, Sun, June, July, Aug to Sept 17, Mons April 17, May 8, 29, Aug 28 (10.30-4.30). Private parties of 20 and over welcome, please* **Tel 01246 432042**

The Riddings Farm ✂❀ (The Spencer Family) Kirk Ireton between Ashbourne and Wirksworth. Leave Kirk Ireton via Gorsey Lane (close to Barley Mow). Turn L at T-junction onto Broom Lane. 1st R into Hays Lane. Alternatively, a pleasant ½m lakeside walk from Severn - Trents Millfields Car Park. Informal hillside garden, about ¾ acre, created since 1979 and still developing, with lovely views over Carsington Water. Emphasis on foliage, yr-round colour and wildlife habitats. Unusual plants propagated for adjacent nursery. TEA. *Adm £1 Chd free. Sun April 30 (2-5). Private visits welcome, please* **Tel 01335 370331**

Shottle Hall Guest House (Mr & Mrs P Matthews) Belper. Off B5023 Duffield to Wirksworth Rd. 200yds N of Xrds (Railway Inn) with A517 Ashbourne to Belper Rd. 2½ acres natural garden featuring shrubs; roses; bedding plants; bulbs; small herbaceous border and lawns. Cream TEAS. *Adm £1 Chd under 12 free. Suns April 9, July 23 (2-5)*

¶Stainsborough Hall ♿❀ (Mr & Mrs Twogood) Wirksworth. On B5035 Wirksworth to Ashbourne Rd. 1½m W of Wirksworth take L turning to Kirk Ireton, house ¼m on R. Set in a wide valley to the N of Carsington Water, this country garden abounds with flowers and birds. The stone house and buildings merge delightfully with lawns, shrubs, roses and flower beds designed informally on different levels to provide meandering walks and pleasantly sited resting places. Covering some 2 acres, the garden incl many young trees, shrubs, herbaceous borders and rose beds. A duck pond with a variety of domestic ducks adds to the tranquillity of the scene. TEAS. *Adm £1 Chd free. Sat July 1 (2-6)*

¶Sudbury HM Prison ♿✂❀ (Farms & Gardens Dept) Sudbury. 9m S of Ashbourne where the junction of A515 (Ashbourne Rd) meets the A50 (Burton/Stoke rd) signposted on the A50. Come and see a wide variety of plant species in approx 10 ha of relaxingly landscaped prison grounds. Featuring large pond and waterfall, bog garden, herbaceous border and kitchen garden (under construction). Special interests May - flowering trees and shrubs, alpine garden, laburnum arch, bulbs, spring bedding, herbaceous border and viburnum and berberis border. June - over 50 varieties of species roses and bedding roses, herbaceous border. July - summer bedding, cut and dried flower border, plus a rose budding demonstration will be held at 3.00 & 4.00 pm. Plants & produce for sale. TEAS. *Adm £1.50 Chd free. Sats May 6, June 24, July 29 (2-5)*

Thatched Farm ♿✂❀ (Mr & Mrs R A Pegram) Radbourne. Exit A52 Derby-Ashbourne road. 2m N of Derby Ring Road. A 2-acre plant lover's garden created from meadowland since 1987 and still being developed. The garden and courtyard surround a C17 listed farmhouse set in tranquil parkland. Many rare and unusual plants grown from seed collected from around the world. Mediterranean and island beds, troughs and alpines in raised beds, wild garden. Trees, shrubs and herbaceous perennials, extensive collection of tender perennials. 2 ponds and bog garden. Home-made Devonshire TEAS. *Adm £1.50 Chd free (Share to RELATE® May 14 & Cancer Research Campaign® June 4). Suns May 14, June 4 (2-6). Private parties also welcome, please* **Tel 01332 824507**

Tissington Hall ✂❀ (Sir Richard FitzHerbert, Bt) N of Ashbourne. E of A515. Large garden; roses, herbaceous borders. Tea available in village. Please park considerately. *Adm £1 Chd free. Sat July 22, Mon Aug 28 (2-5). Parties by written appt only on other days*

Tudor House Farm ✂❀ (Mr & Mrs G Spencer) Kirk Langley. 4½m N of Derby on A52 Ashbourne Rd. Take turning opp Meynell Arms Hotel, garden 400yds on R. ¼-acre garden on two levels. Mixed beds of shrubs and perennials; small fish and lily pond; heathers and alpine troughs. TEAS. *Adm £1 Chd free. Sun June 25 (2-5)*

Valezina Hillside ✂❀ (Mr & Mrs P Bowler) Heage. Between Ripley and Belper, further details on arranging appt. A butterfly/wildlife garden of ½ acre adjacent to open countryside. In parts steeply sloping, can be slippery. Mini-habitats incl a buddleia wilderness and wildlife pond. A hillside meadow and woodland garden are overlooked by a cottage garden rich in butterfly nectar plants. Essentially kept wild (but controlled) in order to maintain a permanent breeding habitat for over 20 species of butterfly who have been encouraged to stay since 1985. Totally informal with a profusion of wild flowers. TEA. *Adm £1 Chd free. Private visits welcome May to Sept. Butterflies most numerous in July and Aug but numbers vary greatly with weather trends. Please* **Tel 01773 853099**

Devon

Hon County Organiser:	Mervyn T Feesey Esq., Woodside, Higher Raleigh Rd, Barnstaple EX31 4JA Tel 01271 43095
Assistant County Organisers:	
Exeter & E Devon	Mrs Ruth Charter, Ravenhill, Long Dogs Lane, Ottery St Mary EX11 1HX Tel 01404 814798
Tiverton & N E Devon	Mrs Diane Rowe, Little Southey, Northcott, Nr Cullompton EX15 3LT Tel 01884 840545
Bovey Tracey & Central Devon	Miss Elizabeth Hebditch, Bibbery, Higher Bibbery, Bovey Tracey TQ13 9RT Tel 01626 833344
Torbay & Dartmouth	Major David Molloy, Mulberry House, Kingswear TQ6 OBY Tel 01803 752307
Kingsbridge & South Devon	Mrs Sheila Blake, Higher Homefield, Sherford, Kingsbridge TQ7 2AT Tel 01548 531229
Plymouth & SW Devon	Mrs Sharin Court, Westpark, Yealmpton, Nr Plymouth PL8 2HP Tel 01752 880236

DATES OF OPENING

By appointment

For telephone numbers and other details see garden descriptions. Private visits welcomed

Addisford Cottage, nr Dolton
Andrew's Corner, nr Okehampton
Bibbery, Bovey Tracy Gardens
Bickham House, Kenn, nr Exeter
Blackpool House, Stoke Fleming
Bramble Cottage, West Hill
Bundels, Sidbury
Castle Tor, Torquay
The Cider House, Yelverton
Cleave House, Sticklepath
Clovelly Court, Clovelly
Croftdene, Ham, nr Dalwood
Didcot, nr Chardstock
Farrants, Kilmington
The Gate House, Lee Ilfracombe
The Glebe House, Whitestone, nr Exeter
Greenlands, Ash Thomas & Brithem Bottom Gardens
Higher Knowle, nr Bovey Tracey
Higher Spriddlestone, Brixton, nr Plymouth
Holywell, Bratton Fleming
Kerscott House, nr Swimbridge
Little Cumbre, Exeter
The Lodge, Mannamead
Lower Coombe Royal, Kingsbridge
20 Monmouth Avenue. Topsham Gardens, nr Exeter
The Moorings, nr Lyme Regis
16 Moorland View, Derriford
Mulberry House, Barbican Terrace, Barnstaple
Mulberry House, Kingswear-Ridley Hill Gardens
Oare Manor Cottage, Oare, Lynton
The Old Mill, Blakewell
The Old Rectory, Clayhidon
The Old Rectory, Woodleigh
The Orchard, Kenn
Orchard Cottage, Exmouth
38 Phillipps Avenue, Exmouth
The Pines, Salcombe
Priors, Abbotskerswell
Purple Hayes, Halberton
Quakers, Membury
51 Salters Road, nr Exeter
Silver Copse, nr Marsh Green
Spillifords, nr Tiverton
Sowton Mill, Dunsford
Stone Lane Gardens, nr Chagford
Vicar's Mead, East Budleigh
Warren Cottage, nr Ermington
96 Wasdale Gardens, Plymouth
Weetwood, nr Honiton
Westpark, Yealmpton
Withleigh Farm, nr Tiverton
Woodside, Whimple, nr Exeter

Parties only

Barton House, Nymet Rowland
Broadhembury House, Broadhembury
Court Hall, North Molton
Fardel Manor, nr Ivybridge
Fast Rabbit Farm, Ash, Dartmouth
1 Feebers Cottage, Westwood
Grattons Field Cottage, Northlew
Hamblyn's Coombe, Dittisham
Higher Warcombe, Kingsbridge
Lee Ford, Budleigh Salterton
Membland Villa, Newton Ferrers
Monks Aish, South Brent
Mothecombe House, Holbeton
The Old Glebe, Eggesford
Pleasant View Nursery, nr Newton Abbot
Robin Hill, Exeter
Sunrise Hill, Withleigh

Regular openings

For details see garden descriptions

Avenue Cottage, Ashprington. Tues to Sats April 4 to Sept 30
Bickham Barton, Roborough. Suns April 2 to June 14
Bicton College of Agriculture. Daily except Dec 25
Burrow Farm Garden, Dalwood. Daily April to Sept 30
The Croft, Yarnscombe. Mons April 3 to Oct 30
Crosspark, Northlew. Suns, Mons April 30 to July 3
Docton Mill, nr Hartland. Daily March to Oct
The Downes, Monkleigh. Daily April 16 to June 11
Flete, Ermington, Ivybridge. Weds, Thurs afternoons, May to end Sept
The Garden House, Yelverton. Daily March 1 to Oct 31
Hill House, nr Ashburton. Open daily
Lukesland, Ivybridge. Suns, Weds April 23 to June 4 incl May Bank Hol Mons
Marwood Hill, nr Barnstaple. Daily except Christmas Day
Plant World, nr Newton Abbot. March to Oct daily
Rosemoor Gardens, Great Torrington. Open daily
Tapeley Park & Garden, Instow. For dates see text
Wylmington Hayes, nr Honiton. Suns, Bank hols Mons to end of June
Yonder Hill, Colaton Raleigh. For dates see text

March 18 Saturday
The Pines, Salcombe

March 19 Sunday
Ash Thomas & Brithem Bottom Gardens
Bickham House, Kenn, nr Exeter
Higher Knowle, nr Bovey Tracey
The Pines, Salcombe
Westpark, Yealmpton

March 22 Wednesday
Bickham House, Kenn, nr Exeter
Westpark, Yealmpton

March 26 Sunday
1 Feebers Cottage, Westwood
Higher Knowle, nr Bovey Tracey
Kingswear-Ridley Hill Gardens

April 1 Saturday
The Pines, Salcombe

April 2 Sunday
Dippers, Shaugh Prior, nr Plymouth
Higher Knowle, nr Bovey Tracey
Mothecombe House, Holbeton
38 Phillipps Avenue, Exmouth
The Pines, Salcombe

April 9 Sunday
Higher Knowle, nr Bovey Tracey
Meadow Croft, Plympton
Penrose, Crediton
38 Phillipps Avenue, Exmouth
Saltram House, Plymouth

April 14 Friday
Grattons Field Cottage, Northlew
Wylmington Hayes, nr Honiton

April 15 Saturday
Wylmington Hayes, nr Honiton

April 16 Sunday
Bickham House, Kenn, nr Exeter
Fast Rabbit Farm, Ash, Dartmouth
Grattons Field Cottage, Northlew
Higher Knowle, nr Bovey Tracey
The Pines, Salcombe
Silver Copse, nr Marsh Green
Wylmington Hayes, nr Honiton

April 17 Monday
Bickham Barton, Roborough
1 Feebers Cottage, Westwood
Higher Knowle, nr Bovey Tracey
Membland Villa, Newton Ferrers
The Pines, Salcombe
Silver Copse, nr Marsh Green
Wylmington Hayes, nr Honiton

April 19 Wednesday
Bickham House, Kenn, nr Exeter

April 20 Thursday
Whitmore, nr Chittlehamholt

April 23 Sunday
Andrew's Corner, nr Okehampton
Coleton Fishacre, Kingswear
Hartland Abbey, Hartland
Higher Knowle, nr Bovey Tracey
Killerton Garden, Broadclyst
Meadow Croft, Plympton
Membland Villa, Newton Ferrers

38 Phillipps Avenue, Exmouth

April 27 Thursday
Greenway Gardens, Churston Ferrers
Lee Ford, Budleigh Salterton
Little Cumbre, Exeter

April 29 Saturday
Dartington Hall Gardens, nr Totnes

April 30 Sunday
Castle Drogo, Exeter
Dartington Hall Gardens, nr Totnes
Dippers, Shaugh Prior, nr Plymouth
Fast Rabbit Farm, Ash, Dartmouth
Gorwell House, nr Barnstaple
Higher Knowle, nr Bovey Tracey
Holywell, Bratton Fleming
Knightshayes Gardens, nr Tiverton
38 Phillipps Avenue, Exmouth

May 1 Monday
Little Upcott Gardens, Marsh Green

May 4 Thursday
Greenway Gardens, Churston Ferrers

May 6 Saturday
Mothecombe House, Holbeton
The Old Glebe, Eggesford
Starveacre, nr Axminster

May 7 Sunday
Andrew's Corner, nr Okehampton
Bicton College of Agriculture
Bramble Cottage, West Hill
Broadhembury House, Broadhembury
Bundels, Sidbury
Flete, Ermington, Ivybridge
Hamblyn's Coombe, Dittisham
Higher Knowle, nr Bovey Tracey
Holywell, Bratton Fleming
The Lodge, Mannamead
Lukesland, Ivybridge
Mothecombe House, Holbeton
The Old Glebe, Eggesford
38 Phillipps Avenue, Exmouth
Silver Copse, nr Marsh Green
Topsham Gardens, nr Exeter
Woodside, Barnstaple

May 8 Monday
Bickham Barton, Roborough
Bicton College of Agriculture
Bramble Cottage, West Hill
Broadhembury House, Broadhembury
Hamblyn's Coombe, Dittisham
Higher Knowle, nr Bovey Tracey
Membland Villa, Newton Ferrers
The Old Glebe, Eggesford
Silver Copse, nr Marsh Green
Topsham Gardens, nr Exeter

May 9 Tuesday
Meadowcroft, Plympton

May 10 Wednesday
Bundels, Sidbury
Cleave House, Sticklepath

May 13 Saturday
Wood Barton, Kentisbeare

May 14 Sunday
Arlington Court, nr Barnstaple
Broadhembury House, Broadhembury
The Cider House, Yelverton
Cleave House, Sticklepath
Delamore, Ivybridge
Fast Rabbit Farm, Ash, Dartmouth
Higher Knowle, nr Bovey Tracey
Higher Warcombe, Kingsbridge
Holywell, Bratton Fleming
Ivy Cottage, Heanton, nr Braunton
Little Southey, Culm Valley, nr Culmstock
The Orchard, Kenn
Ottery St Mary Gardens
38 Phillipps Avenue, Exmouth
Saltram House, Plymouth
Wood Barton Kentisbeare

May 15 Monday
Little Southey, Culm Valley, nr Culmstock

May 20 Saturday
Sunrise Hill, Withleigh
Vicar's Mead, East Budleigh
Withleigh Farm, nr Tiverton

May 21 Sunday
Addisford Cottage, nr Dolton
Bickham House, Kenn, nr Exeter
Broadhembury House, Broadhembury
Coleton Fishacre, Kingswear
1 Feebers Cottage, Westwood
Lukesland, Ivybridge
Meadow Court, Slapton
Meadow Croft, Plympton
Ottery St Mary Gardens
38 Phillipps Avenue, Exmouth
Withleigh Farm, nr Tiverton

May 24 Wednesday
Bickham House, Kenn, nr Exeter

May 25 Thursday
Lee Ford, Budleigh Salterton
Little Cumbre, Exeter

May 27 Saturday
Ash Thomas & Brithem Bottom Gardens
Dicot, nr Chardstock
Little Upcott Gardens, Marsh Green
Monks Aish, South Brent
Wolford Lodge, nr Honiton

May 28 Sunday
Addisford Cottage, nr Dolton
Andrew's Corner, nr Okehampton
Bicton College of Agriculture
Bramble Cottage, West Hill
Broadhembury House, Broadhembury
Bundels, Sidbury
Chevithorne Barton, nr Tiverton
Croftdene, Ham, nr Dalwood
Dicot, nr Chardstock
Dippers, Shaugh Prior, nr Plymouth
Fast Rabbit Farm, Ash, Dartmouth
The Glebe House, Whitestone, nr Exeter
Gorwell House, nr Barnstaple
Holywell, Bratton Fleming
Lee Ford, Budleigh Salterton
Little Upcott Gardens, Marsh Green
Lukesland, Ivybridge
Monks Aish, South Brent
The Old Parsonage, Warkleigh
The Orchard, Kenn
38 Phillipps Avenue, Exmouth
Purple Hayes, Halberton
Robin Hill, Exeter
Silver Copse, nr Marsh Green
Twitchen Mill, nr South Molton
Vicar's mead, East Budleigh

May 29 Monday
Alswood, nr George Nympton
Bickham Barton, Roborough
Bicton College of Agriculture
Bramble Cottage, West Hill
Broadhembury House, Broadhembury
Little Upcott Gardens, Marsh Green
Membland Villa, Newton Ferrers
Silver Copse, nr Marsh Green
Vicar's Mead, East Budleigh

May 30 Monday
Vicar's Mead, East Budleigh

May 31 Wednesday
Bundels, Sidbury
Little Upcott Gardens, Marsh Green
Stone Lane Gardens, nr Chagford

June 3 Saturday
Hayne Old Manor, Moretonhampstead
Pleasant View Nursery, nr Newton Abbot

June 4 Sunday
Addisford Cottage, nr Dolton
Andrew's Corner, nr Okehampton
Broadhembury House, Broadhembury
Glebe Cottage, nr Warkleigh
The Glebe House, Whitestone, nr Exeter
Grattons Field Cottage, Northlew
Hayne Old Manor, Moretonhampstead
Overbecks, Salcombe
Pleasant View Nursery, nr Newton Abbot

June 10 Saturday
Bovey Tracy Gardens

Bramble Cottage, West Hill
Little Upcott Gardens, Marsh Green

June 11 Sunday
Addisford Cottage, nr Dolton
Bovey Tracy Gardens
Bramble Cottage, West Hill
Broadhembury House, Broadhembury
The Croft, Yarnscombe
Fast Rabbit Farm, Ash, Dartmouth
1 Feebers Cottage, Westwood
The Glebe House, Whitestone, nr Exeter
Grattons Field Cottage, Northlew
Holywell, Bratton Fleming
Ivy Cottage, Heanton, nr Braunton
Little Upcott Gardens, Marsh Green
Mothecombe House, Holbeton
The Old Mill, Blakewell
38 Phillipps Avenue, Exmouth
Woodside, Whimple nr Exeter

June 14 Wednesday
Little Upcott Gardens, Marsh Green

June 16 Friday
Vicar's Mead, East Budleigh

June 17 Saturday
Little Upcott Gardens, Marsh Green

June 18 Sunday
Addisford Cottage, nr Dolton
Andrew's Corner, nr Okehampton
Bickham Barton, Roborough
Bickham House, Kenn, nr Exeter
Broadhembury House, Broadhembury
Castle Drogo, Exeter
The Glebe House, Whitestone, nr Exeter
Heddon Hall, Parracombe
Kerscott House, nr Swimbridge
Little Upcott Gardens, Marsh Green
The Lodge, Mannamead
Lower Kerse, Thurleston
Membland Villa, Newton Ferrers
16 Moorland View, Derriford
The Old Parsonage, Warkleigh
Penrose, Crediton
Priors, Abbotskerswell
Riversbridge, nr Dartmouth
Topsham Gardens, nr Exeter
Woodside, Barnstaple

June 21 Wednesday
Bickham House, Kenn, nr Exeter
Scypen, Ringmore
Stone Lane Gardens, nr Chagford
Winkfield, Colyford

June 23 Friday
Dippers, Shaugh Prior, nr Plymouth

June 24 Saturday
Bundels, Sidbury
Little Upcott Gardens, Marsh Green

June 25 Sunday
Ash Thomas & Brithem Bottom Gardens
Broadhembury House, Broadhembury
Bundels, Sidbury
Cleave House, Sticklepath
The Croft, Yarnscombe
Croftdene, Ham, nr Dalwood
Fast Rabbit Farm, Ash, Dartmouth
1 Feebers Cottage, Westwood
Glebe Cottage, nr Warkleigh
The Glebe House, Whitestone, nr Exeter
Gorwell House, nr Barnstaple
Little Upcott Gardens, Marsh Green
Little Webbery, Alverdiscott
The Old Parsonage, Warkleigh
Overbecks, Salcombe
38 Phillipps Avenue, Exmouth
Priors, Abbotskerswell
Purple Hayes, Halberton
Riversbridge, nr Dartmouth
Scypen, Ringmore
Sowton Mill, Dunsford

June 28 Wednesday
Bundels, Sidbury
Little Upcott Gardens, Marsh Green
Membland Villa, Newton Ferrers

June 29 Thursday
Bundels, Sidbury
Lee Ford, Budleigh Salterton
Little Cumbre, Exeter

July 1 Saturday
Barton House, Nymet Rowland
Whitmore, nr Chittlehamholt

July 2 Sunday
Addisford Cottage, nr Dolton
Alswood, nr George Nympton
Barton House, Nymet Rowland
The Glebe House, Whitestone, nr Exeter
Knightshayes Gardens, nr Tiverton
The Old Parsonage, Warkleigh
Priors, Abbotskerswell
Robin Hill, Exeter
Sowton Mill, Dunsford

July 3 Monday
Barton House, Nymet Rowland

July 5 Wednesday
Court Hall, North Molton
Little Upcott Gardens, Marsh Green

July 8 Saturday
Glebe House, Whitstone
Kerscott House, nr Swimbridge
Mulberry House, Barbican Terrace, Barnstaple

July 9 Sunday
Addisford Cottage, nr Dolton
Arlington Court, nr Barnstaple
Court Hall, North Molton
The Croft, Yarnscombe
Fast Rabbit Farm, Ash, Dartmouth
The Glebe House, Whitestone, nr Exeter
Kerscott House, nr Swimbridge
Killerton Garden, Broadclyst
Mulberry House, Barbican Terrace, Barnstaple
38 Phillipps Avenue, Exmouth
Winkfield, Colyford

July 12 Wednesday
The Garden House, Yelverton
Stone Lane Gardens, nr Chagford

July 15 Saturday
Little Upcott Gardens, Marsh Green
Membland Villa, Newton Ferrers

July 16 Sunday
Andrew's Corner, nr Okehampton
Bickham House, Kenn, nr Exeter
The Cider House, Yelverton
1 Feebers Cottage, Westwood
The Glebe House, Whitestone, nr Exeter
Higher Warcombe, Kingsbridge
Ivy Cottage, Heanton, nr Braunton
Little Upcott Gardens, Marsh Green
Portington, nr Lamerton
Silver Copse, nr Marsh Green
Starveacre, nr Axminster
Twitchen Mill, nr South Molton

July 17 Monday
Silver Copse, nr Marsh Green

July 19 Wednesday
Bickham House, Kenn, nr Exeter
Little Upcott Gardens, Marsh Green

July 23 Sunday
Addisford Cottage, nr Dolton
Bicton College of Agriculture
The Croft, Yarnscombe
The Lodge, Mannamead
The Old Mill, Blakewell
38 Phillipps Avenue, Exmouth
Portington, nr Lamerton
Woodside, Whimple, nr Exeter

July 24 Monday
Fardel Manor, nr Ivybridge

July 26 Wednesday
Sunrise Hill, Withleigh

July 29 Saturday
Dicot, nr Chardstock
Little Upcott Gardens, Marsh Green

July 30 Sunday
Addisford Cottage, nr Dolton
Ash Thomas & Brithem Bottom Gardens

Dicot, nr Chardstock
Glebe Cottage, nr Warkleigh
Gorwell House, nr Barnstaple
Little Upcott Gardens, Marsh Green
Membland Villa, Newton Ferrers

August 2 Wednesday
Sunrise Hill, Withleigh

August 6 Sunday
Addisford Cottage, nr Dolton
Glebe Cottage, nr Warkleigh
Grattons Field Cottage, Northlew
Longham, nr Lydford Gorge
Membland Villa, Newton Ferrers
Penrose, Crediton
38 Phillipps Avenue, Exmouth

August 12 Saturday
Little Upcott Gardens, Marsh Green

August 13 Sunday
Grattons Field Cottage, Northlew
Little Upcott Gardens, Marsh Green
Longham, nr Lydford Gorge
Mulberry House, Barbican Terrace, Barnstaple

August 16 Wednesday
The Garden House, Yelverton
Little Upcott Gardens, Marsh Green

August 20 Sunday
Bickham House, Kenn, nr Exeter
Mulberry House, Barbican Terrace, Barnstaple
38 Phillipps Avenue, Exmouth
Purple Hayes, Halberton
Woodside, Barnstaple

August 23 Wednesday
Bickham House, Kenn, nr Exeter

August 27 Sunday
Alswood, nr George Nympton
Fast Rabbit Farm, Ash, Dartmouth
Glebe Cottage, nr Warkleigh
Kerscott House, nr Swimbridge
Silver Copse, nr Marsh Green
Whitmore, nr Chittlehamholt
Woodside, Whimple nr Exeter

August 28 Monday
Membland Villa, Newton Ferrers
Silver Copse, nr Marsh Green

September 2 Saturday
Pleasant View Nursery, nr Newton Abbot

September 3 Sunday
Gorwell House, nr Barnstaple
38 Phillipps Avenue, Exmouth
Pleasant View Nursery, nr Newton Abbot

September 17 Sunday
Bickham House, Kenn, nr Exeter
Bicton College of Agriculture
1 Feebers Cottage, Westwood
Membland Villa, Newton Ferrers

September 20 Wednesday
Bickham House, Kenn, nr Exeter

September 24 Sunday
Glebe Cottage, nr Warkleigh
Woodside, Whimple, nr Exeter

October 1 Sunday
1 Feebers Cottage, Westwood
Gorwell House, nr Barnstaple

October 15 Sunday
1 Feebers Cottage, Westwood
Starveacre, nr Axminster

DESCRIPTIONS OF GARDENS

Addisford Cottage ✲❀ (Mr & Mrs R J Taylor) West Lane, Dolton. ½m W of Dolton. From village centre past Royal Oak for ½m to bottom of valley, gate on R across ford. 1-acre garden surrounding picturesque thatched cottage in secluded wooded valley. Natural stream, large pond and water garden with hardy moisture loving and woodland plants. Extensive herbaceous borders, densely planted for sun and shade alongside many wild species. Large collection of geraniums. TEAS Suns only. *Adm £1 Chd free. Suns May 21, 28 June 4, 11, 18, July 2, 9, 23, 30, Aug 6 (11-5); also every Tues June, July. Private visits welcome, please* **Tel 018054 365**

¶Alswood ♿❀ (Bob & Marjorie Radford) George Nympton. 2m S of S Molton, halfway between the villages of George Nympton and Alswear. Ample parking in adjoining field. 2-acre developing garden designed and maintained by owners. Set in rural area with extensive view of the Crooked Oak Valley. Wide variety of herbaceous plants, many unusual ornamental trees, shrubs, heathers and conifers, small pond and stream. TEAS. *Adm £1 Chd free (Share to St George's Church & Heart Foundation Fund®). Mon May 29, Suns July 2, Aug 27 (2-5.30)*

Andrew's Corner ♿✲❀ (H J & Mr & Mrs R J Hill) Belstone, 3m E of Okehampton signed to Belstone. Parking restricted but may be left on nearby common. Plantsman's garden 1,000ft up on Dartmoor, overlooking Taw Valley; wide range unusual trees, shrubs, herbaceous plants for year round effect inc alpines, rhododendrons, bulbs, dwarf conifers; well labelled. TEAS. *Adm £1 Chd free. Suns April 23; May 7, 28; June 4, 18; July 16; (2.30-6); also private visits welcome, please* **Tel 01837 840332**

Arlington Court ♿✲ (The National Trust) Shirwell, nr Barnstaple. 7m NE of Barnstaple on A39. Rolling parkland and woods with lake. Rhododendrons and azaleas; fine specimen trees; small terraced Victorian garden with herbaceous borders and conservatory. Regency house containing fascinating collections of objet d'art. Carriage collection in the stables, carriage rides. Restaurant. *Adm garden only £2.40 Chd £1.20. Suns May 14, July 9 (11-5.30)*

Ash Thomas and Brithem Bottom Gardens ✲ 5m SE of Tiverton, 2m S of Halberton. Take A361 from junction 27 on M5 signposted Tiverton but leave in ½m signposted Halberton. In 3m turn L signposted Ash Thomas. 1st garden 1m. A route map to each garden will be available on open days. TEAS at Greenlands. *Combined adm £1.50 Chd 25p. Sat May 27, Suns March 19, June 25, July 30 (2.30-6.30)*

Greenlands ♿❀ (Dr & Mrs J P Anderson) Ash Thomas. ⅓-acre garden in open rural setting with far-reaching views. Alpine beds and troughs, herbaceous borders, roses and rustic screening, spring bulbs, annuals, herbs, fruit garden, vegetable plot, pond and wild areas. Parking in surrounding lanes, except disabled. Plants for sale in adjacent nursery. TEAS. *(Share to St Francis Hospital, Katete, Zambia©). Private visits also welcome March to Sept, please* **Tel 01884 821257**

Lower Beers ♿ (Mr & Mrs G Nicholls) Brithem Bottom. Listed C16 longhouse fronts a developing 3-acre hidden garden, incl ornamental herb and vegetable garden, herbaceous beds, woodland dell and large open area leading to stream. Parking in adjoining yard

Lower Coombe Farm (Mr & Mrs M Weekes) Brithem Bottom. Large cottage garden with an interesting selection of plants, old roses and a ditch garden situated behind C17 farmhouse. Parking in farmyard

Avenue Cottage ♿ (Mr R J Pitts & Mr R C H Soans) Ashprington. A381 from Totnes to Kingsbridge. 3m SE Totnes, from centre of village uphill past church for 400yds, drive on R. 11 acres of garden with woodland. Part of listed C18 landscape. Secluded valley site undergoing re-creation. Large collection of young and mature planting. *Adm £1 Chd 25p. Collecting box. Tues to Sat April 4 to Sept 30 (11-5). Private visits welcome, please* **Tel 01803 732769**. *No coaches*

Barton House ✿❀ (Mr and Mrs A T Littlewood) Nymet Rowland. 9m NW of Crediton. Follow signs to Nymet Rowland from A377 at Lapford or B3220 at Aller Bridge. Garden opposite C15 church. 1-acre garden designed and maintained by owners. Beautiful views to Dartmoor. Individual areas developed with varied character. Herbs; pond; herbaceous; yew garden; ferns, grotto, roses and fountain pool. Cream TEAS. *Adm £1 Chd 50p (Share to St Bartholomew's Church, Nymet Rowland®). Sat, Sun, Mon July 1, 2, 3 (2-6) Garden societies by appt*

Bickham Barton ✿❀ (Helen Lady Roborough) Roborough, 8m N of Plymouth. Take Maristow turn on Roborough Down, ½-way between Plymouth and Tavistock, then follow poster directions. Bus stop: Maristow sign on Roborough Down; posters at Maristow turning 1m from house. Shrub garden; camellias; rhododendrons; azaleas; cherries; bulbs; trees. Lovely views. *Adm £1 Chd 50p. Every Sun April 2 to June 4 and June 18; Mons April 17, May 8, 29 (2-5.30); also private visits welcome until end of June, please* **Tel 01822 852478**

Bickham House ♿✿❀ (Mr & Mrs John Tremlett) Kenn. 6m W of Exeter 1m off A38. Plymouth-Torquay rd leave dual carriage-way at Kennford Services, follow signs to Kenn. 1st R in village, follow lane for ¾m to end of no-through rd. Ample parking. No shade for dogs. 5-acre garden in peaceful wooded valley. Lawns, mature trees and shrubs; naturalised bulbs, mixed borders. Conservatory, small parterre, pond garden; 1-acre walled kitchen garden; lake. Cream TEAS. *Adm £1.50 Chd 50p. Suns March 19, April 16, May 21, June 18, July 16, Aug 20, Sept 17; Weds March 22, April 19, May 24, June 21, July 19, Aug 23, Sept 20 (2-5). Private visits also welcome, please* **Tel 01392 832671**

Bicton College of Agriculture ♿✿❀ Entrance to the College is by Sidmouth Lodge, half-way between Budleigh Salterton and Newton Poppleford on B3178. Proceed up famous monkey puzzle avenue with fine views of the parkland and trees. From the top of the drive follow signs to garden car park. The gardens are linked to the old Georgian mansion and extend via the arboretum to the old walled garden and glasshouses, being the centre of the Horticultural Dept. Rich variety of plants in beds and borders, laid out for teaching and effect; including NCCPG national collections of agapanthus & pittosporum; arboretum extends for ½m with various trees and shrubs incl magnolia, camellia and flowering cherries. Parking in gardens car park, short walk to gardens. Entrance tickets obtainable at Plant Centre. When plant centre closed please use box by gate. Plant centre closes 4.30pm. Garden and arboretum guides available. TEAS. *Adm £2 Chd free. Suns, Mons May 7, 8, 28, 29, Suns July 23, Sept 17 (10-5). Gardens also open daily throughout year, except Christmas day (10.30-5.00). Private parties welcome, please* **Tel 01395 568353**

Blackpool House ✿ (Lady A Newman) Stoke Fleming, 4½m SW of Dartmouth. Opp car park at Blackpool Sands. Shrub garden, on steep hillside, containing many rare, mature and tender shrubs. Beautiful sea views. Tea Blackpool Sands take-away on sands. *Adm £1 Chd free. Private visits welcome, spring & summer, please* **Tel 01803 770261**

Bovey Tracey Gardens Gateway to Dartmoor. A382 midway Newton Abbot to Moretonhampstead. Teas locally. *Combined adm £1.75 Chd 25p. Sat, Sun June 10, 11 (2-6)*

Bibbery ❀ (Misses E & A Hebditch) Higher Bibbery. B3344 to Chudleigh Knighton. Cul-de-sac behind Coombe Cross Hotel. Plantspersons small garden, sheltered corners harbouring interesting shrubs and tender plants. *Also private visits welcome, please* **Tel 01626 833344**

Church View ❀ (Mr & Mrs R Humphreys) East Street. B3344 opp St Peter & St Paul's Church. Small garden, but many unusual plants, incl secluded vegetable area. Disabled parking

Smithays Cottage (Mr & Mrs Arthur Mann) Fore Street. Small traditional walled cottage garden

Sunnyside (Mr & Mrs Green) Hind Street. Near town centre off A382. Opp Baptist church. Well established enclosed garden; trees and shrubs; herbaceous and colourful conservatory; productive vegetable area. Parking nearby

¶Thuja (Mr & Mrs Bowman) Hind Street. Experienced plantswomen, started new garden in small enclosed space with mediterranean feel, spot plantings in chippings

Bramble Cottage ✿❀ (Captain & Mrs Brian Norton) Lower Broad Oak Rd, West Hill, Ottery St Mary. From A3052 Exeter-Sidmouth rd turn N at Halfway Inn on B3180 for 2m, then right at Tipton Cross, then left fork and continue down hill to turn left at bottom into Lower Broad Oak Rd to second house on right. ¾-acre semi-woodland garden, plus ½-acre woodland, ponds and bog area; interesting shrubs; troughs; primulas a special feature in late spring. *Adm £1 Chd 15p. Suns, Mons May 7, 8, 28, 29; Sat, Sun June 10, 11 (11-5); also private visits welcome May to June, please* **Tel 01404 814642**

Broadhembury House ✿❀ (Mr & Mrs W Drewe) Broadhembury. 5m equidistant on A373 from Honiton-Cullompton signed Broadhembury. 2-acre informal garden in C16 picturesque thatched village. A spring garden with rhododendrons and azaleas, daffodils and bluebells. Ample parking in village square. TEAS. *Adm £1.25 Chd 50p (Share to Muscular Dystrophy Group®). Suns, Mons May 7, 8, 14, 21, 28, 29; Suns June 4, 11, 18, 25 (2-5). Larger groups welcome by appt during May and June, please* **Tel 0140484 1326**

By Appointment Gardens. These owners do not have a fixed opening day usually because they do not like crowds or have insufficient parking space. Owner will often give guided tour.

Bundels ♿❀ (Mr & Mrs A Softly) Ridgway, Sidbury. From Sidmouth B3175 turn left at free Car Park in Sidbury. From Honiton A375, turn right. Garden 100yds up Ridgway on left. 1½-acre organic garden inc small wood and pond set round C16 thatched cottage (not open); over 100 varieties of old-fashioned and other shrub roses. Typical cottage garden with accent on preservation of wild life. GRBS Gift stall. Teas in village. *Adm £1 Chd 20p. Suns May 7, 28, June 25; Weds May 10, 31, June 28; Thurs June 29; Sat June 24 (2-6). Private visits also welcome May to July for parties of 4 and over, please* **Tel 01395 597312**

Burrow Farm Garden ♿❀ (Mr & Mrs John Benger) Dalwood, 4m W of Axminster. A35 Axminster-Honiton rd; 3½m from Axminster turn N near Shute Garage on to Stockland Rd; ½m on right. Secluded 5-acre garden with magnificent views has been planned for foliage effect and includes woodland garden in a dell with rhododendrons, azaleas etc; large bog garden; pergola walk with rose-herbaceous borders. Nursery adjoining. Cream TEAS (Suns, Weds & Bank Hols). *Adm £2 Chd 50p. April 1 to Sept 30 daily (2-7). Private visits also welcome in the morning, please* **Tel 01404 831285**

Castle Drogo ♿✲❀ (The National Trust) Drewsteignton. W of Exeter, S of A30. Medium-sized garden with formal beds and herbaceous borders; shrubs, woodland walk overlooking Fingle Gorge. Wheelchair available. Plant centre. Restaurant. Tea room. *Adm gardens only £2 Chd £1. For NGS Suns April 30, June 18 (10.30-5.30)*

Castle Tor (Leonard Stocks) Wellswood, Torquay. From Higher Lincombe Rd turn E into Oxlea Rd. 200yds on right, entrance identified by eagles on gate pillars. Spectacular scenic listed garden superbly designed and laid out under the influence of Lutyens in the mid-30s. Stepped terraces, orangery, paved work and ornamental water. *Adm £1 Chd 25p. Private visits welcome for parties of 5 and over, please* **Tel 01803 214858**

Chevithorne Barton ❀ (Michael Heathcoat Amory Esq) Chevithorne. 3m NE of Tiverton. A terraced walled garden and further informal planting in woodland of trees and shrubs incl NCCPG National Oak Collection. In spring the garden features magnolias, rhododendrons and azaleas. *Adm £1 Chd 50p (Share to CPRE®). Sun May 28 (2-6)*

The Cider House ♿✲❀ (Mr & Mrs M J Stone) Buckland Abbey, Yelverton. From A386 Plymouth-Tavistock, 100yds S of Yelverton roundabout follow NT signs to Buckland Abbey. At Xrds before Abbey entrance turn N signed Buckland Monachorum. Drive 200yds on L, or short walk for visitors to Abbey. Peaceful and secluded garden with restrained planting complementing mediaeval house, part of a Cistercian monastery. Terrace borders and herbs, former Abbey walled kitchen garden with fruit, vegetables and flowers. Unspoilt aspect over wooded valley surrounded by NT land. Cream TEAS. *Adm £1 Chd 50p. Suns May 14, July 16 (2-6). Private visits welcome, please* **Tel 01822 853285**

Regular Openers. See head of county section.

Cleave House ✲❀ (Ann & Roger Bowden) Sticklepath, 3½m E of Okehampton on old A30 towards Exeter. Cleave House on left in village, on main road just past small right turn for Skaigh. ½-acre garden with mixed planting for all season interest. National Collection of hostas with 300 varieties, 100 of these are for sale. Partially suitable for wheelchairs. *Adm 50p. Wed May 10; Suns May 14, June 25 (10.30-5.30). Private visits also welcome April to Oct, please* **Tel 0183784 0481**

Clovelly Court ♿❀ (The Hon Mrs Rous) Clovelly. 11m W of Bideford. A39 Bideford to Bude turn at Clovelly Cross Filling Station, 1m lodge gates and drive straight ahead; also 'Long Walk' pedestrian entrance 200yds from top of village (back rd) at large green gate shared with entrance to coastal footpath. 25 acres parkland with beautiful open views through woodlands towards sea. 1-acre walled garden with borders, fruit and vegetables. 500yds walk from village (through green gate) along path lined with ancient trees and rhododendrons. Medieval Manor adjacent C14 Church nr coastline. Free parking in drive. Directions at Garden entrance, blue doors in Church Path. *Adm £1 Chd 20p (Share to NSPCC®; Braunton Cheshire Home®). Private visits and coach parties welcome May 1 to Sept 30, please* **Tel 01237 431215**

Coleton Fishacre ✲❀ (The National Trust) 2m NE of Kingswear. 20-acre garden planted and developed according to personal taste of the D'Oyly Carte family during 1926-1947 and unaltered by subsequent owners, now under restoration; wide range of tender and uncommon trees and shrubs in spectacular coastal setting. TEAS weather permitting. Unusual plants sale. *Adm £2.80 Chd £1.40. Suns April 23, May 21 (10.30-5.30)*

Court Hall ✲❀ (Mr & Mrs C Worthington) North Molton. 2½m N from A361 Barnstaple-Tiverton rd. In N Molton drive up the hill into the square with church on your L take the only drive beside the old school buildings and Court Hall is just round the bend. A very small south facing walled garden; large conservatory; rose, clematis, honeysuckle arbours surround a swimming pool garden with tender plants, rock wall and table. *Adm £1 Chd 20p. Wed July 5, Sun July 9 (2-5.30). Private visits of 20 or over also welcome June 25 to July 9, please* **Tel 015984 740224**

The Croft ♿✲❀ (Mr & Mrs Jewell) Yarnscombe. From A377, 5m S of Barnstaple turning W opposite Chapelton Railway Stn. for 3m. Drive on L at village sign. From B3232 ¼m N of Huntshaw TV mast Xrds, turn E for 2m. 1-acre plantswoman's garden on edge of village with unspoilt distant views to West. Alpine area and wide selection of unusual plants and shrubs. Island beds, much herbaceous material, ponds and bog area. No toilets. Cream TEAS Suns & Bank Hols. *Adm £1 Chd free (Share to St. Andrews Church®). Suns June 11, 25, July 9, 23 (2-6). Private visits also welcome Mons April 3 to Oct 30 (2-5) by appt, please* **Tel 01769 60535**

By Appointment Gardens. Avoid the crowds. Good chance of a tour by owner. See garden description for telephone number.

Croftdene ✿❀ (Joy and Phil Knox) Ham Dalwood. Between Axminster and Honiton. From A35 3½m W of Axminster turn N nr Shute Garage signed Dalwood and Stockland. Keep L up Stockland Hill until just past television mast. Turn R signed Ham. 1½m to Ham Cross. Park by telephone box. From A30 5m E of Honiton turn R signed Axminster and Stockland 3m to televsion mast turn L to Ham. 1½-acre garden in the making since 1988 with further 1 acre of natural woodland. Wide range of shrubs; herbaceous; ericaceous; alpines; woodland and water plants. Island beds; rock garden; peat beds; stream-side and pond. Featured on TV 'Gardens For All 1991'. TEAS at **Burrow Farm**. *Adm £1 Chd free. Suns May 28, June 25 (2-6). Private visits also welcome, please* **Tel 01404 831271**

Crosspark ♿✿❀ (Mrs G West) Northlew. From Okehampton follow A30 for 1m turn R to Holsworthy drive for 6m past Flare Garage turn R signposted Northlew, over bridge, turn L to Kimber, we are 3m along this rd on L, or 2½m from Highampton on the Northlew Rd. 1-acre plantswoman's garden by colour theme; herbaceous borders; ponds, incl wildlife pond; bog garden; rockery heathers and conifers. Wide range of plants. Featured on BBC Gardeners World and ITV. Large variety of unusual plants for sale. TEA. *Adm 75p Chd 20p. Suns, Mons April 30 to July 3 (1-5). Private visits also welcome for parties of 50 and over, coaches welcome also, please* **Tel 01409 221518**

Dartington Hall Gardens ♿✿❀ (Dartington Hall Trust) Approx 1½m NW of Totnes. From Totnes take A384, turn R at Dartington Parish Church. 28-acre garden surrounds C14 Hall and Tiltyard. Plant sales shop and nursery. *Adm (donation) £2.00 recommended.* ▲*Sat, Sun April 29, 30 (dawn to dusk)*

Delamore ♿ (Mrs F A V Parker) Cornwood, Ivybridge. A38; leave at turning for Lee Mill and Cornwood 6m E of Plymouth. 4-acre garden with flowering shrubs, lawns and mature trees. Swimming pool available. TEAS. *Adm £1 Chd 50p. Sun May 14 (2-5)*

¶Dicot ✿ (Mr & Mrs F Clarkson) Chardstock. Axminster to Chard A358 at Tytherleigh to Chardstock. R at George Inn, L fork to Hook, R at Burridge, 2nd house on L. 3-acre enthusiasts garden, trees unusual shrubs and conifers, bog orchids in May. Stream, mixed borders, fish pool, features. TEAS. *Adm £1 Chd 50p (Share to St Andrews Church, Chardstock®). Sats, Suns May 27, 28, July 29, 30 (2-5.30) Private visits welcome, please* **Tel 01460 220364**

Dippers ✿❀ (Mr & Mrs R J Hubble) Shaugh Prior. 8m NE of Plymouth on edge of Dartmoor. From A38 take Ivybridge exit and follow signs to Cornwood, continue on same rd to Shaugh Prior. From A386 follow signs to Bickleigh from Roborough then signs to Shaugh. Garden approx 100yds down lane opp church near top of village. Park in village or at White Thorn public house. No parking in lane. ¾-acre informal garden with further 1 acre being developed as nature reserve with stream and small bluebell wood. Emphasis on foliage contrast with varied collection of dwarf rhododendrons, azaleas, dwarf conifers and shrubs together with herbaceous and heathers; peat-bed; wildlife pond. Extensive collection of alpines, dwarf willows, gentians in raised beds, scree and 18 troughs. Special interest in pinks; scented pink walk. NCCPG National collection of dianthus. Choice alpines and unusual herbaceous for sale. *Adm £1 Chd free (Share to Ruth Murray's Badger Sanctuary©). Suns April 2, 30, May 28, Fri June 23 (11-5)*

Docton Mill and Garden ❀ (Mr & Mrs M G Bourcier) Spekes Valley nr. Hartland. Off A39: From N Devon via Clovelly Cross & Hartland to Stoke, or from N Cornwall via Kilkhampton to the West Country Inn. On either route turn L and follow Elmscott signs towards Lymebridge in Spekes Valley for 3½m. A garden for all seasons (depicted on BBC TV in Spring, Summer and Autumn) with working water mill dated 1249, situated in one of Devon's outstanding beauty spots where garden blends with natural landscape. Nearly 8 acres of sheltered wooded valley 1500yds from Spekes Mill Mouth coastal waterfalls and beach. Mill pond, leats, trout stream crossed by footbridges and smaller streams. Cultivated areas including bog garden, rockery, outcrops, woodland, and orchard. Displays in their seasons of narcissi, primulas, shrub roses, specimen trees, shrubs and herbaceous plants beside a profusion of wild primroses, bluebells, foxgloves and ferns. Devon cream TEAS at mill. *Adm £2 Chd 50p. Daily March to Oct (10-5). Parties by prior arrangement* **Tel 01237 441369**

The Downes ✿❀ (Mr & Mrs R C Stanley-Baker) 4½m S of Bideford; 3m NW of Torrington. On A386 to Bideford turn left (W) up drive, ¼m beyond layby. 15 acres with landscaped lawns; fine views overlooking fields and woodlands in Torridge Valley; many unusual trees and shrubs; small arboretum; woodland walks. Featured in Homes and Gardens June 1993. TEA Sats, Suns only. *Adm £1 Chd 20p. Daily April 16 to June 11 (all day); private visits also welcome June to Sept, please* **Tel 01805 622244**

Fardel Manor ♿✿❀ (Dr A G Stevens) 1¼m NW of Ivybridge; 2m SE of Cornwood; 200yds S of railway bridge. 5-acre, all organic garden, maintained with conservation and wildlife in mind. Partly reticulated. 2½ acres developed over past 10 years with stream, pond and lake. Also, small courts and walled gardens around C14 Manor, with orangery, herbaceous borders, formal pond and shrub garden. TEAS. *Adm £1.50 Chd 50p (Share to Frame®). Mon July 24 (11-4.30). Parties welcome by appt, please* **Tel 01752 892353**

Farrants ❀ (Mrs B Richards) Kilmington. 2m W of Axminster. A35, turn S at Kilmington Cross into Whitford Rd; garden about ¼m on left. 1-acre garden with stream planted since 1963; mostly shrubs and ground cover for colour contrast around C16 cottage. *Adm £1 Chd free. Private visits usually welcome May to July, please* **Tel 01297 32396**

By Appointment Gardens. These owners do not have a fixed opening day usually because they do not like crowds or have insufficient parking space. Owner will often give guided tour.

Fast Rabbit Farm ✤❀ (Mr & Mrs Mort) Ash Cross. 1½m from Dartmouth off the Dartmouth-Totnes rd pass park and ride. Turn L at Rose Cottage. Opp direction, from Totnes or Kingsbridge, pass Woodland Park on R, drive past Norton Park on L turn R at Rose Cottage. Newly created garden in sheltered valley with natural stream. Several ponds and lake; partially wooded; rockery; extensively planted; extends 8 acres with new woodland planting and walks being created through woodland at head of valley. Small specialist nursery open daily. Car park. Some level walks. 'Invalids' please phone prior to visit. TEAS. *Adm £1 Chd 50p. Suns April 16, 30, May 14, 28, June 11, 25, July 9, Aug 27 (11-5). Parties welcome by appt, please* **Tel 01803 712437**

1 Feebers Cottage ♿✤❀ (Mr & Mrs M J Squires) Westwood. 2m NE of Broadclyst from B3181 (formerly A38) Exeter-Taunton, at Dog Village bear E to Whimple, after 1½m fork left for Westwood. A modern cottage garden, a little of everything set in ¾ of an acre, with a maze of pathways; specialising in plants which tolerate heavy clay soil (alpines are in raised beds) and with a section of plants introduced by Amos Perry. Nursery. Cream TEAS July 16 only, tea and biscuits on other days. *Adm £1 Chd free. Sun March 26, Mon April 17, Suns May 21, June 11, 25, July 16, Sept 17, Oct 1, 15 (2-6). Private visits of 30 and over also welcome, please* **Tel 01404 822118**

Flete ✤ (Country Houses Association) Ermington, 2m W of Modbury on A379 Plymouth-Kingsbridge rd. Entrance adjacent to Sequers Bridge. 5 acres of gardens overlooking R Erme and valley. Landscaped in 1920's by Russell Paige and incl an Italian garden and water garden which Lawrence of Arabia helped to construct. Many fine trees and shrubs. Interesting cobbled terrace to W face of original Tudor manor. TEA. *Adm £1.50 Chd 75p (Share to Country Houses Assoc®). House and gardens open every Weds, Thurs pm May to end Sept. For NGS Sun May 7 (2.30-4.30).* **Tel 01752 830308**

The Garden House ✤❀ (The Fortescue Garden Trust) Buckland Monachorum, Yelverton. W of A386, 10m N of Plymouth. 8-acre garden of interest throughout year; inc 2-acre walled garden, one of finest in the country; fine collections of herbaceous and woody plants in glorious S Devon landscape. Coaches and parties by appt only. TEAS. *Adm £2.75 Chd 50p (Share to NGS®). March 1 to Oct 31 daily. For NGS Weds July 12, Aug 16 (10.30-5)*

The Gate House ✤ (Mr & Mrs D Booker) Lee Coastal Village. 3m W of Ilfracombe. Park in village car park. Take lane alongside The Grampus public house. Garden is 50yds past inn buildings. Peaceful streamside garden with a range of habitats; bog garden (with a National Collection of Rodgersia), woodland, herbaceous borders, patio garden with hardy 'exotics'. 2¼ acres, where no chemicals are used, only a few minutes walk from the sea and dramatic coastal scenery. Good food at the Grampus. *Collecting box. Private visits welcome, please* **Tel 01271 862409**

Regular Openers. See head of county section.

Glebe Cottage ✤❀ (Mrs C Klein) Warkleigh. From N Devon link rd or A377. Halfway between S Molton and Umberleigh on B3227 at Homedown Cross. S for Chittlehamolt, straight on for 2m entrance 100yds beyond Xrds. Garden featured on BBC 'Gardeners World', 'Garden Club' and ITV West Country. Chelsea Gold Medal Winners 1992, 93, 94. 1-acre cottage garden. recently redesigned with new features and exciting new plantings. S sloping, terraced. Wide collection of plants in different situations. Stumpery with ferns to sheltered formal beds and cottage garden plantings. Wide variety of unusual plants available from adjoining nursery open Tuesday to Friday. Cream TEAS on fine days. *Adm £1 Chd free. Suns June 4, 25, July 30, Aug 6, 27, Sept 24 (2-5)*

The Glebe House ✤ (Mr & Mrs John West) Whitestone. 2½-acre mature garden at 650ft S facing with outstanding views ranging from Exe estuary to Dartmoor. Garden on 3 levels; lower level with extensive lawns, mature trees and lge heather garden; middle level where house walls and buildings covered by climbing roses, clematis, honeysuckles and jasmines; upper level, given over to lawns with families of trees, acer, birch and eucalyptus underplanted with many types of rose. Over 300 varieties of rose most notable being Rosa filipes 'Kiftsgate', probably largest rose in UK, stretching over 130ft along Tithe Barn in courtyard and close to its equally vigorous double seedling 'St Catherine'. Former Rectory part C14 with Georgian frontage (not open). C14 Tithe Barn (Ancient Monument). C13/14 Church adjoins. Parking in lanes around Church, unsuitable for large coaches. *Adm £1 Chd free (Share to Whitestone Church®). Suns May 28, June 4, 11, 18, 25, July 2, 9, 16; Sat July 8 (2-6). Private visits also welcome, please* **Tel 01392 811200**

Gorwell House ♿❀ (Dr J A Marston) 1m E of Barnstaple centre, on Bratton Fleming rd, drive entrance between two lodges on left. 4 acres of trees and shrubs, walled garden; mostly created since 1982; small temple; summer house with views across estuary to Lundy and Hartland Point. TEAS except April 30, Oct 1. *Adm £1 Acc chd free. Suns April 30, May 28, June 25, July 30, Sept 3, Oct 1 (2-6)*

Gratton's Field Cottage ✤❀ (Mrs C F Luxton) Northlew. 8m W of Okehampton. Northlew Square towards Highampton. ½m from village on L. Small cottage garden; spring bulbs; shrubs; fuchsias; fish pond. Recent additional tree and shrub planting. TEA. *Adm 75p. Easter Fri, Sun April 14, 16; Suns June 4, 11, Aug 6, 13 (11-5). Private visits also welcome for parties of 20 and over, please* **Tel 01409 221361**

Greenway Gardens ❀ (Mr & Mrs A A Hicks) Churston Ferrers, 4m W of Brixham. From B3203, Paignton-Brixham, take rd to Galmpton, thence towards Greenway Ferry. Partly suitable for wheelchairs; 30 acres; old-established garden with mature trees; shrubs; rhododendrons, magnolias and camellias. Recent plantings; commercial shrub nursery. Woodland walks by R Dart. Limited parking, partly suitable for wheelchairs. TEA and biscuits. *Adm £1 Chd 50p. Thurs April 27, May 4 (2-6).* **Tel 01803 842382**

iamond Cottage, Powys. A hillside garden having beautiful views to the Berwyn Mountains.
hotograph by Jackie Newey.

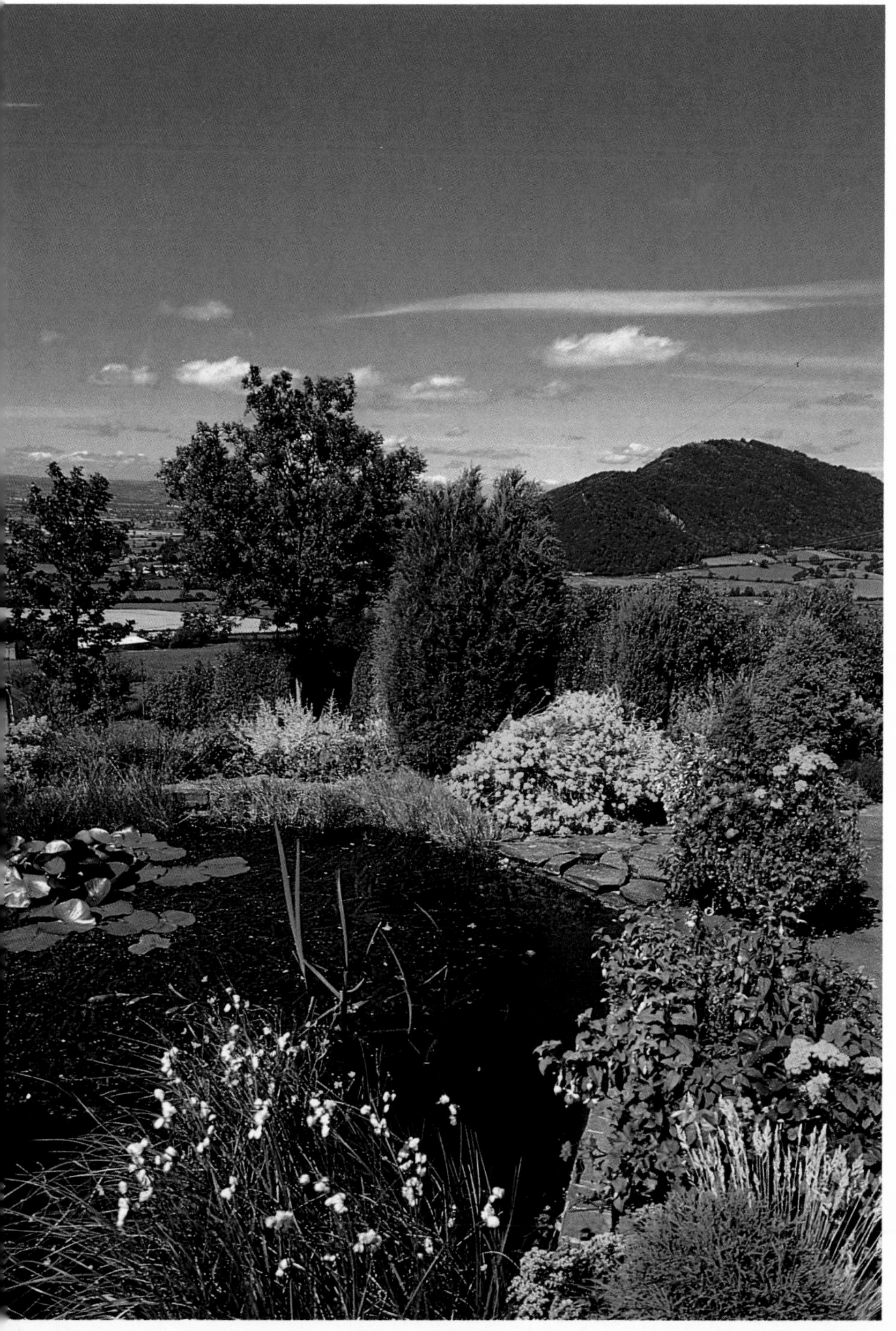

Winkworth Arboretum, Surrey. Superb colours blaze in this garden in spring and autumn.
Photograph by John Glover.

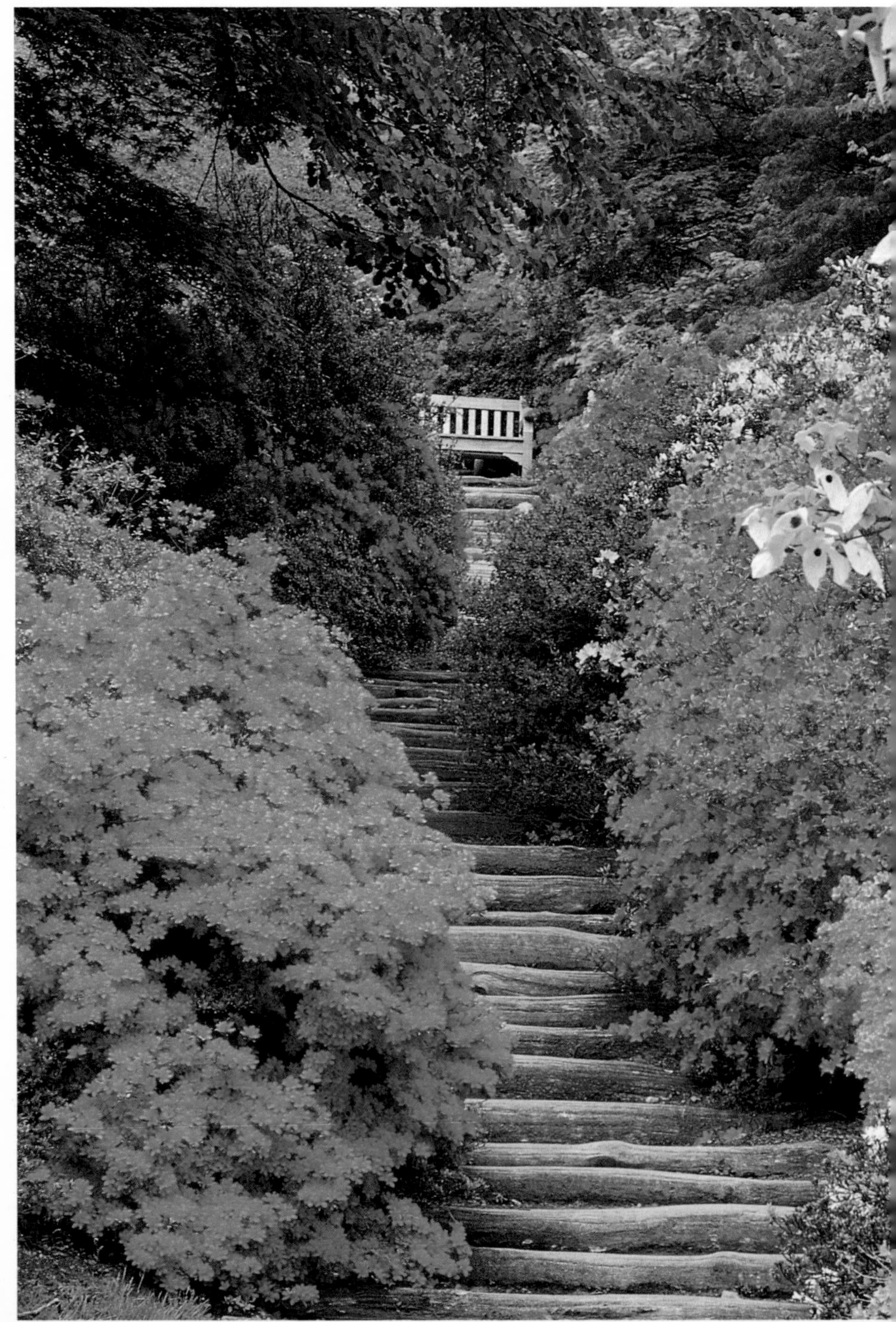

ight **Madron, Avon.** Plant and .olour associations feature in a ‹arden overlooking the Avon alley.
'hotograph by Eric Crichton.

elow **Gilling Castle, Yorkshire.** n 1995 this terraced garden has een opening for the National ;ardens Scheme for 61 years.
'hotograph by Jane Baldwin.

left **The Garden House, Buckland, Devon.** Contains a 2-acre walled garden.
Photograph by Andrew Lawson.

below **Hoveton Hall Gardens, Norfolk.** A variety of gardens in one.
Photograph by Brian Chapple.

left **Great Thurlow Hall, Suffolk.** Drifts of daffodils and blossom in a spring garden.
Photograph by Brian Chapple.

below **Abbey Dore Court, Hereford & Worcester.** This garden holds the National Collection of Euphorbia.
Photograph by Brian Chapple.

right **Grafton Cottage, Staffordshire.** A plant lovers cottage garden.
Photograph by Trish Walters.

below **Gothic House, Charlbury Gardens, Oxfordshire.** Sculptures, trellis work and false perspectives are unusual features of the photographer's own garden.
Photograph by Andrew Lawson.

Abbotswood, Gloucestershire. Massed plantings of spring bulbs in a formal garden.
Photograph by Ron Evans.

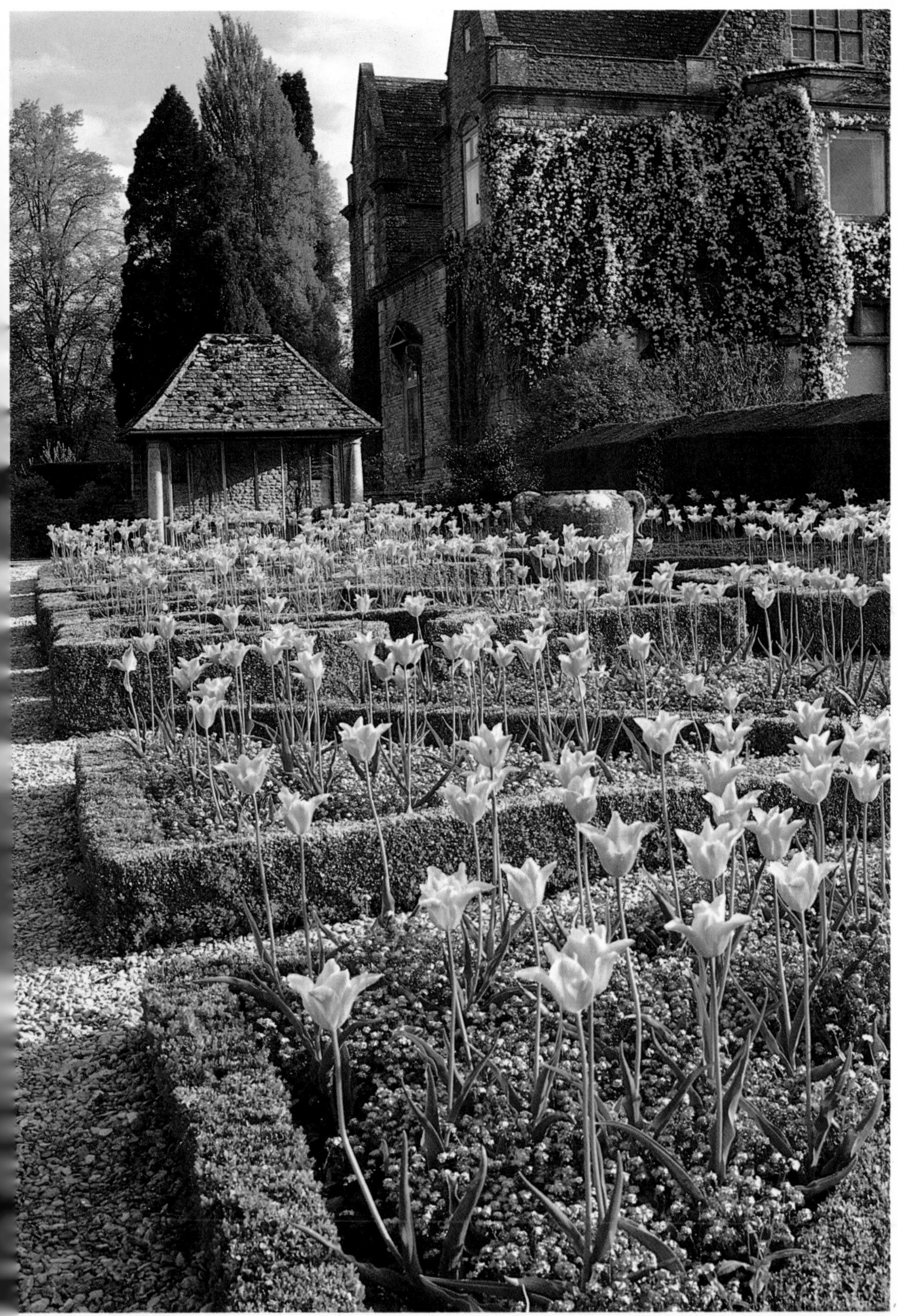

Raby Castle, County Durham. This garden has opened for the National Gardens Scheme for 60 years.
Photograph by Brian Chapple.

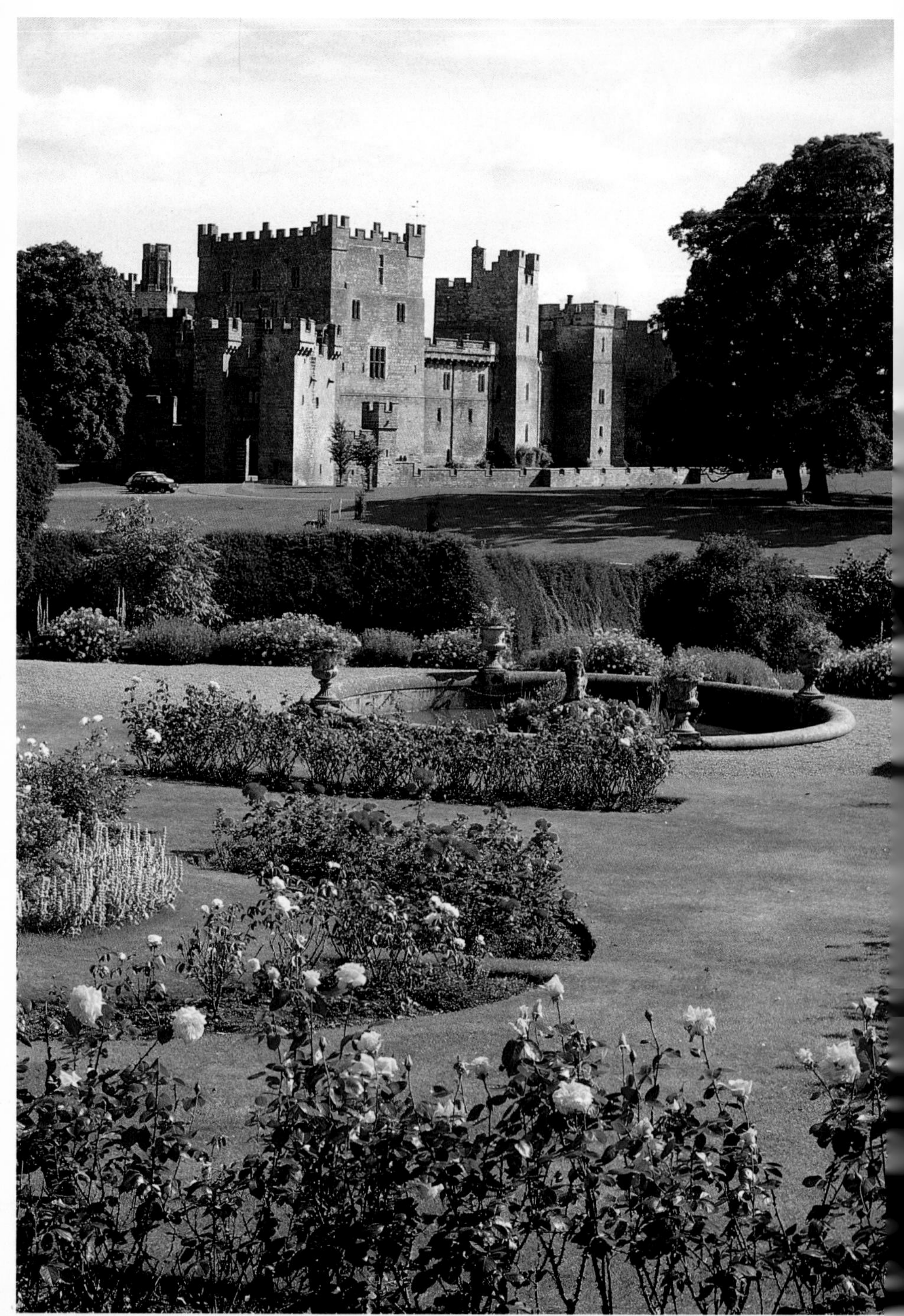

Hamblyn's Coombe (Capt R S McCrum RN Ret'd & Mrs B McCrum) Dittisham. From B3207 to Dittisham, turn sharp R at Red Lion Inn, along The Level. After public car park on L fork R up steep private rd. Field car park signposted at top. 10 min very pretty walk to garden. 7 acres sloping steeply to R Dart, with dramatic view across river to Greenway House. Extensive planting of trees and shrubs; wild meadows and mature broad-leaf woods. Woodland walks, stream and ponds and long river foreshore at bottom of garden. Sculpture by Bridget McCrum around garden. Ideal for children and dogs. TEA. *Adm £1.50 Chd free (Share to National Hospital for Neurology & Neurosurgery®). Sun, Mon May 7, 8 (2-6). Parties welcome by appt, please* **Tel 01803 722228**

Hartland Abbey ✣ (Sir Hugh Stucley & the Hon Lady Stucley) Hartland. Turn off A39 W of Clovelly Cross. Follow signs to Hartland through town on rd to Stoke and Quay. Abbey 1m from town on right. 2 woodland shrubberies with camellias, rhododendrons; wildflower walk through bluebell woods to remote Atlantic cove (Private walled gardens also open for NGS). TEAS. *Adm £1 Chd 50p (Share to St Nectan's Church, Hartland®).* ▲ *Sun April 23 (2-5.30). Tel The Administrator* **01237 441264**

¶Hayne Old Manor (Mr & Mrs R L Constantine) Moretonhampstead. ¼m S of Moretonhampstead on A382. 5 acres with lake and walled garden, shrubs and herbaceous borders. Recent landscaping and new plantings, extensive views. TEAS. *Adm £1.50 Chd free. Sat, Sun June 3, 4 (2-5.30)*

Heddon Hall ❀ (Mr & Mrs W H Keatley) Parracombe. 10m NE of Barnstaple off A39. 400yds N up hill from village centre. Entrance to drive on R. Ample parking 200yds. Garden of former rectory on edge of Exmoor under restoration extending to 3 acres. Walled garden with formal layout and herbaceous beds; sheltered flower garden; semi shaded S sloping shrubbery with paths leading down to natural stream and water garden. Cream TEAS. *Adm £1 Chd 50p. Sun June 18 (2-6)*

Higher Knowle (Mr & Mrs D R A Quicke) Lustleigh, 3m NW of Bovey Tracey A382 towards Moretonhampstead; in 2½m L at Kelly Cross for Lustleigh; in ¼m L/R at Brookfield along Knowle Rd; in ½m steep drive on left. 3-acre steep woodland garden; rhododendrons, camellias, magnolias on a carpet of primroses, bluebells; water garden and good Dartmoor views. Teas in village. *Adm £2 Chd free. Suns March 19, 26; April 2, 9, 16, 23, 30; May 7, 14; Mons April 17, May 8 (2-6). Private visits welcome, please* **Tel 0164 77 275**

Higher Spriddlestone ♿ (Mr & Mrs David Willis) Brixton, nr Plymouth. A379 5m E from Plymouth, S at Martin's Garden Centre sign, ¾m to top of hill, R opp Spriddlestone sign, entrance 50yds on L. 1½-acre developing garden in rural setting. Level area around house, with borders, informal wildlife and kitchen gardens and ponds. Teas at Martin's Garden Centre. *Adm £1 Chd free. Private visits welcome Weds, please* **Tel 01752 401184**

Higher Warcombe ✣❀ (Mr & Mrs A Treverton) Nr Kingsbridge. 2m N of Kingsbridge on the B3194 between Sorley Green Cross and Stumpy Post Cross. Take 1st turning L signposted Warcombe, house and garden approx ½m down lane. 1-acre garden on SW facing slope started in 1982 incl lawns, trees, rhododendrons, shrubs and herbaceous. Two steep banks planted for ground cover are a special feature and there is a pretty courtyard with container planting and a small walled garden. TEAS. *Adm £1 Chd 50p. Suns May 14, July 16 (2-5.30). Parties welcome by appt, please* **Tel 01548 550 280**

Hill House Nursery & Gardens ♿❀ (Mr & Mrs R Hubbard) Landscove. Between Dartington & Ashburton signed A38 or A384 Buckfastleigh-Totnes. Old Vicarage beside church both designed by John Loughborough Pearson, architect of Truro Cathedral. The 3 acre garden was the subject of 'An Englishman's Garden' by Edward Hyams, a previous owner. Also featured in 'English Vicarages and Their Gardens' and several times on TV. Said by many well known horticulturists to be one of the finest collections of plants anywhere. TEAS. *Free entrance open all year, Tea Room Mar to Oct. Collection box for NGS (11-5)*

Holywell ✣❀ (Mr & Mrs R Steele) Bratton Fleming. 7m NE of Barnstaple. Turn W beside White Hart Inn (opp White Hart Garage) signed Village Hall. At 300yds fork L for Rye Park. Entrance drive ¼m at sharp L. Parking at house. Garden on edge of Exmoor in woodland setting of mature trees, in all about 25 acres. Stream, ponds and borders. Woodland walk to Lower River meadow and old Lynton Railway Track. Many unusual plants for sale. TEAS. *Adm £1 Chd free. Suns April 30; May 7, 14, 28; June 11 (2-5). Private visits also welcome, please* **Tel 01598 710213**

¶Ivy Cottage ✣ (John Turner) Heanton Punchardon. 4m W of Barnstaple off A361 to Ilfracombe at Chivenor Roundabout. Head for church clearly visible on brow of hill. Garden adjacent. Parking in church car park. C17 thatched cottage with small typical cottage garden with wind tolerant planting giving shelter from exposure to coastal winds. Mixed tender shrubs, ornamental trees, wall climbers and small secret courtyard. Filtered view over estuary of R Taw. TEA. *Adm £1 Acc chd free (Share to St Augustines Church, Heanton®). Suns May 14, June 11, July 16 (12-5)*

Kerscott House ♿✣❀ (Mrs J Duncan) Swimbridge. Barnstaple-South Molton (former A361) 1m E of Swimbridge, R at top of hill, immediate fork L, 100yds on L, 1st gate past house. Developing 6-acre garden surrounding C16 farmhouse in peaceful rural setting. Ornamental trees, wide selection of shrubs, herbaceous and tender perennials, pond and bog garden. *Adm £1 Chd free. Suns June 18, July 9, Aug 27, Sat July 8 (2-6). Private visits also welcome during July, please* **Tel 01271 830943**

Killerton Garden ♿✣❀ (The National Trust) 8m N of Exeter. Via B3181 Cullompton Rd (formerly A38), fork left in 7m on B3185. Garden 1m follow NT signs. 15 acres of spectacular hillside gardens with naturalised bulbs sweeping down to large open lawns. Delightful walks through fine collection of rare trees and shrubs; herbaceous borders. Wheelchair and 'golf' buggy with driver available. Restaurant. Tea room, plant centre. *Adm gardens only £2.80 Chd £1.40. For NGS Suns April 23, July 9 (10.30-5.30)*

Kingswear-Ridley Hill Gardens From Torquay and Paignton A379 S towards Brixham, at Hillhead B3205 follow signs to Lower Ferry. At Kingswear one-way circuit up hill to Y fork, L into Higher Contour Rd. ½m keep to R at fork down Ridley Hill. After 100yds turn L into drive. Parking at Mulberry House 100yds on L. From Dartmouth cross river on Lower Ferry. 30yds hard R up church hill. 200yds at 1st junction L into Ridley Hill. A close-knit group of medium-sized terraced gardens in spectacular setting overlooking the estuary of the R Dart, dating from 2nd half of the C19. Wide range of shrubs, camellias, herbaceous perennials and bulbs. TEAS. *Combined adm £2.50 Chd 25p (Share to Army Benevolent Fund®). Sun March 26 (2-6)*

The Chart House (Mrs D Curry)
The Coach House (Mrs B Stannard)
Mount Ridley (Mr & Mrs Farmer)
Mulberry House ❀ (Major & Mrs Molloy) *Private visits welcome, please* **Tel 01803 752307**
Ridley Gate (Mrs C Byass)

Knightshayes Gardens ♿✂❀ (The National Trust) 2m N of Tiverton. Via A396 Tiverton-Bampton; turn E in Bolham, signed Knightshayes Court; entrance ½m on left. Large 'Garden in the Wood', 50 acres of landscaped gardens with pleasant walks and views over the Exe valley. Choice collections of unusual plants, incl acers, birches, rhododendrons, azaleas, camellias, magnolias, roses, spring bulbs, alpines and herbaceous borders; formal gardens; Wheelchair available. Restaurant. *Adm garden only £2.80 Chd £1.40. Suns April 30, July 2 (10.30-5.30)*

Lee Ford ♿❀ (Mr & Mrs N Lindsay-Fynn) Budleigh Salterton. Bus:DG, frequent service between Exmouth railway station (3½m) and Budleigh Salterton, alight Lansdowne corner. 40 acres parkland, formal and woodland gardens with extensive display of spring bulbs, camellias, rhododendrons, azaleas and magnolias. Adam pavilion. Picnic area. Car park free. Home made cream TEAS (3-5.30) and charity stalls. *Adm £1.40 OAPs £1 Chd 60p Special rate for groups 20 or more £1 (Share to other charities). Sun May 28 (1.30-5.30); also by prior appt for parties of 20 or over* **Tel 01395 445894**

Little Cumbre ✂ (Dr & Mrs John Lloyd) Exeter. At top of Pennsylvania Rd, 50yds below telephone kiosk on same side. Extensive views of Dartmoor and the Exe Estuary. ½-acre 9-yr-old mixed shrub and herbaceous garden. Collection of hellebores, clematis and small ornamental trees chosen for bark. Ample parking in rd. *Adm £1 Chd 50p. Thurs April 27, May 25, June 29 (2-6). Private visits also welcome for parties of 2 and over, please* **Tel 01392 58315**

Little Southey ♿✂❀ (Mr & Mrs S J Rowe) Northcott, Nr Culmstock. Uffculme to Culmstock rd, through Craddock then turn R at 6'6 restriction sign, Little Southey ½m on L. Culmstock to Uffculme turn L at restriction sign to Blackborough, right at Xrds to Northcott. House on R. Garden surrounding C17 farmhouse. Wide variety of plants grown for round the year interest. Limited parking if wet. Plant sale partly in aid of NCCPG. TEAS May 14 only. *Adm £1 Chd free. Sun May 14 (2-6); Mon May 15 (2-4)*

Little Upcott Gardens ♿✂❀ (Mr & Mrs M Jones) Marsh Green signposted off A30 Exeter to Honiton rd 4m E of M5 junction 29. Also signposted off B3180 and then from village. Informal 2-acre garden with many features of visual interest on different levels, featured on TV in 1992. Sensitive combination of plant styles and colour and unusual varieties of conifers, shrubs, perennials and alpines, some of which are available for sale. The original cottage garden is also open and there is a newly landscaped water feature with ornamental ducks. Plenty of seats available and assistance given to disabled incl partially sighted, by prior arrangement. Parties welcomed with cream teas, available by appt. TEAS. *Adm £1.50 Chd 50p (Share to Cats Protection League, Ottery Branch). Sat, Sun, Mon, Wed May 1, 27, 28, 29, 31; Sats, Suns, Weds June 10, 11, 14, 17, 18, 24, 25, 28; Sats, Suns Weds July 5, 15, 16, 19, 29, 30; Sat, Sun, Wed Aug 12, 13, 16 (1.30-5.30). Private visits also welcome, please* **Tel 01404 822797**

Little Webbery ♿✂ (Mr & Mrs J A Yewdall) Webbery Cross, Alverdiscott. Approx 2½m E of Bideford. Accessible either from Bideford (E The Water) along the Alverdiscott Rd or from the Barnstaple to Torrington Rd B3232 taking the rd to Bideford at Alverdiscott and passing through Stoney Cross. Parking adjacent Xrds. Approx 3-acre garden with two large borders near the house with lawns running down a valley, a pond, mature trees on either side and fields below which are separated by a Ha Ha. It has a walled garden with box hedging, which is partly used for fruit, vegetables, and incl a greenhouse; lawns; rose garden and trellises; shrubs and climbing plants. There is a tennis court below and a lake beyond. TEA 70p. *Adm £1.50 Chd free. Sun June 25 (2-6)*

The Lodge ♿❀ (Mr & Mrs M H Tregaskis) Hartley Ave, Mannamead, Plymouth. 1½m from City Centre via Mutley Plain. Turn right at Henders Corner into Eggbuckland Rd, 3rd right at Tel kiosk to end of cul de sac. ½-acre S sloping aspect with variety of unusual shrubs, conifers, camellias and ground cover plants. Former L.A. Nursery with range of lean-to glasshouses for fruit and tender subjects. Featured on TV 'Gardens For All'. TEA. *Adm £1.20 Chd 20p (Share to St. Luke's Hospice®). Suns May 7, June 18, July 23, (2-5.30). Private visits also welcome, please* **Tel 01752 220849**

¶Longham ✂❀ (Jennie Hale & Andrew Osborne) Coryton. Nr Lydford Gorge. A30, turn onto A386 Tavistock. 5m to Dartmoor Inn, signed to Lyford, past Lydford Gorge (NT). 3m R for Chillaton, 500yds R to Liddaton, downhill to Liddaton Cross, sharp R, 400yds over railway bridge, immed R into T sign rd, ½m downhill, L over small bridge, signed Longham Farm. Follow short track to the cottage. Ample parking. Small cottage garden with colourful mass herbaceous planting, ornamental grasses, shrubs, unusual perennials and climbers, vegetable garden, raised beds and polytunnel. Beautiful rural setting in wooded valley. TEAS. *Adm £1 Chd 50p. Suns Aug 6, 13 (2-6)*

By Appointment Gardens. Avoid the crowds. Good chance of a tour by owner. See garden description for telephone number.

Lower Coombe Royal ✂❀ (Mr & Mrs H Sharp) Kingsbridge. ½m N of Kingsbridge on Loddiswell Rd. Sign at gate. Historic woodland garden with rhododendrons, camellias, azaleas, magnolias and rare trees; terraces with tender and unusual shrubs; lawns, herbaceous borders; eucalypts. (Commercial shrub nursery open daily.) *Adm 50p Chd 25p. Private visits welcome, please* **Tel 01548 853717**

Lower Kerse ❀ (Mr & Mrs S O Parker-Swift) Thurlestone. Village of Thurlestone is 4m W of Kingsbridge. Garden is on fringe of village signposted Kerse at Kerse Cross before entering village. 7 acres of natural garden set in a delightful valley ½m from the coast, bounded by a stream and 2 ponds. TEAS. *Adm £1 Chd 50p. Sun June 18 (2-6)*

Lukesland (Mr & Mrs B N Howell) Ivybridge. 1½m N of Ivybridge on Harford Rd, E side of Erme valley. 15 acres of flowering shrubs, wild flowers and fine and rare trees with pinetum in Dartmoor National Park. Beautiful setting of small valley around Addicombe Brook with small lakes, numerous waterfalls and pools. Extensive and unusual collection of large and small leaved rhododendrons and one of the largest Magnolia Campbellii in the country. Partially suitable for wheelchairs. TEAS. *Adm £2 Chd 50p (Share to Harford Church® and Wixenford House©). Suns, Weds April 23 to June 4 incl. Bank Hol Mons May 8, 29. For NGS Suns May 7, 21 (2-6). Coaches on application only,* **Tel 01752 893390**

Marwood Hill ♿❀ (Dr J A Smart) Marwood, 4m N of Barnstaple signed from A361 Barnstaple-Braunton rd. In Marwood village, opp church. 20-acre garden with 3 small lakes. Extensive collection of camellias under glass and in open; daffodils, rhododendrons, rare flowering shrubs, rock and alpine scree; waterside planting; bog garden; many clematis; Australian native plants. National Collection astilbe, iris ensata, tulbaghia. Plants for sale between 11-1 and 2-5. Teas in Church Room (Suns & Bank Hols or by prior arrangement for parties). *Adm £2 OAP £1.50 Acc chd under 12 free. Daily except Christmas Day (dawn-dusk)*

Meadow Court ♿ (Ken & Heather Davey) Slapton. Entering the village of Slapton from the A379 at the Memorial on the beach. Take 2nd R and 1st L to house and garden in middle of village. Large free parking area. Level garden of 1 acre created in the last 12 yrs and maintained by the owner. Large pond with waterfall; Gunnera and marginals, water hens nest here. Large lawned area with trees and shrubs; heathers and shrub roses. TEAS. *Adm £1 Chd 50p. Sun May 21 (2-6)*

Meadowcroft ♿❀ (Mrs G Thompson) 1 Downfield Way, Plympton. From Plymouth left at St Mary's Church roundabout, along Glen Rd, 3rd right into Downfield Drive; garden on right. From A38, Plympton turn-off L at 1st roundabout, R at 2nd down Hillcrest Drive and Glen Rd, L at bottom of hill. Opp Dillons into Downfield Drive. Downfield Way on R. Medium size; stream; rhododendrons, azaleas, trees, flowering shrub borders. TEAS. *Adm 80p Chd 10p. Suns April 9, 23, May 21; Tues May 9 (1.30-5)*

Membland Villa ✂❀ (Mr & Mrs L J Hockaday) Newton Ferrers. 10m E of Plymouth. A374 Plymouth-Kingsbridge. At Yealmpton, S to Newton Ferrers. Sharp L at Widey Cross to Bridgend, then L to Membland. 2nd house on L from top of Membland Hill. Small 'Revelstoke' house set in country garden. Laid out and planted over 22yrs by present owner. Ornamental pond. Old roses, camellias, bulbs, trees, shrubs, climbers, herbaceous. Many unusual plants. Garden incl many acres steep bluebell woods spectacular in the season. TEAS. *Adm £1.25 Chd 25p. Suns April 23, June 18, July 30, Aug 6, Sept 17; Mons April 17, May 8, 29, Aug 28; Weds June 28; Sat July 15 (2-5). Private visits also welcome for parties of 10 and over, please* **Tel 01752 872626**

Monks Aish (Capt & Mrs M J Garnett) 1m W of South Brent, near the hamlet of Aish, off B3372 W of village. Follow signposts to Aish. After going under Aish railway bridge up hill, 3rd house on L next to Great Aish. [Grid Ref 688603.] A very attractive 1-acre garden with stream, a little different from most with varieties of shrubs, trees, flowers, fruit and vegetables. TEA. *Adm £1 Chd under 12 50p (Share to The Missions to Seamen®). Sat, Sun May 27, 28 (2-5). Private visits of 8 or over welcome, please* **Tel 01364 73102**

The Moorings ❀ (Mr & Mrs A Marriage) Rocombe, Uplyme, 2m NW of Lyme Regis. From Lyme Regis, about 1m on A3070, turn R signposted Rocombe, over Xrds, take narrow lane signposted Rocombe 4th house on R, drive beyond house. From Axminster, straight at Hunters Lodge then fork R twice, straight at Xrds and R again. ¾m on L. 3-acre peaceful woodland garden, developed since 1965, on hillside with terraced paths, overlooking unspoilt countryside. Fine trees inc many species eucalyptus, unusual pines, nothofagus; flowering shrubs inc some rare; daffodils and other spring flowers, ground cover, many ferns, autumn colour. *Adm 75p Chd free. Private visits welcome, please* **Tel 01297 443295**

16 Moorland View ✂ (Mr & Mrs G E J Wilton) Derriford, Plymouth. From Plymouth or A38 take A386 Tavistock Rd. After Derriford roundabout 1st L into Powisland Drive, 1st R into Roborough Ave, then L at bottom. Garden is approx 4m from Plymouth City centre. Small town garden with variety of plants. A typical lady's garden. TEA. *Adm £1 Chd 25p. Sun June 18 (2-5). Private visits also welcome, please* **Tel 01752 708800**

Mothecombe House ♿✂❀ (Mr & Mrs A Mildmay-White) Holbeton, SE of Plymouth 4m. From A379, between Yealmpton and Modbury, turn S for Holbeton. Queen Anne house (not open). Walled gardens, herbaceous borders. Orchard with spring bulbs; camellia walk and flowering shrubs. Newly planted bog garden; streams and pond; bluebell woods leading to private beach. Walk through picturesque thatched cottages to the Old School Teahouse and along the coastal footpath to the stunning Erme Estuary. TEAS. *Adm garden £1.50 Chd free (Share to Holbeton Church®). Sat May 6, Suns April 2, May 7, June 11 (2-5). Parties welcome by appt, please* **Tel 0175 530444**

Mulberry House ♿❀ (Dr & Mrs David Boyd) Barbican Terrace, Barnstaple. From the new rd (A361) follow signs to the Barbican Industrial Estate. This takes you L past a corner shop down Summerland St. At the end R into Barbican Terrace, Mulberry House 2nd entrance on L. Parking at Trinity Churchyard which is also accessible from the south end. 1-acre varied planting; foliage, especially gold and variegated; climbers and shade plants. TEA. *Adm £1 Chd free. Sat, Sun July 8, 9; Suns Aug 13, 20 (2-6). Private visits also welcome, please* **Tel 01271 45387**

Oare Manor Cottage ✱❀ (Mr & Mrs J Greenaway) Oare. 6m E of Lynton off A39. R after county gate to Oare. 50yds from Oare Church immortalized, in R D Blackmore's 'Lorna Doone'. Sheltered cottage garden in the romantic Oare Valley. Old-fashioned herbaceous borders, unusual shade plants, alpines, roses, Mediterranean pot plants. Fine views of the moor. Parking in lower field or opp church. TEAS. *Adm £1 Chd 50p. Private visits and coach parties welcome, please* **Tel 0159 87 242**

The Old Glebe ♿✱❀ (Mr & Mrs Nigel Wright) Eggesford, 4m SW of Chulmleigh. Turn S off A377 at Eggesford Station (½-way between Exeter & Barnstaple), cross railway and River Taw, drive straight uphill (signed Brushford) for ¾m; turn right into bridle path. 5-acre garden of former Georgian rectory with mature trees and several lawns, courtyard, walled herbaceous borders and a bog garden; emphasis on species and hybrid rhododendrons and azaleas 500 varieties. TEAS. *Adm £1.50 Chd 50p (Share to The Abbeyfield Chulmleigh®). Sat, Sun, Mon May 6, 7, 8 (2-6). Parties welcome by appt, please* **Tel 01769 580632**

The Old Mill ✱ (Mr & Mrs Shapland) Blakewell Muddiford, nr Barnstaple. ½m past hospital off B3230 to Ilfracombe at Blakewell Fisheries. Follow signs to Mill (grade II) at end of lane. A 3-acre south facing garden partly on slope at the rear surrounded by beautiful countryside views. Many varieties of shrubs, herbaceous, conifers and trees. Vegetable, herbs, an orchard, wildlife ponds. A young lime avenue leading to new folly. Parking in field if dry, limited if wet. *Adm £1 Chd free. Suns June 11, July 23 (11-6). Private visits also welcome, please* **Tel 01271 75002**

The Old Parsonage ✱❀ (Mr & Mrs Alex Hill) Warkleigh. 4m SW South Molton on B3226 past Clapworthy Mill (Hancocks Cider) R at stone barn signs to Warkleigh. From S through Chittlehamholt then 2nd R at War Memorial. Telephone kiosk marked on OS landranger sheet 180. 1-acre garden around former C16 Parsonage. Herbaceous border at entrance; enclosed stepped terraced garden behind house with wide range of plants and raised beds. Hillside above planted with trees and shrubs for autumn colour. Cream TEAS. *Adm £1 Chd 50p (Share to NCCPG®). Suns May 28, June 18, 25, July 2 (2-6)*

The Old Rectory, Clayhidon ❀ (Ken Wakeling) 4m from Wellington via South St or M5 exit 26 for Ford St. House next to Half Moon Inn and Church. 3-acres woodland garden with new plantings amid mature native trees; large numbers of naturalized bulbs mainly daffodils and snowdrops. Walled garden with mixed borders, ponds and rockery. *Adm 75p Chd free. Private visits pm usually welcome for parties of 2 and over, please* **Tel 01823 680534**

The Old Rectory, Woodleigh ♿✱ (Mr & Mrs H E Morton) nr Loddiswell. 3½m N of Kingsbridge E off Kingsbridge-Wrangaton Rd at Rake Cross (1m S of Loddiswell). 1½m to Woodleigh. Garden on R in hamlet. C19 Clergyman's garden partly enclosed by stone walls; restored and added to by present owners; mature trees with collection of rhododendrons, camellias and magnolias and other shrubs; large numbers of naturalised bulbs especially crocus and daffodils in early March. *Adm £1 Chd 10p. Private visits usually welcome, please* **Tel 01548 550387**

The Orchard ♿❀ (Mrs Hilda M Montgomery) Kenn. 5m S of Exeter off A38. ¾ acre; mostly trees; variety of conifers, azaleas, camellias, rhododendrons, many shrubs; fishponds and flowerbeds. Masses of spring bulbs. Ample parking nr Church. *Adm £1 OAPs/Chd 50p (Share to Redgate Bird Sanctuary, Exmouth©). Suns May 14, 28 (2-6); private visits also welcome, please* **Tel 01392 832530**

Orchard Cottage ♿❀ (Mr & Mrs W K Bradridge) 30, Hulham Rd, Exmouth, From Exeter A376 L into Hulham Road, just before first set of traffic lights. Entrance lane between Nos 26 and 32 Hulham Rd, opp lower end of Phillips Avenue. ¼-acre typical cottage garden. Parking in Hulham Road or Phillips Avenue. *Adm £1 Chd free. Private visits usually welcome by appt, please* **Tel 01395 278605** *(2.30-5.30)*

Ottery St Mary Gardens Town maps available at each garden. Suggested car park in Brook St will be signposted. *Combined adm £1.50 Chd 50p. Suns May 14, 21 (2-6)*

Little Beaumont, Ridgeway ✱ (Mr & Mrs I A Martin) From town centre, pass church on L (Honiton Rd), take 1st R on bend into Ridgeway. Approx 200yds on R. Partly walled ¼-acre garden with shrubs, trees and herbaceous border

Ravenhill, Longdogs Lane ♿✱❀ (Ruth & Guy Charter) Take Sidmouth Rd from town square, 200yds up Tip Hill turn L up narrow Longdogs Lane, 5th house on R. Medium-sized garden with a wide variety of unusual plants. South aspect, country views; pond; keen NCCPG propagator. Unusual plants for sale (Share to NCCPG®)

10 Slade Close ✱❀ (Betty & Jenny Newell) From town centre take rd towards Seaton. Turn R into Slade Rd, then L into Slade Close and R again. Small garden, mixed shrubs, spring flowers, small pond, scree garden

Overbecks ✱ (The National Trust) Sharpitor 1½m SW of Salcombe. From Salcombe or Malborough follow NT signs. 6-acre garden with rare plants and shrubs; spectacular views over Salcombe Estuary. Tea room same days as museum 12-4.15. *Adm garden only £2 Chd £1. Suns June 4, 25 (10-8 sunset if earlier)*

Regular Openers. Too many days to include in diary. Usually there is a wide range of plants giving year-round interest. See head of county section for the name and garden description for times etc.

Penrose ✠❀ (Mr & Mrs A Jewell) Crediton. A377 main Exeter to Barnstaple road, turn into Park Rd by Hillbrow Residential Home. Garden opp third turning on L. ⅓-acre town garden with small lawns, shrubs and herbaceous borders, pond with waterfall and wishing well, areas for fruit and veg and for growing produce for exhibition. Spring bulbs and summer annuals. TEA. *Adm 60p Chd free. Suns April 9, June 18, Aug 6 (2-5). Private visits of 10 or over welcome, please* **Tel 01363 773587**

38 Phillipps Avenue ♿✠❀ (Mr & Mrs R G Stuckey) Exmouth. From Exeter, turn L into Hulham rd just before 1st set of traffic lights, 1st L into Phillipps Avenue (ample parking). Small, highly specialised alpine and rock garden containing extensive collection of rock plants and minature shrubs, many rare and unusual; peat bed; scree bed; troughs; New Zealand collection. National NCCPG Helichrysum collection. Small alpine nursery. Teashops Exmouth. *Adm 50p Chd free. Suns April 2, 9, 23, May 7, 14, 21, 28; (Helichrysum Day for NCCPG®) June 11, 25; July 9, 23; Aug 6, 20; Sept 3 (2-6). Private visits also welcome, please* **Tel 01395 273636**

The Pines ♿ (R A Bitmead) Main Rd, Salcombe. At junction of Devon and Sandhills rds; lower entrance and parking Sandhills rd. All seasons ¾-acre S facing garden; fine coastal views to Sharpitor Headland and N Sands Valley. Informal garden of surprises; many interesting and unusual shrubs, trees; water gardens; bulbs, camellias, azaleas, heathers. *Adm £1.50 Chd free. Sat, Sun March 18, 19, April 1, 2, 16, Mon April 17 (11-5). Private visits also welcome all year, please* **Tel 01548 842198**

Plant World ❀ (Ray & Lin Brown) St. Mary Church Rd Newton Abbot. Follow brown signs from A380 Penn Inn Roundabout. Car park on L past Water Gardens. 4-acre Hillside Garden, laid out as a map of the world with native plants. Alpines, especially primulas and gentians, shrubs, herbaceous. Himalayan and Japanese gardens. Comprehensive cottage garden with double primroses, auriculas etc. 3 National Primula Collections. Seen on ITV June 1987 and BBC Gardeners World June 1993. Rare and unusual plants sold in adjacent nursery. Picnic area, viewpoint over Dartmoor and Lyme Bay. Collecting box. *Adm £1 Chd free. Open daily March to Oct (9-5). Other times by appt, please* **Tel 01803 872939**

Pleasant View Nursery ♿✠❀ (Mr & Mrs B D Yeo) Two Mile Oak, nr Denbury. 2m from Newton Abbot on A381 to Totnes. R opp 2m Oak Garage signed Denbury. ¾m on L. Large car park. 2-acre plantsman's garden, also 2-acre field planted with individual specimen shrubs, surrounded by open countryside with pleasant views. Wide variety of uncommon shrubs many tender. Began planting in field beside nursery in Autumn 1993. National Collections of Abelia and Salvia. Plants for sale in adjoining nursery (see advert). *Adm £1.20 Chd 25p. Sats, Suns June 3, 4, Sept 2, 3 (2-6). Parties welcome by appt, please* **Tel 01803 813388**

Portington (Mr & Mrs I A Dingle) nr Lamerton. From Tavistock B6632 to Launceston. ¼m beyond Blacksmiths Arms, Lamerton, fork L (signed Chipshop). Over Xrds (signed Horsebridge) first L then L again (signed Portington). From Launceston R at Carrs Garage and R again (signed Horsebridge), then as above. Small garden in peaceful rural setting with fine views over surrounding countryside. Mixed planting with shrubs and borders; woodland walk to small lake. TEAS. *Adm £1 Chd 20p (Share to St Luke's Hospice®). Suns July 16, 23 (2-5.30)*

Priors ♿✠ (Mrs Hunloke) Abbotskerswell. 1½m SW of Newton Abbot on Totnes-Newton Rd, signposted Abbotskerswell. Garden at bottom of village. ⅔-acre enclosed colourful garden, long herbaceous borders, old shrub roses; unusual plants. *Adm £1 Chd 50p. Suns June 18, (Share to Church Roof Fund®) June 25, July 2 (2-5.30). Private visits welcome June to July, please* **Tel 01626 53500**

¶Purple Hayes ✠❀ (Kim & Bruce Thomas) Lake Farm, Halberton. B3391 ¼m SE of Halberton. Plantaholic's garden of 1 acre, started in 1987. Bold herbaceous planting, unusual plants, ornamental grasses, ponds, bog and herb garden. Pigmy goats and ducks. Cream Teas in adjoining farmhouse. *Adm 75p Chd free (Share to Cats Protection League®). Suns May 28, June 25, Aug 20 (11-5). Private visits welcome, please* **Tel 01884 821295**

Quakers ✠❀ (Mr & Mrs T J Wallace) Membury. 3m NW of Axminster. A35 to Honiton, ½m W of Axminster turn N signed Membury. In village go 1m S of the church take sharp L turn. 100yds on L a red front door. Interesting small terraced flower garden around old Quaker Meeting House. 3 acres across lane, more a plantsman's whimsical collection than a garden. Mixed unusual tree and shrub plantings leading down to and over a wooded stream. *Adm £1 Chd free. Private visits welcome April to Nov, please* **Tel 01404 881312**

Riversbridge ♿❀ (Mr & Mrs Sutton-Scott-Tucker) ½m inland from Blackpool sands and signed from A3122. Small walled gardens adjoining farmyard in lovely unspoilt valley with ponds and stream; herbaceous plants, roses and some unusual shrubs. TEAS. *Adm £1 Chd free. Suns June 18, 25 (2-6)*

Robin Hill ✠ (Dr G Steele-Perkins) Deepdene Park, Exeter. From Barrack Rd turn W into Wonford Rd; entry to drive on left beyond Orthopaedic Hospital. ½-acre around house on level ground with variety of ornamental trees and shrubs; wall plants, ground cover and small pond. *Adm £1 Chd free. Suns May 28, July 2 (2-6). Parties welcome by appt, please* **Tel 01392 72861**

Rosemoor Garden ♿✠❀ (The Royal Horticultural Society) Great Torrington. 1m SE of Great Torrington on B3220 to Exeter. Original plantsman's garden started in 1959; rhododendrons (species and hybrid), ornamental trees and shrubs; dwarf conifer collection, species and old-fashioned roses, scree and raised beds with alpine plants, arboretum. The Society is expanding the Garden from 8 acres to 40. The new Garden already contains 2000 roses in 200 varieties, two large colour theme gardens, herb garden, potager, 200 metres of herbaceous border, a large stream and bog garden and a cottage and foliage garden. A fruit and vegetable garden opened in 1994. The new Visitors Centre contains a restaurant, shop, and plant centre selling interesting and unusual plants. *Adm £3 Chd £1 Groups £2.50 per person. Open daily all year (10-6 April to Sept. 10-4 Oct to March) collecting box for NGS*

51 Salters Road ✲❀ (Mrs J Dyke) Exeter. Typical small town garden; specialising in unusual plants inc primulas, auriculas and alpines (owner has for many years been Committee member of Exeter Branch of Alpine Garden Society). *Collecting box for NGS. Private visits welcome, please* **Tel 01392 76619**

Saltram House ♿✲ (The National Trust) Plympton, 3m E of Plymouth, S of A38, 2m W of Plympton. 8 acres with fine specimen trees; spring garden; rhododendrons and azaleas. C18 orangery and octagonal garden house. George II mansion with magnificent plasterwork and decorations, incl 2 rooms designed by Robert Adam. Wheelchair available. Restaurant. *Adm gardens only £2.20 Chd £1.10. For NGS Suns April 9, May 14 (10.30-5.30)*

Scypen ✲❀ (Mr & Mrs John Bracey) Ringmore. 5m S of Modbury. From A379 Plymouth-Kingsbridge S at Harraton Cross on B3392. R at Pickwick Inn (signed Ringmore). Park in Journey's End car park on L opp church. ½-acre coastal garden, integrating design, landscaping and mixed planting for year-round effect and to take advantage of lovely views of church, sea and unspoilt Nat. Trust coast and farmland. Salt and wind tolerant plants; silver wedding garden; organic kitchen garden; chamomile and thyme lawns. Featured on BBC 'Gardener's World'. TEAS. *Adm £1 Chd 25p. Wed June 21, Sun June 25 (2-5)*

Silver Copse ✲❀ (Mrs V E Osmond) nr Marsh Green. From Exeter; A30 to Jack-in-the-Green, R to Rockbeare and Marsh Green, L towards Ottery. Garden ¾m on the R. From Sidmouth; A3052 to Half-way Inn. B3180 N for 1½m L at Xrds towards Marsh Green, garden 200yds on L. 3 acres, all seasons garden, wide selection shrubs, rhododendrons, azaleas, ornamental pools and alpines, as shown T.S.W. *Adm £1 Chd free. Suns, Mons April 16, 17; May 7, 8, 28, 29; July 16, 17; Aug 27, 28 (10-5). Private visits also welcome, please* **Tel 01404 822438**

Sowton Mill ♿✲❀ (A Cooke and S Newton) nr Dunsford. From Dunsford take B3193 S for ½m. Entrance straight ahead off sharp R bend by bridge. From A38 N along Teign Valley for 8m. Sharp R after humpback bridge. 4 acres laid out around former mill, leat and river. Part woodland, ornamental trees and shrubs, mixed borders and scree. Year round interest. TEAS. *Adm £1 Chd free (Share to Cygnet Training Theatre©). Suns June 25, July 2 (2-6). Private visits also welcome, please* **Tel 01647 52347**

Spillifords (Dr Gavin Haig) Lower Washfield. On W bank of R Exe N of Tiverton. A396 Tiverton to Bampton. After 2m L over Iron Bridge, signposted Stoodleigh and Ravenswood. L again following signs to Washfield, after 1m from bridge, garden on L. Please note narrow lanes and limited parking opp house. 1½-acre wildlife and wild flower garden, ideal for those interested in natural history. On steeply sloping bank of R Exe (unsuitable for disabled) in which a wide range of wild flowers, butterflies, birds and other wildlife abound in an ideal arboreal and riverside environment. Frequently featured in media on various wildlife programmes. TEA. *Adm £2 Chd £1. Maximum benefit for visitors would be derived from direct guidance from owner, hence garden open by appointment only. Weds, Sats April to Aug (2-6). Please* **Tel 01884 252422**

Starveacre ✲❀ (Mr and Mrs Bruce Archibold) Dalwood. Leave Axminster on A35 travelling W. After 3m (Shute Xrds) turn R at staggered Xrds signposted Dalwood. Follow signs to Dalwood and go through village, over stream, round sharp L bend. Follow road, ignoring left turn, up steep hill and at top turn L. Under pylons and up hill. After crest, take L turn before white 5-bar gate. Starveacre is at end of lane. A plantsman's garden of 5 acres on a hillside facing S and W with superb views. Mixed plantings of rhododendrons, camellias, conifers, acers, magnolias and much more. TEAS. *Adm £1 Chd under 14 free. Sat May 6; Suns July 16, Oct 15 (2-5)*

Stone Lane Gardens ♿❀ (Kenneth & June Ashburner) Chagford. On NE edge of Dartmoor National park. A382 at Whiddon Down signed Drewsteighton for 1½m. 2nd R (Stone Lane). Parking in farmyards on L. 5-acres informally landscaped specialist arboretum with emphasis on foliage and bark and featuring collections of wild-origin birch and alder from around the northern hemisphere; natural streams and ponds. Open views of Dartmoor. Exhibition of work within garden by sculptors and designers inspired by nature, myth and folklore June-Sept. No coaches. TEA. *Adm £2 Chd £1. Gardens open daily mid-June to mid-Nov (2-6). For NGS Weds May 31, June 21, July 12 (2-6). Private visits also welcome, please* **Tel 01647 231311**

Sunrise Hill ✲❀ (Chris & Sharon Britton) Withleigh. 3m W of Tiverton on B3137 rd to Witheridge and South Molton. Garden reached through Withleigh Nurseries, situated at E end of village. Approx 1 acre of developing colourful garden. Mixed borders, unusual plants, herbaceous, lawns and vegetables. Plants for sale in adjacent nursery (on open days 10% of plant sales for NGS). TEAS. *Adm £1 Chd free. Sat May 20, Weds July 26, Aug 2 (2-5.30). Parties welcome by appt, please* **Tel 01884 253351**

Tapeley Park & Gardens ♿❀ (NDCI Ltd) Instow. On A39 Barnstable-Bideford rd. Italian garden of horticultural interest. Walled kitchen garden; woodland walk to lily pond. Putting, bowls, croquet, picnic area. Lunches & cream TEAS. *Adm £2.50 OAP £2 Chd £1.50. Collecting Box for NGS Easter to end Sept Bank Hol Mons, Tues to Suns incl (10-6), please* **Tel 01271 860 528**

Topsham Gardens 4m from Exeter. Free parking in Holman Way car park. Teas at 20 Monmouth Ave. *Adm 60p each garden Chd free. Suns, Mon May 7, 8, June 18 (2-6)*

4 Grove Hill ♿❀ (Margaret and Arthur Boyce) Off Elm Grove Rd, opp junction with Station Rd. A small town garden with some rare plants, troughs and screes with alpine plants and unusual bulbs

20 Monmouth Avenue ♿❀ (Anne & Harold Lock) Access to Monmouth Ave by footpath on the L after leaving Holman Way car park. ⅓-acre level garden, wide range of unusual plants and shrubs giving year round effect, mixed curved borders, herbaceous, shrubs and bulbs incl a collection of hardy geraniums and alliums. Some old fashioned roses. Featured on TV 'Gardens For All'. TEAS. *Private visits also welcome, please* **Tel 01392 873734**

Twitchen Mill ♿✂❀ (Mr & Mrs G Haydon) 6m NE of South Molton. A361 S Molton to Taunton, 400yds past caravan site on outskirts of town at top of hill, L signed Twitchen for 5m. Straight on at last fork 200yds before Mill. 1-acre level garden on the foothills of Exmoor, in beautiful wooded valley, bordered with leat and clear water stream. Parking on roadside also in field. Wheelchairs only if dry. TEAS. *Adm £1.20 Chd free. Suns May 28, July 16 (10-6)*

Vicar's Mead ♿✂❀ (Mr & Mrs H F J Read) Hayes Lane, East Budleigh, 2m N of Budleigh Salterton. From B3178. Newton Poppleford-Budleigh Salterton, turn off W for East Budleigh; Hayes Lane is opp 'Sir Walter Raleigh'; garden 100yds W of public car park. 3½ acres of informal plantings around a 500yr-old historic former vicarage; wide range of unusual and rare shrubs, trees, bulbs and perennials etc, displayed on a steep terraced escarpment. Hostas and 4 National Collections a feature. Tea in village. *Adm £1 Chd free. Sat, Sun, Mon May 20, 28, 29, Fri June 16 (2-6). Private visits also welcome, please* **Tel 013954 42641**

Warren Cottage ❀ (Margaret Jock & Libs Pinsent) Higher Ludbrook, Ermington, Ivybridge. 1¼m E of Ermington on A3121 turn R signed Higher Ludbrook. 1½-acres started from field 1986, and now, hopefully beginning to look like a garden. Mostly shrubs and small trees with some herbaceous and a few annuals. Small pond usually out of control. *Collecting Box for NGS. Private visits always welcome May to Sept, please* **Tel 01548 830698**

¶96 Wasdale Gardens ✂❀ (David & Colleen Fenwick) Estover, Plymouth. Outskirts of city. From A38 Forder Valley Junction, follow Forder Valley Rd (old A38), R into Novorossisk Rd, L into Miller Way, 3rd L into Keswick Crescent, 1st L into Wasdale Gardens. Car park next to 102 Wasdale Gardens, follow path along top of car park past nos 95 and 94. Garden in front of 93, recognisable by 2 dovecotes. Small council house garden 15m × 11m. Large diversity of plants some unusual. Specialist collection of over 70 crocosmia hybrids. Most landscaping and features constructed using recycled materials. *Adm £1 Chd 25p. Private visits welcome July 10 to Sept 10, please* **Tel 01752 785147**

Weetwood ♿✂ (Mr & Mrs J V R Birchall) Offwell, 2m from Honiton. Turn S off A35 (signed Offwell), at E end of Offwell. 1-acre all seasons garden; rhododendrons, azaleas, shrubs, ornamental pools, rock gardens, collection of dwarf conifers. Teashops Honiton. *Adm 50p Chd 10p (Share to The Forces Help Society, Lord Roberts Workshops). Private visits usually welcome spring, summer & autumn, please* **Tel 01404 831363**

Westpark ✂❀ (Mr & Mrs D Court) Yealmpton, 7m E of Plymouth; on Kingsbridge Rd (A379) Xrds centre of village, turn S on Newton Ferrers rd; park end of Torr Lane. An old fashioned rambling 2-acre garden in peaceful country setting. Year round colour and variety. Old rose, pergola, mulberry (1907), wood with cyclamen, ferns, bulbs, fruit cage, vegetable garden. Interesting C19 narcissi March/April. TEAS. *Adm £1.25 Chd 30p. Sun, Wed March 19, 22 (2-5). Private visits also welcome mid Feb to mid Oct, please* **Tel 01752 880236**

Whitmore ✂❀ (Mr & Mrs Cyril Morgan) Chittlehamholt. 12m SE Barnstaple, house marked on O.S. Landranger 180. From the village take rd S past Exeter Inn and High Bullen Hotel; Whitmore is ¼m further on L down long tree-lined drive. 3-acre garden with ponds, stream and herbaceous borders. An interesting collection of trees and shrubs. Further 3 acres of woodland garden mainly ferns with pleasant sylvan walks, amongst wood warblers and box breeding pied flycatchers and nuthatches. A secluded peaceful garden. TEAS. *Adm £1 Chd 50p. Thurs, Sat, Sun April 20, July 1, Aug 27 (2-5)*

Winkfield see Stop Press on page 334

Withleigh Farm ❀ (T Matheson) Withleigh village. 3m W of Tiverton on B3137, 10yds W of 'Withleigh' sign, entrance to drive at white gate. Peaceful undisturbed rural setting with valley garden, 14 years in making; stream, pond and waterside plantings; bluebell wood walk under canopy of mature oak and beech; wild flower meadow, primroses and daffodils in spring, wild orchids. TEA. *Adm £1 Chd 25p (Share to Cancer & Arthritis Research®). Sat, Sun May 20, 21 (2-5). Private visits also welcome, please* **Tel 01884 253853**

Wolford Lodge ♿ (The Very Rev. the Dean of Windsor and Mrs Patrick Mitchell) Dunkeswell. Take Honiton to Dunkeswell rd. L at Limer's Cross. Drive ½m on L at white entrance gate and lodge. 4 acres semi-woodland with massed rhododendrons, azaleas and camellias. Distant views to S over unspoilt Devon countryside. Woodland walks. *Adm £1 OAP/Chd 50p. Sat May 27 (2-6)*

Wood Barton ♿✂❀ (Mr & Mrs Richard Horton) Kentisbeare. 3m from M5 exit 28. A373 Cullompton to Honiton rd. 2m turn L signed Goodiford for 1m and turn L again at White Cottages. Farm drive, 100yds R. Bull on sign. [Landranger 192. Lat 09 Long 05/06.] 2 acres woodland garden planted 45yrs with species trees on S facing slope. Magnolias, azaleas, camellias, rhododendrons, acers; small pond. TEAS. *Adm £1 Chd 50p. Sat, Sun May 13, 14 (1-5)*

Woodside ✂ (Mr & Mrs Mervyn Feesey) Higher Raleigh Rd, Barnstaple. On outskirts of Barnstaple, A39 to Hospital and Lynton, turn R 300yds above fire station. Semi-woodland, 2 acres S sloping in suburban area with intensive planting incl many ornamental grasses, sedges, bamboos and monocots (Author of RHS Handbook on Ornamental Grasses). Many parts of the garden are shaded and peaceful, offering protection to unusual and tender shrubs. Special interest in New Zealand flora. Raised beds and troughs, variegated, acid loving shrubs, ornamental trees and conifers, all with emphasis on form and colour of foliage, makes this a garden with a difference. *Adm £1 Chd 50p. Suns May 7, June 18, Aug 20 (2-5.30)*

¶Woodside ✂ (Mrs L L Braund) Whimple. Just off A30 rd between Honiton and Exeter. Turn N opp the B3180 turning for Exmouth. 1st L, house 1st on L, signposted Exeter 9m. Honiton 7m. ¾-acre garden 500′ above sea level. Large variety of herbaceous plants, shrubs and roses. Colourful throughout the summer and an excellent example of what can be achieved in late season. TEA. *Adm £1 Chd free. Suns June 11, July 23, Aug 27, Sept 24 (2-5.30) Private visits welcome June to end Sept, please* **Tel 01404 822340**

Wylmington Hayes ✲❀ (Mr and Mrs P Saunders) Wilmington. 5½m NE of Honiton on A30, turn R. Signposted Stockland 3m/Axminster 10m, after 3½m entrance gates on R (before Stockland TV Station) or from A35 3½m W of Axminster turn N nr Shute Garage on to Stockland Road for 3m, entrance on L nr TV mast. Reclaimed gardens, created in 1911. 83 acres of gardens and woodlands with spectacular hybrid rhododendrons, azaleas, magnolias, camellias, acers. Lakes, ponds, topiary, arboretum, woodland walks with abundant wildlife. Interesting collection of ornamental and domestic waterfowl including black swans. Scottish Country Dancing June 4, 11, 18. TEAS. *Adm £2.50 Chd £1. Easter Fri, Sat, Sun, Mon April 14, 15, 16, 17; Suns and Bank Hol Mons until end of June (2-5). Coaches & parties by appt please* **Tel 01404 831751**

Yonder Hill ♿✲❀ (Mrs M H Herbert) Colaton Radleigh. A3052 at Newton Poppleford. B3178 towards Budleigh Salterton. 1m 1st L signposted to Dotton then immed R into small lane. ¼m 1st house on R. Car parking. Part of a small holding set in peaceful countryside with panoramic views, approx 2 acres of fast maturing gardens planted mainly since 1992 with some 2000 different varieties for all-yr interest. Several unusual features, 5 small paddocks with a variety of animals incl Rheas. Rare and unusual plants for sale as available. Easy access to all parts for wheelchairs. *Adm £1 Chd 50p. Fri to Mons March 24, 25, 26, 27, April 21, 22, 23, 24, July 28, 29, 30, 31, Oct 27, 28, 29, 30, Mon to Mon May 22, 23, 24, 25, 26, 27, 28, 29, Tues to Sun Aug 1, 2, 3, 4, 5, 6, Mon to Sat Sept 4, 5, 6, 7, 8, 9, Fri, Sat Sept 29, 30, Sun, Mon Oct 1, 2 (2-4)*

Dorset

Hon County Organiser: Mrs Hugh Lindsay, The Old Rectory, Litton Cheney, Dorchester DT2 9AH Tel 01308 482383

Assistant Hon County Organisers: Mrs Raymond Boileau, Rampisham Manor, Dorchester DT2 0PT Tel 01935 83612

Stanley Cherry Esq., Highbury, Woodside Rd, West Moors, Ferndown BH22 0LY Tel 01202 874372

Mrs G D Harthan, Russets, Rectory Lane, Child Okeford, Blandford DT11 8DT Tel 01258 860703

Mr & Mrs W E Ninniss, 52 Rossmore Road, Parkstone, Poole BH12 3NL Tel 01202 740913

Hon County Treasurer: Michael Gallagher Esq, 6 West Street, Chickerell, Weymouth DT3 4DY

DATES OF OPENING

By appointment

For telephone numbers and other details see garden descriptions. Private visits welcomed

Ashley Park Farm, Damerham
Bladeley House, Buckland Newton ‡
Bridge House Water Garden, Portesham
Bowhay, Iwerne Minster
2 Curlew Rd, Bournemouth
Domineys Yard, Buckland Newton ‡
Edmondsham House, Cranborne
Friars Way, 190 Church Street, Upwey
Highbury, West Moors
Knitson Old Farmhouse, Corfe Castle
Lamorna, Chedington
Langebride House, Long Bredy
Little Platt, Plush
Lower Ware, Lyme Regis
Melbury House, nr Yeovil
Moulin Huet, West Moors
Oakmead, nr Beaminster
The Old Rectory, Fifehead Magdalen
The Old Rectory, Litton Cheney
Old Rectory, Seaborough
The Old Vicarage, Stinsford
Orchard House, Portesham
Pumphouse Cottage, Alweston
46 Roslin Road South, Bournemouth
Smedmore, Kimmeridge
Tara, West Moors
Throop Mill Cottage, Bournemouth
Welcome Thatch, Witchampton
Wincombe Park, nr Shaftesbury
2 Winters Lane, Portesham

Parties only

Bexington, Lytchett Matravers
Boveridge Farm, Cranbourne
Edgeways, Poole
Frith House, Stalbridge
Higher Melcombe, Melcombe Bingham
Long Ash Cottage, nr Dorchester
The Old Rectory, Pulham
52 Rossmore Road, Parkstone
Star Cottage, Wimborne
Sturminster Newton Gardens
Three Bays, Beacon Hill

Regular openings

For details see garden descriptions

Abbotsbury Gardens, nr Weymouth. March 1 to Oct 31
Aurelia Gardens, West Moors. Open Weds, Thurs, Fris, Sats & Suns. All year
Broadlands, Hazelbury Bryan. Every Weds in May, June, July & Aug
Cartref, Stalbridge. Tues, Fris April to Oct. Closed June
Chiffchaffs, Bourton. Open every Sun & Bank Hol weekend, Weds & Thurs
Compton Acres Gardens, Poole. Daily March 1 to Oct 31
Cranborne Manor Gardens, Cranborne. Weds March to Sept incl
Deans Court, Wimborne Minster. For details see text.
Forde Abbey. Daily all year
Heatherwood, Ashington, Wimborne. Daily
Horn Park, Beaminster. Every Tues, Weds, Suns & Bank Hol Mons

Ivy Cottage, Ansty. Every Thurs April to Oct
Kingston Maurward, Dorchester. Easter to Mid Oct
Knoll Gardens, nr Wimborne. Various dates see text
Loscombe House, nr Bridport. Weekends April to Oct
Mapperton Gardens, nr Beaminster. Daily March to Oct
Minterne, nr Cerne Abbas. Daily April to Oct
The Old Mill, Spetisbury. Every Wed May to August
Parnham, Beaminster. Suns, Weds & Bank Hols April 1 to Oct 30
Snape Cottage, Bourton. Every Wed April 5 to Sept 27. Closed Aug
Stapehill Abbey, Wimborne. Open Daily April to Oct. Closed Mon & Tue Nov to March
Star Cottage, Wimborne. See text for dates
Sticky Wicket, Buckland Newton. Thurs June to Sept
Wimborne Minster Model Town and Gardens

March 12 Sunday
Mews Cottage, 34 Easton St, Portland ‡
Witchcroft, 1 Sweet Hill Road, Southwell ‡

March 19 Sunday
Langebride House, Long Bredy

March 26 Sunday
Chiffchaffs, Bourton

April 2 Sunday
Broadlands, Hazelbury Bryan
Frith House, Stalbridge
Langebride House, Long Bredy
Stour House, Blandford

April 5 Wednesday
Edmondsham House, Cranborne

April 9 Sunday
Aller Green, Ansty ‡
Bexington, Lytchett Matravers
Fernhill Cottage, Witchampton ‡‡
Fernhill House, Witchampton ‡‡
Frankham Farm, Ryme Intrinseca
Ivy Cottage, Ansty ‡
1 Manor Close, Stratton ‡‡‡
Manor Orchard, Stratton ‡‡‡
Welcome Thatch, Witchampton ‡‡

April 12 Wednesday
Cranborne Manor Gardens, Cranborne ‡
Edmondsham House, Cranborne ‡
1 Manor Close, Stratton ‡‡
Manor Orchard, Stratton ‡‡

April 15 Saturday
Ashley Park Farm, Damerham

April 16 Sunday
Boveridge Farm, Cranborne
Cartref, Stalbridge
Chiffchaffs, Bourton ‡
Horn Park, Beaminster
The Old Rectory, Litton Cheney
Snape Cottage, Bourton ‡

April 17 Monday
Broadlands, Hazelbury Bryan
Edmondsham House, Cranborne
Thistledown, Alweston

April 19 Wednesday
Edmondsham House, Cranborne

April 20 Thursday
Knitson Old Farmhouse, Corfe Castle

April 23 Sunday
Bladeley House, Buckland Newton ‡
Corfe Barn, Broadstone
Domineys Yard, Buckland Newton ‡
Old Rectory, Seaborough
Thistledown, Alweston

April 26 Wednesday
Edmondsham House, Cranborne

April 27 Thursday
Rampisham Manor, Dorchester

April 30 Sunday
Chiffchaffs, Bourton
Frankham Farm, Ryme Intrinseca
North Leigh House, nr Wimborne
Thistledown, Alweston

May 3 Wednesday
Chedington Court, Chedington ‡
Lamorna, Chedington ‡

May 6 Saturday
Ashley Park Farm, Damerham

May 7 Sunday
Bridge House Water Garden, Portesham
Broadlands, Hazelbury Bryan ‡
Charlton Cottage, Tarrant Rushton
Chiffchaffs, Bourton ‡
Eurocentre Language School, Bournemouth
Pumphouse Cottage, Alweston ‡‡
Snape Cottage, Bourton ‡
Thistledown, Alweston ‡‡

May 8 Monday
Pumphouse Cottage, Alweston ‡
Thistledown, Alweston ‡

May 10 Wednesday
Hilltop Cottage, Woodville

May 14 Sunday
Bexington, Lytchett Matravers
Boveridge Farm, Cranborne
Corfe Barn, Broadstone
Fernhill Cottage, Witchampton ‡
Fernhill House, Witchampton ‡
Friars Way, 190 Church Street, Upwey
Glebe House, East Lulworth
Hilltop Cottage, Woodville
Kesworth, Nr Wareham
46 Roslin Road South, Bournemouth
Thistledown, Alweston
Welcome Thatch, Witchampton ‡

May 17 Wednesday
Glebe House, East Lulworth
Wincombe Park, nr Shaftesbury

May 18 Thursday
Kingston Maurward, Dorchester

May 20 Saturday
Studland Bay House, nr Swanage

May 21 Sunday
Aller Green, Ansty ‡
Cartref, Stalbridge
2 Curlew Road, Bournemouth
Highwood Garden, Wareham ‡‡
Ivy Cottage, Ansty ‡
Kesworth, Nr Wareham ‡‡
Long Ash Cottage, nr Dorchester ‡
Lower Ware, Lyme Regis
Moigne Combe, nr Dorchester
The Old Rectory, Litton Cheney
52 Rossmore Road, Parkstone
Slape Manor, Netherbury
Smedmore, Kimmeridge
Star Cottage, Wimborne
Studland Bay House, nr Swanage
Sturminster Newton Gardens
Thistledown, Alweston
Throop Mill Cottage, Bournemouth

May 24 Wednesday
Throop Mill Cottage, Bournemouth

May 25 Thursday
Knitson Old Farmhouse, Corfe Castle
Melbury House, nr Yeovil

May 27 Saturday
Ashley Park Farm, Damerham

May 28 Sunday
Chiffchaffs, Bourton ‡
Deans Court, Wimborne
Edgeways, Poole
Friars Way, 190 Church Street, Upwey
Highwood Garden, Wareham
Moigne Combe, nr Dorchester
Pumphouse Cottage, Alweston
46 Roslin Road South, Bournemouth
Snape Cottage, Bourton ‡
Tara, West Moors

May 29 Monday
Horn Park, Beaminster
Pumphouse Cottage, Alweston ‡
Tara, West Moors
Thistledown, Alweston ‡

June 1 Thursday
Melbury House, nr Yeovil

June 4 Sunday
7 Church Street, Upwey, Weymouth ‡

Farriers, Puddletown ‡‡
4 Flower Cottage, Lower Waterston, Puddletown ‡‡
Frith House, Stalbridge
Kingston Lacy, nr Wimborne Minster
Portesham House, Portesham
52 Rossmore Road, Parkstone
West Manor, Upwey ‡
Wimborne Minster Model Town & Gardens

June 6 Tuesday
7 Church Street, Upwey, Weymouth

June 7 Wednesday
The Orchard, Blynfield Gate, nr Shaftesbury

June 10 Saturday
Cranborne Manor Gardens, Cranborne
Stepleton, Iwerne Stepleton

June 11 Sunday
Bexington, Lytchett Matravers
Boveridge Farm, Cranborne
Corfe Barn, Broadstone
2 Greenwood Avenue, Ferndown
High Hollow, Corfe Mullen
26 Milestone Rd, Poole
The Old Mill, Spetisbury
The Old Rectory, Fifehead Magdalen
Snape Cottage, Bourton
Waterfalls, Bournemouth

June 14 Wednesday
The Orchard, Blynfield Gate, nr Shaftesbury
Red House Museum and Gardens, Christchurch

June 15 Thursday
Melbury House, nr Yeovil

June 18 Sunday
Bridge House Water Garden, Portesham ‡
Charlton Cottage, Tarrant Rushton
Edgeways, Poole
Fernhill Cottage, Witchampton ‡
Fernhill House, Witchampton ‡
Frankham Farm, Ryme Intrinseca
Friars Way, 190 Church Street, Upwey
Hambledon Cottage, Shaftesbury Rd, Child Okeford
Hyde Farm, Frampton
Long Ash Cottage, nr Dorchester
1 Manor Close, Stratton ‡
Manor Orchard, Stratton ‡
Mews Cottage, 34 Easton St, Portland
The Old Vicarage, Stinsford
Portesham House, Portesham ‡
Pumphouse Cottage, Alweston
Star Cottage, Wimborne
Three Bays, Beacon Hill

June 21 Wednesday
Friars Way, 190 Church Street, Upwey
1 Manor Close, Stratton ‡
Manor Orchard, Stratton ‡
The Orchard, Blynfield Gate, nr Shaftesbury

June 25 Sunday
Chiffchaffs, Bourton
The Cobbles, Shillingstone
2 Greenwood Avenue, Ferndown
Holworth Farmhouse, Holworth
The Priest's House Museum and Garden, Wimborne
Pumphouse Cottage, Alweston ‡
46 Roslin Road South, Bournemouth
Steeple Manor, nr Wareham
Sticky Wicket, Buckland Newton
Thistledown, Alweston ‡
Welcome Thatch, Witchampton
Weston House, Buckhorn Weston

June 28 Wednesday
26 Milestone Rd, Poole
The Orchard, Blynfield Gate, nr Shaftesbury

June 29 Thursday
Melbury House, nr Yeovil

July 2 Sunday
Cherry Tree Cottage, 133 Merley Ways, Wimborne ‡
7 Church Street, Upwey, Weymouth ‡‡
The Cobbles, Shillingstone
Corfe Barn, Broadstone
Edgeways, Poole
Farriers, Puddletown
High Hollow, Corfe Mullen
Rampisham Gardens, Dorchester
Thistledown, Alweston
West Manor, Upwey ‡‡
Wimborne Minster Model Town & Gardens ‡

July 4 Tuesday
7 Church Street, Upwey, Weymouth

July 8 Saturday
Bowhay, Iwerne Minster
Tara, West Moors

July 9 Sunday
Bexington, Lytchett Matravers
Bladeley House, Buckland Newton ‡
Domineys Yard, Buckland Newton ‡
2 Greenwood Avenue, Ferndown
Holworth Farmhouse, Holworth
26 Milestone Rd, Poole
Stour House, Blandford
Tara, West Moors
Thistledown, Alweston
Three Bays, Beacon Hill

July 12 Wednesday
The Old Rectory, Pulham
The Orchard, Blynfield Gate, nr Shaftesbury

July 13 Thursday
Kingston Maurward, Dorchester
Loscombe House, nr Bridport ‡
Melbury House, nr Yeovil
Pear Tree Farm, Loscombe ‡

July 16 Sunday
2 Curlew Road, Bournemouth
Edgeways, Poole
2 Greenwood Avenue, Ferndown
Loscombe House, nr Bridport ‡
Mews Cottage, 34 Easton St, Portland ‡‡
The Old Mill, Spetisbury
The Old Rectory, Pulham
Pear Tree Farm, Loscombe ‡
Portesham Gardens, Portesham
Snape Cottage, Bourton
Three Bays, Beacon Hill
Weston House, Buckhorn Weston
Witchcroft, Southwell ‡‡

July 19 Wednesday
The Orchard, Blynfield Gate, nr Shaftesbury

July 20 Thursday
Knitson Old Farmhouse, Corfe Castle

July 23 Sunday
Higher Melcombe, Melcombe Bingham
Hilltop Cottage, Woodville
Melplash Court, nr Bridport
46 Roslin Road South, Bournemouth

July 26 Wednesday
Hilltop Cottage, Woodville

July 30 Sunday
Chiffchaffs, Bourton
7 Church Street, Upwey, Weymouth
High Hollow, Corfe Mullen ‡
7 Highfield Close, Corfe Mullen ‡
Hilltop Cottage, Woodville
North Leigh House, nr Wimborne

August 1 Tuesday
7 Church Street, Upwey, Weymouth

August 3 Thursday
Melbury House, nr Yeovil

August 6 Sunday
Edgeways, Poole
Farriers, Puddletown
Frith House, Stalbridge
7 Highfield Close, Corfe Mullen

August 13 Sunday
Bexington, Lytchett Matravers
Bladeley House, Buckland Newton ‡
Domineys Yard, Buckland Newton ‡
Stour House, Blandford

August 16 Wednesday
Hilltop Cottage, Woodville

August 19 Saturday
Three Bays, Beacon Hill
August 20 Sunday
High Hollow, Corfe Mullen
Hilltop Cottage, Woodville
Mews Cottage, 34 Easton St, Portland ‡
The Old Rectory, Pulham
Sticky Wicket, Buckland Newton
Three Bays, Beacon Hill
Witchcroft, Southwell ‡
August 27 Sunday
Aller Green, Ansty ‡
Chiffchaffs, Bourton
7 Church Street, Upwey, Weymouth
Ivy Cottage, Ansty ‡
August 28 Monday
7 Church Street, Upwey, Weymouth
September 3 Sunday
Wimborne Minster Model Town & Gardens
September 6 Wednesday
Chedington Court, Chedington ‡
Lamorna, Chedington ‡
September 9 Saturday
Bowhay, Iwerne Minster
September 10 Sunday
Bexington, Lytchett Matravers
Eurocentre Language School, Bournemouth
Fernhill Cottage, Witchampton ‡
Welcome Thatch, Witchampton ‡
September 17 Sunday
Cartref, Stalbridge
Thistledown, Alweston
September 24 Sunday
Aller Green, Ansty ‡
Chiffchaffs, Bourton ‡‡
Ivy Cottage, Ansty ‡
Mews Cottage, 34 Easton St, Portland
The Old Rectory, Litton Cheney
Snape Cottage, Bourton ‡‡
Thistledown, Alweston
October 1 Sunday
Deans Court, Wimborne
Mews Cottage, 34 Easton St, Portland
October 4 Wednesday
Edmondsham House, Cranborne
October 11 Wednesday
Edmondsham House, Cranborne
October 18 Wednesday
Edmondsham House, Cranborne
October 25 Wednesday
Edmondsham House, Cranborne

DESCRIPTIONS OF GARDENS

● **Abbotsbury Gardens** ❀ (Ilchester Estates) 9m NW of Weymouth. 9m SW of Dorchester. From B3157 Weymouth-Bridport, turn off 200yds W of Abbotsbury village, at foot of hill. 20 acres; uniquely mild Mediterranean-type climate, started in 1760 and considerably extended in C19; much replanting during past few years; very fine collection of rhododendrons, camellias, azaleas; wide variety of unusual and tender trees and shrubs. Peacocks. Children's play area, woodland trail, aviaries and plant centre. Partly suitable for wheelchairs. TEAS. *Adm £3.80 OAPs £3 Chd £1, reduced rate in winter. (For party rate* **Tel 01305 871387***) March 1 to Oct 31 (10-5); winter (10-3)*

Aller Green ✤ (A J Thomas Esq) Aller Lane, Ansty, 12m N of Dorchester. From Puddletown take A354 to Blandford; After public house, take 1st L down Long Lane signed Dewlish-Cheselbourne; through Cheselbourne to Ansty then 1st R before Fox Inn down Aller Lane. 1-acre typical Dorset cottage garden; unusual trees, shrubs and perennials in old orchard setting and many perennials grown for Autumn Colour. Garden featured on Channel 4 'Garden Club' 1992. Teas at **Ivy Cottage**. *Combined adm with* **Ivy Cottage** *£2.50 Chd 50p. Suns April 9 (Share to RNLI®); May 21 (Share to the Samaritans®); Aug 27 (Share to Blandford Museum©); Sept 24 (Share to the Red Cross®) (2-5.30)*

Ashley Park Farm ❀ (David Dampney Esq). Damerham. Follow yellow signs off B3078, immediately W of village, 5m from Fordingbridge. Newly created gardens of 5 acres with farm and woodland walks. With many interesting trees, an arboretum in the making although now mature enough for visiting, Eucalyptus grove; wild flower meadow. Many exciting plants for south facing walls, borders. TEAS, also every Sun. *Adm £1 Chd free (Share to Damerham Church®).* ▲*For NGS Sats April 15; May 6, 27 (2-5.30). (See also* **Boveridge Farm***). Private visits welcome, please* **Tel 017254 241**

Aurelia Gardens ♿✤❀ (Mr & Mrs Robert Knight) Newman's Lane, West Moors. N of the village off B3072 Bournemouth-Verwood rd. Heathers, conifers, grasses, variegated and golden foliage plants have been used to create a garden for year round colour. 5-acre level site, incl nursery and an acre of free parking. *Adm 50p. Weds, Thurs, Fris, Sats and Suns all year (9-5)*

Bexington ♿✤❀ (Mr & Mrs Robin Crumpler) Lytchett Matravers. In Lime Kiln Rd, opp old School at W end of village. Colourful garden of ½-acre maintained by owners, with mixed borders of many interesting and unusual plants, shrubs and trees. Bog garden of primulas and hostas etc. Four rockeries of alpines, with walkways over bog area connecting two lawns, making a garden of interest from spring bulbs to autumn colour. Cream TEAS & plant stall for Alzheimer Disease Society & gardening charities. *Adm 70p Chd 20p. Suns April 9, May 14, June 11, July 9, Aug 13, Sept 10 (2-6). Group visits welcome by appt, please* **Tel 01202 622068**

¶**Bladeley House** ✤❀ (Dr & Mrs Peter Sowerby) Buckland Newton. 11m from Dorchester and Sherborne 2m E of A352 or take B3143 from Sturminster Newton. Take 'no through rd' between church and 'Gaggle of Geese' public house next to phone box. Entrance 200 metres on L. Park in lane or in field if available. Approx 1½-acre family garden surrounding Regency house, under renovation. Bordered lawns, kitchen garden, orchard, shrubs, modern conservatory and new woodland. *Combined adm with* **Domineys Yard** *£2 Chd 50p (Share to Leonard Cheshire Foundation West Dorset Care at Home Service ®). Suns April 23, July 9, Aug 13 (2-6). Private visits welcome March to Oct, please* **Tel 01300 345525**

Regular Openers. Too many days to include in diary. Usually there is a wide range of plants giving year-round interest. See head of county section for the name and garden description for times etc.

Boveridge Farm ✿❀ (Mr & Mrs Michael Yarrow) Cranborne. Leave Cranborne on Martin Rd unclass, thence take 2nd R Boveridge Farm. A plantsman's garden of 2 acres on 3 levels, part chalk and part acid; with lawns around old farmhouse, formerly manor house of the Hooper family; in rural surroundings with fine views. Fountain, fern bank and many rare and interesting trees and shrubs. Specimen acer 'Brilliantissimum', prunus 'Shidare Yoshino', prunus 'Pendula Rubra', Paulownia tomentosa. Teas at **Ashley Park**, Damerham (next village 3m). *Adm £1 Chd free (Share to Cranborne Church®). Suns April 16, May 14, June 11 (2-5). (See also* **Ashley Park Farm**). *Group visits welcome by appt, please* **Tel 01725 517241**

¶**Bowhay** ♿✿ (Stephen Ford Esq) Iwerne Minster. Iwerne Minster is connected by two roads to Shaftesbury, 6m to the N; and to Blandford, 6m to the S. Either turn up from the lower A350 rd at the village war memorial, or down from the higher rd at the signed Xrds, to the house or garden sign. Very interesting and exciting 1-acre garden on hill above village, re-designed and re-built in last 4 years. Roses, rockery; pergola, ponds; cascades, terraces and sitting areas with wonderful views. 'Peaceful'. Exhibition of landscape photography and TEAS in aid of Parish Church organ. *Adm £1.50 Chd 20p. Sats July 8, (10-12, 3-7), Sept 9 (10-12, 4-8). Private visits welcome, please* **Tel 01747 811289**

Bridge House Water Garden ✿ (Mr & Mrs G Northcote) 13 Fry's Close, Portesham. 7m W of Weymouth on coast rd, B3157 to Bridport. From Dorchester take A35 W, turn L in Winterborne Abbas and follow signs to Portesham; parking in village. Designed and constructed in 1987 in Japanese manner; featured on BBC2, and in 'Garden Answers!' Stone and ceramic lanterns, 'half-moon', stone and timber bridges, trout stream, borrowed scenery, turtle island, waterfalls; local stone-walled terraces, over 360 plantings suitable for smaller seaside garden; kave-sansui garden, several new rock groupings incl 'Isles of the Blest' feature with further additions planned for 1995; garden planning exhibition in studio. *Adm £1 Acc chd free. Suns May 7, June 18 (2-6). Private visits welcome April to Sept, please* **Tel 01305 871685**

Broadlands ♿✿❀ (Mr & Mrs M J Smith) Hazelbury Bryan. 4m S of Sturminster Newton. From A357 Blandford to Sherborne rd, take turning signed Hazelbury Bryan, garden ½m beyond Antelope public house. An outstanding 2-acre plantsman's garden begun in 1975, designed to give beautiful views at every turn. Woodland, water, courtyard, rose and cottage gardens, mixed beds by colour theme etc contain a remarkable range of the choicest trees, shrubs, perennials, bulbs and alpines to give interest and beauty of foliage and flower at all seasons. TEA. *Adm £1.70 Acc chd free. Sun May 7, every Weds May, June, July and Aug (2-5.30) (Share to NGS). For NGS Sun April 2, Mon Apr 17 (2-5.30) (Share to Dorset Wildlife Trust®).* **Tel 01258 817374**

Cartref ✿❀ (Nesta Ann Smith) Station Rd, Stalbridge. From A30, S at Henstridge for 1m. Turn L opp Stalbridge PO, House 80yds on R. Free car park nearby. A plantsman's garden approx ¼-acre, cottage garden and unusual plants. Small woodland area with choice shade-loving plants. Small potager, organically grown. Plants for sale. TEA. *Adm £1.50 Chd free. Tues (2-6), Fris (10-6) April to Oct 31. For NGS Suns April 16, May 21, Sept 17 (10-5).* **Tel 01963 363705**

Charlton Cottage ♿ (The Hon Penelope Piercy) Tarrant Rushton. 3m SE of Blandford Forum B3082. Fork L top of hill out of Blandford, R at T-junction, first L to Tarrant Rushton, R in village to last thatched cottage on L of st. Garden on both sides st. Herbaceous borders, shrubs, water garden, views of Tarrant valley. *Adm £1.50 (Share to Church of England Childrens Society®). Suns May 7, June 18 (2-6)*

¶**Chedington Court** (Mr & Mrs J P H Chapman) Chedington, Beaminster. 4½m SE of Crewkerne off the A356. Turn at Winyard's Gap Inn, or 4½m NE from Beaminster via A3066. Turn R past Admiral Hood Inn in Mosterton. 10 acres. Mature Victorian garden. Magnificent situation, extensive views. Interesting trees and shrubs. Herbaceous borders, water garden and grotto, giant yew topiary, wild flowers, spring bulbs, mixture of the well-tended and the wild. *Adm £2 Chd 50p. Weds May 3, Sept 6 (11-4.30)*

¶**Cherry Tree Cottage** ♿✿❀ (Mrs T M Osborn) 133 Merley Ways. Take the A349 out of Wimborne towards Poole. Having crossed the river bridge take 1st R and R again into Merley Ways. A ¾-acre garden in tranquil setting half a mile from the centre of Wimborne; having extensive views of the Dorset countryside, ancient bridge and water meadows, with steps leading down to R Stour. Unusual shrubs, secret rose garden, with pineapple scented Moroccan broom. TEA. *Adm £1 Acc chd free. Sun July 2 (2-6)*

Chiffchaffs ✿❀ (Mr & Mrs K R Potts) Chaffeymoor. Leave A303 (Bourton by pass) at junction signposted Gillingham, Blandford and Bourton at W end of Bourton village. A garden for all seasons with many interesting plants, bulbs, shrubs, herbaceous border, shrub roses. Attractive walk to woodland garden with far-reaching views across the Blackmore Vale. Shown on TSW 'Gardens for All' October 92, also in Gardeners World magazine. Nursery open Tues-Sat and on garden open days. TEAS last Sun and Bank Hol weekends. *Adm £1.50 Chd 20p (Share to St Michael's Church, Penselwood®). Open every Sun and Bank Holiday weekend, Weds & Thurs (except for 2nd Sun every month) March 26 to Sept 24. For NGS last Sunday of each month and Suns of Bank Holiday weekends plus 10% of all receipts (2-5.30). Tea/Coffee by arrangement* **Tel 01747 840841**

7 Church Street ♿✿❀ (Ann & Gordon Powell) Upwey, nr Weymouth. ½m from bottom of Ridgeway Hill on A354 Dorchester–Weymouth rd turn R B3159 (Bridport rd) L turn at bottom of hill. Limited parking for disabled only. 3 acres of mixed planting. Main trees planted 1972 with recent additions of shrubs and perennials. Woodland planted early 50's. Teas at Wishing Well. *Adm £1 Chd free. Suns June 4, July 2, 30; Aug 27; Tues June 6, July 4, Aug 1, Mon Aug 28 (2-6)*

The Cobbles ✂❀ (Mr & Mrs A P Baker) Shillingstone. 5m NW of Blandford. In middle of village opp Old Ox Inn, Shillingstone. Plantsman's 1½-acre chalk garden round C17 cottage. Borders thickly planted with a mixture of shrubs, herbs, wild flowers, old roses, foliage plants and perennials incl many hardy geraniums. Small lake, stream and ditch garden. TEAS in aid of Shillingstone Parish Church. *Adm £1 Chd free. Suns June 25, July 2 (2.30-5.30)*

● **Compton Acres Gardens** ♿✂❀ Canford Cliffs Road, Poole. Sign from Bournemouth and Poole. Wilts & Dorset Buses 147, 150, 151. Yellow Buses nos 11 & 12 stop at entrance. Reputed to be the finest gardens in Europe incl Japanese, Italian, Rock and Water, Heather Dell, Woodland Walk and Sub-Tropical Glen. Magnificent bronze and marble statuary. Large selection of plants and stoneware garden ornaments. Refreshments available. Large free car/coach park. *Adm £3.70 Chd £1. March 1 to Oct 31 daily. 10.30-6.30 last admission 5.45pm.* **Tel 01202 700778**

Corfe Barn ✂❀ (John & Kathleen McDavid) Corfe Lodge Rd, Broadstone. From main roundabout in Broadstone W along Clarendon Rd, ¾m N into Roman Rd, after 50yds W into Corfe Lodge Rd. ⅔ acre on three levels on site of C19 lavender farm. Informal country garden with much to interest both gardeners and flower arrangers. Parts of the original farm have been incorporated in the design. A particular feature of the garden is the use made of old walls. TEAS. *Adm 50p Chd 25p. Suns April 23, May 14, June 11, July 2 (2-5)*

Cranborne Manor Gardens ♿✂❀ (The Viscount & Viscountess Cranborne) Cranborne. 10m N of Wimborne on B3078. Beautiful and historic gardens laid out in C17 by John Tradescant and enlarged in C20, featuring several gardens surrounded by walls and yew hedges: white garden, herb and mount gardens, water and wild garden. Many interesting plants, with fine trees and avenues. *Adm £2.50 OAPs £2 (Share to Cranborne Recreation Ground Play Area©). Weds March to Sept incl (9-5). For NGS Wed April 12, Sat June 10 (9-5)*

2 Curlew Road ♿✂❀ (Mr & Mrs Gerald Alford) Strouden Park, Bournemouth. From Castle Lane West turn S into East Way, thence E into Curlew Rd. Small town garden 200′ × 30′ divided into rooms and linked by arches. Conifers, acers, rhododendrons, clematis; spring and summer bedding; three water features. Winner of Bournemouth in Bloom Spring Competition 1993; Best Council Garden 1992–1993; Joint winners of Bournemouth in Bloom Summer Competition 1993. The owners are seriously disabled and their garden is thus of especial interest to other disabled people. *Adm £1 Chd 30p. Suns May 21, July 16 (2-6). Private visits welcome of 2 or more please* **Tel 01202 512627**

Deans Court ♿✂❀ (Sir Michael & Lady Hanham) Wimborne. Just off B3073 in centre of Wimborne. 13 acres; partly wild garden; water, specimen trees, free roaming peacocks. House (open by written appt) originally the Deanery to the Minster. Herb garden with about 150 species chemical free plants for sale. Walled vegetable garden with chemical free produce for sale as available. Free car parking. Morning coffee/TEAS. *Adm £1.50 Chd 70p. Except during Sculpture Exhibition Adm £2 Chd/Students and groups of 15 or more £1.50 incl catalogue. Daffodil weekends with teas Sat, Sun March 18, 19, 25, 26 (2-5). Easter Sun (2-6) Bank Hol Mons (10-6). Last Sun in April, May, July, Aug, Sept and Oct 1 (2-6). Sculpture in the Garden Exhibition June 13-July 3 (10.30-6). For NGS Suns May 28, Oct 1 (2-6)*

Domineys Yard ♿✂ (Mr & Mrs W Gueterbock) Buckland Newton, 11m from Dorchester and Sherborne 2m E of A352 or take B3143 from Sturminster Newton. Take 'no through rd' between church and 'Gaggle of Geese' public house next to phone box. Entrance 200 metres on L. Park in lane or in field if available. 2½-acre garden on chalk, clay and green sand surrounding C17 thatched cottage with adjacent terraced cottages and gardens, with large kitchen garden and lawn tennis court. Developed over 34 years with unusual plants, shrubs and trees incl camellias, clematis, roses, lilies and other bulbs, spring and autumn colour making it a garden for all seasons. Heated swimming pool available for summer openings. TEAS. *Combined adm with* **Bladeley House** *£2 Chd 50p (Share to Leonard Cheshire Foundation West Dorset Care at Home Service®). Suns April 23, July 9, Aug 13 (2-6), also private visits welcome, parties of 4 and over, please* **Tel 01300 345295**

Edgeways ♿✂❀ (Mr & Mrs Gerald Andrew) 4 Greenwood Ave, Poole. From Lilliput Rd nr Compton Acres turn N into Compton Ave, W into Fairway Rd, thence L into Greenwood Ave. Please do not park by roundabout of cul-de-sac. Delightful ⅓-acre garden designed informally on a gentle slope in a setting of mature trees. Extensive range of choice perennials grouped for colour and foliage effect to provide a succession of seasonal pictures. Mixed and herbaceous borders, lawn, grass paths, arbour and a pond reaching into a steep rock area contibute to a variety of interesting vistas. Several seats. 'Lots to admire and inspire.' Dorset Garden Guide. Shown on ITV's Grass Roots. TEA. *Adm 80p Acc chd free. Suns May 28, June 18, July 2, 16, Aug 6 (11.30-5.30). Private parties welcome, please* **Tel 01202 707074**

Edmondsham House ♿✂❀ (Mrs Julia Smith) Edmondsham, nr Cranborne. B3081, turn at Sixpenny Handley Xrds to Ringwood and Cranborne; thereafter follow signs to Edmondsham. Large garden; spring bulbs, trees, shrubs; walled garden with herbaceous border; vegetables and fruit; grass cockpit. Early church nearby. TEAS Easter Mon, TEA Weds. *Adm £1 Chd 50p under 5 free (Share to PRAMA®). Mon April 17, Weds April 5, 12, 19, 26; Oct 4, 11, 18, 25 (2-5); also private visits and parties welcome, please* **Tel 01725 517207**

Eurocentre Language School ♿✂ (Eurocentres (UK)) 22-28 Dean Park Rd, Bournemouth. Off Wimborne Rd (A347) ¼m N of Richmond Hill roundabout. Series of 4 linked gardens, now being restored to reflect the original surroundings of the late Victorian houses. Mature specimen trees and lawns; rhododendrons, small trees and flowering shrubs; spring and summer bedding, climbers, dahlia borders and small fernery. TEA. *Adm 70p Chd 30p (Share to Bournemouth General Hospital Scanner Appeal®). Suns May 7, Sept 10 (2.30-5)*

Farriers ♿❀ (Mr & Mrs P S Eady) 16 The Moor. On the A354 Puddletown-Blandford rd opp the rd to Piddlehinton, close to the Blue Vinney public house, Dorchester 5m. ⅓-acre informal country garden with much to interest gardeners and flower arrangers, designed and maintained by owners; shrubs, herbaceous, dahlias, sweet peas, vegetable plot, greenhouse with collection of begonias and streptocarpus, pond. TEAS. *Joint opening with* **4 Flower Cottage** *on June 6. Adm £1 each garden Chd free. Suns June 4, July 2, Aug 6 (2-5.30)*

Fernhill Cottage ✲❀ (Miss Shirley Forwood) Witchampton. Next to Fernhill House, directions as below. Small thatched cottage garden, interesting perennials, pulmonarias, old roses and cottage plants. *Joint opening with* **Fernhill House.** *Combined adm £1.50, Chd free (Share to Dorset Hospice and Respite Trust®). Suns April 9, May 14, June 18 (2-5). Also Adm 50p Chd free (Share to Witchampton Village Hall©). Sun Sept 10 (2-5)*

Fernhill House ♿✲❀ (Mrs Henry Hildyard) Witchampton. 3½m E of Wimborne B3078 L to Witchampton then L up Lower St. (Blandford rd,) house on R 200yds. Spring bulbs and blossom, roses and herbaceous borders, woodland walk with water garden and shrubs. Teas in Village Hall, June 18. *Joint opening with* **Fernhill Cottage**. *Combined adm £1.50 Chd free (Share to Dorset Hospice and Respite Trust®). Suns April 9, May 14, June 18 (2-5)*

¶4 Flower Cottage ♿✲❀ (Audrey Penniston) Lower Waterston. From Puddletown on the B3142 take the rd between Blue Vinney public house and Old's Garage on way to Piddletrenthide. ⅓-acre cottage garden, with herbaceous borders, scree and vegetables. TEAS. *Joint opening with* **Farriers** *Adm £1 (each garden) Chd free. Sun June 4 (2-6)*

● Forde Abbey ♿❀ (M Roper Esq) 4m SE of Chard. 7m W of Crewkerne; well signed off A30. 'Christies Garden of the Year 1993'. 30 acres; many fine shrubs and some magnificent specimen trees incl post-war arboretum; herbaceous borders, rock and kitchen gardens; in bog garden one of larger collections Asiatic primulas in SW. Refreshments 11-4.30 during summer. *Adm £3.25 OAPs £2.75 Chd under 15 and wheelchairs free. Open daily all year (10-4.30)*

Frankham Farm ♿✲❀ (Mr & Mrs R G Earle) Ryme Intrinseca. A37 Yeovil-Dorchester; 3m S of Yeovil turn E at Xrds with garage; drive ¼m on L. 2 acres started in 1960s; Plantsman's garden with shrubs, trees, spring bulbs, clematis, roses, vegetables & fruit; extensive wall planting. Recently planted unusual hardwoods. TEAS in aid of Ryme Church. *Adm £1.50 Chd free. Suns April 9, 30, June 18 (2-5.30)*

Friars Way ✲❀ (Les & Christina Scott) 190 Church Street, Upwey. Twixt Weymouth and Dorchester on B3159, Martinstown Rd. C17 thatched cottage is opp church car park. ¾ acre steeply sloping, S facing site. Terraces, lawns and woodland area. On-going development of cottage garden. Many unusual plants. TEAS. *Adm £1 Chd free. Suns May 14, 28, June 18, Wed June 21 (2-5.30). Private visits and parties welcome, please* **Tel 01305 813243**

Frith House ♿❀ (Urban Stephenson Esq) Stalbridge. Between Milborne Port & Stalbridge, 1m S of A30. Turn W nr PO in Stalbridge. 4 acres; self-contained hamlet: lawns; 2 small lakes; woodland walks. Terrace in front of Edwardian house, mature cedars; flower borders, excellent kitchen garden. TEAS. *Adm £1.50 Chd free. Suns April 2, June 4, Aug 6 (2-6). Groups welcome by appt, please* **Tel 01963 250 232**

Glebe House ♿❀ (Mr & Mrs J G Thompson) East Lulworth. 4m S of Wool 6m W of Wareham. Take Coombe Keynes Rd to East Lulworth. Glebe House just to E of Weld Arms and War Memorial. Shrub garden with lawns; walks and terrace, 2 acres with interesting and varied planting. TEAS. *Adm £1 Chd free (Share to Wool & Bovington Cancer Relief®). Sun May 14, Wed May 17 (2-6)*

2 Greenwood Avenue ❀ (Mr & Mrs P D Stogden) Ferndown. Off Woodside Rd which is between Ringwood Rd (A348) and Wimborne Rd (C50 ex-A31), E of town centre. ⅓-acre designed and maintained by owners. An interesting and informal garden, with accent on herbaceous plants; many rare and unusual. Hostas, sempervivums and plants for flower arranging are a special interest of the owners. Soft fruits and vegetable garden. Arbour and pergola. Dogs must be kept on leads. TEAS. *Adm £1 Acc chd free. Suns June 11, 25; July 9, 16 (11-5)*

¶Hambledon Cottage ♿✲ (Mr & Mrs D W Schwier) Child Okeford. 6m W of Blandford Forum take L turn at sign for Child Okeford. Drive through village and take the R fork after passing the church. This is Shaftesbury Rd. Hambledon Cottage is ¼m on the L. It is white with a red brick wall surmounted by a white picket fence. The garden was started in Oct 89 and nearly 2 acres of docks and thistles have been transformed into a series of rooms. These rooms contain 700 old English roses and modern roses, sweet pea walks, fishponds, lawns, shrubs, perennials and annuals. The garden is bounded on three sides by an ancient nut hedge and uses Hambledon Hill as a natural backdrop. *Adm £1.50 Chd free. Sun June 18 (2-6)*

Heatherwood ✲❀ (Mr & Mrs Ronald Squires) 1m S of Wimborne. Leave A349 Wimborne-Poole rd at Merley Bridge, signed Ashington, into Merley Park Rd. Thence garden is ¾m on L. ½-acre garden created by present owners from original woodland. Main theme of the garden is heathers (800 in 50 varieties), conifers (300 in 30 varieties), azaleas and acers. Large lawn with ornamental pool and rockery. Featured on TVs 'That's Gardening'. Large car park at adjacent nursery. *Collection box. Daily except Dec 24 to Jan 1 (9-5, Suns 9.30-12)*

High Hollow ✲❀ (Paul & Valerie Guppy) 15 Chapel Close, Corfe Mullen. From Wareham Rd W end of village at Naked Cross turn N into Waterloo Rd; after 1m turn E into Chapel Lane. Please park nearby and not in Chapel Close. Beautiful and colourful exotic garden of ¼ acre surrounding bungalow, full of spiky and unusual plants from many countries. Herbaceous border, ferns and roses. The use of water is a special feature. TEAS. *Adm 50p Chd 25p (Share to the Cats Protection League®). Suns June 11, July 2, 30, Aug 20 (2-5)*

Highbury ♿✂❀ (Stanley Cherry Esq) West Moors, 8m N of Bournemouth. In Woodside Rd, off B3072 Bournemouth-Verwood rd; last rd at N end of West Moors village. Garden of ½ acre in mature setting surrounding interesting Edwardian house (1909 listed). Many rare and unusual plants and shrubs; herb borders; botanical & horticultural interest for gardeners & plantsmen, with everything labelled. Weather station. Seen on T.V. Featured in detail in Blue Guide Gardens of England. TEAS in orchard when fine. *House and garden, organised parties Adm £1 (incl TEA); Otherwise by appt. Garden only 75p (2-6). April to Sept* **Tel 01202 874372**

Higher Melcombe (Lt Col and Mrs J M Woodhouse) Melcombe Bingham. 11m N of Dorchester. From Puddletown A354 to Blandford. After ½m take turning L (after inn). Follow signs to Cheselbourne then to Melcombe. At Xrds in Melcombe Bingham follow signpost 'Private rd to Higher Melcombe'. 1½-acre garden, many annuals. Fine views and setting outside Elizabethan house and chapel. Parking adjoining field. TEAS in chapel. *Adm £1 Chd free (Share to the Old Brewery Hall, Ansty©). Sun July 23 (2-5.30). Parties by appt in June, please* **Tel 01258 880251**

7 Highfield Close ✂❀ (Mr & Mrs Malcolm Bright) Corfe Mullen. From Wareham Rd turn E in Hanham Rd, thence ahead into Highfield Close. Colourful ⅓-acre summer garden designed and made by owners over 15yrs. Bedding plants, fuchsias and pelargoniums interplanted with shrubs; fish pond and ornamental pool. Much to interest gardeners in a small area. TEAS. *Adm 50p Chd 25p. Suns July 30, Aug 6 (2-5)*

Highwood Garden ✂ (H W Drax Esq) Charborough Park, Wareham, 6m E of Bere Regis. Enter park by any lodge on A31; follow signpost to Estate Office, then Highwood Garden. Large garden with rhododendrons and azaleas in woodland setting. TEAS. *Adm £1.50 Chd 50p (7-16 yrs) (Share to Red Post Parish©). Suns May 21, 28 (2.30-6)*

Hilltop Cottage ✂❀ (Mr & Mrs Emerson) approx 5m N Sturminster Newton on B3092 turn R at Stour Provost Xrds, signed Woodville. After 1¼m a thatched cottage on the RH-side. Parking in lane outside. Old cottage garden with a wealth of different and interesting perennials. Very colourful. An inspiration to those with smaller gardens. Includes a small nursery. TEAS. *Adm 50p Chd free. Weds May 10, July 26, Aug 16; Suns May 14, July 23, 30, Aug 20 (2-6)*

Holworth Farmhouse ✂❀ (Anthony & Philippa Bush) Holworth. 7m E of Dorchester, 1m S of A352. Follow signs to Holworth up the hill, through the farmyard, past duck pond on R. After 300yds turn L to the farmhouse. 3 acres of garden surrounding C16 grade II farmhouse on side of hill with lovely views. Main planting from 1980; considerable use of hedges as protection from exposed windy conditions; partially walled garden terraced and replanted in 1990 with a wide variety of herbaceous plants, shrubs and old roses. Also small wood, orchard, vegetable garden and recently excavated pond. Home-made TEAS in aid of Joseph Weld Hospice & 'Fight for Sight'. *Adm £1.50 Chd free. Suns June 25, July 9 (2-7)*

Horn Park ✂❀ (Mr & Mrs John Kirkpatrick) Beaminster. On A3066 1½m N of Beaminster on L before tunnel. Ample parking, toilet. Large garden; magnificent view to sea; listed house built by pupil of Lutyens in 1910 (not open). Worth visiting at all seasons, many rare and unusual plants and shrubs in terraced, herbaceous, rock and water gardens; rhododendrons, camellias and pieris; separate woodland garden. In spring, walk in bluebell woods by ponds; wild flowers and orchids in summer. Teas at Beaminster & Craft Centre, Broadwindsor. *Adm £2.50 Chd free. Open every Tues, Weds, Suns, also Bank Hol Mons April to Oct 1st. For NGS Sun April 16, Bank Hol Mon May 29 (2-6)* **Tel 01308 862212**

Hyde Farm ✂ (Major & Mrs K Hubbard) Frampton. 5½m NW of Dorchester on A356 to Crewkerne. 500yds W of Frampton. 1¼m E of Maiden Newton on S side of rd. ¾-acre chalk garden, sloping to R Frome; courtyard; terrace, summer house garden; conservatory, good plants, shrub roses. 250yds river walk with wild flower area leading to bird watching hide, over footbridge and water meadow to 2½-acre woodland and pond area with hide. Ample car park in field. Picnic area. TEAS. *Adm £1.50 Acc chd 30p. Sun June 18 (11-5)*

Ivy Cottage ✂❀ (Anne & Alan Stevens) Aller Lane, Ansty, 12m N of Dorchester. A354 from Puddletown to Blandford; After pub take 1st L down Long Lane signed Dewlish-Cheselbourne, through Cheselbourne to Ansty then 1st R before Fox Inn, down Aller Lane. 1½-acre excellent plantsman's garden specialising in unusual perennials, moisture-loving plants; specimen trees and shrubs; well laid out vegetable garden. Featured in the book 'The New Englishwoman's Garden'. Meridian TV 'Grass Roots' 1994. TEAS Suns only. *Combined adm with* **Aller Green** *£2.50 Chd 50p. Also every Thurs April to Oct incl (10-5). For NGS Sun April 9 (Share to R.N.L.I®); Sun May 21 (Share to Samaritans®); Sun Aug 27 (Share to Blandford Museum®); Sun Sept 24 (Share to Red Cross®) (2-5.30).* **Tel 01258 880053**

Kesworth (H J S Clark Esq) 1½m N of Wareham. Turn off A351 almost opp school at Sandford, down Keysworth Drive to level Xing. Grounds incl 600-acre wildlife sanctuary at W end of Poole Harbour suitable for picnics, birdwatching, walks through unspoilt woods and marshes amongst fine wild scenery; herd of Galloway cattle. Elegant and colourful small garden round house. Tea Wareham. *Adm £1 Chd free (Share to Sandford Church®). Suns May 14, 21 (12.30-7). Last adm 5.30 pm*

Kingston Lacy ♿✂ (The National Trust) 1½m W of Wimborne Minster on the Wimborne-Blandford rd B3082. The setting landscaped in the C18, to W J Bankes's Kingston Lacy House. Magnificent trees planted over 175 years by Royal and famous visitors; avenue of limes and cedars; 9 acres of lawn; Dutch garden; sunken garden laid out to 1906 plans. TEAS and lunches. *Adm House & Garden £5.50, Gardens £2.20, Chd half price. For NGS Sun June 4 (12-6)*

By Appointment Gardens. See head of county section

Kingston Maurward ♿✲❀ A delightful Edwardian garden set in a C18 landscape. E of Dorchester turning off the roundabout at end of Dorchester by-pass A35. Bus alight Stinsford ¼m. Enter grounds through the farm animal park. Kingston Maurward house is a classical Georgian mansion set in gardens laid out in the C18 incl a 5-acre lake and overlooks the Dorchester watermeadows. An extensive restoration programme is nearing completion in the Edwardian gardens which are divided by hedges and stone balustrading. Each intimate garden contains a wealth of interesting plants and stone features, including the National Collection of salvias and penstemons. In addition an original Elizabethan walled garden is laid out as a demonstration of plants suitable for Dorset. Restaurant, full menu. *Adm £2.50 Chd £1.50. Open Easter to mid-Oct. For NGS Thurs May 18, July 13 (10-6).* **Tel 01305 264 738** *(Mike Hancock)*

Knitson Old Farmhouse ✲❀ (Rachel & Mark Helfer) Knitson. Signposted L off A351 Knitson is approx 1m W of Swanage 3m E of Corfe Castle. Ample parking in yard or in adjacent level field. Approx 1 acre of mature cottage garden. Herbaceous borders, rockeries, climbers, shrubs – many interesting cultivars. Large organic kitchen garden, orchard. TEAS in aid of F.A.R.M. Africa. *Adm £1 Chd 50p. Thurs April 20, May 25, July 20 (2-6). Private visits and parties welcome, please* **Tel 01929 422836**

●¶**Knoll Gardens** ♿✲❀ (Neil Lucas, Esq) Hampreston. 2½m W of Ferndown, ETB brown signs from A31. Gardens on a 6-acre site, now in 25th year. Wide collections of trees, shrubs and herbaceous plants, continually being expanded under new ownership. Water gardens with waterfalls, pools and streams; mixed borders and woodland setting. NCCPG collections of phygelius and ceanothus. Tea rooms and visitor centre, to which entry is free. Large car park. Many plants shown are available in adjacent nursery. TEAS. *Adm £3.45 OAP's £2.90 Students £2.40 Chd £1.70. Group rates on application. Daily, Easter to end Oct (10-5.30). Nov to Easter, Weds to Sats, reduced prices (10-4)*

¶**Lamorna** ✲❀ (Mr & Mrs R Hewitt) Chedington. 5m N of Beaminster. Off A356 Dorchester-Crewkerne rd at Winyards Gap Inn. Drive ½m into village, Lamorna is next to village hall on L, off layby. Nearby is a National Trust woodland walk and the Wessex Division memorial. Approx 1-acre garden in conservation village with extensive views over Axe valley and a backdrop of National Trust woodland. Mixture of the formal and informal with many shrubs and plants incl pond, bog garden, dry shade garden, pergola, banks and other features. TEAS. *Adm £1 Chd free. Weds May 3, Sept 6 with* **Chedington Court**. *Every Sats and Suns in June, July, Aug (11-5). Private visits welcome mid week, please* **Tel 01935 891410**

Langebride House ✲❀ (Mrs John Greener) Long Bredy. ½-way between Bridport and Dorchester, S off A35, well signed. Substantial old rectory garden with many designs for easier management. 200-yr-old beech trees, bi-colour beech hedge, pleached limes and yew hedges, extensive collections of spring bulbs, bulbarium, herbaceous plants, flowering trees and shrubs. Tea in aid of Joseph Weld House. *Adm £1 Chd free. Suns March 19, April 2 (2-5). Private visits welcome March to end July* **Tel 01308 482 257**

Little Platt ✲ (Sir Robert Williams) Plush, 9m N of Dorchester by B3143 to Piddletrenthide, then 1½m NE by rd signed Plush & Mappowder, 1st house on L entering Plush. 1-acre garden created from a wilderness since 1969; interesting collection of ornamental trees and flowering shrubs, incl several daphnes, spiraeas and viburnums; spring bulbs, hellebores, numerous hardy geraniums and unusual perennials. *Adm £1 Chd free. Private visits welcome March to Aug* **Tel 01300 348320**

Long Ash Cottage ♿✲❀ (Mr & Mrs A Case) Milton Abbas. 10m From Blandford-Dorchester on A354, 3m from Milbourne St Andrew on Ansty Rd not Milton Abbas rd. Private ½-acre cottage garden adjoining The Rare Poultry, Pig and Plant Centre, with many unusual and old-fashioned flowers. Also exhibition of paintings by botanical artist Susan Goodricke (June 18). *Adm 85p Chd 25p. Suns May 21 (11-2), June 18 (2-5.30)*

¶**Loscombe House** ✲ (Mr & Mrs Andrewes) Loscombe. N of Bridport. S of Beaminster. Approx 1½m E of A3066. One way traffic as signed from B3163 via Mapperton and A3066 at Melplash opp Half Moon public house. Leave Loscombe via West Milton and you are requested not to approach from this direction. 4-acre woodland garden in a hidden valley, trees and shrubs with herbaceous plants and old-fashioned roses planted on a hillside through which a stream flows and tumbles. *Combined adm with* **Pear Tree Farm** *£2. Open every weekend April to Oct (2-6). For NGS Thurs, Sun July 13, 16 (2-6)*

¶**Lower Ware** ✲ (Mr & Mrs J Bones) Ware Lane, Lyme Regis. Outskirts of Lyme Regis, off A3052 Sidmouth Rd. From the town E 2nd L after Holmbush Carpark; from W, app Lyme Regis, R at Xrds signposted to 'Ware'. Narrow lane, considerate parking please. Attractive 1-acre hillside garden overlooking Lyme Bay, mainly planted since 1989. Individual small gardens on three levels; mixed planting. TEAS. *Adm £1. Sun May 21 (2-6)*

1 Manor Close ♿ (Mr & Mrs W A Butcher) Stratton. 3m NW of Dorchester off A37 to Yeovil, turn into village gardens signed at church. ⅕-acre with alpine garden at front and to the rear a heather garden, perennials and vegetable garden. *Combined adm with* **Manor Orchard** *£1.50 Chd free. Suns, Weds, April 9, 12; June 18, 21 (2.30-5.30)*

Manor Orchard ♿❀ (Mr & Mrs G B David) Stratton. 3m NW of Dorchester off A37 to Yeovil, turn into village, gardens signed at church. 1-acre kitchen garden with fruit arch and topiary; lawns with spring bulbs, herbaceous and shrub borders; pond, roses and vine. Cream TEAS in aid of Stratton Village Hall & Church (Suns only). *Combined adm with* **1 Manor Close** *£1.50 Chd free. Suns, Weds, April 9, 12; June 18, 21 (2.30-5.30)*

Regular Openers. Too many days to include in diary. Usually there is a wide range of plants giving year-round interest. See head of county section for the name and garden description for times etc.

● **Mapperton Gardens** ♿✂❀ (Montagu Family) nr Beaminster. 6m N of Bridport off A35. 2m SE of Beaminster off B3163. Descending valley gardens beside one of Dorset's finest manor houses (C16-C17) House and garden listed Grade I. Gardens featured in Discovering Gardens TV series (1990-91). Magnificent walks and views. Fish ponds, orangery, formal Italian-style borders and topiary; specimen trees and shrubs; car park. Upper levels only suitable for wheelchairs. House open to group tours by appt **Tel 01308 862645**. *Adm garden £2.50 Chd £1.50, under 5 free. March to Oct daily (2-6)*

Melbury House ✂❀ 6m S of Yeovil. Signed on Dorchester-Yeovil rd. 13m N of Dorchester. Large garden; very fine arboretum; shrubs and lakeside walk; beautiful deer park. Garden only. TEAS. *Adm £2 OAPs/Chd £1 (Share to CRMF®). Thurs May 25, June 1, 15, 29; July 13, Aug 3 (2-5). Private visits welcome for parties of 15 min, please* **Tel 01935 83252** *(Richard Squires)*

Melplash Court ♿❀ (Mr & Mrs Timothy Lewis) Melplash. On the A3066 between Beaminster and Bridport, just N of Melplash. Turn W and enter between field gates next to big gates and long ave of chestnut trees. While the gardens as they exist today were originally designed by Lady Diana Tiarks they continue to evolve and consist of park planting, bog garden, croquet lawn and adjacent borders. Formal kitchen garden and herb garden, ponds, streams and lake; new borders and areas of interest are added and opened up each year. TEAS in aid of Melplash Church. *Adm £2 Chd free. Sun July 23 (2-6)*

¶**Mews Cottage** ✂❀ (Mr & Mrs P J Pitman) 34 Easton Street, Portland. Situated in the 1st village on the top of the Island of Portland, Mews Cottage is in the main street of Easton, some 50yds past the Punchbowl Inn on the L. Park in the main street, walk up the small unmade lane between the Vet and the cake shop, Mews Cottage is at R angles to the lane and well marked. The garden is laid out in the cottage style, with a pond and a good mix of herbaceous plants and unusual shrubs, particularly in Spring a good collection of hellebore and spring bulbs. In the summer some 140 named varieties of Penstemon (incl many alpine varieties), a large crinodendron hookerianum and callestemon. Autumn colour is achieved with a large collection of nerine bowdenii in various shades of pink. TEAS in aid of St Georges Church. *Adm £1 Chd free. Suns March 12, June 18, July 16, Aug 20, Sept 24, Oct 1 (2-5)*

26 Milestone Road ✂❀ (Mr & Mrs P M Fraser) Oakdale. At Oakdale, Poole traffic lights on Wimborne Rd, turn S into Vicarage Rd then 1st L into Milestone Rd. ¼-acre town garden, divided into three rooms. Features include ornamental ponds and waterfall, pergola with roses and other climbing plants, natural wooded area with wild flowers and ferns and many interesting shrubs. TEAS. *Adm 75p Chd 25p. Suns June 11, July 9, Wed June 28 (1-5)*

● **Minterne** (The Lord Digby) Minterne Magna. On A352 Dorchester-Sherborne rd. 2m N Cerne Abbas; woodland garden set in a valley landscaped in the C18 with small lakes, cascades and rare trees; many species and hybrid rhododendrons and magnolias tower over streams and water plants. *Adm £2 Acc chd and parking free. Open daily April 1 to Oct 31 (10-7)*

Moigne Combe (Maj-Gen H M G Bond) 6m E of Dorchester. 1½m N of Owermoigne turn off A352 Dorchester-Wareham Rd. Medium-sized garden; wild garden and shrubbery; heathers, azaleas, rhododendrons etc; woodland paths and lake walk. Tea Wyevale Garden Centre, Owermoigne. *Adm £1. 1st chd 25p thereafter 10p. Suns May 21, 28 (2-5.30)*

Moulin Huet ♿✂❀ (Harold Judd Esq) 15 Heatherdown Rd, West Moors. 7m N of Bournemouth. Leave A31 at West Moors Garage into Pinehurst Rd, take 1st R into Uplands Rd, then 3rd L into Heatherdown Rd. thence into cul-de-sac. ⅓-acre garden made by owner from virgin heathland after retirement. Considerable botanical interest; collections of 90 dwarf conifers and bonsai; many rare plants and shrubs; alpines, sink gardens, rockeries, wood sculpture. Featured on TV 'Gardeners World' 1982. Garden News Gardener of the Year Award 1984. *Adm 75p Chd free. Private visits and parties welcome, please* **Tel 01202 875760**. *Also 2 days in May locally advertised*

North Leigh House ❀ (Mr & Mrs Stanley Walker) Colehill, 1m NE of Wimborne. Leave B3073 (formerly A31) nr Sir Winston Churchill public house into North Leigh Lane, thence ¾m. 5 acres of informal parkland with fine trees, small lake, rhododendrons; ornamental shrubs; specimen magnolia grandiflora and Green Brunswick fig; colony of orchis morio and naturalised spring bulbs in lawns; Victorian features include balustraded terrace, fountain pool, walled garden and superb conservatory, all being restored and maintained by owners. Dogs on leads welcome. Suitable wheelchairs in parts. NCCPG plant stalls May. Teas in Bothy Cottage. *Adm £1 Chd 20p (Share to Animal Aid®, May; Bournemouth & District Animal Ambulance Service© July). Suns April 30, July 30 (2-6)*

Oakmead ♿ (Mr & Mrs P D Priest) Mosterton. On A3066 N of Beaminster in centre of village. Roadside parking. ⅔-acre 'all seasons' garden. The skilful design incorporates traditional herbaceous border, fine heather bed, azaleas, camellias, shrub rose border, modern roses with lawns and gravel beds. Its bold sweeps of colour, interesting trees, shrubs and unusual plants make it 'a model of modern gardening' (Anna Pavord in The Independent) and 'should be high on anyone's visiting list' (The Dorset Garden Guide). *Private visits welcome, please* **Tel 01308 868466**

The Old Mill ♿❀ (The Rev & Mrs J Hamilton-Brown) Spetisbury, Spetisbury Village opposite school on A350 3m SE of Blandford. 2 acres mainly water garden by R Stour; rockery; choice trees and plants. TEAS in aid of Spetisbury Church. *Adm £2 Chd free. Every Wed May to Aug (2-5). For NGS Suns June 11, July 16* **Tel 01258 453939**

The Old Rectory, Fifehead Magdalen ♿❀ (Mrs Patricia Lidsey) 5m S of Gillingham just S of the A30. Small garden with interesting shrubs and perennials; pond; plant stall. *Adm 80p Chd free. Sun June 11 (2-6) also private visits welcome, please* **Tel 01258 820293**

The Old Rectory, Litton Cheney ❀ (Mr & Mrs Hugh Lindsay) 1m S of A35, 10m Dorchester. 6m Bridport. Limited parking for infirm and elderly, otherwise park in centre of village and follow signs. Greatly varied garden with small walled garden recently redesigned; 4 acres beautiful natural woodland on steep slope with streams and ponds, primulas, native plants; wild flower lawn; (stout shoes recommended). TEAS in aid of Red Cross and other charities. *Adm £1.50 Chd 20p. Easter Sun April 16; Suns May 21, Sept 24 (2-6). Private visits welcome April to June, please* **Tel 01308 482383**

The Old Rectory, Pulham ♿❀ (Rear Admiral Sir John and Lady Garnier) On B3143 turn E at Xrds in Pulham. 13m N of Dorchester. Sherborne and Sturminster Newton both 8m. 3 acres with mature trees and shrubs; herbaceous borders, shrub roses, clematis, exuberantly planted terrace, pots, lawns, hedges and beautiful view towards Bulbarrow. 2 ponds and recently planted 4½-acre wood with shrubs and mown rides. TEAS. *Adm £1.50 Chd free. Wed July 12, Suns July 16, Aug 20 (2-6). Parties welcome, please* **Tel 01258 817595**

Old Rectory, Seaborough ❀ (Mr & Mrs C W Wright) 3m S of Crewkerne. Take B3165, after derestriction sign 2nd L, ¾m 1st R, then after 2½m 2nd L in village. 2-acre garden constructed since 1967; splendid views; rare trees, conifers, magnolias, flowering shrubs, roses, Himalayan plants, bulbs throughout the year, ferns; over 1000 species and cultivars. TEAS in aid of Church. *Adm £1 Chd 20p. Sun April 23 (2-6); also private visits welcome all year, please* **Tel 01308 868426**

The Old Vicarage, Stinsford ♿✲❀ (Mr & Mrs Antony Longland) Off roundabout at E end of Dorchester bypass A35. Follow signs for Stinsford Church 400yds. Use church car park. 1¼ acres incl an Italianate garden, herbaceous and mixed borders with unusual plants and shrubs, nearly 200 roses, lawns, terraces with exuberant pots, and fruit. Thomas Hardy, C Day Lewis and Cecil Hanbury, creator of gardens at La Mortola and Kingston Maurward, commemorated in church next door. TEAS. *Adm £1.50 Chd 50p. Sun June 18 (2-6). Private visits welcome for parties of 4 and more, please* **Tel 01305 265 827**

The Orchard ✲❀ (Mr & Mrs K S Ferguson) Blynfield Gate. 2m W of Shaftesbury on the rd to Stour Row. From Shaftesbury take the B3091 to St James's Church then onto the Stour Row rd. A 3-acre country garden, orchard and native flower and grass meadow on SE slope of Duncliffe Hill developed by the owners since 1981. Lawns, paths and grass walks link formal, informal and wild areas. Numerous colourful mixed borders and island beds are stocked with a wide variety of plants, several chosen for their intermingling qualities and lengthy flowering period. Hedgebanks of hardy geraniums, interesting trees and shrubs, small natural pond and plenty of seats. Home-made TEAS. *Adm £1.50 to incl descriptive guide Chd free (Share to Red Cross®). Weds June 7, 14, 21, 28; July 12, 19 (2-6)*

● **Parnham** ♿ (Mr & Mrs John Makepeace) ½m S of Beaminster on A3066, 5m N of Bridport. 14 acres extensively reconstructed early this century; much variety of form and interest, topiary; terraces; gazebos; spring fed water rills; small lake; fine old trees; grand herbaceous borders featured in Discovering Gardens (1990/91). Old roses in formal front courtyard; riverside walk and woodland; many unusual plants. House (Grade 1 listed, dating from 1540) exhibitions of contemporary craftsmanship, also John Makepeace furniture workshops. Restaurant, coffee, lunches. TEAS. *Adm to whole site £4 Chd 10-15 £2 under 10 free. April 1 to Oct 30 every Sun, Wed & Bank Hol incl. Good Friday (10-5).* **Tel 01308 862204**

¶**Pear Tree Farm** ✲ (Major & Mrs John Poe) Loscombe. N of Bridport. S of Beaminster. Approx 1½m E of A3066. One way traffic (narrow lanes) as signed from B3163 via Mapperton and A3066 at Melplash (opp Half Moon Public House). Leave Loscombe via West Milton. You are requested not to approach from this direction. ½ acre garden started in 1989 making best use of limited space with sub dividing into different areas. Wide and interesting variety of shrubs, herbaceous plants, shrub roses with wild flowers and bulbs in long grass area. Conservatory with exotic plants. New developments and plants added every year. *Combined adm with* **Loscombe House** *£2 Acc chd free. Thurs, Sun July 13, 16 (2-6)*

Portesham Gardens 7m W of Weymouth on coast rd, B3157 to Bridport. From Dorchester take A35 W, turn L in Winterborne Abbas and follow signs to Portesham; parking in village. TEAS at **Orchard House** in aid of Possum FEZ WIK. *Combined adm £1.50. Sun July 16 (2-6)*

Orchard House ♿❀ (Mr & Mrs F J Mentern) ⅓-acre walled cottage garden; organic and wild garden, ground cover, herbs; unusual old-fashioned perennials; rockeries and water garden; fruitful veg area, working greenhouses run as a small nursery open daily for charity. *Also private visits and parties welcome May to July, please* **Tel 01305 871611**

2 Winters Lane ✲❀ (Mr & Mrs K Draper) Portesham. Winters Lane is signposted in village to Coryates. ¼-acre garden with ponds and water features. Many ideas for smaller gardens such as small herb garden; container garden. 50 varieties of clematis, wishing well and miniature village; most plants labelled. *Private visits and parties welcome June and July, please* **Tel 01305 871316**

Portesham House ♿✲❀ (Mrs G J Romanes) Portesham. 7m W of Weymouth on coast rd, B3157 to Bridport. From Dorchester take A35 W, turn L in Winterborne Abbas and follow signs to Portesham; parking in village. Home of Admiral Sir Thomas Masterman Hardy with 300-yr-old mulberry tree; over an acre of family garden with excellent modern dry stone walling, old walls and stream. Paeonies and unusual trees and shrubs. Teas at Millmead Country Hotel. *Adm £1 Chd free. Suns June 4, 18 (2-6)*

The Priest's House Museum and Garden ✲❀ (The Priest's House Museum Trust) 23 High St, Wimborne. Public car parks nearby. Old 'borough plot' garden of ½ acre, at rear of local museum, in historic town house. Extending to mill stream and containing many unusual plants, trees and exhibits. Tea-room daily. *Adm £1.50 OAP/Students £1 Chd 50p. ▲Sun June 25 (2-5).* **Tel 01202 882533**

Pumphouse Cottage ❀ (Mr & Mrs R A Pugh) Mundens Lane. Alweston is 3m SE of Sherborne on A3030 to Blandford. Take L turning 50yds after PO marked Mundens Lane. 1st cottage on L. ½-acre cottage garden with erratic stream, collection of old roses, herbaceous borders, and spring bulbs. *Adm £1 Chd free. Suns, Mons May 7, 8, 28, 29; June 18, 25 (2-6). Private visits very welcome throughout the year, please* **Tel 01963 23535**

Rampisham Gardens ✲❀ Dorchester. 9m S of Yeovil take A37 to Dorchester. 7m turn R signed Evershot follow signs to Rampisham. 11m NW Dorchester take A37 to Yeovil, 4m turn L A356 signed Crewkerne; at start of wireless masts R to Rampisham. Small unspoilt village deep in rural Dorset with C14 church. Cream TEAS. Plant and cake stalls in aid of Church and Village Hall at Manor. *Combined adm £2.50 Chd free. Sun July 2 (2-6)*

Broomhill (Mr & Mrs D Parry) A family garden of 1 acre with trellised entrance leading to mixed borders and island beds with a great variety of plants. The lawns slope down to a large wild life pond

¶**Leigh Hill** (Mr & Mrs P Thomas) Approx ½-acre Countryman's garden using large local stones to form sculptured rockeries, a raised 'wild' pond complex and scented garden with fine views across an unspoilt valley

Rampisham Manor (Mr & Mrs Boileau) 2½ acres of spacious lawns, formal white rose beds, hedged walks, shrubs mixed with English roses and herbaceous planting. new pond and grasses bed. Ornamental kitchen garden. *Adm £1 Chd free. Also open Thurs April 27 (2-5)*

Red House Museum and Gardens ♿✲❀ (The Hampshire Museum Service) Quay Road, Christchurch. Tranquil setting in heart of town's conservation area. Gardens of ½ acre developed from early 1950's to complement Museum; plants of historic interest; herb garden with sunken lawn, south garden with lawns, herbaceous and woodland plants; old rose border. Gardens used as gallery display area for sculpture exhibitions. Admission to Museum and Art Gallery included. TEAS. *Adm £1 OAP/Chd 60p (under 5 free) (Share to the Mayor of Christchurch's Appeal of the Year©). ▲For NGS Wed June 14 (10-5)*

46 Roslin Road South ✲❀ (Dr & Mrs Malcolm Slade) Bournemouth. W of N end of Glenferness Ave in Talbot Woods area of Bournemouth. ⅓-acre walled town garden of yr-round interest with unusual plants in attractive settings. Features include rose pergola, 2 pools, sunken lawn, with many colourful and mature herbaceous and shrub plantings. Carefully tended fruit and vegetable garden. *Adm 60p Chd 20p. Suns May 14, 28, June 25, July 23 (1.30-5). Also private visits welcome from May to July, please* **Tel 01202 510243**

52 Rossmore Road ✲❀ (Mr & Mrs W E Ninniss) Parkstone, Poole. From A348 Poole-Ringwood rd turn SE into Rossmore Rd, thence ¼m. ⅓-acre interesting town garden designed in rooms; containing many rare and unusual plants; small knot garden; scree garden; herb garden. Featured on TVS 'That's Gardening' 1991. TEAS. *Adm 80p Chd 25p. Suns May 21, June 4 (2-6). Parties welcome, please* **Tel 01202 740913**

Slape Manor ♿❀ (Mr & Mrs Antony Hichens) Netherbury. 1m S of Beaminster turn W off A3066 to village of Netherbury. House ⅓m S of Netherbury on back road to Bridport. River valley garden – extensive lawns and lake. Azaleas, rhododendrons; specimen trees. TEAS in aid of Netherbury Village Hall. *Adm £1.50 Chd 50p under 5 free. Sun May 21 (2-6)*

Smedmore ♿❀ (Dr Philip Mansel) Kimmeridge, 7m S of Wareham. Turn W off A351 (Wareham-Swanage) at sign to Kimmeridge. 2 acres of colourful herbaceous borders; display of hydrangeas; interesting plants and shrubs; walled flower gardens; herb courtyard. *Adm £2 Chd £1. Sun May 21 (2.15-5.15). Private visits welcome, please* **Tel 01929 480 719** *(Mr T Gargett)*

Snape Cottage ✲❀ (Mr & Mrs I S Whinfield) Leave A303 (Bourton bypass) at junction signposted Gillingham, Blandford and Bourton. Garden at W end of Bourton village; lane signed Chaffeymoor. Opp Chiffchaffs. ½-acre plantsman's country garden full of old-fashioned and uncommon plants, most labelled. Beautiful views, wildlife pond. Plants and herbs for sale. Windsor chairmaker's workshop and pole-lathe on view. *Adm £1 Chd free. Every Wed April 5 to Sept 27 (closed Aug) (2-6). For NGS Suns April 16; May 7, 28; June 11; July 16, Sept 24.* **Tel 01747 840330** *(evenings only please)*

● **Stapehill Abbey** ✲❀ Wimborne Rd West, Ferndown. 2½m W of Ferndown on the old A31, towards Wimborne, ½m E of Canford Bottom roundabout. Early C19 Abbey, its gardens and estate restored and renovated to lawns, herbaceous borders; rose and water gardens; victorian cottage garden; lake and orchid house. Mature trees. Busy working Craft Centre; Countryside Museum featuring the National Tractor Collection, all under cover. Refreshments available in former refectory throughout the day. Licensed coffee shop. Large free car/coach park. *Adm £4.50 OAPs £4 Chd £2.50. Open daily April to Oct (10-5); Nov to Easter (10-4); except Mons and Easter. Closed Christmas Eve to Feb 1.* **Tel 01202 861686**

Star Cottage ✲❀ (Lys de Bray) 8 Roman Way, Cowgrove, Wimborne. Leave B3082 at Wimborne Hospital, along Cowgrove Rd for approx 1½m to Roman Way on R. Created in 1992 from a field, the garden is rapidly becoming another 'living library' of botanical artist and author Lys de Bray, lately of Turnpike Cottage, Wimborne. Visitors will have an opportunity of meeting Miss de Bray and seeing a specialised garden in the making. The owner is a RHS gold medallist whose botanical drawings and paintings are on permanent exhibition in her working studio which is open throughout the year at weekends and bank holidays. *Adm 75p Chd 40p. Garden and Studio open Sats and Suns all year. Easter to end Oct (2-6). End Oct to end March (2-4). For NGS Suns May 21, June 18 (2-6). Private visits and parties welcome, please* **Tel 01202 885130**

Regular Openers. Too many days to include in diary. Usually there is a wide range of plants giving year-round interest. See head of county section for the name and garden description for times etc.

Steeple Manor ♿✂❀ (Mr Julian & the Hon Mrs Cotterell) Steeple, 5m SW of Wareham in Isle of Purbeck. Take Swanage rd from Wareham, or bypass, R in Stoborough. A beautiful garden designed by Brenda Colvin 1920's round C16/17 Purbeck stone manor house (not open); lovely setting in folds of Purbeck hills in small hamlet of Steeple next to ancient church, specially decorated for the occasion. Approx 5 acres, the garden includes walls, hedges, enclosed gardens, ponds, stream, bog garden and meadow, collection old roses; many interesting and tender plants and shrubs for the plantsman. Parts garden suitable for wheelchairs. Free parking. Cream TEAS. *Adm £2.50 (to include written guide) OAPs £1.50 Chd under 16 free. Sun June 25 (1.30-6.30)*

Stepleton ♿✂❀ (Mr & Mrs Derek Coombs) Iwerne Stepleton. Stepleton House is situated 4m N of Blandford Forum on the A350. Approx 1m N of Stourpaine. Grade I park and garden on English Heritage register undergoing extensive restoration. 27 acres incl C18 lake, river walk and walled garden; rose pergola, interesting shrubs and perennials; the park was replanted in 1987 under the guidance of Alan Mitchell VMH. TEAS in aid of Action Research. *Adm £1.50 Chd 50p. Sat June 10 (2-5)*

Sticky Wicket ♿✂❀ (Peter & Pam Lewis) Buckland Newton. 11m from Dorchester and Sherborne. 2m E of A352 or take B3143 from Sturminster Newton. T-junction midway Church, School and Gaggle of Geese public house. 1½-acre garden created since 1987, unusual designs, well documented, showing wild life interest; fragrant cottage garden planting with many perennials and herbs. Features incl the Round Garden, a 'floral tapestry' of gently flowing colours, informal white garden. Featured on TV and in 'English Private Gardens' and other publications. TEAS. *Adm £1.50 Chd £1. Every Thurs June to Sept incl (10.30-8). For NGS Suns June 25, Aug 20 (2-6).* **Tel 01300 345476**

Stour House ♿✂❀ (T S B Card Esq) East St, Blandford. On 1-way system, 100yds short of market place. 2½-acre town garden, half on a romantic island in R Stour reached by a remarkable bridge; bulbs; borders well planted with perennials and many rare shrubs; river views. TEAS. *Adm 80p Chd 20p (Teas and share to Blandford Parish Church, July). Suns April 2 (2-5) July 9, Aug 13 (2-6)*

Studland Bay House ♿❀ (Mrs Pauline Ferguson) Studland. On B3351 5m E of Corfe Castle. Through village, entrance on R after Studland Bay House. Ample parking (no coaches). From Bournemouth, take Sandbanks ferry, 2½m, garden on L after Knoll House Hotel. 6-acre spring garden overlooking Studland Bay. Planted in 1930's on heathland; magnificent rhododendrons, azalea walk, camellias, magnolias, ferns and stream; recent drainage and replanting, garden suitable for wheelchairs. Cream TEAS in aid of Joseph Weld Hospice. *Adm £1.50 Chd free. Sat, Sun May 20, 21 (2-5)*

By Appointment Gardens. Avoid the crowds. Good chance of a tour by owner. See garden description for telephone number.

Sturminster Newton Gardens ♿✂ Off A357 between Blandford and Sherborne take turn opp Nat West Bank. Park in car park or behind Stourcastle Lodge. Walk down Penny St for **Ham Gate** and Goughs Close for **Stourcastle Lodge**. TEAS at **Ham Gate**. *Combined adm £1.50 Chd free. Sun May 21 (2-6). Parties by appt please,* **Tel 01258 472462** *or* **01258 472320**

Ham Gate (Mr & Mrs H E M Barnes) Informal 2-acre garden with shrubs, trees, lawns running down to R Stour, pleasant woodland views across water meadows, over the last few years Pam Lewis has helped redesign the garden

Stourcastle Lodge (Jill & Ken Hookham-Bassett) A S facing secluded cottage style garden, well stocked with herbaceous plants and shrubs with laid out vegetable garden

¶Tara ♿❀ (Mr & Mrs W H Adams) 66 Elmhurst Rd, West Moors. 7m N of Bournemouth. Leave A31 at West Moors Garage (Horizon Motors) into Pinehurst Rd and take 4th R into Elmhurst Rd. Carefully tended garden 130′ x 40′ lawns with island beds, formal pool, statuary features, ivy topiary and bonsai. Featured in Amateur Gardening and Garden News, the garden is also used in its advertising by an organic fertiliser manufacturer. Plants and Teas and other stall in aid of animal charities. *Adm 50p Chd 20p. Sun, Mon, May 28, 29; Sat, Sun July 8, 9 (10-4.30). Private visits welcome, please* **Tel 01202 877686**

Thistledown ♿✂❀ (Mr & Mrs E G Gillingham) Alweston 3m SE of Sherborne. From main A3030, turn into Mundens Lane by Oxfords Bakery. Garden 100yds along lane on R; park in drive/lane, 1-acre plant enthusiast's garden with views to Bulbarrow Hill; garden planted for yr-round interest with spring bulbs, rhododendrons, shrubs, herbaceous borders by colour theme, conifers, old-fashioned and modern roses, clematis, ornamental trees and ponds. *Adm £1 Chd free. Suns April 23, 30, May 7, 14, 21, June 25, July 2, 9, Sept 17, 24, Mons April 17, May 8, 29 (1.30-5)*

Three Bays ✂❀ (Mr & Mrs Christopher Garrett) 8, Old Wareham Rd, Beacon Hill, (nr Limberlost junction with A350) 1½m SW of Corfe Mullen. Garden of ½ acre made and maintained by owners. There is a Japanese flavour to the garden, with stone lanterns, dovecot and water features. Fuchsias are a special interest of the owners and there is a covered fuchsia garden. New rose garden 1993. Shrubs and herbaceous borders with much use of sloping site. TEAS. *Adm £1 Chd 50p (Share to Cancer Research Campaign®). Suns June 18, July 9, 16 (10-5). Illuminated garden Adm 50p Sat, Sun Aug 19, 20 (8.30-10.30). Private visits welcome for parties of 40 and over, please* **Tel 01202 623352**

Throop Mill Cottage (Dr & Mrs James Fisher) Throop Rd, Bournemouth. Turn N from Castle Lane (A3060) at Broadway public house. After ½m Broadway Lane turns R into Throop Rd. Car park in field next to cottage. 1-acre riverside garden separated from fields by ha-ha, notable for its design rather than its planting. Bulbs and spring flowers, water plants, interesting collection of ferns. TEAS. *Adm £1 Chd 25p. Sun May 21, Wed May 24 (2-6). Private visits welcome, please* **Tel 01202 515781**

Waterfalls ✲ (Roger Butler Esq) 59 Branksome Wood Rd, Bournemouth. 1m W from Bournemouth Square, nr Coy Pond Rd. ⅓-acre redesigned garden. Made by owner over past 11 years utilising a steeply inclined site and featuring a series of waterfalls and a new koi pond. Mature trees provide a setting for ericaceous plants and ferns against a woodland background. *Adm 75p Chd 25p. Sun June 11 (2-6)*

Welcome Thatch ✲❀ (Mrs Diana Guy) Witchampton. 3½m E of Wimborne, B3078 L to Witchampton, thence through village past church & shop to last but one on R. Listed thatched house with well-planted ⅔-acre cottage garden. Featured in Amateur Gardening Jan 1993. Plantsperson's borders, wild area with poultry, potager, timber decking with exotics, summerhouse, small wildlife pond and bog, silver garden, small woodland area. Not suitable for elderly, infirm or very young children. TEA. *Adm £1 Chd free. Suns April 9, May 14, June 25, Sept 10 (2-5.30). Private visits also welcome, please* **Tel 01258 840894**

West Manor ♿✲ (Mr & Mrs R Bollam) Church St, Upwey. ½m from bottom of Ridgeway Hill on A354 Dorchester-Weymouth rd. Turn R on B3159 (Bridport rd). At bottom of hill turn L, Church St. Limited parking for disabled only. ¾-acre low maintenance garden, worked on organic principles; lawns, borders, shrubs, woodland, small pond and vegetable garden. Teas at Wishing Well. *Adm £1 Chd free. Suns June 4, July 2 (2-6)*

Weston House ♿❀ (Mr & Mrs E A W Bullock) Buckhorn Weston. 4m W of Gillingham and 4m SE of Wincanton. From A30 turn N to Kington Magna, continue towards Buckhorn Weston and after railway bridge take L turn towards Wincanton. 2nd on L is Weston House. 1 acre; old and English roses; herbaceous and mixed borders; lawns; views of Blackmore Vale; woodland and wild flower meadow areas. TEAS in aid of Buckhorn Weston Parish Church. *Adm £1 Chd free. Suns June 25, July 16 (2-6)*

Wimborne Minster Model Town & Gardens ♿✲❀ (The Wimborne Minster Model Town Trust®). King St 200yds W of Minster, opp. public car park. 1½-acre grounds with 1⁄10 scale models of the town in early fifties, surrounded by landscaped gardens. Herbaceous borders, alpines, herbs, heather and rose gardens, with many rare and unusual plants, with pools and fountain, making a colourful pleasure garden. Many seats and views over Stour valley. Refreshments daily. *Adm £2 OAPs £1.75 Chd £1 (3-15) under 3 free. For NGS Suns June 4, July 2, Sept 3 (10-5).* **Tel 01202 881924**

Wincombe Park ❀ (The Hon M D Fortescue) 2m from Shaftesbury. Off A350 to Warminster signed to Wincombe and Donhead St Mary. Plantsman's garden surrounding house set in parkland; raised beds, shrubs, perennials; walled kitchen garden; view of valley with lake and woods. Unusual plants for sale. TEAS. *Adm £1.50 Chd free. Weds May 17 (2-5.30), also private visits and groups by appt* **Tel 01747 852161**

¶Witchcroft ✲❀ (Mr & Mrs Rowland & Pamela Reynolds) 1 Sweet Hill Rd, Southwell. On arriving on to the island of Portland (A354) follow the signs for Portland Bill. Enter the village of Southwell, pass the Eight Kings public house on your L, proceed a further 300yds up the rd to the junction of Sweet Hill Rd and Southwell St, 'Witchcroft' is the green roofed bungalow situated on your L. Small cottage garden with pond, shrubs, and herbaceous borders and open rural views. In spring there are bulbs and hellebores, in summer new and old-fashioned roses. Park in main st. TEAS. *Adm 60p Chd free (Share to the Cancer and Leukaemia in Childhood Trust®). Suns March 12, July 16, Aug 20 (2-5.30)*

County Durham

Hon County Organiser: Mrs Ian Bonas, Bedburn Hall, Hamsterley, Bishop Auckland DL13 3NN Tel 01388 488231

DATES OF OPENING

By appointment
For telephone numbers and other details see garden descriptions. Private visits welcomed

173 Gilesgate, Durham
Westholme Hall, Winston

Parties only
Barningham Park, nr Barnard Castle

Regular openings
For details see garden descriptions

Raby Castle, Staindrop. See text for details
St Aidan's College, Durham
University of Durham Botanic Garden, Durham

April 16 Sunday
Birkheads Cottage Garden & Nursery

May 21 Sunday
Langdale, nr Melsonby, Richmond, N Yorks

May 28 Sunday
Barningham Park, nr Barnard Castle
Birkheads Cottage Garden & Nursery
Westholme Hall, Winston

June 11 Sunday
Eggleston Hall Gardens, nr Barnard Castle

June 18 Sunday
17 The General's Wood, Harraton

July 2 Sunday
Merrybent Gardens
Ravenside, East Heddon, Heddon on the Wall
Westholme Hall, Winston

July 9 Sunday
Bedburn Hall, Hamsterley

July 16 Sunday
Brancepeth Gardens, Durham
10 The Chesters, Ebchester

July 23 Sunday
Westholme Hall, Winston
Whorlton Village Gardens

July 30 Sunday
Birkheads Cottage Garden & Nursery

August 27 Sunday
Westholme Hall, Winston

DESCRIPTIONS OF GARDENS

Barningham Park ❀ (Sir Anthony Milbank) 6m S of Barnard Castle. Turn S off A66 at Greta Bridge or A66 Motel via Newsham. Woodland walks, trees and rock garden. House (not open) built 1650. Home-made cream TEAS. *Adm £2 Chd free (under 14). Sun May 28 (1-6). Also by appt for parties April-June (incl) and Sept-Oct (incl), please* **Tel 01833 621202**

Bedburn Hall ♿ (Ian Bonas Esq) Hamsterley, 9m NW of Bishop Auckland. From A68 at Witton-le-Wear, turn off W to Hamsterley; turn N out of Hamsterley-Bedburn and down 1m to valley. From Wolsingham on B6293 turn off SE for 3m. Medium-sized garden; terraced garden on S facing hillside with streams; lake; woodland; lawns; rhododendrons; herbaceous borders; roses. TEAS. *Adm £1.50 Chd 50p. Sun July 9 (2-6)*

¶Birkheads Cottage Garden & Nursery ✲❀ (Christine Liddle) Nr Sunniside. From A1M N or S take A692 or A693 on to A6076 rd between Sunniside and Stanley. Birkheads Nursery is signposted 1m S of Tanfield Steam Railway. It is exactly 1m from signed junction to Nursery. Look out for the beehive! Over 4,000 different hardy plants in garden of 1½ acres incl pond, formal topiary garden, rockeries, gravel garden, herbaceous borders set in S facing open countryside. Beautiful views. Small specialist nursery featured on TV 2 yrs ago. *Adm £1.50 Chd 50p. Suns April 16, May 28, July 30 (10-5)*

Brancepeth Gardens ♿❀ 6m SW of Durham on A690 between villages of Brandon and Willington. An attractive sandstone village consisting of a few Georgian and later houses at the gates of the Castle & Church which originate from late C12. TEAS. *Adm £2 Chd 50p. Sun July 16 (2-5.30)*

Quarry Hill Attractively renewed landscaped garden containing many tender and southern hemisphere plantings surrounding Elizabethan house

¶10 The Chesters ♿❀ (Dianne Allison) Ebchester, Nr Consett. S end of village on A694, signposted, 2m from Consett. Small 'cottage-style' garden, with the National Collection of Polemoniums among a wide variety of plants. National Trust woodland walk nearby for dog walking etc. Lectures and group visits by appointment. TEAS. *Adm £1 Chd free/donation. Sun July 16 (2-5)*

Eggleston Hall Gardens ♿✲❀ (Sir William Gray) Eggleston, NW of Barnard Castle. Route B6278. Large garden with many unusual plants; large lawns, rhododendrons, greenhouses, mixed borders, fine trees, large extension of kitchen garden (all organically grown). Garden centre open. Homemade TEAS. *Adm £1.50 Chd free. Sun June 11 (2-5). Private visits welcome, please* **Tel 01833 650553**

¶17 The General's Wood ✲ (Bob & Doreen Wigham) Harraton. From A1M at Chester-Le-Street take rd signposted Fatfield. In 1m turn R into Bonemill Lane; after lm turn R into The General's Wood. ⅓rd acre mature garden in woodland setting with large pond area. TEA. *Adm 50p. Sun June 18 (2-5)*

¶173 Gilesgate ♿ (Dr Anne Sullivan) Durham. Leave Durham Market Place to roundabout at top of Claypath. 3rd exit (marked Hild & Bede College) then immed 1st L. 173 is first house - phonebox outside. ½-acre garden of lawns, mixed herbaceous borders, with small formal herb garden, quiet 'cottage' garden, and small area of formal boxed beds, shade borders. *Adm £1.50 Chd 50p. Private visits welcome, please* **Tel 0191 3866402**

¶Langdale ♿ (Mr & Mrs J Pratt) Melsonby, Richmond, N Yorks. 10m W of Darlington on A66, turn R to Melsonby through village ½m turn L. 2 acres formal garden, lawns, herbaceous borders, roses and bedding plants. Beyond garden woods are a mass of daffodils, bluebells followed by rhododendrons. TEAS. *Adm £1.50 Chd 50p. Sun May 21 (2-5.30)*

Merrybent Gardens ♿ (Mrs D Hunter) 42 Merrybent. On A67 2½m W of Darlington within easy reach of town centre. An opportunity to explore a number of small and up to 1-acre private gardens of great variety close to R Tees. Home-made TEAS. *Combined adm £1.50 Chd free. Sun July 2 (2-5.30)*

● Raby Castle ♿✲ (The Rt Hon The Lord Barnard) Staindrop, NW of Darlington. 1m N of Staindrop on A688 Barnard Castle-Bishop Auckland. Buses: 75, 77 Darlington-Barnard Castle; 8 Bishop Auckland-Barnard Castle; alight Staindrop, North Lodge, ¼m. Large walled garden; informal garden with ericas; old yew hedges; shrub and herbaceous borders; roses. Castle also open, principally C14 with alterations made 1765 and mid-C19; fine pictures and furniture. Collection of horse-drawn carriages and fire engines. Garden only suitable wheelchairs. TEAS at Stables. Special terms for parties on application. *Adm Castle Gardens and carriages £3.50 OAPs £3.20 Chd £1.50; Gardens & carriages only £1 OAPs/Chd 75p. Sat to Wed April 15 to 19, May 1 to June 30, Weds, Suns only; July 1 to Sept 30 daily (except Sats); also Bank Hol weekends, Sat to Tues (Castle 1-5; garden and park 11-5.30, last adm 4.30); also by appt for parties* **Tel 01833 660202**

¶Ravenside ✲❀ (Mrs J Barber) East Heddon. 9m from Newcastle on the A69 take the Heddon on the Wall B 6258 turn off, at end of slip rd turn R under bridge then L to East Heddon. 3rd house on R. ⅓-acre plantswoman's garden filled with shrubs, shrub roses, herbaceous borders, alpine, many in troughs and pond with bog area. TEAS. *Adm £1.50 Chd free. Sun July 2 (2-5)*

St Aidan's College ♿ (By kind permission of the Principal) Durham. 1m from City centre. A1050 N towards Durham City; turn W at South End House, where St Aidan's College signposted. St Aidan's College was designed by Sir Basil Spence and the grounds laid out according to a plan by Prof Brian Hackett about 1966. The maturing garden (3 acres) includes shrub planting, rose beds and raised beds; several specimen trees of interest incl cedrus libani, have been planted. From the garden there are unequalled views of Durham Cathedral, Durham City and Durham University Observatory, designed by Anthony Salvin. In porter's lodge are available, booklets £1 & postcards 20p. *Gardens open all year except Christmas and Easter. Please arrange with Bursar* **Tel 0191 374 3269.** *Donations to NGS*

University of Durham Botanic Garden ♿✲❀ 1m from centre of Druham. Turn off A167 (old A1) at Cock O'The North roundabout, direction Durham for 1m; turn R into Hollingside Lane which is between Grey and Collingwood Colleges; gardens 600yds on R. 18 acres on a beautiful SW facing hillside features 15-yr-old North American Arboretum planted 1980, woodland and ornamental bog garden, winter heather beds and tropical and desert display glasshouses. The Prince Bishop's garden contains 6 statues. TEAS in Visitor Centre. *Adm £1 Chd 50p. March 1 to Oct 31 (10-5), Nov 1 to Feb 28 every afternoon weather permitting. Private parties welcome, please* **Tel 0191 374 2670**

Westholme Hall ♿❀ (Mr & Mrs J H McBain) Winston. 11m W of Darlington. From A67 Darlington-Barnard Castle, nr Winston turn N onto B6274. 5 acres of gardens and grounds laid out in 1892 surround the Jacobean house (not open). Rhododendrons, flowering shrubs, mixed borders, old-fashioned rose garden. The croquet lawn leads on to an orchard, stream and woodland. Home made TEAS. *Adm £1.50 Chd 50p. Suns May 28; July 2, 23; Aug 27 (2-6)*

¶Whorlton Village Gardens ✲ Barnard Castle. A67 from Darlington, westwards for 12m, turn L at sign to Whorlton. A group of gardens in a small attractive village above the Tees. TEAS. *Adm £2 Chd 50p (Share to Whorlton Village Community Assoc®). Sun July 23 (2-5)*

Dyfed

See separate Welsh section beginning on page 314

Essex

Hon County Organisers: Mrs Hugh Johnson, Saling Hall, Great Saling, Braintree CM7 5DT
Assistant Hon County Organiser: Mrs Jill Cowley, Park Farm, Great Waltham, Chelmsford CM3 1BZ (Publicity)
Mrs Rosemary Kenrick, The Bailey House, Saffron Walden CB10 2EA
Hon County Treasurer: Eric Brown Esq, 19 Chichester Road, Saffron Walden CB11 3EW

DATES OF OPENING

By appointment
For telephone number and other details see garden description

8 Dene Court, Chelmsford
Edelweiss, Hornchurch
Folly Faunts House, Goldhanger
Lower Dairy House, Nayland
Olivers, nr Colchester
Perrymans, Boxted
Pound Farmhouse, Rayne
Reed House, Great Chesterford
Volpaia, Hockley
Warwick House, Great Dunmow

Parties only
Beth Chatto Gardens, Elmstead Market
6 Fanners Green, Great Waltham
Feeringbury Manor, Feering
The Fens, Langham
Horkesley Hall, Little Horkesley
The Magnolias, Brentwood
Park Farm, Great Waltham
Saling Hall, Great Saling
Saling Hall Lodge, Great Saling
Shore Hall, Cornish Hall End
Stamps and Crows, Layer Breton Heath

Regular openings
For details see garden descriptions

Beth Chatto Gardens, Elmstead Market. March 1 to Oct 31 Mons to Sats Nov 1 to March 1 Mons to Fris. Closed all Bank Hols
Feeringbury Manor, Feering. Weekday mornings May 1 to July 28. Closed weekends & Bank Hols
The Fens, Langham. Thurs, Sats March to Aug
Glen Chantry, Wickham Bishops. Fris, Sats June & July
Hyde Hall RHS Garden, Rettendon. Sats, Suns, Weds, Thurs & Bank Hols March 26 to Oct 29
Volpaia, Hockley. Thurs, Suns April 16 to June 25
Warwick House, Great Dunmow. Sats, Suns April 15 to July 9

March 26 Sunday
The Magnolias, Brentwood

April 1 Saturday
Lower Dairy House, Nayland
Olivers, Colchester

April 2 Sunday
Lower Dairy House, Nayland
The Magnolias, Brentwood
Olivers, Colchester

April 5 Wednesday
Olivers, Colchester
April 8 Saturday
Lower Dairy House, Nayland
April 9 Sunday
The Fens, Langham
Lower Dairy House, Nayland
April 12 Wednesday
Olivers, Colchester
April 15 Saturday
Lower Dairy House, Nayland
April 16 Sunday
Glen Chantry, Wickham Bishops
Lower Dairy House, Nayland
The Magnolias, Brentwood
Park Farm, Great Waltham
April 17 Monday
Glen Chantry, Wickham Bishops
Lower Dairy House, Nayland
Park Farm, Great Waltham
April 19 Wednesday
Olivers, Colchester
April 23 Sunday
The Magnolias, Brentwood
Saling Hall Lodge, Great Saling
April 26 Wednesday
Olivers, Colchester
April 29 Saturday
Lower Dairy House, Nayland
Olivers, Colchester
April 30 Sunday
The Fens, Langham
Lower Dairy House, Nayland
Olivers, Colchester
Park Farm, Great Waltham
May 1 Monday
Olivers, Colchester
Park Farm, Great Waltham
May 3 Wednesday
Olivers, Colchester
Saling Hall, Great Saling
May 6 Saturday
Lower Dairy House, Nayland
May 7 Sunday
6 Fanners Green, Great Waltham ‡
Glen Chantry, Wickham Bishops
Lower Dairy House, Nayland
Lyston Mill, Liston
The Magnolias, Brentwood
Park Farm, Great Waltham ‡
May 8 Monday
6 Fanners Green, Great Waltham ‡
Glen Chantry, Wickham Bishops
Lower Dairy House, Nayland
Park Farm, Great Waltham ‡
May 10 Wednesday
Olivers, Colchester
Saling Hall, Great Saling
May 14 Sunday
The Magnolias, Brentwood
Old Hill House, Aldham
Saling Hall Lodge, Great Saling
May 17 Wednesday
Olivers, Colchester
Saling Hall, Great Saling
May 20 Saturday
Lower Dairy House, Nayland
May 21 Sunday
1 Coronation Villa, Feering
Lower Dairy House, Nayland
May 24 Wednesday
Olivers, Colchester
Saling Hall, Great Saling
May 27 Saturday
Lower Dairy House, Nayland
May 28 Sunday
Folly Faunts House, Goldhanger
Glen Chantry, Wickham Bishops
Lower Dairy House, Nayland
The Magnolias, Brentwood
Park Farm, Great Waltham
May 29 Monday
Edelweiss, Hornchurch
Glen Chantry, Wickham Bishops
Lower Dairy House, Nayland
Park Farm, Great Waltham
May 31 Wednesday
Olivers, Colchester
Saling Hall, Great Saling
June 3 Saturday
Lower Dairy House, Nayland
June 4 Sunday
8 Dene Court, Chelmsford
Lower Dairy House, Nayland
The Old Rectory, Boreham
Park Farm, Great Waltham
June 5 Monday
Park Farm, Great Waltham
June 7 Wednesday
Olivers, Colchester
Saling Hall, Great Saling
June 10 Saturday
Amberden Hall, Widdington
Lower Dairy House, Nayland
Stamps & Crows, Layer Breton Heath
June 11 Sunday
Amberden Hall, Widdington
Cobbs, Howe Street ‡
The Dower House, Castle Hedingham
Fanners Farm, Great Waltham ‡
6 Fanners Green, Great Waltham ‡
The Fens, Langham
Glen Chantry, Wickham Bishops
Lower Dairy House, Nayland
Park Farm, Great Waltham ‡
Stamps & Crows, Layer Breton Heath
June 12 Monday
Cobbs, Howe Street
Fanners Farm, Great Waltham ‡
6 Fanners Green, Great Waltham ‡
Park Farm, Great Waltham ‡
June 14 Wednesday
Amberden Hall, Widdington
Olivers, Colchester
Saling Hall, Great Saling
Stamps & Crows, Layer Breton Heath
June 17 Saturday
Lower Dairy House, Nayland
June 18 Sunday
Lofts Hall, Elmdon, nr Saffron Walden
Lower Dairy House, Nayland
The Magnolias, Brentwood
Park Farm, Great Waltham
Pound Farmhouse, Rayne
Shore Hall, Cornish Hall End
June 19 Monday
Park Farm, Great Waltham
June 21 Wednesday
Olivers, Colchester
Saling Hall, Great Saling
June 24 Saturday
Lower Dairy House, Nayland
June 25 Sunday
Clavering Gardens, Saffron Walden
1 Coronation Villa, Feering
8 Dene Court, Chelmsford
Edelweiss, Hornchurch
Lower Dairy House, Nayland
Park Farm, Great Waltham
Saling Hall, Great Saling ‡
Saling Hall Lodge, Great Saling ‡
June 26 Monday
Park Farm, Great Waltham
June 28 Wednesday
Olivers, Colchester
Saling Hall, Great Saling
July 1 Saturday
Lower Dairy House, Nayland
Olivers, Colchester
July 2 Sunday
Glen Chantry, Wickham Bishops
Lower Dairy House, Nayland
The Old Vicarage, Rickling
Olivers, Colchester
July 5 Wednesday
Saling Hall, Great Saling
July 8 Saturday
Lower Dairy House, Nayland
July 9 Sunday
8 Dene Court, Chelmsford
Littlebury Gardens, Saffron Walden
Lower Dairy House, Nayland
Park Farm, Great Waltham
July 10 Monday
Park Farm, Great Waltham
July 12 Wednesday
Saling Hall, Great Saling
July 19 Wednesday
Saling Hall, Great Saling
July 23 Sunday
8 Dene Court, Chelmsford

The Magnolias, Brentwood

July 26 Wednesday

Saling Hall, Great Saling

July 30 Sunday

Edelweiss, Hornchurch

August 6 Sunday

8 Dene Court, Chelmsford

August 20 Sunday

The Magnolias, Brentwood

August 27 Sunday

Edelweiss, Hornchurch

September 3 Sunday

Glen Chantry, Wickham Bishops

September 10 Sunday

Lyston Mill, Liston

September 17 Sunday

Glen Chantry, Wickham Bishops

September 24 Sunday

The Magnolias, Brentwood

October 22 Sunday

The Magnolias, Brentwood

DESCRIPTIONS OF GARDENS

Amberden Hall ♿✲❀ (Mr & Mrs D Lloyd) Widdington. 6m from Saffron Walden. E off B1383 nr Newport. Follow signs to Mole Hall Wildlife Park. Drive ½m beyond park on R. Medium-sized walled garden with collection of unusual hardy plants, shrubs and ivy allée. Raised vegetable garden. TEAS. *Adm £2 Chd free (Share to St Mary's Church, Widdington®). Sat, Sun, Wed June 10, 11, 14 (2-6)*

● **Beth Chatto Gardens** ✲❀ (Mrs Beth Chatto) On A133, ¼m E of Elmstead Market. 5 acres of attractively landscaped garden with many unusual plants, shown in wide range of conditions from hot and dry to water garden. The recently made gravel garden converted from the original car park, has been planted with drought-tolerant plants to help gardeners who have hose-pipe watering bans. Books available by Beth Chatto The Dry Garden, The Damp Garden, Beth Chatto's Garden Notebook, The Green Tapestry. Adjacent nursery open. *Adm £2 Chd free. March 1 to Oct 31, every Mon to Sat but closed Bank Hols (9-5); Nov 1 to end of Feb every Mon to Fri but closed Bank Hols (9-4). Parties by appt*

Clavering Gardens ♿✲❀ Clavering. On B1038 7m N of Bishops Stortford. Turn W off B1368 (old A11) at Newport. TEAS in Cricket Pavilion on village green in aid of Clavering Cricket Club. *Adm £2.50 Chd free. Sun June 25 (2-5.30)*

Brooklands (Mr & Mrs John Noble) Walled garden, herbaceous and shrub borders, rustic rose trellis. 15-yr-old arboretum. Newly planted orchard area 1½ acres

Clavering Court (Mr & Mrs S R Elvidge) Approx 1½ acres fine trees, shrubs and borders. Walled garden, Edwardian greenhouse

Piercewebbs (Mr & Mrs B R William-Powlett) Includes old walled garden, shrubs, lawns, ha ha, yew and stilt hedges, pond and grass tennis court. Extensive views. Best amateur garden in Country Gardens Competition. Trellised rose garden, plant stall

Shovellers (Miss J & Miss E Ludgate) Stickling Green. 3-acre extended cottage garden, orchard and meadow

Cobbs ♿✲ (Mr & Mrs St Aubyn) Howe Street, nr Chelmsford. Take old A130 6m N from Chelmsford to Gt Waltham through village approx 1m to village of Howe Street. Turn R down Parsonage Lane, over river 1st L (no through rd). House on L. Approx 1-acre garden, large herbaceous border; bog garden; kitchen garden and roses. *Adm £1 Chd free under 16. Sun, Mon June 11, 12 (2-6)*

¶**1 Coronation Villa** ✲❀ (Mr Colin Smith) Feering. 9m W of Colchester. 4m E of Witham, signposted off the A12 ½m NE from The Bell Inn on R-hand side towards The Teys. ⅓-acre informal garden consisting of a variety of trees, shrubs, climbing plants and perennials. With a pond, gazebo, pergola and sink gardens to add extra interest to the garden. TEAS. *Adm £1 Chd free. Suns May 21, June 25 (2-5.30)*

8 Dene Court ✲❀ (Mrs Sheila Chapman) Chelmsford. W of Chelmsford (Parkway). Take A1060 Roxwell Rd for 1m. Turn R at traffic lights into Chignall Rd, Dene Court 3rd exit on R. Parking in Chignall Rd. Well maintained and designed compact garden (250 sq yds) circular lawn surrounded by many unusual plants incl wide variety of clematis, roses, ferns and grasses; ornamental well; three pergolas; rose-covered perimeter wall. Featured in Essex Homes and Living and Garden News. *Adm £1 Chd free (Share to Audrey Appleton Trust for the Terminally Ill®). Suns June 4, 25, July 9, 23, Aug 6 (2-5.30). Private visits welcome, please* **Tel 01245 266156**

¶**The Dower House** ✲❀ (Mr & Mrs John Allfrey) Castle Hedingham on B1058. 5m from Halstead A604. 1m NE of Sible Hedingham. Follow signs to Hedingham Castle. Garden 50yds from entrance. Terraced plantsman's garden of 1½ acres overlooking Tudor church and village. Mixed borders developed since 1987 with flower arranging in mind. TEAS. *Adm £1.50 Chd free (Share to St Nicholas Church, Castle Hedingham®). Sun June 11 (2-6)*

¶**Edelweiss** ✲❀ (Joan H Hogg, Pat F Lowery) 20 Hartland Road, Hornchurch. From Romford head in an easterly direction along the A124 past Tesco on L, turn R into Albany Rd opp church on corner of Park Lane on the L. Go to the bottom of Albany Rd, humps all the way down, turn L at the end into Hartland Rd. A small town garden approx 200′ × 25′ very colourful and maintained to a high standard. Laid out to maximise use of small narrow plot and featuring many containers, baskets, seasonal bedding and mixed borders. Tiny prize-winning garden to the front of the property. White garden doves (fantails) and poultry add interest and the rear garden has access to Harrow Lodge Park with miniature golf course, boating lake, leisure centre, swimming pool and fishing lake. Owners sell home-made produce, eggs etc. Narrow access and steps at side and rear not really suitable for push-chairs. TEAS. *Adm £1 Chd free. Mon May 29, Suns June 25, July 30, Aug 27. Private visits welcome, June - Aug please* **Tel 01708 454610**

Regular Openers. See head of county section.

Fanners Farm ♿✂ (Mr & Mrs P G Lee) 4m N of Chelmsford. In Great Waltham turn into South Street opp One Step Beyond restaurant (Six Bells Inn). Garden 1¼m on R. Informal garden of approx 2 acres surrounding C14 house (not open). Conservatory featured in The Garden, Feb 1990. Small collection of vintage cars. TEAS Sun only. *Adm £1 Chd free. Sun, Mon June 11, 12 (2-6)*

6 Fanners Green ✂❀ (Dr & Mrs T M Pickard) 4m N of Chelmsford. In Great Waltham turn into South Street opp One Step Beyond restaurant (Six Bells Inn). Garden 1¼m on the R. A 15-yr-old small country garden of ⅓ acre divided into different formal areas with informal planting. Herb garden and conservatory. *Adm £1 Chd free. Suns, Mons May 7, 8; June 11, 12, (2-6). Parties by appt May to July, please* **Tel 01245 360035**

Feeringbury Manor ♿ (Mr & Mrs G Coode-Adams) Coggeshall Rd, Feering, on rd between Coggeshall and Feering. 7-acre garden bordering R Blackwater. Many unusual plants including wide variety of honeysuckles, clematis, old-fashioned roses; rare bog-loving plants, border ponds and streams; small Victorian water wheel. Featured in Country Life 1994 and The Passionate Gardener. *Adm £1.50 Chd £1. Weekday mornings May 1 to July 28 (8-1) closed weekends and Bank Hols. Also parties by appt, please* **Tel 01376 561946**

The Fens ♿✂❀ (Mrs Ann Lunn) Old Mill Rd, Langham. 5m N of Colchester off A12. Old Mill Rd starts at T-junction with High St and is an extension of Chapel Rd, leading to Boxted-Dedham Rd. Undulating 2-acre cottage garden maintained with pond; by owners, shade and ditch gardens recreated after 1987 storm; primulas and a wide variety of interesting plants; nursery open. TEAS for charity. *Adm £1 Chd 50p. Thurs, Sat March to Aug. Suns April 9, 30, (2-5) June 11, (2-6). Also parties by appt, please* **Tel 01206 272259**

Folly Faunts House ♿❀ (Mr & Mrs J C Jenkinson) Goldhanger. On B1026 between Colchester and Maldon. 5-acre garden divided into 7 different settings and incl water and formal rose gardens, island herbaceous and shrub borders with unusual and rare plants and specimen trees. A further 15 acres of varied park and woodland divided by 6 avenues of specialised trees. 1st prize for best large country garden 1994. Unusual and interesting plants for sale. Large car park. TEAS. *Adm £1.50 Chd 50p. Sun May 28 (2-5). Also private visits welcome, please* **Tel 01621 788213**

Glen Chantry ♿✂❀ (Mr & Mrs W G Staines) Wickham Bishops 1½m SE of Witham. Take Maldon Rd from Witham and 1st L to Wickham Bishops. Pass Benton Hall Golf Course: cross narrow bridge over R Blackwater and turn immediately L up track by side of Blue Mills. 3-acre garden with emphasis on mixed borders with unusual perennials and shrub roses. Limestone rock gardens with associated ponds form a dominant feature, formal specialist white garden and foliage beds with grasses and hostas; range of plants for sale. TEAS. *Adm £1 Chd 50p. Suns April 16; May 7, 28; June 11; July 2; Sept 3, 17; Mons April 17, May 8, 29 (2-5) Fris, Sats June and July (10-4). Also parties by appt, please* **Tel 01621 891342**

¶Horkesley Hall ♿ (Mr & Mrs Richard Eddis) Colchester. From A134 Sudbury - Colchester Rd travelling towards Colchester. Shortly after Nayland turn R into Water Lane signed to Little Horkesley and into village with The Beehive on R. Go straight across Xrds and after approx 200 yds go down drive on R, leaving church on R. This is a young garden within the setting of a classical house, 2 old fishponds and some fine old trees around the perimeter. Its creation began in 1990/91 and the emphasis is on shrubs and trees chosen for colour and effect and incl some which are unusual and rare. The total area is about 4-5 acres. TEA by special arrangement. *Adm £2 Chd £1 (Share to Co-workers of Mother Theresa®). Parties of 20 and over May - Aug week-days preferred, please* **Tel 01206 272067**

● Hyde Hall Garden ♿✂❀ (Royal Horticultural Society) Rettendon. 7m SE of Chelmsford; 6m NE of Wickford. Signed from A130. Flowering trees, shrubs, perennials, roses, bulbs, ornamental greenhouses and ponds; all-yr-round colour. Restaurant. *Adm £2.50 Chd 50p 6-14. Parties 20+ £2. Every Sat, Sun, Wed, Thurs and Bank Hols March 26 to Oct 29 (11-6) Sept, Oct (11-5)*

Littlebury Gardens ✂ 2m from Saffron Walden, opp Littlebury church on B1383 1m N of Audley End House, entrance in Littlebury Green Rd. TEAS. *Combined adm £1.25 Chd free. Sun July 9 (2-5.30)*

Granta House ♿❀ (Mr & Mrs R A Lloyd). Old walled garden of 1 acre; unusual shrubs, herbaceous plants and roses

North House (Mr & Mrs B G Sanders) opp Granta House. Mixed borders, herb garden and roses

Lofts Hall ♿✂❀ (Maj & Mrs C R Philipson) Elmdon. 8m E of Royston. 5m W of Saffron Walden off B1039. Large garden, 6 acres; roses; herbaceous and shrub borders; kitchen garden; lake and C16 carp pond. Early C17 dovecote (reputedly 2nd largest in England), stud farm. TEAS. *Adm £1.50 Chd 50p. Sun June 18 (2-6)*

Lower Dairy House ♿✂❀ (Mr & Mrs D J Burnett) 7m N of Colchester off A134. Turn L at bottom of hill before Nayland village into Water Lane, signed to Little Horkesley. Garden ½m on L past farm buildings. Plantsman's garden approx 1½ acres. Natural stream with waterside plantings; rockery and raised beds; lawns; herbaceous borders; roses. Many varieties of shrubs and ground cover plants. Garden made and maintained by owners for yr-round colour and variety. Good spring bulbs and blossom. Tudor House (not open). TEAS. *Adm £1.50 Chd 50p Sats, Suns, Mons April 1, 2, 8, 9, 15, 16, 17, 29, 30; May 6, 7, 8, 20, 21, 27, 28, 29; June 3, 4, 10, 11, 17, 18, 24 25; July 1, 2, 8, 9 (2-6). Also private visits welcome please* **Tel 01206 262 220**

¶Lyston Mill ♿❀ (Mrs E Bevington-Smith) Liston. Turn W off Long Melford High Street, signposted sports field Garden is approx ¾m on R. 2-acre garden with river; assorted beds and rare trees; newly established bog garden. TEAS. *Adm £1. Suns May 7 (2-5.30) Sept 10 (2-5)*

By Appointment Gardens. See head of county section

The Magnolias ✲❀ (Mr & Mrs R A Hammond) 18 St John's Ave, Brentwood. From A1023 turn S on A128; after 300yds R at traffic lights; over railway bridge; St John's Ave 3rd on R. ½-acre well-designed informal garden with particular appeal to plantsmen; good collection spring bulbs; ground-cover; trees and shrubs incl maples, rhododendrons, camellias, magnolias and pieris. Koi ponds and other water interests. Featured on Garden Club in 93. TEA. *Adm £1 Chd 50p. Suns March 26; April 2, 16, 23; May 7, 14, 28; June 18; July 23; Aug 20; Sept 24; Oct 22 (10-5). Parties by appt March to Oct incl, please* **Tel 01277 220019**

Old Hill House ♿✲ (Mr & Mrs J S d'Angibau) Aldham. On A604, 5m W of Colchester; top of Ford Street Hill. From A12 and A120, turn off at Marks Tey; N past Marks Tey Station, R at Xrds by Aldham Church. 1-acre garden with mixed shrubs and herbaceous borders and formal herb garden, maintained by owners for yr-round interest. TEAS. *Adm £1 Chd free (Share to NSPCC®). Sun May 14 (2-5.30)*

¶The Old Rectory ♿✲ (Sir Jeffery & Lady Bowman) Boreham. 4m NE of Chelmsford. Take 1137 to Boreham Village, turn into Church Rd at Red Lion Public House. ½m along on R opp church. 2½-acre garden with ponds, stream, interesting trees and shrubs, herbaceous borders and kitchen garden. TEAS. *Adm £1 Chd free. Sun June 4 (2-6)*

The Old Vicarage ✲❀ (Mr & Mrs James Jowitt) Rickling. 7m from Saffron Walden: from Newport take B1038 W to Wicken Bonhunt. In village turn L to Rickling, The Old Vicarage is on the L after 1m. 2-acre garden with herbaceous and mixed borders; rose garden and shrubbery. TEAS in aid of Rickling Church. *Adm £1.50 Chd free. Sun July 2 (2-6)*

Olivers ♿✲❀ (Mr & Mrs D Edwards) 3m SW of Colchester, between B1022 & B1026 From Colchester via Maldon Rd, turn L into Gosbecks Rd at Leather Bottle public house; R into Olivers Lane (signposted Roman River Centre). C18 house (not open) overlooks Roman river valley, surrounded by terrace and yew backed borders; closely planted with wide variety of plants, many unusual and for varying conditions. Lawns; 3 lakes; meadow; woodland with fine trees underplanted with shrubs including rhododendrons and old roses; spring bulbs and bluebells. TEA. *Adm £1.50 Chd free. Sat, Sun April 1, 2, 29, 30; July 1, 2 (2-6) Mon May 1; Weds April May June (2-5). Also private visits welcome, please* **Tel 01206 330575**

Park Farm ✲❀ (Mrs J E M Cowley & Mr D Bracey) Great Waltham. Take B1008 N from Chelmsford through Broomfield Village. On Little Waltham bypass turn L into Chatham Hall Lane signposted Howe Street; Park Farm ½m on L. 2 acres of garden in separate 'rooms' formed by yew hedges with climber-obscured old farmhouse and dairy in centre. Many different species of bulbs; shrubs; roses and herbaceous perennials; designing still proceeding with new projects underway. Featured in magazines and on TV. TEAS. *Adm £1 Chd 50p. Suns, Mons April 16, 17, 30: May 1, 7, 8, 28, 29; June 4, 5, 11, 12, 18, 19, 25, 26; July 9, 10, (2-6). Parties by appt* **Tel 01245 360871**

¶Perrymans ♿✲❀ (Mr & Mrs H R J Human) Boxted. 4m NE from Colchester Station to Boxted Cross. Follow Dedham Rd, drive entrance on R 200yds past village shop. 7-acre undulating garden created from scratch since 1970, lakes, newly planted rose garden, holly collection, and borders. *Adm £1.50 Chd free. Private visits welcome, please* **Tel 01206 272297**

¶Pound Farmhouse ♿✲ (Mr & Mrs J F Swetenham) Rayne. 3m W of Braintree. Take Shalford Rd NW from A120 in Rayne. Drive 9/10 m through back of village and Duck End Green. House is on R, park in field on L before house. 1st prize in the ½ acre to 3 acres category of 1994 Country Garden Competition. This garden has been planted over the last 25 yrs and can be enjoyed all yr either for the blossom and bulbs in the spring, the roses and pond a little later, the flame border in July or the later summer border in Sept and Oct. TEAS in aid of All Saints Church, Rayne, Fabric Fund. *Adm £1.50 Chd 50p. Sun June 18 (2-5.30). Private visits welcome, please* **Tel 01376 326738**

Reed House ♿✲ (Mrs W H Mason) Great Chesterford. 4m N of Saffron Walden and 1m S of Stump Cross, M 11. On B184 turn into Great Chesterford High Street. Then L at Crown & Thistle public house into Manor Lane. ¾-acre garden with collection of unusual plants developed in the last 6 years. Featured in Essex Homes and Living. *Adm £1.50 Chd 50p. Private visits welcome, please* **Tel 01799 530312**

Saling Hall ♿✲ (Mr & Mrs H Johnson) Great Saling, 6m NW of Braintree. A120; midway between Braintree-Dunmow turn off N at the Saling Oak. 12 acres; walled garden dated 1698; small park with fine trees; extensive new collection of unusual plants with emphasis on trees; water gardens. Hugh Johnson is 'Tradescant' of the RHS. TEAS Sun only. *Adm £2 Chd free (Share to St James's Church, Great Saling®). Weds in May, June, July (2-5). Sun June 25 with* **Saling Hall Lodge** *Combined adm £2.50 (2-6). Also parties by appt*

Saling Hall Lodge ♿✲❀ (Mr & Mrs K Akers), Great Saling. 6m from Braintree. Turn N off A120 between Braintree and Dunmow at the Saling Oak public house. Drive at end of village on L, please park in village. Well-designed and maintained ½-acre garden with pond, limestone rock garden, small peat garden, tufa bed and sinks. As seen on Channel 4 and Anglia TV. TEAS. *Adm £1 Chd free. Suns April 23, May 14, (2-5). Combined adm with* **Saling Hall** *£2.50 Sun June 25 (2-6). Also parties by appt please,* **Tel 01371 850683**

Shore Hall ✲❀ (Mr & Mrs Peter Swete) Cornish Hall End, nr Braintree. 2½m NE of Finchingfield. ½m W of Cornish Hall End on Gt Sampford Rd. Long drive with poplars. 3½-acre garden surrounding C17 house (not open) with several enclosed formal areas and interesting shrubs. 100-yr-old box hedges enclose formal beds planted with herbaceous and old roses; rose garden surrounding lily ponds; newly planted ornamental vegetable and fruit garden and many young rare trees. TEAS in aid of Cornish Hall End Church Restoration Fund. *Adm £1.50 Chd free. Sun June 18 (2-5). Parties welcome of 20 and over, May to July, please* **Tel 017995 86411**

Stamps and Crows ♿❀ (Mr & Mrs E G Billington) Layer Breton Heath. 5½m S of Colchester on B1022 take L fork signposted Birch and Layer Breton. Garden on R side of Layer Breton Heath. 2½ acres of moated garden surrounding C15 farmhouse (not open). Herbaceous borders, mixed shrubs, old roses and good ground cover. Recently created bog garden and dovecote. Highly commended in Essex Country Garden Competition. Fine views towards Layer Marney Tower. TEAS (Sun only). *Adm £1 Chd free (Share to St. Mary's Church, Layer Breton®). Sat, Sun, Wed June 10, 11, 14 (2-6). Parties by appt, please* **Tel 01206 330220**

● **Volpaia** ✲❀ (Mr & Mrs D Fox) 54 Woodlands Rd, Hockley. 2¾m NE of Rayleigh. B1013 Rayleigh-Rochford, turn S from Spa Hotel into Woodlands Rd. On E side of Hockley Woods. 1-acre containing many exotic trees, rhododendrons, camellias besides other shrubs. Carpets of wood anemones and bluebells in spring, underplanting is very diverse especially with woodland, liliaceous plants and ferns. Home of Bullwood Nursery. TEA. *Adm £1 Chd 30p (Share to Essex Group of NCCPG®). All Thurs & Suns from April 16 to June 25 (2.30-6). Also private visits welcome, please* **Tel 01702 203761**

● **Warwick House** ♿✲❀ (Mr & Mrs B Creasey) Easton Lodge. 1m N of Great Dunmow on B184, take rd to Lt Easton, ½m turn L to Easton Lodge, 1¼m to white gates marked Easton Lodge, pass through these; gardens ½m on R. Originally wing of Easton Lodge, home of Countess of Warwick; old house now demolished and gardens of 6 acres created since 1972 on much of old house site. Includes recently acquired 4.5 acres of the abandoned gardens designed by Harold Peto at the turn of the century, now under restoration. Features incl C18 dovecote; conservatory; cobbled, herringbone courtyard with fountain; ponds with koi and water fowl. History of Easton Lodge and occasionally American Air Force Exhibits. TEA. *Adm £1.50 (Share to Five Parishes®). Sats, Suns April 15 to July 9 (2-6). Private visits welcome, please* **Tel 01371 873305**

Glamorgan

See separate Welsh section beginning on page 314

Gloucestershire

Hon County Organisers:	Mr & Mrs Witold Wondrausch, The New Inn, Poulton, Cirencester GL7 5JE Tel 01285 850226
Assistant Hon County Organisers:	Mr Guy Acloque, Alderley Grange, Wotton-under-Edge GL12 7QT Mrs Wendy Dare, Old Mill Dene, Blockley, Moreton-in-Marsh GL56 9HU Mrs Jennie Davies, Applegarth, Alstone, nr Tewkesbury GL20 8JD Mrs Sally Gough, Trevi, Over Old Road, Hartpury GL19 3BJ Mr A V Marlow, Greenedge, 32 Dr Browns Road, Minchinhampton GL6 9BT Mrs Elizabeth-Ann Pile, Ampney Knowle, nr Cirencester GL7 5ED
Hon County Auditor:	Mr H J Shave, ACCA (Bradings) 31 Castle Street, Cirencester GL7 1QD

DATES OF OPENING

By appointment

For telephone numbers and other details see garden descriptions. Private visits welcomed

Ami Yume Teien, Blockley
Ampney Knowle, Barnsley
Barnsley House, nr Circencester
Beverston Castle, Tetbury
Bhardonna, nr Newent
Blundells, Broadwell, nr Stow-on-the-Wold
25 Bowling Green Road, Cirencester Gardens
Burnside, Prestbury Gardens
Camp Cottage, Highleadon, nr Newent
Casa Mia, Clifford Manor, nr Newent
Cerney House, North Cerney
Cecily Hill House, Cirencester Gardens
The Chipping Croft, Tetbury
Cotswold Farm, nr Cirencester
Ewen Manor, nr Cirencester
Grove Cottage, Lower Lydbrook, nr Cinderford
Hartpury College, nr Gloucester
Hodges Barn, Shipton Moyne, nr Tetbury
Home Farm, Huntley, nr Newent
Hunts Court, North Nibley, Dursley
8 Hyatts Way, Bishops Cleeve
Jasmine House, Bream, nr Lydney
Laurel Cottage, Brockweir Gardens,nrChepstow
13 Merestones Drive, Cheltenham
Millend House, nr Coleford
Moor Wood, Woodmancote, nr Cirencester
The New Inn, Poulton Gardens
Old Chapel Garden & Studio, Chalford Gardens
The Old Manor Twyning
Old Mill Dene, Blockley
The Old Rectory, Duntisbourne Rous
Orchard Cottage, Gretton, nr Winchcombe
Painswick Rococo Garden, Painswick

Priors Mesne Cottage, Aylburton, nr Lydney
The Red House, Staunton, nr Gloucester
Redwood, Eastcombe & Bussage Gardens
Redwood House, Halmore, nr Berkeley
The Rock House, Chalford Gardens
Rookwoods, Waterlane, nr Bisley
Rodmarton Manor, nr Cirencester
St Francis, Minchinhampton Gardens
20 St Peters Road, Cirencester
Sunningdale, Grange Court, nr Westbury
Threeways, Brockweir Gardens, nr Chepstow
153 Thrupp Lane, nr Stroud
Tin Penny Cottage, Whiteway, nr Stroud
Upton Wold, nr Moreton-in-Marsh
Willow Lodge, nr Longhope, Gloucester

Parties only
Boilingwell, Sudeley Hill, nr Winchcombe
Cinderdine Cottage, Dymock, nr Newent
Frampton Court, Frampton-on-Severn Gardens
Green Cottage, Lydney
Kiftsgate Court, nr Chipping Campden
Misarden Park, Miserden, nr Cirencester
Ryelands House, Taynton,nr Newent
Stanway House, nr Winchcombe
Trevi Garden, Hartpury, nr Gloucester
Westbury Court Gardens, Westbury-on-Severn

Regular openings
For details see garden descriptions

Barnsley House, nr Cirencester
Batsford Arboretum, nr Moreton-in-Marsh
Bourton House Garden, Bourton-on-the-Hill
Cerney House, North Cerney
Ewen Manor, nr Cirencester
Grove Cottage, Lower Lydbrook, nr Cinderford
Hodges Barn, Shipton Moyne, nr Tetbury
Kiftsgate Court, nr Chipping Campden
Lydney Park, Lydney
Misarden Park, Misarden, nr Cirencester
The Old Manor, Twyning
Painswick Rococo Garden, Painswick
Rodmarton Manor, nr Cirencester
Sezincote, nr Moreton-in-Marsh
Stanway House, nr Winchcombe
Sudeley Castle Gardens, Winchombe
Tin Penny Cottage, Whiteway, nr Stroud
Trevi Garden, Hartpury, nr Gloucester

February
Tin Penny Cottage, Whiteway, nr Stroud. Every Wed

February 2 Thursday
Home Farm, Huntley, nr Newent

February 6 Monday
The Old Rectory, Duntisbourne Rous

February 9 Thursday
Cinderdine Cottage, Dymock, nr Newent

February 14 Tuesday
Cinderdine Cottage, Dymock, nr Newent

February 16 Thursday
Cinderdine Cottage, Dymock, nr Newent
Home Farm, Huntley, nr Newent

February 19 Sunday
Cinderdine Cottage, Dymock, nr Newent
Minchinhampton Gardens

February 21 Tuesday
Cinderdine Cottage, Dymock, nr Newent

February 23 Thursday
Cinderdine Cottage, Dymock, nr Newent

February 26 Sunday
Camp Cottage, Highleadon, nr Newent

February 27 Monday
The Old Rectory, Duntisbourne Rous

March
Camp Cottage, Highleadon, nr Newent. Every Sun
The Old Manor, Twyning. Every Mon
Tin Penny Cottage, Whiteway, nr Stroud. Every Wed

March 2 Thursday
Home Farm, Huntley, nr Newent

March 5 Sunday
Green Cottage, Lydney

March 12 Sunday
Green Cottage, Lydney
Grove Cottage, Lower Lydbrook, nr Cinderford

March 16 Thursday
Home Farm, Huntley, nr Newent
Trevi Garden, Hartpury, nr Gloucester

March 19 Sunday
Green Cottage, Lydney
Grove Cottage, Lower Lydbrook, nr Cinderford
Tin Penny Cottage, Whiteway, nr Stroud

March 23 Thursday
Trevi Garden, Hartpury, nr Gloucester

March 26 Sunday
Boilingwell, Sudeley Hill, nr Winchcombe
Brockweir Gardens, nr Chepstow ‡
Green Cottage, Lydney ‡
Grove Cottage, Lower Lydbrook, nr Cinderford
Painswick Rococo Garden, Painswick

March 27 Monday
The Old Rectory, Duntisbourne Rous

March 30 Thursday
Home Farm, Huntley, nr Newent
Trevi Garden, Hartpury, nr Gloucester

April
Grove Cottage, Lower Lydbrook, nr Cinderford. Every Sun
The Old Manor, Twyning. Every Mon
Tin Penny Cottage, Whiteway, nr Stroud. Every Weds
Trevi Garden, Hartpury, nr Gloucester. Every Thurs

April 2 Sunday
Newark Park, nr Wotton-under-Edge
North Rye House, Broadwell, nr Moreton-in-Marsh
Ryelands House, Taynton, nr Newent
Tin Penny Cottage, Whiteway, nr Stroud
Trevi Garden, Hartpury, nr Gloucester

April 9 Sunday
Beverston Castle, nr Tetbury
Bredon Manor, nr Tewkesbury
Minchinhampton Gardens
Misarden Park, Miserden, nr Cirencester ‡
Pinbury Park, nr Cirencester ‡
Ryelands House, Taynton, nr Newent
Westonbirt Gardens at Westonbirt School

April 10 Monday
Berverston Castle, nr Tetbury

April 13 Thursday
Home Farm, Huntley, nr Newent

April 16 Sunday
Bhardonna, nr Newent ‡
Camp Cottage, Highleadon, nr Newent ‡

Cinderdine Cottage, Dymock, nr Newent ‡
Hodges Barn, Shipton Moyne, nr Tetbury
Jasmine House, Bream, nr Lydney
Ryelands House, Taynton, nr Newent ‡
Trevi Garden, Hartpury, nr Gloucester

April 17 Monday
Ashley Gardens, nr Tetbury
Bhardonna, nr Newent ‡
Camp Cottage, Highleadon, nr Newent ‡
Grove Cottage, Lower Lydbrook, nr Cinderford
Jasmine House, Bream, nr Lydney
Ryelands House, Taynton, nr Newent ‡
Tin Penny Cottage, Whiteway, nr Stroud
Trevi Garden, Hartpury, nr Gloucester

April 18 Tuesday
Camp Cottage, Highleadon, nr Newent

April 22 Saturday
Sudeley Castle Gardens, Winchombe

April 23 Sunday
Ami Yume Teien, Blockley ‡
Boilingwell, Sudeley Hill, nr Winchcombe
Camp Cottage, Highleadon, nr Newent ‡‡
The Chipping Croft, Tetbury
Lydney Park, Lydney
Old Mill Dene, Blockley ‡
Pigeon House, Southam, nr Cheltenham
Redwood House, Halmore, nr Berkeley
Ryelands House, Taynton, nr Newent ‡‡
Stanway House, nr Winchcombe
Upton Wold, nr Moreton-in-Marsh ‡

April 24 Monday
The Old Rectory, Duntisbourne Rous

April 25 Tuesday
Camp Cottage, Highleadon, nr Newent

April 26 Wednesday
The Chipping Croft, Tetbury
Redwood House, Halmore, nr Berkeley

April 27 Thursday
Home Farm, Huntley, nr Newent

April 30 Sunday
Ampney Knowle, Barnsley ‡
Blockley Gardens, nr Moreton-in-Marsh
Brockweir Gardens, nr Chepstow
Camp Cottage, Highleadon, nr Newent ‡‡
Cerney House, North Cerney
Clover House, Winson, nr Cirencester ‡
Nympsfield Gardens, nr Nailsworth
Ryelands House, Taynton, nr Newent ‡‡
Trevi Garden, Hartpury, nr Gloucester

May
Camp Cottage, Highleadon, nr Newent. Every Sun, Tues
Ewen Manor, nr Cirencester. Every Wed, Thurs, Fri
Grove Cottage. Lower Lydbrook, nr Cinderford. Every Sun
The Old Manor, Twyning. Every Mon
Tin Penny Cottage, Whiteway, nr Stroud. Every Wed
Trevi Garden, Hartpury, nr Gloucester. Every Thurs

May 1 Monday
Trevi Garden, Hartpury, nr Gloucester

May 4 Thursday
Jasmine House, Bream, nr Lydney

May 6 Saturday
Barnsley House, nr Circencester

May 7 Sunday
Abbotswood, nr Stow-on-the-Wold
Eastcombe Bussage and Brownshill Gardens
Green Cottage, Lydney ‡
Hidcote Manor Garden, Chipping Campden
Jasmine House, Bream, nr Lydney ‡
Millend House, nr Coleford ‡
Snowshill Manor, nr Broadway
Tin Penny Cottage, Whiteway, nr Stroud
Trevi Garden, Hartpury, nr Gloucester

May 8 Monday
Camp Cottage, Highleadon, nr Newent
Eastcombe Bussage and Brownshill Gardens
Grove Cottage, Lower Lydbrook, nr Cinderford ‡
Jasmine House, Bream, nr Lydney ‡
Millend House, nr Coleford ‡

May 10 Wednesday
Lydney Park, Lydney

May 11 Thursday
Home Farm, Huntley, nr Newent

May 13 Saturday
Kiftsgate Court, nr Chipping Campden

May 14 Sunday
Batsford Arboretum, nr Moreton-in-Marsh
Ewen Manor, nr Cirencester
Green Cottage, Lydney ‡
Priors Mesne Cottage, Aylburton, nr Lydney ‡
Redwood House, Halmore, nr Berkeley
Stowell Park, nr Northleach

May 15 Monday
Camp Cottage, Highleadon, nr Newent
The Old Rectory, Duntisbourne Rous

May 17 Wednesday
Redwood House, Halmore, nr Berkeley

May 20 Saturday
Hartpury College, Gloucester

May 21 Sunday
Abbotswood, nr Stow-on-the-Wold
Boddington Manor, nr Cheltenham
Boilingwell, Sudeley Hill, nr Winchcombe
Green Cottage, Lydney ‡
Millend House, nr Coleford ‡
Thrupp Lane Gardens, nr Stroud
Upper Cam Gardens, nr Dursley

May 22 Monday
Camp Cottage, Highleadon, nr Newent

May 24 Wednesday
Daylesford House, nr Stow-on-the-Wold

May 25 Thursday
Bourton House Garden, Bourton-on-the-Hill
Home Farm, Huntley, nr Newent
Jasmine House, Bream, nr Lydney

May 28 Sunday
Bourton-on-the-Hill Gardens
Brockweir Gardens, nr Chepstow ‡
Eastington Gardens, nr Northleach
Green Cottage, Lydney ‡
Jasmine House, Bream, nr Lydney ‡
Millend House, nr Coleford ‡
Nympsfield Gardens, nr Nailsworth
The Red House, Staunton, nr Gloucester
Tin Penny Cottage, Whiteway, nr Stroud
Trevi Garden, Hartpury, nr Gloucester
Willow Lodge, nr Longhope, Gloucester

May 29 Monday
Brackenbury, Coombe, nr Wotton-under-Edge

Camp Cottage, Highleadon, nr Newent
Eastington Gardens, nr Northleach
Grove Cottage, Lower Lydbrook, nr Cinderford ‡
Jasmine House, Bream, nr Lydney ‡‡
Millend House, nr Coleford ‡‡
The Red House, Staunton, nr Gloucester ‡‡‡
Trevi Garden, Hartpury, nr Gloucester ‡‡‡
Willow Lodge, nr Longhope, Gloucester ‡

June

Camp Cottage, Highleadon, nr Newent. Every Sun, Mon, Tues
Ewen Manor, nr Cirencester. Every Wed, Thurs, Fri
Grove Cottage, Lower Lydbrook, nr Cinderford. Every Sun
The Old Manor, Twyning. Every Mon
Tin Penny Cottage, Whiteway, nr Stroud. Every Wed
Trevi Garden, Hartpury, nr Gloucester. Every Sun, Thurs

June 3 Saturday

Barnsley House, nr Circencester
Blundells, Broadwell, nr Stow-on-the-Wold

June 4 Sunday

Blundells, Broadwell, nr Stow-on-the-Wold
25 Bowling Greed Road, Circencester
The Chestnuts, nr Minchinhampton
Green Cottage, Lydney
High Bank, 59 Bourne Drive, Brimscombe
Hodges Barn, Shipton Moyne, nr Tetbury
Pigeon House, Southam, nr Cheltenham
Stancombe Park, Stinchombe, nr Dursley
Stanway House, nr Winchcombe
Sunningdale, Grange Court, nr Westbury

June 5 Monday

Camp Cottage, Highleadon, nr Newent

June 7 Wednesday

Green Cottage, Lydney

June 8 Thursday

Home Farm, Huntley, nr Newent

June 10 Saturday

Rodmarton Manor, nr Cirencester

June 11 Sunday

25 Bowling Green Road, Circencester
The Chipping Croft, Tetbury
Frampton-on-Severn Gardens
Green Cottage, Lydney
Hillesley House, Hillesley, nr Wotton-under-Edge ‡
Hunts Court, North Nibley, Dursley ‡
Icomb Place, nr Stow-on-the-Wold
Millend House, nr Coleford
Pitt Court, North Nibley, nr Dursley ‡
Prestbury Gardens, nr Cheltenham
Redwood House, Halmore, nr Berkeley
Tetbury Gardens
Willow Lodge, nr Longhope, Gloucester

June 12 Monday

Camp Cottage, Highleadon, nr Newent
The Old Rectory, Duntisbourne Rous
Willow Lodge, nr Longhope, Gloucester

June 14 Wednesday

Green Cottage, Lydney
13 Merestones Drive, Cheltenham

June 15 Thursday

Ami Yume Teien, Blockley ‡
Jasmine House, Bream, nr Lydney
Old Mill Dene, Blockley ‡

June 17 Saturday

Tin Penny Cottage, Whiteway, nr Stroud

June 18 Sunday

Adlestrop Gardens, nr Stow-on-the-Wold
Boilingwell, Sudeley Hill, nr Winchcombe
Cotswold Farm, nr Cirencester
Green Cottage, Lydney ‡
Hunts Court, North Nibley, Dursley
Jasmine House, Bream, nr Lydney ‡
Poulton Gardens, nr Cirencester
The Red House, Staunton, nr Gloucester
Willow Lodge, nr Longhope, Gloucester
Witcombe Gardens, nr Gloucester

June 19 Monday

Camp Cottage, Highleadon, nr Newent ‡
Willow Lodge, nr Longhope, Gloucester ‡

June 21 Wednesday

Green Cottage, Lydney

June 22 Thursday

Ami Yume Teien, Blockley ‡
Home Farm, Huntley, nr Newent ‡‡
Old Mill Dene, Blockley ‡
Sunningdale, Grange Court, nr Westbury ‡‡

June 25 Sunday

Blockley Gardens, nr Moreton-in-Marsh
25 Bowling Green Road, Circencester
Brackenbury, Coombe, nr Wotton-under-Edge ‡
Brockweir Gardens, nr Chepstow
Chalford Gardens, nr Stroud
Grange Farm, Evenlode, nr Moreton-in-Marsh ‡‡
Green Cottage, Lydney
Hunts Court, North Nibley, Dursley ‡
Millend House, nr Coleford
North Rye House, Broadwell, Moreton-in-Marsh ‡‡
Pitt Court, North Nibley, nr Dursley ‡
Stanton Gardens, nr Broadway
Stowell Park, nr Northleach
Sunningdale, Grange Court, nr Westbury ‡‡
Willow Lodge, nr Longhope, Gloucester ‡‡

June 26 Monday

Camp Cottage, Highleadon, nr Newent
The Old Rectory, Duntisbourne Rous
Willow Lodge, nr Longhope, Gloucester

June 28 Wednesday

13 Merestones Drive, Cheltenham
Moor Wood, Woodmancote, nr Cirencester

June 29 Thursday

Ami Yume Teien, Blockley ‡
Bourton House Garden, Bourton-on-the-Hill ‡
Jasmine House, Bream, nr Lydney
Old Mill Dene, Blockley ‡

July

Camp Cottage, Highleadon, nr Newent. Every Sun, Tues
Grove Cottage, Lower Lydbrook, nr Cinderford. Every Sun
The Old Manor, Twyning. Every Mon
Tin Penny Cottage, Whiteway, nr Stroud. Every Wed
Trevi Garden, Hartpury, nr Gloucester. Every Thurs

July 2 Sunday

Beverston Castle, nr Tetbury ‡
25 Bowling Green Road, Circencester ‡‡
Camp Cottage, Highleadon, nr Newent
Combend Manor, Elkstone, nr Cheltenham
High Bank, 59 Bourne Drive, Brimscombe

Hunts Court, North Nibley, Dursley
Jasmine House, Bream, nr Lydney
Misarden Park, Miserden, nr Cirencester
The Old Rectory, Great Rissington
Orchard Cottage, Beverston, nr Tetbury ‡
20 St Peters Road, Cirencester ‡‡
Quenington Gardens, nr Fairford
Upton Wold, nr Moreton-in-Marsh

July 3 Monday
Berverston Castle, nr Tetbury ‡
Camp Cottage, Highleadon, nr Newent
Orchard Cottage, Beverston, nr Tetbury ‡

July 5 Wednesday
Ewen Manor, nr Cirencester
Rookwoods, Waterlane, nr Bisley

July 6 Thursday
Ami Yume Teien, Blockley ‡
Old Mill Dene, Blockley ‡

July 7 Friday
Ewen Manor, nr Cirencester

July 9 Sunday
Campden House, Chipping Campden ‡
Casa Mia, Clifford Manor, nr Newent ‡‡
Hodges Barn, Shipton Moyne, nr Tetbury
Hunts Court, North Nibley, Dursley ‡‡‡
Pitt Court, North Nibley, nr Dursley ‡‡‡
The Red House, Staunton, nr Gloucester
Rockcliffe, nr Upper Slaughter
Sezincote, nr Moreton-in-Marsh ‡
Sunningdale, Grange Court, nr Westbury ‡‡
Tin Penny Cottage, Whiteway, nr Stroud
Willow Lodge, nr Longhope, Gloucester ‡‡

July 10 Monday
Camp Cottage, Highleadon, nr Newent
Willow Lodge, nr Longhope, Gloucester

July 11 Tuesday
Cinderdine Cottage, Dymock, nr Newent

July 12 Wednesday
Rookwoods, Waterlane, nr Bisley

July 13 Thursday
Ami Yume Teien, Blockley ‡
Jasmine House, Bream, nr Lydney
Old Mill Dene, Blockley ‡

July 16 Sunday
Boilingwell, Sudeley Hill, nr Winchcombe
Broad Campden Gardens, nr Chipping Campden
25 Bowling Green Road, Cirencester ‡
Casa Mia, Clifford Manor, nr Newent ‡‡
Cirencester Gardens ‡
Gardeners Way, Kings Stanley, nr Stroud
Jasmine House, Bream, nr Lydney
Millend House, nr Coleford
20 St Peters Road, Cirencester ‡
Willow Lodge, nr Longhope, Gloucester ‡‡

July 17 Monday
Willow Lodge, nr Longhope, Gloucester

July 20 Thursday
Casa Mia, Clifford Manor, nr Newent

July 23 Sunday
25 Bowling Greed Road, Cirencester ‡
Casa Mia, Clifford Manor, nr Newent ‡‡
Pinbury Park, nr Cirencester ‡
Willow Lodge, nr Longhope, Gloucester ‡‡

July 24 Monday
The Old Rectory, Duntisbourne Rous
Willow Lodge, nr Longhope, Gloucester

July 25 Tuesday
Cinderdine Cottage, Dymock, nr Newent

July 27 Thursday
Bourton House Garden, Bourton-on-the-Hill

July 30 Sunday
Brackenbury, Coombe, nr Wotton-under-Edge
Brockweir Gardens, nr Chepstow ‡
Millend House, nr Coleford ‡
Minchinhampton Gardens

July 31 Monday
Minchinhampton Gardens

August
Camp Cottage, Highleadon, nr Newent. Every Sun, Tues
Grove Cottage, Lower Lydbrook, nr Cinderford. Every Sun
The Old Manor, Twyning. Every Mon
Tin Penny Cottage, Whiteway, nr Stroud. Every Wed
Trevi Garden, Hartpury, nr Gloucester. Every Thurs

August 3 Thursday
Jasmine House, Bream, nr Lydney

August 6 Sunday
25 Bowling Greed Road, Circencester
Jasmine House, Bream, nr Lydney
Redwood House, Halmore, nr Berkeley
Sunningdale, Grange Court, nr Westbury ‡
Tin Penny Cottage, Whiteway, nr Stroud
Trevi Garden, Hartpury, nr Gloucester
Willow Lodge, nr Longhope, Gloucester ‡

August 7 Monday
Willow Lodge, nr Longhope, Gloucester

August 8 Tuesday
Cinderdine Cottage, Dymock, nr Newent

August 13 Sunday
Boilingwell, Sudeley Hill, nr Winchcombe
25 Bowling Greed Road, Circencester
Millend House, nr Coleford
Sunningdale, Grange Court, nr Westbury ‡
Willow Lodge, nr Longhope, Gloucester ‡

August 14 Monday
Willow Lodge, nr Longhope, Gloucester

August 17 Thursday
Sunningdale, Grange Court, nr Westbury

August 19 Saturday
Kiftsgate Court, nr Chipping Campden

August 20 Sunday
Westonbirt Gardens at Westonbirt School

August 22 Tuesday
Cinderdine Cottage, Dymock, nr Newent

August 24 Thursday
Jasmine House, Bream, nr Lydney

August 27 Sunday
Brockweir Gardens, nr Chepstow ‡
Eastington Gardens, nr Northleach
Jasmine House, Bream, nr Lydney ‡
Millend House, nr Coleford ‡
Trevi Garden, Hartpury, nr Gloucester

August 28 Monday
Brackenbury, Coombe, nr Wotton-under-Edge
Camp Cottage, Highleadon, nr Newent
Eastington Gardens, nr Northleach
Jasmine House, Bream, nr Lydney ‡
Millend House, nr Coleford ‡
Tin Penny Cottage, Whiteway, nr Stroud

Trevi Garden, Hartpury, nr Gloucester

August 30 Wednesday

The Chipping Croft, Tetbury

August 31 Thursday

Bourton House Garden, Bourton-on-the-Hill

September

Grove Cottage, Lower Lydbrook, nr Cinderford. Every Sun

The Old Manor, Twyning. Every Mon

Tin Penny Cottage, Whiteway, nr Stroud. Every Wed

September 3 Sunday

Green Cottage, Lydney

Westbury Court Gardens, Westbury-on-Severn

Westonbirt Gardens at Westonbirt School

September 7 Thursday

Jasmine House, Bream, nr Lydney

Trevi Garden, Hartpury, nr Gloucester

September 9 Saturday

Sudeley Castle Gardens, Winchombe

September 10 Sunday

Boilingwell, Sudeley Hill, nr Winchcombe

Cinderdine Cottage, Dymock, nr Newent

Hillesley House, Hillesley, nr Wotton-under-Edge

Jasmine House, Bream, nr Lydney

Redwood House, Halmore, nr Berkeley

September 14 Thursday

Trevi Garden, Hartpury, nr Gloucester

September 21 Thursday

Trevi Garden, Hartpury, nr Gloucester

September 24 Sunday

Tin Penny Cottage, Whiteway, nr Stroud

September 25 Monday

The Old Rectory, Duntisbourne Rous

September 28 Thursday

Bourton House Garden, Bourton-on-the-Hill

October

The Old Manor, Twyning. Every Mon

Tin Penny Cottage, Whiteway, nr Stroud. Every Wed

October 8 Sunday

Boilingwell, Sudeley Hill, nr Winchcombe

Painswick Rococo Garden, Painswick

October 16 Monday

The Old Rectory, Duntisbourne Rous

November

Tin Penny Cottage, Whiteway, nr Stroud. Every Wed

December

Tin Penny Cottage, Whiteway, nr Stroud. Every Wed

February 1996

Cinderdine Cottage, Dymock, nr Newent. Tues, 8,13, 20. Thurs 15, 22, Sun 18 (12-4)

DESCRIPTIONS OF GARDENS

Abbotswood (Dikler Farming Co) 1m W of Stow-on-the-Wold, nr Lower Swell. Beautiful, extensive heather and stream gardens; massed plantings of spring bulbs and flowers; rhododendrons, flowering shrubs, specimen trees; extensive herbaceous borders, roses, formal gardens; fine example of garden landscape. Buses not allowed in grounds. TEAS. Car park free. *Adm £2 Chd free. Suns May 7, 21 (1.30-6)*

Adlestrop Gardens ♿❀ 3m E of Stow-on-the-Wold, off A436. A delightful small village made famous by Jane Austen and the poet Edward Thomas. A variety of gardens will be on show. Produce and plant stalls in aid of Church Fabric Fund. TEAS in aid of village hall. *Adm £1.50 Chd free. Sun June 18 (2-6)*

¶**Ami Yume Tein** ✄ (Mr Tim Brown) Blockley. On the Chipping Campden rd almost opp St Georges Hall and the School. A unique example of a Japanese kare sansui teien (dry landscape garden) set in the improbable context of an old Cotswold village. The garden is a small rectangle within a 25sq metre space bounded by two interesting types of Japanese fencing. It is crossed by rectilinear paths (an example of mino ishi) which create five sub-rectangles. Looks interesting in all weathers. TEAS at Old Mill Dene. *Combined adm with* **Old Mill Dene** *£2.50 Chd 50p (Share to Glos Churches Preservation Trust®). Sun April 23, Thurs June 15, 22, 29, Thurs July 6, 13 (2-6). Private visits welcome £1, please* **Tel 01386 701026**

Ampney Knowle ❀ (Mr & Mrs Richard Pile) nr Cirencester. 4m NE Cirencester B4425 ¼m S of Barnsley on Ampney Crucis rd. Medium-sized garden around C18 farmhouse with plant packed terrace; walled gardens, mixed borders and old shrub roses. Woodland garden with indigenous wild flowers and 40-acre bluebell wood. Picnic site. TEAS in aid of Royal British Legion Women's Section. *Adm £1.50 Chd free. Sun April 30 (12-6). Private visits welcome, please* **Tel 01285 740230**

Ashley Gardens 3m NE of Tetbury on A433, turn R through Culkerton to Ashley. TEA. *Combined adm £2 Chd free (Share to Ashley Church®). Mon April 17 (2-5)*

Ashley Grange ♿✄ (Miss A L Pearson) Old garden of one-time Georgian/Victorian rectory with fine landscape views. Shrubs and herbaceous borders. Sensitively redesigned for easier upkeep

Ashley Manor ✄ (Mr & Mrs M J Hoskins) Old garden next to church redesigned by present owners and imaginatively planted. Mature yew hedges divide 4 separate gardens and are the backdrop to a collection of clematis, shrub roses and herbaceous plants. Sweet-smelling herb terrace and kitchen garden

Barnsley House ♿✄❀ (Mrs Rosemary Verey) Barnsley 4m. NE of Cirencester on B4425. Mature garden with interesting collection of shrubs and trees; ground cover; herbaceous borders; pond garden; laburnum walk; knot and herb gardens; formal kitchen garden; C18 summer houses. C17 house (not open). *Adm £2 OAPs £1 Chd free (no charge Dec-Feb). Mons, Weds, Thurs & Sats (10-6). Parties by appt only* **Tel 01285 740281**. *For NGS (Share to Barnsley Church®). Sats May 6, June 3 (2-6)*

Batsford Arboretum ❀ (The Batsford Foundation Registered Charity No 286712) 1½m NW of Moreton-in-Marsh, A44/A429 intersection. Arboretum & wild gardens; over 1500 named trees (many rare) and shrubs; magnolias, flowering cherries, bulbs; beautiful views from Cotswold escarpment. House not open. TEAS at Garden Centre. *Adm £2 OAPs and parties of 12 and over £1.50 Chd under 14 free. Open daily, mid March to 1st week in Nov (10-5). For NGS Sun May 14 (2-5)*

Beverston Castle ♿❀ (Mrs L Rook) Beverston. 2m W of Tetbury on A4135. Overlooked by romantic C12-15 castle ruin the overflowingly planted paved terrace leads from C17 house across moat to sloping lawn with spring bulbs in abundance and full herbaceous and shrub borders. Large walled kitchen garden and greenhouses. TEA (April 9) TEAS (July 2). Plants for sale July. *Adm £1.50 OAPs £1 Chd under 14yrs 50p (Share to Tetbury Hospital®). Suns, Mons, April 9, 10; July 2, 3 (2-6). Private visits by written appt all year*

Bhardonna ♿❀ (Mr & Mrs G W Webb) 1m N of Newent on Ledbury-Dymock rd B4215. Recently created landscaped garden of 1½ acres rich in colour and plant interest. Shrubs; spring bulbs; borders; fish ponds; collection of horse ploughs. Plants for sale on open days. TEA. *Adm £1 Chd free. Sun, Mon April 16, 17 (2-6). Private visits welcome May 1 to Sept 30, please* **Tel 01531 822169**

Blockley Gardens ✂❀ NW of Moreton-in-Marsh. A44 Moreton-Broadway; turning E. Some gardens not safe for small children. TEAS at St George's Hall. *Combined adm £2.50 or 50p per garden Chd free. Suns April 30, June 25 (2-6)*

Elm Barns (Sir Thomas & Lady Skyrme) Shrubs; lawns; pool; beautiful views

The Garage (Mr & Mrs Stuart-Turner) Unusual garden making the best of a difficult slope; varied plantings *Sun June 25 only*

Grange Cottage (Mrs J Moore) Small garden with unusual plants

Holly House ✂❀ (Simon Ford & Robert Ashby) Secluded garden 'rooms', lovely views, unusual trees, small formal kitchen garden

Malvern Mill (Mr & Mrs J Bourne) Converted mill with pond and stream; 1-acre incl orchard

Old Mill Dene (Mr & Mrs B S Dare) 2½-acre garden with terraced slopes and mill pool. *For additional openings and full desc see main entry*

Paxton House (Mr & Mrs Peter Cator) Walled garden on different levels; unusual plants, spring bulbs, shrub roses

Pear Trees (Mrs J Beckwith) Small secluded, walled cottage garden with unusual plants

Rodneys (Mr & Mrs T Q Abell) Newly designed formal walled garden. *Sun June 25 only*

> **Regular Openers.** Too many days to include in diary. Usually there is a wide range of plants giving year-round interest. See head of county section for the name and garden description for times etc.

Blundells ♿❀ (Mr & Mrs Joe Elliott) Broadwell 1m N of Stow-on-the-Wold off A429. Medium-sized garden with large variety of hardy plants and alpines, trees, shrubs, herbaceous borders, lilies, 25 plus old stone sinks and troughs planted with alpines. Cream TEAS. *Adm £1.50 Chd free (Share to GRBS®). Sat, Sun June 3, 4 (2-6). Private visits welcome, please* **Tel 01451 830549**

Boddington Manor ♿❀ (Robert Hitchins Ltd) Boddington 3m W of Cheltenham off the A4019 Cheltenham to Tewkesbury rd. After crossing the M5 motorway take first turning L which is signed to Boddington. Old garden altered and restored since 1985 incl wild flower woodland walk, mature specimen trees, extensive lawns and lakes with recently planted bog garden, and large collection of conifers. Neo-gothic manor house (not open). Cream TEAS in aid of Church Funds and NGS. *Adm £1 Chd free. Sun May 21 (11-5)*

Boilingwell ❀ (Canon & Mrs R W Miles) Sudeley 1½m SE of Winchcombe. Take Castle St. out of Winchcombe, or Rushley Lane on Broadway road (signed Guiting Power); ¼m up hill beyond Sudeley Castle North Lodge. 1½-acre garden, with no room for grass, featuring a wide variety of species intensively planted for year round colour and easy maintenance; a wildish garden in a fairly formal setting. TEAS. *Adm £1.50 Chd free (Share to Stanley Pontlarge Church®). Suns March 26, April 23, May 21, June 18, July 16, Aug 13, Sept 10, Oct 8; (2-5). Parties welcome, please* **Tel 01242 603337**

Bourton House Garden ✂❀ (Mr & Mrs R Paice) Bourton-on-the-Hill 2m W of Moreton-in-Marsh on A44. This handsome C18 Cotswold village house (not open) with fine views is enhanced by a medium-sized garden largely created under the present ownership. Well kept lawns, quiet fountains, a knot garden and stone walls set off a number of imaginatively planted herbaceous borders. A recently planted 7 acre field opp will provide added interest in years to come. DIY TEAS in C16 Tithe Barn. *Adm £2.50 Chd free. Every Thurs & Fri May 25 to Sept 29. Also Bank hols Mon May 29, Sun Mon Aug 27, 28 (12-5). For NGS last Thurs of every month. May to Sept (12-5). Also in conjunction with* **Bourton-on-the-Hill Gardens** *parties welcome, please* **Tel 01386 700121**

Bourton-on-the-Hill Gardens ✂❀ 2m NW Moreton-in-Marsh A44 to Broadway. Wide selection of gardens of varied character in charming hillside village. Plant stall. TEAS (2-5). *Gardens adm £2.50 (including* **Bourton House** *as above) Chd free (Share to village Old School®). Sun May 28 (1-6)*

The Chantry (Mr & Mrs J Coram-James) Large lawns with mixed borders – excellent views

Glebe House (Sir Peter & Lady Herbert) Ex rectory garden. Mixed borders. Views

Hillcrest (Mr & Mrs M Gaden) Small garden, mixed borders

Porch House (Mr & Mrs A Firth) Established terraced garden next to Churchyard

Springwood (Mr & Mrs D Storey) Cottage garden. Mixed borders

Tawnies (Mr & Mrs P Hayes) Raised beds with ericaceous plants. Long lawn

25 Bowling Green Road (Fr & Mrs John Beck) Cirencester. Take A417 to Gloucester just to traffic lights, cross or turn R into The Whiteway then 1st L to no 25 on R of rd bend. Please respect neighbours' driveways, no pavement parking. Fast developing new garden of owners recently moved from well-known garden in Cecily Hill. Many perennials, roses and clematis, and some plant surprises. Featured Channel 4 TV Garden Club and BBC 1 Big Day Out. *Adm £1 Chd under 16 free. Suns June 4, 11, 25, July 2, 23, Aug 6, 13 (2-5). Open with* **Cirencester Gardens** *(2-6). Private visits welcome, please* **Tel 01285 653778**

Brackenbury ❀ (Mr & Mrs Peter Heaton) Coombe, 1m NE of Wotton-under-Edge. From Wotton Church ½m on Stroud rd (B4058) turn right (signed Coombe); from Stroud left off B4058, 300yds past Wotton-under-Edge sign; house 300yds on right. ⅔-acre terraced plantsman's and flower arranger's garden; foliage a special feature. Well stocked mixed borders, cottage garden, pool; 700 different hardy perennials and 200 different shrubs. Fruitcage, vegetables on deep-bed system. National Collection of Erigeron cultivars. Best in June and July. Home-made TEAS. *Adm £1 Chd free (Share to Cotswold Care Hospice®). Mon May 29, Suns June 25, July 30, Mon Aug 28 (2-6)*

Bredon Manor ✂ (Mr & Mrs Richard George) 3m from Tewkesbury on the B4080. The house is next to the NT Tithe Barn in Bredon. 5 acres of well stocked formal gardens incl a ½ acre walled kitchen garden, a walled rose garden, sunken garden of various shrub roses and hostas, water garden with C17 monks fishpond and riverside meadows. Cream TEAS in aid of Save the Children. *Adm £2 Chd free. Sun April 9 (2-5)*

Broad Campden Gardens ♿❀ 5m E of Broadway 1m SE of Chipping Campden. TEAS at Village Hall. *Combined adm £2.50 or 60p each garden Chd free. Sun July 16 (2-6). Free car park. Coaches by appt only* **Tel 01386 840467**

The Angel House (Mr & Mrs Bill Boddington) Garden in old damson and apple orchard, with view of church and C17 and C18 cottages

Briar Hill House (Sir Geoffrey and Lady Elerton) Shrubs, roses, heathers and conifers

Cherry Orchard Cottage (Mr & Mrs David Brook) ¾-acre orchard, shrub bank and secret garden

The Farthings (Mr & Mrs John Astbury) Terraced cottage garden

¶**Hillside** (Mr John Wilkinson) Garden (old orchard) under reclamation within ½ acre of lawns, meadow and old fruit trees

The Malt House (Mr & Mrs Nick Brown) Sheltered garden with small stream, being gradually replanted with shrubs from herbaceous for simplified management

Manor Barn (Mr Michael Miles & Mr Christopher Gurney) 1½-acres. Formal terraces, sweeping cultivated meadow, newly planted woodland and shrubbery, boundary of wandering stream with falls

Oldstones (Mr & Mrs H R Rolfe) A new ¾-acre garden, started 1989. Designed and constructed with the exception of the stone walling by the owners; terraced garden leading down to a stream with lawns, shrubs and roses

Pinders (Mr & Mrs Ian Dunnett) 1-acre garden on several levels, rare shrubs and trees

Sharcomb Furlong (Mr & Mrs Basil Hasberry) ¾-acre; wide range of shrubs, shrub roses and trees

Withy Bank (Mr & Mrs Jim Allen) ½-acre; acers and shrubs

Brockweir Gardens ♿✂❀ (2m Tintern Abbey) From A466 Chepstow to Monmouth rd, cross R Wye to Brockweir, ¾m uphill take L turning to Coldharbour. TEAS at Laurel Cottage or Fernleigh. *Adm 75p each garden. Suns March 26, April 30, May 28, June 25, July 30, Aug 27 (2-6)*

Fernleigh (Capt & Mrs J P Gould) 2½ acres of well established garden situated at an altitude of 500′. Many old trees, camellias and spring bulb collection. A peaceful garden with splendid views across the valley of the R Wye. *Not open March 26, Aug 27*

Laurel Cottage (David & Jean Taylor) Informal 1-acre cottage garden with lovely views over Offas Dyke. Dry stone walling creates gardens within a garden with lawns, herbaceous flowers and spring bulbs. Interesting selection of unusual shrubs and plants. Outside the main garden are a small vegetable garden, arboretum and orchard. *Private visits welcome all year, please* **Tel 01291 689565**

Threeways (Iorrie & Gwen Williams) Follow signs from A466 Brockweir Bridge or from B4228 at Hewelsfield Xrds: also on foot from Laurel Cottage. 2-acre garden developed since 1984. Former paddock planted with unusual shrubs and trees. Small woodland area, bog garden and stream. Formal area with water feature and well stocked herbaceous borders. *Private visits welcome, please* **Tel 01291 689686**

Camp Cottage ✂❀ (Les Holmes & Sean O'Neill) Highleadon, nr Newent. 6m NW of Gloucester. From Glos take A40 Ross rd, turn R onto B4215 Newent rd, 2½m along turn R at sign for Upleadon. The cottage is about 100yds up lane on L hand side. A plant lovers garden with C17 thatched cottage (not open). About 1 acre overflowing with old roses, climbing plants, snowdrops, hellebores and many unusual plants from all over the world mostly grown from seed and cuttings. Pergola, arches and short shrubland walk to bog garden. Widely featured on TV 'Gardeners' World' and Channel 4, radio, magazines, books plus 1995 gardens series on BBC2. TEA on Suns and some weekdays. *Adm £1 Chd 50p. Suns Feb 26, March 5 to 26 (11-3) April 16 to Aug 27, Mons May 22 to July 10, Tues April 18 to Aug 29. Bank Hols April 17, May 8, 29, Aug 28. Private visits welcome all year, please* **Tel 01452 790352**

Campden House ♿❀ (Mr & Mrs Philip Smith) Chipping Campden. Drive entrance on Chipping Campden to Weston Subedge rd, about ¼m SW of Campden. 2-acre garden with mixed borders of plant and colour interest; fine parkland; manor house with C17 tithe barn in hidden valley. TEAS and plant stall in aid of the Gloucestershire Macmillan Nurses. *Adm £1.50 Chd free. Sun July 9 (2-6)*

By Appointment Gardens. See head of county section

Casa Mia ♿❀ (Mr & Mrs Bryan Jones) Clifford Manor, nr Newent. Off B4216 Newent to Huntley rd approx 2½m from Newent turn R signposted May Hill. Garden is on L about ¾m. Enthusiast's 1½-acre garden in idyllic setting. Mixed shrub and herbaceous borders, with a variety of plants, some unusual. Plants labelled. Mature trees, stream and vegetable garden. TEAS. Parking available within grounds. *Adm £1 Chd free. Suns July 9, 16, 23; Thurs July 20 (2-6). Groups by appt July only, please* **Tel 01452 830404**

Cerney House ✂❀ (Sir Michael & Lady Angus) North Cerney. 4m N of Cirencester on A435 Cheltenham rd. Turn L opp Bathurst Arms, past church to top of hill, pillared gates on R. Romantic walled garden filled with old-fashioned roses and herbaceous borders. This is a working kitchen garden with a scented garden and well-labelled herb garden. Spring bulbs in abundance all around the wooded grounds. TEAS. *Adm £1.50 Chd free. Tues, Weds, Fris, Feb to Oct (2-6). For NGS Sun April 30 (2-6). Private visits welcome, please* **Tel 01285 831300**

Chalford Gardens ✂ 4m E of Stroud on A419 to Cirencester. Gardens are high above the Chalford Vale and reached on foot by steep climb from car park on main rd or from New Red Lion Inn in High St. *Combined adm £2 Chd free. Sun June 25 (2-6)*

The Old Chapel (F J & F Owen) Artists' 1-acre Victorian chapel garden on precipitous hillside. A tiered tapestry of herbaceous borders, formal potager, small orchard, pond and summer house, old roses. Gothic pergola and rose tunnel, many unusual plants all laid out on terraced S-facing Marle Cliff. Featured in Gardens Illustrated and Cotswold Life. Old Chapel Garden and Studio *open for private visits May 1 to July 12, please* **Tel 01453 886587**. *Also open with Art Exhibition Mon June 19 to Sat June 24, Adm £1*

¶**The Rock House** (Mr & Mrs George Edwards) 1-acre, S facing old garden, recently reconstructed. Dramatic 40' cliff and cave provide backdrop for climbing roses, clematis, shrubbery, rockery, lawn and herbaceous borders. *Private visits welcome for parties of 2 and more (May-July), please* **Tel 01453 886363**

The Chestnuts ✂❀ (Mr & Mrs E H Gwynn) Minchinhampton. From Nailsworth by Avening rd (B4014) L Weighbridge Inn ¼m up hill. From Minchinhampton 1m via New Rd or Well Hill. ⅔-acre walled garden; shrubs; bulbs; roses; clematis; rock garden; pool garden; wildflower lawn. ⅔-acre arboretum, planted since 1972 with wide variety of unusual trees and shrubs inc many sorbus species and shrub roses. Lovely views of hills, woods and fields. Featured in Channel 4 TV Garden Club. *Adm £1.50 Chd free (Share to Gloucestershire Wildlife Trust®). Sun June 4 (2-6)*

The Chipping Croft – See Tetbury Gardens

¶**Cinderdine Cottage** ♿✂❀ (John & Daphne Chappell) Dymock. 3m NE of Newent. Turn off the B4215 Newent to Ledbury rd just S of Dymock village towards Ryton/Ketford. Cottage ¾m on R of lane. ½-acre garden in the heart of daffodil country belonging to 2 plant-aholics. Combining the formal and informal in a white garden and single-colour borders for summer and early autumn and sheltered spots for woodland plants in winter and early spring, incl our huge collection of species and hybrid snowdrops. *Adm £1 Chd free. Tues, Thurs, Suns, Feb 9, 14, 16, 19, 21, 23 (12-4). TEA. Suns, Tues April 16, July 11, 25, Aug 8, 22, Sept 10 (2-6). Parties welcome, please* **Tel 01531 890265**

Cirencester Gardens Cecily Hill is on W side of Cirencester near gates into Park and open air swimming pool. TEAS at 42 Cecily Hill. *Combined adm £2.50 Chd under 16 free. Sun July 16 (2-6)*

25 Bowling Green Road ❀ (Fr & Mrs John Beck) From Cirencester take A417 to Gloucester just to traffic lights, cross or turn R into The Whiteway then 1st L to no 25 on R of rd bend. See full desc in main entry. Please respect neighbours' driveways, no pavement parking. Fast developing new garden of owners recently moved from well-known garden in Cecily Hill. *Also open Suns June 4, 11, 25; July 2, 23, Aug 6, 13 Adm £1 (2-5)*

40 Cecily Hill. Exhibition of botanical pictures and china by Annette Firth, NDD, SBA

42 Cecily Hill (Mr & Mrs A Graham) Medium-sized walled family garden. Clematis, roses, herbaceous border; shrubs, rock garden

Cecily Hill House ♿ (Mr & Mrs Rupert de Zoete) Walled town garden with tranquil atmosphere; herbaceous and shrub borders; small ornamental kitchen garden. *Private visits also welcome mid June to July 31, please* **Tel 01285 653766**

20 St Peters Road ✂❀ (Meg and Jeff Blumsom) Off Cricklade St. turn R into Ashcroft Rd then L then R For description see main entry. *Also open Suns May to Sept Adm 50p (2-6). Private visits welcome, please* **Tel 01285 657696**

Clover House ♿✂ (Mrs Kenneth Kemble) Winson B4425 6½m from Cirencester. Take Cirencester-Burford rd, then N to Winson just W of Bibury. 4-acres; spring blossom and bulbs; lawns, mixed borders and roses. R Coln flows alongside the garden. *Adm £1.50 Chd free. Sun April 30 (2-6)*

Combend Manor ✂❀ (Mr & Mrs Noel Gibbs) Elkstone On A417 halfway between Cirencester and Cheltenham turn R signed Elkstone immediately R through pillars 1m on R. 3-acre mature garden in beautiful setting, partly laid out by Gertrude Jekyll; a variety of gardens within the main garden incl an arboretum, water garden, old-fashioned roses, heather garden. TEAS. *Adm £2 Chd free (Share to Elkstone Parish Church®). Sun July 2 (2-6)*

Cotswold Farm ✂ (Major & Mrs P D Birchall) 5m N of Cirencester on A417; signed immediately W of Five Mile House Inn. Cotswold garden in lovely position on different levels with a terrace designed by Norman Jewson in 1938; shrubs, mixed borders, alpine border, spring flowers, shrub roses; walled kitchen garden. TEAS. *Adm £2 Chd free. Sun June 18 (2-6). Private visits welcome May, June and July, please* **Tel 01285 653856**

Regular Openers. Too many days to include in diary. Usually there is a wide range of plants giving year-round interest. See head of county section for the name and garden description for times etc.

Daylesford House ♿✂❀ (Sir Anthony & Lady Bamford) Daylesford. Between Stow-on-the-Wold and Chipping Norton off A436. Magnificent lakeside and woodland walks amidst unusual shrubs and trees and massed bluebells. Large decorative formal fruit and vegetable walled garden with orchid house, peach house and working glasshouses. Trellised rose garden on raised terrace. Grounds immediately around the Grade 1 house not open. *Adm £1.50 Chd free (Share to swings and roundabouts appeal Kingham Village©). Wed May 24 (2-6). Coaches by appt,* **Tel 01608 659777**

Eastcombe, Bussage & Brownshill Gardens 3m E Stroud. 2m N of A419 Stroud to Cirencester on turning signposted to Bisley and Eastcombe. Cream TEAS at Bussage Village Hall. *Combined adm £2.50 Chd free (Share to Glos Macmillan Nurses Appeal®). Sun, Mon, May 7, 8 (2-6)*

Eastcombe:

Ashcroft (Mr & Mrs H T Cornell) Small garden with many bulbs, primulas and year-round colour

¶Beggars Roost ♿ (Mr & Mrs D R Page) Landscaped 12yrs ago using trees, shrubs and rare conifers. Conservatory houses over 900 cacti and succulent plants. Experimental 'O' gauge railway in part of garden

Brewers Cottage ♿ (Mr & Mrs T G N Carter) Easily managed hillside garden with laburnum covered pergola, shady & sunny borders and a small hidden courtyard. All year colour. Featured in 'Over the Hills from Broadway' and 'Amateur Gardening'

21 Farmcote Close ♿❀ (Mr & Mrs R Bryant) A housing estate garden, designed with curved beds to soften appearance. Nearly 350 varieties of interesting perennials, bulbs, shrubs and old roses on various colour themes. Espalier fruit

Fidges Hill House (Mr & Mrs R Lewis) Tranformed from building site with knee high weeds to cottage garden; secluded and lovely view. No car access, please park in village

Glenview (Mr & Mrs J Carroll) Cottage garden; colour scheme of yellow, blue and white with two exceptions.

¶Highlands (Mr & Mrs J Page) Small, tranquil and colourful cottage garden with views across the Toadsmoor Valley

Jasmine Cottage (Mr & Mrs K Hopkins) Very colourful cottage garden with view of the beautiful Toadsmoor valley

Vatch Rise ♿❀ (Mr & Mrs R G Abbott) Small garden with beautiful view. Extensive and interesting collection of bulbous plants, alpines and unusual perennials. A real plantsmans garden

Brownshill:

Beechcroft ♿ (Mr & Mrs R H Salt) Garden surrounds Edwardian House bounded by meadow. Mature trees, shrubs, borders, vegetables, fruit, conservatory and wild area

Bovey End (Sir Norman & Lady Wakefield) Brownshill. A large, informal garden sloping steeply with beautiful views across the Golden and Toadsmoor Valleys; many trees and shrubs

Bussage:

Pine Corner (Mr & Mrs W Burns-Brown) ¾-acre terraced garden overlooking Toadsmoor Valley. Spring bulbs, shrubs, alpines; kitchen & herb garden

Redwood ❀ (Mr & Mrs D F Collins) Terraced garden with 3 small ponds and many unusual trees, shrubs, bulbs, alpines and herbaceous plants. Vegetables and cordon fruit trees. Nearly 1000 plants for sale. *Private vists welcome April to July, please* **Tel 01453 882595**

Spindrift, The Ridge ♿ (Mr & Mrs B Wilson) Small garden on housing estate devoted largely to plant breeding experiments including a foxglove mutation

Eastington Gardens 1m SE of Northleach (A40). Charming Cotswold village with lovely views. TEAS at **Middle End**. *Combined adm £1.50 Chd free (Share to Northleach Church®). Suns, Mons May 28, 29, Aug 27, 28 (2-6)*

Bank Cottage (Mr & Mrs E S Holland) Lower End. Colourful cottage garden

Middle End ❀ (Mr & Mrs Owen Slatter) Medium-sized garden of general interest

Yew Tree Cottage (M Bottone Esq) Hardy plants for sun and shade

Ewen Manor ♿❀ (Lady Gibbs) 4m S of Cirencester via A429 3m from Cirencester turn at signpost Ewen 1m. Profusely planted series of gardens with architectural features, mature yew hedges, fine lawns, big borders, plant-filled terrace and containers, lily pool, cedar trees over 200yrs old and woodland area all around. Georgian Cotswold manor (not open). TEAS Sun only. *Adm £1.50 Chd free. Weds, Thurs, Fri May 3 to July 7 (11-4.30) Sun May 14 (Share to Glos Association for Mental Health®) (2-6). Also private visits welcome, please* **Tel 01285 770206**

Frampton-on-Severn Gardens ♿ SW of Gloucester nr Stonehouse 2m from M5 junction 13. TEAS in Village Hall in aid of WI. *Adm 80p per garden Chd free (Share to Gloucestershire Wildlife Trust and International League for Protection of Horses and NCCPG, Glos®). Sun June 11 (2-6)*

Buckholt (Brigadier & Mrs C E H Sparrow) 200yds beyond the S end of the village green on the L. Walled garden of about 1-acre, mature trees, shrubs and herbaceous borders, lavender garden with roses

Frampton Court (Mrs P F S Clifford) L hand side of village green. Fine view of Gothic orangery, 1750, standing at the end of a formal canal with water lilies and mixed shrub border on one side. Mature trees. *Groups welcome, please* **Tel 01452 740267**

Frampton Manor (Mr & Mrs Rollo Clifford) R hand side of village green. Fragrant walled garden with yew and lavender hedges. Mixed shrub and herbaceous borders. C15 timbered house, reputed birthplace of 'Fair Rosamund'

Gardeners Way ✂❀ (GRBS) Kings Stanley, 3m W of Stroud off A419, 2nd turn R after church in village. The ten bungalows provided by the Gardeners' Royal Benevolent Society for retired gardeners are a colourful showpiece of gardening skills. The gardens are all of individual design and character and contain many interesting plants and ideas. Gardening questions gladly answered. TEA. *Adm £2 OAP's £1 Chd free (Share to the GRBS®). Sun July 16 (2-6)*

¶Grange Farm (Lady Aird) Evenlode, nr Moreton-in-Marsh. Evenlode 3mls from Morton-in-Marsh and Stow-on-the-Wold. E of the A429 Fosseway and 1½m from Broadwell. The medium sized garden has been considerably developed over the past few years but the old house and apple trees provide a delightful setting for the newer water and sunken gardens while mature shrubs conceal hidden corners. TEAS. *Adm £1.50 Chd free (Share to Evenlode Church®). Sun June 25 (2-6)*

Green Cottage ♿❀ (Mr & Mrs F Baber) At far end of Lydney from Gloucester on A48 turn R into narrow lane just after derestriction sign. Garden 50 yds on R. Ample shady car park. An informal country garden of approx 1 acre with planted stream bank, hostas, hellebores, iris and cottage garden. Many herbaceous paeonies, incl the National Reference Collection of pre and early post 1900 cultivars (1824-1918). Large wayward specimen of clematis montana rubens (May). Specie and officinalis paeonies (May). National Collection 60-70 cultivars (June) Hellebores (Feb, March). Cream TEAS Suns May, June & Sept only. *Adm £1.50 Chd free. Suns March 5, 12, 19, 26 (12.30-4.00) (Hellebores), May 7, 14, 21, 28, June 4, 11, 18, 25, Sept 3 (2-6) Weds June 7, 14, 21 (11-5). Private visits for parties in June, please* **Tel 01594 841918**

Grove Cottage ✲❀ (Graham Birkin & Allan Thomas) Forge Hill, Lower Lydbrook. 5m NW of Cinderford. Leave car in public car park by river, mount facing flight of 115 steps to Forge Hill: garden 2nd L from top step. 2-acre garden packed with both common and little known plants suitable for this precipitous slope overlooking the Wye valley. Most plants are shade loving or shade tolerant and are set off by being grown in raised beds constructed in natural stone by the present owners. Also peat beds, ponds, herbaceous borders, shrub borders, and ¼-acre rockery all linked by a series of steep paths and natural stone steps. Extenisve collections of hellebores and irises. Not suitable for small children. TEA Suns only. *Adm £1 Chd 50p. Every Sun March 12 to Sept 24, Mons April 17, May 8, 29 (2-6). Private visits welcome, parking at garden by appt, please* **Tel 01594 860544**

Hartpury College ♿✲❀ Hartpury House, 5m N of Gloucester on A4l7 Gloucester-Ledbury. An extensive and historically important garden still retaining many of the original features created by its designers, notably Alfred Parsons and, later, Thomas Mawson. 17 acres of landscaped grounds incl a Victorian walled garden, terraced borders, glasshouses, herbaceous and alpine borders, and a collection of old apple and pear varieties as well as an extensive tree and shrub collection. TEA. *Adm £1.50 Chd free. Sun May 20 (2-5). Private visits welcome for parties of 6, please* **Tel 01452 700283**

Hidcote Manor Garden ♿✲❀ (The National Trust) 4m NE of Chipping Campden. Series of formal gardens, many enclosed within superb hedges, incl hornbeam on stems. Many rare trees, shrubs, plants. Coffee, lunches and teas. *Adm £5 Chd £2.50. Daily except Tues & Fri, April to Oct 31 (11-7); no entry after 6 or an hour before dusk if earlier). For NGS Sun May 7 (11-6)*

Regular Openers. See head of county section.

¶High Bank, 59 Bourne Drive ✲❀ (Mr & Mrs Malcolm Buckenham) Brimscombe. 2m E of Stroud on A419 on L, opp Golden Valley Cars sales showroom, up short footpath to 2nd gate on L. Intensely planted ¼-acre terraced hillside garden with herbaceous beds hosting a variety of interesting plants and offering fine views across the Golden Valley. Created in 4yrs and featuring sunken dell, pergolas, formal pool, enclosed rose garden, small gazebo, rockery and many unusual containers; also roses and clematis. TEAS. *Adm £1.50 Chd free. Suns June 4, July 2 (2-6)*

¶Hillesley House ❀ (Mr & Mrs J Walsh) Hillesley. 3m from Wotton-under-Edge on rd to Hawkesbury Upton and the A46. 1st house on L entering Hillesley from Wotton. 4 acres surrounding Tudor house (not open), walled garden; borders in sun and shade; roses. Innovative perennial plantings by Noël Kingsbury under development. TEA. *Adm £1.50 Chd free. Suns June 11, Sept 10 (2-6)*

Hodges Barn ♿❀ (Mr & Mrs C N Hornby) Shipton Moyne 3m S of Tetbury on Malmesbury side of Shipton Moyne. Very unusual C15 dovecot converted into a family home. Cotswold stone walls act as host to climbing and rambling roses, clematis, vines and hydrangeas; and together with yew, rose and tapestry hedges they create the formality of the area around the house; mixed shrub and herbaceous borders, shrub roses and a water garden; woodland garden planted with cherries, magnolias and spring bulbs. Featured in Country Life, Homes and Gardens, Sunday Telegraph and Sunday Times. Also open for NGS; adjoining garden of **Hodges Farmhouse,** by kind permission of Mr & Mrs Clive Lamb. *Combined adm £2.50 Chd free. Mons, Tues & Fris April 3 to Aug 18 (2-5). For NGS Suns April 16, June 4, July 9 (2-5). Private visits and parties welcome, teas by arrangement, please* **Tel 01666 880202**

Home Farm (Mrs T Freeman) Huntley. On the B4216 ½m from the A40 in Huntley travelling towards Newent. The house and gardens are in an elevated position with exceptional views over the Vale of Gloucester and up to the Cotswold escarpment. Over 1m of woodchip paths winding through woods to show carpets of spring flowers. Snowdrops, wood anemones, daffodils, bluebells and orchids. Enclosed garden with heather bed and fern border. One wood recently planted with rhododendrons and azaleas. *Adm £1 Chd free. Thurs Feb 2, 16, March 2, 16, 30, April 13, 27, May 11, 25, June 8, 22 (2-6 or dusk). Private visits welcome for parties of 2 and over, please* **Tel 01452 830209**

Hunts Court ♿✲❀ (Mr & Mrs T K Marshall) North Nibley, Dursley. 2m NW of Wotton-under-Edge. From Wotton B4060 Dursley rd turn R in Nibley at Black Horse; fork L after ¼m. Unusual shrubs, 450 varieties old roses, large collection of penstemons in peaceful 2½-acre garden with lawns set against tree clad hills and Tyndale monument. Superb views. House (not open) possible birth place of William Tyndale. Picnic area. Home-made TEAS (Suns only). *Adm £1 Chd free. Garden and Nursery open Tues-Sat all year ex Aug; also Bank Hol Mons. For NGS Suns June 11, 18, 25; July 2, 9 (2-6); Private visits welcome, please* **Tel 01453 547440**

8 Hyatts Way ✇❀ (Mr & Mrs P M Herbert and Paul Herbert) Bishops Cleeve, 4m N of Cheltenham; take A435 towards Evesham, at roundabout take road to Bishops Cleeve; at Bishops Cleeve turn R past Esso Garage, follow road to school, turn L, then 2nd R. Small plantsman's garden, slightly untidy but featuring over 500 varieties, incl digitalis and salvia species; many other unusual plants and alpines in sinks. *Adm 80p Chd 25p. Private visits welcome April 8 to Aug 5, please* **Tel 01242 673503**

Icomb Place ✇ (Mr & Mrs T L F Royle) 4m S of Stow-on-the-Wold; after 2m on A424 Burford rd turn L to Icomb village. 100-year-old sizeable garden extensively restored. Featuring woodland walk through mature & young trees in arboretum; rhododendrons & azaleas; grotto; pools, stream and water garden; parterre; lawned garden with extensive views. C14 manor house (not open). TEAS. *Adm £2 Chd £1 (Share to Deus Laudamus Trust®). Sun June 11 (2-6)*

Jasmine House ♿✇❀ (Mr & Mrs V M Bond) Bream. In picturesque Royal Forest of Dean. From Lydney take B4231 Bream rd; in 3 miles turn R to village; immediately after Xrds turn R into concealed lane Blue Rock Crescent opp. school; house 200yds on L. Approx 1 acre garden divided into rooms. Many interesting and unusual plants and old varieties to discover. Featured in Amateur Gardening. *Adm £1 Chd free. Suns April 16; May 7, 28; June 18; July 2, 16; Aug 6, 27; Sept 10. Bank Hol Mons April 17; May 8, 29; Aug 28. Thurs May 4, 25; June 15, 29; July 13; Aug 3, 24; Sept 7 (2-6). Private visits welcome all the year. Garden clubs especially welcome, please* **Tel 01594 563688**

Kiftsgate Court ✇❀ (Mr & Mrs J G Chambers) 3m NE of Chipping Campden, adjacent to Hidcote Nat Trust Garden. 1m E of A46 and B4081. Magnificent situation and views; many unusual plants and shrubs; tree paeonies, hydrangeas, abutilons, species and old-fashioned roses, inc largest rose in England, R.filipes Kiftsgate. TEAS (April 29 to Aug 31). Buses by appt. *Adm £3 Chd £1. Suns, Weds, Thurs & Bank Hols Mons April 2 to Sept 28. Also Sats in June & July (2-6). For NGS (Share to Sue Ryder Home, Leckhampton Court®) Sats May 13, Aug 19, (2-6).* **Tel 01386 438777**

Lydney Park ❀ (Viscount Bledisloe) Lydney. On A48 Gloucester-Chepstow rd between Lydney & Aylburton. Drive is directly off A48. 8 acres of extensive valley garden with many varieties of rhododendron, azaleas and other flowering shrubs; trees and lakes. Garden round house; magnolias and daffodils (April). Roman Temple Site and Museum. Deer park with fine trees. TEAS; also picnic area (in park). *Adm £2 Weds £1 (Acc chd & cars free). Easter Sun & Mon; Every Sun, Wed & Bank Hol from Sun April 2 to June 4 except May 21 (garden closed). Every day Sun May 28 to June 4 (11-6). For NGS Sun April 23, Wed May 10 (11-6).* **Tel 01594 842844**

¶13 Merestones Drive ❀ (Mr Dennis Moorcraft) Cheltenham. Merestones Drive is a turning off The Park reached by following signs to Gloscat (a technical college). Nearest main rd is A46 from Stroud. From Stroud turn L at traffic lights after Cheltenham town sign into Moorend Rd and take 3 further L turns. Limited parking in Merstones Drive. Small town garden shaded by large trees; hostas and ferns a speciality; many unusual plants; scree garden; small brook. TEAS. *Adm £1.50 Chd 50p. Weds June 14, 28 (2-6). Private visits welcome, please* **Tel 01242 578678**

Millend House ✇❀ (Mr & Mrs J D'A Tremlett) Coleford. 1½m SW out of Coleford on the Newland road, centre of Coleford clocktower signposted (Newland 2m). Magnificently located with beautiful valley views, the 2-acre hillside garden contains many unusual herbaceous plants and shrubs, both shade and sun loving, many of which are for sale. There are also scree and fern beds, a gazebo, ornamental pond, small vegetable and soft fruit garden, and a walk round a 200yr-old wood. TEAS in aid of Glos Macmillan Nurses. *Adm £1.50 Chd free. Suns, Mons, May 7, 8, 21, 28, 29; June 11, 25; July 16, 30; Aug 13, 27, 28 (2-6). Private groups welcome May 1 to Sept 30, please* **Tel 01594 832128**

Minchinhampton Gardens ✇❀ Minchinhampton 4m SE Stroud. From Market Sq down High St 100yds; then right at Xrds; 300yds turn left. Free car parking. Over 8 acres of adjacent gardens. Cream TEAS except Feb TEA. *Combined adm £2 Chd free (Share to Minchinhampton Centre for the Elderly®). Suns Feb 19 (2-4.30) April 9, July 30, Mon July 31 (2-6)*

Derhams House (Mr & Mrs Mark Byng) Garden created since 1957; water garden; shrubs, herbaceous borders; snowdrops and crocus

Lammas Park (Mr & Mrs P Grover) Lawns, herbaceous borders, wild garden, restored 'hanging gardens'. Superb views

St Francis (Mr & Mrs Peter Falconer) Garden made in old park round modern Cotswold stone house. Fine beech avenue; terraced garden; trough gardens; bonsai trees; unusual plants; giant snowdrops (spring); C18 ice-house. Picnickers welcome. *Also private visits welcome, please* **Tel 01453 882188**

Misarden Park ♿✇❀ (Maj M T N H Wills) Miserden 6m NW of Circencester. Follow the signs off the A417 or B4070 from Stroud. Spring flowers, shrubs, fine topiary (some designed by Sir Edwin Lutyens) and herbaceous borders within a walled garden; roses; fine specimen trees; C17 manor house (not open) standing high overlooking Golden Valley. Garden Nurseries open daily except Mons. *Adm £2 Chd free. April 4 to Sept 28 every Tues, Wed & Thurs (9.30-4.30). For NGS (Share to St Andrews Church, Miserden®). TEAS Suns April 9, July 2 (2-6).* **Tel 01285 821303**

¶Moor Wood ✇ (Mr & Mrs Henry Robinson) Woodmancote, nr Cirencester. 3½m from Cirencester turn L off A435 to Cheltenham at North Cerney signed 'Woodmancote 1¼m': entrance in village on L beside lodge with white gates. 2 acres of shrub, orchard and wildflower gardens in isolated valley setting. Holder of the National Collection of rambler roses. TEA. *Adm £1.50 Chd free. Wed June 28 (2-6). Private visits welcome for parties of 4 and more, please* **Tel 01285 831397**

The New Inn see **Poulton Gardens**

Newark Park (Mr & Mrs Christopher Howe) Ozleworth, 1½m E of Wotton-under-Edge, 1½m S of junction A4135/B4058. Steeply terraced romantic woodland garden in 10 acres around C16 hunting lodge house. Spring bulbs and cyclamen on hillside leading down to carp pond and C18 walled garden and summer house. Garden under restoration. Spectacular views. TEAS. *Adm £1.50 Chd 50p (Share to Muscular Dystrophy®). Sun April 2 (2-5)*

North Rye House ♿✲❀ (Mr & Mrs Peter Stoddart) nr Broadwell, Moreton-in-Marsh. On A429 Fosse Way halfway between Moreton-in-Marsh and Stow-on-the-Wold. Also signed from Broadwell village. Recently created and still developing 3-acre garden with modern ha-ha designed to blend scenically into its surrounding parkland setting with mature trees. Spring bulbs, mixed borders, shrub roses, alpines, small vegetable garden and gardener's cottage garden provide continuous colour and interest. TEAS in aid of Glos Macmillan Nurses. *Adm £1.50 Chd free. Suns April 2, June 25 (2-5)*

Nympsfield Gardens ✲❀ 3m NW of Nailsworth. Signed from B4066 Stroud-Dursley rd. TEAS in village hall. *Combined adm £1.50 Chd free (Share to St Bartholomews Church and Nympsfield Village Hall©). Suns April 30, May 28 (2-6)*

- **Barberi Cottage** ❀ (Mrs F Mack) Small garden with alpines
- **Bath Road Farm** (Mr & Mrs K Wright) Windswept cottage garden under construction; interesting wild plants, pond, vegetables
- **Candle Cottage** (Mr & Mrs A N Pearce) Small landscaped cottage garden. *May 28 only*
- **The Coach House** (Mr & Mrs R Overton) Small tree-lined garden. Unusual plants all labelled
- **Four Wells** (Mr J Price) Small cottage garden. *May 28 only*
- **Highlands** (Mr & Mrs R Easton) Garden on sloping windswept site
- **Pen-y-Banc** (Mr Philip Reynolds) adjoining above garden
- **The Post Office** (Mr & Mrs B Westwood) Small garden featuring heathers & violas
- **White Hart Court** (Mr & Mrs M Reynolds) Small formal garden with pool. C16 Coach House (part open)

The Old Manor ♿✲❀ (Mrs Joan Wilder) Twyning. 3m N of Tewkesbury via A38 to Worcester; follow sign to Twyning; garden opposite T-junction at top end of village. 2 acres, walled garden full of interest. Unusual shrubs, trees, herbaceous, alpines; two areas of developing arboretum; pool; terrace plantings; troughs. Field walks for picnics. Featured in TV 'Gardeners World'. Small nursery, all stock from garden (catalogue 30p and large SAE). TEA on Bank Hol Mons only. *Adm £1.50 Acc chd free (Share to GRBS & RGOF®). Every Mon March 6 to Oct 30 (2-5, or dusk if earlier) Private visits welcome except Suns including winter months, please* **Tel 01684 293516** *evenings*

Old Mill Dene, Blockley ✲❀ (Mr & Mrs B S Dare) School Lane, Blockley. From A44, Bourton-on-the-Hill, take the turn to Blockley. 1m down hill turn left behind 30mph sign, labelled cul de sac. 2½-acre garden with steep lawned terraces facing south and a mill-pool in a frost pocket with stream. Vegetable garden parterre with views over the hills. Dangerous for young children. Recently featured in Sunday Times and the Gardener. TEAS. *Combined adm with* **Ami Yume Teien** *£2.50 Chd 50p (Share to Glos Churches Preservation Trust®). Sun April 23, Thurs June 15, 22, 29; July 6, 13 (2-6). Also open with* **Blockley Gardens** *Suns April 30, June 25. Private visits welcome (not August) Adm £2 please* **Tel 01386 700457**

¶The Old Rectory, Duntisbourne Rous ✲ (Charles & Mary Keen) NW of Cirencester at Daglingworth take valley rd for the Duntisbournes. After ½m no through rd joins from R at entrance to Old Rectory. Writer and designer's own 1½ acre Cotswold family garden in the making, now in its 3rd yr. Beautiful setting nr Saxon church. Planted for atmosphere and all-yr-interest, this small garden has ten distinct areas and moods. Winter flowers, tender plants and unusual pelargoniums a speciality. *Adm £1.50 Chd free. Mons Feb 6, 27, March 27, April 24 (10-3) May 15, June 12, 26, July 24 (10-6) Sept 25, Oct 16 (10-3). Private visits by written appt welcome. Charges negotiable*

¶The Old Rectory, Great Rissington ♿ (Captain & Mrs Richard Turner). Off A429 through Bourton on the Water. Turn R to Great Rissington. At village green, Lamb Inn, turn R to bottom of hill, where Old Rectory is next to church. 1½-acre garden, with large borders, incl a yellow border. Secluded white, blue and pink garden. Roses, shrubs, vegetable garden leading to 2-acre woodland walk through 4,500 newly planted trees. (Woodland walk is not suitable for wheelchairs.) Cream TEAS. *Adm £1.50 Chd free. Sun July 2 (2-6)*

Orchard Cottage, Beverston ✲❀ (Mr & Mrs H L Pierce) 2m W of Tetbury on A4135 rd to Dursley. On corner by memorial garden. Nr Beverston Castle. ⅔-acre space used to the full with mixed borders, trees, shrubs, climbers, ferns and other shady plants, together with kitchen garden, wall and cordon fruit and herb interest in sheltered back garden. Lawns mown with mulching mower, *Adm £1 Chd free. Sun, Mon July 2, 3 (2-6)*

Orchard Cottage, Gretton ✲❀ (Mr Rory Stuart) 2m N of Winchcombe. Up Duglinch Lane beside Bugatti Inn in the middle of Gretton. Approx 300yds up lane turn R after Magnolia Grandiflora and opp black railings. Approx 1½-acres. Romantically overplanted, owner-maintained garden, created largely by the late Mrs Nancy Saunders. Always some interest. Teas in Winchcombe. *Adm £1. Open all year. By appt only, please* **Tel 01242 602491**

Painswick Rococo Garden ❀ (Painswick Rococo Garden Trust Reg no 299792) ½m outside village on B4073. Unique C18 garden restoration from the brief Rococo period combining contemporary buildings, vistas, ponds and winding woodland walks. Coach House restaurant for coffee, lunches, TEAS. 'Present Collection' shop. *Adm £2.60 OAP £2.20 Chd £1.30. Jan 11 to Nov 30. Weds to Sundays and Bank Hol Mons (11-5). For NGS Suns March 26, Oct 8 (11-5)* **Tel 01452 813 204**

Pigeon House ✗ (Mr & Mrs Julian Taylor) Southam Lane, Southam. 3m from Cheltenham off B4632 toward Winchombe. Revitalised 2-acre garden surrounding C14 manor house. Small lake and bubbling water garden with fish and bog plants. Wide range of flowering shrubs and borders designed to create multitude of vistas and plant interest. TEAS in aid of Southam Church of the Ascension. *Adm £1.50 Chd free. Suns April 23, June 4 (2-6)*

Pinbury Park (Mr & Mrs John Mullings) Cirencester 6½m. Signed off Sapperton-Winstone rd between A419 and A417. 5-acres; topiary, yew avenue, lawns, spring bulbs incl shoals of daffodils and anemones, impressive view, gazebo. Rose garden and many varieties of clematis. Tudor Manor house (not open) former Royal residence of King Penda. *Adm £1.50 Chd 50p. Suns April 9, July 23 (2-5)*

Pitt Court ♿✗❀ (Mr & Mrs M W Hall) North Nibley. Turn E off the B4060 at North Nibley past the Black Horse Inn into Barrs Lane. Continue for approx ¾m. A small garden of approx ⅓ acre, interesting use of 'hard' features; paving, dwarf walls, etc. variety of smaller trees, shrubs and herbaceous borders; conifers; lawn and alpine area. Limited car parking. Teas at **Hunts Court** open nearby with plenty of parking (½m). *Adm 75p Chd free. Suns June 11, 25, July 9 (2-6)*

Poulton Gardens ♿ 5m E of Cirencester on A417. Cream TEAS at **Poulton Manor**. *Combined adm £2 Chd free. Sun June 18 (2-6)*

Almas Cottage (Mr & Mrs G Lavin) Tiny garden overflowing with traditional cottage plants

The New Inn ❀ (Mr & Mrs Witold Wondrausch) On A417 opp sign to Quenington/Bibury. An acre behind erstwhile pub transformed into idiosyncratic collection of plants; spring bulbs; cottagey flowers, climbing plants, wild garden with pond, vegetable patch. *Private visits by groups or individuals very welcome, please* **Tel 01285 850226**

The Old School (Mr & Mrs Derek Chalk) Small walled garden with interesting shrubs, clematis, roses, herbaceous plants

Poulton House (Mr & Mrs Tom Boyd) 1½-acre Cotswold garden; herbaceous border, rose border, pond, shrubs, kitchen garden and specimen trees

Poulton Manor ❀ (Mrs Anthony Sanford) 2 acres reconstructed for minimal maintenance; old yew hedges, hornbeam avenue, mixed borders, herb parterre, walled kitchen garden, natural area with trees, pond and bog garden. Charles II house (not open)

Sarnia (Mr & Mrs W M Young) ½-acre garden with shrubs and perennials to give colour and interest throughout the year

Prestbury Gardens ✗ 3m NE of Cheltenham, off B4632 to Winchcombe. TEAS in aid of St Mary's Prestbury Church Fund. *Combined adm £2 Chd free. Sun June 11 (2-6)*

Burnside ❀ (Mr & Mrs John Anton-Smith) Mill Lane. 1½-acre working garden specialising in plant-breeding of Hellebores, Pulsatillas, Geraniums, Erodiums and other plants, and production of unusual herbaceous plants. Stock beds, large rockery, stream. *(Share to NCCPG Glos Group®). Private visits welcome, please* **Tel 01242 244645**

¶Lane End ♿ (Mr & Mrs Jim Readings) A former ⅔-acre paddock with walnut trees, soft fruit and shrubs. Rockery with small water garden

The Lower Mill ♿ (Mr & Mrs W R Marsh) Mill St. Mature ¾-acre country garden on varying levels with mill stream and waterfalls surrounded by specimen trees, big borders of shrubs and herbaceous plants, and old shrub roses

¶Mansard House ♿ (Michael and Elspeth Holland) Colourful perennials, shrubs, old fruit trees and an ancient mulberry in a small secluded garden

¶Pellon 24 High Street (Mrs Jean Thompson) Small patio with unusual tub plants, interesting herbaceous borders, lilies, hostas and variety of shrubs and trees all in ½-acre

Tatchley House ♿ (Dr & Mrs R W Lyle) Tatchley Lane. Small walled family garden sculptured by shrubs and perennial borders about lawn, pond and bricked patio areas

Priors Mesne Cottage ❀ (Mr & Mrs T F Cox) Aylburton 4m S of Lydney. Take A48 towards Chepstow. In Aylburton take 1st right at The George, Church Rd. 2m up hill to junc, left at sign to Alvington and Woolaston, entrance 1st on right. Woodland walk to remains of romantic 2-acre wild garden with three pools, fine trees, azaleas, bamboos. Subject of the book A Gloucestershire Wild Garden (1899) written by the Indian Army Officer who developed it. *Adm £1 Chd free. Sun May 14 (2-6). Private visits welcome, please* **Tel 01594 562454**

Quenington Gardens ♿❀ 2m N of Fairford, E of Cirencester. Peaceful Cotswold riverside village with church renowned for Norman doorways. TEAS in aid of The Home Farm Trust at **The Old Rectory**. *Combined adm £2.50 Chd free. Sun July 2 (2-6)*

Apple Tree Cottage (Mrs P Butler-Henderson) Interesting small cottage garden protected by its own 'micro-climate'. Conservatory with unusual plants

Court Farm (Mr & Mrs Frank Gollins) Natural riverside landscape; part of historic grounds of Knights Hospitallers with dovecote, woodland walk and water garden

Mallards (Mrs Joyce Roebuck) Summer flowers, large well-stocked fish pond, aquatics and walled vegetable garden

¶Mawley Field (Mr & Mrs N Collins) Secluded 1-acre Cotswold garden; orchard, mixed herbaceous borders, rose garden, kitchen garden

The Old Rectory (Mr & Mrs David Abel-Smith) Picturesque and varied riverside garden with herbaceous border and wilderness; extensive organic vegetable garden

Pool Hay (Mr & Mrs A W Morris) Small is beautiful. Picturesque riverside cottage garden

Quenington House (Mr & Mrs Geoffrey Murray) Walled gardens, pergolas, old shrub roses, wide herbaceous borders. Lots of clematis, salvias and penstemons

By Appointment Gardens. Avoid the crowds. Good chance of a tour by owner. See garden description for telephone number.

The Red House ✻❀ (Mr & Mrs W K Turner) Pillows Green, Staunton, 8m NW of Gloucester on A417; from Staunton Xrds ½m off B4208. Split level 2 acre organic garden and wildlife garden with herbaceous borders; rockery and terrace with containers; parterre; also flower meadow. C17 House (part open). Garden designed & maintained by owners. All plants for sale grown from garden stock. TEA. *Adm £1.50 Chd free (Share to Glos Wildlife Trust®). Sun, Mon May 28, 29; Suns June 18, July 9 (2-6). Private visits welcome, please* **Tel 01452 840505**

Redwood House ♿✻❀ (Mr & Mrs Eric Sadler) Halmore. 2½m NE Berkeley and SW Slimbridge. Turn off A38 at The Prince of Wales and follow signs to Halmore. First R out of Halmore into Slimbridge Lane for ½m to garden on L handside of sharp bend. ⅓ acre. 700 different cottage garden perennials and herbs, all labelled; old roses, shrubs and trees planted for scent and wildlife. *Adm £1 Chd free. Suns, Weds April 23, 26; May 14, 17, Suns June 11, Aug 6, Sept 10 (2-6). Private visits welcome all year, please* **Tel 01453 811421**

Rockcliffe ✻❀ (Mr & Mrs Simon Keswick) nr Lower Swell. On B4068. From Stow-on-the-Wold turn R into drive 1½m from Lower Swell. 5-acre garden incl herbaceous borders, pink and white and blue gardens, rose terrace, walled kitchen garden and orchard. TEAS in aid of St Peters Church, Upper Slaughter. *Adm £1.50 Chd free. Sun July 9 (2-6.30)*

Rodmarton Manor ♿✻❀ (Mr & Mrs Simon Biddulph) Cirencester. Between Cirencester and Tetbury off A433. House designed by Ernest Barnsley. Gardens laid out in the 1920's and made famous by Mary Biddulph during the 1960's-1980's. Many separate areas of distinctive character and a wide range of plants, shrubs, topiary, hedging, alpines and the well known herbaceous borders. TEAS (June 10 only). *Adm £1.50 Sats, £2 any other time Chd free. Every Sat May 13 to Aug 26 (2-5). For NGS (Share to Rodmarton PCC®) Sat June 10 (2-6). Private visits welcome, please* **Tel 01285 841253**

Rookwoods ✻ (Mr & Mrs R Luard) Waterlane, Oakridge, 5m E of Stroud, 7m W of Cirencester just N of A419. 1¼m SE of Bisley. 3-acre well structured garden with herbaceous borders to colour themes. Pleached Whitebeam around recently designed pool area. Wide variety of old-fashioned and modern climbing and shrub roses (labelled), water gardens and outstanding views. TEAS. *Adm £1.50 Chd free. Weds July 5, 12 (2-6). Coaches by appt. Private visits welcome May and July, please* **Tel 01452 770747**

Ryelands House ❀ (Capt & Mrs Eldred Wilson) Taynton, 8m W of Gloucester. ½-way between Huntley (A40) and Newent (B4215) on B4216. Renowned spring garden with great variety of bulbs, many rare. Trees, shrubs, waterside plants, pools, herbs surrounding a grade II listed house in peaceful idyllic setting in own 100 acres. Also unique and very popular country and woodland walk. Outstanding views and abundance of wild flowers; famed for wild daffodils. 2-acre lake in beautiful setting. Good selection quality plants for sale. Dogs welcome on walk. TEAS. *Adm £2 Chd free. Suns April 2, 9, 16, 23, 30; Mon April 17, (2-5.30). Parties welcome in April, please* **Tel 01452 790251**

20 St Peters Road ✻❀ (Meg & Jeff Blumson) Cirencester. Off Cricklade St. turn R into Ashcroft Rd them L then R. Small town garden entirely remade without grass; herbaceous, clematis, rockery, pond. *Adm 50p Chd free. Suns July 2, 16 (2-6). Private visits welcome, please* **Tel 01285 657696**

Sezincote ✻ (Mr & Mrs David Peake) 1½m SW of Moreton-in-Marsh. Turn W along A44 towards Evesham; after 1½m (just before Bourton-on-the-Hill) take turn left, by stone lodge with white gate. Exotic oriental water garden by Repton and Daniell with lake, pools and meandering stream, banked with massed perennial plants of interest. Large semi-circular orangery, formal Indian garden, fountain, temple and unusual trees of vast size in lawn and wooded park setting. House in Indian manner designed by Samuel Pepys Cockerell was insipiration for Brighton Pavilion. TEAS (NGS day only). *Adm £2.50 Chd £1 under 5 free. Open every Thurs Fri & Bank Hols (except Dec) (2-6). For NGS Sun July 9 (2-6)*

Snowshill Manor ✻ (The National Trust) 3m SW of Broadway. Small terraced garden in which organic and natural methods only are used. Highlights include tranquil ponds, old roses, old-fashioned flowers and herbaceous borders rich in plants of special interest. House contains collections of fine craftmanship incl musical instruments, clocks, toys, bicycles. *Adm house & gdn £5 Chd £2.50. Family ticket £13.75. House & garden are open April & Oct Sats, Suns (1-5), Easter Sat to Mon open (1-6); May to end Sept Wed to Sun and Bank Hol Mon (1-6 or sunset if earlier). For NGS Sun May 7 (1-6)*

Stancombe Park ♿❀ (Mrs B S Barlow) Stinchcombe, nr Dursley. ½-way between Dursley and Wotton-under-Edge on B4060. Bus stop: 30yds from gates. Here are 2 gardens. One is a tranquil formal garden with recently created herbaceous borders of delicate colour interest, a pleached limewalk, young trees and shrubs. The second is a vast and secret Folly Garden of early C19 date which is a short but steep walk away along the hidden valley where there are 3 lakes, a temple, a grotto, tunnels and hiding places amidst magic mature woods. Cream TEAS. *Adm £2 Chd 50p (Share to Garden History Society®). Sun June 4 (2-6)*

Stanton ♿❀ Nr Broadway. One of the most picturesque and unspoilt C17 Cotswold villages with many gardens to explore (15 open in 1994) ranging from charming cottage to large formal gardens of appeal to visitors of all tastes. Plant stall. Car park £1. TEAS from 3-5.30. *Adm £2 Chd free (Share to Stanton Village Church®). Sun June 25 (2-6)*

Stanway House (Lord Neidpath) 1m E of B4632 Cheltenham-Broadway rd on B4077 Toddington to Stow-on-the-Wold rd. 20 acres of planted landscape in early C18 formal landscape setting. Arboretum, historic pleasure grounds with specimen trees inc pinetum; remains of ornamental canal and cascade; chestnut and oak avenue; folly; daffodils and roses in season. Striking C16 manor with gatehouse, tithe barn and church. Tea at The Bakehouse, Stanway. *Adm gardens only £1 Chd 50p; House and Gardens £3 OAP £2.50 Chd £1. Also house open Tues & Thurs June to Aug (2-5). For NGS (Share to Glos Aids Trust®) Suns April 23, June 4 (2-5).* **Tel 01386 584469**

Stowell Park ✇ (The Lord & Lady Vestey) 2m SW of Northleach. Off Fosseway A429. Large garden, lawned terraces with magnificent views over the Coln Valley. Fine collection of old-fashioned roses and herbaceous plants, with a pleached lime approach to the House. Two large walled gardens contain vegetables, fruit, cut flowers and ranges of greenhouses, also a long rose pergola and wide, plant-filled borders divided into colour sections. House (not open) originally C14 with later additions. TEAS. *Adm £2 Chd free (Share to St John's Ambulance Brigade and Royal British Legion®). Suns May 14, June 25 (2-5)*

Sudeley Castle Gardens ♿✇❀ (Lord and Lady Ashcombe) Winchcombe. The gardens of historic C15 castle, home of Queen Katherine Parr. The Queen's Garden, with double yew hedges, has been replanted with old-fashioned roses, herbs and perennials. Richard III's Banqueting Hall is backdrop for romantic 'ruined' garden while the Tithe Barn displays an impressive collection of species roses. Also formal pools, extensive lawns with fine trees and spring bulbs; magnificent views. 'Sudeley Castle Roses'. Specialist plant centre, with old roses, topiary, herbs and other unusual plants. Restaurant. TEAS. *Garden adm £3.35 OAPs £2.95 Chd £1.60. Open daily March 1 to 31 (10.30-3.30) April 1 to Oct 31 (10.30-5.30). For NGS Suns April 22; Sept 9, (10.30-5.30).* **Tel 01242 602308**

Sunningdale ✇❀ (Mr J Mann Taylor) Grange Court. 2m S of Huntley. Turn off the A40 in the middle of Huntley, signposted to Westbury-on-Severn., ¾-acre. Q up-queue up! Your quest for quintessence quickly quenched. Quality and quantity epitomises this quiet, quaint quarter, with its quota of quatrefoils and quinquefoliates in all its quadrants; created by a quixotic quinquagenarian ready for a quizzical quip or quote. All quibbles quickly quelled without question. Have no qualms; no quirks; no quagmires. (The National Collection of Phlomis should be at its best in June/July). Teas in Westbury. *Adm £1.50 Chd 50p. Suns June 4, 25; July 9; Aug 6, 13; Thurs June 22, Aug 17 (2-5). Private visits welcome, please* **Tel 01452 760268**

Tetbury Gardens, Tetbury. *Combined adm £2.50 Chd free. Sun June 11 (2-6)*

The Chipping Croft ❀ (Dr & Mrs P W Taylor) At bottom of Chipping Hill approached from market place. 2-acre, secluded, walled town garden on three levels, with mature trees, shrubs, herbaceous borders, rose beds and unusual plants; spring blossom and bulbs. A series of formal gardens, incl fruit and vegetable/flower potager all informally planted; also a water garden. C17 Cotswold house (not open). TEAS Suns only at Chipping Croft in aid of Action Research for the Crippled Child and Leighterton Church. *Also open Sun April 23, Weds April 26, Aug 30 (2-6) Adm £2. Private visits welcome, please* **Tel 01666 503178**

The Old Stables (Brigadier and Mrs J M Neilson) Enter New Church St B3124 from Long St at Xroads signed to Stroud and Dursley. Turn L at Fire station into Close Gardens. Small walled garden on two levels in old stable yard of a town house. Flowering shrubs; clematis; bonsai; water garden; paved area with alpines in troughs

¶Thrupp Lane Gardens ✇ nr Stroud. Turn L off A419 into Thrupp Lane 1m E of Stroud and drive on for approx ½m. Small hillside gardens with panoramic views. Cream TEAS at Hillside. *Combined adm £2 Chd free. Sun May 21 (2-6)*

¶Hillside, 85 Thrupp Lane (Mr & Mrs J P Heymans) Created by its owners, a ⅓-acre organic garden of many levels and sections. Incl a wide variety of plants together with a small lily pond, orchard and tiered vegetable plot

¶115 Thrupp Lane (Mr & Mrs P Hugo) A garden on a garage! Super views. Sloping flower and fruit garden behind the house

¶138 Thrupp Lane (Mr & Mrs K A Beard) Imaginatively planned small sloping garden containing colourful covered patio, ponds (one for frogs, one for fish), ornamental garden with rockery, and miniature working vineyard. TEA

153 Thrupp Lane ❀ (Mr & Mrs D Davies) ⅓-acre on sloping site, full of interesting and unusual plants, rockeries, shrubs and ponds - all planted to encourage wild life. Good winter interest. *Private visits welcome, please* **Tel 01453 883580**

¶Thrupp Primary School ❀ (The Head Teacher) Small wildlife conservation area in the school grounds created and looked after by the children with a little bit of help!

Tin Penny Cottage ✇❀ (E S Horton) Whiteway, near Miserden, 6m NE Stroud between Birdlip & Stroud on B4070. At Fostons Ash Public House take rd signed Bisley then immediately L to Whiteway ½m; 300yd walk to garden. Enthusiast's medium-sized garden on cold clay. Designed to be visually attractive and grow a wide variety of hardy plants, many unusual and rarely seen, and incl a collection of Sempervivum. TEAS in Village Hall Bank Hol Mon April 17, Suns May 28, Aug 6, Mon Aug 28. *Adm £1 Chd free. Weds all year. Bank Hol Mons April 17, Aug 28, Sat June 17. Suns March 19, April 2, May 7, 28, July 9, Aug 6, Sept 24 (2-6). Private visits welcome all year, please* **Tel 01285 821482**

Trevi Garden ♿❀ (Gilbert & Sally Gough) Hartpury 5m NW of Gloucester via A417. In village sharp back right into Over Old Road before War Memorial. 1 acre of gardens within a garden; winding water garden; laburnum/clematis walk, shrubberies, herbaceous borders, collection of hardy geraniums/penstemons; newly designed formal vegetable/flower garden; all-yr interest. Garden completely designed by owners. Featured in NGS video 1. TEAS Thurs, Suns May 7, Aug 6. *Adm £1.50 Chd free. Suns, Mons April 2, 16, 17, 30; May 1, 7, 28, 29; Suns June 4, 11, 18, 25; Suns, Mon Aug 6, 27, 28; also open every Thurs March 16 to Sept 21 (2-6); coaches/groups by appt on other dates* **Tel 01452 700370**

Upper Cam Gardens ✇❀ 1m W of Dursley. Grouped around St George's Church. Upper Cam signposted from B4066. TEAS. *Combined adm £1.50 Chd free. Sun May 21 (2-6)*

Bell Courts (Mr & Mrs E W V Acton) ¾-acre; shrubs, herbaceous plants and kitchen garden

Cleveland (Mr & Mrs R Wilkinson) Plant enthusiast's small garden on windy site. Shrubs, herbaceous and unusual plants. Vegetable plot

17 Everlands (T Edwards) Small new garden, bowl's green; ducks; R Cam flows through the garden
Homefield House (Mr & Mrs Grove) Little garden with shrubs, colourful flowers, pond and kitchen garden
16 Springhill (Old Court) (Mr & Mrs J E Beebee) Mature garden with open aspect. Shrubs, herbaceous and rock plants, pond. Display of complementary stained glass
The Vicarage (Rev Chris & Mrs Gill Malkinson) Small walled garden recently replanted; trees; shrubs and spring/summer rockery with labelled plants

Upton Wold ✾❀ (Mr & Mrs I R S Bond) 5m W of Moreton-in-Marsh, on A44 1m past A424 junction at Troopers Lodge Garage. Recently created garden architecturally and imaginatively laid out around C17 house with commanding views. Yew hedges; old shrub roses; herbaceous walk; some unusual plants and trees; vegetable garden; pond garden and woodland garden. Cream TEAS. *Adm £2 Chd free (Share to Chipping Norton Theatre Trust®). Suns April 23, July 2 (10-6). Private visits welcome May to July, please* **Tel 01386 700667**

Westbury Court Garden ♿✾ (The National Trust) Westbury-on-Severn 9m SW of Gloucester on A48. Formal Dutch style water garden, earliest remaining in England; canals, summer house, walled garden; over 100 species of plants grown in England before 1700. *Adm £2.30 Chd £1.15. April to end Oct. Wed to Sun & Bank Hol Mon (11-6) Closed Good Fri. Other months by appt only. For NGS Sun Sept 3 (11-6)*

Westonbirt Gardens at Westonbirt School ♿ 3m S of Tetbury. A433 Tetbury-Bristol. 22 acres. Formal Victorian Italian garden now Grade 1 listed, terraced pleasure garden, rustic walks, lake redredged & stocked with carp. Rare, exotic trees and shrubs. Tea at Hare & Hounds Hotel, Westonbirt ½m, (to book for parties **Tel 01666 880233**). *Adm £1.50 Chd 25p. Suns April 9, Aug 20, Sept 3 (2-5.30)*

Willow Lodge ♿✾❀ (Mr & Mrs John H Wood) on A40 between May Hill & Longhope 10m W of Gloucester, 6m E of Ross-on-Wye. Plantsman's garden with unusual and rare plants incl colour themed herbaceous borders, shrubs, an alpine walk, stream and pools with water features, several greenhouses, organic vegetable garden, newly planted small arboretum with over 200 trees and shrubs from around the world, and wild flowers in the 4-acre grounds. Plants labelled. TEAS. *Adm £1 Chd free. Suns, Mons, May 28, 29; June 11, 12, 18, 19, 25, 26; July 9, 10, 16, 17, 23, 24; Aug 6, 7, 13, 14 (2-6). Groups and private visits welcome, please* **Tel 01452 831211**

Witcombe Gardens ♿ 4m E of Gloucester on A417 turn R at 12 Bells Inn for Church Cottage and Witcombe Park; ½m up A417 from Inn turn L signed **Court Farm House.** TEAS **Witcombe Park**. *Combined adm £1.50 Chd free. Sun June 18 (2-6)*
Church Cottage ✾❀ (Sir Christopher & Lady Lawson) Great Witcombe. More than 2 acres of country garden with shrubs, trees and lawns. Stream and two ponds. Rose arbour. Old clipped yews. Further beds of roses, herbaceous borders, and several seats for resting. Soft drinks
Court Farm House ✾❀ (Mr & Mrs Andrew Hope) Little Witcombe. An informal family garden of 1 acre. Shrubs, roses, herbaceous perennials and self-seeding annuals; pond, pergola; wild garden, rock garden, herb garden, scree bed, play area; children welcome
Witcombe Park ✾ (Mrs W W Hicks Beach) Great Witcombe. A plant connoisseur's medium-sized garden set in beautiful Cotswold scenery. Richly planted borders, flowering shrubs, roses; walled garden, cottage garden area and hidden sunken water garden; C17 gazebo

Regular Openers. Too many days to include in diary. Usually there is a wide range of plants giving year-round interest. See head of county section for the name and garden description for times etc.

By Appointment Gardens. These owners do not have a fixed opening day usually because they do not like crowds or have insufficient parking space. Owner will often give guided tour.

Gwent & Gwynedd

See separate Welsh section beginning on page 314

Hampshire

Hon County Organiser: Central West: Mrs A R Elkington, Little Court, Crawley nr Winchester SO21 2PU Tel 01962 776365

Assistant Hon County Organisers: South-East: Mrs R J Gould, Ewell House, 44 Belmore Lane, Lymington SO41 3NN
East: Mrs D Hart Dyke, Hambledon House, Hambledon PO7 4RU
South: Mrs J S M Jones, Elms House, Twyford, Winchester SOZ1 IQF
North: J J Morris Esq, The Ricks, Rotherwick, Nr Basingstoke RG27 9BL
North-East: Mrs B Powell, Broadhatch House, Bentley, Nr Farnham GU10 5JJ
Central-East: Mrs W F Richardson, Hill House, Old Alresford SO24 9DY
South-West: C K Thornton Esq, Merrie Cottage, Woodgreen, Nr Fordingbridge SP6 2AT
North-West: M H Walford Esq, Little Acre, Down Farm Lane, Headbourne Worthy, Winchester SO23 7LA

Hon County Treasurer: S Every Esq, The White House, Crawley, Winchester SO21 2PR

DATES OF OPENING

By appointment

For telephone numbers and other details see garden descriptions. Private visits welcomed

Abbey Cottage, Itchen Abbas
Beechenwood Farm, nr Odiham
Brandy Mount House, Alresford
Broadhatch House, Bentley
Croft Mews, Botley
Fairfield House, Hambledon
Hambledon House, Hambledon
John Hine's Studios, Aldershot
53 Ladywood, Eastleigh
60 Lealand Rd, Drayton
Little Barn Garden & Barnhawk Nursery, Woodgreen, nr Fordingbridge
The Little Cottage, Lymington
Little Court, Crawley
Longparish Gardens, nr Andover
Manor Lodge, Crawley
Marycourt, Odiham
Merdon Manor, Hursley
Merrie Cottage, Woodgreen
Old Meadows, Silchester
Paddocks Way, Brook, Lyndhurst
Pylewell Park, Lymington
Rowans Wood, Ampfield
South End House, Lymington
Spinners, Boldre
Springfield, Hayling Island
22 Springvale Road, Kingsworthy
Warwick House, Wickham

Parties only

Bramdean House, Bramdean, nr Alresford
Bramdean Lodge, Alresford
Cheriton Cottage, Cheriton
The Clock House, Sparsholt
Little Coopers, Eversley Gardens
Croylands, nr Romsey
Durmast House, Burley
The House-in-the-Wood, Beaulieu
Lake House, Northington
Lymore Valley Herbs, Milford-on-Sea
The Old House, Silchester
Mylor Cottage, Droxford
Rumsey Gardens, Clanfield
Sowley House, Sowley, Lymington
Vernon Hill House, Bishop's Waltham
West Silchester Hall, nr Reading

Regular openings

For details see garden descriptions

Exbury Gardens, nr Southampton. Open daily Feb 11 to Oct 24
Furzey Gardens, Minstead. Daily except Dec 25 & 26
Greatham Mill, Greatham, nr Liss
Highclere Castle, nr Newbury. Open Wed to Suns, July, Aug, Sept, Easter & Bank Hols
Sir Harold Hillier Arboretum, Nr Romsey. Daily
Jenkyn Place, Bentley. Thurs to Suns & Bank Hols, April 13 to Sept 10
The Little Cottage, Lymington. Tues May 30 to Sept 26
Long Thatch, Warnford. Weds Mar 1 to Aug 30
Lymore Valley Herbs, Milford-on-Sea. Daily except Dec 25 to Mar 1
Macpenny Woodland Garden & Nurseries, Bransgore. Daily except Dec 25, 26 & Jan 1
Spinners, Boldre. For details see text
Stratfield Saye House. Daily May 1 to Sept 24

February 11 Saturday
Brandy Mount House, Alresford

March 5 Sunday
Long Thatch, Warnford

March 12 Sunday
Long Thatch, Warnford

March 19 Sunday
Bramdean House, Bramdean, nr Alresford ‡‡
Brandy Mount House, Alresford ‡‡
Long Thatch, Warnford
Pennington Chase, Lymington ‡
Sadlers Gardens, Lymington ‡
Sowley House, Sowley, Lymington

March 26 Sunday
Durmast House, Burley
Eversley Gardens, Eversley
Little Court, Crawley

March 27 Monday
Little Court, Crawley

March 28 Tuesday
Little Court, Crawley

April 2 Sunday
Abbey Cottage, Itchen Abbas
Copperfield, Dogmersfield
Mylor Cottage, Droxford Gardens
Longparish Gardens
Paddocks Way, Brook, Lyndhurst
White Windows, Longparish

April 9 Sunday
Appleshaw Manor, nr Andover ‡
Bramley Lodge, nr Appleshaw ‡
Crawley Gardens, nr Winchester
East Lane, Ovington ‡‡
The Old House, Silchester
Tichborne Park, Alresford ‡‡

April 10 Monday
Crawley Gardens, nr Winchester
Manor Lodge, Crawley

April 11 Tuesday
Little Court, Crawley

April 16 Sunday
Bramdean House, Bramdean, nr Alresford ‡
The Cottage, Chandlers Ford
60 Lealand Road, Drayton
Rowans Wood, Ampfield

Woodcote Manor, Alresford ‡

April 17 Monday

Beechenwood Farm, nr Odiham
Bramdean House, Bramdean, nr Alresford
The Cottage, Chandlers Ford
Rowans Wood, Ampfield

April 23 Sunday

Abbey Road Gardens, Fareham
Brandy Mount House, Alresford
Fairfield House, Hambledon
Hall Place, West Meon
The Old House, Silchester
Rumsey Gardens, Clanfield

April 30 Sunday

North Ecchinswell Farm, Nr Newbury
Rowans Wood, Ampfield

May 7 Sunday

Abbey Cottage, Itchen Abbas ‡
Brandy Mount House, Alresford ‡
Chilland, Martyr Worthy ‡
Coles, Privett, nr Alton
Eversley Gardens, Eversley
Ewell House, Lymington ‡‡
Fernlea, Chilworth, Southampton
Greatham Mill, Greatham, nr Liss
Manor Lodge, Crawley
The Old House, Silchester
Pennington Chase, Lymington
South End House, Lymington ‡‡
Tylney Hall Hotel, Rotherwick
Vernon Hill House, Bishop's Waltham

May 8 Monday

Abbey Cottage, Itchen Abbas ‡
Chilland, Martyr Worthy ‡
Coles, Privett, nr Alton
Fernlea, Chilworth, Southampton
The House-in-the-Wood, Beaulieu
Manor Lodge, Crawley
Rookley Manor, Up Somborne
Stratfield Saye House, Basingstoke
Vernon Hill House, Bishop's Waltham

May 10 Wednesday

The Clock House, Sparsholt
Exbury Gardens, nr Southampton

May 13 Saturday

Coles, Privett, nr Alton

May 14 Sunday

The Clock House, Sparsholt
Coles, Privett, nr Alton
The Dower House, Dogmersfield
Hackwood Park, (Spring Wood), Basingstoke
Heathlands, Locks Heath
53 Ladywood, Eastleigh
60 Lealand Rd, Drayton
Lithend, Crawley ‡
Little Barn Garden & Barnhawk Nursery, Woodgreen
Little Court, Crawley ‡
Pylewell Park, Lymington
Rowans Wood, Ampfield

May 15 Monday

Lithend, Crawley Gardens ‡
Little Court, Crawley ‡

May 16 Tuesday

Little Court, Crawley

May 20 Saturday

Coles, Privett, nr Alton
Littlewood, Hayling Island
Paddocks Way, Brook, Lyndhurst
Verona Cottage, 6 Webb Lane, Hayling Island

May 21 Sunday

Bramdean House, Bramdean, nr Alresford
Coles, Privett, nr Alton
The Cottage, Chandlers Ford
Crossways, Woodgreen Common
The Dower House, Dogmersfield
Eversley Gardens, Eversley
Hambledon House, Hambledon ‡‡
Littlewood, Hayling Island
The Old House, Silchester
Pylewell Park, Lymington ‡
RumseyGardens, Clanfield
Verona Cottage, 6 Webb Lane, Hayling Island
Walhampton, Lymington ‡
White Cottage, Hambledon ‡‡
The Wylds, Liss Forest

May 22 Monday

Hambledon House, Hambledon ‡
White Cottage, Hambledon ‡

May 26 Friday

Warwick House, Wickham

May 28 Sunday

Croylands, nr Romsey
Long Thatch, Warnford
Monxton Gardens, nr Andover
Rowans Wood, Ampfield
West Silchester Hall, nr Reading

May 29 Monday

Long Thatch, Warnford
Monxton Gardens, nr Andover

May 31 Wednesday

The Clock House, Sparsholt
Croylands, nr Romsey

June 4 Sunday

Beechenwood Farm, nr Odiham
Croylands, nr Romsey
Jenkyn Place, Bentley
Tichborne Park, Alresford
Tylney Hall Hotel, Rotherwick

June 7 Wednesday

Croylands, nr Romsey

June 11 Sunday

Applecroft, Woodgreen
Croft Mews, Botley ‡
Croylands, nr Romsey
Durmast House, Burley
53 Ladywood, Eastleigh
Longparish Gardens
Merrie Cottage, Woodgreen
Old Timbers, Alresford
Southview, Eversley Cross
Vernon Hill House, Bishop's Waltham ‡
Warwick House, Wickham ‡

June 12 Monday

Applecroft, Woodgreen ‡
Croft Mews, Botley
Longparish Gardens
Merrie Cottage, Woodgreen ‡

June 14 Wednesday

The Clock House, Sparsholt
Croylands, nr Romsey

June 17 Saturday

Upham Gardens, Southampton

June 18 Sunday

Apple Court, nr Lymington
Bramdean House, Bramdean, nr Alresford ‡‡
Bramdean Lodge, Alresford ‡‡
Brandy Mount House, Alresford ‡‡
Broadhatch House, Bentley ‡
Closewood House, Waterlooville
Cranbury Park, Otterbourne
Croylands, nr Romsey
Droxford Gardens
The Garden House, Lymington ‡‡‡
Glevins, Lymington ‡‡‡
60 Lealand Road, Drayton
Longstock Park and Water Garden, Stockbridge
Quoin Cottage, Denmead
Rosewood Farm, Frenchmoor
Westbrook House, Holybourne ‡

June 19 Monday

Broadhatch House, Bentley

June 21 Wednesday

Closewood House, Waterlooville
Croylands, nr Romsey
Pullens,West Worldham, Nr. Alton
Quoin Cottage, Denmead

June 24 Saturday

Hinton Ampner, Alresford

June 25 Sunday

Abbey Road Gardens, Fareham
Appleshaw Gardens, nr Andover
Cliddesden Gardens, nr Basingstoke
Crookley Pool, Horndean
Fairfield House, Hambledon ‡
Hambledon House, Hambledon ‡
Hinton Ampner, Alresford
Holt End House, Ashford Hill
John Hine's Studio, Aldershot
Lake House, Northington
Long Thatch, Warnford
Marycourt, Odiham
Mottisfont Abbey, nr Romsey
Oakdene, Sandleheath
Old Meadows, Silchester
Shalden Park House, Shalden
Southview, Eversley Cross

June 27 Tuesday
Oakdene, Sandleheath
June 28 Wednesday
Crookley Pool, Horndean
Pullens, West Worldham, Nr Alton ‡
Wheatley House, Kingsley Bordon ‡
July 1 Saturday
Manor Lodge, Crawley
Merebimur, Mockbeggar, Ringwood
July 2 Sunday
Abbey Cottage, Itchen Abbas
Brocas Farm, Lower Froyle ‡
Burkham House, nr Alton
Cheriton Cottage, Cheriton
Downgate Farm, Steep Marsh
Fritham Lodge, nr Lyndhurst ‡‡
Jenkyn Place, Bentley ‡
Manor Lodge, Crawley ‡‡‡‡‡
Marycourt, Odiham
Merebimur, Mockbeggar, Ringwood
Moth House, Brown Candover ‡‡‡
Moundsmere Manor, Preston Candover ‡‡‡
Paddocks Way, Brook, Lyndhurst ‡‡
Paige Cottage, Crawley ‡‡‡‡‡
Vernon Hill House, Bishop's Waltham ‡‡‡‡
Waldrons, Brook ‡‡
Warwick House, Wickham ‡‡‡‡
July 3 Monday
Downgate Farm, Steep Marsh
July 5 Wednesday
Manor Lodge, Crawley
Marycourt, Odiham
Merdon Manor
July 9 Sunday
Broadhatch House, Bentley
Colemore House, Nr Alton
John Hine's Studio, Aldershot
Merdon Manor, Hursley
July 10 Monday
Broadhatch House, Bentley
July 16 Sunday
Apple Court, nr Lymington ‡‡‡
Bramdean House, Bramdean, nr Alresford ‡
Bramdean Lodge, Alresford ‡
Fernlea, Chilworth, Southampton
Heathlands, Locks Heath ‡‡
Highclere Castle, nr Newbury
53 Ladywood, Eastleigh ‡‡
Robins Return, Tiptoe ‡‡‡
Tunworth Old Rectory, nr Basingstoke
July 19 Wednesday
Robins Return, Tiptoe
July 22 Saturday
3 St Helens Road, Hayling Island
July 23 Sunday
Highclere Castle, nr Newbury
John Hine's Studio, Aldershot
Little Mead, Hambledon ‡
Long Thatch, Warnford ‡
3 St Helens Road, Hayling Island
The Vyne, Sherborne St John
July 29 Saturday
12 Rozelle Close, Littleton
July 30 Sunday
Little Court, Crawley ‡
Littleton House, Crawley ‡
12 Rozelle Close, Littleton ‡
July 31 Monday
Little Court, Crawley
August 6 Sunday
The Barn House, Church Oakley
Bohunt Manor, Liphook
Elbow Corner, Basingstoke
Hill House, Old Alresford
Martyr Worthy Gardens, nr Winchester
Oakley Manor, Church Oakley
West Silchester Hall, nr Reading
August 7 Monday
Chilland, Martyr Worthy
West Silchester Hall, nr Reading
August 13 Sunday
Cheriton Cottage, Cheriton
Elbow Corner, Basingstoke
Highclere Castle, nr Newbury
Little Court, Crawley
August 14 Monday
Little Court, Crawley
August 15 Tuesday
Little Court, Crawley
August 20 Sunday
Bramdean House, Bramdean, nr Alresford ‡
Bramdean Lodge, Alresford ‡
Highclere Castle, nr Newbury
Malt Cottage, Upper Clatford
Somerley, nr Ringwood
August 27 Sunday
Abbey Cottage, Itchen Abbas
Fernlea, Chilworth, Southampton
Long Thatch, Warnford
August 28 Monday
Abbey Cottage, Itchen Abbas
Fernlea, Chilworth, Southampton
September 2 Saturday
Wonston Lodge, Wonston
September 3 Sunday
Cheriton Cottage, Cheriton
Copperfield, Dogmersfield
Greatham Mill, Greatham, nr Liss
Wonston Lodge, Wonston
September 10 Sunday
Hambledon House, Hambledon
September 16 Saturday
Hinton Ampner, Alresford
September 17 Sunday
Hinton Ampner, Alresford
Little Court, Crawley
September 18 Monday
Little Court, Crawley
September 23 Saturday
Mill Court, Alton
September 24 Sunday
Mill Court, Alton
October 1 Sunday
Paddocks Way, Brook, Lyndhurst
October 7 Saturday
Coles, Privett, nr Alton
October 8 Sunday
Coles, Privett, nr Alton
Pennington Chase, Lymington
October 15 Sunday
Abbey Cottage, Itchen Abbas
Elbow Corner, Basingstoke

DESCRIPTIONS OF GARDENS

Abbey Cottage ♿✂❀ (Colonel P J Daniell) Rectory Lane, Itchen Abbas. Turn off B3047 Alresford-Kingsworthy Rd, 1m E of Itchen Abbas. Interesting and inspiring walled garden and meadow of 1½ acres with trees, designed, created and maintained by owner. Featured on BBC TV 'The Great British Gardening Show'. *Adm £1.50 Chd free (Share to Winchester Cathedral®). Suns April 2, July 2, Oct 15; Sun Mon May 7, 8, Aug 27, 28 (12-5.30). Private visits welcome, please* **Tel 01962 779575**

¶Abbey Road Gardens From M27 Junction 9 travel on A27 towards Fareham. At top of hill past Titchfield Gyratory, turn L into Highlands Rd. Take 4th turning R into Blackbrook Rd. Abbey Rd is 4th turning on L. *Combined adm £1.50 Chd 50p. Suns April 23, June 25 (11-5.30)*

¶80 Abbey Road ✂❀ (Brian & Vivienne Garford) Very small garden with developing collection of herbs and plants of botanical and historical interest. 2 small ponds, miniscule meadow area, but no lawn

¶86 Abbey Road ♿✂❀ (Tricia & Don Purseglove) Small developing garden started in 1991. Mixed planting and trellis work for breezy position. Small vegetable plot and Japanese garden. TEA

Apple Court & Apple Court Cottage ♿✂❀ (Mrs D Grenfell, Mr R Grounds & Mrs M Roberts) Lymington. From the A337 between Lymington and New Milton turn N into Hordle Lane at the Royal Oak at Downton Xrds. Formal 1½-acre garden being created by designer-owners within the walls of former Victorian kitchen garden. Four National Reference Collections incl small leafed hosta. White garden, daylily display borders, collection of ferns and grasses. Small specialist nursery. Adjoining small cottage garden with variegated catalpa. TEAS. *Adm £1.50 Chd 25p (Share to All Saints Church, Hordle®). Suns June 18, July 16 (2-5.30)*

Applecroft ✂ (Dr G T Creber) Brook Lane, Woodgreen. 3m N of Fordingbridge on A338 turn E to Woodgreen. Turn R at Horse and Groom and R again along the edge of the common. Park on common and walk down through 5-barred gate. Small garden created over 9 yrs with distant view to the SW over the Avon Valley. Mixed planting incl annuals and vegetables in the cottage style. Shady arbour and pond. TEA (Mon). *Adm 50p Chd free Sun, Mon June 11, 12 (2-5.30)*

¶**Appleshaw Gardens** ✂ Take A342 Andover to Marlborough Rd, turn to Appleshaw 1m W of Weyhill, fork L at playing field. TEAS. *Combined adm £3 (Share to Appleshaw Church). Sun June 25 (2-5)*

¶**Hillfield Cottage** (Dr & Mrs P Drake) ½-acre terraced garden developed over 7 yrs for low maintenance; lavender and potentilla hedges; roses; vegetables with plants for picking, framed by trees & shrubs

The Old Vicarage (Sir Dermot & Lady De Trafford) 2-acre walled garden, mature trees, bush and rambler roses, shrub borders, shrubs and trees in grass; fruit and herb garden with box hedges

¶**Rose Hill** (Mr & Mrs H McCall) 2 acres surrounded by paddocks grazed by thoroughbred horses. Mature trees; herbaceous borders; small orchard and kitchen garden

Appleshaw Manor ✂ (The Hon Mrs Green) Nr Andover. Take A342 Andover-Marlborough Rd. Turn to Appleshaw 1m W of Weyhill. Fork L at playing field. Entrance on R after ½m next to white Church. 7-acre garden and grounds surrounded by wall. Shrubs, herbaceous, roses, wood garden, arboretum. Notable beech and yew hedges. Spring bulbs. TEAS. *Adm £2 Chd free (Share to St Peter in the Wood Church; Appleshaw®). Sun April 9 (2-5)*

Ashley Park Farm. See Dorset

The Barn House ✂❀ (Brigadier & Mrs H R W Vernon) Rectory Rd, Oakley. 5m W of Basingstoke. From Basingstoke towards Whitchurch on B3400. Turn L at Station Rd ½m W of Newfound and follow signs. Bus No 55a, 55b Basingstoke to Oakley. Small garden, with view of church. Borders, alpines and uncommon plants, large collection of clematis, informal planting in cottage style. Tea at **Oakley Manor**. *Combined adm with* **Oakley Manor** *£2 Chd free. Free parking at Manor. Sun Aug 6 (2-5.30)*

Beechenwood Farm ♿✂❀ (Mr & Mrs M Heber-Percy) Hillside, Odiham; turn S into King St. from Odiham High St. Turn L after cricket ground for Hillside. Take 2nd turn R for Roke after 1m. Modern house ½m. Garden in many parts incl woodland garden, rock garden, pergola, conservatory, herb garden with exuberant planting, belvedere with spectacular views over Odiham. Newly planted 8 acre wood, open from 1pm for picnics. WI TEAS. *Adm £1.50 Chd free. Mon April 17 (2-5); Sun June 4 (2-6); also private visits welcome April to July, please* **Tel 01256 702300**

¶**Bohunt Manor** ♿✂❀ (Lady Holman) Liphook. On old A3 in 30m area in Liphook nr station. Flowering shrubs, herbaceous borders, lakeside and woodland walks, rhododendrons, bulbs, wild flowers and vegetable garden. Tame waterfowl will eat out of children's hands. Specimen trees. About ¾hr to walk round, lake 3½ acres. *Adm £1.50 OAP £1 Chd free. Sun Aug 6 (10-6)*

Bramdean House ✂ (Mr & Mrs H Wakefield) In Bramdean village on A272. Carpets of spring bulbs. Walled garden with famous herbaceous borders, working kitchen garden, large collection of unusual plants. TEAS. *Adm £1.50 Chd free (Share to Bramdean Parish Church®). Mon April 17; Suns March 19, April 16, May 21, June 18, July 16, Aug 20, (2-5); also private parties welcome, please* **Tel 01962 771214**

Bramdean Lodge ♿ (Hon Peter & Mrs Dickinson) Bramdean village, on A272 (car park and TEAS as for Bramdean House). 1¾ acres around Victorian Gothic house. Walled garden. Borders densley planted. Style evolved rather than planned. Many oddities. Over 100 varieties of clematis, and 250 of roses, all labelled. *Adm £1 Chd free. Suns June 18, July 16, Aug 20 (2-5). Parties by appt* **Tel 01962 771324**

¶**Bramley Lodge** ♿✂❀ (Mrs J D Ward) Fyfield. From A342 Andover/Marlborough Rd take turning opp Appleshaw turning. Immed turn L into Dauntsey Drove, turn R under bridge 100yds on R. Long 1-acre garden framed and sheltered by old railway embankment, with many shrubs in curving beds, underplanted with drifts of spring bulbs; pond and bog garden, lime tolerant heathers and conifers. Plants in aid of Stroke Assoc. Teas at **Appleshaw Manor** 1½m. *Adm £1.50 Chd free. Sun 9 April (2-5)*

Brandy Mount House ♿❀ (Mr & Mrs M Baron) Alresford centre, first R in East St before Sun Lane. Please leave cars in Broad St. 1-acre informal plantsman's garden, spring bulbs, hellebores, species geraniums, snowdrop collection, daphne collection, clematis, herbaceous and woodland plants. Featured in Gardeners World Feb 1993. *Adm £1.50 Chd free. Sat Feb 11 (2-4.30); Suns March 19, April 23, May 7, June 18 (2-5). Also private visits welcome on Sats, please* **Tel 01962 732189**

Broadhatch House ♿✂❀ (Bruce & Lizzie Powell) Bentley; 4m NE of Alton; on A31 between Farnham/Alton; Bus AV452; go up School Lane. 3½ acres formal garden, double herbaceous borders; rose gardens, old-fashioned roses; unusual flowering shrubs. Included and illustrated in 'Rose Gardens of England'. *Adm £1.50 Chd free (Share to Killoran Trust®). Suns June 18, July 9, (2-5.30); Mons June 19, July 10 (2-5.30). Also private visits welcome in June/July, please* **Tel 01420 23185**

Brocas Farm ✲❀ (Mrs A A Robertson) Lower Froyle. ½m up road to Lower Froyle from A31 turning just W of Bentley; C18 House (not open) and old timber barn. 2-acre garden surrounded by open country views. Large yew hedges, roses, herbaceous. Interesting ground cover planting. Maturing arboretum. TEAS. *Adm £1.50 Chd 75p (Share to CRMF®). Sun July 2 (2-6)*

Burkham House (Mr & Mrs D Norman) nr Alton. 5m NW of Alton from A339 between Basingstoke and Alton. On Alton side of Herriard, turn off W for Burkham. 10 acres of beautiful mature trees, azaleas, acers, spring flowers, lake, and new arboretum, cottage garden and herbaceous borders. TEAS. *Adm £1.50 Chd 25p. Sun July 2 (2-6)*

Cheriton Cottage ♿✲ (Mrs I Garnett-Orme) Cheriton. 3m S of New Alresford on B3046 on R behind brick wall. Garden created over 44 yrs with chalk streams of R Itchen, planting to blend with surrounding countryside and for all seasons, small plantations of specimen trees 4 to 5 acres. Home-made teas in Village Hall. *Adm £1 Chd 50p. Suns July 2, Aug 13, Sept 3 (2-5). Parties welcome, please* **Tel 01962 771276**

Chilland ♿✲(Mr & Mrs John Impey) Martyr Worthy. Midway between Winchester and Alresford on B3047. 4-acre garden with stream at bottom overlooking R Itchen watermeadows with woods and farmland beyond. Large collection of mature shrubs planned for their yr-round colour effects. Many fine trees incl huge plane and ancient mulberry, nutwalk, spring bulbs, clematis and herbaceous borders. *Adm £1.50 Chd free. Sun, Mon May 7, 8 with* **Abbey Cottage,** *Mon Aug 7 (2-5.30). Also Sun Aug 6 with* **Martyr Worthy Gardens**

¶Cliddesden Gardens ✲❀ 2m S of Basingstoke. Take A339 (Basingstoke to Alton Rd) Turn R into Farleigh Rd (B3046) Gardens situated about 1m on L. TEAS. *Combined adm £1.50 Chd free. Sun June 25 (2-5.30)*

Sussex House (Molley & Bob Jones) ⅓-acre garden with herbaceous borders and embryonic rose beds. Pond stocked with Koi and Orfe bordered by a small rock garden partly enclosed with dwarf conifers. *(Share to St Michael's Hospice, Basingstoke®)*

Yew Tree Cottage ♿ (Jean & Peter Matthews) Cottage garden in ⅓-acre. Areas of different character. Thatched well-head with roses, white garden, stream and pool. *(Share to Local Primary School Garden Project)*

The Clock House ♿✲ (Mr & Mrs David Gibbs) Northwood Park, Sparsholt, 3m W of Winchester. Turn off A272 Winchester-Stockbridge Rd opp railings and sign for Sparsholt College. Converted stables in a courtyard, with a walled garden (11ft high). Created on clay and chalk over the past 10 years with many unusual shrubs and varied climbers on the walls; Paul's Himalayan musk rose envelops a fallen apple tree. Specimen trees. Laburnum and wisteria arcade, far reaching views, large Victorian greenhouse. TEAS Sun only. *Adm £1.50 Chd free. Sun May 14 (Share to St John's Ambulance®) (2-6); Weds May 10, 31, June 14 (11-7)*

¶Closewood House ♿ (Mr & Mrs Peter Clowes) Waterlooville. Take Closewood Rd to the W of the B2150 between Waterlooville and Denmead. L at T-junction after ½m. Signs to car park after 300 metres. 1½ acres, surrounded by farmland, looking towards Portsdown Hill. Good collection of scented roses and flowering shrubs. Unusual trees. Car park. TEAS (Sun) TEA (Wed). *Adm £1.50 Chd free. Sun June 18, Wed June 21 (2-6)*

Colemore House ♿✲❀ (Mr & Mrs S de Zoete) Colemore. 5m S of Alton. Take A32 towards Petersfield then L to Colemore just beyond East Tisted. A 2½-acre garden with a wide variety of unusual plants. Mixed herbaceous and shrub borders, new yellow and blue garden. Many different roses, salvias, penstemons, and tender plants. Crab apple walk and excellent lawns. Garden being redesigned. TEAS. *Adm £1.50 Chd free. Sun July 9 (2-6)*

Coles ✲❀ (W B S Walker) Privett, Nr Alton. From Alton take A32 S to Fareham. Approx 6m after Farringdon and 3m after East Tisted turn L at small Xrds on brow of gentle hill signposted Froxfield. Just past the Xrds on R is the Lawns/Pig and Whistle public house. Continue for just under ½m then at T-junction turn L to Froxfield and continue just under 1m. Turn L at small Xrds by bungalow and continue up lane. Turn R after 350yds at entrance marked car park. If approaching from S turn R off A32 to Froxfield just after Pig and Whistle/Lawns public house. 26 acres of spectacular secluded gardens set out over undulating grounds. Extensive lawns with paths and clearings opening onto diverse views. Beech and other woodland; a wide variety of acid loving plants including unusual varieties of azaleas and rhododendrons, acers, 2 ponds one in a secret garden. *Adm £2.50 Chd £1. Sun, Mon May 7, 8; Sats, Suns May 13, 14, 20, 21; Oct 7, 8 (2-5.30)*

¶Copperfield ♿ (John Selfe) Dogmersfield. Turn N off Odiham-Farnham A287 to Dogmersfield. Turn L by Queens Public House. 1½ acres laid out to heathers, specimen conifers, shrubs and ornamental trees for all-yr colour and easy maintenance. *Adm £1 Chd free. Suns April 2, Sept 3 (2-5.30)*

The Cottage ✲❀ (Mr & Mrs H Sykes) 16 Lakewood Rd, Chandler's Ford. 6m S of Winchester. Leave M3 at junction 12, follow signs to Chandler's Ford. At Hanrahans Public House on Winchester Rd, turn R into Merdon Ave, then 3rd rd on L. ¾-acre garden planted for yr-round interest with spring colour from bulbs, camellias, rhododendrons, azaleas and magnolias. Woodland, conifers, herbaceous borders, bog garden, ponds, fruit and vegetable garden; bantams. TEAS. *Adm £1.50 Chd 10p (Share to British Heart Foundation®). Sun, Mon April 16, 17; Sun May 21 (2-6)*

Cranbury Park ♿❀ (Mr & Mrs Chamberlayne-Macdonald) Otterbourne, 5m S of Winchester. 2m N of Eastleigh; main entrance on old A33 between Winchester-Southampton, by bus stop at top of Otterbourne Hill. Entrance also in Hocombe Rd, Chandlers Ford. Extensive pleasure grounds laid out in late C18 and early C19; fountains; rose garden; specimen trees; lakeside walk. Family carriages will be on view and collection of prams. TEAS. *Adm £1.50 Chd 50p. Sun June 18 (2-5)*

Crawley Gardens 5m NW of Winchester, off A272 Winchester-Stockbridge Rd. Gardens signed from centre of village. Please park nr church. TEA Sun only. *Combined adm £2.50 Chd free. Sun, Mon April 9, 10 (2-5.30)*

Glebe House ♿ (Lt-Col & Mrs John Andrews) 1½-acres. Bulbs, shrubs and herbaceous borders.

Lithend ♿✿❀ (Mrs F L Gunner) Small cottage garden. *Also open Sun, Mon May 14, 15 (Share to Gift of Sight®) (2-5.30) Mon (2-7). Combined adm £2 Chd free with* **Little Court**

Little Court ♿✿❀ (Professor & Mrs A R Elkington) *Also open on Sun, Mon, Tues, March 26, 27, 28, Sun, Mon, July 30, 31, Aug 13, 14, 15. See separate entry*

Manor Lodge ♿✿❀ (Mr & Mrs K Wren) See separate entry. Cream Teas in aid of St Mary's Church, Crawley. *Also open July 9, 10*

Croft Mews ♿❀ (Captain & Mrs W T T Pakenham) Botley. 2m N of Botley on B3354, on L under trees (M27 exit 7). A recently created garden of about 2 acres with much older buildings and walls, standing in the grounds of an old country house. Walled garden, lawns and mixed borders, woodland area, kitchen garden. Many interesting ideas and features including (new) ha ha with views over meadows. An exhibition of figurative sculpture will be on display during the opening. TEAS in aid of NSPCC. *Adm £1 Chd free. Sun June 11 (2-6) Mon June 12 (11-5). Private visits welcome during June and July, please* **Tel 01703 692425**

Crookley Pool ♿✿❀ (Mr & Mrs F S K Privett) Horndean. Turn up Blendworth Lane by the main bakery from the centre of Horndean. House 200yds before church on L. Off the A3 5m S of Petersfield. Medium sized garden surrounded by parkland. Mixed borders with unusual plants, with a special interest in colour and plants for hot dry situations. Wisteria covered walls and terraces overlooking pool garden. Walled kitchen garden. TEAS. *Adm £1 Chd 25p. Sun, June 25 (2-6); Wed June 28 (2-6)*

Crossways ✿❀ (J Egerton-Warburton) Woodgreen Common. 3m N of Fordingbridge on A338 turn E to Woodgreen, bear L in village and R immediately after the Horse and Groom, on to the common turn R. Parking on the common. Colourful spring garden with bulbs and azaleas. TEAS in aid of Barnardo's. *Adm £1 Chd free. Sun May 21 (2-6)*

Croylands ♿✿❀ (The Hon Mrs Charles Kitchener) Old Salisbury Lane, Romsey. From Romsey take A3057 Stockbridge Rd, L after 1m at Dukes Head, fork L after bridge, 1m on R. Wheelwright's cottage on Florence Nightingale's Family Estate, surrounded by 2 acres unusual, interesting trees, shrubs and plants. Peony garden. TV appearances. TEAS. *Adm £1.50 Chd free. Sun May 28, June 4, 11, 18; Weds, May 31, June 7, 14, 21 (2-6). Also parties welcome mid-May and all June, please* **Tel 01794 513056**

The Dower House ♿ (Mr & Mrs Michael Hoare) Dogmersfield. Turn N off A287. 6-acre garden including bluebell wood with large and spectacular collection of rhododendrons, azaleas, magnolias and other flowering trees and shrubs; set in parkland with fine views over 20-acre lake. TEAS. *Adm £1.50 Chd free (Share to Dogmersfield Church Organ Fund®). Suns May 14, 21 (2-6)*

¶**Downgate Farm** ✿ (Mr & Mrs R J Sinclair) Steep Marsh. 2m NE of Petersfield. Turn L off A3 Northbound to Steep Marsh. From Sheet Village follow signs N past church, ½m on R. 2 acres of gardens and lawns surrounding C17 Farmhouse and outbuildings with free range chicken Farm. Sunken rose and lavender garden, herbaceous borders, mature shrubs and trees, greenhouses, naturalised pond. Extensive views of beech hangers. TEAS. *Adm £1.50 Chd free. Sun, Mon July 2, 3 (2-5)*

Droxford Gardens 4½m N of Wickham on A32 approx mid-way between Alton-Portsmouth. *Combined adm £2.50 Chd 50p 1 garden £1. Sun June 18 (2-6)*

Fir Hill ❀ (Mrs Derek Schreiber) 4½ acres; roses, shrubs, herbaceous and shrub borders. Home-made TEAS. Car park

The Mill House ♿ (Mrs C MacPherson) Garden of 2 acres; shrubs, flower beds, orchard, mill stream, roses, pond. Car park

Mylor Cottage ♿❀ (Dr & Mrs Martin ffrench Constant) ½m S of Droxford on the Swanmore Rd. Car park. Trees, shrubs and herbaceous border. *Also open Sun April 2 (2-5) see under* **Mylor Cottage**

Park View ♿ (Mrs F V D Aubert) Small town garden, flowers, shrubs and very small wooded walk. Home-made TEAS

Durmast House ♿❀ (Mr & Mrs P E G Daubeney). 1m SE of Burley, nr White Buck Hotel. 4-acre garden designed by Gertrude Jekyll in 1907 in the process of being restored from the original plans. Formal rose garden edged with lavender, 130-yr-old Monterey pine, 100-yr-old cut leaf beech and large choisya. Victorian rockery, lily pond, coach-house, large wisteria and herbaceous border. *Adm £1 Chd 50p (Share to Hampshire Garden Trust and Delhi Commonwealth Women's Assoc Clinic®). Suns March 26, June 11 (2.30-5.30). Private parties welcome, please* **Tel 01425 403527**

East Lane (Sir Peter & Lady Ramsbotham) Ovington A31 from Winchester towards Alresford. Immediately after roundabout 1m west of Alresford, small sign to Ovington turn sharp L up incline, down small country rd to Ovington. East Lane is the only house on left, 500yds before Bush Inn. 4 acres, spring bulbs, mixed herbaceous and shrubs; woodland plantings; walled rose garden. Terraced water garden. Ample parking. *Adm £1.50 OAPs £1 Chd free. Sun April 9 (2.30-6)*

¶**8 Elbow Corner** ✿❀ (Mr Michael Penfold) off Church Square, Basingstoke. Park in Churchill Way Car Park off Churchill Way in centre of Basingstoke. Walk via Lower Church St to Elbow Garden, adjacent to St Michael's Church. A short terrace of houses covered with hanging baskets with the small front gardens planted with annuals to give a blaze of colour in the centre of town. A winner of 'Basingstoke in Bloom' competition. TEA. *Adm £1 Chd 50p. Suns Aug 6, 13 (10-5)*

Eversley Gardens ❀ On B3016. Signposted from A30 (just west of Blackbush Airport) and from B3272 (Formerly A327). E of the cricket ground at Eversley Cross. *Combined adm £2 Chd free. Suns March 26 (2-5); May 7, 21 (2-6)*

Kiln Copse (A Jervis O'Donohue Trust) 8 acres; wide variety of spring flowering bulbs, bluebell wood and foxgloves. Good collection of rhododendrons, azaleas and roses; lake with bog-side plants, large mixed borders, round garden with gazebo and plants climbing into the trees. Kitchen garden and greenhouses

Kiln Copse Cottage Small garden of perennials and shrubs in the grounds of Kiln Copse

Little Coopers (Mr & Mrs J K Oldale) 10-acre garden. Drifts of daffodils in March and new small heather garden. A woodland walk meanders through bluebells, rhododendrons, azaleas and unusual shrubs most of which are labelled. Shaded by mature trees, walk leads to water & bog garden with ponds and stream, then onto extensive lawn in front of house surrounded by Mediterranean and rose gardens. Small Japanese garden by the house. Featured on TV Channel 4 Garden Club 1993. TEAS in aid of Arthritis and Rheumatism Research. *Parties by appt, please* **Tel 01252 872229**

Ewell House ♿❀ (Mr & Mrs R J Gould) 44 Belmore Lane, Lymington. 100yds downhill on R from exit off Waitrose car park. Town garden of ⅓ acre completely replanned and replanted in 1986. New planting still taking place but has acquired maturity. Large variety of interesting shrubs include camellias and small rhododendrons. TEAS at **South End House** (q.v.) Plants at Ewell House. *Combined adm £2 Chd free. Sun May 7 (2-5.30)*

● **Exbury Gardens** ♿❀ (Exbury Gardens Trust) Exbury, 2½m SE of Beaulieu; 15m SW of Southampton. Via B3054 SE of Beaulieu; after 1m turn sharp R for Exbury. 200 acres of woodland garden incorporating the Rothschild Collection of azaleas, rhododendrons, magnolias, maples and camellias. Luncheons and teas. Plant Centre and Gift Shop. *Spring Season: Sat Feb 12 to mid April Adm £3 OAPs £2.50. Parties of 15 or more £2.50 Chd 10-16 £2. Adm mid April-early June £4 OAPs & groups £3.50 (OAPs reduced 50p Weds and Thurs) Chd 10-16 £3. (All main season prices except OAPs increase by 50p weekends and Bank Hols). Mid June to July 10 Adm £3 OAPs £2.50. Parties £2.50 Chd £2. Gardens N of Gilbury Lane Bridge open Summer July 11 to Sept 16 Adm adults & parties £2.50 OAPs & Chd 10-16 £1.50. Autumn Sept 17 to Oct 24. Adm £2.50 OAPs & groups £2 Chd 10-16 £1.50. Open daily 10- 5.30/dusk. For NGS Wed May 10*

Fairfield House ♿✿❀ (Mrs Peter Wake) Hambledon. 10m SW of Petersfield. Hambledon village. 5-acre informal garden on chalk, with extensive walls, fine mature trees; large collection of shrubs and climbing roses mixed with wide variety of small trees and interesting perennials. Adjacent car park and wild flower meadow. Featured in 'A Heritage of Roses' by Hazel Le Rougetel, 'The Rose Gardens of England' by Michael Gibson, 'The Latest Country Gardens' by George Plumptre. TEAS. *Adm £1.50 Chd free. Suns, April 23, June 25 (2-6). Also private visits welcome anytime by appt; suitable for groups, please* **Tel 01705 632431**

By Appointment Gardens. Avoid the crowds. Good chance of a tour by owner. See garden description for telephone number.

Fernlea ✿❀ (Mr & Mrs P G Philip) Chilworth. N of Southampton on A27 at junction of M3 and M27, take A27 towards Romsey. After 1m turn L at Clump Inn (Lunches available). Proceed along Manor Rd into Chilworth Drove for about ½m. 15-acre organic garden created to encourage wild life, with many birds and butterflies, and woodland, meadow and heathland habitats. Many Mediterranean plants, specially Cistus with informal planting. Views to the Isle of Wight and large specimen trees. Garden merges into woodland. 15 acres in all. Picnics welcome. TEAS. *Adm £1.50 Chd free. Suns May 7, July 16, Aug 27; Mons May 8, Aug 28 (12-5)*

Fritham Lodge ♿❀ (Christopher and Rosie Powell) Fritham, nr Lyndhurst. 3m NW of Cadnam junction 1 on M27. Follow signs to Fritham, after approx 3m, turn into Fritham village, turn down gravel track low sign Fritham Lodge only; parking in field. Set in heart of New Forest. Approx 1-acre; old walled garden surrounding C17 listed house (not open) originally one of Charles II's hunting lodges. Parterre of old roses, potager with wide variety of vegetables, herbs and fruit trees, pergola, herbaceous and blue and white mixed borders, ponds, walk across hay meadows to woodland and stream. TEAS. *Adm £1.50 Chd free. Sun July 2 (2-5)*

● **Furzey Gardens** ♿✿❀ (Furzey Gardens Charitable Trust) Minstead, 8m SW of Southampton. 1m S of A31; 2m W of Cadnam and end of M27; 3½m NW of Lyndhurst. 8 acres of informal shrub garden; comprehensive collections of azaleas and heathers; water garden; fernery; summer and winter flowering shrubs. Botanical interest at all seasons. Also open (limited in winter) Will Selwood Gallery and ancient cottage (AD 1560). Highclass arts and crafts by 150 local craftsmen. Tea Honey Pot ¼m. *Adm £3 OAPs £2.50 Chd £1.50 March to Oct. £1.50 OAPs £1 Chd 75p winter. Daily except Dec 25 & 26 (10-5; dusk in winter).* **Tel 01703 812464**

The Garden House ✿❀ (Mr & Mrs C Kirkman) Lymington. Off Lymington High St opp Woolworths. An explosion of unusual herbaceous, roses, grasses, house leeks agaves and shrubs, interspersed with a riot of annuals, punctuated by 2 ponds and an ornamental kitchen garden. Prime example of close boscage. TEAS with extravagent portions of clotted cream. *Adm £2 Chd free incl* **Glevins** *q.v. (Share to Oakhaven Hospice®). Sun June 18 (2-6)*

Glevins ♿✿❀ (Mrs Clarke) Lymington. Situated off Lymington High St. between Lloyds Bank and Nat West Bank. ½-acre small walled garden with wide view of the Solent and Yarmouth I.O.W. Mixed borders, small rockery, conservatory. *Adm £2 Chd free including* **The Garden House.** *Sun June 18 (2-6)*

Greatham Mill ♿✿❀ (Mr & Mrs E Groves) Greatham, nr Liss. 5m N of Petersfield. From A325, at Greatham turn onto B3006 towards Alton; after 600yds L into 'No Through Rd' lane to garden. Interesting garden with large variety of plants surrounding mill house, with mill stream and nursery garden. Home-made TEAS. *Adm £1 Chd free. April 14 to end of Sept, every Sat and Sun and Bank Hols. NGS Suns May 7, Sept 3 (2-6). Private visits welcome, please* **Tel 01420 538245**

Hackwood Park (The Spring Wood) ✲❀ (The Viscount and Viscountess Camrose) 1m S of Basingstoke. Entrance off Tunworth Rd. Signed from A339 Alton-Basingstoke. 80 acres delightful C17-C18 semi-formal wood with pavilions, cockpit, walks, glades; magnificent ornamental pools, amphitheatre, interesting trees and bulbs. Home-made TEAS and produce. *Adm £2 OAPs £1 Chd free (Share to St Leonard's Church, Cliddesden and St Mary's Church, Herriard®). Suns April 2 (2-6) Oct 8 (1.30-5.30). For NGS Sun May 14 (2-6)*

Hall Place ♿ (Mr & Mrs Dru Montagu) West Meon. 7m W of Petersfield. From A32 in West Meon, take rd to East Meon, garden on R. Parking in drive. Large collection of rare and unusual daffodils in 8 acres of garden designed by Lanning Roper 30 years ago. Grass walks, spring bulbs, many varieties of trees and shrubs; walled kitchen garden. *Collecting box. Sun April 23 (2-6)*

Hambledon House ✲❀ (Capt & Mrs David Hart Dyke) Hambledon. 8m SW of Petersfield. In village centre behind George Hotel. Approx 2 acres partly walled garden with unusual plants, shrubs suited to chalk soil and to give colour and interest through the seasons. Centred around 150-yr-old copper beech. Special interest in grasses, salvias, penstemons. Featured on TV 1992. TEAS (Suns). *Adm £1.50 Chd free. Suns May 21, June 25, Sept 10, Mon May 22 (2-6); also private visits welcome, please* **Tel 01705 632380**

Heathlands ♿ (Dr John Burwell) 47 Locks Rd, Locks Heath. Locks Rd runs due S from Park Gate into Locks Heath. No 47 is 1m down on the R hand side [Grid Ref 513 069]. 1-acre garden designed & developed by the owner since 1967. An attempt has been made to give yr-round interest against a background of evergreens and mature trees. Spring bulbs, rhododendrons, paulownias. cyclamen, ferns and some less usual plants. Topiary, small herbaceous border and scree bed. National Collection of Japanese anemones. 'A treat for garden visitors' Stefan Buczacki TVS. TEAS. *Adm £1 Chd free. Suns May 14, July 16 (2-5.30)*

Highclere Castle ♿✲ (The Earl of Carnarvon) Nr Newbury. Entrance on A34 4½m S of Newbury. Spectacular Charles Barry Mansion set in park designed by Capability Brown. Superb cedars, orangery with exotic and edible plants. Secret garden with tranquil herbaceous planting. C18 walled garden; beautiful views. Picnics welcome. TEAS. *Adm £3 (garden only). Weds-Suns July, Aug, Sept, Suns & Mons Easter, May & Aug Bank Hols. For NGS Suns July 16, 23, Aug 13, 20 (2-6) last entry 5pm*

Hill House, Old Alresford ♿ (Maj & Mrs W F Richardson) From Alresford 1m along B3046 towards Basingstoke, then R by church. 2 acres with large old-fashioned herbaceous border and shrub beds, set around large lawn; kitchen garden. TEAS. *Adm £1.20 Chd free. Sun Aug 6 (2-5.30)*

Regular Openers. Too many days to include in diary. Usually there is a wide range of plants giving year-round interest. See head of county section for the name and garden description for times etc.

● **Sir Harold Hillier Arboretum** ♿✲❀ Jermyns Lane, Ampfield. Situated between Ampfield and Braishfield, 3m NE of Romsey. Signposted from A31 and A3057. From M27 junction 3, follow signs to Romsey. Parking at the gardens. 160-acres containing the finest collection of hardy trees and shrubs in the UK. Home to 9 national collections quercus, carpinus, cornus, cotoneaster, ligustrum, lithocarpus, corylus, photinia, pinus. Pond, scree beds, heather garden, peat garden, centenary border and acer valley. Wonderful spring and autumn colour with guided tours at 2pm every Suns and Weds in May and Oct. Fine collections of magnolias, azaleas and rhododendrons. TEAS. *Adm March to Nov £4 OAP £3.50 Chd £1 (Group rate 30+ £3.50); Dec to Feb £3, OAP £2.50 Chd £1. Daily April 1 to Oct 31 (10.30-6); Nov 1 to March 31 (10.30-5 or dusk)*

Hinton Ampner ♿✲ (The National Trust) S of Alresford. On Petersfield-Winchester Rd A272. 1m W of Bramdean village. 12-acre C20 shrub garden designed by Ralph Dutton. Strong architectural elements using yew and box topiary, with spectacular views. Bold effects using simple plants, restrained and dramatic bedding. Orchard with spring wild flowers and bulbs within formal box hedges; magnolia and philadephus walks. Dell garden made from chalk pit, now restored and maturing. Shrub rose border dating from 1950s. Special interest viburnum, buddleia, cotinus, foxgloves. TEAS. *Adm £2.40 Chd £1.20. Sats, Suns June 24, 25; Sept 16, 17 (1.30-5)*

Holt End House ✲❀ (Maj & Mrs J B B Cockcroft) Ashford Hill, Newbury. Ashford Hill is on B3051 between Kingsclere and Tadley. The garden is in the village on the R going E. 3-acre garden with extensive collection of labelled roses, with many climbers on unusual tree hosts. Substantial mature shrub planting. Large ginkgo biloba. Area of SSI woodland. TEAS. *Adm £1.50 Chd free (Share to St Paul's Church, Ashford Hill®). Sun June 25 (2-6)*

House-in-the-Wood ✲ (Countess Michalowska) 1½m from Beaulieu; signed from Motor Car Museum, Beaulieu. R turn to Southampton off B3056 Beaulieu-Lyndhurst Rd. 13-acre woodland garden; rhododendrons and azaleas. *Adm £2 Chd 50p. Mon May 8 (2.30-6.30). Parties of 15 or more by appt.* **Tel 01590 612346**

Jenkyn Place ♿✲❀ (Mrs G E Coke) Bentley. 400yds N of Xrds in Bentley. Heritage sign on A31. Bus: Guildford-Winchester, alight Bentley village, 400yds. Well designed plantsman's garden, many interesting shrubs and perennials, double herbaceous borders. Featured in NGS video 1. Car park free. Disabled may set down at gates (Coaches only by prior appt). *Adm £2 Chd 75p. Thurs, Fris, Sats, Suns & Bank Hol Mons April 13 to Sept 10 (2-6). For NGS Suns June 4, July 2 plus 5 per cent of other receipts*

John Hines Studios ♿✲ (Mr John Hine) 2 Hillside Rd, Aldershot. From A31 take exit off large roundabout on E side of Farnham signed Farnborough A325 and Basingstoke A30. At next roundabout take 3rd exit signed Aldershot B3007. After 1m, with railway bridge ahead, rd bends sharply L and becomes Eggars Hill. Hillside Rd is 400yds on L. Garden is 2nd entrance on R. A small newly created courtyard garden (approx 50′ × 60′) surrounded by a restored C17 barn (open). Garden is planted with a wide range of climbers & herbaceous plants to give maximum colour and interest over a long season. Garden also includes hanging baskets, window boxes, containers and a dovecote. TEAS in traditional English tea room. *Adm £1 Chd 50p. Suns June 25, July 9, 23 (10.30-4.30). Private visits welcome, please* **Tel 01252 334672**

53 Ladywood ✲❀ (Mr & Mrs D Ward) Eastleigh. Leave A33/M3 at junction 12, signed A335 Eastleigh N and follow A335 towards Eastleigh. R at roundabout into Woodside Ave, 2nd R into Bosville. Ladywood is 5th R off Bosville, please park in Bosville. A plant lover's very small garden, 45′ × 45′, developed by the owners over the last 6 yrs, giving many ideas for the small garden featured in Gardener's World 1994. Over 1000 different plants labelled. Rustic fences have been built to give vertical space for clematis and climbing roses. A secluded shade garden, a pond garden and a tiny lawn; collections of hardy geraniums, pulmonarias, asters for the small garden and many foliage plants. TEAS (2-5). *Adm £1 Chd 50p. Suns May 14, June 11, July 16, (10-5). Private visits welcome May to July Thursday afternoons, please* **Tel 01703 615389**

Lake House ♿❀ (Lord & Lady Ashburton) Northington, Alresford. 4m N of Alresford off B3046. Follow English heritage signs to The Grange. From Winchester take A33 N turning R at Lunway Inn follow signs to Northington and The Grange. Large garden in Candover Valley. 2 large lakes set off by mature woodland with waterfalls formed by streams, abundant bird life and long landscape vistas. Sizeable walled garden with rose pergola leading to moon gate, large herbaceous border, formal flower and kitchen gardens, also numerous flowering pots. Wide range of plants, many choice and unusual. Gardening experts to answer questions. Picnicking by lakes. Visit can conveniently be continued with seeing The Grange, an English Heritage property in the Greek revival style. TEAS. *Adm £2 Chd free. Sun June 25 (1-5). Parties welcome for 10 and over, please* **Tel 01962 734426**

Landford Lodge Landford see Wiltshire

60 Lealand Road ♿✲❀ (Mr F G Jacob) Drayton. 2m from Cosham E side of Portsmouth. Old A27 (Havant Rd) between Cosham and Bedhampton. Small prize winning garden created and designed by owner since 1969. Featured in National Gardening Magazines. Exotic plants with rockery, ponds, dwarf conifers and collection of grasses, cacti and other exotics in greenhouse. TEA. *Adm 75p Chd 25p. Suns April 16, May 14, June 18 (11-5). Also private visits welcome, please* **Tel 01705 370030**

Lithend ♿✲❀ (Mrs F L Gunner) For directions see under **Crawley Gardens** *open April 9. Also open with* **Little Court, Crawley** *Combined adm £1.50 Chd free. Sun, Mon May 14, 15 (2-5.30)*

Little Barn Garden & Barnhawk Nursery ♿❀ (Drs R & V A Crawford) Woodgreen. 3m NE of Fordingbridge via A338. Turn E to Woodgreen; bear L in village; R immediately past Horse and Groom, continue for 1¼m; 2½ acres of mature informal garden with all year interest in form, colour and texture; rhododendron; azalea; camellia; magnolia; acer and collector's plants with peat, scree, rock, woodland, bog and water area. *Adm £1 Chd 25p. For NGS Sun May 14 (2-6). Also private visits welcome, please* **Tel 01725 512213**

The Little Cottage ✲❀ (Lyn & Peter Prior) In Lymington on A337; opp Toll House Inn. ¼ acre garden divided into 7 small formal rooms by hedges or ivy clad fences and each with intricate paving, box and topiary and pot and urn collections. Each garden has a precise colour scheme - blue/yellow, blue/white, pink/lime, mauve/silver, apricot/copper, red/purple and white courtyard garden with tender white climbers on S-facing cottage wall. Most main paths have a specific feature/construction to complete the picture and mark their end. Completion of 4/5 or more further feature/constructions is expected before re-opening in 1995. Article in RHS 'The Garden' Sept 1993. *Adm £1. Visitors welcome each Tuesday from May 30 to Sept 26 (10-1 & 2-dusk). Visitors are usually 'taken around the gardens' and therefore telephoning first is preferred.* **Lymington 01590 679395**

Little Court ♿✲❀ (Prof & Mrs A R Elkington) Crawley 5m NW of Winchester off A272 in Crawley village; 300yds from either village pond or church. Please park near church. Sheltered walled chalk garden. Naturalised bulbs; informal planting for peaceful effect-mostly herbaceous. Special interests incl euphorbia, geraniums, eryngiums. Traditional walled kitchen garden. Beautiful views to Farley Mount. Bantams and geese. TEAS Suns only. *Adm £1.50 (Combined with* **Lithend** *£2; with* **Crawley Gardens** *£2.50). Sun, Mon, Tues March 26, 27, 28; April 9, 10, 11; May 14, 15, 16; (Share to Gift of Sight®). Sun. Mon, July 30, 31, Sun, Mon, Tues Aug 13, 14, 15; Sun, Mon, Sept 17, 18 (Suns 2-5.30, Mons & Tues 2-7). Also private visits welcome, please* **Tel 01962 776365**

¶Little Mead ♿✲ (Mr & Mrs K C Moon) 4m NW of Waterlooville on B2150 opp Hartridges at W end of village. Garden of ⅐ acre, intensively cultivated. Outstanding herbaceous borders. Shrubs, clematis and other climbers. Many unusual, tender and foliage plants; vegetables. Featured on TV in 1985 and 1992 and in 'Garden News' in 1993. *Adm £1 Chd free. Sun July 23 (2-6)*

Littleton House ♿✲ (Mr & Mrs James Butler) Crawley 5m NW of Winchester, off A272 Winchester-Stockbridge Rd. 1m from Littleton Church towards Crawley. 4 acres lawns; pergola; borders; vegetable garden; conservatory. TEA. *Adm £1 Chd free. Sun July 30 (2-5)*

Littlewood ♿✲❀ (Steven and Sheila Schrier) 163 West Lane, Hayling Island. From A27 Havant/Hayling Island roundabout, travel S 2m, turn R into West Lane. Travel 1m and Littlewood is on R in a wood. 2½-acre woodland garden protected from the sea winds by multi barrier hedge. Woodland walk and access to Hayling Billy harbour trail. Rhododendrons, azaleas, camellias and many other shrubs. Features incl pond, bog garden watered from roof of comfortable conservatory with many house plants. Picnickers welcome. Easy access for elderly and wheelchair bound. TEAS. *Donations. Sat, Sun May 20, 21 (11-6)*

Longparish Gardens ♿❀ 5m E of Andover off A303 to village centre on B3048. *Combined adm £2.50 Chd free. Sun, Mon June 11, 12 (2-5.30)*

Longmead House ♿❀ (Mr & Mrs J H Ellicock) 2½-acre organic garden. Large hedged vegetable garden with deep beds, polytunnel, fruit cage and composting display. A fishpond and wildlife pond, wildflower meadow, herbaceous and shrub borders, trees. Shetland pony, angora goats, dairy goat and chickens. TEAS. *Private visits welcome, please* **Tel 01264 720386**

White Windows ✻❀ (Mr & Mrs B Sterndale-Bennett) ⅔-acre with unusual range of hardy perennials, trees and shrubs planted for yr-round foliage interest and colour blendings in garden rooms, including many hellebores, hardy geraniums and euphorbias. Garden featured on TV, in 'Hortus' and 'English Private Gardens'. TEA. *Also open Sun April 2 (2-6). Adm £1.50. Private visits welcome Weds April to Sept, please* **Tel 01264 720222.**

Longstock Park Gardens ♿✻❀ (Leckford Estate Ltd; Part of John Lewis Partnership) 3m N of Stockbridge. From A30 turn N on to A3057; follow signs to Longstock. A water garden of repute with extensive collection of aquatic and bog plants set in 7 acres of woodland with rhododendrons and azaleas. A walk through the park leads to an arboretum, herbaceous border and nursery. The water garden has featured in several TV programmes and gardening books. *Adm £2 Chd 50p. Sun June 18 (2-5)*

Long Thatch ♿✻❀ (Mr & Mrs P Short) Warnford. 1m S of West Meon on A32 turn R from N or L from George & Falcon, 100yds turn R at T-junction, continue for ¼m; thatched C17th house on R, parking opp house. Interesting 2-acre plantsman's garden rolling down to the R. Meon. Plantings being continually being enhanced with good selection of rare trees and shrubs. A large display of Helleborus Orientalis with over 50 named cultivars; alpine and bog gardens, pond and riverside plantings. Fine lawns with herbaceous borders designed to give maximum colour through the seasons. *Adm £1.50 Chd free. Open for NGS Suns March 5, 12, 19 (2-5); Sun, Mon May 28, May 29; Suns June 25, July 23, Aug 27 (2- 6). Also private visits by Societies and individuals welcome. We also open Weds Mar 1 to Aug 30 (10-6) please* **Tel 01730 829285**

Lymore Valley Herbs ♿✻❀ (N M Aldridge) Braxton Farm. 3m W of Lymington. From A337 at Everton take turning to Milford-on-Sea, 70yds on L is Lymore Lane. Turn into Lane and gardens are at Braxton courtyard on L. Attractive courtyard with raised lily pool and dovecote. Restored C19 barn leading into formal walled garden. Spring bulbs incl galanthus, narcissi and fritillaria. Extensive summer and autumn borders; knot garden and lawns. Horticultural societies welcome. Special evening visits. TEA. Shop, plants nursery, no dogs in courtyard or walled garden (dog rings & water provided). *Donations. Open 9-5 all year round except Dec 25 to March 1st.* **Tel 01590 642008**

By Appointment Gardens. See head of county section

Macpenny Woodland Garden & Nurseries ❀ (Mr & Mrs T M Lowndes) Burley Road, Bransgore. Midway between Christchurch and Burley. From Christchurch via A35, at Cat and Fiddle turn left; at Xrds by The Crown, Bransgore turn R and on ¼m. From A31 (travelling towards Bournemouth) L at Picket Post, signed Burley; through Burley to Green Triangle then R for Bransgore and on 1m beyond Thorney Hill Xrds. 17 acres; ¾-acre gravel pit converted into woodland garden; many choice, rare plants incl camellias, rhododendrons, azaleas, heathers. Large selection shrubs and herbaceous plants available. Tea Burley (Forest Tearooms) or Holmsley (Old Station Tea Rooms). *Collecting box. Daily except Dec 25 & 26 and Jan 1. (Mons-Sats 9-5; Suns 2-5)*

¶Malt Cottage ✻ (Mr & Mrs Richard Mason) Turn into Upper Clatford off the Andover-Stockbridge or Andover-Salisbury Rd. Park behind village hall. Garden is down short lane, opposite Crook & Shears Public House. Formal garden blending into natural water meadows with ¼-m chalk stream boundary to 6 acres. Lakes, bog garden; uncommon trees and shrubs. TEA available in aid of another charity. *Adm £2 Chd free. Sun Aug 20 (2-5)*

Manor Lodge ♿✻❀ (Mr & Mrs K Wren) Crawley. Signposted from A272 and near the village pond. Drive with many specie roses growing through yew trees; shrub borders. Walled garden with low maintenance, mixed border; over 50 varieties old and new roses incl 3 chinenis mutabilis. Considered colour combinations; thatched summer house; small courtyard. Converted barn with small garden; ancient walnut tree. Cream TEAS in garden room in aid of St Mary's Church, Crawley (April) WWF (July). Parking outside House only. *Adm £1.50 Sat, Sun May 7, 8; July 1, 2 (2-5.30) Wed July 5 (2-7). Also open with* **Crawley Gardens** *April 9, 10 (2-5.30); also private visits welcome, please* **Tel 01962 776372**

Martyr Worthy Gardens Midway between Winchester and Alresford on B3047. Gardens joined by Pilgrims Way through Itchen Valley, approx ½m. TEAS in Village Hall (Aug 6 only). *Adm £1.50 per garden Chd free. Sun Aug 6 (2-5.30)*

Chilland ♿ (Mrs L A Impey) Mature garden. Fine situation. Shrub borders designed for foliage colour. Many interesting plants. *Also open Sun, Mon May 7, 8, Mon Aug 7*

Manor House ♿ (Cdr & Mrs M J Rivett-Carnac) Large garden, roses, mixed borders, lawns, shrubs and fine trees, next to C12 church

Marycourt ♿✻❀ (Mr & Mrs M Conville) Odiham 2m S of Hartley Wintney on A30 or Exit 5 on M3; In Odiham High St. 1-acre garden and paddocks. Old garden roses; shrubs; ramblers dripping from trees. Silver/pink border, long shrubaceous and colourful herbaceous borders; hosta beds and new delphinium planting. Dry stone wall/alpines thriving. Grade II starred house. *Adm £2 Chd free (Share to Jonathan Conville Memorial Trust®). Suns June 25, July 2 (2-6); Wed July 5 (all day) also private visits welcome, please* **Tel 01256 702100**

Meadow House, nr Newbury See Berkshire

Merdon Manor ♿✂❀ (Mr & Mrs J C Smith) Hursley, SW of Winchester. From A3090 Winchester-Romsey, at Standon turn on to rd to Slackstead; on 2m. 5 acres with panoramic views; herbaceous and rose borders; small secret walled water garden (as seen on TV). Ha-ha and sheep. TEAS. *Adm £1.50 Chd 25p. Sun July 9 (2-6); also private visits welcome, please* **Tel 01962 775215** *or* **775281**

¶**Merebimur** ♿❀ (Mr & Mrs C Snelling) Mockbeggar. 3m N of Ringwood on the A338, turn E to Mockbeggar at The Old Beams Inn. Turn L at the next small Xrds and next L into New Rd. Limited parking at garden but parking on verge opp the end of New Rd with very short walk. ½-acre owner maintained garden with pond, lawns, pergola and mixed borders with many unusual plants. TEAS. *Adm £1 Chd free. Sat, Sun July 1, 2 (2-6). Private visits welcome, please* **Tel 01425 473116**

Merrie Cottage ♿✂ (Mr & Mrs C K Thornton) Woodgreen 3m N of Fordingbridge on A338 turn E to Woodgreen. Fork R at PO towards Godshill. Entrance 200 yds on L. Limited parking for disabled or park on common and walk down footpath. 60ft gingko and huge pollarded beech dominate part of garden. There is no longer a Merrie. The irregular sloping shape offers vistas with a profusion of iris and primulas May and June, followed by seed-grown lilies and wide variety of moisture lovers. There is no hard landscape or colour theme but interest is held throughout year. TEAS (Sun) TEA (Mon) at Applecroft. *Adm £1 Chd free. Sun, Mon June 11, 12 (2-5.30). Private visits welcome, please* **Tel 01725 512273**

¶**Mill Court** ♿❀ (Leila Viscountess Hampden) Alton. 2m E of Alton on A31. Signpost opp Hen & Chicken. 24 acres with 3 acres garden, woodland and river walk. Walled herbaceous border. Mixed shrubbery, vegetable garden and greenhouses. All surrounding Tudor barn. TEA. *Adm £1.50 Chd free. Sat, Sun Sept 23, 24 (2-6)*

Monxton Gardens ♿✂❀ 3m W of Andover, between A303 and A343; in Monxton cream TEAS in village hall in aid of Church. *Combined adm £2 Chd free. Sun, Mon May 28, 29 (2-5.30)*

¶**Field House** (Dr & Mrs Pratt) 2-acre garden made by owners, herbaceous borders, orchard, chalk pit garden with ponds and kitchen garden

Hutchens Cottage (Mr & Mrs R A Crick) ¾-acre cottage garden with old roses, clematis, shrubs, mature trees, small orchard; mixed thyme patch and kitchen garden

¶**White Gables** (Mrs & Mrs D Eaglesham) Cottage style garden of ⅓ acre, leading down to Pill Hill Brook. Interesting shrubs, old roses and herbaceous

¶**Moth House** ❀ (Mrs I R B Perkins) Brown Candover. On B3046 from Alresford toBasingstoke in Brown Candover Village. 5m from Alresford, just past village green on L. 2- acre garden. Gold and silver garden. Herbaceous borders and shrub walk. Speciality - roses. TEAS. *Adm £1.50 Chd free. Sun July 2 (2-5.30)*

Mottisfont Abbey & Garden ♿✂❀ (The National Trust) Mottisfont, 4½m NW of Romsey. From A3057 Romsey-Stockbridge turn W at sign to Mottisfont. 4 wheelchairs and battery car service available at garden. 30 acres; originally a C12 Priory; landscaped grounds with spacious lawns bordering R Test; magnificent trees; remarkable ancient spring pre-dating the Priory; walled garden contains NT's large collection of old-fashioned roses. Tea Mottisfont PO. *Adm £3.50 Chd £1.75. April 2 to Oct 31 Sat to Wed (12-6) June only Sat to Thurs (12-8.30). For NGS Sun June 25 (12-8.30), last adm 7.30 pm*

Moundsmere Manor ✂ (Mr & Mrs Andreae) 6m S of Basingstoke on B3046. Drive gates on L just after Preston Candover sign. 20 acres, incl formal rose gardens; herbaceous borders, large greenhouses, unusual trees and shrubs. Coaches by appt. *Adm £2 Chd £1. Sun July 2 (2-6)*

Mylor Cottage ♿❀ (Dr & Mrs Martin ffrench Constant) Droxford. ½m S of Droxford on the Swanmore Rd. Car park. Gardener's garden; April: anemone blanda, cyclamen, spring bulbs and cherries; June: interesting foliage beds and specimen trees, colourful herbaceous borders. *Adm £1 Chd 50p. (Share to Multiple Sclerosis®). Sun April 2 (11-5) Sun June 18 open with* **Droxford Gardens** *(2-6) (Combined adm £2.50 Chd 50p). Parties welcome, please* **Tel 01489 877462**

North Ecchinswell Farm ♿✂❀ (Mr & Mrs Robert Henderson) Nr Newbury. Turn S off A339 Newbury-Basingstoke rd. House 1m from turning (sign-posted Ecchinswell and Bishops Green) on L-hand side. Approx 6-acre garden. Shrub borders, woodland garden with small lake, woodland walks, many bog plants, shrubs and bulbs, fine trees incl an exceptional lime, small arboretum. *Adm £2 Chd free. Sun April 30 (2.30-5.30)*

¶**Oakdene** ♿✂❀ (Mr & Mrs Christopher Stanford) Sandleheath. Just into Sandleheath on the B3078, 1 from Fordingbridge on the RH-side immed beyond small church. Garden of nearly 2 acres with roses of all types incl rambler covered long pergola, 'white' and 'red' herbaceous beds, orchard with free-range hens, flower-bordered productive organic vegetable garden, dovecote with resident doves. TEAS in aid of the New Forest Children's Hospice Appeal. *Adm £1.50 Chd 50p. Sun June 25, Tue June 27 (2-6). Private visits welcome, please* **Tel 01425 652133**

Oakley Manor ♿✂❀ (Mr & Mrs Priestley) Rectory Rd, Oakley. 5m W of Basingstoke. From Basingstoke towards Whitchurch on B3400 turn L Station Rd and follow signs. Bus 55a, 55b Basingstoke to Oakley. Large 5-acre garden surrounded by open farmland with comprehensive planting incl a conservation area. Mature trees, shrubs, perennials and annuals. Thatched Wendy House. TEA. Free parking at the Manor. *Combined adm with* **The Barn House** *£2 Chd free. Sun Aug 6 (2-5.30)*

The Old House ♿❀ (Mr & Mrs M Jurgens) Bramley Road, Silchester; entrance next to Silchester (Calleva) Roman Museum. Queen Anne rectory with large garden. Fine specimen and unusual trees and shrubs. Well labelled collections of specie and hybrid rhododendrons, azaleas, camellias and shrub roses. Very colourful spring garden dating from 1920's incl dell and pergola walk, bluebell woodland, ponds and paddock. Spring bulbs. Easy walk to Roman town walls and Amphitheatre, medieval Church. TEAS in aid of church. *Adm £1.50 Chd 50p (Share to St Mary The Virgin Church, Silchester®). Suns April 9 (2-6) 23; May 7, 21 (11-6). Private parties welcome April to May, please* **Tel 01734 700240**

Old Meadows ♿✂❀ (Dr & Mrs J M Fowler) Silchester. Off A340 between Reading and Basingstoke. 1m S of Silchester on rd to Bramley, signposted at Xrds. 5 acres including walled potager. Herbaceous borders, meadow walk. TEAS. *Adm £1.50 Chd free (Share to North Hampshire Medical Fund®). Sun June 25 (11-6). Private visits welcome, July to Aug, please* **Tel 01256 881450**

Old Timbers ♿✂ (Mr & Mrs J Leask) Mill Hill, Alresford, Park in Broad St in town centre; Mill Hill at bottom of Broad St on L. C16 cottage with herbaceous garden. TEAS. *Adm £1 Chd 50p. Sun June 11 (2-6)*

¶Paddocks Way ♿✂❀ (Mr & Mrs K Elcock) Brook. 1m W from junction 1 M27 (on B3078) turn L into Canterton Manor Drive before Green Dragon. Country garden of ¼ acre. Maintained solely by plant loving owners. Mixed borders and island beds containing many interesting and unusual herbaceous perennials, grasses and shrubs grown for flower and foliage effect. Kitchen garden containing vegetables, fruit, greenhouse and frames. TEAS. *Adm £1 Chd 50p. Suns April 2, July 2, Oct 1, Sat May 20 (11-5.30). Private visits welcome, please* **Tel 01703 813297**

Paige Cottage ✂ (Mr & Mrs T W Parker) Next to Crawley village pond. Signposted from A272. 1 acre of traditional English country garden with large shrub and herbaceous borders and including grass tennis court and walled Italian style swimming pool; roses climbing into apple trees. *Adm £1 Chd free. Sun July 2 (2-5.30)*

Pennington Chase ♿✂❀ (Mrs V E Coates) 2m SW Lymington L off A337, at Pennington Cross roundabout. 4 acres, flowering shrubs, azaleas and rhododendrons with some unusual trees in fine state of maturity. TEAS 50p. *Adm £1 Chd 50p. Suns March 19, May 7, Oct 8 (2-7)*

Pullens ♿✂❀ (Mr & Mrs R N Baird) W Worldham. From Alton take B3006 SE on the Selborne Rd. After 2½m turn L to W Worldham. By church turn R. Pullen 100yds on R behind wall. Approx 1-acre plantsmans garden on greensand surrounded by hedges and walls. Particular emphasis on colour and yr-round interest. Tranquil atmosphere. TEAS. *Adm £1 Chd free. Weds June 21, 28 (12-5)*

Pylewell Park ♿❀ (The Lord Teynham) 2½ m E of Lymington beyond IOW car ferry. Large garden of botanical interest; good trees, flowering shrubs, rhododendrons, lake, woodland garden. *Adm £2 Chd 50p (Share to Wessex Regional Medical Oncology Unit®). Suns May 14, 21 (2-6). Private visits welcome, please* **Tel 01590 673010**

¶Quoin Cottage ✂❀ (Col & Mrs W Vernon-Harcourt) Denmead. 300yds from village centre on the Southwick Rd and off the B2150. A small garden with quite a wide variety of mature shrubs, and an interesting collection of climbing, rambler and shrub roses, and small trees. *Adm £1 Chd free. Sun, Wed June 18, 21 (2-6)*

Regular Openers. See head of county section.

Robins Return ♿✂❀ (John & Marjorie Ingrem) Tiptoe. 2m NE of New Milton. Take B3055, at Xrds by Tiptoe Church. Turn into Wootton Rd (signposted to Wootton). Garden 400yds on L. ⅔-acre garden. Wisteria pergola (35 yds long). An abundance of miniature roses and box edgings; ornamental pool and rock gardens; newish fern garden, greenhouses, organic kitchen garden. TEAS Sun only. *Adm £1 Chd free. Sun, Wed July 16, 19 (2-5)*

Rookley Manor ♿❀ (Lord & Lady Inchyra) Up Somborne. 6m W of Winchester. From A272 Winchester-Stockbridge Rd. At Rack and Manger turn L towards Kings Somborne. 2m on R. 2 acres; spring bulbs, flowers and blossom; herbaceous, shrub roses, kitchen garden. TEAS. *Adm £1.50 Chd 20p. Mon May 8 (2-6)*

Rosewood Farm ♿✂❀ (Mr & Mrs D Bowman) Frenchmoor, West Tytherley. 10m E of Salisbury, 10m NW of Romsey. From A30 4½m W of Stockbridge take turn S signed West Tytherley - Norman Court. Continue through village on rd to West Dean after ½m L signed to Frenchmoor. Attractive 1-acre informal garden with pond, waterfall and unusual trees, plants and shrubs surrounded by lovely views. Adapted from a field 7 yrs ago. Cream TEAS. *Adm £1.50 Chd free. Sun June 18 (2-6)*

Rowans Wood ♿✂❀ (Mrs D C Rowan) Straight Mile, Ampfield, on A31 (S side); 2m E of Romsey. 2m W of Potters Heron Hotel. Parking on service Rd. Woodland garden planted for yr-round interest. Camellias, rhododendrons, flowering trees, spring bulbs followed by azaleas, hostas and other perennials. Views. TEAS Sun only. *Adm £1.50 Chd free (Share to Winchester & Romsey Branch RSPCA®). Suns April 16, 30, May 14, 28, Mon April 17 (2-5.30). Also private visits welcome, please* **Tel 01794 513072**

12 Rozelle Close ✂ (Margaret & Tom Hyatt) Littleton. Turn E off A272 Winchester to Stockbridge Rd. Just inside Winchester 40 mph zone. 1m Hookers Nursery on R. Rozelle Close 150yds on L just short of Running Horse public house. ⅓-acre spectacular display of herbaceous and 10,000 bedding plants; tubs; troughs; hanging baskets; 2 ponds; 3 greenhouses; vegetables. *Donations. Sat, Sun July 29, 30 (9.30-5.30)*

Rumsey Gardens ♿✂❀ (Mr & Mrs N R Giles) 117 Drift Rd, Clanfield, 6m S of Petersfield. Turn off A3 N of Horndean, signed Clanfield. Planting of garden from a cornfield began during 1956 in poor shallow chalk soil. Acid beds have been constructed enabling lime hating shrubs and plants to be grown. Rock garden, heather beds, pools and bog gardens have been laid out. Collection of cotoneasters. TROBI/NCCPG. *Adm £1 Chd 50p. Suns April 23, May 21 (11-5). Private visits by societies welcome, please* **Tel 01705 593367**

Sadlers Gardens ♿❀ (Nicholas & Marilyn Lock) Lymington. Take A337, S out of Lymington. Turn L at Pennington Cross roundabout. ½m down lane on R. Quantities of rare and half hardy shrubs and trees; herbaceous beds; densely planted in 3 acres. Plantsman's garden created in 1976 by the owner; rhododendrons, camellias, magnolias and acers; spring and summer bulbs. Nursery open. *Adm £1.50 Chd free. Sun March 19 (2-6)*

3 St Helens Road ♿❀ (Mr & Mrs Norman Vaughan) Hayling Island. From Beachlands on seafront, turn R 3rd turning on R into Staunton Avenue, then 1st L. Parking in drive. ⅓-acre ornamental garden with conifers in variety. Interesting trees and shrubs; water garden; old roses. Prizewinning garden featured in 'Amateur Gardening' 1992. TEAS. *Adm by donation. Sat, Sun July 22, 23 (11-6)*

¶Shalden Park House ♿ (Michael D C C Campbell) Shalden. Take B3349 from either Alton or M3 intersection 5. Turn W at X-rds by The Golden Pot Public House marked Herriard, Lasham, Shalden. Garden is ¼m on L. 4-acre woodland garden with extensive views. Pond with duckhouse. Walled kitchen garden. Herbaceous borders. Beds of annuals. Glasshouses. Embryonic arboretum with wild flower walk. Lunchtime picnickers welcome. TEAS. *Adm £1.50 Chd free (Share to The Treloar Trust®). Sun June 25 (11-6)*

Somerley ✲ (The Earl & Countess of Normanton) 2m N of Ringwood off A338 between Ringwood & Ibsley. Turn to Ellingham Church and follow sign to Somerley House. From bus alight Ellingham Cross. Country house garden with herbaceous and rose borders, pergola and herb gardens and gift shop. Wonderful views over R Avon Valley and fine specimen trees in parkland. *Adm £1. Sun Aug 20 (2-6)*

South End House ♿❀ (Mr & Mrs Peter Watson) Lymington. At town centre, turn S opp St Thomas Church 70yds, or park free behind Waitrose and use walkway. Walled town garden to Queen Anne house, home of garden lecturer and writer Elizabeth Watson. ¼-acre, architecturally designed as philosophers' garden. Pergolas, trellises and colonnade attractively planted with vines, clematis, wisteria and roses, combine with sculpted awnings to form 'outdoor rooms', enhanced by fountains, music and lights. Wide pavings, easy access, extensive seating. Featured on TV 'That's Gardening' and NGS video 2. TEAS. Opening with **Ewell House, 44 Belmore Lane, q.v.** Plants for sale at Ewell House. *Combined adm £2 Chd free. Sun May 7 (2-5.30). Private visits welcome, please* **Tel 01590 676848**

Southview ✲❀ (Mr & Mrs Mark Trenear) Chequers Lane, Eversley Cross. Signposted from A30 (W of Blackbush Airport) and from B3272 2m W of Yateley. Turn up Chequers Lane alongside the Chequers Inn. Car park signposted. A plantsman's garden with well designed areas incl old pinks Roman garden, white garden, herbaceous areas and many unusual plants. Featured on TV twice in 1993. TEAS in aid of St Mary's Church Extension Fund. *Adm £1 Chd 50p. Suns June 11, 25 (2-6)*

Sowley House ♿✲❀ (Mr & Mrs O Van Der Vorm) Sowley. At Lymington follow signs to I.O.W. ferry. Continue E on this rd past the ferry nearest to the Solent for 3m until Sowley pond on L. Sowley House is opp the pond. Old garden in country setting approx 4-5 acre with far reaching views over the Solent to the I.O.W. Walled herb garden, with many old roses, clematis, herbaceous and shrub borders, cottage, gardens. Orchard, woodland and bog garden still in the making. Famous for its drifts of daffodils mixed with wild primroses and violets. Stream walk down to the Solent where you might spot kingfishers. TEAS. *Adm £1.50 Chd free (Share to Oakhaven Hospice Lymington®). Sun March 19 (2-5). Parties welcome, please* **Tel 01590 626231**

Spinners ✲❀ (Mr & Mrs P G G Chappell) Boldre. Signed off the A337 Brockenhurst-Lymington Rd (do not take sign to Boldre Church). Azaleas, rhododendrons, magnolias, hydrangeas, maples etc interplanted with a wide range of choice herbaceous plants and bulbs. Nursery specialises in the less common and rare hardy shrubs and plants. *Adm £1.50 Chd under six free. April 14 to Sept 14 daily (10-5) except Suns and Mons (but open Suns in May). Nursery and part of garden open at the same times over the winter. Private visits welcome, please* **Tel 01590 673347**)

Springfield ✲ (Vice-Adm Sir John & Lady Lea) 27 Brights Lane, Hayling Island. From Havant take main rd over Hayling bridge, 3m fork R at roundabout into Manor Rd, Brights Lane ¼m on R. Bus: from Havant, ask for Manor Rd, Hayling Island, alight at Manor Rd PO. This medium sized walled Victorian cottage garden, seen several times on TV, has been gradually altered over the years to produce borders massed with unusual as well as traditional plants surrounding the central lawn and young mulberry tree. The productive vegetable areas and greenhouses keep some of the cottage garden feel. Plants for sale depending on stocks. Partially suited for wheelchairs. *Adm by donation. Private visits welcome, please* **Tel 01705 463801**

¶22 Springvale Road ✲ (Mr & Mrs Fry) Kingsworthy. N end of Springwell Rd. Kingsworthy almost opp Dairiall's shop. ¾ acre of lawns with shrub beds and small trees, underplanted with bulbs. Kitchen garden. 3 best seasons:- End March, early April for magnolias, snowdrops, crocuses and daffodils. Late June for a major display of agapanthus. These were acquired from Lewis Palmer, late President of RHS, who bred them at Headbourne Worthy. This collection of Headbourne hybrids is thought to be the most comprehensive in the country. Sept for drifts of cyclamen, heathers and fine display of foliage. *Adm by Donation. Private visits welcome, please* **Tel 01962 882288**

● **Stratfield Saye House** ♿ (Home of the Dukes of Wellington) Off A33, equidistant between Reading and Basingstoke. House built 1630; presented to the Great Duke in 1817; unique collection of paintings, prints, furniture, china, silver and personal mementoes of the Great Duke. Special Wellington Exhibition; Great Duke's funeral carriage. 3½-acre walled garden with fruit, vegetables, herbs and greenhouses. Large rose garden. Early C19 garden created by the 1st Duke with many plants of American origin: leading to Park with magnificent specimen trees incl Wellingtonia, and riverside walk with wild fowl. Refreshments. Also, nearby, Wellington Country Park with woodlands, meadowlands and lake. TEAS. *Adm £4.50 Chd £2.25 special rates for 20 or more.* **Tel 01256 882882**. *Open daily (except Fri) May 1 until the last Sun in Sept. House (12-4), grounds (11.30-6). For NGS Mon May 8. Adm to grounds £2 Chd £1 (11.30-6)*

Swallowfield Park, nr Reading see Berkshire

Tichborne Park ♿❀ (Mrs J Loudon) Alresford. 1m S off A31 New Alresford on B 3046. 2m N of the A272 New Cheriton on B 3046. Approx 10-acres. Lake, River Itchen, large lawns, trees, shrubs, daffodils, kitchen gardens, glasshouse. Large collection of fuchsias. TEAS. *Adm £1.50 OAP/Chd £1. Suns April 9, June 4 (2-5)*

Tunworth Old Rectory ♿❀ (The Hon Mrs Julian Berry) 5m SE of Basingstoke. 3m from Basingstoke turn S off A30 at sign to Tunworth. Garden laid out with yew hedges, enclosing different aspects of the garden i.e. swimming pool, double rose and mixed border; ruby wedding garden; pleached hornbeam walk; lime avenue, ornamental pond, interesting trees incl beech lined walk to church. TEAS. *Adm £2 OAP £1 Chd free (Share to Church Roof Fund All Saints Church Tunworth®). Sun July 16 (2-5.30)*

Tylney Hall Hotel ♿✽❀ From M3 Exit 5 Via A287 and Newnham, M4 Exit 11 via B3349 and Rotherwick. Large garden. 67 acres surrounding Tylney Hall Hotel with extensive Woodlands and fine vistas now being fully restored with new plantings; fine avenues of Wellingtonias; rhododendron and azaleas; Italian Garden; lakes; large water and rock garden and dry stone walls originally designed with assistance of Gertrude Jekyll. TEA. *Adm £1.50 Chd free. Suns May 7, June 4 (2- 6)*

Upham Gardens ✽ 3m Bishops Waltham on A333, small R turn to Upham by Woodmans Public House. TEAS. *Combined adm £2 or £1 per garden Chd free. Sat June 17 (2-5)*

The Old Rectory ❀ (Mr & Mrs J R Vail) beside church. Enclosed village garden, small woodland area, newly laid out, kitchen parterre, mixed borders, knot garden

Upham Farm ♿ (Mr & Mrs J Walker) Garden made over last 10 yrs; herbaceous, trellis garden of old roses. Walk to small lake with ornamental ducks, wild fowl

Vernon Hill House ❀ (Mr & Mrs Fryer) 1m from Bishop's Waltham. Turn off Beeches Hill. Attractive 6-acre spring and summer garden; wild garden with bulbs growing informally; fine trees, roses, unusual shrubs; kitchen garden. Picnickers welcome. TEA. *Adm £1.25 Chd 25p. Sun, Mon May 7, 8; Suns June 11, July 2 (2-7); also private parties welcome May to early July, please* **Tel 01489 892301**

Verona Cottage ✽❀ (David J Dickinson Esq) 6 Webb Lane, Mengham, Hayling Island. Entrance to garden opp Rose in June public house. Walled garden in 3 parts 500 metres from sea and subject to occasional strong salt winds. Wide variety of tender and Mediterranean plants incl Carpenteria Californica and modern floribunda roses. TEA (Sun). *Adm £1 Chd free. Sat, Sun May 20, 21 (11-6)*

The Vyne ♿✽❀ (The National Trust) Sherborne St John, 4m N of Basingstoke. Between Sherborne St John and Bramley. From A340 turn E at NT signs. 17 acres with extensive lawns, lake, fine trees, herbaceous border, display of tools and machinery. Gardener available to answer questions. TEAS. *Adm house & garden £4 Chd £2; garden only £2 Chd £1. Sun July 23 (12.30-5.30)*

Waldrons ♿✽❀ (Major & Mrs J Robinson) Brook, Lyndhurst. 1m W from exit 1 M27 (on A3079). 1st house L past the Green Dragon public house and directly opp the Bell Inn. A C18 listed cottage with a conservatory, in a garden of 1 acre, containing lawns; a herbaceous border, shrubs and flower beds created around old orchard trees. Small duck pond (free roaming call ducks); fruit cage, herb garden, arbour, rose trellis, raised circular alpine garden and a small stable yard. TEAS. *Adm £1 Chd free. Sun July 2 (2-5.30)*

Walhampton ♿✽ (Walhampton School Trust) Lymington. 1m along B3054 to Beaulieu. 90 acres with azaleas; rhododendrons; lakes; shell grotto. TEAS. *Adm £1 Chd 50p. Sun May 21 (2-6)*

¶Warwick House ✽❀ (Mrs Lucy Marson) Wickham. 2½m N of Fareham on A32. Park in square or signed car park. Warwick House is at the SE corner of the square in Bridge St. Teas available in the Square. ⅛-acre intimate walled town garden with interesting and contrasting planting. Paved courtyard, troughs. Ornamental vegetable and herb garden. *Adm £1 Chd free. Fri May 26, Sun June 11, Sun July 2 (11-6). Private visits welcome until July 2, please* **Tel 01329 832313**

West Silchester Hall ♿❀ (Mrs Jenny Jowett) Bramley Rd, Silchester. Off A340 between Reading and Basingstoke. 1½ acres, plantsman's garden, a good collection of herbaceous plants, rose and shrub borders, rhododendrons and many acid loving plants, small pond and bog garden, and interesting display of half hardies, kitchen garden, and owner maintained. Exhibition of Jenny Jowett's botanical paintings. TEAS. *Adm £1.50 Chd 50p. Suns May 28, Aug 6, Mon Aug 7 (2-6). Parties by appt March-Sept, please* **Tel 01734 700278**

Westbrook House ✽❀ (Andrew Lyndon-Skeggs) Howards Lane, Holybourne. Turn off A31 at roundabout immed to NE of Alton towards Holybourne/Alton 1st R to Holybourne. 1st L up towards Lane on R. Mature 2½ acre garden with stream and pond. Mature trees; herbaceous and shrub borders; orchard; parterre kitchen garden. Redesigned by present owner. CREAM TEAS. *Adm £1 Chd free. Sun June 18 (2.30-5.30)*

¶Wheatley House ♿✽❀ (Mr & Mrs Michael Adlington) Kingsley Bordon. Wheatley is a small hamlet between Binsted and Kingley 4m E of Alton, 5m SW of Farnham. From Alton follow signs to Holybourne and Binsted. At the far end of Binsted turn R signed Wheatley. Wheatley House is ¾m down this narrow farm lane on the L. Magnificent setting with panoramic views over fields, Alice Holt Forest and many miles beyond. Sweeping herbaceous and mixed borders, shrubberies, roses and rockery. Covering about 1½ acres the garden has been designed by the owner, who, as an artist, has given particular emphasis to colour and form. TEA. *Adm £1.50 Chd free. Wed June 28 (2-7)*

By Appointment Gardens. These owners do not have a fixed opening day usually because they do not like crowds or have insufficient parking space. Owner will often give guided tour.

White Cottage ✗ (Mr & Mrs A W Ferdinando) Speltham Hill, Hambledon. Find Speltham Hill 'tween 'George' and shop. Park in street or at hill-top. You will see an ancient cottage small, climbers clinging to its wall. Gain garden, hillside very steep; two-fifty steps to help you peep at covered ground, plants large and small, alpines, shrubs, trees dwarf and tall. A tea-house of the East afar provides a hide, alas no char. Dragons, bridges, pagoda new, pools and fish, vista and view. *Donations. Sun, Mon May 21, 22 (2-6)*

Wonston Lodge ♿ (Mr & Mrs N J A Wood) Wonston. A34 or A30 to Sutton Scotney. At War Memorial turn to Wonston-Stoke Charity; ¾m in Wonston centre. 3 acres, owner maintained. Pond with aquatic plants and ornamental ducks; shrub roses; clematis; topiary. TEAS in barn (with pigeon loft). *Adm £1.50 Chd free (Share to Wessex Medical Trust®). Sat, Sun Sept 2, 3 (2-6)*

Woodcote Manor ♿ (Mrs J S Morton) Bramdean, SE of Alresford. On A272 Winchester-Petersfield Rd, ½m E of Bramdean. Woodland garden; bulbs, shrubs. C17 manor house (not open). *Adm £1.50 OAPs £1 Chd free (Share to Winchester and Central Hampshire Intestinal Cancer Trust®). Easter Sun April 16 (2-5)*

The Wylds ♿ (Gulf International) Warren Rd, Liss Forest. 6m N of Petersfield; follow signs from Greatham on A325 and Rake on A3. 40 acres; 10-acre lake; 100 acres of woodland; rhododendrons, azaleas, heathers; many other shrubs and trees. TEA. *Adm £1.50 Chd 50p. Sun May 21 (2-6)*

Hereford & Worcester

Hon County Organisers:
(Hereford) Lady Curtis, Tarrington Court, nr Hereford
(Worcester) Mrs Graeme Anton, Summerway, Torton, nr Kidderminster Tel 01299 250388

Assistant County Organisers
(Worcester) Jeremy Hughes Esq. Hillwood Farm, Eastham, Tenbury Wells, Worcs WR15 8PA Tel 01584 781366
(Worcester) Mrs William Carr, Conderton Manor, nr Tewkesbury, Glos GL20 7PR
(Hereford) Mr & Mrs Roger Norman, Marley Bank, Whitbourne, Worcester WR6 5RU Tel 01886 821576
(Hereford) Dr J A F Evans, The Lawns, Nunnington, Hereford HR1 3NJ Tel 01432 850664

DATES OF OPENING

By appointment
For telephone numbers and other details see garden descriptions. Private visits welcomed

Arrow Cottage, nr Weobley
Barnard's Green House, Malvern
Bredon Pound, Ashton under Hill
Brilley Court, nr Whitney-on-Wye
Brook House, Colwall
Brookside, Bringsty
Chennels Gate, Eardisley
Churchfield Cottage, Whitbourne
Dial Park, Chaddesley Corbett
Frogmore, nr Ross-on-Wye
Grantsfield, nr Leominster
28 Hillgrove Crescent, Kidderminster
Ivytree House, Clent
Keepers Cottage, Alvechurch
Kingstone Cottages, Rudhall
Kyre Park, Tenbury Wells
Lower Hope, Ullingswick
The Manor House, Birlingham
Marley Bank, Whitbourne
Nerine Nursery, Welland
Orchard Bungalow, Bishops Frome
Pedwardine Cottage, Brampton Bryan
Red House Farm, Bradley Green
St Egwins Cottage, Norton, Evesham
St Michael's Cottage, Broadway
Stone House, Scotland, Wellington
Strawberry Cottage, Hamnish
21 Swinton Lane, Worcester
Torwood, Whitchurch
Well Cottage, Blakemere
Westwood Farm, Hatfield
White Cottage, Stock Green
Whitfield, Wormbridge
Windyridge, Kidderminster

Parties only
Abbey Dore Court, nr Hereford
The Bannut, Bringsty, Bromyard
Bell's Castle, Kemerton
Bodenham Arboretum, Wolverley
Brook Cottage, Lingen
Caves Folly Nursery, Colwall Green
Conderton Manor, nr Tewkesbury
The Cottage Herbery, Boraston, Tenbury Wells
Hartlebury Castle, nr Kidderminster
Kyre Park, Tenbury Wells
Lingen Nursery, Lingen
Moccas Court, nr Hereford
Monnington Court, Hereford
Overbury Court, nr Tewkesbury
The Priory, Kemerton
Whitlenge House Cottage, Hartlebury
Yew Tree House, Ombersley

Regular openings
For details see garden descriptions

Abbey Dore Court, nr Hereford. Daily except Weds March 4 to Oct 22
Barnard's Green House, Malvern. Every Thurs April to Sept incl
The Cottage Herbery, Boraston, Tenbury Wells. Every Sun April 23 to Sept 17
Dinmore Manor, Wellington. All year
Eastgrove Cottage Garden Nursery, nr Shrawley. For dates see text
Hergest Croft Gardens, Kington. Daily Fri April 14 to Sun Oct 29
How Caple Court, Ross-on-Wye. Mon to Sat April 1 to Oct 31

Kingstone Cottages, Rudhall. Mons to Fris except Bank Hols May 8 to July 14
Lingen Nursery and Garden, Lingen. Daily Feb to Oct
The Manor House, Birlingham. Thurs May 4 to July 27 incl, Aug 31 to Sept 28 incl, Weds June & July ‡
The Marsh Country Hotel, Eyton. Thurs, Fris, Suns April 2 to Oct 29
The Picton Garden, Colwall. Weds to Suns April 1 to Oct 29 incl
The Priory, Kemerton. Every Thurs May 25 to Sept 28 incl ‡
Stone House Cottage Gardens, Stone. Wed, Thurs, Fri and Sats March to Oct
Strawberry Cottage, Hamnish. Every Sun, 1st, 2nd, 4th Thurs, Bank Hol Mons April 30 to Sept 10
White Cottage, Stock Green, nr Inkberrow. For dates see text
Whitlenge House Cottage, Hartlebury. Thurs, Fris, Sats and some Suns March 1 to Sept 30

February 23 Thursday
Dial Park, Chaddesley Corbett

March 19 Sunday
Holland House, Cropthorne
Robins End, Eastham

March 26 Sunday
Kyre Park, Tenbury Wells
Little Malvern Court, nr Malvern
Overbury Court, nr Tewkesbury
Whitlenge House Cottage, Hartlebury

April 2 Sunday
Marley Bank, Whitbourne

April 9 Sunday
Eastgrove Cottage Garden Nursery, nr Shrawley
Garnons, nr Hereford
Lower Hope, Ullingswick
Ripple Hall, nr Tewkesbury
Wind's Point, Malvern

April 12 Wednesday
Arrow Cottage, nr Weobley

April 13 Thursday
Conderton Manor, nr Tewkesbury

April 14 Friday
Spetchley Park, nr Worcester
White Cottage, Stock Green, nr Inkberrow

April 15 Saturday
White Cottage, Stock Green, nr Inkberrow

April 16 Sunday
Arrow Cottage, nr Weobley
Brookside, Bringsty ‡
Churchfield Cottage, Whitbourne ‡
Marley Bank, Whitbourne ‡
White Cottage, Stock Green, nr Inkberrow
Whitlenge House Cottage, Hartlebury
Witley Park House, Great Witley

April 17 Monday
Stone House Cottage Gardens, Stone ‡
White Cottage, Stock Green, nr Inkberrow
Whitlenge House Cottage, Hartlebury ‡

April 18 Tuesday
White Cottage, Stock Green, nr Inkberrow

April 19 Wednesday
Arrow Cottage, nr Weobley

April 20 Thursday
Eastgrove Cottage Garden Nursery, nr Shrawley

April 23 Sunday
Arrow Cottage, nr Weobley
Barbers, Martley, nr Worcester
6 Elm Grove, nr Stourport-on-Severn
Lakeside, Whitbourne ‡
Tedstone Court, nr Bromyard ‡

April 27 Thursday
21 Swinton Lane, Worcester

April 30 Sunday
Arley House, Upper Arley, nr Bewdley
Barnard's Green House, Malvern
Brookside, Bringsty
Dinmore Manor, Wellington
Eastgrove Cottage Garden Nursery, nr Shrawley
Stone House, Scotland, Wellington
Whitlenge House Cottage, Hartlebury
Windyridge, Kidderminster

May
White Cottage, Stock Green, nr Inkberrow. Daily except Weds, Thurs and Sun 21

May 4 Thursday
The Manor House, Birlingham

May 5 Friday
The Manor House, Birlingham

May 7 Sunday
Arrow Cottage, nr Weobley
Churchfield Cottage, Whitbourne ‡
Madresfield Court, nr Malvern
Marley Bank, Whitbourne ‡
Staunton Park, Staunton-on-Arrow
Stone House Cottage Gardens, Stone
Whitlenge House Cottage, Hartlebury
Windyridge, Kidderminster

May 8 Monday
The Cottage Herbery, Boraston, Tenbury Wells
Stone House Cottage Gardens, Stone ‡
Whitlenge House Cottage, Hartlebury ‡

May 11 Thursday
Dial Park, Chaddesley Court
The Manor House, Birlingham

May 14 Sunday
Brookside, Bringsty
Eastgrove Cottage Garden Nursery, nr Shrawley
Lingen Nursery and Garden, Lingen
Priors Court, Long Green
Spetchley Park, nr Worcester
Stone House Cottage Gardens, Stone

May 15 Monday
Ivytree House, Clent

May 17 Wednesday
Ivytree House, Clent
Torwood, Whitchurch

May 18 Thursday
Conderton Manor, nr Tewkesbury ‡
The Manor House, Birlingham ‡

May 21 Sunday
Arrow Cottage, nr Weobley
Bodenham Arboretum, Wolverley
Churchfield Cottage, Whitbourne ‡
28 Hillgrove Crescent, Kidderminster ‡
Marley Bank, Whitbourne ‡
St Egwins Cottage, Norton, Evesham
Stone House, Scotland, Wellington
Stone House Cottage Gardens, Stone ‡

May 24 Wednesday
St Egwins Cottage, Norton, Evesham

May 25 Thursday
The Manor House, Birlingham

May 28 Sunday
Arrow Cottage, nr Weobley
Caves Folly Nursery, Colwall Green
Lingen Nursery and Garden, Lingen
Lower Hope, Ullingswick
The Priory, Kemerton
Red House Farm, Bradley Green
Stone House Cottage Gardens, Stone ‡
Whitlenge House Cottage, Hartlebury ‡

May 29 Monday
The Cottage Herbery, Boraston, Tenbury Wells
The Manor House, Birlingham
Stone House Cottage Gardens, Stone ‡

Whitlenge House Cottage, Hartlebury ‡

May 31 Wednesday
Arrow Cottage, nr Weobley

June
The Manor House, Birlingham. Every Weds and Thurs
White Cottage, Stock Green, nr Inkberrow. Daily except Weds, Thurs and Suns 4, 18

June 1 Thursday
21 Swinton Lane, Worcester

June 3 Saturday
Woodmancote, Wadborough

June 4 Sunday
Arrow Cottage, nr Weobley
Ash Farm, Much Birch
Chennels Gate, Eardisley
Churchfield Cottage, Whitbourne ‡
Frogmore, nr Ross-on-Wye
Marley Bank, Whitbourne ‡
Stone House Cottage Gardens, Stone
Tedstone Court, nr Bromyard ‡
Whitfield, Wormbridge
Woodmancote, Wadborough

June 7 Wednesday
Torwood, Whitchurch

June 11 Sunday
Brookside, Bringsty
Cedar Lodge, Blakeshall, nr Wolverley
Hartlebury Castle, nr Kidderminster
How Caple Court, Ross-on-Wye
Lingen Nursery and Garden, Lingen
Moccas Court, nr Hereford
Pershore College of Horticulture
St Egwins Cottage, Norton, Evesham
Stone House Cottage Gardens, Stone
Torwood, Whitchurch

June 14 Wednesday
St Egwins Cottage, Norton, Evesham

June 18 Sunday
Arrow Cottage, nr Weobley
Astley Horticultural Society, Astley Cross
The Bannut, Bringsty, Bromyard
Bell's Castle, Kemerton ‡
Birtsmorton Court, nr Malvern
Churchfield Cottage, Whitbourne ‡
Lakeside, Whitbourne ‡
Marley Bank, Whitbourne ‡
The Old Vicarage, Overbury ‡
Orchard Bungalow, Bishops Frome
St Michael's Cottage, Broadway
Staunton Park, Staunton-on-Arrow
Stone House, Scotland, Wellington
Stone House Cottage Gardens, Stone
Upper Court, Kemerton ‡

June 19 Monday
Ivytree House, Clent

June 21 Wednesday
Ivytree House, Clent

June 22 Thursday
Conderton Manor, nr Tewkesbury

June 24 Saturday
Hergest Croft Gardens, Kington

June 25 Sunday
Arrow Cottage, nr Weobley
Berrington Hall, Leominster ‡
Brook Cottage, Lingen ‡‡
Brook House, Colwall
Croft Castle, Kingsland ‡
28 Hillgrove Crescent, Kidderminster
Lingen Nursery and Garden, Lingen ‡‡
Linton Hall, Gorsley
Pedwardine Cottage, Brampton Bryan
The Priory, Kemerton
Red House Farm, Bradley Green
Shucknall Court, Hereford
Stone House Cottage Gardens, Stone ‡
Torwood, Whitchurch
Well Cottage, Lingen ‡‡
Westwood Farm, Hatfield
Whitlenge House Cottage, Hartlebury ‡
Witley Park House, Great Witley
Yew Tree House, Ombersley

June 26 Monday
Westwood Farm, Hatfield

June 28 Wednesday
Linton Hall, Gorsley
St Egwins Cottage, Norton, Evesham

June 29 Thursday
Grantsfield, nr Leominster
21 Swinton Lane, Worcester

July
The Manor House, Birlingham. Every Weds and Thurs

July 2 Sunday
Chennels Gate, Eardisley
Grantsfield, nr Leominster
Marley Bank, Whitbourne
Snowshill Road Gardens, Broadway
Spetchley Park, nr Worcester

July 5 Wednesday
St Egwins Cottage, Norton, Evesham
Shucknall Court, Hereford
Torwood, Whitchurch

July 8 Saturday
28 Cornmeadow Lane, Claines, Worcester

July 9 Sunday
Bredenbury Court (St Richards), Bredenbury
Hanbury Hall, nr Droitwich
Holland House, Cropthorne
Lower Hope, Ullingswick
Torwood, Whitchurch

July 15 Saturday
Broadfield Court, Bodenham
Eastgrove Cottage Garden Nursery, nr Shrawley

July 16 Sunday
Arley Cottage, Upper Arley, nr Bewdley
Arrow Cottage, nr Weobley
The Bannut, Bringsty, Bromyard ‡
Brampton Bryan Hall, nr Knighton
Churchfield Cottage, Whitbourne ‡
Marley Bank, Whitbourne ‡
Orchard Bungalow, Bishops Frome
The Priory, Kemerton
Stone House, Scotland, Wellington

July 17 Monday
Ivytree House, Clent

July 19 Wednesday
Ivytree House, Clent
St Egwins Cottage, Norton, Evesham

July 23 Sunday
Arrow Cottage, nr Weobley
Lingen Nursery and Garden, Lingen

July 26 Wednesday
Arrow Cottage, nr Weobley

July 27 Thursday
21 Swinton Lane, Worcester

July 30 Sunday
Arrow Cottage, nr Weobley
Red House Farm, Bradley Green
Whitlenge House Cottage, Hartlebury

August 6 Sunday
Brookside, Bringsty ‡
Churchfield Cottage, Whitbourne ‡
28 Hillgrove Crescent, Kidderminster
Marley Bank, Whitbourne ‡
The Priory, Kemerton
Torwood, Whitchurch

August 9 Wednesday
Torwood, Whitchurch

August 13 Sunday
The Bannut, Bringsty, Bromyard
St Egwins Cottage, Norton, Evesham

August 16 Wednesday
St Egwins Cottage, Norton, Evesham

August 20 Sunday
Brookside, Bringsty

August 24 Thursday
21 Swinton Lane, Worcester

August 26 Saturday
Monnington Court, Hereford
Pedwardine Cottage, Brampton Bryan

August 27 Sunday
Arrow Cottage, nr Weobley
Barnard's Green House, Malvern
Churchfield Cottage, Whitbourne
Marley Bank, Whitbourne
Monnington Court, Hereford
Pedwardine Cottage, Brampton Bryan
The Priory, Kemerton
Stone House Cottage Gardens, Stone ‡
Whitlenge House Cottage, Hartlebury ‡

August 28 Monday
Monnington Court, Hereford
Pedwardine Cottage, Brampton Bryan
Stone House Cottage Gardens, Stone ‡
Whitlenge House Cottage, Hartlebury ‡

August 31 Thursday
The Manor House, Birlingham

September 3 Sunday
Arrow Cottage, nr Weobley

September 7 Thursday
The Manor House, Birlingham

September 10 Sunday
Eastgrove Cottage Garden Nursery, nr Shrawley
The Priory, Kemerton

September 14 Thursday
The Manor House, Birlingham

September 16 Saturday
White Cottage, Stock Green, nr Inkberrow

September 17 Sunday
Churchfield Cottage, Whitbourne ‡
Marley Bank, Whitbourne ‡
White Cottage, Stock Green, nr Inkberrow

September 21 Thursday
Dial Park, Chaddesley Corbett
The Manor House, Birlingham

September 24 Sunday
Eastgrove Cottage Garden Nursery, nr Shrawley
Kyre Park, Tenbury Wells
Whitlenge House Cottage, Hartlebury

September 28 Thursday
The Manor House, Burlingham

September 30 Saturday
White Cottage, Stock Green, nr Inkberrow

October 1 Sunday
Dinmore Manor, Wellington

October 8 Sunday
Eastgrove Cottage Garden Nursery, nr Shrawley

October 15 Sunday
Nerine Nursery, Welland

DESCRIPTIONS OF GARDENS

● **Abbey Dore Court** ♿✿❀ (Mrs C L Ward) 11m SW of Hereford. From A465 midway between Hereford-Abergavenny turn W, signed Abbey Dore; then 2½m. 5 acres bordered by R. Dore of rambling and semi formal garden with unusual shrubs, perennials and many clematis in large borders. Pond and rock garden made in a field recently enlarged. River walk with ferns and hellebores leading to a fairly new area, on the site of an old barn and roadway, planted for foliage colour. Large collection of late summer anemones. NCCPG Euphorbia collection. Featured in NGS video 1. Many unusual plants for sale. Out of the ordinary gift gallery. Coffee, lunch and TEAS (11-5). *Adm £1.75 Chd 50p (Share to Mother Theresa®). Sat March 4 to Sun Oct 22 daily except Weds (11-6). Earlier visits for hellebores welcome, please* **Tel 01981 240419**

Arley Cottage ♿ (Woodward family) Upper Arley, nr Bewdley. 5m N of Kidderminster off A442. Small country garden with lawns bordered by interesting shrubs and collection of rare trees. Cream TEAS. *Adm £1 Chd free (Share to Lane-Fox Unit, St Thomas' Hospital, London SE1®). Sun July 16 (2-5)*

Arley House ✿ (R D Turner Esq) Upper Arley, 5m N of Kidderminster. A442. Arboretum containing specimen conifers and hardwoods, rhododendrons, camellias, magnolias, heathers; Italianate garden; greenhouses with orchids, alpines. Aviary with ornamental pheasants, budgerigars. TEA. *Adm £1.50 Chd free (Share to St Peter's, Upper Arley®). Sun April 30 (2-7)*

Arrow Cottage ✿❀ (Mr & Mrs L Hattatt) nr Weobley. From Weobley take unclassified rd direction Wormsley (Kings Pyon/Canon Pyon). After 1m, turn L signposted Ledgemoor. 2nd R (no through rd). 1st house on L. Formal design elements link a series of carefully planted garden rooms in this 2-acre plantsman's garden. A newly developed gothic garden is in addition to C19 shrub roses, white and green gardens, kitchen garden, herbaceous borders and natural stream, all maintained to a high standard. Featured on Channel 4 TV 1991 and Central TV 1993 and incl in the Good Gardens Guide. Rare and beautiful hardy plants are propogated for sale. The garden is unsuitable for children. TEAS if fine. *Adm £1.50. Weds April 12, 19, May 31, July 26; Suns April 16, 23, May 7, 21, 28, June 4, 18, 25, July 16, 23, 30, Aug 27, Sept 3 (2-5). Private visits welcome, please* **Tel 01544 318468**

Ash Farm ✿ (David & Alison Lewis) Much Birch. From Hereford take A49 S to Much Birch (approx 7m). After the Pilgrim Hotel take 1st turning R at Xrds into Tump Lane. Garden is on L. Ample parking. Small walled farmhouse garden and ½-acre new garden created from old fold yard for all year interest over past 5 yrs. Small trees, herbaceous borders, blue and white borders. TEA. *Adm £1 Chd free. Sun June 4 (2-6)*

Astley Horticultural Society ♿❀ 3m W of Stourport on Severn on the B4196 to Worcester. Start the trail around the 3 villages from the Parish Room. Ploughmans and Teas at Parish Room. Cream TEAS at Woodlands Farm. *Combined adm £2.50 (Share to Parkinson Disease Soc®). Sun June 18 (11-5.30)*

Koi Cottage Superb Koi carp in a Japanese setting

Pool House Lge country garden with romantic pools, long herbaceous border, mature trees and shrubs

Astley Towne C16 house with lge garden being replanted. Herbaceous borders, rhododendrons, rose arches, formal vegetable garden

St Peters Church Bell ringing, flowers, Songs of Praise (7pm) in beautiful C12 church

Little Yarhampton Fine country house overlooking wonderful Severn valley. Delightful garden with woodland trail

White House, Dunley. An acre of delight based on Christopher Lloyds 'The Well Chosen Garden'
Swevenings, Dunley. A developing garden in mature setting. Interestingly terraced on steep slope
6 Elm Grove, Astley Cross. A garden for all seasons, mature borders, raised pool, old and new favourites
The Conifers, Astley Burf. Modern bungalow, dripping with hanging baskets. A garden of colour
Woodlands Farm Delicious cream teas on the lawn of old farmhouse
Woodstock Inspiring mixture of rhododendrons, herbaceous borders, roses surrounding an interesting bungalow in old orchard

The Bannut ♿❀ (Mr Maurice & Mrs Daphne Everett) Bringsty. 3m E of Bromyard on A44 Worcester Rd. (½m E of entrance to National Trust, Brockhampton). A 1-acre garden, planted with all year colour in mind; mainly established by the present owners since 1984. Mixed borders and island beds of trees, shrubs and herbaceous plants and a small 'damp' garden. Walls, pergola, and terraces around the house are used to display unusual climbers and colourful pots and urns. The heather garden designed around a Herefordshire cider mill and an unusual heather knot garden with water feature have appeared in several gardening magazines. Plants for sale. TEAS. *Adm £1.50 Chd free. Suns June 18, July 16, Aug 13 (2-5). Also groups by appt, please* **Tel 01885 482206**

Barbers ♿✂❀ (Mr & the Hon Mrs Richard Webb) Martley 7m NW of Worcester on B4204. Medium-sized garden with lawns, trees, shrubs, pools and wild garden. Cowslip and fritillary lawn. Home-made TEAS. *Adm £1 Chd free (Share to Martley Church®). Sun April 23 (2-6)*

Barnard's Green House ♿✂❀ (Mr & Mrs Philip Nicholls) 10 Poolbrook Rd, Malvern. On E side of Malvern at junction of B4211 and B4208. 3-acre cultivated garden; herbaceous, rockeries, heather beds, woodland/water garden, vegetable plot; several unusual plants and shrubs; 2 fine cedars, lawns. Mrs Nicholls is a specialist on dried flowers, on which she has written a book. Half-timbered house (not open) dates from 1635; home of Sir Charles Hastings, founder of BMA. Coach parties by appt. TEAS. *Adm £1.50 Acc chd free (Share to Save the Children Fund®). Suns April 30, Aug 27 and every Thursday April to Sept incl. (2-6). Also private visits welcome, please* **Tel 01684 574446**

Bell's Castle (Lady Holland-Martin) Kemerton, NE of Tewkesbury. 3 small terraces with battlements; wild garden outside wall. The small Gothic castellated folly was built by Edmund Bell (Smuggler) c1820; very fine views. *Adm £1 Chd free. Sun June 18 (2-6). Parties welcome, please* **Tel 01386 725333**

Berrington Hall ♿✂ (The National Trust) 3m N of Leominster on A49. Signposted. Bus Midland Red (W) x 92, 292 alight Luston, 2m. Extensive views over Capability Brown Park; formal garden; wall plants, unusual trees, camellia collection, herbaceous plants, wisteria. Woodland walk, rhododendrons, walled garden with apple collection. Light lunches and TEAS. *Adm house & garden £3.60 Chd £1.80. Grounds only £2 Chd £1. ▲For NGS Sun June 25 (12.30-6)*

Birtsmorton Court ♿✂ (Mr & Mrs N G K Dawes) nr Malvern. 7m E of Ledbury on A438. Fortified manor house (not open) dating from C12; moat; Westminster pool, laid down in Henry V11's reign at time of consecration of Westminster Abbey; large tree under which Cardinal Wolsey reputedly slept in shadow of ragged stone. Topiary. Motor Museum extra. Featured in NGS video 1. TEAS. *Adm £1.75 Chd 25p (Share to St John Ambulance®). Sun June 18 (2-6)*

Bodenham Arboretum (Mr & Mrs J D Binnian) 2m N of Wolverley; 5m N of Kidderminster. From Wolverley Church follow signs. 134 acres landscaped and planted during the past 21 years; 2 chains of lakes and pools; woods and glades with over 1600 species and shrubs; Laburnum tunnel; Grove and Swamp Cypress in shallows of 3-acre lake. Bring wellingtons or strong boots. Partly suitable for wheelchairs. TEA. NO COACHES. *Adm £1.50 Chd free (Share to The Kemp House Trust, Home Care Hospice®). Sun May 21 (2-6). Private visits welcome for parties of 10 and over at other times of the year* **Tel 01562 850382**

Brampton Bryan Hall @ (Mr & Mrs Christopher Harley) Bucknell. 6m E of Knighton on A4113 Knighton-Ludlow rd. Medium-sized garden; large lawns, old cedars, limes and fine yew hedges and collection of interesting trees. Medieval castle in garden. C18 house. TEAS. *Adm £2 Chd 50p. Sun July 16 (2-5)*

Bredenbury Court (St Richards) ♿❀ (Headmaster: R E H Coghlan Esq) Bredenbury, 3m W of Bromyard. On A44 Bromyard-Leominster rd; entrance on right (N) side of rd. 5-acre garden; 15 acres parkland with fine views. Simple rose garden and herbaceous borders. Picnics allowed. Use of swimming pool 30p extra. TEAS. *Adm £1.50 Chd 50p (Share to St Richards Hospice®). Sun July 9 (12-6)*

Bredon Pound ✂ (Mr & Mrs David King) Ashton under Hill. 6m down the Cheltenham Rd from Evesham. A recently landscaped garden at the foot of Bredon Hill with fine views over the Vale of Evesham to the Cotswold Hills. Shrub roses, heathers and an interesting collection of trees and shrubs. TEAS. *Adm £1 Chd free (Share to Spastics Society®). Private visits welcome May to Sept, please* **Tel 01386 881209**

Brilley Court ♿✂ (Mr & Mrs D Bulmer) nr Whitney-on-Wye 6m E Hay-on-Wye. 1½m off main A438 Hereford to Brecon Rd signposted to Brilley. Medium-sized walled garden spring and herbaceous. Valley stream garden; spring colour. Ornamental kitchen garden. Large quantity of roses. Wonderful views. *Adm £1.50 OAPs £1 Chd 50p. Private visits welcome, please* **Tel 01497 831467**

Broadfield Court ♿❀ (Mr & Mrs Keith James) Bodenham 7m SE Leominster A49 from Leominster or Hereford & A417 to Bodenham; turn left to Risbury signposted at Bodenham. 4 acres of old English gardens; yew hedges; spacious lawns; rose garden; herbaceous. Picnic area. 17 acres of vineyard; wine tasting included in entrance charge. TEAS. *Adm £2 Chd free. Sat July 15 (11-5.30)*

¶**Brook Cottage** (Dorothy Phillips) Lingen. 5m NE of Presteigne. 15m SW of Ludlow. 15m NE of Leominster. On B4362 (Mortimers Cross to Presteigne) take N turn 2m from Presteigne centre marked Kinsham and Lingen. Garden in centre of Lingen village at top of lane opp the Royal George. 1¾ acres woodland and field garden with brook developed over 10 yrs by owner for yr-round interest and low maintenance. Old apple trees draped in roses; shrubs and trees for foliage colour and shape plus herbaceous plants of the more robust type suitable for a sheltered, frost pocket garden. Parking at Lingen Nursery Garden. TEAS. *Combined adm with* **Lingen Nursery Garden** *and* **Well Cottage** *£2 Chd under 10 free. Sun June 25 (2-6)*

Brook House ♿ (Mr J Milne) Colwall. 3m SW Malvern and 3m E of Ledbury on B2048. ½-way between Malvern/Ledbury via Wyche Cutting; opp Horse & Jockey Hotel. Water garden; flowering trees and shrubs; walled garden. Old Herefordshire farmhouse with mill stream. TEAS. *Adm £1.50. Sun June 25 (2-6). Private visits welcome, please* **Tel 01684 540283**

Brookside ✂❀ (Mr & Mrs John Dodd) Bringsty; 3m E of Bromyard via A44 10m W of Worcester; Bringsty Common turn down track to 'Live & Let Live'; at PH carpark bear left to Brookside. C16 cottage with 1½-acre garden designed by Denis Hoddy; specimen trees and shrubs in grass sloping to lake; mixed beds with all year interest. Unusual plants. Small alpine collection. Parties by arrangement only. TEAS on terrace. *Adm £1 Chd 20p (Share to Save the Children Fund®). Suns April 16, 30, May 14, June 11, Aug 6, 20 (2-5.30). Private visits welcome, please* **Tel 01886 821835**

Caves Folly Nursery ♿✂❀ (Mr Leaper & Miss Evans) Evendine Lane, off Colwall Green. 3m SW Malvern and 3m E of Ledbury on B2048. Small nursery established 11 yrs. Specialising in herbaceous and alpine plants, some unusual. All plants are grown organically in peat-free compost. Also a selection of Guernsey goats, ducks, chickens, plus recently planted herbaceous borders and a wildflower meadow. TEAS. *Adm £1 Chd free. Sun May 28 (2-6). Private visits welcome for 50 or over, please* **Tel 01684 540631**

Cedar Lodge ✂❀ (Mrs Barbara Andrews) Blakeshall. 4m N of Kidderminster off B4189. 1½m from Wolverley village. ¾-acre prize-wining garden with extensive range of trees, shrubs and plants. Shade borders, gravel garden, small pool and large mixed borders which are in harmony with the beautiful rural setting adjoining Kinver Edge. Featured in NGS Video 3. TEAS. *Adm £1.20 Chd free (Share to St Peter's Church, Cookley®). Sun June 11 (2-5.30)*

Chennels Gate ♿✂❀ (Mr & Mrs Kenneth Dawson) Eardisley. 5m S of Kington. ½m from Tram Inn on Woodseave Lane. Signposted. A 2-acre plantsman's cottage garden, set in 15 acres with newly planted woodland and orchards. Rose and herb gardens; herbaceous borders; water gardens, one with water fowl; conservatory with planted beds. Interesting selection of plants for sale. TEAS in aid of St Mary Magdelene Church, Eardisley. *Adm £1.50 Chd free. Suns June 4, July 2 (2-6). Private visits welcome, please* **Tel 01544 327288**

Churchfield Cottage ♿✂❀ (Peter & Barbara Larner) Turn off A44 at Wheatsheaf public house. 5m E of Bromyard. Through village, down hill, turn R at bottom. 200 yds past Church on L. 1-acre garden extended and replanted since 1985 around some mature shrubs and trees. Large mixed borders, all-yr interest, many unusual plants. Ponds, bog garden, conservatory. TEA. *Adm £1 Chd free. Suns April 16, May 7, 21, June 4, 18, July 16, Aug 6, 27, Sept 17 (2-5.30). Private visits welcome, please* **Tel 01886 821495**

Conderton Manor ♿✂ (Mr & Mrs William Carr) 5½m NE of Tewkesbury. Between A435 & B4079. 7-acre garden with magnificent views of Cotswolds; many trees and shrubs of botanical interest. 100yd long mixed borders, rose walks and formal terrace. Teas available at the Silk Shop in the village. *Adm £2 Chd 25p. Thurs April 13, May 18, June 22 (2-6). Also private visits welcome, please* **Tel 01386 725389**

28 Cornmeadow Lane ✂❀ (Rev P J Wedgwood) Claines is a northern suburb of Worcester; follow signpost Claines at roundabout junction of A449 and M/way link rd; R at church. House beside 3rd hall on L about ½m down Cornmeadow Lane. Parking in Church Hall grounds. Small town garden packed with rare and tropical plants with plenty of colour. TEAS. *Adm £1 Chd free. Sat July 8 (2-6)*

The Cottage Herbery ✂❀ (Mr & Mrs R E Hurst) 1m E of Tenbury Wells on A456, turn for Boraston at Peacock Inn, turn R in village, signposted to garden. Half timbered C16 farmhouse with fast-flowing Cornbrook running close to its side and over ford at the bottom of garden. ½-acre of garden specializing in a wide range of herbs, aromatic and scented foliage plants, planted on a cottage garden theme; also unusual hardy perennial and variegated plants; early interest bulbs, pulmonarias, euphorbias, symphytums. Nursery sells large selection of herbs. Organic garden. Chelsea Medallists 1992 & 93. Featured in Central TV Gardening Time. Gold Medal Winners '94. No toilets. TEAS (served in garden). *Adm £1 Chd free. Every Sun April 23 to Sept 17, also Bank Hol Mons May 8, 29 (11-5). Private visits welcome for 10 and over, please* **Tel 0158 781575**

Croft Castle ♿✂❀ (The National Trust) 5m NW of Leominster. On B4362 (off B4361, Leominster-Ludlow). Large garden; borders; walled garden; landscaped park and walks in Fishpool Valley; fine old avenues. Light lunches and Teas Berrington Hall. *Adm £3.10 Family £8.50 Chd £1.60. For NGS Sun June 25 (1.30-4.30)*

¶**Dial Park** ✂❀ (Mr & Mrs David Mason) Chaddesley Corbett. 4½m from Kidderminster, 4½m from Bromsgrove on A448. 150yds towards Kidderminster from turn into Chaddesley Corbett village. Approx ¾-acre garden developed since 1990 containing interesting and unusual plants with yr-round interest. Incl collections of snowdrops, sambucus and hardy ferns. Also small collection of country bygones. *Adm £1 Chd free. Thurs Feb 23 (1-5) May 11, Sept 21 (2-6). Private visits welcome, please* **Tel 01562 777451**

Dinmore Manor ♿✂❀ (R G Murray Esq) Hereford, 6m N of Hereford. Route A49. Bus: Midland Red Hereford-Leominster, alight Manor turning 1m. Spectacular hillside location. A range of impressive architecture dating from C14-20; chapel; cloisters; Great hall (Music Room) and extensive roof walk giving panoramic views of countryside and beautiful gardens below; stained glass. TEAS for NGS. Unusual plants for sale. *Adm £2.50 Acc chd free. For NGS Suns April 30, Oct 1 (10-5.30). Open throughout the year (10.30-5.30)*

● **Eastgrove Cottage Garden Nursery** ♿✂❀ (Mr & Mrs J Malcolm Skinner) Sankyns Green, Shrawley. 8m NW of Worcester on rd between Shrawley (on B4196) and Great Witley (on A443). Set in 5 acres unspoilt meadow and woodland, this unique 1-acre garden and nursery is of particular interest to the plantsman. Very fine collection of hardy and tender perennial plants in old world country flower garden with much thought given to planting combinations both of colour and form, outstanding at all times. C17 half-timbered yeoman farmhouse (not open). Garden and nursery maintained since 1970 by owners who are always available for help and advice. Featured in Country Life and The Times and BBC TV. Wide range of well grown less usual plants for sale, all grown at Nursery. *Adm £1.50 Chd 20p. April 1 to July 31 Thurs, Fri, Sat, Sun, Mon. Closed Tues & Weds.* **Closed throughout August.** *Sept 1 to Oct 14; Thurs, Fris, Sats only and Suns Sept 10, 24, Oct 8 (2-5)*

The Elms School see Wych & Colwall Horticultural Society Show

6 Elm Grove ♿✂❀ (Michael Ecob) Astley Cross. W of Stourport on Severn. Turn S on B4196 towards Worcester-Bewdley. ⅓-acre garden with mature trees, borders, patio area, pool and small conservatory. Spring time in a cottage garden with many unusual bulbs and plants amongst old favourites: small vegetable area used for show produce. *Adm 80p Chd 20p. Sun April 23 (1-6)*

Frogmore ♿✂❀ (Sir Jonathan & Lady North) Pontshill. 4m SE of Ross-on-Wye. 1m S of A40 through Pontshill. 2-acre garden with fine mature trees and many unusual young trees and shrubs. Mixed borders with nut walk and ha ha. Mown walk along stream and to spinney. TEAS (in aid of Hope Mansel Church). Hardy geranium nursery, open Mons only 10-6 April to Sept or private visits welcome, please **Tel 01989 750214**. *Adm £1.50 Chd free. Sun June 4 (2-6)*

Garnons ♿❀ (Sir John & Lady Cotterell) 7m W of Hereford on A438; lodge gates on right; then fork left over cattle grid. Large park landscaped by Repton; attractive spring garden. House is remaining wing (1860) of house pulled down in 1957. TEA. *Adm part of house & garden £2 Chd free; garden only £1 Chd 50p (Share to Byford Church®). Sun April 9 (2-5.30)*

Grantsfield ♿✂❀ (Col & Mrs J G T Polley) nr Kimbolton, 3m NE of Leominster. A49 N from Leominster, turn right to Grantsfield. Car parking in field; not coaches which must drop and collect visitors at gate. Contrasting styles in gardens of old stone farmhouse; wide variety of unusual plants and shrubs, old roses, climbers; herbaceous borders; superb views. 4-acre orchard and kitchen garden with flowering and specimen trees. Spring bulbs. TEAS. *Adm £1.20 Chd free (Share to St John Ambulance®). Thurs, June 29, Sun July 2 (2-5.30). Private visits welcome April to end Aug, please* **Tel 01568 613338**

Hanbury Hall ♿✂ (The National Trust) Hanbury, 3m NE of Droitwich, 6m S of Bromsgrove. Signed off B4090. Recreation of C18 formal garden by George London. Victorian forecourt with detailed planting. William & Mary style brick house of 1701 with murals by Thornhill; contemporary Orangery and Ice House. TEAS. *Adm house & garden £3.70 Chd £1.80. Sun July 9 (2-6)*

Hartlebury Castle ♿✂ (The Rt Revd The Lord Bishop of Worcester) Medieval moated castle reconstructed 1675, restored 1964. Many Tudor and Hanoverian Royal connections. Herbaceous borders, terraced garden. Wheelchairs ground floor. *Adm gardens & state rooms 75p Chd 25p. Sun June 11 (2-5). Private visits welcome for parties of 30, please* **Tel 01299 250410**

● **Hergest Croft Gardens** ♿❀ (W L Banks Esq & R A Banks Esq) ½m off A44 on Welsh side of Kington, 20m NW of Hereford: Turn left at Rhayader end of bypass; then 1st right; gardens ¼m on left. 50 acres of garden owned by Banks' family for 4 generations. Edwardian garden surrounding house (not open); Park wood with rhododendrons up to 30ft tall; old-fashioned kitchen garden with spring and herbaceous borders. One of finest private collections of trees and shrubs; now selected to hold National Collections Maples and Birches. TEAS for NGS day. *Adm £2.50 Chd under 15 free (Share to NCCPG®). Fri April 14 to Sun Oct 29 daily. For NGS Sat June 24 (1.30-6.30).* **Tel 01544 230160**

28 Hillgrove Crescent ✂❀ (Mr & Mrs D Terry) Kidderminster. Crescent linking Chester Rd (A449) & Bromsgrove Rd (A448). A town garden designed to maximize the planting areas without losing a feeling of space. Many unusual plants including alpines, herbaceous, shrubs, ferns and clematis planted with skilful use of colour. *Adm £1.50 Chd free (Share to CRMF®). Suns May 21, June 25, Aug 6 (2-6). Also private visits welcome, please* **Tel 01562 751957**

Holland House ✂ (Warden: Mr Peter Middlemiss) Main St, Cropthorne, Pershore. Between Pershore and Evesham, off A44. Car park at rear of house. Gardens laid out by Lutyens in 1904; thatched house dating back to 1636 (not open). TEAS. *Adm £1 Chd 30p (Share to USPG®). Suns March 19, July 9 (2.30-5)*

How Caple Court ❀ (Mr & Mrs Peter Lee) How Caple, 5m N of Ross on Wye 10m S of Hereford on B4224; turn right at How Caple Xrds, garden 400 yds on left. 11 acres; Edwardian gardens set high above R. Wye in park and woodland; formal terraces: yew hedges, statues and pools; sunken florentine water garden under restoration; woodland walks; herbaceous and shrub borders, shrub roses, mature trees: Mediaeval Church with newly restored C16 Diptych. Nursery specialising in old rose varieties and apple varieties, unusual herbaceous plants. Shop open for gifts, fabric and menswear. TEAS. *Adm £2.50 Chd £1.25. Open Mon to Sat, April 1 to Oct 31. Also Suns April 1 to Oct 31 (10-5). For NGS Sun June 11 (10-5).* **Tel 01989 86612**

Ivytree House ❀ (Dr & Mrs H Eggins) [OS139 91.79] Bromsgrove Rd, Clent. 3m SE of Stourbridge and 5m NW of Bromsgrove, off A491 Stourbridge to Bromsgrove dual carriageway. Car parking next door at Woodman Hotel. Over 1,000 varieties of small trees, shrubs and herbaceous plants in approx ½-acre plantsman's cottage garden; tree ivies and ivytrees, collection of aucubas, small conservatory with fuchsia trees, pond garden, fruit and vegetables, bantams and bees. *Adm £1 Chd free. Mons May 15, June 19, July 17; Weds May 17, June 21, July 19 (2-5). Also private visits welcome, please* **Tel 01562 884171**

Keepers Cottage ✣❀ (Mrs Diana Scott) Alvechurch. Take main A441 rd through Alvechurch towards Redditch. Turn opp sign to Cobley Hill and Bromsgrove for 1m over 2 humpback bridges. 3-acre garden at 600ft with fine views towards the Cotswolds; rhododendrons, camellias; old-fashioned roses; unusual trees and shrubs; rock garden; 2 alpine houses; paddock with donkeys. *Adm £1 Chd 50p. Private visits welcome in May and June, please* **Tel 01214 455885**

Kingstone Cottages ❀ (Michael & Sophie Hughes) A40 Ross-Gloucester, turn L at Weston Cross to Bollitree Castle, then L to Rudhall. Informal 1½-acre cottage garden containing National Collection of old pinks and carnations and other unusual plants. Terraced beds, ponds, grotto, summerhouse, lovely views. Some areas now replanted incl a new parterre containing the Collection. Dianthus and other plants for sale, also garden furniture designed and made on premises. The garden has featured in several magazines and Channel 4 programmes. *Adm £1 Chd free. Mons to Fris May 8 to July 14 (except Bank Hols) (9-4). Private visits welcome, please* **Tel 01989 565267**

¶Kyre Park ❀ (Mr & Mrs M H Rickard & Mr & Mrs J N Sellers) Kyre. 4m S of Tenbury Wells or 7m N of Bromyard. Follow signs to Kyre Church off B4214. Approx 29 acres, shrubbery walk, 5 lakes, waterfalls, hermitage, picturesque views, mature trees, Norman dovecote and Jacobean tithe barn. Landscaped in 1754 but neglected for several decades, now in early stages of restoration. A rare example of a Georgian shrubbery hardly touched for 240yrs. Stout shoes advised. Ferns for sale at Richards Hardy Fern Nursery. TEAS. *Adm £1.50 Chd 50p. For NGS Suns March 26, Sept 24 (11-5). Private visits welcome, please* **Tel 01885 410282**

Lakeside ✣❀ (Mr D Gueroult & Mr C Philip) Gaines Rd, Whitbourne. 9m W of Worcester off A44 at County boundary sign (ignore sign to Whitbourne Village). 6-acres, large walled garden with many mixed beds and borders; spring bulbs, climbers, unusual shrubs and plants, heather garden, bog garden, newly extended lake walk, medieval carp lake with fountain. Uncommon plants for sale. Steep steps and slopes. TEAS in aid of Red Cross. *Adm £1.50 Chd free. Suns April 23, June 18 (2-6)*

Regular Openers. Too many days to include in diary. Usually there is a wide range of plants giving year-round interest. See head of county section for the name and garden description for times etc.

Lingen Nursery and Garden ✣❀ (Mr Kim Davis) Lingen. 5m NE of Presteigne take B4362 E from Presteigne, 2m turn L for Lingen, 3m opposite Chapel in village. 2 acres of specialist alpine and herbaceous nursery and general garden intensively planted giving a long period of interest having large areas of rock garden and herbaceous borders, a peat bed, raised screes and an Alpine House and stock beds, together with 2 acres of developing garden where picnics are welcome. Many unusual plants with comprehensive labelling. Wide range of plants for sale from the nursery frames. Catalogue available. National collection of Iris Sibirica held for NCCPG. TEAS (NGS days only). *Adm £1 Chd free. Suns May 14, 28; June 11, 25; July 23 (2-6). Combined adm with* **Brook Cottage** *and* **Well Cottage** *£2 Sun June 25 (2-6) for NGS. Also open Feb-Oct everyday (10-6). Coach parties by appt* **Tel 01544 267720**

Linton Hall ✣❀ (Mr & Mrs Sanders & Mr & Mrs Berrington) Gorsley. 5m E of Ross-on-Wye, junction 3 off M50 toward Newent. Entrance ½m on RH-side on county boundary. 8½ acres of woodland and gardens undergoing construction. Mature trees including wellingtonias; orchard; croquet lawn; old-fashioned roses. TEAS. *Adm £1.50 Chd 50p. Sun, Wed June 25, 28 (2-6)*

Little Malvern Court ✣❀ (Mrs T M Berington) 4m S of Malvern on A4104 S of junction with A449. 10 acres attached to former Benedictine Priory, magnificent views over Severn valley. An intriguing layout of garden rooms, and terrace round house. Newly made and planted water garden below, feeding into chain of lakes. Wide variety of spring bulbs, flowering trees and shrubs. Notable collection of old-fashioned roses. TEAS. *Adm £2.50 Chd 50p (5-14) (Share to SSAFA). Sun March 26 (2-6)*

Lower Hope ♿✣❀ (Mr & Mrs Clive Richards) Ullingswick. From Hereford take the A465 N to Bromyard. After 6m this road meets the A417 at Burley Gate roundabout. Turn L on the A417 signposted Leominster. After approx. 2m take the 3rd turning on the R signposted Lower Hope and Pencombe. Lower Hope is 0.6m on the LH-side. 5-acre garden facing S and W constitutes principally herbaceous borders, rose borders, water gardens, woodland walks; in addition other features include a Laburnum Walk, conservatories and greenhouses, a fruit and vegetable garden. Surrounding the gardens are paddocks in which the prize-winning Herd of Pedigree Poll Hereford cattle and flock of Pedigree Suffolk sheep are grazed. TEAS. *Adm £2 Chd £1 (Share to St John Ambulance®). Suns April 9, May 28, July 9 (2-6). Also private visits welcome, please* **Tel 01432 820557**

Madresfield Court ♿ (The Hon Lady Morrison) Nr Malvern. 60 acres formal and parkland garden incl rare species of mature trees, Pulhamite rock garden, maze, majestic avenues and a mass of wild flowers. TEAS. *Adm £2 Chd 50p (Share to St John Ambulance®). Sun May 7 (2-6)*

The Manor House ✣❀ (Mr & Mrs David Williams-Thomas) Birlingham, nr Pershore off A4104. Very fine views of Bredon Hill, frontaging on the R Avon. Walled white and silver garden, gazebo as featured in 'Practical Gardening'

Aug 1993 and 'House & Garden' Aug 1994. Visitors are invited to picnic by the river. TEAS. *Adm £1 Chd free. Every Thurs May 4 to July 27 incl (11-5.30), Aug 31 to Sept 28 incl (11-5.00). Every Weds June, July. Fri May 5, Mon May 29 (11-5.30). Private visits welcome, please* **Tel 01386 750005**

Marley Bank ✲❀ (Mr & Mrs Roger Norman) From A44 (5m E Bromyard) follow Whitbourne & Clifton-on-Teme signs for 1.2m. 1½-acre garden with a wide range of plants to give all-yr interest, set in 3.5 acres old orchard; good views. Steep paths and steps. Trees, shrubs, mixed borders, alpine terraces, troughs, peat beds, naturalised snowdrops & daffodils. TEA. *Adm £1.50 Chd free. First and third Sun April to Sept and Aug 27 (2-5.30). Closed Sun July 2, Augut 20, Sept 3. Private visits welcome, please* **Tel 01886 821576**

The Marsh Country Hotel ✲❀ (Mr & Mrs Martin Gilleland) Eyton. 2m NW of Leominster. Signed Eyton and Lucton off B4361 Richard Castle Rd. A 1½-acre garden created over the past 6 years. Herbaceous borders, small orchard, lily pond, herb garden and stream with planted banks and walk. Vegetable plot. Landscaped reed bed sewage treatment system. Featured in 'The Gardener' 1994. C14 timbered Great Hall listed grade II* (not open). TEAS. *Adm £1.50 Chd 50p. Suns, Thurs, Fris April 2 to Oct 29 (11-5)*

Moccas Court ♿ (Trustees of Baunton Trust) 10m W of Hereford. 1m off B4352. 7-acres; Capability Brown parkland on S bank of R. Wye. House designed by Adam and built by Keck in 1775. TEAS in village hall. *Adm house & garden £1.95 Chd £1 (Share to Moccas Church®). Sun June 11 (2-6). By appt for groups of 20 or over, please* **Tel 01981 500381**

Monnington Court (Mr & Mrs John Bulmer) Monnington. The ¾m lane to Monnington on Wye to Monnington Court is on the A438 between Hereford and Hay 9m from either. Approx 10 acres. Lake, pond and river walk. Sculpture garden (Mrs Bulmer is the sculptor Angela Conner); various tree lined avenues including Monnington Walk, one of Britain's oldest, still complete mile long avenues of Scots pines and yews, made famous by Kilvert's Diary; collection of swans and ducks; Foundation Farm of the British Morgan Horse - a living replica of ancient horses seen in statues in Trafalgar Square, etc; working cider press; FREE horse and carriage display at 3.30 each of open days. The C13, C15, C17 house including Mediaeval Moot Hall is also open. Barbecue on fine days, lunches. TEA 10.30-6.30. Indoor horse display and films on rainy days. *Adm house and garden £3.50 Chd £2.50, garden only £2.50 Chd £1.50 (Share to British Morgan Horse Foundation Farm®). Sat, Sun, Mon Aug 26, 27, 28 (10.30-7). Private visits for 10 or over welcome, please* **Tel 01981 500264**

Nerine Nursery ❀ (Mr & Mrs I L Carmichael) Brookend House, Welland, ½m towards Upton-on-Severn from Welland Xrds (A4104 × B4208). Internationally famous reference collection of Nerines, 30 species and some 800 named varieties in 5 greenhouses and traditional walled garden with raised beds, hardy nerines. Coaches by appt only. TEAS. *Adm £1.50 Chd free. Sun Oct 15 (10-5). Private visits welcome, please* **Tel 01684 594005**

¶The Old Vicarage ❀ (Mr & Mrs M J MacKinlay MacLeod) Overbury. 5m NE of Tewkesbury. 2½m N of Teddington Hands roundabout where A438 crosses A435. 1-acre garden commanding lovely long distance views. Under creation by present owners since 1988. Interesting mixed borders and wide range of planted containers. Semi-walled vegetable garden. *Adm £1 Chd free. Sun June 18 (2-6)*

¶Orchard Bungalow ✲❀ (Mr & Mrs Robert Humphries) Bishops Frome. 14m W of Worcester. A4103 turn R at bottom of Fromes Hill, through village of Bishops Frome on B4214. Turn R immediately after de-regulation signs along narrow track for 250yds. Ample parking in field 200yds from garden. ½-acre garden with conifers, trees, shrubs and herbaceous borders. Over 200 roses incl many old varieties, 4 ponds, small stream, 3 aviaries and dovecote. 1993 winner of Garden News water garden competition. TEAS. *Adm £1 Chd free. Suns June 18, July 16 (2-6). Private visits welcome, please* **Tel 01885 490273**

Overbury Court ♿❀ (Mr & Mrs Bruce Bossom) 5m NE of Tewkesbury, 2½m N of Teddington Hands Roundabout, where A438 crosses A435. Georgian house 1740 (not open); landscape gardening of same date with stream and pools. Daffodil bank and grotto. Plane trees, yew hedges. Shrub, cut flower, coloured foliage, gold and silver, shrub rose borders. Norman church adjoins garden. Home-made TEAS in aid of Village Hall. *Adm £1.50 Chd free. Sun March 26 (2-6). By appt for groups of 15 or more*

¶Pedwardine Cottage ✲ (Robert Milne) On rd to Lingen, 1m S of Brampton Bryan which is 12m W of Ludlow. ⅛-acre organic kitchen garden. Efficient design. 17th yr of intensive cropping. Informative written guide and plan. *Adm £1.20 Chd free. Daily in July (2-6). For NGS Sun June 25, Sat, Sun, Mon Aug 26, 27, 28 (10-7). Private visits welcome, please* **Tel 01568 86489**

Pershore College of Horticulture ♿✲❀ 1m S of Pershore on A44, 7m from M5 junction 7. 180-acre estate; ornamental grounds; arboretum; fruit, vegetables; amenity glasshouses; wholesale hardy stock nursery. Plant Centre open for sales. West Midlands Regional Centre for RHS. Plant Centre open for gardening advice. TEA. *Adm £1 Chd 50p. Sun June 11 (2-4)*

The Picton Garden ♿✲❀ (Mr & Mrs Paul Picton) Walwyn Rd, Colwall. 3m W of Malvern on B4218. 1½-acres W of Malvern Hills. A plantsman's garden extensively renovated in recent years. Rock garden using Tufa. Moist garden. Rose garden with scented old and modern varieties. Mature interesting shrubs. Large herbaceous borders full of colour from early summer. NCCPG National Reference collection of asters, michaelmas daisies, occupies its own vast borders and gives a tapestry of colour from late Aug through Sept and Oct. If wet there will be a small display of Asters under cover. *Adm £1.50 Chd free. Open Wed to Sun April 1 to Oct 29 inc (10-1; 2.15-5.30). Private parties of 10 or over welcome, please* **Tel 01684 540416**

Priors Court ✤❀ (Robert Philipson-Stow) Long Green. From Tewkesbury take A438 to Ledbury. Exactly 5m pass under M50. Garden on hill on L of A438. From Ledbury, Worcester or Gloucester aim for Rye Cross (A438 and B4208) then take A438 for Tewkesbury. Priors Court is approx 3m from Rye Cross on R. 3-acre garden established in 1920s by owner's parents surrounding C15 house (not open). Rock, herb and vegetable gardens, also mature trees and shrubs, herbaceous and rose borders; stunning views. Norman church 250yds over field will be open. TEAS. *Adm £1.50 Chd 50p (Share to Berrow & Pendock Parish Church®). Sun May 14 (2-6)*

The Priory ♿❀ (The Hon Mrs Peter Healing) Kemerton, NE of Tewkesbury B4080. Main features of this 4-acre garden are long herbaceous borders planned in colour groups; stream, fern and sunken gardens. Many unusual plants, shrubs and trees. Featured in BBC2 'Gardeners' World' and 'The Garden magazine'. Small nursery. TEAS Suns only. *Adm £1.50 Chd over 7 yrs 50p (Share to St Richard's Hospice® Aug 27, SSAFA® Sept 11). Every Thurs May 25 to Sept 28; also Suns May 28, June 25, July 16, Aug 6, 27, Sept 11 (2-7). Private visits welcome, please* **Tel 01386 725258**

Red House Farm ✤❀ (Mrs M M Weaver) Flying Horse Lane, Bradley Green. 7m W of Redditch on B4090 Alcester to Droitwich. Turn opp The Red Lion. Approx ½-acre plant enthusiast's cottage garden containing wide range of interesting herbaceous perennials; roses; shrubs; alpines. Garden and small nursery open daily offering wide variety of plants mainly propogated from garden. *Adm £1 Chd free. Sun May 28, June 25, July 30 (11-5). Private visits welcome, please,* **Tel 01527 821269**

Ripple Hall ♿ (Sir Hugo Huntington-Whiteley) 4m N of Tewkesbury. Off A38 Worcester-Tewkesbury (nr junction with motorway); Ripple village well signed. 6 acres; lawns and paddocks with donkeys; walled vegetable garden; cork tree and orangery. TEAS. *Adm £1.50 Acc chd free (Share to St John Ambulance®). Sun April 9 (2-5)*

Robins End ✤❀ (Mr & Mrs A Worsley) Eastham. 15m W of Worcester, turn L off A443 2m after Eardiston to Eastham. ½m turn R to Highwood, 1st gate on L. Queen Anne Rectory garden in peaceful surroundings. Splendid display of snowdrops and daffodils. TEAS. *Adm £1.25 Chd free (Share to Eastham Parish Church®). Sun March 19 (2.30-5.30)*

St Egwins Cottage ✤❀ (Mr & Mrs Brian Dudley) Norton. 2m N of Evesham on A435. 300 yds past 'Little Chef'. Park in St Egwins Church car park. Walk through churchyard to Church Lane (50yds). Please do not park in Church Lane. ⅕-acre plantsman's garden, many unusual plants; mainly perennials including hardy geraniums, campanulas and salvias. Small thatched cottage next to C12 church (open). TEAS. *Adm £1 Chd free. Suns, May 21, June 11, August 13; Weds May 24, June 14, 28, July 5, 19; Aug 16 (2-5). Also private visits welcome April to September, please* **Tel 01386 870486**

By Appointment Gardens. See head of county section

St Michael's Cottage ❀ (Mr & Mrs K R Barling) Broadway. 5m SE of Evesham. Thatched cottage opp St Michael's Parish Church, 200yds along rd from The Green to Snowshill. (Public car park nearby, via Church Close.) Approx ⅓-acre of intensively planted cottage style and herbaceous garden planned in colour groups, including a small white sunken garden. Modest informal fishpond; close to Cotswold Way. Cream TEAS and home-made cakes. *Adm £1 Acc chd free. Sun June 18 (2-5.30). Private visits also welcome during June. Please* **Tel 01386 852639**

Shucknall Court ✤ (Mr & Mrs Henry Moore) 5½m E of Hereford off A4103, sign-posted Weston Beggard. Garden 100yds from main rd. Large collection of specie, old-fashioned and shrub roses. Mixed borders in the old walled farmhouse garden. Wild garden, small stream garden, vegetables and fruit. Partly suitable for wheelchairs. Cream TEAS. *Adm £1.50 Chd free (Share to St. John Ambulance®). Sun, Wed June 25, July 5 (2-6)*

¶Snowshill Road Gardens ♿✤❀ All 6 gardens are on Snowshill Rd out of Broadway. TEAS. *Combined adm £2 Chd free (Share to Lifford Hall, Broadway®). Sun July 2 (2-6)*

Far Bunchers (Mrs A Pallant) A recently developed mixed garden of about 1 acre with an emphasis on shrub roses and organic vegetable growing

¶Meadowside (Mrs Patricia A Bamford)

The Mill (Mrs & Mrs Hugh Verney) 2½-acre paddock, bounded by 2 streams, transformed since 1975 into an attractive garden which will support a variety of wild life. Informal planting of trees, shrub roses and other shrubs, moisture loving plants and bulbs. Minimal annual maintenance required

Mill Hay Cottage (Dr & Mrs W J A Payne) The garden approx 2 acres is of relatively recent origin and is still being developed. Informally planted terraces, orchard areas and wild garden. A special feature is the number of rare fruiting plants and an attempt is being made to accommodate these with the demands of wild life

¶The Old Orchard (Major I F Gregory)

¶Pye Corner (Mr Michael J Naylor)

Spetchley Park ♿✤❀ (R J Berkeley Esq) 2m E of Worcester on A422. 30-acre garden containing large collection of trees, shrubs and plants. Red and fallow deer in nearby park. TEAS. *Adm £2.20 Chd £1.10. Good Fri April 14 (11-5) & Suns May 14, July 2 (2-5)*

Staunton Park ♿❀ (Mr E J L & Miss A Savage) Staunton-on-Arrow. 3m from Pembridge; 6m from Kington on the Titley road. 18m from Hereford; 11m from Leominster; 16m from Ludlow. Signposted. 14-acres of garden, specimen trees, herbaceous borders, herb garden, rock garden, hosta border, lake, lakeside garden, woodland walk, spring bulbs. New scented border for enjoyment of the blind. Wild flower area. Ice-house. TEAS. *Adm £1.50 Chd free. Weds, Suns April to end Sept. Easter and Bank Holidays. For NGS Suns May 7, June 18 (2-5.30)*

Stone House ❀ (Peter & Sheila Smellie) Scotland, Wellington. A49 6m N of Hereford, end of dual carriageway, turn L for Westhope. ¾m turn R up narrow track. Parking ¼m. Parking difficult in wet conditions. 1-acre S sloping garden with magnificent views over countryside. Winding paths traverse the bank and terraced areas which contain a wide selection of unusual shrubs and herbaceous plants. *Adm £1.50 Chd 50p. Suns April 30, May 21, June 18, July 16 (12-6). Private visits welcome, please* **Tel 01432 830470**

● Stone House Cottage Gardens ♿✂❀ (Maj & the Hon Mrs Arbuthnott) Stone, 2m SE of Kidderminster via A448 towards Bromsgrove next to church, turn up drive. 1-acre sheltered walled plantsman's garden with towers; rare wall shrubs, climbers and interesting herbaceous plants. In adjacent nursery large selection of unusual shrubs and climbers for sale. Featured in The Garden, Country Life and Hortus. Coaches by appt only. *Adm £1.50 Chd free. Suns May 7, 14, 21, 28; June 4, 11, 18, 25; Aug 27; Mons April 17, May 8, 29; Aug 28 (10-6); also open March to Oct every Wed, Thurs, Fri, Sat (10-6). Private visits welcome during November, please* **Tel 01562 69902**

Strawberry Cottage ✂❀ (Mr & Mrs M R Philpott) Hamnish. 3m E of Leominster. A44 E from Leominster, turn L at 1st Xrds to Hamnish. A 2-acre cottage garden created by the present owners since 1988. Part of garden on steep slope with large rockeries and heather beds. Wide variety of plants and shrubs, many unusual. Over 250 roses. Mixed and herbaceous borders. Beds with single colour themes. Pond and wild garden area, herb and large kitchen garden. Spring bulbs. Superb position with spectacular views. Interesting selection of plants for sale. TEAS. *Adm £1.20 Chd free (Share to Leominster Community Hospital®). Every Sun and 1st, 2nd, 4th Thurs and Bank Hol Mons April 30 to Sept 10 (2-5.30). Private visits welcome, please* **Tel 01568 760319**

21 Swinton Lane ✂❀ (Mr A Poulton & Mr B Stenlake) Worcester. 1½m W of City Centre off A4103 Hereford Rd turning into Swinton Lane between Portabello public house and Boughton Golf Course. ⅓-acre town garden featuring a wide variety of plants. Herbaceous borders, silver garden and red border. Many interesting tender plants are used both in the garden and in containers for the summer. *Adm £1 Chd free. Thurs April 27, June 1, 29, July 27, Aug 24 (11-6). Also private visits welcome, please* **Tel 01905 422265**

Tedstone Court ❀ (Mrs N C Bellville) Approx 17m from Hereford. From Bromyard take road for Stourport B4203 for 3m. Turn R signed Whitbourne, Tedstone Delamere. Spring garden, daffodils, rhododendrons; rockery; kitchen garden; fine views. Plants for sale. In June tour of deer farm. Calves arriving (separate charge). TEAS. *Adm £2 Chd 25p. Suns April 23, June 4 (2-6)*

Torwood ♿✂❀ (Mr & Mrs S G Woodward) Whitchurch, Ross-on-Wye. A40 turn to Symonds Yat W. Garden adjacent village school and roundabout. Interesting and colourful, shrubs, conifers, herbaceous plants, bulbs, etc. Featured by Central TV 'My Secret Garden'. TEAS. *Adm £1 Chd free. Suns June 11, 25, July 9, Aug 6, Weds May 17, June 7, July 5, Aug 9 (2-6). Private visits welcome, please* **Tel 01600 890306**

Upper Court ♿ (Mr & Mrs W Herford) Kemerton, NE of Tewkesbury B4080. Take turning to Parish Church from War Memorial; Manor behind church. Approx 13 acres of garden and grounds inc a 2-acre lake where visitors would be welcome to bring picnics. The garden was mostly landscaped and planted in 1930s. TEAS. *Adm £1.50 Chd free. Sun June 18 (2-6)*

Well Cottage ♿✂ (R S Edwards Esq) Blakemere. 10m due W of Hereford. Leave Hereford on A465 (Abergavenny) rd. After 3m turn R towards Hay B4349 (B4348). At Clehonger keep straight on the B4352 towards Bredwardine. Well Cottage is on L by phone box. ¾-acre garden of mixed planting plus ½ acre of wild flower meadow suitable for picnics. There is a natural pool with gunnera and primulae. Good views over local hills and fields. Featured in Diana Saville's book 'Gardens for Small Country Houses' and Jane Taylor's 'The English Cottage Garden'. *Adm £1 Chd free. Private visits welcome May to Aug, please* **Tel 01981 500475**

¶Well Cottage ❀ (Mrs A Turnbull) Lingen. 5m NE of Presteigne. 15m SW of Ludlow. 15m NE of Leominster. On B4362 (Mortimers Cross to Presteigne), take N turn 2m from Presteigne Centre marked Kinsham and Lingen. Garden is next to Lingen Alpine Nursery. Approx ½-acre cottage garden with stream. Entirely managed by OAP! *Combined adm with* **Brook Cottage** *and* **Lingen Nursery** *£2 Chd under 10 free. Sun June 25 (2-6)*

Westwood Farm (Mr & Mrs Caspar Tremlett). From Bromyard take A44 towards Leominster. R turn to Hatfield and Bockleton 2m R turn down Westwood Lane. First Farm. From Leominster, take A44 toward Worcester 6m L to Hatfield and Bockleton. [Map ref OS sheet 149 60.59.] ¾ acre of cottage type garden with unusual plants and trees, small conservatory and pond with waterside plants. Dogs can be exercised in car park field. TEAS. *Adm £1 Chd free (Share to St John Ambulance®). Sun, Mon June 25, 26 (2-6). Also private visits welcome May to June, please* **Tel 01885 410212**

White Cottage ♿✂❀ (Mr & Mrs S M Bates) Earls Common Rd, Stock Green. A422 Worcester-Alcester; turn L at Red Hart PH (Dormston) 1½m to T junc in Stock Green. Turn L. 2-acre garden, developed since 1981; large herbaceous and shrub borders, many unusual varieties; specialist collection of hardy geraniums; stream and natural garden carpeted with primroses, cowslips and other wild flowers; nursery; featuring plants propagated from the garden. When fine teas at Coneybury Plant Centre. *Adm £1 OAPs 75p Chd free. April 14, 15, 16, 17, 18, 21, 22, 24, 25, 28, 29, 30. May daily except Weds, Thurs and Sun 21. June daily except Weds, Thurs and Suns 4, 18. July 1, 3, 4, 7, 8, 9 only. Sats, Suns, Mons Aug 26, 27, 28. Sept 16, 17, 30. Oct 1. (10-5), Nursery open daily April 1 to Oct 9. Private visits welcome by prior appt only, please* **Tel 01386 792414**

Whitfield ♿ (G M Clive Esq) Wormbridge, 8m SW of Hereford on A465 Hereford-Abergavenny Rd. Parkland, large garden, ponds, walled kitchen garden, 1780 gingko tree, 1½m woodland walk with 1851 Redwood grove. Picnic parties welcome. TEAS. *Adm £1.50 Chd 50p (Share to St John Ambulance®). Sun June 4 (2-6). Private visits welcome, please* **Tel 0198 121 202**

Whitlenge House Cottage ♿✂❀ (Mr & Mrs K J Southall) Whitlenge Lane, Hartlebury. S of Kidderminster on A449. Take A442 (signposted Droitwich) over small island, ¼m, 1st R into Whitlenge Lane. Follow signs. Professional landscaper's own demonstration garden with over 400 varieties of trees, shrubs, conifers, herbaceous, heathers and alpines, giving year-round interest. Small water features, rustic work, twisted pillar pergola, gravel gardens surrounded by rockeries and stone walls. Evolved over 10 years over 2 acres of informal plantsman's garden and incorporating an adjacent nursery specialising in large specimen shrubs. TEAS. *Adm £1.50 Chd free. Suns March 26, April 16, 30, May 7, 28, June 25, July 30, Aug 27, Sept 24. Every Thurs, Fri, Sat March 1 to Sept 30 (10-5) Bank Hol Mons April 17, May 8, 29, Aug 28 (10-5). Private visits welcome for parties of 10 and over, please* **Tel 01299 250720**

Wind's Point ✂ (Cadbury Trustees) British Camp. 3m SW of Malvern on Ledbury Rd. Medium-sized garden; unusual setting, lovely views. Last home of great Swedish singer Jenny Lind and where she died 1887. TEA. *Adm £1 Chd free. Sun April 9 (12-5)*

Windyridge ✂❀ (Mr P Brazier) Kidderminster. Turn off Chester Rd N (A449) into Hurcott Rd, then into Imperial Avenue. 1-acre spring garden containing azaleas, magnolias, camellias, rhododendrons, mature flowering cherries and davidia. Please wear sensible shoes. *Adm £1 Chd free. Suns April 30, May 7 (2-6). Private visits welcome, please* **Tel 01562 824994**

Witley Park House ♿ (Mr & Mrs W A M Edwards) Great Witley. 9m NW of Worcester. On A443 1m W of Little Witley. Garage on L coming from Worcester and Droitwich. 18 acres incl pool, lakeside and woodland walk, water fowl, many varieties young trees, shrubs and roses. TEAS. *Adm £1 Chd 25p (Share to Worcester Swan Rescue Service®). Suns April 16 (2-5), June 25 (2-6)*

¶Woodmancote ♿❀ (Ila & Ian Walmsley) Wadborough. 1½ m S of Stoulton, which is on A44 between Worcester and Pershore. A garden of approx ¾ acre acquired and developed in stages since 1986 by the present owners. 2 ponds, wide variety of shrubs and herbaceous plants in mixed borders, to give interest for most of the yr, heather beds and lawns. Please park considerately at The Mason Arms 400yds. TEAS in aid of St Peter's Church. *Adm £1 Chd free. Sat, Sun June 3, 4 (2-6)*

● **Wych & Colwall Horticultural Society Show**. The Elms School ♿✂ (L A C Ashley, Headmaster) Colwall Green. Medium-sized garden, herbaceous borders, fine views of Malvern Hills. Interesting exhibits of perennials, shrubs and crafts. Classes for flowers, vegetables, art & handicrafts. TEAS. *Adm to show and garden 80p. Share to NGS Sat July 29 (2-6)*

Yew Tree House ♿ (Mr & Mrs W D Moyle) Ombersley. Turn off A449 up Woodfield Lane R at T-junction. 2½-acre garden with many rare herbaceous plants and shrubs. Pretty walled garden with alpines and lily pond, numerous old-fashioned roses. Mature plantings of blue, pink and white borders around tennis court and other yellow and white beds. Orchard, copse and lawns with lovely views set around c1640 timber framed house. TEA. *Adm £2 Chd free. Sun June 25 (2-6)*

Regular Openers. Too many days to include in diary. Usually there is a wide range of plants giving year-round interest. See head of county section for the name and garden description for times etc.

Hertfordshire

Hon County Organiser: Mrs Antony Woodall, The Old Rectory, Wyddial, Buntingford SG9 0EN
Assistant Hon County Organisers: Mrs Edward Harvey, Wickham Hall, Bishop's Stortford CM23 1JQ
Mrs Hedley Newton, Moat Farm House Much Hadham SG10 6AE
Mrs Leone Ayres, Patmore Corner, Albury, Ware, Herts SG11 2LY
Hon County Treasurer: Mrs John Lancaster, Manor Cottage, Aspenden, Nr Buntingford SG9 9PB

DATES OF OPENING

By appointment

For telephone numbers and other details see garden descriptions. Private visits welcomed

The Abbots House, Abbots Langley
Garden Cottage, Abbots Langley
1 Gernon Walk, Letchworth
Hill House, Stanstead Abbotts
Hunton Park, Kings Langley
Lamer Lodge, Wheathamstead
Lane House, Patmore Heath
13 Little Gaddesden, Berkhamsted
St Paul's Walden Bury, Hitchin
Waterdell House, Croxley Green
23 Wroxham Way, Harpenden

Parties only

Ashridge Management College, Little Gaddesdon Gardens
Deansmere, West Hyde, Rickmansworth
Fanhams Hall, Ware
Pelham House, Brent Pelham
Queenswood School, Hatfield
West Lodge Park, Hadley Wood

Regular openings

For details see garden descriptions

Benington Lordship, nr Stevenage. For dates see text
Capel Manor Gardens, Enfield. For dates see text
The Manor House, Ayot St Lawrence. Suns May 7 to Aug 31

West Lodge Park, Hadley Park.
Every Wed

April 2 Sunday
Holwell Manor, Nr Hatfield

April 16 Sunday
Pelham House, Brent Pelham
St Paul's Walden Bury, Hitchin

April 23 Sunday
The Abbots House, Abbots Langley
Great Munden House, nr Ware
Odsey Park, Ashwell
Old Brickfields, New Road, Guilden Morden

May 14 Sunday
The Abbots House, Abbots Langley
Hipkins, Broxbourne
Pelham House, Brent Pelham

May 20 Saturday
Cockhamsted, Braughing, nr Ware

May 21 Sunday
Cockhamsted, Braughing, nr Ware
St Paul's Walden Bury, Hitchin
Wrotham Park, Barnet

May 28 Sunday
Great Sarratt Hall, Rickmansworth
Queenswood School, Hatfield

May 29 Monday
Queenswood School, Hatfield

June 4 Sunday
Moor Place, Much Hadham
West Lodge Park, Hadley Wood

June 10 Saturday
Cockhamsted, Braughing, nr Ware

June 11 Sunday
Cockhamsted, Braughing, nr Ware
Hill House, Stanstead Abbotts
Little Gaddesdon Gardens
Pelham House, Brent Pelham
St Paul's Walden Bury, Hitchin

June 18 Sunday
The Abbots House, Abbots Langley
Hunton Park, Kings Langley
The Gardens of Mackerye End, Harpenden

June 20 Tuesday
The Abbots House, Abbots Langley

June 24 Saturday
The Barn, Abbots Langley ‡
Bennington Lordship, nr Stevenage
Serge Hill, Abbots Langley ‡

June 25 Sunday
Bennington Lordship, nr Stevenage
Odsey Park, Ashwell
Old Brickfields, New Road, Guilden Morden
Rushmead, Abbots Langley

July 2 Sunday
Hunton Park, Kings Langley
St Paul's Walden Bury, Hitchin
Waterdell House, Croxley Green

July 9 Sunday
The Mill House, Tewin, Nr Welwyn

July 16 Sunday
Deansmere, West Hyde, Rickmansworth
Hunton Park, Kings Langley
The Manor House, Ayot St Lawrence

July 19 Wednesday
Deansmere, West Hyde, Rickmansworth

August 27 Sunday
The Abbots House, Abbots Langley

October 1 Sunday
Knebworth House, Stevenage

October 15 Sunday
Capel Manor Gardens, Enfield
Hunton Park, Kings Langley

October 22 Sunday
Fanhams Hall, Ware
West Lodge Park, Hadley Wood

DESCRIPTIONS OF GARDENS

The Abbots House ♿✻❀ (Dr & Mrs Peter Tomson) 10, High Street, Abbots Langley NW of Watford (5m from Watford). Junction 20 M25, junction 6 M1. Parking in free village car park. 1¾-acre garden with interesting trees; shrubs; mixed borders; sunken garden; ponds; conservatory. Nursery featuring plants propagated from the garden. TEAS. *Adm £1.50 Chd free (Share to Friends of St Lawrence Church®). Suns, April 23, May 14, June 18; Tues June 20, Sun Aug 27 (2-5). Also at other times by appt* **Tel 01923 264946**

The Barn ♿✻❀ (Tom Stuart-Smith and family) Abbots Langley. ½m E of Bedmond in Serge Hill Lane. 1-acre plantsman's garden. Small sheltered courtyard planted with unusual shrubs and perennials, contrasts with more open formal garden with views over wild flower meadow. Tea at Serge Hill. *Combined adm £3 with* **Serge Hill** *(Share to Tibet Relief Fund UK®). Sat June 24 (2-5)*

Benington Lordship ✻❀ (Mr & Mrs C H A Bott) Benington. 5m E of Stevenage, in Benington Village. Hilltop garden on site of Norman castle overlooking lakes. Ruins, spectacular spring bulbs, roses, rock/water garden, herbaceous borders, ornamental kitchen garden. *Adm £2.40 Acc chd free (Share to St Peters Church®). Spring and Summer Bank Hol Mons, Weds April to Sept 27, Thurs July to Aug (12-5). Suns April to Aug 27, Sun Oct 22 (2-5) For NGS TEAS and Floral Festival in Church adjoining garden. Sat, Sun June 24, 25 (12-6). Private visits of 20 and over, please* **Tel 01438 869668**

Capel Manor Gardens ♿ (Horticultural & Environmental Centre) Bullsmoor Lane, Enfield, Middx. 3 mins from M25 junction M25/A10. W at traffic lights. Nearest station Turkey Street - Liverpool Street line (not Suns). 30 acres of historical and modern theme gardens, Japanese garden, large Italian style maze, rock and water features. 5 acre demonstration garden run by Gardening Which? Walled garden with rose collection, display glasshouses and woodland walks. TEAS. *Adm £3 OAP £2 Chd £1.50. Open daily (10-5.30 - check for winter opening times). For NGS (Share to Horticultural Therapy©) Sun Oct 15 (10-5.30). For other details* **Tel 0181 3664442**

Cockhamsted ♿✻❀ (Mr & Mrs David Marques) Braughing. 2m E of village towards Braughing Friars (7m N of Ware). 2 acres; informal garden; shrub roses surrounded by open country. Island with trees surrounded by water-filled C14 moat. TEAS in aid of Leukaemia Research. *Adm £2 Chd free. Sat, Sun May 20, 21; June 10, 11 (2-6)*

By Appointment Gardens. These owners do not have a fixed opening day usually because they do not like crowds or have insufficient parking space. Owner will often give guided tour.

Deansmere ♿✂❀ (Mr & Mrs Derek Austen) Old Uxbridge Rd, West Hyde. 3m SW of Rickmansworth, off A412. Leaving M25 junction 17, follow the sign 'Maple Cross'. In 200yds at roundabout take 2nd exit; across traffic lights at Maple Cross (A412), at mini roundabout turn L (signposted 'Harefield'), in 100yds at T junction turn L, 100yds. Deansmere is opposite St. Thomas's Church. 2-acre garden full of variety and interest. Perennials, bedding plants, containers, bulbs, heather, shrubs, trees: summerhouses; aviary; rhododendron bed; pergola; vegetables, fruit trees; two small ponds; dell; viola and penstemon collections. TEAS. *Adm £1.25 Chd 50p (Share to Harrow Ciné & Video Society®). Sun, Wed July 16, 19 (2-6). Private parties welcome with tea, please* **Tel 01923 778817**

¶Fanhams Hall ♿✂ (Sainsburys Business Training Centre) Ware. Situated on Fanhams Hall Road 1½m NE of Ware Town Centre. 27 acres of park and gardens which incl many rare trees; also incl Queen Anne garden and Japanese house and garden. (Autumn colour is very special). *Adm £1.50 Chd 50p. Sun Oct 22 (12-5). Private visits welcome, please* **Tel 01920 460511**

Garden Cottage (Anthony House) 85 Furtherfield, Abbots Langley. NW of Watford 5m from Watford junction 20 M25 junction 6 M1. A small plantsman's garden in total 100′ long by 20′ wide; planted in 1991, filled with unusual perennials and interesting features all year. TEA. *Adm £1 Chd 50p. Private visits welcome, please* **Tel 01923 260571**

1 Gernon Walk ✂ (Miss Rachel Crawshay) Letchworth (First Garden City). Tiny town garden (100ft long but only 8ft wide in middle) planned and planted since 1984 for year-round and horticultural interest. *Collecting box. Private visits only, please* **Tel 01462 686399**

Great Munden House ✂❀ (Mr & Mrs D Wentworth-Stanley) 7m N of Ware. Off A10 on Puckeridge by-pass turn W; or turning off A602 via Dane End. 3½-acre informal garden with lawns, mixed shrub and herbaceous borders; variety shrub roses, trees; kitchen and herb garden. Plant stall. TEAS in aid of NE Herts NSPCC. *Adm £1.50 Chd 50p. Sun April 23 (2.30-5.30)*

Great Sarratt Hall ♿✂❀ (H M Neal Esq) Sarratt, N of Rickmansworth. From Watford N via A41 (or M1 Exit 5) to Kings Langley; and left (W) to Sarratt; garden is 1st on R after village sign. 4 acres; herbaceous and mixed shrub borders; pond, moisture-loving plants and trees; walled kitchen garden; rhododendrons, magnolias, camellias; new planting of specialist conifers and rare trees. TEAS. *Adm £2 Chd free (Share to Courtauld Institute of Art Fund©). Sun May 28 (2-6)*

Hill House ✂❀ (Mr & Mrs R Pilkington) Stanstead Abbotts, near Ware. From A10 turn E on to A414; then B181 for Stanstead Abbotts; left at end of High St, garden 1st R past Church. Ample car parking. 8 acres incl wood; species roses, herbaceous border, water garden, conservatory, aviary, woodland walk. Lovely view over Lea Valley. Modern Art Exhibition in loft gallery (20p extra). Unusual plants for sale. Home-made TEAS. *Adm £2 Chd 50p (Share to St Andrews Parish Church of Stanstead Abbotts®). Sun June 11 (2-5.30). Private visits and parties welcome, please* **Tel 0192 0870013**

Hipkins ♿✂❀ (Michael Goulding Esq) Broxbourne. From A10 to Broxbourne turn up Bell or Park Lane into Baas Lane, opposite Graham Avenue. 3-acre informal garden with spring fed ponds; azaleas and rhododendrons; shrub and herbaceous borders specialising in plants for flower arrangers; many unusual plants; fine trees and well kept kitchen garden. TEAS. *Adm £1.50 Chd 50p. Sun May 14 (2-6)*

Holwell Manor ✂❀ (Mr & Mrs J Gillum) Nr Hatfield. On W side of B1455, short lane linking A414 with B158 between Hatfield (3m) and Hertford (4m). B1455 joins the A414 roundabout and is signposted Essendon. Holwell is 500yds from this roundabout. Natural garden with large pond, mature trees, river walks; approx 2-3 acres. Island in pond covered with daffodils and narcissi in spring. TEAS. *Adm £1.50 Chd 50p. Sun April 2 (2-5)*

¶Hunton Park ❀ Kings Langley. 1m S of Junction 20 of M25 and 3m N of Watford. On exiting from Junction 20 follow signs to Watford (A41), turn L at traffic lights after ½m signposted Abbots Langley. Follow Bridge Rd for ½m up hill and Hunton Park is to be found on the RH-side. 22 acres of terraced lawns, gardens, pond and woodlands incl mature trees and ancient yews. First established in the 1840s the present grounds staff are working to return the gardens to their original setting comprising herbaceous borders, heather gardens, woodland plants and rose garden. A picnic area is provided for lunches. TEAS. *Adm £1.50 Chd free. Suns June 18, July 2, 16, Oct 15 (12-5). Private visits welcome, please* **Tel 01932 261511**

Knebworth House ♿✂ (The Lord Cobbold) Knebworth. 28m N of London; direct access from A1(M) at Stevenage. Station and Bus stop: Stevenage 3m. Historic house, home of Bulwer Lytton; Victorian novelist and statesman. Lutyens garden designed for his brother-in-law, the Earl of Lytton, comprising pleached lime avenues, rose beds, herbaceous borders, yew hedges restored mazeand various small gardens in process of restoration; Gertrude Jekyll herb garden. Restaurant and TEAS. *Adm £1.50 Chd £1. ▲For NGS Sun Oct 1 (12-5)*

Lamer Lodge ♿ (Mr & Mrs J Wilson) Wheathampstead. 6m N of St Albans on B651; from roundabout N of Wheathampstead continue N on Lamer Lane for ½m towards Kimpton. House 1st on R at drive entrance. 2½ acres of informal garden, woodland paths, lawns, varied trees, shrubs and roses; countryside surroundings. TEAS by arrangement. *Adm £1.50 Chd free. Private visits welcome April to end of June, please* **Tel 01582 832113**

¶Lane House ✂❀ (Mrs Diana Fernsby) Patmore Heath, Albury. M11 Bishops Stortford. Follow A120 towards Puckeridge. At traffic lights in Little Hadham, turn to Albury. 2m from lights, at Catherine Wheel Inn turn R. 30yds turn R again. Follow the rd round the heath to a high brick wall on R. Lane on R leads to house. Please park carefully on heath. Small garden of approx 1 acre. Wonderful views over surrounding countryside. Garden developed over last 28yrs by present owners, still being altered and developed as ideas change. Interesting collection of herbaceous plants, trees, shrubs and semi-hardy plants. *Adm £1.50 Chd free (Share to Oast House Trust®). Private visits welcome, please* **Tel 01279 771 322**

¶**13 Little Gaddesden** (Mrs G Catchpole) Berkhampsted. Approach from Hemel Hempstead along Leighton Buzzard Rd or from centre of Berkhampsted N of Station. The village hall is in Church Rd in centre of village, which is 2m N of Berkhampsted or 3½m W of Hemel Hempstead. Cottage next to village shop. ⅓-acre cottage garden. Spring best season-many bulbs. *Adm £1 Chd free (Share to Oast House Trust®). Private visits welcome March to May, please* **Tel 01442 842202**

¶**Little Gaddesden Gardens** Approach from Hemel Hempstead along Leighton Buzzard Rd or from centre of Berkhampsted N of Station. The village hall is in Church Rd in centre of village, which is 2m N of Berkhampsted or 3½m W of Hemel Hempstead. Plants and Teas at village hall in aid of ARC. *Combined adm £2.50 Chd 50p. Sun June 11 (11-5)*

¶**Ashridge Management College** From hall down Church Rd to Village Rd and straight over to Ashridge Rd. Through gates into Ashridge College. 180 acreage approx/features as on map. The pleasure gardens were planned by Capability's disciple Humphry Repton (1813). Mount garden, circular rose garden and grotto. A new rock and water garden rhododendron walk

¶**1 Home Farm** (Mr & Mrs D E A Tucker) From village hall, down to main village rd L SE towards Nettleden ¾m to Home Farm Cottage and Shepherds Cottage on L. 4yr old garden with some mature trees, herbaceous borders, roses, clematis, water feature; a cottage garden

¶**Nettleden** (Mr & Mrs Allsop) From village hall down main Village Rd to Nettleden 1½m on R. Approx 4 acres comprising extensive lawns, herbaceous borders, ornamental lake and cascade, rhododendrons, magnolias, acers and many unusual plants. A plantsman's garden

¶**Shepherds Cottage** (Mr & Mrs G A B Ward) Small walled garden of interesting design. Unusual plants, water feature

The Gardens of Mackerye End (Mr & Mrs David Laing) Harpenden. A1 junc 4 follow signs for Wheathampstead then Luton. Garden ½m from Wheathampstead on R. M1 junct 10 follow Lower Luton Rd (B653) to Cherry Tree Inn. Turn L to Wheathampstead. A 1550 Grade 1 manor house set in 11 acres of gardens and park. Front garden set in framework of formal yew hedges with a long border (best in early summer) and a fine C17 tulip tree. Victorian walled garden now divided into smaller sections; path maze; cutting garden; quiet garden; vegetables. Newly created W garden enclosed by pergola walk of old English roses and vines. Lunches and TEAS. *Adm £2.50 Chd £1 (Share to Macintyre®), and incl* **Hollybush Cottage** (Mrs & Mrs John Coaton) delightful cottage garden around this listed house. *Sun June 18 (12-5)*

The Manor House Ayot St Lawrence (Mrs Andrew Duncan) Bear R into village from Bride Hall Lane, ruined Church on L and the Brocket Arms on R. On bend there is a pair of brick piers leading to drive - go through green iron gates. The Manor house is on your L. New garden, with formal garden, mixed borders and nut grove, large walled garden and orchard. TEAS NGS days only. *Adm £2 OAP/Chd £1 (under ten free). Open every Sun May 1 to Aug 31. Also by appt for parties, please* **Tel 01438 820943**. *For NGS Sun July 16 (2-6)*

The Mill House (Dr and Mrs R V Knight) Tewin, nr Archers Green. 3½m W of Hertford and 3½m E of Welwyn on B1000. Parking at Archers Green which is signposted on B1000. On the banks of the R Mimram. Approx 20 acres; mature gardens incl fine hedges, woodlands, many rare trees labelled, shrub and herbaceous borders, spring fed water gardens, with an abundance of wildlife in a lovely valley setting. Plants and TEAS in aid of Hospice Care, E Herts. *Adm £2 Chd under 10 free. Sun July 9 (2-6)*

Moor Place (Mr & Mrs Bryan Norman) Much Hadham. Entrance either at war memorial or at Hadham Cross. 2 C18 walled gardens. Herbaceous borders. Large area of shrubbery, lawns, hedges and trees. 2 ponds. Approx 10 acres. TEAS. *Adm £1.50 Chd 50p. Sun June 4 (2-5.30)*

Myddelton House see London

Odsey Park (Mr & The Hon Mrs Jeremy Fordham) Ashwell. Situated equidistant between Royston and Baldock 4½m each way. On N carriageway of A505 enter by Lodge and drive into park as signposted. Recently remade medium-sized garden originally dating from 1860 with walled garden, set in park with mature trees, spring bulbs, tulips; small colourful herbaceous border, roses, shrubs and small herb garden. Car parking free. TEA April 23 only. TEAS June 25 only. *Adm £1.50 Chd free (Share to Ashwell Church Restoration Fund®). Suns April 23 (1-5); June 25 (2-6)*

Old Brickfields (Mr & Mrs Robert Rosier) New Rd. Guilden Morden. Approx. 4m N of the A505 Baldock to Royston rd. Old Brickfields is ¼m out of the village on the L on the Wendy-Shingay rd. A 1 acre friendly garden of lawns, 'shrubaceous' borders with interesting labelled plants and vegetable garden. 1½ acres of wild flower meadow and lge pond. Pondside picnic area. *Adm £1.50 Chd free. Suns April 23, June 25 (11-5)*

Pelham House (Mr David Haselgrove & Dr Sylvia Martinelli) Brent Pelham. On E side of Brent Pelham on B1038. When travelling from Clavering immed after the village sign. 3½-acre informal garden on alkaline clay started by present owners in 1986. Plenty of interest to the plantsman. Wide variety of trees and shrubs especially birches and oaks. Bulb frames, raised beds with alpines and acid-loving plants and small formal area with ponds. Many daffodils and tulips. *Adm £1.50 Chd free (Share to Brent Pelham Church®). Suns April 16, May 14, June 11 (2-5)*

Queenswood School Shepherds Way. From S: M25 junction 24 signposted Potters Bar. In ½m at lights turn R onto A1000 signposted Hatfield. In 2m turn R onto B157. School is ½m on the R. From N: A1000 from Hatfield. In 5m turn L onto B157. This year is a special year for Queenswood as it celebrates its Centenary. 120 acres informal gardens and woodlands. Rhododendrons, fine specimen trees, shrubs and herbaceous borders. Glasshouses; fine views to Chiltern Hills. Picnic area. Lunches and TEAS. *Adm £1.50 OAP's/Chd 75p. Sun, Mon May 28, 29 (11-6)*

Rushmead ✂❀ (Mr & Mrs Brian Munnery) Abbots Langley. Garden sited midway between Abbots Langley and Bedmond on main Watford-Leverstock Green Rd. M25 junction 20 or M1 junction 6. A ¼-acre garden with variety of shrubs, trees and perennials; a lge, deep pond (care needed with children) with ornamental lilies and fish. Plants propagated from the garden. *Adm £1.50 Chd free (Share to Ovingdean Hall School®). Sun June 25 (2-5)*

St Paul's Walden Bury ♿❀ (Simon Bowes Lyon and family) Whitwell, on B651 5m S of Hitchin; ½m N of Whitwell. Formal woodland garden listed Grade 1. Laid out about 1730, influenced by French tastes. Long rides and avenues span about 40 acres, leading to temples, statues, lake and ponds. Also more recent flower gardens and woodland garden with rhododendrons, azaleas and magnolias. Dogs on leads. TEAS. *Adm £1.50 Chd 75p (Share to St Pauls Walden Church®). Suns April 16, May 21, June 11 (2-7), July 2 (2-6) followed by lakeside concert 7pm. Also other times by appt* **Tel 01438 871218** *or* **871229**

Serge Hill ✂❀ (Murray & Joan Stuart-Smith) Abbots Langley. ½m E of Bedmond. The house is marked on the OS map. Regency house in parkland setting with fine kitchen garden of ½ acre. A range of unusual wall plants, mixed border of 100yds. New small courtyard garden and wall garden planted with hot coloured flowers. TEAS. *Combined adm £3 with* **The Barn** *(Share to Herts Garden Trust©). Sat June 24 (2-5)*

Tarn, Oxhey Drive South, Northwood *see* London.

Waterdell House ♿✂❀ (Mr & Mrs Peter Ward) Croxley Green. 1½m from Rickmansworth. Exit 18 from M25. Direction R'worth to join A412 towards Watford. From A412 turn left signed Sarratt, along Croxley Green, fork right past Coach & Horses, cross Baldwins Lane into Little Green Lane, then left at top. 1½-acre walled garden developed and maintained over many years to accommodate growing family; mature and young trees, topiary holly hedge, herbaceous borders; modern island beds of shrubs, old-fashioned roses; vegetable and fruit garden. New pond garden. TEA 50p, TEAS 80p. *Adm £1.50 OAPs/Chd £1. Sun July 2 (2-6) and private visits welcome May-mid July (2-6), please* **Tel 01923 772775**

West Lodge Park ♿ (T Edward Beale Esq) Cockfosters Rd, Hadley Wood. On A111 between Potters Bar and Southgate. Exit 24 from M25 signed Cockfosters. Station: Cockfosters underground (Piccadilly Line); then bus 298 to Beech Hill. Beale Arboretum, set in 10-acre section of West Lodge Park, consists of splendid collection of trees, some 500 varieties, all labelled; many original and interesting specimens, some old-established as well as scores planted since 1965; magnificent leaf colour. TEA (or lunch if booked in advance in adjoining hotel). *Adm £1.50 Chd 30p (Share to GRBS®). Suns June 4 (2-5.30); Oct 22 (12-4), Weds every week (2-5). Organised parties anytime by appt. Collecting box.* **Tel 0181 4408311**

Wrotham Park ♿❀ (Mr Robert Byng) M25 Junction 23, take A1081 towards Barnet, first left to Bentley Heath into Dancers Hill Rd. Lodge in village 1½m on R opp church. 30 acres in Parkland setting. Woodland, rhododendrons, azaleas, herbaceous. Picnic area. TEA. *Adm £2 OAPs/Chd 50p. Sun May 21 (2-6)*

¶23 Wroxham Way ✂❀ (Mrs M G M Easter) Harpenden. NE Harpenden off Ox Lane. M1 Junction 6 + A1081 or Junction 10a + A1081. A1 Junction 4 or 5 and B653 Lower Luton Road. Plantsman's garden 70′ × 35′ backing on to mini nature reserve. Sloping site with steps and walls. Large mixed border at front. Planted for yr round interest, especially galanthus, crocus, pulmonaria, helleborus, dianthus, diascia, penstemon, thymus. Alpine scree and camomile lawn. Herbs. *Adm £1 Chd £1 (Share to Gt Ormond St Children's Hospital®). Open selected Thurs, Sats and Suns Feb to Sept by appt only (2-5.30). Please* **Tel 01582 768467**

Humberside

Hon County Organiser: Peter Carver Esq., The Croft, North Cave, East Yorkshire HU15 2NG
Tel 01430 422203

DATES OF OPENING

By appointment

For telephone numbers and other details see garden descriptions. Private visits welcomed

The Chimney Place, Bilton Grange
The Croft, North Cave
Evergreens, 119 Main Road
Grange Cottage, Cadney
54a Keldgate, Beverley
Lanhydrock Cottage, Skerne
Saltmarshe Hall, Saltmarshe
8 Welton Old Road, Welton

Parties only

The Cottages, Barrow-Haven, nr Barton
Houlton Lodge, Goxhill
Laburnum Cottage, Cadney
5 Lockington Road, Lund
The Old Rectory, Nunburnholme
The White Cottage, Halsham

Regular opening

For details see garden descriptions

Burton Agnes Hall, Driffied. April 1 to Oct 31

April 16 Sunday
The Croft, North Cave

April 17 Monday
Castle Farm, Nurseries, Barmby Moor

Croft House, Ulceby

May 7 Sunday
Evergreens, 119 Main Road ‡
Il Giardino, Bilton ‡

May 8 Monday
The White Cottage, Halsham

May 17 Wednesday
The Chimney Place, Bilton Grange

May 20 Saturday
The Chimney Place, Bilton Grange

May 21 Sunday
8 Welton Old Road, Welton

May 28 Sunday
Castle Farm Nurseries, Barmby Moor
The Cottages, Barrow-Haven, nr Barton
High Farm, Bilton ‡
Il Giardino, Bilton ‡
The Old Rectory, Nunburnholme

May 29 Monday
The Cottages, Barrow-Haven, nr Barton

June 10 Saturday
Burton Agnes Hall, Driffield, Gardener's Fair

June 11 Sunday
Burton Agnes Hall, Driffield, Gardener's Fair
The Cottages, Barrow-Haven, nr Barton
Houlton Lodge, Goxhill
Saltmarshe Hall, Saltmarshe

June 14 Wednesday
The Chimney Place, Bilton Grange

June 17 Saturday
The Chimney Place, Bilton Grange

June 18 Sunday
54a Keldgate, Beverley
Lullaby, Hull
The White Cottage, Halsham

June 24 Saturday
Wincroft, Swanland

June 25 Sunday
Grange Cottage, Cadney ‡
The Green, Lund ‡‡
Laburnum Cottage, Cadney ‡
5 Lockington Road, Lund ‡‡

July 2 Sunday
Evergreens, 119 Main Road ‡
High Farm, Bilton ‡
Il Giardino, Bilton ‡
Lullaby, Hull ‡

July 9 Sunday
Boynton Hall, Bridlington
The Cottages, Barrow-Haven, nr Barton
The Croft, North Cave

July 12 Wednesday
The Chimney Place, Bilton Grange

July 15 Saturday
The Chimney Place, Bilton Grange

July 16 Sunday
Houlton Lodge, Goxhill
Wincroft, Swanland

August 27 Sunday
The Cottages, Barrow-Haven, nr Barton

August 28 Monday
The Cottages, Barrow-Haven, nr Barton

September 10 Sunday
Evergreens, 119 Main Road
The White Cottage, Halsham

DESCRIPTIONS OF GARDENS

Boynton Hall ♿❀ (Mr & Mrs R Marriott) Bridlington. On B1253 2m W of Bridlington S from Boynton Xroads. Lawn and yew hedge around Elizabethan house and lovely old walled garden with shrubs and roses; also gate house and knot garden (recently created). House Tour and TEAS in aid of church. *Adm £1.50 Chd £1. Sun July 9 (1.30-5)*

Burton Agnes Hall ♿❀ (Mr & Mrs N Cunliffe-Lister) nr Driffield. Burton Agnes is on A166 between Driffield & Bridlington. 8 acres of gardens incl lawns with clipped yew and fountains, woodland gardens and a walled garden containing a potager, herbaceous and mixed borders; maze with a thyme garden; jungle garden; campanula collection garden and coloured gardens containing giant games boards also collections of hardy geraniums, clematis, penstemons and many unusual perennials. 'Gardeners Fair' Adm £2.30 Chd £1 Sat, Sun June 10, 11; specialist nurseries; gardening advice; dried flower & herb craft. TEAS. *Adm £1.80 Chd 80p. April 1 to Oct 31 (11-5)*

Castle Farm Nurseries ♿✲❀ (Mr & Mrs K Wilson) Barmby Moor. Turn off A1079 Hull/York rd, ¾m from Barmby Moor at Hewson & Robinson's Garage, towards Thornton; ½m on R is sign for nursery. 13yr-old garden of 1¼ acres created and maintained by owners; incl trees, mixed borders, herbaceous border, rock garden, rhododendrons and water garden; emphasis on heather and conifer beds. Nursery open. Cream TEAS in aid of local Methodist Church. *Adm £1 Chd free. Mon April 17; Sun May 28 (2-5.30)*

The Chimney Place, 23 Parthian Road ✲❀ (Mrs Paddy Forsberg) Bilton Grange. In E Hull take Holderness Rd, R into Marfleet Lane, Staveley Rd, L into Griffin Rd. Parthian Rd immed on R. A small secluded (hedged all round) 30yr-old established garden, designed by a keen flower arranger with the welfare of birds, butterflies and fish in mind. Several Victorian chimney pots act as containers for alpine and other non invasive plants. Situated in the heart of an urban housing estate it demonstrates what can be achieved in a very restricted area. Delightful. *Adm 75p Chd free. Wed, Sat May 17, 20; June 14, 17; July 12, 15 (1.30-4.30). Private visits welcome, please* **Tel 01482 783804**

The Cottages ✲❀ (Mr & Mrs E C Walsh) 4m due E of Barton-on-Humber, adjacent to Barrow-Haven Railway Station. Turn L 3m E of Barton. Variable shrub-lined walks adjacent to reed bed hides. Large range of trees, shrubs, perennials, insects, birds and butterflies abound. Organic vegetable garden, photographic hides. An all-the-year-round garden created in 11yrs on 1¼ acres, of a once derelict tile yard. Runner up in 'Birdwatching' Large Garden Competition in 1989. Large selection of plants for sale, hostas, lobelia etc. Partly suitable for wheelchairs. TEAS. *Adm £1 OAPs £1 Chd free. Suns, Mons May 28, 29; June 11, July 9, Aug 27, 28 (11-5). Also private visits for 40 and over welcome, please* **Tel 01469 531614**

The Croft ♿✲❀ (Mr & Mrs Peter Carver) North Cave. On B1230 (1½m from exit 38, M62). Entrance 100yds S War Memorial in village centre (towards South Cave). Celebrating their centenary this year. Stewardship by same family since Queen Victoria's reign pervades this large garden of much pleasure and permanence. Recent additions include jardin potager, yew hedging (1985) and 'Tapis Vert' statue garden (1991). Included in garden books; subject of press articles and featured on BBC TV with Geoffrey Smith 3 times and ITV with Susan Hampshire. Featured in NGS video 2. Private car parking. TEAS in aid of St John Ambulance. *Adm £1.50 Acc chd free. For NGS Suns April 16 (Easter), July 9 (2-5). Private visits welcome, please* **Tel 01430 422203**

Croft House ♿❀ (Mr & Mrs Peter Sandberg) Ulceby. At War Memorial turn into Front Street follow sign to Pitmoor Lane. 2 acres plantswoman's garden largely created and solely maintained by present owners. Mixed borders; bulbs; lawns, fine trees; hedging. Victorian vinery, many interesting plants. TEAS in aid of St Nicholas' Church, Ulceby. *Adm £1.50 Chd free. Mon April 17 (2-5)*

Evergreens ♿✂❀ (Phil & Brenda Brock) Bilton. 5m E of Hull. Leave city by A165. Exit B1238. Bungalow ¼m on L nearly opposite the Asda Store. Over 1 acre developed since 1984. Features incl mosaics and sundials; raised beds; rockeries and landscaped pond; Japanese garden; conifer, heather and mixed beds. Collection of potentillas and more than 150 dwarf conifers, many labelled. Photographs showing development of garden; small conifer/plant nursery open. Yorkshire recipe TEAS in aid of Family Conciliation Service. *Adm £1 Acc chd free. Suns May 7, July 2, Sept 10 (2-5). Private visits welcome May to Sept* **Tel 01482 811365**

● **Giardino** ♿✂❀ (Peter & Marian Fowler) Bilton. 5m E of Hull City Centre. Take A165 Hull to Bridlington Rd. Turn off; take B1238 to Bilton Village. Turn L opp. St Peter's Church. "Il Giardino" is at bottom of Limetree Lane on L. No. 63. Once neglected garden approx ⅓ acre redesigned and revived over last 7yrs by present owners. Features incl mixed borders and island beds stocked with many unusual plants, shrubs and trees. Attractive beech hedge, small allotment, herb garden, orchard of old apple trees; pear; plum; cherries; medlar and filberts; cedarwood greenhouse with many pelargoniums; fuchsias; grapevine; fig tree; meyer lemon and other less common plants. TEAS. *Adm 75p Chd free. Suns May 7, 28, July 2 (12-5)*

Grange Cottage ✂❀ (Mr & Mrs D Hoy) Cadney. 3m S of Brigg. In Brigg turn L into Elwes St; follow rd to Cadney. From Market Rasen to Brigg Rd, turn L in Howsham on to Cadney Rd. ⅓-acre cottage garden; many unusual and old-fashioned plants; old roses; pond; orchard; conservatory with interesting tender plants. TEAS. *Adm £1 Chd free. Sun June 25 (1-5). Private visits also welcome May to July, please* **Tel 01652 678771**

The Green ♿✂❀ (Mr & Mrs Hugh Helm) Lund. 7m N of Beverley. Off B1248 Beverley Malton Rd. ¼-acre cottage garden; pool, rockery; climbing roses; shrubs; herbaceous plants, natural gravel garden. Established 10yrs in this delightful award winning "Britain in Bloom" village. Also open **5 Lockington Road.** *Adm £1 Chd free. Sun June 25 (2-5)*

¶**High Farm** ✂❀ (Mr & Mrs G R Cooper) Bilton. 5m E of Hull City Centre, take A165 Brid Rd, turn off at Ganstead Lane, onto B1238 to Bilton. Turn L opp Church. High Farm is at the bottom of Limetree Lane. Drive straight up the drive past the house, where parking is available in paddock. A mature garden of approx 1½ acres, harmoniously created and maintained by its present owners around a Georgian farmhouse. Many trees, shrubs, old species and climbing roses, herbaceous plants, as well as the thriving traditional kitchen garden. Flower arrangers will find much to interest them in the many unusual and rare plants to be found in the numerous beds and borders. TEAS. *Adm £1.50 Chd free. Suns May 28, July 2 (2-6)*

Houlton Lodge ♿✂❀ (Mr & Mrs M Dearden) Goxhill. 6m E of Barton-on-Humber. Follow signs to Goxhill, do not go into village centre but straight on over railway bridge and take 5th turning on R. Houlton Lodge is about 100yds from junction on LH-side. Park cars outside property. A well established very neat garden approx ¾ acre. Shrub rose and mixed borders; large island bed and rockery and conifer bed. TEAS in aid of Goxhill Methodist Church. *Adm £1 Chd free. Suns June 11, July 16 (2-6). Private parties of 10 and over, please* **Tel 01469 531355**

¶**54a Keldgate** ♿✂ (Lenore & Peter Greensides) Beverley. Half-way between the double mini roundabout at SW entrance to Beverley on the B1230 and Beverley Minster. No private parking. ½-acre 'secret' garden within the charming town of Beverley. Largely created and solely maintained by the present owners over the last 17yrs. Clematis in variety, herbaceous plantings and shrubs, an inner garden of old roses, underplanted with peonies and geraniums; a recently redesigned kitchen garden, fruit trees and irises. TEAS in aid of Shelter. *Adm £1 Chd free. Sun June 18 (2-5). Private visits welcome, please* **Tel 01482 866708**

Laburnum Cottage ♿✂ (Colin & Jessie Lynn) Cadney. 3m S of Brigg. In Brigg turn L into Elwes St, follow rd to Cadney. from Market Rasen to Brigg Rd turn L in Howsham on to Cadney Rd. 1-acre, herbaceous and mature shrub borders; island beds; smaller separate gardens within the garden; rose covered walk leading to shrub roses; wild flowers and small orchard; wildlife and formal pond. TEAS in aid of Blue Cross Animal Hospital. *Adm £1 Chd free. Sun June 25 (1-5). Private parties of 10 and over welcome, please* **Tel 01652 678725**

Lanhydrock Cottage ✂❀ (Mrs Jan Joyce) Skerne. 3m SE Driffield; follow signs to Skerne. Delightful small cottage garden of much interest and love, old-fashioned roses, herbs, fragrant perennials and wild flowers etc. Light refreshments. *Adm £1 Chd free. Private visits welcome, please* **Tel 01377 253727**

5 Lockington Road ♿✂ (Miss E Stephenson) Lund. Lund is off B1248 Beverley-Malton Rd. Small walled garden converted from old fold yard on edge of village with old-fashioned roses and cottage garden plants. "Charmingly English". Also open **The Green.** *Adm £1 Chd free. Sun June 25 (2-5). Private parties of 10 and over welcome, please* **Tel 01377 217284**

¶**Lullaby** ✂❀ (Michael Whitton) Hull. From the A165 (Holderness Rd), travel along Saltshouse Rd towards Sutton Village. Turn R into Dunvegan Rd, R into Barra Close and R again, no 22 on L. Created by the owners from a building site, this compact 40′ × 60′ garden has developed over the last 6yrs into a peaceful retreat welcoming fox, squirrel, butterflies, frogs and a large variety of birds among its visitors. A curving lawn leads the eye from a paved terrace, around herbaceous borders and an island bed and incl a pergola and a summerhouse. Development continues with a small courtyard garden and a water feature. TEA. *Adm 75p Chd free. Suns June 18, July 2 (2-5)*

The Old Rectory ♿✲ (Martin & Jean Stringer) Nunburnholme. A1079 Hull-York rd, turn to Nunburnholme in Hayton and follow signposts. Owner maintained, large garden for chalk loving plants, with stream and herbaceous borders blending into surrounding countryside. Field parking. TEAS. *Adm £1 Chd free. Sun May 28 (1.30-5.30). Private parties welcome May to Aug, please* **Tel 01759 302295**

Saltmarshe Hall ♿✲❀ (Mr & Mrs Philip Bean) Howden. N bank of R Ouse, Approx 3½m E of Howden. Follow signs to Laxton through Howdendyke and then signs to Saltmarshe. House in park west of Saltmarshe village. Approx 10 acres beautifully situated on the banks of the R Ouse. Fine old trees, woodland, walled garden and courtyards. Recent planting includes herbaceous borders and old roses. TEAS in aid of Laxton Church. *Adm £1.50 Chd free. Sun June 11 (2-5.30). Private visits welcome, please* **Tel 01430 430199**

8 Welton Old Road ❀ (Dr & Mrs O G Jones) Welton. In village of Welton 10m W of Hull off A63. Coming E turn L to village past church, turn R along Parliament St. and up hill. House 50yds on R opp Temple Close. From E take A63 and turn off at flyover to Brough; turn R for Welton and follow above instructions. Roadside parking in village. Informal 1-acre garden developed by owners over 30yrs. Imaginative planting with unusual shrubs, plants and less common trees; natural pond and lily pond. TEAS in aid of Leukaemia Research. *Adm £1 Chd free. Sun May 21 (2-5). Private visits welcome May to July* **Tel 01482 667488**

The White Cottage ✲❀ (Mr & Mrs John Oldham) Halsham. 1m E of Halsham Arms on B1362, Concealed wooded entrance on R. Parking available in grounds. The garden was created by its owners 25yrs ago and is surrounded by open countryside. Delightful specialised and unusual planting in island beds. Natural pond; vegetable and herb garden; architect designed sunken conservatory. Recently erected traditional pergola. Featured with Geoffrey Smith on BBC2 in 1992. Teas at Halsham Church. *Adm £1.50 Chd free (Share to Dove House Hospice, Hull®). Mons May 8, Suns June 18, Sept 10 (2-5). Parties welcome, please* **Tel 01964 612296**

¶Wincroft ♿✲ (Mrs Mary Good) Swanland. From Humber Bridge N roundabout take A164 N to Beverley. After 1m turn L into Tranby Lane and proceed to 'Garden Open' signs on L. Park on roadside. Formal garden approx 1¼ acres laid out in and around attractive balustrading formerly at Swanland Manor. Long herbaceous border with good 'plant association' leads the eye towards views of the Humber estuary and beyond. Plants & TEAS in aid of Christ Church, Swanland, June 24 only. *Adm £1 Chd free. Sat June 24, Sun July 16 (2-5)*

Isle of Wight

Hon County Organiser: Mrs John Harrison, North Court, Shorwell I.O.W. PO30 3JG
Hon County Treasurer: Mrs S Robak, Little Mead, Everard Close, Freshwater Bay, I.O.W. PO40 9PT

DATES OF OPENING

By appointment
For telephone numbers and other details see garden descriptions. Private visits welcomed

Blackwater Mill, Newport
Fountain Cottage, Bonchurch, nr Ventnor
Highwood, Cranmore Gardens, Cranmore
North Court Gardens, Shorwell
Owl Cottage, Mottistone
Rock Cottage, Blackwater
Westport Cottage, Yarmouth
Yaffles, Bonchurch

Parties only
Nunwell House, Brading

April 16 Sunday
Kings Manor, Freshwater

April 23 Sunday
Woolverton House, St Lawrence

May 7 Sunday
Yaffles, Bonchurch

May 10 Wednesday
North Court Gardens, Shorwell

May 14 Sunday
Brook Edge, Binstead

May 21 Sunday
North Court Gardens, Shorwell

May 24 Wednesday
North Court Gardens, Shorwell

May 28 Sunday
Blackwater Mill, Newport ‡
Rock Cottage ‡

May 29 Monday
The Watch House, Bembridge

May 31 Wednesday
North Court Gardens, Shorwell

June 4 Sunday
Badminton, Clatterford Shute, Carisbrooke ‡
Charlestown, 25 Fieldfare Rd, Carisbrooke ‡

June 7 Wednesday
Mottistone Manor Garden, Mottistone ‡
North Court Gardens, Shorwell ‡

June 11 Sunday
Colwell Cottage, Freshwater ‡
Kirknewton House, Totland Bay ‡
Meadowside, Freshwater ‡

June 18 Sunday
Nunwell House, Brading

June 25 Sunday
The Six Gardens of Cranmore, Cranmore

July 2 Sunday
Pitt House, Bembridge

July 9 Sunday
Waldeck, Brighstone

July 16 Sunday
Cassies, Billingham

DESCRIPTIONS OF GARDENS

¶**Badminton** ❀ (Mr & Mrs G S Montrose) Clatterford Shute. Parking in Carisbrooke Castle car park. Public footpath in corner of car park leads down to the garden. ¾-acre garden with natural chalk stream. Mixed borders planted by owners during last 20 yrs, for all-yr interest. Lovely views. *Adm 75p Chd 25p. Sun June 4 (2.30-5)*

Blackwater Mill ♿✂❀ (Mrs Jacque Humphreys) Newport. Take the main Sandown rd from Newport, turn R at the junction to Blackwater. Pass the garage on your L and the garden open is approx 200yds on the R by the bus stop. Look for the Blackwater Mill Retirement Home sign. Garden set in 6 acres incl 2-acre lake with waterfowl; river walk and bridges; lge selection of shrubs; herbaceous, grasses, trees, conifers and heathers; scree bed, spring bulbs and many unusual plants. Easy walks around. TEA. *Combined adm with* **Rock Cottage** *£1.50 Chd free. Sun May 28 (2.30-5). Private visits by appt, please* **Tel 01983 526208**

Brook Edge ✂ (Dr & Mrs Philip Goodwin) Binstead, at the bottom of Binstead Hill to Ryde rd. Parking available at factory car-park. 2½ acres of undulating garden on edge of old quarry with 2 streams flowing through. Fine woodland trees, waterside plants and shrubs. TEAS. *Adm £1 Chd 20p. Sun May 14 (2.30-5)*

¶**Cassies** ❀ (Barbara Smith) Billingham. Between Chillerton and Chale Green on the Newport Rd. From Newport bottom of Berryshute on L side. 2 fields from Billingham Manor. An organic cottage garden still developing on site of old sandpit. Approx 1 acre, borders, shrubs and herbaceous; ponds. Cliff walk through wild garden. Vegetable garden with raised beds. TEAS. *Adm £1.50 Chd free (Share to Peter Smith Wavenden Student Award©). Sun July 16 (2-6)*

¶**Charlestown** ✂ (Mr & Mrs D Trevan) 23 Fieldfare Rd, Carisbrooke. From Newport take the R turn into Gunville Rd at the mini roundabout by the Waverley Inn, then turn R at Argos and MFI. This leads into Fieldfare Rd. Charlestown at the junction of Kingfisher Close. Small, suburban, new corner plot gardens with unusual shrubs, climbers and pond. *Adm 75p Chd 25p (Share to Isle of Wight Branch of NCCPG®). Sun June 4 (2.30-5)*

¶**Colwell Cottage** ♿ (Mr & Mrs Roger Pyrah) Freshwater. Coming on main rd from Yarmouth to Totland, last driveway on L after Colwell Bay Inn and immed before Colwell Lane. A charming cottage garden featuring ponds and small artificial stream, informally planted with a wide variety of perennials and shrubs overlooking Colwell Common. Small patio garden. TEAS at Kirknewton House. *Combined adm £1.50 Chd 20p with* **Kirknewton House**. *Sun June 11 (2.30-5)*

The Six Gardens of Cranmore ♿✂❀ Cranmore Ave is approx halfway between the town of Yarmouth and the village of Shalfleet on the A3054. From Yarmouth the turning is on the L hand side, opp a bus shelter approx 3m out of Yarmouth on an unmade rd. TEAS at Cranmore Farm Cottage. *Combined adm £1.50 Chd 50p. Sun June 25 (2-6)*

Cranmore Lodge (Mr & Mrs W Dicken). This is a garden in the making. Approx 1 acre with perennials, shrub roses and climbers. A small pond and woodland area

¶**Enborne** A garden of approx 1 acre divided by shrubs, trees and flowers. Woodland area and ponds

Freshfields (Mr & Mrs O Butchers) Approx 1-acre garden, patio, pond with marginal planting, raised bed and an interesting display of fuschias and a wild garden

Funakoshi (Mr & Mrs D Self) A 1-acre garden divided by an aviary, patio, greenhouses and tunnels into areas of shrubs, perennials, climbers and conifers

Halcyon A smaller garden consisting of a conservatory of unusual plants and colourful shrubs and perennials

Highwood ❀ (Mr & Mrs Cooper) 10-acre site with approx 4 acres under cultivation; woodland area, pond with marginal planting with many unusual trees, shrubs and perennials. *Private visits welcome March to Oct, please* **Tel 01983 760 550**

Fountain Cottage ✂ (Mr & Mrs P I Dodds) Bonchurch. Approx ½m E from central Ventnor at junction of Bonchurch Village Rd, Trinity Rd and St Boniface Rd. Reasonable parking in these rds and on forecourt of garage/ stable opposite. Originally a gardener's cottage with approx 2 acres formerly part of a country estate landscaped in the 1830's with ponds, stream, waterfalls and fountains being a feature. S facing slope, partly wooded and terraced. Really a spring garden but with hydrangea and roses providing colour later in the year. Light refreshments if required. *Adm £1 Chd free. Private visits welcome April to end Aug, please* **Tel 01983 852 435**

¶**Kings Manor** ♿✂ (Mrs Jamie Sheldon) Freshwater. Head E out of Yarmouth over R Yar Bridge. Approx 1m turn L at top of Pixleys Hill. Entrance on L at top of next hill. 3-acre informal garden with shrubs and spring bulbs and frontage onto marshes. Special features - views of estuary and saltings - formal garden around lily pond. TEAS. *Adm £1.50 Chd free. Sun April 16 (2.30-5)*

¶**Kirknewton House** ♿✂❀ (Mrs Sarah Willetts) Totland Bay. Heading towards Totland after the Hurst View Point roundabout take the 3rd turning on L into Kendal Rd. Garden opp the top of Kendal Rd. Parking along Uplands Rd (unmade rd) or car park just off Totland Broadway. Varied 1-acre garden on E facing slope overlooking the Downs. Planted largely in the last few yrs with hardy perennials and shrubs. Dried flowers a speciality. TEAS. *Combined adm £1.50 Chd 20p with* **Colwell Cottage**. *Sun June 11 (2.30-5)*

¶**Meadowside** ♿✂❀ (Dr & Mrs G Walker) Freshwater. Entering Afton Rd from Freshwater Bay 50yds past Afton Farm Shop on L. ½ acre SW facing garden with mature trees. Planted in past 5 yrs with shrubs. Next to local nature reserve. *Adm £1 Chd 20p. Sun June 11 (2.30-5)*

By Appointment Gardens. Avoid the crowds. Good chance of a tour by owner. See garden description for telephone number.

Mottistone Manor Garden ❀ (The National Trust) Mottistone. 8m SW Newport on B3399 between Brighstone and Brook. Medium-sized formal terraced garden, backing onto mediaeval and Elizabethan manor house, set in wooded valley with fine views of English Channel and coast between Needles and St. Catherine's Point. *Adm £1.80 Chd 90p. Wed June 7 (2-5.30)*

North Court Gardens ♿✲❀ (Mrs C D Harrison, Mr & Mrs J Harrison, Mr & Mrs L Harrison) Shorwell 4m S of Newport on B3323, entrance on R after rustic bridge, opp thatched cottage. 14 acres; 3 varied gardens consisting of landscaped terraces, stream and water garden, woodland, walled rose garden, herbaceous borders, shrubs surrounding Jacobean Manor House (part open). TEAS. *Combined adm £1.50 Chd 20p. Sun May 21 (2.30-5). Weds May 10, 24, 31; June 7, 14 (4-5.30)*

Nunwell House ✲❀ (Col & Mrs J A Aylmer) Brading. 3m S of Ryde; signed off A3055 in Brading into Coach Lane. 5 acres beautifully set formal and shrub gardens with fountains. Exceptional view of Solent. House developed over 5 centuries, full of architectural interest. Coaches by appt only. TEAS. *Adm £1.50 Chd 20p incl Home Guard Museum; House £1.30 Chd 40p extra (Share to The Prince's Trusts Isle of Wight Appeal®). Sun June 18 (2-5)*

Owl Cottage ♿❀ (Mrs A L Hutchinson) Hoxall Lane, Mottistone. 9m SW of Newport, from B3399 at Mottistone turn down Hoxall Lane for 200yds. Interesting cottage garden, view of sea. Home-made TEAS. Plant sale. *Adm £1.50 Chd 20p. Visits by appointment only May, June, July, Aug, parties of 10 up to 30 (2.30-5.30)* **Tel 01983 740433** *after 6pm*

Pitt House ♿✲ (L J Martin Esq) Bembridge. NE of Bembridge Harbour. Enter Bembridge Village, pass museum and take 1st L into Love Lane. Continue down lane (5 min walk) as far as the bend; Pitt House is on L. Enter tall wrought iron gates. If coming by car enter Ducie Ave 1st L before museum. Pitt House at bottom of ave, on the R. Parking in lane. Approx 4 acres with varied aspects and points of interest. A number of sculptures dotted around the garden; also victorian greenhouse, mini waterfall and 4 ponds. *Adm £1.20 Chd 50p. Sun July 2 (10.30-5)*

Rock Cottage ✲ (Mary & Cliff Pain) Blackwater. From Newport take main rd to Ventnor. Park in Blackwater on/off main rd **but not** in Sandy Lane. Short walk, approx 200yds, up Sandy Lane to Rock Cottage. ⅓-acre. Cottage garden. Some flowering shrubs, spring bulbs, numerous clematis and hardy perennials; fruit and vegetables. Lawn and numerous small plots divided by grass paths. Tea at Blackwater Mill. *Combined adm with* **Blackwater Mill** *£1.50 Chd free. Sun May 28 (2.30-5). Also private visits by appt for max 10, please* **Tel 01983 525845**

Waldeck ✲ (Mr & Mrs G R Williams) Brighstone. 8m SW of Newport. Take Carisbrooke-Shorwell rd, then B3399 to Brighstone. Through village centre, turn R off main rd into Moor Lane. Limited parking in lane. ¾-acre garden informally planted to provide some colour and interest from trees, shrubs and perennial plants throughout the year. Special emphasis placed on foliage and shade tolerant plants such as acers, ferns, hostas, etc. Teas available. *Adm £1 Chd free (Share to Society for the Blind®). Sun July 9 (2.30-5.30)*

The Watch House ✲ (Sir William Mallinson) Bembridge. Most easterly part of I of W. St Helens-Bembridge. Before ascending hill by Pilot Inn turn L to Silver Beach Cafe. Last house on R. ¾-acre garden best known for its garden architecture and sea views (house built for the Admiralty). Formal garden at rear of house with fruit trees, rose arches and box hedges. *Adm £1 Chd 20p (Share to Bembridge Lifeboat®). Mon May 29 (2-5)*

Westport Cottage ♿❀ (M Fisher & K Sharp) Situated 100yds up Tennyson Close off Tennyson Rd, entrance to R of field gate into gravelled yard. ½-acre garden to S behind red rat trap walls, divided into quarters. One formal with small pond fountains and aquatics, trees and shrubs. An orchard quarter with apples, pears and nuts, with shrub borders. A working vegetable quarter for the owners and guests use. Also the swimming pool and patio area with shrubs and greenhouse. Semi-hardy and unusual plants grown. Plants and cuttings for sale. *Adm £1 Chd 20p. Private visits welcome, please* **Tel 01983 760751**

Woolverton House (Mr & Mrs S H G Twining) St Lawrence. 3m W of Ventnor; Bus 16 from Ryde, Sandown, Shanklin. Flowering shrubs, bulbs, fine position. Home-made TEAS. *Adm £1.50 Chd 20p (Share to St Lawrence Village Hall®). Sun April 23 (2-5)*

Yaffles ❀ (Mrs Wolfenden) The Pitts. The garden may be approached through Bonchurch Village, up the hill past the parish church 1st on L or from the top rd (Shanklin 2m to the E) turn L down the Bonchurch Shute, garden is immediately above St Boniface Church and next to the cul de sac The Pitts. Park in the rd. A 60′ flowering cliff sculptured into glades; it is full of interesting plants and commands excellent views of the Channel. Only suitable for wheelchairs on the top level where the teas and toilet are situated. Joan Wolfenden's book the Year from Yaffles is sold in aid of the NGS. Coffee and TEAS in aid of church. *Adm £1.50 Chd free. Open all year. For NGS May 7 (3-5.30). Private visits welcome. Parties of 10 or more preferred. Please* **Tel 01983 852193** *after 12 noon*

Kent

Hon County Organiser: Mrs Valentine Fleming, Stonewall Park, Edenbridge TN8 7DG
Assistant Hon County Organisers: Mrs Jeremy Gibbs, Upper Kennards, Leigh, Tonbridge TN11 8RE
Mrs Nicolas Irwin, Hoo Farmhouse, Minster, Ramsgate CT12 4JB
Mrs Richard Latham, Stowting Hill House, nr Ashford TN25 6BE
Miss E Napier, 447 Wateringbury Road, East Malling ME19 6JQ
Mrs M R Streatfeild, Hoath House, Chiddingstone Hoath, Edenbridge TN8 7DB
Mrs Simon Toynbee, Old Tong Farm, Brenchley TN12 7HT
Hon County Treasurer: Valentine Fleming Esq, Stonewall Park, Edenbridge TN8 7DG

DATES OF OPENING

By appointment only
For telephone number and other details see garden descriptions. Private visits welcomed

Cares Cross, Chiddingstone Hoath
Everden Farmhouse, Alkham, nr Dover
Flint Cottage, Bourne Park, Bishopsbourne
Greenways, Berry's Green, nr Downe
115 Hadlow Road, Tonbridge
43 Layhams Road, West Wickham
The Old Parsonage, Sutton Valence
The Pear House, Sellindge
Saltwood Castle, nr Hythe

Regular openings
For details see garden descriptions

Cobham Hall, Cobham
Doddington Hall, nr Sittingbourne
Finchcocks, Goudhurst
Geddesden, Rolvenden Layne
Goodnestone Park, Wingham, nr Canterbury
Great Comp, Borough Green
Groombridge Place, Groombridge
Hault Farm, Waltham, nr Canterbury
Hever Castle, nr Edenbridge
Marle Place, Brenchley
Mount Ephraim, Hernhill, Canterbury
Owl House, Lamberhurst
Penshurst Place, Penshurst
The Pines Garden and Bay Museum, St Margaret's Bay
Riverhill House, Sevenoaks
Squerryes Court, Westerham
Woodlands Manor, Adisham

February 12 Sunday
Goodnestone Park, Wingham, nr Canterbury ‡
Woodlands Manor, Adisham ‡

March 5 Sunday
Great Comp, Borough Green

March 12 Sunday
Great Comp, Borough Green
Weeks Farm, Egerton Forstal

March 19 Sunday
Goodnestone Park, Wingham, nr Canterbury ‡
Woodlands Manor, Adisham ‡

March 26 Sunday
Church Hill Cottage, Charing Heath
Copton Ash, Faversham
Tanners, Brasted
Woodlands Manor, Adisham

April 2 Sunday
Church Hill Cottage, Charing Heath
Coldham, Little Chart Forstal
Crittenden House, Matfield
Woodlands Manor, Adisham

April 7 Friday
Haydown, Great Buckland, nr Cobham

April 8 Saturday
Sissinghurst Place, Sissinghurst

April 9 Sunday
Church Hill Cottage, Charing Heath ‡
Cobham Hall, Cobham
Godmersham Park, nr Ashford
Hole Park, Rolvenden
Luton House, Selling
190 Maidstone Road, Chatham ‡‡
Mere House, Mereworth ‡‡‡
Parsonage Oasts, Yalding ‡‡‡
Sissinghurst Place, Sissinghurst
Spilsill Court, Staplehurst
2 Thorndale Close, Chatham ‡‡
39 Warwick Crescent, Borstal ‡‡
Weeks Farm, Egerton Forstal ‡

April 10 Monday
Sissinghurst Place, Sissinghurst

April 11 Tuesday
Groombridge Place, Groombridge

April 16 Easter Sunday
Church Hill Cottage, Charing Heath
Copton Ash, Faversham
Crittenden House, Matfield
Edenbridge House, Edenbridge
Godinton Park, Ashford
Hault Farm, Waltham, nr Canterbury
Hole Park, Rolvenden
Jessups, Mark Beech, nr Edenbridge
Ladham House, Goudhurst
Longacre, Selling
Pines Garden and Bay Museum, St Margaret's Bay
Street End Place, nr Canterbury
Withersdane Hall, Wye

April 17 Monday
Brewhouse, Boughton Aluph
Church Hill Cottage, Charing Heath
Copton Ash, Faversham
Crittenden House, Matfield
Longacre, Selling
Street End Place, nr Canterbury

April 22 Saturday
Pett Place, Charing

April 23 Sunday
Collingwood Grange, Benenden
Egypt Farm, nr Plaxtol ‡
Hamptons Farm, nr Plaxtol ‡
New Barns House, West Malling
Pett Place, Charing
Sea Close, Hythe
Stoneacre, Otham, Maidstone
2 Thorndale Close, Chatham ‡‡
Torry Hill, nr Sittingbourne
39 Warwick Cresent, Borstal, nr Rochester ‡‡
Woodlands Manor, Adisham

April 26 Wednesday
Hole Park, Rolvenden
Sissinghurst Garden, Sissinghurst
Stoneleigh House, Stone Street, nr Canterbury
Westview, Hempstead, Gillingham

April 28 Friday
Great Maytham, Rolvenden

April 29 Saturday
Westview, Hempstead, Gillingham

April 30 Sunday
Amber Green Farmhouse, Chart Sutton
Beech Court, Challock
Bradbourne House, East Malling

Church Hill Cottage, Charing Heath
Crittenden House, Matfield
Hole Park, Rolvenden
Longacre, Selling
Maurice House, Broadstairs
Mount Ephraim, Hernhill, Faversham
Owl House, Lamberhurst
Oxley House, nr Lenham
St Michael's House, Roydon, Peckham Bush
Swan Oast, Stilebridge, Marden
Turkey Court, Maidstone
Woodlands Manor, Adisham

May 3 Wednesday
Amber Green Farmhouse, Chart Sutton
Penshurst Place, Penshurst
Rock Farm, Nettlestead
Stoneleigh House, Stone Street, nr Canterbury

May 4 Thursday
Geddesden, Rolvenden Layne

May 6 Saturday
Peddars Wood, St Michaels, Tenterden
Riverhill House, Sevenoaks
Rock Farm, Nettlestead

May 7 Sunday
Beech Court, Challock
Charts Edge, Westerham
Church Hill Cottage, Charing Heath
Doddington Place, nr Sittingbourne
Edenbridge House, Edenbridge
Hole Park, Rolvenden
Ladham House, Goudhurst
Meadow Wood, Penshurst
Mere House, Mereworth
Stonewall Park, nr Edenbridge
Swan Oast, Stilebridge, Marden

May 8 Monday
Brewhouse, Boughton Aluph
Church Hill Cottage, Charing Heath
Longacre, Selling
Meadow Wood, Penshurst

May 10 Wednesday
Rock Farm, Nettlestead
Stoneleigh House, Stone Street, nr Canterbury

May 11 Thursday
Geddesden, Rolvenden Layne

May 13 Saturday
Emmetts Garden, Ide Hill
Rock Farm, Nettlestead

May 14 Sunday
Beech Court, Challock
Bilting House, Ashford
Charts Edge, Westerham
Copton Ash, Faversham
Crittenden House, Matfield
Doddington Place, nr Sittingbourne ‡
Greencroft, Hildenborough
Larksfield, Crockham Hill ‡‡
Larksfield Cottage, Crockham Hill ‡‡
Little Trafalgar, Selling ‡‡‡
Longacre, Selling ‡‡‡
The Red House, Crockham Hill ‡‡
Swan Oast, Stilebridge, Marden
2 Thorndale Close, Chatham ‡‡‡‡
Torry Hill, nr Sittingbourne
Updown Farm, Betteshanger
39 Warwick Crescent, Borstal ‡‡‡‡
Woodlands Manor, Adisham

May 17 Wednesday
Abbotsmerry Barn, Penshurst
Hault Farm, Waltham, nr Canterbury
Hole Park, Rolvenden
Rock Farm, Nettlestead
Stoneleigh House, Stone Street, nr Canterbury
Waystrode Manor, Cowden
Westview, Hempstead, Gillingham

May 18 Thursday
Geddesden, Rolvenden Layne

May 19 Friday
Haydown, Great Buckland, nr Cobham

May 20 Saturday
The Anchorage, West Wickham
Rock Farm, Nettlestead
Sissinghurst Place, Sissinghurst
Westview, Hempstead, Gillingham

May 21 Sunday
The Anchorage, West Wickham
Brenchley Gardens
Church Hill Cottage, Charing Heath
Doddington Place, nr Sittingbourne
Everden Farmhouse, Alkham, nr Dover
Finchcocks, Goudhurst
Goudhurst Gardens
Larksfield, Crockham Hill ‡
Larksfield Cottage, Crockham Hill ‡
Mill House, Hildenborough
Pevington Farm, Pluckley
Ramhurst Manor, Leigh, Tonbridge
The Red House, Crockham Hill ‡
St Michael's House, Roydon, Peckham Bush
Sea Close, Hythe
Sissinghurst Place, Sissinghurst
Town Hill Cottage, West Malling
Woodlands Manor, Adisham

May 24 Wednesday
Edenbridge House, Edenbridge
Rock Farm, Nettlestead
Stoneleigh House, Stone Street, nr Canterbury

May 25 Thursday
Geddesden, Rolvenden Layne

May 26 Friday
Kypp Cottage, Biddenden
Rosefarm, Chilham

May 27 Saturday
Kypp Cottage, Biddenden
Riverhill House, Sevenoaks
Rock Farm, Nettlestead
Rosefarm, Chilham

May 28 Sunday
Beech Court, Challock
The Beehive, Lydd ‡
Church Hill Cottage, Charing Heath
Crittenden House, Matfield
Flint Cottage, Bishopsbourne
Hole Park, Rolvenden
Kypp Cottage, Biddenden
Ladham House, Goudhurst
Little Trafalgar, Selling ‡‡
Longacre, Selling ‡‡
Marle Place, Brenchley
Olantigh, Wye
Oxon Hoath, nr Hadlow
Pines Garden and Bay Museum, St Margaret's Bay
29 The Precincts, Canterbury
Vine House, Lydd ‡
Walnut Tree Gardens, Little Chart
Waystrode Manor, Cowden
Woodlands Manor, Adisham

May 29 Monday
The Beehive, Lydd ‡
Brewhouse, Boughton Aluph
Church Hill Cottage, Charing Heath
Forest Gate, Pluckley ‡‡
Kypp Cottage, Biddenden
Little Trafalgar, Selling ‡‡‡
Longacre, Selling ‡‡‡
Mere House, Mereworth
29 The Precincts, Canterbury
Scotney Castle, Lamberhurst
The Silver Spray, Sellindge
Vine House, Lydd ‡
Walnut Tree Gardens, Little Chart ‡‡

May 30 Tuesday
Kypp Cottage, Biddenden

May 31 Wednesday
Belmont, Throwley, nr Faversham
Kypp Cottage, Biddenden
Rock Farm, Nettlestead
Stoneleigh House, Stone Street, nr Canterbury

June 1 Thursday
Geddesden, Rolvenden Layne

June 3 Saturday
Peddars Wood, St Michaels, Tenterden
29 The Precincts, Canterbury

Rock Farm, Nettlestead

June 4 Sunday
Abbotsmerry Barn, Penshurst
Congelow House, Yalding
Kypp Cottage, Biddenden
Northbourne Court, nr Deal
29 The Precincts, Canterbury
2 Thorndale Close, Chatham
Walnut Tree Gardens, Little Chart
Waystrode Manor, Cowden
Whitehill, Wrotham

June 5 Monday
Kypp Cottage, Biddenden

June 6 Tuesday
Ightham Mote, nr Sevenoaks
Kypp Cottage, Biddenden

June 7 Wednesday
Hole Park, Rolvenden
Knole, Sevenoaks
Kypp Cottage, Biddenden
Rock Farm, Nettlestead
Sissinghurst Garden, Sissinghurst
Stoneleigh House, Stone Street, nr Canterbury
Westview, Hempstead, Gillingham

June 8 Thursday
Geddesden, Rolvenden Layne
Lantern Cottage, Bitchett Green, nr Sevenoaks
Penshurst Place, Penshurst

June 10 Saturday
Lantern Cottage, Bitchett Green, nr Sevenoaks
29 The Precincts, Canterbury
Rock Farm, Nettlestead
Westview, Hempstead, Gillingham

June 11 Sunday
Horton Priory, Sellindge
Kypp Cottage, Biddenden
Little Trafalgar, Selling ‡
Longacre, Selling ‡
Lullingstone Castle, Eynsford
Nonington and Woodnesborough Gardens
Northbourne Court, nr Deal
29 The Precincts, Canterbury
Shipbourne Gardens
Updown Farm, Betteshanger
Walnut Tree Gardens, Little Chart
Whitehurst, Chainhurst, Marden
Woodlands Manor, Adisham

June 12 Monday
Kypp Cottage, Biddenden

June 13 Tuesday
Kypp Cottage, Biddenden

June 14 Wednesday
Kypp Cottage, Biddenden
Rock Farm, Nettlestead
Slip Mill, Hawkhurst
Stoneleigh House, Stone Street, nr Canterbury
Upper Pryors, Cowden

June 15 Thursday
Geddesden, Rolvenden Layne

June 17 Saturday
Downs Court, Boughton Aluph
The Old Parsonage, Sutton Valence
Rock Farm, Nettlestead
The Silver Spray, Sellindge

June 18 Sunday
The Anchorage, West Wickham
Battel Hall, Leeds, nr Maidstone
Downs Court, Boughton Aluph
Edenbridge House, Edenbridge
Egerton Gardens ‡
Everden Farmhouse, Alkham, nr Dover
Forest Gate, Pluckley ‡‡
Goudhurst Gardens
Groome Farm, Egerton ‡
Hartlip Gardens, nr Sittingbourne
Kypp Cottage, Biddenden
Long Barn, Weald, Sevenoaks
Northbourne Court, nr Deal
Old Place Farm, High Halden
Oxley House, nr Lenham
Pevington Farm, Pluckley ‡‡
St Michael's House, Roydon, Peckham Bush
Slip Mill, Hawkhurst
2 Thorndale Close, Chatham
Town Hill Cottage, West Malling ‡‡‡
Walnut Tree Gardens, Little Chart ‡‡
Went House, West Malling ‡‡‡

June 19 Monday
Kypp Cottage, Biddenden

June 20 Tuesday
Kypp Cottage, Biddenden
The Old Parsonage, Sutton Valence

June 21 Wednesday
Brewhouse, Boughton Aluph
Kypp Cottage, Biddenden
Rock Farm, Nettlestead
Stoneleigh House, Stone Street, nr Canterbury
Waystrode Manor, Cowden
Wyckhurst, Aldington

June 22 Thursday
Geddesden, Rolvenden Layne

June 23 Friday
The Old Parsonage, Sutton Valence

June 24 Saturday
Pett Place, Charing
Rock Farm, Nettlestead
Tanners, Brasted

June 25 Sunday
Kypp Cottage, Biddenden
Little Trafalgar, Selling ‡
Longacre, Selling ‡
Northbourne Court, nr Deal
Olantigh, Wye
The Old Parsonage, Sutton Valence
Pett Place, Charing
Placketts Hole, Bicknor, nr Sittingbourne
Plaxtol Gardens
Rogers Rough, Kilndown
Sibton Park, Lyminge
The Silver Spray, Sellindge
Smiths Hall, West Farleigh
Walnut Tree Gardens, Little Chart
Waystrode Manor, Cowden
Woodlands Manor, Adisham
Wyckhurst, Aldington

June 26 Monday
Kypp Cottage, Biddenden

June 27 Tuesday
Kypp Cottage, Biddenden

June 28 Wednesday
Kypp Cottage, Biddenden
Rock Farm, Nettlestead
Stoneleigh House, Stone Street, nr Canterbury

June 29 Thursday
Geddesden, Rolvenden Layne
Walnut Tree Gardens, Little Chart

June 30 Friday
Great Maytham Hall, Rolvenden

July 1 Saturday
Rock Farm, Nettlestead
Womenswold Gardens

July 2 Sunday
Kypp Cottage, Biddenden
Northbourne Court, nr Deal
St Clere, Kemsing
South Hill Farm, Hastingleigh
Swan Oast, Stilebridge, Marden
Torry Hill, nr Sittingbourne
Walnut Tree Gardens, Little Chart
Went House, West Malling
Whitehurst, Chainhurst, Marden
Womenswold Gardens
Worth Gardens

July 3 Monday
Kypp Cottage, Biddenden

July 4 Tuesday
Kypp Cottage, Biddenden

July 5 Wednesday
Chartwell, Westerham
Kypp Cottage, Biddenden
Rock Farm, Nettlestead
The Silver Spray, Sellindge

July 6 Thursday
Geddesden, Rolvenden Layne

July 8 Saturday
Peddars Wood, St Michaels, Tenterden
Rock Farm, Nettlestead
The Silver Spray, Sellindge

July 9 Sunday
Bilting House, Ashford
Field House, Staplehurst
Godinton Park, Ashford
Kypp Cottage, Biddenden
Ladham House, Goudhurst
Little Trafalgar, Selling ‡

Longacre, Selling ‡
Nettlestead Place, Nettlestead
Northbourne Court, nr Deal
2 Thorndale Close, Chatham
Walnut Tree Gardens, Little Chart
Withersdane Hall, Wye

July 10 Monday
Kypp Cottage, Biddenden

July 11 Tuesday
Kypp Cottage, Biddenden

July 12 Wednesday
Chiddingstone Hoath Gardens
Kypp Cottage, Biddenden
Rock Farm, Nettlestead
Sissinghurst Garden, Sissinghurst
Stoneleigh House, Stone Street, nr Canterbury

July 13 Thursday
Geddesden, Rolvenden Layne

July 15 Saturday
Haydown, Great Buckland, nr Cobham
Rock Farm, Nettlestead

July 16 Sunday
Edenbridge House, Edenbridge
Goodnestone Park, Wingham, nr Canterbury
115 Hadlow Road, Tonbridge
Kypp Cottage, Biddenden
Northbourne Court, nr Deal
Owl House, Lamberhurst
Ringfield, Knockholt
Squerryes Court, Westerham
Swan Oast, Stilebridge, Marden
Walnut Tree Gardens, Little Chart
Woodlands Manor, Adisham

July 17 Monday
Kypp Cottage, Biddenden

July 18 Tuesday
Kypp Cottage, Biddenden

July 19 Wednesday
185 Borden Lane, Sittingbourne
Kypp Cottage, Biddenden
Rock Farm, Nettlestead
The Silver Spray, Sellindge

July 20 Thursday
Geddesden, Rolvenden Layne

July 22 Saturday
Rock Farm, Nettlestead
The Silver Spray, Sellindge

July 23 Sunday
Coldham, Little Chart Forstal
Everden Farmhouse, Alkham, nr Dover
Little Trafalgar, Selling ‡
Long Barn, Weald, Sevenoaks
Longacre, Selling ‡
190 Maidstone, Chatham ‡‡
Northbourne Court, nr Deal
Rogers Rough, Kilndown
Sea Close, Hythe
Spilsill Court, Staplehurst
2 Thorndale Close, Chatham ‡‡
Thornham Friars, Thurnham
Walnut Tree Gardens, Little Chart

July 26 Wednesday
Rock Farm, Nettlestead
Stoneleigh House, Stone Street, nr Canterbury

July 27 Thursday
Geddesden, Rolvenden Layne

July 29 Saturday
Rock Farm, Nettlestead

July 30 Sunday
185 Borden Lane, Sittingbourne
Copton Ash, Faversham
Northbourne Court, nr Deal
Swan Oast, Stilebridge, Marden
Turkey Court, Maidstone
Walnut Tree Gardens, Little Chart

August 2 Wednesday
185 Borden Lane, Sittingbourne
Knole, Sevenoaks

August 3 Thursday
Geddesden, Rolvenden Layne

August 5 Saturday
Peddars Wood, St Michaels, Tenterden

August 6 Sunday
Chevening, Sevenoaks
Field House, Staplehurst
Little Trafalgar, Selling
Marle Place, Brenchley
Northbourne Court, nr Deal
Orchard Cottage, Bickley, Bromley
Walnut Tree Gardens, Little Chart
Withersdane Hall, Wye

August 9 Wednesday
Stoneleigh House, Stone Street, nr Canterbury

August 10 Thursday
Geddesden, Rolvenden Layne

August 13 Sunday
Church Hill Cottage, Charing Heath
Northbourne Court, nr Deal
Swan Oast, Stilebridge, Marden
Walnut Tree Gardens, Little Chart

August 17 Thursday
Geddesden, Rolvenden Layne

August 20 Sunday
Church Hill Cottage, Charing Heath
Cobham Hall, Cobham
Coldharbour Oast, Tenterden
Finchcocks, Goudhurst
Goodnestone Park, Wingham, nr Canterbury
Northbourne Court, nr Deal
Squerryes Court, Westerham
West Studdal Farm, nr Dover

August 23 Wednesday
The Silver Spray, Sellindge

August 24 Thursday
Geddesden, Rolvenden Layne

August 25 Friday
Rosefarm, Chilham

August 26 Saturday
Rosefarm, Chilham

August 27 Sunday
The Beehive, Lydd ‡
Church Hill Cottage, Charing Heath
Copton Ash, Faversham
115 Hadlow Road, Tonbridge
Little Trafalgar, Selling ‡‡
Longacre, Selling ‡‡
Northbourne Court, nr Deal
Oswalds, Bishopsbourne
Pines Garden & Bay Museum, St Margaret's Bay
Sea Close, Hythe
Swan Court, Stilebridge, Marden
Vine House, Lydd ‡

August 28 Monday
The Beehive, Lydd ‡
Church Hill Cottage, Charing Heath
Copton Ash, Faversham
Little Trafalgar, Selling ‡‡
Longacre, Selling ‡‡
Oswalds, Bishopsbourne
The Silver Spray, Sellindge
Vine House, Lydd ‡

August 31 Thursday
Geddesden, Rolvenden Layne

September 3 Sunday
185 Borden Lane, Sittingbourne
Oswalds, Bishopsbourne
Withersdane Hall, Wye

September 10 Sunday
Groome Farm, Egerton
Little Trafalgar, Selling ‡
Longacre, Selling ‡
Nettlestead Place, Nettlestead

September 17 Sunday
Oxley House, nr Lenham

September 24 Sunday
Hault Farm, Waltham, nr Canterbury
Horton Priory, Sellindge
Little Trafalgar, Selling
Mount Ephraim, Hernhill, Faversham
39 Warwick Crescent, Borstal
Weeks Farm, Egerton Forstal

September 27 Wednesday
Edenbridge House, Edenbridge

September 29 Friday
Great Maytham Hall, Rolvenden
Haydown, Great Buckland, nr Cobham

October 1 Sunday
Beech Court, Challock
Hole Park, Rolvenden
Owl House, Lamberhurst
Sea Close, Hythe
Whitehurst, Chainhurst, Marden

October 7 Saturday
Emmetts Garden, Ide Hill

October 8 Sunday
Beech Court, Challock
Everden House, Alkham, nr Dover
Hole Park, Rolvenden
Marle Place, Brenchley
Stoneacre, Otham, Maidstone
Whitehurst, Chainhurst, Marden

October 15 Sunday
Hole Park, Rolvenden

October 22 Sunday
Copton Ash, Faversham

October 29 Sunday
Tanners, Brasted

November 5 Sunday
Great Comp, Borough Green

DESCRIPTIONS OF GARDENS

¶Abbotsmerry Barn ✗ (Mr & Mrs K H Wallis) Salmans Lane, Penshurst. Between Penshurst and Leigh on B2176: 200yds N of Penshurst turn L, 1m down lane with speed ramps. 5-acre garden with widely varied planting on S-facing slope overlooking the Eden valley. Teas in Penshurst. *Adm £2 Acc chd free. Wed May 17; Sun June 4 (2-5.30)*

Amber Green Farmhouse ✗❀ (Mr & Mrs J Groves) Chart Sutton, 7m SE of Maidstone. Turn W off A274 onto B2163, in 1m turn L at Chart Corner, next R is Amber Lane, house ½m W. C17 listed weatherboarded farmhouse (not open) in 1-acre garden. Peaceful cottage garden with hardy perennials and old-fashioned roses, 2 old ponds and a small cob platt. *Adm £1 Acc chd free. Sun April 30; Wed May 3 (2–5.30)*

The Anchorage ✗❀ (Mr & Mrs G Francis) 8 Croydon Road, W Wickham. 4m SW of Bromley. 100yds from A232 and A2022 roundabout; enter from A232 opp Manor House public house, as rd is one way. ⅓-acre garden, lovingly created since 1988, inspired by Sissinghurst, comprising small compartments individually designed for colour within recently-planted hedges; old-fashioned roses, irises & large collection of unusual perennials; herb garden, walled garden, vegetables, trained fruit trees; conservation & wild-life area incl pond, woodland & meadow flowers. Featured on BBC Gardeners World 1993. TEAS. *Adm £1.50 Chd 25p (Share to Coney Hill School Appeal; Shaftesbury Society®). Suns May 21, June 18 (2-5.30)*

Battel Hall ♿✗ (John D Money Esq) Leeds, Maidstone. From A20 Hollingbourne roundabouts take B2163 S (signed Leeds Castle), at top of hill take Burberry Lane, house 100yds on R. Garden of approx 1 acre created since 1954 around medieval house; roses, herbaceous plants, shrubs and ancient wisteria. TEAS. *Adm £1.50 Chd £1 (Share to Macmillan Fund for Cancer Relief®). Sun June 18 (2-6)*

Beech Court ♿✗❀ (Mr & Mrs Vyvyan Harmsworth) Challock, 7m N of Ashford; entrance on A252, Challock being midway between Charing and Chilham. Informal woodland garden with a fine collection of acers, rhododendrons, azaleas, conifers and shrubs set in 7 acres. TEAS. *Adm £1.50 Chd 50p. Suns April 30, May 7, 14, 28, Oct 1, 8 (2-5.30); also private visitors and tours welcome, please* **Tel 01233 740641**

The Beehive ✗ (C G Brown Esq) 10 High Street, Lydd. S of New Romney on B2075, in centre of Lydd opp Church. Small walled garden, tucked behind village street house dating from 1550, with over 200 varieties of plants. There are paths and cosy corners in this cottage garden with pond and pergola; a pool of seclusion; the busy world outside unnoticed passes by. Teas usually available in the church. *Adm £1 Chd 50p (Share to Horder Centre for Arthritis, Crowborough®). Suns, Mons May 28, 29, Aug 27, 28 (2-5)*

Belmont ♿❀ (The Harris (Belmont) Charity) Throwley 4m SW of Faversham. Take A251 (Faversham-Ashford Rd), from Badlesmere follow brown tourist signs. Walled pleasure garden and orangery; small pinetum; long yew walk and folly; Victorian grotto; pets' cemetery. House by Samuel Wyatt c.1792. TEAS. ▲*Adm £2 Chd 75p (Share to St Michaels Church, Throwley©). Wed May 31 (2-5)*

Bilting House ♿✗ (John Erle-Drax Esq) A28, 5m NE of Ashford, 9m from Canterbury. Wye 1½m. Old-fashioned garden with ha-ha; rhododendrons, azaleas; shrubs. In beautiful part of Stour Valley. TEAS. *Adm £1.50 Chd 50p (Share to BRCS®). Suns May 14, July 9 (2-5.30)*

185 Borden Lane ♿✗❀ (Mr & Mrs P A Boyce) ½m S of Sittingbourne. 1m from Sittingbourne side of A2/A249 junction. Small informal garden with many varieties of fuchsia; hardy perennials; shrubs; pond; fruit, vegetable and herb garden. Home-made TEAS. *Adm £1 Acc chd free. Suns July 30, Sept 3; Weds July 19, Aug 2 (2-5.30); also private visits welcome, please* **Tel 01795 472243**

Bradbourne House Gardens ♿ (East Malling Trust for Horticultural Research & Horticulture Research International) East Malling, 4m W of Maidstone. Entrance is E of New Road, which runs from Larkfield on A20 S to E Malling. The Hatton Fruit Garden consists of demonstration fruit gardens of particular interest to amateurs, in a walled former kitchen garden and incl intensive forms of apples and pears. Members of staff available for questions. TEAS. *Adm Gardens £1.50; House £1 (to East Malling Church Restoration Appeal) Acc chd free. Sun April 30 (2-5)*

Brenchley Gardens 6m SE of Tonbridge. From A21 1m S of Pembury turn N on to B2160, turn R at Xrds in Matfield signed Brenchley. *Combined adm £2 Acc chd free. Sun May 21 (2-6)*

Holmbush ♿✗ (Brian & Cathy Worden Hodge) 1½-acre informal garden, mainly lawns, trees and shrub borders, planted since 1960

Portobello ✗ (Barry M Williams Esq) 1½ acres, lawn, trees, shrubs incl azaleas and shrub roses; walled garden. C17 barn containing 1936 Dennis fire engine in running order. House (not open) built by Monckton family 1739

Puxted House ♿❀ (P J Oliver-Smith Esq) 1½ acres with rare and coloured foliage shrubs, water and woodland plants. Alpine and rose garden all labelled. Present owner cleared 20yrs of brambles in 1981 before replanting. TEAS

Brewhouse ✂❀ (Mrs J A H Nicholson) Malthouse Lane, Boughton Aluph, 3m N of Ashford, off Pilgrims Way. ¼m N and signed from Boughton Lees village green, on A251 Ashford-Faversham. 1-acre plantsman's garden. C16 farmhouse (not open) with fine views of open chalkland. Collections of old roses, other old-fashioned flowers, herbaceous and foliage plants. TEAS (in aid of All Saints Church; not April 17, May 8). *Adm £1.50 Acc chd free. Mons April 17, May 8, 29; Wed June 21 (2-5.30) also by appt, please* **Tel 01233 623748**

Cares Cross ♿❀ (Mr & Mrs R L Wadsworth) Chiddingstone Hoath. [Ordnance Survey Grid ref. TQ 496 431.] Landscaped garden around C16 house (not open). Dramatic views to N Downs over fields with old oaks, restored hedgerows, wildfowl lake and vineyard. Garden features old roses; water garden; innovative ground cover; rare shrubs and trees; speciality American plants. Featured on BBC Gardeners World 1990. TEAS. *Adm £2.50 OAPs £2 Acc chd free. By appt to groups of 5-20, weekdays only May 15 to July 30; and under* **Chiddingstone Hoath Gardens** *on Wed July 12 (2-6)*

Charts Edge ♿ (Mr & Mrs John Bigwood) Westerham, ½m S of Westerham on B2026 towards Chartwell. 7-acre hillside garden being restored by present owners; large collection of rhododendrons, azaleas, acers & magnolias; specimen trees & newly-planted mixed borders; Victorian folly; walled vegetable garden; rock garden. Fine views over N Downs. Dressage display, if riders available, at 3.30pm. TEAS. *Adm £1.50 Chd 25p (Share to BHS Dressage Group©). Suns May 7, 14 (2-5)*

Chartwell (The National Trust) 2m S of Westerham, fork L off B2026 after 1½m, well signed. 12-acre informal gardens on a hillside with glorious views over Weald of Kent. Fishpools and lakes together with red-brick wall built by Sir Winston Churchill, the former owner of Chartwell. The avenue of golden roses given by the family on Sir Winston's golden wedding anniversary will be at its best. Self-service restaurant serving coffee, lunches and teas. *Adm £2 Chd £1. ▲Wed July 5 (11-4.30)*

Chevening ♿ (By permission of the Board of Trustees of Chevening Estate and the Rt Hon Douglas Hurd) 4m NW of Sevenoaks. Turn N off A25 at Sundridge traffic lights on to B2211; at Chevening Xrds 1½m turn L. 27 acres with lawns and woodland garden, lake, maze, formal rides, parterre. Garden being restored. TEAS in aid of Kent Church Social Work and overseas charities. *Adm £1.50 OAPs £1 Chd 50p. Sun Aug 6 (2-6)*

Chiddingstone Hoath Gardens 4m E of Edenbridge, via B2026, at Cowden Pound turn E to Mark Beech. Old Buckhurst is 1st house on R after leaving Mark Beech on Penshurst Rd. Maps will be provided. *Combined adm £2.50 OAPs £2 Acc chd free (Share to St Mary's Church®). Wed July 12 (2-5.30)*

Cares Cross ♿❀ (Mr & Mrs R L Wadsworth) For garden description, see individual entry

Old Buckhurst (Mr & Mrs J Gladstone) Chiddingstone Hoath Rd, Mark Beech. 1-acre garden surrounding C15 farmhouse (not open). Part walled ornamental & kitchen gardens designed & planted 1988 onwards. 'New English' shrub roses; range of clematis, shrubs & herbaceous plants. Parking in 1-acre paddock

Church Hill Cottage ♿✂❀ (Mr & Mrs Michael Metianu) Charing Heath, 10m NW of Ashford. Leave M20 at junction 8 (Lenham) if Folkestone-bound or junction 9 (Ashford West) if London-bound: then leave A20 dual carriageway ½m W of Charing signed Charing Heath and Egerton. After 1m fork R at Red Lion, then R again; cottage 250yds on R. C16 cottage surrounded by garden of 1½ acres, developed & planted by present owners since 1981. Several separate connected areas each containing island beds & borders planted with extensive range of perennials, shrubs, spring bulbs, ferns and hostas. Gardens & nursery open every day except Mons. Picnic area. Lunches/snacks at Red Lion. *Adm £1.50 Acc chd free (Share to Paula Carr Trust®). For NGS Suns March 26, April 2, 9, 16, 30, May 7, 21, 28, Aug 13, 20, 27; Mons April 17, May 8, 29, Aug 28 (11-5): also private visits welcome, please* **Tel 01233 712522**

Cobham Hall ♿✂ (Westwood Educational Trust), Cobham. next to A2/M2 8m E of junction 2 of M25, midway between Gravesend and Rochester. Beautiful Elizabethan mansion in 150 acres landscaped by Humphry Repton at end of C18. Acres of daffodils and flowering trees planted in 1930s; grounds now being restored by Cobham Hall Heritage Trust. TEAS. *Adm House £2.50 OAP/Chd £2 Garden £1 (Share to Cobham Hall Heritage Trust®). ▲For NGS Suns April 9; Aug 20 (2-5). For details of other open days, please* **Tel 01474 823371/824319**

Coldham ♿✂❀ (Dr & Mrs J G Elliott) Little Chart Forstal, 5m NW of Ashford. Leave M20 at junction 8 (Lenham) if Folkestone-bound or junction 9 (Ashford West) if London-bound: then leave A20 at Charing by road signposted to Little Chart, turn E in village, ¼m. 2-acre garden developed since 1970 in setting of old walls; good collection of rare plants, bulbs, alpines, mixed borders. C16 Kent farmhouse (not open). TEA on July 23. *Adm £2 Chd 50p. Suns April 2, July 23 (2-5.30)*

Coldharbour Oast ♿✂❀ (Mr & Mrs A J A Pearson) Tenterden. 300yds SW of Tenterden High St (A28), take lane signed West View Hospital, after 200yds bear R on to concrete lane signed Coldharbour, proceed for 600yds. Garden started in late 1987 from ¾-acre field in exposed position. Pond; dry stream; unusual shrubs and perennials maintained by owners. TEA in aid of Norwegian Locomotive Trust. *Adm £1.25 Acc chd free. Sun Aug 20 (12.30-5.30)*

Collingwood Grange ♿✂❀ (Mrs Linda Fennell), Benenden, SE of Cranbrook, 100yds on E of rd to Iden Green from village centre. Bus: Cranbrook-Tenterden. Flowering cherries; rhododendrons, incl large collection of dwarf kinds; autumn colour. Former home of the late Capt Collingwood 'Cherry' Ingram. Special botanical interest. TEAS. *Adm £1.50 Acc chd free. Sun April 23 (2-5)*

Congelow House ♿ (Mrs D J Cooper) Yalding, 8m SW of Maidstone. Approx mid-way between Tonbridge and Maidstone, and S of Yalding. 4-acre garden created from an orchard since 1973; backbone of interesting ornamental trees planted about 1850, with recent plantings; walled vegetable garden; pleasure gardens incl rhododendrons, azaleas, irises, roses, shrub roses. TEAS. *Adm £1.50 Chd 50p. Sun June 4 (2-5.30)*

Copton Ash ♿✂❀ (Mr & Mrs John Ingram & Drs Tim & Gillian Ingram) 105 Ashford Rd, Faversham, 1m. On A251 Faversham-Ashford rd opp E-bound junction with M2. 1½-acre plantsman's garden developed since 1978 on site of old cherry orchard. Wide range of plants in mixed borders and informal island beds; incl spring bulbs, alpine and herbaceous plants, shrubs, young trees and collection of fruit varieties. Special interest in plants from Mediterranean-type climates. Good autumn colour. TEAS. *Adm £1 Acc chd free (Share to National Schizophrenia Fellowship, East Kent Group®). Suns March 26, April 16, May 14, July 30, Aug 27, Oct 22; Mons April 17, Aug 28 (2-6)*

Crittenden House ✂ (B P Tompsett Esq) Matfield, 6m SE of Tonbridge. Bus: MD 6 or 297, alight Standings Cross, Matfield, 1m. Garden around early C17 house completely planned and planted since 1956 on labour-saving lines. Featuring spring shrubs (rhododendrons, magnolias), roses, lilies, foliage, waterside planting of ponds in old iron workings, of interest from early spring bulbs to autumn colour. Rare young trees mentioned in Collins Guide to Trees in UK and Europe, by Alan Mitchell. Subject of article in *R.H.S. Journal*, 1990. Tea Cherry-trees, Matfield Green. *Adm £2 Chd (under 12) 25p. Suns April 2, 16, 30, May 14, 28; Mon April 17 (2-6)*

Doddington Place ♿❀ (Richard Oldfield Esq) 6m SE of Sittingbourne. From A20 turn N opp Lenham or from A2 turn S at Teynham or Ospringe (Faversham) (all 4m). Large garden, landscaped with wide views; trees and yew hedges; woodland garden with azaleas and rhododendrons, Edwardian rock garden; formal garden planted for late summer interest. TEAS, restaurant, shop. *Adm £2 Chd 25p (Share to Kent Assoc for the Blind and Doddington Church®). Every Wed and Bank Holiday Mon from Easter to end Sept; Suns in May only. For NGS Suns May 7, 14, 21 (11-6)*

Downs Court ♿✂❀ (Mr & Mrs M J B Green) Boughton Aluph, 4m NE of Ashford off A28. Take lane on L signed Boughton Aluph church, fork R at pillar box, garden is next drive on R. Approx 3 acres with fine downland views, sweeping lawns and some mature trees and yew hedges. Mixed borders largely replanted by owners in last 10 years; shrub roses. TEAS Sunday only in aid of National Hospital Development Foundation®. *Adm £1.50 Chd 50p. Sat, Sun June 17, 18 (2-6)*

Edenbridge House ♿❀ (Mrs M T Lloyd) Crockham Hill Rd, 1½m N of Edenbridge, nr Marlpit Hill, on B2026. 5-acre garden of bulbs, spring shrubs, herbaceous borders, alpines, roses and water garden. House part C16 (not open). TEAS. *Adm £1.50 OAPs £1 Chd 25p. Suns April 16, May 7, June 18, July 16 (2-6); Weds May 24, Sept 27 (1-5); also private visits welcome for groups, please* **Tel 01732 862122**

Regular Openers. Too many days to include in diary. Usually there is a wide range of plants giving year-round interest. See head of county section for the name and garden description for times etc.

¶Egerton Gardens ✂ 10m W of Ashford. From A20 at Charing Xrds take B2077 direction Biddenden; at Pluckley turn R to Egerton, then R at George Inn. Start at Glebe Cottage, next to church; maps available. A group of cottage gardens reflecting the owners' tastes and needs. TEAS. *Combined adm £2 Chd 25p (Share to St James's Church, Egerton). Sun June 18 (2-6)*

Egypt Farm (Mr & Mrs Francis Bullock) Hamptons, 6m N of Tonbridge, equidistant from Plaxtol and Hadlow. From Hadlow take Carpenters Lane, at end turn L at T-junction, R at next Xrds, next turning L (Pillar Box Lane), R at next junction, oast house on L 100yds N of Artichoke Inn. Undulating garden of 4 acres designed by owners; spring bulbs, terrace, water garden lovely views. **Hamptons Farm** open same day. TEA. *Adm £1.50 Acc chd free (Share to W. Peckham Church). Sun April 23 (2-6)*

Emmetts Garden ♿ (The National Trust) Ide Hill, 5m SW of Sevenoaks. 1½m S of A25 on Sundridge-Ide Hill Rd. 1½m N of Ide Hill off B2042. 5-acre hillside garden. One of the highest gardens in Kent, noted for its fine collection of rare trees and shrubs; lovely spring and autumn colour. TEAS. *Adm £2.50 Chd £1.30. March Sats, Suns; April to end Oct every Wed to Sun. Open Bank Hol Mons. For NGS Sats May 13, Oct 7 (1-6) last adm 5, or sunset if earlier*

¶Everden Farmhouse ✂❀ (Martinez family) Alkham, 4m W of Dover. Follow signs to Alkham Valley, turn R opp Hoptons Manor to Everden, then follow 'Gardens Open' signs. Designer's garden created from field since 1990, exposed hillside, alkaline soil. Many unusual plants combined with colour and form in mind. TEAS. *Adm £1.50 Chd 50p. Suns May 21, June 18, July 23, Oct 8 (2-6); also private visits welcome, please* **Tel 01303 893462**

Field House ♿✂❀ (Mr & Mrs N J Hori) Clapper Lane, Staplehurst. W of A229, 9m S of Maidstone and 1½m N of Staplehurst village centre. A 'Garden of the Mind'. Approx 1½ acres designed in the tradition of contemplative and paradise gardens. Good plant collection on Wealden clay, also 1-acre, species-rich meadow with pond. TEAS. *Adm £1.50 Chd 50p. Suns July 9, Aug 6 (2-6)*

Finchcocks ♿✂❀ (Mr & Mrs Richard Burnett) Goudhurst. 2m W of Goudhurst, off A262. 4-acre garden surrounding early C18 manor, well-known for its collection of historical keyboard instruments. Spring bulbs; mixed borders; autumn garden with unusual trees & rare shrubs; recently restored walled garden on lines of C18 pleasure garden. TEAS. *Adm £4.80 House & garden, £1.50 Garden, Chd £3.20 & 50p. Suns Easter to Sept 24; Bank Hol Mons; Aug every Wed to Sun (2-6). ▲For NGS Suns May 21, Aug 20 (2-6)*

Flint Cottage ✂❀ (Mr & Mrs P J Sinnock) Bourne Park, Bishopsbourne, 4m S of Canterbury turn off A2 to Bridge, through village turn W at church, follow garden signs. Small garden; alpines in gravel beds, sink gardens; water feature; mixed borders and small heather beds; herb garden. TEAS. *Adm £1 Chd 50p (Share to Foundation for the Study of Infant Death®). Sun May 28 (2-6); also private visits welcome, please* **Tel 01227 830691**

Forest Gate ♿✂❀ (Sir Robert & Lady Johnson) Pluckley, 8m W of Ashford. From A20 at Charing take B2077 to Pluckley village; turn L signed Bethersden, continue 1m to garden 100yds S of Pluckley station. 2-acre garden on heavy clay; well stocked mixed borders, laburnum tunnel, ponds and interesting herb collection. Many plants labelled. C17 house (not open). Picnics allowed in meadow. TEAS. *Adm £1.30 Acc chd free (Share to Cystic Fibrosis Trust®). Mon May 29, Sun June 18 (1-6)*

Geddesden ♿✂❀ (Mr & Mrs J R Hunt) Friezingham Lane, Rolvenden Layne: At junction 4m S of Tenterden, follow sign Rolvenden Layne, in village turn L 30yds on from Wooden Tops shop into Friezingham Lane; garden 1st drive L. Garden started in 1985 on sloping N-facing site on clay with rose, heather, bog and pond gardens; flowers for all seasons, azaleas, rhododendrons, cherries, Jekyll-style summer borders, autumn colour. *Adm £1.50 Chd 75p. Open Fris, Sats, Suns from May 4 to Aug 31. For NGS every Thurs from May 4 to Aug 31 (1.30-4.30)*

Godinton Park ✂ (Alan Wyndham Green Esq) Entrance 1½m W of Ashford at Potter's Corner on A20. Bus: MD/EK 10, 10A, 10B Folkestone-Ashford-Maidstone, alight Hare & Hounds, Potter's Corner. Formal and wild gardens. Topiary. Jacobean mansion with elaborate woodwork. Unique frieze in drawing room depicting arms drill of Kent Halbardiers 1630. *Adm garden only 70p, house & garden £2, Chd under 16 70p.* ▲*Suns April 16, July 9 (2-5)*

Godmersham Park ♿❀ (John B Sunley Esq) off A28 midway between Canterbury and Ashford; garden signed from either end of Park loop rd. Early Georgian mansion (not shown) in beautiful downland setting. 24 acres formal and landscape gardens, superb daffodils, restored wilderness; topiary; rose beds; herbaceous borders. Associations with Jane Austen. TEA. *Adm £1.50 Chd 75p (Share to Godmersham Church®). Sun April 9 (11-6)*

Goodnestone Park ♿✂❀ (The Lady FitzWalter) nr Wingham, Canterbury. Village lies S of B2046 rd from A2 to Wingham. Sign off B2046 says Goodnestone. Village St is 'No Through Rd', but house and garden at the terminus. Bus: EK13, 14 Canterbury-Deal; bus stop: Wingham, 2m. 5 to 6 acres; good trees; woodland garden, snowdrops, spring bulbs, walled garden with old-fashioned roses. Connections with Jane Austen who stayed here. Picnics allowed. TEAS available. *Adm £2 OAP £1.80 Chd under 12 20p (Disabled people in wheelchair £1). Suns April 2 to Oct 15 (12-6); Mons, Weds to Fris March 27 to Oct 27 (11-5). For NGS Suns Feb 12 (snowdrops), March 19 (spring bulbs and helebores), July 16, Aug 20 (12-5). Closed Tues and Sats*

Goudhurst Gardens 4m W of Cranbrook on A262. TEAS. *Combined adm £2 Acc chd free. Suns May 21, June 18 (1-6)*

Crowbourne Farm House ♿✂ (Mrs S Coleman) 2-acre farmhouse garden in which replanting started in 1989. Established cottage garden; shrub roses; vegetable garden; and areas newly planted with trees and shrubs. Former horse pond now stocked with ornamental fish

¶**Garden Cottage** (Mr & Mrs Peter Sowerby) ¾-acre garden with small trees, shrubs, perennials and grass, to provide year-round softly coloured foreground to outstanding views of Teise valley. First laid out in 1930s with extensive planting in 1970s

Tara ♿✂❀ (Mr & Mrs Peter Coombs) 1¼ acres redesigned in 1982 into a number of linked garden areas, including a formal herb garden, each providing a different atmosphere, using an interesting range of plants and shrubs

Tulip Tree Cottage ♿✂❀ (Mr & Mrs K A Owen) 1½ acres with sweeping lawn, established trees in herbaceous and shrub borders; 90ft Liriodendron tulipifera, said to be one of finest in country, also fine Cedrus atlantica glauca. In May azalea garden of ½-acre, established 1902

Great Comp Charitable Trust ♿✂❀ (R Cameron Esq) 2m E of Borough Green. A20 at Wrotham Heath, take Seven Mile Lane, B2016; at 1st Xrds turn R; garden on L ½m. Delightful 7-acre garden skilfully designed by the Camerons since 1957 for low maintenance and yr-round interest. Spacious setting of well-maintained lawns and paths lead visitors through a plantsman's collection of trees, shrubs, heathers and herbaceous plants. From woodland planting to more formal terraces good use is made of views to plants, ornaments and ruins. Good autumn colour. Early C17 house (not shown). TEA on Suns, Bank Hols and NGS days (2-5). *Adm £2.50 Chd £1. Open Suns in March and every day April 1 to Oct 31 (11-6). Openings for NGS (Share to Tradescant Trust®) Suns Mar 5, 12 (for hellebores, heathers and snowflakes); Nov 5 (for autumn colour) (11-6)*

Great Maytham Hall ✂ (Country Houses Association) Rolvenden, 4m SW of Tenterden. On A28 in Rolvenden turn L at church towards Rolvenden Layne; Hall ½m on R. Lutyens house (not open) and garden, 18 acres of parkland with bluebells, daffodils and flowering trees in spring; formal gardens incl blue and silver border, roses, hydrangeas and autumn colour. Walled garden inspired Frances Hodgson Burnett to write her novel 'The Secret Garden'. TEAS. *Adm £1.50 Chd 75p (Share to Country Houses Association©). Fris April 28, June 30, Sept 29 (2-5)*

Greencroft ✂ (Dr & Mrs A Marr) Nizels Lane, Hildenborough, 3½m S of Sevenoaks. Take A225, at Riverhill roundabout take B245, Nizels Lane 1st R. 2-acre plantsman's garden. Trees, shrubs, mixed borders. Interesting planting to screen Tonbridge by-pass; water and woodland garden, being developed by owner-gardeners with view to easy maintenance. TEA. *Adm £1.50 Acc chd free. Sun May 14 (2-6)*

Greenways ♿✂❀ (Mr & Mrs S Lord) Single Street, Berry's Green, nr Downe. Gardener's garden; interesting design ideas; willows, jasmines, honeysuckles and alpines; large collection of bonsai; collection of miniature gardens; gardens combining fruit and vegetables, trees, shrubs and flowers; small pool, conservatory and pottery. *Adm £1.50 Chd 50p (Share to Save the Children Fund®). Private visits welcome, anytime, please* **Tel 01959 574691**

Groombridge Place ♿✂❀ (Andrew de Candole Esq) 4m SW of Tunbridge Wells. Take A264 towards E. Grinstead, after 2m take B2110: Groombridge Place entrance on L, past the church. C17 formal walled gardens with medieval moat, ancient topiary and fountains. Canal boat rides to Enchanted Forest; children's garden and birds of prey displays. TEAS. *Adm £3.50 OAPs £3 Chd £2.25. Groups by arrangement. Open daily April 1 to Dec 17 (10am-6pm); Dec 18 to March 31 weekends & Bank Hols (not Christmas Day) (noon-dusk). For NGS Tues April 11 (10-6)*

Groome Farm ♿✂❀ (Mr & Mrs Michael Swatland) Egerton, 10m W of Ashford. From A20 at Charing Xrds take B2077 Biddenden Rd. Past Pluckley turn R at Blacksmiths Tea Rooms; R again, until Newland Green sign on L, house 1st on L. 1½ acres; still being developed around C15 farmhouse and oast (not open). Interesting collection trees, shrubs, roses and herbaceous plants; also water, heather and rock gardens. Picnics welcome in field. TEAS. *Adm £1.50 Acc chd free. Suns June 18, Sept 10 (2-6)*

115 Hadlow Road ✂ (Mr & Mrs Richard Esdale) in Tonbridge. Take A26 from N end of High St signed Maidstone, house 1m on L in service rd. ½-acre unusual terraced garden with roses, herbaceous border, clematis, hardy fuchsias, shrub borders, alpines, kitchen garden and pond; well labelled. TEA. *Adm £1 Acc chd free. Suns July 16, Aug 27 (2-6); also private visits welcome, please* **Tel 01732 353738**

Hamptons Farm House ♿✂ (Mr & Mrs Brian Pearce) Plaxtol. Between Plaxtol, Hadlow, Shipbourne and W Peckham. In a hamlet opp Artichoke Inn; signed from the 4 villages. Garden of 3 acres; stream and pond; trees, shrubs and old barn; fine views. **Egypt Farm** open same day. *Adm £1.50 Acc chd free. Sun April 23 (2-6)*

Hartlip Gardens 6m W of Sittingbourne, 1m S of A2 midway between Rainham and Newington. Parking for Craiglea in village hall car park and The Street. TEAS at Hartlip Place for Kent Gardens Trust. *Combined adm £2 Acc chd free. Sun June 18 (2-6)*

Craiglea ♿✂ (Mrs Ruth Bellord) The Street. Small cottage garden crammed with interesting shrubs and plants; vegetable garden; tiny pond

Hartlip Place ✂ (Lt-Col & Mrs J R Yerburgh) Secret garden concealed by rhododendrons, planted with old roses; shrub borders; wilderness walk; sloping lawns; pond

Hault Farm ♿✂❀ (Mr & Mrs T D Willet) 7m S of Canterbury, between Petham and Waltham. From B2068 turn R signed Petham/Waltham; 1m on L. Victorian house on site of Knights Templar property once occupied by Crusader Sir Geofrey de Hautt. Plantaholic's 4 acres of woodland, bog, herbaceous, rose and scree areas. TEAS. *Adm £2 Chd £1. Suns and Bank Hols from April 16 to July, and Sept 3, 10, 24. For NGS Suns April 16, Sept 24; Wed May 17 (2-5) Groups welcome at any time by appt, please* **Tel 01227 700263**

¶Haydown ✂ (Dr & Mrs I D Edeleanu) Great Buckland, nr Cobham, 4m S of A2. Take turning for Cobham, at war memorial straight ahead down hill, under railway bridge to T-junction, turn R, after 200yds take L fork, follow narrow lane for 1½m. Entrance on L after riding stables. North Downs 9-acre hillside garden developed since 1980, with woodland and meadowland, incl native and unusual trees, shrubs, small vineyard, orchard, ponds, bog garden; patio with terracing; roses and good autumn colour. TEA. *Adm £1.50 Acc chd free (Share to Rotary Charities). Fris April 7, May 19, Sept 29; Sat July 15 (2-6)*

● Hever Castle ♿❀ (Broadland Properties Ltd) 3m SE of Edenbridge, between Sevenoaks and E. Grinstead. Signed from junctions 5 and 6 of M25, from A21 and from A264. Formal Italian gardens with statuary, sculpture and fountains; large lake; rose garden and Tudor style gardens with topiary and maze. New Tudor herb garden opening this year. Romantic moated castle, the childhood home of Anne Boleyn, also open. No dogs in castle, on lead only in gardens. Refreshments available. *Open every day from March 14 to Nov 5 (11-6 last adm 5, Castle opens 12 noon). Adm Castle and gardens £5.70 OAPs £5.20 Chd £2.90 Family (2 adults 2 chd) £14.30; gardens only £4.30 OAPs £3.80 Chd £2.50 Family (2 adults 2 chd) £11.10*

Hole Park ♿✂ (D G W Barham Esq) Rolvenden–Cranbrook on B2086. Beautiful parkland; formal garden with mixed borders, roses, yew hedges and topiary a feature, many fine trees. Natural garden with daffodils, rhododendrons, azaleas, conifers, dell and water gardens; bluebell wood in spring. Autumn colour. *Adm £2 Chd under 12 50p (Share to St Mary's Church, Rolvenden©). Suns April 9, 16, 30, May 7, 28, Oct 1, 8, 15; Weds April 26, May 17, June 7 (2-6)*

Horton Priory ✂ (Mrs A C Gore) Sellindge, 6m SE of Ashford. From A20 Ashford-Folkestone, 1m from Sellindge, turn E along Moorstock Lane, signed Horton Priory. Bus: EK/MD 10, 10A, 10B Maidstone-Ashford-Folkestone; alight Sellindge, 1m. Herbaceous and rose border, lawn, pond and rock garden. Priory dates back to C12; church destroyed in reign of Henry VIII, but remains of W doorway and staircase to S aisle of nave can be seen by front door. Along W front Norman buttresses (all genuine) and C14 windows (some restored); one genuine small Norman window. Outer hall only open to visitors. TEAS. *Adm £1 Chd 50p. Suns June 11, Sept 24 (2-6)*

Ightham Mote ♿✂❀ (The National Trust) Ivy Hatch. 6m E of Sevenoaks, off A25 and 2½m S of Ightham [188: TQ584535] Buses: Maidstone & District 222/3 from BR Borough Green: NU-Venture 67/8 Sevenoaks to Plaxtol passing BR Sevenoaks: alight Ivy Hatch ½m walk to Ightham Mote. 14-acre garden and moated medieval manor c.1340. Mixed borders with many unusual plants; lawns; courtyard; newly-planted orchard; water features incl small lake, leading to woodland walk with rhododendrons and shrubs. TEAS. ▲*Adm £2 Chd £1. Tues June 6 (11.30-5). Special opening of garden, house not open; NT members to pay*

Regular Openers. See head of county section.

Jessups ♿❀ (The Hon Robin Denison-Pender) Mark Beech. 3m S of Edenbridge. From B2026 Edenbridge-Hartfield rd turn L opp Queens Arms signed Mark Beech, 100yds on L. Small established garden, spring bulbs and shrubs, fine views to Sevenoaks Weald. Small wood. Wildfowl pond (25 different breeds). TEAS. *Adm £1.50 Acc chd free. Sun April 16 (2-5)*

Knole ♿✻ (The Lord Sackville; The National Trust) Sevenoaks. Station: Sevenoaks. Pleasance, deer park, landscape garden, herb garden. TEAS. *Adm Car park £2.50: garden 50p Chd 30p; house £4 Chd £2. Weds June 7, Aug 2 (11-4.30 last adm 4)*

Kypp Cottage ✻❀ (Mrs Zena Grant) Woolpack Corner, Biddenden. At Tenterden Rd A262 junction with Benenden Rd. Cottage garden (planted and maintained by owner) started about 1964 from rough ground; extensive collection of interesting plants; enjoy perfumed, shady nooks provided by over 200 climbing and shrub roses, intertwined with clematis; variety of geraniums and other ground cover plants. Good examples of trees suitable for small gardens. Morning coffee & home-made TEAS. *Adm £1 Chd 30p (Share to NSPCC®). Suns May 28, June 4, 11, 18, 25, July 2, 9, 16; Mons May 29, June 5, 12, 19, 26, July 3, 10, 17; Tues May 30, June 6, 13, 20, 27, July 4, 11, 18; Weds May 31, June 7, 14, 21, 28, July 5, 12, 19; Fri, Sat May 26, 27 (Suns 2-6, weekdays 10.30-6); also private visits welcome all season, please* **Tel 01580 291480**

Ladham House ❀ (Betty, Lady Jessel) Goudhurst. On NE of village, off A262. 10 acres with rolling lawns, fine specimen trees, rhododendrons, camellias, azaleas, shrubs and magnolias. Arboretum. Spectacular twin mixed borders; fountain and bog gardens. Fine view. Subject of many magazine articles. TEAS. *Adm £2 Chd under 12 50p. Suns April 16, May 7, 28, July 9 (11-5.30); open other times for private visits and for coaches*

¶Lantern Cottage ✻ (Mr & Mrs Handcock) Bitchett Green, 4m SE of Sevenoaks. Take A225 towards Tonbridge, turn L along St Julians Rd to Bitchett Green. From Seal on A25, take Park Lane then 1st L (Grove Rd) to sign to Bitchett Green; park in lane by cricket field. Japanese Hill Garden approx ½ acre with ponds, tea house, wells, sand paths, shrubs and trees, being restored by present owners. TEA. *Adm £2 Chd 50p. Thurs June 8; Sat June 10 (2-4.30)*

Larksfield ♿✻ (Mr & Mrs P Dickinson) Crockham Hill, 3m N of Edenbridge, on B269 (Limpsfield-Oxted). Octavia Hill, a founder of the NT, lived here and helped create the original garden; fine collection of azaleas, shrubs, herbaceous plants, rose beds and woodlands; views over Weald and Ashdown Forest. **The Red House** and **Larksfield Cottage** gardens open same days. TEAS at The Red House. *Combined adm £2.50 OAPs £2 Chd 50p. Suns May 14, 21 (2-6)*

Larksfield Cottage ♿✻❀ (Mr & Mrs J Mainwaring) Crockham Hill, 3m N of Edenbridge, on B269. An enchanting garden redesigned in 1981 with attractive lawns and shrubs. Views over the Weald and Ashdown Forest. **Larksfield** and **The Red House** gardens also open same days. *Combined adm £2.50 OAPs £2 Chd 50p. Suns May 14, 21 (2-6)*

43 Layhams Road ♿✻ (Mrs Dolly Robertson) West Wickham. Semi-detached house recognisable by small sunken flower garden in the front. Opp Wickham Court Farm. A raised vegetable garden, purpose-built for the disabled owner with easy access to wide terraced walkways. The owner, who maintains the entire 24ft × 70ft area herself, would be pleased to pass on her experiences as a disabled gardener so that others may share her joy and interest. *Collecting box. Private visits welcome all year, please* **Tel 0181-462 4196**

Little Trafalgar ♿✻❀ (Mr & Mrs R J Dunnett) Selling, 4m SE of Faversham. From A2 (M2) or A251 make for Selling Church, then follow signs to garden. ¾-acre garden of great interest both for its wealth of attractive and unusual plants, and its intimate, restful design. Emphasis is placed on the creative and artistic use of plants. TEAS. *Adm £1 Acc chd free (Share to Council for the Protection of Rural England (Kent branch) ®). Suns May 14, 28, June 11, 25, July 9, 23, Aug 6, 27, Sept 10, 24; Mons May 8, 29, Aug 28 (2-6); also private visits welcome, please* **Tel 01227 752219**

Long Barn ✻ (Brandon & Sarah Gough) Weald, 3m S of Sevenoaks. Signed to Weald at junction of A21 & B245. Garden at W end of village. 1st garden of Harold Nicolson and Vita Sackville-West. 3 acres with terraces and slopes, giving considerable variety. Dutch garden designed by Lutyens, features mixed planting in raised beds. Teas in village. *Adm £2 OAPs £1 Chd 50p under 5 free (Share to Hospice at Home®). Suns June 18, July 23 (2-5)*

Longacre ♿✻❀ (Dr & Mrs G Thomas) Perry Wood, Selling, 5m SE of Faversham. From A2 (M2) or A251 follow signs for Selling, passing White Lion on L, 2nd R and immediately L, continue for ¼m. From A252 at Chilham, take turning signed Selling at Badgers Hill Fruit Farm. L at 2nd Xrds, next R, L and then R. Small plantsman's garden with wide variety of interesting plants, created and maintained entirely by owners. Lovely walks in Perry Woods adjacent to garden. TEAS in aid of local charities. *Adm £1 Acc chd free (Share to Canterbury Pilgrims Hospice®). Suns April 16, 30, May 14, 28, June 4, 25, July 9, 23, Aug 27, Sept 10; Mons April 17, May 8, 29, June 11, Aug 28 (2-5); also private visits welcome, please* **Tel 01227 752254**

Lullingstone Castle ♿✻❀ (Mr & Mrs Guy Hart Dyke) In the Darenth Valley via Eynsford on A225. Eynsford Station ½m. All cars and coaches via Roman Villa. Lawns, woodland and lake, mixed border, small herb garden. Henry VII gateway; Church on the lawn open. TEAS. *Adm garden £1.50 OAPs/Chd £1; house 50p extra. Sun June 11 (2-6)*

Luton House ✻ (Sir John & Lady Swire) Selling, 4m SE of Faversham. From A2 (M2) or A251 make for White Lion, entrance 30yds E on same side of rd. 4 acres; C19 landscaped garden; ornamental ponds; trees underplanted with azaleas, camellias, woodland plants. *Adm £1.50 Acc chd free. Sun April 9 (2-6)*

¶190 Maidstone Road ✲ (Dr M K Douglas) Chatham. On A230 Chatham-Maidstone, about 1m out of Chatham and 7m from Maidstone. Informal ¼-acre garden; herbaceous borders on either side of former tennis court; scree garden and pool; many snowdrops and other spring bulbs. *Adm £1.50 Acc chd free. Suns April 9, July 23 (2-6); private visits welcome, please* **Tel 01634 842216**

Marle Place ♿✲❀ (Mr & Mrs Gerald Williams) Brenchley, 8m SE of Tonbridge, signed from Brenchley, or take B2162, 1m S of Horsmonden and 1½m NW of Lamberhurst. Turn W on Marle Place Rd. Victorian gazebo; plantsman's shrub borders; walled scented garden, large herb rockery and herb nursery. Woodland walk; collection of bantams. C17 listed house (not open). TEAS. *Adm £2 Chd £1.50. Every day April 1 to Oct 31 (10-5.30). For NGS Suns May 28, Aug 6, Oct 8 (10-6)*

Maurice House ♿ (The Royal British Legion Residential Home) Callis Court Rd, Broadstairs. From Broadstairs Broadway take St Peter's Park Rd; turn R under railway arch into Baird's Hill; join Callis Court Rd entrance on R, 100yds beyond Lanthorne Rd turning. Well-maintained 8-acre garden; lawns, flowering trees, shrubs; formal flower beds; rose and water gardens; orchard. Spring bedding displays of wallflowers, tulips, polyanthus; wide variety of herbaceous plants and shrubs especially suited to coastal conditions. TEAS. *Adm £1 Chd 25p (Share to the Royal British Legion®). Sun April 30 (2-5.30)*

Meadow Wood ♿ (Mr & Mrs James Lee) Penshurst. 1¼m SE of Penshurst on B2176 in direction of Bidborough. 1920s garden, on edge of wood with long southerly views over the Weald, and with interesting trees and shrubs; azaleas, rhododendrons and naturalised bulbs in woods with mown walks. TEAS. *Adm £2 Chd £1 (Share to Relate®). Sun, Mon May 7, 8 (2-6)*

Mere House ♿✲ (Mr & Mrs Andrew Wells) Mereworth, midway between Tonbridge & Maidstone. From A26 turn N on to B2016 and then into Mereworth village. 6-acre garden with C18 lake; ornamental shrubs and trees with foliage contrast; lawns, daffodils; Kentish cobnut plat. TEAS. *Adm £1 Chd 25p. Suns April 9, May 7; Mon May 29 (2.30-6)*

Mill House ♿✲❀ (Dr & Mrs Brian Glaisher) Mill Lane, ½m N of Hildenborough, 5m S of Sevenoaks. From B245 turn into Mill Lane at Mill garage. 3-acre garden laid out in 1906; herbaceous and mixed borders; new secluded herb garden; old shrub roses and climbers; clematis and many fine trees. Formal garden with topiary; ruins of windmill and conservatory with exotics. *Adm £1.50 Chd 25p. Sun May 21 (2-6)*

Mount Ephraim (Mrs M N Dawes and Mr & Mrs E S Dawes) Hernhill, Faversham. From M2 and A299 take Hernhill turning at Duke of Kent. Herbaceous border; topiary; daffodils and rhododendrons; rose terraces leading to a small lake; Japanese rock garden with pools; water garden; small vineyard. TEAS daily except Tues; lunches only Bank Hol Suns & Mons. *Adm £2 Chd 50p. Open April to Sept (1-6). For NGS Suns April 30, Sept 24 (1-6)*

Nettlestead Place ♿✲ (Mr & Mrs Roy Tucker) Nettlestead, 6m W/SW of Maidstone. Turn S off A26 onto B2015 then 1m on L (next to Nettlestead Church). C13 manor house set in 7-acre garden; garden on different levels, defined by ragstone walls and yew hedges with fine views of open countryside; garden in course of further development, including pond garden, new terraces and plant collections. TEAS. *Adm £1.50 Acc chd free (Share to St Mary's Church, Nettlestead®). Suns July 9, Sept 10 (2-6)*

New Barns House ♿✲❀ (Mr & Mrs P H Byam-Cook) West Malling. Leave M20 at Exit 4 to West Malling. In High Street turn E down Waters Lane, at T-junction turn R, take bridge over by-pass, follow lane 400yds to New Barns House. 1-acre garden with fine trees and flowering cherries. Walled garden, mixed borders and shrubs. TEAS. *Adm £1.50 Acc chd free. Sun April 23 (2-6)*

Nonington & Woodnesborough Gardens ♿✲ 6m & 3m from Sandwich respectively on Sandwich-Woodnesborough-Nonington Road. *Combined adm £2.50 Acc chd free (Share to Macmillan Fund for Cancer Relief®). Sun June 11 (2-6)*

Birnam (Mr & Mrs Douglas Miller) Hamill Road, ½m SW of Woodnesborough. ¾-acre garden on clay, designed in 1963 by Anthony du Gard Pasley for a windswept site. Interesting trees, shrubs, roses. TEA

Gooseberry Hall Cottage (Mr Edward & Dr Audrey Carey) Nonington. From A2 take B2046 at Barham, after 300yds turn R for Nonington, proceed for 3m, passing disused Snowdon Colliery through Nonington village to mini-roundabout, turn R, house further ¾m on L. Cottage garden, with special-interest hedges and croquet lawn

Gooseberry Hall Farm (Mr & Mrs F McL Hayward) Nonington. 400yds from **Gooseberry Hall Cottage** down Gooseberry Lane on R. ½-acre garden surrounding Grade II thatched hall house. Herbaceous borders, lawns, climbing and hybrid roses, mature elms and small vegetable garden aimed at self sufficiency

Northbourne Court ✲ (The Hon Charles James) W of Deal. Signs in village. Great brick terraces, belonging to an earlier Elizabethan mansion, provide a picturesque setting for a wide range of shrubs and plants on chalk soil; geraniums, fuchsias and grey-leaved plants. *Adm £2.50 OAPs/Chd £1.50 (Share to National Art Collections Fund®). All Suns in June, July, Aug (2-5)*

Olantigh ✲ (J R H Loudon Esq) Wye, 6m NE of Ashford. Turn off A28 either to Wye or at Godmersham; ¾m from Wye on rd to Godmersham. Edwardian garden in beautiful setting; water garden; rockery; shrubbery; herbaceous border; extensive lawns. *Adm £1.50 Chd 50p. Suns May 28, June 25 (2-5)*

The Old Parsonage ♿✲❀ (Dr & Mrs Richard Perks) Sutton Valence, 6m SE of Maidstone. A274 from Maidstone or Headcorn, turn E into village at King's Head Inn and proceed on upper rd through village; climb Tumblers Hill and entrance at top on R. 4-acre labour-saving garden planted since 1959 with emphasis on ground cover; trees, shrubs and mixed borders; cranesbills and shrub roses. Ancient nut plat now developed as a wild garden. Fine views over Low Weald. In grounds is Sutton castle, C12 ruined keep, permanently open to the public. *Adm £1.50 Chd 50p. Sat June 17, Tue June 20, Fri June 23, Sun June 25 (2-6); also private visits welcome, please* **Tel 01622 842286**

Old Place Farm ♿✂❀ (Mr & Mrs Jeffrey Eker) High Halden, 3m NE of Tenterden. From A28 take Woodchurch Rd (opp Chequers public house) in High Halden, and follow for ½m. 3½-acre garden, mainly designed by Anthony du Gard Pasley, surrounding period farmhouse & buildings with paved herb garden & parterres, small lake, ponds, lawns, mixed borders, cutting garden, old shrub roses, lilies & foliage plants; all created since 1969 & much new planting in 1995. Featured in *Country Life*, & *House & Garden* in 1990. TEAS in aid of St Mary's Church, High Halden. *Adm £1.50 Chd 50p. Sun June 18 (2-6)*

Orchard Cottage ♿✂❀ (Professor & Mrs C G Wall) 3 Woodlands Road, Bickley, 1½m E of Bromley, about 400 yds from the A222. From Bickley Park Road turn into Pines Road, then 1st R into Woodlands Road, no 3 is 1st house on L. Attractive ⅓-acre garden in course of development; mixed borders with many interesting herbaceous plants and shrubs; scree beds and troughs with alpines and other small plants. TEAS. *Adm £1.50 Acc chd free (Share to Downs Syndrome Association: SE Branch ®). Sun Aug 6 (2-5.30)*

Oswalds ♿✂❀ (Mr & Mrs J C Davidson) Bishopsbourne, 4m S of Canterbury. Turn off A2 at B2065, follow signs to Bishopsbourne, house next to church. 3-acre plantsman's garden created since 1972 by present owners. Yr-round interest includes bulbs, spring garden; mixed borders; rockeries; pools; bog garden; potager; pergola; old roses; and many fruit varieties. NCCPG National Collections of *photinia* and *zantedeschia*. House (not open) has interesting literary connections. Teas at village hall nearby. *Adm £1.50 Chd 50p (Share to Kent Gardens Trust®). Suns Aug 27, Sept 3; Mon Aug 28 (2-5.30); also private visits welcome, July to Sept only, please* **Tel 01227 830340**

¶Owl House ♿❀ (Maureen, Marchioness of Dufferin and Ava) Lamberhurst. 1m W of A21, signposted from Lamberhurst. 16½-acre woodland garden surrounding C16 wool smuggler's cottage: water gardens, unusual roses climbing into woodland trees; daffodils, rhododendrons, azaleas, magnolias, camellias, roses, irises, good autumn colour. TEA on NGS days. *Adm £3 Chd £1 (Share to Maureen's Oast House for Arthritics®). Open all year except Christmas Day and New Year's Day. For NGS Suns April 30, July 16, Oct 1 (11-6)*

Oxley House ♿✂❀ (Dr & Mrs I D H McMullen) Boughton Road, Sandway, 8m from Ashford or Maidstone. From Lenham Square take Headcorn Road, 1st L after station, house 300yds on L, before 'White Horse'. About 1½ acres on heavy clay and sand, largely developed since 1987 storm, surrounding Queen Anne & Victorian house; wide variety of perennials, shrubs and old roses; small woodland garden with bulbs and hellebores. *Adm £1.50 Chd 50p (Share to Heart of Kent Hospice®). Suns April 30, June 18, Sept 17 (2-5)*

Oxon Hoath ♿✂❀ (Mr & Mrs Henry Bayne-Powell) nr Hadlow, 5m NE of Tonbridge. *Car essential.* Via A20, turn off S at Wrotham Heath onto Seven Mile Lane (B2016); at Mereworth Xrds turn W, through West Peckham. Or via A26, in Hadlow turn off N along Carpenters Lane. 10 acres, landscaped with fine trees, rhododendrons and azaleas; woodland walk; replanted cedar avenue; formal parterre rose garden by Nesfield. Large Kentish ragstone house (not shown) principally Georgian but dating back to C14; Victorian additions by Salvin. Once owned by Culpeppers, grandparents of Catherine Howard. View over C18 lake to Hadlow Folly. TEAS in picnic area if fine. *Adm £1.50 Chd 50p (Share to W. Peckham Church©). Sun May 28 (2-7)*

Parsonage Oasts ✂❀ (Mr & the Hon Mrs Raikes) Yalding, 6m SW of Maidstone. Between Yalding village and station turn off at Anchor public house over bridge over canal, continue 100yds up the lane. ¾-acre riverside garden with walls, shrubs, daffodils. TEAS in aid of The Fifth Trust for Mentally Handicapped Adults. *Adm £1 Chd 50p. Sun April 9 (2-5.30)*

The Pear House ✂❀ (Mrs Nicholas Snowden) Sellindge, 6m E of Ashford. Turn L off A20 at Sellindge Church towards Brabourne into Stone Hill. ⅔ acre developed by present owner; still evolving. Contains smaller gardens with informal planting; bulbs, roses (mostly old-fashioned), shrubs, small orchard with climbing roses, pond garden, shady areas. *Adm £1.50 Chd 50p. Private visits welcome only April 29 to July 9, please* **Tel 01303 812147**

Peddars Wood ♿✂❀ (Mr & Mrs B J Honeysett) 14 Orchard Rd, St Michaels, Tenterden. From A28, 1m N of Tenterden, turn W into Grange Rd at Crown Hotel, take 2nd R into Orchard Rd. Small plantsman's garden created by present owner since 1984. One of the best collections of rare and interesting plants in the area, incl over 100 clematis, 50 climbing roses, lilies and ferns. TEAS. *Adm £1 Chd 20p (Share to Baptist Minister's Help Society). Sats May 6, June 3, July 8, Aug 5 (2-6); also private visits welcome, please* **Tel 015806 3994**

Penshurst Place ✂ (Viscount De L'Isle), S of Tonbridge on B2176, N of Tunbridge Wells on A26. 10 acres of garden dating back to C14; garden divided into series of 'rooms' by over a mile of clipped yew hedge; profusion of spring bulbs: herbaceous borders; formal rose garden; famous peony border. All yr interest. TEAS and light refreshments. *Adm House & Gardens £4.95 OAPs £4.50 Chd £2.75 Family Ticket £13: Gardens £3.50 OAPs £3 Chd £2.25 Family Ticket £9.80. Open daily April 1 to Oct 1. For NGS Wed May 3, Thurs June 8 (11-6)*

Pett Place ✂❀ (Mrs I Mills, C I Richmond-Watson Esq & A Rolla Esq) Charing, 6m NW of Ashford. From A20 turn N into Charing High St. At end turn R into Pett Lane towards Westwell. Four walled gardens covering nearly 4 acres. Within formal framework of old walls, much planting has been carried out since 1981 to make a garden of different, pleasing vistas and secret places. A ruined C13 chapel is a romantic feature beside the manor house (not open), which was re-fronted about 1700 and which Pevsner describes as 'presenting grandiloquently towards the road.' TEAS. *Adm £1.50 Chd 50p (Share to Kent Gardens Trust®). Sats, Suns April 22, 23, June 24, 25 (2.30-5)*

Pevington Farm ♿❀ (Mr & Mrs David Mure) Pluckley, 3m SW of Charing. From Charing take B2077 towards Pluckley, before Pluckley turn R towards Egerton. Pevington Farm ½m on. From SW go through Pluckley, turn L for Egerton. ¾-acre garden with wonderful views over the Weald. Mixed borders with many interesting plants. PLOUGHMAN'S LUNCH & TEAS on May 21 for Friends of St Nicholas Church, Pluckley: on June 18 for Pluckley School Building Fund. *Adm £1.50 Chd 50p. Suns May 21, June 18 (11-5); also private visits welcome, please* **Tel 01233 840317**

The Pines Garden & The Bay Museum ♿❀ (The St Margaret's Bay Trust) Beach Rd, St Margaret's Bay, 4½m NE of Dover. Beautiful 6-acre seaside garden. Water garden. Statue of Sir Winston Churchill complemented by the Bay Museum opposite. Fascinating maritime and local interest. TEAS. *Adm £1 Chd 50p. Gardens open daily except Christmas Day. Museum open May to end Aug (closed Mon and Fri). For NGS Suns April 16, May 28, Aug 27 (10-5)*

Placketts Hole ♿✿❀ (Mr & Mrs D P Wainman) Bicknor 5m S of Sittingbourne, and W of B2163. Owners have designed and planted 2-acre garden around charming old house (C16 with Georgian additions); interesting mix of shrubs, large borders, rose garden, a formal herb garden and sweet- smelling plants. TEAS. *Adm £1.50 Acc chd free (Share to Bicknor Church®). Sun June 25 (2-6.30)*

Plaxtol Gardens 5m N of Tonbridge, 6m E of Sevenoaks, turn E off A227 to Plaxtol village. TEAS. Tickets and maps available at all gardens. Parking at Spoute Cottage. *Combined adm £2.50 Acc chd free (Share to Friends of Plaxtol Church©). Sun June 25 (2-6)*

- **¶Ducks Farm** ✿ (Mr & Mrs H Puleston Jones) Dux Lane. 2 acres, in course of restoration, surrounding medieval/Victorian farmhouse. Mixed herbaceous borders, walled garden, vegetable garden, herb garden
- **Malling Well House** ♿ (Mr & Mrs Cedric Harris) The Street, Plaxtol; next to Papermakers Arms. An open garden of about 1¼ acres, created over last 18 years by present owners; herbaceous border, pond, marsh garden and large vegetable plot
- **Spoute Cottage** ✿❀ (Mr & Mrs Donald Forbes) situated at the bottom of Plaxtol St on L side opp Hyders Wrought Iron Works. ¾ acre of mixed borders of contrasting flowering and foliage plants, especially for flower arranging; small pond & stream. New Japanese garden. Plant nursery attached
- **¶Watermead** ✿❀ (Mr & Mrs M Scott) Long Mill Lane. A 6-yr-old garden of ¼ acre. Borders themed with the aim of having flower or foliage interest all year round

29 The Precincts ✿❀ (The Archdeacon of Canterbury & Mrs T Till) Canterbury. Enter Cathedral Precincts by main (Christ Church) gate, follow path round W end of Cathedral into cloister, entry through gate N side of cloister. **No access for cars; please use public car parks**. ¾-acre of medieval walled garden with perpetual presence of the Cathedral soaring above. Enter Cellarer's Hall beneath earliest known carving of Thomas Becket, past a noble descendant of the mulberry tree in whose shade (allegedly) Becket's murderers washed their hands. TEAS. *Adm £1 Chd 50p (Share to L'Arche Overseas®). Sun, Mon May 28, 29; Sats, Suns June 3, 4, 10, 11 (2-5.30)*

Ramhurst Manor ♿ (The Lady Rosie Kindersley) Powder Mill Lane, Leigh, Tonbridge. Historic property once belonged to the Black Prince and Culpepper family. Formal gardens; roses, azaleas, rhododendrons, wild flowers. TEA. *Adm £1.50 Acc chd free. Sun May 21 (2.30-6)*

The Red House ♿✿ (K C L Webb Esq) Crockham Hill, 3m N of Edenbridge. On Limpsfield-Oxted Rd, B269. Formal features of this large garden are kept to a minimum; rose walk leads on to 3 acres of rolling lawns flanked by fine trees and shrubs incl rhododendrons, azaleas and magnolias. Views over the Weald and Ashdown Forest. TEAS. **Larksfield** and **Larksfield Cottage** gardens also open same days. *Combined adm £2.50 OAPs £2 Chd 50p (Share to The Schizophrenia Association of Great Britain®). Suns May 14, 21 (2-6)*

Ringfield ♿ (Professor Sir David Smithers) Knockholt. Via A21 London-Sevenoaks; from London turn at Pratts Bottom roundabout, also reached from Orpington-Bromley turn off from M25 or from Sevenoaks at Dunton Green (Rose & Crown). Rhododendrons, over 4,000 rose trees, incl recent varieties, and wide vistas. TEAS. *Adm £1.50 Chd 40p. Sun July 16 (2-6)*

Riverhill House ✿ (The Rogers family) 2m S of Sevenoaks on A225. Mature hillside garden with extensive views; specimen trees, sheltered terraces with roses and choice shrubs; bluebell wood with rhododendrons and azaleas; picnics allowed. TEAS. *Adm £2 Chd 50p (Share to RNIB®). Every Sun in April, May & June and Bank Hol weekends in this period (12-6). For NGS Sats May 6, 27 (12-6)*

Rock Farm ♿✿❀ (Mrs P A Corfe) Nettlestead. 6m W of Maidstone. Turn S off A26 onto B2015 then 1m S of Wateringbury turn R. 2-acre garden set around old Kentish farmhouse and farm buildings in beautiful setting with lovely views; created since 1968 with emphasis on all-year interest and ease of maintenance. Plantsman's collection of shrubs, trees and perennials for alkaline soil: extensive herbaceous border, vegetable area, bog garden and plantings around two large natural ponds. Plant nursery adjoining garden. *Adm £2 Chd 50p (Share to St Mary's Church, Nettlestead®). Every Wed & Sat from May 3 to July 29 (11-5)*

¶Rogers Rough ♿✿❀ (Richard and Hilary Bird) Kilndown, Cranbrook 10m S of Tonbridge. From A21 2m S of Lamberhurst turn E into Kilndown; take 1st R down Chick's Lane until rd divides. Garden writer's 1½-acre garden, mainly herbaceous borders, but also rock gardens, shrubs, a small wood and pond. Extensive views. TEAS in aid of Christ Church Kilndown Restoration Fund. *Adm £1.50 Chd 50p. Suns June 25, July 23 (2-5.30)*

Rosefarm ♿✿❀ (Dr D J Polton) 1m NW of Chilham. 6m equidistant Canterbury and Faversham. ¼m along narrow lane. Signed 'Denne Manor' at Shottenden Xrds. ½-acre garden with interesting and unusual plants. *Adm £1 Acc chd free. Fris, Sats May 26, 27, Aug 25, 26 (2-6)*

St Clere ♿✻ (Mr & Mrs Ronnie Norman) Kemsing, 6m NE of Sevenoaks. Take A25 from Sevenoaks toward Ightham; 1m past Seal turn L signed Heaverham and Kemsing; in Heaverham take rd to R signed Wrotham and West Kingsdown; in 75yds straight ahead marked Private rd; 1st L and follow rd to house. 4-acre garden with herbaceous borders, shrubs, rare trees. C17 mansion (not open). TEAS. *Adm £2 Chd 75p. Sun July 2 (2-6)*

St Michael's House ♿❀ (Brig & Mrs W Magan) Roydon Road, Seven Mile Lane, 5m NE Tonbridge, 5m SW Maidstone. On A26 at Mereworth roundabout take S exit (A228) signed Paddock Wood, after 1m turn L at top of rise (signed Roydon). Gardens ¼m up hill on L. Old vicarage garden of ¾ acre enclosed by shaped yew hedge; tulips; roses, climbing roses, irises; 6-acre meadow with extensive views. TEAS. *Adm £2 OAPs £1 Chd 50p. Suns April 30 (tulips), May 21 (irises), June 18 (roses) (2-6)*

● **Saltwood Castle** (The Hon Mrs Clark) 2m NW of Hythe, 4m W of Folkestone; from A20 turn S at sign to Saltwood. Medieval castle, subject of quarrel between Thomas a Becket and Henry II. C13 crypt and dungeons; armoury; battlement walks and watch towers. Lovely views; spacious lawns and borders; courtyard walls covered with roses. Picnics allowed. Saltwood Castle closed to the general public in 1995. *Private parties of 20 or more weekdays only, please write for appt*

Scotney Castle ♿✻ (Mrs Christopher Hussey; The National Trust) On A21 London-Hastings, 1¼m S of Lamberhurst. Bus: (Mon to Sat) M & D 246 & 256, Tunbridge Wells-Hawkhurst; alight Spray Hill. Famous picturesque landscape garden, created by the Hussey family in the 1840s surrounding moated C14 Castle. House (not open) by Salvin, 1837. Old Castle open May – mid-Sept (same times as garden). Gift Shop. Picnic area in car park. Tea Goudhurst. *Adm £3.20 Chd £1.60; Pre-booked parties of 15 or more (Wed-Fri) £2 Chd £1; April 1-end Oct, daily except Mons & Tues, but open Bank Hol Mons (closed Good Fri). Wed-Fri (11- 6), Sats & Suns 2-6 or sunset if earlier; Bank Hol Mons & Suns preceeding (12-6). For NGS (Share to Trinity Hospice, Clapham Common®) Mon May 29 (12-6)*

Sea Close ✻❀ (Maj & Mrs R H Blizard) Cannongate Rd, Hythe. A259 Hythe-Folkestone; ½m from Hythe, signed. A plantsman's garden; 1¼ acres on steep slope overlooking the sea; designed, laid out & maintained by present owners since 1966. Approx 1000 named plants & shrubs, planted for visual effect in many varied style beds of individual character. Cold refreshments. Teas Hythe. *Adm £1 Acc chd free (Share to Royal Signals Benevolent Fund®). Suns April 23, May 21, July 23, Aug 27 (2-5), Oct 1 (2-4.)*

Shipbourne Gardens 3m N of Tonbridge, 5m E of Sevenoaks on A227. TEAS in village hall. Maps available at gardens and village hall. Parking on village green. *Combined adm £2.50 Acc chd free. Sun June 11 (2-6)*

1 Batey's Cottage ♿✻ (Mr & Mrs E Martin) Stumble Hill. Small cottage garden with vegetable patch, herbaceous borders, shrubs

Brookers Cottage ♿✻❀ (Ann & Peter Johnson) Back Lane. ⅔-acre garden with natural pond, herbaceous borders and island beds; large collection of hardy geraniums (cranesbills); small fruit and vegetable patch

The Coach House ✻❀ (Mrs Ann Buckett) The Grange. Small informal garden, ⅓ acre, in former orchard; herbaceous and shrub borders with roses growing through apple trees; small pond; vegetable garden

¶**Plantation House** (Mr & Mrs A Primarolo) Reeds Lane. ¾-acre garden originally a Kent cobnut orchard, with island herbaceous borders; herbs, conifers, heathers, roses, old apple trees, azaleas, small vegetable garden

Yew Tree Cottage ✻ (Susan & Ian Bowles) The Green. Small cottage garden, partially walled, with herbaceous border, small gravel garden and old roses. Studio of wild life artist Ian Bowles will be open

Sibton Park ♿✻ (Mrs Ridley-Day & Mr & Mrs C Blackwell) Lyminge, 8m NW of Folkestone. Off Elham Valley road, N of Lyminge, turn L for Rhodes Minnis, ¼m on L. Landscaped garden with spacious lawns, 30 feet high yew hedges and topiary; old walled garden; children's adventure playground (own risk). TEAS. *Adm £1.50 OAP £1 Chd 50p. Sun June 25 (2-6)*

The Silver Spray ♿✻❀ (Mr & Mrs C T Orsbourne) Sellindge. 7m SE of Ashford on A20 opposite school. 1-acre garden developed and planted since 1983 and maintained by owners. Attractively laid out gardens and wild area combine a keen interest in conservation (especially butterflies) with a love of unusual hardy and tender plants. TEAS. *Adm £1 Acc chd free (Share to St Mary's Church, Sellindge®). Mons May 29, Aug 28; Weds July 5, 19, Aug 23; Sats June 17, July 8, 22; Sun June 25 (2-5)*

Sissinghurst Garden ♿✻❀ (Nigel Nicolson Esq; The National Trust) Cranbrook. Station: Staplehurst. Bus: MD5 from Maidstone 14m; 297 Tunbridge Wells (not Suns) 15m. Garden created by the late V. Sackville-West and Sir Harold Nicolson. Spring garden, herb garden. Tudor building and tower, partly open to public. Moat. **Because of the limited capacity of the garden, daily visitor numbers are restricted; timed tickets are in operation and visitors may have to wait before entry.** Lunches and TEAS. *Adm £5 Chd £2.50 (Share to Charleston Farmhouse Trust®). Garden open April 1 to Oct 15. (Closed Mons incl Bank Hols). Tues to Fri 1-6.30 (last adm 6pm); Sats and Suns 10-5.30 (last adm 5pm). For NGS Weds April 26, June 7, July 12 (1-6.30)*

Sissinghurst Place ♿✻ (Mr & Mrs Simon macLachlan) Sissinghurst, 2m N of Cranbrook, E of village on A262. Large garden of herbaceous beds, lawns, rhododendrons, fine trees, daffodils, shrubs and roses; herbs and climbers in ruin of original house, wild spring garden and pond. TEAS May openings only. *Adm £1.25 Chd 25p. Sats, Suns April 8, 9, May 20, 21; Mon April 10 (2-6)*

Slip Mill ✻❀ (Mrs Sheila Doyle) Hawkhurst, 3½m S of Cranbrook. From A21 at Flimwell take A268 signed Hawkhurst; turn 1st L after hospital, garden ½m on. 1½ acres with lawns; herbaceous plants; roses and established trees bounded on two sides by streams. TEAS/coffee. *Adm £1.50 Chd 25p. Wed June 14; Sun June 18 (10-6)*

Smith's Hall ♿ (Mr and Mrs Stephen Norman) West Farleigh, 4½m W of Maidstone, turn S off A26 Maidstone-Tonbridge rd at Teston Bridge, turn W at T-junction, garden on L. Roses, herbaceous borders, woodland walk. TEA. *Adm £1.50 Acc chd free. Sun June 25 (2-5)*

South Hill Farm ♿✂❀ (Sir Charles Jessel Bt) Hastingleigh, E of Ashford. Turn off A28 to Wye, go through village and ascend Wye Downs, in 2m turn R at Xrds marked Brabourne and South Hill, then first L. Or from Stone Street (B2068) turn W opp Stelling Minnis, follow signs to Hastingleigh, continue towards Wye and turn L at Xrds marked Brabourne and South Hill, then first L. 2 acres high up on N Downs, C17/18 house (not open); old walls; ha-ha; formal water garden; old and new roses; unusual shrubs, perennials and foliage plants. TEAS. *Adm £1.50 Chd 25p. Sun July 2 (2-6)*

Spilsill Court ♿✂❀ (Mr & Mrs C G Marshall) Frittenden Road, Staplehurst. Proceed to Staplehurst on A229 (Maidstone-Hastings). From S enter village, turn R immediately after Elf garage on R & just before 30mph sign, into Frittenden Rd; garden ½m on, on L. From N go through village to 40mph sign, immediately turn L into Frittenden Rd. Approx 4 acres of garden, orchard and paddock; series of gardens including those in blue, white and silver; roses; lawns; shrubs, trees and ponds. Small private chapel. Jacob sheep & unusual poultry. TEA. *Adm £1.50 Chd under 16 50p (Share to Gardening for the Disabled Trust®). Suns April 9, July 23 (11-5)*

Squerryes Court ♿ (Mr & Mrs John Warde) ½m W of Westerham signed from A25 Edenbridge Rd. 15 acres incl lake & woodland; well documented historic garden laid out in 1689; owners restoring the formal garden in William & Mary style; parterres, borders, 300-yr-old lime trees, dovecote, gazebo, cenotaph commemorating Gen Wolfe. TEAS. *Adm £2 Chd £1 (House & garden £3.50 Chd £1.60). Weds, Sats, Suns from April 1 to Sept 30 (2-6). For NGS (Share to St Mary's Church, Westerham©). Suns July 16, Aug 20 (2-6)*

Stoneacre ✂ (Mrs Rosemary Alexander; The National Trust) Otham, 4m SE of Maidstone, between A2020 and A274. Old world garden recently replanted. Yew hedges; herbaceous borders; ginkgo tree. Timber-framed Hall House dated 1480. Subject of newspaper and magazine articles. (National Trust members please note that this opening in aid of the NGS is on a day when the property would not normally be open, therefore adm charges apply). TEA. Open Weds & Sats April-Oct 28 (2-5) *Adm £1.50 Chd 50p (Share to Garden History Society®). For NGS Suns April 23, Oct 8 (2-5); private visits welcome, please* **Tel 01622 862871**

¶Stoneleigh House ♿✂❀ (John Martin Esq) Stone Street, 6m S of Canterbury on B2068, 7m N of M20 junction 11. About 6 acres including 3 acres of lawns, herbaceous plants and roses, specimen trees. 3-yrs-old but is maturing rapidly with computerised irrigation system. *Adm £2 Chd £1. Weds April 26, May 3, 10, 17, 23, 31, June 7, 14, 21, 28, July 12, 26, Aug 9 (11-5); also private visits welcome, please* **Tel 01227 700761**

Stonewall Park Gardens (Mr & Mrs V P Fleming) Chiddingstone Hoath, 5m SE of Edenbridge. ½-way between Mark Beech and Penshurst. Large walled garden with herbaceous borders. Extensive woodland garden, featuring species and hybrid rhododendrons and azaleas; wandering paths, lake. **North Lodge** (Mrs Dorothy Michie) traditional cottage garden full of interest. TEA. *Adm £2 Acc chd free. Sun May 7 (2-5.30)*

Street End Place ♿ (Mr & Mrs R Baker White) Street End. 3m S of Canterbury-Hythe rd (Stone St). Drive gates at Granville Inn. Long established garden incl walled garden, in pleasant setting; large area of naturalised daffodils with lawns of flowering shrubs; fine trees. *Adm £1.50 Chd 50p. Sun, Mon April 16, 17 (2-4.30)*

Swan Oast ♿✂ (Mr & Mrs Bedford) Stilebridge, Marden, 6m S of Maidstone. On A229 (Maidstone-Hastings) ½m S of Stilebridge inn, 2m N of Staplehurst. 20-year-old 1¾-acre garden, incl ¼ acre of water, landscaped with shrubberies, rockeries, with dwarf conifers and heathers, raised beds of seasonal bedding, kitchen garden; also ornamental fish and small collection of waterfowl. TEA. *Adm £1.50 Acc chd free (Share to The Mike Colinwood Trust®). Suns April 30, May 7, 14, July 2, 16, 30, Aug 13, 27 (2-6)*

Tanners ✂❀ (Lord & Lady Nolan) Brasted, 2m E of Westerham, A25 to Brasted; in Brasted turn off alongside the Green and up the hill to the top; 1st drive on R opp Coles Lane. Bus stop Brasted Greeen and White Hart 200yds. 5 acres; mature trees and shrubs; maples, magnolias, rhododendrons and foliage trees; water garden; interesting new planting, mainly labelled. Teas in Village Tearoom, High Street, Brasted. *Adm £1.50 Chd 50p. Suns March 26 (2-6), Oct 29 (1-5); Sat June 24 (2-6); parties welcome by appt, please* **Tel 01959 563758**

2 Thorndale Close ♿✂❀ (Mr & Mrs L O Miles) Chatham. From A229 Chatham-Maidstone rd turn E opp Forte Posthouse into Watson Ave, next R to Thorndale Close. Minute front and rear gardens of 11 × 18ft and 20 × 22ft. Plantsman's garden with alpines, pool, bog garden, rockery, peat and herbaceous beds. *Adm £1 Acc chd free. Suns April 9, 23, May 14, June 4, 18, July 9, 23 (2-6); also private visits welcome, please* **Tel 01634 863329**

Thornham Friars ♿✂ (Geoffrey Fletcher Esq) Pilgrims Way, Thurnham, 4m NE of Maidstone. From M20 or M2 take A249, at bottom of Detling Hill turn into Detling and 1m along Pilgrims Way to garden. 2-acre garden on chalk. Distant views across parkland. Many unusual shrubs; trees; lawns with special beds for ericaceous shrubs. Tudor house. *Adm £1.50 Chd 25p. Sun July 23 (2-5.30)*

Torry Hill ♿✂❀ (Lord & Lady Kingsdown) 5m S of Sittingbourne. Situated in triangle formed by Frinsted, Milstead and Doddington. Leave M 20 at junction 8 for A20, at Lenham turn N for Doddington; at Great Danes N for Hollingbourne and Frinsted (B2163). From M2 Intersection 5 via Bredgar and Milstead. From A2 and E turn S at

Ospringe via Newnham and Doddington. 8 acres; large lawns, specimen trees, flowering cherries, rhododendrons, azaleas and naturalised daffodils; walled gardens with lawns, shrubs, roses, herbaceous borders, wild flower areas and vegetables. Extensive views to Medway and Thames estuaries. TEA. *Adm £1.50 Chd over 12 50p (Share to St Dunstan's Church, Frinsted©). Suns April 23, May 14, July 2 (2-5)*

Town Hill Cottage ✿❀ (Mr & Mrs P Cosier) 58 Town Hill, West Malling. From A20 6m W of Maidstone, turn S onto A228. Top of Town Hill at N end of High St. Part walled small village garden of C16/C18 house, with many interesting plants. Hardy ferns for sale. TEAS. *Adm £1 Chd 50p. Suns May 21, June 18 (2-5)*

Turkey Court ♿✿❀ (Mr & Mrs Peter Young) Ashford Road, Maidstone. Leave M20 at exit 7 to town centre, then A20 E for ½m. Large garden 1st established in early C17, now with lawns, lake, river and waterfall. Walled garden, beautiful trees, herbaceous borders and shrubs; yr-round interest. TEAS. *Adm £1.25 Chd 30p. Suns April 30, July 30 (2-6)*

Updown Farm ♿✿ (Mr & the Hon Mrs Willis-Fleming) Betteshanger, 3m S of Sandwich. From A256 Sandwich-Dover, turn L off Eastry by-pass SE of Eastry, signed Northbourne, Finglesham. Again 1st L; house 1st on R. 3-acre garden begun in 1975 and now showing promise of its eventual maturity. One of the most extensive figgeries in East Kent; cherry and plum orchards with old roses and climbers; terrace garden; herbaceous borders, unusual trees and shrubs. TEAS in aid of Save the Children Fund & Kent Multiple Sclerosis Therapy Centre. *Adm £1.50 OAP 80p Chd 30p. Suns May 14, June 11 (2-6)*

Upper Pryors ♿✿ (Mr & Mrs S G Smith) Cowden, 4½m SE of Edenbridge. From B2026 Edenbridge-Hartfield, turn R at Cowden Xrds and take 1st drive on R. 10 acres recently redesigned to incorporate parkland and a water garden. The terrace, with courtyard and wisteria walkway leads out onto large lawns, borders and open views. TEAS. *Adm £1.50 Chd 50p. Wed June 14 (2-5)*

Vine House ♿✿❀ (Dr & Mrs Peter Huxley-Williams) 62 High St, Lydd. S of New Romney on B2075, past the church in High St on R-side. Informal gardens of about 1 acre surrounding C16 farmhouse; many unusual small trees & shrubs; ponds with waterfall; vineyard; new planting of old roses. Teas usually available in the church. *Adm £1 Acc chd free (Share to All Saints Church, Lydd®). Suns, Mons May 28, 29, Aug 27, 28 (2.30-5)*

Walnut Tree Gardens ♿✿❀ (Mr & Mrs M Oldaker) Swan Lane, Little Chart. 6m NW of Ashford. Leave A20 at Charing signed to Little Chart. At Swan public house turn W for Pluckley, gardens 500yds on L. Romantic 4-acre garden set within and around walls dating from early C18. Large collection of old roses; extensive range of unusual and interesting plants, shrubs and young trees. TEAS subject to weather. *Adm £1.50 Acc chd free (Share to German Shepherd Dog Rescue©). Suns May 28, June 4, 11, 18, 25 (Rose Day), July 2, 9, 16, 23, 30, Aug 6, 13; Mon May 29; Thurs June 29 (Rose Day) (2-5) Coaches by appt, please* **Tel 01233 840214**

39 Warwick Crescent ✿❀ (Mr & Mrs J G Sastre) Borstal, Rochester. From A229 Maidstone-Chatham at 2nd roundabout turn W into B2097 Borstal-Rochester rd; turn L at Priestfields, follow Borstal St to Wouldham Way, 3rd turning on R is Warwick Cres. Small front & rear plantsperson's gardens; most plants labelled; alpine terraces, peat & herbaceous beds; rockery with cascade & pool, bog garden, borders. Featured in NGS video 2. *Adm £1 Acc chd free. Suns April 9, 23, May 14, Sept 24 (2-5.30); also private visits welcome, please* **Tel 01634 401636**

Waystrode Manor ♿✿❀ (Mr & Mrs Peter Wright) Cowden, 4½m S of Edenbridge. From B2026 Edenbridge-Hartfield, turn off at Cowden Pound. Station: Weekdays Cowden; Suns Oxted or East Grinstead. 8 acres; large lawns, small grey garden, borders, ponds, bulbs, shrub roses and clematis. Subject of many magazine articles. All plants and shrubs labelled. House C15 (not open). Last entry ½-hour before closing time. TEAS. Gift shop. *Adm £2 Chd 50p. Suns May 28, June 4, 25 (2-6), Weds May 17, June 21 (1.30-5.30); also private visits welcome for groups*

Weeks Farm ♿✿ (Robin & Monica de Garston) Bedlam Lane, Egerton, Forstal, 3½m E of Headcorn. Take Smarden Road out of Headcorn, Bedlam Lane is 3rd turning on L, Weeks Farm approx 1½m on R. 1½-acre garden on Wealden clay, showing varied use of badly drained site; double herbaceous borders flanking gateway, vista a feature; orchard with crocus & fritillaria. Pond with abundance of wild life. TEAS. *Adm £1.50 Acc chd free. Suns March 12, April 9, Sept 24 (12-6)*

Went House ♿❀ (Mrs Robin Baring) Swan Street, West Malling. From A20, 6m W of Maidstone turn S onto A228. Turn E off High Street in village towards station. Queen Anne house with secret garden surrounded by high wall. Interesting plants, water gardens, woodland and parterre. TEAS. *Adm £1.50 Acc chd free (Share to Lane-Fox Respiratory Patients Assoc, St Thomas's Hospital®). Suns June 18, July 2 (2-6)*

West Studdal Farm ♿❀ (Mr & Mrs Peter Lumsden) West Studdal, N of Dover half-way between Eastry and Whitfield. From Eastry take A256, after 2½m pass Plough & Harrow, then 2nd L and 1st R, entrance ¼m on L. From Whitfield roundabout take A256, after 2½m pass High & Dry public house, ¼m fork R at 3-way junction, entrance ½m on R. Medium-sized garden around old farmhouse set by itself in small valley; herbaceous borders, roses and fine lawns protected by old walls and beech hedges. TEAS in Duodecagonal folly. *Adm £1.50 Chd 50p (Share to The Friends of St Thomas's Hospital®). Sun Aug 20 (2-6)*

Westview ❀ (Mr & Mrs J G Jackson) Spekes Rd, Hempstead. From M2 take A278 to Gillingham; at 1st roundabout follow sign to Wigmore, proceed to junction with Fairview Av, turn L & park on motorway link rd bridge, walk into Spekes Rd, Westview 3rd on L. ¼-acre town garden on very sloping site with many steps; good collection of plants & shrubs suitable for a chalk soil; designed by owners for all-year interest and low maintenance. Good autumn colour. TEAS. *Adm £1 Acc chd free. Weds April 26, May 17, June 7; Sats April 29, May 20, June 10 (2-5); also private visits welcome, please* **Tel 01634 230987**

Whitehill (Mrs Henderson) Wrotham. On A20 at Wrotham, between junctions 2A (M26) and 2 (M20). 3-acre garden, incl 1½ acres with design by Gertrude Jekyll in 1919, now carefully restored from original plans. *Adm £1.50 Chd 50p (Share to Kent Air Ambulance©). Sun June 4 (2-5.30); private visits welcome, please* **Tel 01732 882521**

Whitehurst (Mr & Mrs John Mercy) Chainhurst, 3m N of Marden. From Marden station turn R into Pattenden Lane and under railway bridge; at T-junction turn L; at next fork bear R to Chainhurst, then second turning on L. 1½ acres of trees, roses & water garden. Tree walk. Exhibition of root dwellings. TEAS. *Adm £1 Chd 50p (Share to Stroke Assoc®). Suns July 2, Oct 1, 8; Wed June 11 (2-5.30)*

Withersdane Hall (University of London) Wye College, 3m NE of Ashford. A28 take fork signed Wye. Bus EK 601 Ashford-Canterbury via Wye. Well-labelled garden of educational and botanical interest, containing several small carefully designed gardens; flower and shrub borders; spring bulbs; herb garden. Rain-fed garden. Free guide book with map available. TEAS. *Adm £1.50 Chd 50p. Suns April 16, July 9, Aug 6, Sept 3 (2-5)*

¶Womenswold Gardens Midway between Canterbury and Dover, SE of A2, take B2046 signed Wingham at Barham crossover, after about ¼m turn R at Armada beacon, follow signs for gardens. Five diverse and colourful cottage gardens within easy walking distance. St Margaret's Church will be open, with flower display. TEAS. *Combined adm £2.50 Acc chd free (Share to St Margaret's Church). Sat, Sun July 1, 2 (2-6)*

Woodlands Manor (Mr & Mrs Colin B George) Adisham, 5m SE of Canterbury. On A2 Canterbury-Dover, leave at sign to **Barham** ⅔m; at bottom of exit rd turn sharp L, follow signs marking rd to house, 1m. Approaching from E, from Adisham village turn R at end of The Street; ¾m on, follow signs. Small Georgian house of architectural interest (not open) set in old walled gardens. Spring garden a speciality; pleached lime and woodland walks; sunny corners; rose garden; gazebo. Good vistas; park. Picnics allowed. TEAS. *Adm £1.50 Acc chd under 12 free. Suns Feb 5, 19, April 9 (2-5), May 7, June 4, 18, July 2 (2-5.30). For NGS Suns Feb 12, March 19, 26, April 2, 23, 30 (2-5), May 14, 21, 28, June 11, 25, July 16 (2-5.30)*

Worth Gardens 2m SE of Sandwich and 5m NW of Deal, from A258 signed Worth. A group of cottage gardens in wide variety in peaceful village setting. Maps and tickets available at each garden. TEAS. *Combined adm £1.50 Chd 25p. Sun July 2 (2-5)*

Wyckhurst (Mr & Mrs C D Older) Mill Road, Aldington, 4m SE of Ashford. Leave M20 at junction 10, on A20 travel S to Aldington turning; proceed 1½m to Aldington village hall, 'Walnut Tree' take rd signed to Dymchurch, after ¼m turn R into Mill Road is on R. C16 cottage (not open) surrounded by 1-acre cottage garden; old roses; herbaceous borders; unusual perennials. Extensive views across Romney Marsh. TEAS in aid of Bonnington Church. *Adm £1.50 Chd 50p. Wed June 21; Sun June 25 (11-6)*

Lancashire, Merseyside & Greater Manchester

Hon County Organisers: Mr & Mrs R Doldon, Old Barn Cottage, Greens Arms Road, Turton Nr Bolton BL7 OND Tel 01204 852139

Assistant Hon County Organiser: J Bowker Esq, Swiss Cottage, 8 Hammond Drive, Read, Burnley

DATES OF OPENING

By appointment

For telephone numbers and other details see garden descriptions. Private visits welcomed

Catforth Gardens, Catforth
Cross Gaits Cottage, Blacko
Frigham Cottage, Trawden
Lindeth Dene, Silverdale
Mill Barn, Salmesbury Bottoms
Old Barn Cottage, Turton
The Ridges, Limbrick, nr Chorley
Stonestack, nr Turton
Swiss Cottage, Read
Windle Hall, St Helens

Parties only

Loxley, Wrightington
Speke Hall, Liverpool

April 14 Friday

The Ridges, Limbrick, nr Chorley

April 16 Sunday

Lindeth Dene, Silverdale

April 17 Monday

The Ridges, Limbrick, nr Chorley

May 1 Sunday

Swiss Cottage, Read

May 7 Sunday

Bank House, Borwick
Spring Bank House, Cow Ark

May 21 Sunday

191 Liverpool Road South, Maghull
Loxley, Wrightington

May 28 Sunday

Catforth Gardens, Catforth
Cross Gaits Cottage, Blacko
Lindeth Dene, Silverdale
191 Liverpool Road South, Maghull
Loxley, Wrightington
Old Barn Cottage, Turton

May 29 Monday

Cross Gaits Cottage, Blacko
Old Barn Cottage, Turton

June 4 Sunday

Bank House, Borwick
Rufford Old Hall, Rufford, nr Ormskirk

June 11 Sunday

Mill Barn, Salmesbury Bottoms
Speke Hall, The Walk, Liverpool

June 18 Sunday

Higher Parrock House, Barrowford

June 21 Wednesday
Higher Parrock House, Barrowford
June 25 Sunday
Catforth Gardens, Catforth
Mill Barn, Salmesbury Bottoms
Swiss Cottage, Read
July 2 Sunday
Bank House, Borwick
Lindeth Dene, Silverdale
Spring Bank House, Cow Ark
Windle Hall, St Helens
July 9 Sunday
Frigham Cottage, Trawden
Weeping Ash, Glazebury
July 16 Sunday
Cross Gaits Cottage, Blacko
Montford Cottage, Fence
July 30 Sunday
Catforth Gardens, Catforth
August 6 Sunday
Bank House, Borwick
August 28 Monday
The Ridges, Limbrick, nr Chorley
September 3 Sunday
Bank House, Borwick
Windle Hall, St Helens
September 10 Sunday
Weeping Ash, Glazebury
October 1 Sunday
Bank House, Borwick
Mill Barn, Salmesbury Bottoms

DESCRIPTIONS OF GARDENS

Bank House ✲❀ (Mr & Mrs R G McBurnie) Borwick. 2m NE of Carnforth off A6. Leave M6 at junction 35. Plantsman's garden of 2 acres designed to provide all year round shape, colour and form. Divided into different areas of interest including shady borders, sunny gravel area with old-fashioned roses, arboretum, fruit and vegetables. Island beds, silver and gold borders. Collection of carnivorous plants. Featured in 'English Private Gardens'. TEAS. *Adm £1 Chd 25p. Suns May 7, June 4, July 2, Aug 6, Sept 3, Oct 1 (2-6)*

Catforth Gardens ♿❀ Leave M6 at junction 32 turning N on A6. Turn L at 1st set of traffic lights; 2m to T-junction, turn R. Turn L at sign for Catforth, L at next T-junction, 1st R into Benson Lane. Bear L at church into Roots Lane. Includes adjoining garden of Willowbridge Farm with access through Catforth Gardens Nursery as seen on Gardeners World 1993, featured in the Good Gardens Guide. TEAS NGS days only. *Combined adm £1.50 Chd 20p. Suns May 28, June 25, July 30 (12-5) adjacent nursery open March 18 to Sept 17 (10.30-5). Parties by appt, please* **Tel 01772 690561/690269**

Catforth Gardens Nursery (Mr & Mrs T A Bradshaw) 1-acre informal country garden, planted for year round interest and colour. Wide variety of unusual shrubs; trees; rhododendrons, azaleas; unusual and rare herbaceous plants including euphorbias, dicentras, pulmonarias; ground cover plants; national collection of hardy geraniums; 2 ponds with bog gardens, large rockery and woodland garden

Willow Bridge Farm (Mr & Mrs W Moore) ¼-acre garden planted with a wide variety of herbaceous perennials (many rare & unusual). Planted with particular attention to colour from spring to autumn, giving a cottage garden effect, plus an acre garden in the making, large ponds, sunny banks and long herbaceous borders

Cross Gaits Cottage ✲❀ (Mr & Mrs S J Gude) Take M65 exit junction 13. Follow Barrowford signs then Barnoldswick signs. Garden 1½m on Barnoldswick Road opp Cross Gaits Inn. ⅔-acre walled cottage garden, shrub and herbaceous borders. 2 ornamental ponds. 700ft above sea level; fine view of Pennines. TEA/coffee. *Adm £1 Chd 50p. Sun, Mon May 28, 29; Sun July 16 (1-5). Private visits welcome, please* **Tel 01282 617163**

¶Frigham Cottage ❀ (Sue & Alec Rumbold) Trawden. 3m SE of Colne. From the A6068, follow the B6250 into Trawden. Turn L at church, then straight on for 1m. No parking at the house on open day - visitors have a 600yd walk. ⅓-acre of recently developed garden on the lower slopes of Boulsworth Hill at 850ft above sea level. Divided into several small gardens and secret corners to give an element of surprise; water features and a wide variety of shrubs and plants. TEAS. *Adm £1 Chd free. Sun July 9 (11-5). Private visits welcome May to July (with parking at the house), please* **Tel 01282 870581**

¶Higher Parrock House ✲ (J S Thornton Esq) Barrowford. M65 motorway. Take turning to Fench at junction 13, R after 600yds to top of Parrock Rd. 2 acres of mature gardens on S facing slope. Spring flowering trees and shrubs, mature conifers, gardens within gardens, ponds and water features, rambling roses. TEAS (Sun June 18 TEA (Wed June 21). *Adm £1. Sun June 18 (11-5), Wed June 21 (2-6)*

Lindeth Dene ✲❀ (Mrs B M Kershaw) 38 Lindeth Rd, Silverdale. 13m N of Lancaster. Take M6 to junction 35, turn L (S) on A6 to Carnforth traffic lights. Turn R follow signs Silverdale. After level crossing ¼m uphill turn L down Hollins Lane. At T junction turn R into Lindeth Rd. Garden is 4th gateway on L, park in rd. Approx 1¼ acres overlooking Morecombe Bay on W facing slope. Large limestone rock garden, trees, shrubs, hardy perennials, troughs, pools, heather garden, veganic kitchen garden with raised beds. Collections of saxifrages, geraniums, Elizabethan primroses, New Zealand plants. Teas and toilets available in village. *Adm £1 Acc chd free. Suns April 16, May 28, July 2 (2-5). Private visits welcome by app, please* **Tel 01524 701314**

191 Liverpool Rd South ♿❀ (Mr & Mrs D Cheetham) Maghull. From A59 take turning for Maghull Town Centre. Turn L at traffic lights and veer R over canal bridge. Garden ¼m on R. ½-acre suburban garden; rhododendrons, azaleas, camellias, rockery, pool, sink gardens, primulas, a variety of trees (some unusual), shrubs, bulbs and herbaceous plants for all year colour in the smaller garden. TEA or coffee. *Adm £1 Acc chd free. Suns May 21, 28 (1.30-5.30)*

By Appointment Gardens. Avoid the crowds. Good chance of a tour by owner. See garden description for telephone number.

Loxley ✲❀ (Mr & Mrs D Robinson) Robin Hood Lane, Wrightington, nr Wigan. Situated 1m from junction 27 of the M6. Continue past Wrightington Hospital to Xrds, turn R by the garage ½m up the rd situated on the L. ¼-acre garden designed on two levels with water feature & ornamental fish pond. Variety of shrubs, conifers, rhododendrons, azaleas and perennials. Barbecue, weather permitting. TEA. *Adm £1 Acc chd free. Suns May 21, 28 (12-5). Parties welcome, please* **Tel 01257 54120**

Mill Barn ♿❀ (Dr C J Mortimer) Goose Foot Close, Samlesbury Bottoms, Preston. 6m E of Preston. From M6 junction 31 2½m on A59/A677 B/burn. Turn S. Nabs Head Lane, then Goose Foot Lane 1m. 1½-acre tranquil, terraced garden on the site of C18 corn and cotton mills along the banks of the R Davwen. Varied planting with many uncommon herbaceous perennials. A maturing garden that is still being developed and extended. TEAS. *Adm £1 Chd free. Suns June 11, 25 (2-6), Oct 1 (2-5). Private visits of 4 and over welcome, please* **Tel 01254 853300**

Montford Cottage ♿✲❀ (C Bullock & A P Morris) Fence, nr Burnley. Situated on the B6248 between Brierfield & Fence. From the M65 junction 13, take the A6068 (signs for Fence) and in 2m turn L onto the B6248 (signs for Brierfield). Proceed down the hill for ½m, entrance to garden is on L (near dangerous bend-drivers please take care). Walled garden ⅔-acre developed over last 10 yrs and now maturing, with many unusual plants of particular interest to flower arrangers and plantsmen. Particular emphasis on variety of foliage, with varied shrubs, trees, herbaceous plants and pools and featuring new oriental garden. No coaches. TEAS. *Adm £1 Chd 50p. Sun July 16 (2-6)*

Old Barn Cottage ♿❀ (Ray & Brenda Doldon) Greens Arms Rd, Turton. Midway between Bolton and Darwen on B6391 off A666, or through Chapeltown Village High St (B6391). 1-acre developing garden on moorland site. Spring flowering trees; shrubs; azaleas, rhododendrons; water gardens; heathers; conifers, herbaceous beds; moorland views. As seen on TV Garden Club 1993. TEAS in aid of St Ann's Church (Sun), Beacon Counselling Service (Mon). *Adm £1 Chd free. Sun, Mon, May 28, 29 (1-5). Private visits welcome by app (May to Aug), please* **Tel 01204 852139**

¶The Ridges ♿✲❀ (Mr & Mrs J M Barlow) Limbrick, nr Chorley. Approx 2m SE of Chorley Centre. M6 junction 27 approx 10m. M61 from Manchester Chorley S junction 6 app 6m, passing through Adlington and taking Long Lane to Limbrick. Passing Black Horse follow the rd to L and uphill on L. Chorley N junction 8 from Preston and N, take Cowling Rd out of Chorley towards Rivington approx 1½m on R. C17 house with Georgian additions with 2¼-acre gardens. Incl old walled kitchen garden/orchard, now converted to cottage style garden with lawn, large well stocked herbaceous borders, and area for growing annual flowers, and grasses to dry (of particular interest to flower arrangers). Also small fish pond with patio; laburnum arch leads to large formal lawn, surrounded by long established rhododendrons, flowering shrubs and natural woodland. TEAS. *Adm £1 Chd 50p. Fri, Mons April 14, 17, Aug 28 (11-5). Private visits for 5 & over welcome, please* **Tel 01257 279981**

Rufford Old Hall ♿ (The National Trust) Rufford. On A59 Liverpool to Preston rd in village of Rufford, 7m N of Ormskirk. Set in 14 acres of garden and woodland. Informal garden and walks. Spectacular in May and June for spring flowering rhododendrons and azaleas. TEAS. *Adm £1.60 Chd 80p (Garden only). Sun June 4 (12-4.30)*

Speke Hall ♿✲ (The National Trust) Liverpool. 8m SE of Liverpool adjacent to Liverpool Airport. Follow signs for Liverpool Airport. A formal garden with herbaceous border, rose garden; moated area with formal lawns. A stream garden now open this yr. A wild wood is included. Approx size of estate 35 acres. TEAS. *Adm £1 Chd 50p. (Garden only). Sun June 11 (1-5.30). Parties of 20 or over welcome, please* **Tel 0151 4277231**

Spring Bank House ✲❀ (Joan & Philip Lord) Cow Ark. Situated 6m NW of Clitheroe between Bashall Eaves and Whitewell within ½m of Browsholme Hall, which is well signposted. From Clitheroe take Longridge Rd (B6243) then take 1st R after Edisford Bridge Hotel. A country garden of 6½-acres, made and maintained by the owners since 1975. Stretching away from the house, 2 acres of informal garden are planted with a large variety of trees, shrubs and herbaceous plants, many of them unusual, to provide yr-round interest; while the remaining 4½ acres make up the woodland garden. This steeply wooded valley planted with species rhododendrons, acers, magnolias and other woodland plants, together with many native wild flowers. TEAS in aid of St Michael's Church, Whitewell. *Adm £1 Chd 50p. Suns May 7, July 2 (1-5.30)*

Stonestack ♿❀ (Frank Smith Esq) 283 Chapeltown Rd, Turton; 4½m N of Bolton, via A666 leading to B6391 nr Turton Tower. 2½-acre garden; shrubs, rhododendrons, azaleas; herbaceous borders; rockeries, waterfall, ornamental fishpond, fountain, rose garden, bog garden, fuchsias and abutilons a special feature; sweet peas, soft fruit area; orchard, greenhouses and plant houses. As seen on BBC Gardener's World 1985 and BBC Look North TV Aug 88. *Private visits welcome July & August, please* **Tel 01204 852460**

Swiss Cottage ❀ (James & Doreen Bowker) 8 Hammond Drive, Read. 3m SE of Whalley on A671 Whalley to Burnley Road, turn by Pollards Garage, up George Lane to T junction, L into Private Rd. 1½-acre Hillside Garden designed on two levels in mature woodland setting. Variety of shrubs, trees, rhododendrons, azaleas, perennials and alpines. Stream and bog garden feature. Featured in Lancashire Life. TEAS. *Adm £1 Chd free. Suns May 1, June 25 (1-5). Private visits welcome by appt, please* **Tel 01282 774853**

Regular Openers. Too many days to include in diary. Usually there is a wide range of plants giving year-round interest. See head of county section for the name and garden description for times etc.

Weeping Ash ✲ (John Bent Esq) Glazebury. ¼m S A580 (East Lancs Rd Greyhound Motel roundabout, Leigh) on A574 Glazebury/Leigh Boundary. 2-acre garden of year long interest on heavy soil. A broad sweep of lawn with deep mixed borders of shrubs and herbaceous perennials gives way to secret areas with pools, rose beds and island beds, new for 1995, a rockery with alpines, a ruined Doric temple, elevated viewing points to enable one to see broad sweeps of the garden, plus industrial Lancashire landscape. A hot area with mediterranean planting and a further extensive lawn. Teas 100yds N at Garden Centre. *Adm £1 Chd 50p (Share to Macmillan Leigh Home Care Unit®). Suns July 9, Sept 10 (2-6)*

Windle Hall ♿❀ (The Lady Pilkington) N of E Lancs Rd, St Helens. 5m W of M6 via E Lancs Rd, nr Southport junction. Entrance by bridge over E Lancs Rd. 200yr-old walled garden surrounded by 5-acres of lawns, rock and water garden; Victorian thatched cottage. Tufa stone grotto; herbaceous borders, pergola and rose gardens containing exhibition blooms, miniature ornamental ponies, pheasants; greenhouses. TEAS. *Adm £1 Chd 50p. Suns June 2, Sept 3 (2-5). Private visits welcome for 10 and over, please* **Tel 01744 23534**

Regular Openers. See head of county section.

Leicestershire & Rutland

Hon County Organisers: (Leicestershire) Mr John Oakland, Old School Cottage, Oaks-in-Charnwood, nr Loughborough LE12 9YD Tel 01509 502676
(Rutland) Mrs R Wheatley, Clipsham House, Oakham LE15 7SE Tel 01780 410238

Hon County Treasurer (Rutland): A Whitamore Esq., The Stockyard, West Street, Easton-on-the-Hill, Stamford, Lincs PE9 3LS

DATES OF OPENING

By appointment
For telephone number and other details see garden descriptions. Private visits welcomed

Brooksby College, nr Melton Mowbray
Burrough House, Melton Mowbray
The Cottage, Keyham
6 Dennis Road, Burbage Gardens
7 Hall Road, Burbage Gardens
Long Close, Woodhouse Eaves
Orchards, Walton, nr Lutterworth
18 Park Road, Birstall
Rose Cottage, Owston Gardens, Oakham
Stepping Stones Old Farm, Little Beeby
Whatton House, Loughborough

Parties only
Burrough House, Melton Mowbray
7 Hall Road, Burbage Gardens, Burbage
Paddocks, Shelbrook, Ashby-de-la-Zouch
Stoke Albany House, Market Harborough
University of Leicester Botanic Garden, Oadby
Vine Cottage, Sheepy Magna Gardens
Wartnaby, nr Melton Mowbray

Regular openings
For details see garden descriptions

Arthingworth Manor, Market Harborough. Every Weds, June, July
Burrough House, Melton Mowbray. Bank Hol Suns, Mons Easter to Aug. Every Sun, Thurs June, July, Aug
1700 Melton Road, Rearsby. Daily March to Oct

April 2 Sunday
Long Close, Woodhouse Eaves

April 6 Thursday
Burbage Gardens, Burbage

April 15 Saturday
Paddocks, Shelbrook, Ashby-de-la-Zouch

April 16 Sunday
Paddocks, Shelbrook, Ashby-de-la-Zouch

April 18 Tuesday
Whatton House, Loughborough

April 23 Sunday
Ashwell Lodge, Oakham

April 30 Sunday
Hoby Gardens, Hoby, nr Melton Mowbray ‡
Reservoir Cottage, Knipton ‡

May 4 Thursday
Burbage Gardens, Burbage

May 7 Sunday
Long Close, Woodhouse Eaves ‡
19 The Ridgeway, Rothley ‡

May 9 Tuesday
Whatton House, Loughborough

May 13 Saturday
Wakerley Manor, Uppingham

May 14 Sunday
Burrough House, Melton Mowbray
Paddocks, Shelbrook, Ashby-de-la-Zouch
18 Park Road, Birstall
Wakerley Manor, Uppingham

May 17 Wednesday
Paddocks, Shelbrook, Ashby-de-la-Zouch

May 18 Thursday
18 Park Road, Birstal

May 21 Sunday
Owston Gardens, Oakham
Wartnaby, nr Melton Mowbray

May 28 Sunday
Long Close, Woodhouse Eaves

May 30 Tuesday
Whatton House, Loughborough

June 4 Sunday
Park Farm, Bottesford, (see Nottinghamshire)
Woodyton Farmhouse, Coalville

June 11 Sunday
Burbage Gardens, Burbage
Prebendal House, Empingham
19 The Ridgeway, Rothley

June 18 Sunday
Arthingworth Manor, Market Harborough
Beeby Manor, Beeby ‡

The Old Rectory, Teigh
Orchards, Walton, nr Lutterworth
Queniborough Gardens ‡

June 20 Tuesday
Beeby Manor, Beeby

June 21 Wednesday
Orchards, Walton, nr Lutterworth

June 24 Saturday
Plungar Gardens, The Vale of Belvoir
Sheepy Magna Gardens

June 25 Sunday
Ashwell Gardens, Oakham ‡
Hoby Gardens, Hoby, nr Melton Mowbray ‡‡
Langham Lodge, Oakham ‡
The Old Vicarage, Granby (see Nottinghamshire)
18 Park Road, Birstall
Plungar Gardens, The Vale of Belvoir
Sheepy Magna Gardens
Wartnaby, nr Melton Mowbray ‡‡
Woodyton Farmhouse, Coalville

July 2 Sunday
Hickling Gardens, nr Melton Mowbray (see Nottinghamshire)
Manton Grange, Oakham
Paddocks, Shelbrook, Ashby-de-la-Zouch
The Priory, Ketton
Sutton Bonington Hall, Sutton Bonington

July 4 Tuesday
Stoke Albany House, Market Harborough

July 5 Wednesday
Paddocks, Shelbrook, Ashby-de-la-Zouch
Stoke Albany House, Market Harborough

July 6 Thursday
Burbage Gardens, Burbage

July 9 Sunday
Market Overton Gardens
Stoke Albany House, Market Harborough

July 11 Tuesday
Stoke Albany House, Market Harborough

July 12 Wednesday
Stoke Albany House, Market Harborough

July 16 Sunday
Fenny Drayton Gardens
South Luffenham Hall, nr Stamford

July 23 Sunday
University of Leicester Botanic Garden, Oadby
Wartnaby, nr Melton Mowbray

July 30 Sunday
The Cottage, Keyham

August 13 Sunday
Paddocks, Shelbrook, Ashby-de-la-Zouch

August 16 Wednesday
Paddocks, Shelbrook, Ashby-de-la-Zouch

August 20 Sunday
Woodyton Farmhouse, Coalville

September 3 Sunday
Brooksby College, nr Melton Mowbray

September 10 Sunday
Barnsdale Plants & Gardens, Oakham ‡
1 Cumberland Road, Loughborough
Little Froome, Fenny Drayton Gardens
Hill House, Market Overton Gardens ‡

September 17 Sunday
Whatton House, Loughborough

October 1 Sunday
1700 Melton Road, Rearsby
19 The Ridgeway, Rothley

October 8 Sunday
Whatton House, Loughborough

DESCRIPTIONS OF GARDENS

Arthingworth Manor ♿ (Mr & Mrs W Guinness) 5m S of Market Harborough. From Market Harborough via A508 at 4m L to Arthingworth; from Northampton via A508. At Kelmarsh turn R at bottom of hill for Arthingworth. In village turn R at church 1st L. 6 to 7-acre beautiful garden; collection shrub roses; white garden; delphiniums, herbaceous and mixed borders; greenhouses. Newly planted 3-acre arboretum. Original house now restored. Art gallery, British Modern Pictures. TEAS. Limited wheelchair access. *Adm £1.50 Chd 50p (Share to St John Ambulance, Northants®). Weds, June, July; Sun June 18 (2-5)*

Ashwell Gardens ♿✂ 3m N of Oakham, via B668 towards Cottesmore, turn L for Ashwell. TEAS at Ashwell House. *Combined adm £2 Chd 50p (Share to St Mary's Church®). Sun June 25 (2-6)*

Ashwell House (Mr & Mrs S D Pettifer) 1½-acre vicarage garden, 1812; vegetable garden; almost original format partly given over to specialist flowers for drying. Pleasure garden with summer pavilion in classical style and architectural features by George Carter. TEAS. Home-made produce stall

The Old Hall (Mrs N L McRoberts) Medium-sized garden, mixed borders, good variety of shrubs, climbers and herbaceous plants

¶Thistles ❀ (Mr & Mrs M Hope) Small new plantsman's garden with over 280 named varieties (many unusual) in bog, pond, scree, shade and raised beds. Borders and climbers on pergolas and fences

Ashwell Lodge ♿✂❀ (Mrs B V Eve) Ashwell, 3m N of Oakham. From Al, 10m N of Stamford, turn W through Greetham and Cottesmore; then turn R for Ashwell. Park in village st. Medium-sized garden redesigned by Percy Cane c.1973; spring bulbs; herbaceous borders, paved rose garden, shrubs, greenhouse. As featured in 'Country Life' Nov 1990. TEAS. *Adm £1 Chd 25p (Share to Forces Help Soc & Lord Roberts Workshops®). Sun April 23 (2-6)*

¶Barnsdale Plants & Gardens ♿✂❀ (Mr Geoff & Mr Nick Hamilton) The Avenue, Exton. Turn off Stamford/Oakham rd A606 at Barnsdale, signposted Cottesmore. 1m down avenue. 1 acre of small gardens within a larger garden. Good mix of perennials, shrubs, trees, bog garden and stream. *Adm £1.50 Chd 25p (Share to Plant Life®). Sun Sept 10 (10-4)*

Beeby Manor ♿✂❀ (Mr & Mrs Philip Bland) Beeby. 8m E of Leicester. Turn off A47 in Thurnby and follow signs through Scraptoft. 3-acre mature garden with venerable yew hedges, walled herbaceous border, lily ponds, rose towers and box parterre. Plus the start of a 1-acre arboretum. C16 and C18 house (not open). TEAS. *Adm £1.70 Chd free (Share to Village Tree Project©). Sun, Tues June 18, 20 (2-6)*

Brooksby College ♿✂❀ 6m SW of Melton Mowbray. From A607 (9m from Leicester or 6m from Melton Mowbray) turn at Brooksby; entrance 100yds. Bus: Leicester-Melton Mowbray-Grantham; alight Brooksby turn, 100yds.

Grounds incl extensive lawns, lake, ornamental brook, flowering shrub borders, heather bed, large collection young trees; other ornamental features; glasshouses, nursery. Church built 1220 open. TEA. *Adm £2 Chd free. Sun Sept 3 (1-5). Private visits welcome, please* **Tel 01664 434291**

Burbage Gardens ❀ From M69 junction 1, take B4109 signed Hinckley. TEA (Thurs only). *Combined adm £1 Chd 20p (Share to LOROS®). Thurs April 6, May 4, July 6 (2-5) Combined adm £1.50 Sun June 11 (11-5)*

6 Denis Road ✲❀ (Mr & Mrs D A Dawkins) Sketchley Manor Estate. 1st L after roundabout. Small garden planted for scent with alpine house, scree area, alpines in troughs, herbaceous borders with old roses; collection of clematis and spring bulbs

7 Hall Road Burbage (Mr & Mrs D R Baker) Sketchley Manor Estate. 1st roundabout 1st L to Sketchley Lane; 1st R; 1st R; 1st R again; 1st L to Hall Rd. Medium-sized garden; mixed borders; alpines; sink gardens; scree area; collection of hellebores and hosta; unusual plants; foliage plants. *Private visits welcome, please* **Tel 01455 635616**

The Long Close Bullfurlong Lane ♿ (Mr & Mrs A J Hopewell) Burbage. 1st R onto Coventry Road 2nd R onto Bullfurlong Lane, garden on L. Limited parking, park if poss on Coventry Rd. ½-acre family garden. Mixed borders; 'natural' ponds; vegetable plot; greenhouse and cool orchid house. Local orchid society in attendance. Cream TEAS, ploughman's lunches; toilets. *Open Sun June 11 only*

11 Primrose Drive (Mr & Mrs D Leach) Take 2nd turning on R into Sketchley Rd. 1st L into Azalea Drive, 1st R into Marigold Drive, 1st L Begonia Drive, 1st R into Primrose Drive. No 11 is on L on bend. Small cottage garden. Spring interest camellias and rhododendrons, summer interest paeonies and clematis. Plants and pressed flower work for sale

Burrough House ♿✲❀ (Mrs Barbara Keene) Burrough on the Hill. 6m W of Oakham, 5m S of Melton Mowbray. From A606 at Langham, take rd signposted to Cold Overton and Somerby, continue through Somerby to Burrough on the Hill. Approx 5½ acres of garden with an interesting small collection of rhododendrons and azaleas in late May; spring bulbs highlighted in 2 woodland walks; a timber, thatch- roofed Bower House used by the Prince of Wales and Mrs Simpson; cascading water pools and rose garden. The garden was created by an enthusiastic plantsman, Sir Raymond Greene in the early 1920's and retains much of his original structural concepts. New white garden under construction. TEAS. *Adm £1.50 weekdays, £2 weekends Chd free (St Mary's Church Roof Appeal®). Bank Hols Suns, Mons, Easter to Aug (11-5). Every Sun and Thurs June, July, Aug (2-5). For NGS Sun May 14 (2-5). Private visits welcome, please* **Tel 01664 77226**

¶**The Cottage** ♿ (Mrs Ainsley Poole) Keyham. 6m E of Leicester. Turn off A47 in Thurnby and follow signs through Scraptoft to Keyham. 2½ acre informal garden with herbaceous and shrub borders, vintage fruit trees and mature conifers, interesting topiary; recently enlarged pond contains a variety of fish. *Adm £1.50 Chd free. Sun July 30 (10-5). Private visits welcome, please* **Tel 01533 595235**

¶**1 Cumberland Road** ♿❀ (Mr & Mrs R Peddle) Loughborough. On A512 into Loughborough, 1m E of M1 junction 23, 1st L turn 300yds after Ring rd roundabout. Parking in Cumberland Rd and adjacent streets. Plant enthusiast's small walled town garden, herbaceous borders, scree, climbers, pots. Planted for sun and shade. TEAS. *Adm £1 Chd free (Share to NCCPG®). Sun Sept 10 (1-5)*

¶**Fenny Drayton Gardens** Situated approx 3m N of Nuneaton on the A444, crossing the A5 at The Royal Red Gate Inn and MSF Garage junction. Teas and Flower Festival in St Michael's Church. *Combined adm £1.50 Chd free (Share to St Michael's Church®). Sun July 16 (2-6)*

¶**4 Drayton Lane** ✲❀ (Mr & Mrs G Wright) ½ acres of lawn, with heather conifer beds, inlaid with bedding, plant areas, rockeries and pond

¶**Little Froome** ♿❀ (Mr & Mrs G J Cookes) Drayton Lane. 1½-acre garden, mature trees and wide variety of conifers. Landscaped with heathers at their best in Sept, large pond with bridge. *Also open Sun Sept 10 (2-6).* TEA

¶**4 Rookery Close** ✲❀ (Mr & Mrs J Dowse) Average sized garden with pond and waterfall. Abundance of hanging baskets and tubs. Very good selection of perennials and shrubs

¶**Crofters** ♿ (Mr & Mrs G M Heaton) 16 Rookery Close. Neat tidy garden front and year, mostly lawns and flower beds. Open views of Leicestershire countryside at rear

¶**19 Rookery Close** ♿ (Mr & Mrs Ratcliffe) Small garden lots of colour

¶**Gem Cottage** ✲ (Alan & Jane Priest) 4 Church Lane. ⅓-acre cottage side and rear gardens. Trees, shrubs and plants with pool and fish. Chimney pots and cart filled to brim with colour

¶**12 Church Lane** ♿ (Mr & Mrs M Ambrose) ½-acre garden, ornamental walls and borders with rockeries, pond and waterfall. *Private visits of 6 and over welcome, please* **Tel 01827 713257**

¶**Five Corners** ♿✲ (Mr & Mrs Perrin) ¼-acre garden, mainly lawns with mixed shrubbery borders and evergreen hedges

Hoby Gardens ✲ 8m NE of Leicester, 1m NW of A607 Leicester-Melton rd. Turn at Brooksby Agricultural College. *Combined adm £1.50 Chd free (Share to St John's Ambulance® and FSID®). Suns April 30, June 25 (2-6)*

Glebe House ♿❀ (Mr & Mrs S Horsfield) Church Lane. 1 acre of shrubs and herbaceous mixed borders, created since 1977, mainly within lovely C18 wall; paddock. Pleasing views over glebe land. TEAS

Rooftree Cottage (D Headly Esq) Main Street. Small garden to a medieval cruck cottage. The site slopes down towards the R Wreake and the garden is planned to lead to pastoral views across the valley. Traditional and indigenous plantings

Langham Lodge ♿✲❀ (Mr & Mrs H N Hemsley) Oakham. ½m out of Langham on Burley Rd. 1 acre; shrubs; interesting foliage; stone walls; shrub roses. Light lunches in aid of Langham Church. *Adm £1 Chd free. Sun June 25 (11-6)*

Long Close ❀ (Mrs George Johnson) 60 Main St, Woodhouse Eaves, S of Loughborough. From A6, W in Quorn B591. 5 acres rhododendrons (many varieties), azaleas, flowering shrubs, old shrub roses, many rare shrubs, trees, heathers, conifers, forest trees; lily pools; fountain; terraced lawns, herbaceous borders. Featured in *Country Life*. TEA May 7. TEAS and specialist plant sale April 2, May 28. *Adm £1.50 Chd 20p. Suns April 2, (2-5), May 7, 28 (2-6). Also private visits welcome March to June, please* **Tel 01509 890616** *business hrs*

Manton Grange ✂❀ (Mr & Mrs M Taylor) Manton. Turn off A6003 halfway between Uppingham and Oakham to Manton Village. Recently redesigned garden still undergoing improvements. Good mix of foliage, shrubs, rose garden with gazebo and fountain. Good trees and spectacular view. TEAS. *Adm £1.50 Chd 20p (Share to Manton Village Hall®). Sun July 2 (2-6)*

Market Overton Gardens ✂ 6m N of Oakham beyond Cottesmore; 5m from the A1 via Thistleton; 10m E from Melton Mowbray via Wymondham. TEAS. *Combined adm £2.50 Chd 50p (Share to Market Overton Play Area Assoc®). Sun July 9 (2-6)*

31 Bowling Green Lane (Richard Hirst) Secluded cottage garden, approx ⅓-acre, varied plants and shrubs

Church Cottage ♿ (Mr & Mrs W M Cox) Well hidden partly-walled ½-acre old-fashioned garden surrounding thatched cottage; climbing and shrub roses, clematis, peonies, shrubs, perennials and lawns

Hill House ❀ (Brian & Judith Taylor) ½-acre plantsman's garden mainly of mixed herbaceous beds for yr-round colour and texture and comprising many uncommon hardy and half hardy perennials. Unusual plants for sale. *Also open Sun Sept 10 (2-6). TEAS. Adm £1 Chd 50p*

The Old Hall (Mr & Mrs P Hart) Newly designed S facing 3-acre garden. lovely views, flowing lawns on 2 levels; herbaceous borders, climbing roses; pond; unusual trees

1700 Melton Road ✂❀ (Hazel Kaye) Rearsby, N of Leicester on A607. In Rearsby, on L.H. side from Leicester. 1-acre garden with wide range of interesting herbaceous plants; some shrubs and trees. Nursery. *Adm 25p Chd 10p. Daily March to Oct (Wed to Sat 10-5.30, Sun 10- 12). Also SPECIAL OPEN DAY Sun Oct 1 (2-5.30). Adm £1 Chd 10p. TEAS Oct 1 only.* **Tel 01664 424578**

The Old Rectory ♿❀ (Mr & Mrs D B Owen) Teigh. 5m N of Oakham. Between Wymondham and Ashwell; or from A1 via Thistleton and Market Overton. Medium-sized walled garden; mixed borders; good variety shrubs, herbaceous and climbing plants. House and garden to be featured in BBC's new production of 'Pride and Prejudice' as Mr Collin's Parsonage. Unusual C18 church next door. TEAS. *Adm £1.50 Chd 25p (Share to Holy Trinity Church, Teigh®). Sun June 18 (2-6)*

Orchards ✂❀ (Mr & Mrs G Cousins) Hall Lane, Walton, nr Lutterworth. 8m S of Leicester via the A50 take a R turn just after Shearsby (sign-posted Bruntingthorpe); thereafter follow signs for Walton. A garden of surprises. It is full of rare and unusual plants which are grown in colour-theme garden 'rooms'. Featured on TVs Garden Club. Views of countryside. TEAS June 18, TEA June 21. *Adm £1.20 Chd free. Sun, Wed June 18, 21 (2-5.30). Also private visits welcome June to Sept, please* **Tel 01455 556958**

Owston Gardens ♿❀ 6m W of Oakham via Knossington, 2m S of Somerby. From Leicester turn L 2m E of Tilton. TEAS. *Combined adm £1.50 Chd free (Share to Owston Church®). Sun May 21 (2-6)*

The Homestead (Mr David Penny) ⅓ acre with lawn, clematis, ponds, borders, containers, alpine garden, views and photographs. Plants and sundries stalls

Rose Cottage (Mr & Mrs John Buchanan) Undulating 1¾ acres; shrub and flower borders; spring bulbs, roses, alpines, ponds, waterfall, fine views. *Private visits welcome, please* **Tel 01664 77545**

Paddocks ♿✂❀ (Mrs Ailsa Jackson) Shelbrook. 1½m W of Ashby-de-la-Zouch on B5003 towards Moira. A plantaholic's garden with over 2000 varieties in 1 acre incl snowdrops, hellebores, astrantias and many less common herbaceous plants & shrubs. Plants propagated from garden for sale. NCCPG collection of old named double and single primulas. Silver medallist at Chelsea and Vincent Square. TEA. *Adm £1 Chd free. Sat April 15, Suns and Weds April 16; May 14, 17, July 2, 5; Aug 13, 16 (2-5). Also private visits welcome, please* **Tel 01530 412606**

18 Park Road ♿❀ (Dr & Mrs D R Ives) Birstall. Turn off A6 into Park Rd at crown of the hill on Leicester side of Birstall. Local buses stop at end of Park Rd. Approx 1-acre of lawn, trees, shrubs and other mixed planting incl hellebores, aquilegias, bluebells etc with emphasis on foliage and scent. TEAS. *Adm £1 Chd 25p (Share to COPE® Thurs May 18 only). Sun, Thurs May 14, 18 (2-5.30). Private visits welcome April, May and June, please* **Tel 01533 675118**

Plungar Gardens (in The Vale of Belvoir) ♿❀ 16m E of Nottingham take A52, turn R 1m after Bingham. 12m N of Melton Mowbray via Scalford, Eastwell and Stathern. Art exhibition in church. Lunches and TEAS. *Combined adm £2 incl car park Chd free (Share to St Helen's Church®). Sat, Sun June 24, 25 (11-6)*

Church House (Mr & Mrs M S B Cross) Newly landscaped garden, shrubs, flowers, trees (converted barn)

Cordwainer's Cottage (Mr & Mrs D A Wells) Shrubs, lawn, mixed borders, stream, vegetables

Elsian Deane (Mr & Mrs D Marriott) Cottage garden, mixed borders, annuals, vegetables

The Old Barn Gardens (G W Miller Esq & Mr & Mrs A E Pear) Trees, shrubs, lawns, view of small lake

Other gardens open

Prebendal House ♿ (Mr & Mrs J Partridge) Empingham. Between Stamford & Oakham on A606. House built in 1688; summer palace for the Bishop of Lincoln. Recently improved old-fashioned gardens incl water garden, topiary and kitchen gardens. TEAS. *Adm £1.50 Chd 50p. Sun June 11 (2-6)*

¶The Priory ♿✂❀ (Mr & Mrs J Acton) Ketton. 4m W of Stamford. Take A6121 to Ketton, turn at Xrds in Ketton, down Church Rd, opp the churchyard. Newly created 2-acre garden; herbaceous border; water garden; alpines. Over 150 different roses. 2 courtyard gardens with mixed planting. TEAS. *Adm £1.50 Chd 50p (Share to Rutland Dyslexia Assoc®). Sun July 2 (2-6)*

Queniborough Gardens ✂❀ A607 N out of Leicester. 6m from Leicester. 9m from Melton Mowbray. *Combined adm £1 Chd free. Sun June 18 (11-5).*

5 Barkby Road (Mr & Mrs A R B Wadd) Small cottage garden containing herbs, pond, herbaceous borders. Small orchard with greenhouse, collection of scented leaved pelargoniums

40 The Ringway (Mr & Mrs W D Hall) Small redesigned garden with alpine scree, tufa bed, alpine house. Large pond and bog, herbaceous plants and greenhouse. Parking can be difficult; if possible, please leave cars on main rd and walk 100 yds

8 Syston Road (Mrs R A Smith) Plant enthusiasts cottage style garden; old and new English roses, small pond with frogs and newts; organic vegetable garden

Reservoir Cottage ♿ (Lord & Lady John Manners) Knipton, 7m W of Grantham. W of A1; between A52 and A607; nr Belvoir Castle. Medium-sized country garden with lovely views over the lake. TEA. *Adm £1 Chd free. Sun April 30 (2-6)*

19 The Ridgeway ✂❀ (Mr & Mrs J K Mensley) Rothley. Take B5328 to Rothley off A6 midway Leicester-Loughborough. After ½m turn R opp Rothley Court Hotel into Ridings then 1st L. Parking available. ¾-acre garden, wide variety of trees and shrubs. Redesigned with gravel area instead of grass, alpines, grasses, ferns, pond life. TEA. *Adm £1 Chd 25p (Share to Rainbow Hospice, Loughborough®). Suns May 7, June 11 (2-6), Oct 1 (2-5)*

Sheepy Magna Gardens ♿✂ B4116 2½m N of Atherstone on Atherstone to Twycross Rd. Cream TEAS in aid of Sheepy Magna Church. *Combined adm £2 Chd 30p. Sat, Sun June 24, 25 (2-6)*

Gate Cottage ❀ (Mr & Mrs O P Hall) Church Lane. Opp church. Approx ½-acre cottage garden; mixed herbaceous borders; greenhouse; vegetable garden; several specimen trees; lawns and patio

The Grange (Mr & Mrs V Wetton) Main Rd. ¼m from shop towards Twycross opp entrance to trout ponds farm. Spacious Edwardian garden redeveloped since 1989. Extensive lawns; mature specimen trees; ponds; massed roses; heather beds; mixed borders

Vine Cottage ❀ (Mr & Mrs T Clark) 26 Main Rd. Opp shop. Approx ¾-acre cottage garden; mixed herbaceous borders with many unusual plants; alpine gardens; ponds; vegetable plot with greenhouse. Cream TEAS. *Also private visits welcome Adm £1.50. May to Sept, please* **Tel 01827 880529**

South Luffenham Hall ♿✂❀ (Dr & Mrs G Guy) South Luffenham on 6121 between Stamford and Uppingham. Turn off A47 at Morcott. 3-acre garden around 1630 house (not open), featured in 'The Perfect English Country House'. Shrubs, roses, herbaceous borders, lawns, pleached lime hedge and terrace with alpines and lilies. TEAS. *Adm £1.50 Chd 50p (Share to St Marys Church, S Luffenham®). Sun July 16 (2-6)*

Stepping Stones ♿✂ (Mr Clem Adkin) Little Beeby. 8m E of Leicester off A47 at Thurnsby, through Scraptoft, R at Beeby Xrds, 1st R Hungarton Lane (signed No Rd). 2-acre garden on site of deserted medieval village (part excavated). Stream, arboretum, shrub roses, spring bulbs in variety. Spring blossom, surprise features, autumn colour. More than 2000 additional bulbs this year. C14 church and ancient medieval well in nearby village. Lovely countryside. TEA. *Adm £1.50 Chd 50p. Private visits welcome Feb To Nov, please* **Tel 01533 595677** *or just arrive. Welcome assured*

Stoke Albany House ♿❀ (Mr & Mrs A M Vinton) 4m E of Market Harborough via A427 to Corby; turn to Stoke Albany; R at the White Horse (B669); garden ½m on L. Large garden with fine trees; shrubs; herbaceous borders and grey garden. TEAS on Sun only. *Adm £1.50 Chd free. Sun July 9 (2-5.30); Tues, Weds July 4, 5, 11, 12 (2-5). Private parties welcome May to July, please* **Tel 01858 535227**

Sutton Bonington Hall ♿❀ (Anne, Lady Elton) Sutton Bonington, 5m NW of Loughborough; take A6 to Hathern; turn R (E) onto A6006; 1st L (N) for Sutton Bonington. Conservatory, formal white garden, variegated leaf borders. Queen Anne house (not open). Picnics. TEA. *Adm £1.20 Chd 50p (Share to St Michael's and St Ann's Church, Sutton Bonington®). Sun July 2 (12-5.30)*

University of Leicester Botanic Garden ♿✂❀ Stoughton Drive South, Oadby. SE outskirts of city opp race course. 16-acre garden inc grounds of Beaumont Hall, The Knoll, Southmeade and Hastings House. Wide variety of ornamental features and glasshouses laid out for educational purposes incl NCCPG collections of aubrieta, hardy fuchsia and skimmia. TEA. *Adm £1.50 Chd free (Share to Friends of Gardens). Sun June 25 (2-5). For NGS Sun July 23 (2-6)*

Wakerley Manor ♿❀ (A D A W Forbes Esq) 6m Uppingham, R off A47 Uppingham-Peterborough through Barrowden, or from A43 Stamford to Corby rd between Duddington and Bulwick. 4 acres lawns, shrubs, herbaceous; kitchen garden; 3 greenhouses. TEAS. *Adm £1 Chd 10p (Share to South Luffenham Church®). Sat, Sun May 13, 14 (2-6)*

Wartnaby ♿❀ (Lord & Lady King) Wartnaby. 4m NW of Melton Mowbray. From A606 turn W in Ab Kettley, from A46 at Durham Ox turn E on A676. Medium-sized garden, shrubs, herbaceous borders, a good collection of old-fashioned roses, small arboretum and newly designed vegetable garden. TEAS. *Adm £2 Chd 20p (Share to Marie Curie Nurses®). Suns May 21, June 25, July 23 (2-6). Private parties welcome, please* **Tel 01664 822296 business hours**

Regular Openers. Too many days to include in diary. Usually there is a wide range of plants giving year-round interest. See head of county section for the name and garden description for times etc.

Whatton House ♿❀ (Lord Crawshaw) 4m NE of Loughborough on A6 between Hathern and Kegworth; 2½m SE of junc 24 on M1. 15 acres; shrub and herbaceous borders, lawns, rose and wild gardens, pools; arboretum. Nursery open. TEAS. Teas in Old Dining Room. Catering arrangements for pre-booked parties any day or evening. *Adm £1.50 OAP/Chd 75p. Open Suns and Weds from Easter to end August. Also Bank Hol Mons. For NGS Tues April 18, May 9, 30 (2-6). Special plant sales Suns Sept 17, Oct 8. Also private visits welcome, please* **Tel 01509 842268**

Woodyton Farmhouse ♿✲❀ (Mr & Mrs F A Slater) Coalville. On A512, 6m E of Ashby de la Zouch, 6m W of Loughborough, 3m W of M1 junction 23. ¼-acre garden, herbaceous borders, shrub roses, hydrangeas, scree and shade. TEA. *Adm £1 Chd free. Suns June 4, 25, Aug 20 (2-6)*

Lincolnshire

Hon County Organiser: Mrs Patrick Dean, East Mere House, Lincoln LN4 2JB Tel 01522 791371
Assistant Hon County Organisers: Lady Bruce-Gardyne, The Old Rectory, Aswardby, Spilsby, Lincs PE23 4JS Tel 01790 752652
Mrs Julian Gorst, Oxcombe Manor, Horncastle, Lincs LN9 6LU Tel 01507 533227

DATES OF OPENING

By appointment
For telephone numbers and other details see garden descriptions. Private visits welcomed

21 Chapel Street, Hacconby
Crowmarsh Cottage, Holbeach St Matthews
East Mere House, nr Lincoln
Hall Farm, Harpswell
83 Halton Road, Spilsby
Luskentyre, Roman Bank, Saracens Head, nr Spalding
The Old Rectory, East Keal
2 School House, Stixwould
The Villa, South Somercotes, Louth
Walnut Cottage Careby
Westcombe, 25 High Street, Rippingale

Parties only
Fulbeck Hall, nr Grantham
The Manor House, Bitchfield
Park House Farm, Walcott

Regular openings
For details see garden descriptions

Harlaxton Manor Gardens, Grantham. April 1 to Oct. Closed Mons except Bank Hols

---

February 18 Saturday
21 Chapel Street, Hacconby ‡
Manor Farm, Keisby, Bourne ‡
Westcombe, 25 High Street, Rippingale ‡

February 19 Sunday
21 Chapel Street, Hacconby ‡
Manor Farm, Keisby, Bourne ‡
Westcombe, 25 High Street, Rippingale ‡

March 2 Thursday
21 Chapel Street, Hacconby

April 16 Sunday
21 Chapel Street, Hacconby

April 17 Monday
East Mere House, Lincoln

April 23 Sunday
Grimsthorpe Castle Gardens, Bourne

April 30 Sunday
83 Halton Road, Spilsby

May 4 Thursday
21 Chapel Street, Hacconby

May 6 Saturday
Belton House, Grantham

May 14 Sunday
Doddington Hall, nr Lincoln

May 21 Sunday
Grantham House, Grantham
Holton cum Beckering Gardens

May 28 Sunday
Harston Village Gardens
Westcombe, 25 High Street, Rippingale

June 1 Thursday
21 Chapel Street, Hacconby

June 3 Saturday
Bishop's House, Lincoln

June 4 Sunday
Crowmarsh Cottage, Holbeach St Matthews ‡
Holly House, Fishtoft Drove, Boston
Luskentyre, Roman Bank, Saracens Head, nr Spalding ‡
Park Farm, Bottesford (see Nottinghamshire)

June 11 Sunday
Fulbeck Hall, Grantham

June 18 Sunday
83 Halton Road, Spilsby ‡
Little Ponton Hall, Grantham
The Old Rectory, East Keal ‡

June 22 Thursday
Grimsthorpe Castle Gardens, Bourne

June 24 Saturday
Hall Farm, Harpswell

June 25 Sunday
Gunby Hall, Burgh-le-Marsh
Park House Farm, Walcott
The Villa, South Somercotes, Louth

July 2 Sunday
Aubourn Hall, Aubourn
Onslow House, Long Sutton

July 6 Thursday
21 Chapel Street, Hacconby

July 9 Sunday
Harrington Hall, Spilsby

July 23 Sunday
Belton House, Grantham

July 30 Sunday
Harlaxton Manor Gardens, Grantham
Marston Hall, nr Grantham

August 3 Thursday
21 Chapel Street, Hacconby
August 20 Sunday
Crowmarsh Cottage, Holbeach St Matthews
Luskentyre, Roman Bank, Saracens Head, nr Spalding
September 2 Saturday
Belton House, Grantham
September 3 Sunday
Hall Farm, Harpswell
September 7 Thursday
21 Chapel Street, Hacconby
September 24 Sunday
Harlaxton Manor Gardens, Grantham
October 5 Thursday
21 Chapel Street, Hacconby
1996
February 17 Saturday
21 Chapel Street, Hacconby
February 18 Sunday
21 Chapel Street, Hacconby

DESCRIPTIONS OF GARDENS

Aubourn Hall ♿✗ (Sir Henry Nevile) Aubourn. 7m SW of Lincoln. Signposted off A606 at Harmston. Approx 3 acres. Lawns, mature trees, shrubs, roses, mixed borders. C11 church adjoining. Wheelchairs in dry weather only. TEAS. *Adm £1.50 Chd 50p (Share to St. Peters Church Aubourn-repairs®). Sun July 2 (2-6)*

Belton House ♿✗ (The National Trust) 3m NE of Grantham on the A607 Grantham to Lincoln rd. Easily reached and signed from the A1 (Grantham N junction). 32 acres of garden incl formal Italian and Dutch gardens, and orangery by Sir Jeffrey Wyatville. TEAS. *Adm house & garden £4.30 Chd £2.10. ▲Sun July 23, Sats May 6, Sept 2 (11-5.30)*

Bishop's House ♿✗ (Bishop of Lincoln) Lincoln. Approaching Lincoln from N take A15 towards Cathedral. Enter Bailgate via Newport Arch, turn L into Eastgate. Bishop's House last on L before Eastgate Hotel. Various car parks in city. Approx 1½ acres walled town garden of lawns, trees, shrubs and herbaceous borders. Vegetable garden. *Adm £1 Chd 50p. Sat June 3 (2-5)*

21 Chapel Street ✗❀ (Cliff & Joan Curtis) A15 3m N of Bourne, turn E at Xrds into Hacconby. Small village garden with alpine house, rockeries, scree bed, old stone troughs planted as miniature gardens. Herbaceous borders with climbing roses and numerous clematis, collections of snowdrops, primula allionii, lewisia, rhodohypoxis. Featured on TV. TEAS. *Adm £1 Chd free (Share to Marie Curie Memorial Foundation®). Sat, Sun Feb 18, 19 (11-4) Sun April 16 (11-6) Thurs March 2, May 4, June 1, July 6, Aug 3, Sept 7, Oct 5 (2-6). Sat, Sun Feb 17, 18, 1996 (11-4). Private visits and parties welcome, please* **Tel 01778 570314**

Crowmarsh Cottage ❀ (Les & Janet Doy) Holbeach St Matthews. 9m E of Spalding. From A17 at Holbeach take Pennyhill turning and follow Holbeach St Matthews signs (approx 3m). A cottage garden recently redeveloped with natural pond. Large selection of foliage plants and shrubs; also wide selection of perennials. TEAS. *Adm £1 Chd free. Suns June 4, Aug 20 (1-6). Priate visits and parties welcome, please* **Tel 01406 32424**

Doddington Hall ♿✗ (Antony Jarvis Esq) 5m SW of Lincoln. From Lincoln via A46, turn W on to B1190 for Doddington. Superb walled gardens; thousands of spring bulbs; wild gardens; mature trees; Elizabethan mansion. Free Car Park. Lunches and TEAS available from 12 noon in fully licensed garden restaurant. *Adm house & garden £3.60 Chd £1.80. Garden only £1.80 Chd 90p (Share to Lincolnshire Old Churches Trust© and St Peter's Church Doddington®). ▲Sun May 14 (2-6)*

East Mere House ♿✗❀ (Mr & Mrs Patrick Dean) Lincoln. 3m S of Lincoln on A15. 1m E on B1178. Mixed shrubs, roses and herbaceous borders, vegetable and herb gardens, spring bulbs. TEAS. *Adm £1 Chd 50p. Mon April 17 (2-5). Private visits welcome May to end July, please* **Tel 01522 791371**

Fulbeck Hall ♿✗❀ (Mrs M Fry) Grantham. On A607 14m S of Lincoln, 11m N of Grantham. 1m S of Xrds of old A17 at Leadenham. 11 acres incl formal Edwardian garden with yew hedges, tulip tree, cedars and venetian well head. Recent planting of old roses, shrubs and unusual herbaceous within the Edwardian design. TEAS. *Adm £1.50 Chd 50p Sun June 11 (2-5)*

Grantham House ♿✗ (Lady Wyldbore-Smith) Castlegate, opp St Wulframs Church, Grantham. An old English garden of approx 5 acres of bulbs, many unusual shrubs and trees; river walk and water garden. TEAS. *Adm £1 Chd 50p. Sun May 21 (2-6)*

Grimsthorpe Castle Gardens ♿❀ (Grimsthorpe and Drummond Castle Trust) 8m E of A1 on the A151 from the Colsterworth junction, 4m W of Bourne. 15 acres of formal and woodland gardens which incl bulbs and wild flowers. The formal gardens encompass fine topiary, roses, herbaceous borders and an unusual ornamental kitchen garden. TEAS. *Adm £2 OAP/Chd £1. Combined adm castle and garden £4 OAP/Chd £2. ▲Sun April 23, Thurs June 22 (11-6)*

Gunby Hall ♿❀ (Mr & Mrs J D Wrisdale; The National Trust) 2½m NW of Burgh-le-Marsh; S of A158. 7 acres of formal and walled gardens; old roses, herbaceous borders; herb garden; kitchen garden with fruit trees and vegetables. Tennyson's 'Haunt of Ancient Peace'. House built by Sir William Massingberd 1700. Plant centre, games. TEAS. *Adm garden only £1.50 Chd 70p (Share to St Barnabas Hospice (Lincoln)®). ▲Sun June 25 (2-6)*

Hall Farm ♿❀ (Pam & Mark Tatam) Harpswell. 7m E of Gainsborough on A631. 1½m W of Caenby Corner. ¾-acre garden with mixed borders of trees, shrubs, roses and perennials (many of the plants are unusual). Over 80 varieties of rose - mainly old varieties. Sunken garden, pond and recently constructed courtyard garden. Short walk to old moat and woodland. Free seed collecting in garden Sept 3. TEAS. *Adm £1 Chd 25p. Sat June 24, Sun Sept 3 (2-6). Private visits welcome, please* **Tel 0142 7668412**

83 Halton Road ✲❀ (Jack & Joan Gunson) Spilsby. In Spilsby take B1195 towards Wainfleet; garden on L. Limited parking on Halton Rd, free car park Post Office Lane, Spilsby. ¼-acre town garden and hardy plant nursery, divided into a series of smaller gardens featuring densely planted mixed borders, incl many unusual plants and hardy geranium collection of approx 130 varieties. Spring bulbs a feature, many unusual. Featured in 'The Times' and 'Practical Gardening'. TEAS. *Adm £1 Chd free. Suns April 30, June 18 (2-6). Private visits welcome, please* **Tel 01790 752361**

Harlaxton Manor Gardens (University of Evansville) Grantham. 1m W of Grantham off A607 Melton Mowbray rd. Historically important 110-acre formal gardens and woodland currently undergoing restoration. 6½-acre walled gardens, extremely ornate walls; plantsman's and theme gardens. Harlaxton Manor was built by Gregory Gregory and the house and garden built to rival anything in Europe. The restoration project is being monitored for a television series. Formal gardens built as a walk around European styles, Dutch canal, Italian gardens, French terracing, views. Partially suitable for wheelchairs. TEAS. *Adm £2.50 Chd £1.25. April 1 to Oct closed Mons except Bank Hol Mons. For NGS Suns July 30, Sept 24 (11-5)*

Harrington Hall ✲❀ (Mr & Mrs David Price) Spilsby. 6m NW of Spilsby. Turn off A158 (Lincoln-Skegness) at Hagworthingham, 2m from Harrington. Approx 5-acre tudor & C18 walled gardens, incl recently designed kitchen garden with herbaceous borders, roses and other flowering shrubs. High terrace mentioned in Tennyson's 'Maud'. TEAS. *Adm £1 Chd 25p. Sun July 9 (2-5)*

¶Harston Village Gardens ✲ 6½m W of Grantham off A607. Turn R into Denton. Follow rd through village, fork L signposted to Harston. Cream TEAS. *Combined adm £1.50 Chd 50p. Sun May 28 (2-6)*

¶Algar House (Mr & Mrs D Morton) Informal garden, approx ½-acre with beautiful view of the surrounding countryside

¶Bretton House (Mr & Mrs J B Grice) A new garden only 9yrs old, built on hillside with a superb view. Approx ½-acre. Terraces, herbaceous borders, raised beds, fish pond, pergola etc, arranged in a formal manner to compliment the Jacobean style house

Harston House ❀ (Mr & Mrs R E Gardiner) Mature peaceful hillside garden of 2½ acres with spectacular view, trees, shrubs, roses and herbaceous

¶Holly House ♿✲❀ (Sally & David Grant) Fishtoft Drove, Boston. Fishtoft Drove is an unclassified rd approx 3m N of Boston and 1m S of Frithville on the W side of the West Fen Drain. Approx 1-acre informal gardens with mixed borders, scree beds, old sinks with alpines and steps leading down to a large pond with cascade and stream. Softly curving beds are full of unusual and interesting herbaceous plants. TEAS. *Adm £1 Chd free (Share to Pilgrim Heart and Lung Fund®). Sun June 4 (2-6)*

> **By Appointment Gardens.** These owners do not have a fixed opening day usually because they do not like crowds or have insufficient parking space. Owner will often give guided tour.

¶Holton-Cum-Beckering Gardens Take A158 E from Lincoln. 2m past Langworth turn L on B1399. Village in 2m. TEAS at Grangemead in aid of Save the Children. *Combined adm £1.50 Chd free. Sun May 21 (11-6)*

¶Amber Lea ✲❀ (Mr & Mrs W H Fehnert) Mature, country cottage style garden. Approx ⅓-acre, lawns, orchard, vegetable garden, variety of perennials, shrubs, trees, bulbs, palm tree, yucca tree, beech hedges. Small pond with fountain and fish. Environmentally friendly and natural

Grangemead ♿ (Mr Howard Crapp) 2-acre landscaped garden. Plantsman's collection of 130 conifers some 30yrs old. See how your conifers will look when they grow up! Alpine troughs and rock garden. Flowering shrubs, 2 ponds

¶The Holt ♿✲ (D W Stubbings) Small low maintenance garden in various stages of development. Patio, conservatory, pergola and pond with waterfall. Conifer, heather area. Bonsai area containing about 50 bonsai at various stages of training. Espalier fruit trees, vegetable patch, trees, grass and wildlife area

¶Upfield ♿ (Allan & Irene Wakeman) A new garden approx ⅕-acre, 18 months old. Herbaceous and shrub borders with unusual plants and alpines. Gravel area

Little Ponton Hall ♿❀ (Mr & Mrs Alastair McCorquodale) Grantham 3m. ½m E of A1 at S end of Grantham bypass. 3 to 4-acre garden. Spacious lawns with cedar tree over 200yrs old. Many varieties of old shrub roses; borders and young trees. Stream with spring garden; bulbs and river walk. Kitchen garden and listed dovecote. Adjacent to Little Ponton Hall is St Guthlacs Church which will be decorated and all visitors welcome. TEAS. *Adm £1.50 Chd under 12 free (Share to St Guthlacs Church, Little Ponton). Sun June 18 (2-6)*

Luskentyre ✲❀ (Mr & Mrs C Harris) 7m E of Spalding signed from A17 at Saracen's Head. Attractive small garden extensively planted with a wide range of interesting plants mainly chosen for their ability to withstand dry conditions and give yr-round interest, also fine display of fuchsia. *Adm £1 Chd free. Suns June 4, Aug 20 (1-5). Private visits welcome, please* **Tel 01406 423987**

Manor Farm ✲❀ (Mr & Mrs C A Richardson) Keisby. 9m NW of Bourne, 10m E of Grantham, signed to Keisby from Lenton and Hawthorpe. ½-acre plantsman's garden. Snowdrop collection and hellebores. *Adm £1 Chd free (Share to Stamford and Bourne CRMF®). Sat, Sun Feb 18, 19 (11-4)*

The Manor House ✲ (John Richardson Esq) Bitchfield; 6m SE of Grantham, close to Irnham and Rippingale. A52 out of Grantham to Spital Gate Hill roundabout; take B1176 to Bitchfield; House on R after public house. 1½ acres entirely re-created in 1972; essentially a shrub rose garden (96 varieties) with shrubs and other perennials; 50 by 40ft pond planted spring 1985; small box hedged formal garden; ha-ha, new large garden room with fountain and over 100 plants. *Adm £2. Parties of 20 or more welcome by appointment only after June 1 to mid-July. Please* **Tel Ingoldsby 261**

Marston Hall ♿❀ (The Rev Henry Thorold) 6m N of Grantham. Turn off A1, 4½m N of Grantham; on 1½m to Marston. Station: Grantham. Notable trees; wych elm and laburnum of exceptional size. House C16 continuously owned by the Thorold family. Interesting pictures and furniture. TEAS. *Adm house & garden £2.50 Chd £1 (Share to Hougham Church Restoration Fund®). ▲Sun July 30 (2-6)*

¶**The Old Rectory** ❀ (John & Ruth Ward) East Keal. 2m SW of Spilsby on A16. Turn into Church Lane by PO. A rambling cottage garden with a variety of mixed borders, incl shrubs, roses, climbers, perennials and annuals. Ponds and rock garden. TEAS. *Adm £1.20 Chd free. Sun June 18 (2-6). Private visits welcome, please* **Tel 01790 752477**

¶**Onslow House** ♿✲ (Mr & Mrs Julian Proctor) ¾m S of Long Sutton A17 bypass, on B1390. Parking on L of B1390, garden on R. A 3-acre garden with topiary, lawns, lily pond, rose garden and herbaceous borders, C18 dovecote and mature trees. TEAS in aid of British Diabetic Assoc. *Adm £1.50 Chd 50p. Sun July 2 (2-6)*

Park House Farm ♿✲❀ (Mr & Mrs Geoffrey Grantham) Walcott. 16m S of Lincoln on B1189 between Billinghay and Metheringham. Traditional farm buildings adapted to make a series of garden rooms; with half-hardy climbers, gravel. Winter and white garden. Featured in Garden Club 1993 with Roy Lancaster. *Adm £1 Chd 50p. Sun June 25 (2-6)*

¶**2 School House** ✲❀ (Andrew & Sheila Sankey) Stixwould. 1½m N of Woodhall Spa. ¼-acre garden, redesigned in Oct 1994 and in process of being developed to incl front garden with unusual perennials and shrubs, herb garden, vegetable garden. Owners are garden designers. TEAS. *Adm £1 Chd free (Share to Sick Children's Trust®). Private visits welcome by appt only May to Sept, please* **Tel 01526 352453**

The Villa ✲❀ (Michael & Judy Harry) South Somercotes. 8m E of Louth. Leave Louth by Eastfield Rd. Follow signs to S Cockerington. Take rd signposted to North & South Somercotes. House on L 100yds before church. ¼-acre densely planted in the cottage style; large collection of herbs, old-fashioned and unusual perennials; orchard with interesting old varieties of fruit trees. Livestock incl flock of Lincoln Longwool Sheep. TEAS. *Adm £1 Chd free. Sun June 25 (2-6). Private visits welcome, preferably May and September. Please,* **Tel 01507 358487**

Walnut Cottage ❀ (Roy & Sue Grundy) Careby. 6m N of Stamford on B1176. 5m E of A1 at Stretton. Situated approx ⅓m at end of Main St on L. ½-acre developing garden with interesting herbaceous borders. Herb garden, small shade and gravel areas, water garden with S facing slope leading to small woodland feature with natural pond. TEA. *Adm £1 Chd free. Private visits welcome Tues and Sat, May to Sept, please* **Tel 01780 410660**

¶**Westcombe** ♿❀ (Mr & Mrs R Beddington) 25 High St, Rippingale. On A15 5m N of Bourne. Turn E at Xrds into Rippingale. No 25, Westcombe is 5th house on R. ½-acre village garden. Borders, island beds, ponds and vegetable garden. Yr-round interest. Hellebores and snowdrops in spring. TEA (Feb). TEAS (May). *Adm £1 Acc chd free. Sat, Suns Feb 18, 19 (11-4) May 28 (11-6)*

London (Greater London Area)

Hon County Organiser: Mrs Maurice Snell, Moleshill House, Fairmile, Cobham, Surrey KT11 1BG Tel 01932 864532

Assistant Hon County Organisers: Mrs Stuart Pollard, 17 St Alban's Rd, Kingston-upon-Thames, Surrey Tel 0181 546 6657

Mrs C G Wall, Orchard Cottage, 3 Woodlands Road, Bickley, Kent Tel 0181 467 4190

Mrs V West, 11 Woodlands Rd, Barnes, SW13 0JZ Tel 0181 876 7030

Miss Alanna Wilson, 38 Ornan Road, London NW3 4QB Tel 0171 794 4071

DATES OF OPENING

By appointment

For telephone numbers and other details see garden descriptions. Private visits welcome

39 Boundary Road, NW8
65 Castelnau, Barnes SW13. Suns in July
101 Cheyne Walk, SW10
51 Cholmeley Crescent, N6
133 Crystal Palace Road, East Dulwich, SE22
The Elms, Kingston-on-Thames
Elm Tree Cottage, 85 Croham Road, S Croydon
49 & 51 Etchingham Park Road, N3
16 Eyot Gardens, Chiswick Mall, W4
7 The Grove, N6
133 Haverstock Hill, NW3
1 Lister Road, E11
Little Lodge, Thames Dtton
13 Mercers Road, N19
33 Mundania Road, SE22
26 Nassau Road, Barnes Gardens, SW13
26 Northchurch Road, N1
Flat 1, 1F Oval Road, NW1 ‡
Regents College, NW1 ‡
19 St Gabriel's Road, NW2
7 St George's Road, Twickenham
St Michael's Convent, Ham
14 Sebright Road, High Barnet
South London Botanical Institute, SE24

Southwood Lodge, N6
Tarn, Oxhey Drive South, Northwood
15 Upper Grotto Road, Twickenham
10 Wildwood Road, NW11
7 Woodstock Road, W4

Parties only
43 Brodrick Road, SW17
15a Buckland Crescent, NW3
37 Heath Drive, NW
60 St Pauls Road, Canonbury Gardens, N1
57 St Quintin Avenue, W10

Regular openings
For details see garden descriptions

Barbican Conservatory, EC2. Sats, Suns, Bank Hols all year
Chelsea Physic Garden, SW3. Suns April 2 to Oct 29, Weds April 5 to Oct 25, Mon to Fri May 22 to May 26, Mon to Fri June 5 to June 9
Myddelton House, EN2. Mon to Fri (except Bank Hols). Last Sun in month

---

March 18 Saturday
The Elms, Kingston-on-Thames
March 19 Sunday
The Elms, Kingston-on-Thames
April 2 Sunday
Chelsea Physic Garden, SW3
April 8 Saturday
Lambeth Palace, SE1
April 9 Sunday
Ham House, Richmond
April 16 Sunday
29 Deodar Road, SW15
April 17 Monday
Tarn, Oxhey Drive South, Northwood
April 22 Saturday
The Elms, Kingston-on-Thames
April 23 Sunday
Chiswick Mall, W4
Eccleston Square, SW1
The Elms, Kingston-on-Thames
St Mary's Convent and Nursing Home, Chiswick
7 Woodstock Road, W4
April 29 Saturday
1 Hocroft Avenue, NW2
Trinity Hospice, SW4
April 30 Sunday
39 Boundary Road, NW8
51 Cholmeley Crescent, Highgate, N6
9 Eland Road, Battersea, SW11 ‡
51 Gloucester Road, Kew
7 The Grove, Highgate Village, N6
1 Hocroft Avenue, NW2
17 Park Place Villas, W2
Trinity Hospice, SW4 ‡
7 Upper Phillimore Gardens, W8
47 Winn Road, Lee, SE12
May 7 Sunday
5 Burbage Road, SE24
2 Millfield Place, N6
Southwood Lodge, N6
The Water Gardens, Kingston-on-Thames
May 8 Monday
26 Nassau Road, Barnes Gardens, SW13
May 10 Wednesday
12 Lansdowne Road, W11
May 13 Saturday
The Elms, Kingston-on-Thames
Highwood Ash, NW7
May 14 Sunday
54 Burnfoot Avenue, SW6
133 Crystal Palace Road, East Dulwich, SE22
Edwards Square, W8
The Elms, Kingston-on-Thames
5 Greenaway Gardens, NW3 ‡
37 Heath Drive, NW3 ‡
Highwood Ash, NW7
Malvern Terrace, N1
43 Ormeley Road, SW12
43 Penerley Road, SE6
131 Upland Road, SE22
May 21 Sunday
Chiswick Mall, W4
49 & 51 Etchingham Park Road, N3
Hall Grange, Croydon
117 Hamilton Terrace, NW8
3 Radnor Gardens, Twickenham
66 Woodbourne Avenue, Streatham, SW16
May 28 Sunday
22 Loudoun Road, NW8
Myddelton House, EN2
Regents College, NW1
South London Botanical Institute, SE24
June 4 Sunday
Barbican Conservatory, EC2
Canonbury Gardens, N1 ‡
8 College Cross, N1 ‡
29 Deodar Road, SW15
Eccleston Square, SW1
Museum of Garden History, Tradescant Trust, SE1
15 Norcott Road, N16
7 St George's Road, Twickenham
June 9 Friday
Flat 1, 1F Oval Road, NW1
June 10 Saturday
Lambeth Community Care Centre, SE11
Flat 1, 1F Oval Road, NW1
Trinity Hospice, SW4
June 11 Sunday
Albion Square Gardens E8 ‡
Barbican Conservatory, EC2
Barnes Gardens, SW13
28 Barnsbury Square, N1
43 Brodrick Road, SW17
5 Burbage Road, SE24
37 Creighton Avenue, N10
De Beauvoir Gardens, N1 ‡
Ealing Gardens, W5
Elm Tree Cottage, 85 Croham Road, S Croydon
70 Gloucester Crescent, NW1 ‡‡
11 Hampstead Way, NW11 ‡‡‡
5 Hillcrest Avenue, NW11 ‡‡‡
Lambeth Community Care Centre, SE11
15 Lawrence Street, SW3
20 Lessingham Avenue, Tooting Bec, SW17
Little Lodge, Thames Ditton
17 Navarino Road, E8 ‡
2 Northbourne Road, SW4
Flat 1, 1F Oval Road, NW1 ‡‡
Southwood Lodge, N6
103 Thurleigh Road, SW12
Trinity Hospice, SW4
Trumpeters' House and Lodge Garden, Richmond
June 15 Thursday
12a Selwood Place, SW7
June 17 Saturday
5 Greenaway Gardens, NW3
29 Mostyn Road, SW19
June 18 Sunday
33 Balmuir Gardens, Putney, SW15 ‡
15a Buckland Crescent, NW3
The Coach House, SW6
Fenton House, NW3
Highgate Village, N6
17 Gwendolen Avenue, SW15 ‡
Leyborne Park Gardens, Kew
4 Macaulay Road, SW4
29 Mostyn Road, SW19 ‡‡
North Ruislip Gardens, Ruislip, Middx
Osterley Park, Isleworth
78 Palace Road, SW2
43 Penerley Road, SE6
7 St George's Road, Twickenham
Wimbledon Gardens, SW19 ‡‡
June 25 Sunday
22 Cambridge Road, Teddington, TW11
101 Cheyne Walk, SW10
133 Crystal Palace Road, East Dulwich, SE22
20 Eatonville Road, SW17
12 Greenheys Close, Northwood
117 Hamilton Terrace, NW8
133 Haverstock Hill, NW3
125 Honor Oak Park, SE23
Hornbeams, Stanmore

10 Lawn Road, NW3
13 Mercers Road, N19
Ormeley Lodge, Richmond
South London Botanical Institute, SE24
103 Thurleigh Road, SW12
13 Trecastle Way, N7
3 Wellgarth, Road, NW11
47 Winn Road, Lee, SE12
66 Woodbourne Avenue, Streatham, SW16

July 1 Saturday
19 St Gabriel's Road, NW2

July 2 Sunday
65 Castelnau, Barnes, SW13 (by appt)
10 Chiltern Road, Eastcote, Pinner
Goldsborough, Blackheath, SE3
21a The Little Boltons, SW10
10a The Pavement, Chapel Road, SE27
3 Radnor Gardens, Twickenham ‡
15 Upper Grotto Road, Twickenham ‡
10 Wildwood Road, NW11

July 9 Sunday
32 Atney Road, SW15
65 Castelnau, Barnes, SW13 (by appt)
17 Fulham Park Gardens, SW6
37 Heath Drive, NW3
3 Radnor Gardens, Twickenham ‡
15 Upper Grotto Road, Twickenham ‡

July 16 Sunday
65 Castelnau, Barnes, SW13 (by appt)
29 Deodar Road, SW15
5 Greenaway Gardens, NW3
36 Marryat Road, Wimbledon, SW19
35 Perrymead Street, SW6 ‡
9 Ranelagh Avenue, SW6 ‡
Ranulf Road Gardens, NW22
14 Sebright Road, High Barnet

July 22 Saturday
Trinity Hospice, SW4
27 Wood Vale, N10

July 23 Sunday
29 Addison Avenue, W11
65 Castelnau, Barnes, SW13 (by appt)
10 Chiltern Road, Eastcote, Pinner
15 Norcott Road, N16
Trinity Hospice, SW4
27 Wood Vale, N10

July 30 Sunday
65 Castelnau, Barnes, SW13 (by appt)
2 Millfield Place, N6
57 St Quintin Avenue, W10 ‡
66 Wallingford Avenue, W10 ‡

August 6 Sunday
235, Eastcote, Road, North Ruislip Gardens, Ruislip, Middx

August 20 Sunday
73 Forest Drive East, E11 ‡
1 Lister Road, E11 ‡
65 Wilmot Road, E10 ‡
47 Winn Road, Lee, SE12

August 28 Sunday
3 Radnor Gardens, Twickenham

September 9 Saturday
Trinity Hospice, SW4

September 10 Sunday
43 Penerley Road, SE6
Trinity Hospice, SW4

September 17 Sunday
17 Fulham Park Gardens, SW6

September 24 Sunday
Myddelton House, EN2
14 Sebright Road, High Barnet

October 8 Sunday
The Water Gardens, Kingston-on-Thames

October 29 Sunday
Chelsea Physic Garden, SW3

February 25 Sunday 1996
Myddelton House, EN2

DESCRIPTIONS OF GARDENS

29 Addison Avenue, W11 ✄❀ (Mr & Mrs D B Nicholson) No entry for cars from Holland Park Avenue; approach via Norland Square and Queensdale Rd. Station: Holland Park. Bus 12, 94. Small prizewinning town garden with country feel. Lawn, fruit trees, unusual wall shrubs and perennials. Phlox paniculata a speciality: over 25 varieties in shades of pink, mauve, purple and red. *Adm £1 Chd 50p (Share to the Tradescant Trust®). Sun July 23 (2-6)*

The Anchorage see Kent

¶Albion Square Gardens, E8 ✄ 2m N of Liverpool St Station (BR & tube). 1m S of Dalston/Kingsland Station (BR). Buses 22, 67, 149, 243. By car approach from Queensbridge Rd turning L into Albion Drive then 1st R. *Combined adm £1.50 Chd 50p. Sun June 11 (2-5.30)*

¶24 Albion Square (Mr David French) 80′ town garden designed to unfold as a series of views and focal points divided by a yew hedge. Emphasis on foliage plants rather than flowers. Secluded seating areas, fountain

¶25 Albion Square (Sandy Maclennan) 80′ informal walled garden on two levels with pond beside camomile patch and features mainly, ornamental shrubs and trees creating interest in foliage, form and colour

32 Atney Road, SW15 ✄ (Sally Tamplin) Off Putney Bridge Rd. Tubes, Putney Bridge or East Putney. Bus 14, 22, 37, 74, 80, 85, 93, 220. Mixed borders, terrace with pots, lawn, woodland area all compressed into 90′ L-shaped garden perpetually changing to accommodate needs of obsessive gardener with too little time for gardening, TEAS. *Adm £1 (Share to All Saints' Church®). Sun July 9 (2-6)*

¶33 Balmuir Gardens, SW15 ✄❀ (Mrs Gay Wilson) Putney. 5 mins walk from Putney SR Station. Off the Upper Richmond Rd on corner with Howards Lane. Bus 37, 74, 14. A designer's garden on a corner plot that is continually evolving. Secluded, on different levels, tiny mixed borders backed by stained beams. Pots, fruit trees and a formal pond with a waterfall through moose antlers. A passionate plantswoman who tries out different colour combinations before using them on clients. All crammed into 80′ x 38′ at widest only 16′ at narrowest. *Adm £1 Chd 50p (Share to The Berith Foundation®). Sun June 18 (2-6)*

Barbican Conservatory, EC2 ♿✄❀ Silk Street, nearest tube station Barbican and Moorgate. City of London's largest conservatory, part of the Barbican Centre; collection of temperate plants incl palms, orchids and climbers. Large collection of cactus and succulents with many rare varieties. Time allowed approx 1½ hours, but many other gardens with interesting plants to be seen in the locality. TEAS in restaurant. *Adm £1 OAP/Chd 60p Family (2 adults, up to 2 chd) £2.40. Sats, Suns, Bank Hols all year. Telephone Operational Services Department* **0171 638 4141** *for opening times. For NGS Suns June 4, 11 (12-5.30)*

Barnes Gardens Barnes, SW13. TEAS at 25 Castelnau. *Adm £4 for 5 gardens or £1 each garden, OAP £2 for 5 gardens or 50p each garden, Chd free. Sun June 11 (2-6)*

25 Castelnau ✲ (Dr & Mrs P W Adams) Castelnau is on the main route from Hammersmith Bridge. The garden is approx 120′ × 40′ designed in 1978 by Malcolm Hillier and the late Colin Hilton, well known for their books on flowers and garden design. The garden was planned for ease of maintenance and family living. There is a good variety of herbaceous plants, some attractive roses and a compact working vegetable area and screened swimming pool. TEAS

29 Lonsdale Road ✲ (Mrs R Morris) Over Hammersmith Bridge first R or Underground Hammersmith. Bus 9, 33, 72. ⅓-acre S facing walled garden with York terrace. Designed to give all yr interest. A plantsman's garden with herbaceous borders. Old English roses, clematis, peonies, iris, lilies and flowering shrubs, lavender walk with spring bulbs and hostas

26 Nassau Road ♿❀ (Captain & Mrs Anthony Hallett) 26 Nassau Road lies midway between the Thames and Barnes Pond and is approached via Lonsdale Rd or Church Rd in Barnes. Long, slim, terraced garden with tallest wisteria in Barnes, shrouded on all sides by weigela, philadelphus, pittosporum, chaemomeles, ceanothus with borders of hebe, cistus, rose, delphiniums, potentilla and spiraea. New borders of blue and yellow; white and red perennials; cool phlox; red hot lilies and campanula abound. 200ft of dense green and gold arranged in 'rooms', add to the excitement. Plants for sale. *Adm £1. Also open on Mon May 8 (2-6). Private visits welcome, please* **Tel 0181 748 5940**

8 Queen's Ride ♿ (His Honour Judge White & Mrs White) Train: Barnes Station, turn R down Rocks Lane, then L along Queen's Ride. Bus, 22 terminus at Putney Hospital; 3 minutes walk W along Queen's Ride. House is at the junction of Queen's Ride and St Mary's Grove. ⅔-acre garden facing Barnes Common. Croquet lawn with herbaceous and mixed borders and a small history of the rose garden. TEA

12 Westmoreland Road ✲❀ (Mr & Mrs Norman Moore) From Hammersmith take Bus 9, 33, or 72 to the Red Lion. Briefly retrace steps along Castelnau turn L into Ferry Rd then L at Xrds. Small garden with raised stone terrace planted with choisya, convolvulus, euonymus, honeysuckle and decorative herbs, leading to lower lawn. Borders densely planted with wide variety of flowering shrubs and pretty pool with fountain. Gravel garden with lilies, agapanthus, diascia and lady's mantle. *(Share to St Mary's Churchyard®)*

28 Barnsbury Square, N1 ✲ (F T Gardner Esq) Islington N. 1¾m N of King's Cross off Thornhill Rd. Bus stop: Islington Town Hall, Upper St or Offord Rd, Caledonian Rd, Tube Highbury and Islington. Small prize-winning Victorian garden; gazebo; pond; grotto; roses, shrubs, plants of interest throughout yr. *Adm £1 Chd free (Share to CRMF®). Sun June 11 (2-6)*

39 Boundary Road, NW8 ✲ (Hermoine Berton) St John's Wood. Between Finchley Rd and Abbey Rd. Buses 13, 113, 82, 46, 159; ask for Boundary Rd or 6 min walk between Swiss Cottage and St John's Wood station. Unusual walled garden closely planted to provide wild life sanctuary for birds, frogs, newts, toads, squirrels; accent on foliage, texture, fern and perfume; includes ponds, waterfall and rocks. As seen on Gardeners World 1992 and filmed for 'Inside Britain' 1993. *Adm £1.50 Chd 30p (Share to London Lighthouse Aids Centre®). Sun April 30 (2-6). Private visits welcome April to Sept please* **Tel 0171 624 3177**

43 Brodrick Road, SW17 ✲ (Helen Yemm) Wandsworth Common. Approx 1m S of Wandsworth Bridge, off Trinity Rd. A long (110′), tranquil garden of a typical Victorian terrace house, surrounded by mature trees. Its length is broken by a bank of shrubs and a pond, overhung by an ancient rose-clad apple tree. Elsewhere the garden is stuffed with flowering shrubs, herbaceous planting for semi-shade, clematis and roses - distinctly un-urban. Featured in Sainsbury's Magazine and Sunday Times in 1994. *Adm £1 Chd 50p (Share to Alzheimers Disease Soc®). Sun June 11 (2-6). Small groups (min 5, max 15) welcome by appt. May to mid July.* **Tel 0181 672 1473**

15a Buckland Crescent, NW3 ♿✲❀ (Lady Barbirolli) Swiss Cottage Tube. Bus: 46, 13 (6 mins) or Hampstead Hoppa (request stop nearby). ⅓-acre; interesting collection of shrubs and trees in well-designed garden featured in Country Life Nov 88, also in books 'Private Gardens of London' by Arabella Lennox Boyd and 'Town Gardens' by Caroline Boisset. *Adm £1 Chd over 12 50p (Share to RUKBA®). Sun June 18 (2.30-6.30). Private visits welcome for parties of 25 and over, please* **Tel 0171 586 2464**

¶5 Burbage Road, SE24 ✲❀ (Crawford & Rosemary Lindsay) Nr junction with Half Moon Lane. BR Station Herne Hill, 5 mins walk. Buses 2, 3, 37, 40, 68, 196. Garden of member of The Society of Botanical Artists. 150′ × 40′ with large and varied range of plants. Herb garden, woodland area, herbaceous borders for sun and shade, terraces, climbing plants, selection of potters' plant containers, lawns. TEAS. *Adm £1 Chd free. Suns May 7, June 11 (2-5)*

54 Burnfoot Avenue, SW6 ✲ (Lady Jocelyn) nearest tube Parson's Green, then walk W on Fulham Rd, R up Munster Rd, 3rd street on L of Munster Rd. 14 bus along Fulham Rd. directions as above; 11 bus along Dawes Rd and walk down through Filmer Rd. 74 bus along Fulham Palace Rd walk through to Burnfoot Ave. Small walled paved garden 20′ × 30′ with raised beds, the emphasis on leaf shapes and colours; fruit trees; climbing plants; frequently changing due to deaths and new ideas; the garden is used as an extra room of the house. *Adm £1 Chd free (Share to St Joseph's Hospice Hackney®). Sun May 14 (2-6)*

¶22 Cambridge Road ♿✲ (Sheila & Roger Storr) Teddington. S turning off Teddington High St. Buses 281, 285. A family garden of approx ⅙-acre. Designed to give the long garden a feeling of width. Many unusual shrubs and herbaceous perennials. A tree house has been built around an old pear tree incl a drawbridge and flying fox. The water feature allows children to paddle in it. At the end of the garden is a large vegetable and soft fruit plot. TEA. *Adm 50p Chd free. Sun June 25 (2-6)*

Canonbury Gardens, N1 ✿❀ Station: Highbury & Islington. Bus: 4, 19, 30, 43, 104, 279 to Highbury Corner or Islington Town Hall, 30 to New Crown public house stops outside 60 St Paul's Rd. A1 runs through Canonbury Sq. *Combined adm £1.75 or £1 each garden Chd 75p or 50p each garden. Sun June 4 (2-6)*

37 Alwyne Road ♿✿❀ (Mr & Mrs J Lambert) Bordering the New River Walk. A garden writer's garden with open informal views and an enclosed formal hidden garden. Old-fashioned roses if it hasn't been too hot, lilies if it hasn't been too cold. TEAS. (Share to British Red Cross®)

46 Canonbury Square, NI ♿❀ (Miss Peggy Carter) Station: Highbury & Islington Bus: 4, 19, 30, 43, 104, 279 to Highbury Corner or Islington Town Hall. A1 runs through Canonbury Sq. Walled garden lying behind 2 end-of-terrace Georgian houses with statuary; pool; waterfall; spring blossom.

60 St Paul's Road ✿❀ (John & Pat Wardroper) This typical back-of-terrace town garden, has been planted chiefly for shade, and to create a quiet, green enclosed atmosphere just off a busy street; designed on 3 levels with paved patios, border of flowering shrubs. *Private visits welcome for parties of 4 and over, please* **Tel 0171 2267767**

Capel Manor Farm and Gardens see Hertfordshire

65 Castelnau, SW13 ✿ (Prof & Mrs G Teeling Smith) Barnes. From Hammersmith, buses 9A, 33, 72 to Castelnau library. No 65 is 50yds S of library. Two Londoners' idea of a country garden. Herbaceous border, roses, shrubs, grass and behind a high clipped hedge, a small kitchen garden with narrow box edged beds where vegetables and flowers for cutting are grown. *Adm £1. Sundays in July by appt only. Please* **Tel 0181 748 4254**

Chelsea Physic Garden, SW3 ♿✿❀ (Trustees of the Garden) 66 Royal Hospital Rd, Chelsea. Bus 239 (Mon-Sat) alight outside garden (Cheyne Court). Station: Sloane Square (10 mins). Cars: restricted parking nr garden weekdays; free Sundays, or in Battersea Park (across river) weekdays. Entrance in Swan Walk (except wheelchairs). Second oldest Botanic Garden in UK; 3.8 acres; medicinal and herb garden, incl an ethnobotanical 'Garden of World Medicine' perfumery border; family order beds; historical walk, glasshouses and over 5,000 trees, shrubs and herbaceous plants, many rare or unusual. TEAS. *Adm £3.50 Students/Chd £1.80. Suns April 2 to Oct 29 (2-6); Weds April 5 to Oct 25 (2-5); also in Chelsea Flower Show week Mon-Fri May 22-26 and in Chelsea Festival Week Mon-Fri June 5-9 (12-5). For NGS Suns April 2, Oct 29 (2-6)*

101 Cheyne Walk, SW10 ✿❀ (Malcolm Hillier Esq) The garden is situated just to the W of Battersea Bridge on Cheyne Walk. Parking on Sunday is possible in Millman St, Beaufort St and in the wider parts of Cheyne Walk with a single yellow line or in residents spaces. The garden is long and narrow 115′ × 18′ and is strongly layered with a structure of evergreen hedges and topiaries leading from a Mediterranean terrace through shady ferns to a winding path set about with old roses, perennials and many rare and tender shrubs. A raised arbour covered with scented climbers looks back down the length of the garden. TEAS. *Adm £1 Chd 50p. Sun June 25 (1-6). Private visits welcome for parties of 5 and over, please* **Tel 0171 352 9031**

¶10 Chiltern Road ✿❀ (Mrs G Creswell) Eastcote, Pinner. Off Bridle Rd-Eastcote Rd between Francis Rd and Cheney St. Please park in Francis Rd. Plantswoman's garden ⅓-acre, mature trees, mixed shrubs and herbaceous plantings. Plants for sale propagated from the garden. TEAS. *Adm £1.50 Chd free. Suns July 2, 23 (2-5)*

Chiswick Mall, W4 ✿❀ Station: Stamford Brook (District Line). Bus: 290 to Young's Corner from Hammersmith. By car A4 Westbound turn off at Eyot Gdns S, then R into Chiswick Mall. *Suns April 23 (2-6), May 21 (2-7)*

16 Eyot Gardens ✿ (Dianne Farris) Between Great West Road and river, at junction of Chiswick Mall and Hammersmith Terrace. If coming from outside London go down to river at Hogarth roundabout. Small town garden at end of terrace of houses. Front has mostly yellow, blue and white flowers, a lot of pink in the back garden with raised beds and a terrace. Planting and design with the help of Anthony Noel. TEAS. *Adm £1 Chd free. Private visits by appt please,* **Tel 0181 741 1370**

Walpole House ✿❀ (Mr & Mrs Jeremy Benson) Plantsman's garden; specie and tree peonies; water garden; spring flowers. Features in 'The Englishman's Garden'. Mid C16 to early C18 house, once home of Barbara Villiers, Duchess of Cleveland. Seeds and some plants for sale. *Adm £1.50 OAP/Chd 50p (Share to Chiswick House Friends Cascade Appeal®)*

51 Cholmeley Crescent, N6 ✿ (Ernst & Janet Sondheimer) Highgate. Between Highgate Hill and Archway Rd, off Cholmeley Park. Nearest tube Highgate. Approx ⅙-acre garden with many alpines in screes, peat beds, tufa and greenhouse; shrubs, rhododendrons, camellias, magnolias, pieris, ceanothus etc. Clematis, bog plants, roses, primulas. TEA. *Adm £1 Chd 50p. Sun April 30 (2-6). Private visits welcome please* **Tel 0181 340 6607**

The Coach House, SW6 ✿❀ (Dr John Newton) Landridge Rd. Nearest underground station Putney Bridge. Across New Kings Rd into Burlington Rd, R into Rigault Rd. The garden is at the end of Rigualt Rd behind the white wall. Small 34′ × 36′ walled garden with pond, fountain; herbaceous borders, surrounding small lawn designed to have yr-round flowering. *Adm £1 Chd 50p. Sun June 18 (2-5.30)*

¶8 College Cross, N1 ✿ (Anne Weyman & Chris Bulford) Nearest Station Highbury and Islington. Buses to Highbury Corner or Islington Town Hall. Walled town garden, 70′ x 20′, many shrubs and herbaceous plants, incl perennial geraniums; walls covered with climbers. *Adm £1 Chd 50p (Share to National Children's Bureau®). Sun June 4 (2-6)*

By Appointment Gardens. See head of county section

37 Creighton Avenue, N10 ✲❀ (Tim Elkins & Margaret Weaver) Muswell Hill. Buses 43, 134, 243 from Highgate tube to Muswell Hill Broadway-Fortis Green Rd, along Tetherdown, turn R into Creighton Ave at mini-roundabout. S facing rear garden 120′ × 30′. Two alpine beds, well stocked mixed borders of delphiniums, kniphofias, lupins, foxgloves, rhododendrons, azaleas, acers and many evergreen shrubs. Ornamental trees and grapevine. Patio with pots. TEAS. *Adm £1 Chd 30p (Share to CHICS®). Sun June 11 (2-5)*

¶133 Crystal Palace Road, SE22 ✲❀ (Miss S Hillwood-Harris) East Dulwich. Nearest Station Peckham Rye and East Dulwich. Buses 176, 185, coming S 2nd stop Lordship Lane, up Northcross Rd, turn R into Crystal Palace Rd. House on L. Bus 12 coming S 2nd stop Barry Rd, up Upland Rd, turn L into Crystal Palace Rd. Inspirational Victorian town house garden 17′ x 36′ each inch packed with winding charm. Formal, but with a strong wilful dash of indiscipline. Roses, wisteria, shrubs, herbs and shade loving plants. Original Victorian wall a victim of gales, but now reborn as a central circular terrace. A garden of character and surprises. TEAS. *Adm 50p Chd 25p (Share to Crusaid®). Suns May 14, June 25 (2-6). Private visits welcome, please* **Tel 0181 693 3710**

¶De Beauvoir Gardens, N1 Islington-Hackney border. *Combined adm £1.50 Chd 50p. Sun June 11 (2-6)*

¶51 Lawford Road ✲❀ (Mrs Carol Lee) Lawford Rd (formerly called Culford Rd) is a cul-de-sac with entrance for cars from Downham Rd. Parking fairly restricted. Downham Rd runs between Kingsland and Southgate Rd. Buses Kingsland Rd 149, 243, 22A/B and 67, Southgate Rd 141. A small garden 16′ x 45′ at rear of a typical Victorian terraced house. Bricked with different levels, lots of pots and a pond with waterfalls. Hostas, ferns and fuchsias greatly favoured. TEAS. *(Share to National Deaf Children's Soc®). Sun June 11 (2-6)*

¶26 Northchurch Road ✲ (Mrs Kathy Lynam) Angel tube then Buses 38, 73, 56, 30, 171A down Essex Rd, alight bus stop after Essex Rd Station just before Northchurch Rd. Cross over and proceed down Northchurch Rd (petrol stn on corner) to lower end near church. House on L. By car from Angel down Essex Rd. R into Halliford St past lights at Southgate Rd. Turn L 1st rd Upton Rd, then R at bottom, house on L. Walled back garden, approx 70′ x 30′ with 2 old apple trees, greenhouse and lawn, mixed borders with clematis, roses and lots of perennials. Places to sit and ponder. TEA. *Private visits welcome, please* **Tel 0171 254 8993**

29 Deodar Road, SW15 ✲❀ (Peter & Marigold Assinder) Putney. Off Putney Bridge Rd Bus: 14, 22, 37, 74, 80, 85, 93, 220. Tubes: Putney Bridge and East Putney. Small garden 130ft × 25ft running down to Thames with lovely view. Camellias, wide range of variegated shrubs, hardy geraniums. Featured in Private Gardens of London by Arabella Lennox Boyd 1990. Cuttings and visits at other times by arrangement **Tel 081 788 7976**. TEA. *Adm £1 Chd 50p (Share to Royal Marsden Hospital®). Suns April 16, June 4, July 16 (2-5)*

¶Ealing Gardens, W5 ✲❀ Ealing Broadway Station (Central and District Lines). Bus 65 from Kingston and Richmond. Two gardens within a few mins walk of the station and each other. TEAS in aid of Action Research for the Crippled Child. *Combined adm £1.50 Chd 25p. Sun June 11 (2-6)*

52 Mount Park Road (Mr & Mrs Paddy O'Hagan) 100′ x 50′ triangular garden on two levels. Designed for wildlife in 1989 by Chris Baines. Woodland walk, terrace, decorative vegetable plot and glass fountain, pond and bog area, many architectural and tender plants densely planted. Conservatory with unusual euphorbias. Classical music

23 Woodville Road (Jill & Taki Argyropoulos) Mediterranean style part-paved front garden with lots of tubs and pots, planted for yr round colour (prize winner in 1994 Ealing in Bloom Competition). Secluded, walled garden at rear 100′ x 40′, well stocked with flowering shrubs, climbers and many herbaceous plants. Small fish pond with waterfall and bog garden, vegetable and herb area

20 Eatonville Road, SW17 ❀ (Pamela Johnson & Gethyn Davies) Tooting. 400yds from Tooting Bec tube (Northern Line). Off Trinity Rd and Upper Tooting Park. Bus stop on Trinity Rd at top of Eatonville Rd Nos. 249, 219, 349 or on Balham High Rd outside tube Nos. 155, 355. 42′ × 23′ S facing garden. Filled with an imaginative variety of plants to give yr-round colour and form. Mixed borders, climbing plants, containers and small pond. Also tiny front garden. TEAS. *Adm £1 Chd 50p. Suns June 25 (2-6)*

Eccleston Square, SW1 ♿❀ (Garden Manager Roger Phillips) Central London; just off Belgrave Rd near Victoria Station, parking allowed on Suns. 3-acre square was planned by Cubitt in 1828. The present Garden Committee have worked intensively over the last 12 years to see what can be created despite the inner city problems of drought, dust, fumes, shade and developers. Within the formal structure the garden is sub-divided into mini-gardens incl camellia, iris, rose, fern, and container garden. A national collection of ceanothus incl more than 50 species and culitvers is held in the square. TEAS. *Adm £1.50 Chd 75p. Suns April 23, June 4 (2-5)*

Edwardes Sq, W8 ♿✲ (Edwardes Sq Garden Committee) Edwardes Sq is off Kensington High Street. Accessible by bus and underground. Car parking is allowed on Sundays. 3-acres laid out circa 1815. Spring flowering trees, shrubs and bulbs. *Adm £1 Chd 50p. Sun May 14 (2-6)*

¶9 Eland Road ✲ (Nancye Nosworthy) Battersea. Off Lavender Hill backing onto Battersea Arts Centre. 45a, 77 and 77a bus stop at top of st. Clapham Junction Station and buses 19, 49, 319, 137a nearby. Small London garden designed by Christopher Masson. A series of gentle terraces, pool and fountain. Many unusual shrubs providing yr-round interest. *Adm £1 Chd free. Sun April 30 (2-5)*

¶Elm Tree Cottage ✲ (Wendy Witherick & Michael Wilkinson) 85 Croham Rd, S Croydon. Off B275 from Croydon. Off A2022 from Selsdon. A gently sloping plantsperson's garden with fine views of Croham Hurst and Croham Valley. This cottage garden designed, built and maintained by present owners is now 5 yrs old. It has many rare and unusual roses, perennials, shrubs and pond. A novel bog garden in pots! 120 roses, 50 helianthemums, 70 hardy geraniums, 50 clematis, 20 tree and herbaceous peonies as well as many other plants. TEA. *Adm £1 Chd free. Sun June 11 (12-5.30). Private visits welcome, please* **Tel 0181 681 8622**

The Elms ✄❀ (Prof & Mrs R Rawlings) Kingston-on-Thames entry via Manorgate Rd. 1m E Kingston on A308. Buses to Kingston Hospital: LT 213, 85, 57, K3, K5, K6, K8, K10, 718: BR Norbiton Station 100yds. Enter via garages in Manorgate Rd which is off A308 at foot of Kingston Hill. Wheelchairs limited to the tea area. Small (55′ × 25′) compact town-house rear garden, of special interest to horticulturists and plant lovers. Truly a collector's garden with numerous rare and unusual plants, particularly featuring rhododendrons, magnolias, camellias, dwarf conifers and a wide range of evergreen and deciduous shrubs. Small trees, herbaceous, ground cover plants, a two-level pool with geyser and well planted margins, roses, clematis and other choice and tender climbers, alpine trays are also featured. This small garden even bears some fruit namely, plum, pear, and soft fruits. Seeds and plants available. The garden has been featured on the radio and in various publications. TEAS in aid of Home Farm Trust and Princess Alice Hospice. *Adm £1 Chd 50p. Sats, Suns March 18, 19; April 22, 23; May 13, 14 (2-5). Private visits by appt, please* **Tel 0181 546 7624**

49 & 51 Etchingham Park Rd N3 ♿✄❀ (Robert Double, Gilbert Cook and Diane & Alan Langleben) Finchley. Off Ballards Lane overlooking Victoria Park. Station: Finchley Central. 2 rear gardens. ⅝-acre; lawn, small orchard, shrubs, large selection of hostas. Sculpture by Wm Mitchell, new ornamental vegetable garden. Exhibition and sale of water colour paintings by Robert Double. TEAS. Live music. *Adm £1 Chd free. Sun May 21 (2-6). Private visits by appt, please* **Tel 0181 346 4924**

Fenton House, NW3 ✄ (The National Trust) 300yds from Hampstead Underground. Entrances: top of Holly Hill and Hamstead Grove. 1½-acre walled garden in its first decade of development. It is on three levels with compartments concealed by yew hedges and containing different plantings, some still in the experimental stage. The herbaceous borders are being planned to give yr-round interest while the recently brick paved sunken rose garden is already donning the patina of age. The formal lawn area contrasts agreeably with the rustic charm of the orchard and kitchen garden. *Adm £1.50 Chd 50p. For NGS Sun June 18 (11-6)*

Frogmore Gardens see Berkshire

73 Forest Drive East, E11 ✄❀ (A J Wyllie) Leytonstone. Into Whipps Cross Rd, then SW into James Lane. 1st L into Clare Rd, 1st R into Forest Drive East. By bus to Whipps Cross Hospital or tube to Leytonstone and bus to James Lane. 20′ × 65′ country garden in miniature, but with full-sized plants, behind a terraced house. Small lawn with mixed borders leading to a shrub and woodland area. Two fountains and various unusual plants. Also 20′ front garden informally planted round formal paths and centre piece. TEA. *Adm £1 Chd 50p (Share to The Margaret Centre, Whipps Cross Hospital®). Sun Aug 20 (11-5)*

17 Fulham Park Gardens, SW6 ✄ (A Noel Esq) Putney Bridge Tube. Refer to A-Z. Up Kings Road L at Threshers Off- licence, (Elysium St.) into Fulham Park Gardens. Turn R, on RH-side. 40ft × 17ft romantic silver and white garden, with interesting variety of plants in harmoniously designed form. An oasis of peace in a hostile environment. Featured in Sunday Times and on ITV. *Adm £2, OAPs £1. Suns July 9, Sept 17 (2.30-6)*

¶70 Gloucester Crescent NW1 ✄ (Lucy Gent & Malcolm Turner) Nr junction Gloucester Crescent and Oval Rd 600yds SW of Camden Town Tube Station. A square in front, a triangle at the side, a wedge at the back, lots of inherited character: quite a challenge. Visitors welcome to see work in progress. Albanian Folk music (3-4). *Adm £1 Chd 50p (Share to Faik Konica, local Albanian Community Centre©). Sun June 11 (2-5)*

¶51 Gloucester Road ✄❀ (Mrs Lindsay Smith) Kew. 10 mins walk from Kew Gardens Tube Station. Travel towards S Circular along Leybourne Park Rd, cross main rd, down Forest Rd 1st L into Gloucester Rd. House ½-way down on R. A small square cottage garden. Many interesting plants and shrubs. Wallflowers and bulbs in spring. TEAS. *Adm £1 Chd 50p. Sun April 30 (2-6)*

Goldsborough, SE3 ♿✄ 112 Westcombe Park Rd, Blackheath. Located between Greenwich Village Centre and The Standard Blackheath. N of Blackheath Heath and E of Greenwich Park. Nearest BR Westcombe Park (10 mins walk) or Maze Hill (15 mins walk). Buses to the Standard from Central London and surrounding areas. Hoppa buses stop directly outside. Westcombe Park Rd situated in A-Z of London. Car parking available. Community garden for close care and nursing home residents. Approx ½ acre of landscaped gardens, incl walkways of rose-covered pergolas; fish ponds; herbaceous borders and colourful annuals. A very sheltered and peaceful garden. TEAS. *Adm £1 Chd 50p. Sun July 2 (2-5)*

5 Greenaway Gardens, NW3 ✄ (Mrs Marcus) Tube equidistant (½ mile) Hampstead or Finchley Road Stations. Buses: Finchley Road, West End Lane stop, nos. 13, 82, 113. From Finchley Road, turn up Frognal Lane, 2nd on L. Unusually large and varied London garden landscaped on three levels with year-round interest. Terrace with variety of climbing plants; water feature and swimming pool; steps to large lawn surrounded by borders with wide variety of trees, shrubs and herbaceous perennials, decorative urns and furniture. Partially suitable for wheelchairs. TEAS July 16 only. *Adm £1 Chd free. Sun May 14, Sat June 17, Sun July 16 (2-6)*

Regular Openers. Too many days to include in diary. Usually there is a wide range of plants giving year-round interest. See head of county section for the name and garden description for times etc.

12 Greenheys Close ✿❀ (Mrs Joan G Moody) Murray Rd, Northwood. 10min walk from Northwood Met Line. L into Green Lane, L at Maxwell Rd, L again at Murray Rd (Police St on corner). Greenheys Close on L past pillar box. From M25 at junction 18, take 404 Rickmansworth direction, after Mount Vernon Hospital, go over lights at Green Lane, Northwood, take 2nd on L into Murray Rd, Greenheys Close on R. A well-maintained town garden - plus! Accent on colour through the yr. Extensive collection of healthy roses flowering over a long period, unusual bulbs, climbers and shrubs, many herbaceous and annual plants. Open plan garden in a Neo-Georgian Close. *Adm £1 Chd 50p. Sun June 25 (2-5)*

7 The Grove, N6 ♿✿ (Thomas Lyttelton Esq) The Grove is between Highgate West Hill & Hampstead Lane. Stations: Archway or Highgate (Northern Line, Barnet trains) Bus: 210, 271 to Highgate Village. ½-acre designed for maximum all-yr interest with minimum upkeep. TEA April 30 only. *Adm £1 OAPs/Chd 50p. Suns April 30 (2-6), June 18 (2-5). Private visits welcome, please* **Tel 0181 340 7205**

¶17 Gwendolen Avenue ♿✿ (Mrs Philippa Conville) Putney. 5 mins walk W of Putney High St. Off Upper Richmond Rd. 10 mins walk E, Putney Tube Station. On the slopes of Putney Hill ¼ acre of partly walled family garden enclosed by trees and mixed borders, with a wide variety of plants, some unusual to provide all-yr interest. Everything in the garden planted by present owner over 25 yrs. TEAS. *Adm £1 Chd 50p (Share to MS Society®). Sun June 18 (2-6)*

Hall Grange ♿✿ (Methodist Home for the Aged) Croydon. Situated in Shirley Church Rd near to junction with Upper Shirley Rd. From N leave A232 at junction of Shirley Rd and Wickham Rd. From S leave A212 at junction of Gravell Hill and Shirley Hills Rd. The garden was laid out circa 1913 by Rev William Wilkes secretary to the RHS and breeder of the Shirley Poppy. Approx 5 acres of natural heathland is planted with azaleas, rhododendrons, heathers and shrubs and remains unchanged. A grassy area contains many wild flowers and is mown only once a year to permit natural reproduction. No parking at garden. TEAS. *Adm £1 Chd free. Sun May 21 (2-5.30)*

¶Ham House ♿✿ (The National Trust) Richmond. Midway between Richmond and Kingston W of A307 on the Surrey bank of the R Thames. Signposted with Tourism brown signs. Restored C17 garden, gravel terrace, paths dividing eight large grass plats; wilderness; parterre. TEAS. *Adm House £4 Chd £2 Garden free. For NGS Sun April 9 (11.30-6)*

117 Hamilton Terrace, NW8 ♿✿ (Mrs K Herbert and the Tenants Association) Hamilton Terrace is parallel with Maida Vale to the E. Buses from Marble Arch 16, 16a, 8, go up Edgeware Road to Maida Vale. Alight at Elgin Avenue, cross Maida Vale and go up Abercorn Place. 117 is to the L. There is room in Hamilton Terrace to park cars. 117 is the opp end of Hamilton Terrace from Lords nearly opp St Mark's Church. This is a large garden for London. The lawn at the back is kept partly wild with different grasses and wild flowers. There is a tiny garden in memory of Dame Anna Neagle who lived in the house. There is a standard rose near the house given in her memory. TEA. *Adm £1 Chd 20p (Share to the Spastics Society®). Suns May 21, June 25 (2-6)*

11 Hampstead Way, NW11, ✿❀ (Mr & Mrs R L Bristow) Nearest tube station Golders Green, 10 minute walk up North End Road, L into Wellgarth Road, R up Hampstead Way. ¼-acre prize winning garden, water features. unusual plants around lawns in the front and patio at the back. TEAS. *Adm £1 Chd 50p. Sun June 11 (2-6)*

133 Haverstock Hill, NW3 ✿❀ (Mrs Catherine Horwood) Belsize Park Tube Station turn L out of station. Buses C11, C12, 168 (Haverstock Arms stop). Prizewinning 120ft long narrow garden divided into rooms. Design features incl paved terrace, beds of old and English roses with clematis and cottage garden companion planting, and soft fruit garden. Many unusual tender perennial and scented plants; wildlife pond. Featured in Country Life and Wonderful Window-boxes. Highly Commended in The Gardener Magazine Gardener of the Year competition. *Adm £1 Chd free. Sun June 25 (2-6). Private visits welcome from April to July by written appt*

37 Heath Drive, NW3 ♿✿❀ (Mr & Mrs C Caplin) Station: Finchley Rd; buses: 82, 13 & 113 Heath Drive. Many uncommon plants; lawn; pond; rockery; ferns. Unusual treatment of fruit trees, greenhouse and conservatory. 1982, 1983, 1987, 1988, 1989, 1991, 1993 winner of Frankland Moore Trophy. Featured in Arabella Lennox-Boyd's Private Gardens of London. TEA. *Adm £1 Chd 50p. Suns May 14, July 9 (2.30-6). Parties welcome by appt, please* **Tel 0171 435 2419**

Highgate Village, N6 ✿ The Grove is between Highgate West Hill & Hampstead Lane Stations: Archway or Highgate (Northern Line, Barnet trains). Bus: 210, 271, 211 to Highgate Village. TEAS in aid of local Scouts, per cent to NGS, at **5 The Grove**. *Adm £1 each garden Chd 50p. Sun June 18 (2-5)*

4 The Grove (Cob Stenham Esq) 2-tiered with formal upper garden; view across Heath; orchard in lower garden

5 The Grove (Mr & Mrs A J Hines) Newly-designed garden on 2 levels

7 The Grove see separate entry

Highwood Ash, NW7 ❀ (Mr & Mrs R Gluckstein) Highwood Hill, Mill Hill. From London via A41 (Watford Way) to Mill Hill Circus; turn R up Lawrence St; at top bear L up Highwood Hill; house at top on R. Stations Totteridge and Whetstone or Edgware (Northern Line). Stanmore (Jubilee Line) Arnos Grove (Piccadilly Line). Bus from all these 251 (Sat only). 3¼-acre incl rose garden, shrub and herbaceous borders, rhododendrons, azaleas, lake with waterfall, a mixture of formal and informal. TEAS. *Adm £1 Chd 50p (Share to The North London Hospice®). Sat, Sun May 13, 14 (2-6)*

5 Hillcrest Avenue NW11 ✿❀ (Mrs R M Rees) Hillcrest Ave is off Bridge Lane. By bus to Temple Fortune, Buses 82, 102, 260. Nearest Tube Golders Green or Finchley Central. Walk down Bridge Lane. Small labour saving colourful garden with many interesting features; rockery, fish pond, conservatory, tree fern. Low maintenance, yr-round interest, acid bed. TEAS. *Adm 80p Chd 40p (Share to ADS®). Sun June 11 (2-6)*

1 Hocroft Avenue NW2 ♿✿❀ (Dr & Mrs Derek Bunn) 113 bus (stop at Cricklewood Lane). Travelling N from the Finchley Rd on the Hendon Way (A41), take 3rd turn on L into Hocroft Ave. Easy parking. Prize-winning garden with yr-round interest, especially in the spring. Front garden shown on BBC Gardeners' World, in their Front Garden series. Black and white bed featured in The Independent and The Evening Standard. Mixed borders in the back garden with a wide variety of plants against a background of trees. Subject of an article by Tony Venison in Country Life focusing on plant sales in the NGS. Home-made TEAS. *Adm £1.50 Chd free (Share to Hampstead Counselling Service®). Sat, Sun April 29, 30 (2-6)*

The Holme ♿✿ (Lesses of The Crown Estate Commissioners) Positioned in Inner Circle, Regents Park opp Open Air Theatre. Nearest tube stations Regents Park and Baker St. 4-acre garden bordering the Regents Park Lake with many mature trees, shrubs and much new planting. Secluded grotto and formal rose garden. Teas available in Park Cafe adjacent. *Adm £2 Chd £1. For opening dates see local press or* **Tel NGS 01483 211535**

125 Honor Oak Park SE23 ✿❀ (Mrs Heather West) BR station: Honor Oak Park turn R. Off South Circular (A205) via Honor Oak Rd. Small 75′ × 45′ multifarious froth on two levels: the lower shady with small beds, the upper sunny with grass, verandah and pots. TEAS in aid of BHHI. *Adm £1 Chd 50p. Sun June 25 (2-6)*

Hornbeams ♿✿❀ (Dr & Mrs R B Stalbow) Priory Drive, Stanmore. 5m SE of Watford; underground: Stanmore; Priory Drive private rd off Stanmore Hill (A4140 Stanmore-Bushey Heath Rd). ½-acre slightly wild cottage-style garden where everyday plants and rare treasures mingle happily. Shrub roses, alpines, species bulbs. Conservatory shaded by muscat grape. Kitchen garden. Many unusual plants propogated for sale. TEAS. *Adm £1 Chd 50p (Share to Jerusalem Botanic Garden©). Sun June 25 (2.30-6)*

Lambeth Community Care Centre, SE11 ♿✿❀ Monkton Street. Tube or buses to Elephant and Castle, cut behind Leisure Centre and follow Brook Drive. Turn into Sullivan Rd at Bakery, through passage to Monkton St. Buses 3, 109, 159 (or drive) to Kennington Road. At The Ship turn into Bishop's Terrace and 1st R to Monkton St. ⅔-acre garden ideal for people in wheelchairs to see all aspects of garden. Mixed shrubs, trees, small rose garden, herbs, interesting walkways and mixed borders. Part of award winning hospital designed by Edward Cullinan Architects. Indoor planted area also open. 1st prize winner in London Hospital Gardens Competition. TEAS. *Adm £1 OAP/Chd 50p (Share to St. Thomas's Trustees for the garden®). Sat, Sun June 10, 11 (2-5)*

Lambeth Palace, SE1 ♿✿❀ (The Archbishop of Canterbury & Mrs Carey) Waterloo main line and underground, Westminster, Lambeth and Vauxhall tubes all about 10 mins walk. 3, 10, 44, 76, 77, 159, 170, 507 buses go near garden. Entry to garden on Lambeth Palace Rd (not at gatehouse) 2nd largest private garden in London. Land in hand of Archbishops of Canterbury since end C12. Work on garden carried out over last 100 years but significant renewal has taken place during last 6 years; restored rose walk, new border beneath wall by Beth Chatto, herb garden, shrub border, rhododendrons, spring bulbs and camellias. TEA. *Adm £2 OAP/Chd 10-16 £1 (Share to Lambeth Palace Garden©). Sat April 8 (2-5)*

12 Lansdowne Rd, W11 ♿ (The Lady Amabel Lindsay) Holland Park. Turn N off Holland Park Ave nr Holland Park Station; or W off Ladbroke Grove ½-way along. Bus: 12, 88, GL 711, 715. Bus stop & station: Holland Park, 4 mins. Medium-sized fairly wild garden; border, climbing roses, shrubs; mulberry tree 200 yrs old. *Adm £1 Chd 50p. Wed May 10 (2-6)*

10 Lawn Road, NW3 ♿✿❀ (Mrs P Findlay) Tube to Belsize Park or go up Haverstock Hill. Turn R at Haverstock Arms then L. House 200yds on R, with blue door. ⅒-acre approx; uniquely curvaceous design of intersecting circles, set in rectangular format. Organically cultured garden, very heavily stocked; many unusual and native species plants. *Adm £1 Chd 50p. Sun June 25 (2.30-6)*

15 Lawrence Street, SW3 ✿ (John Casson Esq) Between King's Rd and the river down Old Church St S from King's Rd to the river, turn L round the statue of Sir Thomas More then L (behind garden) into Lawrence St. Garden at top of street on L. Nearest tubes: Sloane Square and South Kensington. Prize winning small Chelsea cottage type garden, old-fashioned flowers, clematis, roses and some unusual plants. Plants to cover each season. Featured in Rosemary Verey's Secret Gardens. House built c1790, not open except for access to garden. *Adm £1 Chd 50p (Share to Chelsea Physic Garden®). Sun June 11 (2-6)*

¶20 Lessingham Avenue, SW17 ✿ (George Hards) Tooting Bec underground (Northern Line). Buses 155, 219. Tranquil green and white small town garden 20′ x 40′ with water feature. Closely planted to provide yr-round variety, interesting plants incl trachelospermum jasminoides, catalpa bungei, auralia elata variegata, romneya coulteri. TEAS. *Adm 50p (Share to Imperial Cancer Research Fund®). Sun June 11 (2-6)*

Leyborne Park Gardens ✿❀ Two minute walk from Kew Gardens station. Take exit signposted Kew Gardens. On leaving station forecourt bear R past shops. Leyborne Park is 1st rd on R. Bus 391, R68 to Kew Gdns station. Bus 65 to Kew Gdns, Victoria Gate. Access by car is from Sandycombe Rd. TEAS. *Combined adm £1.50 Chd free (Share to Arthritis and Rheumatism Council for Research®). Sun June 18 (2-5.30)*

36 Leyborne Park (David & Frances Hopwood) 120ft long mature, family garden; architect designed for minimum upkeep with maximum foliage effects; patio; imaginative children's play area; huge eucalyptus. TEAS

38 Leyborne Park ❀ (Mr & Mrs A Sandall) 120ft long organic family garden; lawn with mixed borders; containers; long established vine; alliums, lavenders, eryngiums, scented pelargoniums, bamboos; plants for the dry garden

40 Leyborne Park (Debbie Pointon-Taylor) 120ft long garden; heather and conifer garden; lawn and mixed borders; mature shrubs; patio with containers

1 Lister Road, E11 ✿❀ (Myles Challis Esq) Leytonstone underground station (central line). 5 mins to High Rd Leytonstone. Hills garage marks corner of Lister Rd which is directly off High Rd. Garden designer's unexpected, densely planted sub-tropical garden containing a mixture of tender plants such as daturas, gingers, cannas, tree ferns, bananas and hardy exotics including gunneras, bamboos, cordylines, phormiums and large leaved perennials in a space unbelievably only 40′ × 20′. *Adm £1 Chd 50p. Sun Aug 20 (11-5). Private visits welcome for parties of 15 and over, please* **Tel 0181 556 8962**

21a The Little Boltons, SW10 ❀ (Mrs D Capron) Between Fulham and Old Brompton Rd off Tregunter Rd, next to The Boltons. Nearest tube Earls Court, buses 30, 14, 74. 70ft prize winning herbaceous plant collection. Portrayed in the book 'Private Gardens of London' by Arabella Lennox-Boyd. *Adm £1 Chd 25p. Sun July 2 (2-6)*

Little Lodge ♿✿❀ (Mr & Mrs P Hickman) Watts Rd, Thames Ditton (Station 5 mins). A3 from London; after Hook underpass turn left to Esher; at Scilly Isles turn R towards Kingston; after 2nd railway bridge turn L to Thames Ditton village; house opp library after Giggs Hill Green. A cottage style informal garden within 15m of central London. Many British native plants. Garden has an atmosphere of tranquillity, featuring plants with subtle colours and fragrance; small brick-pathed vegetable plot. TEAS. *Adm £1 Chd free (Share to Cancer Research®). Sun June 11 (11.30-6). Private visits welcome, please* **Tel 0181 398 5550**

22 Loudoun Road, NW8 ✿ (Ruth Barclay) 3 to 4 min walk to St. John's Wood tube station. Lies between Abbey Road and Finchley Rd serviced by buses, minutes from bus stop. Small front garden, well matured, started from scratch 9 years ago. A strong emphasis on design with leaf and flowers subtle colour combination, water, arbour garden within a garden. Back Italianate courtyard, romantic and mysterious. Interesting water features, incl Grotto with water cascading down mussel shells surrounded by ferns and tree ferns. Prizewinner for 4 consecutive years. Featured in 'Town Gardens'. TEA. *Adm £1 Chd 25p. Sun May 28 (2-6.30)*

4 Macaulay Road, SW4 ♿✿❀ (Mrs Diana Ross) Clapham Common Tube. Buses 88, 77, 77A, 137, 137A, 37, 45. Prize-winning garden whose owner appeared on the TV programme 'An Englishwoman's Garden' in 1993. The garden 80′ × 50′ was revamped last yr and now combines its original formal outline with roses, clematis and herbaceous perennials jockeying for space between exotic foliage and architectural plants. Mini-grotto surrounded by a growing collection of ferns. Music and TEAS in aid of Trinity Hospice. *Adm £1.50 OAPs £1. Sun June 18 (2-6)*

Malvern Terrace, N1 ♿❀ Barnsbury. Approach from S via Pentonville Rd into Penton St, Barnsbury Rd; from N via Thornhill Rd opp Albion public House. Tube: Highbury & Islington. Bus: 19, 30 to Upper St Town Hall. Unique London terrace of 1830s houses built on site of Thos Oldfield's dairy and cricket field. Cottage-style gardens in cobbled cul-de-sac; music. Victorian plant stall. Home-made TEAS. Music. *Combined adm £1.50 Chd free (Share to International Spinal Research Trust®). Sun May 14 (2-5.30)*

1 Malvern Terrace (Mr & Mrs Martin Leman)
2 Malvern Terrace (Mr & Mrs K McDowall)
3 Malvern Terrace (Mr & Mrs A Robertson)
4 Malvern Terrace
5 Malvern Terrace (Mr & Mrs J J Broad)
6 Malvern Terrace (Dr B A Lynch)
7 Malvern Terrace (Mr & Mrs Mark Vanhegan)
8 Malvern Terrace (Mr & Mrs R Le Fanu)
10 Malvern Terrace (Dr & Mrs P Sherwood)

36 Marryat Road, SW19 ✿❀ (R P Finch Esq) 1m N from Wimbledon Station. 93 Bus. Up the hill turn R at far end of High St in Wimbledon village. Access for wheelchairs ltd to terrace. 1-acre garden with large area of mixed borders for yr-round interest. Unusual plants, special feature of containers on terrace. TEAS. *Adm £1 Chd free. Sun July 16 (1-5.30)*

13 Mercers Road N19 ✿❀ (Dr & Mrs N Millward) off Holloway Rd (A1) N of Odeon Cinema. 30′ × 15′ front garden featuring cool whites, greys and greens. 30′ × 20′ rear garden on two levels. Profusion of pastel shades from April to Sept. Many small-flowered clematis, pink schizophragma, rosa soulieana and other interesting climbers and perennials. Teas at **13 Trecastle Way**. *Adm £1 Chd 50p. Sun June 25 (2-6). Private visits welcome for small groups and individuals please* **Tel 0171 281 2674**

2 Millfield Place, N6 ♿✿ Garden is off Highgate West Hill, E side of Hampstead Heath. Buses 210, 271 to Highgate Village or C2, C12, 214 to Parliament Hill Fields terminus. Nearest train stations Kentish Town, Tufnell Park and North London BR line to Gospel Oak. 1½-acre spring and woodland garden with camellias and rhododendrons. Long mixed herbaceous border with some formal bedding schemes; small orchard. TEAS. *Adm £1 Chd 50p. Suns May 7, July 30 (2-6)*

29 Mostyn Road SW19 ✿❀ (Chris & Sue Spencer) Merton Park is 1m N of Wimbledon. From London cross Wimbledon Common, through Wimbledon Village, down Wimbledon Hill into The Broadway. Follow one-way system after Wimbledon Station following it round to the L before turning L into Hartfield Rd. Turn R at the end of Hartfield Rd cross level crossing. Mostyn Rd is 3rd on L. Greystones is 200 metres on R. ⅕-acre small garden laid out by Gertrude Jekyll in 1913 with further plantings added by her between 1913 and 1922. The garden has been restored by the present owners. Re-planting was carried out in 1992 using Jekyll's original plant lists. The garden is far from mature and the owners are still in the process of trying to arrange plantings to Jekyllian principles. The garden has been featured in Traditional Homes and Period House and Its Garden. Also BBC Television's Gardeners' World. TEAS. *Adm £1 Chd 50p (Share to St Mary's The Virgin®). Sat, Sun June 17, 18 (2-6)*

33 Mundania Road SE22 ✿❀ (Ms Helen Penn) 63 bus to Honor Oak. Nearest BR station Peckham Rye. Plantswoman's mature garden; 15′ × 40′ shaded N facing front garden, small woodland plants some unusual; 100′ × 40′ S facing back garden with variety of bulbs, herbaceous plants and shrubs. Small pond with native grasses. Conservatory with tender plants. 50′ × 20′ organic vegetable and herb garden adjoining. TEA. *Adm £1.25 Chd free. Private visits welcome May to June, please* **Tel 0181 693 4741**

Museum of Garden History, The Tradescant Trust ♿❀ St Mary-at-Lambeth, Lambeth Palace Road, SE1. Bus: 507 Red Arrow from Victoria or Waterloo, alight Lambeth Palace. 7,450 sq ft. replica of C17 garden planted in churchyard with flowers known and grown by John Tradescant. Tombs of the Tradescants and Admiral Bligh of the 'Bounty' in the garden. Opened by HM the Queen Mother in 1983. Museum being established in restored church of St Mary-at-Lambeth saved from demolition by The Trust. TEA. *Adm £1 OAPs/Chd 25p (Share to Museum of Garden History®). ▲For NGS Sun June 4 (10.30-5)*

Myddelton House Gardens ♿✿❀ (Lee Valley Park) Bulls Cross, Enfield. Situated a short distance S of junction 25 of M25, off W section of Bullsmoor Lane which crosses the A10. Pass Capel Manor, then bear L to Bulls Cross. The entrance to the Gardens is a few hundred yds further along, but it is partly concealed - please approach with care. The 4 acres of garden were created by Edward A Bowles, author of gardening trilogy 'My Garden in Spring, Summer, Autumn and Winter'. The gardens feature a diverse and unusual plant collection including a large selection of many species and varieties of naturalised bulbs, as well as the national collection of award winning bearded irises. The grounds have a large pond with terrace, two conservatories and interesting historical artefacts. TEA and plants for sale on NGS days and Suns only. *Adm £1.20 Concessions 60p. Open Mon-Fri (10-3.30)(except Bank Hols) (2-5) selected Suns. For NGS Sun May 28, Sept 24, Feb 25 1996. No concessions on NGS days & Suns.* **Tel 01992 713838**

¶17A Navarino Road, E8 ✿❀ (John Tordoff Esq) situated between Dalston and Hackney and connects Graham Rd with Richmond Rd. Buses 38, 22A, 22B, 277, 30. A formal Italian garden of clipped box and yew. Rambler roses make a spectacular display over arches and a pergola. The Japanese garden begun 2yrs ago features a large informal pond, ornamental bridge, miniature teahouse and Mount Fuji. Plantings of azaleas, acers and bamboo. TEA. *Adm £1 Chd 50p. Sun June 11 (12-6)*

15 Norcott Road, N16 ✿❀ (Amanda & John Welch) Buses 73, 149, 76, 67, 243 (see bus map and A to Z) Clapton or Stoke Newington Stations (Rectory Rd closed Suns). Largish (for Hackney) walled back garden. Pond, herbs, herbaceous plants especially irises, geraniums and campanulas. TEAS. *Adm 70p Chd 50p (Share to St Joseph's Hospice®). Suns June 4, July 23 (2-6)*

North Ruislip Gardens ✿ Ruislip, Middlesex. *Combined adm £1.50 Chd free. Sun June 18 (2-5)*

235 Eastcote Road ❀ (T & J Hall) From Ruislip High Street take the B466 (Eastcote Road) nearest tube Ruislip Manor. Parking off Eastcote Rd in Evelyn Ave please. Medium sized suburban garden. 115ft × 80ft. Contains a wide variety of herbaceous perennials and shrubs, shady patio area and ponds. Home-made TEAS. *Adm £1 Chd free. Also open Sun Aug 6 (1-5)*

82 Evelyn Avenue (Mr & Mrs K Morgan) Refer to A-Z. Nearest Underground Station – Ruislip Manor. Turn R out of Station. Continue up and over the hill; cross the Eastcote Rd and turn 1st R into Evelyn Ave. Suburban garden 40ft × 170ft. Curving borders and island beds planted with shrubs and herbaceous plants to give yr-round interests. Lawns and mature trees

86 Evelyn Avenue (Isabel & Frank Thornton) Med-sized working garden approx 180′ × 40′. Pond, productive vegetable plot, soft fruit, shrubs and herbaceous plants to give continuing interest. Mature fruit trees

2 Northbourne Road SW4 ♿✿ (Mr & Mrs Edward A Holmes) Claphan Common tube. Buses 137, 137A, 37. W facing, walled garden 36′ × 56′ with good architectural planting and rose pergola. Designed with a young family in mind and planted in Feb 1991. Featured in Sainsbury's The Magazine Nov '93. *Adm £1 OAPs/Chd 50p (Share to the Foundation for the Study of Infant Deaths®). Sun June 11 (2-6)*

Orchard Cottage see Kent

Ormeley Lodge ✿ (Lady Annabel Goldsmith) Ham Gate Avenue, Richmond. From Richmond Park, exit at Ham Gate into Ham Gate Avenue. 1st house on R. From Richmond A307, 1½m past New Inn on R, first turning on L. House is last on L. Bus: 65. Large walled garden in delightful rural setting on Ham Common. Newly designed formal garden, wide herbaceous borders, box hedges. Walk through to newly planted orchard with wild flowers. Vegetable garden. Secluded swimming pool area, trellised tennis court with roses and climbers. TEA. *Adm £1 Chd 20p. Sun June 25 (3-6)*

43 Ormeley Road SW12 ✿❀ (Richard Glassborow & Susan Venner) Nearest tube and BR station Balham, 5 mins walk, off Balham High Rd. Big ideas in a small garden 30′ × 18′ approx, SW facing, full of unusual plants. *Adm £1 Chd free (Share to Friends of the Earth®). Sun May 14 (2-6)*

¶Osterley Park House ♿ (The National Trust) Jersey Rd. 8m W of Piccadilly Circus. 3m E of Heathrow Airport in W London. Access is via Thornbury Rd on N side of A4 (Great West Rd) between Gillette Corner and Osterley Tube Station. Nearest station Osterley (Piccadilly Line) then 20 mins walk. Car Park free. Set in 140-acres of landscaped park, Osterley is one of the last great houses with an intact estate in Greater London. The pleasure grounds which were the part of the park reserved for the cultivation of shrubs and flowers are currently being restored. The NGS fund is contributing a substantial part of the cost of replanting the early C19 garden which stood in front of Rupert Adams's elegant semi-circular garden house. TEAS. *Adm £1.50 Chd free. For NGS Sun June 18 (11-4)*

Flat 1, 1F Oval Road, NW1 ✼ (Sheila Jackson) Tube station Camden Town. Buses: any bus to Camden Town, C2 and 274 stop very near. Parking difficult near centre on Sunday. A small side garden approaches an illustrator's very small hidden back garden approx 24ft × 20ft which abuts the Euston railway line. A great variety of plants, mainly in pots, are banked to create interesting shapes, making use of a variety of levels. This garden is the subject of the book 'Blooming Small, A City Dwellers Garden' *Adm £1 Chd 50p. Fri, Sat June 9, 10 (6-9) Sun June 11 (2-5). Also private visits welcome, please* **Tel 0171 267 0655**

78 Palace Road SW2 ✼❀ (Mr & Mrs D S Senior) BR station Streatham Hill 15min walk (NB Tulse Hill BR closed Sundays). Buses 2, 68, 196 to Tulse Hill station. By car S Circular Rd, just W of Tulse Hill one-way system. Located corner Palace Rd and Northstead Rd. 90′ × 60′ garden planted mainly for foliage effect and yr-round interest. Shrubs, bamboos, grasses, some interesting small trees. Part planted with Mediterranean plants to suit hot dry conditions, areas left wild to encourage wildlife, pond. *Adm £1 Chd free. Sun June 18 (2-6)*

17 Park Place Villas, W2 (Little Venice) ✼ (H C Seigal Esq) Park Place Villas is off Maida Ave which runs along Regent's Canal from Maida Vale to Warwick Ave. Station: Warwick Ave. Garden (⅛-acre) is one of an internal square of small gardens each belonging to a single house; rhododendrons, azaleas, woodland plants, alpines in raised beds and sinks; small pond with aquatic and bog plants; grass. *Adm 50p OAPs/Chd free. Sun April 30 (2-6)*

10A The Pavement SE27 ✼❀ (Brendan Byrne) Chapel Rd. Located off Ladas Rd down alleyway behind All Seasons Fish Bar. Buses 68 to Knights Hill alight at S London College or W Norwood Bus Garage. No. 2 to bus garage or Gypsy Rd. BR W Norwood. Come out Knights Hill, turn L. Chapel Rd is 10 mins walk on L after passing bus garage. Possibly the smallest garden in London (entry restricted to 5 people at any one time). A hidden oasis behind houses and shops. Collection of plants and shrubs incl roses, blackberries, raspberries, sweet peas, wild flowers, herbaceous and bedding plants, daturas. Plants and shrubs in containers, hanging baskets, window boxes. Featured in 'The Observer'. *Adm 80p Chd free (Share to Horses & Ponies Protection Assoc®). Sun July 2 (10-12, 2-6)*

43 Penerley Rd SE6 ♿✼❀ (Mr & Mrs E Thorp) BR stations Catford, Catford Bridge (15 mins walk). Buses 36, 36B, 47, 54, 75, 124, 160, 172, 180, 181, 185, 202, 208, 284, 306, (5 mins walk). Off A21 just S of S Circular Rd. Plant lover's shady garden 33′ × 100′, full of interesting and unusual plants. Formal lawns, informal planting, paved areas with ferns, hostas and other foliage plants in pots. TEAS in aid of St Laurence Church. *Adm £1 Acc chd free. Suns May 14, June 18, Sept 10, (2-5.30)*

35 Perrymead St, SW6 ✼ (Mr & Mrs Richard Chilton) Fulham. New King's Rd W from Chelsea; 1st on L after Wandsworth Bridge Rd. Stations: Fulham Broadway or Parsons Green; bus 22 from Chelsea; 28 from Kensington. Small paved garden with ornamental feature; surrounded by mature trees. Shrubs, climbers (especially clematis) interspersed with summer planting suitable for shade. *Adm £1 Chd 50p. Sun July 16 (2-6)*

3 Radnor Gardens ✼❀ (Ms Jill Payne) Twickenham. BR station Twickenham underground or N London line to Richmond then bus 90, R70 to Heath Rd, or 33, R68 to Twickenham junction or Popes Grotto, also 267. Turn off Heath Rd into Radnor Rd by Tamplins garage and R into Radnor gardens. Small garden of an 11′ 6″ wide terraced house owned by a compulsive plant collector. Front garden – raised bed and terracotta pots. Back garden – 45′ long, 6′ × 6′ patio, winding brick path and two tiny ponds. Garden crammed with a motley collection ranging from native wild flowers to tender plants. Small conservatory. *Adm 50p Chd 20p. Suns May 21 (11-5) July 2, 9; Aug 28 (2-6)*

9 Ranelagh Avenue SW6 (Mrs P Tham) Nearest tube Putney Bridge. Approx 60′ × 40′. A semi-formal two level garden featuring shade tolerant plants, incl many hostas and trees; arbutus, judas, magnolia, crab apple. Small patio with container grown plants; datura, hostas, vegetables. A resident but crowd-shy-toad! *Adm £1 Chd 50p. Sun July 16 (2-5.30)*

Ranulf Road Gardens NW2 ✼❀ At junction of Finchley Rd with Platts Lane and Fortune Green Rd enter Ardwick Rd and bear L into Ranulf Rd, nos. 9 and 11 are on L at brow of hill. Junction is 150yds S of junction of Finchley Rd and Hendon Way. Buses 13, 113, 82 from Finchley Rd station, 13, 82, 28, 139 from Golders Green, 28 from West Hampstead station. Home-made TEAS. *Combined adm £2 Chd free (Share to Hampstead Church Music Trust©). Sun July 16 (2-6)*

> **9 Ranulf Road** (Sir Patrick Garland) S facing terraced garden with open view; varied interest with vines, fruit, vegetables, conservatory and cactus collection; pots and troughs on terraces; lawn
>
> **11 Ranulf Road** (Mr & Mrs Jonathan Bates) Medium-sized garden, surrounded by trees, full of colour; herbaceous borders, roses, lilies, fuchsias, bedding plants and many geranium filled pots

Regents College, NW1 ❀ Regents Park. Regents College is located at the junction of York Bridge and the Inner Circle opp Queen Mary's Rose Garden in Regents Park. Baker Street tube is on the Bakerloo, Jubilee, Metropolitan, Hammersmith & City and Circle lines and is 5 mins walk. Buses: 1, 2, 2B, 13, 27, 30, 74, 159. Enter via gate on York Bridge Rd or the Garden Gate which is reached via the footbridge at Clarence Gate. The college and grounds occupy a site of approx 10 acres. The large lawns and mature trees echo the surrounding parkland. This landscape gives way to more ornamental planting near the buildings; special features incl a quadrangle garden, a gold border; folly garden on lake edge, herb area with bees. The focus will be on the more intimate former Botany Garden, a quiet and fairly secluded place, landscaped in a more traditional decorative style with pond, pergola, arbour, rock garden and herbaceous plants. TEA. *Adm £1 Concessions/Chd 50p. Sun May 28 (12-5). Private visits welcome, please* **Tel 0171 487 7494**

19 St Gabriel's Road NW2 ♿ (Mrs Penelope Mortimer) St Gabriel's Rd is a short walk from Willesden Green Tube (Jubilee Line). When Penelope Mortimer moved here in 1991 she brought two van-loads of plants from her Cotswold garden. With the help of a splendid balsam poplar, a great deal of muck and hard work, what was 150ft of exhausted grass and rubbish is now a miniature country garden brimming with old roses and rare herbaceous plants. "A sanctuary!" *Adm £1 Chd under 14 free. Sat July 1 (2.30-6.30). Private visits welcome, please* **Tel 0181 452 8551**

7 St George's Rd ✄❀ (Mr & Mrs Richard Raworth) St Margaret's, Twickenham. Off A316 between Twickenham Bridge and St Margarets roundabout. ½-acre maturing town garden backing onto private parkland. Garden divided into 'rooms' by yew, thuja and hornbeam hedges. Unusual shrubs, clematis and old English roses. Large conservatory with rare plants and climbers. Knot garden with herbs. Sink garden. Pergola covered in roses and rare clematis. New sunken paved garden with Pithari pot and planting. Small gravel garden. Mist propagation. Propagated specimens and unusual plants for sale. Featured in several books including Penelope Hobhouse's 'Garden Style' and 'Private Gardens of London' by Arabella Lennox Boyd, and Homes & Garden. TEAS. *Adm £1 Chd 50p. Suns June 4, 18 (2-6) or private visits welcome, please* **Tel 0181 892 3713**

St Mary's Convent & Nursing Home, W4 ♿❀ (Sister Jennifer Anne) Chiswick. Exit W from London on A4 to Hogarth roundabout. Take A316 signposted Richmond. St Mary's is 500yds down on L. Parking in Corney Rd, 1st turning L after Convent. 2½-acre walled garden with fine specimen trees; herbaceous borders and shrub borders being planted for yr-round interest, incl spring flowering shrubs and bulbs. TEAS. *Adm £1 Chd free. Sun April 23 (2-5)*

St Michael's Convent, Ham ♿✄❀ (Community of The Sisters of The Church) 56 Ham Common. From Richmond or Kingston, A307, turn onto the common at traffic lights nr the New Inn, 100 yds on the R adjacent to Martingales Close. 4-acre walled organic garden. Bible garden and circle garden of meditation. Extensive herbaceous borders, two orchards, wild life areas, working kitchen garden, vinehouse and ancient mulberry tree. *Collection Box. Private visits welcome please* **Tel 0181 940 8711**

57 St Quintin Avenue, W10 ✄❀ (H Groffman Esq) 1m from Ladbroke Grove/White City Underground. Turn into North Pole Rd from Wood Lane (White City, Shepherds Bush or Harrow Road approaches) or L into Cambridge Gdns, R from Cambridge Gds into St Marks Rd, then L into Qunitin Ave. From Ladbroke Grove station. Bus; 7, 220 to North Pole Road, or 72, 283 to Du Cane Road. 30ft × 40ft walled garden; yr-round selection of shrubs, perennials, summer bedding schemes. Patio; small pond; hanging baskets. 11 times winner Brighter Kensington & Chelsea Gardens competition. 3 gold medals and 1992 Banksian Medal award from London Gardens Society in 1993. Featured in Channel 4's Flowering Passions, LWT's Gardening Roadshow and 'Learn How to Create Your Perfect Garden' video in May 1994 edition of Ideal Home magazine. TEAS. *Adm £1.30 Chd 70p. Sun July 30 (2-6.30). Private visits welcome for paties of 10 and over, please,* **Tel 0181 969 8292**

14 Sebright Road ♿✄❀ (Julian Bishop & Rhian Morgan) High Barnet. Short walk W of Barnet High St. From M25 junction 23, follow A1081 to Barnet. Take 3rd R, into Alston Rd, 2nd R into Puller Rd and follow one way system to Sebright Rd. Parking possibly difficult - public car park at junction of Stafford Rd and Staplyton Rd, 3 min walk. Nearest tube High Barnet, 20 mins. Small 120′ × 20′ newly designed town garden, with traditional herbaceous borders, vegetable patch, fruit trees and little wildlife pond. Many old-fashioned roses, honeysuckles, unusual foxgloves and geraniums. TEAS. *Adm £1 Chd 25p (Share to Cat Protection League®). Sun July 16 (11-6) Sept 24 (2-6). Please ring* **0181 440 2042** *before visiting; owners may be moving house. Private visits welcome.*

12a Selwood Place, SW7 ♿ (Mrs Anthony Crossley) South Kensington, adjacent to 92 Onslow Gardens (cul-de-sac). South Kensington tube 8 mins walk, no. 14 bus down Fulham Rd (Elm Place request stop). Long green and white border; pink border in L-shaped walled garden; collection of roses, peonies, camellias, iris, lilies, poppies, vegetables; terraced herb garden. Suitable for wheelchairs only if dry. *Adm 70p Chd 35p. Thurs June 15 (2.30-6)*

South London Botanical Institute, SE24 ✄❀ 323 Norwood Rd. From South Circular Rd (A205) at Tulse Hill, turn N into Norwood Rd; Institute is 100yds on R. Small botanic garden, formally laid out; many rare and interesting species; over 200 labelled plants. TEA. *Adm £1 Chd 50p (Share to South London Botanical Institute®). Suns May 28, June 25 (2- 5). Private visits welcome, please* **Tel 0181 674 5787**

Southwood Lodge, N6 ✄❀ (Mr & Mrs C Whittington) 33 Kingsley Place. Off Southwood Lane. Buses 210, 271. Tube Highgate. A romantic, hidden garden laid out last century on a steeply sloping site, now densely planted with a wide variety of shrubs, bulbs, roses and perennials. Pond, waterfall, frogs. Many unusual plants are grown and propagated for sale. Featured in Gardeners Illustrated Sept '94. *Adm £1 Chd 40p (Share to North London Hospice®). Suns May 7, June 11 (2-6). Private visits welcome, please* **Tel 0181 348 2785**

Tarn ✄❀ (Mr & Mrs R Solley) Oxhey Drive South, Northwood. From Northwood Station turn R into Green Lane. At mini roundabout (signposted NATO Headquarters) follow sign turning L into Watford Rd, take 3rd R into Sandy Lane; at top U-turn into Oxhey Drive South, 2nd house on L. Approx ⅓-acre garden of special interest to horticulturists and plant lovers. Featured by Francesca Greenoak in 'The Times' Saturday Gardening Page April 1993, entitled 'Harmony in Variety'. Visited by the International Camellia Society, and the Garden Club of Milan. Many unusual shrubs, trees and plants; large collection of rhododendrons; camellias; magnolias and allied species. Spring blossom, drifts of bulbs including wild cyclamen, anemones, erythronium; bluebells; primroses etc. Greenhouses with camellias and many rare plants. Large collection of clematis and climbing roses growing informally through trees. Old world terrace with pond. Very old standard wisteria. Much of the garden was 'tree lifted' by present owner from Hampstead in 1970 where it had a mention by the late Lanning Roper in the 'Sunday Times'. *Adm £1.50 Chd 50p. Mon April 17 (2-5.30). Also private visits welcome Feb to June, please* **Tel 01923 828373**

¶103 Thurleigh Road ♿✻❀ (Charles MacKinnon) Clapham S Tube Station (Northern Line) is 5 mins walk. Thurleigh Rd runs parallel to Nightingale Lane, between Clapham Common (Wside) and Wandsworth Common (Bollingbroke Grove). A 140′ x 120′ walled garden surrounded by pleached limes. Very deep herbaceous beds enable some large plants to flourish eg crambe, mallow. Careful planting to minimise upkeep and to balance my dreams of Sissinghurst with my children's footballs. TEAS. *Adm £1.50 Chd 50p. Suns June 11, 25 (11-6)*

13 Trecastle Way N7 ✻❀ (Mrs Vera Quick) Carleton Rd. Camden Rd buses 29, 253 to Dalmeny Ave. 1st R from Dalmeny Ave into Trecastle Way (nr Holloway Prison). A very pretty garden. Small in size approx 60′ × 30′ . Full of colour, lots of interesting plants, ornamental pond and waterfall. Bedding plants grown from seeds and cuttings. TEAS. *Adm 80p Chd free. Sun June 25 (2-6)*

Trinity Hospice ♿✻❀ 30 Clapham Common North Side, SW4. Tube: Clapham Common. Bus: 37, 137, 45 stop outside. 2-acre park-like garden restored by Lanning Roper's friends as a memorial to him and designed by John Medhurst. Ricky's sculpture a feature. TEAS. *Adm £1 Chd free. Sats, Suns April 29, 30; June 10, 11; July 22, 23; Sept 9, 10 (2-5)*

Trumpeters' House (Miss Sarah Franklyn) & **Trumpeter's Lodge** ♿✻❀ (Mrs Pamela Franklyn) Old Palace Yard, Richmond. Off Richmond Green on S side. Car parking on the green and in car parks. Approx 3 acres, lawns, established old trees. Many old roses; shrubs; ponds; knot garden; mixed borders; aviary for doves. Featured in House & Garden, Country Life and in NGS Calendar 1995 (July). NCCPG collection of old-fashioned pinks (Dianthus). TEAS. *Adm £2 OAP's £1 Chd 50p. Sun June 11 (2-6)*

131 Upland Road ♿✻ (Ms G Payne & Ms P Harvey) East Dulwich. Nearest BR Peckham Rye. Buses 78, 12, 63. 78, 12 to Barry Rd. Get off 1st stop opp Peckham Rye Common. Upland Rd 50yds on L. House ¼m on L. 63 to Peckham Rye Common. Get off Forest Hill Rd. Cross over to Piermont Green leading to Upland Rd. Turn L house 50yds on L. Small garden full of surprises. Unusual, semi-oriental-style stone rear garden with pond and waterfall plus 2 'dinosaur eggs'! Informal planted areas incl varieties of clematis, acers, rhododendrons and NZ natives. 20′ × 40′ designed for effect and low maintenance. Front and side areas incl shade loving plants, bamboos, camellias, magnolias and viticellas. TEAS. *Adm 75p Chd 25p. Sun May 14 (2-6)*

15 Upper Grotto Road ✻❀ (Jeane Rankin) Strawberry Hill, Twickenham. Stations Strawberry Hill or Twickenham. Buses R68, 33 to Pope's Grotto, then Pope's Grove 1st R into Radnor Rd, 1st L Upper Grotto Rd or 90B, 267, 281, 290 to Heath Rd, into Radnor Rd, 2nd R into Upper Grotto Rd. Small sunken suntrap courtyard garden designed and constructed with advancing age and arthritis in mind; raised borders with small shrubs, herbaceous perennials, self sown annuals and some half-hardy annuals for infill; wall shrubs, clematis and other climbers; plants in pots and tiny fountain over pebbles. TEA. *Adm 50p Chd 25p. Suns July 2, 9 (2-6). Private visits welcome. Please,* **Tel 0181 891 4454**

7 Upper Phillimore Gardens W8 ✻❀ (Mr & Mrs B Ritchie). From Kensington High St take either Phillimore Gdns or Camden Hill Rd; entrance Duchess of Bedford Walk. 100′ × 35′ garden; rockery, sunken garden; Italian wall fountain, ground cover planting, pergola. TEA. *Adm 75p Chd 35p. Sun April 30 (2.30-6)*

66 Wallingford Avenue (off Oxford Gdns), W10 ✻ (Mrs R Andrups). Nearest underground station: Latimer Rd and Ladbroke Grove. Nearest bus stop Oxford Gdns (7) or Ladbroke Grove (7, 52, 70, 295, 302). Small garden 20′ × 40′. Raised beds, mixed borders, ponds, conservatory. Yr-round garden. 7 times winner Brighter Kensington & Chelsea Gardens Competition. Refreshments 30p. *Adm £1 Chd 50p. Sun July 30 (2-6)*

The Water Gardens ✻ Warren Road, Kingston (Residents' Association). From Kingston take the A308 (Kingston Hill) towards London about ½m on R turn R into Warren Road. Japanese landscaped garden originally part of the Coombe Wood Nursery, approx 9 acres with water cascade features. *Adm £1.50 Chd 50p. Suns May 7, Oct 8 (2-5)*

3 Wellgarth Road, NW11 ✻❀ (Mr & Mrs A M Gear) Hampstead Garden Suburb. Approx 4m N of London centre. Turning off the North End Road which runs between Hampstead and Golders Green, (buses 268, 210 stop quite near). Golders Green tube station (Northern Line) is the nearest, 7 mins walk and is also a terminal for buses from many parts of London. Medium-size garden. A walk all round the house, swathe of grass with long borders of bushes, trees and climbers now established and not too difficult to maintain. Close planting, herbaceous beds, roses, heathers and lavenders: herbs and mints, some uncommon plants. Paving, pots, tubs and old oak tree; and now the small pond with bubbling water is becoming established. Winner several times of Hampstead Gardens Competition and of the All London Championship. Home-made TEAS. *Adm £1 (Share to Friends of Queen Mary's©). Sun June 25 (2-6)*

10 Wildwood Rd NW11 ♿ (Dr J W McLean) Hampstead. Wildwood Rd is between Hampstead Golf Course and N end of Hampstead Heath. From North End Rd turn by Manor House Hospital into Hampstead Way, then fork R. Garden planned and maintained by owner; one of finest herbaceous borders in North London, pond, HT roses; owner-grown prize winning delphiniums and seedlings. TEA. *Adm £1 Chd free. Sun July 2 (2-7). Private visits welcome for parties of 10 and over, please* **Tel 0181 455 2808**

¶65 Wilmot Road ✻ (Ms Jan Sellers) Leyton. From Leyton Tube Station, turn R onto Leyton High Rd, after ¾m follow one-way system into Grange Park Rd. Wilmot Rd is 1st L by GP surgery. Buses 69, 158, 58, 97 stop on Leyton High Rd just before Grange Park Rd (no car access to Wilmot Rd direct from Oliver Rd). Tiny 17′ x 17′ green haven which brings the tranquillity of the Japanese garden to an urban terraced house. *Adm 50p Chd 20p (Share to Motor Neurone Disorder Assoc®). Sun Aug 20 (11-5)*

Wimbledon Gardens ♿✂ SW19 Train: BR or underground 10 mins walk turning R out of Wimbeldon station. 2nd L into Worple Rd then 4th R into Spencer Hill which becomes Murray Rd, or 5th R into Denmark Avenue which leads to Denmark Rd. Maps will be available for those visiting Somerset Rd (15 mins walk). To go directly to Somerset Rd see directions below. Morning coffee and TEAS etc Murray Rd and Somerset Rd. *Combined adm £2 £1 per garden Chd free. Sun June 18 (11-5)*

10 Denmark Road (Mr & Mrs Eadie) Tiny courtyard garden of interesting design with raised beds and containers. Wall fountain and pool; dovecote. Denmark Rd is a street of mid C19 cottages, with interesting front gardens

3 Murray Road SW19 ♿ (Mr & Mrs Michael Waugh) On the corner of St Johns Rd opp St Johns Church. A continuous narrow plot approx 308 sq yds, round 3 sides of house. Informal cottage-garden planting of small shrubs, fruit trees, climbing roses, herbaceous and ground cover plants easily grown and maintained with sunny position and very dry soil pond redesigned; some replanting. TEAS and morning coffee

¶21 Somerset Road (Mr & Mrs John Perring) By train BR or underground, turn R take Bus 93 at bottom of Wimbledon Hill ask for Calonne Rd bus stop then walk on and take next R into Somerset Rd, garden a short way on L. Or walk 1½m up hill through village along Parkside to Somerset Rd on R. Partly walled garden in ⅓-acre with 2 fine speciman cedars, shrubs herbaceous, groundcover, climbing plants and small herb area around a lawn with lots of pine needles in it. TEAS and morning coffee

47 Winn Road SE12 ♿❀ (Mr & Mrs G Smith) Lee. 8m SE central London. 15mins walk from either BR Lee station (Sidcup Line to Dartford) or Grove Park (Orpington Line) from Charing Cross. By car, ½m from A20 Sidcup bypass or A205 S Circular. ⅓-acre mature plantsman's garden maintained by owners. Mixed borders, alpine beds, fruit and vegetables, 3 greenhouses featuring colourful displays of pelargoniums, fuchsias, begonias, cacti and succulents and other interesting plants. TEAS. *Adm £1 Chd 50p (Share to The Fifth Trust©). Suns April 30, June 25, Aug 20 (2-5)*

27 Wood Vale, N10 ✂❀ (Mr & Mrs A W Dallman) Muswell Hill 1m. A1 to Woodman public house; signed Muswell Hill; Muswell Hill Rd sharp R Wood Lane leading to Wood Vale; Highgate tube station. ¾-acre garden with herbaceous borders; ponds; orchard and kitchen garden. Unusual layout full of surprises. Numerous shrubs, roses, trees and conifers; greenhouses. Visitors may also wander in neighbouring gardens, all of which are of high standard. TEAS. *Adm £1 Chd under 14 free (Share to British Legion and Meeting Point For St Georges Church®). Sat, Sun July 22, 23 (2-6)*

¶66 Woodbourne Avenue ♿✂ (Mr Brian Palmer & Mr Keith Simmonds) Streatham. Off A23 in Streatham High Rd. Woodbourne Ave runs W from PO. By car enter from Garrads Rd by Tooting Bec Common. Easy parking. Numerous bus routes to Streatham (alight Odeon Cinema-S, WH Smiths-Woolworths-N) BR Streatham Hill 10-15 mins walk. Approx 40′ x 60′ front garden, cottage style mix of roses and herbaceous planting with spring bulbs and irises a focal point. Rear garden approx 40′ x 80′ has been created by the owners over the last 5 yrs. Has a softer more informal country house estate in miniature look. There are 4 magnolias, various shrubs, herbaceous plants, gazebo with orientally-sourced plants surrounding pool. Shady border and numerous unusual plants; always being added to! TEAS. *Adm £1 Chd 50p (Share to Crusaid ®). Suns May 21, June 25 (2-6)*

7 Woodstock Road, W4 ✂ (Mr & Mrs L A Darke) Buses 94, 27. Underground district line to Turnham Green. (Piccadilly line stops Sunday). Turn R from station and over zebra crossing into Woodstock Rd. No. 7 is on L side beyond Sydney House flats and Bedford Rd. Victorian garden with large original rockery behind Norman Shaw house in Bedford Park, the earliest garden suburb. Wide selection of fine flowering trees; shrubs; herbaceous plants, roses and bulbs made over 40 years by present owners. A variety of hardy ferns is being planted. Featured in 'London's Pride', the 1990 exhibition of the history of the capital's gardens in the Museum of London. *Adm £1 Chd free. Sun April 23 (2-5). Private vists welcome, please* **Tel 0181 994 2234**

Open by appointment Please do not be put off by this notation. The owner may consider his garden too small to accommodate the numbers associated with a normal opening or, more often, there may be a lack of car parking space. It is often more rewarding than a normal opening as the owner will usually give a guided tour of the garden. The minimum size of party is either stated in the garden description or can be found out when making the appointment; usually 2. If the garden has normal open days, the entrance fee is as stated in the garden description.

Norfolk

Hon County Organisers: Lady Blofeld, Hoveton House, Nr Wroxham, Norwich NR12 8JE
Tel 01603 782202
Mrs Neil Foster, Lexham Hall, King's Lynn PE32 2QJ
Assistant County Organisers: Mrs David Mcleod, Park House, Old Hunstanton, King's Lynn PE36 6JS
Mrs David McCosh, Baconsthorpe Old Rectory, Holt NR25 6LU
Hon Treasurer: Denzil Newton Esq OBE, Briar House, Gt Dunham, King's Lynn PE32 2LX

DATES OF OPENING

By appointment

For telephone numbers and other details see garden descriptions. Private visits welcomed

Besthorpe Hall, Attleborough
Breccles Hall, Attleborough
72 Branthill Cottages, Wells-next-the-Sea
Cubitt Cottage, Sloley
Elmham House Gardens, North Elmham
Gillingham Hall, Beccles
4 Green Lane, Mundford
Lanehead, Garboldisham
The Mowle, Ludham Gardens
Orchards, Raveningham Gardens
Rainthorpe Hall, Tasburgh, S of Norwich
Wretham Lodge, East Wretham

Parties only

Elsing Hall, nr Dereham
Lake House, Brundall
Lexham Hall, Litcham
Stow Hall, Stow Bardolph

Regular openings

For details see garden descriptions

Hoveton Hall Gardens, nr Wroxham. For dates see text
Norfolk Lavender Ltd, Heacham. Daily (closed 3 weeks over Christmas)
The Old Vicarage, East Ruston. Every Wed from June 7 to Sept 27 incl
The Plantation Garden, Norwich. Suns April to Oct
Raveningham Hall, nr Beccles. Suns, Weds & Bank Hols March 19 to Sept 17
Sandringham Grounds. Daily April 1 to Oct 2, but see text for exceptions

---

April 9 Sunday
Gayton Hall, King's Lynn

April 16 Sunday
Lake House, Brundall

April 17 Monday
Lake House, Brundall ‡
The Old House, Ranworth ‡

April 23 Sunday
The Birches, Top Row
Grove House, Erpingham

April 30 Sunday
Minns Cottage, Potter Heigham
The Plantation Garden, Norwich

May 7 Sunday
Lake House, Brundall
Raveningham Hall, nr Beccles
Ryston Hall, Downham Market
Wretham Lodge, East Wretham

May 8 Monday
Lake House, Brundall

May 12 Friday
Hoveton Hall Gardens, nr Wroxham

May 14 Sunday
Breccles Hall, Attleborough
Burgh House, Aylsham ‡‡
Elmham House, North Elmham
Hoveton House, nr Wroxham ‡
How Hill Farm, Ludham ‡
86 Hungate Street, Aylsham ‡‡

May 21 Sunday
The Mowle, Ludham Gardens
Rippon Hall, Hevingham
Sheringham Park, Sheringham

May 28 Sunday
Aylsham Gardens, Aylsham
Lexham Hall, Litcham
Rainthorpe Hall, Tasburgh
Selborne House, Harleston

May 29 Monday
Rainthorpe Hall, Tasburgh
Selborne House, Harleston

June 4 Sunday
Besthorpe Hall, Attleborough
Cubitt Cottage, Sloley
Letheringsett Gardens, Holt
Sheringham Park, Sheringham

June 11 Sunday
The Garden in an Orchard, Bergh Apton
Gillingham Hall, Beccles
Mannington Hall, nr Aylsham
The Old Rectory, South Acre
Southgate House, South Creake

June 14 Wednesday
Mannington Hall, nr Aylsham
The Old Vicarage, East Ruston

June 18 Sunday
Bayfield Hall, nr Holt
72 Branthill Cottages, Wells-next-the-Sea ‡
Ludham Gardens, Ludham
Southgate Barn, South Creake ‡
Stow Hall, Stow Bardolph
Wootton Road Gardens, King's Lynn

June 25 Sunday
Conifer Hill, Starston
Cubitt Cottage, Sloley
Felbrigg Hall, Roughton
Raveningham Hall Gardens
Wretham Lodge, East Wretham

July 2 Sunday
Elsing Hall, Dereham
Hoveton House, nr Wroxham
Wicken House, Castle Acre

July 9 Sunday
Minns Cottage, Potter Heigham

July 16 Sunday
Blicking Hall, Aylsham
Cubitt Cottage, Sloley
Easton Lodge, Easton

July 23 Sunday
Felbrigg Hall, Roughton
The Lodge, Old Lakenham ‡
Oak Tree House, Thorpe ‡
Oxburgh Hall Garden, Oxburgh
Raveningham Hall Gardens

July 30 Sunday
The Garden in an Orchard, Bergh Apton
The Plantation Garden, Norwich

August 6 Sunday
Oxburgh Hall Garden, Oxburgh

August 13 Sunday
Blicking Hall, Aylsham
Minns Cottage, Potter Heigham

August 20 Sunday
The Birches, Top Row

August 27 Sunday
Barningham Hall, Matlaske
Oak Tree House, Thorpe

August 30 Wednesday
The Old Vicarage, East Ruston

September 3 Sunday
Hoveton Hall, Gardens, nr Wroxham

September 14 Thursday
Holkham Hall, Wells-next-the-Sea

DESCRIPTIONS OF GARDENS

Aylsham Gardens *Combined adm £3.50 Chd 50p*

5 Cromer Road (Dr & Mrs James) Aylsham. 100yds N of Aylsham Parish Church down old Cromer Rd on LH-side. Approx 1 acre of semi-wild garden nr town centre with large willow trees and grass. Shrubs and small natural pond. Mixed borders, heathers and vegetable garden. *Sun May 28 (2-6)*

Dell Farm (Mrs M J Monk) Aylsham. Approx ¼m W of centre of Aylsham turn L off Blickling Rd on to Heydon Rd (signposted Oulton). 400yds on to copper beech arching rd. Turn R through gate onto gravelled yard. 4-acre garden, Magnificent mature trees and shrubs. Various rose collections, rhododendrons, azaleas, heathers. Spring bulbs, primroses etc in old orchard and wild flower garden. TEA. *Sun May 28 (2-6). (Also private visits welcome especially for spring bulbs, please* **Tel 01263 732 277** *Adm £1 Chd 50p)*

10 St Michael's Close (M I Davies Esq) Aylsham NW on B1354 towards Blickling Hall; 500yds from market place, turn R, Rawlinsons Lane, then R again. Front gravelled area with mixed shrub and herbaceous border; small rockery. Back garden with large variety of shrubs, herbaceous plants, bulbs, small lawn, roses, azaleas. Plant, pond. Aviary, guinea pigs. TEAS. *Adm £1.50 Chd free. Sun May 28 (11-6). Private visits welcome, please* **Tel 01263 732174**

West Lodge (Mr & Mrs Jonathan Hirst) Aylsham. ¼m NW of market square on N side of B1354 (entrance in Rawlinsons Lane) Large 9-acre garden with lawns, mature trees, rose garden, herbaceous borders, ornamental pond and walled kitchen garden; Georgian House (not open) and outbuildings incl a well-stocked toolshed (open) and greenhouses. TEAS in aid of Aylsham Church. *Adm £1.50 Chd free. Sun May 28 (2-6)*

Barningham Hall (Lady Mott-Radclyffe) Matlaske, NW of Aylsham. Medium-sized garden, vistas, lake. TEAS. *Adm £2 Chd free. Sun Aug 27 (2-6.30)*

Bayfield Hall (Mr & Mrs R H Combe) 1m N of Holt, off A148. Formal but simple pleasure gardens with medieval church ruin. Old-fashioned roses, herbaceous and shrub borders; magnificent view over lake and park. Wildflower centre adjacent to garden. Church Fete stalls and entertainment in aid of St Martins Church, Glandford. TEA. *Adm £1.50 Chd 50p. Sun June 18 (2-5)*

Besthorpe Hall (John Alston Esq) 1m E of Attleborough. On Attleborough-Bunwell Rd; adjacent to Besthorpe Church. Garden with shrubs, trees and herbaceous borders within Tudor enclosures; walled kitchen garden; tilting ground. Coach parties by appt. TEAS. *Adm £2 Chd free (Share to Besthorpe Church®). Sun June 4 (2-5). Also private visits welcome, please* **Tel 01953 452138**

The Birches (Mr & Mrs J McCarthy) Top Row. 8m S of Norwich on B1113 Norwich-New Buckenham Rd. Take 1st turning L ¼m after Bird in Hand Restaurant. 1¼-acre garden landscaped with lawns, herbaceous, shrub and rose beds. Rockery, pond and alpine scree garden, orchard with naturalized bulbs. Vegetable garden, greenhouses and conservatory. TEAS. *Adm £1.50 Chd free. Suns April 23, Aug 20 (2-6)*

Blickling Hall (The National Trust) 1¼ miles NW of Aylsham on N side of B1354. 15m N of Norwich (A140). Large garden, orangery, crescent lake, azaleas, rhododendrons, herbaceous borders. Historic Jacobean house. Wheelchairs available. TEAS and lunches. *Adm £2.50 Chd £1.25. Suns July 16, Aug 13 (11-5)*

72 Branthill Cottages (Timothy Leese Esq.) Wells-next-the-Sea. 2m from Wells. Off Fakenham-Wells rd. At Xrds unmarked by signpost, turn L, opp yellow sign to Branthill Farm ¼m down lane, cottage on LH-side. NGS posters and signposts on open day. Around a farm cottage, a ¼ acre of rather impractical garden, rigidly laid out and informally planted over the last 9 yrs. Not uncommon flowers, old roses and shrubs, closely planted to make garden appear larger, and to cut down on weeding. Very light alkaline soil. TEAS. *Adm £1 Chd free (Share to Wells Cottage Hospital®). Sun June 18 (2-6). Private vists welcome, please* **Tel 01328 711273**

Breccles Hall (Major & Mrs R J Archdale) Attleborough. On the B1111 midway between East Harling and Watton. Approx 10-acre garden, fine Elizabethan house (not open) surrounded by walled gardens incl rose garden and herbaceous borders. Wild garden with rhododendrons, bulbs and mature trees. Ploughmans lunches, exceptional TEAS. *Adm £1.50 Chd free (Share to St Margaret's Church, Breckels®). Sun May 14 (11.30-5). Private vists welcome, please* **Tel 01953 498234**

Burgh House (Mr & Mrs Richard Burr) Aylsham. Off A140 between Norwich and Cromer. 300yds E of Aylsham town square. Free public car park in Burgh Rd. Very old 4-acre mixed deciduous woodland with ponds. A slow project to uncover its history and reclaim paths, areas of bulbs etc. Haven for small birds. TEAS. *Adm £1.50 Chd free. Sun May 14 (12-6)*

Conifer Hill (Mr & Mrs Richard Lombe Taylor) Starston, Harleston. 18m S of Norwich. A140 to Pulham Xrds. Turn L to B1134. 1m NW of Harleston, off B1134. Take Redenhall Rd out of Starston. Conifer Hill on L ½m out of village. Steep bend and white gates. 4-acre Victorian garden. Lawns, shrubs, roses, herbaceous and kitchen garden. ½-acre pinetum, in steep escarpment of old quarry. TEAS. *Adm £1.50 Chd free. Sun June 25 (2-6)*

Cubitt Cottage (Mrs Janie Foulkes) Sloley. 11m N of Norwich just off B1150 Coltishall to North Walsham Rd. 2nd R after Three Horseshoes public house at Scottow. Into village, then Low Street, R at next signpost. 1-acre garden with lawns, herbaceous and shrub border, over 100 varieties of old roses, clematis and unusual plants; wildflower meadow; wild life pond and bog garden; vegetable garden and greenhouses. TEAS. *Adm £2 Chd free. Suns June 4, 25 (2-6). Also private visits welcome, please* **Tel 01692 538295**

Regular Openers. Too many days to include in diary. Usually there is a wide range of plants giving year-round interest. See head of county section for the name and garden description for times etc.

Easton Lodge ❀ (J M Rampton Esq) Easton, 6m W Norwich. Cross the new Southern Norwich Bypass at the Easton Roundabout and take the Ringland Rd. Large garden in magnificent setting above river surrounded by fine trees; walks amongst interesting shrubs, roses, plants; herbaceous border; walled kitchen garden. Late Georgian house with Jacobean centre portion (not open). TEAS. *Adm £1.50 Chd free. Sun July 16 (2.30-5.30)*

Ellingham Hall nr Bungay. See Suffolk for details

Elmham House ♿✾❀ (Mr & Mrs R S Don) North Elmham, 5m N of East Dereham, on B1110. Entrance opp Church. Medium-sized garden; wild garden; C18 walled garden; view of park and lake; vineyard, tours of winery. TEAS. *Adm £2 Chd free (Share to St Mary's Church N Elmham®). Sun May 14 (2-6). Private visits by appt only to incl vineyard, please* **Tel 01362 668363**

Elsing Hall ✾❀ (Mrs D Cargill) Dereham. 2m E of Dereham off A47; sign to Elsing. Medieval house surrounded by moat. Over 200 varieties of old-fashioned roses; wild flower lawn, walled kitchen garden with roses, fruit trees & clematis. Many water plants by moat and fish stew. Rare and interesting trees in arboretum; newly planted formal garden with clipped box, lavender, sage, santolina and thyme. Suitable wheelchairs in places. TEAS. *Adm £2 Chd free (Share to Elsing Church restoration fund®). Sun July 2 (2-6). Private parties welcome, please* **Tel 01362 637224**

Felbrigg Hall ♿✾ (The National Trust) Roughton, 2½m SW of Cromer, S of A148; main entrance from B1436; signed from Felbrigg village. Large pleasure gardens; mainly lawns and shrubs; orangery with camellias; large walled garden restored and restocked as fruit, vegetable and flower garden; vine house; dovecote; dahlias; superb colchichum; wooded parks. 2 Electric wheelchairs available. Lunches, pre booking essential. TEAS. *Adm £1.80 Chd 80p. For NGS Suns June 25, July 23 (11-5)*

The Garden in an Orchard ♿❀ (Mr & Mrs R W Boardman) Bergh Apton, Norwich. 6m SE of Norwich off A146 at Hellington Corner signed to Bergh Apton. Down Mill Rd 300 yds. 3½-acre garden set in an old orchard. Many rare and unusual plants set out in an informal pattern of wandering paths. ½-acre of wild flower meadows, many bamboos, specie roses, 9 species of eucaplyptus. In all a plantsman's garden. TEAS. *Adm £1.50 Chd free. Suns June 11, July 30 (11-6)*

Gayton Hall ♿❀ (Mr & Mrs Julian Marsham) 6m E of King's Lynn off B1145; signs in Gayton village. 20 acres; wild woodland, water garden. Bulbs, TEAS. *Adm £2 Chd free (Share to St John Ambulance®). Sun April 9 (2-5). Private visits welcome, please* **Tel 01553 636259**

Gillingham Hall ♿✾❀ (Mr & Mrs Robin Bramley) Beccles. 16m SE of Norwich, 1½m from Beccles off A146. 14-acre garden with lake, lawns, borders, rose garden, specimen plane trees, wild flower areas, bulbs; Mansion house (not open) c1600. TEAS. *Adm £1.50 Chd 50p (Share to Church Restoration Funds®). Sun June 11 (2-5). Parties welcome, please* **Tel 01502 713294**

4 Green Lane ♿✾❀ (Mr & Mrs Dennis Cooper) Mundford. From main Mundford roundabout take A1065 to Swaffham. After ¼m turn L down Green Lane. Divided into 'rooms' giving a cottage garden effect, a 1-acre garden filled with island beds, intensively planted with unusual perennials and cottage garden plants. Ponds and planted gravel areas. Wide variety of unusual plants available from adjoining nursery. *Adm £1 Chd free. Open by appt any day May, June, July, Aug (9-6), please* **Tel 01842 878496**

Grove House ♿❀ (Mr & Mrs John Alston) Erpingham. On A140 4m N Aylsham by Alby Crafts, parking by Alby Crafts car park. 4-acre garden. Primroses, spring bulbs, irises, hellebores, old-fashioned roses, mixed borders, 4 ponds (1 with wild flower and conservation area). Plantsman's garden. TEAS. *Adm £1.50 Chd free. Sun April 23 (10-5). Parties welcome, please* **Tel 01263 761226**

Holkham Hall ♿ (The Earl of Leicester) Wells-next-the-Sea. 2m W of Wells off A149. Arboretum with many rare specimens of trees and shrubs; shell house. TEAS. *Adm 50p Chd 20p. ▲For NGS Thurs Sept 14 (1.30-4.40)*

Hoveton Hall Gardens ♿✾❀ (Mr & Mrs Andrew Buxton) nr Wroxham. 8m N of Norwich; 1m N of Wroxham Bridge on A1151 Stalham Rd. Approx 10-acre gardens and grounds featuring principally daffodils, azaleas, rhododendrons and hydrangeas in a woodland setting and a large, mature, walled herbaceous garden. Water plants, a lakeside walk and walled kitchen garden provide additional interest. Early C19 house (not open). TEAS. *Adm £2 Chd 50p. Gardens open, every Wed, Fri, Sun and Bank Hols, Easter Sun to Sept 17 incl (11-5.30). For NGS Fri May 12, Sun Sept 3 (Share to Multiple Sclerosis Society Research®) (11-5.30)*

Hoveton House ♿✾❀ (Sir John & Lady Blofeld) 9m N Norwich, ½m Wroxham on B1062, Horning-Ludham Rd. Interesting old-fashioned walled garden; herbaceous and other borders; rock garden; many unusual plants and bulbs. Established rhododendron grove. Kitchen garden. Lawns, walks etc. William & Mary House (not open.) Plants for sale May only. TEAS. *Adm £2 Chd free (Share to St John's Church©). Suns May 14 (2-5), July 2 (2-6)*

How Hill Farm ✾ (P D S Boardman Esq) 2m W of Ludham on A1062; then follow signs to How Hill; Farm Garden – S of How Hill. Very pretty garden started in 1968 in water garden setting with three ponds; recent 3-acre broad (dug as conservation project) with variety of water lilies and view over the R Ant; fine old mill. Winding paths through rare conifers; unusual and rare rhododendrons with massed azaleas; other ornamental trees and shrubs; a few herbaceous plants and lilies; collection of English holly, ilex aquifolium (over 50 varieties). Collection of bamboos. Partly suitable for wheelchairs. TEA. *Adm £1.50 Chd free (Share to How Hill Trust©). Sun May 14 (2-5)*

¶86 Hungate Street ✾ (Mrs Sue Ellis) Aylsham. From Norwich towards Cromer on A140. Turn L at roundabout S of Aylsham towards Stonegate, turn R into Hungate St. Proceed along for ¾m to row of white cottages on L. A small town garden 95′ × 45′ laid out in a semi-formal style, consisting of sunken lawns, raised beds and pergolas. A plantswoman's garden densely planted with small specimen trees/shrubs. Rhododendrons, roses, primulas, ornamental pond. Raised vegetable area with propagation frame, greenhouse, enclosed by beech and laurel hedge. *Adm £1.50 Chd 50p. Sun May 14 (12-6)*

Lake House ❀ (Mr & Mrs Garry Muter) Brundall. Approx 5m E of Norwich on A47; take Brundall turn at Roundabout. Turn R into Postwick Lane at T-junction. An acre of water gardens set among magnificent trees in a steep cleft in the river escarpment. Informal flower beds with interesting plants; a naturalist's paradise; unsuitable for young children or the infirm. Wellingtons advisable. 'Unusual plants for sale.' TEAS. *Adm £2 Chd free (Share to Water Aid©). Easter Sun & Mon April 16, 17; Sun, Mon May 7, 8 (11-5). Private parties welcome, please* **Tel 01603 712933**

Lanehead ♿ (Mrs N A Laurie) Garboldisham, 8m W of Diss off A1066 at village Xrds take the A111 for ½m to 1st R. Medium-sized garden created by owner; featured in a television programme, visited by many horticultural groups; well designed natural walks with shrubs and specimen trees; colour co-ordinated borders for all-year interest; water and bog garden; roses and woodland. Coffee, TEAS. *Adm £1.50 Chd free (Share to Garboldisham Church Fabric Fund®). Private visits welcome by appt April to Sept, please* **Tel 01953 81380**

Letheringsett Gardens ♿ 1m W of Holt on A148. Car park King's Head, Letheringsett for disabled near church. TEAS. *Combined adm £2 Chd free. Sun June 4 (2-5.30)*

Hall Cottage (Mr David Mayes) Attractive, easily-managed garden with 2 ponds

The Glebe ♿❀ (The Hon Beryl Cozens-Hardy) Medium-sized riverside garden, with island, wild flowers, water garden, shrub borders, clematis

Letheringsett Hall (Mrs English) Home for the Elderly; medium-sized garden and river

Letheringsett Estate Garden (Mr & Mrs Robert Carter) Large garden; wooded walks, fountain, lake, water plants, wild flowers. Hydraulic rams 1852 and 1905

The Old Foundry House (Peter Miller Esq) Small unusual garden. Roses

Lexham Hall ♿✿❀ (Mr & Mrs Neil Foster) 2m W of Litcham off B1145. Fine 17th/18th century Hall (not open); parkland with lake and river walks. Formal garden with terraces, yew hedges, roses and mixed borders. Traditional kitchen garden with crinkle-crankle wall. 3-acre woodland garden with azaleas, rhododendrons, spring bulbs and rare trees. TEAS. *Adm £2 Chd free (Share to St Andrews Church, E. Lexham®). Sun May 28 (2-6). Also groups by appt May 1 to July 31 (weekdays only), please* **Tel 01328 701288**

The Lodge ✿❀ (Mr & Mrs P J E Smith) Old Lakenham. SE of Norwich just off ring rd (Barrett Rd). Turn out of city at Mansfield Lane traffic lights. 200yds on L opp St John's Church (also open). 1½-acres of contoured garden in beautiful setting leading down to R Yare. Herbaceous and shrub borders, enclosed croquet lawn, 1920's sunken garden, muscovy and other ducks. TEAS. *Adm £1.50 Chd free (Share to St John's Church®). Sun July 23 (2-6)*

Ludham Gardens ✿❀ B1062 Wroxham to Ludham 7m. Turn R by Ludham village church into Staithe Road. Gardens ¼m from village

The Dutch House (Mrs Peter Seymour) Long narrow garden designed and planted by the painter Edward Seago, leading through marsh to Womack Water. Approx 2½ acres. New project in hand to re-create C17 herbaceous borders. TEAS. *Adm £1.50 Chd free. Sun June 18 only*

The Mowle (Mrs N N Green) Approx 2½ acres running down to marshes. Interesting shrub borders, unusual trees etc including tulip trees and a golden catalpa. TEAS and plants May opening only. *Adm £1.50 Chd free. Suns May 21, June 18 (2-6). Private visits welcome, please* **Tel 01692 678213**

Mannington Hall ♿✿❀ (The Lord & Lady Walpole) 2m N of Saxthorpe; 18m NW of Norwich via B1149 towards Holt. At Saxthorpe (B1149 & B1354) turn NE signed Mannington. 20 acres feature roses, shrubs, lake and trees. Heritage rose, scented and walled gardens. Extensive countryside walks and trails. C15 moated manor house (not open). Saxon church with C19 follies. Coffee, lunches and TEAS in aid of St Mary's Church, Itteringham. *Adm £2.50 OAPs/students £2 Chd free. Sun June 11 (12-5), Wed June 14 (11-5)*

Minns Cottage ♿✿❀ (Mr & Mrs Derek Brown) Chapel Rd, Potter Heigham. From Norwich take A1151 then A149 to Potter Heigham Xrds. Turn L into Station Rd on to T junction, turn L into School Rd. Turning into Green Lane. At telephone box turn R into Chapel Rd. Approx 1¼-acres winding lawns leading through pergola's to rose garden with old English roses and other small gardens with mixed borders, recently planted woodland area with rhododendrons and bulbs. A garden to walk round peacefully at all seasons. TEAS. *Adm £1.50 Chd free. Suns April 30 (2-5), July 9, Aug 13 (2-6)*

Norfolk Lavender Ltd ♿❀ Caley Mill, Heacham. On A149 13m N of Kings Lynn. National collection of lavenders set in 2 acres (lavender harvest July-Aug); herb garden with many varieties of native herbs; rose garden. TEA. *Adm free. Collecting box. Daily to Christmas (10-5). Closed for three weeks Christmas holiday.* **Tel 01485 570384**

Oak Tree House ✿❀ (W R S Giles Esq) 6 Cotman Rd, Thorpe. E of Norwich off A47 Thorpe Rd. ¼m from Norwich Thorpe Station. From Yarmouth direction follow one way system towards City Centre, turn R at traffic lights opposite Min. of Fisheries & Agric. Approx 300yds on, turn L opposite Barclays Bank. Botanical illustrators interesting plantsmans garden, of approx ½-acre on a hillside. Containing a mixture of hardy and tender plants giving a strong subtropical Mediterranean influence, containing tree ferns, bamboos, palms, bananas, cannas, agaves and many more. Also traditional herbaceous borders and a woodland garden with fernery. This garden has appeared in various TV programmes, magazines and books. TEAS. *Adm £1.60, Chd 30p. Suns July 23, Aug 27 (1.30-5.30)*

The Old House, Ranworth (Mr Francis & The Hon Mrs Cator) 9m NE of Norwich off B1140. Turn L in S Walsham to Ranworth on inner broad below church. Attractive linked and walled gardens alongside beautiful, peaceful Ranworth inner broad. Bulbs, shrubs, potager, mown rides through recently established arboretum where dogs may be walked on leads, pond with many species of ducks and geese. ½m of woodland walk adjacent to Norfolk Naturalist Trust Conservation Centre and Nature Trail (entrance extra). Historic church nearby. TEA. *Adm £1.50 Chd free. Easter Monday April 17 (2-5)*

¶**The Old Rectory** ♿❀ (Mrs Clive Hardcastle) South Acre. 3m NW of Swaffham off A1065 opp Southacre Church. 3-acre garden with splendid views of Castle Acre Priory. Mixed borders, shrubs, small vineyard, herb garden, pool and old-fashioned rose garden. Interesting Saxon church. TEAS. *Adm £1.50 Chd 50p. Sun June 11 (2-5.30)*

¶**The Old Vicarage** ♿✿❀ (Alan Gray and Graham Robeson) East Ruston. Off A149 3m N of Stalham on Stalham to Walcott Rd (ignore all 3 signposts to East Ruston). At Xrds turn R 200 yds just N of East Ruston Church. 12-acre exotic coastal garden and grounds incl impressive herbaceous borders, autumn border, tropical border incl bananas and palms, sunken garden, walled garden, Mediterranean garden and wild flower meadows and walks. TEAS. *Adm £2.50 Chd £1. Open every Wed from June 7 to Sept 27 incl. For NGS Wed June 14, Aug 30 (2-5)*

Oxburgh Hall Garden ♿✿ (The National Trust) 7m SW of Swaffham, at Oxburgh on Stoke Ferry rd. Hall and moat surrounded by lawns, fine trees, colourful borders; charming parterre garden of French design. Lunches. Cream TEAS. *Adm £2 Chd 50p. For NGS Suns July 23, Aug 6 (12-5)*

The Plantation Garden ♿✿❀ (Plantation Garden Preservation Trust) 4 Earlham Rd, Norwich. Entrance between Crofters and Beeches Hotels, nr St John's R C Cathedral. 3-acre Victorian town garden created 1856-96 in former medieval chalk quarry. Still undergoing restoration by volunteers, remarkable architectural features include 60ft Italianate terrace and unique 30ft Gothic fountain. Surrounded by mature trees. 10 min walk city centre, beautifully tranquil atmosphere. *Adm £1.50 Chd free (Share to Plantation Garden Preservation Trust©). Suns April to Oct (2-5). For NGS TEAS Suns April 30, July 30 (2-5)*

Rainthorpe Hall ♿✿ (Mr & Mrs Alastair Wilson) Tasburgh. Approx 8m S of Norwich, just off the A140 - turn by garage in Newton Flotman. On 1m to red brick pillars and gates on L. Elizabethan/Victorian/Country House (not open) prettily set in interesting variety of gardens, incl knot hedge (said to be as old as the house) and hazel coppice (said to be older). Fine trees and collection of bamboos. [Croquet and bowls available, but *not* to high standard]. TEAS. *Adm £2.50 Chd free. Sun, Mon, May 28, 29 (2-6). Private visits welcome, please* **Tel 01508 470618**

¶**Raveningham Gardens** ♿❀ 14m SE of Norwich, 4m from Beccles off B1136. *Suns June 25, July 23 (2-5)*

Raveningham Hall ♿❀ (Sir Nicholas Bacon) Large garden specialising in rare shrubs, herbaceous plants, especially euphorbia, agapanthus and shrub roses. Victorian conservatory and walled vegetable garden, newly planted Arboretum. *Adm £2 Chd free. Nursery open 9-5 every day except weekends in November, December, January, February. Garden open every Sunday, Bank Hols and Weds March 19 to September 17 (2-5) Weds (1-4). For NGS TEAS Suns June 25, July 23 (2-5)*

¶**Cossey Corner Farm** (Mr & Mrs M Myhill) From Norwich, ¼m before Hall. ¼-acre herbaceous and large variety of bedding plants. Colourful and delightful garden. *Combined adm with* **Orchards** *£1 Chd free*

¶**Orchards** (Priscilla Lady Bacon) From Norwich, ¼m before Hall. New garden planted over last 10 yrs. Plantsman's garden. *Combined adm with* **Cossey Corner Farm** *£1 Chd free. Private visits welcome, please* **Tel 01508 548 322/206**

Rippon Hall ♿❀ (Miss Diana Birkbeck) Hevingham, 8m N of Norwich. From A140 Norwich-Aylsham rd, turn R (E) at Xrds just N of Hevingham Church. Rhododendrons and azalea borders. Large herd of rare breed of British White Cattle. TEAS. *Adm £1.50 Chd 25p. Sun May 21 (2-5.30)*

Ryston Hall ♿✿ (Mr & Mrs Piers Pratt) Downham Market. 1m S of Downham Market off A10. 6-acre garden with azaleas and rhododendrons; orangery; walled kitchen garden being restored and woodland walk. TEAS. *Adm £1.50 OAPs/Chd £1.* ▲*For NGS Sun May 7 (2-6)*

Sandringham Grounds ♿✿❀ By gracious permission of H.M. The Queen, the House, Museum and Grounds at Sandringham will be open. 60 acres of informal gardens, woodland and lakes, with rare plants and trees. Donations are given from the Estate to various charities. For further information see p 13. TEAS. *Adm House and Grounds £4 OAPs £3 Chd £2; Grounds only £3 OAPs £2.50 Chd £1.50. April 1 to Oct 2 daily. House closed July 19 to Aug 4 incl & Grounds closed July 23 to Aug 3 incl. Hours House 11-4.45; Grounds 10.30-5*

¶**Selborne House** ✿❀ (Mr & Mrs Walland) Approx 5m off A140 Norwich to Ipswich Rd. Turn off to Harleston and follow one way signs or 8m from Scole A143. ¾-acre town garden, off Market Square opp. Magpie Hotel. Old Wellingtonia Spruces in front garden; rock garden and pond; clematis a speciality; mixed borders; plantsman's garden. TEAS. *Adm £1.50 Chd free. Sun May 28, Mon May 29 (2-5)*

Sheringham Park ♿ (The National Trust) 2m SW of Sheringham. Access for cars off A148 Cromer to Holt Road, 5m W of Cromer, 6m E of Holt (signs in Sheringham Town). 50-acres of species rhododendron, azalea and magnolia. Also numerous specimen trees incl handkerchief tree. Viewing towers, waymarked walks, sea and parkland views. Special walk way and WCs for disabled. Teas at Felbrigg Hall nearby. *Adm £2.30 per car. For NGS Suns May 21, June 4 (dawn to dusk).* **Tel 01263 823778**

Southgate Barn ✂❀ (Mrs Philip Anley) South Creake. 5m N of Fakenham off B1355 to Burnham Market. 100yds past turning to R signed Waterden turn L down lane. Entrance 100yds on L. Small garden of approx 2 acres made 10 yrs ago around a converted barn. Shrubs and trees in front. At back large terrace, roses, pergola, herbaceous border. Cream TEAS. *Adm £1.50 Chd free (Share to Rumanian Relief for Children in Orphanages®). Sun June 18 (2-6)*

Southgate House ♿✂❀ (Mr & Mrs Harry Schulman) South Creake. 5m NW of Fakenham. Follow B1355 towards Burnham Market. Just after sign to Waterden on R, turn L at signs. Entrance approx 200yds. A challenging garden of approx 1½ acres developed from 3 paddocks 7 yrs ago. Many interesting trees and unusual shrubs, plants and bulbs. A must for anyone discouraged by wind and lack of shelter. Cream TEAS. *Adm £1 Chd free (Share to St Mary's Church, North Creake®). Sun June 11 (2-6)*

¶Stow Hall ♿❀ (Lady Rose Hare) Stow Bardolph. 2m N of Downham Market on A10, village of Stow Bardolph signposted to the E of the A10. Approx 6 acres of garden with many mature trees, high walls, climbing plants and shrub roses. Walled kitchen garden contains very old varieties of apple and pear trees one of which - Golden Noble Apple is mentioned in The English Apple by Rosanne Sanders as having been raised at Stow in 1820. Young apple trees with East Anglian interest are being planted. Newly landscaped gardens on site of old Hall. TEAS. *Adm £1.50 Chd free (Share to Holy Trinity Curch, Stow Bardolph®). Sun June 18 (2-6). Private parties welcome, please* **Tel 01366 383194**

Wicken House ♿✂❀ (Lord & Lady Keith) Castle Acre, 5m N of Swaffham off A1065; W at Newton to Castle Acre; then 2m N off the rd to Massingham. Large walled garden planted in sections with many roses and unusual herbaceous plants; gravel paths and greenhouses; swimming pool garden; spring and wild gardens. Fine views. Approx 6 acres. Rare plants for sale. Home-made cream TEAS. *Adm £1.50 Chd free (Share to the Friends of Castle Acre Church®). Sun July 2 (2-6)*

Wootton Road Gardens ✂ E side King's Lynn between Gaywood (clock) and The New Inn traffic lights. Both gardens are together opp Mobil Garage. Plant and cake stalls. *Combined adm £1.50 Chd free (Share to St Margaret's Church Funds, Kings Lynn®). Sun June 18 (2-6)*

260 Wootton Road (Miss Janet Dent) Delightfully landscaped garden, with wide number of species of shrubs, conifers and heathers. Impressive lawns and water features, incl informal rockery

262 Wootton Road ♿❀ (Mr & Mrs L Dyer) Average size suburban/town garden comprising wide range of established trees/shrubs and conifers all informally landscaped for colour, shape and easy maintenance

Wretham Lodge ♿✂❀ (Mrs Anne Hoellering) East Wretham. A11 E from Thetford; L up A1075; L by village sign; R at Xrds then bear L. In spring masses of specie tulips, hellebores, fritillaries, daffodils and narcissi; bluebell walk, apple blossom. In June hundreds of old specie and climbing roses, lillies. Walled garden, trained fruit trees, interesting mixed borders, extensive lawns. Fine old trees. TEAS. *Adm £2 Chd free (Share to Norfolk Churches Trust in May, and Wretham Church in June®). Suns May 7, June 25 (2.30-5.30). Also private visits and coach parties welcome, please write or* **Tel 01953 498366**

Northamptonshire

Hon County Organiser: Mrs John Boughey, Butts Close, Farthinghoe, Brackley NN13 5NY Tel 01295 710411

Asst Hon County Organisers: Mrs John Bussens, Glebe Cottage, Titchmarsh, Kettering NN14 3DB Tel 01832 732510
Mrs R H N Dashwood, Farthinghoe Lodge, Nr Brackley, Northants NN13 5NX
Mrs R Blake, Lodge Lawn, Fotheringhay, Peterborough PE8 5HZ

Hon County Treasurer: R H N Dashwood Esq Farthinghoe Lodge, nr Brackley, Northants NN13 5NX Tel 01295 710377

DATES OF OPENING

By appointment

For telephone numbers and other details see garden descriptions. Private visits welcomed

Bradden House, nr Towcester
Bulwick Rectory, Bulwick
Evenley Wood Garden, Brackley
Falcutt House, Brackley
Irthlingborough, nr Wellingborough
Great Addington Manor, nr Kettering
72 Larkhall Lane, Harpole Gardens, Northampton
Maidwell Hall, Northampton
19 Manor Close, Harpole Gardens, Northampton
The Old Barn, Weedon Lois Gardens, nr Towcester.
The Old Rectory, Sudborough
Spring House, nr Banbury
The Walnuts, King's Cliffe
Wisteria Cottage, Maidwell Gardens
13 Whytewell Road, Wellingborough

Parties only

Guilsborough & Hollowell Gardens
Versions Farm, nr Brackley.

Regular openings

For details see garden descriptions

Coton Manor, Guilsborough. Open Weds to Suns & Bank Hols, Easter to end Sept
Cottesbrooke Hall, nr Creaton. Open Thurs & Bank Hol Mons, Easter Mon to end Sept

April 2 Sunday
The Old Rectory, Sudborough
April 9 Sunday
Charlton, nr Banbury
April 16 Sunday
Evenley Wood Garden, Brackley
April 17 Monday
Evenley Wood Garden, Brackley
Titchmarsh Gardens, nr Thrapston
April 19 Wednesday
Great Addington Manor, nr Kettering
April 23 Sunday
Great Addington Manor, nr Kettering
Maidwell Hall, Northampton
The Menagerie, Horton, nr Northampton
April 30 Sunday
Finedon Gardens, nr Wellingborough
May 7 Sunday
Aldwincle Gardens, nr Thrapston
Falcutt House, Brackley
The Haddonstone Show Garden, nr Northampton
May 8 Monday
The Haddonstone Show Garden, nr Northampton
May 14 Sunday
Deene Park, nr Corby
Great Brington Gardens, nr Northampton
Holdenby House, Northampton
May 21 Sunday
Guilsborough & Hollowell Gardens
Litchborough Gardens, Towcester
The Walnuts, King's Cliffe
May 24 Wednesday
The Walnuts, King's Cliffe
May 25 Thursday
Coton Manor, Guilsborough
May 28 Sunday
Badby & Newnham Gardens, nr Daventry
Chacombe Gardens, nr Banbury
Slapton Gardens, nr Towcester
May 29 Monday
Titchmarsh Gardens, nr Thrapston
May 31 Wednesday
Badby & Newnham Gardens, nr Daventry
June 4 Sunday
Benefield House, Lower Benefield, nr Oundle
Cottesbrooke Hall, nr Creaton
Falcutt House, Brackley ‡
Gamekeepers Cottage, nr Creaton
Lois Weedon House, nr Towcester ‡
Preston Capes Gardens
Sholebroke Lodge, Towcester
Stoke Park, Stoke Bruerne, Towcester
June 10 Saturday
Canons Ashby House, Daventry
June 11 Sunday
Evenley Gardens, Brackley
Turweston Mill, Turweston Gardens, Brackley
Versions Farm, nr Brackley
June 12 Monday
Evenley Gardens, Brackley
June 17 Saturday
Flore Gardens, nr Northampton
June 18 Sunday
Cottingham & Middleton Gardens
Flore Gardens, nr Northampton
Great & Little Harrowden Gardens, nr Wellingborough
Kilsby Gardens, nr Rugby
Maidwell Gardens
Sulgrave Gardens, Banbury
June 21 Wednesday
Great & Little Harrowden Gardens, nr Wellingborough
June 24 Saturday
The Old Vicarage, Great Cransley, nr Kettering
June 25 Sunday
The Old Vicarage, Great Cransley, nr Kettering
Turweston Gardens, Brackley
Weedon Lois Gardens, nr Towcester
Wilby Gardens, nr Wellingborough
June 29 Wednesday
Bradden House, nr Towcester
July 2 Sunday
Bulwick Rectory, Bulwick
Easton Neston, Towcester
Harpole Gardens, Northampton
West Haddon Gardens, nr Northants
July 9 Sunday
Guilsborough Court, Guilsborough
July 16 Sunday
Castle Ashby House, nr Northampton
1 The Green, Kingsthorpe Village, Northampton
Guilsborough Court, Guilsborough
Ravensthorpe Gardens
July 19 Wednesday
1 The Green, Kingsthorpe Village, Northampton
Ravensthorpe Nursery, Ravensthorpe Gardens
August 6 Sunday
Bulwick Gardens, nr Corby
August 20 Sunday
The Old Rectory, Sudborough
September 3 Sunday
Cottesbrooke Hall, nr Creaton
Gamekeepers Cottage, nr Creaton
Haddonstone Show Garden, nr Northampton
September 7 Thursday
Coton Manor, Guilsborough
September 10 Sunday
Canons Ashby House, Daventry
September 24 Sunday
Hill Grounds, Evenley Gardens, Brackley
October 1 Sunday
Bulwick Rectory, Bulwick

DESCRIPTIONS OF GARDENS

Aldwincle Gardens ♿✗ 4m S of Oundle; 3m N of Thrapston on A605. Turn at The Fox at Thorpe Waterville. Aldwincle village 1½m. TEAS. *Combined adm £1.50 Chd free. Sun May 7 (2-6)*

The Maltings (Mr & Mrs N Faulkner) ¾-acre old farm house garden incl farm yard; walled garden, lawns, mixed borders, scree bed, tender wall shrubs; many plants in containers; spring bulbs, small tree plantation

Regular Openers. See head of county section.

Old School House (Mr & Mrs R Raymond-Anderson) Small secluded mainly walled garden. Previously a rough lawn and vegetable patch; present design started in 1989, care being taken to preserve old box hedge and trees

¶Badby & Newnham Gardens ❀ TEAS at Church Hill. *Combined adm £2 Chd free. Sun, Wed May, 28, 31 (2-6)*

Church Hill ✗ (Dr & Mrs C M Cripps) 3m S of Daventry on E side of A361. Close to Badby Woods and Fawsley Park (suitable for walks and picnics). Medium-sized country garden on an irregular sloping site, parts of which have been recently redesigned. Yew hedges, mixed borders thickly planted in colour groups. Some interesting plants, shady border, greenhouse and conservatory

¶**Newnham Grounds** (Mr & Mrs R Hodges) 1m E of Newnham on B4037. 2 acres mature garden planted in late 20's on 3 levels with lovely view. Had been allowed to lapse but being reclaimed in recent yrs. Interesting shapes and paths, lime avenue, rose garden, early spring rockery *(Share to St Michael & All Angels, Newnham)*

Benefield House ♿✂ ❀ (Mr & Mrs John Nicholson) Lower Benefield. 3m W Oundle off A427. Oundle-Corby Rd. 2½-acre garden. Shrubbery and large herbaceous border with interesting plants. Old walled kitchen garden containing vegetables and flowers. TEA. *Adm £1.50 Chd free (Share to St Mary's Church®). Sun June 4 (2-6)*

¶**Bradden House** ✂❀ (Keith Barwell Esq) Bradden. 5m W of Towcester. 25 acres of garden with ornamental woodland and lake, the walled garden of Edwardian origin the rest has been laid out by present owners since 1991. Good mixed borders with colour themes, long rose pergola and rose garden planted with new English roses around an ornamental pool, vegetable, herb and fruit gardens. Walk through newly planted park and flower meadow with ponds. TEAS. *Adm £1.80 Chd 50p (Share to Home Farm Trust®). Wed June 29 (2-6). Private visits welcome March to Sept, please* **Tel 01327 860902**

Bulwick Gardens Bulwick village 7m NE of Corby, 10m SW of Stamford, ½m off A43. TEAS. *Combined adm £2 Chd free (Share to Multiple Sclerosis®). Sun Aug 6 (2-5.30)*

Bulwick Park ♿ (Mr & Mrs G T G Conant) In Bulwick Village turn in Red Lodge Rd, enter park over cattle grid. Formal terraced 8-acre walled garden leading to river and island. 50 metre double herbaceous borders. 100 metre holly walk ending at attractive C18 wrought iron gates. C19 orangery and colonnade; large newly planned kitchen garden; fine mature trees; peacocks. TEAS

The Shambles ✂❀ (Mr & Mrs M R Glithero) Approx ⅓-acre garden, mixed herbaceous borders, vegetable garden with fruit and an original village well; variety of flowering plants in pots and tubs

Bulwick Rectory ♿✂❀ (Revd & Mrs Mervyn Wilson) Bulwick. 8m NE of Corby; 13m NE of Kettering; next to Bulwick Church. 1½-acre old rectory garden largely remade and replanted since 1978 as a number of gardens with vistas and surprises. Dovecote; folly; stonewalls. Shrubs, old roses, mixed borders with wide variety of plants. Fruit trees 30 varieties of apple, 15 of pear and 12 of plum in various forms of training and quince medlar and vegetables cultivated on organic principles. TEAS and plants July only. *Adm £1 Chd 50p (Share to St Nicholas Church®). Suns July 2, Oct 1 (2-5). Private visits welcome, please* **Tel 01780 485 249**

Canons Ashby House ♿✂❀ (The National Trust) nr Daventry. Formal gardens enclosed by walls being developed. Gate piers from 1710; fine topiary; axial arrangement of paths and terraces; wild flowers, old varieties of fruit trees, newly planted gardens. Home of the Dryden family since C16, Manor House 1550 with contemporary wall paintings and Jacobean plastering. Plants (June 10 only). TEAS. *Adm £3.20 Chd £1.60 (includes house). Reduced party rate. For NGS Sat June 10, Sun Sept 10 (12-5.30)*

Castle Ashby House ♿❀ (The Marquis of Northampton) 6m E of Northampton. 1½m N of A428 Northampton-Bedford; turn off between Denton and Yardley Hastings. Parkland incl avenue planted at suggestion of William III in 1695; lakes etc by Capability Brown; Italian gardens with orangery; extensive lawns and trees. Nature trail. Elizabethan house (not open). TEA. *Adm £2 Chd & OAPs £1. For NGS Sun July 16 (11-5)*

Chacombe Gardens 4m NE of Banbury. On A361 from Banbury centre turn R signed to Chacombe. TEAS **17 Silver St**. *Combined adm £1.50 Chd free (Share to St Peter & St Paul Church®). Sun May 28 (2-6)*

Cartmel ✂ (Mr & Mrs John Willis) Small informal elevated garden with herbaceous plants, spring bulbs, roses, shrubs and small trees; pond and rockery with wide variety of plants. Greenhouse with tender plants for summer planting. Surrounded on three sides by hedges and old stone walls

Pear Tree House (Capt & Mrs Peter Northey) A 1-acre garden leading up to church with spring bulbs, mature trees and shrubs surrounding an extended C17 cottage

Poplars Farm ❀ (Mr & Mrs Geoff Jones) 4 acres mixed borders; streamside borders with ferns, species primulas and bog plants; kitchen garden; dry garden with alpines; wild areas with some growing willow for fuel, spring and summer meadow areas being developed, greenhouse with cacti and carnivorous plants. Thatched 1654 farmhouse (not open)

17 Silver St (Dr & Mrs Stephen Large) 2 acres under development; paddocks with shetland ponies; wild stream-side; mixed borders; rose garden with wall plantings; small court

Charlton ♿ 7m SE of Banbury, 5m W of Brackley. From A41 turn off N at Aynho; or from A422 turn off S at Farthinghoe. Home-made TEAS **The Cottage**. *Combined adm £1.50 Chd 75p (Share to Charlton Playing Fields©). Sun April 9 (2-6)*

The Cottage (Lady Juliet Townsend) Flowering shrubs, spring bulbs, roses, lawns, woodland walk, stream and lakes. House in village street

Holly House (The Hon Nicholas Berry) Walled garden with beautiful views. C18 house (not open)

Coton Manor ♿❀ (Mr & Mrs Ian Pasley-Tyler) 10m N of Northampton. 11m SE of Rugby nr Ravensthorpe Reservoir. From A428 & A50 follow Tourist signs. C17 stone manor house with water gardens, herbaceous borders, rose garden, old holly and yew hedges; interesting variety of foliage plants; collection of ornamental waterfowl, cranes and flamingoes. Home-made Lunches and TEAS. *Adm £2.70 OAPs £2.20 Chd £1. Open daily Weds to Suns & Bank Hols. April to end Sept. For NGS Thurs May 25, Sept 7 (12-6). Private parties welcome, please* **Tel 01604 740219**

Cottesbrooke Hall ♿✂❀ (Captain & Mrs J Macdonald-Buchanan) 10m N of Northampton, nr Creaton on A50, nr Brixworth on A508. (A14 link rd A1/M1). Car park free. Notable gardens of great variety incl fine old cedars and specimen trees, herbaceous borders, water and wild gardens. TEAS. *Adm house & gardens £3.50 Gardens only £2 Chd half price. Open Easter Mon to Sept every Thurs and Bank Hol Mons (2-5.30). For NGS Combined adm with* **Gamekeepers Cottage** *£2 Chd £1. House £2 extra (Share to All Saints Church®). Suns June 4, Sept 3 (2-6).* **Tel 01604 505808**

¶Cottingham & Middleton Gardens ✂❀ 4m W of Corby on B607. Off A427 Corby to Market Harborough rd. Cream TEAS at Cottingham Methodist Chapel in aid of the Lakeside Hospice, Corby. *Combined adm £2 Chd free. Sun June 18 (2-6)*

¶4 Church Street (Miss Susan Hall & Mr Christopher Owen) A small cottage/plantswoman's garden containing some vegetables, a formal herb garden, soft fruits and pots. The garden adjoins a C17 house in the old part of the village

¶Fosse Way House (Mr & Mrs R H Newman) Garden created in 1968. Well stocked with mature trees and herbaceous plants. Small pond and greenhouse. Hidden areas reached by an intriguing network of paths

¶Clairmont (Mr & Mrs N J Henson) ½-acre garden developed since 1986, situated on a very steep slope with magnificent views over the Welland Valley. Island beds with many unusual shrubs and plants

Deene Park ♿✂ (Edmund Brudenell Esq) 5m N of Corby on A43 Stamford-Kettering Rd. Large garden; long mixed borders, old-fashioned roses, rare mature trees, shrubs, natural garden, large lake and waterside walks. Parterre designed by David Hicks echoing the C16 decoration on the porch stonework. Interesting Church and Brudenell Chapel with fine tombs and brasses. TEAS. *Adm £2 Chd 50p. Sun May 14 (2-5)*

Easton Neston ♿✂❀ (The Lord & Lady Hesketh) Towcester. Entrance on Northampton Rd (old A43). Hawkesmoor's only Private house. Large formal garden; ornamental water, topiary; walled garden; woodland walk with C14 church (not open) in grounds. TEA. *Adm £2 Chd 50p. Sun July 2 (2-6)*

Evenley Gardens From Brackley 1m S on A43. Teas at Evenley Hall. *Combined adm £1.40 Chd 40p. Sun, Mon June 11, 12 (2-6)*

15 Church Lane (Mr & Mrs K O'Regan) ⅓-acre garden, newly built terrace, pond, mixed borders and vegetable garden

Five Gables ✂❀ (Mr & Mrs M Bosher) SE facing sloping garden of 1½ acres. Designed in 'compartments' and still being developed

Hill Grounds ♿❀ (Mr & Mrs C F Cropley) 2-acres S facing sheltered garden re-developed since 1982; mature trees, 200yds of yew hedge; terrace; old roses, winter garden; wide range of unusual plants. TEA. *Adm £1 Sun Sept 24 (2-6). Harvest Flower Festival in adjoining church*

The Manor House (Mr & Mrs H Bentley) Established garden on ½-acre sloping site; topiary and an ambience in harmony with fine Elizabethan Manor House (not open)

Evenley Wood Garden (R T Whiteley) Brackley. A43 ¾m S turn L to Evenley straight through village towards Mixbury 1st turning L. A woodland garden spread over a 60-acre mature wood. Acid and alkaline soil. Magnolias, rhododendrons, azaleas, malus, quercus, acers, euonymus collection and many other species. A large collection of bulbous plants. TEAS. *Adm £2 Chd £1. Suns, Mons April 30, May 1, 28, 29 (2-7). For NGS Sun, Mon April 16, 17 (2-7). Private visits welcome, please* **Tel 01280 703329**

¶Falcutt House ♿✂❀ (Paul & Charlotte Sandilands) Helmdon. 4m N of Brackley, 2m to the W of A43, ½m SE of Helmdon Village Church. 3-acre garden in secluded rural setting; fine hedges incl yew topiary; mixed borders; lilacs, ancient mulberry tree; garden in process of being restored; young tree plantation. Small nursery with unusual plants. TEAS. *Adm £1.50 Chd free. Suns May 7, June 4 (2-6)*

Finedon Gardens ✂ Wellingborough. 2m NE of Wellingborough on the A510, 6m SE Kettering on the A6. Teas in aid of Finedon Church, at Finedon Antique Centre. *Combined adm £1.50 Chd free. Sun April 30 (2-6)*

4 Harrowden Lane ♿ (Mr & Mrs D J West) ½-acre garden on a steep slope, created since 1982 from waste land; lawns, rose and flower beds; ornamental fish pond with cascade fountain, aviary and greenhouses

¶23 Regent Street ✂ (Mr & Mrs G Perkins) ½-acre garden with raised lawn, mature trees, fruit trees. 2 large ponds with koi carp, golden orfe and terrapins; inc filter system. Aviaries, ducks and numerous pets. Free-flying budgerigars

Thingdon Cottage (Mrs M A Leach) 4½ acres of garden, originally Finedon Hall grounds. Lawns, ancient trees, shrubs, spring flowers, brook, hillside pasture with unique view of Finedon Hall and Church

Flore Gardens 7m W of Northampton, 5m E of Daventry on A45. Flower Festival at All Saints Church and U.R Chapel incl light lunches, Teas, plants, etc. *Combined adm £2 Chd free (Share to Flower Festival®). Sat, Sun June 17, 18 (11-6)*

Beech Hill ✂ (Dr & Mrs R B White) The garden of approx 1 acre is on a hillside facing S over the Nene Valley. It is laid out to lawns, herbaceous and shrub borders with mature trees. There is a vegetable garden and an orchard, an alpine house and cool greenhouse. The terrace has hanging baskets and tubs

The Croft (John & Dorothy Boast) ⅓-acre garden of C17 cottage with mature trees, shrubs, lawns and interesting perennials

The Grange ✂ (Mr & Mrs C R Buswell) Mature 2½-acre garden with lawns, trees, herbaceous beds, shrubs and pond. Partly suitable for wheelchairs

The Manor House ✂ (Richard & Wendy Amos) 1-acre garden with established lawns and herbaceous border surrounded by mature trees. Formal pond and walled kitchen garden. Partly suitable for wheelchairs

The Old Manor ✂ (Mr & Mrs Keith Boyd) Early C18 house (not shown) with medium-sized garden, comprising lawn, herbaceous border, rose garden, vegetables and fruit. Pleasant views over the Nene valley. Also paddock with pond and shrubs

6 Thornton Close (Mr & Mrs D L Lobb) Medium-sized garden; trees, shrubs, herbaceous plants, conifers and alpines. 2 small ponds with fish

The White Cottage ♿✗ (Mr & Mrs G Menzies) Large cottage garden. Approx 1 acre; lawns, shrubs, perennial beds; fruit trees and vegetable garden

Gamekeepers Cottage Garden ♿✗❀ (Mr & Mrs D Daw) Cottesbrooke. 10m W of Northampton, nr Creaton on A50; nr Brixworth on A508. Cottage garden featuring unusual herbaceous plants, flowers for drying, fruit, vegetables. *Combined adm £1.50 Chd 50p with* **Cottesbrooke Hall**. *Suns June 4, Sept 3 (2-6)*

¶**Great Addington Manor** (Mr & Mrs G E Groome) Great Addington. 7m SE of Kettering, 4m W Thrapston, A510 exit off A14 signed Finedon and Wellingborough. Turn 2nd L to the Addingtons. 4½-acre manor gardens with lawns, mature trees, mulberry, yew hedges, pond and spinney. Spring daffodils. A garden being rejuvenated. Teas in Village Hall. *Adm £1.50 Chd over 5yrs 50p (Share to Great Addington Church Maintenance Fund®). Wed, Sun April 19, 23 (2-6). Private visits welcome during April only, please* **Tel 01536 330204**

Great Brington Gardens ✗ 7m NW of Northampton off A428 Rugby rd. 1st L turn past main gates of Althorp. Tickets/maps at church. Gardens signed in village. Parking facilities. Lunches, TEAS. Exhibition and plant stall at various village venues in aid of St Mary's Church. *Combined adm £1.50 Chd free. Sun May 14 (11-5)*

Brington Lodge ♿✗ (Mr & Mrs P J Cooch) An old garden on the edge of the village, approx ¾ acre, partially walled with a number of spring flowering trees and shrubs

Dairy Farm ♿✗ (Ian & Alex Ward) ½-acre garden comprising lawn with mixed borders, cottage garden, rose garden, secret garden; orchards, vegetables and pond; also farmyard animals

Folly House ✗ ❀ (Capt & Mrs L G Bellamy) Early C18 house (not shown) 1-acre garden, lawns, herbaceous, shrubs and vegetable garden. Interesting setting using different levels with the church as background

30 Great Brington ♿✗ (Mr & Mrs John Kimbell) Interesting small garden attached to old stone cottage, well-stocked with shrubs, climbers and perennials. Small pond with bog area, secret garden

The Last Straw ♿✗ (Mr & Mrs A Johnson) C15 thatched cottage with cottage garden. Pleasant views of Althorp. Newly-planted herbaceous borders, summer house

New Cross ♿✗ (R J Kimbell) ½-acre old country garden surrounding a mellow Northamptonshire stone house. Mature trees and shrubs with many spring flowering bulbs

Ridgeway House ✗ (Mr & Mrs John Gale) 1½ acres with lawns, herbaceous borders and many spring-flowering shrubs and bulbs

¶**Rose Cottage** ♿ (Mr David Green) 2yr old estate cottage garden designed, built and planted by owner. Variety of fan fruit trees, rockery and brick terrace with pagoda

Great & Little Harrowden Gardens On A509 2m N of Wellingborough on the L. 5m S of Kettering on the R. TEAS in aid of ARC. *Combined adm £2 Chd free. Sun, Wed June 18, 21 (2-6)*

Dolphins ♿✗❀ (Mr & Mrs R C Handley) Gt Harrowden. 2-acre country garden surrounding old stone house. Many old roses grown among interesting trees, shrubs and a wide range of hardy perennials

Great Harrowden Lodge ♿✗❀ (Mrs J & Mr R M Green) 1¼-acre garden on a dry exposed site, recently extended. Wide variety of herbaceous perennials

South View ♿✗ (Mr & Mrs D W Osborne) Little Harrowden. Small lane off Main St near to church. Recently constructed terraced garden, with S facing rural aspect. Herbaceous and shrub borders, interesting kitchen garden encl by different varieties of trained fruit trees, wild flower area

¶**1 The Green** ✗❀ (Mr & Mrs D Nightingale) Kingsthorpe Village. 2m N of Northampton Town Centre. Turn off A508 into Mill Lane at Cock Hotel, taking 2nd turn R. ⅓-acre well-established garden on steep slope, partly terraced. Planned for yr-round interest with a variety of shrubs, herbaceous and climbing plants; to be explored with many surprises. TEAS. *Adm £1 Chd 50p. Sun July 16 (12-5) Wed July 19 (2-6)*

Guilsborough Court ♿❀ (Mr & Mrs John Lowther) Guilsborough. 10m N of Northampton off A50. 10m NE of Daventry; 10m E of Rugby; ¼m outside Guilsborough on Cold Ashby rd. 4-acre garden, many fine mature trees, beautiful views, interesting shrubs, large lawn and herbaceous borders. Good plant sales area. TEAS. *Adm £1.50 Chd free. Suns July 9, 16 (2-6)*

Guilsborough and Hollowell Gardens 10m NW of Northampton between A50 - A428. 10m E of Rugby. Cream TEAS at **Dripwell House** by Guilsborough WI. Teas at Hollowell Village Hall. *Combined adm £1.50 Chd free. Sun May 21 (2-6). Private visits welcome for parties of 12 and over*

Dripwell House ✗❀ Guilsborough (Mr & Mrs J W Langfield, Dr C Moss, Mr & Mrs P G Moss) 2½-acre mature garden; many fine trees and shrubs on partly terraced slope. Rock garden, herbaceous border, herb garden. Some unusual shrubs and many rhododendrons and azaleas in woodland garden. Cream TEAS in garden. **Tel 01604 740140**

Gower House (Peter & Ann Moss) Small garden evolving since 1991 on part of Dripwell vegetable garden. A plantsman's garden with herbaceous alpine, climbing plants and shrubs. **Tel 01604 740755**

Rosemount, Hollowell ✗❀ (Mr & Mrs J Leatherland) In centre of village, up hill behind bus shelter towards Church, entrance 100yds on R. ½-acre plantsman's garden reconstructed in 1982, unusual plants and shrubs, alpine garden, fish pond, small collections of clematis, conifers, camellias, daphne and abutilons. Partly suitable for wheelchairs. Car parking and teas at village hall behind Church, **Tel 01604 740354**

By Appointment Gardens. Avoid the crowds. Good chance of a tour by owner. See garden description for telephone number.

The Haddonstone Show Garden, East Haddon Manor ♿✂❀ (Mr & Mrs R Barrow) 10m N of Northampton, 12m S of Rugby, from A50. Walled garden on different levels, old shrub roses, ground cover plants, conifers, clematis and climbers; swimming pool surrounded by Haddonstone Colonnade, over 30 planted pots and containers. Refreshments. TEAS. *Adm £2.50 Chd free (Share to NSPCC®) Garden Festival Weekend Sun, Mon May 7, 8, (10-5). Adm £2 Chd free. Sun Sept 3 (2-5).* Special autumn plant sale

Harpole Gardens 4m W Northampton on A45 towards Weedon; turn R at 'The Turnpike' into Harpole. TEAS at **The Close**. *Combined adm £1 Chd free. Sun July 2 (2-6)*

The Close ♿✂❀ (Mr & Mrs Orton Jones) 68 High Street. Old-fashioned English country garden with large lawns, herbaceous borders and mature trees; stone house, various plant stalls

Darnley ✂ (Mr & Mrs Peter Rixon) 47b High St. An enclosed garden of ⅙th acre, consisting of cottage garden borders, a rockery, pond, rose and herb areas; a Japanese style feature and a large collection of cacti and succulents

72 Larkhall Lane ✂ (Mr & Mrs R G Murton) ⅙-acre well designed garden for all seasons; a flower to bloom everyday of the year; shrubs; variety of conifers and alpines. *Private visits welcome, please* **Tel 01604 830680**

19 Manor Close ✂ (Mr & Mrs E Kemshed) 40yd × 10yd flower arranger's garden on new estate; cultivated by present owners since 1975. *Private visits welcome, please* **Tel 01604 830512**

Holdenby House ♿✂ (Mr & Mrs James Lowther) 7m W of Northampton. Signposted from A50 and A428. Impressive remains of terrace gardens of Holdenby Palace, where Charles I was imprisoned; Elizabethan garden; fragrant and silver borders. Rare breeds farm animals; museum, falconry centre. TEAS. *Adm £2.75 (groups of 25 or more £2.25) OAP £2.25 Chd £2. ▲For NGS Sun May 14 (2-6). House open by appt for groups of 25 or more Adm £3.75*

Irthlingborough ♿✂❀ (Mr & Mrs D Ingall) 49 Finedon Rd. 5m E of Wellingborough, off the A6. A garden of approx 1 acre full of interest and unusual plants, incl herbaceous border, shrubs, pools, gravel bed and rock, wild and scented areas. Also fruit and vegetables. TEAS. *Adm £1 Chd free. Private visits welcome between Easter and end of July, please* **Tel 01933 650343**

Kilsby Gardens 5m SE of Rugby on A428 turn R on B4038 through village. 6m N of Daventry on A361. Flower Festival at St Faith's Church and UR Chapel. Teas in village hall. *Combined adm £2 Acc chd free. Sun June 18 (2-6)*

Croft Close (Mr & Mrs P Couldrey) Rugby Rd. Herbaceous beds, shrubs, pond and rockery. Productive vegetable garden, soft fruit, greenhouse

¶Elms House ♿✂ (Mr & Mrs D Willis) Middle St. The house was semi-derelict. The garden which was completely overgrown and derelict has been rebuilt and refurbished over the past 2yrs. Approx ⅓-acre it was laid out in early spring 1994 and planted through that year with lawns, 2 small fish ponds, conifer and heather bed, ornamental grasses, rose bed with David Austen roses, small herb garden, various shrubs and a bed of perennials. Small walled vegetable garden, greenhouse

The Haven ♿ (Mr & Mrs Arthur Old) Essen Lane. ½-acre walled garden of listed cottage

Lawn House ✂ (Mr & Mrs Morris) 7 The Lawns. Small walled garden with no grass (despite name of house); formal pond; mixture of surfaces; paving, cobbles, shingle; climbing and rock plants; variety of containers

¶Lynn Cottage ✂ (Mr & Mrs G Burton) Manor Rd. Small cottage garden with pond, thatched summer house, containers and hanging baskets

The Old Vicarage ♿ (Mr & Mrs P G B Jackson) On A5 opp George Hotel. 1-acre; lawns, mature trees, shrubs, herbaceous border, small water garden, vegetable garden

Pytchley ♿✂❀ (Mr & Mrs T F Clay) 14 Main Rd. 1-acre mature garden; lawns; trees; island beds; vegetable garden; 3 fish ponds; wild garden

Rainbow's End ♿✂ (Mr & Mrs J J Madigan) Middle St. Approx ⅛-acre mixed garden with large pond feature and own design of pergola patio

15 Smarts Estate (Mr & Mrs R Collins) Mature, small garden with shrubs, climbers, herbaceous border, pond and vegetable garden, fruit. Greenhouse

¶The White House ✂ (John & Lesley Loader) Chapel St. ½-acre partly walled garden with ponds and stream, heather bed, herbaceous border, vegetable garden with raised beds

Litchborough Gardens ✂ Nr Towcester, Litchborough village is mid-way between Northampton and Banbury. Teas in WI Hall, Farthingstone Rd. *Combined adm £2 Chd free (Share to St Martins Church®). Sun May 21 (2-6.30)*

Bruyere Court, Farthingstone Rd ♿ (Mr & Mrs R Martin) 4 acres of landscaped garden featuring lawns; 2 ornamental lakes with rock streams and fountain; shrub borders; rhododendron and azalea borders; herbaceous border; old-fashioned rose hedge; ornamental trees and conifers

Good Reste ❀ (Mr & Mrs J B Guy) Banbury Rd. An unusual late Victorian/Edwardian acre, with lawns, sunken stone gardens and grotto linked by York stone paths to shaded walks under old trees and shrubs incl venerable magnolia; thatched gazebo. Kitchen garden and orchard. Original layout intact with general renewal and replanting underway

The Hall ♿ (A R Heygate Esq) Large garden with open views of parkland; laid to lawns and borders with clipped hedges around the house; the extensive wild garden has large numbers of specimen trees and shrubs; walks wind through this area and round the lakes

The Old Rectory (Mr & Mrs T R Sykes) Partly walled garden approx 1 acre with small fishpond, mixed herbaceous and shrub borders, established heather bank surrounds newly planted raised beds. Small kitchen garden area. The garden is still being developed with new features each year

Orchard House ❀ (Mr & Mrs B Smith) Banbury Rd, Landscape architects country garden designed for low maintenance; orchard, pools, conservatory and working pump

Lois Weedon House ❀ (Sir John & Lady Greenaway) Weedon Lois. 7m from Towcester on the edge of Weedon Lois village. Pass through village going E towards Wappenham; as you leave village Lois Weedon House entrance on R, further on is 2nd entrance which has a lodge. Medium-sized garden with terraces and fine views; lawns; pergola; water garden; mature yew hedges; large pond. TEAS. *Adm £1.50 Chd free (Share to Lois Weedon PCC®). Sun June 4 (2-6). Private visits welcome, please* **Tel 01327 860472**

¶Maidwell Gardens ✠ 8m N of Northampton on A508, 6m S of Market Harborough. TEAS. *Adm £2 Chd free. Sun June 18 (2-6)*

¶The Old Bake House (Ken & Angela Palmer) Small walled garden with herbaceous borders, shrubs, old fruit trees and a large gravel courtyard under redevelopment. Many plants are grown for preserving or drying for arrangements

¶The Old Barn ♿❀ (Mr & Mrs John Groocock) ¾-acre garden developed around an old stone barn. Mixed herbaceous and shrub borders. Newly-planted area surrounding gazebo with clematis and roses

¶School Farmhouse ♿ (Mr & Mrs D J Carter-Johnson) ¾-acre walled cottage garden brimful of traditional mid-summer flowering perennials

¶Wisteria Cottage ✠❀ (Mr & Mrs P J Montgomery) A plantsman's cottage garden of approx ½ acre, developed over the last 6 yrs. A series of rooms in themed colours, sunken garden, water feature, knot garden, herbaceous borders. *Private visits welcome for 2 and over, please* **Tel 01604 686308**

Maidwell Hall ♿❀ (Mr & Mrs P R Whitton, Maidwell Hall School) A508 N from Northampton, 6m S of Market Harborough, entrance via cattle grid on S fringe of Maidwell village. 45 acres of lawns, playing fields, woodland. Colourful display of spring bulbs, magnolias and early flowering shrubs; mature rose garden; lake and arboretum. TEA. *Adm £2 Chd free (Share to St Mary's Church, Maidwell®). Sun April 23 (2-6). Private visits welcome April to July, Sept to Oct, please* **Tel 01604 686234**

The Menagerie ♿✠❀ (Mr G Jackson-Stops & Mr I Kirby) On B526, 6m S of Northampton, 1m beyond Horton, turn L at lay-by, across field. These newly developed gardens are set around an C18 folly. Most recently completed is the Wetland Garden, planted with native material from the Horton park. The Vernal garden, now in its 3rd year, uses spring bulbs, hellebores and early perennials under a canopy of spring flowering trees and shrubs. TEAS. *Adm £2.50 Chd £1. Thurs (10-4). House, garden and shell grotto open to parties by written appt. For NGS Sun April 23 (2-6)*

The Old Rectory, Sudborough ♿✠❀ (Mr & Mrs Huntington) Corby exit off A14. Village just off A6116 between Thrapston & Brigstock. Classic English country garden containing many rare and unusual plants which fill this 3-acre plantsman's garden surrounding a fine Georgian Rectory (not open). Features incl colour themed mixed and herbaceous borders; formal rose garden; shrubberies and pond; woodland walk; intricate potager designed by Rosemary Verey and developed by the owners with Rupert Golby. Many well planted containers; in March a comprehensive display of helleborus x orientalis (Lenten Rose) can be seen massed with spring bulbs. Featured in House & Garden, June 93. TEA April 2, TEAS Aug 20. *Adm £2 Chd free (Share to All Saints Church, Sudborough®). Suns March 19, 26, April 16, May 7, June 4, 18, 25; Mons April 17, May 8 (2-6). For NGS Suns April 2, Aug 20 (2-6). Private visits welcome, please* **Tel 01832 733247**

The Old Vicarage ✠ (Mr & Mrs M J Percival) Great Cransley. 3m SW of Kettering off A43 signposted to Broughton and 1m to Great Cransley. 1½ acres of English country garden with lawns, mature trees and hedges; mixed herbaceous and shrub borders. TEAS. *Adm £1.50 Chd free (Share to St Andrews Church®). Sat, Sun June 24, 25 (2-6)*

Preston Capes Gardens ✠ Approx 7m S of Daventry, 3m N of Canon's Ashby. Homemade TEAS at **Old West Farm**. TEAS and plants in aid of St Peter's & St Paul's Church. *Combined adm £2 Chd 50p. Sun June 4 (2-6)*

Archway Cottage (Mr & Mrs King) Approx ½-acre garden, with outstanding views over Northants countryside. Lawns with specimen shrubs, herbaceous borders and ornamental fish pond. Sloping plot being converted to nature garden, with natural pond, marginal plants and berry-bearing trees and shrubs

City Cottage ♿❀ (Mr & Mrs Gavin Cowen) A mature garden in the middle of an attractive village, with a walled herbaceous border, rose beds, flowering shrubs, wisteria and a newly planted sunken garden with unusual shrubs

Old West Farm ♿❀ (Mr & Mrs Gerard Hoare) Little Preston. Between Charwelton (A361) and Maidford. 2-acre garden re-designed since 1980. Woodland area underplanted with shrubs and bulbs. Roses and borders designed for yr-round interest

Ravensthorpe Gardens Halfway between Rugby and Northampton. Signposted Ravensthorpe 1½m from the A428. TEAS in aid of Riding for the Disabled at Ravensthorpe Nursery. *Combined adm £1.50 Chd free. Sun July 16 (2-6)*

32 The High St (Mr & Mrs J Patrick) Moderate size garden planted over the last 6yrs. Mostly perennials but some shrubs and roses; also greenhouse and vegetables

Lingles Farm ♿ (Mr & Mrs A Mold) Large garden with mixed island beds

Ravensthorpe Nursery ♿❀ (Mr & Mrs Richard Wiseman) Approx 1-acre new show garden being developed to display plants; wide range of shrubs, trees and hardy perennials, incl shrub rose and mixed borders with fine views; also private ¼-acre owners' plantsman's garden. *Also open Wed July 19 (6.30-9).* **Tel 01604 770548**

Sholebroke Lodge ♿❀ (A B X Fenwick Esq) Whittlebury, 3m S of Towcester. Turn off A413 Towcester end of Whittlebury village. 5-acres informal garden; large herbaceous borders and walks. Through shrub plantings with view of lake. Garden shop in old barn. Home-made TEAS. *Adm £1 Chd 50p. Sun June 4 (2-6)*

Slapton Gardens ✽❀ Slapton, a tiny village 4m W of Towcester ¼m N of the Towcester to Wappenham Rd. Superb small 13/14th century church. TEAS & car park at Slapton Lodge. *Combined adm £2 Chd free. Sun May 28 (2-6)*

¶**Fellyard** (Mr & Mrs R Owen) Mature 1½-acre garden with orchard, herbaceous and walled garden areas. Stream walk, new ha-ha and rose plantings. Some unusual specimen trees and shrubs

The Old Royal Oak (Mrs D Mumford) A garden for the gardener and plantsman, approx ⅓-acre, started from bare site 1989. Imaginative use of layout to take in different levels and difficult soil conditions. Trees, flowering shrubs, (many unusual) herbaceous, alpines and lawn; large cottage borders

Slapton Lodge ♿ (Mr & Mrs Webster) In beautiful grounds and parkland

The Spring House ✽ (Mr & Mrs C Shepley-Cuthbert) Mill Lane, Chipping Warden on A361 between Banbury and Daventry. Garden originally laid out by Miss Kitty Lloyd Jones in the thirties and now mature. Approx 3 acres app through a 16′ tapestry hedge. April-May spring flowers, bulbs and blossom. June-Sept bog and water garden at its most colourful. Other times unconventional borders, shrub roses and specimen trees with many new plantings. Ploughmans lunches and Teas available for groups & clubs by arrangement. *Private visits welcome, please* **Tel 01295 86261**

Stoke Park ♿ (A S Chancellor Esq) Stoke Bruerne, Towcester. Stoke Bruerne village lies 1m off A508 between Northampton and Stony Stratford. Stoke Park is down a private road ¾m, 1st turning L, ¼m beyond village. Approx 3-acres. Terraced lawn with ornamental basin, orchard, herb garden, shrub and other borders, as setting to two C17 pavillions and colonnade. TEA. *Adm £1 Chd 50p.* ▲*Sun June 4 (2-6)*

¶**Sulgrave Gardens** ✽ Off B4525 rd from Banbury to Northampton, 7m NE of Banbury. TEAS at Sulgrave Manor. *Combined adm £2 Chd free. Sun June 18 (2-6)*

¶**Church Cottage** (Mr & Mrs H R Lloyd) Church St. Nr church on S-side. [Map ref SP557453] ½-acre garden. Mixed shrubs, old shrub, rambling and climbing roses, herbaceous borders

¶**The Cottage** ♿ (Mrs Jean Garton) Magpie Rd. Small terraced garden with roses

¶**Ferns** ♿❀ (George & Jane Metcalfe) Helmdon Rd. ⅙-acre garden containing a wide range of plants, many of them unusual

¶**Forge Cottage** (Mrs B Burke) School St. Informal cottage garden, tubs and containers. Partially suitable for wheelchairs

¶**Mayfield** ♿ (Mr & Mrs Brian Hart) Manor Rd. Approx ½-acre family garden, mixed borders, fruit and vegetable gardens, greenhouse, small stream, lovely setting

¶**Apple Acre** (Mr & Mrs P Flynn) Manor Rd. Medium-sized garden comprising lawns, shrubs, mixed borders, pond, pergola and fruit trees. Partially suitable for wheelchairs

¶**Harrys Cottage** ♿ (Mr & Mrs R Jeffery) Manor Rd. Tiny walled cottage garden

¶**Sulgrave Manor** (The Sulgrave Manor Board) Formal gardens designed by Sir Reginald Bloomfield in the 1920's. Ancient orchard, herbaceous borders, herb garden in the form of an Elizabethan knot. Partially suitable for wheelchairs. Manor open. *Adm £3 extra*

Titchmarsh Gardens 2m N of Thrapston, 6m S of Oundle on A605, Titchmarsh signposted as turning to E. TEAS. *Combined adm £2 Chd free (Share to St Marys Church, Titchmarsh©). Mons April 17, May 29 (2-6)*

Glebe Cottage ♿✽ (Mr & Mrs J Bussens) ⅓ acre; NE aspect; informal herbaceous and shrub borders and beds. Clematis in a variety of situations

16 Polopit ✽ (Mr & Mrs C Millard) ½ acre. Developed since 1984; rockeries, ornamental and herbaceous borders; fruit decorative shrubs

¶**Swallows** ✽ (Mr & Mrs W Melvin) ⅓-acre informal garden with rockery, fish and lily ponds, mixed beds leading to vegetable area. Panoramic view of open countryside

Titchmarsh House ♿✽ (Mr & Mrs Ewan Harper) 4 acres extended and laid out since 1972; cherries, magnolias, herbaceous irises; shrub roses, clematis, range of wall shrubs, walled borders

Turweston Gardens A43 from Oxford, in Brackley turn R at traffic lights. A422 towards Buckingham, 1m turn L signposted Turweston. Teas in village hall. *Combined adm £2 Chd 50p (Share to St Mary's Restoration Fund®). Sun June 25 (2-6)*

¶**The Old School House** (Mr & Mrs Hugh Carey) ¼-acre walled garden. Formal with potager and featuring planters

Spring Valley ✽❀ (Mr & Mrs A Wildish) 1-acre terraced garden leading to formal and informal ponds, bog garden, herbaceous borders

Turweston Barn (Mr & Mrs A J M Kirkland) 2 acres informal planting, mixed herbaceous and shrub borders, lawns, woodland and walled garden

Turweston House (Mrs Octavian von Hofmannsthal) 5½ acres landscaped garden; walled garden and lake

Turweston Mill ✽ (Mr & Mrs Harry Leventis) 5 acres, mill stream, water garden, lawns. Also open with **Versions Farm**. *Combined adm £1.50 Chd free. Sun June 11 (2-6)*

Versions Farm ♿✽❀ (Mrs E T Smyth-Osbourne) Brackley 2m N of Brackley on the Turweston Rd. 3-acres plantsman's garden; old stone walls; terraces; old-fashioned rose garden; iris border; shrubs and trees some unusual; pond. Conservatory. Cream TEAS. *Combined adm £1.50 Chd free with* **The Mill House, Turweston** *(Share to Whitfield Church®). Sun June 11 (2-6). Parties welcome by appt May to July, please* **Tel 01280 702412**

¶**The Walnuts** ♿ (Mr & Mrs Martin Lawrence) King's Cliffe. 7m NE of Oundle, 7m SW of Stamford, 4m W of Wansford from A1 and A47; last house on L leaving King's Cliffe on rd to Apethorpe. 2½-acre country garden with lawns, mature trees and hedges, mixed herbaceous and shrub borders, newly planted sunken rose garden. Mown pathway through meadow to pond, R Willowbrook and woodland walk. TEAS. *Adm £1.50 Chd free (Share to King's Cliffe Village Hall®). Sun, Wed May 21, 24 (2-6). Private visits welcome, please* **Tel 01780 470312**

Regular Openers. See head of county section.

Weedon Lois Gardens Nr Towcester. 8m W of Towcester. TEAS. *Combined adm £1.50 Chd free. Sun June 25 (2-6)*

Elizabeth House (Mr & Mrs A Cartwright) A C17 vicarage garden of 1½ acres. Herbaceous beds, a walled vegetable garden and wild wooded area

The Leys (Mr & Mrs Peter French) A garden of 1-acre sloping away from the house; designed to incl attractive vistas; separate areas and styles formed to suit, water, alpine screes, Japanese gravel gardens and mixed borders

Lois Weedon Farm (Mr & Mrs W J Richards) 1½ acres; lawns; woodland; conservation area; vegetables; orchard; ha-ha; pool, lilies, goldfish; views S over fields. Church worth a visit

The Old Barn (Mr & Mrs John Gregory) Small ⅓-acre plantsman's garden designed by the owners to compliment converted C18 barn; with interesting selection of herbaceous perennials, climbing plants, shrub roses and gravel gardens. Many unusual plants for sale, incl white varieties. *Private visits welcome June to July, please* **Tel 01327 860577**

West Haddon Gardens As seen on BBC TV in 1992. The village is on the A428 between Rugby and Northampton and lies 4m E of M1 exit 18. Teas in village hall. *Combined adm £2 Chd free (Share to West Haddon Parish Church and West Haddon Baptist Church©). Sun July 2 (2-6)*

¶Beech Trees (Gerald & Daphne Kennaird) Small partially walled garden with views over rolling Northamptonshire countryside. Terrace, lawns, mixed borders and small pond

The Bungalow West Haddon Hall (John and Jean Terry) Small secluded informal garden surrounded by mature trees with rockery; lawns; mixed borders; two aviaries and pond

Crystal House (Pat and Dick Hughes) ¼-acre of landscaped garden, mostly walled, informal terrace areas, lawn and mixed borders, many containers and hanging baskets, new summerhouse and vegetable garden

Lime House (Leslie and David Roberts) ½-acre of walled garden with rockeries, herbaceous borders, walk-through shrubbery, rose beds; croquet lawn. Summerhouse and patio with greenhouse

The Mews (Rob and Jane Dadley) ½-acre of secluded walled garden including lawns, secret garden, herbaceous border, formal and informal ponds, statuary and pergolas

Well Cottage (Sandra and Roger Woodcock) Very small walled garden on various levels displaying many containers, pond and a variety of plants

West Cottages (Geoff and Rosemary Sage) ⅔-acre of mixed borders and lawns; informal pond; lawn tennis court and kitchen garden. Newly acquired additional land; garden under construction. Open views

¶13 Whytewell Road (Mrs H S Talbot) 1m N of Wellingborough. 1st turn R on the A509 Wellingborough to Kettering rd. Approx ¼-acre garden with unusual shrubs, old-fashioned roses and clematis. Many varieties of spring flowering bulbs, herbaceous plants incl azaleas. *Adm £1. Private visits for parties of 1-4 welcome March to June, please* **Tel 01933 222661**

Wilby Gardens. 3m SW of Wellingborough on the A4500 to Northampton signposted Wilby. TEAS at **Glebe Farmhouse.** *Combined adm £1.50 Chd free. Sun June 25 (2-6)*

Glebe Farmhouse (Mr & Mrs K B Shipp) Medium-sized garden with shrub and herbaceous borders

7 Mears Ashby Road (Mr & Mrs K H Coleman) Small garden containing shrubs and herbaceous borders. Variety of plants in containers, plenty of colour

Wilby Cottage (Mrs B K Gale) Well established cottage garden, surrounded by walls and hedge, shrubs, herbaceous border, rockery and tubs, a plantsman's garden

Northumberland & Tyne and Wear

(including 3 Berwickshire gardens open under Scotland's Garden Scheme)

Hon County Organiser: Mrs G Baker Cresswell, Preston Tower, Chathill, Northumberland NE67 5DH Tel 01665 589210

Assistant Hon County Organiser: Mrs T Sale, Ilderton Glebe, Ilderton, Alnwick, Northumberland NE66 4YD Tel 01668 217293

DATES OF OPENING

By Appointment

For telephone numbers and other details see garden descriptions. Private visits welcomed

Ashfield, Hebron, Morpeth
Berryburn, Ancroft
Bridge House, Fox Covert Lane, Ponteland
Mindrum, Cornhill on Tweed

Parties only

Kirkley Hall College, Ponteland
Loughbrow House, Hexham

Regular openings

For details see garden descriptions

Bughtrig, nr Leitholm, Coldstream. Open June to Sept
Chipchase Castle, Wark-on-Tyne. For dates see text
The Hirsel, Coldstream. Open all year
Northumbria Nurseries, Walled Gardens, Ford, Berwick-upon-Tweed. For dates see text

April 16 Sunday
Netherbyres, Eyemouth

April 30 Sunday
Preston Tower, Chathill

May 14 Sunday
Wallington, Morpeth

May 21 Sunday
Belsay Hall, Castle & Gardens
Lilburn Tower, Alnwick

May 31 Wednesday
Bide-a-Wee Cottage, Netherwitton, Morpeth

June 4 Sunday
Chipchase Castle, Wark-on-Tyne
Meldon Park, Morpeth

June 11 Sunday
Bradley Gardens, Wylam

June 18 Sunday
Chesters, Humshaugh, nr Hexham
Hexham Herbs, Chesters Walled Garden, Humshaugh, nr Hexham

June 22 Thursday
Herterton House, Morpeth

June 24 Saturday
Kirkley Hall College, Ponteland

June 25 Sunday
Berryburn, Ancroft
Chillingham Castle, Chillingham
Kirkley Hall College, Ponteland
Mindrum, Cornhill on Tweed

July 2 Sunday
Bughtrig, nr Leitholm, Coldstream
Hartford Bridge House, nr Bedlington
Northumbria Nurseries, Walled Gardens, Ford, Berwick-upon-Tweed

July 5 Wednesday
Bridge House, Fox Covert Lane, Ponteland
66 Darras Road, Ponteland

July 9 Sunday
49 Coronation Terrace, Ashington

July 12 Wednesday
Bridge House, Fox Covert Lane, Ponteland
66 Darras Road, Ponteland

July 16 Sunday
Cragside, Rothbury
Kirkwhelpington Village Gardens
Netherbyres, Eyemouth

July 19 Wednesday
Bridge House, Fox Covert Lane, Ponteland
66 Darras Road, Ponteland

July 20 Thursday
Herterton House, Morpeth

July 26 Wednesday
Bide-a-Wee Cottage, Netherwitton, Morpeth
Bridge House, Fox Covert Lane, Ponteland
66 Darras Road, Ponteland

July 30 Sunday
Kiwi Cottage, Scremerston

August 10 Thursday
Herterton House, Morpeth

September 10 Sunday
Belsay Hall, Castle & Gardens

DESCRIPTIONS OF GARDENS

¶Ashfield ✲❀ (B & R McWilliam) Hebron. S side of Hebron 3m N of Morpeth. Hebron is ½m E of the A1 on a minor rd C130 which is the 1st junction to the E, N of the Morpeth by-pass and A697 (Wooler) junction. The garden extends to 5 acres and is in course of development. The area close to the house has many bulbs, a collection of alpines, herbaceous and mixed borders. A woodland garden is being developed and collections of sorbus, acer and betula are planned. TEAS. *Adm £1 Chd free. Private visits welcome, please* **Tel 01670 515616**

Belsay Hall, Castle & Gardens ♿❀ (English Heritage) Ponteland. Belsay village lies 14m NW of Newcastle-upon-Tyne, on the A696 [OS map 88. Ref NZ 082785]. 30-acres newly restored C19 garden incl formal terraces; large heather garden; rhododendrons, rare trees & shrubs. Quarry garden covering several acres. Belsay Hall & Castle within the grounds. TEAS and refreshments. *Adm (incl Hall and Castle) £2.40 Concessions £1.80 Chd £1.20. Suns May 21, Sept 10 (10-6). Private parties welcome, please* **Tel 01661 881636**

Berryburn ✲❀ (Mr & Mrs W J Rogers-Coltman) Ancroft. 5m S of Berwick. Take Ancroft Mill Rd off A1 for 1m; drive entrance 2nd turn on R beside council bridge. 4 acres created from wilderness since 1981. Mixed borders; shrubs; shrub roses; woodland walk alongside burn with progressive tree planting. Partially suited for wheelchairs. TEA. *Adm £1.50 Chd free. Sun June 25 (2-5). Private visits welcome, please* **Tel 01289 87332**

Bide-a-Wee Cottage ✲❀ (M Robson) Netherwitton. 7m NNW of Morpeth. Turn L off A192 out of Morpeth at Fairmoor. Stanton is 6m along this road. Both a formal and informal garden developed out of a small stone quarry as well as some surrounding higher land. Natural rock is featured as are water and marsh areas. Garden contains mixed planting with a large number of perennial species. *Adm £1.50. Weds May 31, July 26 (1.30-5). Parties by appt, please* **Tel 01670 772262**

Bradley Gardens ❀ (Mr & Mrs J Hick) Sled Lane, Wylam. Along A695 between Crawcrook and Prudhoe. Approx ½m W from Crawcrook, R.A.C. signposted. A69 through Wylam, over bridge S of R Tyne, 3rd turning R, ¼m up lane. Signposted from Wylam. Approx 2 acres walled garden formerly kitchen garden to Bradley Hall. We specialise in herbs, both pot grown and fresh cut. Display beds of herbs, herbaceous border, childrens play area and greenhouse to view. Cottage garden plants and a selection of shrubs and bedding also available. Scented garden and shop. TEAS in aid of Church. *Adm £1.50 Chd free. Sun June 11 (9-5)*

Bridge House ♿✲❀ (Dr & Mrs J C White) Fox Covert Lane, Ponteland. 8m NW of Newcastle. Just off A696, last L turn before leaving Ponteland village (travelling W). ¼m down Fox Covert Lane. 1¼-acre garden, only 9 yrs old. Incl riverside planting, vegetable garden, herbs, mixed borders and summer meadow. Winner of 'Northumbria in Bloom' 1993 – Best Garden open to the public. TEAS. *Adm £1.50 Chd free. Weds July 5, 12, 19, 26 (2-5). Private visits welcome, please* **Tel 01661 23780**

Bughtrig ♿ (Major General & The Hon Mrs Charles Ramsay) Near Leitholm, Coldstream. Interesting Georgian house about 1790. New porch, roof balustrades and other features after 1875. Old roses, shrubs, herbaceous. Cars free. Small picnic area available. ¼m E of Leitholm on B6461. Produce stalls. Tea in house. *Adm £1.50 Chd 50p (Share to Leitholm Parish Church© and Christ Church, Duns©). Sun July 2 (2.30-5). Open daily June to Sept (11-5) or by appt, please* **Tel 01890 840678** *donation to Scotland's Gardens Scheme*

Chesters ✼❀ (Major & Mrs J E Benson) Humshaugh. 5m N of Hexham. ½m W of Chollerford on B6318. Curved terraced border in front of C18 house with 1891 wings designed by Norman Shaw. Herbaceous borders, rock garden, lawns overlooking ha-ha and parkland with fine views over the North Tyne. TEA. *Combined adm with* **Hexham Herbs, Chesters Walled Garden** *£1.50 Chd under 10 free. Sun June 18 (1-5)*

Chillingham Castle ✼ (Sir Humphry Wakefield) Chillingham. N from Alnwick, S from Berwick-upon-Tweed. Parkland landscaped with avenues and lodges by Sir Geoffrey de Wyattville fresh from his Royal triumph at Windsor in 1828. Lake and woodland walks with finest specimen trees in the region. Moats removed and gardens brought up to castle 1752. Italian and French topiary garden with largest herbaceous border in Northern England all restored with urns and fountains. TEAS. *Adm £3.30 OAPs/Chd £2.50. ▲For NGS Sun June 25 (1.30-5).* **Tel 01668 215359**

¶Chipchase Castle ♿✼❀ (Mrs P J Torday) Wark-on-Tyne. Situated on the E banks of the North Tyne, 10m N of Hexham, between Barrasford and Wark. It can be approached via A68, taking the exit to Hexham-Barrasford N of Corbridge or via A69 turning onto the A6079, then take minor rd to Barrasford. Approx 3 acres; incl a walled vegetable garden and orchard, woodland garden, pond and formal borders. The gardens are approached through a second walled garden which is dedicated to the sale of specialist herbaceous plants. *House open Adm £2. June only (2-5). Thurs, Fri, Sat, Sun April 1 to Oct 15 incl Bank Hol Mons (10-5). For NGS Adm £1.50 Chd 50p. Sat June 4 (10-5)*

¶49 Coronation Terrace ✼❀ (Mr Sean Murray) Ashington. From Ashington Town Centre, go straight down North Seaton Rd until you come to a small roundabout, turn L and then you come to the North Seaton Hotel, opp this is a small car park, which you are able to park in. Created since 1989 from scratch. Approx 100′ × 20′, contains a wide selection of hostas and perennials, filled with approx 200 plants. Winner of the Champion of Champions, Wonsbeck Council Gardening prize for the past 3 yrs. TEAS. *Adm £1.50 Chd 50p. Sun July 9 (2-5)*

Cragside ✼ (The National Trust) Rothbury, 13m SW of Alnwick (B6341); 15m NW of Morpeth (B6344). Open for the first time in 1992 Lord Armstrong's original formal garden, incl orchard house, fernery, terraces and rose loggia. Extensive grounds of over 1000 acres on S edge of Alnwick Moor; famous for magnificent trees; rhododendrons and beautiful lakes. House designed by Richard Norman Shaw, famous Victorian architect; built 1864-1895; contains much original furniture designed by Shaw; also pictures and experimental scientific apparatus (it was 1st house in the world to be lit by electricity generated by water power). Restaurant. Shop. Grounds, Power Circuit and Armstrong Energy Centre. TEAS. *Adm House, Garden & Grounds £5.50; Garden & Grounds £3.50 Chd half price. Family ticket House, Garden & Grounds (2 adults & 2 chd) £14. For NGS Sun July 16 (10.30-5.30). Large parties by appt, please,* **Tel 01670 774691**

¶66 Darras Road ✼ (Mr & Mrs D J Goodchild) Ponteland. SW of A696 at Ponteland. Turn L after crossing the R Pont. Travelling W, signposted Darras Hall. 1m on R. Medium-sized garden, owner designed and maintained, with herbaceous and shrub borders incl some unusual varieties. Conifers, kitchen garden, water garden and greenhouses. TEA. *Adm £1.50 Chd 50p. Weds July 5, 12, 19, 26 (2-5)*

Hartford Bridge House ✼❀ (Dr & Mrs F J B Taylor) Bedlington. On A1068/A192 where it crosses R Blyth, opposite Plessey Woods Country Park. 2m S of Bedlington. Parking as directed on the day. 1¼-acre garden sloping down to river with a large variety of trees and shrubs and a newly planted woodland walk; old-fashioned roses; herbaceous beds, rock garden and pond. TEAS. *Adm £1.50 Chd free. Sun July 2 (2-5)*

Herterton House ✼❀ (Frank Lawley Esq) Hartington. Cambo, Morpeth. 2m N of Cambo on the B6342 signposted to Hartington. (23m NW of Newcastle-on-Tyne). 1 acre of formal garden in stone walls around a C16 farmhouse. Incl a small topiary garden, physic garden, flower garden and a nursery garden. Planted since 1976. *Adm £1.40 Chd free. ▲For NGS Thurs June 22, July 20, Aug 10 (1.30-5.30)*

Hexham Herbs, Chesters Walled Garden ♿✼❀ Chollerford. 6m N of Hexham, just off the B6318. ½m W of Chollerford roundabout, past the entrance to Chesters Roman Fort, take L turning signposted Fourstones and immediately L through stone gateposts. 2-acre walled garden containing a very extensive collection of herbs. Raised thyme bank, home to the National Thyme Collection, Roman garden; National Collection of Marjoram. Elizabethan-style knot garden, gold and silver garden and collection of dye plants. Herbaceous borders contain many unusual plants and old-fashioned roses. Outside the walled garden is a newly-planted wildflower meadow and woodland walk. Hexham Herbs won a large gold medal at National Garden Festival, Gateshead 1990 and featured on BBC2's 'Gardener's World' and Channel 4's 'Over the Garden Wall'. Shop sells herbal gifts, honey and dried flowers. TEA. *Combined adm with* **Chesters** *£1.50 Chd under 10 free. Sun June 18 (1-5)*

The Hirsel ♿ (Lord Home of the Hirsel) Coldstream. Immediately W of Coldstream on A697. Snowdrops and aconites in Spring; daffodils in March/April; rhododendrons and azaleas in late May/early June, and magnificent autumn colouring. Walks round the lake, Dundock Wood and Leet valley. Marvellous old trees. Dogs on leads, please. Homstead Museum, Craft Centre and Workshops. Tearoom - under new management (parties please book). *Parking charge only. Open daily all year (reasonable daylight hours). Donation to Scotland's Gardens Scheme*

By Appointment Gardens. These owners do not have a fixed opening day usually because they do not like crowds or have insufficient parking space. Owner will often give guided tour.

Kirkley Hall College ♿✂❀ (Dr R McParlin) Ponteland. 2½m NW of Ponteland on C151 to Morpeth. Turn L at main college entrance. Turn R ¼m further on at the Horticultural centre signboard. Car park. These beautiful gardens and Victorian Walled Garden form a showcase for the gardening enthusiast. Inside the Walled Garden are climbers, salad potager garden, wall-trained fruit trees, borders and unusual and colourful herbaceous plants all grouped and labelled. Grounds contain skilfully shaped island beds following the contours of the land each composed for variety of profile and continuity of colour. The terrace garden with its outstanding array of beautifully planted containers leads down to the front lawn and then to a most attractive sunken garden planted with a wide range of dwarf conifers. TEAS. *Adm £1.50 OAPs 70p family £3 Chd under 8 free. Sat, Sun June 24, 25 (10-5). Private visits welcome, please* **Tel 01661 860808**

Kirkwhelpington Village Gardens ✂❀ On A696 approx 10m N of Belsay. Turn R into village. A number of small gardens in an attractive village. Each garden entirely different with something of interest for everyone. Teas in village hall. *Combined adm £1.50 Chd 50p tickets at village hall (Share to village hall fund®). Sun July 16 (2-5)*

Cliff House (Mr & Mrs I Elliot)
3 The Green (Mrs K Buchanan)
The School House (Mr & Mrs F Young)
Sike View (Prof & Mrs D Kinniment)
Welburn (Prof D Wise)
Whitridge House (Mr & Dr C Keating)

Kiwi Cottage ♿✂❀ (Col J I M Smail) Scremerston. Kiwi Cottage is in the village of Scremerston, about 2½m due S of Berwick-upon-Tweed. It is the 1st house on the R hand side of the village, off the A1 rd coming from the S and the last house on the L hand side of the village when travelling S from Berwick-upon-Tweed. Entrance through gateway next to War Memorial. Please drive in and do not park on the rd. 3-acre garden with lawns, annuals, herbaceous plants, providing colour and interest throughout the year. Shrubs, orchard and large vegetable garden TEA. *Adm £1.50 Chd 50p. Sun July 30 (2.30-5.30)*

Lilburn Tower ✂ (Mr & Mrs D Davidson) Alnwick. 3m S of Wooler on A697. 10 acres of walled and formal gardens including conservatory and large glass house. About 30 acres of woodland with walks and pond garden. Also ruins of Pele Tower and C15 Chapel. Rhododendrons and azaleas. TEA. *Adm £1.25 Chd 25p under 5 free. Sun May 21 (2-6)*

Loughbrow House ♿✂❀ (Mrs K A Clark) Hexham. Take B6306 from Hexham fork R, lodge gates in intersection of 2nd fork, ½m up drive. 5 acres; woodland garden; herbaceous borders, roses, wide lawns; kitchen garden. *Adm £1.50 Chd 50p. Private visits welcome, please* **Tel 01434 603351**

Meldon Park ♿✂ (M J B Cookson Esq) Morpeth. Situated 6m W of Morpeth on B6343. Victorian and Edwardian laid out garden, with walled kitchen garden, herbaceous borders, roses and woodland walk with azaleas and rhododendrons. TEAS. *Adm £2 Chd 50p. Sun June 4 (2-5)*

Mindrum ❀ (Hon P J Fairfax) Cornhill on Tweed. On B6352, 4m from Yetholm, 5m from Cornhill on Tweed. Old-fashioned roses; rock and water garden; shrub borders. Wonderful views along Bowmont Valley. Approx 2 acres. TEAS. *Adm £1.50 Chd 50p. Sun June 25 (2-6). Private visits welcome, please* **Tel 01890 85246**

Netherbyres ♿ (Col S J Furness & GRBS) Eyemouth. Eyemouth ¼m on A1107. Unique C18 century elliptical walled garden, with a new house built inside. Daffodils and wild flowers in the spring. Annuals, roses, herbaceous borders and coloured borders during the summer. Produce stall. Teas in house. *Adm £1.50 Chd 50p (Share to British Red Cross Society (Berwickshire branch)® April 16; Eyemouth Museum Trust® July 16). Suns April 16, July 16 (2-6)*

Northumbria Nurseries, Walled Gardens ♿❀ (Northumbria Nurseries) Ford. Follow the flower signs on the brown Ford Etal Heritage signs to Ford village, 10m N of Wooler, off A697. 1¾-acre walled garden incl display beds and growing areas. Teas available in village. *Open all year Mon to Fri (8-6, or dusk), March to Oct Sat, Sun (10-6, or dusk). Donations for NGS Sun July 2 (10-6)*

Preston Tower ♿✂❀ (Maj & Mrs T Baker Cresswell) Chathill. 7m N of Alnwick, take the turn to the R ¼m beyond Esso garage and Little Chef, signed to Preston and Chathill. Preston Tower is at the top of a hill, in 1¼m. Mostly shrubs and woodland; daffodils and azaleas. C14 Pele Tower with great views from the top. TEAS. *Adm £1.50 Chd 50p (Share to local church). Sun April 30 (2.30-5). Parties by appt, please* **Tel 016655 89210**

Wallington ♿ (The National Trust) Cambo. From N 12m W of Morpeth (B6343); from S via A696 from Newcastle, 6m W of Belsay, B6342 to Cambo. Walled, terraced garden with fine shrubs and species roses; conservatory with magnificent fuchsias; 100 acres woodland and lakes. House dates from 1688 but altered and interior greatly changed c.1740; exceptional rococo plasterwork by Francini brothers; fine porcelain, furniture, pictures, needlework, dolls' houses, museum, display of coaches. Restaurant. Shop. *Adm to House and Garden £4.60; Walled garden, garden and grounds £2.30 Chd half price. Last admission (5). For NGS Sun May 14 (10.30-7)*

Nottinghamshire

Hon County Organisers: Mr & Mrs A R Hill, The White House, Nicker Hill, Keyworth, Nottinghamshire NG12 5EA Tel 0115 9372049

Assistant Hon County Organisers: Mr & Mrs J Nicholson, 38 Green Lane, Lambley, Nottingham NG4 4QE Tel 0115 9312998

Hon County Treasurer: Mr J Gray, 43 Cliffway, Radcliffe-on-Trent, Nottinghamshire NG12 1AQ Tel 0115 9334272

DATES OF OPENING

By appointment
For telephone number and other details see garden descriptions.

17 Bridle Road, Burton Joyce Gardens
Field House Nursing Home, Radcliffe-on-Trent
38 Green Lane, Lambley
Gringley Hall, Gringley on the Hill Gardens
Holmes Villa, Walkeringham
37 Loughborough Road, Ruddington
Mill Hill House, East Stoke
Oakland House, Oxton Road, Southwell
Springwell House, Brinkley
14 Temple Drive, Nuthall
Willowholme Herb Farm, Upton & Headon Gardens
The White House, Keyworth

Parties only
Felley Priory, Underwood
Hazel Cottage, Treswell, nr Retford
Morton Hall, Ranby
The Willows, Radcliffe-on-Trent

Regular openings
For details see garden descriptions

Felley Priory, Underwood. For dates see text
Hodsock Priory, Blyth. For dates see text
Holme Pierrepont Hall, Holme Pierrepont. For dates see text

April 5 Wednesday
The Willows, Radcliffe-on-Trent

April 9 Sunday
Morton Hall, Ranby
Skreton Cottage, Screveton
Southwell, Bishops Manor

April 12 Wednesday
Hazel Cottage, Treswell, nr Retford
Springwell House, Brinkley

April 17 Monday
Holme Pierrepont Hall, Holme Pierrepont

April 23 Sunday
Felley Priory, Underwood
37 Loughborough Road, Ruddington

April 27 Thursday
Field House Nursing Home, Radcliffe-on-Trent

April 30 Sunday
Hodsock Priory, Blyth

May 3 Wednesday
The Willows, Radcliffe-on-Trent

May 7 Sunday
Gringley on the Hill Gardens
Mill Hill House, East Stoke
Morton Hall, Ranby
St Helen's Croft, Halam
14 Temple Drive, Nuthall

May 8 Monday
The White House, Keyworth

May 10 Wednesday
Hazel Cottage, Treswell, nr Retford
Oakland House, Oxton Road, Southwell

May 13 Saturday
7 Barratt Lane, Attenborough

May 14 Sunday
7 Barratt Lane, Attenborough
Holme Pierrepont Hall, Holme Pierrepont
Morton Hall, Ranby

May 17 Wednesday
38 Green Lane, Lambley

May 21 Sunday
Bracken House, Caythorpe ‡
Gringley on the Hill Gardens
144 Lambley Lane, Burton Joyce ‡
Springwell House, Brinkley

May 24 Wednesday
Rose Cottage, 82 Main Road, Underwood

May 27 Saturday
Epperstone Gardens, Epperstone

May 28 Sunday
Epperstone Gardens, Epperstone
Mill Hill House, East Stoke
Papplewick Gardens, Papplewick

June 4 Sunday
Cream Cottage, Misterton ‡
Holmes Villa, Walkeringham ‡
Park Farm, Normanton
Woodborough Manor, Woodborough

June 5 Monday
The White House, Keyworth

June 8 Thursday
7 Barratt Lane, Attenborough

June 11 Sunday
7 Barratt Lane, Attenborough
Mill Hill House, East Stoke
Rose Cottage, 82 Main Road, Underwood
Skreton Cottage, Screveton

June 12 Monday
7 Barratt Lane, Attenborough
The White House, Keyworth

June 14 Wednesday
38 Green Lane, Lambley

June 18 Sunday
Field House Nursing Home, Radcliffe-on-Trent
Gardeners Cottage, Papplewick
1 Hilltop Cottage, Thurgarton
Hodsock Priory, Blyth
14 Temple Drive, Nuthall

June 19 Monday
The White House, Keyworth

June 21 Wednesday
Gardeners Cottage, Papplewick
Oakland House, Oxton Road, Southwell

June 24 Saturday
Plungar Gardens in the Vale of Belvoir, see Leics

June 25 Sunday
Felley Priory, Underwood
Flintham Hall, Flintham, nr Newark
37 Loughborough Road, Ruddington
The Old Vicarage, Granby
Plungar Gardens in the Vale of Belvoir, see Leics
Sutton Bonington Hall, Sutton Bonington

June 26 Monday
The White House, Keyworth

June 28 Wednesday
Hazel Cottage, Treswell, nr Retford

July 2 Sunday
12 Dunster Road, West Bridgford

Hickling Gardens
Thrumpton Hall, Nottingham
Upton and Headon Gardens

July 5 Wednesday
The Willows, Radcliffe-on-Trent

July 9 Sunday
Burton Joyce Gardens
Greenways, Bathley
Holme Pierrepont Hall, Holme Pierrepont
Rose Cottage, 82 Main Road, Underwood

July 16 Sunday
Brackenhurst College, Southwell
Mill Hill House, East Stoke
The Old Rectory, Kirkby in Ashfield

July 23 Sunday
The White House, Keyworth

August 2 Wednesday
Mill Hill House, East Stoke

August 13 Sunday
1 Hilltop Cottage, Thurgarton
Rose Cottage, 82 Main Road, Underwood

September 6 Wednesday
The Willows, Radcliffe-on-Trent

September 10 Sunday
Mill Hill House, East Stoke
Rose Cottage, 82 Main Road, Underwood
St Helen's Croft, Halam

October 4 Wednesday
Hazel Cottage, Treswell, nr Retford

October 15 Sunday
Morton Hall, Ranby
Springwell House, Brinkley

October 22 Sunday
St Helen's Croft, Halam

DESCRIPTIONS OF GARDENS

7 Barratt Lane ♿❀ (Mrs D Lucking & Mr & Mrs S J Hodkinson) Attenborough. Beeston, 6m SW of Nottingham. Off A6005 nr Attenborough Station. ¾-acre established plantsman's garden featured in 'Garden Answers' 1992 & 1993. Mature trees, unusual flowering shrubs, bulbs, hostas and bearded irises. *Adm £1 Chd 40p (Share to 2nd Attenborough Scout Group®). Sat, Sun May 13, 14 (11-1 & 2-6) Thurs June 8, (3-8) Sun June 11 (11-1 & 2-6) Mon June 12 (3-8)*

¶Bracken House ♿✂ (Mr & Mrs A Wheelhouse) Caythorpe. Approx 9m NE Nottingham. A612 to Lowdham at Magna Carta Inn. Follow signs Caythorpe, immed over level-Xing turn L Caythorpe Rd. Through village 1½m past Black Horse Inn, Brackenhill Lane on L. Park at bottom on main rd. Last house up Brackenhill. Approx ¼-acre garden. Re-designed 1991. Colourful densely planted mixed borders and rockeries with shrubs and bulbs, small pond. Picturesque views over open countryside and Trent valley. TEA in aid of St Aidens Church, Caythorpe. *Adm £1 Chd free. Sun May 21 (2-5.30)*

Brackenhurst College ♿❀ (The Secretary) Southwell. Brackenhurst 1m S of Southwell on A612. Ornamental shrubs, lawns, rose, sunken, and walled gardens, glasshouses, views. Organic vegetable plot. Wheelchair users please notify in advance. Careers information. TEAS. *Adm £1.50 Chd 50p. Sun July 16 (2-6)*

Burton Joyce Gardens Situated about 6m NE of Nottingham off A612 to Southwell. In Burton Joyce turn L onto Main St at 1st Xrds. L again within 100yds onto Lambley Lane. Bridle Rd is ½m on R and is an impassable-looking rd. *Combined adm £1.80 Chd 60p (Share to St Helen's Church, Burton Joyce®). Sun July 9 (2-6)*

17 Bridle Road ✂❀ (Mr & Mrs C P Bates) Burton Joyce, Nottingham. 1-acre mixed borders, woodland slopes, stream and water garden with naturalised ferns, primulas, hostas and moisture loving plants. Terrace and orchard with spring and summer bulbs in grass. TEAS. *Also private visits welcome at weekends, please* **Tel 0115 9313725**

61 Lambley Lane ❀ (Mr & Mrs R B Powell) Approx ⅔-acre of spring flowering plants; shrubs; azaleas; bulbs and trees; mixed borders

¶Cream Cottage ✂❀ (Susan & Philip Cross) Misterton. Approx 7m NW Gainsborough. Follow the A161 to Goole, continue through Misterton, Cream Cottage on R, approx ⅕m after church. Walled cottage garden. Cottage dates from early C18. Re-designed and planted 1992 by present owners. Contains many traditional and some unusual cottage garden plants in mixed borders incl selection of hardy geraniums and species clematis. Herb bed, evergreen border, wildlife pond and formal fish pond. TEAS. *Adm £1 Chd free. Sun June 4 (2-6)*

¶12 Dunster Road ✂❀ (Mr & Mrs M Jones) West Bridgford. Approx 2m S of Nottingham. From Trent Bridge follow A606 Melton Rd. Approx 1m turn L into Burleigh Rd, 400yds turn 4th R into Dunster Rd. 90′ × 30′ garden developed from overgrown plot since 1989. Mixed borders with many varied trees, shrubs and perennials especially penstemons, pinks, rhododendrons, alpines and climbers. Small woodland bed, patio and summerhouse, numerous containers. *Adm £1 Chd 25p (Share to Alzheimer's Disease Society®). Sun July 2 (2-5)*

Epperstone Gardens 8m NE Nottingham off A6097 between Lowdham and Oxton. Parking opp Cross Keys. TEAS. *Combined adm £1.50 Chd free (Share to Epperstone Village Hall Fund©). Sat, Sun May 27, 28 (2-6)*

Field House ✂ (Mr & Mrs G H Gisborne) ⅓-acre attractively laid out garden incl foliage, alpines, bulbs, water; lovely view of surrounding countryside

Hazelwych (Mr & Mrs P J Clark) ½-acre, trees, shrubbery, pond and alpine terrace

¶The Old Rectory (Mr & Mrs Cedric Coates) Enter from churchyard. Approx 2 acres mature garden in superb setting incl lawns, borders, spring bulbs, mature yews forming 'The Dark Walk'. Lovely sculptured large box hedge

Felley Priory ♿❀ (The Hon Mrs Chaworth Musters) Underwood. 8m SW Mansfield, leave M1 junction 27, take A608, entrance is ½m W of M1. Old-fashioned garden round Elizabethan house. Orchard of daffodils, herbaceous borders, pond. Topiary, rose garden, featured in Good Garden Guide; unusual plants for sale. TEAS. *Adm £1.50 Chd free. Weds Feb 8, 22, March 8, 22, April 12, 26 May 10, 24, June 14, 28, July 12, 26, Aug 9, 23, Sept 13, 27, Oct 11, 25 (9-4). For NGS Suns April 23, June 25 (11-4). Private visits welcome for parties of 15 min, please* **Tel 01773 810230**

Field House Nursing Home ♿✿❀ (Mr & Mrs C Pring) 11 Main Road, Radcliffe-on-Trent. 6m E Nottingham. Follow A52 and turn N into Radcliffe-on-Trent. Opp Co-op supermarket, turn into Radcliffe Health Centre car park. Nursing Home adjoins car park. 1-acre garden with many specimen conifers and rare shrubs. Large conservatory, colourful bedding schemes; thatched cottage reconstructed from old materials in 1987 within grounds; and set in a typical cottage garden. Cream TEAS. *Adm £1 Chd 25p (Share to Residents' Comfort Fund©). Thurs April 27, Sun June 18 (2.30-6). Private visits welcome, please* **Tel 0115 9335811**

Flintham Hall ❀ (Myles Thoroton Hildyard Esq) 6m SW of Newark on A46. Fine trees, park and lake, wilderness, aviary, unique conservatory, herbaceous borders, woodland walk. Featured 'Country Life' Sept 89. Picnics allowed. TEAS. *Adm £1.50 Chd 50p (Share to St Augustines Church, Flintham PCC®). Sun June 25 (2-5)*

Gardeners Cottage ♿✿❀ (Mr & Mrs J Hildyard) Papplewick; nr Papplewick Hall. 6m N of Nottingham off A60. Interesting old-fashioned garden of 1½ acres with 150yd long border, shrub and rhododendrons; shrub rose garden. Large rockery and water feature; scree beds. Many unusual plants for sale. TEAS. *Adm £1.50 Chd 50p (Share to St. James Church Window Fund®). Sun, Wed June 18, 21 (2-6)*

The Gardens of Plungar – see Leicestershire & Rutland

38 Green Lane ✿❀ (Mr & Mrs J E Nicholson) Lambley. 6m N of Nottingham. Take B684 Woodborough Rd turn R to Lambley. Main St turn L into Church St, R into Green Lane. Small cottage garden densely planted, spring bulbs, herbaceous beds, shrub roses, varied climbers, secret corners and surprises. Separate formal vegetable garden. Beautiful views across open countryside. TEA. *Adm £1.20 Chd free. Weds May 17, June 14 (1-5). Private group visits welcome, please* **Tel 0115 9312998**

Greenways ♿✿❀ (Mr & Mrs D Smith) Bathley. 1m A1. B6325 North Newark. 1½-acre, mixed trees; shrubs; enclosed rose garden; formal beds; orchard and vegetables. Newly planted pergola; alpine troughs; newly completed tennis court. TEAS. *Adm £1.50 Chd free (Share to Arthritis Care, Newark Branch®). Sun July 9 (2-6)*

Gringley On The Hill Gardens 6m E of Bawtry, 5m W of Gainsborough on A631. TEAS in aid of Gringley Church. *Combined adm £2 Chd 50p. Suns May 7, 21 (2-6)*

Gringley Hall ♿✿❀ (Mr & Mrs I Threlfall) 2-acre English country garden with several mixed borders with different colour themes; old roses; water garden and a newly created potager. *Private visits welcome Weds and Suns, please* **Tel 01777 817262**

Honeysuckle Cottage ✿❀ (Miss J E Towler) Approx ¼-acre traditional small terraced cottage garden with rose bed and mixed borders. Interesting loose laid chevron brick wall; paths of river boulders and brick

Hazel Cottage ♿✿❀ (Mr & Mrs M J Rush) Treswell. Treswell is approx 6m E of Retford; 4½m NW of A57 at Dunham-on-Trent. Parking in village st. ½-acre packed plantsman's garden containing many unusual trees, shrubs and herbaceous plants; spring bulbs, collection of old roses, clematis and climbing plants on pergolas; small pond and gravelled areas to give pleasure in every season. Featured on Yorkshire TV 'Great Little Gardens' 1993. Paintings by garden owners for sale in small gallery. TEA. *Adm £1 Chd free. Weds April 12, May 10, June 28, Oct 4 (1-5.30). Private group visits welcome, please* **Tel 01777 248089**

¶Hickling Gardens ♿ 10m SE of Nottingham. From junction of A46 and A606 head for Melton Mowbray. At Hickling Pastures turn L Hickling (2m). In village turn R for Elm House, L for The Old Rectory. Art Exhibition in church. TEAS in aid of Village Hall. *Combined adm £1.50 Chd free. Sun July 2 (2-6)*

¶Elm House ❀ (Mr & Mrs D Chambers) Main St. A developing 2-acre garden created from a field 4yrs ago and maintained entirely by owners. Knot garden, mixed borders, pond, island beds, vegetables, many varieties of magnolias

¶The Old Rectory (Commander & Mrs K Cadogan-Rawlinson) 1-acre developing old-fashioned style country garden round lovely mellow old building. Features herbaceous borders and in keeping with atmosphere, old-fashioned roses incl ramblers and climbers, fruit arch and newly cleared puddled pond

1 Hilltop Cottage ✿❀ (Zoe Richmond & Gary Dixon) Thurgarton. Situated approx 3m S of Southwell on the main A612 Nottingham-Southwell Rd. Long narrow cottage-style garden designed and developed since 1990. Mixed herbaceous borders, many unusual plants, container garden area, rose arch and walk way through different garden 'rooms'. TEA & plant sales in aid of Dr Hadwen Trust. *Adm £1 Chd free. Suns June 18, Aug 13 (2-6)*

Hodsock Priory ♿✿❀ (Sir Andrew & Lady Buchanan) Blyth. Off B6045, Blyth-Worksop rd approx 2m from A1. 5 acres bounded by dry moat. Grade 1 listed gatehouse circa 1500. Victorian mansion (not open). Mature cornus, indian bean, tulip tree, swamp cypress; small lake; bog garden; snowdrops and spring bulbs; mixed borders; roses old and new. Established beech and holly hedges; featured in 'Shell Garden Guide', 'Country Life, 'Good Garden Guide' (starred) and other magazines. TEAS. *Adm £2 Wheelchairs/Acc chd under 16 free. Daily Feb 1 to March 1 (weekends 10-4) (weekdays 1-4) Suns, Tues, Weds, Thurs April 1 to July 30 (2-5). For NGS Sun April 30, June 18 (2-5)*

By Appointment Gardens. These owners do not have a fixed opening day usually because they do not like crowds or have insufficient parking space. Owner will often give guided tour.

Regular Openers. Too many days to include in diary. Usually there is a wide range of plants giving year-round interest. See head of county section for the name and garden description for times etc.

Holme Pierrepont Hall ♿✂❀ (Mr & Mrs Robin Brackenbury) Follow the signs from the A52 Nottingham-Grantham rd to the National Water Sports centre and continue for 1½m. The courtyard garden enclosed on 3 sides by the house with the church on the 4th side is a formal, listed garden laid out in 1875 with lawns, flower beds and elaborate box parterre probably influenced by Nesfield. In this 'Secret Garden' repeat flowering shrub roses, herbs and herbaceous plants have replaced Victorian hybrid tea roses and annuals, showing how contemporary planting fits into an earlier authentic framework. There is a second garden to the E of the house, clipped yews and shrubs with a long June border of old-fashioned roses. The parkland is grazed by Jacob sheep. TEAS. *Adm £1.50 Chd 50p. Every Sun June; Thurs, Suns July; Tues, Thurs, Fris, Sun Aug (2-6); Sat, Sun June 24, 25 (all day). For NGS Mon April 17, Suns May 14, July 9 (2-6)*

Holmes Villa ♿✂❀ (Sheila & Peter Clark) Holmes Lane, Walkeringham; NE Retford and within 4m Gainsborough. Take A620 from Retford or A631 from Bawtry/Gainsborough and A161 to Walkeringham and then towards Misterton. Turn at sign R. Trent and follow signs for last mile. Interesting plantsman's and flower arranger's garden created and maintained by owners incl collections of ivies, alliums and many unusual herbaceous plants; new wild life pond and rhododendron bank. TEAS in aid of Notts Wildlife Trust. Specialist plant and craft stalls. *Adm £1 Chd free. Sun June 4 (1.30-5.30). Also private visits welcome, please* **Tel 01427 890233**

144 Lambley Lane ❀ (Mr & Mrs B P Collyer) Burton Joyce. In Burton Joyce turn N off A612 Nottingham to Southwell Rd, up Lambley Lane to top. Sloping ½-acre garden with mature trees, spring flowering shrubs, conifers, rockeries, troughs, containers and wild garden. TEA. *Adm £1 Chd free (Share to St Helens Church Centre®). Sun May 21 (2-6)*

37 Loughborough Road ✂ (Mr & Mrs B H C Theobald) Ruddington. 4m S of Nottingham. From Nottingham take A60 Loughborough Rd, cross A52 ring road at Nottingham Knight. Take 1st L 400 yds beyond roundabout and immed L again up old Loughborough Rd. 1-acre garden with broad lawns and long borders, extensively developed in last 7 yrs. Shady walk with ferns, hostas etc, island beds, specimen trees and walled patio garden. Planting based on mixture of bulbs, perennials, shrubs and small trees. *Adm £1 Chd free. Suns April 23, June 25 (2-5.30). Also private visits welcome, please* **Tel 0115 984 1152**

Mill Hill House ❀ (Mr & Mrs R J Gregory) Elston Lane, East Stoke. 5m S of Newark on A46 turn E to Elston. Garden ½m on R. Entrance through nursery car park. ½-acre plantsman's garden for all seasons, wide selection of unusual hardy plants; mixed borders, alpines, shade plants. Teas in Newark. *Adm £1 (Share to NCCPG®). Suns, May 7, 28; June 11; July 16; Sept 10; Wed Aug 2 (2-6). Also private visits welcome, please* **Tel 01636 525460**

Morton Hall ❀ (Lady Mason) Ranby, 4m W of Retford. Entrance on Link Rd from A620 to S bound A1. Medium-sized woodland garden, flowering shrubs, rhododendrons, azaleas, specimen trees; pinetum in park, cedars and cypresses. Bulbs, autumn colour. Picnics. Partly suitable for wheelchairs. TEAS in aid of Ranby Church. *Adm £2 per car or £1.25p per person whichever is the least. Open May 21. For NGS Suns April 9, May 7, 14, (2-6), Oct 15 (2-5). Also groups by appt, please* **Tel 01777 701142**

Oakland House ✂❀ (Dr & Mrs D Skelton) Southwell. 12m NE Nottingham, 12m E Newark. From Southwell E on B6386 to Oxton. 3m on from Southwell on the R. 2½-acre garden created from paddock since 1986 incl large water feature and bog plants, ornamental garden for all yr round interest; alpine and cottage gardens together with extensive fruit and vegetable areas mainly organically managed, many unusual plants, trees and shrubs. *Adm £1.20 Chd free. Weds May 10 (2-5), June 21 (2-5 & 6-9). Also private visits welcome, please* **Tel 0115 9652030**

The Old Rectory ✂❀ (Mr & Mrs M F Brown) Kirkby in Ashfield. Adjacent to St Wilfrids Church on B6018, 1½m W of Kirkby town centre. Ample parking. 2½-acre garden restored and developed. Maturing nicely. Much to see; many features. Several gardens in one. Quality plants and TEAS in aid of St Wilfrid's Church. *Adm £1.50 Chd free. Sun July 16 (2-6)*

¶The Old Vicarage ✂❀ (Dr & Mrs M A Hutson) Granby. 14m E of Nottingham (on A52 Nottingham-Grantham) turn S 1m E of Bingham signposted Granby 2½m. At Xrds in centre of village (church on corner) turn L into Sutton Lane, Old Vicarage on L. Large country garden with old-fashioned and English roses, herbaceous borders, conservatory, large pond. Courtyard garden with raised pond. *Adm £1.50 Chd free. Sun June 25 (1.30-5.30)*

Papplewick Gardens North end of Papplewick Village on B683, 7m N of Nottingham off the A60. Parking at Hall only. *Combined adm £2 Chd free (Share to St James Church, Papplewick®). Sun May 28 (2-6)*

Altham Lodge ♿ (C G Hill Esq) Lovely garden of rhododendrons; azaleas and spring flowers

Papplewick Hall ♿✂ (Dr & Mrs R B Godwin-Austen) Woodland garden of approx 8 acres underplanted with rhododendrons; spring bulbs and hostas

Park Farm ♿✂ (Mr & Mrs John E Rose) Normanton, Bottesford. Park Farm is half way between Bottesford and Long Bennington on A1 side of Normanton village and sited on the old Normanton Airfield. 2½-acre garden, developed since 1987 comprising formal and mixed borders; natural and formal ponds; scree gardens and small woodland area. Mature trees moved by JCB to flat open field prior to the creation of this garden. Large scented, colour co-ordinated herb garden, now complete. *Adm £1.50 Chd free. Sun June 4 (2-6)*

Rose Cottage ✂❀ (Mr & Mrs Allan Lowe) 82 Main Rd, Underwood. 1½m from junction 27 M1. Take B608 to Heanor. Join B600; after about 200-300yds turn R into Main Rd by large sign for 'the Hole in the Wall' Inn.

Flower arrangers' cottage garden with ponds; shrubs; small secret garden. Rear garden of approx 1,000 sq yds with surprise features, partly developed from a field very recently; goat and other animals. Bed of show spray chrysanthemums; greenhouses. TEAS. *Adm £1.20 Chd free. Wed May 24, Suns June 11, July 9, Aug 13, Sept 10 (2-6)*

St Helen's Croft ♿✂❀ (Mrs E Ninnis) Halam. A614 Nottingham-Doncaster, turn off at White Post roundabout to Southwell and Halam. ½m beyond Halam Village, towards Edingley. 3m W of the lovely Southwell Minster worth a visit in its own right. 9 acres in all. A tranquil plantsman's country garden beside an English meadow; cowslips, wild fritillaries and violets grow; primroses abound in copses planted with trees for superb autumn colour and berries. Mown roadway within meadow for disabled sticker cars. Teas in Southwell. *Adm £1.20 Chd free. For NGS Suns May 7, Sept 10, Oct 22 (2-5)*

Skreton Cottage ♿❀ (Mr & Mrs J S Taylor) Screveton, 8m SW of Newark, 12m E of Nottingham. From A46 Fosse Rd turn E to Car Colston; L at green and on for 1m. 1¾-acre mature garden, created during the last 30yrs to be a 'garden for all seasons' with separate areas of different character. Fine display of spring bulbs followed by old and English roses and a wide variety of trees, shrubs and herbaceous plants; spacious lawns, pool, orchard, kitchen garden, greenhouses and many interesting design features. Set in delightful unspoilt village. TEAS and plants in aid of St Wilfrid's Church, Screveton. *Adm £1 Chd free. Suns April 9, June 11 (2-6)*

Southwell, Bishops Manor ♿ (The Rt Rev the Lord Bishop of Southwell & Mrs Harris) End of Bishops Drive on S side of Minster. Turn R for free parking on recreation ground. The house is built into a part of the old medieval Palace of the Archbishops of York. The ruins form a delightful enclosed garden, lawns, 4 seasons tree garden, orchard and vegetable garden. Rockery, spring flowers and attractive borders in an unusual setting. TEAS (Share to Mirasol Charitable Trust). *Adm £1.50 Chd free. Sun April 9 (2-5)*

Springwell House ✂❀ (Mrs Celia Steven) Brinkley. In Southwell turn off A612 by The White Lion towards Fiskerton. Springwell House ¾m on RH-side. Approx 2 acres, many unusual trees and shrubs; perennials in informal beds. Lovely country setting. Part of garden incl pond and waterfall redeveloped by disabled students from Portland Training College. Collection of daffodils featuring local names supplied by world famous specialist. Autumn foliage colour; selection of plants; climbers and trees available from adjoining nursery. *Adm £1 Chd 25p. Wed April 12, Suns May 21, Oct 15 (2-5). Private visits welcome, please* **Tel 01636 814501**

Sutton Bonington Hall ♿❀ (Anne, Lady Elton) 5m NW of Loughborough, take A6 to Kegworth, turn R (E) onto A6006. 1st L (N) for Sutton Bonington into Main St. Conservatory, formal white garden, variegated leaf borders. Queen Anne house (not open). Plant stall consisting shrubby, herbaceous and some alpine plants. Picnics. TEA. *Adm £1.20 Chd 25p (Share to St Michael's & St Ann's Church, Sutton Bonington®). Sun June 25 (12-5.30). Also open for Leicestershire*

14 Temple Drive ♿✂❀ (Mr & Mrs T Leafe) Nuthall. 4m N W of Nottingham. From M1 leave at junction 26 and take A610 towards Nottingham. Circle 1st roundabout in A6002 lane and leave on minor rd marked 'Cedarlands and Horsendale'. From Nottingham take A610, turning off at the Broxtowe Inn, Cinderhill. Parking restricted, use Nottingham rd. ⅓-acre garden with herbaceous borders; informal island beds, ornamental trees and shrubs; troughs; old-fashioned roses; clematis. Mostly labelled. Colour all seasons of year. Fruit and vegetable garden. TEAS and cake stall. *Adm £1.20 Chd 50p (Share to Cats Protection League®). Suns May 7, June 18 (2-5.30). Also private visits by appt, please* **Tel 0115 9271118**

Thrumpton Hall ♿❀ (The Hon Mrs Rosemary Seymour) 8m SW of Nottingham. W of A453; 3m from M1 at Exit 24. Large lawns; massive yew hedges; rare shrubs; C17 larches, cedars, planted to commemorate historic events since George III. Lake. Early Jacobean house shown. NO DOGS in house. TEA. *Adm to Garden £1 Chd 50p; House £2 extra Chd £1 (Share to The Tradescant Trust, London®). Sun July 2 (2.30-6)*

Upton and Headon Gardens ❀ South Retford on A638 and turn L to Grove, or in Eaton village, turn L to Upton. TEAS at Willowholme Herb Farm. *Combined adm £1.50 Chd free. Sun July 2 (2-6)*

Headon

- **Greenspotts** ♿ (Mr & Mrs Dolby) A well designed and colourful garden with rose covered pergolas, clematis, hostas and conifers, old-fashioned roses
- **The Holmestead** ♿ (Mr & Mrs Brailsford) Small cottage garden, lovingly tended. 2-acre wild flower meadow walk

Upton

- **Manor House** ♿ (Mr & Mrs Walker) Cottage garden with mixed borders, old orchard and vegetables. Plants in aid of Headon Church
- **Willowholme Herb Farm** (Mr & Mrs Farr) Cottage garden, with established herb garden containing culinary, aromatic and medicinal herbs. *Private visits welcome, please,* **Tel 01777 248053**

The White House ✂❀ (Mr & Mrs A R Hill) Nicker Hill, Keyworth. Approx 8m SE Nottingham. From A606 at Stanton-on-the-Wolds, by Shell Garage, turn into Browns Lane. Follow Keyworth signs into Stanton Lane, and continue into Nicker Hill. Great diversity of very unusual plants (many available on stall) of interest to the plantsman, grown in informal mixed beds in this ¾-acre garden, esp. euphorbia, primula, penstemon, grasses, geranium, tender perennials. Designed and developed by owners since 1987 incl brick pergola with climbers, extensive water and bog garden, newly developing raised area for choice woodlanders. Many interesting plants in pots. Featured on video 2. *Adm £1.20 Chd free. Bank Hol Mon May 8, Sun July 23 (2-5.30). Also private visits welcome, March (esp primulas, hellebores) to Sept (esp asters) incl, please* **Tel 0115 9372049**. *Also owner guided tours (strictly pre-phone booked to limit nos.) Mons June 5, 12, 19, 26 - 7pm prompt start £2.30 incl coffee and home-made cake*

The Willows ✿❀ (Mr & Mrs R A Grout) 5 Rockley Ave, Radcliffe-on-Trent. 6m E of Nottingham; Radcliffe-on-Trent is N of A52; from High St PO turn into Shelford Rd; over railway bridge, 300yds opp green seat turn L into Cliff Way, then 2nd R. Restricted parking. Designed 1982 62yds × 12yds garden; a quart in a pint plot; featured 'Gardeners World' TV 1986 and Yorks TV 'Great Little Gardens' 1992. Many rare and unusual plants; collections of hostas, hellebores, pulmonarias, paeonies, clematis, snowdrops. Holders of National Collection of Crocus Chrysanthus Cultivars. Colour planned island beds throughout the year. Coaches strictly by appt **Tel 0115 9333621.** TEAS. *Adm £1 Chd free (Share to NCCPG®). Weds April 5, May 3, July 5, Sept 6 (2-5.30)*

Woodborough Manor ♿❀ (Mr & Mrs C R Hanson) Woodborough. 7m NE of Nottingham. Turn R off the B684 down Bank Hill, turn R at bottom. Approx 1.6 acres. A woodland frontage features mature trees incl giant wellingtonias, azaleas, rhododendrons, hostas, herbaceous borders, large kitchen garden. *Adm £1.50 Chd free (Share to Happy Start Blind Baby Unit®). Sun June 4 (2-6)*

Oxfordshire

Hon County Organisers:	Col & Mrs J C M Baker, Hartford Greys, Sandy Lane, Boars Hill Oxford, OX1 5HN Tel 01865 739360
Hon County Treasurer:	Col J C M Baker
Assistant Hon County Organisers:	
Vale of the White Horse (Abingdon, Wantage & Faringdon areas)	Mrs D J Faulkner, Haugh House, Longworth, Abingdon, Oxon OX13 5DX Tel 01865 820286
N Oxon (Chipping Norton & Banbury areas)	Mr & Mrs B A Murphy, Hundley Cottage, Hundley Way, Charlbury OX7 3QU Tel 01608 810549
S Oxon (Henley, Wallingford & Thame areas)	Mrs J Kimberley, Baracca, Sheep Street, Burford, Oxon OX18 4LT Tel 01993 822256
	Mr & Mrs R J Baldwin, Northfield Cottage, High Street, Long Wittenham, Oxon OX14 4QJ Tel 01865 407258
E Oxon (Oxford & Bicester areas)	Mrs M Curtis, Bradwell, Blackditch, Stanton Harcourt, Witney OX8 1SB Tel 01865 881957
W Oxon (Bampton, Burford & Steeple Aston areas)	Mrs H H Atkinson, Ampney Lodge, High Street, Bampton OX18 2JN Tel 01993 850120

DATES OF OPENING

By appointment

For telephone numbers and other details see garden descriptions. Private visits welcomed

23 Beech Croft Road, Summertown, Oxford
Broadwell House, nr Lechlade ‡
Brook Cottage, Alkerton, nr Banbury
Buckland, nr Faringdon
Carinya, Goring Road, Woodcote
Clematis Corner, Shillingford
Clock House, Coleshill
Epwell Mill, nr Banbury
Faringdon House, Faringdon
Friars Court, Clanfield
Greystone Cottage, Kingwood Common, nr Henley
Hearns House, Gallows Tree Common
Heron's Reach, Whitchurch, nr Pangbourne
Holywell Manor, Oxford
Home Close, Garsington
Home Farm, Balscote Gardens, nr Banbury
Home Farm House, Steeple & Middle Aston Gardens
Kingston Lisle Park, nr Wantage
14 Lavender Place, Carterton ‡
Little Place, Clifton Hampden
Magdalen College, Oxford
Mount Skippet, Ramsden ‡
New College, Oxford
4 Northfield Cottages, Water Eaton, Oxford
Nutford Lodge, nr Faringdon
The Old Rectory, Albury
The Old Rectory, Salford Gardens, nr Chipping Norton
Rewley House, Oxford
Rofford Manor, Little Milton
Seven Bells Cottage, Garsington
Shucklets, Ramsden ‡
Stansfield, Stanford-in-the-Vale
Sunnyside, Hornton Gardens, nr Banbury
Templeton College, Kennington, Oxford
Town Farm Cottage, Kingston Blount
Wilcote House, nr Finstock ‡
Yeomans, Tadmarton

Parties Only

Clifton Hampden Manor
Dundon House, Minster Lovell
Greys Court, nr Henley
Hethersett, Benson Gardens
Manor Farm, Old Minster Lovell
The Mill House, Sutton Courtenay
40 Osler Road, Headington Gardens, Oxford
Pusey House, Pusey
St. Hilda's College, Oxford
Swyncombe House, nr Nettlebed
Wardington Manor, Wardington Gardens

Regular openings

For details see garden descriptions

Brook Cottage, Alkerton, nr Banbury. Mon to Fri April 1 to Oct 31 incl Bank Hol

4 Northfield Cottages, Water Eaton, Oxford. Every Tues, Fri, Sat April 1 to Sept 16
Salford Gardens, nr Chipping Norton. 1st Tues of every month April to Sept
Stansfield, Stanford-in-the-Vale
Stanton Harcourt Manor. For dates see text

March 5 Sunday
Greystone Cottage, Kingwood Common, nr Henley

March 26 Sunday
Magdalen College, Oxford ‡
St Hilda's College, Oxford ‡ ‡
Wadham College, Oxford

April 2 Sunday
Ashbrook House, Blewbury
Bampton & Weald Gardens
Buckland, nr Faringdon
The Mill House, Sutton Courtenay
Taynton House, nr Burford
Pettifers, Wardington Gardens

April 9 Sunday
Broughton Poggs & Filkins Gardens
Epwell Mill, nr Banbury
Haseley Court, SE Oxford
The Old Rectory, Coleshill
Quarry Bank House, Gibralter Hill, nr Tackley

April 16 Sunday
Clifton Hampden Manor
Faringdon House, Faringdon
Shotover House, nr Wheatley
Stanton Harcourt Manor

April 17 Monday
Broadwell Gardens, nr Lechlade
Brook Cottage, Alkerton, nr Banbury
Kencot Gardens, nr Lechlade

April 23 Sunday
Barton Abbey, Steeple Barton
Kingston Bagpuize House
Lime Close, Drayton
Loreto, Ewelme ‡
The Mill House, Stadhampton ‡
Swyncombe House, nr Nettlebed

April 30 Sunday
Bottom House, Bix, nr Henley
Garsington Manor, nr S Oxford ‡
Kingston Lisle Park, nr Wantage
St Hugh's College, Oxford
Town Farm Cottage, Kingston Blount Gardens
Wick Hall, Radley, nr Abingdon
Wilcote House, nr Finstock

May 7 Sunday
Adderbury Gardens
Charlbury Gardens
Checkendon Court, nr Reading ‡
Greystone Cottage, Kingwood Common, nr Henley ‡
The Old Rectory, Albury
40 Osler Road, Headington Gardens, Oxford
Wolfson College, Oxford

May 8 Monday
Brook Cottage, Alkerton, nr Banbury
Denton House, Denton

May 12 Friday
Hearns House, Gallows Tree Common

May 13 Saturday
Hearns House, Gallows Tree Common

May 14 Sunday
Clock House, Coleshill
Epwell Mill, nr Banbury
Foxcombe End, Boars Hill ‡
Hearns House, Gallows Tree Common ‡‡
The Manor House, Sutton Courtenay
Sue Ryder Home, Joyce Grove, Nettlebed ‡‡
Wood Croft, Boars Hill ‡
Woodperry House, nr Beckley, Oxford

May 20 Saturday
Greys Court, nr Henley

May 21 Sunday
Balscote Gardens, nr Banbury
Dundon House, Minster Lovell
Headington Gardens, Oxford
Seven Bells Cottage, Garsington, nr S Oxford
Wardington Gardens
Westwell Manor, nr Burford

May 24 Wednesday
Towersey Manor, nr Thame

May 28 Sunday
Adwell House, nr Tetsworth
Hornton Gardens, nr Banbury
Nutford Lodge, nr Faringdon

May 29 Monday
Brook Cottage, Alkerton, nr Banbury
Nutford Lodge, nr Faringdon
The Old Vicarage, Weston-on-the-Green
Sparsholt Manor, nr Wantage
Swerford Park, nr Chipping Norton
Wroxton Gardens

June 4 Sunday
South Newington Gardens, nr Banbury
Stansfield, Stanford-in-the-Vale
Stratton Audley Gardens
University Arboretum, Nuneham Courtenay

June 11 Sunday
Bloxham Gardens, nr Banbury
Friars Court, Clanfield
Haseley Court, SE Oxford
Hill Farm, Elsfield, nr Oxford
Kingston Blount Gardens
Lime Close, Drayton
Pettifers, Wardington Gardens
Waterperry Gardens, nr Wheatley

June 17 Saturday
Hill Court, Tackley

June 18 Sunday
Adwell House, nr Tetsworth
Clock House, Coleshill
Goring-on-Thames Gardens
Hill Court, Tackley
Kiddington Hall, nr Woodstock
The Mill House, Sutton Courtenay
Sibford Gower Gardens

June 21 Wednesday
Sibford Gower Gardens
Towersey Manor, nr Thame

June 25 Sunday
Broadwell House, Broadwell Gardens, nr Lechlade
Broughton Castle, nr Banbury
Green College, Oxford ‡
Green Place, Rotherfield Greys
Iffley Gardens, S Oxford
Kencot House, Kencot Gardens, nr Lechlade
Manor Farm, Kencot Gardens, nr Lechlade
Manor Farm, Old Minster Lovell
The Manor House, Wheatley
Querns, Goring Heath ‡
Salford Gardens, nr Chipping Norton
Sibford Ferris Gardens
Souldern Gardens
White's Farm House, Letcombe Bassett

June 28 Wednesday
New College, Oxford

July 2 Sunday
Exeter & New Colleges, Oxford
Great Rollright Gardens, nr Chipping Norton
Heron's Reach
New College, Oxford
Steeple & Middle Aston Gardens
Westwell Manor, nr Burford

July 5 Wednesday
Broughton Castle, nr Banbury

July 9 Sunday
Hornton Gardens, nr Banbury
Manor Barn House, Wendlebury, nr Bicester
Stanton Harcourt Manor

July 16 Sunday
Benson Gardens
Chastleton Gardens, nr Moreton-in-Marsh
Headington Gardens, Oxford
Home Farm, Balscote Gardens, nr Banbury

Seven Bells Cottage, Garsington, nr S Oxford
Shutford Gardens
Sibford Gower Gardens
Stonewalls, Hempton, nr Deddington
Swinbrook Gardens, nr Burford
Tusmore Park, between Bicester & Brackley
White's Farm House, Letcombe Bassett
Wroxton Gardens

July 23 Sunday
Adwell House, nr Tetsworth
Chivel Farm, Heythrop, nr Chipping Norton
Queen's & Wadham Colleges, Oxford
Stansfield, Stanford-in-the-Vale

July 30 Sunday
Ashbrook House, Blewbury
Churchill Gardens, nr Chipping Norton
Rewley House, Oxford

August 6 Sunday
Broughton Castle, nr Banbury
East Oxford Gardens

August 13 Sunday
Christ Church, Corpus Christi & Trinity Colleges
Colegrave Seeds Ltd, West Adderbury
Friars Court, Clanfield
Headington Gardens, Oxford
Thames-Side Court, Shiplake
Waterperry Gardens, nr Wheatley

August 20 Sunday
Pusey House, nr Faringdon
Woodperry House, nr Beckley, Oxford
Wootton Hill, Boars Hill

August 27 Sunday
Blenheim Palace, Woodstock
Loreto, Ewelme
Nutford Lodge, nr Faringdon
Pusey House, nr Faringdon

August 28 Monday
Blenheim Palace, Woodstock
Broadwell House, Broadwell Gardens, nr Lechlade
Brook Cottage, Alkerton, nr Banbury
Kencot Gardens, nr Lechlade
Loreto, Ewelme
Nutford Lodge, nr Faringdon
The Old Vicarage, Weston-on-the-Green

September 3 Sunday
Templeton College, Kennington, Oxford

September 10 Sunday
Charlbury Gardens
Clock House, Coleshill ‡
The Old Rectory, Coleshill ‡
Rofford Manor, Little Milton
Tadmarton Gardens, nr Banbury

September 16 Saturday
Tadmarton Gardens, nr Banbury

September 17 Sunday
Epwell Mill, nr Banbury

October 1 Sunday
Garsington Manor, nr S Oxford
Hook Norton Manor, nr Banbury
The Mill House, Sutton Courtenay

October 8 Sunday
Wilcote House, nr Finstock

DESCRIPTIONS OF GARDENS

Adderbury Gardens On A4260, 3m S of Banbury. A large village with many quaint lanes and a beautiful church. TEAS. *Combined adm £2 Chd free. Sun May 7 (2-6)*

West of A423

Berry Hill House ♿✿ (Mr & Mrs J P Pollard) Berry Hill Rd, off A4260 signed Milton, Bloxham, W Adderbury. 2-acre garden reclaimed since 1982. Mature trees; lawns; shrubbery; mixed herbaceous and shrub borders. Kitchen garden

Briarwood (Mr & Mrs W Johnson) Berry Hill Road. ¼-acre cottage style garden with interesting collection of shrubs and herbaceous plants. No dogs

Crosshill House (Mr & Mrs Gurth Hoyer Millar) Manor Rd. 4-acre classic Victorian walled gardens around stone Georgian House

The Old Vicarage (Mr & Mrs Philip Allan) 1-acre garden (and kitchen garden) overlooking flood meadows. No dogs

Adwell House ♿✿ (Mr & Mrs W R A Birch-Reynardson) Nr Tetsworth, 4m SW of Thame. From London leave M40 at exit 6, turn L in Lewknor. From Oxford A40, turn R in Tetsworth. Roses, formal and water gardens, ornamental lakes, fine trees, lawns; new tree and shrub planting. Commemorative garden with monument. Recently designed potager. TEAS not July 23. Plant sale (subject to availability). *Adm £2 Chd free (Share to Adwell Church PCC©). Suns May 28, June 18, July 23 (2.30-5.30)*

Arboretum see Oxford University Gardens

Ashbrook House ✿❀ (Mr & Mrs S A Barrett) Blewbury. 4m SE of Didcot on A417; 3½-acre chalk garden with small lake, stream, spring bulbs. Teas Lantern Cafe April, Ashbrook House July. *Adm £1 Chd free. Suns April 2, July 30 (2-6)*

Balscote Gardens ♿❀ Pretty hill village ½m off A422 5m W of Banbury. TEAS (May only) at a nearby garden in aid of Church (C14 St Mary Magdalene). *Combined adm £2 Chd free. Sun May 21 (2-6)*

Home Farm (Mr & Mrs G C Royle) C17 house and barn with attractive views from ½-acre closely planted elevated garden designed for year-round interest with contrasting foliage, flowering shrubs, bulbs, heathers, alpines, herbaceous, roses, lilies, young trees. Featured in Maison et Jardin, No 19 Spring 1992 and R.H.S. The Garden July 1992. *Also open Sun July 16. Teas at Shutford. Adm £1.50. Private visits also welcome by appt April 1 to Oct 31, please* **Tel 01295 738194**

Homeland (Dr & Mrs J S Rivers) ¾-acre, developed since 1982 with shrubs, roses, perennials and rock garden, includes field adjacent to church, planted with trees

Bampton & Weald Gardens On A4095 Witney-Faringdon rd. TEAS at **Weald Manor.** *Combined adm £1.50 Chd free. Sun April 2 (2-5.30)*

Bampton Manor ♿❀ (Earl & Countess of Donoughmore) Interesting wild spring garden with beautiful views of church. Masses of varied spring flowers. *(Share to Dr Clark Memorial Fund)*

Weald Manor ♿ (Maj & Mrs R A Colvile) Medium-sized old garden; woodland area with many spring bulbs; topiary and shrub borders; fine trees; small lake *(Share to Bampton Church Spire Fund®)*

Barton Abbey ♿✂❀ (Mrs R Fleming) On B4030; 1m Middle Barton; ½m from junction of A4260 and B4030. 4 acres lawns; 3 acres of lake; fine trees; kitchen garden and glasshouses; prize rosette display. Plants and home produce stall. TEAS. *Adm £1.50 Chd free. Sun April 23 (2-6)*

23 Beech Croft Road ✂ (Mrs A Dexter) Summertown, Oxford. A 23yd by 7yd, south-facing, plant lover's paved garden of a terraced house has been made secluded by planting evergreen shrubs, roses and clematis all round the brick walls; the 2 herbaceous, 2 alpine, 2 shady beds all contain many unusual plants, shrubs, ferns; troughs filled with small alpines. NO push-chairs. *Adm £2.50. Private visits welcome April to Sept 30* **Tel 01865 56020**

Benson Gardens Off High St. Benson off A4074 Oxford-Henley, 2m from Wallingford. Parking in High St. TEAS at **Mill Lane House**. *Combined adm £1.50. Sun July 16 (2-6)*

Hethersett ❀ (Dr Anne Millar) ½-acre garden on natural chalk stream; climbing plants and bog area; colour co-ordination and plant-form a feature of mixed beds. *Private visits welcome for parties of 15 and over, please* **Tel 01491 838116**

Mill Lane House ✂ (Marion & Geoff Heywood) ¼-acre garden with alpine rockeries and banks sloping to stream, pond, small island and spring. Dried flower crafts display

Blenheim Palace ✂ (His Grace the Duke of Marlborough) Woodstock, 8m N of Oxford. Bus: 44 Oxford-Chipping Norton-Stratford, alight Woodstock. Original grounds and garden plan by Henry Wise. Park landscaped and lake created by 'Capability' Brown in late C18. Maze; butterfly house; cafeteria; adventure play area; *Adm charge not available on going to press.* ▲*For NGS Sun, Mon Aug 27, 28 (10.30-4.45)*

Bloxham Gardens ✂❀ A large village near Banbury on A361 to Chipping Norton. Has a fine church with a 198ft spire. TEAS in village by WI. *Combined adm £1.50 Chd free. Sun June 11 (2-6)*

25 The Avenue (Miss E Bell-Walker) A small informal garden with emphasis on small shrubs; sub shrubs and herbaceous plants

71 Courtington Lane ❀ (Mr P Sheasby) About ⅓ acre with herbaceous borders, shrubs, rockeries and small peat beds; there is a small pond and a series of alpine troughs; the greenhouse contains cacti and a large succulent collection especially Lithops, Haworthia and Echeveria; a wide range of herbaceous species are grown

¶Frog Lane Cottage ❀ (Mr & Mrs R Owen) An artists and a plantsmans garden. Steeply terraced on many levels, mixture of shrubs and herbaceous plants, incl camomile lawn, wonderful views across valley

Rose Cottage ❀ (Mr & Mrs David Willmott) Small cottage garden on elevated site incl alpines, herbaceous bed and climbing roses

Bottom House ♿✂❀ (Mrs G Scouller) Bix, 1½m NW of Henley-on-Thames on A4130 (dual carriageway) 2-acre family garden, spring bedding, tulips, many unusual plants. Small formal garden with topiary; yellow and white garden. "Considered one of the most beautiful gardens in Oxfordshire" (Oxford Mail). TEAS. *Adm £1 Chd free. Sun April 30 (2-6)*

Broadwell Gardens 5m NE Lechlade, E of A361 to Burford. Delightful Cotswold village with interesting church. TEAS. *Combined adm with* **Kencot** *£2 Chd free. Mons April 7, Aug 28. £1.50 Chd free. Sun June 25 (2-6)*

Broadwell House ♿❀ (Brigadier & Mrs C F Cox) Mature 2-acre garden planted for colour throughout the year. Many interesting trees and shrubs including wellingtonia, ginkgo, acers, aralias, salix, cornus, clematis. Topiary, rare plants, many golden, silver and variegated; unusual grasses, penstemons and osteospermums, also many hardy geraniums. Featured in 'Over the Hills from Broadway'. Listed house and old barn. Gardening clubs welcome. *Mons April 7, Aug 28; Sun June 25 (2-6). Private visits welcome, please* **Tel 01367 860230**

Broadwell Old Manor ✂ (Mr & Mrs M Chinnery) 1-acre garden with listed house. Shrub borders, courtyard and topiary garden. Pleached lime hedge, old mulberry tree, young tulip and sorbus trees. *April 17 only*

Brook Cottage ❀ (Mr & Mrs D Hodges) Alkerton, 6m W of Banbury. From A422, Banbury-Stratford, turn W at sign to Alkerton, L opp Alkerton War Memorial, into Well Lane, R at fork. 4-acre hillside garden, formed since 1964, surrounding C17 house. Wide variety of trees, shrubs and plants of all kinds in areas of differing character; water garden; alpine scree; one-colour borders; over 200 shrub and climbing roses; many clematis. Interesting throughout season. DIY Tea & Coffee. Refreshments for groups by arrangement. *Adm £2 OAPs £1.50 Chd free. Mon to Fri April 1 to Oct 31 incl Bank Hols (9-6). Evenings, weekends and all group visits by appt* **Tel 01295 670303** *or* **670590**

Broughton Castle ♿❀ (Lord Saye & Sele) 2½m W of Banbury on Shipston-on-Stour rd (B4035). 1-acre shrub, herbaceous borders, walled garden, roses, climbers seen against background of C13-C16 castle surrounded by moat in open parkland. House also open, extra charge. TEAS. *Adm Garden only £1.50 Chd 75p.* ▲*For NGS Suns June 25, Aug 6; Wed July 5 (2-5)*

Broughton Poggs & Filkins Gardens ♿ Enchanting limestone villages between Burford and Lechlade, just E of A36l. A number of gardens varying in size from traditional cottage garden to over 2 acres, growing wide variety of plants. TEAS. *Combined adm £2 Chd free. Tickets from* **The Court House, Broughton Hall** *or* **Little Peacocks** *(Share to Broughton & Filkins Church Funds®). Sun April 9 (2-5.30)*

Broughton Poggs:

Broughton Hall (Mr & Mrs C B S Dobson)
Corner Cottage (Mr & Mrs E Stephenson)
The Court House (Richard Burls Esq)
The Garden Cottage (Mr & Mrs R Chennells)
The Old Rectory (Mrs E Wansbrough)
Rose Cottage (Mr & Mrs R Groves)

Filkins:
Fox House (Lady Cripps)
Little Peacocks (Colvin & Moggridge, Landscape Consultants)
St Peter's House (John Cambridge Esq)

Buckland ❀ (Mrs Richard Wellesley) Signposted to Buckland off A420, lane between two churches. Beautiful lakeside walk; fine trees; daffodils; shrubs. Norman church adjoins garden. TEAS. *Adm £1 Chd free. Sun April 2 (2-7). Private visits welcome Tues and Thurs, please* **Tel 01367 87203**

Carinya ✲❀ (Mrs S J Parsons) Goring Rd, Woodcote. 8m NW of Reading; 5m SE of Wallingford on SW edge of Village on B471. ⅓-acre plant lover's cottage style garden, densely planted with a wide variety of plants, many rare or unusual with interest at all times of the year. *Adm £1 Chd free. Private visits and parties welcome by appt April 1 to Sept 30, please* **Tel 01491 680663**

Charlbury Gardens ✲❀ Large historic village on B4022 Witney-Enstone. TEAS. *Combined adm £1.50 Chd 50p (Share to Wytham Hall Sick Bay for Medical Care of Homeless®). Suns May 7, Sept 10 (2-6)*
Gothic House (Mr & Mrs Andrew Lawson) Near Bell Hotel. ⅓-acre walled garden, planted for sculpture display and colour association. False perspective, pleached lime walk with bulbs, trellis, alpine pyramid, terrace pots
The Priory ♿ (Dr D El Kabir and others) Adjacent church. A collector's garden in the making. Over 1 acre planted with many fine specimens of trees and shrubs in a formal topiary garden with terraced beds incorporating colour scheme foliage

Chastleton Gardens 3m SE of Moreton-in-Marsh and W of Chipping Norton off A44. TEAS in aid of Chastleton Church. *Combined adm £2 Chd free. Sun July 16 (2-6)*
Chastleton Glebe ♿❀ (Prue Leith) 1m from village on lane to Moreton-in-Marsh. 5 acres; old trees; terraces (one all red); small lake, island; Chinese-style bridge, pagoda; formal vegetable garden; Cotswold house; views; new rose tunnel
Kitebrook End Farm ♿ (Mr & Mrs W G Bamford) Directions as for Chastleton Glebe. ½-acre garden created in 1988 from derelict farm yard. Designed to be labour-saving; walls; paving and shaped borders around a lawn. Massed shrubs and herbaceous planting for ground cover and colour, southerly aspect, opened up with raised ha-ha wall
The Old Post Office ❀ (Prof & Mrs Griffith Edwards) in Chastleton. ⅔-acre roses, shrubs and perennials in attractive sheltered setting below historic Chastleton House

Checkendon Court ♿✲ (Sir Nigel Broackes) Checkendon, NW of Reading. 2m NE of Woodcote on B479 nr Checkendon church. 15 acres, attractively laid out with yew hedges, herbaceous borders, roses, kitchen garden; work continues to woodland areas. New rhododendrons and azalea planting and new laburnum pergola walk now complete. TEAS at **Greystone Cottage.** *Adm £2 Chd free. Sun May 7 (2-5)*

Chivel Farm ♿✲❀ (Mr & Mrs J D Sword) Heythrop, 4m E of Chipping Norton, off A44 or A361. High and open to extensive view, medium-sized garden designed for continuous interest. Colour schemed borders with many unusual shrubs, roses, herbaceous plants; small formal white garden, conservatory. TEAS. *Adm £1.50 Chd free. Sun July 23 (2-6)*

Christ Church See Oxford University Gardens

Churchill Gardens Churchill 3m SW of Chipping Norton on B4450. From Burford, W for Churchill via A361. TEAS in aid of village church. *Combined adm £1.50 Chd free. Sun July 30 (2-6)*
Haughton House ♿ (Mr & Mrs A D Loehnis) Medium-sized garden recently reclaimed. Terrace with fine views, borders, formal white garden, meadow. All season interest. Also fine kneelers in nearby church
Rynehill Farm ♿✲❀ (Mr & Mrs M D Bell) On B4450 1m S of Churchill. 1-acre farmhouse garden. Well-stocked kitchen garden, walled area, mixed borders, annuals, roses

¶Clematis Corner ♿✲❀ (Mike & Dorothy Brown) 15 Plough Close. At Shillingford roundabout (10m S of Oxford on A4074), take A329 towards Warborough and Thame. Clematis Corner is 200yds from roundabout, 1st on L inside Plough Close, just round sharp L bend. ¼ acre garden. Specialising in clematis (approx 200 varieties) grown in a variety of ways. Enthusiastic amateurs, propagating and raising new varieties. TEA. *Adm £1 Chd 50p. Private visits welcome May 1 to Sept 30, please* **Tel 01865 858721**

Clifton Hampden Manor ♿✲❀ (Mr C Gibbs) 4m E of Abingdon on A415. 4-acre romantic C19 garden above R. Thames with statuary and far-reaching views; long pergola, new lime tunnel, herbaceous borders, bulbs, wild riverside walks, much new planting in progress. TEAS in aid of St Michael's and All Angels Church. *Adm £2 Chd free. Sun April 16 (2.30-5.30). Parties welcome, please* **Tel 0130 7720**

Clock House ♿✲❀ (Michael & Denny Wickham & Peter Fox) Coleshill, 3½m SW of Faringdon on B4019. Garden at top of village. Planted around site of Coleshill House, which was burnt down in the 50's, the main floor plan has been laid out and is being planted as a memorial to this famous house. Walled garden in old laundry drying ground; with big greenhouse, unusual plants, vegetables and herbs; good views across Vale of the White Horse and parkland. Toilets not suitable disabled. TEAS. *Adm £1.50 Chd free. Open every Thurs May to Sept (2-5). Suns May 4, June 18, Sept 10 (2-6). Private visits welcome, please* **Tel 01793 762476**

Colegrave Seeds Ltd ♿✲ Milton Rd, West Adderbury off A423 Banbury-Oxford Rd. From M40 travelling S leave at junction 11: travelling N leave at junction 10. In Adderbury head for Milton and Bloxham. Trial grounds ½m on right. Seed trials grounds and patio display gardens containing thousands of summer flowering annuals and perennials. Many new items in trial prior to introduction. A festival of colour unique in Oxfordshire. Covered display area of hanging baskets and containers. (Note strictly wholesale; no retail sales). Parking. Light lunches and TEAS. *Adm £2 Chd free (Share to RNLI®). Sun Aug 13 (11-5)*

Corpus Christi College (see Oxford University Gardens)

Denton House ♿✂❀ (Mr & Mrs J Luke) Denton. SE of Oxford. 1m E Garsington between A40 and B480. 3-acre walled garden; large lawns; many mature trees and shrubs; spring bulbs incl fritillaria; wild garden; walled vegetable garden; interesting stable yard. Gothic windows from Brasenose Chapel in high stone wall surrounding garden. TEAS in aid of Cuddesdon Church and Village Hall. *Adm £1 Chd free. Mon May 8 (2-6)*

Dundon House ♿✂❀ (Mr & Mrs W Pack) In Old Minster Lovell, charming Cotswold village on R Windrush. Off B4047 Witney-Burford Rd opp White Hart, signed to Minster Lovell Hall, 1st drive on R, parking in field to L. Disabled parking at house. Mainly C16 house, (not open), owned in C18 by the Dundons, a notorious family of highwaymen; moved in 1930s to old quarry. Beautiful views across Windrush valley. 4-acre terraced garden built over last 12yrs. Yew hedges and stone walls enclose flower, shrub rose and wild gardens. Planted pool and new woodland gardens. TEAS by WI. *Adm £1.50 OAPs £1 Chd free (Share to Garden History Society®). Sun May 21 (2-6). Parties welcome by appt, please* **Tel 01993 775092**

East Oxford Gardens ♿❀ Off Cowley Rd, Oxford 1m E from the Plain. Parking at **Restore**. TEAS at **Restore** and **St John's Home**. *Combined adm £1 Chd free (Share to Restore and St John's Home®). Sun Aug 6 (2-5)*

Restore Manzil Way N off Cowley Rd leading to E Oxford Health Centre. A town garden and plant nursery run as a mental health rehabilitation project. Sample beds of shrubs, perennials, herbs, alpines and annuals. Large range of plants for sale, also hand-made crafts and cards

St John's Home St Mary's Rd, off Leopold St S of Cowley Rd. 3-acre grounds of All Saints Convent and St John's Home for the Elderly. Mature trees, lawns, secluded prayer garden; cherry orchard and vegetable garden. Comper chapel open

Epwell Mill ♿❀ (Mr R A Withers) Epwell, 7m W of Banbury, between Shutford and Epwell. Medium-sized garden, interestingly landscaped in open country, based on former water-mill; terraced pools; bulbs; azaleas. TEAS. *Adm £1 Chd free (Share to Epwell Church®). Suns April 9, May 14, Sept 17 (2-6). Please apply in writing for groups outside opening dates*

Exeter College see Oxford University Gardens

Faringdon House ♿❀ (Dr S Zinovieff) Faringdon. Large garden; spring bulbs; autumn borders; orangery; park; lakeside walk; fine trees; Norman church adjoining. TEAS in aid of All Saints Church. *Adm £1 Chd free. Sun April 16 (2-5). Private visits welcome, please* **Tel 01367 240240**

Foxcombe End ♿❀ (Mr & Mrs R Stevens) Foxcombe Lane, Boars Hill, 3 m S of Oxford. From roundabout at junction of ring rd with A34 S of Oxford follow signs to Wootton and Boars Hill. Foxcombe Lane is 1st on L after entering Boars Hill. Parking at Foxcombe End reserved for disabled **only**. 11 acres of natural garden, incl a nature trail, a pasture with a donkey and an abundance of wild flowers, particularly orchids. Extensive oak woodlands, within which are magnolia and azalea gardens and rhododendrons. Yew walk and ornamental yew hedges around the house. TEAS in aid of Sobell House Hospice. *Adm £1 Chd free. Sun May 14 (2-6)*

Friars Court ♿ (Mr & Mrs J H Willmer) Clanfield. A4095 Faringdon to Witney, S of Clanfield [OS 285009]. C16 part moated farmhouse. New/mature gardens and woodland walks. Working displays on alternative energy. Cream TEAS. *Adm £1.50 Chd under 12 free. Suns June 11, Aug 13 (2-6)*

Garsington Manor ❀ (Mr & Mrs L V Ingrams) SE of Oxford N of B480. House C16 of architectural interest (not open). Monastic fish ponds, water garden, dovecot c.1700; flower parterre and Italian garden laid out by Philip and Lady Ottoline Morrell; fine trees and yew hedges. Free car park. TEAS. *Adm £2 Chd free. Suns April 30, Oct 1 (2-6)*

Goring-on-Thames Gardens 5m S of Wallingford, where B4009 crosses wooden bridge over Thames, a beautiful old village backed by steep wooded hills. TEAS at **The Old Farmhouse**. *Combined adm £2 Chd free. Sun June 18 (2-6)*

Coney Berry ✂❀ (Mr & Mrs H F Armstrong) Elvendon Road, running E from B4009 n of Goring, parallel to B4626 Goring-Crays Pond Rd. Informal garden with woodland backing on thin soiled chalk hill. Trees and hedges planted at turn of century, shrubs, roses, ground cover for easy maintenance; white border, large herb border, old fashioned roses. *(Share to Arthritis & Rheumatism Council®)*

Manor Field ♿✂❀ (Mr & Mrs D L Watts) Manor Road. An interesting ½-acre garden of a modern bungalow. Collection of rock plants, some in troughs. Unusual shrubs and tender plants, vegetable garden. *(Share to The Reading Abbeyfield House Appeal®)*

The Mill Cottage ♿✂ (Mr & Mrs M J H Weedon) By St Thomas Church. 1-acre riverside garden of C17 timbered cottage with its own small bridge and island, dramatic views over the Thames. *(Share to Rampage Trust©)*

The Old Farmhouse ♿❀ (Mr & Mrs J F Denny) Station Road. A walled village garden of approx 1 acre. It surrounds square 1809 house and incl lawns, herbaceous, roses, shrubs; swimming pool (visitors invited to use pool for charge of 50p); kitchen garden; lily pond and attractive varied layout. *(Share to St John Ambulance®)*

Great Rollright Gardens 3m N of Chipping Norton, off A34 or A361. TEAS at **Old Rectory** in aid of St Andrews Church Restoration Fund. *Adm £2 Chd free. Sun July 2 (2-6)*

Barston House ♿✂ (Miss E L Jackson) 1-acre, formal garden with herbaceous borders, shrubs; kitchen garden; views

¶**Brasenose Cottage** ♿ (Mr & Mrs M Freeman) Walled cottage garden S facing, walled sheltered garden with lawn. ⅓-acre round C17 cottage replanted in 1994.

Duck End ✲ (Mr & Mrs J Lively) Informal ½-acre cottage garden, surrounding listed C17 farmhouse with dovecote; streams, yew hedges, shrub roses; parking available in adjoining paddock only

The Old Beer House (Mr & Mrs B A Tucker) ½-acre village garden with small knot garden and conservatory; orchard

The Old Rectory ♿✲ (Mr Michael & Lady Joanna Stourton) 3 acres with beautiful views to south. Herbaceous border, lawns, knot garden; tree walk; water garden with brook, small lake; many specimen trees

Green College see Oxford University Gardens

Green Place ♿✲❀ (Mr & Mrs R P Tatman) Rotherfield Greys. 3m W of Henley-on-Thames next to Greys War Memorial. Extensive views towards the E from secluded 1-acre garden containing a pergola walk, herbaceous borders, rose beds and many varieties of fuchsia. Teas by WI in nearby village hall. *Adm £1. Sun June 25 (2-6)*

Greys Court ✲❀ (Lady Brunner; The National Trust) Rotherfield Greys, 3m W of Henley-on-Thames on rd to Peppard. 8 acres amongst which are the ruined walls and buildings of original fortified manor. Rose, cherry, wisteria and white gardens; lawns; kitchen garden; ice house; Archbishop's maze. Jacobean house open with C18 alterations on site of original C13 house fortified by Lord Grey in C14. Donkey wheel and tower. Large sale of unusual plants. TEAS. *Adm garden £3 Chd £1.50 House £1 extra, Chd 50p extra. For NGS Sat May 20 (2-5.30)*

Greystone Cottage ♿✲❀ (Mr & Mrs W Roxburgh) Colmore Lane, Kingwood Common. Between B481 Nettlebed-Reading rd and Sonning Common-Stoke Row rd; turn N at 'Unicorn'. 2-acre garden in woodland setting. Many unusual shrubs and plants, including varied collection of hostas, geraniums, grasses, fritillary species, ferns and old fashioned roses. Woodland walk with azaleas, narcissus, hellebores, bilberries and cistus. 80-year-old arched pear tree walk, wildlife ponds, sink gardens, small Mediterranean garden, golden garden. Planted for year round interest. Featured in 'Practical Gardening', 'Good Gardeners Guide' and Gardeners Year Book. Small nursery. TEAS. *Adm £1 Chd free. Suns March 5, May 7 (2-6). Private visits welcome March 1 to Sept 1, please* **Tel 01491 628559**

Haseley Court ♿✲❀ (Mr & Mrs D Heyward) SE of Oxford. From London M40 exit 7, L to A329, 1st L to Great Haseley then to Little Haseley. From Oxford A40, L on A418 to Aylesbury, 1st R onto A329 and over M40. Topiary chess set in box and yew. Hornbeam and laburnum tunnels, walled garden with box hedges. Collection of old roses. Potager, woodland with many spring flowers. Ornamental canal. TEAS. *Adm £2 Chd free. Suns April 9, June 11 (2-6)*

Headington Gardens ✲❀ East Oxford, off London Road, ¾m W of ring road. TEAS in parish hall, Dunstan Rd (plants only May 21, July 16). TEAS (May 7 TEAS in garden). *Adm £1. Sun May 7,* **40 Osler Rd** *only. Combined adm £1.80 Chd free. Suns May 21, July 16, Aug 13 (2-6)*

2 Fortnam Close (Mr & Mrs D Holt) Off Headley Way. Winner best back garden, Oxford in Bloom 1991 and 1993. Featured on TV. ¼-acre garden on 3 levels, trees, shrubs including heathers, azaleas and a large wisteria. Roses, bearded iris and other herbaceous plants in a planned layout which includes a pond and pergola. There are watercolour paintings and pressed flower arrangements to view if you wish. *May 21, July 16, Aug 13*

40 Osler Road (Mr & Mrs N Coote) ⅔-acre 'secret garden' in built-up area on the edge of Old Headington. Semi-formal design with statuary and decorative pots with tender shrubs and plants supporting Mediterranean atmosphere of house. Luxuriant spring display. Plants for dry soil (neutral sand), many chosen for foliage effect, some rare or unusual, many late flowering. Featured in English Private Gardens, the Garden, Garden Source Book and Gardener's Yearbook. *May 7, 21, July 16, Aug 13. No plant stall May 7, Aug 13. Private visits for groups welcome, please* **Tel 01865 67680 (after dark)**

Pumpkin Cottage ♿ (Mr & Mrs M Davis) 6 St Andrew's Lane, Old Headington, off St Andrew's Rd, nr to Church. Small garden, 20m × 16m, enclosed within stone walls situated at rear of Grade II listed cottage. Small pool and rockery; mixed planting; paved areas with some container grown plants. Small cobble paved front garden. Wheelchair access possible by arrangement. *May 21, July 16, Aug 13*

1 Stoke Place ♿ (Mrs Sarah McCabe) The garden takes its shape from a network of old stone walls which happen to have survived in the area. A scattering of trees blending with stone work provides a framework for a linked series of paths and flower beds which gives an atmosphere of seclusion. A number of small pools and many contrasting shrubs and plants provide variety and do not diminish the sense of privacy of the whole garden. The area is just short of an acre. *Open May 21 only (Share to Toxiplasmosis Trust®)*

Hearns House ♿❀ (Mr & Mrs J Pumfrey) Gallows Tree Common, 5m N of Reading, 5m W of Henley. From A4074 turn E at The Fox, Cane End. Limited car parking in the garden so additional Friday and Saturday openings. Architects house in 2-acre garden in woodland setting. Designed for maintenance by two people with full time careers. Featured in Amateur Gardening. Emphasis on design, good foliage and single colour areas with paved courtyard and shady walks. New small garden. Unusual plants for sale. TEAS or coffee in aid of Water Aid. *Adm £1 Chd free. Fri, Sat, Sun May 12, 13, 14, (10-12; 2-5); private visits also welcome in Sept, please* **Tel 01734 722848**

Heron's Reach ❀ (Mr & Mrs B Vorhaus) Eastfield Lane, Whitchurch. From Pangbourne take tollbridge rd over Thames to Whitchurch; at The Greyhound turn R into Eastfield Lane. 1 acre in beautiful Thames-side setting with views to the Chiltern hills; woodland garden with pond, stream and waterfall; shrubs, and herbaceous borders. TEA. *Adm £1.50 Chd free. Sun July 2 (2-6). Private visits also welcome in July, please* **Tel 01734 843140**

Hill Court ♿✂❀ (Mr & Mrs Andrew Peake) Tackley. 9m N of Oxford. Turn off A4260 at Sturdy's Castle. Walled garden of 2 acres with clipped yew cones at the top of the terrace as a design feature by Russell Page in the 1960s. Terraces incl silver, pink and blue plantings, white garden, herbaceous borders, shrubberies, orangery. Many rare and unusual plants. Entry incl History Trail (not suitable for wheelchairs) with illustrated leaflet giving notes on unique geometric fishponds (1620), C17 stables and pigeon house, C18 lakes, icehouse etc (stroll of at least 1hr). TEAS. Pied Pipers recorder group (Sun only) *Adm £1.50 Chd free (Share to Sir Michael Sobell House, M E Association and Tackley Church Bell Appeal®). Sat, Sun June 17, 18 (2-6)*

Hill Farm ✂❀ (Mr & Mrs J Garson) Elsfield. 5m N of Oxford. A40 flyover signed Marston and Elsfield. Mixed borders, shrubs, trees; good view of Oxford. TEAS. *Adm £1 Chd free (Share to Elsfield Church®). Sun June 11 (2-6)*

Home Close ✂ (Mrs M Baker) Southend, Garsington. SE of Oxford, N of B480. 2-acre garden, being redeveloped, surrounding C17 listed bailiff's house and granary. Mixed borders; walled garden with water feature; herb garden; pergola; kitchen garden; orchard; woodland areas. *Adm £1. Private visits welcome April to Sept 30, please* **Tel 01865 361394**

Hook Norton Manor ❀ (Mr & Mrs N Holmes) SW of Banbury. From A361, 1m from Chipping Norton turn N and follow signs. 2½-acres terraced lawns leading down to streams; trees, shrubs and bog garden. TEAS in aid of St Peter's Church. *Adm 80p Chd free. Sun Oct 1 (2-5.30)*

Hornton Gardens 6m NW of Banbury. Between A422 and B4100. An attractive village known for its quarry which produced Hornton stone for the neighbourhood. Fine old buildings around the village green. TEAS in aid of Hornton School May 28; Hornton Cubs and Brownies July 9. *Combined adm £1.50 Chd free. Suns May 28, July 9 (2-6)*

Bellevue ✂❀ (Mr & Mrs E W Turner) Bell St. Approx 1½-acre hillside garden of many aspects. Bordered walks; a 'surprise' garden leading to water falling to pools, flower beds and the finest views of Hornton Village. Added attraction miniature windmill ⅓ scale of original at Hornton

Sunnyside ♿✂❀ (Philip Williams Esq) A cottage garden of approx ½-acre with attractive borders of mixed perennials; shrub planting and pond area. Created from rough ground over 7 years and still adding. *Private visits welcome, please* **Tel 0129 587763**

West End House ❀ (The Hon William & Mrs Buchan) Small, pretty garden designed for maximum interest. Old fashioned roses, herbs

Iffley Gardens ✂❀ S Oxford. Secluded old village within Oxford's ring road, off A4158 from Magdalen Bridge to Littlemore roundabout. Renowned Norman church, featured on cover of Pevsner's Oxon guide. Short footpath from Mill Lane leads to scenic Iffley Lock and Sandford-Oxford towpath. TEAS from 3-5 at thatched village hall, Church Way (to avoid queues, timed tea tickets should be obtained in gardens). Plant stall in aid of the White House Nursery. *Combined adm £2 OAPs £1.50 Chd free. Sun June 25 (2-6)*

8 Abberbury Road ♿ (F S Tordoff Esq) Off Church Way. ½-acre plantsman's garden developed since 1971. Mature trees, shrubs, coloured and variegated foliage, many old and modern shrub roses and climbers

24 Abberbury Road ♿ (Mr & Mrs E Townsend-Coles) ½-acre family garden with fruit, flowers and vegetables

65 Church Way ❀ (Mrs J Woodfill) Small cottage garden planted with shrubs, perennials and herbs, many of them grown for their historical associations

71 Church Way (Mrs M L Harrison) A small, low maintenance professionally designed, front garden with mixed shrubs and herbaceous plantings

122 Church Way (Sir John & Lady Elliott) Small secluded cottage style garden with trees, shrubs, roses and herbaceous plants behind listed house with view of church tower

The Mill House ♿ (Mrs P A Lawrence) 30 Mill Lane. A terraced garden dropping westwards to the river at the old mill-race

Rosedale ♿❀ (Mrs T Bennett) Mill Lane, off Church Way. ½-acre garden on different levels, hidden behind walls. A mixture of trees, shrubs, roses and herbaceous plants with a large rockery and tiny woodland garden

Kencot Gardens ♿✂❀ 5m NE of Lechlade, E of A361 to Burford. A most charming Cotswold village with interesting church. TEAS. *Combined adm with* **Broadwell** *£2 Chd free. Mons April 17, Aug 28. £1.50 Chd free (Share to RSPB®). Sun June 25*

De Rougemont (Mr & Mrs D Portergill) ½-acre garden with very varied planting: over 350 named plants; beds for perennials, conifers, fuchsias, herbs and roses; spring bulbs; vegetables and fruit trees; soft fruit cage; greenhouse with vine; well. *Mons April 17, Aug 28*

The Gardens (Lt-Col & Mrs J Barstow) ¼-acre cottage garden featuring spring bulbs, iris, roses, herbaceous, rock plants, old apple trees and a well. *Mons April 17, Aug 28*

Ivy Nook (Mr & Mrs W Gasson) Cottage garden; rockeries, lawns, mixed borders. *Sun April 10, Mon Aug 28*

Kencott Cottage (Mrs M Foster) Very small garden with spring bulbs and bedding, also bonsai trees. *Mons April 17, Aug 28*

Kencot House (Mr & Mrs A Patrick) 2-acre garden with lawns, trees, borders; quantities of daffodils and other spring bulbs; roses and over 50 different clematis; notable ginkgo tree. Interesting carved C13 archway. *Mons April 17, Aug 28, Sun June 25*

Manor Farm (Mr & Mrs J R Fyson) 2-acre garden with lawns and herbaceous borders; naturalised spring bulbs; incl long-established fritillaries; clipped yew, pleached lime walk, pergola with rambling and gallica roses. Mature orchards. C17 listed farmhouse. *Mon April 17, Sun June 25*

¶Pinnocks (Mr & Mrs J Coxeter) ¾-acre garden with spring bulbs, flowering trees, roses and bedding plants. *Mons April 17, Aug 28*

Kiddington Hall ✿❀ (Hon Maurice & Mrs Robson) 4m NW of Woodstock. From A44 Oxford-Stratford, R at Xrds in Kiddington and down hill; entrance on L. Partly suitable for wheelchairs. Large grounds with lake, parkland designed by Capability Brown; terraced rose garden and orangery beside house designed by Sir Charles Barry; C12 church, C16 dovecote and large walled kitchen garden. TEAS in aid of St Nicholas Church, Kiddington. *Adm £1.50 Chd free. Sun June 18 (2-6)*

Kingston Bagpuize House ♿✿ (Lady Tweedsmuir) Kingston Bagpuize, A415/A420, 5½m W of Abingdon. Flowering shrubs, bulbs; woodland garden; herbaceous plants; hydrangeas. Charles II Manor house. House not suitable wheelchairs. TEAS. *Adm house & garden adults £3, OAPs £2.50, Chd £2 (under 5 not admitted to house). Garden only £1, under 5's free (Share to British Red Cross and Lucy Faithful House). Suns, Bank Hols Mons April 1 to Sept 30 (2.30-5.30). For NGS Sun April 23 (2.30-5.30). Last adm 5pm. Parties welcome by appt*

Kingston Blount Gardens 4m S of Thame, 4m NE of Watlington 1½m NE of junction 6, M40. Kingston Blount on B4009. TEAS at **Town Farm Cottage**. *Combined adm £1.50 Chd free. Sun June 11 (2-6)*

Moat Manor ♿(Mr & Mrs A O Hunt) Pretty 1½-acre garden surrounding C17 listed house. Herbaceous, roses; lawns and small lake

Town Farm Cottage ♿✿❀ (Mr & Mrs J Clarke) For details see main text

Kingston Lisle Park (Mr & Mrs J L S Lonsdale) nr Wantage. 5m W of Wantage along B4507. 12 acres of gardens incl a shrubbery, pleeched limes, an avenue leading up to an ornamental pond and a replica of Queen Mary's rose garden in Regents Park. 3 acres of lakes. Guided tour of house on the hour. TEAS. *Adm £5 (incl house) Chd under 16 free. Mons April 17, May 8, 29, Aug 28. For NGS Sun April 30 (1.30-5) Parties welcome by appt, please* **Tel 01367 820599**

¶14 Lavender Place ✿ (Mrs Angela Chambers) Carterton. 4m SE of Burford on B4020. After entering Carterton from Burford, turn R at lights into Upavon Way (towards Alvescot & Faringdon). Lavender Place fourth L. Plant enthusiast's tiny 35′ square garden behind small modern house. Clematis and other climbers provide secluded setting for densely packed collection of unusual and exotic perennials. Small pond, shaded area, raised beds. Colour and interest all year. Combine with visit to **Broadwell House**, less than 2m away. *Adm 80p Chd free. Private visits welcome by appt, please* **Tel 01993 843216**

Lime Close ♿❀ (Miss de Laubarede) 35 Henleys Lane, Drayton. 2m S of Abingdon. 3-acre mature garden with very rare and unusual trees, shrubs, perennials and bulbs. Raised beds, rock garden and troughs with alpines, Creation of new borders and much new planting in progress. New ornamental kitchen garden with pergola under construction. Herb garden designed by Rosemary Verey. Listed C16 house (not open). Unusual plants for sale from Green Farm Plants. TEAS in aid of Alzheimer Disease, Oxon Branch. *Adm £1.50 Chd 50p. Suns April 23, June 11 (2-6)*

Little Place ✿ (His Honour Judge & Mrs Medd) Clifton Hampden. 5m E of Abingdon. Leaving Abingdon on A415, At Clifton Hampden turn R at traffic lights and take 1st turning R. Garden 200yds on R. 1½-acre terraced garden originally made at turn of century (part possibly designed by Gertrude Jekyll) but replanned by present owners; with small woodland garden. *Adm £2 Chd free (Share to Barristers Benevolent Association®). Private visits welcome March to Sept, please* **Tel 01865 407702**

Loreto ♿✿❀ (Mr & Mrs R J Styles) Between Ewelme and Benson off B4009 NE of Wallingford. 5 acres; extensively replanted and developed since 1974. Emphasis on water gardens, shrubs and conifers, herbaceous and bedding plants. TEAS. *Adm £2 Chd free. Suns April 23, Aug 27, Mon Aug 28 (2-6)*

Magdalen College. See Oxford University Gardens

Manor Barn House ♿❀ (Mr & Mrs Charles Swallow) Wendlebury. 12m NE of Oxford off A421 to Bicester. Small barn converted in 1979. Garden and field 3½ acres developed over last 15 years from neglected farmyard and adjoining land. Large pond, dug in 1985 and fed from roofs and high water table. Variety of rushes and aquatic plants, trout, crayfish. Rose walk, specimen trees and shrubs. Homemade TEAS, ice cream and plants for sale in aid of Wendlebury Church. *Adm £1 Chd 50p. Sun July 9 (2-6)*

Manor Farm ♿❀ (Sir Peter & Lady Parker), Old Minster Lovell, beautiful Cotswold village in Windrush valley. Off B4047 Witney-Burford rd; turn R at sign to Old Minster Lovell and Leafield; in ¼m cross Windrush bridge, turn R at Old Swan; no parking in village, follow signs to large free car park. 5-acre garden around small Cotswold farmhouse adjoining churchyard and ruins of Minster (open); mediaeval barns divide garden into sections; pools, informal herbaceous areas; shrubs and specie roses. C14 dovecote. Owner is author of book about her garden: 'Purest of Pleasures'. TEAS by WI. *Adm £1.50 Chd free. Sun June 25 (2-5). Parties welcome by appt*

The Manor House ♿✿❀ (The Hon David Astor) Sutton Courtenay. 4m S of Abingdon. Out of Abingdon on the A415. Turn off to Culham – Sutton Courtenay. From A34 going N come into Milton Village take last rd on R to Sutton Courtenay. 10 acres of garden approx 100 acres of land. ½m R Thames Bank. TEAS. *Adm £1.50 Chd 50p. Sun May 14 (2-6)*

The Manor House Wheatley ✿❀ (Mr & Mrs T G Hassall) 26 High St, Wheatley. Off A40 E of Oxford. 1½-acre garden of Elizabethan manor house; formal box walk, established fruit trees, incl espalier apples; herb garden, cottage garden with rose arches and a shrubbery with old roses. TEAS in aid of Wheatley Windmill Restoration Society. *Adm £1 Chd free. Sun June 25 (2-6)*

The Mill House, Stadhampton ♿ (Mr & Mrs F A Peet) A329/B480, 8m SE of Oxford. 1-acre family garden with old mill and stream. Mill not working but machinery largely intact and wheel turning with pumped water. Parking on green; parking for disabled only at house. TEAS in aid of Stadhampton Church Restoration Fund. *Adm £1 Chd free. Sun April 23 (2-5.30)*

The Mill House, Sutton Courtenay ♿✂❀ (Mrs J Stevens) S of Abingdon. Approx 8½ acres; R Thames runs through garden which is on several islands with mill pond and old paper mill. TEAS. *Adm £2 Chd £1; under 4's free. Suns April 2, June 18, Oct 1 (2-6). Parties of 10 and over welcome, please* **Tel 01235 848219**

Mount Skippet ♿✂❀ (Dr & Mrs M A T Rogers) Ramsden, 4m N of Witney. At Xrds turn E towards Finstock; after 30yds, turn R (sign-post Mount Skippet). After 400yds turn L (No Through Way sign) for 75yds. 2 acres; 2 rock gardens; alpine house; stone troughs; shrubs; herbaceous beds; primulas; conservatory; many rare plants. Fine views. Cotswold stone house largely C17. Teas for groups by prior arrangement. *Adm £1 Chd free. Private visits welcome April 1 to Sept 30, please* **Tel 01993 868253**

New College. See Oxford University Gardens

4 Northfield Cottages ♿❀ (Miss S E Bedwell) Water Eaton, nr Kidlington. From Sainsbury Roundabout S of Kidlington on A4260 take exit for A34 N. Take 1st R Water Eaton lane opp Kings Arms. Then 1st L following signs for Northfield Farm. A cottage garden of approx ¼-acre designed over last 7yrs. Mainly herbaceous, unusual plants, fruit, vegetables and greenhouse. *Adm £1. Every Tues, Fri, Sat, March 25 to Sept 16 (2-5). Private visits welcome all year, please* **Tel 01865 378910**

Nutford Lodge ♿❀ (Mrs P Elmore) In Longcot Village next to The King & Queen public house. 1m S of A420 between Faringdon and Shrivenham. 1½ acres with ornamental vegetable plot, herb and alpine rockeries, colour schemed borders, sculpture trail with many interesting features. Ponds and scree garden. An indoor gallery. *Adm 75p Chd free (Share to Headway in Oxford). Suns, Mons May 28, 29; Aug 27, 28 (2-6). Also private visits welcome for parties of 4 and over, please* **Tel 01793 782258**

The Old Rectory, Albury ♿✂❀ (Mr & Mrs J Nowell-Smith). Nr Tiddington. 4m W of Thame, at end of cul-de-sac off A418 Wheatley-Thame rd. Approx 5 acres incl lawns and borders wooded walk around lake. TEAS and plants in aid of St Helens Church. *Adm £1.50 Chd free. Sun May 7 (2-6). Private visits welcome, please* **Tel 01844 339650**

The Old Rectory, Coleshill ♿ (Mr & Mrs Martin) 3m W of Faringdon. Coleshill (a Nat Trust village) is on B4019, midway between Faringdon and Highworth. Medium-sized garden; lawns and informal shrub beds; wide variety shrubs, incl old-fashioned roses; 40-yr-old standard wisteria. Distant views of Berkshire and Wiltshire Downs. House dates from late C14. TEAS. *Adm £1 Chd free. Suns April 9 (2-6), Sept 10 (2-5)*

Regular Openers. Too many days to include in diary. Usually there is a wide range of plants giving year-round interest. See head of county section for the name and garden description for times etc.

The Old Rectory, Farnborough nr Wantage. See Berkshire

The Old Vicarage ♿❀ (Mrs T A Laurie) Weston-on-the-Green 4½m SW of Bicester, take Bletchingdon turn into village centre. 2½-acre old-fashioned vicarage garden imaginatively restored keeping its tranquil secluded atmosphere. Many unusual plants and colour combinations. Stream in a woodland walk and lily ponds. Something of interest for everyone. TEAS in aid of St Mary's Church. *Adm £1 Chd free. Mons May 29, Aug 28 (2-6)*

Oxford see also 23 Beech Croft Road, East Oxford, Headington, Iffley

Oxford University Gardens

Christ Church ✂ **Masters' Garden** Entrance on Christ Church Meadow (through War Memorial garden on St Aldates'). Created in 1926, has herbaceous borders and a new border with some unusual shrubs. A walk through the newly designed and replanted Pocock Garden, past Pocock's plane, an oriental plane planted in 1636, leads to the Cathedral Garden. *Adm £1 Chd free Combined adm £2.50 with* **Corpus Christi** *and* **Trinity College** *gardens. Sun Aug 13 (2-5)*

Corpus Christi ♿✂ Entrance from Merton St or Christ Church **Fellows' garden**. Several small gardens and courtyards overlooking Christchurch meadows. Fellows private garden not normally open to the public. *Adm £1 Combined adm £2.50 with* **Christ Church** *and* **Trinity College** *gardens. Sun Aug 13 (2-5)*

Exeter College ✂ **Rector's Lodgings** The Turl, between High & Broad Sts, Oxford. Small enclosed garden, herbaceous and shrubs, especially clematis. *Combined adm with* **New College** *£1.50 Chd free. Sun July 2 (2-5)*

Green College ♿✂ Woodstock Rd, next to Radcliffe Infirmary. 3 acres; lawns, herbaceous borders, medicinal garden with notes on traditional usage of plants. Radcliffe Observatory (Tower of the Winds) open for views of Oxford and TEAS. *Adm £1 OAP's 50p Chd free (incl Observatory). Sun June 25 (2-6)*

Holywell Manor ✂ (Balliol College) Central Oxford at corner of Manor Rd and St Cross Rd on L of St Cross Church opp law library. College garden of about 1 acre, not normally open to the public. Imaginatively laid out 50 yrs ago around horse chestnut to give formal and informal areas. Mature ginkgo avenue, spinney with spring flowers and bulbs. *Adm £1 Chd free. Please* **Tel 01865 271501** *any time of the year*

Magdalen College and Fellows' Garden (and **President's Garden** not normally open to the public) ♿✂ High Street Oxford. Entrance in High St. 60 acres including deer park, college lawns, numerous trees 150-200 yrs old, notable herbaceous and shrub plantings; Magdalen Meadows containing the deer herd is surrounded by Addison's Walk, a tree lined circuit by the R Cherwell developed since the late C18. TEAS. *Adm £1.50 Child £1. Sun March 26 (12-5). Private visits welcome by arrangement with Home Bursar* **Tel 01865 276000**

New College ✲ **Warden's Garden** Entered from New College Lane, off Catte St. Secret walled garden, replanted 1988 with interesting mix of herbaceous and shrubs. *Adm £1 Chd free. Wed June 28. Combined adm with* **Exeter College** *£1.50. Sun July 2 (2-5). Private visits welcome for parties of 4 and over, please* **Tel 01865 249002**

Queens College, Provost's, Fellows' and Nuns' Gardens High Street. ½ acre with splendid herbaceous borders, rose garden, high old stone walls; large ilex tree. Magnificent statues set in wall of Hawkesmoor's library (viewed from Provost's garden). Teas 43 St Giles (in their garden if fine). *Combined adm with* **Wadham College** *£1.50. Sun July 23 (2-5)*

Rewley House ♿✲ (Oxford University Dept for Continuing Education) Wellington Sq., St John Street. Roof Garden, 60ft × 26ft, and courtyard gardens, planted by townscaper, Jeanne Bliss, with variegated shrubs, climbers, trailing plants in mobile boxes on wheels. Maintained by the University Parks under the direction of Walter Sawyer. TEA. *Adm 75p Chd free. Sun July 30 (2-5). Private visits welcome, please* **Tel 01865 270375**

¶St Hilda's College ♿✲❀ Approx 15 mins walk E from city centre. Cross Magdalen Bridge and turn R at roundabout into Cowley Place. College Lodge at end on R. Or park in public car park at St Clements. Approx 5 acres laid to lawns and flower beds with flood plain meadow containing interesting wild flowers. TEAS. *Adm £1 Chd free. Sun March 26 (2-5)*

St Hugh's College ♿✲❀ At intersection of St Margaret's Rd and Banbury Rd, N of city centre. 10 acres comprising main garden, Principal's and Fellow's gardens largely developed from grounds of 3 early C19 houses with some original features remaining. Fine trees, many shrubs, herbaceous plants; dell garden developed from Victorian fernery; large terrace. TEAS. *Adm £1 Chd free. Sun April 30 (2-5.30)*

Templeton College ♿❀ Kennington. The College is signposted off the A423 S ring rd and Abingdon Rd out of Oxford. It is situated in the triangle between A34 and A423. Landscaped for ease of maintenance by Alan Mitchell, well known author of Collins 'A Field Guide to the Trees of Britain & Northern Europe', the College's 37 acres have been planted with more than 20,000 trees during the past 25yrs and are ringed with footpaths. Alan's mastery of shape, colour and form in trees and shrubs is noticeable in this low maintenance layout. Informal pond and cottage garden plantings designed by Stephanie Carter to harmonise with the uncompromisingly modern main buildings and the more traditional graduate residences at Egrove Farmhouse. Formal herb garden designed by Paul Edwards. TEAS. *Adm £1.50 Chd free. Sun Sept 3 (2-5.30). Private visits welcome, please* **Tel 01865 735422**

Trinity College ♿✲❀ **President's Garden**. Entrance in Broad St. Surrounded by high old stone walls, recently redesigned, has mixed borders of herbaceous and shrubs, and statuary. Historic main college gardens with specimen trees incl 200-yr-old forked catalpa and splendid fraxinus, fine long herbaceous border and handsome garden quad originally designed by Wren. **Fellows' Garden** Small walled terrace, herbaceous borders; water feature formed by Jacobean stone heraldic beasts. On display for first time. TEAS in aid of local charities. *Adm £1 Chd free Combined adm £2.50 with* **Christ Church** *and* **Corpus Christi College** *gardens Sun Aug 13 (2-5)*

University Arboretum ✲❀ 6m S of Oxford on A4074 (formerly A423), 400yds S of Nuneham Courtenay. 55 acres incl informal rhododendron walks, camellia, bamboo and acer collections, natural woodland and oak woodland, meadow with pond and associated aquatics and marginals; fine collection of mature conifers; many 150 yrs old. Staff available to answer queries. Large sale of unusual plants. Plant stall in aid of Oxford University Botanic Garden. *Adm £1 Chd free. Sun June 4 (2-5)*

Wadham College: ♿✲ **Fellows' Private Garden & Warden's Garden** Parks Rd. 5 acres, best known for trees and herbaceous borders. In the Fellows' main garden, fine ginkgo and Magnolia acuminata, etc; in the Back Quadrangle very large Tilia tomentosa 'Petiolaris'; in Mallam Court white scented garden est 1994; in the Warden's garden an ancient tulip tree; in the Fellows' private garden Civil War embankment with period fruit tree cultivars, recently established shrubbery with unusual trees and ground cover amongst older plantings. Teas 43 St Giles (July 23 only). *Adm £1 Chd free. Sun March 26. Combined adm with* **Queen's College** *£1.50, Sun July 23 (2-5)*

Wolfson College ♿❀ End of Linton Rd, off Banbury Rd, between city centre and Summertown shops. 9 acres by R Cherwell; garden developed in recent years with comprehensive plant collection tolerant of alkaline soils, grown in interesting and varied habitats both formal and informal, around a framework of fine mature trees; award winning building designed by Powell & Moya; President's garden. TEAS. *Adm £1 Chd free. Sun May 7 (2-6)*

¶Pusey House ♿✲ (Mr & Mrs R J Montague) Pusey. 1m S of A420. 12m W of Oxford. 5m from Faringdon. 38-acres. C18 setting, lawns, fine trees, lake, walled gardens, herbaceous borders, water garden, large collection of shrubs. *Adm £2 Chd free. Suns Aug 20, 27 (10-4). Parties welcome by appt, please* **Tel 01367 87491**

Quarry Bank House ♿✲ (Mr & Mrs D J Smith) nr Tackley. 2m E of Woodstock. From A4260 take A4095 to Bicester; entrance at bottom of Gibraltar Hill on sharp bend of river bridge. 8 acres with abundance of early spring flowers in sheltered situation on R. Cherwell; lawns, fine cedar, orchard and banks of trees and shrubs; attractive walks in natural quarry setting. TEAS in aid of The Muscular Dystrophy Group. *Adm £1 Chd free. Sun April 9 (2-6)*

Queen's College see Oxford University Gardens

Querns ♿✲❀ (Mr M & the Hon Mrs Whitfeld) Goring Heath. 3m NE of Pangbourne. Take B4526 from A4074 Reading-Oxford Rd. After ½m follow signs. 2-acre garden: shrub and herbaceous borders, rose garden, shrub rose garden, courtyard and formal pond. Listed house dating from early C16 with large thatched C17 barn. TEAS. *Adm £1.25 Chd free. Sun June 25 (2-6)*

Rewley House see Oxford University Gardens

Rofford Manor ♿✲❀ (Mr & Mrs J L Mogford) Little Milton. 10m SE of Oxford. 1m from Little Milton on Chalgrove Rd. Signposted Rofford only. 2 acres of gardens, within old walls laid out since 1985. Vegetable, herb, rose and swimming pool gardens. Box garden with raised pool. Yew hedges and pleached limes. Twin herbaceous borders planted Autumn 1989 flanking lawn leading to recently constructed ha-ha. TEAS. *Adm £2 Chd free. Sun Sept 10 (2-6). Private visits welcome, please* **Tel 01865 890238**

St Hilda's College and **St Hugh's College** see Oxford University Gardens

Salford Gardens ✲ 2m W of Chipping Norton. Off A44 Oxford-Worcester. TEAS. *Combined adm £1.50 Chd free. Sun June 25 (2-6). Also open 1st Tuesday of month April to Sept (2-6)*

Old Rectory ♿❀ (Mr & Mrs N M Chambers) 1½-acre garden mainly enclosed by walls. A garden of year round interest with unusual plants in mixed borders, many old roses, orchard and traditional vegetable garden. Small nursery. *Private visits welcome, please* **Tel 01808 643969**

Willow Tree Cottage ❀ (Mr & Mrs J Shapley) Small walled twin gardens; one created by owners since 1979 with shrub and herbaceous borders, many clematis; other created 1985 from old farmyard with heathers and large alpine garden. Featured in 'Successful Gardening'

Seven Bells Cottage ♿✲❀ (Dr & Mrs M Pusey) Garsington. SE of Oxford, N of B480. 1-acre garden of surprises developed since 1986, with views to Berkshire Downs and the Chilterns. A diversity of interesting trees, shrubs, plants, vegetables and herbs. Herbaceous border, island beds, wildlife areas, ponds and bog garden. Garden sculptures. Small C16 thatched farmhouse. TEAS in aid of St Mary's Church. *Adm £1. Suns May 21, July 16 (2-6). Private visits welcome, please* **Tel 01865 361488**

Shotover House ♿❀ (Lt-Col Sir John Miller) Wheatley, 6m E of Oxford on A40. Bus: Oxford-Thame or Oxford-High Wycombe-London; alight Islip turn. Large unaltered landscape garden with ornamental temples, lawns and specimen trees. Also small collection of rare cattle, sheep and birds. TEAS (in arcade with view of lake). *Adm £1 Chd free. Sun April 16 (2-6)*

Shucklets ✲❀ (Dr & Mrs G Garton) High Street Ramsden. 3m N of Witney off B4022, near centre of village. Plantsman's garden of 2 acres, with a variety of different areas: rock garden, raised beds, troughs; foliage plants, shrubs, old-fashioned roses; ornamental vegetable garden, small vineyard. Teas for large parties by WI in village hall. *Adm £1.50 Chd free. Private visits welcome April 1 to Sept 30, please* **Tel 01993 868659**

Shutford Gardens ♿✲❀ An unspoilt village 5m W of Banbury, between A422 to Stratford and B4035 to Shipston. TEAS. *Combined adm £2 Chd free. Sun July 16 (2-6)*

Fiveways Cottage (Dr & Mrs M R Aldous) Just over ½ acre in present form started 1986. Essentially cottage garden style, with shrubs, roses and many herbaceous plants, small fish pond edged by alpine bed and troughs, many trees still immature

Shutford Manor (Mr & Mrs N D Cadbury) 1½-acre walled garden of dramatic C16 house with pastoral view. Yellow and white border; formal beds with modern shrub roses; avenue of poplars

Sibford Ferris Gardens ✲ Near the Warwickshire border, S of B4035 (Banbury 6½m, Shipston-on-Stour 7½m). TEAS in aid of Sibford Primary School PTA. *Combined adm £1.50 Chd free. Sun June 25 (2-6)*

Back Acre ❀ (Mr & Mrs F A Lamb) Almost an acre, much of which is wild woodland and rough grass with wild flowers; rockery and pond, constructed about 100 years ago and restored over the last few years

Home Close (Mr & Mrs P A Randall) Cotswold stone house fronting formal 1¼-acre garden designed by Baillie-Scott in 1911, under restoration. Courtyard with ornamental fountain and Roman-style stone recesses. Terraced garden, large variety of shrubs including rare species

¶**Maria's House** ♿ (Mr & Mrs B R Mills) ¼-acre old cottage garden, surrounded and subdivided by low stone walling. Features incl box hedge porch, small pond, rockeries and herbaceous borders

¶**Sibford School** ❀ (The Manor Walled Gardens) 1½ acres of walled gardens, completely reconstructed and replanted since 1984. Designed with central pergola covered pathways, with many varieties of climbing roses and clematis. The garden is subdivided to provide vegetable plots, soft fruit, greenhouses and herb garden. The gardens are used for the teaching of horticulture and are maintained by students at the school

Sibford Gower Gardens Near the Warwickshire border, S of B4035 (Banbury 7m, Shipston-on-Stour 7m) Superlative views and numerous intriguing tucked away lanes are features of this village. TEAS.

Sun, Wed June 18, 21 *(2-6) Combined adm £1.50 Chd free*

Handywater Farm ✲❀ (Mr & Mrs W B Colquhoun) ½m N of Sibford Gower on rd to Epwell; 1½ acre family garden in process of creation since 1980. Lovely setting in open rolling countryside. Westerly sloping lawns, stream and ponds, shrub and herbaceous beds

Meadow Cottage ♿✲❀ (Mr & Mrs Roger Powell) 6 The Colony. At S end of village. A 1.3-acre garden started from a field in 1988. Large 'shrubaceous' borders; over 1300 different plants; many unusual. Conifers; shrub roses and alpines in raised beds; budding arboretum and series of waterfalls leading to stream. Views

Sun July 16 *(2-6) Combined adm £1.50 Chd free*

Carters Yard (Mr & Mrs W J S Clutterbuck) Next to Wykeham Arms. ⅓-acre very private cottage garden. Various beds and rockeries in soft colours

Meadow Cottage (as described for earlier dates)

Temple Close ♿❀ (Mr & Mrs E Jones) E of Wykeham Arms. 1¼ acres with rockery, various beds of shrubs, roses, perennials and herbs; paved streamside walk running through extensive water garden between two ponds with fountains; pets paddock; good view

Souldern Gardens ❀ Between Banbury (8m) and Bicester (7m) off B4100. 5 gardens in picturesque 'Best Kept' prizewinning village. TEAS. *Combined adm £2 Chd free (Share to Souldern Trust®). Sun June 25 (2-6)*

The Barn (Mr J Talbot) Sheltered garden with pond; wide mixed borders

Great House Close ♿❀ (Mrs C E Thornton) Long, varied garden and orchard framed by old farm buildings

The Old Forge (Mr & Mrs D Duthie) Resourceful, densely planted cottage garden with stone walling

Souldern House ♿ (Maj & Mrs A H Gray) Walled garden round C17 house; gazebo dated 1706, ancient yew hedge; bantams

Souldern Manor ♿✲ (Mr & Dr C Sanders) 25 acres of C17 house with much fresh development. Linked ponds, rock garden, waterfall, fountains, temple, pavilions and view of Cherwell valley are enhanced by many newly planted mature trees. Children's play area and pony rides

South Newington Gardens A small village 1½m from Bloxham, nr Banbury on A361 to Chipping Norton. It has a fine church, with superb mediaeval wall paintings. TEA at the village hall with stalls. 3 gardens within easy walking distance. *Combined adm £1.50. Sun June 4 (2-6)*

Applegarth ✲ (Mr & Mrs Kenneth Butcher) ¾-acre cottage garden with a rose walk featuring old-fashioned roses and lavenders; herbaceous borders and mixed borders with some unusual shrubs and young trees; small water garden and pond

The Barn ♿✲ (Mrs Rosemary Clark) Green Lane. 1 acre of lawns and mixed borders with outdoor chess game, croquet lawn, vine walk and vegetable patch

The Little Forge ♿ (Mr M B Pritchard) Small garden with shrubs; trees and vegetable patch

Sparsholt Manor (Sir Adrian & Lady Judith Swire) Off B4507 Ashbury Rd 3½m W of Wantage. Spring garden, lakes and wilderness. Teas in village hall. *Adm £1 Chd free (Share to St John Ambulance, Wantage Division®). Mon May 29 (2-6)*

Stansfield ✲❀ (Mr & Mrs D Keeble) 49 High St, Stanford-in-the-Vale. 3½m SE of Faringdon. Turn off A417 opp Vale Garage into High St 300yds. Park in street. Plantsman's 1¼-acre garden on alkaline soil. Wide range of plants, many uncommon. Scree bed, sinks and troughs, damp garden, herbaceous borders, ornamental grasses. Copse underplanted with hellebores and shade loving plants. Aromatic plants. Unusual trees and shrubs. Yr-round interest. Wide range of plants for sale. Listed in Good Gardens Guide. Featured in TV's Secret Garden 95. TEAS. *Adm £1 Chd free. Every Tues April 4 to Sept 26 (10-4) Suns June 4, July 23 (2-6). Private visits also welcome, please* **Tel 01367 710340**

Stanton Harcourt Manor ♿❀ (Mr Crispin & The Hon Mrs Gascoigne) W of Oxford on B4449. Picturesque stone manor house with unique C15 Great Kitchen, Chapel and Pope's Tower. Formal gardens leading to woodland area with remains of moat and medieval stew ponds. *Adm House and garden £3 Chd/OAP's £2. Garden only £1.50 Chd/OAP's £1. Thurs April 27, May 11, 25, June 8, 22, July 6, 20, Aug 10, 24, Sept 7, 21, Suns April 16, 30, May 7, 14, 28, June 11, 25, July 9, 23, Aug 13, 27, Sept 10, 24, Bank hol Mons April 17, May 1, 8, 29, Aug 28. For NGS Suns April 16, July 9 (2-6)*

Steeple & Middle Aston Gardens. Beautiful stone villages midway between Oxford & Banbury, ½m off A4260. Villages bordering Cherwell valley; interesting church and winding lanes with a variety of charming stone houses and cottages. Map available at all gardens. TEAS at Canterbury House. *Combined adm £2 Chd free. Sun July 2 (1-6)*

Home Farm House ✲❀ (Mr & Mrs T J G Parsons) Opp Middle Aston House, ¾m N of Steeple Aston, opp Middle Aston House. 1-acre informal garden surrounding C17 farmhouse, fine view. Mixed planting, incl unusual perennials, shrubs and roses. Vegetables and Jacob sheep. Interesting small nursery. *Private visits welcome May to Sept, please* **Tel 018693 40666**

Middle Aston House ✲ (Mr & Mrs B C Box) ¾m N of Steeple Aston. 20 acres of grounds landscaped in C18 by William Kent, incl 2 lakes, granary and icehouse

Canterbury House (Mr & Mrs M G Norris) Former rectory in 2-acre garden intersected by walls. Mature trees, herbaceous borders, lavender, herb garden, rose garden

The Longbyre (Mr & Mrs V Billings) Hornton stone house in ¼ acre. Garden constructed out of old orchard. Water feature, mixed perennials, shrubs, tubs on different levels

Kralingen (Mr & Mrs Roderick Nicholson) 2-acre informal garden designed for low maintenance without any professional help. Great variety of interesting trees and shrubs. Water garden and wild flower area

Willow Cottage ❀ (Mr & Mrs M Vivian) The Dickredge, opp White Lion. Hornton stone cottage with ½-acre garden. Old-fashioned shrub roses, many unusual plants in garden and conservatory. Fish pond with Koi

Rowans ♿✲❀ (Mr & Mrs M J Clist) The Dickredge, opp White Lion. An acre of orchard and mixed garden, incl shrubs, herbaceous borders, alpines, vegetables and small streamside area

Stonewalls ♿✲ (Mr & Mrs B Shafighian) Hempton. 1½m W of Deddington on B4031. A plantsman's garden of 1½ acres divided into many interesting areas, incl shrubbery, herbaceous border, conifer and heather bed, nearly 200 clematis and climbers. Sunken pool. TEA. *Adm £1 Chd free. Sun July 16 (2-6)*

Stratton Audley Gardens ♿❀ 3m NE of Bicester, off A421 to Buckingham. Village dates from Roman times. Church is largely mediaeval with spectacular late C17 tomb. TEAS *Combined adm £1.50 Chd free (Share to Helen House Hospice®). Sun June 4 (2-6)*

1 Church Cottages ✲ (Mr & Mrs L Sweetman) About ½-acre. A proper country cottage garden with rockery pools and stonework, vegetables, seasonal bedding, orchids

Mallories (Mr P Boyd) Mainly walled garden of ¾ acre behind row of C17 cottages converted to house. Sunny and shady herbaceous borders, old roses and other shrubs, wall plants and climbers, small conservatory. A new iris border has been planted

Manor Farm ♿✿ (Mrs H M Gosling) A recently constructed garden at Old Manor Farm House of approx ¾ acre. Shrub borders, raised beds and tree plantings, a small pond with running water and a nice view southwards into the hills

¶**Sue Ryder Home** ♿✿❀ (The Sue Ryder Foundation) Joyce Grove, Nettlebed. 5m NW of Henley-on-Thames. At Nettlebed take B481 towards Reading. Entrance 200yds on R. Ample parking. Garden of over 26 acres surrounds large Edwardian house dating from 1904. Fine selection of rhododendrons; some rare trees over 200yrs old; large lawns to rear of house slope down to pond and summer house. Italian terrace and dell. Plants and TEAS in aid of Sue Ryder Home. *Adm £1 Chd free. Sun May 14 (2-5.30)*

Swerford Park (Mr & Mrs J W Law) 4m NE of Chipping Norton, just off A361 to Banbury, ½m W of Swerford Church. In extensive parkland setting with lakeside walks, garden of Georgian house overlooks spectacular wooded valley with series of lakes linked by waterfalls. Approach along front drive where signed; parking at rear only, may not be very close. TEAS. *Adm £1 Chd free. Mon May 29 (2-6)*

Swinbrook Gardens ♿✿ 2½m E of Burford, off A40. Unspoilt Cotswold village in Windrush Valley with interesting church. TEAS. *Combined adm £1.50 or £1 each garden Chd free (Share to Swinbrook PCC®). Sun July 16 (2-6)*

Swinbrook House (Mr & Mrs J D Mackinnon) 1½m N of Swinbrook on Shipton-under-Wychwood Rd. Large garden; herbaceous border; shrubs; shrub roses; large kitchen garden; fine views. Picnics allowed

Swinbrook Manor Farm (Mrs S Freund) Medium-sized garden in exceptionally pretty surroundings next to church

Swyncombe House ♿❀ (Mr W J Christie-Miller) Cookley Green on B481 Nettlebed-Watlington. Tranquil setting in a large park; rare trees; many mature flowering shrubs and spring bulbs in woodland. C11 church in grounds. TEA (in aid of St Botolph's Church). *Adm £1 Chd under 12 free. Sun April 23 (2-7). Private visits welcome for parties of 30 and over, please* **Tel 01491 641119**

Tadmarton Gardens 5m SW of Banbury on B4035. Refreshments (1-5) at village hall in aid of St Nicholas Church, Tadmarton (1-5pm). *Combined adm £1.50 Chd free. Sun Sept 10, Sat Sept 16 (12-5)*

¶**The Arches** ♿✿ (Mr & Mrs J Bolland) ⅕-acre garden hidden at back of 30's house, lovingly designed for disabled occupant. Stone paths, open air 'rooms', summer houses. No parking

¶**Buxton House** ♿✿ (Mr & Mrs J Steele) Small garden created in last 10yrs incl a waterfall and two fountains

Tadmarton Manor ♿❀ (Mr & Mrs R K Asser) Old established 2½-acre garden; beautiful views of unspoilt countryside; fine trees, great variety of perennial plants and shrubs; wild cyclamen, tunnel arbour; C15 barn and C18 dovecote

Taynton House ♿✿❀ (Mr & Mrs David Mackenzie) Taynton, off A424 Burford to Stow-on-the-Wold. Medium-sized garden behind listed stone house in delightful Cotswold village with interesting church. Stream and copse with thousands of daffodils and spring flowers. TEAS. *Adm £1 Chd free (Share to St John's Church, Taynton®). Sun April 2 (2-6)*

Templeton College see Oxford University Gardens

Thames-Side Court ♿❀ (Mr U E Schwarzenbach) Shiplake. Take A4155 (Reading Rd) out of Henley-on-Thames to Shiplake memorial (approx 2 mls). Turn into Station Rd go over level Xing. Turn immed L into Bolney Rd, and continue to the end of this rd. Car park available within the estate. Spend hrs in these 8 acres of outstanding riverside gardens; sunken, Japanese and water gardens, dramatic tropical glasshouse, greenhouses. Children and adults are invited to ride on superb steam trains along a magnificently landscaped track and to have the chance to play croquet and boule. TEAS. *Adm £5 OAPs/Chd £2.50. Sun Aug 13 (11-5)*

Towersey Manor ♿❀ (Mr & Mrs U D Barnett) Towersey, 1½m SE of Thame, 300 yds down Manor Rd from Xrds in middle of village. Main 2-acre garden lying behind house, has all been laid out and planted within last 18 years. Formal hornbeam hedges frame smaller informal areas incorporating many shrubs, trees and old-fashioned and modern shrub roses. TEAS in fine old timbered barn. *Adm £1.50 Chd free. Weds May 24, June 21 (2-6)*

Town Farm Cottage ♿✿❀ (Mr & Mrs J Clark) Kingston Blount. 4m S of Thame. 4m NE of Watlington. 1½m NE of junction 6, M40 on B4009. 1-acre colourful garden developed over 6 yrs by present owners. Herbaceous borders, rockeries, scree beds and shrubs, rare English native black poplar trees by small lake. Many unusual plants. TEAS June only. *Adm £1 Chd free. Sun April 30. Combined adm with* **Moat Manor** *£1.50 Chd free, Sun June 11 (2-6). Private visits also welcome please* **Tel 01844 352152**

Trinity College see Oxford University Gardens

Tusmore Park ♿❀ (Tusmore Park Holdings) On A43, Baynards Green 2m, Brackley 3½m. About 20-acres of lawns, herbaceous borders, woodland garden and terraces; 6-acre lake, 3 greenhouses. TEAS. *Adm £1 Chd free. Sun July 16 (2-6)*

University Arboretum see Oxford University Gardens

Wadham College see Oxford University Gardens

Wardington Gardens 5m NE of Banbury. TEAS. *Combined adm £2.50 Chd free. Sun May 21*

Pettifers ♿✿❀ (Mr J & the Hon Mrs Price) Lower Wardington C17 village house. 1-acre plantsman's garden frames an exceptional view of sheep pastures and wooded hills. A lot of new planting, with some areas reaching maturity. Unusual plants for sale. Teas (2-6). *Adm £1 Chd free. Also open Suns April 2, June 11*

Wardington Manor ♿✿ (The Lord & Lady Wardington) 5-acre garden with topiary, rock garden, flowering shrub walk to pond. Carolean manor house 1665 (2-5.30). *Private visits by parties also welcome adm £2, please* **Tel 01295 750202**

Waterperry Gardens ♿❀ 2½m from Wheatley M40 Junction 8. 50m from London, 62m from Birmingham, 9m E of Oxford. Gardens well signed locally with Tourist Board 'rose' symbol. 20-acres; ornamental gardens, nurseries, parkland; many interesting plants; shrub, herbaceous and alpine nurseries; glasshouses and comprehensive fruit section. High quality plant centre, garden shop (**Tel 01844 339226**). TEA SHOP, Art and Craft Gallery. Saxon church with famous glasses and brasses in grounds. *Adm Gardens & Nurseries £2.20 OAPs £1.70 Chd £1 under 10 free.* **OPEN DAILY** *except Christmas and New Year hols and July 13 to 16. Coach parties by appt only* **Tel 01844 339254**. ▲*For NGS (Share to NCCPG®). Suns June 11, Aug 13 (10-6)*

Weald Manor see Bampton & Weald Gardens

Westwell Manor ✻❀ (Mr & Mrs T H Gibson). 2m SW of Burford, from A40 Burford-Cheltenham, turn L after ½m on narrow rd signposted Westwell. Unspoilt hamlet with delightful church. 6 acres surrounding old Cotswold manor house, knot and water gardens, potager, shrub roses, herbaceous borders, topiary, moonlight garden. *Adm £2 Chd 50p (Share to St Mary's Church Westwell®). Suns May 21, July 2 (2-6.30)*

White's Farm House ♿❀ (Dr & Mrs M Shone) Letcombe Bassett 3m SW of Wantage. Take B4507 signed Ashbury, then through Letcombe Regis. 2½ acres; mixed borders; wild garden with 30 yrs growth of chalk-tolerant trees, shrubs, unusual herbaceous plants, summer bulbs. Gravel scree bed, plants in pots and tubs, pond, playground and monster adventure walk. TEAS in C18 barn. *Adm £1.50 Chd free. Suns June 25, July 16 (2-6)*

Wick Hall & Nurseries ♿✻❀ (Mr & Mrs P Drysdale) Between Abingdon & Radley on Audlett Drive. Parking for disabled at house, some off-street parking. Approx 10 acres lawns and wild garden; topiary; ericaceous bed; pond garden; rockeries; walled garden enclosing knot garden. Young arboretum. Early C18 house, barn and greenhouses garden restored and developed since 1982. TEAS. *Adm £1 Chd free. Sun April 30 (2-5)*

Wilcote House ♿❀ (The Hon C E & Mrs Cecil) Finstock. Between Finstock & North Leigh. East of B4022 Witney-Charlbury Road. 4 acres set in parkland surrounding an early C17-C19 Cotswold stone house. Shrub and herbaceous borders, old-fashioned rose garden and 40yd laburnum walk (planted 1984). Old orchard being replanted as an arboretum. Spring bulbs, flowering trees, sheep and lovely views. TEAS. *Adm £1.50 Chd free (Share to Homelife DGAA & British Legion®). For NGS Suns April 30, Oct 8 (2-5.30). Private visits also welcome, please contact Mr Pollard on* **Tel 01993 868 606**

Wolfson College see Oxford University Gardens

Wood Croft ✻❀ (St Cross College) Foxcombe Lane, Boars Hill, S of Oxford. From ring rd follow signs to Wootton and Boars Hill. From junction at top Hinksey Hill, house first on L. 1½ acres designed and planted by the late Prof G E Blackman FRS. Rhododendrons, camellias, azaleas, many varieties primula in woodland and surrounding natural pond; fine trees. TEA. *Adm £1 Chd free (Share to Royal Marsden Hospital Development Appeal®). Sun May 14 (2-6)*

Woodperry House ♿✻❀ (Mr & Mrs Robert Lush) nr Stanton St John. 4m E of Oxford off B4027 on road from Headington to Horton-cum-Studley. C18 house of architectural interest (not open). Approx 5 acres including lime tree avenue, formal garden, 1 acre of walled vegetable garden. Large herbaceous and shrub borders. Water gardens under construction. Good views and country walks (Aug). TEAS in aid of Cancer Research Campaign (May) in aid of Stanton St John Parish Church (Aug). *Adm £1.50 Chd free. Suns May 14, Aug 20 (2-5). Private visits welcome for parties of 10 and over please* **Tel 01865 351204**

¶Wootton Hill ✻❀ (Mr & Mrs A Ellis) Boars Hill. From B4017 to Abingdon Rd take 1st L 50yds after Bystander Pub (Wootton Village). Colourful 7 acres with large herbaceous border. Extensive lawns, pond and natural woodland. Wonderful mulberry tree; beautiful views to The Ridgeway. TEAS. *Adm £2 Chd 50p. Sun Aug 20 (2-6)*

Wroxton Gardens 3m NW of Banbury off A422. Grounds of Wroxton Abbey open free. Teas at village fete May. TEAS **Laurels Farm** July. *Combined adm £1.30 Chd free. Mon May 29, Sun July 16 (1-6)*

6 The Firs Stratford Rd ♿❀ (Mr & Mrs D J Allen) Approx ⅓-acre family garden with island beds, shrubs, herbaceous perennials and alpines incl large collection of cranesbill geraniums

Laurels Farm ❀ (Mr & Mrs R Fox) ½-acre with island beds, shrubs, old roses and herbaceous perennials. *(Share to Katherine House Hospice)*

Yeomans ✻❀ (Mrs A E Pedder) Tadmarton 5m SW of Banbury on B4035. Small garden on 4 levels, featured in 'Easy Plants for Difficult Places' by Geoffrey Smith; C16 thatched cottage. Colourful from spring to autumn; wide variety annuals, perennials, shrubs; many climbers inc roses, clematis; shrub roses with hips. *Adm £1 Chd free (Share to Katharine House Hospice Trust®). Private visits welcome for 2 and over, by appt, please. April to Sept* **Tel 01295 780285**

Powys

See separate Welsh section beginning on page 314

Rutland

See Leicestershire

Shropshire

Hon County Organisers: Mrs J H M Stafford, The Old Rectory, Fitz, Shrewsbury SY4 3AS Tel 01743 850555
Mr & Mrs James Goodall, Rectory Cottage, Chetton, Bridgnorth, Shropshire WV16 6UF

Hon County Treasurer: Mrs P Trevor-Jones, Preen Manor, Church Preen, nr Church Stretton SY6 7LQ

DATES OF OPENING

By appointment

For telephone numbers and other details see garden descriptions. Private visits welcomed

Adcote School, Little Ness
Ashford Manor, nr Ludlow
Badger Farmhouse, Badger, nr Shifnal
Bakers House, Bromley, nr Bridgnorth
Brownhill House, Ruyton XI Towns
Church Bank, Westbury
Cricklewood Cottage, Plox Green
Farley House, Much Wenlock
Field House, Clee St Margaret, nr Ludlow
Hartshill Gardens
Haye House, nr Bridgnorth
Limeburners, Ironbridge
Millichope Park, Munslow
Oteley, Ellesmere
The Patch, Acton Pigot
Radnor Cottage, Clun,

Parties only

Erway Farm House, Dudleston Heath
Gate Cottage, English Frankton
Hatton Grange, Shifnal
Herbert Lewis Garden, Merton Nurseries, Bicton
Lower Hall, Worfield
Preen Manor, nr Church Stretton
Ruthall Manor, Ditton Priors
Swallow Hayes, Albrighton
Walcot Hall, Lydbury North
Wollerton Old Hall, Market Drayton

Regular openings

For details see garden descriptions

Field House, Clee St Margaret. Please see text
Nordybank Nurseries, nr Ludlow. Easter to mid-Oct Mons, Weds & Suns
Weston Park, Shifnal. Easter to Sept.
Wollerton Old Hall, Market Drayton. Please see text

February 12 Sunday
The Patch, Acton Pigot

February 26 Sunday
Erway Farmhouse, Dudleston Heath

March 12 Sunday
The Patch, Acton Pigot

March 26 Sunday
Erway Farmhouse, Dudleston Heath

March 28 Tuesday
Radnor Cottage, Clun

April 9 Sunday
Badger Farmhouse, Badger, nr Shifnal

April 12 Wednesday
Cricklewood Cottage, Plox Green

April 15 Saturday
Erway Farm House, Dudleston Heath

April 16 Sunday
Erway Farm House, Dudleston Heath

April 17 Monday
Erway Farm House, Dudleston Heath

April 23 Sunday
Field House, Clee St Margaret, nr Ludlow
New Hall, Eaton-under-Heywood

April 30 Sunday
Erway Farmhouse, Dudleston Heath
Morville Hall Gardens, Nr Bridgnorth
New Hall, Eaton-under-Heywood
Swallow Hayes, Albrighton

May 7 Sunday
Adcote School, Little Ness
Gatacre Park, Six Ashes

May 10 Wednesday
Cricklewood Cottage, Plox Green

May 14 Sunday
Brownhill House, Ruyton XI Towns
Gatacre Park, Six Ashes
Swallow Hayes, Albrighton

May 15 Monday
Mawley Hall, nr Cleobury Mortimer

May 21 Sunday
Adcote School, Little Ness
Hatton Grange, Shifnal
Willey Park, Broseley

May 23 Tueday
Radnor Cottage, Clun

May 27 Saturday
Brownhill House, Ruyton XI Towns

May 28 Sunday
Bitterley Court, Ludlow
Brownhill House, Ruyton XI Towns
Erway Farmhouse, Dudleston Heath
Longnor Hall, nr Dorrington
Swallow Hayes, Albrighton
Upper Shelderton House, Clungunford
Walcot Hall, Lydbury North

May 29 Monday
Dudmaston, nr Bridgnorth
Longnor Hall, nr Dorrington
Oteley, Ellesmere
Walcot Hall, Lydbury North

June 1 Thursday
Preen Manor, nr Church Stretton

June 2 Friday
Wollerton Old Hall, Market Drayton

June 4 Sunday
Adcote School, Little Ness
The Old Rectory, Fitz
The Old Vicarage, Cardington

June 6 Tuesday
Radnor Cottage, Clun

June 9 Friday
Wollerton Old Hall, Market Drayton

June 11 Sunday
Adcote School, Little Ness
Gate Cottage, English Frankton
Lower Hall, Worfield
The Old Vicarage, Cardington

June 13 Tuesday
The Patch, Acton Pigot
Radnor Cottage, Clun
Weston Park, Shifnal

June 14 Wednesday
Cricklewood Cottage, Plox Green

June 15 Thursday
Preen Manor, nr Church Stretton

June 16 Friday
Wollerton Old Hall, Market Drayton

June 17 Saturday
Hartshill Gardens, Oakengates
Peplow Hall, Hodnet

June 18 Sunday
Brownhill House, Ruyton XI Towns
Hartshill Gardens, Oakengates
Lower Hall, Worfield
Nordybank Nurseries, nr Ludlow
The Old Vicarage, Cardington
Peplow Hall, Hodnet

June 19 Monday
Mawley Hall, nr Cleobury Mortimer

June 23 Friday
Wollerton Old Hall, Market Drayton

June 24 Saturday
Whittington Village Gardens, nr Oswestry

June 25 Sunday
Benthall Hall, Broseley
Bitterley Court, Ludlow
David Austin Roses Ltd, nr Wolverhampton
Erway Farmhouse, Dudleston Heath
Harnage Farm, Cound, Shrewsbury
Herbert Lewis Garden, Merton Nurseries, Bicton
The Mill Cottage, Cound, Shrewsbury
Millichope Park, Munslow
Morville Hall Gardens, Nr Bridgnorth
Nordybank Nurseries, nr Ludlow
The Old Vicarage, Cardington
Whittington Village Gardens, nr Oswestry
Wollerton Old Hall, Market Drayton

June 29 Thursday
Preen Manor, nr Church Stretton

June 30 Friday
Moortown, nr Wellington
Wollerton Old Hall, Market Drayton

July 1 Saturday
Moortown, nr Wellington

July 2 Sunday
Field House, Clee St Margaret nr Ludlow
Glazeley Old Rectory, Glazeley
Moortown, nr Wellington
Nordybank Nurseries, nr Ludlow
The Old Vicarage, Cardington

July 7 Friday
Wollerton Old Hall, Market Drayton

July 9 Sunday
Herbert Lewis Garden, Merton Nurseries, Bicton
Linley Hall, nr Bishop's Castle
Nordybank Nurseries, nr Ludlow
The Old Vicarage, Cardington

July 11 Tuesday
Weston Park, Shifnal

July 12 Wednesday
Burford House Gardens, nr Tenbury Wells
Cricklewood Cottage, Plox Green

July 13 Thursday
Preen Manor, nr Church Stretton

July 14 Friday
Wollerton Old Hall, Market Drayton

July 15 Saturday
Brownhill House, Ruyton XI Towns
Ruthall Manor, Ditton Priors

July 16 Sunday
Astley Abbotts House, Bridgnorth
Brownhill House, Ruyton XI Towns
Nordybank Nurseries, nr Ludlow
The Old Vicarage, Cardington

July 17 Monday
Mawley Hall, nr Cleobury Mortimer

July 21 Friday
Wollerton Old Hall, Market Drayton

July 23 Sunday
Church Bank, Westbury
Nordybank Nurseries, nr Ludlow

July 25 Tuesday
Radnor Cottage, Clun

July 27 Thursday
Preen Manor, nr Church Stretton

July 28 Friday
Wollerton Old Hall, Market Drayton

July 30 Sunday
Erway Farmhouse, Dudleston Heath
Herbert Lewis Garden, Merton Nurseries, Bicton
Nordybank Nurseries, nr Ludlow

August 2 Wednesday
Herbert Lewis Garden, Merton Nurseries, Bicton
Morville Hall Gardens, Nr Bridgnorth

August 4 Friday
Wollerton Old Hall, Market Drayton

August 5 Saturday
Hawkstone Hall, Shrewsbury
Hodnet Hall Gardens, nr Market Drayton

August 6 Sunday
Hawkstone Hall, Shrewsbury

August 9 Wednesday
Burford House Gardens, nr Tenbury Wells
Cricklewood Cottage, Plox Green

August 11 Friday
Wollerton Old Hall, Market Drayton

August 12 Saturday
Hodnet Hall Gardens, nr Market Drayton

August 20 Sunday
Church Bank, Westbury

August 25 Friday
Wollerton Old Hall, Market Drayton

August 27 Sunday
Erway Farmhouse, Dudleston Heath
Herbert Lewis Garden, Merton Nurseries, Bicton

September 10 Sunday
Brownhill House, Ruyton XI Towns
Limeburners, Ironbridge

September 13 Wednesday
Burford House Gardens, nr Tenbury Wells
Cricklewood Cottage, Plox Green

September 24 Sunday
Erway Farmhouse, Dudleston Heath
Herbert Lewis Garden, Merton Nurseries, Bicton
Oteley, Ellesmere

October 1 Sunday
Preen Manor, nr Church Stretton

DESCRIPTIONS OF GARDENS

Adcote School ✗ (Adcote School Educational Trust Ltd) Little Ness, 8m NW of Shrewsbury via A5 to Montford Bridge, turn off NE follow signs to Little Ness. 20-acres; fine trees incl beeches, tulip trees, oaks (American and Evergreen); atlas cedars, Wellingtonia etc; rhododendrons, azaleas; small lake; landscaped garden. House (part shown) designed by Norman Shaw RA; Grade 1 listed building; William Morris windows; De Morgan tiles. TEAS. *Adm £1.20 Acc chd free. Suns May 7, 21, June 4, 11 (2-5). Other times strictly by appt only* **Tel 01939 260202**

Ashford Manor ♿❀ (Kit Hall Esq) Ashford Carbonel, 2¾m S of Ludlow. E of A49 Ludlow-Leominster. Garden of 2 acres, herbaceous foliage and shrubs grown in the hope of maintaining interest through the entire year, hence very few flowers. Worked entirely by owner. Picnic area – Dogs welcomed. Reasonably level ground. *Adm 50p. Private visits welcome all year, please* **Tel 01584 872100**

Astley Abbotts House ❀ (Mrs H E Hodgson) 2m NW of Bridgnorth. B4373 from Bridgnorth turn R at Cross Lane Head. Bus: Bridgnorth-Broseley or the Smithies; alight Cross Lane Head ½m. 10 acres, 5 acres PYO lavender, bee village; herbs; wild woodland garden; fine trees; lawns; rhododendrons. Only partly suitable for wheelchairs. TEAS. *Adm £1.50 Chd free (Share to Wolverhampton Eye Infirmary®). Sun July 16 (11-6)*

Badger Farmhouse (Mr & Mrs N J D Foster) Badger. From A464 Shifnal to Wolverhampton Rd turn S to Burnhill Green. In Burnhill Green turn W to Beckbury. At T junction in Beckbury turn S, ¾m on R. 3-acre garden. Over 200 varieties of daffodils and narcissi in a mature setting. Mainly in three orchards, one of apple one pear and plum and one of cherry. Also fine trees, shrubs and roses. TEAS. *Adm £1.50 Chd free (Share to Brockton Court Riding for the Disabled®). Sun April 9 (2-6). Private visits welcome, please* **Tel 01746 783222**

Bakers House ✲ (Miss L M North) Bromley. 2m from Bridgnorth. From Bridgnorth to Wolverhampton Rd (A454) signposted Bromley approx 1m from B'th or Bridgnorth to Telford Rd (A442) signposted Bromley approx 2m from Bridgnorth, Timbered cottage opp phone box. Approx ½-acre cottage garden with unusual and interesting perennials, shrubs and old roses. Scree garden for alpines, alpine house; peat bed and stone troughs; informal planting in cottage garden style in a very pretty rural setting. Best months May & June. *Adm £1 Chd 25p. Parties welcome. Private visits welcome April to July (10-7) please* **Tel 01746 763296**

Benthall Hall ♿✲ (Mr & Mrs James Benthall; The National Trust) 1m NW of Broseley, 4m NE of Much Wenlock (B4375); turning up lane marked with brown sign. Garden 3-acres; shrub roses; rockery banks; lawns; former kitchen garden; wild garden. Interesting plants and fine trees. C16 house also open. *Adm £2 Chd £1 (House & Garden £3 Chd £1). Sun June 25 (1.30-5.30)*

Bitterley Court ♿❀ (Mr & Mrs J V T Wheeler) Ludlow. Next to Bitterley Church. Follow A4117 E from Ludlow and turn off to Bitterley after about 2m. 5m from Ludlow altogether. A 6-acre garden comprising mainly lawns, specimen trees and shrubs, shrub roses and some borders. TEAS in aid of Marie Curie and Cancer Research. *Adm £1.50 Chd free. Suns May 28, June 25 (2-6)*

Brampton Bryan Hall see Hereford and Worcester

Brownhill House ✲❀ (Roger & Yoland Brown) Ruyton XI Towns. 10m NW of Shrewsbury on B4397, in village. Park at Bridge Inn. Unusual and distinctive hillside garden bordering River Perry; which has been shown on BBC2 'Gardeners World'. Great variety of features and style including laburnum walk; parterre; formal terraces; extensive shrub planting; woodland paths; glasshouses; fruit and large kitchen garden. New developments every year. TEAS. *Adm £1.50 Chd free. Sun May 14; Sat, Sun May 27, 28 Sun June 18, Sat, Sun July 15, 16, Sun Sept 10 (1.30-5.30). Private visits welcome May to Aug, please* **Tel 01939 260626**

Burford House Gardens ♿✲❀ (Treasures of Tenbury) 1m W of Tenbury Wells. 400yds S of A456. Bus: CM Ludlow-Tenbury Wells. 4-acre garden designed in 1954 by owner in beautiful surroundings on R Teme. Flowering shrubs, herbaceous plants, extensive lawns. National Clematis Collection (held on behalf of NCCPG). Nursery specializing in clematis, herbaceous, many unusual shrubs and climbers. Fine church adjacent containing Cornwall monuments. Gift shop. DOGS on lead, nursery only. TEAS; light lunches. *Adm £2.50 Chd £1. Weds July 12, Aug 9, Sept 13 (10-5)*

Church Bank ✲❀ (Mr & Mrs B P Kavanagh) Rowley 12m SW of Shrewsbury on B4386 Montgomery Rd continuing through Westbury. After ⅓m turn R for Rowley. After 3½m turn L at Xrds for Brockton. Church Bank is on L after 120yds. A plant enthusiast's, S facing garden set in a beautiful and little known part of the county, begun 5 years ago and continuing to develop and change. *Adm £1 Chd free. Suns July 23, Aug 20 (2-6); also private visits welcome May to Sept, please* **Tel 01743 891661**

Cricklewood Cottage ✲❀ (Paul & Debbie Costello) Plox Green. On A488 1m SW of Minsterley. Park on grass verge opposite. Pretty ⅓-acre cottage garden, bordered by trout stream with waterfalls and natural bog garden; colour-schemed borders of shrubs and perennials, all packed with plants, particularly shrub roses, day lilies and hardy geraniums. Featured in Your Garden, Dec 94. TEAS. *Adm £1 Chd free (Share to League of Friends of Shrewsbury Hospitals®). Weds April 12, May 10, June 14, July 12, Aug 9, Sept 13 (1.30-5.30). Private visits also welcome, please* **Tel 01743 791229**

David Austin Roses ♿❀ (Mr & Mrs David Austin) Bowling Green Lane, Albrighton, 8m NW of Wolverhampton. 4m from Shifnal (A464) left into Bowling Green Lane; or junc 3, M54 to Albrighton, right at sign 'Roses & Shrubs', Bowling Green Lane 2nd R. Famous nursery and gardens; 900 varieties old roses, English roses, shrub, species and climbing roses; rose breeding trials; rose fields; small herbaceous display garden. Private garden recently redesigned with many plants. Sculpture by Pat Austin. TEAS. *Adm £1.20 Chd free. Sun June 25 (2-6)*

Dudmaston ♿✲❀ (Sir George & Lady Labouchere; The National Trust) 4m SE of Bridgnorth on A442. Bus stop at gates ½m. 8 acres with fine trees, shrubs; lovely views over Dudmaston Pool and surrounding country. Dingle walk. TEAS. *Adm £2.50 Chd £1. Mon May 29 (2-6)*

Erway Farm House ✲❀ (Mr & Mrs A A Palmer) 3m N of Ellesmere, 2m S of Overton on Dee. Signposted from B5068 Ellesmere-St Martins Rd and B5069 Overton-Oswestry rd. 1-acre Plantswoman's garden packed with rare and interesting plants. Hellebores in profusion, many varieties of snowdrop. Later, hardy geranium and other shade loving plants. Sunny gravel garden, and new wild garden in the making. Permanent display of garden sculpture. Unusual plants from garden for sale. *Adm £1 Chd 50p. Sat, Sun, Mon April 15, 16, 17 (2-6), also last Sun in every month Feb to Sept (2-6) (February 1-5). Coach parties by appt, please* **Tel 01691 75479**

Farley House ✂ (Mr & Mrs R W Collingwood) From A458 at Much Wenlock turn N on to A4169 signed Ironbridge; house 1m on L. 1-acre garden made since 1980 by owners; alpines, herbaceous island beds, shrubs and trees. Gardening clubs and WI welcome. *Adm £1 Chd free. Open by appt April to Oct, please* **Tel 01952 727017**

Field House ♿✂❀ (Dr & Mrs John Bell) Clee St Margaret. 8m NE of Ludlow. Turning to Stoke St Milborough and Clee St Margaret. 5m from Ludlow, 10m from Bridgnorth along B4364. Through Stoke St Milborough to Clee St Margaret. Ignore R turn to Clee Village. Carry on to Field House on L. Parking. 1-acre garden created since 1982 for yr-round interest. Mixed borders; rose walk; pool garden; herbaceous borders; organic vegetable garden; spring bulbs and autumn colours. TEAS (July 2 only). *Adm £1.50 Chd 50p. Garden and nursery open Fri, Sat, Sun, Bank Hol Mons March 31 to Oct 15 (12-5). For NGS Suns April 23, July 2 (12-5). Private visits welcome, please* **Tel 01584 823242**

Gatacre Park ♿❀ (Lady Thompson) Six Ashes, 6m SE of Bridgnorth on A458. Stourbridge-Bridgnorth Rd. 8 acres. Originally a Victorian garden partly redeveloped over the last 56 years by present owner. Flowering shrubs, fine trees, incl 100ft tulip tree and manna ash; topiary walk; large woodland garden with pieris, azaleas, rhododendrons inc many interesting species now fully grown. Lovely views over Park. TEA. *Adm £1.50 Chd free (Share to Tuck Hill Church, Six Ashes®). Suns May 7, 14 (2-6)*

¶**Gate Cottage** ✂❀ (G W Nicholson & Kevin Gunnell) nr Ellesmere 10m N of Shrewsbury on A528. At village of Cockshutt take rd signposted English Frankton. Garden is 1m on R. Parking in adjacent field. A developing garden at present about 2 acres. Informal mixed plantings of trees, shrubs, herbaceous of interest to flower arrangers and plantsmen. Pool and rock garden; informal pools. Large collection of hostas; old orchard with roses. TEA. *Adm £1.50 Chd 50p. Sun June 11 (12-5). Parties by appt at other times, please* **Tel 01939 270606**

Glazeley Old Rectory ♿✂❀ (Mr & Mrs R Arbuthnott) 3½m S of Bridgnorth on B4363 Bridgnorth-Cleobury Mortimer Rd. 2½-acre garden; soil pH 6.5; largely herbaceous borders with some cottage beds; bulbs, shrubs; old-fashioned roses, shady, paved and bog gardens. Very beautiful, natural setting. Award winning garden 1990. TEAS. *Adm £1.50 Chd 50p. Sun July 2 (2-6)*

Harnage Farm ♿✂ (Mr & Mrs Ken Cooke) Cound. 8m SE of Shrewsbury on A458. Turn to Cound 1m S of Cross Houses. Harnage Farm 1m, bearing L past church. ½-acre farmhouse garden; well stocked with unusual herbaceous plants, shrubs and climbers and a collection of old roses. Extensive views over beautiful Severn Valley. TEAS. *Combined adm with* **The Mill Cottage** *£2 Chd 50p (Share to Ward 21, Nurses Fund, Shrewsbury Hospital©). Sun June 25 (2-6)*

¶**Hartshill Gardens** ✂❀ Oakengates E of Shrewsbury. Follow local signs to Oakengates. Situated in town centre, once within the Telford/Wrekin district. TEA. *Combined adm £1 Chd 50p. Sat, Sun June 17, 18 (2-5.30)*

¶**Longmede** ♿ (Mr & Mrs D J Steele) 13 Hartshill Road. Approx ½-acre ornamental garden with specimen trees, shrubs and raised alpine beds. Yr round interest. *Private visits welcome (April-Oct), please* **Tel 01952 612710**

¶**Northcote** (Mr & Mrs R A Woolley) 15 Hartshill Road. ¼-acre garden with vegetables, flowers and shrubs. *Private visits welcome (April-Oct), please* **Tel 01952 613644**

Hatton Grange ♿❀ (Mrs Peter Afia) Shifnal. Lodge gate entrance on A464, 2m S of Shifnal. 1m up drive. Large dingle with pools, rhododendrons, azaleas, fine old trees; shrubbery; rose-garden; lily pond garden. TEAS. *Adm £1.20 Chd 50p (Share to CRMF®). Sun May 21 (2-7). Parties by appt, please* **Tel 01952 460415**

Hawkstone Hall (Redemptorist Study Centre) 13m NE of Shrewsbury. 6m SW of Market Drayton on A442. Entrance from Marchamley. Large formally laid out garden. Features include ornamental flower beds; herbaceous border; rockery; pools and magnificent trees. Georgian mansion (open) with courtyard garden and winter garden. TEAS. *Adm garden only £1 Chd 50p.* ▲*Sat, Sun Aug 5, 6 (2-5)*

Haye House ♿✂❀ (Mrs Paradise) Eardington. 2m S of Bridgnorth, sign Highley B4555. 1m through village Eardington. 1-acre garden especially planted by the owner, for her work as a National & International flower demonstrator. Grade 2 listed house (not open). TEAS. *Adm £1.50 Chd free. Private visits welcome, April to Oct (10-6), please* **Tel 01746 764884**

Herbert Lewis Garden, Merton Nurseries ♿✂❀ (Herbert Lewis & Family) Bicton. 3m NW of Shrewsbury on B4380 (old A5) towards Oswestry. The Herbert Lewis is attached to Merton Nurseries. The acre of garden is a plantsman's collection of widely available and unusual plants. It is a garden for all seasons containing over 200 varieties of conifers and heathers for autumn and winter interest. However the outstanding feature is the vast collection of herbaceous perennials growing in borders and island beds. A woodland garden contains rhododendrons and azaleas as well as a selection of moisture and shade loving plants incl magnificent specimens of gunnera manicata. Open for hospice rest of the year. Guided tours if required; coach parties. TEAS in aid of Shropshire Hospice. *Adm £1.50 Chd free. Weds Aug 2, Suns June 25, July 9, 30; Aug 27; Sept 24 (11-6). Private evening visits welcome, please* **Tel 01743 850773**

Hodnet Hall Gardens ♿❀ (Mr & the Hon Mrs A Heber-Percy) 5½m SW of Market Drayton; 12m NE Shrewsbury; at junc of A53 and A442. 60-acre landscaped garden with series of lakes and pools; magnificent forest trees, great variety of flowers, shrubs providing colour throughout season; featured on TV and Radio. Unique collection of big-game trophies in C17 tearooms. Gift shop and kitchen garden. TEAS; parties to pre-book. Free car-coach park. *Adm £2.60 OAP £2.10 Chd £1. April 1 to end of Sept (Tues to Sat 2-5; Suns & Bank Hols 12-5.30). Reduced rates for organised parties of 25 or over* **Tel 01630 685 202**. *For NGS Sats Aug 5, 12 (2-5)*

Limeburners ♿✂ (Mr & Mrs J E Derry) Lincoln Hill. On outskirts of Ironbridge, Telford. From Traffic Island in Ironbridge take Church Hill and proceed up hill for ½m, garden on L 300yds below The Beeches Hospital. Prize Winning garden formerly site of a rubbish tip developed by owners as a Nature garden to attract wildlife. Many unusual shrubs giving year round interest. Featured on TV Channel 4, Garden Club. TEAS in aid of Arthritis & Rheumatism Council for Research. *Adm £1.50 Chd free. Sun Sept 10 (2-6). Private visits also welcome April to Sept, please* **Tel 01952 433715**

Lingen Nursery, Lingen Village see Hereford and Worcester

Linley Hall ♿❀ (Justin Coldwell Esq) 3m NE of Bishop's Castle. Turn E off A488 nr Lydham. Parkland; lawns, rose garden, herbaceous border; lake; temple. TEAS. *Adm £1.50 Chd free. Sun July 9 (2-6)*

Longnor Hall ♿✂❀ (Mr & Mrs A V Nicholson) Longnor. Take A49 road S of Shrewsbury to Longnor. Entry to Longnor Hall garden through grounds of Longnor Church. 70-acre garden and parkland. Interesting varieties of trees; herbaceous borders, yew and beech hedges; walled kitchen garden; stable yard and C17 house (not open); sheep and deer; Cound Brook; views of The Lawley and Caer Caradoc hills. Adjacent C13 Longnor Church. TEAS. *Adm £1.50 Chd 50p (Share to St. Mary's Church, Longnor®). Sun, Mon May 28, 29 (2-6)*

Lower Hall ♿❀ (Mr & Mrs C F Dumbell) Worfield, E of Bridgnorth, ½m N of A454 in village centre. 4 acres on R Worfe; stream, pool; shrub and woodland garden. Tudor half-timbered house (not open). Plant sales to local charity. TEAS. *Adm £2 OAPs £1.50 Chd free. Suns June 11, 18 (2-6). Private visits welcome. By appt – Coach parties May to Aug and evening parties with local catering.* **Tel 0174 64607**

Mawley Hall ♿❀ (Mr & Mrs R A Galliers-Pratt) 2m NE of Cleobury Mortimer. On A4117 Bewdley-Ludlow Rd. Bus: X92, alight at gate. A natural garden in beautiful country with magnificent views; designed for wandering amongst roses, herbs, flowering shrubs; fine old trees. TEAS. *Adm £1.50 OAPs £1 Chd under 15, 50p. Mons May 15, June 19, July 17 (2-6)*

The Mill Cottage ♿✂❀ (Mrs A J Wisden & Miss J M Hawkes) Cound. 8m SE of Shrewsbury on A458. Turn to Cound 1m S of Cross Houses. Mill Cottage 300yds on L. ¼-acre cottage garden. Many unusual & lovely herbaceous & alpine plants. Good & varied collection of hostas and ferns. *Combined adm with* **Harnage Farm** *£2 Chd 50p (Share to Ward 21, Nurses Fund, Shrewsbury Hospital©). Sun June 25 (2-6)*

Millichope Park (Mr & Mrs L Bury) Munslow, 8m NE of Craven Arms. From Ludlow (11m) turn L off B4368, ¾m out of Munslow. 13-acre garden with lakes; woodland walks; fine specimen trees, wild flowers; herbaceous borders. TEAS. *Adm £1.50 Chd 50p. Sun June 25 (2-6). Private visits welcome, please* **Tel 0158 476234**

Moortown ♿✂❀ (David Bromley Esq) 5m N of Wellington. Take B5062 signed Moortown 1m between High Ercall and Crudgington. Approx 1-acre plantsman's garden. Here may be found the old-fashioned, the unusual and even the oddities of plant life, in mixed borders of 'controlled' confusion. *Adm £2 Chd 50p. Fri, Sat, Sun June 30, July 1, 2 (2-5.30)*

Morville Hall Gardens ♿❀ nr Bridgnorth. 3m NW of Bridgnorth on A458 at junction with B4368. TEA, Hall, Dower House, Gatehouse Gardens Sun June 25. *Combined adm £2 Chd 50p. Dower House, Gate House only Sun April 30 and Wed, Aug 2 £1.50 Chd 50p (Share to Morville Church®) (2-6)*

The Dower House (Dr K Swift) 1½-acre formal garden begun 1989; incl ornamental kitchen garden and knot garden

The Gate House (Mr & Mrs A Rowe) Mature 0.4-acre garden with cottage, formal and woodland sections together with small vineyard

Morville Hall (Mr & Mrs John Norbury & The National Trust) Recently restored 2-acre garden with newly planted parterre and vineyard; C12 Church, Elizabethan House (not open) in fine setting

New Hall ❀ (Mrs R H Treasure) Eaton-under-Heywood, 4m SE of Church Stretton. Between B4368 and B4371. 10 acres of woodland with grass walks, pools, wild flowers, streams. Wellingtons needed if wet. Garden suitable for wheelchairs only in dry weather. *Adm £1.20 Chd 50p. Suns April 23, 30 (2-5)*

Nordybank Nurseries ❀ (Polly Bolton) Clee St Margaret. 7½m NE of Ludlow. Turning to Stoke St Milborough and Clee St Margaret 5m from Ludlow, 10m from Bridgnorth along B4364, through Stoke St Milborough on the Lane to Clee St Margaret. 1-acre cottage garden, densley planted with shrubs, trees, old roses and herbaceous plants including many rare varieties. Also wildflowers, herbs and foliage plants. The garden has wonderful views of Wenlock Edge and the Long Mynd and has been landscaped since 1980 on the site of an old cider orchard. Also a 'Field Garden' with over 700 varieties of herbaceous plants and a 'Rose Garden' with 60 varieties of old roses which are open Easter to mid-Oct Mons, Weds and Suns. TEAS. *Adm £1.50 Chd 50p. For NGS Suns June 18, 25, July 2, 9, 16, 23, 30 (11-6)*

The Old Rectory ✂❀ (Mrs J H M Stafford) Fitz; A5 NW of Shrewsbury; turn off at Montford Bridge, follow signs; from B5067 turn off at Leaton, follow signs. 1¼-acre botantists garden; shrub roses, vegetables; water garden. TEAS. *Adm £1.50 Chd 20p. Sun June 4 (12-6)*

The Old Vicarage ♿ (W B Hutchinson Esq) Cardington, 3m N of B4371 Church Stretton-Much Wenlock Rd, signed, or turn off A49 Shrewsbury-Ludlow Rd at Leebotwood, 2½-acre scenic garden; trees, shrubs, roses, primulas, alpines, water and bog garden. Lunch and tea picnics allowed; on site parking. *Adm £1.20 Chd free. Suns June 4, 11, 18, 25; July 2, 9, 16 (12-5.30)*

Regular Openers. See head of county section.

Oteley ❀ (Mr & Mrs R K Mainwaring) Ellesmere 1m. Entrance out of Ellesmere past Mere, opp Convent nr to A528/495 junc. 10 acres running down to Mere, incl walled kitchen garden; architectural features many interesting trees, rhododendrons and azaleas, views across Mere to Ellesmere Church. Wheelchairs only if dry. TEAS (For NSPCC). *Adm £1.50 Chd 50p. Mon May 29 (2-6), Sun Sept 24 (1-5). Private visits also welcome, please* **Tel 01691 622514**

The Patch ♿✂❀ (Mrs J G Owen) Acton Pigot. 8m SE of Shrewsbury between A49 and A458. Take Cressage Rd from Acton Burnell. Turn L after ½m, signpost Acton Pigot. This is not a garden in the strict sense but an unconventional developing patch for the plant connoisseur. Early spring bulbs, hellebores, primulas, National Collection of Epimediums. June early herbaceous, shrubs and trees. Plants in aid of St. Anthony's Cheshire Home. *Adm £1.50 Chd free. Sun Feb 12 (11-5), Sun Mar 12 (2-5), Tue June 13 (2-6). Private visits also welcome, please* **Tel 01743 718846**

Penwardine Cottage see Hereford and Worcester

Peplow Hall ♿❀ (The Hon & Mrs R V Wynn) 3m S of Hodnet via A442; turn off E. 10-acre garden with lawns, azaleas, rhododendrons, etc; roses, herbaceous borders; walled kitchen garden; 7-acre lake. TEAS. *Adm £2 Chd 50p. Sat, Sun June 17, 18 (2-5.30)*

Preen Manor ✂❀ (Mr & Mrs P Trevor-Jones) Church Preen, nr Church Stretton; 5m SW of Much Wenlock. On B4371 3m turn R for Church Preen and Hughley; after 1½m turn L for Church Preen; over Xrds, 1¼m drive on R. 6 acres on site of C12 Cluniac monastery, later Norman Shaw mansion (now demolished); garden restored and replanned now contains a variety of different gardens: walled, terraced, wild, water, kitchen and chess gardens; fine trees in park; woodland walks. C12 monastic church with oldest yew tree in Europe. Featured in NGS video 1. TEAS (except Oct 2 TEA). *Adm £2 Chd 50p. Thurs June 1, 15, 29, July 13, 27 (2-6); Sun Oct 1 (2-5). Private visits of min 15 and coach parties by appt June & July only* **Tel 01694 771207**

Radnor Cottage ✂❀ (Pam and David Pittwood) Clun. 8m W of Craven Arms, 1m E of Clun on B4368 midway between Clunton and Clun. 2 acres S-facing slope, overlooking Clun Valley. Recently developed for all-year-round interest. Daffodils; cottage garden borders; dry stone wall and terracing with herbs and alpines; stream and bog garden with willow collection; native trees, orchard, wild flower meadow. TEAS. *Adm £1 Chd 50p (Share to Christian Aid®). Tues Mar 28, May 23, June 6, 13, July 25 (2-6). Private visits welcome, please* **Tel 01588 640451**

Ruthall Manor ♿✂ (Mr & Mrs G T Clarke) Ditton Priors, Bridgnorth. Weston rd from village church 2nd L, garden ¾m. 1-acre garden with pool and specimen trees. Designed for easy maintenance with lots of ground-covering and unusual plants. Old Shires Tea Room in village open (10-5) daily except Weds. *Adm £1.50 Chd free. Sat July 15 (2.30-6). Parties welcome April to Sept, please* **Tel 01746 712 216/608**

Swallow Hayes ♿❀ (Mrs P Edwards) Rectory Rd, Albrighton WV7, 7m NW of Wolverhampton. M54 exit 3 Rectory Rd 1m towards Wolverhampton off A41 just past Roses and Shrubs Garden Centre. 2-acres; planted since 1968 with emphasis on all-the-year interest and ease of maintenance; National collection of Hamamellis and Russell Lupins. Nearly 3000 different plants, most labelled. TEAS. *Adm £1.20 Chd 10p (Share to Compton Hospice®). Suns April 30; May 14, 28 (2-6); also by appt for parties, please* **Tel 01902 372624**

Upper Shelderton House ✂❀ (Mr & Mrs G W McKelvie) 3m SW of Craven Arms. From A49 turn W at Craven Arms or at Bromfield, sign posted. From Clungunford on B4367 turn E. Azaleas, rhododendrons, trees and shrubs approx 4½ acres. Beautiful views. TEAS in aid of St Cuthbert's Church. *Adm £1.50 Chd 50p. Sun May 28 (2-6)*

Walcot Hall ♿❀ (The Hon Mrs E C Parish) Bishops Castle 3m. B4385 Craven Arms to Bishops Castle, turn L by Powis Arms, in Lydbury N. Arboretum planted by Lord Clive of India's son, now undergoing restoration. Cascades of rhododendrons, azaleas amongst specimen trees and pools. Fine views of Sir William Chambers Clock Towers, with lake and hills beyond. TEAS. *Adm £1.50 Chd 15 and under free (Share to Lydbury North Church Bell Appeal©). Sun, Mon May 28, 29 (2-6). Also by appt for parties, please* **Tel 0158 88232**

Weston Park ♿ (The Weston Park Foundation) Shifnal. 7m E of Telford on the A5 in the village of Weston-under-Lizard. Easy access junction 12 M6 and junction 3 M54. Free car/coach park. 28 acres Capability Brown landscaped gardens and arboretum, incl fine collection of nothofagus, rhododendrons and azaleas. Formal gardens of SW terrace recently restored to original C18 design, together with colourful adjacent Broderie Garden. Wide variety of trees, shrubs and flowers provides colour throughout the season. C17 house open (adm £1.50). TEAS and light meals available in The Old Stables restaurant. *Adm £3.50, OAP's £2.50, Chd £2, reduced rates for parties of 20 or more. Open Easter to September (enquiries for dates and times,* **Tel 01952 850207***). For NGS Tues June 13, July 11 (11-5)*

Whittington Village Gardens ♿❀ Daisy Lane Whittington. 2½m NE of Oswestry. Turn off B5009 150yds NW of church into Top St then into Daisy Lane. Car parking at Whittington Castle and Top St. Special features in individual gardens incl shrubs for walls, a newly restored cottage garden, a family play area, and a collection of old-fashioned and unusual herbaceous perennials. TEAS at 'The Bramleys', Top St. *Combined adm £1.50 Chd free. Sat, Sun June 24, 25 (1-5.30)*

Willey Park ✂❀ (The Lord & Lady Forester) Broseley 5m NW of Bridgnorth. Turn W off B4373. Much Wenlock 4m. 6-acre formal garden set in extensive parkland. Fine views. 10-acre woodland rhododendron/azalea walk. Magnificent mature trees. Recently planted herbaceous borders. Spectacular azalea bed near house. TEAS. *Adm £2 Chd/OAP 50p (Share to Willey & District Social Centre®). Sun May 21 (2-6)*

Wollerton Old Hall ✂❀ (John & Lesley Jenkins) Wollerton. From Shrewsbury take A53 to Hodnet 13m. Follow same road out towards Market Drayton. Turn R just after 'Wollerton' sign. Go 300 yards over a bridge to a brick pound. Garden ahead on L. 2-acre garden created around a C16 house (not open). A combination of formal design, plant associations, and intensive cultivation of perennials; a number of separate gardens with different atmospheres. Wide range of plants, some unusual and rare. Continuing expansion of garden. Featured in NGS video 1. Partly suitable wheelchairs. Light lunches, TEAS. *Adm £2 Chd 50p. Every Sat June 3 to Aug 26. For NGS every Fri June 2 to Aug 25 and Suns June 25, Aug 6 (1-5). Private visits welcome, please* **Tel 01630 84769**

Somerset

Hon County Organiser: Mrs Lyn Spencer-Mills, Hooper's Holding, Hinton St George, Somerset TA17 8SE Tel 01460 76389

Assistant Hon County Organisers: Mrs M R Cooper, 21 Lower St, Merriott, Somerset
Miss P Davies-Gilbert, Coombe Quarry, West Monkton, Taunton
Mrs Alison Kelly, The Mount, Wincanton, Tel 01968 32487

Somerset Leaflet: Mrs B Hudspith, Rookwood, West St, Hinton St George, Somerset TA17 8SA Tel 01460 73450

Hon County Treasurer: John A Spurrier Esq, Tudor Cottage, 19 Comeytrowe Lane, Taunton, Somerset TA1 5PA Tel 01823 333827

DATES OF OPENING

By appointment

For telephone numbers and other details see garden descriptions. Private visits welcomed

Abbey Farm, Montacute Gardens
Benchmark, Wells
Birdwood, Wells
Butleigh House, Butleigh
Broadview, Crewkerne
Cannington College Gardens
Chinnock House, Middle Chinnock
Clapton Court, Crewkerne
Cobbleside, Milverton Gardens
3 The College, Milverton Gardens
Copse Hall, Brent Knoll
Dodington Hall, Nether Stowey
Elworthy Cottage, Elworthy
Fig Tree Cottage, Hinton St George, Crewkerne
Forge House, Oake
Garden Cottage, Milverton Gardens
Gaulden Manor, Tolland
Gerbestone Manor, Wellington
Greencombe, Porlock
Hadspen Garden, nr Castle Cary
Hooper's Holding, Hinton St George Gardens, Crewkerne
Kingsdon, Somerton
Kites Croft, Westbury-sub-Mendip
Landacre Farm, Withypool
Leaside, Bruton
Littlecourt, West Bagborough
The Mill, Cannington
The Mill, Henley Lane, Wookey
The Mount, West Hill, Wincanton
Shepton Nursery Garden, Shepton Mallet
Stone Allerton Gardens, nr Wedmore
Walnut Farm, Yarley, nr Wells
Wayford Manor, Crewkerne
Withey Lane Farmhouse, Barton St David
Wootton House, Butleigh Wootton

Parties only

Ash House, Rimpton
Clapton Court, Crewkerne
Hatch Beauchamp Gardens
Marlpit Cottage, Wrangway Gardens
Peart Hall, Spaxton

Regular openings

For details see garden descriptions

Elworthy Cottage, Elworthy. Every Tues and Thurs mid March to mid Oct (except Aug)
Greencombe, Porlock. Sats to Tues, April to July
Hadspen Garden, nr Castle Cary. Thurs to Suns & Bank Hol Mons, March 1 to Oct 1
Hatch Court, Hatch Beauchamp Gardens. See text
Lower Severalls, Crewkerne. Open April 1 to Sept 30
Milton Lodge, Wells. Daily (not Sats) April 14 to Oct 31
Watermeadows, Clapton. Open Mon to Sat, April to Sept

April 2 Sunday
Elworthy Cottage, Elworthy
Peart Hall, Spaxton
Smocombe House, Enmore

April 8 Saturday
Stowleys, Porlock

April 9 Sunday
Wayford Manor, Crewkerne

April 14 Friday
Beryl, Wells

April 15 Saturday
Greeencombe, Porlock

April 16 Sunday
Barrington Court, Ilminster
Broadview, Crewkerne
Fairfield, Stogursey
Gerbestone Manor, Wellington
Hangerige Farm, Wrangway Gardens

April 17 Monday
Broadview, Crewkerne

April 22 Saturday
Higher Luxton Farm, Churchinford
Pear Tree Cottage, Stapley

April 23 Sunday
Clapton Court, Crewkerne
Higher Luxton Farm, Churchinford
Pear Tree Cottage, Stapley

April 29 Saturday
The Mount, West Hill, Wincanton

April 30 Sunday
Broadview, Crewkerne
7 Little Keyford Lane, Frome
The Mount, West Hill, Wincanton
Wayford Manor, Crewkerne

May 2 Tuesday
Shepton Nursery Garden, Shepton Mallet

May 3 Wednesday
Shepton Nursery Garden, Shepton Mallet

May 6 Saturday
Kingsdon, Somerton

May 7 Sunday
Broadview, Crewkerne
Forge House, Oake
Kingsdon, Somerton
Spaxton Gardens, Spaxton
West Bradley House, Glastonbury

May 8 Monday
Broadview, Crewkerne

May 13 Saturday
Clapton Court, Crewkerne
The Mount, West Hill, Wincanton

May 14 Sunday
Cannington College Gardens
Court House, East Quantoxhead
Elworthy Cottage, Elworthy
Lovibonds Farm, Burrowbridge
Milton Lodge, Wells
The Mount, West Hill, Wincanton
Smocombe House, Enmore
Wayford Manor, Crewkerne

May 17 Wednesday
Elworthy Cottage, Elworthy

May 21 Sunday
7 Little Keyford Lane, Frome

May 27 Saturday
The Mount, West Hill, Wincanton

May 28 Sunday
Broadview, Crewkerne ‡
Chinnock House, Middle Chinnock ‡
Greencombe, Porlock
Hinton St George Gardens, Crewkerne ‡
The Mill House, Castle Cary
Milton Lodge, Wells
The Mount, West Hill, Wincanton
Stone Allerton Gardens, nr Wedmore
Wayford Manor, Crewkerne
Westhay, Kingston St Mary

May 29 Monday
Broadview, Crewkerne ‡
Chinnock House, Middle Chinnock ‡
Hinton St George Gardens, Crewkerne ‡
The Mill House, Castle Cary
Stone Allerton Gardens, nr Wedmore

May 31 Wednesday
Hapsford House, nr Frome

June 3 Saturday
Ashmead, Halse
Kingsdon, Somerton
The Mill, Cannington

June 4 Sunday
Ashmead, Halse
Drayton Gardens, Langport
Kingsdon, Somerton
Landacre Farm, Withypool
The Mill, Cannington
Montacute House, Montacute

June 6 Tuesday
Shepton Nursery Garden, Shepton Mallet

June 7 Wednesday
Shepton Nursery Garden, Shepton Mallet

June 10 Saturday
Higher Luxton Farm, Churchinford
Pear Tree Cottage, Stapley

June 11 Sunday
Broadview, Crewkerne ‡
Clapton Court, Crewkerne ‡
Forge House, Oake
Hestercombe House, Taunton
Higher Luxton Farm, Churchinford
Kites Croft, Westbury-sub-Mendip
7 Little Keyford Lane, Frome
Lovibonds Farm, Burrowbridge
Lower Severalls, Crewkerne ‡
Magnolias, Thurloxton
Milton Lodge, Wells
The Mount, Chelston, Wellington
Pear Tree Cottage, Stapley

June 14 Wednesday
Kites Croft, Westbury-sub-Mendip
Magnolias, Thurloxton

June 17 Saturday
The Old Rectory, Swell
Park Wall House, Bruton
Pendower House, Hillcommon, nr Taunton
Wellesley Park Gardens, Wellington

June 18 Sunday
Gaulden Manor, Tolland
Hatch Beauchamp Gardens, Taunton
Montacute Gardens, nr Yeovil
The Mount, Chelston, Wellington ‡
The Old Rectory, Swell
Park Wall House, Bruton
Pendower House, Hillcommon, nr Taunton
Stogumber Gardens, Taunton
Wellesley Park Gardens, Wellington ‡

June 21 Wednesday
Elworthy Cottage, Elworthy
Wellesley Park Gardens, Wellington

June 24 Saturday
Greencombe, Porlock
The Mount, West Hill, Wincanton
Stapleton Manor, Martock
Stowleys, Porlock

June 25 Sunday
Ashwick Gardens, Oakhill, nr Shepton Mallet
Hassage House, Faulkland
The Mount, West Hill, Wincanton

June 26 Monday
Broadview, Crewkerne

June 28 Wednesday
Hapsford House, nr Frome

July 1 Saturday
Kingsdon, Somerton
Leaside, Bruton

July 2 Sunday
Ash House, Rimpton
Broadview, Crewkerne
Butleigh House, nr Street
Elworthy Cottage, Elworthy
Field Farm, Shepton Mallet
Kingsdon, Somerton
Leaside, Bruton
Pendower House, Hillcommon, nr Taunton

July 4 Tuesday
Shepton Nursery Gardens, Shepton Mallet

July 5 Wednesday
Shepton Nursery Gardens, Shepton Mallet

July 8 Saturday
Wrangway Gardens, Wellington

July 9 Sunday
Barford Park, nr Bridgwater
Milton Lodge, Wells
Wrangway Gardens, Wellington

July 15 Saturday
Hadspen Garden, nr Castle Cary
Holywell House, Holywell

July 16 Sunday
Brent Knoll Gardens, Highbridge
Broadview, Crewkerne
Fernhill, nr Wellington
Forge House, Oake
Holywell House, Holywell
7 Little Keyford Lane, Frome
Sutton Hosey Manor, Long Sutton

July 19 Wednesday
Fernhill, nr Wellington
Tintinhull House, nr Yeovil

July 23 Sunday
Barrington Court, Ilminster ‡
Fernhill, nr Wellington
Greencombe, Porlock
Magnolias, Thurloxton
Milverton Gardens, Taunton
Stapleton Manor, Martock ‡

July 30 Sunday
Broadview, Crewkerne
Walnut Farm, Yarley, nr Wells

August 1 Tuesday
Shepton Nursery Garden, Shepton Mallet

August 2 Wednesday
Shepton Nursery Garden, Shepton Mallet

August 3 Thursday
Dunster Castle, nr Minehead

August 5 Saturday
The Mill, Cannington

August 6 Sunday
Broadview, Crewkerne
Landacre Farm, Withypool
The Mill, Cannington
August 13 Sunday
Fernhill, nr Wellington
August 16 Wednesday
Fernhill, nr Wellington
August 20 Sunday
Birdwood, Wells
August 27 Sunday
Broadview, Crewkerne
August 28 Monday
Beryl, Wells
Broadview, Crewkerne
September 3 Sunday
Fernhill, nr Wellington
September 10 Sunday
Kites Croft, Westbury-sub-Mendip
September 13 Wednesday
Kites Croft, Westbury-sub-Mendip
September 16 Saturday
7 Little Keyford Lane, Frome
September 17 Sunday
Elworthy Cottage, Elworthy
7 Little Keyford Lane, Frome
October 1 Sunday
Glencot House, nr Wells
October 21 Saturday
Pendower House, Hillcommon, nr Taunton
October 22 Sunday
Pendower House, Hillcommon, nr Taunton

DESCRIPTIONS OF GARDENS

¶Ash House ♿ (Mr & Mrs Malcolm Shennan) Rimpton. 3m from Sherborne turn off B3148 at White Post Inn down hill to Rimpton. 1st house on L after ½ m. Garden laid out and planned in 1988/1989. 1½ acres of mainly mixed borders, small pond, collection of ornamental garden trees. Mainly rare and interesting plants. TEAS. *Adm £1.50 Chd free. Sun July 2 (2-6)*

¶Ashmead ♿ ✿❀ (Mr & Mrs O D West) Halse. Approx 7m W of Taunton off A358, about 1 SW Bishop's Lydeard and W Somerset Railway Station. Follow signs to Halse. On LH-side before reaching village. Approx 1½ acres informal garden with mixed borders; lge rockery; stream, pond and bog gardens, developed from a meadow over past 5-6 years. Also raised vegetable bed. TEAS in aid of Halse Church. *Adm £1.25 Chd 50p (under 12 free). Sat, Sun June 3, 4 (2-6)*

¶Ashwick Gardens ✿❀ ¾m N of Oakhill beside Ashwick Church. From A367, turn into Oakhill. Take 1st R and after ¼m R fork following signs to Ashwick. 2 adjoining country gardens set in Mendip Hills with beautiful views. TEAS and plants in aid of Ashwick Church. *Combined adm £2 Chd £1. Sun June 25 (2-6)*

¶Ashwick Court (Mr & Mrs C Beatson-Hird) Formal gardens with listed buildings surrounded by parkland and trees. Newly created pond garden. Approx 3 acres

¶Heckley Lodge (Mr & Mrs E Beatty) ¾-acre cottage garden with established herbaceous borders and kitchen garden. Many unusual plants of interest to flower arrangers

Barford Park ♿ (Mr & Mrs M Stancomb) Spaxton. 4½m W of Bridgwater, midway between Enmore and Spaxton. 10 acres including woodland walk. Formal garden, wild garden and water garden, surrounding a Queen Anne house with park and ha ha. TEAS. *Adm £1.50 Chd free. Sun July 9 (2-5.30)*

Barrington Court ♿ ✿❀ (The National Trust) Ilminster. NE of Ilminster. Well known garden constructed in 1920 by Col Arthur Lyle from derelict farmland (the C19 cattle stalls still exist). Gertrude Jekyll approved of the design and layout; paved paths with walled iris, white and lily gardens, large kitchen garden. Licensed restaurant, plant sales and garden shop. Lunches and TEAS. *Adm £3 Chd £1.50. Suns April 16, July 23 (11-5.30)*

¶Benchmark ✿❀ (Mr & Mrs Terence Whitman) 99 Portway, Wells. On A371 Cheddar Rd out of Wells, ½m from city centre on L. ¾-acre mature garden with mixed borders, an ornamental but productive potager, interesting perennials incl more than 50 varieties of penstemon and an orchard containing friendly geese! *Adm £1. Private visits welcome, April to Sept, please* **Tel 01749 677155**

Beryl ♿ ❀ (Mr & Mrs E Nowell) 1m N of Wells off B3139 to Bath. Left at Hawkers Lane. Victorian park created in 1842. Walled vegetable garden broken into quadrangles with box hedging and double flower picking borders. More recent planting of trees and shrubs and creation of walks and vistas. Morning coffee and TEAS. *Adm £1 OAP/Chd 50p. Fri, Mon April 14, Aug 28 (11-5.30).* **Tel 01749 678738**

Birdwood ✿❀ (Mr & Mrs R A Crane) 1½m NE Wells on B3139. Last house in Wells on edge of Mendip Hills nr double bend sign. House has long stone garden wall close to rd. Traditional Victorian garden with stone walls, lawns, herbaceous border, organic vegetable garden, small wood and wild area with conservation in mind. Special features incl many stone walls and terraces at different levels and interesting trees. TEAS. *Adm £1 Chd free. Sun Aug 20 (11-6). Private visits for parties of 25 or more welcome, please* **Tel 01749 679250**

Brent Knoll Gardens off A38 2m N of Highbridge and M5 exit 22. A mixture of 3 colourful country gardens. TEAS at Copse Hall in aid of Parish Hall. *Combined adm £2.50 Chd free. Sun July 16 (2-6)*

Cherry Trees ♿ (Group Captain D Wood)

Copse Hall ❀ (Mrs S Boss & Mrs N Hill) Terraced gardens, crinkle crankle kitchen garden wall, kiwi fruit. Display and sale of fuchsias by Brent Knoll Friendly Fuchsia Society. *Private visits welcome, please* **Tel 01278 760856** *evenings*

¶Orchard ♿ (Mr & Mrs R Brafield) Much new planting

Broadview ✿❀ (Mr & Mrs R Swann) East Street, Crewkerne. Take the A30 Yeovil Rd out of Crewkerne approx 200 yds on the left hand side. Please enter drive by turning R from the E Yeovil side. 1-acre terraced garden on elevated site with panoramic views over Crewkerne. Interesting plants and shrubs, many for sale. *Adm £1 Chd free. Suns, Mons April 16, 17, 30, May 7, 8, 28, 29, June 11, 26, July 2, 16, 30, August 6, 27, 28 (11-5). Also private visits welcome, please* **Tel 01460 73424**

Butleigh House ♿❀ (Sir Dawson & Lady Bates) Butleigh. 4m SE of Glastonbury and N of B3153 at Kingweston. Turn down High St in centre of village. About 3 acres of well laid out garden. Large herbaceous borders with chosen colours; fine trees; high semi-circular yew hedge; many roses and other good plants. TEAS in aid of St Leonard's Church, Butleigh. *Adm £1.50 Chd free. Sun July 2 (2-6). Private visits welcome June, July, please* **Tel 01458 50383**

Cannington College Gardens ♿✂❀ Cannington, 3m NW of Bridgwater. On A39 Bridgwater-Minehead Rd. Old College: Benedictine Priory 1138; fine Elizabethan W front; 7 old sandstone walled gardens protect wide range of plants, inc many less hardy subjects, ceanothus, Fremontias, Wistarias etc; 10 very large greenhouses contain exceptionally wide range of ornamental plants. New College (built 1970); magnificent views to Quantocks; tree and shrub collections; ground cover plantings; lawn grass collection and trials; horticultural science garden; one of the largest collections of ornamental plants in SW England including 8 national plant collections. TEA. *Adm for both College grounds £1.50 Chd (& organised parties of OAPs) 75p. Special rates for party bookings. For NGS Sun May 14 (2-5)*

Chinnock House ♿✂❀ (Guy & Charmian Smith) Middle Chinnock. Off A30 between Crewkerne and Yeovil. 1½-acre walled gardens, silver, white and herbaceous; recently redesigned. TEAS. *Adm £1.50 Chd free. Sun, Mon May 28, 29 (2-6). Private visits welcome for parties of 2 or over, please* **Tel 01935 881229**

Clapton Court ✂❀ (Mr & Mrs Philip Giffin) 3m S of Crewkerne on B3165 to Lyme Regis, in Clapton village opposite petrol station. 10 acres; many rare and unusual plants, shrubs and trees of botanical interest in formal and woodland settings; largest and oldest ash in Great Britain. *Adm £3 Chd free. Suns April 23, June 11, Sat May 13 (11-5). Private visits welcome, please* **Tel 01460 73220/72200**

Court House ♿❀ (Sir Walter & Lady Luttrell) East Quantoxhead 12m W of Bridgwater off A39; house at end of village past duck pond. Lovely 5-acre garden; trees, shrubs, roses and herbaceous. Views to sea and Quantocks. Partly suitable for wheelchairs. Teas in Village Hall. *Adm £2 Chd free. Sun May 14 (2-5.30)*

Dodington Hall ✂❀ (Grania & Paul Quinn) A39 Bridgwater-Minehead. 2m W of Nether Stowey turn at signpost opp Castle of Comfort. ¼m turn R. Entrance through churchyard. Reclaimed 1½-acre terrace garden; clematis, shrub roses, bulbs; Tudor house (part open). TEAS in aid of Meningitis Research. *Adm £1.50 Chd 50p. Private visits welcome, please* **Tel 01278 741400**

Drayton Gardens ½m S of A378 between Curry Rivel and Langport. TEAS at Podgers Orchard. *Combined adm £1.50. Sun June 4 (2-6)*

Bicknells Farm (Mrs Beryl Phillips) Garden on L going towards Muchelney, 100yds past PO on opp side of rd. ¾-acre garden. Lawns and shrubs either side of drive; wild flower garden in old orchard behind outbuildings; wild life pond next to small wood, with wild bank covered in foxgloves, etc; also rose bank; walled cottage garden behind house; contemporary outdoor sculptures, not usually associated with country gardens; stable now gallery for contemporary artwork

Podgers Orchard ♿ (Kate Selbourne) 1-acre cottage garden with part wild orchard; some rare herbaceous plants and shrubs featured in Homes and Gardens 1992

Dunster Castle ♿✂ (The National Trust) On A396 3m SE of Minehead. Terraces of sub-tropical plants, shrubs and camellias surrounding the fortified house of the Luttrells for 600 years; fine views. Self-drive battery operated car available. Teas in village. *Adm Garden Only £2.70 Chd £1.30. Family ticket £6.50. For NGS Thurs Aug 3 (11-5)*

Elworthy Cottage ✂❀ (Mike & Jenny Spiller) Elworthy, 12m NW of Taunton. Leave Taunton on A358 signed Minehead. In 5m turn L onto B3224 signed Monksilver. After 6m turn R into Elworthy village. 5m N of Wiveliscombe. 1-acre informal garden, yr-round, cottage-style plantings, island beds. Many unusual herbaceous plants. Large collection of hardy geraniums (over 200 varieties); pulmonarias, campanulas, penstemons, michaelmas daisies, grasses and plants for foliage effect. Wide selection of plants from the garden for sale. *Adm £1 Chd free (Share to Cancer and Leukaemia in Childhood Trust®). Nursery open Tues and Thurs afternoons mid March to mid Oct (closed Aug). Garden open Suns April 2, May 14, July 2, Sept 17, Weds May 17, June 21 (1.30-5.30). Parties welcome, please* **Tel 01984 656427**

Fairfield ♿ (Lady Gass) Stogursey, 11m NW of Bridgwater 7m E of Williton. From A39 Bridgwater-Minehead turn N; garden 1½m W of Stogursey. Woodland garden with bulbs and shrubs; paved maze. Views of Quantocks. Dogs in park and field only. TEA. *Adm £1.50 Chd free (Share to Stogursey Church®). Easter Sun April 16 (2-5.30)*

¶Fernhill ✂❀ (Mr & Mrs P Bowler) White Ball, Wellington. W on A38 from Wellington. Past Beam Bridge Hotel on L. Look for garden signs on L just before dual carriageway. Mature well-wooded garden with many specimen trees in approx 2 acres. Relandscaped and extensively restocked by present owners. Alpine, water and bog gardens leading to terraced arbour. Interesting shrub and herbaceous borders, one with walkway through from rose garden. Ha-ha with views to Wellington Monument. TEAS. *Adm £1.50 Chd free. Suns, Weds July 16, 19, 23, Aug 13, 16, Sept 3 (2-6)*

Field Farm ❀ (Mr & Mrs D R Vagg) ½m S Shepton Mallet on A371 Cannards Grave Rd. Large farmhouse garden with lovely mixed planting; old and climbing roses, variegated plants, water garden, large rockery; many old stone features. TEAS. *Adm £1.50 Chd free (Share to Doulting Church©). Sun July 2 (2-6)*

By Appointment Gardens. Avoid the crowds. Good chance of a tour by owner. See garden description for telephone number.

Forge House ♿✲❀ (Peter & Eloise McGregor) Oake. East of Taunton midway between Taunton & Wellington. On A38 take signpost for Bradford-on-Tone, Oake. 1st house on R entering village. ¾-acre informal country garden with some interest in all seasons incl pond and wildlife area. Emphasis on colour borders and fragrance. TEAS. *Adm £1 Chd 50p. Suns May 7, June 11, July 16 (2-6). Disabled & parties especially welcome by appt May to July, please* **Tel 01823 461 500**

Gaulden Manor ♿✲❀ (Mr & Mrs J Le G Starkie) Tolland. Nr Lydeard St Lawrence. 9m NW Taunton off A358. Medium-sized garden made by owners. Herb; bog; scent and butterfly gardens. Bog plants, primulas and scented geraniums. Partly suitable for wheelchairs. Cream TEAS. *Adm house & garden £3, garden only £1.50, Chd £1.50. Sun June 18 (2-5.30)*

¶Gerbestone Manor ♿✲❀ (Mr & Mrs B Lord) Wellington. 2½m E of Wellington. ½m E of junction 26 on M5. Take directions for Ford Street. The drive will be found after a short distance on the L. The garden extends to 2½ acres. Features incl a walled garden, pergola walk and sunken garden; also a pond and fountain feature and traditional beds and borders. Sadly neglected for many years; refurbishing has recently got underway. New plantings are ongoing as work continues. A more extensive, non-wheelchair walk will also be marked out to include a wooded pack rd and lake. TEAS. *Adm £2 Chd 50p. Sun April 16 (1.30-6). Private visits welcome, please* **Tel 01823 662665**

¶Glencot House ✲ (Mrs Jenny Attia) Wookey Hole. ½m SW of Wells. From Wells follow the signs to Wookey Hole. Through the village, past the Wookey Hole Caves and take 1st turning L into Titlands Lane. Proceed for approx ½m and the entrance to Glencot Cricket field is on LH-side. Drive across field and park to L of bridge. 18 acres of parkland of which approx 4 acres are formal gardens with frontage to R Axe. Herbaceous borders, rose walk and terraced walk with a water feature. TEAS. *Adm £1.50 Chd 50p. Sun Oct 1 (2-5)*

Greencombe ♿✲❀ (Miss Joan Loraine, Greencombe Garden Trust) ½m W of Porlock, left off road to Porlock Weir. 49 year old garden on edge of ancient woodland, overlooking Porlock Bay. Choice rhododendrons, azaleas, camellias, maples, roses, hydrangeas, ferns, small woodland plants and clematis. National collection of Polystichum, the 'thumbs up' fern, and of Erythronium, Vaccinium and Gaultheria. Completely organic, with compost heaps on show. Featured in NGS video 1. *Adm £2.50 Chd under 16 50p. Sats, Suns, Mons, Tues April, May, June & July (2-6); private visits welcome by appt, please* **Tel 01643 862363**. *For NGS Sats April 15, June 24, Suns May 28, July 23 (2-6)*

Hadspen Garden ♿✲❀ (N & S Pope) 2m SE of Castle Cary on A371 to Wincanton. 5-acre Edwardian garden featuring a 2-acre curved walled garden with extensive colourist borders of shrub roses and choice herbaceous plants; woodland of fine specimen trees; meadow of naturalised native flowers and grasses. National Rodgersia Collection. Lunches, TEAS Thurs, Fri, Sat, TEAS only Sun & Bank Hol Mon. *Adm £2 Chd 50p (Share to Garden History Society®). Garden and Nursery open Thurs, Fri, Sat, Sun & Bank Hol Mon (9-6); private visits welcome, March 1 to October 1, please* **Tel 01749 813707** *(after 6pm). For NGS Sun July 15 (2-6)*

Hapsford House ♿ (Mr & Mrs R Enthoven) Great Elm. 1m out of Frome on A362 to Radstock. 1st road on L to Great Elm, Hapsford and Mells. Approx ½m house on L. 8-acre C19 grade II listed garden runs from Regency house (not open) to R Mells. Woodland, riverside and meadow walks. Unrestored grotto on island of flowers. Extensive laburnum walk to main house. Garden is in its 5th yr of restoration and replanting incl many species and shrub roses. *Adm £2.50 Chd £1. Weds May 31, June 28 (11-6)*

Hassage House ✲❀ (Mr & Mrs J Donnithorne) Faulkland. 8m S of Bath on Trowbridge-Radstock Rd A 366, 1½m West Norton St Philip, 1m E Faulkland. Turn off at Tuckers Grave Inn. 300yds turn R, house at end of lane. 1½-acres of informal garden; shrubs, herbaceous, roses; lily pond; small bog garden; conservatory. Cream TEAS. *Adm £1.50 Chd free. Sun June 25 (1.30-6)*

Hatch Beauchamp Gardens 5m SE of Taunton (M5 junction 25) off A358 to Ilminster. Turn L in village of Hatch Beauchamp at Hatch Inn. Parking at Hatch Court. TEAS. *Combined adm £2 Chd £1 under 12 free. Sun June 18 (2.30-5.30)*

Hatch Court ♿✲ (Dr & Mrs Robin Odgers) Turn L in village at Hatch Inn. 5-acre garden with 30 acres of parkland and deer park surrounding a perfect 1750 Palladian mansion. Extensive, recent and continuing restoration, redesign and replanting. Magnificent walled kitchen garden, fine display of roses, shrubs, clematis and many young trees. Glorious views and a lovely setting. TEAS Thurs only. *Adm Garden only £1.50, Chd £1.00 under 12 free, house and garden £3. Tues, Wed, Thurs and Bank hol Mons May 2 to Sept 28 (garden) Thurs June 15 to Sept 14 and Aug Bank Hol Mon (house) (2.30-5.30). For NGS Sun June 18*

Hatch Court Farm ♿✲ (John Townson Esq) ⅓-acre walled garden with mixed borders created over recent years from derelict farm buildings. Also wild area with large pond surrounded by wood and parkland. Woodland walk

Hestercombe House (Somerset Fire Brigade) Cheddon Fitzpaine. Situated 3m N of Taunton. Signposted from Monkton Heathfield. Historic gardens designed by Sir Edwin Lutyens and Gertrude Jekyll. The terraced gardens are an exquisite blend of good architecture and subtle planting schemes. Long pergola and fine orangery; the borders have been restored using Jekyll's original plans. TEA. *Adm £2 OAP £1.50 Chd free. May to Sept Mon to Fri (9-5) Sat, Sun (2-5). For NGS Sun June 11 (2-5)*

Higher Luxton Farm ✲ (Mr & Mrs Peter Hopcraft) 1½m out of Churchingford on Honiton Rd. Over county boundary into Devon past thatched farmhouse on R; next turning on L before Xrds. 9m S of Taunton, 9m N of Honiton. Approx 1 acre with species trees and bulbs; walls with clematis; ponds with primula; lovely views. Pony stud. Partially suitable for wheelchairs. TEAS (June only). *Adm £1 Chd free. Sats, Suns April 22, 23 ;June 10, 11 (2-6)*

Hinton St George Gardens 2m NW of Crewkerne. N of A30 Crewkerne-Chard; S of A303 Ilminster Town Rd, at roundabout signed Lopen & Merriott, then R to one of Somerset's prettiest villages. TEAS & dog park provided at Hooper's Holding. *Combined adm £2.50 Chd free. Sun, Mon May 28, 29 (2-6)*

Fig Tree Cottage ♿✗ (Mr & Mrs Whitworth) Old walled cottage garden and courtyard of stables made from kitchen garden of neighbouring rectory, over the past 16 years by owners inspired by Margery Fish. Ground cover, shrubs, old-fashioned roses. Three giant fig trees, all perennials. *Private visits welcome, please* **Tel 01460 73548**

Holly Oak House (Mr & Mrs Michael O'Loughlin) Gas Lane. ½-acre garden with terraced lawns and south facing views. A mixture of flower beds, shrubs and herbaceous borders

Hooper's Holding ♿❀ (Ken & Lyn Spencer-Mills) High St. ⅓-acre garden, in a formal design; lily pool; dwarf conifers, rare herbaceous and shrubby plants; NCCPG National Collection of Hedychiums; fancy poultry. TEAS in aid of Cats Protection League. (Hedychiums flowering Sept and Oct). *Private visits welcome, please,* **Tel 01460 76389**

Rookwood ♿ (Ian & Betty Hudspith). ¼-acre, modern garden, herbaceous borders, pond, greenhouse, vegetable garden and fruit cage

Springfield House ♿❀ (Capt & Mrs T Hardy) 1½-acres; semi-wild wooded dell, mature trees framing view to Mendips, shrubs, herbaceous plants, bulbs

¶Holywell House ✗ (Mr & Mrs Ronald D N Somerville) Yeovil. Take the A30 Yeovil to Crewkerne for 2m. Pass the Yeovil Court Hotel then 1st L to North Coker & Hardington. Pass Foresters Arms on the L. Holywell House is next drive on R. 3-acre garden in the making; in beautiful setting with 2 streams, lge pond and lovely mature trees; variety of micro-climates used to create a range of planting with extended flowering season. Pond is fed by a spring and surrounded by bamboos. Stream and banks a special feature. Fine collection of ferns and many plants of special interest. TEAS. *Adm £1.50 Chd free. Sat, Sun July 15, 16 (2-6)*

Iford Manor see Wiltshire

Kingsdon ♿✗❀ (Mr & Mrs Charles Marrow) 2m SE of Somerton off B3151 Ilchester Rd. From Ilchester roundabout on A303 follow NT signs to Lytes Cary; left opp gates ½m to Kingsdon. 2-acre plantsman's garden and nursery garden. Over 500 varieties of unusual plants for sale. Teas in Village Hall. *Adm £2 Chd free. Sats, Suns May 6, 7; June 3, 4; July 1, 2, (2-7). Private visits welcome, please* **Tel 01935840 232**

Kites Croft ✗❀ (Dr & Mrs W I Stanton) Westbury-sub-Mendip 5m NW of Wells. At Westbury Cross on A371 turn uphill, right to square and left up Free Hill to Kites Croft 2-acre garden with fine views to Glastonbury Tor. Winding paths lead from the terrace to different levels; lawn, ponds, rockery, herbaceous borders, shrubs and wood. Many unusual plants of interest to the flower arranger and cottage gardener. As featured on TV. *Adm £1.50 Chd free. Sun June 11, Wed June 14, Sun Sept 10, Wed Sept 13 (2-5); also private groups welcome, please* **Tel 01749 870328.** *No coaches*

Landacre Farm ♿✗❀ (Mr & Mrs Peter Hudson) Withypool, nr Minehead. On the B3223 Exford/S. Molton Rd 3m W of Exford not in Withypool village. 9m NW of Dulverton ¼m above Landacre Bridge. ½-acre terraced garden 1000ft up on Exmoor. Developed from a field over past 19yrs by present owners; rockery, stream and bog garden, octagonal pergola, rhodedendrons and shrub roses. Exposed position with fantastic views of Barle Valley and open moorland; specializing in climbers and hardy perennials. TEAS. *Adm £1. Chd free. Suns June 4, Aug 6 (2-5.30). Private visits welcome, please* **Tel 0164 383 223**

Leaside ♿❀ (Mr & Mrs M Hedderwick) Bruton. 1m SE of Bruton on B3081 (signposted Wincanton) turn E to Stourton 1st cottage on R. 1-acre field transformed into a nature garden with nearly 1000 fragrant shrubs and trees. Informal pond and old-fashioned roses. Worth seeing in each season. TEAS. *Adm £1 Chd free (Share to Bristol Area Kidney Patients Association®). Sat, Sun July 1, 2. Private visits welcome, please* **Tel 01749 813759**

¶7 Little Keyford Lane ✗❀ (Duncan Skene) Frome. From the Frome bypass (A361) app Frome from the S on the B3092. On the outskirts, Little Keyford Lane is the first sharp L and no.7 is approx 300metres. 7yr-old ½-acre garden featuring recent landscaping and planting; perennials galore, native plants, unusual trees, children's play area. Edge of town location with views of local landmarks. Partially suitable wheel chairs. TEAS. *Adm £1 Chd free (Share to Oxfam®). Suns April 30, May 21, June 11, July 16; Sat, Sun Sept 16, 17 (2-6)*

Littlecourt ♿✗ (Jane Kimber & John Clothier) West Bagborough. 7m N of Taunton signed from A358. 6-acre garden in fine setting with woodland and water; spectacular new borders, interesting and extensive planting; wonderful views. *Adm £2 Private visits only, please* **Tel 01823 432281**

Lovibonds Farm ♿✗❀ (Mr & Mrs J A Griffiths) Burrowbridge. A361 from Taunton to Glastonbury, in village of Burrowbridge turn L immediately over bridge ½m on. 3-acre garden reclaimed from derelict farmyard; herbaceous; shrub; bog garden; ponds and woodland walk; small lake with ornamental duck and geese. TEAS in aid of Burrowbridge WI. *Adm £1.50 Chd free. Suns May 14, June 11 (2-5.30)*

Lower Severalls ♿✗❀ (Howard & Audrey Pring) 1½m NE of Crewkerne. Turning for Merriott off A30; or Haselbury from A356. 2-acre plantsman's garden beside early Ham stone farmhouse. Herbaceous borders incl collection of salvias and herbaceous geraniums. Herb gardens. Shrub borders. Nursery (open daily March 1 to Oct 31 10-5, Suns 2-5) Closed all day Thurs.) Sells herbs, unusual herbaceous plants and half-hardy conservatory plants. TEAS on Suns June 11, July 9, Aug 13. *Adm £1.50 Chd free. Coaches by appointment. Garden open daily for NGS April 1 to Sept 30. (2-5).* **Tel 01460 73234**

Magnolias ♿✂❀ (Mr & Mrs Peter Brown) Thurloxton. 4m N of Taunton, just off A38. Next to Maypole Inn. 1 acre of informal mixed borders planted since 1986, winding grassy paths, very wide range of shrubs and small trees incl many rare varieties such as 70 different hollies. Small ornamental kitchen garden; acidified areas. TEAS in aid of St Giles Church. *Adm £1 Chd free. Sun June 11, Wed June 14, Sun July 23 (2-6)*

The Mill ♿✂❀ (Peter & Sally Gregson) Wookey. 2m W of Wells off A371. Turn L into Henley Lane, driveway 100 yds on L. 2½ acres beside R Axe. Traditional and unusual cottage plants informally planted in formal beds with roses, pergola, lawns and 'hot red border'. As seen on TV. Ornamental kitchen garden adjoining Nursery. Wide selection of plants from garden for sale. TEA. *Adm 75p Chd free. Private visits welcome, please* **Tel 01749 676966**

The Mill ✂❀ (Mr & Mrs J E Hudson) 21 Mill Lane, Cannington. 4m W of Bridgwater on A39. Turn opposite Rose & Crown. ¼-acre cottage type plantsman's garden with waterfall and pond, over 70 clematis and National Caltha Collection. Featured in NGS video 1. TEA in aid of Cannington W.I. *Adm £1.50 Chd free (Share to NCCPG®). Sats June 3, Aug 5 (2-6), Suns July 4, Aug 6 (11-5). Private visits welcome, by appt please* **Tel 01278 652304**

The Mill House ♿✂❀ (Mr & Mrs P J Davies) Castle Cary. Do not go into Castle Cary Town Centre, but follow signs to Torbay Rd Industrial Estate (W). Entrances to Trading Estate on L proceed E along Torbay Rd about 200yds. Garden on the R. Approx 1-acre terraced sloping garden, with stream and waterfalls. Emphasis on Natural look. Many interesting plants mingled with native flora. Bog garden; small orchard and vegetable plot. TEAS and plants in aid of Oncology Centre BRI Bristol. *Adm £1.50 Chd free. Sun, Mon May 28, 29 (2-6)*

Milton Lodge ✂❀ (D C Tudway Quilter Esq) ½m N of Wells. From A39 Bristol-Wells, turn N up Old Bristol Rd; car park first gate on L. Mature Grade II listed terraced garden with outstanding views of Wells Cathedral and Vale of Avalon. Mixed borders; roses; fine trees. Separate 7-acre arboretum. TEAS: Suns & Bank Hol Mons April to Sept. *Adm £2 Chd under 14 free (Share to Somerset Gardens Trust®). Open daily (2-6) ex Sats, Good Friday to end Oct; parties by arrangement. For NGS Suns May 14, 28, June 11, July 9 (2-6). Private visits welcome, please* **Tel 01749 672168**

Milverton Gardens 9m W of Taunton on the new B3227 (old A361) L at roundabout to Milverton. *Combined adm £1.50 Chd free. Sun July 23 (2-6)*

Cobbleside ♿✂ (Mr & Mrs C Pine) ¾-acre walled garden incl newly laid out herb garden and potagere. Completely redesigned, with photographs illustrating the old layout. *Private visits welcome May to Sept please* **Tel 01823 400404**

3 The College ✂ (Mr Eric Thresher) Small interesting garden, featuring fireplaces amongst shrubs and borders; interesting water features. *Private visits welcome, please* **Tel 01823 400956**

Garden Cottage ♿✂❀ (Mr & Mrs R Masters) Interesting plantsman's garden with many unusual plants for sale. TEAS in aid of Milverton Surgery Fund. Primroses in variety and other spring flowers for visitors by appt. *Private visits welcome April to Sept, please* **Tel 01823 400601**

Montacute Gardens 4m from Yeovil follow A3088, take slip road to Montacute, turn L at T-junction into village. TEAS. *Combined adm £2 Chd free. Sun June 18 (2-5.30)*

Abbey Farm ❀ (Mr & Mrs G Jenkins) Turn R between Church and Kings Arms (no through Rd). 2½-acre of mainly walled gardens on sloping site provide setting for mediaeval Priory gatehouse. Roses; herbaceous borders. Garden recently extended and improved. About half the garden suitable for wheelchairs. Parking available. TEAS in aid of St Catherine's Church Fund. *Private visits welcome, please* **Tel 01935 823572**

Park House ❀ (Mr & Mrs Ian McNab) Turn L (signposted Tintinhull) after red brick council houses and immediately R. Approx 2-acres, spacious lawns; shrubs; walled garden with herbaceous borders and vegetable garden at present being redesigned. The literary Powys family lived here during their father's lifetime. Cream TEAS in aid of St Catherines Church Fund

Montacute House ♿✂❀ (The National Trust) Montacute. NT signs off A3088 4m W of Yeovil and A303. Magnificent Tudor House with contemporary garden layout. Fine stonework provides setting for informally planted mixed borders and old roses; range of garden features illustrates its long history. Lunch and TEAS. *Adm Garden only £2.70 Chd £1.20. For NGS Sun June 4 (11.30-5.30)*

The Mount ✂❀ (Jim & Gilly Tilden) Chelston. Off M5 1m NW of junction 26. At A38 Chelston roundabout take Wellington rd. After 200yds turn R to Chelston. 1st house on R. Enclosed garden with herbaceous borders and shrubs; trees, old roses, more shrubs and pond outside. 1 acre altogether. TEAS in aid of Wellington Stroke Club. *Adm £1 Chd free. Suns June 11, 18 (2-6)*

The Mount ✂❀ (Alison & Peter Kelly) Wincanton. Follow one-way system round lower half of town, bear L at signposted Castle Cary, on up hill, house on L. 1¼-acre. Plantswomans garden with hidden surprises. Alpine lawn and garden, half terraced shrub borders, gravel bed, rock garden and pond. TEAS Suns. *Adm £1.50 Chd free. Sats April 29, May 13, 27, June 24; Suns April 30, May 14, 28, June 25 (2-5.30). Private visits welcome at weekends April to end June, please* **Tel 01963 32487** *after sundown*

Oare Manor Cottage (see Devon)

The Old Rectory ♿❀ (Cdr & Mrs J R Hoover) Swell. 4m W of Langport on A378; signposted Swell, ½m S of A378. Mature informal garden of approx 1½ acres. Good trees; pool/bog plants; old-fashioned roses; a stone belfry from nearby ancient Church of St Catherine. TEAS in aid of St Martin's Church, Fivehead. *Adm £1.50 Chd 50p. Sat, Sun June 17, 18 (2-5.30)*

¶Park Wall House ♿❀ (Capt & Mrs J J Howard) Bruton. ¼m SE of Bruton. Take B3081 out of Bruton towards Wincanton. 300yds after railway bridge on R. 1 acre (and expanding) multi-interest garden. Wide variety of mature trees, shrubs and roses. Herbaceous borders, pond, wild garden and pergola walk. Spectacular views. TEAS. *Adm £1.50 Chd 75p. Sat, Sun June 17, 18 (2-6)*

Pear Tree Cottage ♿❀ (Mr & Mrs C R Parry) Stapley. 9m S of Taunton nr Churchingford. Charming cottage garden leading to 2½-acre newly made park; well planted with interesting trees and shrubs leading to old leat and mill pond. TEAS. *Adm £1 Chd 50p. Sat, Sun April 22, 23; June 10, 11 (2-6)*

Peart Hall (Mr & Mrs J Lawrence-Mills) Spaxton. Bridgwater 6m. Take West Street (signposted Spaxton) off dual carriageway Broadway (A39) in Bridgwater. In village, take Splatt Lane opp school, then L to church and garden. Extensive gardens include rockeries sloping to trout stream, riverside walk with weirs, waterfalls; Victorian herb garden; daffodils; many rare trees. TEAS in aid of SCOPE. *Adm £1.50 Chd free. Sun April 2 (2-5)*

¶Pendower House ✿❀ (Mrs O M Maggs) Hillcommon. 5m W of Taunton off B3227 (old A361) turn R at Oake Xrds. 1st on R, parking on L verge. 1-acre landscaped garden created since 1980 on fairly level site. Shrub and herbaceous borders, collection of ceonothus. Fine display of roses, incl old-fashioned. Lge variety of young specimen and mature trees incl acers. Good autumn colour. Cream TEAS in aid of Heathfield Church. *Adm £1.50 Chd free. Sats, Suns June 17, 18, July 2 (2-5.30) Oct 21, 22 (2-4)*

Shepton Nursery Garden ♿✿❀ (Mr & Mrs P W Boughton) Old Wells Rd, Shepton Mallet. Signs to Shepton Community Hospital off B3136 Glastonbury Rd. Yr-round informal country garden built over small concrete farmyard. Closely planted with interesting and colourful shrubs and plants. Old roses, numerous container plantings. *Adm £1. Tues, Weds May 2, 3; June 6, 7; July 4, 5; Aug 1, 2 (all day). Private visits welcome at other times, please* **Tel 01749 343630**

Smocombe House ✿❀ (Mr & Mrs Dermot Wellesley Wesley) Enmore. 4m W of Bridgwater take Enmore Rd, 3rd L after Tynte Arms. 5-acres S facing in Quantock Hills. Lovely woodland garden rising up hill behind the house; views down to stream and pool below; rhododendron woodland and waterside stocked with wide variety of interesting plants for spring display; 100 tree arboretum designed by Roy Lancaster; charming old kitchen garden. TEAS in aid of Enmore Parish Church. *Adm £1.50 Chd free. Suns April 2, May 14 (2-6)*

Spaxton Gardens ♿❀ Take A39 and Spaxton Rd W from Bridgwater. In village take Splatt Lane opp school. TEAS in aid of Spaxton Church. *Combined adm £1.50 Chd free. Sun May 7 (2.30-5.30)*

Old Mill House ✿❀ (Mr & Mrs W Bryant) 2-acre beautiful, peaceful plantsman's garden beside a weir and trout stream. Many interesting plants. *(Plant stall in aid of RAF Benevolent Fund)*

Tuckers ✿❀ (Mrs John Denton) ½-acre delightful cottage garden with orchard leading over leat to Old Mill House. One way system to Old Mill House from Tuckers

Stapleton Manor ♿✿❀ (Mr & Mrs G E L Sant) 1m N of Martock on B3165 Long Sutton Rd. 2½-acres of roses, shrubs; herbaceous and mixed borders; pool/bog garden; dahlia walk; grass area with small trees and shrubs; fine mature trees. Scheduled Georgian Hamstone house (not open). *Adm £1.50 Chd free. Sat June 24, Sun July 23 (12-6)*

Stogumber Gardens ✿❀ A358 NW from Taunton for 11m. Sign to Stogumber W near Crowcombe. Eight delightful gardens of interest to plantsmen in lovely village at edge of Quantocks. TEAS. *Combined adm £2 Chd free. Sun June 18 (2-6)*

Brook Cottage ♿✿ (Mrs M Field) Good plants incl lilies in a lovely setting; small pond for added interest

Butts Cottage (Mr & Mrs J A Morrison) Cottage garden with old roses, old-fashioned perennials, alpines, pond, small vine house and vegetable garden

Cridlands Steep (Mrs A M Leitch) Large and interesting garden with young collection of trees

Manor House (Mr & Mrs R W Lawrence) Large garden with borders and beds planted to give yr-round interest and colour

Manor Linney (Dr F R Wallace) A medium-sized walled garden full of colour and interest

¶Manor Mill (Mr G Dyke) A colourful garden on a slope bounded by a stream

Orchard Deane ✿❀ (Mr & Mrs P H Wilson) Medium-sized garden, beds and borders with wide variety of hardy plants, bulbs and alpines

Wynes ✿ (Mr & Mrs L Simms) Large garden with orchard; shrubs; ponds; perennials; alpines and vegetable garden

Stone Allerton Gardens 11m NW of Wells, 2m from A38, signposted from Lower Weare. TEAS. *Combined adm £1.50 Chd free. Sun May 28, Mon May 29 (2-6)*

Manor Farm ♿✿❀ (Mr & Mrs P Coate) 1-acre of mixed herbaceous and shrub beds, foliage bed, wall borders, water garden. Old orchard and many climbing plants, a painter's garden. Listed C18 House (not open). TEAS. *Private visits welcome, please* **Tel 01934 713015**

Mill House ♿✿❀ (Mr & Mrs B W Metcalf) ¼-acre cottage style, plantsman's garden with unusual and a great variety of plants. Extensive views over levels to Quantocks. *Private visits welcome, please* **Tel 01934 712459**

¶Stowleys ♿❀ (Rev R L Hancock) Bossington Lane, Porlock. NE of Porlock off A39. 6m W of Minehead. Med-size garden, approx 2 acres with magnificent views across Porlock Bay and Bristol Channel. Daffodils, roses, unusual tender plants incl leptospermum, drimys and embothrium. Parking in paddock next door to garden. TEA and plants June only. *Adm £1 Chd free (Share to Bath and Wells Diocesan Project in Zambia®). Sats April 8, June 24 (2-6)*

Sutton Hosey Manor ♿✂ (Roger Bramble Esq) On A372 just E of Long Sutton. 2-acres; ornamental kitchen garden, lily pond, pleached limes leading to amelanchier walk past duck pond; rose and juniper walk from Italian terrace; Judas tree avenue; new ptelea walk. TEA. *Adm £2 Chd over 3 yrs 50p. Sun July 16 (2.30-6)*

Tintinhull House ♿✂ (The National Trust) NW of Yeovil. NT signs on A303, W of Ilchester. Famous 2-acre garden in compartments, developed 1900-1960, influenced by Gertrude Jekyll and Hidcote; many good and uncommon plants. C17 & C18 house (not open). TEAS in aid of St Margaret's Church. *Adm £3.30 Chd £1.60 (Party rate £2.60 Chd £1.20). For NGS Wed July 19 (12-6)*

Walnut Farm ✂❀ (Angela & John Marsh) Yarley. 3m W of Wells. On B3139 turn L at Yarley Cross. Island site 200yds up Yarley Hill. ⅔-acre plantsman's garden developed over 5 yrs. Many unusual and traditional plants. Informal and mixed planting. 2 ponds and bog garden. Yr-round interest. Splendid views of Mendips. Conservatory. Small conservation area in adjoining field. TEA and plants in aid of British Diabetic Assoc. *Adm £1.50 Chd 50p. Sun July 30 (2-6). Private visits welcome for parties of 2 and over, please* **Tel 01749 676942**

Watermeadows ♿❀ (Mr & Mrs R Gawen) 2½m S of Crewkerne on B3165 Lyme Regis Rd. A sophisticated cottage garden made from a field over 16yrs. There is something of everything including one hundred and twenty of the old-fashioned roses. Car park. TEA on request. *Adm £1 Chd free. Open Mon to Sat April to Sept (10-5). Private parties welcome, please* **Tel 01460 74421**

Wayford Manor ❀ (Mr & Mrs Robin L Goffe) SW of Crewkerne. Turning on B3165 at Clapton; or on A30 Chard-Crewkerne. 3 acres, noted for magnolias and acers. Bulbs; flowering trees, shrubs; rhododendrons. Garden redesigned by Harold Peto in 1902. Fine Elizabethan manor house (not open). TEAS. *Adm £1.50 Chd 50p. Suns April 9, 30, May 14, 28 (2-6); also private parties welcome, but please* **Tel 01460 73253**

¶Wellesley Park Gardens ♿✂❀ Wellington. ½m from centre of Wellington on S side, or can be found by turning down Hoyles Rd off the Wellington Relief Rd and taking 3rd rd L. 4 gardens situated just below the brow of the hill. TEAS. *Combined adm £2. Sat, Sun, Wed June 17, 18, 21 (2-5)*

¶Greenlands (Jack & Pat Kenney) A ½-acre 1930's town garden in process of refurbishment, planted in cottage garden style with herbaceous plants and shrubs, all organically grown. Small wildlife pond

¶Miraflores (Dr & Mrs R W Phillips) ½-acre town garden with more than 60 specimens of old roses, lawn with pond, herbaceous border, vegetable garden and small orchard

¶48 Wellesley Park (John & Julie Morton) Approx ⅕-acre small town garden. Front low maintenance with trees. Rear designed for pleasing views from house and to give breadth to garden. Central rockery and pond. Trees, shrubs and herbaceous plants augmented by pots and baskets. Screened fruit and vegetable area

¶Long Close (John & Judith Macrae) 1930's foliage garden with established trees, shrubs, pergola and sunken garden

West Bradley House ♿❀ (Mr & Mrs E Clifton-Brown) Glastonbury. 2½m due E of Glastonbury. Turn S off A361 (Shepton Mallet/Glastonbury Rd) at W Pennard. C17 octagonal stone house in 3-acre open garden next to church. 3 old carp ponds at different levels, with waterfall between 2. Range of unusual perennial and waterside plants. 70 acres of apple orchards around house, hopefully in full blossom when garden open. Visitors welcome to walk (or even drive) through orchards. Parking available. TEAS in aid of W Bradley Church. *Adm garden & orchards £1.50 Chd 50p (Share to National Listening Library®). Sun May 7 (2-6)*

Westhay ♿✂❀ (Mr & Mrs T Thompson) Kingston St Mary Taunton. 1st house on the R up the hill after the White Swan Inn, Kingston St Mary. Landscaped walled garden, bog garden, small lake; wood walk; spring daffodil lawn; streams and informal shrubberies. Suitable for wheelchairs in parts. Cream TEAS. *Adm £1.50 Chd free. Sun May 28 (2-6)*

Withey Lane Farmhouse ♿✂❀ (Sqn Ldr & Mrs H C Tomblin) Barton St David. 4m E of Somerton, turn off B3153 in Keinton Manderville. Turn R in Barton at Barton Inn. 200yds turn L at Manor House. 300yds turn R into small lane; farmhouse 300yds on right. ½-acre plantsman's garden with many unusual and interesting plants; herbaceous beds with shrubs; raised alpine beds; old roses; climbing plants; vegetables grown organically in deep beds 1½-acre old cider orchard. TEA. *Adm £1 Chd 50p. Private visits welcome all year, please* **Tel 01458 50875** *(2-5.30)*

Wootton House ♿✂ (The Hon Mrs John Acland-Hood) Butleigh Wootton, 3m S of Glastonbury. Herbaceous borders; rose garden; shrubs, trees, spring and autumn bulbs; rock garden; woodland garden. C17 house (not open). *Adm £2 Chd under 5 free. Private visits welcome, please* **Tel 01643 83586**

Wrangway Gardens ✂ Wellington 1m off A38 bypass signposted Wrangway. 1st L towards Wellington Monument over motorway bridge 1st R. TEA at Hangeridge Farm. *Combined adm £1.50. Sat, Sun July 8, 9 (2-6)*

Hangeridge Farm ♿❀ (Mr & Mrs S J Chave) Wrangway. 1-acre garden, herbaceous borders, flowering shrubs and heathers, raised rockeries, spring bulbs. Lovely setting under Blackdown Hills. *Also April 16 (2-6) Adm £1*

Marlpit Cottage ✂ (Mr & Mrs John Manning) Wrangway. 200 yds above **Hangridge Farm**. An 8yr-old ½-acre garden. Informal mixed herbaceous borders, many interesting plants colour coordination is attempted. ¾-acre garden with good views, easy parking. *Private visits welcome for parties of 25 or over, please* **Tel 01826 666130**

Staffordshire & part of West Midlands

Hon County Organisers: Mr & Mrs D K Hewitt, Arbour Cottage, Napley, Market Drayton, Shropshire TF9 4AJ Tel 01630 672852

Assistant Hon County Organiser: Mrs L Standeven, The Covert, Pheasant Walk, Burntwood, Loggerheads, Market Drayton TF9 2QZ Tel 01630 672677

DATES OF OPENING

By appointment

For telephone numbers and other details see garden descriptions. Private visits welcome

Arbour Cottage, Napley, Market Drayton
The Covert, nr Market Drayton
12 Darges Lane, Great Wyrley
Heath House, nr Eccleshall
Lower House, Sugnall Parva, Eccleshall
Manor Cottage, Chapel Chorlton, Newcastle
Moseley Old Hall, Fordhouses, Wolverhampton
Park Farm, High Offley
Wedgwood Memorial College, Barlaston
Wightwick Manor, Compton
The Wombourne, Wodehouse

Parties only

Bleak House, Bagnall
The Garth, Milford, Stafford

Regular openings

For details see garden descriptions

Arbour Cottage, Napley, Market Drayton. Fris April 21 to July 28
Manor Cottage, Chapel Chorlton, Newcastle. Mons April 17 to 25 Sept

---

Sunday 9 April
Park Farm, High Offley

Monday 8 May
Park Farm, High Offley

Wednesday 10 May
Edgewood House, nr Kinver

Sunday 14 May
Hales Hall, nr Market Drayton
Little Onn Hall, Church Eaton, nr Stafford
Moor Croft, Pattingham

Sunday 21 May
The Bradshaws, Codsall
Heath House, nr Eccleshall
Wedgwood Memorial College, Barlaston
Wightwick Manor, Compton

Sunday 28 May
The Wombourne Wodehouse

Sunday 4 June
Edgewood House, nr Kinver
The Garth, Milford, Stafford
Park Farm, High Offley

Saturday 10 June
Lower House, Sugnall Parva, Eccleshall

Sunday 11 June
The Hollies Farm, Pattingham
Little Onn Hall, Church Eaton, nr Stafford
Lower House, Sugnall Parva, Eccleshall

Sunday 25 June
Eastfield House, Kings Bromley
The Garth, Milford, Stafford
Grafton Cottage, Barton-under-Needwood
Moseley Old Hall, Fordhouses, Wolverhampton

Saturday 1 July
Park Farm, High Offley

Sunday 2 July
Bleak House, Bagnall
Eccleshall Castle Gardens
Grafton Cottage, Barton-under-Needwood
Park Avenue Gardens, Stafford

Sunday 9 July
The Covert, nr Market Drayton

Sunday 16 July
Heath House, nr Eccleshall

Sunday 23 July
Biddulph Grange Garden, Biddulph

Sunday 30 July
12 Darges Lane, Great Wyrley

Sunday 6 August
Grafton Cottage, Barton-under-Needwood
The Willows, Trysull

Sunday 27 August
Grafton Cottage, Barton-under-Needwood

Sunday 24 September
Biddulph Grange Garden, Biddulph

Sunday 8 October
Wightwick Manor, Compton

Sunday 15 October
Wedgwood Memorial College, Barlaston

DESCRIPTIONS OF GARDENS

Arbour Cottage ♿✗❀ (Mr & Mrs D K Hewitt) Napley. 4m N of Market Drayton. Take A53 then B5415 signed Woore, turn L 1¾m at telephone box. Cottage garden 2 acres of alpine gardens, grasses, shrub roses and many paeonias, bamboos etc. Colour all yr from shrubs and trees of many species. Featured in NGS Video III. TEAS. *£1.50 Chd 50p. Fris April 21 to July 28 (2-5.30). Private visits welcome, please* **Tel 01630 672852**

Biddulph Grange Garden ✗ (The National Trust) Biddulph. 3½m SE of Congleton, 7m N of Stoke-on-Trent on A527. An exciting and rare survival of a high Victorian garden extensively restored since 1988. Conceived by James Bateman, the 15 acres are divided into a number of smaller gardens designed to house specimens from his extensive plant collection. An Egyptian Court; Chinese Pagoda, Willow Pattern Bridge; Pinetum and Arboretum together with many other settings all combine to make the garden a miniature tour of the world. TEAS. *Adm £3.90 Chd £1.95 Family £9.75. April 1 to Oct 29 Wed to Fri (12-6); Sat to Sun (11-6). For NGS Suns July 23, Sept 24 (11-6)* **Tel 01782 517999**

¶Bleak House ✗❀ (Mr & Mrs J H Beynon) Bagnall. A5009 to Milton Xrds turn for Bagnall. 2m up hill past golf course to corner opp Highlands Hospital. 1-acre plantswoman's garden on 3 levels with roses, herbaceous borders. Quarry pool and terraces under construction.

TEAS. *Adm £1.50 Chd free. Sun July 2 (2-6). Parties welcome, please* **Tel 01782 534713**

The Bradshaws ♿✂❀ (Mrs R Smith & Miss S Smith) Oaken. 5m NW of Wolverhampton on A41 Wolverhampton-Newport Rd, 5m S off junction 3 M54. Mature 15-acre landscaped garden, rhododendrons and azaleas. Pools with wildfowl; specimen trees. **Dower Cottage** nearby with conservatory and cottage garden. TEAS. *Combined adm £1.50 Chd free (Share to Leonard Cheshire Foundation®). Sun May 21 (2-6)*

The Covert ✂❀ (Mr & Mrs Leslie Standeven) Burntwood Loggerheads. On Staffordshire/Shropshire borders. Turn off A53 Newcastle-Market Drayton Rd onto Burntwood at Loggerheads Xrds. A plantsman's cottage garden of approx ¾ acre, pool; bog garden, yucca bank; Tuffa Boulders; mixed borders and scree beds. Featuring many architectural, rare and unusual plants, shrubs and trees. Partially suitable for wheelchairs. TEAS. *Adm £2 Chd 50p. Sun July 9 (2-6). Private visits welcome, please* **Tel 01630 672677**

12 Darges Lane ✂❀ (Ann and Ken Hackett) Great Wyrley. From A5 take A34 towards Walsall. Darges Lane is 1st turning on R (over brow of hill). House on R on corner of Cherrington Drive. ¼-acre well stocked plantsman's and flower arranger's garden. Foliage plants a special feature. Mixed borders including trees, shrubs and rare plants giving yr-round interest. As featured in Channel 4 Garden Club Sept 93. TEAS. *Adm £1 Chd 50p. Sun July 30 (2-6). Also private visits welcome, please* **Tel 01922 415064**

¶Eastfield House ♿✂❀ (Mr & Mrs A Rogers) Kings Bromley. Kings Bromley lies 5m N of Lichfield on A515 Lichfield to Ashbourne rd and 3m W of the A38 on the A513 Tamworth to Rugby rd. Eastfield House is ½m E of the village centre on the A513. 2-acre garden surrounding a Victorian House, shrubs, lawns herbaceous plants, pond and bog garden. TEA. *Adm £1.50 Chd 50p. Sun June 25 (2-5.30)*

Eccleshall Castle Gardens ♿ (Mr & Mrs Mark Carter) ½m N of Eccleshall on A519; 6m from M6, junction 14 (Stafford); 10m from junction 15 (Stoke-on-Trent). 20 acres incl wooded garden with moat lawns around William and Mary mansion house; herbaceous, rose garden, wide variety of trees and shrubs; also recently renovated C14 tower. Home-made cream TEAS. Free car/coach parking. *Adm £1.50 Chd 50p. ▲For NGS Sun July 2 (1.30-5.30)*

¶Edgewood House ❀ (Mr & Mrs G E Fletcher) Stourton. 4m W of Stourbridge 11m E of Bridgnorth. Take A458 from Stew Poney Junction on A449 (Wolverhampton/Kidderminster) towards Bridgnorth. 1st lane on R (Greenforge Lane). ¾m along lane on L. 12 acres of woodland with winding paths through bluebells (in May) and assorted trees from cultivated natural garden with small pools. Rhododendrons and azaleas. TEAS. *Adm £1.50 Chd 50p. Wed May 10, Sun June 4 (2-6)*

The Garth ❀ (Mr & Mrs David Wright) 2 Broc Hill Way, Milford, 4½m SE of Stafford. A513 Stafford-Rugeley Rd; at Barley Mow turn R (S) to Brocton; L after 1m. ½-acre; shrubs, rhododendrons, azaleas, mixed herbaceous borders, naturalized bulbs; plants of interest to flower arrangers. Rock hewn caves. Fine landscape setting. Coach parties by appt. TEAS. *Adm £1 Chd 50p. Suns June 4, 25 (2-6). Private parties welcome, please* **Tel 01785 661182**

Grafton Cottage ✂ (Margaret & Peter Hargreaves) Bar Lane, Barton-under-Needwood. 5m N of Lichfield. Take B5016 between Barton-under-Needwood and Yoxall. Bar Lane is ½m W of Top Bell public house. ¾m along lane. A plant lover's cottage garden. ¼-acre. Designed and maintained by owners. Trellises with old roses and clematis; mixed borders, wide range of perennials with all-summer interest, stream and vegetables. TEAS. *Adm £1.50 Chd free (Share to RNIB, Midland Region®). Suns June 25, July 2, Aug 6, 27 (1.30-5.30)*

Hales Hall ✂❀ (Mr & Mrs R Hall) Hales. Signposted to Hales due S from A53 between Market Drayton & Loggerheads. C18 house (not open) in beautiful setting. 15 acres of mixed garden particularly rhododendrons, azaleas, woodland and wild garden. Partially suitable for wheelchairs by prior arrangement. Bring picnic lunches to have in park beforehand. TEAS. *Adm £2 Chd 50p. Sun May 14 (2-5.30)*

Heath House ✂❀ (Dr & Mrs D W Eyre-Walker) Nr Eccleshall. 3m W of Eccleshall. Take B5026 towards Woore. At Sugnall turn L, after 1½m turn R immediately by stone garden wall. After 1m straight across Xrds. 1½-acre garden. Borders, bog garden, woodland garden. Many unusual plants. Car parking limited and difficult if wet. TEAS. *Adm £1.50 Chd free (Share to Parish Church®). Suns May 21, July 16 (2-6). Also private visits welcome, please* **Tel 01785 280318**

The Hollies Farm ✂❀ (Mr & Mrs J Shanks) Pattingham. From Wolverhampton A454 W, follow signs to Pattingham. Cross traffic lights at Perton, 1½m R for Hollies Lane. From Pattingham take Wolverhampton Rd 1m turn L to Hollies Lane. 2-acre plantsman's landscaped garden with interesting trees and shrubs. TEAS in aid of NSPCC. *Adm £1.50 Chd free. Sun June 11 (2-6)*

Little Onn Hall ♿ (Mr & Mrs I H Kidson) Church Eaton, 6m SW of Stafford. A449 Wolverhampton-Stafford; at Gailey roundabout turn W on to A5 for 1¼m; turn R to Stretton; 200yds turn L for Church Eaton; or Bradford Arms - Wheaton Aston & Marston 1¼m. 6-acre garden; herbaceous lined drive; abundance of rhododendrons; formal paved rose garden with pavilions at front; large lawns with lily pond around house; old moat garden with fish tanks and small ruin; fine trees; walkways. Paddock open for picnics. TEAS. *Adm £1.50 Chd 50p. Suns May 14, June 11 (2-6)*

Lower House ♿❀ (Mr & Mrs J M Treanor) Sugnall Parva, Eccleshall. 2m W of Eccleshall. On B5026 Loggerheads Rd turn R at sharp double bend. House ½m on L. Large cottage garden with all yr colour and interest, mixed borders, shrubs, pond and rockery in rural setting. TEAS. *Adm £1.50 Chd free. Sat, Sun June 10, 11 (1-6). Also private visits welcome, please* **Tel 01785 851 378**

Manor Cottage ♿❀ (Mrs Joyce Heywood) Chapel Chorlton. 6m S of Newcastle-U-Lyme. On A51 Nantwich to Stone Rd turn behind Cock Inn at Stableford; white house on village green. The garden is full of interesting and unusual plants especially fern, euphorbias, grasses and geraniums. TEAS. *Adm £1.50 Chd 50p. Mons April 17 to Sept 25 (2-5). Also private visits welcome, please* **Tel 01782 680206**

Moor Croft ✲ (Mr & Mrs Peter Hollingsworth) Pattingham. Take the A454 signed to Bridgnorth. Follow signs to Pattingham. Cross traffic lights at Perton, 1m turn L Gt Moor Rd. Coming from Pattingham follow main rd to Wolverhampton for 1½m. Turn R at top of small rise for Great Moor. An interesting landscaped garden of mixed beds and trees leading to an old water meadow with stream. Fine old willows and alders together with more recent plantings. *Adm £1 Chd 50p. Sun May 14 (2-6)*

Moseley Old Hall ♿✲❀ (The National Trust) Fordhouses, 4m N of Wolverhampton, between A460 & A449 south of M54 motorway; follow signs. Small modern reconstruction of C17 garden with formal box parterre; mainly includes plants grown in England before 1700; old roses, herbaceous plants, small herb garden, arbour. Late Elizabethan house. TEAS. *Adm House & Garden £3.30 Chd £1.65; Garden £1.60 Chd 80p. For NGS Sun June 25 (2-5.30)*

Park Avenue Gardens ✲ Rising Brook. Leave M6 at Junction 13, A449 towards Stafford, approx 2m, past Royal Oak on R, past Westway on L, next turn L. From Stafford A449 over railway bridge, 4th turn on R. TEA. *Combined adm £1 Chd free. Sun July 2 (2-5.30)*

36 Park Avenue (Mr & Mrs M Harper) ⅛-acre, traditional garden with roses, shrubs and mixed borders

38 Park Avenue ❀ (Mr & Mrs E V Aspin) Small suburban mixed garden from nearly formal to nearly wild. Good collection of old roses with shrubs, clematis, fruit trees etc. Many unusual plants. Secluded brook in residential setting

Park Farm ♿✲❀ (Mr & Mrs Peter Celecia) High Offley. 4m W of Eccleshall. Take A519 towards Newport. At Woodseaves sign turn R into Back Lane, at T-junction turn R Park Lane 1m on R. A developing informal country cottage garden of 1 acre. Interesting trees, shrubs, mixed borders; pool and vegetable garden. TEA. *Adm £1.50 Chd free (Share to Multiple Sclerosis®). Suns April 9, June 4; Mon May 8; Sat July 1 (2-6). Parking available off High Offley Rd (see signs). Private visits and parties welcome at other times, please* **Tel 01785 284248** *evenings*

Wedgwood Memorial College ❀ Station Rd, Barlaston. In centre of Barlaston Village 5m S of Stoke on Trent. Leave M6 at junctions 14 or 15 take A34. Extensive grounds and gardens, the main feature being the aboretum with nearly 400 species of tree incl cherry, sorbus, and maple. Contemporary sculpture garden incorporated in the grounds and arboretum. TEAS. *Adm £1.50 Chd 50p. Suns May 21 (2-5), Oct 15 (2-4.30); also private visits welcome May to Oct, please* **Tel 01782 372105**

Wightwick Manor ♿ (The National Trust) Compton, 3m W of Wolverhampton A454, Wolverhampton-Bridgnorth, just to N of rd, up Wightwick Bank, beside Mermaid Inn. Partly suitable for wheelchairs. 17-acre, Victorian-style garden laid out by Thomas Mawson; yew hedges; topiary; terraces; 2 pools; rhododendrons; azaleas. House closed. TEAS. *Adm £2 Chd £1. For NGS Suns May 21, Oct 8 (2-6)*

The Willows ♿✲❀ (Mr & Mrs Nigel Hanson) Trysull. 7m SW of Wolverhampton. From A449 at Himley B4176 towards Bridgnorth, 2¼m turn R to Trysull. ¾m on L. 2-acre garden created and maintained by owners since 1981. Natural pool, hostas, rhododendrons, salvias, old-fashioned roses, colour theme borders with a wide range of interesting and unusual plants. Teas in village hall. *Adm £1.50 Chd free. Sun Aug 6 (2-6)*

The Wombourne Wodehouse ♿✲❀ (Mr & Mrs J Phillips) 4m S of Wolverhampton just off A449 on A463 to Sedgley. 18-acre garden laid out in 1750. Mainly rhododendrons, herbaceous and iris border, woodland walk, water garden. TEAS. *Adm £1.50 Chd free (Share to Cancer Research®). Sun May 28 (2-6); also private visits welcome, please* **Tel 01902 892202**

Suffolk

Hon County Organisers:	
(East)	Mrs Robert Stone, Washbrook Grange, Washbrook, Nr Ipswich Tel 01473 730244
(West)	Lady Mowbray, Hill House, Glemsford, Nr Sudbury CO 10 7PP Tel 01787 281930
Asst Hon County Organiser: (East)	Mrs R I Johnson, The Old Farmhouse, Flixton Road, Bungay NR35 1PD
(West)	Mrs M Pampanini, The Old Rectory, Hawstead, Bury St Edmunds IP29 5NT Tel 01284 386 613
Hon County Treasurer: (West)	Sir John Mowbray

DATES OF OPENING

By appointment

For telephone numbers and other details see garden descriptions. Private visits welcomed

Chequers, Boxford
4 Church Street, Hadleigh
Felsham House, Bury St Edmunds
Gable House, Redisham
Garden House Farm, Drinkstone
Grundisburgh Hall, Woodbridge
Pippin Cottage, nr Newmarket
Reydon Grove House, Reydon
Rosedale, Bures, nr Sudbury
Rosemary, East Bergolt
Thrift Cottage, Cowlings, nr Newmarket
Thumbit, Walsham-Le-Willows
25 Westbury Avenue, Bury St Edmunds

Parties only

The Abbey, Eye
The Priory, Stoke by Nayland
The Rookery, Eyke

Regular openings

For details see garden descriptions

Akenfield, 1 Park Lane, Charsfield. Daily Easter to Sept 30
Blakenham Woodland Gardens. Daily except Sats, March 1 to June 30
Euston Hall, nr Thetford. See text

April 2 Sunday
Barham Hall, Barham, Ipswich
Great Thurlow Hall, Haverhill

April 16 Sunday
The White House, Clare

April 17 Monday
The White House, Clare

April 23 Sunday
Garden House Farm, Drinkstone

April 30 Sunday
The Abbey, Eye
Blakenham Woodland Garden, Little Blakenham

May 3 Wednesday
Blakenham Woodland Garden, Little Blakenham

May 7 Sunday
13 Drapers Lane, Ditchingham
Magnolia House, Yoxford

May 8 Monday
13 Drapers Lane, Ditchingham
Letheringham Watermill, Woodbridge

May 13 Saturday
Warwick House, Bury St Edmunds

May 14 Sunday
The Rookery, Eyke
Warwick House, Bury St Edmunds

May 21 Sunday
The Abbey, Eye
Battlies House, Rougham
Keepers Cottage, Lawshall

May 28 Sunday
Felsham House, Bury St Edmunds
The Priory, Stoke by Nayland
Washbrook Grange, nr Ipswich
Woottens, Wenhaston

May 29 Monday
Washbrook Grange, nr Ipswich

May 31 Wednesday
Felsham House, Bury St Edmunds

June 11 Sunday
Clipt Bushes, Cockfield ‡
Hengrave Hall, Hengrave
Hillside, Freston
Moat Cottage, Great Green, Cockfield ‡
The Old Rectory, Brinkley, nr Newmarket
Rosemary, East Bergolt
Somerleyton Hall, Lowestoft
The Spong, Groton
Stour Cottage, East Bergholt
Wyken Hall, Stanton

June 18 Sunday
The Abbey, Eye
21 Bederic Close, Bury St Edmunds
Ellingham Hall, nr Bungay
Gable House, Redisham
Little Thurlow Hall, Haverhill
Pippin Cottage, nr Newmarket
The Rookery, Eyke
Woottens, Wenhaston

June 25 Sunday
Cavendish Hall, Cavendish
Denston Hall, Denston
Highfield Farm, Bures ‡
North Cove Hall, Beccles
Reydon Grove House, Reydon
Rosedale, Bures, nr Sudbury ‡
Tollemache Hall, Offton

June 28 Wednesday
Highfield Farm, Bures
Thumbit, Walsham-Le-Willows

July 2 Sunday
Long Melford Gardens
Thumbit, Walsham-Le-Willows

July 9 Sunday
Redisham Hall, Beccles

July 16 Sunday
Holbecks, Hadleigh
25 Westbury Avenue, Bury St Edmunds
Woottens, Wenhaston

July 23 Sunday
Highfield Farm, Bures ‡
Rosedale, Bures, nr Sudbury ‡

July 30 Sunday
Porters Lodge, Caversham

August 6 Sunday
The Beeches, Walsham-le-Willows
Ruggs Cottage, Reydon

August 13 Sunday
Akenfield, 1 Park Lane, Charsfield
Woottens, Wenhaston

August 14 Monday
Akenfield, 1 Park Lane, Charsfield

August 15 Tuesday
Akenfield, 1 Park Lane, Charsfield

August 16 Wednesday
Akenfield, 1 Park Lane, Charsfield

August 17 Thursday
Akenfield, 1 Park Lane, Charsfield

August 18 Friday
Akenfield, 1 Park Lane, Charsfield

August 19 Saturday
Akenfield, 1 Park Lane, Charsfield

August 20 Sunday
Akenfield, 1 Park Lane, Charsfield
21 Bederic Close, Bury St Edmunds
Washbrook Grange, nr Ipswich

August 28 Monday
Letheringham Watermill, Woodbridge

September 3 Sunday
Ickworth House, Park & Gardens, Horringer

September 17 Sunday
Chequers, Boxford

DESCRIPTIONS OF GARDENS

The Abbey ✤❀ (Mrs K Campbell) Eye. 6m S of Diss, Norfolk. Leaving Eye on B1117 passing Eye Church on L cross River Dove and The Abbey is immediately on the L with ample parking. Marked remains of Benedictine Priory on some maps. The garden is approx 3 acres and surrounds a red brick and flint timber framed house incorporating a Benedictine Abbey founded in the 11th century. The remains of the church such as are above ground make for interesting gardening with walls and courtyards. Raised beds and sink gardens and 2 large glasshouses. Unusual plants, many double primroses and auriculas, iris and roses and a large herbaceous collection. Miniature geraniums and succulents are in the glasshouses. Ample parking. TEAS. *Adm £1.50 OAP & Chd 75p. Suns April 30, May 21, June 18 (2-5.30). Parties welcome by appt May to July, please* **Tel 01379 870263**

Akenfield, 1 Park Lane ✲❀ (Mrs E E Cole) Charsfield, 6m N of Woodbridge. On B1078, 3m W of Wickham Market. ½-acre council house garden; vegetables, flowers for drying, 2 greenhouses; small fishponds with water wheel; many pot plants etc. In village of Charsfield (known to many readers and viewers as Akenfield). TEA Sunday only. *Adm £1 OAPs 75p Chd free. Daily from Easter to Sept 30. For NGS Sun Aug 13 daily to Sun Aug 20 (10.30-7). Parties welcome by appt, please* **Tel 01473 737402**

Barham Hall ♿✲❀ (Mr & Mrs Richard Burrows) Barham. Ipswich to A45 going W. 4m sign Great Blakenham to roundabout beneath motorway. Leave by 3rd turning to Claydon. Through Claydon, after decontrolled signs turn R up Church Lane to Barham Green. ½m up Church Lane. Barham church on L.h.s Barham Hall behind long brick wall. 7 acres of undulating gardens mainly recreated during the last 5yrs. 3 herbaceous borders, a lake surrounded by azaleas and bog plants, a woodland shrub garden full of spring flowers; a very considerable collection of victorian roses set in well kept lawns with mature trees; a water garden and many other interesting features. St Mary's and St Peter's Church open with famous Henry Moore sculpture. TEA. *Adm £1.50 OAPs £1 Chd 25p (Share to St Mary's & St Peters Church Barham®). Sun April 2 (2-5)*

Battlies House ♿✲ (Mr & Mrs John Barrell) Bury St Edmunds. Turn N off the A14 at the GT Barton and Rougham industrial estate turning, 3m E of Bury St Edmunds. In ½m turn R by the lodge. 8-acre garden laid out to lawns; shrubberies; woodland walk with a variety of old trees; rhododendrons; elms and conifers. TEAS. *Adm £1.50 Chd free (Share to St Nicholas' Hospice®). Sun May 21 (2-5.30)*

21 Bederic Close ✲❀ (Mrs S Robinson) Bury St Edmunds. Leave A14 at exit for Bury St Edmunds (E) and Sudbury. Proceed N and at 1st roundabout (Sainsbury's entrance) turn L into Symonds Rd. After R angled turn at end take 1st R into Bederic Close. ⅙ acre surburban garden enthusiastically developed over 10yrs with rockery and water garden. Over 500 old-fashioned, unusual rare plants and shrubs. Emphasis on conservation to encourage wildlife. Finalist in Gardener of the Year Competition. *Adm £1.50 Chd free. ▲For NGS Suns June 18, Aug 20 (2.30-6). Private visits welcome, please* **Tel 01284 764310**

The Beeches ♿ (Dr & Mrs A J Russell) Walsham-le-Willows. 10m NE of Bury St Edmunds; signed Walsham-le-Willows off A143. At Xrds in village pass Church on L, after 50yds turn L along Grove Rd. Pink house behind Church. 3 acres; lawns, herbaceous border, mature and newly-planted trees. Potager, thatched summer house with ornamental pond, gazebo and wild garden by stream. TEAS. *Adm £1.50 Chd under 14 free (Share to St Mary's Church, Walsham-le-Willows©). Sun Aug 6 (2-6)*

By Appointment Gardens. These owners do not have a fixed opening day usually because they do not like crowds or have insufficient parking space. Owner will often give guided tour.

Blakenham Woodland Garden ✲ Little Blakenham. 4m NW of Ipswich. Follow signs from 'The Beeches' at Lt Blakenham, 1m off the old A1100, now called B1113. 5-acre bluebell wood densely planted with fine collection of trees and shrubs; camellias, magnolias, cornus, azaleas, rhododendrons, roses, hydrangeas. *Adm £1 Chd £1. Open daily (1-5) except Sats, March 1 to June 30. For NGS Suns April 30, Wed May 3 (1-5). Parties welcome by appt, please* **Tel 01473 830344**

¶Cavendish Hall ♿✲ (Mrs T S Matthews) Cavendish. Entrance on A1092 midway between Cavendish and Clare, about 7m NW of Sudbury. Fine views overlooking Stour Valley woodland walks, old roses, paeonies, shrubs in encircling borders. TEAS. *Adm £1.50 Chd under 12 free. Sun June 25 (2-6)*

Chequers ♿ (Miss J Robinson) Boxford, 5m W of Hadleigh via A1071. From Sudbury A134 then A1071. From Ipswich A1071, from Colchester A134. 2-3-acre plantsman's walled and stream gardens full of rare plants. TEA. *Adm £1.50 Chd under 14 free. Sun Sept 17 (2-5). Private visits welcome, please* **Tel 01787 210295**

4 Church Street ✲❀ (Lewis Hart) Hadleigh. Approx 6m W of Ipswich on the A1071. 25yds from St Mary's Church. ⅓-acre old walled garden. Wide range of lesser known plants. Many clematis, penstemon, iris, euphorbia, alpines; crocosmias, kniphofias, trees and shrubs incl sorbus, skimmia, indigofera, daphnes. Collection of plants in sinks and tubs. *Donation box. Private visits welcome, please* **Tel 01473 822418**

¶Clipt Bushes ♿ (Mr & Mrs H W A Ruffell) Cockfield. Just off the A1141 8m S of Bury St Edmunds and 3m N of Lavenham. Ample parking. Farmhouse gardens, approx 2 acres designed for easy maintenance. Shrubberies, specimen trees and old roses. TEAS. *Combined adm with* **Moat Cottage** *£2 Chd free. Sun June 11 (2-6)*

¶Denston Hall ♿ (Mr & Mrs R Macaire) Denston. Approx 10m from Bury St Edmunds and Newmarket. Denston is 1m SE of A143. Denston Hall is situated at end of cul de sac in centre of village. Approx 10-acre garden newly renovated to a very high standard set in parkland with large walled garden, lake, old fish ponds and many fine trees. TEAS. *Adm £1.50 Chd 50p. Sun June 25 (2-6)*

13 Drapers Lane ✲❀ (Mr & Mrs Borrett) Ditchingham. 1¼m Bungay off the B1332 towards Norwich. ⅓-acre containing many interesting, unusual plants including 80 plus varieties of hardy geraniums, climbers and shrubs. Herbaceous perennials a speciality. Owner maintained. TEAS. *Adm £1 Chd free. Sun, Mon May 7, 8 (10-4)*

Ellingham Hall ♿✲❀ (Col & Mrs H M L Smith) On A143 between Beccles 3m and Bungay 2m. Georgian house set in parkland. An enormous amount of tree planting and conservation work has been carried out since 1984. The 2-acre garden has been restored and laid out. Designed by Sue Gill (see Great Campston, Gwent). It is now planted in deep borders with a wide and unusual variety of plants and trees. Walled garden with fan trained fruit trees. Exhibition of garden sculptures by Nick Deans. TEAS. *Adm £1.50 Chd under 12 free (Share to St Mary's Church, Ellingham®). Sun June 18 (2-6)*

●Euston Hall ✻ (The Duke & Duchess of Grafton) on the A1088 12m N of Bury St Edmunds. 3m S of Thetford. Terraced lawns; herbaceous borders, rose garden, C17 pleasure grounds, lake. C18 house open; famous collection of paintings. C17 church; temple by William Kent. Craft shop. Wheelchair access to gardens, tea-room and shop only. TEAS in Old Kitchen. *Adm house & garden £2.50 OAPs £2, Chd 50p Parties of 12 or more £2 per head (Share to NGS®). Thurs June 1 to Sept 28; Suns June 25 & Sept 3 (2.30-5)*

Felsham House ♿✻❀ (The Hon Mrs Erskine) Felsham 7m SE of Bury St Edmunds off A134, 8m W of Stowmarket via Rattlesden. 5 acres incl meadow with wild flowers, established trees, shrubs, roses; herb garden. TEAS. *Adm £1.50 Chd 50p. Sun, Wed May 28, 31 (2-6). Private visits of 6 and over welcome, please* **Tel 01449 736326**

Gable House ♿✻❀ (Mr & Mrs John Foster) Redisham. 3½m S of Beccles. Mid-way between Beccles and Halesworth on Ringsfield-Ilketshall St Lawrence Rd. Garden of 1 acre, mixed borders, alpines, fruit and vegetables. Home-made TEAS. *Adm £1 (Share to St Peters Church Redisham, Beccles, Suffolk®). Sun June 18 (2-5.30). Private visits welcome Suns from May to Sept* **Tel 01502 575298**

¶Garden House Farm ✻ (Mrs Seiffer) Drinkstone. A45 now A14. Turn off at Woolpit, go through village and follow signs to Drinkstone and then Drinkstone Green, past Cherry Tree Inn and then 1st L, Rattlesden Rd. After ¾m turn L down lane and drive to end. 3m from Woolpit. Formerly the gardens of Barcock's Nursery. The woodland garden is particularly delightful in Spring with many camellias, magnolias and Spring flowers. This is a plantsman's garden with many rare and unusual plants, trees and shrubs. 11 acres incl pond and lake. New owners are currently creating new areas of interest. *Adm £1.50 Chd free. Sun April 23 (2-5.30). Private visits welcome, please* **Tel 01449 736434**

Great Thurlow Hall ♿ (Mr & Mrs George Vestey) Haverhill. N of Haverhill. Great Thurlow village on B1061 from Newmarket; 3½m N of junction with A143 Haverhill-Bury St Edmunds rd. 20 acres. Walled kitchen garden, herbaceous borders, shrubs, roses, spacious lawns, river walk, trout lake. Daffodils and blossom. TEA. *Adm £1.50 Chd free. Sun April 2 (2-5)*

Grundisburgh Hall ♿✻ (Lady Cranworth) 3m W of Woodbridge on B1079, ¼m S of Grundisburgh on Grundisburgh to Ipswich Rd. Approx 5 acres walled garden with yew hedges; wisteria walk and mixed borders. Old rose garden; lawns and ponds. TEAS. *Adm £2 Chd free (Share to St Marys Grundisburgh, St Botolphs Culpho®). Private visits welcome May 20 to July 20, please* **Tel 01473 735 485**

Hengrave Hall ♿✻❀ Hengrave. 3½m NW Bury St Edmunds on A1101. Tudor mansion (tours available). Lake and woodland path. 5-acre formal garden with spacious lawns. Mixed borders with some unusual plants. Kitchen garden. TEAS in aid of Hengrave Bursary Fund. *Adm £2 OAPs £1 Chd free. Sun June 11 (2-6)*

¶Highfield Farm ♿ (Mr John Ineson) Bures. 6m SE of Sudbury. From Bures Church take Nayland Rd. In 2m turn L signposted Assington. Take 1st R Tarmac Drive. From other directions take Assington-Wormingford rd. Approx 1½-acre plantsman's garden started in 1984 with mixed borders, shrubs and herbaceous. Various features incl lily pond, wildlife pond and folly. TEA. *Adm £1.50 Chd under 16 free. Suns, Wed June 25, 28, July 23 (10-6)*

Hillside ✻❀ (Mr & Mrs J M Paul) Freston. 3m S of Ipswich on the S bank of the R Orwell on the B1456 to Shotley just before the Freston Boot public house on the R. Approx 3 acres of gently sloping garden on well-drained light land. A wide variety of trees, shrubs and herbaceous plants, incl some more tender species due to the proximity to the R Orwell and lack of hard frosts. Vegetable garden, greenhouses and newly developed swimming pool garden. TEAS. *Adm £2 Chd free (Share to Suffolk Historic Churches Trust®). Sun June 11 (2.30-5.30)*

Holbecks ❀ (Sir Joshua & Lady Rowley) Hadleigh. From Hadleigh High St turn into Duke St signed to Lower Layham; immediately over bridge go right up concrete rd to top of hill. 3 acres; early C19 landscape terraced and walled gardens, flowerbeds, roses and ornamental shrubs. TEA. *Adm £1.50 Chd free (Share to Suffolk Historic Churches Trust®). Sun July 16 (2-5.30)*

Ickworth House, Park & Gardens ♿✻ (The National Trust) Horringer. 3m SW of Bury St. Edmunds on W side of A143 [155:TL8161] 70 acres of garden. South gardens restored to stylized Italian landscape to reflect extraordinary design of the house. Fine orangery, agapanthus, geraniums and fatsias. North gardens informal wild flower lawns with wooded walk; the Buxus collection, great variety of evergreens and Victorian stumpery. New planting of cedars. The Albana Wood, a C18 feature, initially laid out by Capability Brown, incorporates a fine circular walk. Restaurant TEAS. *Adm £4.50 (house, park and garden) Chd £2. £1.50 (park and garden) Chd 50p. Sun Sept 3 (10-5.30). Private visits of 15 and over welcome, please* **Tel 01284 735288**

Keepers Cottage ♿✻❀ (Mr & Mrs P Coy) Bury Rd Lawshall. 6m S of Bury St Edmunds; from A134 Bury St Edmunds to Sudbury turn R at Lawshall signpost; proceed for 2½m through village to T junction turn R on Bury Road and proceed for ½m. Pretty ½-acre garden surrounding a C15 thatched cottage in delightful woodland setting; many pretty borders containing unusual and interesting shrubs and perennials, with lawns, shady areas and pool. TEAS. *Adm £1.50 Chd free. Sun May 21 (2-6)*

¶Letheringham Watermill ♿✻❀ (Mr & Mrs Rod Allen) Woodbridge. 7m N of Woodbridge. Letheringham turn off B1078, 1m W of Wickham Market. 5 acres of garden and river walks. Aviary. Watermill has picture gallery and restored waterwheel. Unusual plants for sale. Home-made TEAS. *Adm £1.50 OAP's £1 Chd free. Open every Sun April, May, July, Aug (2-6). For NGS Mons May 8, Aug 28 (2-6)*

Regular Openers. See head of county section.

Little Thurlow Hall ♿❀ (Mr & Mrs E Vestey) Thurlow. On B1061 between Newmarket and Haverhill, in the middle of village. A re-made garden started in 1987; herbaceous and lily borders; sunken garden; rose garden, ancient canals; orchard, formal box edged herb and kitchen gardens, greenhouses and conservatory, shrubberies, many unusual plants; woodland and lakeside walks woodland stream garden under construction. Approx 20 acres in all. Paddocks with horses. TEAS. *Adm £1.50 Chd 50p. Sun June 18 (2-6)*

Long Melford Gardens TEAS at Sun House. Long Melford is 3½m N of Sudbury on A134. *Combined adm £3 Chd free (Share to Long Melford Community Trust©). Sun July 2 (2-6)*

¶**Conduit House** ♿ (Sir Harold and Lady Atcherley) The Green. 50yds S of Black Lion off A1096 to Clare; on the Green. Approx 1 acre of partly walled garden, old-fashioned roses mixed borders

Ely House ♿ (Miss Jean M Clark) Church Walk. Small walled garden; mixed borders; ponds and fountains

Sun House ♿✗ (Mr & Mrs John Thompson) Centre of village opp Cock and Bell Inn. Two attractive adjacent walled gardens with roses, shrubs and herbaceous borders. Interesting collection of clematis. Water and architectural features. Prize winning garden 1994

Magnolia House ✗ (Mr Mark Rumary) On A1120 in centre of Yoxford. Small, completely walled village garden. Mixed borders with flowering trees, shrubs, climbers, bulbs, hardy and tender plants. Featured in UK and foreign gardening books and magazines. *Adm £1.50 Chd free. Sun May 7 (2.30-6)*

Moat Cottage ✗ (Stephen & Lesley Ingerson) Great Green. Cockfield. Take A134 S from Bury St Edmunds. After Sicklesmere village turn sharp L for Cockfield Green and R at 1st Xrds. Follow winding rd through Bradfield St Clare. At Great Green fork L Moat Cottage is opp garage at far end. 1 acre of enchanting cottage garden created over the last 8yrs and forever changing. The garden is divided into smaller areas incl white, herb and rose gardens, herbaceous borders, with a kitchen garden that provides the owners with all year round vegetables. Teas at Clipt Bushes (½m). *Combined adm with* **Clipt Bushes** *£2 OAPs £1 Chd free. Sun June 11 (2-6)*

North Cove Hall ♿❀ (Mr & Mrs B Blower) Beecles. Just off A146 3½m E of Beecles on Lowestoft Rd. Take sign to North Cove. 5 acres of garden; large pond; new water feature; mature and interesting young trees. Walled kitchen garden; shrub roses; herbaceous borders; woodland walks. Home-made TEAS. *Adm £1.50 Chd free. Sun June 25 (2-5.30)*

The Old Rectory, Brinkley ✗ (Mr & Mrs Mark Coley) 6m S of Newmarket B1061, then B1052. After Brinkley post office, 1st left down Hall Lane, Old Rectory at bottom on R with white gates. 2-acre garden created over last 15yrs; mixed borders and some interesting trees. TEA. *Adm £1.50 Chd 50p. Sun June 11 (2-6)*

Pippin Cottage ♿✗❀ (Mr & Mrs Sanders) Woodditton. Leave E end of Newmarket on B1061 for Haverhill, almost immediately fork L (signpost Woodditton) continue approx 3m and at 2nd Xroads turn R. Garden is 2nd thatched cottage on L nearly opposite Three Blackbirds public house. 1½-acre garden designed and planted by owners, surrounding a C17 cottage; large collection of trees, shrubs, hardy perennials, shrub roses etc; natural pond and paved areas covered with alpines, paddock and small wooded area; TEA. *Adm £1.50 Chd 30p. Suns June 18 (2-6). Also open by appointment* **Tel 01638 730857**

¶**Porters Lodge** ♿ (Mr Craig Wyncoll) Cavenham. 5m W of Bury St Edmunds; 1m SW of Cavenham on the rd to Kentford. 2 acres of woodland walks surrounding an acre of semi-formal ponds, mixed borders and lawns laid out during the last 6 yrs. TEAS. *Adm £1.50 Chd free. Sun July 30 (2-6)*

The Priory ♿❀ (Mr & Mrs H F A Engleheart) Stoke-by-Nayland (1m); 8m N of Colchester, entrance on B1068 rd to Sudbury. Interesting 9-acre garden with fine views over Constable countryside, with lawns sloping down to small lakes & water garden; fine trees, rhododendrons & azaleas; walled garden; mixed borders & ornamental greenhouse. Wide variety of plants; peafowl. TEAS. *Adm £1.50 Chd free. Sun May 28 (2-6). Private visits welcome, please* **Tel 01206 262216**

Redisham Hall ♿✗ (Mr Palgrave Brown) SW of Beccles. From A145 1½m S of Beccles, turn W on to Ringsfield-Bungay Rd. Beccles, Halesworth or Bungay, all within 6m. 5 acres; parkland and woods 400 acres. Georgian house C18 (not shown). Safari rides. TEAS (3.30-5 only). *Adm £1.50 Chd free (Share to East Suffolk Macmillan Nurses®). Sun July 9 (2-6)*

¶**Reydon Grove House** ♿❀ (Cmdr & Mrs J Swinley) Reydon. Situated ½m N of Reydon Church. Turnings off the Wangford-Southwold rd. 1½-acre mature garden. Large herbaceous borders, many interesting and unusual shrubs, plants, old-fashioned roses. Large vegetable garden. TEAS. *Adm £1.50 Chd free (Share to Suffolk Historic Churches Trust®). Sun June 25 (2-6) Private visits welcome June to Sept, please* **Tel 01502 723655**

The Rookery ♿✗❀ (Captain & Mrs Sheepshanks) Eyke. 5m E of Woodbridge turn N off B1084 Woodbridge-Orford Rd when sign says Rendlesham. 10-acre garden; planted as an arboretum with many rare specimen trees and shrubs; landscaped on differing levels, providing views and vistas; the visitor's curiosity is constantly aroused by what is round the next corner; ponds, bog garden, shrubbery, alpines, garden stream, bulbs, herbaceous borders and a 1-acre vineyard. Wine tastings and farm shop. Home-made TEAS. *Adm £1.50 Chd 50p. Suns May 14, June 18 (2-5.30). Private visits welcome for parties of 10 and over, please* **Tel 01394 460271**

¶**Rosedale** ✗❀ (Mr & Mrs Colin Lorking) 40 Colchester Rd, Bures. 9m NW of Colchester on B1508. As you enter the village of Bures, garden is on the L or 5m SE of Sudbury on B1508, follow signs through village towards Colchester, garden is on the R as you leave village. Approx ⅓-acre, plantsman's garden; many unusual plants, herbaceous borders, pond, woodland area, rose beds. TEA. *Adm £1.50 Acc chd free. Suns June 25, July 23 (12-6). Private visits welcome, please* **Tel 01787 227619**

Rosemary ♿✂❀ (Mrs N E M Finch) Rectory Hill. Turn off the A12 at East Bergholt and follow rd round to church. Rosemary is 100yds down from the church on L. Mature 1-acre garden adapted over 20yrs from an old orchard loosely divided into several smaller gardens; mixed borders; herb garden; over 80 old roses, unusual plants. TEAS. *Adm £1 Chd free. Sun June 11 (2-6) and private visits welcome May & June, please* **Tel 01206 298241**

Ruggs Cottage ♿✂ (Mrs Patricia Short) Raydon. 12m NE of Colchester and 11m S of Ipswich, off A12 between Colchester and Ipswich. Turn N on B1070 towards Hadleigh. Raydon is 2m from A12. Car park available at Chequers Inn. Ruggs Cottage is on R just before Chequers Inn. ¾-acre designer plantsman's garden with wide selection of flowering shrubs and trees, herbaceous and unusual plants, new chequered board herb garden, grassy walks, roses and bulbs, small greenhouse with mimosa. TEAS by PCC. *Adm £1.50 Chd free. Sun Aug 6 (2-6)*

Somerleyton Hall ♿✂ (The Lord & Lady Somerleyton) 5m NW of Lowestoft. Off B1074. Large garden; famous maze, beautiful trees and avenue. House C16 remodelled in 1840's. Grinling Gibbons' carving, library, tapestries. Mentioned in Domesday Book. Miniature railway. Light lunches & TEAS. *Adm £3.75 Chd £1.75. House open 2-5 Gardens 12.30-5.30: Easter Sun to end Sept, Thurs, Suns, Bank Hol Mons; Tues, Weds, July and Aug; in addition miniature railway will be running on most days*

The Spong ❀ (Joseph Barrett Esq & John Kirby Esq) Groton, Boxford. 5m W of Hadleigh on A1071. Leave Boxford via Swan Street, bear R at Fox and Hounds follow main road past Groton Church, take next R. The Spong is the pink house at the bottom of the hill. 9-yr-old garden of ⅔-acre; approached over stream; planned as a series of small gardens due to irregular shape; ever changing with mixed herbaceous/shrubs; ponds; pergola. TEAS. *Adm £1.50 Chd 50p. Sun June 11 (2-6)*

Stour Cottage ✂ (Mr J H Gill) East Bergholt. Halfway between Ipswich and Colchester on the A12, turn at the sign for E Bergholt, follow rd around to the R towards the village centre. Car parking in the centre of the village. Take the lane to the R by the post office and Stour Cottage Garden entrance is the first large gate on the L side of lane. Formal walled garden of about ⅓-acre, Italianate in feeling. Many unusual half hardy shrubs and climbers. Features incl fountain and water garden. Comprehensive collection of herbaceous perennials. *Adm £1 Chd free. Sun June 11 (2-6)*

Thrift Farm ♿✂❀ (Mrs J Oddy) Cowlinge. 7m SE of Newmarket, centrally between Cowlinge, Kirtling and Gt Bradley. On the Gt Bradley rd from Kirtling. Picturesque thatched house set in a cottage style garden extending to approx 1½ acres. After the 1987 storm the garden took on its new mantle of island beds filled with herbaceous plants amongst shrubs and ornamental trees in great variety. It is a garden which encourages you to walk round but many will just sit and enjoy the vistas. TEAS. *Adm £1.50 Chd 50p. Private visits welcome, please* **Tel 01440 783274**

Thumbit ♿ (Mrs Ann James) Walsham-le-Willows. 10m NE of Bury St Edmunds. Leave A143 at Walsham-le-Willows sign and continue to Xrds by church at centre of village. Take Badwell Rd to outskirts of village (½m). House is part of thatched C16 one-time inn. Shared driveway - (please do not drive in). Small informal cottage-style garden with strong emphasis on structural design and plant association for subtlety of form and colour. Pergola, pool, topiary. 500 choice herbaceous plants and shrubs, roses and climbers. Featured in Weekend Telegraph and Practical Gardening. TEA. *Adm £1.50 Chd free. Wed Sun June 28, July 2 (2-6). Private visits also welcome June-Oct adm £1.50 OAPs £1 Chd free. Please* **Tel 01359 259 414**

Tollemache Hall ♿✂ (Mr & Mrs M Tollemache) Offton, nr Ipswich. S of the B1078 opp the Ringshall turning. 4 acres of recently renovated garden in a lovely rural setting. Shrubs, rose and knot gardens. A large walled garden with interesting herbaceous borders. Also woodland walk planted with many conifer species. TEAS. *Adm £1.50 Chd free. Sun June 25 (2-6)*

Warwick House ♿❀ (Dr & Mrs H Parris) Bury St Edmunds. Entrance in Westgate St opp R C Church; this st runs E from double roundabout at junction of A134 and A143 in Bury St Edmunds. ⅓-acre walled hidden garden in centre of Bury St Edmunds behind C17 house, but redesigned to given several vistas and different places to sit and relax. Wall fountain, conservatory and some unusual herbs, plants and specimen trees, chosen whenever possible for scent. *Adm £1.50 (Share to National Council of Women®). Sat, Sun, Mon May 13, 14, 29 (11-6)*

¶Washbrook Grange ✂❀ (Mr & Mrs Robert Stone) From Ipswich take A1071 to Hadleigh. L at 1st roundabout and then 1st R to Chattisham. ½m on L. 5 acres with small lake, ornamental vegetable garden, maple walk, herbaceous borders, roses, iris, shrubs and trees both old and new; woodland walk. TEAS. *Adm £1.50 Chd 75p. Suns May 28, Aug 20, Mon May 29 (2-6)*

25 Westbury Avenue ♿✂❀ (Mr & Mrs D J Payne) Bury St Edmunds. 1m West of town centre. Parkway roundabout (Kings Rd)-Queens Rd-Westbury Ave. ½-acre to lawns, shrubs and trees, many spring flowers and bulbs. Heathers, conifers, fuschias. Patios and sunken garden; Mediterranean area. Water features, seasonal beds, borders, pots and hanging baskets, greenhouse. TEAS. *Adm £1.50 Chd under 14 free. Sun July 16 (11-6) also private visits (and parties March to Sept) welcome, please* **Tel 01284 755 374**

¶The White House ♿ (Lady Verney) Clare. From W on A604, approach into Clare is up a long straight street, Nethergate St, with row of beeches on R. Entrance to the garden of The White House (1st house on R after beeches) is from footpath running behind beeches and through door in flint wall. From E take A1092 from Long Melford, Sudbury direction and drive through Clare and along Nethergate St as though leaving town. The White House is opp Clare Hotel. A large village garden, bounded by high flint walls on 2 sides with the R Stour forming the southern boundary. It extends for about 1½ acres on different levels and has all manner of trees, shrubs and borders, plus an ancient orchard. TEAS. *Adm £1.50 Chd under 16 free (Share to Suffolk Historic Churches Trust®). Sun, Mon April 16, 17 (2-6)*

Woottens ♿✂❀ (M Loftus) Blackheath Rd. Woottens is situated between A12 and B1123 follow signposts to Wenhaston. Woottens is a small romantic garden with attached plantsman nursery, in all about 1-acre; scented leafed pelargoniums, violas, cranesbills, lilies, salvias, penstemons primulas, etc. Featured in Gardens Illustrated and RHS Journal. *Adm £1 OAPs 50p Chd 20p. Suns May 28, June 18, July 16, Aug 13 (2-6)*

Wyken Hall ♿❀ (Mr & Mrs K Carlisle) Stanton, 9m NE from Bury St Edmunds along A143. Follow signs to Wyken vineyards on A143 between Ixworth and Stanton. 4-acre garden much developed recently; with knot and herb gardens; old-fashioned rose garden; wild garden; nuttery, gazebo and maze, herbaceous borders and old orchard. Woodland walk, vineyard. TEAS. *Adm £2 OAPs £1.50 Chd free. Sun June 11 (10-6)*

Surrey

Hon County Organiser: Lady Heald, Chilworth Manor, Guildford GU4 8NL Tel 01483 61414

Assistant Hon County Organisers: Mrs J Foulsham, Vale End, Albury, Guildford GU5 9BE Tel 01483 202296
Miss C Collins, Knightsmead, Rickman Hill Rd, Chipstead, Surrey CR5 3LB Tel 01737 551694
Mrs P Karslake, Oakfield Cottage, Guildford Road, Cranleigh GU6 8PF Tel 01483 273010
Mrs D E Norman, Spring Cottage, Mannings Hill, Cranleigh GU6 8QN Tel 01483 272620
Mrs J Pearcy, Far End, Pilgrims Way, Guildford GU4 8AD Tel 01483 63093

Hon County Treasurer: Mr Ray Young, Paddock View, 144 Dorking Road, Chilworth, Guildford GU4 8RJ Tel 01483 69597

DATES OF OPENING

By appointment

For telephone number and other details see garden descriptions. Private visits welcomed

Brookwell, Bramley
Chauffeur's Flat, Tandridge
Chilworth Manor, Guildford
2 Court Avenue, Old Coulsdon
Coverwood Lakes and Gardens, Ewhurst
High Meadow, Churt
The Homestead, Old Lodge Lane, Kenley
Knightsmead, Chipstead
22 Knoll Road, Dorking
Park House, Chiddingfold
Pinewood House, Worplesdon Hill, Woking
Postford House, Chilworth
Pyrford Court, nr Woking
Rise Top Cottage, Mayford
South Park Farm, South Godstone
Spring Cottage, Cranleigh
Stuart Cottage, East Clandon Gardens
Street House, Thursley
Unicorns, Farnham
6 Upper Rose Hill, Dorking
Vann, Hambledon
Woodside, Send
Yew Tree Cottage, Haslemere

Parties only

Brockhurst, The Green, Chiddingfold
Four Aces, Pirbright
Lodkin, Hascombe
Park House, Chiddingfold
Pyrford Court, nr Woking
South Park Farm, South Godstone
Stonywood, Haslemere
Walton Poor, Ranmore Common
Westland Farm, Ewhurst
Woodlands, 67 York Road, Cheam

Regular openers

For details see garden descriptions

Crosswater Farm, Churt. Daily May 1 to May 31
25 Little Woodcote Estate, Wallington. Every Weds & Sats April 15 to Sept 30
Painshill, Cobham. Suns April 9 to Oct 15
Ramster, Chiddingfold. Daily April 15 to July 30

February 5 Sunday
Wintershall Manor, Bramley

March 5 Sunday
Wintershall Manor, Bramley

March 12 Sunday
Maryland, Worplesdon

March 19 Sunday
27 Foley Road, Claygate ‡
90 Foley Road, Claygate ‡

April 2 Sunday
Whinfold, Hascombe ‡
Wintershall Manor, Bramley ‡

April 8 to 12 Saturday to Wednesday
Chilworth Manor, Guildford

April 9 Sunday
Lodkin, Hascombe

April 16 Sunday
High Meadow, Churt

April 17 Monday
High Meadow, Churt

April 18 to 23 Tuesday to Sunday
Vann, Hambledon

April 19 Wednesday
The Coppice, Reigate
Knightsmead, Chipstead

April 22 Saturday
Woodside, Send

April 23 Sunday
Coverwood Lakes and Gardens, Ewhurst
27 Foley Road, Claygate ‡
90 Foley Road, Claygate ‡
Highlands, Givons Grove, Leatherhead
Munstead Wood, nr Godalming
Vann, Hambledon
Woodside, Send

April 26 Wednesday
The Coppice, Reigate
April 30 Sunday
Compton Lodge, Moor Park, Farnham
Coverwood Lakes and Gardens, Ewhurst
22 Knoll Road, Dorking
Street House, Thursley
Vann, Hambledon
Westland Farm, Ewhurst
May 1 to 6 Monday to Saturday
Vann, Hambledon
May 3 Wednesday
22 Knoll Road, Dorking
May 6 to 10 Saturday to Wednesday
Chilworth Manor, Guildford
May 6 Saturday
Greathed Manor, Dormansland
May 7 Sunday
Coverwood Lakes and Gardens, Ewhurst
Feathercombe, nr Hambledon
Highlands, Givons Grove, Leatherhead
Malthouse Farm, Hambledon
Westbourn, Virginia Water
Winkworth Arboretum, Hascombe
Wintershall Manor, Bramley
May 8 Monday
Feathercombe, nr Hambledon
Malthouse Farm, Hambledon
Walton Poor, Ranmore Common
May 9 Tuesday
Malthouse Farm, Hambledon
May 10 Wednesday
Malthouse Farm, Hambledon
Westland Farm, Ewhurst
May 11 Thursday
Malthouse Farm, Hambledon
May 12 Friday
Malthouse Farm, Hambledon
May 13 Saturday
The Old Croft, South Holmwood
Pyrford Court, nr Woking
May 14 Sunday
Claremont Landscape Garden, Esher
Compton Lodge, Moor Park, Farnham
Copt Hill Shaw, Kingswood, Tadworth
Coverwood Lakes and Gardens, Ewhurst
Montfleury, Virginia Water
The Old Croft, South Holmwood
Polesdon Lacey, Bookham
Postford House, Chilworth
Pyrford Court, nr Woking
41 Shelvers Way, Tadworth
Snowdenham House, Bramley
Street House, Thursley
87 Upland Road, Sutton
Whinfold, Hascombe
May 21 Sunday
Coverwood Lakes and Gardens, Ewhurst
Olivers, Church Road, Hascombe
Postford House, Chilworth
Stonywood, Haslemere
May 24 Wednesday
Coverwood Lakes and Gardens, Ewhurst
May 27 Saturday
Crosswater Farm, Churt
Merrist Wood College, Worplesdon
May 28 Sunday
Brook Lodge Farm Cottage, Blackbrook
Coverwood Lakes and Gardens, Ewhurst
Crosswater Farm, Churt
Feathercombe, nr Hambledon
High Meadow, Churt
15 Highview Road, Lightwater
Merrist Wood College, Worplesdon
Munstead Wood, nr Godalming
Postford House, Chilworth
May 29 Monday
Crosswater Farm, Churt
Feathercombe, nr Hambledon
High Meadow, Churt
Merrist Wood College, Worplesdon
May 30 to June 4 Tuesday to Sunday
Vann, Hambledon
May 31 Wednesday
Brook Lodge Farm Cottage, Blackbrook
June 3 to 7 Saturday to Wednesday
Chilworth Manor, Guildford
June 3 Saturday
Hatchlands Park, East Clandon
Hookwood Farm House, West Horsley
June 4 Sunday
2 Chinthurst Lodge, Wonersh
Dovecote, Cobham
Hookwood Farm House, West Horsley
Painshill, Cobham
Vann, Hambledon
Walton Poor, Ranmore Common
Wintershall Manor, Bramley
June 7 Wednesday
Spring Cottage, Cranleigh
Walton Poor, Ranmore Common
June 10 Saturday
Brookwell, Bramley
June 11 Sunday
Brookwell, Bramley
27 Foley Road, Claygate ‡
90 Foley Road, Claygate ‡
37 Hare Lane, Claygate ‡
Ridings, 56 Cross Road, Tadworth ‡‡
41 Shelvers Way, Tadworth ‡‡
Spring Cottage, Cranleigh
June 14 Wednesday
27 Foley Road, Claygate ‡
37 Hare Lane, Claygate ‡
June 17 Saturday
South Park Farm, South Godstone
June 18 Sunday
Brockhurst, The Green, Chiddingfold
Brook Lodge Farm Cottage, Blackbrook
Four Aces, Pirbright
Haslehurst, Haslemere
High Hazard, Blackheath
Merrist Wood College, Worplesdon
South Park Farm, South Godstone
Thanescroft, Shamley Green
6 Upper Rose Hill, Dorking
Yew Tree Cottage, Haslemere
June 19 Monday
Four Aces, Pirbright
South Park Farm, South Godstone
June 21 Wednesday
Brook Lodge Farm Cottage, Blackbrook
June 24 Saturday
Knightsmead, Chipstead
The Moorings, Horley
June 25 Sunday
Four Aces, Pirbright
High Meadow, Churt
Knightsmead, Chipstead
Mitchen Hall Shackleford, Godalming
The Moorings, Horley
Street House, Thursley
Titsey Place Gardens, Titsey
Vale End, Albury
June 26 Monday
High Meadow, Churt
The Moorings, Horley
July 1 Saturday
Little Mynthurst Farm, Norwood Hill
July 2 Sunday
Addlestone Gardens
Little Mynthurst Farm, Norwood Hill
Maryland, Worplesdon
White House, nr Guildford
Wintershall Manor, Bramley
July 8 to 12 Saturday to Wednesday
Chilworth Manor, Guildford
July 15 Saturday
The Old Croft, South Holmwood
July 16 Sunday
The Old Croft, South Holmwood
41 Shelvers Way, Tadworth

Woodlands, 67 York Road, Cheam

July 19 Wednesday
Brockhurst, The Green, Chiddingfold
Woodlands, 67 York Road, Cheam

July 22 Saturday
The Homestead, Old Lodge Lane, Kenley

July 23 Sunday
Brook Lodge Farm Cottage, Blackbrook
Chiddingfold House, Chiddingfold
The Homestead, Old Lodge Lane, Kenley
Lodkin, Hascombe
Vale End, Albury

July 26 Wednesday
Brook Lodge Farm Cottage, Blackbrook

July 29 Saturday
Street House, Thursley

August 2 Wednesday
The Coppice, Reigate

August 3 Thursday
Park House, Chiddingfold

August 5 to 9 Saturday to Wednesday
Chilworth Manor, Guildford

August 6 Sunday
Odstock, Bletchingley
Park House, Chiddingfold

August 19 Saturday
East Clandon Gardens

August 20 Sunday
Brook Lodge Farm Cottage, Blackbrook
East Clandon Gardens

August 27 Sunday
High Meadow, Churt

August 28 Monday
High Meadow, Churt

September 24 Sunday
Claremont Landscape Garden, Esher
Haslehurst, Haslemere
Maryland, Worplesdon
Munstead Wood, nr Godalming

October 1 Sunday
Albury Park, Albury

October 8 Sunday
Walton Poor, Ranmore Common
White House, nr Guildford

October 15 Sunday
Pyrford Court, nr Woking
Winkworth Arboretum, Hascombe

October 22 Sunday
Coverwood Lakes and Gardens, Ewhurst

November 5 Sunday
Lodkin, Hascombe

DESCRIPTIONS OF GARDENS

¶Addlestone Gardens ✲❀ Situated within ½m of each other, 5m NE of Woking off B3121. From M25 junction 11 take A320 signposted Woking then L into B3121 or A317 signposted Weybridge and R into B3121 and follow yellow signs. Maps available at each garden. TEAS in aid of St Paul's Church Roof Fund. *Combined adm £2 Chd free. Sun July 2 (10-5).*

¶Charton (Daphne & John Clarke-Williams) Ongar Hill. ⅓-acre upward sloping mature garden, with trees, shrubs, climbing plants, hardy perennials and sink gardens, pond and vegetable garden. Extensive use of home-made compost

¶106 Liberty Lane (Mrs Ann Masters) 100′ × 30′ suburban garden belonging to self confessed 'plantaholic' imaginatively laid out, some design, new acquisitions permitting; containing an interesting mix of shrubs, grasses, hardy perennials, climbers and hardy geraniums, a pond and some unusual plants. Very interested in propagation

¶St Keverne (Mr & Mrs Julian Clarke-Willams) ⅓-acre garden created by owners over last 5 yrs. Inspired use of companion planting. Hardy perennials-specialising in geraniums and alliums; many trees, shrubs and roses. Gravel and pots a feature

Albury Park Garden ♿✲ (Trustees of Albury Estate) Albury 5m SE of Guildford. From A25 take A248 towards Albury for ¼m, then L up New Rd, entrance to Albury Park immediately on L. 14-acre pleasure grounds laid out in 1670's by John Evelyn for Henry Howard, later 6th Duke of Norfolk. ¼m terraces, fine collection of trees, lake and river. The gardens of Albury Park Mansion also open (by kind permission of Country Houses Association Ltd). TEAS. *Adm £1.50 Chd 50p. Sun Oct 1 (2-5)*

¶Brockhurst ♿❀ (Prof & Mrs C F Phelps) Chiddingfold. On the Green at Chiddingfold A283. Entrance through small gate RH-side of Manor House. Parking around Village Green. A series of surprising gardens, tucked behind the village green, beginning with an old walled cottage border and expanding successively into 2½ acres of lawns, shrubs, walkways and flower beds. Within the garden created over the last 10 yrs by the present owners are many species and foliage plants, incl lilies and clematis; fruit and vegetable garden. TEAS. *Adm £1.50 Chd free. Sun June 18, Wed July 19 (2-6). Private visits welcome for parties of 10 and over May, June, July, Aug, please* **Tel 01428 683092**

Brook Lodge Farm Cottage ♿✲❀ (Mrs Basil Kingham) Blackbrook, 3m S of Dorking. Take L-hand turning for Blackbrook off A24, 1m S of Dorking 500yds past Plough Inn. 3½-acre 45-year-old plantsman's garden made by present owner. Entrance provides vista of spacious lawns, curving borders of shrubs, flowering trees and shrub roses; hosts of unusual plants frame main house. Fine collection of conifers cradles summer-house. Swimming pool, hidden by Hoathly stone wall leads to waterfall and rockery with woodland walk beyond. On leaving garden, pass herbaceous borders, roses, herb and kitchen gardens, greenhouses and 2 cottage gardens full of interest. Light lunches Weds, TEAS on Suns. *Adm £1.50 Chd free (Share to St Catherine's Hospice, Crawley®). Weds May 31, June 21, July 26 (11-3). Suns May 28, June 18, July 23, Aug 20 (2-6)*

Brookwell ♿✲❀ (Mr & Mrs P R Styles) 1½m S of Bramley on A281; turn R into private road-bridleway in Birtley Green. 2-acre garden with lake and woodland. Mixed borders, sunken garden, and knot garden planted with scented flowers and herbs. Collection of old roses, fruit tunnel and vegetable garden; greenhouses and conservatory. TEA. *Adm £1 Chd 25p. Sat, Sun June 10, 11 (2-6) also private visits welcome June, July, please* **Tel 01483 893423** *(evenings)*

Chauffeur's Flat ✲ (Mr & Mrs Richins) Tandridge. Tandridge Lane lies 1m W of Oxted off the A25. Drive adjacent to church ½m from A25. Pass Lodge to your R. Fork R. Continue through to Courtyard. A hidden romantic garden set in just under 1 acre of land with superb views, it uses an abundant variety of trees and shrubs intermingled with wild and cultivated plants. Mainly set on two levels as a series of mini gardens the upper having a more natural woodland feel, the lower using informal planting within a formal framework. Only for the surefooted. *Adm £1 Chd 25p (Share to Waylands Special Needs Unit©). Private visits welcome Sats to Suns May 20 to 28, June 17 to 25 (10-5), please* **Tel 01883 715937** *between 7-9.30am or 7-9.30pm*

Chiddingfold House ✿ (Mr & Mrs J R Morrison) Chiddingfold. In Chiddingfold turn E at top of village green on rd marked to Dunsfold. Chiddingfold House about 500 yds from green on N side of rd. A large and interesting garden divided into many smaller ones incl a beautifully underplanted Pergola; rose garden; fish pond. Very fine lawns. *Adm £1.50 Chd free. Sun July 23 (2-5)*

Chilworth Manor ♿✿ (Lady Heald) 3½m SE of Guildford. From A248, in centre of Chilworth village, turn up Blacksmith Lane. Bus: LC 425 Guildford-Dorking; alight Blacksmith Lane. Station: Chilworth. House C17 with C18 wing on site of C11 monastery recorded in Domesday Book; stewponds in garden date from monastic period. Garden laid out in C17; C18 walled garden added by Sarah, Duchess of Marlborough; spring flowers; flowering shrubs. Featured in NGS video 1. Flower decorations in house (Sats, Suns): May 6-10 Michael Kemp, June 3-7 Merrow Floral and Garden Club, July 8-12 St Catherine's Flower Arrangement Club, Aug 5-9 Haselmere Flower Club. Free car park in attractive surroundings open from 12.30 for picnicking. TEAS (Sat, Sun, only). *Adm to garden £1.50 Chd free. Adm to house £1 Sat & Sun only (Share to Marie Curie Foundation Guildford Branch®); Open Sats to Weds April 8 to 12, May 6 to 10, June 3 to 7, July 8 to 12, Aug 5 to 9 (2-6); also private visits welcome, please* **Tel 01483 61414**

2 Chinthurst Lodge ♿✿❀ (Mr & Mrs M R Goodridge) Wonersh. 4m S Guildford, A281 Guildford-Horsham. At Shalford turn E onto B2128 towards Wonersh. Just after Wonersh rd sign, before village, garden on R. 1-acre yr-round garden, herbaceous borders, large variety specimen trees and shrubs incl Parrotia Persica; kitchen garden; fruit cage; two wells; ornamental pond and conservatory. TEAS. *Adm £1 Chd free (Share to Guildford Branch Arthritis & Rheumatism Council®). Sun June 4 (2-6)*

Claremont Landscape Garden ♿✿ (The National Trust) 1m SE of Esher; on E side of A307 (No access from A3 by-pass). Station: Esher. Bus GL 415, alight at entrance gates. One of the earliest surviving English landscape gardens; begun by Vanbrugh and Bridgeman before 1720; extended and naturalized by Kent; lake; island with pavilion; grotto and turf amphitheatre; viewpoints and avenues. TEAS 11-5.30. *Adm £2.60 Chd £1.30.* ▲*For NGS Suns May 14, Sept 24 (10-7)*

Compton Lodge ✿❀ (Mr & Mrs K J Kent) Farnham. 2m E of Farnham along A31 Hogs Back (new rd) follow signs Runfold. Turn S down Crooksbury Rd at Barfield School signposted Milford & Elstead. 1m on R Compton Way, Compton Lodge 2nd house on R. 1¼-acre S-facing sloping garden. Mature rhododendrons and azaleas; mature trees; raised herbaceous border with rose and clematis trellis; rose border. 2 ponds; heather bed and mixed beds; conservatory. TEAS. *Adm £1.50 Chd 50p (Share to Waverley Victim Support®). Suns April 30, May 14 (11-5)*

Cooksbridge, Fernhurst (See Sussex)

The Coppice ❀ (Mr & Mrs Bob Bushby) Reigate. M25 to junction 8. A217 (direction Reigate) down Reigate Hill, immediately before level Xing turn R into Somers Rd cont as Manor Rd. At very end turn R into Coppice Lane 'The Coppice' approx 200yds on L. Partly suitable wheelchairs. 6½ acres redeveloped in last 6yrs. Mixed borders with interesting and unusual plants giving yr-round interest. Pergola and conservatory, 2 large ornamental ponds. Fritillarias and spring bulbs, April to May. Partially suitable for wheelchairs. TEAS. *Adm £1.50 Chd 50p (Share to Winged Fellowship®). Weds April 19, 26; Aug 2 (2-5)*

Copt Hill Shaw ✿❀ (Mr & Mrs M Barlow) Alcocks Lane, Kingswood. 6m S of Sutton off the A217. 1st turn on L after Burgh Heath traffic lights, Waterhouse Lane, signposted Kingswood Station and Coulsdon. Alcocks Lane 1st on L. Parking in Furze Hill, courtsey of Legal and General. A formal garden of 1½ acres laid out in 1906. Fine yew hedges and topiary with azaleas, mature trees and rhododendrons and pergola of old roses and clematis, spring bulbs, geraniums, alliums, small collection of unusual plants. Fruit and vegetable garden. TEAS. *Adm £1 Chd 50p. Sun May 14 (2-5.30)*

2 Court Avenue ♿✿ (Dr K Heber) Old Coulsdon. Approach from London-Brighton Rd. A23 from S or M23/25, turn R B276 Old Coulsdon; from N after leaving Purley turn L B2030 Old Coulsdon. Follow rd to top of hill, immediately past parade of shops. Garden opp Tudor Rose public house (food available). Flat compact garden approx ⅓-acre filled with herbaceous plants and shrubs in cottage garden layout; small ponds; good selection of unusual plants. Gives ideas for small gardens and use of foliage. *Adm £1 Chd 50p (Share to Coulsdon Rotary International Charities®). Private visits welcome, please* **Tel 017375 54721**

Coverwood Lakes and Gardens ♿✿❀ (Mr & Mrs C G Metson) Peaslake Rd, Ewhurst. 7m SW of Dorking. From A25 follow signs for Peaslake; garden ½m beyond Peaslake. Landscaped water, bog garden and cottage gardens in lovely setting between Holmbury Hill and Pitch Hill; rhododendrons, azaleas, primulas, fine trees. 3½-acre Arboretum planted March 1990. Featured in NGS video 1. Marked trail through working farm to see herd of pedigree Poll Hereford cattle and flock of sheep. (Mr & Mrs Nigel Metson). Home-made TEAS. *Adm £2 Chd £1 car park and Chd under 5 free (Share to NGS®). Gardens Suns April 23, 30, May 7, 14, 21, 28; Wed May 24 (2-6); Sun Oct 22 hot soup and sandwiches (11-4.30). Also private visits welcome, please* **Tel 01306 731103/1**

By Appointment Gardens. These owners do not have a fixed opening day usually because they do not like crowds or have insufficient parking space. Owner will often give guided tour.

Crosswater Farm ♿✂❀ (Mr & Mrs E G Millais) Churt. Farnham and Haslemere 6m, from A287 turn E into Jumps Road ½m N of Churt village centre. After ¼m turn acute L into Crosswater Lane and follow signs for Millais Nurseries. 6-acre woodland garden surrounded by NT Property. Plantsman's collection of rhododendrons and azaleas including many rare species collected in the Himalayas, and hybrids raised by the owners. Ponds, stream and companion plantings. Plants for sale from specialist Rhododendron nursery. TEAS in aid of Frensham Church Restoration on NGS days only. *Adm £1.50 Chd free. Daily May 1 to 31. For NGS Sat, Sun, Mon May 27, 28, 29 (10-5). Private parties welcome, please* **Tel 01252 792698**

Dovecote ✂❀ (Mr & Mrs R Stanley) Cobham. Off A307 Esher to Cobham rd near A3 bridge. Turn R from Cobham, L from Esher into Fairmile Lane. Then 4th L into Green Lane. ⅓-acre plot surrounding extended bothy. Secluded plant lovers yr-round garden with natural boundaries of mature trees, shrubs and hedges developed by present owners to incl many hardy plants on light sandy soil. TEA. *Adm £1.50 Chd free. Sun June 4 (10.30-5.30)*

East Clandon Gardens ♿❀ This C16 hamlet, public house and C12 church is well worth a visit. Situated 4m E of Guildford on the A246 or from A3 via Ripley, turing L in centre of Ripley, Rose Lane, then 2nd R. East Clandon is 4m. Home-made TEAS. *Combined adm £1.50 Chd free (Share to Cherry Trees, respite care for handicapped children®). Sat and Sun Aug 19 (2-6), 20 (11-6)*

Stuart Cottage (Mr & Mrs J M Leader) ½-acre partly walled garden with rose walk, herbaceous beds with some colour co-ordination and unusual planting. 2 water features, paved areas with planting incl small sunken garden shaded by old apples trees. A collection of old chimney pots offering a later flower display, reflects the charm of this C16 flint and brick cottage. *Adm £1. Private visits welcome from mid June - Aug, please* **Tel 01483 222689**

3 The Tithe Barn (Mr & Mrs L Wharrad) As a contrast to the Stuart Cottage garden, No 3 The Tithe Barn in Ripley Rd provides a fine example of a small walled courtyard garden. The clever use of setts in circular patterns which lead to a small fountain and the many containers of plants are particularly worth noting

The Elms Kingston-on-Thames (see London)

Feathercombe ❀ (Miss Parker) nr Hambledon, S of Godalming. 2m from Milford Station on Hambledon Rd, turn to Feathercombe off rd between Hydestile Xrds and Merry Harriers. 12-acre garden designed and made by Surrey author and journalist Eric Parker and his wife Ruth (née Messel) of Nymans, 1910 onwards. Mature rhododendrons, azaleas and trees. Fine views of Blackdown, Hindhead and Hogs Back. House (not open) Ernest Newton, now lived in and maintained by his daughter Mary Parker, and grandchildren, Wielers and Campbells. Picnic area at garden. Tea Winkworth Arboretum. *Adm £1.50 Chd 10p (Share to Order of St John, Surrey®). Suns, Mons May 7, 8; 28, 29 (2-6)*

27 Foley Road ✂❀ (Mr & Mrs D Love) Drive into Claygate from Esher, Hook or Hinchley Wood and follow signs. Small, informal garden with some unusual plants and ornamental grasses of particular interest to the flower arranger. TEAS. *Adm 80p Chd Free. Suns March 19, April 23, June 11; Wed June 14 (2-5)*

90 Foley Road ❀ (Mr & Mrs B Mathew) Drive into Claygate from Esher, Hinchley Wood, Hook or Chessington and follow signs from Foley Arms. A plantsman's garden specialising in bulbs. The owner is the author of 15 books. Collection of species irises. *Adm 80p Chd free. Suns March 19, April 23, June 11 (2-5)*

Four Aces ✂❀ (Mr & Mrs R V St John Wright) 5m NW of Guildford on A322 Bagshot Road. Just before Brookwood arch, directly opp West Hill Golf Club, turn L into Cemetery Pales. After 9/10m turn sharp L after village sign into Chapel Lane. Four Aces is 5th house on R. Overflow parking in village green car park, 250yds. Approx ⅔-acre 9yr-old garden with 2 ponds, terraces with pergolas, loggias and pots; mixed borders with shrubs, perennials and old roses planted in informal cottage garden style. TEAS. *Adm £1 Chd 50p. Suns June 18, 25 (12-6) Mon June 19 (11-3) Private visits welcome May to July, please* **Tel 01483 476226**

¶Greathed Manor ✂❀ (Country Houses Association) Lingfield. 2½m SE of Lingfield, follow the B2028, Lingfield/Edenbridge rd to the Plough Inn, Dormansland and take the private rd, Ford Manor Rd opp and follow the signs for about 1m to Greathed Manor (not open) and Gardens. Parkland with sunken garden. Stepped terraces and flower beds surround an oval pool set in decorative paving which is enclosed by a balustraded sandstone wall attributed to Harold Peto early this century. 4 acres of attractive garden set in parkland with rhododendrons, azaleas, specimen trees, and many other spring flowers. TEAS. *Adm £1.50 Chd free (Share to Country Houses Association®). Sat May 6 (2-6)*

Hall Grange, Croydon (see London)

37 Hare Lane ✂❀ (Mr & Mrs C Ingram) Claygate; 100yds on Esher side of railway bridge, 3 mins walk from Claygate Station. Entrance and parking in Loseberry Rd. Originally a narrow garden, and designed by the owner to overcome this, more land was acquired in 1991 and has been incorporated for fruit and vegetables; hardy geraniums, cistus, roses; some interesting green ideas; designed to be labour saving. TEAS. *Adm 80p Chd free (Share to National Schizophrenia Fellowship®). Sun, Wed June 11, 14 (2-5)*

Haslehurst ✂❀ (Mrs W H Whitbread) Bunch Lane, Haslemere. Turn off High St into Church Lane, leave church on L, carry on to T-junction, turn R, Hazelhurst, 2nd on L. 2½ acres; lawns, superb trees, rhododendrons, azaleas; various shrubs; paved rose garden, double herbaceous border; woodland rockery & waterfall. C15 Barn. See **Yew Tree Cottage**. TEA. *Adm £1 Chd 50p (Share to Queen Mary's Clothing Guild®). Suns June 18, Sept 24 (2.15-6)*

¶Hatchlands Park ♿✂ (The National Trust) Situated near East Clandon, off A246. If using A3 from London direction, follow signposts to Ripley to join A247 and proceed via West Clandon to A246. If coming from Guildford take A25 and then A246 towards Leatherhead at West Clandon. The garden and park were designed by Repton in 1800 and there are 3 newly restored walks in the park. On the S side of the house is a parterre designed by Gertrude Jekyll in 1913. This has been restored to Jekyll's original design. The house is not open to the public on this day. TEA. *Adm £1 Chd 50p.* ▲*For NGS Sat June 3 (12 noon-5.30)*

High Hazard ♿❀ (Mr & Mrs P C Venning) Blackheath, Guildford. 4½m SE of Guildford from A281 Guildford to Horsham at Shalford turn E on B2128 towards Wonersh, at entry to Wonersh, turn L into Blackheath Lane, straight on at Xrds in village. Access to garden is 300yds on R. Park in Heath car park a further 150yds up lane. (No access to front of house which faces the cricket ground in use). ½-acre garden designed and laid out by the present owners 12 yrs ago. Herbaceous and mixed borders containing interesting and some unusual herbaceous perennial plants, a large number of which are for sale on the premises. TEAS. *Adm £1 Chd free (Share to St Joseph's Centre for Addiction, Holy Cross Hospital, Haslemere®). Sun June 18 (2-6)*

High Meadow ✂❀ (Mr & Mrs J Humphries) Tilford Rd, Churt. From Hindhead A3 Xrds take A287 signposted Farnham. After ½m take R fork signposted Tilford. 1.9m to Avalon PYO farm. Park here, short walk to garden. Disabled visitors park on grass verge in drive. Approx 1 acre maintained by owners. Large collection of rare and unusual plants attractively planted to provide all-year interest; large collection of old and modern shrub roses and David Austin English Roses; pergola walk, sunken garden with pond, colour co-ordinated borders, alpines in troughs; featured in Daily Mail and Woman's Weekly. TEAS. *Adm £1.50 Chd free (Share to G.U.T.S. at Royal Surrey County Hospital). Suns, Mons April 16, 17; May 28, 29; June 25, 26; Aug 27, 28 (2-6). Groups welcome, please* **Tel 01428 606129**

Highlands ✂❀ (Mr & Mrs R B McDaniel) Givons Grove, Leatherhead. From Leatherhead By-pass (A24) at roundabout by Texaco garage 1m S of Leatherhead turn into Givons Grove and proceed up hill (The Downs) for ¾m, ignoring side turnings. Highlands is on the R. Chalk garden of 1 acre on a steep slope. Large rock garden, alpine house and sinks; mixed borders; orchard; pond; fruit and vegetable garden. Fine views over Mole Valley. TEAS in aid of Cystic Fibrosis. *Adm £1 Chd free. Suns April 23, May 7 (2-6)*

15 Highview Road ✂❀ (Mr & Mrs J Pearce) Lightwater. Camberley 4m, Chobham 4m, 1½m S of junction (3) M3, off Macdonald Road Lightwater. ½-acre garden on hillside incl rock; water; heather and Japanese garden. A good example of a steeply terraced layout. (Many steps). As seen on Channel 4 Garden Club Aug 1993. TEAS. *Adm £1 Chd free. Sun May 28 (2-6)*

The Homestead ♿✂❀ (Mr & Mrs P Wallace) Kenley. 3rd dwelling down Old Lodge Lane from Wattendon Arms at junction on Old Lodge Lane (SE off A23 Brighton Road at Reedham Station) and Hayes Lane. (SSW from A22 Godstone Road at Kenley Station). Arrangements made for parking & catering to be available for garden visitors throughout day at Wattendon Arms, (end of Old Lodge Lane Purley), ½m walk up hill (Old Lodge Lane Kenley). Designed, developed and maintained by present (amateur) owners. ½-acre prize-winning suburban garden on edge of Green Belt, close to Kenley Airfield (Battle of Britain fame). Lawns with water feature, colourful beds and borders, well stocked with shrubs and flowers, vegetable garden and greenhouses; patio with outstanding display of hanging baskets, tubs, troughs etc. TEA. *Adm £1 Chd free. Sat, Sun July 22, 23 (10-5). Private visits welcome July, Aug, please* **Tel 0181 660 9816**

Hookwood Farm House ♿✂❀ (Mr & Mrs E W Mason) West Horsley. Approx 7m E of Guildford off A246 Guildford-Leatherhead Rd. From Guildford turn R into Staple Lane (sign-posted Shere) at end of dual carriageway. At top of Staple Lane turn L and then take 1st L into Shere Rd. (sign-posted West Horsley) then L into Fullers Farm Rd. From Leatherhead turn L into Greendene (sign-posted Shere) follow this for approx 2½m then R into Shere Rd. The garden made and maintained by the owners over the last 20yrs approx 1½ acres in size, is situated on a S facing slope of the North Downs. Large variety of interesting and unusual plants including alpines; herbaceous plants particularly geraniums; trees and shrubs. The garden also features a new garden in walled farmyard; a wild area with pond, a small kitchen garden and a Victorian style conservatory. Home-made TEAS in aid of Cystic Fibrosis Research Trust. Plant sales to Spastics Society. *Adm £1.50 Chd free. Sat, Sun June 3, 4 (11-5)*

Knightsmead ✂❀ (Mrs Jones & Miss Collins) Rickman Hill Rd, Chipstead. 1m SW of Coulsdon. 3m SE of Banstead. From A23 in Coulsdon turn W onto B2032. Through traffic lights, L fork into Portnalls Rd. Top of hill at Xrds, turn R into Holymead Rd. R into Lissoms Rd. R into Bouverie Rd. ½-acre plantsman's garden, designed and maintained entirely by owners. Wide variety of shrubs and perennials for yr-round interest; hellebores, spring bulbs and woodland plants; pond; scented roses; raised alpine and peat beds, clematis, hostas, hardy geraniums etc. April soup, tea, coffee. June small craft exhibition. Home-made TEAS in conservatory. All refreshments in aid of Surrey Wildlife Trust. *Adm £1.30 Chd 50p. Wed April 19; Sat, Sun June 24, 25 (2-5.30). Private visits welcome, please* **Tel 01737 551694**

22 Knoll Road ✂❀ (Mr & Mrs D C Drummond) Dorking. S part of Dorking. From one way system after May's Garage turn L up the Horsham rd (A2003 which runs to N Holmwood roundabout A24). Knoll Road is the 4th turning R just beyond The Bush Inn. ⅓-acre town garden with many interesting and unusual plants labelled and with notes available. Mixed borders, raised beds, sinks, mini-meadow and peat bed, fern alley and some fruit and vegetables. A surprising front garden and well stocked conservatory. A comprehensive collection of Arum species for pollination research. (Mostly suitable for wheelchairs if driven to front door). TEAS. *Adm £1 Chd free. Sun April 30, Wed May 3 (10.30-5.30). Private visits welcome, please* **Tel 01306 883280**

Little Lodge, Thames Ditton (see London)

Little Mynthurst Farm ♿✂❀ (Mr & Mrs G Chilton) Norwood Hill. Between Leigh (2m) and Charlwood (3m); from Reigate take A217 to Horley; after 2m turn R just after river bridge at Sidlowbridge; 1st R signed Leigh; then L at T junction. 12-acre garden; walled old-fashioned roses, herbaceous borders and shrubs around old farm house (not open). Kitchen garden with greenhouses and secret garden. TEAS. *Adm £1.50 Chd free. Sat, Sun July 1, 2, (12-5.30). Coach parties welcome on NGS days only by prior arrangement please contact Head Gardener Mark Dobell* **Tel 01293 862639**

25 Little Woodcote Estate ♿✂❀ (Mr & Mrs Brian Hiley) Wallington. Private rd off Woodmansterne Lane. Signed SCC Smallholdings. Woodmansterne Lane joins B278 and A237. An exciting 1-acre plantsman's garden full of many rare unusual, tender and interesting plants; several large herbaceous borders; annual border; extensive collection of stone sinks. A good collection of plant containers, garden and farm bygones. Suitable in parts for wheelchairs. *Adm £1.20 Chd free (Share to Motor Neurone Disease Association®). Every Wed & Sat April 15 to Sept 30 (9-5). Private visits welcome for parties, please* **Tel 0181 647 9679**

Lodkin ❀ (Mr & Mrs W N Bolt) Lodkin Hill, Hascombe, 3m S of Godalming. Just off B2130 Godalming-Cranleigh, on outskirts of Hascombe; take narrow lane off signposted Thorncombe Street. About 5½ acres incl woodland, stream and prolific daffodils and cherries. 4 old Victorian greenhouses have been completely rebuilt and are in full use to produce fruit, flowers and vegetables. Chrysanthemums in November. Much of the old cast staging etc has been retained. In parts suitable for wheel chairs. TEAS. *Adm £1 Chd 50p. Suns April 9, July 23 (2-6), Nov 5 (greenhouses). Adm 75p that day Chd free (2-4). Private parties welcome, please* **Tel 01486 32323**

Malthouse Farm ❀ (Mr & Mrs G Pitt) Hambledon. Take A283 S through Witley at bottom of long downhill straight turn L marked Hambledon; straight on for ½m. Park opp village hall, entrance to garden further 120yds on RH-side. Map ref [SU 964385]. Entrance through picturesque passageway painted by Helen Allingham and Miles Birket Foster and photographed by Gertrude Jekyll (Homes & Gardens). 2-3 acres flowing into landscape of South Downs. Azaleas, flowering trees and shrubs; small water garden and woodland walk to small lake fed by one of the sources of the R Arun. House (not open) C16 with later additions; 1737 Granary on straddle stones. Small collection of Edwardian & vintage cars, old bicycles, motor cycles and lawnmowers. Partially suitable for wheelchairs. Home-made TEAS (Sun & Mon). *Adm £2 Chd 50p. Sun, Mon May 7, 8, Tues to Fri May 9 to 12 (2-6)*

Maryland ♿❀ (Mrs J Woodroffe) Worplesdon. From Guildford (A3) take A322 Bagshot Road. 4-acre mixed garden incl woodland area; large herbaceous border, lawns; mature specimen trees; climbing and wall shrubs and many less common plants. NCCPG National Collection of Veratrum. TEA. *Adm £1 Chd free. Suns March 12 (2-5), July 2, Sept 24 (2-6)*

Merrist Wood College ♿✂❀ Worplesdon 4m NW of Guildford. 40 acres of amenity areas, landscape demonstration gardens, 16 acres nursery stock, house a listed building (Norman Shaw 1877). Only reception hall open. One of the largest colleges of agriculture and horticulture in the UK with students from many countries. Information available for courses in Nursery, Landscape, Agriculture, Arboriculture, Countryside, Equestrian and Golf Studies. TEA. *Donation.* Rare plants for sale. Percentage of Plant Shop takings to NGS. *For NGS Sat, Sun, Mon, May 27, 28, 29, June 18 (10-6) with Surrey Horticultural Federation Summer Flower Show June 18 only. Parties welcome please,* **Tel 01483 232424**

Mitchen Hall ✂❀ (Mr & Mrs Timothy Holland-Bosworth) Shackleford. 7m SW of Guildford on the A3. Take the Hurtmore, Elstead and Shackleford exit. In Shackleford take the rd to Cutmill. House is ¾m outside village. Mitchen Hall is a Carolean house surrounded by interesting old barns set in unspoilt countryside. There are herbaceous and mixed borders; lake and woodland walks (some under construction); vegetable garden and greenhouse. Mostly suitable for wheelchairs. TEAS. *Adm £1 Chd free. Sun June 25 (2-6)*

Montfleury ✂❀ (Cdr & Mrs Innes Hamilton) Christchurch Rd, Virginia Water. From A30 at Virginia Water, opp Wheatsheaf Restaurant, turn down B389. Over roundabout. Last house on R before village. Former National English Tourist Board Award Winners' new small garden. Design, plant assoc propagation. Interesting plant sales. Also wide choice of professional nursery stock for immediate effect. Unlimited parking. TEA. *Adm £1 Chd 10p. Sun May 14 (2-6)*

The Moorings ♿❀ (Dr & Mrs C J F L Williamson) 14 Russells Cres, Horley. Nr town centre between A23 and B2036; 400yds from the railway station. 1-acre secluded country garden in centre of small town; contains all sorts of rare plants, interesting trees, many roses, pleasant vistas. An escapist's garden! See Collins Book of British Gardens. TEA. *Adm £1.25 Chd 25p (Share to St Bartholomew's Church, Horley). Sat, Sun Mon June 24, 25, 26 (2-6)*

29 Mostyn Road, Merton Park (see London)

Munstead Wood ♿❀ (Sir Robert & Lady Clark) nr Godalming. Take B2130 Brighton Rd out of Godalming towards Horsham. After 1m church on R, Heath Lane just thereafter on L. 400yds on R is entrance to Munstead Wood. Parking in Heath Lane. 10 acres of rhododendrons, azaleas, woods and shrub and flower beds. Home until 1931 of Gertrude Jekyll; parts of garden recently refurbished. The architect for the house (not open) was Edwin Lutyens. TEAS. *Adm £2 OAP/Chd £1 (Share to GUTS®). Suns April 23, May 28, Sept 24 (2-6)*

Odstock ♿✂❀ (Mr & Mrs J F H Trott) Bletchingley. Between Godstone 2m and Redhill 3m on A25. Junction 6 off M25 to Godstone. A25 towards Redhill. In Bletchingley from Whyte Harte up hill - Castle Square on L at top of hill. Just off A25. Parking in village. No parking in Castle Square. Bus 409 from Redhill Station alight at Red

Lion public house. ⅔ of an acre maintained by owners and continually being developed for all-yr interest. Covered walk created by training old apple trees plus other climbers. Interesting variety of plants and shrubs with imaginative complementary and contrasting groupings of form and colour. Japanese features; dahlias. No dig, low maintenance vegetable garden. TEAS. *Adm £1.50 Chd free (Share to NSPCC®). Sun Aug 6 (1-5.30). Disabled welcome – please telephone first* **Tel 01883 743100**

The Old Croft ✲❀ (David and Virginia Lardner-Burke) South Holmwood. 3m S of Dorking. From Dorking take A24 S for 3m. Turn L at sign to Leigh-Brockham into Mill Road. ¾m on L, 2 free car parks in NT Holmwood Common. Follow directional signs for 400yds along country walk through woodland to The Old Croft. 4 to 5 acres completely surrounded by NT property; parkland garden with lake, woodland, wild areas, herb garden, wide variety of specimen young trees, mature native trees, rhododendrons, azaleas and shrubs. Garden redeveloped and designed over last 7yrs by Virginia Lardner-Burke. TEAS. *Adm £1.50 Chd free (Share to St Catherine's Hospice, Crawley®). Sats, Suns May 13, 14; July 15, 16 (2-6)*

Olivers ✲❀ (Mr & Mrs Charles Watson) Church Road, Hascombe. On B2130, Godalming to Cranleigh Road (Godalming 3m). Park by White Horse in Hascombe village. Olivers is 50yds up Church Rd, between public house and pond. 2½-acre informal country garden; wide variety, herbaceous borders, interesting trees, shrubs and perennials, some new development areas. All this maintained on 1 day a week. Beautiful village location by historic church. TEAS. *Adm £1 Chd 20p (Share to Church Fabric Fund®). Sun May 21 (2-6)*

Painshill ♿✲ (Painshill Park Trust) 1m W Cobham on A245. Entrance on R, 200yds E of A3/A245 roundabout. Painshill is one of Europe's finest C18 landscape gardens, contemporary with Stourhead & Stowe. Created by the Hon Charles Hamilton between 1738-1773. Ornamental pleasure grounds dominated by 14-acre lake fed from river by immense waterwheel; grotto, ruined Abbey, Temple, Chinese Bridge, castellated Tower, Mausoleum. Turkish tent and newly planted vineyard. In 1981 the Painshill Park Trust was formed and following meticulous restoration the beautiful gardens are now emerging from the wilderness. Suitable for wheelchairs with exceptions. TEA. *Adm £3.50, disabled, students and OAPs £3 Chd 5-16 £2.50 Acc chd under 5 free (Share to Painshill Park Trust®). Suns only April 9 to Oct 15 (11-6). Private groups of 10 and over on other days, please* **Tel 01932 868113.** *For NGS Sun June 4 (11-5)*

¶Park House ♿✲❀ (The Viscount & Viscountess Leathers) Chiddingfold. ½m from top of village green (signposted Dunsfold) in E direction on the Pickhurst Rd. Park House is on the R. Parking by kind permission of Mr & Mrs Stamp. Disabled drive up to the house. A S facing interesting garden of mixed borders featuring many unusual trees and shrubs; agapanthus. Places to sit and relax. 6 acres in all incl woodland and wildlife area. TEAS (Sun Aug 6). *Adm £1.50 Chd 25p (Share to South West Surrey Mobile Physiotherapy Service®). Thurs, Sun Aug 3, 6 (2-6). Private visits and parties welcome, please* **Tel 01428 683222**

Pinewood House ♿✲ (Mr & Mrs J Van Zwanenberg) Heath House Rd, Worplesdon Hill. 3m Woking, 5m Guildford off A322 opp Brookwood Cemetery Wall. 4 acres. Walled garden and arboretum; water garden; bulbs in April. Interesting new house finished in Dec '86 with indoor plants. *Adm house & gardens £2 (Share to Action Research®). Private visits welcome for parties of 2-30 April to Oct, please* **Tel 01483 473241**

Polesden Lacey ♿✲ (The National Trust) Bookham, nr Dorking. 1½m S of Great Bookham off A246 Leatherhead-Guildford rd. 60 acres formal gardens; extensive grounds, walled rose garden, winter garden, lavender garden, iris garden, lawns; good views. House originally a Regency villa dating early 1820's, remodelled after 1906 by the Hon Mrs Ronald Greville, well-known Edwardian hostess; fine paintings, furniture, porcelain and silver, also many photographs from Mrs Greville's albums on display. King George VI and Queen Elizabeth (now the Queen Mother) spent part of their honeymoon here. For wheelchair details **Tel 01372 458203**. Gift shop. Lunch and TEAS in licensed restaurant in grounds (11-6). *Adm garden £2.50, Chd £1.25; house £3 extra; Chd £1.75.* ▲*For NGS garden only Sun May 14 (11-6)*

Postford House ♿❀ (Mrs R Litler-Jones) Chilworth. 4m SE Guildford Route A248 Bus LC 425 Guildford-Dorking alight nr entrance. 25 acres woodland; water garden; stream; rose garden; vegetable garden; rhododendrons, azaleas and shrubs; swimming pool open. Home-made TEAS. *Adm £1.50 Chd free (Share to Cruse Bereavement Care® May 28). Suns May 14, 21, 28 (2-6). Private visits welcome, please* **Tel 01483 202657**

Pyrford Court ♿ (Mr C Laikin) Pyrford Common Rd, 2m E of Woking. B367 junction with Upshott Lane; M25 exit 10 onto A3 towards Guildford off into Ripley signed Pyrford. 20 acres; wild gardens; extensive lawns; azaleas, rhododendrons, wisterias, autumn colour. As well as many fine established species of wisteria, there are several new plantings which together comprise the National Wisteria Collection. TEAS. *Adm £2.50, Chd 80p (Share to Age Concern®). Sat, Suns May 13, 14 (2-6), Oct 15 (12-4). Private visits and parties welcome, please* **Tel 01483 765880**

●Ramster ♿❀ (Mr & Mrs Paul Gunn) Chiddingfold. On A283, 1½m S of Chiddingfold; large iron gates on R. Mature 20-acre woodland garden of exceptional interest with lakes, ponds and woodland walks. Laid out by Gauntlett Nurseries of Chiddingfold in early 1900s. Fine rhododendrons, azaleas, camellias, magnolias, trees and shrubs. Picnic area. TEAS daily in May. *Adm £2 Chd under 16 free (Share to NGS®). Daily for April 15 to July 30 (2-6). Special early morning opening for photographers from 7am May 13, 14. Embroidery for Gardeners Exhibition May 6-19.* **Tel 01428 644422**

Regular Openers. Too many days to include in diary. Usually there is a wide range of plants giving year-round interest. See head of county section for the name and garden description for times etc.

Ridings ♿✂❀ (Mr & Mrs K Dutton) Tadworth. On A217 at large roundabout 6m S of Sutton and 3m N of junction 8 on M25 take B2220 sign posted Tadworth. Take 2nd R into Tadorne Rd; L into Cross Rd. House on corner of Epsom Lane S. ¾-acre informal garden containing interesting trees, shrubs and herbaceous plants with emphasis on colour, texture and foliage; vegetable plot. *Adm £1 Chd 30p. Sun June 11 (2-5.30). Coach parties by prior arrangement, please* **Tel 017378 13962**

Rise Top Cottage ✂❀ (Trevor Bath Esq) On entering Maybourne Rise, take immediate L turn. At the top of rise, turn L along a rough track (about 100yds). There is limited parking by the entrance otherwise, please park tactfully in Maybourne Rise. Trevor Bath is a garden writer and lecturer who began his delightful garden 26 yrs ago; profusion of planting; many unfamiliar varieties of cottage plants and some surprises; special interests incl aquilegias, pulmonarias, herbs, old roses and white flowers; mainly a wide range of hardy geraniums which are the subject of his new book. Home-made TEAS. *Adm £1 Chd free. Private visits welcome mid April and mid July, please* **Tel 01483 764958**

41 Shelvers Way ✂❀ (Mr & Mrs K G Lewis) Tadworth. 6m S of Sutton off the A217. !st turning on R after Burgh Heath traffic lights heading S. 400 yds down Shelvers Way on L. ⅓-acre suburban style with a difference. Cobbled area with bubble fountain and shingle scree leading to colourful herbaceous plantings, azaleas and rhododendrons in spring. Designed and developed entirely by owners for yr-round interest. TEA June, July only in aid of Tadworth and Walton Horticultural Society. *Adm £1.50 Chd free. Suns May 14, June 11 (2-5.30); July 16 (10.30-5)*

Snowdenham House ♿❀ (The Hon Lady Hamilton) Snowdenham Lane, Bramley. S of Guildford A281 from Guildford, R at Bramley mini-roundabout. House is ½m on L. Georgian house, outbuildings and water mill (not open). 9 acres of water, woodland, formal and walled gardens. Wide range of rhododendrons, azaleas and specimen trees and shrubs in woodland garden bordering stream. TEA. *Adm £2 Chd free. Sun May 14 (11.30-5)*

South Park Farm ♿ (Mrs P J Stewart-Smith) South Godstone. Take A22 London to East Grinstead rd and 1m S of railway bridge at South Godstone turn R into Carlton Rd just before Walker's Garden Centre; follow signs for 1m. Medium-sized garden; wide variety of roses; herbaceous border; fine trees and landscape; small lake. C17 (listed) farm house (not open). Peacocks. Home-made TEAS till 6 in large C17 barn. *Adm £1.50 Chd free. Sat, Sun, Mon June 17, 18, 19 (2-6). Also private visits welcome, please* **Tel 01342 892141**

Spring Cottage ♿✂❀ (Mr & Mrs D E Norman) Cranleigh. A281 from Guildford turn L 1m out of Bramley. Turn R at roundabout then immed L, into Smithwood Common Rd; garden 1m on R. 1-acre garden with lovely view; cottage garden; small woodland garden, old roses and new pond. TEAS. *Adm £1.25 Chd free. Wed June 7, Sun June 11 (2-6); private visits welcome, please* **Tel 01483 272620**

Spur Point, nr Fernhurst (See Sussex)

Stonywood ✂❀ (Mr & Mrs Noble) Chase Lane, Haslemere. From centre of town take B2131 E towards Petworth. Take 2nd turning R for Blackdown. At junction of 5 lanes go straight on towards Tennyson's Lane. At next junction (150yds) go straight on. House on L, ⅓m down lane. Parking space very limited in narrow lane. ⅓-acre steeply sloping garden. Many rhododendrons, azaleas, shrubs, spring bulbs; pleasant views across Chase Valley and NT woods. TEAS. *Adm £1 Chd free (Share to Foundation for the study of Infant Deaths®). Sun May 21 (2-5). Private visits welcome for parties of 10 and over, please* **Tel 01428 658583**

Street House ♿❀ (Mr & Mrs B M Francis) Thursley village ½m off A3 between Milford and Hindhead. From A3 100yds past Three Horse Shoes public house. House is on L. Car park is on recreation ground past PO in centre of village. Please park carefully in wet weather. Street House (not open), a listed Regency building and childhood home of Sir Edwin Lutyens where he first met Gertrude Jekyll (not open). Garden of 1¼ acres divided into three separate and individual gardens. Beautiful views towards Devils Punch Bowl. Ancient wall; special features include magnificent specimen cornus kousa; Japanese snowball tree; rare old roses; special rhododendrons and camellias; rubus tridel and many surprises. Special feature Astrological Garden now completed. Home-made TEAS. *Adm £1.50 Chd 50p (Share to Thursley Horticultural Soc®). Suns April 30, May 14, June 25, Sat July 29 (11-5)*

Thanescroft ♿✂ (Mr & Mrs Peter Talbot-Willcox) Shamley Green. 5m S of Guildford, A281 Guildford-Horsham rd, at Shalford turn E onto B2128 to Wonersh and Shamley Green. At Shamley Green Village sign turn R to Lord's Hill, ¾m on L. 4-acres mixed formal and informal garden, incl vegetables; lawns; roses; herbaceous; shrubs and specialist trees. Interesting icehouse; swimming pool. TEAS. *Adm £1 Chd 25p. Sun June 18 (2-6)*

¶Titsey Place Gardens ♿✂ (The Trustees of the Titsey Foundation) Oxted. 2m N of Oxted. On A25 between Oxted and Westerham, turn N into Limpsfield Village. On bend at end of village, turn L (straight on) into Bluehouse Lane. After 100yds, take 1st R into Water Lane. Proceed all the way up Water Lane. Turn R into Titsey Place. Proceed along drive. Signs will direct you to garden car park. 18 acres of landscaped gardens and lakes surrounded by parkland together with a rare opportunity to see a walled garden in the process of restoration. *Adm £2 Chd £1. Sun June 25 (1-5)*

Unicorns ✂❀ (Mr & Mrs Eric Roberts) Long Hill, The Sands, Farnham. Approx 4½m E of Farnham take A31 towards Guildford. 1st slip rd to Runfold turn R, then L into Crooksbury Rd through 's' bend then L turn to The Sands through village past Barley Mow public house on R. Long Hill 1st turning on R. Mainly woodland garden on a sloping site, rhododendrons, azaleas, ferns, plants for ground cover and many other interesting and unusual plants and shrubs. Teas at Manor Farm, Seale. *Adm £1. Private visits welcome from mid April to end of August please* **Tel 01252 782778 after 6pm**. *Due to terrain 2 to 15 adults only*

87 Upland Road (Mr & Mrs David Nunn) 50yds S Carshalton Beeches station into Waverley Way, at shops into Downside Rd, then 1st on L. 0.4-acre secluded suburban plantsman's garden overlaying chalk. Shrubs; herbaceous; orchard; fruit and vegetable garden. Developed and maintained by owners. Exhibition of botanical watercolour paintings. TEAS. *Adm £1.50 Chd free. Sun May 14 (2-6)*

¶6 Upper Rose Hill (Peter & Julia Williams) Dorking. Situated just S of Dorking town centre, A24 from N/S or A25 from E/W to roundabout at A24/A25 junction. Follow signs to town centre and one way system towards Horsham. After ½m take narrow concealed L turn (Rose Hill) after Pizza Piazza on L under cedar tree overhanging rd just before Mays Garage. At top of hill take 2nd R (Upper Rose Hill) No 6 is 3rd on R. Parking available in rd and also in large car park behind Sainsburys in town centre, leave car park by S exit (Rose Hill) and walk 5 minutes up hill following signs. Upper Rose Hill is on the L at top of hill. ½-acre suburban garden, S facing terraced site backing onto St Pauls Church on neutral dry sandy soil. Laid out with rockeries informal mixed flower and shrub borders, with fruit and vegetables for family use and yr-round interest. Wide range of foliage and form, ferns, hardy geraniums, cistus, grasses and herbs, incl some unusual plants, good autumn colour. Top level only, suitable for wheelchairs. TEAS. *Adm £1 Chd 25p (Share to Mole Valley Crossroads for Carers®). Sun June 18 (2-6). Private visits welcome, please* **Tel 01306 881315**

Vale End (Mr & Mrs John Foulsham) Albury, 4½m SE of Guildford. From Albury take A248 W for ¼m. 1-acre walled garden on many levels in beautiful setting; featured in Homes and Gardens 1994; views from terrace across sloping lawns to mill pond and woodland; wide variety herbaceous plants and old roses; attractive courtyard. Ornamental fruit and vegetable garden. Featured in NGS video 2. Morning coffee and home-made TEAS in aid of St Luke's Hospital, Guildford Cancer Appeal. *Adm £1.50 Chd free. Suns June 25, July 23 (10-5)*

Vann (Mr & Mrs M B Caroe) Hambledon, 6m S of Godalming. A283 to Wormley. Turn L at Hambledon Xrds signed 'Vann Lane'. Follow yellow 'Vann' signs for 2m. House on left. GPO box on gate. A listed garden of 4½ acres surrounding Tudor/William & Mary house with later additions and alterations incorporating old farm buildings by W D Caröe 1907-1909. Formal yew walk recently replanted, ¼-acre pond, Gertrude Jekyll water garden 1911, pergola, old cottage garden. Spring bulbs, woodland, azaleas, roses. New vegetable garden borders. Featured in *Architectural Digest 1991, Homes & Gardens* and *World of Interiors 1993.* Maintained by family with 2 days assistance per week. Part of garden suitable for wheelchairs. Party bookings, guided tours, morning coffee, lunches, home-made teas in house from Easter-July by prior arrangement. TEAS (Sun April 30 only). *Adm £2.50 Chd 50p (Share to Hambledon Village Hall®, May 1). Tues-Sun April 18-23 (10-6). Sun April 30 (2-7); Mon-Sat May 1-6 (10-6), Tues-Sun May 30-June 4 (10-6). Private visits welcome, please* **Tel 01428 683413**

Walton Poor (Mr & Mrs Nicholas Calvert) 4m W of Ranmore. From N and W off A246 on outskirts of East Horsley take Greendene 1st fork L Crocknorth Rd. From E take A2003 to Ranmore Rd from Dorking to E Horsley. Approx 3 acres; tranquil, rather secret garden; paths winding between areas of ornamental shrubs; landscaped sunken garden; pond; herb garden. Autumn colour. Extensive range of foliage, scented plants and herbs for sale; garden next to miles of forest paths leading to North Downs with fine views over Tillingbourne valley. TEAS (May and June) (from 3pm). *Adm £1.50 Chd 50p (Share to Leukaemia Research®). Mon May 8, Sun, Wed June 4, 7, Sun Oct 8 (11-5) Herb garden open daily Wed to Sun Easter to Sept 30. Private visits of 10 and over welcome to the main garden, please* **Tel 01483 282273**

Westbourn (Mr & Mrs John Camden) Virginia Water. From Egham 3m S on A30. Turn L into Christchurch Rd opp the Wheatsheaf Hotel. After 200yds turn R into Pinewood Rd; Westbourn is 50yds on the R. 4 acres landscaped woodland on 2 levels extensively planted with unusual trees and shrubs. Rhododendrons and azaleas predominate with over 80 different species and as many hybrids. Other notable collections well represented include acer, prunus, sorbus, hydrangea, ferns, ornamental cherries and hosta. The R Bourne, a narrow winding rivulet, forms the southern boundary of the garden. Soft drinks & biscuits. TEA. *Adm £1 Chd free. Sun May 7 (2-6)*

Westland Farm (Mrs E J Burnet) Ewhurst. 11m SE of Guildford. Join Ockley Rd (B2127) at Bull's Head N of village. Go E for ¾m. See sign on RH-side. 2½ acres plus 14 acres bluebell woodland; rhododendrons, azaleas, other acid-loving plants, lake with woodland walk, spring bulbs; Australian plants and trees around house and cottages. Interesting use of horticultural plastic for low maintenance and growth promotion; established trees and shrubs in garden extension (designer Jan Martinez). Ancient stone well. Australian TEAS and pavlova icecream; dried flower arrangements. *Adm £1.50 Chd free (Share to Gfd Scouts and Ewhurst Infant School). Sun April 30, Wed May 10 (1.30-5.30). Coach parties by prior arrangement, please* **Tel 01483 277270**

Whinfold (Mr & Mrs A Gash) Hascombe. 3½m SE of Godalming. Turn off B2130 at top of Winkworth Hill between Godalming and Hascombe. Woodland garden about 15 acres originally planned by Gertrude Jekyll in 1897. The garden is maintained by the owners with weekend help and includes a pond, herb garden, specimen trees, magnolias, rhododendrons, azaleas and camellias with spring bulbs followed by masses of bluebells. TEA. *Adm £1 Chd free (Share to Hydon Hill Cheshire Home®). Suns April 2, May 14 (2-5)*

White House (Lt Cdr & Mrs Michael Lethbridge) Stringers Common, Guildford. On A320 Guildford to Woking Rd 2m N of Guildford centre just beyond junction with Jacob's Well Rd. 3 acres, shrubs and herbaceous borders in setting of stone walls, roses, old orchard and pond. Quiet garden beside busy rd. Aims to maintain natural surroundings and habitat for birds, insects and wild flowers and to avoid unnecessary chemicals. A 'controlled' wild look. TEA. *Adm £1 Chd free (Share to Jacobs Well Ecological Society®). Suns July 2 (2-6), Oct 8 (2-5.30)*

Winkworth Arboretum (The National Trust) Hascombe, Godalming. Entrances with car parks; Upper 3m SE of Godalming on E side of B2130; Lower 2¼m S of Bramley on Bramley-Hascombe rd, turn R off A281 from Guildford by Bramley Grange Hotel, up Snowdenham Lane. Coaches (by written arrangement) should use Upper car park on B2130. Station: Godalming 3m. 95 acres of hillside planted with rare trees and shrubs; 2 lakes; many wild birds; view over N Downs. Limited suitability for wheelchairs. Disabled visitors use lower car park. TEAS 11-6. *Adm £2 Chd 5-17 £1. ▲Suns May 7, Oct 15 (dawn-dusk)*

Wintershall Manor ✲ (Mr & Mrs Peter Hutley) 3m S of Bramley village on A281 turn R, then next R. Wintershall drive next on L. Bus: AV 33 Guildford-Horsham; alight Palmers Cross, 1m. 2-acre garden and 200 acres of park and woodland; snowdrop walk, acres of bluebell walks in spring; banks of wild daffodils; rhododendrons; specimen trees; several acres of lakes and flight ponds; Domesday yew tree. St Francis Chapel by Chapel Lake. Path commences The Stations of the Cross by contemporary young sculptors leading up the hill to Hollybarn and The Chapel of St Mary, Queen of Peace, with superb views. Partially suitable for wheelchairs. TEA from 3.30 pm. *Adm £2 OAPs £1.50 Chd 4-14 50p. Suns Feb 5, March 5, April 2, May 7, June 4, July 2 (2-4.30)*

Woodlands, 67 York Rd ♿✲❀ (F A Wood Esq) Cheam. York Rd is situated in the Sutton Cheam area and runs between Cheam Rd and Dorset Rd. 67 is located at the S end of York Rd, towards the junction with Dorset Rd, which is a turning off Belmont Rise A217. Mainly walled suburban garden just under 0.2 acres, laid out and developed by the present owner over the past few years. The layout comprises 2 lawned terraces with interesting hard landscaping and footpath patterns, incl raised shrub, heather and flower beds. Good range of plants, incl viburnums, hollies, ferns, ivies and conifers, plus 75′ herbaceous border with wide range of hardy plants. 2 raised ponds, 1 comprising an open roofed water pavilion. Good selection of wall climbers. Dried flowers for sale. TEAS. *Adm £1 Chd free. Sun, Wed July 16, 19 (10-4); also private parties welcome, please* **Tel 0181 642 4260**

Woodside ✲❀ (Mr & Mrs J A Colmer) Send Barns Lane, Send, nr Ripley, 4m NE of Guildford; on A247 (Woking/Dorking Rd) 200yds west (Send side) at junction with B2215. If travelling via M25 leave at junction 10. ⅓-acre garden; main feature rock garden and alpine house; many shrubs incl rhododendrons, ericaceous species etc; herbaceous planting; specialist collection of alpines. *Adm £1 Chd free. Sat, Sun April 22, 23 (2-6). Private visits welcome in May, please* **Tel 01483 223073**

Yew Tree Cottage ✲❀ (Mr & Mrs E E Bowyer) Bunch Lane, Haslemere. Turn off High St into Church Lane, leave church on L, carry on to T junction, turn L, 1st house on L. 2-acre garden created by owners since 1976 on hillside. Large variety of trees and shrubs, water garden, kitchen garden, Jacob and Shetland sheep, rare breed poultry, Shetland pony in paddock beyond garden. See **Haslehurst.** Tea at Haslehurst. *Adm £1 Chd 50p (Share to Haslemere Educational Museum®). Sun June 18 (2.30-6). Coach parties by prior arrangement. Private visits welcome, please* **Tel 01428 644130**

Sussex

Hon County Organisers:

(East & Mid-Sussex)	Mrs Janet Goldsmith, Sunnymead, Durgates, Wadhurst TN5 6RS Tel 01892 783264
(West Sussex)	Mrs Mark Dunn, Wildham, Stoughton, Chichester. Tel 01243 535202

Assistant Hon County Organisers:

(East & Mid-Sussex)	Mrs J Charlesworth, Snape Cottage, Snape Lane, Wadhurst
(West Sussex)	Mrs Nigel Azis, Coke's Barn, West Burton, Pulborough RH20 1HD Tel 01798 831636
(West Sussex)	Mrs Jane Burton, Church Farmhouse, Lavant, nr Chichester
((West Sussex)	Mrs Juliet Tuck, New Barn, Egdean, Pulborough

Hon County Treasurers:

(East & Mid-Sussex)	D C Goldsmith Esq, Sunnymead, Durgates, Wadhurst TN5 6RS
(West Sussex)	W M Caldwell Esq, The Grange, Fittleworth, Pulborough

---

DATES OF OPENING

By appointment

For telephone number and other details see garden descriptions. Private visits welcomed

Bates Green, Arlington
Berri Court, Yapton
Buckhurst Park, Withyham
Casters Brook, Cocking, nr Midhurst
Coates Manor, Fittleworth
Coke's Barn, West Burton, nr Pulborough
Combehurst, Frant
Cooke's House, West Burton
Crown House, Eridge
Gaywood Farm, Pulborough
Ghyll Farm, Sweethaws, Crowborough
Great Allfields, Petworth
6 Hollbrook Park, Northlands Road, nr Horsham
Home Farm House, Buckham Hill, Uckfield. Feb and March
Houghton Farm, nr Arundel
King John's Lodge, Etchingham

Knabbs Farmhouse, Fletching
Lilac Cottage, Duncton
Little Dene, Chelwood Gate
The Manor of Dean, Tillington, Petworth
Mill House, Nutbourne
Neptune House, Cutmill, Bosham
North Springs, Fittleworth
Old Barklye, Heathfield
The Old Chalk Pit, Hove Gardens
64 Old Shoreham Road, Hove Gardens
Palmer's Lodge, West Chiltington Village
Priesthawes Farm, Polegate
Sherburne House, Eartham
Spur Point, nr Fernhurst
Telegraph House, North Marden, nr Chichester
Upper House, West Burton
Warren House, Crowborough
46 Westup Farm Cottages, Balcombe
The White House, Burpham, nr Arundel
Woodstock, West Boyle, Chichester

Parties only
Baker's Farm, Shipley, nr Horsham
Champs Hill, Coldwaltham, nr Pulborough
Chidmere House, Chidmere
Chilsham House, Herstmonceux
Clinton Lodge, Fletching
Cobblers, Crowborough
Cowbeech Farm, Rushlake Green
Crawley Down Gardens
Duckyls, Sharpthorne
Frewen College, Brickwall, Northiam
Frith Lodge, Northchapel
High Beeches Gardens, Handcross
Highdown Gardens, Goring-by-Sea
Ketches, Newick
Malt House, Chithurst, nr Rogate
Merriments Gardens, Hurst Green
Middle Coombe, East Grinstead
The Old Rectory, Newtimber
Palmer's Lodge, West Chiltington Village
Penns in the Rock, Groombridge
Pheasants Hatch, Newick. June to July
Somerset Lodge, North Street, Petworth
Whiligh, Shovers Green, Wadhurst

Regular openings
For details see garden descriptions

Borde Hill Garden, nr Haywards Heath. Daily March 18 to Oct 1
Denmans, Fontwell, nr Arundel. Daily except Dec 25, 26
Great Dixter, Northiam. For dates see text.
Moorlands, nr Crowborough. Weds April to Oct 1
Parham House and Gardens, nr Pulborough. For dates see text
Pashley Manor, Ticehurst. For details see text
West Dean Gardens, nr Chichester. Daily April 1 to Oct 29
Wilderness Farm, Hadlow Down. For details see text

March 5 Sunday
Champs Hill, Coldwaltham, nr Pulborough

March 6 Monday
Denmans, Fontwell, nr Arundel

March 12 Sunday
Champs Hill, Coldwaltham, nr Pulborough

March 25 Saturday
The Manor of Dean, Tillington, Petworth ‡
Parham House and Gardens, nr Pulborough
Petworth House Pleasure Ground ‡

March 26 Sunday
Champs Hill, Coldwaltham, nr Pulborough
The Manor of Dean, Tillington, Petworth
Orchards, Rowfant, nr Crawley Down

March 27 Monday
The Manor of Dean, Tillington, Petworth

April 2 Sunday
Berri Court, Yapton
Champs Hill, Coldwaltham, nr Pulborough
Rymans, Apuldram, nr Chichester

April 3 Monday
Berri Court, Yapton
Northwood Farmhouse, Pulborough

April 4 Tuesday
Northwood Farmhouse, Pulborough

April 9 Sunday
Bates Green, Arlington

April 10 Monday
Little Thakeham, Storrington

April 11 Tuesday
Little Thakeham, Storrington

April 16 Sunday
Bignor Park, nr Pulborough
Chidmere House, Chidmere

April 17 Monday
Bignor Park, nr Pulborough
Chidmere House, Chidmere
Highdown Gardens, Goring-by-Sea
Orchards, Rowfant, nr Crawley Down
Penns in the Rock, Groombridge
Stonehurst, Ardingly

April 22 Saturday
The Manor of Dean, Tillington, Petworth

April 23 Sunday
Cooke's House, West Burton
Ghyll Farm, Sweethaws, Crowborough
Malt House, Chithurst, nr Rogate
The Manor of Dean, Tillington, Petworth

April 24 Monday
Cooke's House, West Burton
The Manor of Dean, Tillington, Petworth

April 25 Tuesday
Cooke's House, West Burton

April 26 Wednesday
West Dean Gardens, nr Chichester

April 29 Saturday
Cedar Tree Cottage, Washington

April 30 Sunday
Coke's Barn, West Burton, nr Pulborough ‡
Duckyls, Sharpthorne
Houghton Farm, nr Arundel ‡
Hove Gardens
Hurst Mill, Petersfield
Malt House, Chithurst, nr Rogate
Newtimber Place, Hurstpierpoint
Rymans, Apuldram, nr Chichester
Wadhurst Park, Wadhurst

May 1 Monday
Coke's Barn, West Burton, nr Pulborough ‡
Duckyls, Sharpthorne
Houghton Farm, nr Arundel ‡

May 2 Tuesday
Coke's Barn, West Burton, nr Pulborough

May 3 Wednesday
Cedar Tree Cottage, Washington

May 6 Saturday
Champs Hill, Coldwaltham, nr Pulborough
Cooksbridge, Fernhurst
High Beeches Gardens, Handcross

May 7 Sunday
Cedar Tree Cottage, Washington
Champs Hill, Coldwaltham, nr Pulborough ‡
Cooke's House, West Burton ‡
Cooksbridge, Fernhurst
Hammerwood House, Iping ‡‡
Malt House, Chithurst, nr Rogate ‡‡
Merriments Gardens, Hurst Green
Moorlands, nr Crowborough
Offham House, Offham, nr Lewes
Orchards, Rowfant, nr Crawley Down ‡‡‡

Puddle House, Cross in Hand
Standen, East Grinstead ‡‡‡

May 8 Monday
Cooke's House, West Burton
Ghyll Farm, Sweethaws, Crowborough
Highdown Gardens, Goring-by-Sea
Malt House, Chithurst, nr Rogate

May 9 Tuesday
Cooke's House, West Burton

May 10 Wednesday
Middle Coombe, East Grinstead
Nyewood House, Nyewood, nr Rogate

May 13 Saturday
Champs Hill, Coldwaltham, nr Pulborough

May 14 Sunday
Berri Court, Yapton
Champs Hill, Coldwaltham, nr Pulborough
Cobblers, Crowborough ‡
Cowdray Park Gardens, Midhurst ‡‡
The Garden In Mind, Stansted Park
Hammerwood House, Iping ‡‡‡
6 Hollbrook Park, Northlands Road, nr Horsham
Malt House, Chithurst, nr Rogate ‡‡‡
Mountfield Court, nr Robertsbridge
New Grove, Petworth ‡‡
Selehurst, Lower Beeding, nr Horsham
Stonehurst, Ardingly
Tinkers Bridge Cottage, Ticehurst
Warren House, Crowborough ‡

May 15 Monday
Berri Court, Yapton
The Garden In Mind, Stansted Park
Mountfield Court, nr Robertsbridge
New Grove, Petworth

May 16 Tuesday
The Garden In Mind, Stansted Park

May 17 Wednesday
Sheffield Park Garden, nr Uckfield

May 18 Thursday
6 Hollbrook Park, Northlands Road, nr Horsham

May 20 Saturday
Champs Hill, Coldwaltham, nr Pulborough ‡
Fittleworth Gardens, Pulborough ‡
Lane End, Midhurst ‡‡
The Manor of Dean, Tillington, Petworth ‡‡

May 21 Sunday
Champs Hill, Coldwaltham, nr Pulborough ‡
Chidmere House, Chidmere
Cowbeech Farm, Rushlake Green
Fittleworth Gardens, Pulborough ‡
Fitzhall, Iping, nr Midhurst ‡‡
Ghyll Farm, Sweethaws, Crowborough ‡‡‡
Greenacres, Crowborough ‡‡‡
Lane End, Midhurst ‡‡
Legsheath Farm, nr Forest Row
Malt House, Chithurst, nr Rogate ‡‡
The Manor of Dean, Tillington, Petworth ‡
Merriments Gardens, Hurst Green
Trotton Old Rectory, nr Rogate ‡‡‡‡
Trotton Place, nr Rogate ‡‡‡‡
Woodstock, West Boyle, Chichester

May 22 Monday
Chidmere House, Chidmere
Lane End, Midhurst ‡
The Manor of Dean, Tillington, Petworth ‡

May 25 Thursday
Houghton Farm, nr Arundel

May 26 Friday
Houghton Farm, nr Arundel

May 27 Saturday
Gaywood Farm, Pulborough
King Edward V11 Hospital, nr Midhurst ‡
Lane End, Midhurst ‡

May 28 Sunday
Baker's Farm, Shipley, nr Horsham
Bumble Cottage, Monkmead Lane, W Chiltington ‡
Gaywood Farm, Pulborough ‡
Lane End, Midhurst ‡‡
Malt House, Chithurst, nr Rogate ‡‡
Manvilles Field, Fittleworth
Moorlands, nr Crowborough ‡‡‡
New Place, Framfield
Northfields Farmhouse, Eastergate
Walland Manor, Wadhurst ‡‡‡
Warren House, Crowborough ‡‡‡
Wilderness Farm, Hadlow Down

May 29 Monday
Bumble Cottage, Monkmead Lane, W Chiltington ‡
Cobblers, Crowborough ‡‡
Highdown Gardens, Goring-by-Sea
Lane End, Midhurst ‡‡‡
Malt House, Chithurst, nr Rogate ‡‡‡
Manvilles Field, Fittleworth ‡
Northfields Farmhouse, Eastergate
Stonehurst, Ardingly
Warren House, Crowborough ‡‡

June 2 Friday
Northfields Farmhouse, Eastergate

June 3 Saturday
Lilac Cottage, Duncton ‡
Somerset Lodge, North St, Petworth ‡

June 4 Sunday
Combehurst, Frant
The Garden In Mind, Stansted Park
Greenacres, Crowborough ‡
Hailsham Grange, Hailsham
Lilac Cottage, Duncton ‡‡
Merriments Gardens, Hurst Green
Moorlands, nr Crowborough ‡
Neptune House, Cutmill, Bosham ‡‡‡
Northfields Farmhouse, Eastergate
Offham House, Offham, nr Lewes
Pembury, Clayton, nr Brighton
Pondfield, Cutmill, Bosham ‡‡‡
Somerset Lodge, North St, Petworth ‡‡
The White House, Burpham, nr Arundel

June 5 Monday
The Garden In Mind, Stansted Park
Little Thakeham, Storrington

June 6 Tuesday
The Garden In Mind, Stansted Park
Little Thakeham, Storrington
Nymans, Handcross

June 7 Wednesday
Lilac Cottage, Duncton ‡
Parham House and Gardens, nr Pulborough
Somerset Lodge, North St, Petworth ‡

June 8 Thursday
Parham House and Gardens, nr Pulborough

June 9 Friday
Northfields Farmhouse, Eastergate

June 10 Saturday
Coombland, Coneyhurst, Billingshurst

June 11 Sunday
Clinton Lodge, Fletching ‡
Coates Manor, Fittleworth ‡‡
Cobblers, Crowborough ‡‡‡
Ebbsworth, Nutbourne, nr Pulborough ‡‡
Frith Hill, Northchapel ‡‡‡‡
Frith Lodge, Northchapel ‡‡‡‡
Greenacres, Crowborough ‡‡‡
Kingston Gardens, nr Lewes
Knabbs Farmhouse, Fletching ‡

Northfields Farmhouse, Eastergate
Nyewood House, Nyewood, nr Rogate

June 12 Monday
Clinton Lodge, Fletching
Coates Manor, Fittleworth ‡
Ebbsworth, Nutbourne, nr Pulborough ‡

June 13 Tuesday
Coates Manor, Fittleworth

June 14 Wednesday
Nyewood House, Nyewood, nr Rogate

June 15 Thursday
Frith Hill, Northchapel ‡
Frith Lodge, Northchapel ‡

June 16 Friday
Northfields Farmhouse, Eastergate

June 17 Saturday
Chantry Green House, Steyning
King John's Lodge, Etchingham ‡
Little Hutchings, Etchingham ‡
Telegraph House, North Marden, nr Chichester
Upper House, West Burton
Winchelsea Gardens

June 18 Sunday
Baker's Farm, Shipley, nr Horsham
Casters Brook, Cocking, nr Midhurst
Chantry Green House, Steyning
Framfield Gardens, Uckfield
Ketches, Newick
King John's Lodge, Etchingham ‡
Little Hutchings, Etchingham ‡
Lye Green House, nr Crowborough
Mayfield Cottage Gardens ‡
Merriments Gardens, Hurst Green
Moat Mill Farm, Mayfield ‡
Northfields Farmhouse, Eastergate ‡‡
Priesthawes Farm, Polegate
Sherburne House, Eartham ‡‡
Telegraph House, North Marden, nr Chichester
Upper House, West Burton
Warren House, Crowborough
Whiligh, Shovers Green, Wadhurst
The White House, Burpham, nr Arundel

June 19 Monday
Clinton Lodge, Fletching
Houghton Farm, nr Arundel ‡
Northwood Farmhouse, Pulborough
Priesthawes Farm, Polegate
Upper House, West Burton ‡
Whiligh, Shovers Green, Wadhurst

June 20 Tuesday
Houghton Farm, nr Arundel
Northwood Farmhouse, Pulborough

June 21 Wednesday
Ashburnham Place, Battle
Bateman's, Burwash
Clinton Lodge, Fletching

June 22 Thursday
Ashburnham Place, Battle

June 23 Friday
Down Place, South Harting
Northfields Farmhouse, Eastergate

June 24 Saturday
Buckhurst Park, Withyham
Chilsham House, Herstmonceux
Coombland, Coneyhurst, Billingshurst
Down Place, South Harting

June 25 Sunday
Ambrose Place Back Gardens, Worthing ‡
Ashburnham Place, Battle ‡‡
Belsize Road Gardens, Worthing ‡
Berri Court, Yapton
Casters Brook, Cocking, nr Midhurst
Chidmere House, Chidmere
Chilsham House, Herstmonceux ‡‡
Cobblers, Crowborough
Down Place, South Harting ‡
The Garden In Mind, Stansted Park
Home Farm House, Buckham Hill, Uckfield ‡‡
Hove Gardens
Hurst Mill, Petersfield ‡
Merriments Gardens, Hurst Green
Northfields Farmhouse, Eastergate
The Old Rectory, Newtimber, nr Hurstpierpoint
The Old Vicarage, Firle, nr Lewes
Pashley Manor, Ticehurst
Pheasants Hatch, Newick
Trotton Old Rectory, nr Rogate ‡‡‡
Trotton Place, nr Rogate ‡‡‡

June 26 Monday
Berri Court, Yapton
Chidmere House, Chidmere
Clinton Lodge, Fletching
The Garden In Mind, Stansted Park
Home Farm House, Buckham Hill, Uckfield ‡
Pheasants Hatch, Newick ‡

June 27 Tuesday
The Garden In Mind, Stansted Park

June 30 Friday
Northfields Farmhouse, Eastergate
St Mary's House, Bramber

July 1 Saturday
St Mary's House, Bramber

July 2 Sunday
Bates Green, Arlington
Northfields Farmhouse, Eastergate
Warren House, Crowborough

July 4 Tuesday
Nymans, Handcross

July 7 Friday
Northfields Farmhouse, Eastergate

July 8 Saturday
Crown House, Eridge
North Springs, Fittleworth

July 9 Sunday
Cobblers, Crowborough ‡
Crown House, Eridge ‡
Fitzhall, Iping, nr Midhurst
Merriments Gardens, Hurst Green
North Springs, Fittleworth
Northfields Farmhouse, Eastergate

July 10 Monday
Merriments Gardens, Hurst Green

July 12 Wednesday
Middle Coombe, East Grinstead

July 14 Friday
Northfields Farmhouse, Eastergate

July 15 Saturday
Buckhurst Park, Withyham
Bumble Cottage, Monkmead Lane, W Chiltington ‡
Gaywood Farm, Pulborough ‡
The Manor of Dean, Tillington, Petworth
Palmer's Lodge, West Chiltington Village ‡
Telegraph House, North Marden

July 16 Sunday
Bumble Cottage, Monkmead Lane, W Chiltington ‡
Chilsham House, Herstmonceux
Gaywood Farm, Pulborough ‡
The Manor of Dean, Tillington, Petworth
Northfields Farmhouse, Eastergate
Nyewood House, Nyewood, nr Rogate ‡‡
Palmer's Lodge, West Chiltington Village ‡
Telegraph House, North Marden ‡‡
Wadhurst Gardens

July 17 Monday
Chilsham House, Herstmonceux
The Manor of Dean, Tillington, Petworth
Wadhurst Gardens

July 19 Wednesday
Nyewood House, Nyewood, nr Rogate

July 21 Friday
Northfields Farmhouse, Eastergate
Wakehurst Place, Ardingly

July 22 Saturday
Bumble Cottage, Monkmead Lane, W Chiltington ‡

Palmer's Lodge, West Chiltington Village ‡

July 23 Sunday

Belsize Road Gardens, Worthing
Bumble Cottage, Monkmead Lane, W Chiltington ‡
Cobblers, Crowborough ‡‡
Frewen College, Brickwall, Northiam
Kingston Gardens, nr Lewes
Moorlands, nr Crowborough ‡‡
Northfields Farmhouse, Eastergate
Palmer's Lodge, West Chiltington Village ‡

July 28 Friday

Northfields Farmhouse, Eastergate

July 30 Sunday

Bignor Park, nr Pulborough ‡
Champs Hill, Coldwaltham, nr Pulborough ‡
Houghton Farm, nr Arundel
Merriments Gardens, Hurst Green
Northfields Farmhouse, Eastergate

July 31 Monday

Merriments Gardens, Hurst Green

August 5 Saturday

Champs Hill, Coldwaltham, nr Pulborough
Cooksbridge, Fernhurst

August 6 Sunday

Bates Green, Arlington
Champs Hill, Coldwaltham, nr Pulborough
Cobblers, Crowborough
Cooksbridge, Fernhurst
Hailsham Grange, Hailsham
Wilderness Farm, Hadlow Down

August 13 Sunday

Champs Hill, Coldwaltham, nr Pulborough
Merriments Gardens, Hurst Green

August 14 Monday

Merriments Gardens, Hurst Green

August 19 Saturday

Champs Hill, Coldwaltham, nr Pulborough ‡
The Manor of Dean, Tillington, Petworth ‡

August 20 Sunday

Champs Hill, Coldwaltham, nr Pulborough ‡
Cobblers, Crowborough
The Manor of Dean, Tillington, Petworth ‡

August 21 Monday

The Manor of Dean, Tillington, Petworth

August 27 Sunday

Chidmere House, Chidmere
Merriments Gardens, Hurst Green
Newtimber Place, nr Hurstpierpoint
Warren House, Crowborough

August 28 Monday

Chidmere House, Chidmere
Cobblers, Crowborough
Houghton Farm, nr Arundel
Merriments Gardens, Hurst Green
Penns in the Rock, Groombridge

September 2 Saturday

High Beeches Gardens, Handcross

September 3 Sunday

Uppark, South Harting
Wilderness Farm, Hadlow Down

September 6 Wednesday

West Dean Gardens, Nr Chichester

September 8 Friday

Northfields Farmhouse, Eastergate

September 10 Sunday

Cowbeech Farm, Rushlake Green
Fitzhall, Iping, nr Midhurst ‡
The Garden In Mind, Stansted Park
Merriments Gardens, Hurst Green
Northfields Farmhouse, Eastergate
Standen, East Grinstead
Uppark, South Harting ‡

September 11 Monday

The Garden In Mind, Stansted Park
Northfields Farmhouse, Eastergate

September 12 Tuesday

The Garden In Mind, Stansted Park
Northfields Farmhouse, Eastergate

September 13 Wednesday

Cowbeech Farm, Rushlake Green

September 16 Saturday

The Manor of Dean, Tillington, Petworth

September 17 Sunday

The Manor of Dean, Tillington, Petworth

September 18 Monday

The Manor of Dean, Tillington, Petworth

September 24 Sunday

The Garden In Mind, Stansted Park
Hurst Mill, Petersfield
Orchards, Rowfant, nr Crawley Down

September 25 Monday

The Garden In Mind, Stansted Park

September 26 Tuesday

The Garden In Mind, Stansted Park
Houghton Farm, nr Arundel

October 1 Sunday

Bates Green, Arlington
Warren House, Crowborough

October 7 Saturday

The Manor of Dean, Tillington, Petworth

October 8 Sunday

The Manor of Dean, Tillington, Petworth

October 9 Sunday

The Manor of Dean, Tillington, Petworth

October 14 Saturday

Great Allfields, Petworth

October 18 Wednesday

Sheffield Park Garden, nr Uckfield

October 23 Monday

Denmans, Fontwell, nr Arundel

October 29 Sunday

Berri Court, Yapton

October 30 Monday

Berri Court, Yapton

DESCRIPTIONS OF GARDENS

Ambrose Place Back Gardens, Richmond Rd ♿✂❀
Worthing 10m E of Bognor, 7m W of Brighton. Take Broadwater Rd into town centre, turn R at traffic lights into Richmond Rd opp Library; small town gardens with entrances on left; parking in rds. TEAS. *Combined adm £1 Chd 25p (Share to Christ Church and St Paul's Worthing®). Sun June 25 (11-1, 2-5)*

No 1 (Mrs M M Rosenberg) Walled garden; shrubs, pond, climbing plants

No 3 (Mr & Mrs M Smyth) Paved garden with climbing plants and lawn

No 4 (Mr & Mrs T J Worley) Paved garden with raised herbaceous borders, lawn and flowering summer plants

¶**No 5** (Mr & Mrs P Owen) Paved with borders

No 6 (Mrs Leslie Roberts) Attractive garden with conservatory

No 7 (Mr M Frost) Patio garden, with conservatory

No 8 (Mr & Mrs P McMonagle) Summer flowering plants and lawn

No 10 (Mrs C F Demuth) Paved garden with roses and interesting trees

No 11 (Mrs M Stewart) Roses, summerhouse, flowering plants

No 12 (Mr & Mrs P Bennett) Original paved small garden with trees

No 14 (Mr & Mrs A H P Humphrey) Roses, flowering plants, greenhouse and bonsai collection

Ambrose Villa (Mr & Mrs Frank Leocadi) Italian style small town garden

Ashburnham Place ♿✂❀ (Ashburnham Christian Trust) Battle. 5m W of Battle on A271 (formerly B2204). 220 acres of beautifully landscaped gardens with glorious views over 3 lakes designed by George Dance and Capability Brown. Extensive 4-acre walled garden being restored incl newly planted scented garden and kitchen gardens. Peaceful woodland walks. Features from several centuries. Cream TEAS in C18 orangery. *Adm £2 Chd 50p. Wed, Thurs, Sun June 21, 22, 25 (2-5.30)*

Baker's Farm ✂❀ (Mr & Mrs Mark Burrell) Shipley, 5m S of Horsham. Take A24 then A272 W, 2nd turn to Dragon's Green, L at George and Dragon then 300yds on L. Large Wealden garden; lake; laburnum tunnel; shrubs, trees, rose walks of old-fashioned roses; scented knot garden and bog gardens. TEAS. *Adm £1.30 Chd 30p (Share to St Mary the Virgin, Shipley®). Suns May 28, June 18 (2-6). Parties by appt, please* **Tel 01403 741215**

Bateman's ♿✂ (The National Trust) Burwash ½m S (A265). From rd leading S from W end of village. Home of Rudyard Kipling from 1902-1936. Garden laid out before he lived in house and planted yew hedges, rose garden, laid paths and made pond. Bridge to mill which grinds local wheat into flour. LUNCHES & TEAS. *Adm £4 Groups 15 or more £3 Chd £2. ▲For NGS Wed June 21 (11-5.30). Parties welcome by appt on open days, please* **Tel 01435 882302**

Bates Green ♿✂❀ (Mr & Mrs J R McCutchan) Arlington. 2½m SW of A22 at Hailsham and 2m S Michelham Priory, Upper Dicker. Approach Arlington passing the 'Old Oak Inn' on R continue for 350yds then turn R along a small lane. [TQ5507.] Plantsman's tranquil garden of over 1 acre gives year-round interest; rockery; water; mixed borders with colour themes, and shaded foliage garden. B & B accommodation. TEAS. *Adm £1.50 Chd free. Suns April 9, July 2, Aug 6, Oct 1 (2.30-5). Private visits welcome, please* **Tel 01323 482039**

¶Belsize Road Gardens ✂❀ Worthing. 10m E of Bognor, 10m W of Brighton. Take Broadwater Rd into town centre. Turn R at traffic lights into Richmond Rd, continue straight for approx 1m. After Heene Rd Xrds/traffic lights take 2nd turning R. Medium-sized part-walled town gardens. TEAS. *Combined adm £1 Chd 25p. Suns June 25, July 23 (1-5)*

¶No 10 (Mr Robin Spare) Combined ornamental and vegetable garden, incl conservatory with vine and small greenhouse

¶No 12 (Mrs Claudia L Pearce) Large variety of perennials, shrubs, climbers, some unusual. Interesting features incl many pots and hanging baskets

Berri Court ♿❀ (Mr & Mrs J C Turner) Yapton, 5m SW of Arundel. In centre of village between PO & Black Dog public house. A2024 Littlehampton-Chichester rd passes. Intensely planted 3-acre garden of wide interest; trees, flowering shrubs, heathers, eucalyptus, daffodils, shrub roses, hydrangeas and lily ponds. *Adm £1.50 Chd free. Suns, Mons April 2, 3; May 14, 15; June 25, 26 (2-5); Oct 29, 30 (12-4). Private visits welcome for 4 and more, please* **Tel 01243 551663**

Bignor Park ❀ (The Viscount & Viscountess Mersey) Pulborough, 5m from Petworth on West Burton rd. Nearest village Sutton (Sussex). 11 acres of trees, shrubs, flowers and magnificent views of the South Downs, from Chanctonbury Ring to Bignor Hill. Music in the temple. TEAS and plants in aid of Bignor and Sutton churches. *Adm £1.50 Chd 25p. Sun, Mon April 16, 17; Sat, Sun July 29, 30 (2-6)*

● Borde Hill Garden ♿❀ (The Borde Hill Garden Co Ltd) 1½m. N of Haywards Heath on Balcombe Rd. Large informal garden of great botanical interest and beauty; rare trees and shrubs; extensive views; woodland and lakeside walks, rhododendrons, azaleas, camellias, magnolias, at its best in the spring. Picnic area. Tea rooms, bar and restaurant. *Adm £3.50 OAPs £3 Chd £1.50. Daily from March 18 to Oct 1 (10-6)*

Buckhurst Park ✂❀ (Earl & Countess De La Warr) Withyham. On B2110 between Hartfield and Groombridge. Drive adjacent to Dorset Arms public house. Historic garden undergoing complete restoration. Repton park, large lake with woodland walk and ornamental waterfall and rocks created by James Pulham. Terraces, ornamental ponds and Pergolas designed by Lutyens and originally planted by Jekyll. Shetland pony stud. TEAS. *Adm £1.50 Chd 50p (Share to Withyham Recreation Association©). Sat June 24, Sat July 15 (2-5.30). Private visits welcome, please* **Tel 01892 77090**

Bumble Cottage ✂ (Mr & Mrs D Salisbury-Jones) West Chiltington. 2m E of Pulborough, 2m N of Storrington. From Pulborough turn off A283 E of Pulborough into W Chiltington Rd then R into Monkmead Lane (signed Roundabout Hotel) follow yellow signs. From Storrington take B2139 W into Greenhurst Lane, R at T Junc. 100yds fork L into Monkmead Lane then 2nd entrance after Hotel. Charming 'all seasons' garden of 1 acre created from a sandy slope. Wide variety of interesting trees, shrubs and plants combined with ponds all set off by very fine lawn. *Adm £1 Chd 25p. Sun, Mon May 28, 29; Sats, Suns July 15, 16; 22, 23 (2-6)*

Cabbages & Kings see Wilderness Farm

Casters Brook ♿✂ (Mr & Mrs John Whitehorn) Cocking; 3m S of Midhurst at Cocking PO on A286 take sharp turn E; garden is 100yds to right. Interesting 2-acre chalk garden full of surprises; slopes to old mill pond; good collection of old roses; fine downland setting. TEAS. *Adm £1.50 Chd free (Share to Cocking Church®). Suns June 18, 25 (2-6). Private visits welcome, please* **Tel 01730 813537**

Regular Openers. Too many days to include in diary. Usually there is a wide range of plants giving year-round interest. See head of county section for the name and garden description for times etc.

Cedar Tree Cottage ✲❀ (Mr & Mrs G Goatcher) Rock Rd, Washington. Turn W off A24 ¼m N. of Washington Roundabout. Park in 'Old Nursery' Car Park. Mixed borders with many unusual shrubs and perennials, leading into newly developing 5 acre arboretum with many rare subjects and also some fine mature trees and shrubs dating from early C19. Fine views of S Downs. Picnics welcome. *Adm £1.50 Chd free. Sat April 29, Wed May 3, Sun May 7 (2-5.30)*

Champs Hill ♿✲❀ (Mr & Mrs David Bowerman) Coldwaltham, S of Pulborough. From Pulborough on A29, in Coldwaltham turn R to Fittleworth Rd; garden 300yds on R. From Petworth turn off B2138 just S of Fittleworth to Coldwaltham, garden approx ½m on L. 27 acres of formal garden and woodland walks around old sand pit. Conifers and acid-loving plants, many specie heathers labelled. Superb views across Arun valley. Special features. March - Winter heathers and spring flowers. May - rhododendrons, azaleas, wild flowers. August - heathers and other specialities. Tea (March, April only), TEAS. *Adm £1.50 Chd free. Suns March 5, 12, 26; April 2; May 7, 14, 21; July 30; Aug 6, 13, 20 (1-6); Sats May 6, 13, 20; Aug 5, 19. Private visits welcome for parties of 10 and over, please* **Tel 01798 831868**

Chantry Green House ✲❀ (Mr R S Forrow & Mrs J B McNeil) Steyning. 5m N of Worthing, 10m NW of Brighton off A283. Turn into Church St from High St opp White Horse Inn. Garden 150yds down on LH-side. Parking on Fletchers Croft car park, entrance opp church. An interesting 1-acre garden, redesigned over the past 5yrs by Jack Grant White. Features incl a wall fountain, herbaceous borders and extensive shrub borders with a predominance of colourful evergreens providing interest throughout the year. There is also a small arboretum and rock and water garden. TEAS and plants in aid of NSPCC. *Adm £1.30 Chd 50p. Sat, Sun June 17, 18 (2-5)*

Chidmere House ♿ (Thomas Baxendale Esq) Chidham, 6m W of Chichester. A259 1m Bus: SD276/200 Chichester-Emsworth. Interesting garden; subject of article in 'Country Life'; yew and hornbeam hedges; bulbs, and flowering shrubs bounded by large mere, now a private nature reserve. C16 house (not open). *Adm £1.50 Chd free under 12. Suns, Mons April 16, 17; May 21, 22 (2-6); June 25, 26; Aug 27, 28 (2-7). Parties welcome, please* **Tel 01243 572287** *or* **573096**

Chilsham House ♿✲❀ (Mr & Mrs P E B Cutler) Herstmonceux. 5m NE of Hailsham. From A271 in Herstmonceux take turning by Woolpack Inn towards Cowbeech after approx ¾m turn R into Chilsham Lane, ¾m on the left. 1½-acre garden, herbaceous border, water garden, old fashioned roses. Small gardens in colour harmony, many unusual plants. Victorian garden. TEAS. *Adm £1.50 Chd free. Sat, Sun June 24, 25; Sun, Mon July 16, 17 (2-5.30). Parties welcome by appt, please* **Tel 01323 832235**

Clinton Lodge ♿❀ (Mr & Mrs H Collum) Fletching, 4m NW of Uckfield; from A272 turn N at Piltdown for Fletching, 1½m. 6-acre formal and romantic garden overlooking parkland with old roses, double herbaceous borders, yew hedges, pleached lime walks, copy of C17 scented herb garden, medieval-style potager, vine and rose allée, wild flower garden. Carolean and Georgian house (not open). TEAS. *Adm £2 Chd 50p (Share to Fletching Church Fabric Fund®). Sun June 11; Mons June 12, 19, 26; Wed June 21 (2-6). Parties welcome, please* **Tel 01825 722952**

Coates Manor ✲❀ (Mrs G H Thorp) nr Fittleworth. ½m S of Fittleworth; turn off B2138 at signpost marked 'Coates'. 1 acre, mainly shrubs and foliage of special interest. Small walled garden with tender and scented plants. Often featured in UK and foreign gardening magazines. Elizabethan house (not open) scheduled of historic interest. TEAS organised by Church of England Children's Society Committee. *Adm £1.50 Chd free. Sun, Mon, Tues June 11, 12, 13 (11-6). Private visits welcome, please* **Tel 01798 865356**

Cobblers ♿✲❀ (Mr & Mrs Martin Furniss) Mount Pleasant, Jarvis Brook, Crowborough. A26, at Crowborough Cross take B2100 towards Crowborough Station. At 2nd Xrds turn into Tollwood Rd for ¼m. 2-acre sloping site designed by present owners since 1968 to display outstanding range of herbaceous and shrub species and water garden, giving all season colour. Subject of numerous articles and TVS 'That's Gardening' programme June 1991. TEAS. *Adm £3 Chd £1 (incl home-made Teas). Suns May 14, June 11, 25, July 9, 23, Aug 6, 20; Mons May 29, Aug 28 (2.30-5.30). Groups welcome by appt, please* **Tel 01892 655969**

Cokes Barn ✲❀ (Mr & Mrs Nigel Azis) West Burton. 5m SW of Pulborough-Petworth. At foot of Bury Hill turn W off A29 to West Burton for 1m then follow signs. Just under 1-acre garden around converted barn (1670 not open) which divides into 2 natural spaces: the yard a sheltered enclosure with gravelled areas, mixed shrubs and roses and other traditional cottage perennials. Walls covered in decorative ivies, vines, roses and clematii. 2nd part of garden subdivided by hedges. Planting follows gentle contours; at far end 2 small pools surrounded by damp loving plants. Conservatory on S side of barn. *Adm £1 Chd 40p. Sun April 30 (2-5); Mon, Tues May 1, 2 (11-5). Private visits welcome for parties of 4 and over, please* **Tel 01798 831636**

Combehurst ♿❀ (Mrs E E Roberts) 3m S of Tunbridge Wells off A267, 400yds S of B2099. 2½-acre beautifully laid out garden; shrubs, trees, plants. TEAS. *Adm £1.50 Chd free. Sun June 4 (2-6). Private visits welcome, please* **Tel 01892 750367**

Cooke's House ♿✲ (Miss J B Courtauld) West Burton, 5m SW of Pulborough. Turn off A29 at White Horse, Bury, ¾m. Old garden with views of the Downs, Elizabethan house (not open); varied interest, spring flowers, topiary, herbaceous borders, herbs. Free car park. *Adm £1 Chd free under 14. Suns, Mons, Tues April 23, 24, 25; May 7, 8, 9 (2-6). Private visits welcome, please* **Tel 01798 831353**

Cooksbridge ✠❀ (Mr & Mrs N Tonkin) Fernhurst. On A286 between Haslemere and Midhurst, ¾m S of Fernhurst Xrds. 6 acres, landscaped garden with glade and woodland walk through adjoining bluebell wood. Pictured in the GRBS 1993 Gardens to remember calendar this plantsman's garden is situated in a fold of the downs beside the R Lodd. Features incl the herbaceous border, vine and ornamental plant houses, lily pond and well stocked shrubberies. The main lawn sweeps down from the terrace to the lake which has an island with weeping willow and several species of waterfowl. TEAS. *Adm £1.50 Chd 50p 5 and under free (Share to Sussex Wildlife Trust®). Sats, Suns May 6, 7; Aug 5, 6 (2-6)*

Coombland ✠❀ (Mr & Mrs Neville Lee) Coneyhurst. In Billingshurst turn off A29 onto A272 to Haywards Heath; approx 2m, in Coneyhurst, turn S for further ¾m. Large garden of 5 acres developed since 1981 with the help and advice of Graham Stuart Thomas. Undulating site on heavy clay. Old shrub-rose beds, rose species and ramblers scrambling up ageing fruit trees; extensive planting of hardy geraniums; herbaceous border with interesting planting. Oak woodland; orchard dell with hybrid rhododendrons; hostas; primulas and meconopsis. Nightingale wood with water area under development, water wheel recently added leading to 1-acre arboretum. National collection of hardy geraniums held here. TEAS. *Adm £1.50 Chd 50p. Sats June 10, 24 (10-5). Nursery open Mon to Fri (2-4). Parties welcome, please* **Tel 01403 741549**

Cowbeech Farm ✠❀ (Mrs M Huiskamp) Cowbeech. 4m NE of Hailsham. A271 to Amberstone turn off N for Cowbeech. 5-acre garden, herb garden, bog garden. Beautiful shrubs and trees. Farmhouse TEAS, plants, cakes, and produce. *Adm £2 Chd £1. Suns May 21, Sept 10, Wed Sept 13 (10-30-12.30 and 2.30-5.30). Parties welcome, please* **Tel 01323 832134**

Cowdray Park Gardens ✠ (The Viscount Cowdray) S of A272. 1m E of Midhurst. Entrance by East Front. Avenue of Wellingtonias; rhododendrons, azaleas; sunken garden with large variety trees and shrubs, Lebanon cedar 300 yrs old; pleasure garden surrounded by ha-ha. *Adm £1. Sun May 14 (2-7)*

Crawley Down Gardens ✠ B2028 8m N of Haywards Heath, 4m W of E Grinstead. 2½m E of M23 (junction 10). TEAS, morning coffee by prior arrangement. *Combined adm £1.50 Chd free*

Bankton Cottage ♿❀ (Mr & Mrs Robin Lloyd) 3½-acre garden, herbaceous borders, shrub and climbing roses. Large 1-acre pond, many terracotta pots planted up round house. Large range on sale. Featured 'Country Living' 1990. *Parties welcome from May to July, please* **Tel 01342 718907**

Yew Tree Cottage ❀ (Mrs K Hudson) ¼-acre garden planted for all year round interest and easy management. Featured in RHS 1989 and book 'Cottage Garden'. *Parties welcome from May to July, please* **Tel 01342 714633**

Crown House ♿✠❀ (Maj L Cave) Eridge, 3m SW of Tunbridge Wells. A26 Tunbridge Wells-Crowborough rd; in Eridge take Rotherfield turn S, then take 1st R, house 1st on L. 1½ acres with pools; alpine garden; herbaceous border; herb garden; aviary. Full size croquet lawn. Prize winner in Sunday Express garden of the year competition. Plant and produce stalls. TEAS. *Adm £1.50 Chd under 14 free (Share to Multiple Sclerosis®). Sat, Sun July 8, 9 (2-6). Private visits welcome May to Aug, please* **Tel 01892 864389** *or* **864605**

Denmans ♿✠❀ (Mrs J H Robinson, Mr John Brookes) Denmans Lane, Fontwell. Chichester and Arundel 5m. Turn S on A27 at Denmans Lane, W of Fontwell Racecourse. Renowned gardens extravagantly planted for overall, all-year interest in form, colour and texture; areas of glass for tender species. Plant Centre, Garden Café for lunches, teas, coffees, refreshments to suit served from 10am. *Adm £2.50 OAPs £2.25 Chd £1.50. Groups over 15 persons £1.95. Open daily all year excl Christmas and Boxing Day. Coaches by appt. For NGS Mons March 6, Oct 23 (9-5)*

Down Place ✠❀ (Mr & Mrs D M Thistleton-Smith) South Harting. ¼m E down unmarked lane below top of hill. 1m SE of South Harting on B2141 towards Chichester. From Petersfield E via B2146 to South Harting. From Chichester via A286 for 4m, N of Lavant turn NW on to B2141. 7-acre hillside chalk garden on N slope of South Downs. Terraced herbaceous and shrub borders, walks through woodland and natural wild flower meadow. Fine views over South Harting. TEAS. *Adm £1.20 Chd 50p (Share to National Asthma Campaign®). Fri, Sat, Sun June 23, 24, 25 (2-6)*

Duckyls ❀ (Lady Taylor) Sharpthorne. 4m SW of E Grinstead. 6m E of Crawley. At Turners Hill take B2028 S 1m fork left to W Hoathly, turn L signed Gravetye Manor. Interesting old 12-acre woodland garden. Partly suitable for wheelchairs. TEAS. *Adm £2 Chd £1 (Share to St Margarets Church, W Hoathly®). Sun, Mon April 30, May 1 (2-6). Parties weclome by appt, please* **Tel 01342 810352**

Ebbsworth ✠ (Mrs F Lambert) Nutbourne nr Pulborough. Take A283 E from junction with A29 (Swan Corner) 2m with 2 L forks signposted Nutbourne. Pass Rising Sun and follow signs to garden. Charming, well-planted, owner maintained cottage garden, surrounding old cottage. Roses and lilies, together with herbaceous borders. Man-made stream and ponds planted with water plants. *Adm £1.50 Chd free. Sun, Mon June 11, 12 (1-5)*

Fittleworth Gardens ♿✠❀ Fittleworth A282 midway Petworth-Pulborough; in Fittleworth turn onto B2138 then turn W at Swan. Car parking available. TEAS. Plants in aid of NSPCC and St Mary's Church, Fittleworth. *Combined adm £1.50 Chd free. Sat, Sun May 20, 21 (2-6)*

The Grange ♿ (Mr & Mrs W M Caldwell) 3-acre garden with island beds of spring flowering shrubs, walled garden, herbaceous borders. Pond and stream being replanted

The Hermitage (Mr & Mrs P F Dutton) Charming informal garden; azaleas, rhododendrons sloping to the R Rother with riverside walk and lovely views to the S Downs

Lowerstreet House (L J Holloway Esq) Small garden with shrubs, bulbs, herbaceous

Fitzhall ✿❀ (Mr & Mrs G F Bridger) Iping, 3m W of Midhurst. 1m off A272, signposted Harting Elsted. 9 acres; herb garden; herbaceous and shrub borders; vegetable garden. Farm adjoining. House (not open) originally built 1550. Garden and teas all year round. *Adm £1.50 Chd 75p. For NGS Suns May 21, July 9, Sept 10 (2-6)*

¶**Framfield Gardens** ♿ Uckfield. *Combined adm £2 Chd free. Sun June 18 (2-6)*

Hailwell House ❀ (Lady Elizabeth Baxendale) On L B2102 towards Uckfield. ½m from church. Beautiful 4-acre garden with attractive shrubs, borders and lake

Hobbs Barton ✿ (Mr & Mrs Jeremy Clark) ¼m E of church turn L off B2102, ½m turn L. House ¾m on L. Attractive garden in 2½ acres with shrubs, specimen trees, roses, herbaceous borders, ponds, walled vegetable and fruit garden. TEAS

Frewen College (Brickwall) ♿❀ (Frewen Charitable Trust) Northiam. 8m NW of Rye on B2088. Tudor home of Frewen family since 1660. Recently featured in the filming of 'Cold Comfort Farm'. Gardens and walls built and laid out by Jane Frewen c1680; chess and lavender gardens; arboretum. Teas at historic Hayes Arms Hotel. *Adm £1.50 Chd under 10 free. Sun July 23 (2-5). Parties welcome of 30 to 50, please* **Tel 01797 223329**

Frith Hill ✿❀ (Mr & Mrs Peter Warne) Northchapel 7m N of Petworth on A283 turn E in centre of Northchapel into Pipers Lane (by Deep Well Inn) after ¾m turn L into bridleway immed past Peacocks Farm. 1-acre garden, comprising walled gardens with herbaceous border; shrubbery; pond; old-fashioned rose garden and arbour. Herb garden leading to white garden with gazebo. Outstanding views of Sussex Weald. TEAS. *Adm £1.50 Chd free (Share to Cystic Fibrosis Research Fund®). Sun, Thurs June 11, 15 (2-6)*

Frith Lodge (Mr & Mrs Geoffrey Cridland) Northchapel. 7m N of Petworth on A283 turn E in centre of Northchapel into Pipers Lane (by Deep Well Inn) after ¾m turn L into bridleway immediately past Peacocks Farm. 1-acre cottage style garden created around pair of Victorian game-keepers cottages. Undulating ground with roses, informal planting with paved and hedged areas; outstanding views of Sussex Weald. *Adm £1 Chd 50p. Sun, Thurs June 11, 15 (2-6). Parties welcome, please* **Tel 01428 707241**

The Garden in Mind ✿❀ (Mr & Mrs Ivan Hicks - Stansted Park Foundation) Stansted Park, Rowlands Castle. From A3 at Horndean follow brown signs for Stansted House. From A27M at Havant follow Stansted House brown signs. Stansted House is 3m NE of Havant, 7m W of Chichester. A surreal symbolic dream garden created within a ½-acre walled garden at Stansted House. Began in 1991 as a concept for BBC2 dream garden series. Extravagant planting combined with sculpture, assemblage, found objects, mirrors and chance encounters. Wide range of plants; sequioa to sempervivum, marigolds to melianthus, grasses, foliage plants, topiary and tree sculpture. Featured in numerous publications and TV – come with an open mind. TEAS. *Adm £1.01 Chd donation. Suns, Mons, Tues May 14, 15, 16; June 4, 5, 6, 25, 26, 27; Sept 10, 11, 12, 24, 25, 26 (2-6)*

Gaywood Farm ♿✿ (Mrs Anthony Charles) nr Pulborough. 3m S of Billingshurst turn L off A29 into Gay Street Lane. After railway bridge at 2nd junction fork L and at T junction turn L signed 'no through rd'. 2-acre garden, surrounding ancient farm house, built between C14 and C18. Fine weeping Ash, black Mulberry, Irish yews and extravagantly planted borders with interesting plant assoc. Large pond surrounded by good planting. TEAS. *Adm £1 Chd free. Sat, Sun May 27, 28; July 15, 16 (2-5). Private visits welcome, please* **Tel 01798 812223**

Ghyll Farm Sweethaws Lane ❀ (Mr & Mrs I Ball) Crowborough. 1m S of Crowborough centre on A26. L into Sheep Plain Lane immed R Sweethaws Lane ½m. 'The Permissive Garden' planted by the late Lady Pearce. 1-acre, azaleas, camellias, woodland bluebell walk; spectacular views. TEAS. *Adm £1 Chd 50p. Suns April 23, May 21; Mon May 8 (2-5.30). Private visits welcome April to end July please* **Tel 01892 655505**

Great Allfields ✿❀ (Lord & Lady Birkett) Balls Cross. 3m N of Petworth. Take 283 out of Petworth, turn 2nd R signed Balls Cross, Kirdford. At Balls Cross take L turn after Stag Inn to Ebernoe, Northchapel (Pipers Lane) 250yds entrance on R. 1 acre of garden, 2 acres of woodland, plus old walls and barns covered with many interesting climbers; autumn colour. TEAS. *Adm £1.50 Chd 50p (Share to Fairbridge®). Sat Oct 14 (10-6). Private visits welcome, please* **Tel 01403 820226**

● **Great Dixter** ✿❀ (Quentin Lloyd) Northiam, ½m N of Northiam, off A28 8m NW of Rye. Buses infrequent 340, 342, 348. Hastings & District. Alight Northiam P Office 500yds. Topiary; wide variety of plants. Historical house open (2-5). *Adm house & garden £3.50 Chd 50p OAPs & NT members (Fris only) £3; garden only £2.50 Chd 25p. April 1 to Oct 8 daily except Mons but open on Bank Hols (2-5); also Oct 14, 15, 21, 22 (2-5); garden open May 27, 28, 29; also Suns in July, Aug; Mon Aug 28 (11-5)*

Greenacres ✿❀ (Mr & Mrs John Hindley) Crowborough. From A26 at Crowborough Cross take B2100 S. At 1st Xrd R into Montagis Way, then 2nd L into Luxford Rd for ⅓m. 2-acre sloping woodland garden maintained wholly by present owners. Developed over the years with interesting water features fed by natural springs: ponds, bog area, naturalised area, raised island beds. Many trees, shrubs and foliage plants. A tranquil garden with views over countryside. TEA. *Adm £1.50 Chd free. Suns May 21, June 4, 11 (11-5.30)*

Hailsham Grange ♿✿❀ (John Macdonald Esq) Hailsham. Turn off Hailsham High St into Vicarage Rd, park in public car park. Formal garden designed and planted since 1988 in grounds of former C17 Vicarage (not open). A series of garden areas representing a modern interpretation of C18 formality; Gothic summerhouse; pleached hedges; herbaceous borders, romantic planting in separate garden compartments. Teas in adjacent church in aid of The Children's Society. *Adm £1.50. Suns June 4, Aug 6 (2-5.30)*

By Appointment Gardens. See head of county section

Hammerwood House ♿ (The Hon Mrs J Lakin) Iping, 1m N of A272 Midhurst to Petersfield Rd. Approx 3m W of Midhurst. Well signposted. Large informal garden; fine trees, rhododendrons, azaleas, acers, cornus, magnolias; wild garden (¼m away), bluebells, stream. TEAS. *Adm £1.50 Chd free. Suns May 7, 14 (1.30-5.30)*

● **High Beeches Gardens** ⚘ (High Beeches Gardens Conservation Trust) Situated on B2110 1m E of A23 at Handcross. 20-acres of enchanting landscaped woodland and water gardens; spring daffodils; bluebell and azalea walks; many rare and beautiful plants; wild flower meadows, glorious autumn colours. Picnic area. Car park. Lunches and TEAS only on special events days April 16, 30, May 28, Aug 20, Oct 15 (10-5). *Daily April, May, June, Sept, Oct (1-5) closed on Weds. Adm £3 Acc chd free (Share to St Mary's Church, Slaugham®). For NGS Sats May 6, Sept 2 (1-5). Also by appt for organised groups at any time, please* **Tel 01444 400589**

Highdown, Goring-by-Sea ⚘ (Worthing Borough Council) Littlehampton Rd (A259), 3m W of Worthing. Station: Goring-by-Sea, 1m. Famous garden created by Sir F Stern situated in chalk pit and downland area containing a wide collection of plants. Spring bulbs, paeonies, shrubs and trees. Many plants were raised from seed brought from China by great collectors like Wilson, Farrer and Kingdon-Ward. *Collecting box.* ▲*Mons April 17, May 8, 29 (10-8). Parties by appt, please* **Tel 01903 239999 ext 2544**

¶**6 Hollbrook Park** ⚘❀ (Mr & Mrs John Pollard) Northlands Road, nr Horsham. 3m N of Horsham. ⅓m N side of A264 Horsham northern bypass. From Horsham drive on to A24 Dorking direction. At roundabout where dual carriage ends on A24 turn R signposted Gatwick. Follow dual carriageway, take 2nd on L marked Northlands Rd. Please park carefully on RH-side of lane. 2½-acre garden on sloping site. Informal areas created in a park-like setting to provide colour and interest throughout the year. Some fine trees, azaleas, rhododendrons, golden shrub border and herbaceous borders; small pond; conservatory. Partially suitable for wheelchairs. TEA. *Adm £1.50 Chd free. Sun, Thurs May 14, 18 (2-6). Private visits welcome Thurs pm, April, May, June, please* **Tel 01403 252491**

Home Farm House ❀ (Mrs P Cooper) Buckham Hill. Uckfield-Isfield back rd. Small attractive cottage garden; interesting shrubs. *Adm £1 Chd free. Sun, Mon June 25, 26 (2-5.30). Private visits also welcome Feb to March to see 20ft mimosa, please* **Tel 01825 763960**. *Also open* **Pheasant Hatch**

Houghton Farm ⚘❀ (Mr & Mrs Michael Lock) Arundel. Turn E off A29 at top of Bury Hill onto B2139 or W from Storrington onto B2139 to Houghton. 1-acre garden with wide variety of shrubs and plants, interesting corners and beautiful views. Tea Houghton Bridge Tea Gardens. *Adm £1 Chd free. Sun April 30, Mon May 1, Thurs, Fri May 25, 26, Mon, Tues June 19, 20, Sun July 30, Mon Aug 28, Tues Sept 26 (2-5). Private visits welcome, please* **Tel 01798 831327**

¶**Hove Gardens** ⚘ Three contrasting gardens nr the junction of Old Shoreham Rd (A270) and Shirley Drive. Ample parking in surrounding streets. TEAS at 9 Shirley Drive in aid of The Tarner Home. *Combined adm £2 Chd 50p. Suns April 30, June 25 (2-6)*

¶**The Old Chalk Pit** ❀ (Mr & Mrs Hugo Martin) 27 Old Shoreham Rd. Unexpected, romantic garden recently redesigned to form 5 differing areas; with white garden; ponds, wildlife and shady places to sit! *Private visits by written request very welcome*

64 Old Shoreham Road (Brian & Muriel Bailey) Small beautifully designed mainly walled garden ⅛ acre on chalk and flint with yr-round interest. 2 ponds with fountain and waterfall, conservatory, arches, pergola, rose arbour, alpine bed, vegetable garden and many potted acid loving plants. *Private visits welcome at weekends adm £1 Chd 40p (2-6), please* **Tel 01273 889247**

9 Shirley Drive (Mr & Mrs P McIntyre) Interesting paved garden with mature conifers, much new planting and welcoming rockery

Hurst Mill ⚘ Hurst. 2m SE of Petersfield on B2146 midway between Petersfield and S Harting 8-acre garden on many levels in lovely position overlooking 4-acre lake in wooded valley with wildfowl. Waterfall and Japanese water garden beside historic mill. Bog garden; large rock garden with orientally inspired plantings; acers, camellias, rhododendrons, azaleas, magnolias, hydrangeas and ferns; shrubs and climbing roses; forest and ornamental trees. TEA. *Adm £2 Chd free. Suns April 30, June 25 (2-6); Sept 24 (2-5)*

Ketches ♿⚘❀ (David Manwaring Robertson Esq) Newick, 5m W of Uckfield on A272. Take Barcombe Rd S out of Newick, house is on right opp turning to Newick Church. 3 acres; lovely old-fashioned roses; specimen trees; shrub and herbaceous borders. TEAS. *Adm £1.50 Chd free. Sun June 18 (2-6). Parties welcome, mid May to mid July, please* **Tel 01825 722679**

King Edward VII Hospital ♿❀ Midhurst. 3m NW of Midhurst. Hospital built early this century, stands in grounds of 152 acres elevated position of great natural beauty; extensive views across Downs. Gardens by Gertrude Jekyll. Aspect over gardens and pine woods little changed. TEA. *Collecting box. Sat May 27 (10-4)*

King John's Lodge ♿⚘❀ (Mr & Mrs R A Cunningham) Etchingham. Burwash to Etchingham on the A265 turn L before Etchingham Church into Church Lane which leads into Sheepstreet Lane after ½m. L after 1m. 3-acre romantic garden surrounding a listed house. Formal garden with water features, wild garden, rose walk, large herbacous borders, old shrub roses and secret garden. B & B accommodation. Garden Statuary for sale. TEAS. *Adm £1.50 Chd free. Sat, Sun June 17, 18 (11-6). Also private visits welcome, please* **Tel 01580 819232**

Regular Openers. Too many days to include in diary. Usually there is a wide range of plants giving year-round interest. See head of county section for the name and garden description for times etc.

Kingston Gardens ❀ 2½m SW of Lewes. Turn off A27 signposted Kingston at roundabout; at 30 mph sign turn R. Home-made TEAS **Nightingales**. *Combined adm (payable at* **Nightingales** *only) £2 Chd free. Suns June 11, July 23 (2-6)*

Nightingales (Geoff & Jean Hudson) The Avenue. Informal sloping ½-acre garden for all-year interest; wide range of plants incl shrub roses, hardy geraniums, perennials, ground cover. Mediterranean plants. Childrens play area. Short steep rough walk or drive, parking limited, to:-

The White House (John & Sheila Maynard Smith) The Ridge. ½-acre garden on a chalk ridge. Shrubs, herbaceous border, alpines; greenhouse with unusual plants

Knabbs Farmhouse ❀ (Mr & Mrs W G Graham) 4m NW of Uckfield; from A272 turn N at Piltdown for Fletching, [TQ430/240] 1½m. Garden at N-end of village and farm. ½-acre informal garden; mixed beds and borders; shrubs, roses, perennials, foliage plants. Good views over ha-ha. TEAS at **Clinton Lodge**. *Adm £1 Chd 20p. Sun June 11 (2-6). Private visits welcome, please* **Tel 01825 722198**

Lane End ✲ (Mrs C J Epril) Sheep Lane, Midhurst. In North St turn L at Knock-hundred Row, L into Sheep lane, L to garden. Park at church or in lane. 2 acres incl wild garden; alpine rockery with pools; rhododendrons, azaleas, heath border. Below ramparts of original castle with fine views over water meadows to ruins of Cowdray House. Tea Midhurst. *Adm £1 Chd free. Sats, Suns, Mons May 20, 21, 22; 27, 28, 29 (11-6)*

Legsheath Farm ♿❀ (Mr & Mrs Michael Neal) Legsheath Lane. 2m W of Forest Row, 1m S of Weirwood Reservoir. Panoramic views over reservoir. Exciting 10-acre garden with woodland walks, water gardens and formal borders. Of particular interest, clumps of wild orchids, a fine davidia, acers, eucryphia and rhododendrons. TEAS. *Adm £1.50 Chd free. Sun May 21 (2-6)*

Lilac Cottage ✲ (Mrs G A Hawkins) Willet Close, Duncton. 3m S of Petworth on the W side of A285 opp St Michaels School. Park in Close where signed. ¼-acre village garden on several levels with shrubs, small trees and approx 90 varieties of shrub and climbing roses and herb garden. TEAS. *Adm 75p. Sat, Sun, Wed, June 3, 4, 7 (2-6). Private visits welcome, please* **Tel 01798 43006**

¶Little Dene ♿✲❀ (Prof & Mrs D Anderson) Chelwood Gate. 8m S of East Grinstead. Take A275 off A22 at Wych Cross, then 1st L and 2nd R. ⅓-acre plantsmans garden yr-round interest. Many unusual shrubs and climbers, over 80 clematis, raised alpine bed. *Adm £1.50. Open April to Mid-Sept (not Fri). Private visits welcome, please* **Tel 01825 740657**

Little Hutchings ♿✲❀ (Mr & Mrs P Hayes) Fontridge Lane, Etchingham. [TQ 708248.] Take A265 to Etchingham from A21 at Hurst Green. 1st turning L after level crossing. R after ½m. Colourful 1½-acre old-fashioned cottage garden laid out over 19 years. At least 300 different roses, over 100 metres of tightly packed herbaceous borders full of many different perennials. Large collection of clematis. Shrubberies containing specimen trees and shrubs. Kitchen garden. TEAS. *Adm £1.75 Chd free. Sat, Sun June 17, 18 (11-6)*

Little Thakeham ✲ (Mr & Mrs T Ratcliff) Storrington. Take A24 S to Worthing and at roundabout 2m S of Ashington return N up A24 for 200yds. Turn L into Rock Rd for 1m. At staggered Xrds turn R into Merrywood Lane and garden is 300yds on R. From Storrington take B2139 to Thakeham. After 1m turn R into Merrywood Lane and garden is 400yds on L. 4-acre garden with paved walks, rose pergola, flowering shrubs, specimen trees, herbaceous borders and carpets of daffodils in spring. The garden laid out to the basic design of Sir Edward Lutyens in 1902 is entering its final year of restoration. All surrounding one of the finest examples of a Sir Edward Lutyens manor house now a luxurious country house hotel. No toilet fac. House closed to public. Partially suitable for wheelchairs. *Adm £2 Chd £1. Mon, Tues April 10, 11; June 5, 6 (2-5)*

Lye Green House ✲ (Mr & Mrs Hynes) Lye Green. Situated just off the B2188 between Groombridge and Crowborough. 6-acre garden restored after long neglect. 4 large ponds, woodland and rockeries; 7 enclosed gardens, herbaceous borders, rose garden, kitchen garden and lime walk. TEAS. *Adm £1.50 Chd free. Sun June 18 (2-6)*

Malt House ❀ (Mr & Mrs Graham Ferguson) Chithurst, Rogate. From A272, 3½m W of Midhurst turn N signposted Chithurst then 1½m; or at Liphook turn off A3 onto old A3 for 2m before turning L to Milland, then follow signs to Chithurst for 1½m. 5 acres; flowering shrubs incl exceptional rhododendrons and azaleas, leading to 50 acres of lovely woodland walks. TEA. *Adm £1.50 Chd 50p (Share to King Edward VII Hospital Midhurst). Suns April 23, 30; May 7, 14, 21, 28; Mons May 8, 29 (2-6); also private visits welcome for parties or plant sales, please* **Tel 01730 821433**

The Manor of Dean ✲❀ (Miss S M Mitford) Tillington, 2m W of Petworth. Turn off A272 N at NGS sign. Flowers, shrubs, specimen trees, bulbs in all seasons. A miniature pony, 2 pigmy goats, Vietnamese pigs, tame lambs. House (not open) 1400-1613. TEA 50p. *Adm £1 Chd over 5 50p. Sats, Suns, Mons March 25, 26, 27; April 22, 23, 24; May 20, 21, 22; July 15, 16, 17; Aug 19, 20, 21; Sept 16, 17, 18; Oct 7, 8, 9 (2-6). Private visits welcome*

Manvilles Field ♿✲❀ (Mrs P J Aschan & Mrs J M Wilson) 2m W of Pulborough take A283 to Fittleworth, turn R on sharp L-hand bend. 2 acres of garden with orchard, many interesting shrubs, clematis, roses, other herbaceous plants. Beautiful views surrounding garden. TEAS Sun in aid of Motor Neurone Disease Assn, Mon in aid of Cystic Fibrosis Trust. *Adm £1 Chd 40p. Sun, Mon May 28, 29 (2-6)*

Mayfield Cottage Gardens ✲ 8m S of Tunbridge Wells on A267. *Combined adm £1.50 Chd 20p. Sun June 18 (2-5.30)*

Courtney Cottage (Mr & Mrs D Clark) ⅕-acre steeply sloping garden

Hopton (E Stuart Ogg Esq) Fletching St. ½-acre, Delphinium Specialist
Knowle Way (J Freeman Esq) West St. S of High St by Barclays Bank. ¼-acre plantsman's garden
The Oast ❀ (Mr & Mrs R G F Henderson) Fletching St. Turn off A267 by garage towards Witherenden ¼m. Charming ½-acre sloping garden, fine views. TEAS

Merriments Gardens ♿✿❀ (Mark & Mandy Buchele) Hawkhurst Rd, Hurst Green. Situated between Hawkhurst and Hurst Green. 2m SW Hawkhurst. Young 4-acre garden with richly planted mixed borders in country setting. Ponds, stream and rare plants give beautiful display all season. TEAS. *Adm £1.50 Chd free. Suns May 7, 21; June 4, 18, 25; July 9, 30; Aug 13, 27; Sept 10; Mons July 10, 31; Aug 14, 28 (12-5). Parties welcome by appt, please* **Tel 01580 860666**

Middle Coombe ♿✿❀ (Andrew & Ann Kennedy) East Grinstead. From E Grinstead 1½m SW on B2110. Turn L into Coombe Hill Rd. ¼m on L. 4½-acre garden and woodland walk with small lake. The garden was created in 16 weeks in 1990. Designed in Victorian rooms using Agriframes. Formal and informal planting to give all year colour. Light lunches and TEAS. *Adm £2 Chd free. Weds May 10, July 12 (2-5). Parties welcome by appt, please* **Tel 01342 328387**

Mill House ✿ (Sir Francis & Lady Avery Jones) Nutbourne, nr Pulborough. Take A283 E from junction with A29 (Swan Corner) 2m with 2 L forks signposted Nutbourne. Pass Rising Sun after 80yds turn R into unmade lane, continue for 200yds. ¾-acre surrounding old miller's house; and wild flower banks; cottage frontage with interesting walled herb garden; sloping down to water garden with stream, spring-fed pools and nearby mill pond. *Adm £1. By appt only, please* **Tel 01798 813314**

Moat Mill Farm ♿❀ (Mr & Mrs C Marshall) Newick Lane, Mayfield. 1m S on Mayfield-Broadoak Rd. 8 acres, formal rose garden, herbaceous border and wild gardens. Nature Trail for Children. Picnic area (12.30-2). TEAS and ice creams. *Adm £1 Chd 40p. Sun June 18 (2-5.30)*

Moorlands ❀ (Dr & Mrs Steven Smith) Friar's Gate, 2m N of Crowborough. St Johns Rd to Friar's Gate. Or turn L off B2188 at Friar's Gate. 3 acres set in lush valley adjoining Ashdown Forest; water garden with ponds and streams; primulas, rhododendrons, azaleas, many unusual trees and shrubs. New river walk. TEAS. *Adm £2 OAPs £1.50 Chd free. Every Wed April to Oct 1 (11-5). Suns May 7, 28, June 4, July 23 (2-6). Private visits welcome, please* **Tel 01892 652474**

Mountfield Court ♿✿ (T Egerton Esq) 2m S of Robertsbridge. On A21 London-Hastings; ½m from Johns Cross. 2-3-acre wild garden; flowering shrubs, rhododendrons, azaleas and camellias; fine trees. Homemade TEAS. *Adm £1 Chd 50p (Share to All Saints Church Mountfield®). Sun, Mon May 14, 15 (2-6)*

Neptune House ✿❀ (The Hon & Mrs Robin Borwick) Cutmill. E from Chichester take A259 to Fishbourne and Bosham, over roundabout at Bosham and after ½m move into reservation in rd and turn R into Newells Lane. 150yds turn L and park. From W take A259 to Emsworth. Turn L after the Bosham Inn at Chidham into Newells Lane. A 2-acre garden with the R Cut forming the NW boundary and a canal from it taking water to the largest of 3 ponds. Planting is being increased by owners in this coastal garden. Parents are warned that water can be dangerous and children must be kept under control near river and canals. **Pondfield** is reached over a small bridge. Live classical music and TEAS on the lawn. *Combined adm with* **Pondfield** *£1.50 Chd 50p. Sun June 4 (2-6). Private visits welcome April 13 to Sept 30, please* **Tel 01243 576900**

New Grove ♿✿ (Mr & Mrs Robert de Pass) Petworth. 1m S of Petworth turn L off A285 and take next L. Follow signs. From the N at Xrds in Petworth straight across into Middle Street then L into High Street follow signs. A mature garden of about 3 acres. Mainly composed of shrubs with all year interest incl a small parterre; magnolias, camellias, azaleas, cornuses, roses etc. lovely views to the South Downs. TEAS in aid of King Edward VII Hospital, Midhurst, or Church of England Childrens Society. *Adm £1.50 Chd free. Sun, Mon May 14, 15 (2-6)*

¶New Place ✿❀ (Mr R H Edmondson) Framfield. 10m NE Lewes. From A26 take B2102 E at Uckfield to Framfield. R 1m down Pump Lane. Extensive formal gardens with topiary, water and rose gardens, herbaceous and raised alpine gardens, new tree and shrub plantings all overlooking lakes and natural woodland with walks. TEAS. *Adm £2 Chd 50p. Sun May 28 (11-6)*

Newtimber Place ♿❀ (Andrew Clay Esq) Newtimber. 7m N of Brighton off A281 between Poynings and Pyecombe. Beautiful C17 moated house. Wild garden, roses, mixed borders and water plants. TEAS in aid of Newtimber Church. *Adm £1.50 Chd 50p. Suns April 30, Aug 27 (2-6)*

North Springs ✿❀ (Mr & Mrs Michael Waring) Fittleworth. Approach either from A272 outside Wisborough Green or A283 at Fittleworth and follow signs. Steep hillside garden with walls, terraces, water gardens and pools, mixed borders containing wide variety of trees, shrubs, herbaceous plants, roses and clematis. *Adm £2 Chd £1. Sat, Sun July 8, 9 (2-6). Private visits welcome May to Aug please,* **Tel 01798 865731**

¶Northfields Farmhouse ✿❀ (Jean & Steve Jackman) Approx 6m Chichester and Bognor, 4m Arundel. Turn off A27 onto A29 at Fontwell roundabout. Garden is 1 m S. Partially flint-walled garden started in Spring 1994. Emphasis on artistic use of foliage colour, shape and texture. Special interest in unusual flower colours, umbellifers, architectural plants, anything sinister, plants attracting insects and self-sown wildings. Collection of pots and containers. Not suitable for children as many poisonous plants. *Adm £1. Sun, Mon May 28, 29, every Fri & Sun from June 2 to Sun July 30 incl; Fri, Sun, Mon Sept 8, 10, 11 (2-5); Fri June 2, 23, 30, July 7, 14 (2-9)*

Regular Openers. See head of county section.

Northwood Farmhouse ♿✂ (Mrs P Hill) Pulborough. 1m N of Pulborough on A29. Turn NW into Blackgate Lane and follow lane for 2m then follow the signs. Cottage Garden with bulbs, roses, pasture with wild flowers and pond all on Wealded clay surrounding Sussex farmhouse dating from 1420. TEA. *Adm £1 Chd £1. Mon, Tues April 3, 4; June 19, 20 (2-5)*

Nyewood House ♿✂❀ (Mr & Mrs Timothy Woodall) Nyewood. From A272 at Rogate take rd signposted Nyewood, S for approx 1¼m. At 40 mph sign on outskirts of Nyewood, turn L signposted Trotton. Garden approx 500yds on R. 3-acre S facing garden recently renovated, with colour planted herbaceous borders, newly planted knot garden, pleaching, rose walk, water feature, and new potager. TEAS. *Adm £1.50 Chd free. Weds May 10, June 14, July 19; Suns June 11, July 16 (2-5.30)*

Nymans ♿✂❀ (The National Trust) Handcross. On B2114 at Handcross signposted off M23/A23 London-Brighton rd, SE of Handcross. Bus: 137 from Crawley & Haywards Heath [TQ265294]. Glorious herbaceous borders, June borders, old-fashioned rose garden, rare trees and shrubs. New Tea Rooms and shop. *Adm £3.80 Chd £1.90. ▲For NGS Tues June 6, July 4 (11-7)*

Offham House ♿❀ (Mr & Mrs H N A Goodman; Mrs H S Taylor) Offham, 2m N of Lewes on A275. Cooksbridge station ½m. Fountains; flowering trees; double herbaceous border; long paeony bed. Queen Anne house (not open) 1676 with well-knapped flint facade. Featured in George Plumptre's Guide to 200 Gardens in Britain. Home-made TEAS. *Adm £2 Chd over 14 25p. Suns May 7, June 4 (2-6)*

Old Barklye ✂❀ (Mr & Mrs G C Atkinson) Heathfield. [TQ 619230] 3½m W of Burwash on A265, N into Swiffe Lane, 100yds on L. 2-acre garden created by owners over past 25 yrs. Planned to be romantic and interesting, situated on hillside with magnificent views. Mixed borders, trees, shrubs, water features, wild flower meadow and area developed in 1992 on semi-formal lines linking gravel garden to lily pond. Refreshments in C18 barn. *Adm £1.50 Chd 50p. Parties welcome, May 28 to July 2, please* **Tel 01435 883317**

The Old Rectory, Newtimber ♿❀ (Lambert & Rosalyn Coles) 7m N of Brighton off A281 between Poynings and Pyecombe. 2 acres with views of South Downs and Newtimber Church. Pond garden, fine tulip tree, perennial borders; combined kitchen and flower garden. TEAS. *Adm £1.50 Chd 50p. Sun June 25 (2-6). Parties welcome by appt, please* **Tel 01273 857288**

The Old Vicarage ✂ (Arabella & Charlie Bridge) Firle. 5m SE Lewes on A27 towards Eastbourne. Sign to Firle. 3½-acre garden with downland views. Walled garden with mixed vegetable and flower borders. TEAS. *Adm £1.30 Chd 20p. Sun June 25 (2-5)*

Orchards ✂❀ (Penelope S Hellyer) Rowfant. Wallage Lane off B2028. 8½m N of Haywards Heath, 4½m W of East Grinstead. Garden created by Arthur and Gay Hellyer after 2nd World War. 6 acres mature trees, herbaceous borders, orchard, bluebell wood, heather/conifer garden, rhododendrons and camellias. Yr-round interest. Restoration, redesign and replanting by their daughter Penelope Hellyer. TEAS. *Adm £2 Acc chd free. Suns March 26, May 7, Sept 24, Mon April 17 (11-4)*

Palmer's Lodge ✂ (R Hodgson Esq) West Chiltington Village. At Xroads in centre of West Chiltington Village opp Queens Head. 2m E of Pulborough 3m N Storrington. A charming plantsman's ½-acre garden with herbaceous and shrub borders. *Adm £1 Chd free. Sats, Suns July 15, 16; 22, 23 (2-6). Parties by appointment (July only), please* **Tel 01798 812751**

Parham House and Gardens ♿ (gdns) ✂ (Hse) ❀ 4m SE of Pulborough on A283 Pulborough-Storrington Rd. Beautiful Elizabethan House with fine collection of portraits, furniture, rare needlework. 4 acres of walled garden; 7 acres pleasure grounds with lake. 'Veronica's Maze' a brick and turf maze designed with the young visitor in mind. Picnic area. Light refreshments. *Open Easter Sun to first Sun in Oct; Weds, Thurs, Suns & Bank Hols. Adm House & garden (1994 rates) £4 OAPs £3.50 Chd £2. Garden £2.50 Chd £1. For NGS. Wed, Thurs June 7, 8. (Garden & picnic area (1-6), House (2-6) last adm 5)*

Pashley Manor ✂❀ (J Sellick Esq) Ticehurst. 10m S of Tunbridge Wells. 1½m SE Ticehurst on B2099. Pashley Manor is a grade 1 Tudor timber-framed ironmaster's house. Standing in a well timbered park with magnificent views across to Brightling Beacon. The 8 acres of formal garden, dating from the C18, were created in true English romantic style and are planted with many ancient trees and fine shrubs, new plantings over the past decade give additional interest and subtle colouring throughout the year. Waterfalls, ponds and a moat which encircled the original house built 1262. TEAS on fine days. *Adm £3 OAPs £2.50 Chd £1 6 to 14 years, under 6 free. Tues, Wed, Thurs, Sat and Bank Hols April 15 to Sept 30. For NGS Sun June 25 (11-5)*

Pembury ♿❀ (Nick & Jane Baker) Clayton. 6m N of Brighton. On B2112, 100yds from junction with A273. Disabled parking at garden, otherwise follow signs. 2-acre garden on clay at foot of South Downs. Fine views; young and mature trees, shrubs, old-fashioned roses and herbaceous planting. Owner maintained; nearby Jack and Jill windmills and Saxon Church with restored wall paintings. Childrens' play area nearby. Teas in village hall in aid of Clayton Church Fund. *Adm £1.50 Chd free. Sun June 4 (11-6)*

Penns in the Rocks ♿❀ (Lord & Lady Gibson) Groombridge. 7m SW of Tunbridge Wells on Groombridge-Crowborough Rd just S of Plumeyfeather corner. Bus: MD 291 Tunbridge Wells-East Grinstead, alight Plumeyfeather corner, ¾m. Large wild garden with rocks; lake; C18 temple; old walled garden. House (not open) part C18. Dogs under control in park only (no shade in car park). TEAS. *Adm £2 – Up to two chd 50p each, further chd free. Bank Hol Mons April 17, Aug 28 (2.30-5.30). Parties welcome, please* **Tel 01892 864244**

Petworth House ♿✂ (The National Trust) Petworth. In centre of Petworth A272/A283. Car park on A283 Northchapel Rd. 30-acre woodland garden of Elizabethan origin and redesigned by 'Capability Brown' in 1751. Millions of daffodils and early wild flowers in March, plus new wild walks through 10,000 trees and shrubs planted since Great Storm. Park also open. 1 guided walk with NT head gardener and staff at 2pm (about 1½hr) starting from car park kiosk. (House closed). *Adm £1.50 Chd free. Sat March 25 (1-4.30)*

Pheasants Hatch ♿❀ (Mrs G E Thubron) Piltdown. 3m NW of Uckfield on A272. 2 acres, rose gardens with ponds and fountains; beautiful herbaceous borders; foliage; wild garden; peacocks. TEAS. *Adm £1 Chd free. Sun, Mon June 25, 26 (2-6.30). Parties welcome June to July, please* **Tel 01825 722960.** *Also open* **Home Farm, Buckham Hill**

Pondfield ✂❀ (Dr & Mrs Peter Sainsbury) Cutmill. E from Chichester, take A259 to Fishbourne and Bosham: over roundabout at Bosham and after ½m move into reservation in rd and turn R into Newells Lane, 150yds turn L and park. From W take A259 to Emsworth. Turn L after the Bosham Inn at Chidham, into Newells Lane. Approx 2 acres laid out by owners with specific emphasis on specimen trees. This garden is very informal with interesting vistas. Neptune House is reached over small bridge. TEAS. *Combined adm with* **Neptune House** *£1.50 Chd 50p. Sun June 4 (2-6)*

Priesthawes ♿✂❀ (Mr & Mrs Andrew Wadman) Polegate. On B2104 2½m. S Hailsham 4m N Eastbourne. 1m N of Stone Cross. C15 listed house of historical interest (not open) surrounded by 2½ acres. Walls used to full advantage with large clematis collection, climbers, old roses, herbaceous borders and pergola. Mainly replanted in the last 10 yrs. Lovely views over farmland. Cream TEAS. *Adm £1.50 Chd free (Share to St Wilfreds Hospice®). Sun, Mon June 18, 19 (2-6). Private visits also welcome mid-May to July, please* **Tel 01323 763228**

Puddle House ✂❀ (Mr & Mrs John Harwood) Cross-in-Hand. Pass through Cross-in-Hand towards Heathfield; before entering Heathfield take the R-hand fork signposted A267 to Eastbourne, then take the 1st turning R into New Pond Hill. 5-acre garden, with lovely views of South Downs. Extensive lawns with interesting trees, shrub and mixed borders and 2 natural ponds. Planting, begun in 1986, incl many unusual varieties, particularly eucalyptus spp, pinus spp, rhododendron spp and old-fashioned roses. TEAS. *Adm £2 (Share to St Thomas of Canterbury Roman Catholic Church, Mayfield®). Sun May 7 (2-5.30)*

Rymans ✂ (Anne, Lady Phillimore) Apuldram, 1½m SW of Chichester. Witterings Rd out of Chichester; at 1½m SW turn R signposted Apuldram; garden down rd on L. Walled and other gardens surrounding lovely C15 stone house (not open); bulbs, flowering shrubs, roses. Tea shops in Chichester. *Adm £1 Chd 50p. Suns April 2, 30, (2-5)*

St Marys House ♿✂ (Mr Peter Thorogood) Bramber. 10m NW of Brighton in Bramber Village off A283 or 1m E of Steyning. Medium-sized formal gardens with amusing topiary, large example of living-fossil Gingko tree and Magnolia Grandiflora; pools and fountains, ancient ivy-clad 'Monk's Walk', all surrounding listed Grade I C15 timber-framed medieval house, once a monastic inn. TEAS. *(House open but not in aid of NGS) Easter to Sept 30, Suns and Mons (2-6) also Suns, Mons, Weds, Thurs in Aug (2-6). For NGS garden only Adm £1 Chd 50p. Fri, Sat June 30, July 1 (2-6)*

Selehurst ♿✂❀ (Mr & Mrs M Prideaux) Lower Beeding, 4½m S of Horsham on A281 opp Leonardslee. Large woodland garden recently extended with a chain of five ponds and a romantic bridge. Fine collection of camellia, azaleas, rhododendrons; walled garden, 60′ laburnum tunnel underplanted with cream and silver, fine views. TEAS. *Adm £1.50 Chd free (Share to St. John's Church, Coolhurst®). Sun May 14 (1-5)*

Sheffield Park Garden ♿✂ (The National Trust) Midway between E Grinstead and Lewes, 5m NW of Uckfield; E of A275. The garden, with 5 lakes, was laid out by Capability Brown in C18, greatly modified early in the C20. Many rare trees, shrubs and fine waterlilies; the garden is beautiful at all times of year. Teas Oak Hall (not NT). *Adm £4 Chd £2. ▲For NGS Weds May 17, Oct 18 (11-6)*

Sherburne House ♿✂ (Mr & Mrs Angus Hewat) Eartham, 6m NE of Chichester, approach from A27 Chichester-Arundel Rd or A285 Chichester-Petworth Rd nr centre of village, 200yds S of church. Chalk garden of about 2 acres facing SW. Shrub and climbing roses; lime-tolerant shrubs; herbaceous, grey-leaved and foliage plants, pots; water feature; small herb garden, kitchen garden potager and conservatory. TEAS. *Adm £1.50 Chd 50p. Sun June 18 (2-6). Private visits welcome June 12 to 23, please* **Tel 01243 814261**

Somerset Lodge (Mr & Mrs R Harris) North St, Petworth. 7m S of Northchapel on A283. 15m N of Chichester on A285 garden on A283 100 yds N of church. Parking in town car park. Charming ½-acre town garden with ponds and walled kitchen garden, small collections of old and English roses and wildflower garden. Cleverly landscaped on slope with beautiful views. *Adm 80p Chd 20p. Sat, Sun June 3, 4 (11-6), Wed June 7 (2-6). Parties by appointment, please* **Tel 01798 43842**

Spur Point ✂ (Mr & Mrs T D Bishop) nr Fernhurst. 3 acres of S facing terraced gardens, created by owners since 1970. Well planted with rhododendrons, azaleas, shrubs and mixed borders. Outstanding views to South Downs. *Adm £2 Chd 50p. Private visits welcome May to June, please* **Tel 01483 211535**

Standen ✂ (The National Trust) 1½m from East Grinstead. Signed from B2110 and A22 at Felbridge. Hillside garden of 10½-acres with beautiful views over the Medway Valley. Partly suitable for wheelchairs. TEAS. *Adm £3 Chd £1.50. ▲Suns May 7, Sept 10 (12.30-6 Last adm 5pm)*

Stonehurst ❀ (Mr D R Strauss) Ardingly. 1m N of Ardingly. Entrance 800yds N of S of England showground, on B2028. 30-acre garden set in secluded woodland valley. Many interesting and unusual landscape features; chain of man made lakes and waterfalls; natural sandstone rock outcrops and a fine collection of trees and shrubs. TEAS. *Adm £2.50 Chd £1 (Share to Homelife®). Mons April 17, May 29, Sun May 14 (11-5)*

Telegraph House ❀ (Mr & Mrs David Gault) North Marden, 9 m. NW of Chichester. Entrance on B2141. From Petersfield to South Harting for 2m. From Chichester via A286 for 4m N of Lavant turn W on to B2I4I. 1-acre enclosed chalk garden 700 ft asl; chalk-tolerant shrubs, shrub roses, herbaceous plants; 1m avenue of copper beeches; walks through 150-acre yew wood; lovely views. House (not shown) in small park, built on site of semaphore keeper's cottage. TEAS. *Adm £1.50 Chd 75p. Sats, Suns June 17, 18; July 15, 16 (2-6). Also private visits welcome May to Aug (2-5), please* **Tel 01730 825206**

¶Tinkers Bridge Cottage ❀ (Mr & Mrs Michael Landsberg) Ticehurst. From B2099 1m W Ticehurst; turn N to Three Leg Cross for 1m R after Bull Inn house at bottom of hill. 12 acres attractively landscaped; stream garden nr the house leading to herbaceous borders, newly planted trees and shrubs, pond, wild flower meadow and woodland with bluebell walk. *Adm £1.50 to incl TEA Chd 25p. Sun May 14 (2.30-5.30)*

Trotton Old Rectory ✠❀ (Captain & Mrs John Pilley) nr Petersfield 3m W of Midhurst on A272. This typical English garden with its rose beds designed by Hazel Le Rougetel, framed in box and yew, has 2 levels with beautiful and interesting trees and shrubs running down to a lake and the R Rother. Plants for sale in the adjoining vegetable garden. *Adm £1.50 Chd 50p. Suns May 21, June 25 (2-6)*

Trotton Place ♿✠ (Mr & Mrs N J F Cartwright) 3½m W of Midhurst on A272. Entrance next to church. Large garden extending to over 4 acres surrounding C18 house (not open). Walled fruit and vegetable garden; C17 dovecote with small knot garden. Fine trees; mature borders with shrub roses; lake and woodland walk. TEAS. *Adm £1.50 Chd free. Suns May 21, June 25 (2-5.30)*

Uppark ♿✠ (The National Trust) 5m SE of Petersfield on B2146, 1½m S of S Harting. Fine late C17 house situated high on the South Downs with magnificent views towards the Solent. Important collection of paintings and decorative art. Dairy and new exhibition on restoration. Garden replanned and replanted since major fire in 1989. Woodland walk. Shop. TEAS. *Adm House, Garden and Exhibition £5, Family ticket £12.50. Collection for NGS Suns Sept 3, 10 (1-5.30)*

Upper House ✠ (Mr & Mrs C M Humber) West Burton. 5m SW of Pulborough, R off A29 at Bury-West Burton Xrds; garden is ½m from Roman Villa at Bignor. Large garden, formal yew lawn, interesting roses, walled garden incl herbs and raised beds, water garden; many unusual plants, shrubs, large Victorian greenhouse. *Adm £1.50 Chd free. Sat, Sun, Mon June 17, 18, 19 (2-6). Private visits welcome, please* **Tel 01798 831604**

Wadhurst Gardens ✠❀ 6m SE of Tunbridge Wells. On B2099, ¾m SE Wadhurst Station. 3 gardens all created by present owners. *Combined adm £2 Chd free. Sun, Mon July 16, 17 (2-5.30)*

Millstones (Mr & Mrs H W Johnson) ½-acre plantsman's garden featuring an exceptionally wide range of shrubs and perennial plants

Robins (Mr & Mrs D G Leney) At NW end Wadhurst turn W off B2099 onto B2100 to Mark Cross. ⅓m on L. ¾-acre garden created in 1991 with many unusual shrubs and beautifully planted natural pond

Sunnymead (Mr & Mrs D Goldsmith) 1¼-acre landscaped garden imaginatively designed for the sporting family, small kitchen garden. TEAS

Wadhurst Park ♿✠ (Dr & Mrs H Rausing) Wadhurst. 6m SE of Tunbridge Wells. Turn R along Mayfield Lane off B2099 at NW end of Wadhurst. L by Best Beech public house, L at Riseden Rd. 800-acres park with 7 different species of deer. Re-created garden on C19 site; restored C19 conservatories. Trailer rides into park. TEAS. *Adm £2 Chd 50p. Sun April 30 (2-5.30)*

Wakehurst Place ♿✠ (National Trust & Royal Botanic Gardens, Kew) Ardingly, 5m N of Haywards Heath on B2028. National botanic garden noted for one of the finest collections of rare trees and flowering shrubs amidst exceptional natural beauty. Walled gardens, heath garden, Pinetum, scenic walks through steep wooded valley with lakes, attractive water courses and large bog garden. Guided tours 11.30 & 2.30 most weekends, also prebooked tours. The ranger **Tel 01444 892701**. Restaurant. *Adm £4 OAPs/Students £2 Chd £1.50 under 5's free. Fri July 21 (10-7)*

¶Walland Manor ✠❀ (Mr & Mrs Malcolm Williams) Wadhurst. Take B2099 SE of Tunbridge Wells. Leaving Wadhurst turn R at Brinkers Lane. Jacobean house (not open) surrounded by 1 acre of garden designed and planted 6 yrs ago in traditional style. TEA. *Adm £1 Chd 30p. Sun May 28 (2-5.30)*

Warren House ✠❀ (Mr & Mrs M J Hands) Warren Rd, Crowborough. From Crowborough Cross take A26 towards Uckfield. 4th turning on R. 1m down Warren Rd. Beware speed ramps. 9-acre garden with views over Ashdown Forest. Series of gardens old and new, displaying a wealth of azaleas, rhododendrons, impressive trees and shrubs. Sweeping lawns framed by delightful walls and terraces, woodlands, ponds and ducks. Planted and maintained solely by owner. TEAS. *Adm £2 OAPs £1.50. Chd free. Suns May 14, 28; June 18; July 2; Aug 27; Oct 1; Mon May 29 (2-5). Private visits welcome, please* **Tel 01892 663502**

West Dean Gardens ♿✠❀ (Edward James Foundation) On A286, 5m N of Chichester. Historic garden of 35 acres in tranquil downland setting. Noted for its 300′ long Harold Peto pergola, mixed and herbaceous borders, rustic summerhouses, water garden and specimen trees. Newly restored 2½-acre walled garden contains fruit collection, 13 Victorian glasshouses, apple store, large working kitchen garden and a tool and mower collection. Circuit walk (2¼m) climbs through parkland to 45-acre St Roches Arboretum with its varied collection of trees and shrubs. TEA. *Adm £3 OAP £2.50 Chd £1.50. Pre-booked parties over 20, £2.50, April 1 to Oct 29 (11-5). For NGS Weds April 26, Sept 6 (11-5)*

¶46 Westup Farm Cottages ✂❀ (Chris & Pat Cornwell) Balcombe. Midway Cuckfield and Crawley. 1¼m Balcombe Station off B2036. Telephone for further directions. Well stocked cottage garden created over 10yrs; to provide yr-round interest in rural setting. *Adm £1 Chd free. Private visits welcome all yr, please* **Tel 01444 811891**

¶Whiligh ✂❀ (Mr & Mrs John Hardcastle) Shovers Green. 1½m E of Wadhurst on N side of B2099. Old garden of 3½ acres with some new features. Mature trees and shrubs and wide selection of herbaceous plants, chosen for colour and form. TEAS. *Adm £1.50. Sun, Mon June 18, 19 (2-5.30)*

The White House ✂ (Elizabeth Woodhouse) Burpham. Turn off A27 Arundel-Worthing Rd ½ S of Arundel. Proceed through Wepham to Burpham for 2m. Charming garden planned and planted by practicing garden designer artist. Great attention to plant forms and colour groupings. New wild garden with pond. TEAS. *Adm £1 Chd 50p (Share to Burpham Church Restoration Fund). Suns June 4, 18 (2.30-6). Private visits welcome, please write for appt*

Wilderness Farm ✂❀ (Andrew & Ryl Nowell of Cabbages and Kings). Hadlow Down. ½m S of A272 from village. Approx 1-acre terraced garden of great charm created from an exposed E facing slope. Richly planted courtyard area with many unusual herbaceous plants and grasses achieving maximum interest with minimum maintenance. Mixed shrubberies and lawns carry the eye from the garden to the superb views of the High Weald. Featured in Gardeners World and Grassroots. The design has developed to show visitors that by using sympathetic plants and materials garden and landscape may effectively be united. Exhibits include constructed features, hand crafted furniture, pots and sculpture. Walks through adjoining fields to Wilderness Wood. TEAS. *Adm £2 Chd £1. Suns May 28, Aug 6, Sept 3 (2-6)*

Winchelsea Gardens ✂ S of Rye. Teas at Three Chimneys. *Combined adm £1.75 Chd 75p. Sat June 17 (2-6)*

Cleveland House (Mr & Mrs S Jempson) 1½-acre semi-formal walled garden; many varied plants, ornamental trees, water feature, beautiful views, swimming in heated pool

Cooks Green (Roger & Tina Neaves) Cottage garden with views to Rye Bay

Nesbit (Mr & Mrs G Botterell) Formal enclosed ¼-acre garden; many and varied plants

The Old Rectory (June & Denis Hyson) ½ acre of open lawn garden with views overlooking the Brede Valley

The Roundal (Lord & Lady Ritchie) Wild garden with views to Rye

Strand Plat (Mrs P Mason) Unusual and colourful walled garden

Three Chimneys (Mr & Mrs Dominic Leahy) Formal town garden. TEAS

No. 1 Trojans Plat (Mr & Mrs Norman Turner) C13 Grade II listed archway providing access to small garden of great variety

Well House (Misses Barbara and Nancy Lyle) Small enclosed town garden

Woodstock ✂ (Group Captain A R Gordon-Cumming) West Broyle. From roundabout N of Chichester take B2178 (Funtingdon) rd NW for 1⅓m. Turn L into Pine Grove and after 100yds R into West Way. Woodstock is at far end. ⅔-acre mainly woodland garden specialising in ground cover plants, camellias, especially asiatic primulas and hostas. Teas at The Spinney in aid of Save the Children Fund. *Adm £1.50 Chd free. Sun May 21 (1.30-5.30). Private visits welcome mid March to mid July, please* **Tel 01243 776413**

Warwickshire & West Midlands

Hon County Organiser: Mrs D L Burbidge, Cedar House, Wasperton, Warwick CV35 8EB
Assistant Hon County Organiser: Mrs C R King-Farlow, 8 Vicarage Road, Edgbaston, Birmingham B15 3EF
Mrs Michael Perry, Sherbourne Manor, Sherbourne, Warwick CV35 8AP
Hon County Treasurer: Michael Pitts, Hickecroft, Mill Lane, Rowington, Warwickshire CV35 7DQ

DATES OF OPENING

By appointment

For telephone numbers and other details see garden descriptions. Private visits welcomed

Brook Farm, Abbots Salford
Elm Close, Welford-on-Avon
The Folly Lodge, Halford
17 Gerrard Street, Warwick
11 Hillwood Common Rd, Four Oaks, Sutton Coldfield
Ilmington Manor, Shipston-on-Stour
Lord Leycester Hospital, Warwick
16 Prospect Rd, Moseley Gardens
Sherbourne Park, nr Warwick
Shrewley Pools Farm, Haseley, Warwick
Silver Trees Farm Gardens, Balsall Common
52 Tenbury Road, Kings Heath, Birmingham
8 Vicarage Road, Edgbaston
50 Wellington Road, Edgbaston
Woodpeckers, Bidford-on-Avon

Parties only

Avon Dassett Gardens
Greenlands, Wellesbourne
Ivy Lodge, Radway
Kissing Tree House, Alveston
Rowington Gardens

Regular openings
For details see garden descriptions

Birmingham Botanical Gardens & Glasshouses, Edgbaston
The Mill Garden, Warwick. Suns & Bank Hols April 15 to Oct 15
Ryton Organic Gardens, nr Coventry. Daily

March 5 Sunday
Birmingham Botanical Gardens & Glasshouses, Edgbaston
March 26 Sunday
Elm Close, Welford-on-Avon
Sherbourne Manor, nr Warwick
March 28 Tuesday
Woodpeckers, Bidford-on-Avon
April 8 Saturday
Kissing Tree House, Alveston
April 9 Sunday
Greenlands, Wellesbourne
63 Green Road, Hall Green Gardens, Birmingham
Ilmington Gardens
Kissing Tree House, Alveston
April 14 Friday
Kissing Tree House, Alveston
April 15 Saturday
Kissing Tree House, Alveston
April 16 Sunday
55 Elizabeth Road, Mosely, Birmingham
Kissing Tree House, Alveston
April 17 Monday
Kissing Tree House, Alveston
April 18 Tuesday
Woodpeckers, Bidford-on-Avon
April 22 Saturday
Castle Bromwich Hall Gardens Trust, Castle Bromwich
The Hiller Garden & Dunnington Heath Farm, nr Alcester
Kissing Tree House, Alveston
April 23 Sunday
Cedar House, Wasperton, nr Warwick ‡
The Hiller Garden & Dunnington Heath Farm, nr Alcester
Ivy Lodge, Radway
Kissing Tree House, Alveston ‡
The Mill Garden, Warwick
Moseley Gardens
April 30 Sunday
Ryton Organic Gardens, nr Coventry
May 7 Sunday
Brook Farm, Abbots Salford
Hunningham Village Gardens
Kissing Tree House, Alveston
Wroxall Abbey School, nr Warwick
May 8 Monday
Hunningham Village Gardens
Kissing Tree House, Alveston
May 9 Tuesday
Woodpeckers, Bidford-on-Avon
May 10 Wednesday
Brook Farm, Abbots Salford
May 14 Sunday
Bodymoor Green Farm, Kingsbury
Greenlands, Wellesbourne
Hall Green Gardens, Birmingham
The Mill Garden, Warwick
52 Tenbury Road, Kings Heath, Birmingham
May 20 Saturday
Sutton Coldfield Gardens
May 21 Sunday
Alscot Park, nr Stratford-on-Avon
Alveston Gardens
Ilmington Manor, Shipston-on-Stour ‡
Pear Tree Cottage, Ilmington ‡
Wroxall Abbey School, nr Warwick
May 28 Sunday
55 Elizabeth Road, Moseley, Birmingham
Loxley Hall, nr Stratford-on-Avon
26 Sunnybank Road, Wylde Green
Warwickshire Constabulary Headquarters, Leek Wootton
May 29 Monday
Kissing Tree House, Alveston
Silver Trees Farm Gardens, Balsall Common
May 30 Tuesday
Woodpeckers, Bidford-on-Avon
June 3 Saturday
Baddesley Clinton
June 4 Sunday
Bodymoor Green Farm, Kingsbury
Maxstoke Castle, nr Coleshill
June 11 Sunday
Brook Farm, Abbots Salford
Elm Close, Welford-on-Avon
Holywell Gardens, nr Claverdon ‡
Shrewley Pools Farm, Haseley, Warwick ‡
June 13 Tuesday
Woodpeckers, Bidford-on-Avon
June 14 Wednesday
Brook Farm, Abbots Salford
The Folly Lodge, Halford
June 17 Saturday
17 Gerrard Street, Warwick
June 18 Sunday
Alscot Park, nr Stratford-on-Avon
Dorsington Gardens
17 Gerrard Street, Warwick
Greenlands, Wellesbourne
Lord Leycester Hospital, Warwick
The Mill Garden, Warwick
Paxford, Leamington Road, Princethorpe, Rugby
Pereira Road Gardens
50 Wellington Road, Edgbaston
Whichford & Ascott Gardens
June 24 Saturday
Rowington Gardens
Sheepy Magna Gardens, see Leics
June 25 Sunday
Bodymoor Green Farm, Kingsbury
The Folly Lodge, Halford
Honington Village Gardens ‡
Ilmington Manor, Shipston-on-Stour
Ivy Lodge, Radway
Roseberry Cottage, Fillongley
Rowington Gardens
St Dennis Farm, nr Shipston-on-Stour ‡
Sheepy Magna Gardens, see Leics
26 Sunnybank Road, Wylde Green
July 2 Sunday
Packwood House, nr Hockley Heath
52 Tenbury Road, Kings Heath, Birmingham
July 5 Wednesday
The Folly Lodge, Halford
52 Tenbury Road, Kings Heath, Birmingham
July 9 Sunday
Alscot Park, nr Stratford-on-Avon
Avon Dassett Gardens
Compton Scorpion Farm, nr Ilmington ‡
Ilmington Manor, Shipston-on-Stour ‡
Moseley Gardens
Upton House, nr Banbury
July 16 Sunday
Brook Farm, Abbots Salford
Fenny Drayton Gardens, see Leics
Martineau Centre Gardens, Edgbaston
Paxford, Leamington Road, Princethorpe, Rugby
Warmington Village Gardens
July 19 Wednesday
Brook Farm, Abbots Salford
Charlecote Park, Warwick
The Folly Lodge, Halford
July 23 Sunday
55 Elizabeth Road, Moseley, Birmingham
Greenlands, Wellesbourne
Hall Green Gardens, Birmingham
The Mill Garden, Warwick
26 Sunnybank Road, Wylde Green
July 25 Tuesday
Woodpeckers, Bidford-on-Avon
August 16 Wednesday
Paxford, Leamington Road, Princethorpe, Rugby
August 19 Saturday
The Hiller Garden & Dunnington Heath Farm, nr Alcester
August 20 Sunday
The Mill Garden, Warwick
The Hiller Garden & Dunnington Heath Farm, nr Alcester

August 22 Tuesday
Woodpeckers, Bidford-on-Avon

August 27 Sunday
Greenlands, Wellesbourne

September 3 Sunday
Sherbourne Manor, nr Warwick

September 10 Sunday
Little Frome, Fenny Drayton Gardens, see Leics
Tysoe Manor, Warwick

September 17 Sunday
The Mill Garden, Warwick

September 24 Sunday
Birmingham Botanical Gardens & Glasshouses, Edgbaston
Ryton Organic Gardens, nr Coventry

September 30 Saturday
Castle Bromwich Hall Gardens Trust, Castle Bromwich

October 14 Saturday
The Hiller Garden & Dunnington Heath Farm, nr Alcester

October 15 Sunday
The Hiller Garden & Dunnington Heath Farm, nr Alcester
The Mill Garden, Warwick

DESCRIPTIONS OF GARDENS

Alscot Park ❀ (Mrs James West) 2½m S of Stratford-on-Avon A34. Fairly large garden; extensive lawns, shrub roses, fine trees, orangery, with C18 Gothic house (not open), river, deer park, lakes. Home-made TEAS on June 18, July 9 only. *Adm £1 Chd free (Share to Warwickshire Assoc. of Boys' Clubs©). Suns May 21, June 18, July 9 (2-6)*

Alveston Gardens ♿✂❀ 2m NE of Stratford-upon-Avon. Turn left at War Memorial off B4086 Stratford-Wellesbourne rd; Alveston ¼m. TEAS at The Malt House in aid of Alveston WI. *Combined adm £1.50 Chd 20p. Sun May 21 (2-6)*

The Bower House (Mr & Mrs P S Hart) 1 acre, owner-designed, unusual trees, water garden and rockeries. Pergolas, alpine sinks, choice shrubs

Court Leys (Mr & Mrs E Barnard) 1 acre; shrubs, trees and herbaceous borders, circular raised brick planters, conservatory

Long Acre (Dr & Mrs N A Woodward) Owner designed, 1 acre; interesting trees, shrubs and roses; rockery, barbecue area, pergola, terraces and ponds

Parham Lodge (Mr & Mrs K C Edwards) 1 acre; designed and maintained by owners. Choice trees, shrubs; plants, bulbs; island beds, heathers, large pond, patios, tubs, rose garden

Avon Dassett Gardens ♿✂❀ 7m N of Banbury off B4100 (use Exit 12 of M40). Car parking in the village and in car park at top of hill. TEAS at **Old Mill Cottage**. *Combined adm £2 Chd free (Share to Myton Hamlet Hospice®). Sun July 9 (2-6). Parties welcome, please* **Tel 01295 690643**

Church Cottage (Mr R & Mrs J Mandle) Pretty cottage garden with colourful beds. Shrubs and herbaceous plants

Hill Top Farm (Mrs N & Mr D Hicks) 1-acre garden. Dramatic display of bedding plants, perennials and roses. Extensive kitchen garden. Greenhouses

Old Mill Cottage (Mr & Mrs M Lewis) Conservation garden of ½ acre with shrub, perennial borders and rockeries. Collection alpines and herbs. Two ponds and kitchen garden. Newly planted tropical garden

Old Pumphouse Cottage (Mr & Mrs W Wormell) Cottage garden with mixed borders featuring varieties of pinks and shrub roses and clematis. Kitchen garden and greenhouse

The Old Rectory (Mrs L Hope-Frost) 2-acre garden surrounding listed building mentioned in Doomsday Book (not open). Large variety of fine trees and shrubs. Small wood

The Old Schoolhouse (Mr & Mrs P Fletcher) Small garden with interesting plants and shrubs; pond; views over parkland

Post Box Cottage Large garden with many fine plants, trees and shrubs. Vegetable garden and pond with waterfowl; hanging baskets

Baddesley Clinton ♿✂ (The National Trust) ¾m W off A4141 Warwick-Birmingham rd near Chadwick End. 7½m NW of Warwick. Mediaeval moated manor house little changed since 1633; walled garden and herbaceous borders; natural areas; lakeside walk. Lunches and TEAS. *Adm Grounds only £2.10 Chd £1.05. Shop and restaurant open from 12.30. ▲For NGS Sat June 3 (12.30-6)*

Birmingham Botanical Gardens & Glasshouses ♿✂❀ 2m SW of Birmingham City Centre, signposted from Hagley Rd (A456). 15 acres; Tropical House with large lily pond and many economic plants. Palm House; Orangery; Cactus House. Outside bedding displays; rhododendrons and azaleas; rose garden; rock garden; 200 trees. Theme, herb, historic and cottage gardens. Fun area for children. Plant centre. Bands play every Sun afternoon. TEAS in the Pavilion. *Adm £3.30 Chd, Students & OAPs £1.70. Open daily. For NGS Suns March 5, Sept 24 (10-6)*

Bodymoor Green Farm ✂❀ (Mr & Mrs P J Maiden) ¾m S of Kingsbury on B4098 to Coventry. Easy approach from junction 9, M42; take A4097 signposted Kingsbury, Nether Whitacre. Traditional C18 farmhouse with courtyard and outbuildings. 1-acre country garden with old roses and herbaceous borders. Formal secret garden with pergola and white roses, silver scheme; ornamental pools, orchard with collection of spring bulbs; large kitchen garden, many interesting features incl treillage; ducks, hens, geese, sheep and lambs. TEAS. *Adm £1.50 Chd free. Suns May 14, June 4, 25 (2-6)*

Brook Farm ♿❀ (Mr & Mrs R B Hughes) Abbots Salford, Salford Priors 5m N of Evesham on B439. 1½ acres; large mixed borders, island beds, pond; bog, scree and peat gardens. Many unusual plants and shrubs. *Adm £1 Chd free. Suns, Weds May 7, 10; June 11, 14; July 16, 19 (2-6). Also private visits welcome all year, please* **Tel 01386 871122**

By Appointment Gardens. These owners do not have a fixed opening day usually because they do not like crowds or have insufficient parking space. Owner will often give guided tour.

Castle Bromwich Hall Garden Trust Chester Rd. ♿❀ 4m E of Birmingham. 1m from junction 5 of the M6 (exit Northbound). An example of the Formal English Garden of the C18. The ongoing restoration, started 6 yrs ago now provides visitors, academics and horticulturalists opportunity of seeing a unique collection of historic plants, shrubs, medicinal and culinary herbs and a fascinating vegetable collection. Guided tours Weds, Sats & Suns. Shop. Refreshments available; meals by arrangement. TEAS. *Adm £2 OAPs £1.50 Chd 50p.* ▲*For NGS Sats April 22, Sept 30 (2-6)*

Cedar House ♿✲ (Mr & Mrs D L Burbidge) Wasperton. 4m S of Warwick on A429, turn R between Barford and Wellesbourne, Cedar House at end of village. 3-acre mixed garden; shrubs, herbaceous borders, ornamental trees, woodland walk. TEAS. *Adm £1.50 Chd free (Share to St John's Church, Wasperton®). Sun April 23 (2-6)*

Charlecote Park ♿✲ (The National Trust) Warwick. 1m W of Wellesbourne signed off A429. 6m S of Warwick, 5m E of Stratford upon Avon. Landscaped park by Capability Brown with Victorian balustrated formal gardens featuring clipped yews and terraces with urns planted with geraniums and lobelia. A C19 orangery (open for teas) and a rustic thatched summer house stand by the cedar lawn. Shakespeare is said to have poached deer in Charlecote Park, and the border close to the orangery has been planted with species mentioned in his plays. The Ladies' Walk on a raised promontory with fine park views and vistas to two churches was created in the C19 by the Lucy family. A park walk (1m) follows a route round the park along the banks of the R. Avon. TEAS. *Special opening for NGS. Adm £2 (incl NT members and Chd).* ▲*Wed July 19 (2-6)*

Compton Scorpion Farm ✲ (Mrs T M Karlsen) nr Ilmington. As for Ilmington Manor then fork L at village hall; after 1½m L down steep narrow lane, house on L. Garden designed and created by owners in 1989 from meadow hillside, aiming at Jekyll single colour schemes. *Adm £1 Chd free. Sun July 9 (2-6)*

Dorsington Gardens ♿❀ 7m SW of Stratford-on-Avon. On A439 from Stratford turn L to Welford-on-Avon, then R to Dorsington. TEAS. *Combined adm £2 Chd free (Share to St Peter's Church, Dorsington®). Sun June 18 (2-5.30)*

- **Aberfoyle** (Mr & Mrs B Clarke)
- **Knowle Thatch** (Mr & Mrs P W Turner)
- **Milfield** (Mr & Mrs P Carey)
- **The Moat House** (Mr & Mrs I Kolodotschko)
- **New House Farm** (Mr & Mrs G Wood-Hill)
- **The Old Manor** (Mr F Dennis) TEAS
- **The Old Rectory** (Mr & Mrs N Phillips)
- **White Gates** (Mrs A G Turner)
- **Windrush** (Mrs M B Mills)

55 Elizabeth Rd ✲❀ (Rob & Diane Cole) Moseley. 4m S of Birmingham City centre, halfway between Kings Heath Centre & Edgbaston Cricket Ground. Off Moor Green Lane. Plantsman's garden 100′ × 30′ on 3 levels, with scree area and mixed borders of alpines, rhododendrons, primulas and many unusual plants. Alpine House & troughs. TEAS. Wide range of plants for sale. *Adm 80p Chd 20p. Suns April 16, May 28, July 23 (2-6)*

Elm Close ♿✲❀ (Mr & Mrs E W Dyer) Binton Rd, Welford-on-Avon. From Stratford-on-Avon, take A4390 towards Evesham; turn L after approx 5m (signed Welford and Long Marston). Elm Close is between Welford Garage and The Bell Inn. ⅔-acre plantsman's garden designed and maintained by owners and stocked for yr-round effect. Herbaceous beds, bulbs and shrubs, alpines in troughs, pool and bog garden, clematis and hellebores a particular speciality. Listed in The Good Gardens Guide. TEAS in aid of Red Cross. *Adm £1.50 Chd free. Suns March 26, June 11 (2-6). Parties other days by appointment, please* **Tel 01789 490803**

¶**The Folly Lodge** ✲❀ (Mrs Susan Solomon) Halford. On A429 (Fosse Way) 9m NE Moreton in Marsh. 9m SE Stratford on Avon. In Halford take turning opp PO to Idlicote. House is 300yds down on R. ⅓-acre designed, constructed and maintained by owners since 1983. Colour themed herbaceous borders and island beds. Roses, shrubs and small pond; wide variety of plants many unusual. TEAS. *Adm £1.50 Chd over 7yrs 50p (Share to Stratford & District Samaritans®). Sun June 25 (2-6), Weds June 14, July 5, 19 (2-5). Private visits welcome May to Aug, please* **Tel 01789 740184**

17 Gerrard Street ✲ (Mr T K Meredith) Warwick. 100yds from castle main gate. Car park at St Nicholas. Small town garden with interesting plants. *Adm 40p Chd free. Sat, Sun June 17, 18 (11-1 & 2-6). Private visits welcome, please* **Tel 01926 496305**

Greenlands ♿❀ (Mr Eric T Bartlett) Wellesbourne. Leave Statford-upon-Avon due E on the B4086. Garden on Xrds at Loxley/Charlecote by airfield. An acre of mature trees; shrubs; shrub roses and herbaceous borders. TEAS. *Adm £1 Chd free. Suns April 9, May 14, June 18, July 23, Aug 27 (11-5). Parties welcome, please* **Tel 01789 840327**

Hall Green Gardens ✲❀ *Adm £1.20 Chd free (Share to Acorns Children's Hospice, St Mary's Hospice®). Suns May 14, July 23 (2-5)*

63 Green Rd (Mrs M Wilkes) Green Rd is W off A34 Hall Green Parade. (Nr Hall Green Station). Narrow suburban garden; 4 pools, bedding plants, herbaceous, shrubs, several distinctive features made by owner. *Also open Sun April 9*

117 Lulworth Road (Mrs J Kimberley) Turn off A34 E at Hall Green Library (traffic lights) down School Rd, then L into Studland Rd, then L into Lulworth Rd. Suburban garden, interesting shrubs, rhododendrons etc. *Only open May 14*

120 Russell Rd ✲❀ (Mr D Worthington) Turn off A34 E at Swithland Motors, Hall Green, down York Rd then L into Russell Rd. Small suburban garden designed by owner; shrubs, herbaceous, climbers, old roses and fountain; tubs, hanging baskets and window boxes. TEA in aid of REAP

¶**The Hillier Garden & Dunnington Heath Farm** ♿✲❀ (Mr & Mrs R Beach) Alcester. On A441 nr junction with A435, 3m S Alecester. 1-acre garden of unusual herbaceous perennials with all-yr interest. A similarly-sized extension will open June 1995 to display old-fashioned and English roses, shrubs and a herb barden. Open all year. 10% of plant sales and TEAS to NGS on NGS days. *Adm by donation. For NGS Sats, Suns Apr 22 (10-5), 23 (10-4); Aug 19 (10-5), 20 (10-4); Oct 14 (10-5) 15 (10-4). Private gardens of* **Dunnington Heath Farm** *(adjacent) also open on NGS days. Adm £1 Chd free*

11 Hillwood Common Road ✿❀ (Mr & Mrs C T Smith) Four Oaks, Sutton Coldfield. From A5127 at Mere Green traffic island take Hill Village Rd. 2nd R into Sherifoot Lane and follow L bend. Straight on into Hill Wood Common Rd. AZ ref 27.4H. ½-acre Japanese style garden with tea house; stone and water feature; Japanese courtyard. Low heeled shoes, please. Ceramics by Janet Cottrell for sale. *Adm £1 Chd 50p. Private visits welcome, please* **Tel 0121 3081180**

Holywell Gardens ♿✿❀ 5m E of Henley-in-Arden, nearest village Claverdon. Coffee and TEAS in aid of Myton Hospice. *Combined adm £1.50 Chd free. Sun June 11 (11-6)*

Holywell Farm (Mr & Mrs Ian Harper) 2½-acre natural garden; lawn, trees, shrubs. Laid out in 1963 for easy maintenance, surrounding C16 half timbered house

Manor Farm (Mr & Mrs Donald Hanson) Cottage type garden surrounding C16 farmhouse with natural duck pond, yew and box hedges, herb garden; white and grey border

Honington Village Gardens ♿✿ 1½m N of Shipston-on-Stour. Take A34 towards Stratford then R signed Honington. TEAS **Honington Hall**. *Combined adm £2 Chd free (Share to All Saints Church, Honington Restoration Fund®). Sun June 25 (2.15-5.30)*

Holts Cottage (Mr & Mrs Whitticase)

Honington Glebe (Mr & Mrs John Orchard) Over 2 acres of informal garden interesting ornamental trees; shrubs and foliage. Parterre and raised lily pool recently laid out in old walled garden

Honington Hall (Lady Wiggin) Extensive lawns; fine trees. Carolean house (not open); Parish Church adjoining house

Honington Lodge (Lord & Lady Tombs)

The Old Cottage (Mrs Wigington)

Old Mullions (Mr & Mrs R Lawton)

Hunningham Village Gardens ♿✿❀ Hunningham. From Leamington Spa B4453 to Rugby. Signposted Hunningham R after Weston-under-Wetherley. Or A425 to Southam at Fosseway (B4455) turn L. At Hunningham Hill turn L then follow signs to church (open). Teas at Vicarage. *Adm £2 Chd free. Sun, Mon May 7, 8 (2-5)*

The Barn (Mr & Mrs M Lambert) Small family garden with hens

High Cross (Mr & Mrs T Chalk) Secluded garden with alpines

Moat Cottage (Mr & Mrs Murchek) New garden with interesting features and planting

The Olde School House (Mr & Mrs G Longstaff) 1 acre of borders, shrubs, pond and wilflife paddock area

Sandford Cottage (Mr & Mrs A Phillips) Village cottage garden

Other gardens may open

Ilmington Gardens ✿❀ 8m S of Stratford-on-Avon, 4m NW of Shipston-on-Stour. Ilmington traditional Morris dancers. Teas in the Village Hall. Start anywhere, all gardens well signed and within walking distance. *Combined adm £3 Chd free (Share to Ilmington Village Hall©). Sun April 9 (2-6)*

Crab Mill (L Hodgkin)

The Bevingtons (N Tustain)

Foxcote Hill (M Dingley)

Foxcote Hill Cottage (A Terry)

Frog Orchard (N Naish)

The Manor (D Flower) (see next entry)

Pear Tree Cottage (Dr & Mrs A F Hobson) See individual entry

Puddocks (H Syme)

Ilmington Manor ♿❀ (Mr D & Lady Flower). 4m NW of Shipston-on-Stour, 8m S of Stratford-on-Avon. Daffodils in profusion (April). Hundreds of old and new roses, ornamental trees, shrub and herbaceous borders, rock garden, pond garden, topiary, fish ponds with geese and ducks. House (not open) built 1600. TEAS. *Adm £2 Chd free. Suns May 21, June 25, July 9 (2-6). Also open Sun April 9 with* **Ilmington Gardens**. *Private visits welcome, please* **Tel 01608 682230**

Ivy Lodge ♿ (Mrs M A Willis) Radway 7m NW of Banbury via A41 and B4086, turn R down Edgehill; 14m SE of Stratford via A422. L below Edgehill. 4-acres; spring bulbs and blossom; wildflower area; climbing roses; site Battle of Edgehill. TEAS. *Adm £1.50 OAP £1 Chd free (Share to Katherine House Hospice, Banbury®). Suns April 23, June 25 (2-6). Also parties welcome May to July and throughout Oct (Autumn colours), please* **Tel 01295 670371** *or* **670580**

¶Kissing Tree House ✿❀ (John & Julie Fenton) Alveston. 2m NE of Stratford-on-Avon on the B4086 Stratford to Wellesbourne Rd. Junction 15 M40 A429 S to Barford & Charlecote B4086 towards Stratford 2m on R. Georgian & Victorian house once owned and lived in by J B Priestley. Set in 32 acres of parkland, woodland walks with spring bulbs. Traditional lawns and herbaceous borders, shrubs and pools in 10 acres of landscaping, many new, contemporary plantings. Large collections of perennials - many for sale from old kitchen garden and glasshouses. TEAS. *Adm £2 Chd 50p (Share to Alveston Village Association®). Sat, Sun April 8, 9, Easter Fri, Sat, Sun, Mon April 14, 15, 16, 17, Sat, Sun April 22, 23 (10-5). Sun May 7 & Bank Hol Mons May 8, 29 (9-6). Parties welcome Mon to Sat June, July, Aug & Sept, please* **Tel 01789 414065**

Lord Leycester Hospital ✿❀ High Street, Warwick. Town centre beside West Gate. Garden adjoins historic C14 Guildhall, Chapel, courtyard, Great Hall and Museum of the Queen's Own Hussars also open to public. 1-acre walled garden, partly under reconstruction, including Norman arch and ancient finial of Nilometer. TEAS. *Adm £1 Chd free. Sun June 18 (11-5). Private visits welcome, please* **Tel 01929 491422**

By Appointment Gardens. See head of county section

Loxley Hall ♿ (Col A Gregory-Hood) 4m SE of Stratford-on-Avon. Turn N off A422 or W off A429 1½m SW of Wellesbourne. Modern sculpture, iris, shrubs, roses, trees. Small Japanese Garden. Old church adjacent can be visited. TEAS. *Adm £1 Chd 20p. Sun May 28 (2-7)*

Martineau Centre Gardens ♿✿❀ (City of Birmingham Education Dept) Priory Rd, Edgbaston. From Birmingham S via A38; R at Priory Rd (lights and box junction); entrance 100yds on R opp Priory Hospital. 2-acre demonstration gardens; hardy ornamentals, vegetables, small orchard; glasshouses; nature reserve/wild garden. Mown field for picnics. TEAS. *Adm £1 Chd 50p. Sun July 16 (10-6)*

Maxstoke Castle ♿✿ (Mr & Mrs M C Fetherston-Dilke) nr Coleshill, E of Birmingham, 2½m E of Coleshill on B4114 take R turn down Castle Lane; Castle Dr 1¼m on R. 4 to 5 acres of garden and pleasure grounds with flowers, shrubs and trees in the immediate surroundings of the castle and inside courtyard; water-filled moat round castle. *Adm £2.50 OAP/Chd £1 under 6 free. Sun June 4 (2-5)*

The Mill Garden ♿✿❀ (Mr A B Measures) 55 Mill St, Warwick off A425 beside castle gate. 1 acre; series of informal, partially enclosed areas, on river next to castle. Superb setting; herb garden; raised beds; small trees, shrubs, cottage plants and some unusual plants. Use St Nicholas Car Park. Tea in Warwick. *Adm £1 Chd free (Share to Lord Leycester Hospital®). Sun & Bank Hols April 15 to Oct 15 (2-6). Open for NGS Suns April 23, May 14, June 18, July 23, Aug 20, Sept 17, Oct 15. Parties welcome, please* **Tel 01926 492 877**

Moseley Gardens ✿❀ Approx 3m from Birmingham City Centre halfway between Kings Heath Centre & Moseley Village. TEA April 23. TEAS July 9. *Combined adm £1.50 Chd free. Suns April 23, July 9 (2-6)*

No 14A Clarence Rd (Ms C Fahy) Small suburban garden with a difference. *July 9 only*

No 16 Prospect Rd ❀ (Mrs S M & Mr R J Londesborough) Small garden with wide range of plants. Registered wildlife garden. *Also private visits welcome all year, please* **Tel 0121 449 8457**

No 19 Prospect Rd (Mr A White) Well planted spring suburban garden. *April 23 only*

No 20 Prospect Rd (Martin Page & Annie Sofiano). Large town garden on 3 levels. *July 9 only*

No 30 Prospect Rd (Mrs J Taylor) South-facing terraced garden incorporating rockery-covered air-raid shelter

No 33 School Rd (Ms J Warr-Arnold) Mixed garden containing plants with interesting histories. *Sun July 9 only*

No 65 School Rd (Mrs W Weston) Small shady garden with patio and pergola. *Sun July 9 only*

Packwood House ♿✿ (The National Trust) 11m SE of Birmingham. 2m E of Hockley Heath. Carolean yew garden representing the Sermon on the Mount. Tudor house with tapestries, needlework and furniture of the period. Teas at Baddesley Clinton (NT) Henley in Arden or Knowle. *Adm garden only £2 Chd £1. ▲For NGS Sun July 2 (2-6)*

Paxford ✿❀ (Mr & Mrs A M Parsons) Princethorpe. 7m SE of Coventry, on B4453 Leamington Rd approx 200yds from junction with A423. A flower arranger's garden with heathers and fuchsias which has been designed and maintained by the owners as a series of rooms. Parking on road on one side only please. *Adm £1 (Share to Stretton-on-Dunsmore Parish Church®). Suns June 18, July 16; Wed Aug 16 (2-6)*

Pear Tree Cottage ❀ (Dr & Mrs A F Hobson) Ilmington 8m S of Stratford-on-Avon, 4m NW of Shipston-on-Stour. Cottage garden with many interesting plants and bulbs. Designed and maintained by owners; rock garden and terrace. Partially suitable for wheelchairs. TEA at **Ilmington Manor**. *Adm 50p Chd 20p. Sun May 21 (2-6). Also open Sun April 10 (2-6) with* **Ilmington Gardens**

Pereira Road Gardens ✿❀ Birmingham A-Z 5c p.72 between Gillhurst Rd and Margaret Grove, ¼m from Hagley Rd or ½m Harborne High St. TEAS at **No. 84** in aid of St Peter's Church Restoration Fund. *Combined adm £1.50 Chd 30p. Sun June 18 (2-5)*

No. 45 (Wyn & Alfred White) Harborne. ⅕ acre on four levels. Spring bulbs, rhododendrons, roses, shrubs, herbaceous borders, ornamental and fruit trees in formal and informal areas. *(Share to CAFOD and Break Through Trust for the Deaf®)*

No. 50 ❀ (Prof M Peil) About ⅕ acre, with a wide range of shrubs and perennials for all seasons; fruit and vegetables. Large bed of plants with African connections, pond. (Plants sold in aid of Catholic Fund for Overseas Development.)

No. 84 ♿ (Mrs R E Barnett) ⅕ acre with 30 degree sloping concreted bank, now extensive rockery, interesting shrubs, herbaceous borders

Roseberry Cottage ♿✿❀ (Mr & Mrs Richard G Bastow) Fillongley. 6m N of Coventry on B4098 Tamworth Road. Go under motorway bridge to top of hill, take Woodend Lane, sign on R. Turn L into Sandy Lane, opp triangle of beech trees. 1st house on R in Sandy Lane. Please use one way system due to restricted parking. Garden of 1¾ acres incl herbaceous border, rock garden, pool, peat and bog area, scree and small herb garden. Stone troughs, orchard with wild flowers, organically grown fruit and vegetables. Herbs for sale, thymes a speciality. TEA. *Adm £1 Chd 30p (Share to NCCPG®). Sun June 25 (2-6)*

Rowington Gardens ♿✿❀ 6m NW of Warwick. 15m SE of Birmingham on B4439 between Hockley Heath and Hatton. Turn into Finwood Rd (signed Lowsonford); at Rowington Xrds 1st L into Mill Lane. TEA. *Combined adm £1.50 Chd 50p (Share to Myton Hospice®). Sat, Sun June 24, 25 (2-5.30)*

Hickecroft (Mr J M Pitts) 2-acre garden reaching maturity following redesigning and replanting; interesting plants, mixed borders. Home to part of the NCCPG Digitalis collection

Woodlands (Mr & Mrs M J O Morley) A medium-sized English country garden with colour schemes surrounding C16 farmhouse. Recent tree planting on large scale

Ryton Organic Gardens ♿✂❀ 5m SE of Coventry (off A45 to Wolston). 8-acre site demonstrating organic gardening methods as seen on Channel 4's 'All Muck and Magic' series: composting display, herb, rose and bee garden; shrub borders; vegetable plots and fruit; garden for the blind and partially sighted; conservation area with pond and wild flowers meadow. Shop; children's play area; award winning restaurant serving organically grown food. Guide dogs allowed. TEAS. *Adm £2.50 Concessions £1.75, Chd £1.25 Family £6.50. Open daily except Christmas period. For NGS Suns April 30, Sept 24 (10-5.30)*

¶St Dennis Farm ✂❀ (Mr & Mrs Motion) Shipston on Stour. 3m NE of Shipston on Stour. Take the 4035 (Banbury) 100yds after Riverbridge L to Tysoe then 1st L and 1st R to Tysoe, St Dennis Farm is 1½m on R. A charming ½-acre farmhouse garden set in the heart of unspoilt Warwickshire countryside; herbaceous and flower borders, rose beds, many old roses. Adjoining cottage garden. TEAS. *Adm £1.50 Chd free. Sun June 25 (2-6)*

Sherbourne Manor ✂❀ (Mr & Mrs M Perry) 2m S of Warwick just off A429 Barford Rd. Large garden contains herbaceous borders; lawns; stream; small lake and large variety of established trees and many new trees; new parterre garden. Paddocks with rare breed sheep. TEAS in aid of All Saints Church, Sherbourne. *Adm £3 OAPs £1 Chd up to 12 free. Suns March 26, Sept 3 (2-5.30)*

Sherbourne Park ♿ (The Hon Lady Smith-Ryland) 3m S of Warwick off A429; ½m N of Barford. Medium-sized garden; lawns, shrubs, borders, roses, lilies; lake; temple; church by Gilbert Scott 1863 adjacent to early Georgian House (not open) 1730. Featured in 'New Englishwoman's Garden' (R Verey) and 'English Gardens' (P Coats). Featured in 1991 & 1992 Gardeners Royal Benevolent Society Calendar. Lunches, teas or coffee for private tours by arrangement. Free car park. *Adm £3 OAPs and Chd (13-16) £2, under 12 free (Share to All Saints Church, Sherbourne®). Open for private tours and coaches by appt only, please* **Tel 01926 624255 624506**

Shrewley Pools Farm ✂ (Mrs C W Dodd) Haseley. 4m NW of Warwick through Hatton. At roundabout turn L along Five Ways Rd, after approx ¾m farm entrance on L opp Audholi poultry farm. ¾m off A4177 from Falcon Inn (Warwick). 1-acre garden, herbaceous borders, rhododendrons, roses, irises, peonies etc. Many interesting shrubs and trees, terrace and garden pool. Farm animals and C17 farmhouse and barn. TEA. *Adm £1.50 Chd 30p. Sun June 11 (2-6). Private visits welcome for 4 and over, please* **Tel 01926 484315**

¶Silver Trees Farm Gardens ♿✂❀ Balsall Common. 5m S of M42/M6 intersection, 6m W of Coventry, 10m N of Warwick, junction of A452 and B4101. From traffic lights of this intersection go W along B4101 towards Knowle for ¾m. Map available for each garden. TEAS at **Silver Trees Farm**. *Combined adm £2 Chd 50p (Share to Helen Lay House, Multiple Sclerosis®). Mon May 29 (2-6). Private visits welcome May & June, please* **Tel 01676 533143**

¶The Bungalow (Mr & Mrs G Johnson) Table Oak Lane, Fen End. 2 acres mixed borders, pond and lawn. New areas developing

¶Meriglen (Mr & Mrs J Webb) Windmill Lane, Balsall Common. ¾-acre mixed borders, small woodland

¶Silver Trees Farm (Mr & Mrs B Hitchens) Balsall Street. 1½ acres, mixed borders, orchard, bog area, woodland garden

¶140 Station Road (Mr & Mrs J Matts) Balsall Common. Small village garden with range of perennials, shrubs and climbing plants

¶White Cottage Farm (Mr & Mrs J Edwards) Holly Lane. 1½ acres cottage garden, mixed borders, pond, sunken garden

¶32 Wootton Green Lane (Dr & Mrs Leeming) Balsall Common. Lawns, water features, greenhouses

26 Sunnybank Road ✂❀ (Chris & Margaret Jones) Wylde Green. ¾m S of Sutton Coldfield. Turn off A5127 towards Wylde Green Station then; 2nd L. Medium-sized town garden on sandy soil, redesigned in mid-80's by present owners as a series of 'rooms'. Yr-long interest achieved by use of bulbs, shrubs and herbaceous plants. Featured on Garden Club Aug 93 (Channel 4), Secret Gardens (BBC) Spring 95, and 'Your Garden' magazine Dec 93. TEAS in aid of Save the Children Fund. *Adm £1 OAPs 50p Chd free. Suns May 28, June 25, July 23 (2-6)*

Sutton Coldfield Gardens ✂ Teas at White Lion Inn. *Combined adm £1 Chd 50p. Sat May 20 (2-6)*

16 Hillwood Common Road (Mr & Mrs John Harrison) Four Oaks. From A5127 at Mere Green traffic island take Hill Village Rd. 2nd R into Sherifoot Lane and follow L bend. Straight on into Hillwood Common Rd. AZ ref 27.4H. A ½-acre garden with interesting trees and shrubs, shrub roses, herbaceous underplanting, borders; kitchen garden

¶125 Hill Village Road (Dr & Mrs E R S Hooper) Four Oaks. Hill Village Rd leaves the A5127 at Mere Green roundabout and re-enters the A5127 nr the TV mast. 125 is half-way along opp Dawny Drive. AZ ref 27 5G. ¾-acre hillside garden, trees, shrubs, spring flowers

¶52 Tenbury Road ♿✂ (Mrs V Grace Darby) Kings Heath. 5m S of city centre off A435 (Alcester Rd). 4¾m from junction 3 off M40. ⅛ of an acre suburban garden in cottage garden style. Informal plantings of mixed beds and borders with interesting and unusual plants, shrubs, climbers. Small vegetable and fruit area, minimum use of chemical pest control. TEAS in aid of Kimmos Drop in Centre (July 2) & Muscular Dystrophy (May 14). TEA July 5. *Adm £1.50 Chd free. Suns May 14, July 2, Wed July 5 (2-6). Private visits welcome April to July, please* **Tel 0121 444 6456**

Tysoe Manor ♿✂❀ (Mr & Mrs W A C Wield) Tysoe. 5m NE of Shipston-on-Stour. Take the 4035 to Banbury. In Brailes turn L to Tysoe. The Manor is the 1st house on the L after reaching Upper Tysoe. 4-acre garden, large lawns with stone walls, herbaceous and flower borders; rose beds and mature ornamental and fruit trees. TEAS in aid of Tysoe Church. *Adm £1.50 Chd free. Sun Sept 10 (2-6)*

Regular Openers. See head of county section.

Upton House ✲❀ (The National Trust) 7m NW of Banbury on A422; 2m S of Edgehill. Terraced garden, rockeries, herbaceous borders, roses, water gardens, lawns. House contains a connoisseur's collection of porcelain, tapestries and paintings. Partially suitable for wheelchairs. Coaches by appt. TEAS. *Adm garden only £2.30 Chd £1.15.* ▲*For NGS Sun July 9 (2-6 last adm 5.30)*

8 Vicarage Rd ♿✲ (Charles & Tessa King-Farlow) Edgbaston, 1½m W of City Centre off A456 (Hagley Rd). ¾-acre retaining in part its Victorian layout but informally planted with mixed borders of interesting and unusual plants; shrub rose border; walled potager and conservatory. *Adm £1 Chd free. Private visits very welcome, please* **Tel 0121 455 0902**

Warmington Village Gardens ♿✲❀ 5m NW of Banbury on B4100. TEAS at **The Glebe House**. *Combined adm £1.50 Chd free (Share to Warmington PCC Restoration Fund®). Sun July 16 (2-6) Car park; coaches welcome, please* **Tel 01295 690 318**

Berka (Mr & Mrs B J Castle) Chapel Street
¶3 Court Close (Mr & Mrs C J Crocker)
The Glebe House (Mr & Mrs G Thornton) Village Road
Holly Cottage (Dr & Mrs T W Martin) The Green
Mews Cottage (Mr & Mrs E J Squire) The Green
Rotherwood (Miss M R Goodison) Soot Lane
Sunnyside (Yvonne Farley & Michael Borlenghi)
Underedge (Mr & Mrs J Dixon) 1 Church Hill

¶Warwickshire Constabulary, Police HQ ❀ Leek Wootton. Mid-way between Warwick and Kenilworth, 1m N of the Gaveston Island, on the Kenilworth Rd, off the A46 Warwick to Coventry by-pass. From Warwick, turn L after Anchor Public House in centre of village, signposted Police Headquarters. Approx 6 acres of mixed garden, large and small shrubs, herbaceous borders, Chinese garden, walk around lakes. *Adm £1.50 Chd free (Share to Warwickshire Constabulary Gala Day Charity©). Sun May 28 (2-6)*

50 Wellington Rd ♿✲❀ (Mrs Anne Lee) Edgbaston. 200yds NE of Edgbaston Old Church on the corner of Ampton Rd & Wellington Rd. 1-acre walled town garden, partly replanted in 1985. Terrace, paving, brick paths & some architectural features. 100-yr-old rhododendrons & large trees with newly opened woodland walk. Two long mixed borders round large lawn, fountain. TEAS. *Adm £1.50 Chd free. Sun June 18 (2-6). Private visits also welcome April to July, please* **Tel 0121 440 1744**

Whichford & Ascott Gardens ✲❀ 6m SE of Shipston-on-Stour. Turn E off A3400 at Long Compton for Whichford. Cream TEAS at **Whichford House**. *Combined adm £2 Chd free (Share to Alzheimers Disease Society®). Sun June 18 (2-6)*

Brook Hollow (Mr & Mrs J A Round) Garden on a bank, stream and water garden
Combe House (Mr & Mrs D C Seel) Hidden garden surrounding house; mature fine trees
The Old House (Mr & Mrs T A Maher) Undulating garden. Natural ponds and wildflower meadow
Rightons Cottage (Col & Mrs C R Bourne) Medium-sized garden planted for quiet enjoyment with minimal upkeep in retirement
Roman Row (Mr & Mrs S C Langdon) Beautiful well kept cottage garden
Stone Walls (Mrs J Scott-Cockburn) Walled garden; paved garden in foundations of old stable
Whichford House (Mr & Mrs J W Oakes) Large undulating garden with extensive views. Mainly shrubs and trees
The Whichford Pottery (Mr & Mrs J B M Keeling) Secret walled garden, unusual plants, large vegetable garden and rambling cottage garden. Adjoining pottery

Woodpeckers ♿✲❀ (Dr & Mrs A J Cox) The Bank, Marlcliff, nr Bidford-on-Avon 7m SW of Stratford-on-Avon. Off the B4085 Between Bidford-on-Avon and Cleeve Prior. 2½-acre plantsman's garden designed and maintained by owners; colour-schemed herbaceous and mixed borders, old roses, meadow garden, alpines in troughs and gravel, pool, knot garden, ornamental kitchen garden. Featured on BBC2 'Gardener's World' and in 'Practical Gardening'. *Adm £1.50 Chd free. Tues March 28, April 18, May 9, 30 June 13, July 25, Aug 22 (2-5). Also private visits welcome all year, best months April to June & Sept, please* **Tel 01789 773416**

Wroxall Abbey School ♿✲ (Mrs J M Gowen, Headmistress) Wroxall 6m NW of Warwick. Nr Fiveways junction on A4141. 27 acres; spring flowers, shrubs, rhododendrons, small enclosed flower garden. 'Nature trail' incl comments on plants, flowers, etc. Work in progress on surveying and re-instatement of historical pleasure grounds, by Warwickshire Garden Trust. Evensong in Chapel 5pm. TEA. *Adm £1.50 Chd 50p (Share to St Leonard's Church, Wroxall®). Suns May 7, 21 (2-5)*

Open by appointment Please do not be put off by this notation. The owner may consider his garden too small to accommodate the numbers associated with a normal opening or, more often, there may be a lack of car parking space. It is often more rewarding than a normal opening as the owner will usually give a guided tour of the garden. The minimum size of party is either stated in the garden description or can be found out when making the appointment; usually 2. If the garden has normal open days, the entrance fee is as stated in the garden description.

Wiltshire

Hon County Organiser: Brigadier Arthur Gooch, Manor Farmhouse, Chitterne, Warminster BA12 OLG
Assistant Hon County Organisers: Mrs David Armytage, Sharcott Manor, Pewsey
Mrs Anthony Heywood, Monkton House, Monkton Deverell, Warminster
Mrs Colin Shand, Ashton House, Worton, Devizes
(& PR) Mrs John Nicolls, Barn Flat, Ark Farm, Old Wardour, Tisbury, Salisbury SP3 6RP
Tel 01747 870162

DATES OF OPENING

By appointment

For telephone numbers and other details see garden descriptions. Private visits welcomed

Ashtree Cottage, Kilmington Common
11 Beechfield, Newton Tony
Bolehyde Manor, nr Chippenham
Bryher, Bromham
Crudwell Court Hotel, nr Malmesbury
Home Covert, Devizes
Lower Farm House, Milton Lilbourne
Luckington Court, nr Chippenham
7 Norton Bavant, nr Warminster
The Old Rectory, Stockton
Ridleys Cheer, Mountain Bower
Sharcott Manor, nr Pewsey
Thompson's Hill, Sherston
Waterdale House, East Knoyle

Parties only

Green Hall, East Grafton
Hillbarn House, Great Bedwyn
Hyde's House, Dinton, nr Salisbury
Landford Lodge, nr Salisbury
Lower Burytown, nr Blunsdon
The Old Bakery, Milton Lilbourne
Spye Park, nr Chippenham

Regular openings

For details see garden descriptions

Bowood Rhododendron Walks & Bowood Gardens, nr Chippenham. See text
Broadleas, nr Devizes. Every Sun, Wed & Thurs April 2 to Oct 29
The Courts, nr Bradford-on-Avon. Daily except Sat April to Oct
Hazelbury Manor, nr Box. See text
Heale Gardens & Plant Centre, Middle Woodford. Open all year
Iford Manor, nr Bradford-on-Avon. See text
Lackham Gardens, nr Chippenham. Daily April 1 to Oct 29
Long Hall Gardens & Nursery, Stockton, nr Warminster. See text
The Mead Nursery, Brokerswood. Feb 1 to Oct 29
Pound Hill House, West Kington. Tues to Sun & Bank Hols Feb to Nov
Sheldon Manor, nr Chippenham. Open Easter Sun & Mon. Every Sun, Thurs & Bank Hols to Oct 1
Stourhead Garden, Stourton, nr Mere. Daily
Stourton House, Mere. Every Sun, Wed, Thurs & Bank Hols April 2 to Nov 30

February 12 Sunday
Great Chalfield Manor, nr Melksham

February 19 Sunday
Lacock Abbey, nr Chippenham

February 26 Sunday
Lacock Abbey, nr Chippenham

March 5 Sunday
Lacock Abbey, nr Chippenham

April 2 Sunday
Corsham Court, nr Chippenham
Crudwell Court Hotel, nr Malmesbury

April 5 Wednesday
Sharcott Manor, nr Pewsey

April 9 Sunday
Broadleas, nr Devizes
Easton Grey House, nr Malmesbury
Fonthill House, nr Tisbury
Kingfisher Mill, Great Durnford
Manor House Farm, Hanging Langford

April 16 Sunday
Lower Farm House, Milton Lilbourne

April 17 Monday
Long Hall Gardens & Nursery, Stockton, nr Warminster.

April 22 Saturday
Stourton House, Mere

April 23 Sunday
Stourton House, Mere

April 26 Wednesday
Home Covert, Devizes

April 30 Sunday
Iford Manor, nr Bradford-on-Avon ‡
Inwoods, nr Bradford-on-Avon ‡
Luckington Manor, nr Malmesbury
Oare House, Pewsey ‡‡
Sharcott Manor, nr Pewsey ‡‡

May 3 Wednesday
Sharcott Manor, nr Pewsey

May 7 Sunday
Lackham Gardens, nr Chippenham
Little Durnford Manor, nr Salisbury
Ridleys Cheer, Mountain Bower
Spye Park, nr Chippenham
Waterdale House, East Knoyle

May 14 Sunday
Ashtree Cottage, Kilmington Common ‡
Hyde's House, Dinton, nr Salisbury ‡‡
Luckington Court, nr Chippenham
Old School House, Baverstock ‡‡
Sheldon Manor, nr Chippenham
Stourhead Garden, Stourton, Mere ‡

May 17 Wednesday
Bryher, Bromham
Home Covert, Devizes

May 21 Sunday
Bowden Park, Lacock, Chippenham
Conock Manor, nr Devizes
7 Norton Bavant, nr Warminster

May 24 Wednesday
Bryher, Bromham

May 28 Sunday
Landford Lodge, nr Salisbury

May 31 Wednesday
Bryher, Bromham

June 3 Saturday
Ark Farm, Old Wardour, nr Tisbury

June 4 Sunday
Ark Farm, Old Wardour, nr Tisbury
Bowood Rhododendron Walks, nr Chippenham
Foscote Gardens, Grittleton
Job's Mill, Crockerton, nr Warminster
Mallards, Chirton, nr Devizes

June 7 Wednesday
Bryher, Bromham

Sharcott Manor, nr Pewsey

June 10 Saturday

Mompesson House, The Close, Salisbury

June 11 Sunday

Edington & Coulston Gardens
Fonthill House, nr Tisbury
Maiden Bradley House, nr Warminster

June 14 Wednesday

Bryher, Bromham

June 18 Sunday

Ashtree Cottage, Kilmington Common
Avebury Manor, Avebury
Bolehyde Manor, nr Chippenham ‡
Chisenbury Priory, nr Upavon
Corsham Court, nr Chippenham ‡
East Kennett Gardens, nr Marlborough
Goulters Mill Farm, Nettleton
Langley House, Chippenham ‡
The Old Rectory, Stockton
Pound Hill House, West Kington ‡‡
Ridleys Cheer, Mountain Bower ‡‡
Thompson's Hill, Sherston
Wedhampton Gardens, nr Devizes

June 21 Wednesday

Bryher, Bromham
Home Covert, Devizes

June 24 Saturday

Hazelbury Manor, nr Box
61 Whitegate, Castle Combe, nr Chippenham

June 25 Sunday

Beech Knoll House, Aldbourne
The Courts, nr Bradford-on-Avon
Green Hall, East Grafton
Hazelbury Manor, nr Box
Kingfisher Mill, Great Durnford
Long Hall Gardens & Nursery, Stockton, nr Warminster ‡
Lower Burytown, nr Blunsdon
Luckington Manor, nr Malmesbury ‡‡
Parks Court, Upton Scudamore ‡
Sharcott Manor, nr Pewsey
Sherston Gardens ‡‡
Sutton Veny Gardens ‡
61 Whitegate, Castle Combe, nr Chippenham

July 2 Sunday

Biddestone Manor, nr Corsham
Chisenbury Priory, nr Upavon ‡
The Grange, Winterbourne Dauntsey ‡‡
Hannington Hall, Highworth, nr Swindon
Little Durnford Manor, nr Salisbury ‡‡
Manningford Bruce Gardens ‡

July 5 Wednesday

Sharcott Manor, nr Pewsey

July 9 Sunday

Ashtree Cottage, Kilmington Common
Courtlands, nr Corsham ‡
Crudwell Court Hotel, nr Malmesbury
Lackham Gardens, nr Chippenham ‡

July 15 Saturday

Great Somerford Gardens

July 16 Sunday

Great Somerford Gardens
Waterdale House, East Knoyle
Worton Gardens, Devizes

July 23 Sunday

Home Covert, Devizes ‡
Mallards, Chirton, nr Devizes ‡

July 30 Sunday

Oare House, nr Pewsey

August 2 Wednesday

Sharcott Manor, nr Pewsey

August 6 Sunday

Heale Gardens & Plant Centre, Middle Woodford
Lower Farm House, Milton Lilbourne ‡
Luckington Manor, nr Malmesbury
The Old Bakery, Milton Lilbourne ‡

August 13 Sunday

Broadleas, nr Devizes
The Mead Nursery, Brokerswood

August 16 Wednesday

Home Covert, Devizes

August 19 Saturday

Stourton House, Mere

August 20 Sunday

Ashtree Cottage, Kilmington Common ‡
Stourton House, Mere ‡

August 27 Sunday

Hyde's House, Dinton, nr Salisbury

August 28 Monday

11 Beechfield, Newton Tony

September 3 Sunday

The Courts, nr Bradford-on-Avon
Pound Hill House, West Kington

September 6 Wednesday

Sharcott Manor, nr Pewsey

September 17 Sunday

Ashtree Cottage, Kilmington Common
Avebury Manor, Avebury
Hillbarn House, Great Bedwyn

October 1 Sunday

Lackham Gardens, nr Chippenham

October 4 Wednesday

Sharcott Manor, nr Pewsey

October 8 Sunday

Great Chalfield Manor, nr Melksham

November 19 Sunday

Heale Gardens & Plant Centre, Middle Woodford

Dates for 1996

February 18 Sunday

Lacock Abbey, nr Chippenham

February 25 Sunday

Lacock Abbey, nr Chippenham

March 3 Sunday

Lacock Abbey, nr Chippenham

DESCRIPTIONS OF GARDENS

Ark Farm ✇❀ (Mr & Mrs Edmund Neville-Rolfe) Tisbury. 9m from Shaftesbury. 2½m from Tisbury. From Tisbury follow English Heritage signs to Old Wardour Castle. Private rd from Castle car park to Ark Farm (400yds). 1¼ acres incl water and woodland gardens, as featured in Country Life and the Daily Telegraph. TEAS. *Adm £2 Chd free (Share to the Wiltshire branch of the Mental Health Foundation®). Sat, Sun June 3, 4 (2-6)*

Ashtree Cottage ✇❀ (Mr & Mrs L J Lauderdale) Kilmington Common. 3½m NW of Mere (A303) on B3092, ½m N of Stourhead Garden. Turn W at sign for Alfred's Tower and follow NGS signs. 1-acre garden created since 1984 by owners, a series of gardens surrounding thatched cottage, with densely planted mixed borders of shrubs, roses and perennials and unusual plants, many of which are available for sale in the garden nursery. TEAS. *Adm £2 Chd 50p (Share to St Margaret's Somerset Hospice & Woodgreen Animal Shelter®). Suns May 14, June 18, July 9, Aug 20, Sept 17 (2-6). Also private visits welcome daily, please* **Tel 01985 844740**

Avebury Manor Garden ✇❀ (The National Trust) Avebury. On A361 9m N of Devizes 2m from Beckhampton roundabout on A4. Entrance to Manor and car park N of the village. This 4-acre garden is undergoing restoration to planting, hedges and walls. Ancient walled garden on site of former priory, divided by stone walls and topiary hedges, incl a rose garden; topiary garden, herb garden. Italian walk and half moon garden. Late mediaeval manor house under restoration (not open). *Adm £2.20 Chd £1.40.* ▲*Suns June 18, Sept 17 (11-5)*

Beech Knoll House ✿❀ (Mr & Mrs Richard Price) Aldbourne. 8m NW of Hungerford, 8m NE of Marlborough M4 exit 14 via Baydon or Hungerford. Park in centre of village by pond and 'Crown' public house. Walk to Church then up lane to R of Church around 'Crooked Corner'. Beech Knoll is on the R. Signs from Church. 2-acre garden has an enclosed London style entrance garden. Large terraced lawns with huge purple beech trees. East facing planting examples, tree peonies and roses. Restoration work recently undertaken on terrace with addition of small pool and decorative fountain; walled Victorian garden with a large fruit cage, beehives and swimming pool (not open). Beautiful plants tumbling over sarsen stone walls near the small conservatory; clipped hedges and wide variety of recently planted shrubs. One page guide available at gate. TEAS in aid of Home Farm Trust. *Adm £1.50 Chd 25p. Sun June 25 (2-6)*

11 Beechfield ✿❀ (J Hindle) Newton Tony. 2m S of A303, off A338; turn SE off A338 into the village to 2nd thatched cottage on R. Limited parking on L further down Beechfield or on Memorial Hall playing field in village. Professionally designed village garden, approx 75′ × 50′ encompassing paved terrace carpeted with alpines, small wildlife pond, clematis bower and rose tunnel, knot garden, herb and vegetable beds, cordon apples and mixed borders of shrubs, old roses and herbaceous perennials. An illusion of size is created by adept use of screening, changes of direction and mood, carefully placed seating and dense planting. Open to coincide with village fête. TEAS in the marquee on the Memorial Hall playing field. *Adm £1 Chd free. Mon Aug 28 (2-6). Private visits welcome, please* **Tel 01980 629323**

Biddestone Manor ♿✿❀ (Mr N Astrup) Biddestone, nr Corsham, 5m W of Chippenham, 3m N of Corsham. On A4 between Chippenham and Corsham turn N; or from A420, 5m W of Chippenham, turn S. Large garden with extensive lawns; small lake; topiary; swimming pool set in attractive rose garden; newly planted orchard and herb garden. Fine C17 manor house (not open) with interesting older outbuildings. TEAS. *Adm £1.20 Chd 60p. Sun July 2 (2-5.30)*

Bolehyde Manor ♿✿❀ (Earl and Countess Cairns) Allington. 1½m W of Chippenham on Bristol Rd (A420). Turn N at Allington crossroads. ½m on R. Parking in field. A series of gardens around C16 Manor House; enclosed by walls and Topiary, densely planted with many interesting shrubs and climbers, mixed rose and herbaceous beds; inner courtyard with troughs full of tender plants; wild flower orchard, vegetable, fruit garden and greenhouse yard. TEAS. *Adm £1.50 Chd 50p (Share to Kingston St Michael Church©). Sun June 18 (2.30-6). Also private visits welcome, please* **Tel 01249 652105**

Bowden Park ♿✿❀ (Bowden Park Estate) Lacock, 5m S of Chippenham. From Lacock village take rd to Bowden Hill, Sandy Lane and Devizes; proceed up hill; (entrance and parking top lodge opp Spye Arch). 12 acres incl horticultural areas, shrubberies; borders; fountains; follies; woodland and water gardens. *Adm £1.50 Chd 50p. Sun May 21 (2-6)*

Bowood Rhododendron Walks ✿❀ (The Earl of Shelburne) nr Chippenham. Entrance off A342 between Sandy Lane and Derry Hill villages. A breath-taking display of rhododendrons and azaleas from the minute detail of the individual flower to the grand sweep of colour formed by hundreds of shrubs, surrounded by a carpet of bluebells. *Open May & June. For NGS Adm £2.50 Sun June 4 (11-6).* **Tel 01249 812102**. *Also open* **Bowood House & Gardens** *Luncheon, TEAS. Garden centre. Adm £4.70 OAP £4 Chd £2.50. April 1 to Oct 29 (11-6)*

Broadleas ❀ (Lady Anne Cowdray) S of Devizes on A360. Bus: Devizes-Salisbury, alight Potterne Rd. Medium-sized garden; attractive dell planted with unusual trees, shrubs, azaleas and rhododendrons; many rare plants in secret and winter gardens. Home-made TEAS (on Sundays). *Adm £2 Chd £1. April 2 to Oct 29 every Sun, Wed & Thurs. For NGS (Share to Animal Health Trust®). Suns April 9, Aug 13 (2-6)*

Bryher ♿✿❀ (Mr & Mrs Richard Packham) Yard Lane Bromham. 4m N of Devizes on A342 to Chippenham turn R into Yard Lane at Xrds. A compact level garden, approx ⅔ acre created around a bungalow home. Borders planted mainly for foliage effect using a wide range of red, gold, silver and variegated plants, with many unusual varieties; short wildlife walk; display greenhouses with small nursery beds. *Adm £1 Chd free. Weds May 17, 24, 31; June 7, 14, 21 (11-5). Also private visits welcome, please* **Tel 01380 850455**

Chisenbury Priory ♿✿ (Mr & Mrs John Manser) 6m SW of Pewsey, turn E from A345 at Enford then N to E Chisenbury, main gates 1m on R. Mediaeval Priory with Queen Anne face (not open) in middle of 5-acre garden on chalk; walled gardens; mature trees; shrubs; lawns; water; fine herbaceous borders; many unusual plants. TEAS. *Adm £2 Chd free. Suns June 18, July 2 (2-6)*

Conock Manor ♿✿❀ (Mr & Mrs Bonar Sykes) 5m SE of Devizes off A342. Mixed borders, flowering shrubs; extensive replanting including new arboretum and woodland walk; collection of eucalyptus trees. C18 house in Bath stone (not shown). TEA. *Adm £1.20 Chd free under 16 (Share to Chirton Church, Chirton, nr Devizes®). Sun May 21 (2-6)*

Corsham Court ♿❀ (James Methuen Campbell Esq) 4m W of Chippenham. S of A4. Park and gardens laid out by Capability Brown and Repton. Large lawns with fine specimens of ornamental trees; rose garden; lily pond with Indian bean trees; spring bulbs; young arboretum; C18 bath house; Elizabethan mansion with alterations. *Adm gardens £2 OAP £1.50 Chd £1 (Share to RNLI®). ▲For NGS Suns April 2, June 18 (2-6)*

Courtlands ♿✿❀ (Mr Julius Silman) 4m S of Chippenham on Corsham-Lacock Road, 2m E of Corsham. 4-acre formal garden divided by splendid yew hedges into three connecting lawned gardens. Features include 2 gazebos; sunken lily pond with fountain, large fish pond with waterfall; walled kitchen garden; greenhouse with vines. Use of heated swimming pool available £1. TEAS. *Adm £1.50 Chd under 10 free. Sun July 9 (2-6)*

The Courts ♿✂ (National Trust) Holt, 2m E of Bradford-on-Avon, S of B3107 to Melksham. In Holt follow National Trust signs, park at Village Hall. 3½-acres different formal gardens divided by yew hedges, raised terraces and shrubberies. Features incl conservatory, lily pond, herbaceous borders, pleached limes with interesting stone pillars, venetian gates and stone ornaments. 3½ acres wildflower and arboretum; many fine trees. NT C15 House (not shown) open every day except Sat April to Oct. Plant sales in aid of Bath Cancer Research Unit in Sept only. Teas (on NGS days only) in church hall in aid of Church Hall Fund. *Adm £2.80 Chd £1.40. For NGS Suns June 25, Sept 3 (2-5)*

Crudwell Court Hotel ♿❀ (Nicholas Bristow Esq) Crudwell. On the A429 between Cirencester and Malmesbury. E of the rd, beside the church. 2½-acre garden surrounding C17 Rectory (now a hotel). Fine specimen 'rivers' beech, blue atlas cedar, magnolias, C12 dovecote surrounded by ancient yew hedges; Victorian sunken pond with wrought iron surround and lavender hedging. Rose garden and spring colour border outside conservatory. Herbaceous; shrub and herb borders; climbing roses; espaliered fruit trees and an Edwardian wooded walk; also newly planted pastel coloured herbaceous border in rose garden. Swimming pool available in July. Coffee, lunch TEAS. *Adm £1 Chd free. Suns April 2, July 9 (11-5). Private visits welcome, please* **Tel 01666 577194**

¶East Kennett Gardens ♿✂❀ 5m W of Marlborough, ½m S of A4. TEAS at Manor Farmhouse in aid of Village Church. *Combined adm £1.50 Chd free. Sun June 18 (2-6)*

East Kennett Manor (Dr & Mrs C B Cameron) 3-acre sarsen stone walled garden, featuring long herbaceous border: shrubs; herbs and several small gardens divided by hedges. C18 house (not open) with stable block and dovecote

¶Manor Farmhouse (Mr & Mrs John Evans) ¾-acre garden opp church. Borders, vegetable and herb garden all made by present owners in 8 yrs. Courtyard with old farm buildings

Easton Grey House ♿✂❀ (Mr & Mrs Sheldon Gordon) 3½m W of Malmesbury on B4040. Intensively cultivated 9-acre garden of beautiful C18 house. Also contains Easton Grey Church with its interesting Norman tower, font etc. Superb situation overlooking R Avon and surrounding countryside; lime-tolerant shrubs; tremendous display of spring bulbs, clematis, many roses; large walled garden containing traditional kitchen garden, large greenhouses, rose garden and borders. Home-made TEAS in garden; produce, cake, and other stalls (in aid of Easton Grey Parish Church). *Adm £2 Chd free. Sun April 9 (2-6)*

Edington and Coulston Gardens 4m Westbury on B3098 halfway between Westbury and West Lavington. Follow signs and park outside The Monastery Garden or in Church car park for The Grange, and walk through churchyard and along path, and for The Old Vicarage walk up hill to B3098. TEAS at The Monastery Garden. *Combined adm £2.50 Chd free (Share to Wiltshire Garden Trust®). Sun June 11 (2-6)*

Bonshommes Cottage (Michael Jones Esq) Through Old Vicarage Garden. ¼-acre garden, formerly part of the Vicarage garden with mixed herbaceous, roses, shrubs. An interesting feature is the control of Japanese knotweed, which divides the garden into different areas

Font House ✂ (Mr & Mrs R S Hicks) Coulston. 1½m E of Edington on B3098 take 1st L to Coulston, 1st house on L. 1-acre garden in rural surroundings which has been restored from a wilderness over past 30yrs and is still evolving; on 2 levels with courtyard, herbaceous borders, shrubs, herb and small specimen trees

The Grange ✂ (Col J S Douglas) Mature ¾-acre garden with interesting plants, shrubs and trees

The Monastery Garden ♿ (The Hon Mrs Douglas Vivian) 2½-acre garden with many varieties of spring bulbs; orchard and shrub roses; mediaeval walls of national importance

The Old Vicarage ♿✂❀ (J N d'Arcy Esq) A 2-acre garden on greensand situated on hillside with fine views; intensively planted with herbaceous borders; shrubs; a small arboretum with a growing range of trees; woodland plants; bulbs; lilies and recently introduced species from abroad. NCCPG National Collection of Evening primroses, over 20 species

Fonthill House (The Lord Margadale) 3m N of Tisbury. W of Salisbury via B3089 in Fonthill Bishop. Large woodland garden; daffodils, rhododendrons, azaleas, shrubs, bulbs; magnificent views; formal garden, limited for wheelchairs. TEAS. *Adm £1.50 Chd 30p (Share to NSPCC® June 11 only). Suns April 9, June 11 (2-6)*

Foscote Gardens ✂❀ Grittleton, 5m NW of Chippenham. A420 Chippenham-Bristol; after 2m turn R on B4039 to Yatton Keynell, fork R for Grittleton; in village for 2m, just over motorway turn R at Xrds; house on right. Home-made TEAS. *Combined adm £1.50 Chd 30p. Sun June 4 (2-6)*

Foscote Stables ✂❀ (Mr & Mrs Barry Ratcliffe) 2½-acres; many clematis; shrub roses; unusual shrubs, trees; small collection ornamental ducks

Foscote Stables Cottage ❀ (Mrs Beresford Worswick) This adjoining garden has been re-designed and replanted but still retains its cottage character. Unusual and some rare plants for sale

Goulters Mill Farm ♿❀ (Mr & Mrs Michael Harvey) Nettleton. On B4039 5m W of Chippenham; 2m NW of Castle Combe, through the Gib. Park at top of 300 metre drive and walk down to garden. Approx ¾-acre cottage garden; mixed perennials, eremurus, old-fashioned roses; water garden and woodland walk. Home-made cream TEAS and plant stall in aid of Russian Immigrants to Israel. *Adm £1 Chd 20p. Sun June 18 (2-6)*

¶The Grange ♿✂❀ (Mr & Mrs Rebdi) Winterbourne Dauntsey. Winterbourne Dauntsey is 4m NNE of Salisbury on the A338. Spacious 6-acre garden, still being developed, with R Bourne running through. Immaculate lawns, clipped box, borders. Laburnum, rose and clematis arched walk; lily pond; vegetable and herb garden. Wild natural area with peacocks. Restored C17 thatched barn (open). TEAS in aid of Winterbourne Glebe Hall. *Adm £2.50 Chd under 16 free. Sun July 2 (2-6)*

Great Chalfield Manor ✲ (The National Trust; Mr & Mrs Robert Floyd) 4m from Melksham. Take B3107 from Melksham then 1st R to Broughton Gifford signed Atworth, turn L for 1m to Manor. Park on grass outside. Garden and grounds of 7 acres laid out 1905-12 by Robert Fuller and his wife; given to NT in 1943, it remains the home of his family. Garden paths, steps, dry walls relaid and rebuilt in 1985 and roses replanted; daffodils, spring flowers; topiary houses, borders, terraces, gazebo, orchard, autumn border. C15 moated manor (not open) and adjoining Church. Harvest Festival Service 6pm Oct 8. TEAS. *Adm £2 Chd free (Share to All Saints Church®). ▲For NGS Sun Oct 8 (2-6)*

¶**Great Somerford Gardens** ♿✲❀ 2m N of M4 between junctions 17 and 18; 2m S of B4042 Malmesbury-Wootton Bassett rd; 3m E of A429 Circencester-Chippenham rd. TEAS. *Combined adm £3, Chd under 12 free (Share to Malmesbury Branch National Osteoporosis Society®). Sat, Sun July 15, 16 (1.30-6)*

¶**Clematis** (Mr & Mrs Arthur Scott) A small but active, charming village garden created about 3 yrs ago. Very well-stocked herbaceous borders, shrubs, fruit trees and a pond, with a collection of about 25 clematis

¶**The Manor** (Mr & Mrs Jeremy Davies) Set in about 2 acres of the original Manor parkland with lovely mature specimen trees. During a period of about 17 yrs, the owners have created extensive herbaceous and rose beds, shrubberies and kitchen garden

¶**Old Church School** (Cdr & Mrs Peter Neate) A ¾-acre garden created over the last 2 yrs from the school playing field. It is centred around a formal yew-hedged area containing a flourishing pool, parterre and shrubs, surrounded by herbaceous, hebe and rose beds, pergolas and arches, rockery and heathers as well as a good collection of trees and shrubs

¶**The Old Maltings** (Mr & Mrs Peter Prophet) The front garden has been recently designed with extensive and interesting herbaceous and shrub borders. Behind the house there is a walk down to and across the R Avon into a conservation area with plantations of young native trees and shrubs. TEAS

¶**Somerford House** (Mr & Mrs Derek Bayliss) The owners and their family over the past 13 yrs have designed and developed a 3-acre garden, which incorporates the original orchard and features roses, shrubs, old wisteria, perennials, rockery and pool, vegetables and soft fruit. A flower arranger's delight

¶**White Lodge** (Major & Mrs Jonathan Oliphant) Startley. A moderate-sized garden, developed gradually over the last 20 yrs and maturing very well. There are traditional herbaceous borders, interesting topiary, old-fashioned roses and planting along a S-facing wall. TEAS

¶**Green Hall** ♿✲❀ (Mr & Mrs John Inge) East Grafton. 8m S of Marlborough, 2m E of Burbage on A338 signposted Hungerford and East Grafton, 8m W of Hungerford. 2½ acres of herbaceous borders, mixed shrub beds, pond area and water garden. Small kitchen garden, dried flower business run from the garden. Plants and dried flowers for sale. TEAS in lovely old converted barn. *Adm £1.50 Chd under 16 50p (Share to St Nicholas Church, East Grafton©). Sun June 25 (2-6). Private parties welcome, please* **Tel 01672 810242**

Hannington Hall ♿ (Mrs A F Hussey-Freke) Hannington. 5m N of Swindon. 2m NW of Highworth; from B4019 Highworth-Blunsdon, at Freke Arms, turn N for Hannington. 3 acres. Interesting trees and shrubs. Walled kitchen garden. Well preserved ice house. Very interesting house built 1653. TEAS. *Adm £1.50 Chd free. Sun July 2 (2-6)*

Hazelbury Manor Gardens ♿✲❀ nr Box. 5m SW of Chippenham; 5m NE of Bath; 3m N of Bradford-on-Avon. From A4 at Box, take A365 to Melksham, L onto B3109; L again at Chapel Plaister; drive immediately on R. 8 acres of Grade II landscaped formal gardens surrounding a charming C15 fortified manor house. An impressive yew topiary and clipped beeches surround the large lawn; herbaceous and mixed borders blaze in summer; laburnums and limes form splendid walkways. Other features include rose garden, stone ring ponds, an enchanting fountain and rockery. Beyond the house is a new plantation of specimen trees. TEA by arrangement. *Adm Gardens only £2.80 OAPs £2 Chd £1. Open Bank Hols, last weekend of the month, Weds from May 27 to Sept 3 (11-5). For NGS Sats, Suns June 24, 25 (2-6).* **Tel 01225 812952**

Heale Gardens & Plant Centre ♿❀ (Mr Guy Rasch & Lady Anne Rasch) Middle Woodford, 4m N of Salisbury on Woodford Valley Rd between A360 and A345. 8 acres beside R Avon; interesting and varied collection of plants, shrubs; and roses in formal setting of clipped hedges and mellow stonework surrounding C17 manorhouse where Charles II hid after the battle of Worcester. Water garden with magnolia and acer frames, an authentic Japanese Tea House and Nikki bridge. Well stocked plant centre. Gift shop. Practical demonstrations Nov 19. Open all year. TEAS in the house on NGS Sunday afternoon Aug 6 only. Hot soup Nov 19. *Adm £2.50 Acc chd under 14 free (Share to Garden History Society®). For NGS Suns Aug 6, Nov 19 (10-5).* **Tel 01722 782504**

Hillbarn House ✲ (Mr & Mrs A J Buchanan) Great Bedwyn, SW of Hungerford. S of A4 Hungerford-Marlborough. Medium-sized garden on chalk with hornbeam tunnel, pleached limes, herb garden; some planting by Lanning Roper; a series of gardens within a garden. Swimming pool may be used (under 12) Topiary. TEA. *Adm £2 Chd 50p. Sun Sept 17 (2-6). Private visits of 10 and over welcome, please* **Tel 01672 870207**

Hodges Barn Shipton Moyne, See Gloucestershire

Home Covert ♿❀ (Mr & Mrs John F Phillips) Roundway Devizes. 1m N of Devizes on minor rd signed Roundway linking A361 to A342. 1m from each main road, house signed. An extensive garden developed since 1960 by present owners, with many unusual trees, shrubs, and hardy plants. Formal herbaceous borders, small garden of pastel colours and foliage and water gardens 80ft below with waterfall, streams and a small lake planted with bog primulas, various waterside plants and fern collection. Also many varieties hydrangeas and late-flowering clematis. Optional woodland walk, ¾m bluebells. Featured in NGS video 2. TEAS on July 23 in aid of St James Church Repair Fund. *Adm £2 Chd free (Share to Dorothy House Foundation®). Weds April 26, May 17, June 21, Aug, 16; Sun July 23 (2-6). Private visits welcome, please* **Tel 01380 723407**

Hyde's House ❀ (George Cruddas Esq) Dinton. 5m W of Wilton, off B3089, next to church. 2 acres of wild and formal garden in beautiful situation with series of hedged garden rooms and numerous shrub and herbaceous borders. Much interest in layout, old and new planting especially shrub roses. Large walled kitchen garden, herb garden and C13 dovecote (open). Charming C16/18 Grade 1 listed house (not open), with lovely courtyard; short walk to lake; TEAS in adjacent thatched 'old school room'. Opening May 14 to coincide with Horticultural Society Garden Fête. *Adm £1.75 Chd under 12 free (Share to St Mary's Church, Dinton©). Suns May 14, Aug 27 (2-5). Private visits of 20 and over welcome, please* **Tel 01722 716203**

Iford Manor (Mr & Mrs Hignett) Off A36 7 miles S of Bath – sign to Iford 1m or from Bradford-on-Avon/Trowbridge via Lower Westwood village (Brown Signs). Entrance & free parking at Iford Bridge. Very romantic Italian-style terraced garden, listed Grade 1, home of Harold Peto between 1898 and 1933. House not shown. *Adm £2 OAPs/Student/Chd 10+ £1.50. Open daily May to Sept (except Mons & Fris), April & Oct Suns only. For NGS Sun April 30 (2-5). Private visits welcome, please* **Tel 01225 863146**

Inwoods ♿✿❀ (Mr & Mrs D S Whitehead) Farleigh Wick, 3m NW of Bradford-on-Avon. From Bath via A363 towards Bradford-on-Avon; at Farleigh Wick, 100yds past Fox & Hounds, R into drive. 5 acres with lawns, borders, flowering shrubs, wild garden, bluebell wood. TEAS in aid of Romanian Orphans. *Adm £1.50 Chd 50p. Sun April 30 (2-6)*

Job's Mill ❀ (Virginia, Marchioness of Bath) Crockerton, 1½m S of Warminster. Bus: Salisbury-Bath, alight Warminster. Medium-sized garden; small terraced garden, through which R. Wylye flows; swimming pool; kitchen garden. TEAS. *Adm £1.50 Chd 50p (Share to WWF®). Sun June 4 (2-6)*

Kingfisher Mill (The Hon Aylmer Tryon) Gt Durnford. 2m Amesbury. From A345 turn W at High Post. Or 1m from Bridge Inn at Upper Woodford. Park in Village Road. Down short avenue of poplars. 3 acres very watery garden on R Avon with primulas and wild garden to encourage butterflies and show beauty of wild flowers. Good daffodils from Lionel Richardson's nursery in Waterford. Spring bulbs and variety of magnolias. In June many athletic roses up willows. Garden begun 1962 from old water meadow by enthusiastic amateur. Tea at Black Horse in village. *Adm £2 Chd free (Share to Wiltshire Wildlife Trust®). Suns April 9, June 25 (2-5.30)*

Lackham Gardens ♿❀ (Lackham College Principal Peter Morris) Lacock, 2m S of Chippenham. Signposted N of Notton on A350. Few mins S of junction 17 on M4. Station: Chippenham. Bus: Chippenham-Trowbridge, alight drive entrance, 1m. Large gardens; walled garden with greenhouses, carnations, alstroemeria, pot plants, warm greenhouse plants, giant fruited Citron tree, propagating house, fuchsias, begonias; lawn paths separating plots well laid out, labelled with great variety of interesting shrubs, usual and unusual vegetables, herbaceous plants, fruit. Modern style Bradstone paved garden and gazebo. Willow pattern bridge and pool. Sculpture exhibition in the gardens. Pleasure gardens featuring a major historical collection of roses depicting the development of the modern rose; mixed borders, herbs, shrubs, lawns; woodland walks down to river; large bird viewing hide. Raffle drawn shortly after demonstrations at 3.30pm; walled garden (May 7) Planting for summer colour. (July 9), Rose budding (propogation). (Oct 1), Hardwood cuttings (propogation). Particulars of Lackham full and part-time courses available. Museum of Agricultural Equipment, RARE breeds. Adventure playground. Coffee shop; TEAS Bookable menu etc on request within coach party organiser pack (11-4). *Adm £3 Chd £1 (Share to Horticultural Therapy of Frome, Somerset®). Open daily April 1 to Oct 29. For NGS Suns May 7, July 9, Oct 1 (2-5)*

Lacock Abbey Gardens ♿✿❀ (National Trust) Chippenham. A350 midway between Melksham-Chippenham Road. Follow National Trust signs. Use public car park just outside the Abbey. 9 acres of parkland surrounding the Abbey with a pond and exotic tree specimens. Display of early spring flowers with carpets of aconites; snowdrops; crocuses and daffodils. C13 Abbey with C18 gothic additions. (Mediaeval cloisters open on NGS days, house closed until April). Teas available in village. *Adm £1.50 Chd free. Suns Feb 19, 26, Mar 5 (2-5). 1996 Suns Feb 18, 25, Mar 3 (2-5). Parties welcome on NGS days only, please* **Tel 01249 730227**

Landford Lodge ♿❀ (Mr & Mrs Christopher Pilkington) 9m SE of Salisbury turn W off A36; garden ½m N of Landford. C18 House (not open) in lovely parkland overlooking lake; many fine trees. Special feature 3-acre wood with rhododendrons and azaleas. Herbaceous; ornamental terrace and swimming pool (open). Tree nursery. 500 varieties of trees planted in alphabetical order in walled garden. TEAS. *Adm £1.50 Chd 50p. Sun May 28 (2-5). Private parties of 30 and over welcome, please* **Tel 01794 390247**

Langley House ♿✿❀ (Mrs A L Scott-Ashe) Langley Burrell. 2m NE of Chippenham on A420; 300yds from Langley Burrell rd junction. 5-acre formal garden and parkland; magnificent old trees; mainly herbaceous with shrubs, old-fashioned roses and lily pool. Lovely old coach house and stabling. C18 Georgian Manor (not open); C12 Saxon Church with Kilvert the diarist connections (open). TEAS. *Adm £1 Chd free (Share to ARMS®). Sun June 18 (2-6)*

Little Durnford Manor ❀ (Earl & Countess of Chichester) 3m N of Salisbury, just beyond Stratford-sub-Castle. Extensive lawns with cedars; walled gardens, fruit trees, large vegetable garden; small knot and herb gardens, terraces, borders, gravel garden, water garden, lake with islands, river walks. Cottage Garden also on view. Home-made TEAS. *Adm £1.50 Chd 50p (Share to Wessex Medical School Trust®). Suns May 7, July 2 (2-6)*

By Appointment Gardens. These owners do not have a fixed opening day usually because they do not like crowds or have insufficient parking space. Owner will often give guided tour.

Long Hall Gardens and Nursery ♿✿❀ (Mr & Mrs N H Yeatman-Biggs) Stockton 7m SE of Warminster; S of A36; W of A303 Wylye interchange. Follow signs to church in Stockton. 4-acre mainly formal garden; a series of gardens within a garden; clipped yews; flowering shrubs, fine old trees; masses of spring bulbs; fine hellebore walk. C13 Hall with later additions (not open). TEAS on NGS days. *Adm £2 Chd free. 1st Sat of every month from May 6 to August 5 (2-6). Private visits welcome, please* **Tel 01985 850424** Adjacent nursery specialising in chalk tolerant plants, all organically grown, many uncommon varieties and new introductions. *Wed to Sun March 22 to Oct 1 (9.30-6) For NGS Mon April 17, Sun June 25 (2-6)*

Lower Burytown ♿✿❀ (Capt Francis Burne) Nr Blunsdon ¾m off B4019 (between Blunsdon and Highworth). 1¼m from A419; 8m from M4 exit 15. Approached by private drive. A 3-acre garden which has been entirely made in last 4 yrs. Herbaceous borders, shrubs and a water garden. TEA. *Adm £1 Chd 50p (Share to St Leonards, Stanton Fitzwarren Parish Church®). Sun June 25 (2-6). Private parties of 10 and over welcome, please* **Tel 01793 796696**

Lower Farm House ♿✿❀ (Mrs John Agate) Milton Lilbourne. E of Pewsey on B3087. Turn down village street by garage at Xrds. Aug only, car park on L opp Manor House. Lower Farm House down village street on L. An enlarged and developing 5-acre landscaped garden designed by Tim Rees and planted over the last 6 yrs with recent new planting. The garden faces S with views to the N edge of Salisbury Plain over 2 ponds with a connecting stream. Winter garden; extensive spring bulbs; water garden; shrubs and herbaceous borders; extensive lawns; young trees chosen for their bark; mature trees; gazebo; kitchen garden. Conservatory; exhibition of plans and photographs showing garden development. Teas at **The Old Bakery**, Milton Lilbourne on Aug 6 only, entrance £1 Chd free. *Adm £1.50 Chd free (Share to Milton Lilbourne Parish Church®). Suns April 16, Aug 6 (2-6). Also private visits welcome March to Sept, please* **Tel 01672 62911**

Luckington Court ♿❀ (The Hon Mrs Trevor Horn) Luckington village, 10m NW of Chippenham; 6m W of Malmesbury. Turn S off B4040 Malmesbury-Bristol. Bus: Bristol-Swindon, alight Luckington. Medium-sized garden, mainly formal, well-designed, amid exquisite group of ancient buildings; fine collection of ornamental cherries; other flowering shrubs. House much altered in Queen Anne times but ancient origins evident; Queen Anne hall and drawing-room shown. TEAS in aid of Luckington Parish Church. *Collecting box. Sun May 14 (2.30-6). Private visits welcome, please* **Tel 01666 840240**

Luckington Manor ♿✿❀ (Mr & Mrs K Stanbridge) NW of Chippenham 7½m SW of Malmesbury on the B4040 Malmesbury-Bristol. 3½ acres, walled flower gardens; many more additions of unusual and special plants, shrubberies; arboretum, sunken rose garden, well garden, herbs and healing plants. Special Spring feature. Garden now organically run attracting more and more wildlife. C17 Manor House (not open) Home-made TEAS and plants in aid of Parish Church Roof Fund. *Adm £2 Senior Citizens £1 Chd free. Suns April 30, June 25 (in conjunction with Luckington Village Fête), Aug 6 (2-6)*

Maiden Bradley House ♿❀ (The Duke & Duchess of Somerset) Maiden Bradley; 7m SW of Warminster, 1m Longleat, 3m Stourhead. Large garden; lawn; trees; herbaceous borders; woodland walk & extensive views. Early C18 house (not open). Church C11 (open). TEAS. Games and Stalls. *Adm £2 Chd 50p (Share to Maiden Bradley Church®). Sun June 11 (2.30-5)*

¶Mallards ♿✿❀ (Mr & Mrs T Papé) Chirton. Chirton is 4½m SE of Devizes just N of A342. Go right through village and garden is on R. 1-acre informal garden beside the upper R Avon with mixed borders, new rose garden, woodland glade and bog garden. Also a woodland walk under development. TEAS in aid of Chirton & Marden Parish Churches. *Adm £1.50 Chd free. Suns June 4, July 23 (2-6)*

Manningford Bruce Gardens ♿❀ 2m SW of Pewsey on A345 on R after Manningford Bruce sign. From Upavon or Devizes 1m after Woodbridge Inn on L. Car park suitable for picnics. TEAS at Manor. *Combined adm £3 Chd free. Sun July 2 (2-6)*

Manningford Bruce House (Maj & Mrs Robert Ferguson) 1½ acres; lawns, shrubbery and walled garden of C17/C18 Rectory (not open). Herbaceous borders with many unusual plants, shrubs and a folly. Small kitchen garden

The Manor (Visconde & Viscondessa de Pereira Machado) 4-acre garden recently refurbished, incl large walled garden with herbaceous borders and great variety of shrubs and plants; tennis court; croquet lawn; conservatory and herb garden. Swimming pool and rustic arbour

Manor House Farm ♿✿ (Miss Anne Dixon) Hanging Langford. 9m NW of Salisbury S of A36 Salisbury-Warminster. 3m SE of A303 Wylye interchange. Follow signs from Steeple Langford. Series of walled gardens with masses of bulbs; herbaceous plants; many shrubs; old- fashioned roses; collection of clematis; paeonies and delphiniums. Ornamental pond; secret garden in walls of old shearing barn, superb walnut, C14/16 Wiltshire manor house (not open). Opening coincides with exhibition of Langford pedigree lambs and sheep ¼m down the road. Teas Hanging Langford Village Hall in aid of Village Hall Fund. *Adm £1.50 Chd free. Sun April 9 (2-6)*

The Mead Nursery ♿✿❀ (Mr & Mrs S Lewis-Dale) Brokerswood. Equidistant Frome and Westbury E of Rudge. Follow signs for Woodland Park. Halfway between Rudge and Woodland Park. 1-acre nursery with display beds. Over 750 varieties of herbaceous perennials and alpines many unusual herbaceous display beds giving ideas on colour and design. Raised beds with planted tufa and sink garden for alpines. Newly planted bog garden. Tufa rock and hypertufa sinks available. TEAS on NGS day only. *Adm £1 Chd 50p to incl teas. Nursery open Feb 1 to Oct 29 Wed to Sat (9-5), Sun (12-5). For NGS Sun Aug 13 (12-5)*

Regular Openers. Too many days to include in diary. Usually there is a wide range of plants giving year-round interest. See head of county section for the name and garden description for times etc.

Mompesson House ♿✂❀ (The National Trust) The Close. Enter Salisbury Cathedral Close via High St Gate and Mompesson House is on the R. The appeal of this comparatively small but attractive garden is the lovely setting in Salisbury Cathedral Close and with a well-known Queen Anne House. Planting as for an old English garden with raised rose and herbaceous beds around the lawn. Climbers on pergola and walls; shrubs and small lavender walk. TEAS. *Adm £1 Chd free.* ▲*Sat June 10 (11-5)*

7 Norton Bavant ♿✂❀ (Mr & Mrs J M Royds) nr Warminster. 2m E of Warminster on A36 turn S to Sutton Veny at Heytesbury roundabout, then R to Norton Bavant. Turn R in village 1st house on R after tall conifer hedge. Alpine plant collector's garden with numerous varieties (many rare). Alpine house, many troughs, borders, dwarf conifers and specialised collection of daphnes. Members of AGS especially welcome. TEAS in aid of Norton Bavant Church. *Adm £1 Chd free. Sun May 21 (2-6). Private parties also welcome April to July, please* **Tel 01985 840491**

Oare House ♿ (Henry Keswick Esq) 2m N of Pewsey on Marlborough Rd (A345). Fine house (not open) in large garden with fine trees, hedges, spring flowers, woodlands; extensive lawns and kitchen garden. TEA. *Adm £1 Chd 20p (Share to The Order of St John®). Suns April 30, July 30 (2-6)*

The Old Bakery ♿✂❀ (Joyce, Lady Crossley) Milton Lilbourne E of Pewsey on B3087. Turn down village street by garage at X-rds. The Old Bakery is opp churchyard. Fairly intensive 1-acre garden. Mixed shrub and herbaceous plantings. 3 small glasshouses; small rock garden; some rare plants. Home-made TEAS. *Adm £1 Chd free. Sun Aug 6 (2-6). Private parties welcome, please* **Tel 01672 62716**

The Old Rectory ♿✂❀ (Mr & Mrs David Harrison) Stockton. 7m SE of Warminster, S of A36 W of A303 Wylye interchange. The Old Rectory is just beyond the church. The 2-acre garden surrounds an attractive C18 house, with lawns and some fine old trees incl a cedar and a magnificent beech, in the front. To the S it splits into several smaller gardens; an entirely walled herb garden with a variety of herbs, leavened with climbers and some fine roses and vines; and the orchard, dominated by a stunning walnut tree, leads to 3 separate smaller walled gardens with a great variety of plants incl roses and peonies. TEAS. *Adm £1.50 Chd free. Sun June 18 (2-6). Private visits welcome, please* **Tel 01985 850607**

¶Old School House ♿❀ (Mr & Mrs Malcolm Lyell) Baverstock. 1m E of Dinton turn N off B3089 for Baverstock. Garden adjoins church. A 1-acre garden created from a meadow since 1989. Ponds and rock garden. Many unusual trees and shrubs incl 13 varieties of magnolias incl a yellow one which will hopefully be in flower. *Adm £1.50 Chd free (Share to Baverstock Church©). Sun May 14 (2-6)*

Parks Court ✂❀ (Michael Upsall Esq) Upton Scudamore. 2m N of Warminster, approach from Warminster bypass or from A36 taking Upton Scudamore signs. Parks Court is 350yds E of church. A 1-acre walled chalk garden surrounding house dating from C14. The garden is enclosed with hedges forming a series of compartments and areas. TEAS and plants in aid of St Mary's Church. *Adm £1.50 Chd free. Sun June 25 (2-6)*

Pound Hill House ♿✂❀ (Mr & Mrs P Stockitt) West Kington. 8m NNW of Chippenham, 2m NE of Marshfield exit 18 on M4 take A420 Chippenham-Bristol road N signed West Kington. At village take No Through Road at Xrds. Around C15 Cotswold Stone House 2-acre garden in charming setting. The garden is made up of small gardens, an old-fashioned rose garden with clipped box, a small Victorian vegetable garden, pergola with wisteria, roses, clematis; a grass walk with large shrub roses, herbaceous borders backed by clipped yew hedges, shade and water garden. Courtyard garden with clipped yews and box, paved area with interesting plants, raised alpine beds. Wide selection of imaginatively planted pots and containers. Very extensive retail plant area with plants drawn from adjacent nursery with 2000 varieties. TEAS in aid of Orchard Vale Trust, June 18. *Open Tues to Sun and bank Hols Feb to Nov. Adm £1.70 Chd £1.10 (Share to West Kington Church®, Sept 3). Suns June 18, Sept 3 (2-6)*

Ridleys Cheer ♿✂❀ (Mr & Mrs A J Young) Mountain Bower, N Wraxall. 8m NW of Chippenham. At 'The Shoe' on A420 8m W of Chippenham turn N then take 2nd L and 1st R. 1½-acre informal garden containing interesting and unusual trees and shrubs; incl acers, rhododendrons, magnolias, salix and zelkova. Some 75 different shrub rose varieties incl hybrid musks, albas and species roses; planted progressively over past 20 yrs; also 2 acres woodland planted 1989, now with more than 20 different oaks suitable for limestone soils. Cream TEAS in aid of N Wraxall Church and Dorothy House Foundation. *Adm £1 Chd 50p. Suns May 7, June 18 (2-6). Private visits welcome, please* **Tel 01225 891204**

Sharcott Manor ♿✂❀ (Capt & Mrs David Armytage) 1m SW of Pewsey via A345. 5 acre garden with water planted for yr-round interest. Many young trees, bulbs, climbers & densely planted mixed borders of shrubs, roses, perennials and unusual plants, some of which are for sale in the small garden nursery. TEAS in aid of IFAW and Wiltshire Air Ambulance appeal. *Adm £2 Chd free. First Weds in every month from April to Oct (11-5) Suns April 30, June 25 (2-6) all for NGS. Also private visits welcome, please* **Tel 01672 63485**

Sheldon Manor ♿ (A Gibbs Esq) 1½m W of Chippenham turn S off A420 at Allington Xrds. Eastbound traffic signed also from A4. Formal garden around C13 house (700-yrs-old); collection of old-fashioned roses in profusion; very old yew trees; many rare, interesting trees and shrubs. Maze of edible plants (in late summer). Home-made BUFFET LUNCHES (licensed) and cream TEAS. *Adm house & garden £3.50 OAPs £3 Chd 11-16 £1. Garden only £2, OAPs £1.75. Easter Sunday & Mon then every Sun, Thur & Bank Hol to Oct. For NGS Sun May 14 (12.30-6)*

Sherston Gardens ✻❀ High Street, Sherston. 5m from Malmesbury. TEAS. *Combined adm £1.50 Chd free. Sun June 25 (2-6)*

Balcony House (Mrs E M J Byrne) Oldest house in Sherston. Small garden with old-fashioned roses, some topiary, small white garden with yew hedge separating it from coloured garden. Acid bed with azaleas, rhododendrons, acers etc. Conservatory *(Share to Multiple Sclerosis®)*

Foresters House ♿❀ (R Creed Esq) Cotswold stone walled garden. Professionally designed for enthusiastic owner, planted 1984. Many interesting plants, particularly herbaceous; pond; pergola. TEAS in aid of Sherston Parish Church

Spye Park ❀ (Mr & Mrs Simon Spicer) nr Chippenham. Take A342 Chippenham and Devizes rd, turn E at Sandy Lane opp 'The George' public house. Turn S after ½m at White Lodge. Follow signs to car park. Exit only through the village of Chittoe. 25-acre woodland walk through carpets of bluebells with paths cut through the wood. Some fine old trees mostly oak and beech, survivors of the 1989 hurricane, incl the remnants of 1000 yr old King Oak with the 900-yr-old Queen still alive. TEAS. *Adm £1 Chd free. Sun May 7 (11-5). Private parties welcome when bluebells are out, please* **Tel 01249 730247**

Stourhead Garden ♿✻ (The National Trust) Stourton, 3m NW of Mere on B3092. One of earliest and greatest landscape gardens in the world; creation of banker Henry Hoare in 1740s on his return from the Grand Tour, inspired by paintings of Claude and Poussin; planted with rare trees, rhododendrons and azaleas over last 240yrs. Open every day of year. Lunch, tea and supper Spread Eagle Inn at entrance. NT shop. Teas (Buffet service Village Hall). *Adm March to Oct £4.20 Chd £2.20 parties of 15 or over £3.60. Nov to Feb £3.20 Chd 1.50. For NGS Sun May 14 (9-7)*

Stourton House ♿✻❀ (Mrs Anthony Bullivant) Stourton. 3m NW of Mere (A303) on rd to Stourhead. Park in NT car park. 4½-acres informal gardens; much to attract plantsmen and idea seekers. Interesting bulbs, plants and shrubs, through all seasons. Speciality daffodils and hydrangeas. Well known for 'Stourton Dried Flowers' whose production interest visitors (BBC Gardeners World '92). Coffee, lunch, TEAS in Stourton House Garden. *April 2 to November 30, Sun, Wed, Thurs and Bank Hols. Adm £2 Chd 50p. Sats, Suns April 22, 23, Aug 19, 20 (11-6), all for NGS. Private visits welcome for parties of 12 and over, please* **Tel 01747 840417**

¶Sutton Veny Gardens ♿✻ 3m SE of Warminster. Turn W off A36 at Heytesbury Roundabout or E off A350 at Longbridge Deverill. TEAS. Plants at Little Newnham. *Combined adm £3 Chd free (Share to Sutton Veny Church). Sun June 25 (2-6)*

¶Glebe Farm (Lt Col & Mrs Charles Simmons) A 1½ acre informal garden around a C17 farmhouse. Fine trees planted at the beginning of the century, with shrubs, herbaceous borders and vegetable garden, all created by the owner over the last 20 yrs

¶1 Greenhill (Mr & Mrs Peter Crane) A 1 acre garden facing SE on 2 levels interconnected by a natural slope with commanding views towards hills and downland through impressive pines. Mixed borders with shrubs and interesting plants, old roses and clematis. Lower level has mixed shrubs underplanted with massed spring bulbs. Area of vegetables and various fruit plots

¶Little Newnham (Mrs Caroline Ellert) Partly walled 1-acre garden overlooked by C17/18 house (not open), referred to in 'The Buildings of England' by Nikolaus Pevsner. The garden with open views to the downs, has been recently restored and recreated. Many old roses, herbaceous borders, kitchen garden and newly planted orchard. Lawn dominated by rare weeping beech

Thompson's Hill ✻❀ (Mr & Mrs J C Cooper) Sherston. 5m Malmesbury-Tetbury. In Sherston village turn L at Church down hill, bear R up Thompson's Hill. ½-acre fully planted, interestingly designed garden made since 1980. Pretty conservatory added to house 1992. Illustrated in 'House & Garden' Magazine, new issue 'The Englishwoman's Garden', 'The English Garden' by Peter Coates and the 'Good Gardens Guide'. *Adm £1.50 Chd 50p (Share to Cancer Research®). Sun June 18 (2-6.30). Private visits welcome, please* **Tel 01666 840766**

Waterdale House ❀ (Mr & Mrs Julian Seymour) Milton, East Knoyle. North of East Knoyle on A350 turn westwards signed Milton, garden signed from village. 4-acre mature woodland garden with rhododendrons, azaleas, camellias, maples, magnolias, ornamental water and bog garden; herbaceous borders and hydrangeas. Gravelled pot garden. TEAS if fine. *Adm £1.50 Chd free. Suns May 7, July 16 (2-5). Private visits welcome April to July, lunches for parties up to 20 if required, please* **Tel 01747 830262**

Wedhampton Gardens ✻❀ 5m SE of Devizes. Off N side of A342 (nr junction with B3098). TEAS. *Combined adm £2.50 Chd free. Sun June 18 (2-5)*

Wedhampton Cottage (Hon K & Mrs Fraser) Large cottage garden, lawns, shrubs, trees, herbaceous beds around unusual "cottage ornée" (not open)

Wedhampton Manor (Mr & Mrs C V C Harris) 2½ acres informal gardens with new and developing borders amongst the long-established. Many fine old and new trees incl remarkable rare cut leaf lime. Herbaceous border, interesting variety of shrubs, herb, vegetable and fruit gardens incl medlar, quince and espaliered apple and pear. Greenhouses and fine William and Mary house (not open)

61 Whitegate ♿❀ (Mr & Mrs C J Pratt) Castle Combe. Chippenham 5m M4 exit 17 S B4039 Chippenham Burton. Large car park clearly signed at top of hill. Originally Norman, now mostly C15, one of England's prettiest villages. Small garden with yr-round planting. An example of care and initiative in achieving variety in a small garden. Teas in village. *Adm 70p Chd free. Sat, Sun June 24, 25 (2-6)*

By Appointment Gardens. See head of county section

Worton Gardens ♿✂❀ Devizes 3m. Devizes-Salisbury A360 turn W in Potterne or just N of West Lavington. From Seend turn S at Bell Inn, follow signs to Worton. TEAS at Ivy House. *Combined adm £2 Chd free. Sun July 16 (2-6)*

Ashton House (Mrs Colin Shand) ½-acre garden in 3 sections with herbaceous borders, many shrubs and birch grove; walled courtyard and raised vegetable garden; lovely views across Avon Vale

Ivy House (Lt Gen Sir Maurice and Lady Johnston) 2-acre series of gardens separated by yew hedges and walls; herbaceous borders; shrubs; pond garden with maples; courtyard garden and many fine trees incl swamp cypress, holm and red oak, medlar and mulberry; interesting vegetable garden interplanted with fruit trees and large greenhouse

Oakley House ❀ (Mr & Mrs Michael Brierley) ½-acre village garden with herbaceous borders, roses, many shrubs; small pond and bog garden within a rockery; planted by owners since 1974

Springfield Cottage (Group Captain & Mrs D N Corbyn) Cottage garden redesigned since 1983 with small pond, herbaceous plants and shrubs

Worcestershire

See Hereford

Yorkshire & Cleveland

Hon County Organisers:

(N Yorks - Districts of Hambleton, Richmond, Ryedale, Scarborough & Cleveland) Mrs William Baldwin, Riverside Farm, Sinnington, York YO6 6RY Tel 01751 431764

(West & South Yorks & North Yorks Districts of Craven, Harrogate, Selby & York) Mrs Roger Marshall, The Old Vicarage, Whixley, York YO5 8AR Tel 01423 330474

DATES OF OPENING

By appointment

For telephone numbers and other details see garden descriptions. Private visits welcomed

Acorn Cottage, Boston Spa Gardens, nr Wetherby
Bankfield, Huddersfield
Brookfield, Oxenhope
Deanswood, Littlethorpe Gardens, nr Ripon
The Dower House, Great Thirkleby
Fairview, Smelthouses
Hemble Hill Farm, Guisborough
Hillbark, Bardsey
50 Hollins Lane, Hampsthwaite
Holly Cottage, Scholes
Hunmanby Grange, nr Scarborough
Inglemere Lodge, Ilkley
Ling Beeches, Scarcroft, nr Leeds
Maspin House, Hillam, nr Selby
Nawton Tower, Nawton
Old Sleningford, Mickley
Otterington Hall, Northallerton
Plum Tree Cottage, Bramham
55 Rawcliffe Drive, York
The Riddings, Long Preston
Ryedale House, Helmsley
10 Sherwood Grove, Acomb, York
Silver Birches, Scarcroft
The Spaniels, Hensall, nr Selby
Stonegate Cottage, nr Keighley
Tan Cottage, Cononley, nr Skipton
106 Vaughan Road, Barnsley
Victoria Cottage, Stainland
Windsong, Osgodby
Woodlands Cottage, Summerbridge
York House, Claxton

Parties only

Fieldhead, Boston Spa
Goddards, York
Harewood House, nr Leeds
30 Latchmere Road, Leeds 16
The Mews Cottage, Harrogate
Millgate House, Richmond
St Nicholas, Richmond
Thorp Perrow Arboretum, Bedale
The White House, Husthwaite
The Willows, nr Brighouse
Windyridge, Bolton Percy
Wytherstone House, nr Helmsley

Regular openings

For details see garden descriptions

Castle Howard, nr York. Daily March 17 to Oct 29
Constable Burton Hall, nr Leyburn. Daily April 1 to Oct 1
Gilling Castle, Gilling East. Daily July to Aug
Harewood House, nr Leeds. Daily March 26 to Oct 31
Land Farm, nr Hebden Bridge. Weekends & Bank Hols May to end of Aug
Newby Hall, Ripon. Daily April to Sept except Mons. (Open Bank Hols)
Shandy Hall, Coxwold. Open every afternoon except Sats
Stockeld Park, Wetherby. Thurs only April 6 to Oct 12. Sun June 25
Thorp Perrow Arboretum. Open all year

March 26 Sunday

Fairview, Smelthouses

April 2 Sunday

Otterington Hall, Northallerton

ight **1 Lister Road, London E11.** A
eature in this town garden densely planted
ith sub-tropical species.
hotograph by Clive Boursnell.

elow **Minterne, Dorset.** Another garden
hat is in its 60th year of opening for the
ational Gardens Scheme.
hotograph by Sheila Orme.

left **Moorlands, Sussex.** Rhododendrons, azaleas and many unusual shrubs feature in this water garden.
Photograph by Sheila Orme.

below **Scarthwaite, Cumbria.** Meryl Evans painting in the garden for the 1994 Cumbrian art exhibition 'Art in the Garden
Photograph by Val Corbett.

Greenacres, Sussex. Mr Fred Carr, Chief Executive of Carr Sheppards, sponsors of the Yellow Book, admiring the garden with the owners. *Photograph by Murray Sanders.*

Old Barn Cottage, Lancashire. A moorland garden with views over the surrounding countryside.
Photograph by Michael Edwards.

top **Spetchley Park, Hereford & Worcester**.
bottom **Ascott, Buckinghamshire.** Both these gardens celebrate their sixtieth anniversary of opening for the National Gardens Scheme. *Photographs by Sheila Orme.*

Lamorran House, Cornwall. One of the beautiful views from this Mediterranean style garden.
Photograph by Brian Chapple.

ght **Barton Abbey, xfordshire.** A garden that has een opening 61 years for the ational Gardens Scheme in 995.
hotograph by Juliette Wade.

elow **Foxbrush, Gwynedd.** ematis climbing through an 'American Pillar" rose.
hotograph by Jackie Newey.

left **Sleightholme Dale Lodge, Yorkshire.** One of the many densely planted borders.
Photograph by Clive Boursnell.

below **The Well House, Cheshire.** A pretty cottage garden divided by a natural stream.
Photograph by Trish Walters.

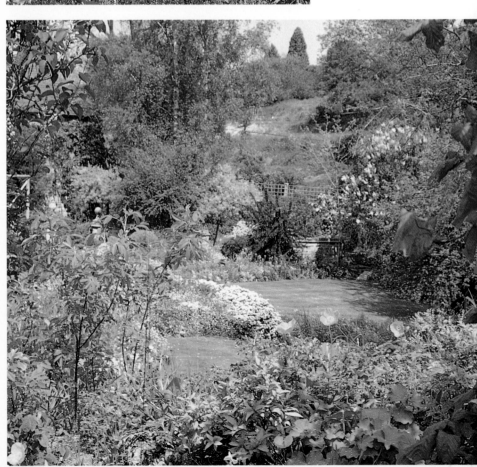

Victoria Cottage, Stainland

April 9 Sunday

Betula & Bolton Percy Cemetery ‡
Harsley Manor, East Harsley
Shandy Hall, Coxwold
Windyridge, Bolton Percy ‡

April 16 Sunday

Netherwood House, Ilkley

April 23 Sunday

Ling Beeches, Scarcroft, nr Leeds
Parcevall Hall, nr Skipton
Plum Tree Cottage, Bramham
St Nicholas, Richmond
Victoria Cottage, Stainland

April 30 Sunday

Boston Spa Gardens

May 6 Saturday

Thorp Perrow Arboretum, Bedale

May 7 Sunday

The Old Vicarage, Whixley

May 10 Wednesday

The Old Vicarage, Whixley

May 13 Saturday

York House, Claxton

May 14 Sunday

Blackbird Cottage, Scampston
Stillingfleet Lodge, nr York
Victoria Cottage, Stainland
York House, Claxton

May 17 Wednesday

Beacon Hill House, nr Ilkley

May 21 Sunday

Fieldhead, Boston Spa ‡
Goddards, York
Hemble Hill Farm, Guisborough
Hillbark, Bardsey ‡
Langdale, Melsonby
Silver Birches, Scarcroft ‡
Wytherstone House, nr Helmsley

May 27 Saturday

Nawton Tower, Nawton
Old Sleningford, Mickley

May 28 Sunday

Brookfield, Oxenhope
Hackness Hall, Hackness
Hunmanby Grange, nr Scarborough
Nawton Tower, Nawton
Old Sleningford, Mickley
Woodcock, Thirsk

May 29 Monday

Nawton Tower, Nawton
Old Sleningford, Mickley
Shandy Hall, Coxwold

June 3 Saturday

Pennyholme, Fadmoor
York Gate, Adel, Leeds 16

June 4 Sunday

Creskeld Hall, Arthington ‡
Elvington Gardens, nr York
Pennyholme, Fadmoor ‡‡
The Riddings, Long Preston
Shadwell Grange, Leeds ‡‡
Sleightholme Dale Lodge, Fadmoor ‡‡
Victoria Cottage, Stainland
York Gate, Adel, Leeds 16 ‡

June 7 Wednesday

Shandy Hall, Coxwold

June 10 Saturday

Pennyholme, Fadmoor

June 11 Sunday

Derwent House, Osbaldwick ‡
Littlethorpe Gardens, nr Ripon
Park House, Moreby, nr York ‡
Pennyholme, Fadmoor ‡‡
55 Rawcliffe Drive, York ‡
Ryedale House, Helmsley ‡‡
10 Sherwood Grove, Acomb, York ‡
Silver Birches, Scarcroft
Snilesworth, Northallerton
The Willows, nr Brighouse

June 18 Sunday

Blackbird Cottage, Scampston
Fieldhead, Boston Spa
Holly Cottage, Scholes
Inglemere Lodge, Ilkley
Parcevall Hall, nr Skipton
Woodlands Cottage, Summerbridge
York House, Claxton

June 21 Wednesday

Windsong, Osgodby

June 25 Sunday

Betula & Bolton Percy Cemetery
Bossall Gardens, Bossall
Fieldhead, Boston Spa ‡
Hillbark, Bardsey ‡
32 Hollybank Road, York
Hovingham Hall, Hovingham
Low Askew, Cropton, Pickering
Ness Hall, Nunnington
Shandy Hall, Coxwold
Skipwith Hall, nr Selby ‡‡
Stillingfleet Lodge, nr York ‡‡
Stockeld Park, Wetherby ‡
Victoria Cottage, Stainland
Windsong, Osgodby ‡‡

June 28 Wednesday

Ness Hall, Nunnington
Wass Gardens, nr Coxwold

July 2 Sunday

Bankfield, Huddersfield ‡
Bridge Cottage, Rievaulx
8 Dunstarn Lane, Adel
Harsley Manor, East Harsley
Millgate House, Richmond
The Old Rectory, Mirfield ‡

July 9 Sunday

Fernwood, Cropton
Hunmanby Grange, nr Scarborough
The Manor House, Tollerton
Norton Conyers, Wath, nr Ripon
Shandy Hall, Coxwold
Springfield House, Tockwith, nr York

July 13 Thursday

Grimston Gardens, Gilling East

July 15 Saturday

St Nicholas, Richmond
Sleightholme Dale Lodge, Fadmoor

July 16 Sunday

Bishopscroft, Sheffield
8 Dunstarn Lane, Adel ‡
Grimston Gardens, Gilling East
30 Latchmere Road, Leeds 16 ‡
55 Rawcliffe Drive, York ‡‡
10 Sherwood Grove, Acomb, York ‡‡
Sleightholme Dale Lodge, Fadmoor ‡‡‡
Wytherstone House, nr Helmsley ‡‡‡

July 19 Wednesday

The Mews Cottage, Harrogate

July 23 Sunday

Beamsley Hall, Bolton Abbey, nr Skipton
30 Latchmere Road, Leeds 16

July 30 Sunday

30 Latchmere Road, Leeds 16
Parcevall Hall, nr Skipton
The Spaniels, Hensall, nr Selby

August 6 Sunday

30 Latchmere Road, Leeds 16

August 27 Sunday

The White House, Husthwaite

September 17 Sunday

Maspin House, Hillam, nr Selby

September 24 Sunday

The Dower House, Great Thirkleby

October 1 Sunday

Betula & Bolton Percy Cemetery
Fairview, Smelthouses

DESCRIPTIONS OF GARDENS

¶Bankfield ✲❀ (Norma & Mike Hardy) Edgerton. 1m N of Huddersfield. From Huddersfield ring rd follow A629 towards Halifax for ½m. Cross traffic lights at Blacker Rd, turn R after 100yds into Queens Rd. From M62, turn S at junction 24 towards Huddersfield on A629. After ¾m pass 30mph sign, turn L after 200yds into Queens Rd. ⅔-acre cottage style garden which has evolved over 11yrs from a neglected Victorian town garden. Large number of perennials incl many unusual and rare of interest to plant collectors. Rambling paths, informal beds, pond, gazebo, conifer arch, terraced beds around lawn. Huddersfield Examiner 'Best Kept Garden'. Featured in Amateur Gardening 1994. TEA. *Adm £1 Chd 50p. Sun July 2 (11-5). Private visits also by appt, please* **Tel 01484 535830**

Beacon Hill House ✲❀ (Mr & Mrs D H Boyle) Langbar. 4m NW of Ilkley. 1¼m E of A59 at Bolton Bridge. Fairly large garden sheltered by woodland, on the southern slope of Beamsley Beacon. Several features of interest to garden historians remain from the original Victorian garden. Early flowering rhododendrons, large shrub roses, mixed borders, unusual hardy and half-hardy shrubs and climbers making use of south facing walls. TEAS. *Adm £1.50. Wed May 17 (2-6.30)*

Beamsley Hall ♿❀ (Marquess & Marchioness of Hartington) Beamsley. 5m E of Skipton. 6-acre traditional English garden with new plantings; including extensive herbaceous border and kitchen garden. Minor restrictions for wheelchairs. TEAS. Also at Bolton Abbey or at Devonshire Arms. *Adm £2 OAPs £1.50 Chd under 15 free. Sun July 23 (1.30-5.30)*

Betula & Bolton Percy Cemetery ✲❀ (Roger Brook Esq) Tadcaster. 5m E of Tadcaster 10m SW of York. Follow Bolton Percy signs off A64. An acre of old village churchyard gardened by Roger Brook, in which garden plants are naturalised and grow wild. Featured in numerous TV programmes, national magazines and publications. The National Dicentra Collection will be on view in Roger Brook's garden and allotment. Light lunches and TEAS in aid of church. *Combined adm with* **Windy Ridge** *£1.50 Chd free Sun April 9. Adm £1 Chd free. Suns June 25, Oct 1 (1-5)*

Bishopscroft ♿❀ (Bishop of Sheffield) Sheffield. 3m W of centre of Sheffield. Follow A57 (signposted Glossop) to Broomhill then along Fulwood Road to traffic lights past Ranmoor Church. Turn Right up Gladstone Rd and then L into Snaithing Lane. Bishopscroft on R at top of hill. 1¼-acres of well-established suburban woodland garden. Small lake and stream; the aim is to present something of the feeling of countryside in the nearby Rivelin Valley; a good variety of elders, brambles and hollies; herbaceous, shrub and rose borders. TEAS. *Adm £1 Chd free (Share to the Church Urban Fund©). Sun July 16 (2-6)*

Blackbird Cottage ♿❀ (Mrs Hazel Hoad) Scampston. 5m from Malton off A64 to Scarborough through Rillington turn L signposted Scampston only, follow signs. ⅓-acre plantswoman's garden made from scratch since 1986. A great wealth of interesting plants, with shrub, herbaceous border. Alpines are a speciality. Please visit throughout the day to ease pressure on a small but inspirational garden. Unusual plants for sale. Morning coffee and TEAS in aid of Scampston Village Hall & Church. *Adm £1 Chd free. Suns May 14, June 18 (10-5)*

Bossall Gardens ♿✲ From York proceed in NE direction on A64 (York to Malton and Scarborough) for 7m and turn R at signpost marked Claxton-Bossall. Go straight across the Xrds in Claxton and you come to Bossall (2m). Gardens adjacent. C12 church will be open. TEAS in aid of Red Cross 125th Birthday. *Combined adm £2.50 Chd free. Sun June 25 (2-5)*

Bossall Hall (Brig I D & Lady Susan Watson) 6-acre garden with moat surrounding C17 hall. Many old trees, lawns, orchard, walled kitchen garden, shrub and rose borders

The Old Vicarage (Mr & Mrs E A K Denison) Approx 2 acres. The garden consists of lawns, borders, shrubs, herbaceous plants and a rose garden all of which has been created over the last 21yrs

Boston Spa Gardens A659 1m S of Wetherby. Church St immed opp Central Garage. TEA at Acorn Cottage. *Combined adm £2.50 incl coffee/tea Chd free (Share to Northern Horticultural Society®). Sun April 30 (11-4)*

Acorn Cottage ✲ (Mr & Mrs C M Froggatt) Garden adjacent to **Four Oaks**. A small walled Alpine rock garden with the plant collection spanning 70 yrs - 2 generations. *Also by appt April to May, please* **Tel 01937 842519**

Four Oaks ✲❀ (Richard Bothamley & Glenn Hamilton) A medium-sized established flower and foliage garden of particular interest to flower arrangers. Pergolas and a series of garden 'rooms' on differing levels create a sense of intimacy. A wide selection of the genera - acer. Terrace with pots and a pool with good waterside plantings

¶Bridge Cottage ✲❀ (Mr & Mrs H Scott) Rievaulx. From Hemsley take the B1257 Stokesley Rd. 1st turning on L to Scawton-Old Byland and follow rd to C18 stone bridge. Cottage is over bridge on R. Approx 1-acre cottage garden with a wide variety of planting on different levels on both sides of Nettlebeck which is crossed by 3 footbridges and joins the R Rye nr the C18 stone bridge. ¼m from the ruins of the Cistercian Abbey of Rievaulx. TEA. *Adm £1.50 Chd free. Sun July 2 (10-30-5)*

Brookfield ✲❀ (Dr & Mrs R L Belsey) Oxenhope. 5m SW of Keighley, take A629 towards Halifax. Fork R onto A6033 towards Haworth. Follow signs to Oxenhope. Turn L at Xrds in village. 200yds after P O fork R, Jew Lane. A little over 1 acre, intimate garden, including large pond with island and mallards. Many varieties of candelabra primulas and florindaes, azaleas, rhododendrons. Unusual trees and shrubs; screes; greenhouse and conservatory. TEA 50p. *Adm £1.50 Chd free. Sun May 28 (2-6). Also by appt, please* **Tel 01535 643070**

Regular Openers. Too many days to include in diary. Usually there is a wide range of plants giving year-round interest. See head of county section for the name and garden description for times etc.

● **Castle Howard** ❀ (The Hon Simon Howard & Castle Howard Estate Ltd) York. 15m NE of York off the A64. 6m W of Malton. Partially suitable for wheelchairs. 300 acres of formal and woodland gardens laid out from the C18 to present day, including fountains, lakes, cascades and waterfalls. Ray Wood covers 50 acres and has a large and increasing collection of rhododendron species and hybrids amounting to 600 varieties. There is also a notable collection of acers, nothofagus, arbutus, styrax, magnolia and a number of conifers. There are walks covering spring, summer and autumn. Two formal rose gardens planted in the mid 1970's include a large assembly of old roses, china roses, bourbon roses, hybrid teas and floribunda. Refreshments are available in the House Restaurant, in the Lakeside Cafe and the Stables Cafe. During the summer months there are boat trips on the lake in an electric launch. There are gift shops in the House and Stable courtyard. Plant centre by the car park. TEAS. *Adm £4 Chd £2. Every day March 17 to Oct 29 (10-4.30)*

● **Constable Burton Hall Gardens** ♿ (Charles Wyvill Esq) 3m E of Leyburn on A684, 6m W of A1. Bus: United No. 72 from Northallerton alight at gate. Large garden, woodland walks; something of interest all spring and summer; splendid display of daffodils; rockery with fine selection of alpines (some rare); extensive shrubs and roses. Beautiful John Carr house (not open) in C18 park. Beautiful countryside at entrance to Wensleydale. *Adm £1 Chd 50p; reduction for large parties. April 1 to Oct 1 daily (9-5.30). Parties of 10 and over welcome, please,* **Tel 016774 50428**

Creskeld Hall ♿✾❀ (The Exors of Lady Stoddart-Scott) Arthington. 5m E of Otley on A659. Well established 3-4-acre large garden with woodland plantings; rhododendrons, azaleas, attractive water garden with canals, walled kitchen and flower garden. TEA. *Adm £1.50 Chd free. Sun June 4 (12-5)*

Derwent House ♿✾❀ (Dr & Mrs D G Lethem) Osbaldwick. On village green at Osbaldwick. 2m E of York city centre off A1079. Approx ¾ acre, a village garden extended in 1984 to provide a new walled garden with yew hedges and box parterres. Conservatories, terraces and herbaceous borders. TEAS. *Adm £1.50 Chd free. Sun June 11 (1.30-5)*

The Dower House ♿❀ (Mrs M J Coupe) Great Thirkleby. 4m from Thirsk on A19 on alternative route avoiding Sutton Bank. Smallholding run as a nature reserve bounded by a stream with ponds, wildflowers, birds, fish, donkeys. Rare trees with autumn colour, fruit and rose hips. TEA. *Adm £1 Chd free (Share to Ripon Choral Soc© and St Leonards Hospice®). Sun Sept 24 (2-6). Private visits (max 20) welcome, please* **Tel 01845 501375**

8 Dunstarn Lane ♿✾ (Mr & Mrs R Wainwright) Adel. Leeds 16. From Leeds ring rd A6120 exit Adel, up Long Causeway. 4th junction R into Dunstarn Lane, entrance 1st R. 28 bus from Leeds centre stops near gate. Entire garden formerly known as The Heath. Featured on YTV and BBC TV. 2 acres of long herbaceous and rose borders incl 60 varieties of delphiniums. Large lawns for picnics. *Adm £1 Chd free. Suns July 2, 16 (2-6)*

Elvington Gardens ✾❀ 8m SE of York. From A1079, immed. after leaving York's outer ring road turn S onto B1228 for Elvington. Light lunches and Teas in Village Hall in aid of village hall. Large free car park. *Combined adm £2.50 Chd free. Sun June 4 (11-5)*

Brook House (Mr & Mrs Christopher Bundy) Old established garden with fine trees; herb garden with rustic summer house; kitchen garden

Elvington Hall (Mr & Mrs Pontefract) 3-4-acre garden; terrace overlooking lawns with fine trees and views; sanctuary with fish pond

Eversfield (David & Helga Hopkinson) Modest sized garden with a wide variety of unusual perennials; grasses and ferns divided by curved lawns and gravel beds. Small nursery. **Tel 01904 608332**

Red House Farm (Dr & Mrs Euan Macphail) Entirely new garden created from a field 10 years ago. Courtyard with interesting plantings and half-acre young wood

Fairview ✾❀ (Michael D Myers) Smelthouses. From B6165 12m NW of Harrogate turn R in Wilsill Village to Smelthouses. Fairview is immed after the bridge on the R. A ⅛-acre small plantsman's garden on a steep slope, packed with unusual bulbs, alpines and woodland plants. 3 NCCPG National Collections; anemone nemorosa, hepatica and primula marginata; alpine house, fernery and tiny pond; small nursery. Due to the situation of the garden there may be some necessary restrictions to entry if busy. TEAS. *Adm £1.50 Chd free. Suns March 26, Oct 1 (12-5). Private visits by appt, please* **Tel 01423 780291**

¶Fernwood ✾❀ (Dick & Jean Feaster) Cropton. 4m NW of Pickering. From A170 turn at Wrelton signed Cropton. 1-acre garden created by the owners in the last 7yrs, containing herbaceous borders, a white garden, a scented garden, species and old roses, a wide variety of interesting plants, with a view of the N Yorkshire moors beyond. Morning coffee & TEAS. *Adm £1 Chd free. Sun July 9 (11-5)*

Fieldhead ✾❀ (Fiona Harrison & Chris Royffe) Boston Spa. Take A659 towards Boston Spa off A1 1m S of Wetherby. Chestnut Avenue on the R after ¾m. Please park on the main rd and walk up the avenue. A ⅓-acre garden recently created around an imposing Victorian house. Interestingly designed with a wide range of spaces, colours and textures; pools, terraces, a rose walk, shade and stone gardens. A large selection of plants; herbaceous, shrubs, ground cover and bamboos. Photographic exhibition showing development. Coffee/TEAS. *Adm £1 Chd free (Share to Northern Horticultural Society®). Suns May 21, June 18, 25 (11-5). Parties by appt please,* **Tel 01937 843513**

Gilling Castle ✾ (The Rt Revd the Abbot of Ampleforth) Gilling East, 18m N of York. Medium-sized terraced garden with steep steps overlooking golf course. Unsuitable for handicapped or elderly. *Adm £1 Chd free. For NGS July & Aug daily (10-4.30). Large parties welcome, please* **Tel 014393 206**

By Appointment Gardens. See head of county section

Goddards ✤❀ (The National Trust Yorkshire Regional Office) 27 Tadcaster Rd, Dringhouses. 2m from York centre on A64, next to Swallow Chase Hotel. National Trust Centenary opening. 1920s garden designed by George Dillistone, herbaceous borders, yew hedges, terraces with aromatic plants, rock gardens, pond. Partially suitable for wheelchairs. Guided tours, TEAS. *Adm £1.50 incl NT members. Sun May 21 (12-5). Large parties by appt May to Sept, please* **Tel 01904 702021**

Grimston Gardens ❀ Gilling East: 17m N of York; 7m S of Helmsley on B1363. Follow sign 1m S of Gilling East. TEA. *Adm £2 Chd free. Thurs, Sun July 13, 16 (2-6)*

Bankside House (Clive & Jean Sheridan) ½-acre garden with sloping lawn, mature trees and shrubs with shaded walk, mixed herbaceous plants, semiformal beds, small Japanese area

Grimston Chase (Mr & Mrs R Clarke) A wooded hillside incorporating a 3-acre woodland garden, flower beds surrounding mature trees and lawns with a stream dividing up the woodland. Variety of flowers with rhododendrons along a woodland path. Magnificent views

Grimston Manor Farm (Richard & Heather Kelsey) ½-acre garden (originally our field) offering all year interest. An intricate design profusely planted with a wide collection of herbaceous plants; trees and shrubs of particular interest to the flower arranger

Hackness Hall ♿✤ (The Lord & Lady Derwent) Hackness. 5m NW of Scarborough A171 Scarborough-Whitby rd turn at Scalby. A170 Scarborough-Pickering turn at Ayton; both signed Hackness. Large garden surrounding beautiful Grade 1 John Carr House (not open) in area of outstanding natural beauty. Many fine and unusual trees; lakeside walk; rhododendrons, shrubs; streams. *Adm £2 Chd 50p. Sun May 28 (1.30-5.30). No coaches except by appt* **Tel 01751 431764**

¶Harewood House ♿❀ (Harewood House Trust) Leeds. 9m N of Leeds on A61. Approx 80 acres of gardens within 1000 acres of Lancelot 'Capability' Brown landscaped parkland, formal terraces recently restored to original Sir Charles Barry design, 2m of box edging surrounding seasonal displays of Victorian bedding enhanced by Italianate fountains and statues, charming informal walks through woods around the lake to the cascade and rock garden with collections of hosta and rhododendrons. TEAS. *Adm £5.95 Chd £3 gardens, grounds, house and bird garden incl. Adm £3.25 Student, Chd £1 gardens & grounds only. March 26 to Oct 31 (10-4.30). For NGS private groups by appt, please* **Tel Michael Walker 0113 2886227**

Harlsey Manor ♿❀ (Mr & Mrs Brian Holey) East Harlsey. Travelling N on the A19 drive past the Cleveland Tontine (A172 turn-off) and take next turn to the L marked East Harlsey. The driveway to Harlsey Manor is about ½m along this rd on the LH-side before the village. 6 acres of garden and woodland walks with wide variety of mature trees and shrubs. Long terrace with formal rose beds and views of Cleveland Hills; extensive replanting of rhododendrons and daffodils carried out in 1993. Herbaceous border replanted Autumn 1994. TEAS in aid of Guide Dogs for the Blind. *Adm £1.25 Chd free. Suns April 9, July 2 (1.30-5.30)*

Hemble Hill Farm ♿❀ (Miss S K Edwards) Guisborough, on A171 between Nunthorpe and Guisborough opp the Cross Keys Inn. Dogs welcome, 7-acre garden facing the Cleveland Hills with formal and informal areas incl lake; young arboretum; heather, rhododendrons, large conservatory. TEAS. *Adm £1.25 Chd free. Sun May 21 (2-6). Private visits welcome June to Sept, please* **Tel 01287 632511**

Hillbark ✤❀ (Malcom Simm & Tim Gittins) Bardsey. 4m SW of Wetherby, turn W off A58 into Church Lane. The garden is 150yds on L just before Church. Please use village hall car park (turn R opp Church into Woodacre Lane). A young 1 acre country garden. Sunday Express 'Large Garden of the Year 1990'. Designed to take advantage of sloping S facing site. Mixed planting with some English roses; paved and gravel terraces; descending to ponds and stream with ducks and marginal planting. TEAS. *Adm £1 Chd 50p (Share to Cookridge Hospital Cancer Research®). Suns May 21, June 25 (11-5). Private visits welcome by appt May to July, please* **Tel 01937 572065**

50 Hollins Lane ✤ (Mr & Mrs G Ellison) Hampsthwaite. 2m W of Harrogate, turn R off A59 Harrogate-Skipton rd. Small ¼-acre garden with limestone rockeries; rhododendrons; azaleas and climbers. Pergolas and pool. Many unusual plants and alpines. TEA. *Adm £1.50 incl tea and biscuits. Private visits and parties May to Aug incl (max 30), please* **Tel 01423 770503**

Holly Cottage ✤❀ (Mr & Mrs John Dixon) Leas Gardens, Scholes. 8m S of Huddersfield on A616. Turn W at signpost to Scholes. ½-acre sloping garden of interest created from a field in 1988 with raised alpine bed and paved area with troughs; pond with small bog garden, rockery and herbaceous borders with good selection of plants. TEA. *Adm £1 Chd free. Sun June 18 (1-5). Private visits by appt, please* **Tel 01484 684 083**

32 Hollybank Road ✤ (Mr & Mrs D Matthews) Holgate. A59 (Harrogate Rd) from York centre. Cross iron bridge, turn L after Kilima hotel (Hamilton Drive East). Fork slightly L (Hollybank Rd) after 400yds. A small town garden 7yds × 28yds planted for year-round interest. Shrubs, small trees, climbing plants, roses, clematis and plants in containers. Cobbled fountain feature, 4 separate patio areas, 2 small ponds, wooden bridge leading to pergola. TEA. *Adm £1 Chd free. Sun June 25 (11-5)*

Hovingham Hall ♿✤❀ (Sir Marcus & Lady Worsley) 8m W of Malton. House in Hovingham village, 20m N of York; on B1257 midway between Malton and Helmsley. Medium-sized garden; yew hedges, shrubs and herbaceous borders. C18 dovecote; riding school; cricket ground. TEAS in aid of Hovingham Church. *Adm £2 Chd free. Sun June 25 (2-6)*

By Appointment Gardens. These owners do not have a fixed opening day usually because they do not like crowds or have insufficient parking space. Owner will often give guided tour.

Hunmanby Grange ♿✿❀ (Mr & Mrs T Mellor) Wold Newton. Hunmanby Grange is a farm 12½m SE of Scarborough, situated between Burton Fleming and Fordon. From Hunmanby take rd to Wold Newton 4m out of village turn R at Xrds towards Fordon garden 200yds on R. From A64 take B1039 towards Filey turn R before Flixton signed Fordon. In Fordon turn L at Xrds to Burton Fleming. Garden 1¼m on L. The garden has been created from exposed open fields over 10 yrs, on top of the Yorkshire Wolds near the coast, hopefully satisfying both a plantswoman's and a young family's needs. Foliage colour, shape and texture have been most important in forming mixed borders, a gravel garden, a rose hedge, pond garden, orchard and laburnum tunnel. Plants also for sale to private visits. TEAS in aid of St Cuthbert's Church, Burton Fleming. *Adm £1 Chd free. Suns May 28, July 9 (11-5). Private visits welcome, please* **Tel 01723 891636**

Inglemere Lodge ✿❀ (Mr & Mrs Peter Walker-Sharp) Ilkley. From Ilkley centre A65 towards Skipton, after ¾m opp post box turn L into Easby Dr. Owner built and maintained ⅙-acre garden surrounding L-shaped bungalow. Unusual layout on sloping site with small pond and large raised bed. Full of colour and interesting plants well displayed and labelled, many of which are for sale during the summer. TEAS. *Adm £1 Chd free (Share to The British Red Cross 125th Birthday®). Sun June 18 (1.30-5). Private visits by appt, please* **Tel 01943 607333**

Land Farm ✿❀ (J Williams Esq) Colden, nr Hebden Bridge. From Halifax at Hebden Bridge go through 2 sets traffic lights; take turning circle to Heptonstall. Follow signs to Colden. After 2¾m turn R at 'no thru' road, follow signs to garden. 4 acres incl alpine; herbaceous, heather, formal and newly developing woodland garden. Elevation 1000ft N facing. Has featured on 'Gardeners' World'. C17 house (not open). Art Gallery. *Adm £2 Chd free. May to end Aug; Open weekends and Bank Hols (10-5). Private visits for groups by appt, please* **Tel 01422 842260**

30 Latchmere Rd ✿❀ (Mr & Mrs Joe Brown) Leeds 16. A660 from City Centre to Lawnswood Ring Rd roundabout; turn sharp left on to ring rd A6120 for ⅓m to 3rd opening on left Fillingfir Drive; right to top of hill, turn right at top by pillar box, then left almost opposite into Latchmere Road, 3rd house on left. Please park in Fillingfir Drive. Bus stop at gate (Bus every 15 mins); 74 & 76 from City Centre; 54 from Briggate; 73 from Greenthorpe. Coaches to park in Latchmere Drive please. A small garden full of interest; fern garden; herbaceous borders; alpine garden; glade; camomile walk; 2 pools; patio built of local York stone; sink gardens; collection of 80 clematis. Featured Sunday Telegraph Magazine & TV with Yehudi Menuhin in *'Fiddling with Nature'* 1985. Gardeners' World, screened 1989. *Adm £1 Chd 50p (Share to GRBS®). Suns July 16, 23, 30, Aug 6 (2.30-5.30). Parties welcome, by written appt*

Ling Beeches ♿✿❀ (Mrs Arnold Rakusen) Ling Lane, Scarcroft 7m NE of Leeds. A58 mid-way between Leeds and Wetherby; at Scarcroft turn W into Ling Lane, signed to Wike on brow of hill; garden ⅓m on right. 2-acre woodland garden designed by owner emphasis on labour-saving planting; unusual trees and shrubs; ericaceous plants, but some species roses, conifers, ferns and interesting climbers. Featured in The English Woman's Garden other publications and TV. TEA. *Adm £2. Sun April 23 (2-5); Private visits also welcome by appt, please* **Tel 01132 892450**

Littlethorpe Gardens ♿✿❀ nr Ripon. Littlethorpe lies 1 ½m SE of Ripon indicated by signpost close to Ripon Racecourse on the B6265 twixt Ripon and the A1. TEAS at **Littlethorpe Hall**. *Combined adm £2.50 Chd free. Sun June 11 (1.30-5.30)*

Deanswood (Mrs J Barber) Garden of approx 1½ acres created during the last 9 years. Herbaceous borders; shrubs; special features streamside garden; 3 ponds with many unusual bog/marginal plants. Adjacent nursery open. *Private visits also welcome, please* **Tel 01765 603441**

¶Field Cottage (Mr & Mrs Richard Tite) A new 1 acre garden under development by owners. Informal herbaceous plantings, raised gravel and sleeper beds, alpines, bulbs and tender perennials. Small walled garden with terrace and an unusual range of plants in pots and containers

Littlethorpe Hall (Mr & Mrs D I'Anson) Mature garden (Victorian). 2 acres of lawns with specimen trees, azaleas; heathers and herbaceous beds. Small lake stocked with fish and a number of interesting waterside plants

Littlethorpe House (Mr & Mrs James Hare) 2 acres with old-fashioned roses; established mixed herbaceous and shrub borders

Langdale, Melsonby see County Durham

Low Askew ✿❀ (Mr & Mrs Martin Dawson-Brown) Cropton. 5m NW of Pickering between the villages of Cropton and Lastingham. Plantsman's garden full of interest incl scree, borders, roses & shrubs. Situated in beautiful countryside with stream and walk to River Seven. Troughs & pots are a speciality, filled with rare & species pelargoniums. Plant stalls by local nurserymen. Picnic area by river. Morning coffee, light lunches & TEAS. *Adm £1.50 Chd free (Share to NSPCC®). Sun June 25 (11-5)*

¶The Manor House ♿✿❀ (Dr & Mrs W D Stone) Tollerton. 10m N of York on A19. Turn L signed Tollerton L at village green. 1-acre walled garden with old brick farm buildings. Plantings of shrubs, roses and climbers. A wide variety of interesting plants. TEA. *Adm £1.50 Chd free. Sun July 9 (2-5.30)*

Maspin House ♿✿❀ (Mr & Mrs H Ferguson) Hillam Common Lane. 4m E of A1 on A63 direction Selby. Turn R in Monk Fryston after Thrust Garage. L at T junction. Maspin House 1m on L. Ample off road parking. Garden of 1½ acres started in 1985 and still evolving. Owner made and maintained. Many unusual and beautiful plants giving good late colour. Lots of features made by handy husband incl paths, patios, ponds and waterfall, raised beds and separate gardens. TEAS in aid of Monk Fryston School. *Adm £1 Chd free. Sun Sept 17 (1.30-5.30). Private visits welcome, by appt please,* **Tel 01977 684922**

The Mews Cottage ✿❀ (Mrs Pat Clarke) 1 Brunswick Drive, Harrogate. W of town centre. From Cornwall Rd, N side of Valley Gardens, 1st R (Clarence Dr), 1st L (York Rd), first L (Brunswick Dr). A small garden on a sloping site of particular interest to hardy planters. Full of unusual and familiar plants but retaining a feeling of restfulness. A courtyard with trompe l'oeil and a gravelled area enclosed by trellising, provide sites for part of a large collection of clematis. TEAS. *Adm £1.50 Chd 50p. Wed July 19 (2-5.30). Private visits for groups, societies and parties also welcome, please* **Tel 01423 566292**

Millgate House ✿❀ (Austin Lynch & Tim Culkin) Richmond Market Place. House is located at bottom of Market Place opp Barclays Bank. SE walled town garden overlooking the R Swale. Although small the garden is full of character, enchantingly secluded with plants and shrubs. Foliage plants incl ferns, hostas; old roses and interesting selection of clematis, small trees and shrubs. Featured in 'Homes & Gardens', 'Dalesman' and 'The Sunday Times'. Full of ideas for small gardens. *Adm £1.50 Chd 50p. Sun July 2 (8am-8pm). Parties welcome, please* **Tel 01748 823571**

Nawton Tower ♿❀ (Mrs D Ward) Nawton, 5m NE of Helmsley. From A170, between Helmsley and Nawton village, at Beadlam turn N 2½m to Nawton Tower. Large garden; heathers, rhododendrons, azaleas, shrubs. Tea Helmsley and Kirbymoorside. *Adm £1 Chd 50p. Sat, Sun, Mon May 27, 28, 29 (2-6); private visits welcome, please* **Tel 01439 771218**

Ness Hall (Hugh Murray Wells Esq) Nunnington, 6m E of Helmsley, 22m N of York. From B1257 Helmsley-Malton rd turn L at Slingsby signed Kirbymoorside, 3m to Ness. Lge walled garden, mixed and herbaceous borders, emphasis on colour and design; orchard with shrubs and climbing roses. *Adm £1.50 Chd free. Sun, Wed June 25, 28 (2-6)*

Netherwood House ♿❀ (Mr & Mrs Peter Marshall) 1m W of Ilkley on A65 towards Skipton; drive on L, car parking adjacent to house. Daffodils, spring flowering shrubs, duck pond; new rockery, bulb and stream plantings. Lovely views up Wharfedale. TEAS. *Adm £1.50 Chd free. Sun April 16 (2-5.30)*

● **Newby Hall & Gardens** ♿✿❀ (R E J Compton Esq) Ripon. 40-acres extensive gardens laid out in 1920s; full of rare and beautiful plants. Winner of HHA/Christie's Garden of the Year Award 1987. Formal seasonal gardens, reputed longest double herbaceous borders to R. Ure and National Collection holder Genus Cornus. C19 statue walk; woodland discovery walk. Miniature railway and adventure gardens for children. Lunches & TEAS in licensed Garden Restaurant. The Newby shop and plant stall. *Adm House & garden £5.20 OAPs £4.50 Disabled/Chd £3, Garden only £3.50, OAPs £3, Disabled/Chd £2.30. April to Sept daily ex Mons (Open Bank Hols) (Gardens 11-5.30; House 12-5). Group bookings and further details from Administrator* **Tel 01423 322583**

Norton Conyers ♿❀ (Sir James Graham) Ripon. 4m NW of Ripon. Take Wath sign off A61 Ripon-Thirsk. Large C18 walled garden of interest to garden historians. Interesting borders and orangery; old-fashioned and unusual hardy plants a speciality. Jacobean House open. TEA. *Collecting box for NGS.* ▲*For NGS Sun July 2 (2-5)*

The Old Rectory, Mirfield ♿✿❀ (G Bottomley Esq) Exit 25 of M62; take A62 then A644 thru Mirfield Village; after approx ½m turn L up Blake Hall Drive, then 1st L, Rectory at top of hill. 1-acre garden surrounding Elizabethan Rectory. Mixed borders, Mulberry tree dating from C16; well, pergola and small ornamental pond. TEAS. *Adm £1 Chd free. Sun July 2 (2-5)*

Old Sleningford ♿❀ (Mr & Mrs James Ramsden) 5m W of Ripon, off B6108. After North Stainley take 1st or 2nd L, follow sign to Mickley for 1m. An excellent example of an early C19 house and garden with original layout of interest to garden historians. Many acres with extensive lawns, interesting trees; woodland walk and Victorian fernery; exceptionally lovely lake and islands, streamside walk; watermill in the walled kitchen garden; long herbaceous border; yew and huge beech hedges. Flowers and grasses grown for drying. Home-made TEAS. *Adm £2 Chd free (Share to N of England Christian Healing Trust®). Sat, Sun, Mon May 27, 28, 29 (1-5). Groups catered for, also private visits by appt, please* **Tel 01765 635229**

The Old Vicarage ✿❀ (Mr & Mrs R Marshall) Whixley, between York and Harrogate. ¾m from A59 3m E of A1. A ¾-acre walled flower garden with mixed borders, unusual shrubs, climbers, hardy plants and bulbs. Courtyard with herb garden. Gazebo. TEAS. *Adm £1.50 Chd free. Sun, Wed May 7, 10 (1-5)*

Otterington Hall ♿❀ (Sir Stephen & Lady Furness) Northallerton. 4m S of Northallerton. On A167 just N of S Otterington Village. 7 acres of garden and woodland walks, flowering shrubs, topiary, wonderful spring and kitchen garden, autumn colour. Designed for all seasons. Wheelchair users and families welcomed. TEAS. *Adm £2 Acc chd free. Sun April 30, Suns, Weds July 16 to Aug 30. For NGS Sun April 2 (2-5). Private visits welcome by appt April to Oct, please* **Tel 01609 772061**

Parcevall Hall Gardens ❀ (Walsingham College (Yorkshire Properties) Ltd) Skyreholme, 12m N of Skipton. From Grassington on B6265 turn S at Hebden Xrds, follow signs to Burnsall, Appletreewick to Parcevall Hall. 20-acres in Wharfedale; shelter belts of mixed woodland, fine trees; terraces; fishponds; rock garden; tender shrubs inc Desfontainea; Crinodendron; camellia; bulbs; rhododendrons; orchard for picnics, old varieties of apples; autumn colour; birds in woodland; splendid views. TEAS. *Adm £2 Chd (5-12 yrs) 50p.* ▲*For NGS Suns April 23, June 18, July 30 (10-5)*

¶**Park House** ♿ (Mr & Mrs A T Preston) Moreby. 6m S of York. Between Naburn and Stillingfleet on B1222. Approx ½-acre, gardened since 1988, set within a 2-acre walled garden using some of the 16′ walls to display a wide variety of wall shrubs and climbers. Some herbaceous and mixed shrub borders. Large conservatory. TEAS. *Adm £1 Chd free. Sun June 11 (2-5.30)*

Pennyholme (Mr C J Wills) Fadmoor, 5m NW of Kirbymoorside. From A170 between Kirbymoorside and Nawton, turn N, ½m before Fadmoor turn L, signed 'Sleightholmedale only' continue N up dale, across 3 cattlegrids, to garden. No Buses. Large, wild garden on edge of moor with rhododendrons, azaleas, primulas, shrubs. TEAS in aid of All Saints, Kirbymoorside. *Adm £1.50 Chd 50p (Share to All Saints, Kirkbymoorside®). Sats, Suns June 3, 4, 10, 11 (11.30-5)*

Plum Tree Cottage ✿❀ (Mr & Mrs G J Rogers) Bramham. 5m S of Wetherby off A1 take 1st L past the Red Lion towards the church. A sloping garden of about ½ acre with particular winter and spring interest. A range of shade- loving plants, epimediums, hellebores, primulas; varieties of spring bulbs; dodecatheons, also magnolia, trees with interesting bark and a small bog garden struggling against wild garlic! TEAS. *Adm £1 Chd free. Sun April 23 (2-5). Also private visits by appt April to July, please* **Tel 01937 843330**

55 Rawcliffe Drive ✿❀ (Mr & Mrs J Goodyer) Clifton. A19 from York centre, turn R at Clifton Green traffic lights (Water Lane). Rawcliffe Drive is 1st L after Clifton Hotel. A 30yd by 10yd suburban garden on 2 levels, which has developed as the family has grown older. Planted for yr-round interest with excellent use of foliage and colour. Many unusual shrubs, herbaceous plants and bulbs; around 90 clematis some varieties of which are in flower March to Nov. *Adm £1.20 Chd free incl TEA. Suns June 11, July 16 (11-5). Also private visits welcome April to July, please* **Tel 01904 638489**

The Riddings ✿❀ (Mr & Mrs T Hague) Long Preston. ¼m W of Long Preston on A65. Turn R over cattle grid up private rd. Parking adjacent to house. Designated wild-life gardens. 10 acres of grounds with mature trees, hollies and conifers. A small formal garden with heathers, alpines and some topiary; a traditional walled kitchen garden with ornamental pond; a delightful walk through rhododendron wood with beck, small waterfalls and bog garden undergoing restoration. TEA. *Adm £1.50 Chd 50p. Sun June 4 (11-5).* **Tel 01729 840231**

Ryedale House ♿ (Dr & Mrs J A Storrow) 41 Bridge Street, Helmsley. On A170, 3rd house on R after bridge into Helmsley from Thirsk and York. ¼-acre walled garden; varieties of flowers, shrubs, trees, herbs. Teashops in Helmsley. *Adm £1 Chd free. Sun June 11 (2-6) also private visits welcome May to July, please* **Tel 01439 770231**

St Nicholas (The Lady Serena James) 1m S of Richmond. On Brompton Catterick Bridge rd, ½ way down hill after leaving Maison Dieu. Bus: Darlington-Richmond; alight The Avenue, 500yds. Medium-large garden of horticultural interest; shrubs, topiary work. *Adm 50p Chd 25p. Suns April 23, Sat July 15 (all day), also by appt parties only*

Shadwell Grange ♿✿❀ (Mr & Mrs Peter Hartley) Shadwell Lane, Leeds 17. Turn L at traffic lights (signed Shadwell) ¼m from Moortown on A6120 (Leeds ring-rd) travelling E. A large 4-acre Victorian garden with established woodlands. Rhododendrons, azaleas, mixed borders and new plantings. Water garden, orchard, wild garden and open views to the S. Parking in paddock. Plant stall, light refreshments in aid of Yorkshire Macmillan Nurse Appeal. *Adm £1.50 Chd (over 5) 50p. Sun June 4 (11.30-4)*

Shandy Hall ✿❀ (The Laurence Sterne Trust) Coxwold, N of York. From A19. 7m from both Easingwold and Thirsk turn E signed Coxwold. C18 walled garden, unusual plants; old roses. 1-acre, with low-walled beds. Newly opened 1-acre wild garden in Quarry adjoining garden. Home of C18 author, Laurence Sterne, who made the house famous. Craft shop in grounds. Unusual plants for sale. Wheelchairs with help. Teas in village, Coxwold (Schoolhouse Tea Room; home baking). *Adm £1.50 Chd 75p (Share to Laurence Sterne Trust®). House open Wed & Sun (2.30-4.30). Garden also open every afternoon except Sat (12-4.30) groups by appt on other days or evenings during the same period. For NGS Suns April 9, June 25, July 9, Mon May 29, Wed June 7 (2-5)*

¶10 Sherwood Grove ✿❀ (Mr & Mrs A C Downes) Acomb. From York on A59, turn L into Beckfield Lane at city boundary sign, before Western Ring Rd. Take 1st R, 2nd L. ¾-acre garden hidden behind suburban semi, developed and extended over 15 yrs. Features rockeries, pond, fruit cage but primarily extensive mixed plantings incl many unusual plants. 3 greenhouses with vines, cactus, succulent & tender plant collections. TEA. *Adm £1 Chd free. Suns June 11, July 16 (10-5)*

Silver Birches ♿❀ (Stanley Thomson Esq) Ling Lane, Scarcroft, 7m NE of Leeds. A58 mid-way between Leeds-Wetherby; at Scarcroft turn W into Ling Lane, signed Wike; garden ½m. 2½-acre woodland garden; foliage trees and shrubs; many conifers, rhododendrons, azaleas; good collection of heaths and heathers; attractive water feature, climbers and roses. TEA. *Adm £1.50 Chd free (Share to Northern Horticultural Society®). Suns May 21, June 11 (2-5.30) also by appt June to Oct, please* **Tel 01132 892335**

Skipwith Hall ♿❀ (Mr & Mrs Nigel Forbes Adam) Selby. From York take A19 to Selby (fork L at Escrick, 4m to Skipwith). From Selby take A19 to York turn R onto A163 to Market Weighton, turn L to Skipwith after approx 2m. An interesting 3-acre garden with well established shrub roses, trees, mixed borders and wall shrubs, large traditional walled kitchen garden. TEAS. *Adm £1.50 Chd 50p. Sun June 25 (2-5.30)*

Sleightholme Dale Lodge ❀ (Mrs Gordon Foster; Dr & Mrs O James) Fadmoor, 3m N of Kirkbymoorside. 1m from Fadmoor. Hillside garden; walled rose garden; herbaceous borders. *Not* suitable for wheelchairs. No coaches. TEAS (Teas and plants not available June 4). *Adm £1.25 Chd 40p. Sun June 4 (11.30-5) Sat, Sun July 15, 16 (2-6)*

Regular Openers. Too many days to include in diary. Usually there is a wide range of plants giving year-round interest. See head of county section for the name and garden description for times etc.

Snilesworth ♿❀ (Viscount & Viscountess Ingleby) Halfway between Osmotherley and Hawnby. From Osmotherley bear L sign posted Snilesworth, continue for 4½m across the moor. 4½m from Hawnby on Osmotherley Rd. Turn R at top of hill. Garden created from moorland in 1957 by present owners father; rhododendrons and azaleas in a 30 acre woodland setting with magnificent views of the Hambleton and Cleveland hills; snowgums grown from seed flourish in a sheltered corner. TEAS. *Adm £1 Chd 20p (Share to Hawnby Church®). Sun June 11 (2-5)*

¶**The Spaniels** ♿✲❀ (Janet & Dennis Tredgett) Hensall. 2m N of M62, 5m S of Selby. Turn E off A19 to Hensall. Field Lane is last turn on R in Hensall Village. A new ¾-acre garden planted over the past 2yrs on previous farmland. Long mixed borders in colour themes, incl young conifers, trees and shrubs, divided by curved lawns with island beds. Small wildlife pond. TEAS. *Adm £1 Chd 50p. Sun July 30 (12-5). Private visits welcome, please* **Tel 01977 661858**

Springfield House ♿✲❀ (Mr & Mrs S B Milner) Tockwith. 5m E of Wetherby; 1m off B1224. Garden at west end of village. 1½ acres. Well established walled garden with herbaceous borders, water and rock gardens. Rose and conifer garden; shrub walk. Wide variety of plants. TEA. *Adm £1 Chd free. Sun July 9 (2-6)*

Stillingfleet Lodge ♿✲❀ (Mr & Mrs J Cook) Stillingfleet 6m S of York, from A19 York-Selby take B1222 signed Sherburn in Elmet. ½-acre plantsman's garden subdivided into smaller gardens, each one based on a colour theme with emphasis on the use of foliage plants. Wild flower meadow and newly constructed pond, holders of National Collection of Pulmonaria. Adjacent nursery will be open. Homemade Teas in village hall in aid of local church. *Adm £1.50 Chd free. Suns May 14, June 25 (1.30-5.30)*

Stockeld Park ♿✲❀ (Mr & Mrs P G F Grant) 2m NW of Wetherby. On A661 Wetherby-Harrogate Rd; from Wetherby after 2m entrance 2nd lodge on left. Bus: Wetherby-Harrogate, alight Stockeld lodge gates (¼m drive). Listed grade 1 house and garden. 4-acres with lawns, grove and flowers, fine trees and roses. House built 1758 for Col Middleton by James Paine (listed Grade 1). C18 pigeon cote. Chapel 1890. Plants for sale June 25. *Open Thurs only April 6 to Oct 12 (2-5). For NGS Sun June 25. Gardens only. TEAS. Adm £1.50 Chd 50p (2-5)*

Stonegate Cottage ✲❀ (Mrs B Smith) Farnhill. 2m W Silsden. From Silsden or A629, follow directions to Farnhill. Stonegate Cottage is situated 100yds from Kildwick Hall towards Skipton. Cottage garden of approx 1 acre, on sloping site. Small pool and rockery. Unusual trees & shrubs. Wide variety of plants incl spring bulbs, herbaceous and roses. *Adm £1.50. Private visits by appt, please* **Tel 01535 632388**

Tan Cottage ✲❀ (Mr & Mrs D L Shaw) West Lane, Cononley. Take A629; turn off to Cononley 2¾m out of Skipton; top of village turn right onto Skipton rd. ¾-acre plantsman's garden adjoining C17 house (not open). Interesting plants, many old varieties; national collection of primroses. *Adm £1. Private visits by appt only, please* **Tel 01535 632030**

¶**Thorp Perrow Arboretum** ♿❀ Bedale. Thorp Perrow is situated off the B6268. 2½m S of Bedale on Bedale-Masham rd. 4m from Leeming Bar on A1. The Arboretum covers 85 acres incl C16 woodland, Victorian Pinetum, lake, woodland walks, tree trails, nature trail. Holds 4 National Tree Collections: Fraxinus, Avercus, Tilia and Juglans. The Arboretum has many plants and trees that are rare or endangered in their natural habitat; Spectacular sights in Spring; thousands of naturalised daffodils and bluebells; magnificent displays of Autumn colour. TEAS. *Adm £2.75 OAP/Chd £1.50. For NGS Sat May 6 (dawn to dusk). Open all year for NGS* **Tel 01677 425323**

106 Vaughan Road ✲❀ (Richard Darlow & Christine Hopkins) Barnsley. 2m NW Barnsley Town centre. From M1 junction 37 take A628 towards Barnsley. After ½m turn L at major Xrds to hospital. Turn L at hospital Xrds into Gawber Rd, after ½m turn L into Vernon Way. Vaughan Rd is 1st cul-de-sac on R. Mediterranean garden to rear 60ft by 30ft. Planted entirely with 'warm climate' trees, shrubs, perennials, incl many tender subjects permanently planted eg palms, cordylines, yuccas, cacti and eucalyptus; spectacular flowering shrubs and exotic plants in pots. Mainly evergreen but most colourful April to Oct. Featured in BBC 2 Gardeners World, and many national magazine publications incl Journal of the European Palm Society and Practical Gardening Magazine. TEA. *Adm £1.50 OAP £1. Private visits welcome by appt only, weekends all yr, also evenings mid summer please* **Tel 01226 291474**. *Not suitable for young children due to many spiky plants!*

Victoria Cottage ✲ (John Bearder Esq) Beestonley Lane, Stainland. 6m SW of Halifax. Take the A629 (Huddersfield) from Halifax and fork R on the B6112 to Stainland. From Huddersfield take A640 Outlane, Sowood and Stainland. Turn at Black Horse Garage in Stainland (Beestonley Lane). ¾-acre plantsman garden, created by the owner from a NE sloping field since 1950. Daffodils; roses, flowering shrubs, some unusual for a hilly and wild part of the Pennines. Scenic setting. *Adm £1 Chd 30p. Suns April 2, 23; May 14, June 4, 25 (10-5). Private visits welcome and parties by appt only, please* **Tel 01422 365215/374280**

¶**Wass Gardens** ✲❀ Nr Coxwold ¼m from Byland Abbey on Coxwold-Ampleforth rd. 6m SW of Helmsley turning from A170. 9m E of Thirsk; turn from A19 signed Coxwold. A variety of gardens in a picturesque hamlet set amid a broad cleft of deep wooded slopes. TEAS in aid of Wass Village Institute. *Adm £2 Chd free. Wed June 28 (12-5)*

The White House ♿✲❀ (Dr & Mrs A H Raper) Husthwaite. 3m N of Easingwold. Turn R off A19 signposted Husthwaite 1½m to centre of village opposite parish church. 1-acre garden created from scratch in 6 years now maturing and of particular interest to the plantswoman, containing herb garden, conservatory, gardens within the garden, herbaceous particularly a late summer 'hot' border; shrubs; borders and many fascinating unusual plants. New landscaping and planting in the old orchard. Do visit throughout the day please to ease pressure. Morning coffee and home-made food all day. Groups by prior arrangement. *Adm £1.50 Chd 25p (Share to St Nicholas Church, Husthwaite©). Sun Aug 27 (11-5)*

The Willows ♿✂❀ (Mr & Mrs Fleetwood) 172 Towngate, Clifton. From M62 exit 25, take A644 towards Brighouse. 1st R to Clifton. L at T junction; house approx 250 yds on L. ¾ acre owner created and maintained garden with oriental features, pools and waterfalls with herbaceous borders with many unusual plants of particular interest to flower arrangers and plantsmen. Containers and sink gardens. A wide variety of plantings in old orchard. TEAS. *Adm £1 Chd 50p. Sun June 11 (1-6). Groups welcome by appt, please* **Tel 01484 716513**

Windsong ❀ (Mr & Mrs Alan Gladwin) Osgodby. Take A63 2m N of Selby off A19, turn L into Sand Lane (signed Osgodby Village). A ½-acre garden created and maintained by the owners over the past 5 yrs. Many unusual features incl a moon gate; hardy plants and tender perennials packed into mixed borders. Ponds and stream-side plantings; orchard area. TEAS. *Adm £1 Chd free. Wed June 21, Sun June 25 (2-5). Private visits welcome by appt please* **Tel 01757 708802**

Windy Ridge ✂❀ (Mr & Mrs J S Giles) Marsh Lane, Bolton Percy. 5m E of Tadcaster. Follw Bolton Percy signs off A64. 10m SW of York. Features a large collection of Barnhaven and Elizabethan primroses; Hose-in-Hose, Jack-in-the-Green, etc. Also wild and unusual hardy plants, grown in a natural cottage garden style sloping down to the Ings, greatly influenced by Margery Fish. Featured in channel 4 'Over the Garden Wall' 1994. Light lunches and teas available in village hall in aid of All Saints Church. *Combined adm with* **Betula and Bolton Percy Cemetery** *£1.50. Sun April 9 (1-5). Private parties welcome by appt, please* **Tel 01904 744264**

Woodcock ♿✂ (Mr & Mrs David Price) ¾m E of Thirsk off A170 (Sutton Bank Rd). Turn R up bridle track. Proceed for 1m. 1½-acre garden laid out with some mature areas, always of interest. Plantings of shrubs, herbaceous, old-fashioned roses, spring bulbs, scree bed and developing camellia walk. Small woodland garden under construction. TEAS. *Adm £1.50 Chd 50p. Sun May 28 (2-5.30)*

¶**Woodlands Cottage** ✂❀ (Mr & Mrs Stark) Summerbridge. ½m W of Summerbridge on the B6165 (Ripley-Pateley Bridge). 1-acre country garden constructed and developed over the past 9yrs by the owners from a sloping site incorporating part of the existing woodland edge, field and natural stone outcrops with an attractive enclosed cottage style garden; herbaceous, formal herb garden, unusual hardy plants and separate vegetable area. Small nursery. TEAS in aid of Muscular Dystrophy Society. *Adm £1 Chd 50p. Sun June 18 (1.30-5). Private visits welcome by appt* **Tel 01423 780765**

Wytherstone House ♿✂❀ (Maj N & Lady Clarissa Collin) Pockley, 3m NE of Helmsley from A170 signpost. Large garden, constantly being improved, consisting of shrubs (some choice and hard to find) shrub roses, perennials, terracotta pots, herb garden, mediterranean garden, beech hedges and magnificent views. The arboretum consisting of rare interesting trees has recently been landscaped with pond and small water garden. Suitable for wheelchairs if someone strong to push. TEAS in aid of Pockley Church and Village Hall. *Adm £2 Chd under 6 free. Over 6 50p. Specialist nursery open Easter to Oct Wed to Sun incl (10-5). Suns May 21, July 16 (11-5.30). Parties welcome, please* **Tel 01439 770012**

York Gate ✂❀ (GRBS) Back Church Lane, Adel, Leeds 16. Behind Adel Church on Otley Rd out of Leeds (A660). Bus: WY 34 Leeds-Ilkley; alight Lawnswood Arms, ½m. A family garden created by father, son and mother. 1 acre of particular interest to the plantsman and containing orchard with pool, an arbour, miniature pinetum, dell with stream and newly constructed root house, folly, nutwalk, peony bed, iris borders, fern border, herb garden, summerhouse, alley, white and silver garden, vegetable garden, pavement maze. Sybil's garden, all within 1-acre! NO COACHES. *Adm £2.50 Chd free. Sat, Sun June 3, 4 (2-6). To be confirmed in local press*

York House ❀ (Mr & Mrs W H Pridmore) Claxton, 8m E of York, off A64. 1-acre plantsmans garden, created by owners since 1975; old roses, herbaceous, shrubs, fruit. Loose gravel drive could be difficult for wheelchairs. TEAS. *Adm £1 Chd 20p (Share to Northern Horticultural Society©). Sat, Suns May 13, 14, June 18 (2-6); private visits welcome, April to Sept please* **Tel 01904 468360**

WALES

Clwyd

Hon County Organisers: Mrs Richard Heaton, Plas Heaton, Trefnant, Denbigh LL16 5AF
North: Tel 01745-730229
Mrs Sebastian Rathbone, Bryn Celyn, Ruthin LL15 1TT Tel 01824 702077
South: Mrs J R Forbes, Pen-y-Wern, Pontblyddyn, nr Mold CH7 4HN
Tel 01978-760531
Hon County Treasurer: A Challoner Esq., 13 The Village, Bodelwyddan LL18 5UR

DATES OF OPENING

By appointment
For telephone numbers and other details see garden descriptions. Private visits welcomed

Abercregan, Llangollen
Alyn View, nr Mold
Bryn Derwen, Mold
Byrgoed, Llandderfel
Castanwydden, Llandyrnog
Donadea Lodge, Babell
Eyarth House, nr Ruthin
The Garden House, Erbistock
Hartsheath, Pontblyddyn
Merlyn, Moelfre, Abergele
Pen-y-Wern, Pontblyddyn
Three Chimneys, Rhostyllen
Trem-Ar-For, Dyserth
Tyn-y-Craig, Llandrillo
2 Woodside Cottages, Halton, Chirk

Parties only
17 Broclywedog, Rhewl
Dolhyfryd, Denbigh
Dolwen, Cefn Coch
The Mount, Higher Kinnerton, Chester

April 9 Sunday
Hawarden Castle, Hawarden
April 16 Sunday
Gardeners Lodge, Trevor Hall
April 17 Monday
Gardeners Lodge, Trevor Hall
April 23 Sunday
Hartsheath, Pontblyddyn
April 26 Wednesday
Hartsheath, Pontblyddyn
April 30 Sunday
Hartsheath, Pontblyddyn
Plas Ffordd Ddwr, Llandyrnog
May 7 Sunday
Bryniau Gardens
Rug, Corwen
May 13 Saturday
Chirk Castle, nr Wrexham
Dibleys Nurseries, Llanelidan
May 14 Sunday
Hawarden Castle, Hawarden
May 21 Sunday
Dolhyfryd, Denbigh
May 24 Wednesday
Dolhyfryd, Denbigh
May 28 Sunday
Bryn Derwen, Mold
Eyarth House, nr Ruthin
2 Woodside Cottages, Halton, Chirk
June 4 Sunday
The Garden House, Erbistock
June 11 Sunday
Abercregan, Llangollen
33 Bryn Twr, Abergele ‡
The Garden House, Erbistock
Lynton, Highfield Park, Abergele ‡
Plas-yn-Rhos, Gellifor
River House, Erbistock
June 18 Sunday
Argoed Cottage, nr Overton-on-Dee
The Garden House, Erbistock
The Old Rectory, Llangynhafal
Plas Nantglyn, nr Denbigh
June 21 Wednesday
Argoed Cottage, nr Overton-on-Dee
June 25 Sunday
Dolwen, Cefn Coch ‡
The Garden House, Erbistock
Gwaenynog, Denbigh
Llangedwyn Hall, Llangedwyn ‡
July 1 Saturday
Cerrigllwydion Hall, Llandyrnog
July 2 Sunday
17 Broclywedog, Rhewl ‡
Bryn Celyn, Llanbedr ‡
The Garden House, Erbistock
July 6 Thursday
17 Broclywedog, Rhewl
July 9 Sunday
The Garden House, Erbistock
Rhyllon, St Asaph
July 13 Thursday
Bryn Hafod, Treuddyn
July 16 Sunday
Cartref, Babell ‡
Donadea Lodge, Babell ‡
The Garden House, Erbistock
July 20 Thursday
Bryn Hafod, Treuddyn
July 23 Sunday
The Garden House, Erbistock
August 6 Sunday
Llanfair T H Village Gardens
August 25 Friday
Erddig Hall Garden, Wrexham
September 17 Sunday
Welsh College of Horticulture, Northop
October 15 Sunday
Three Chimneys, Rhostyllen

DESCRIPTIONS OF GARDENS

Abercregan ♿❀ (Mr & Mrs V Whitworth) Llangollen. A5 150yds Chirk side Llangollen Golf Club. 2½-acre water garden designed in 1985. Roses; herbaceous garden; rhododendrons. Magnificent views of Vale of Llangollen. TEAS in aid of Clwyd Special Riding Trust. *Adm £1 Chd 50p. Sun June 11 (2-6). Private visits welcome May to July, please* **Tel 01978 860205**

¶Alyn View ❀ (Mr & Mrs Smith) nr Mold. Directions on appointment. A cottage garden of 1 acre. A shady private garden and a very sunny open garden. Both areas full of established trees and shrubs. *Private visits welcome, please* **Tel 01352 741771**

Argoed Cottage ♿❀ (Mr & Mrs C J Billington) Overton-on-Dee. App Overton-on-Dee from Wrexham on A528 cross over Overton Bridge and in about ¾m on brow of hill turn L into Argoed Lane. 1¾-acre garden, with new features. Interesting trees and shrubs. Herbaceous beds; roses and vegetable garden. TEAS in aid of Wrexham Hospice Project. *Adm £1 Chd free. Sun June 18, Wed June 21 (2-5.30)*

¶17 Broclywedog ♿❀ (Mr Mel Royles) Rhewl, Ruthin. From Ruthin take A525 to Denbigh. Turn R in Rhewl onto Llandyrnog Rd. 2nd rd on R. A small attractive plantsmans garden packed with unusual varieties of geranium, erodium, sisyrinchium, alpine and others. TEA. *Adm £1 Chd 25p. Sun July 2, Thurs July 6 (2-6). Private groups welcome, please* **Tel 01824 702139**

Bryn Celyn ♿❀ (Mr & Mrs S Rathbone) Llanbedr, Ruthin. [OS Ref SJ 133 603]. From Ruthin take A494 towards Mold. After 1½m at the Griffin Inn turn L onto B5429. 1¼m house and garden on R. 1-acre garden; mixed borders; walled garden; old-fashioned roses. TEAS. *Adm £1 Chd 25p. Sun July 2 (2-6)*

Bryn Derwen ❀ (Roger & Janet Williams) Wrexham Road, Mold. ½m from Mold Cross on Mold-Wrexham rd B5444; opp Alun School and Sports Centre (large car park). ½-acre old walled garden with large sunken area. Plantsmans garden with wide variety of plants for sun and shade, giving interest from spring to autumn; allium, cistus, euphorbia, ferns, hostas, grasses, etc. Japanese garden. Featured on BBC Radio Wales Garddio and in The Good Garden Guide. TEA. *Adm £1 Chd 25p. Sun May 28 (2-5.30). Private visits welcome, please* **Tel 01352 756662**

¶Bryn Hafod ❀ (Rosemary & David Ffoulkes Jones) Treuddyn, Mold. Turn S off A5104 1m W of Treuddyn into Ffordd y Blaenau (signed). Follow lane for 1¼m. Country garden in elevated position of about 1 acre created from pasture 8yrs ago. A wide variety of plants in mixed borders and varied situations. *Adm £1 Chd 50p (Share to Nightingale House Hospice, Wrexham®). Thurs July 13, 20 (11-6)*

Bryn Meifod, see Gwynedd gardens

¶33 Bryn Twr ❀ (Mr & Mrs Colin Knowlson) Abergele. A55 W take slip rd to Abergele. Turn L at roundabout then over traffic lights; 1st L signed Llanfair T H. 3rd rd on L, no.33 is on L. There are 2 connected gardens (Lynton) of approx ¾ acre in total, containing patio and pond areas; mixed herbaceous and shrub borders. TEAS. *Combined adm £2.50 OAPs £2 Chd free (Share to St Michaels, Abergele Scout Group©). Sun June 11 (2-6)*

Bryniau Gardens 2m from Dyserth on A5151 towards Trelawnyd. 1st L out of Dyserth after lay-by on R. TEAS at Craig-y-Castell. *Combined adm £2 OAPs £1 Chd free. Sun May 7 (2-6)*

Appletree Cottage (Mr & Mrs R L Owen) Approx 1½ acres of landscaped gardens with trees; shrubs; alpines and herbaceous plants. Some parts in the process of development and replanting. Features incl a rock quarry garden, a water garden and natural hillside with spring flowers and bulbs

Craig-y-Castell (Mr & Mrs D Watchorn) Site of Dyserth Castle (1241/1263) 4 acres bounded by dry moat and vallum, featuring mature trees, shrubs, rockeries and rose garden. Beautiful views towards Snowdonia. ¾m beyond **Appletree Cottage**

Craig-y-Castell Cottage ❀ (Mr & Mrs Williams) Garden with open views of Dyserth and the Vale of Clwyd. 1 acre of reclaimed wilderness populated by a variety of conifers and shrubs that can withstand ignorant malpractice and planted by the 'ad hoc Topsy' school of garden design and without the aid of squared paper. ¾m beyond **Appletree Cottage**

Byrgoed (Alan & Joy Byrne) Llandderfel. 4½m NE Bala. Off B4401 Bala-Corwen rd. L into village 1st R over stream and up hill. Fork R at old chapel, Byrgoed is ⅝m on L [OS 125 990 372]. Densely stocked terraced cottage garden; thyme lawn, rockery, alpines, roses and fuschias. Yr-round interest. TEAS. *Adm £1 Chd 50p. Private visits welcome March and April; July to Sept, please* **Tel 01678 530270**

¶Cartref (Mrs D Jones) Caerwys Rd Babell, Holywell. Turn off A541 Mold to Denbigh rd at Afonwen signposted Babell. At T-junction turn R, Black Lion Inn turn L, 1st L. 4th house. From Holywell old A55, turn L for Gorsedd then L again. L at Gorsedd Church for Babell, 2m down that rd turn R at Babell Chapel which is now Chapel House, 4th house. Very attractive well-stocked cottage garden; clematis, climbers, vegetables and roses. TEA. *Adm £1 Chd 25p (Share to Cancer Research®). Sun July 16 (2-6)*

Castanwydden ♿❀ (A M Burrows Esq) Fforddlas, Llandyrnog. Take rd from Denbigh due E to Llandyrnog approx 4m. From Ruthin take B5429 due N to Llandyrnog. [OS ref 1264 (sheet 116)]. Approx 1-acre cottage garden with a considerable variety of plants and bulbs. Small nursery growing plants from the garden. TEAS. *Adm £1 Chd 50p. Private visits welcome, please* **Tel 01824 790404**

Cerrigllwydion Hall ❀ (Mr & Mrs D Howard) Llandyrnog. E of Denbigh. B5429 ½m from Llandyrnog village on Ruthin Road. Extensive grounds with mature trees; herbaceous borders; vegetables and greenhouses. TEAS. *Adm £1.50 Chd free (Share to Llanynys Church®). Sat July 1 (2-6)*

Chirk Castle ♿✂ (The National Trust) Chirk 7m SE of Llangollen. Off A5 in Chirk by War Memorial. 4½ acres trees and flowering shrubs, rhododendrons, azaleas, rockery, yew topiary. TEA. *Adm to garden £2 OAPs/Chd £1. Sat May 13 (12-5)*

Dibleys Nurseries ✂❀ (Mr & Mrs R Dibley) Llanelidan. Take A525 to Xrds by Llysfasi Agricultural College (4m from Ruthin, 14m from Wrexham). Turn along B5429 towards Llanelidan. After 1½m turn L at Xrds with houses on the corner. Continue up lane for 1m. Nursery and gardens on the L. 8 acres of mainly young trees and shrubs planted during last 5 yrs. Spectacular views across to the Clwydian range. ¾ acre of glasshouses containing mostly streptocarpus, incl specimen plants ready for Chelsea show. TEAS. *Adm £1 Chd 50p (Share to Action Aid®). Sat May 13 (11-5)*

Dolhyfryd ♿✂❀ (Capt & Mrs H M C Cunningham) The Lawnt, 1m from Denbigh on B5401 to Nantglyn. Several acres of park, woodland and shrub garden with river; magnificent native trees, many azaleas, rhododendrons and bulbs. TEAS. *Adm £2 Chd 50p (Share to Henshaw's Society for the Blind®). Crocuses end of Feb and beginning of March. Sun May 21, Wed May 24 (2-6). Private parties welcome, please* **Tel 01745 814805**

¶Dolwen ✂❀ (Mrs F Denby) Cefn Coch Llanrhaedr-ym-Mochnant. From Oswestry take the B4580 going W to Llanrhaedr. Turn R in village and up narrow lane for 1m. Garden on R. 14m from Oswestry. 4 acres of hillside garden with pools, stream, small wood and many different types of plant and unusual annuals all backed by a stupendous mountain view. TEAS. *Adm £1 Chd free (Share to Oswestry Orthopaedic Hospital®). Every Fri and last Sun in month from May to Sept in aid of local charities. For NGS Sun June 25 (2-5). Private parties welcome, please* **Tel 01691 780 411**

Donadea Lodge ♿✂❀ (Mr & Mrs Patrick Beaumont) Babell. Turn off A541 Mold to Denbigh at Afonwen, signposted Babell; T-junction turn L. A55 Chester to St Asaph take B5122 to Caerwys, 3rd turn on L. Mature shady garden with unusual plants, shrubs, shrub roses and climbing roses. Also clematis; pink, yellow and white beds. Featured in Homes and Gardens 1994, and in The Good Gardens Guide 1995. Cream TEAS. *Adm £1.50 Chd 20p (Share to St Mary's Church, Ysceifiog®). Sun July 16 (2-6). Private visits welcome from May 15 to July 31, please* **Tel 01352 720204**

Erddig Hall ♿✂❀ (The National Trust) 2m S of Wrexham. Signed from A483/A5125 Oswestry Road; also from A525 Whitchurch Road. Garden restored to its C18 formal design incl varieties of fruit known to have been grown there during that period and now includes the National Ivy Collection. TEAS. Tours of the garden by Head Gardener at 1pm, 2.30pm. *Adm £2 Chd £1. NT Shop & plant sales. For NGS Fri Aug 25 (12-4) Garden only*

Eyarth House ✂❀ (Mrs J T Fleming) 2m S of Ruthin off A525. Bus: Ruthin-Corwen, Ruthin-Wrexham. Large garden; rock garden; shrubs and ornamental trees. TEA. *Adm £1 Chd 50p (Share to St Mary's Church®). Sun May 28 (2.30-6) Private visits welcome, please* **Tel 01824 702745**

¶The Garden House ♿❀ (S Dyson-Wingett) Erbistock. 5m S of Wrexham on A528 Wrexham to Shrewsbury. Follow signs to Erbistock Church at Overton Bridge ¾m. Car park at nursery and tea room. Nursery plant centre, organic walled garden, hydrangea avenue. Over 200 species and cultivars (National Collection status applied for); rose pergolas, shrub and herbaceous plantings in monochromatic, analogous and complementary colour schemes. Attractive walk to R Dee. Field grown flowers, Victorian dovecote. 4 acres. TEAS. *Adm £1 Chd free (Share to Frank Wingett Cancer Appeal©). Suns June 4, 11, 18, 25, July 2, 9, 16, 23 (2-6) Private visits welcome, please* **Tel 01978 780958**

Gardeners Lodge ❀ (Mrs M Tomlinson) Trevor Hall, Llangollen. On N side of A539 Rhuabon-Llangollen rd ¼m W of Trevor Village. Yellow direction signs from main rd. Delightful well-stocked ¾-acre cottage garden; herbaceous borders, rockery, shrubs, roses, herbs and spring bulbs. Interesting C18 church with box pews, hatchments etc nearby. TEAS. *Adm £1 Chd 50p (Share to Trevor Church®). Easter Sun, Mon April 16, 17 (1-4)*

Gwaenynog ♿✂❀ (Maj & Mrs Tom Smith & Mrs Richard Williams) Denbigh. 1m W of Denbigh on A543, Lodge on left. 2-acre garden incl the restored kitchen garden where Beatrix Potter wrote the Tale of the Flopsy Bunnies. Small exhibition of some of her work. C16 house visited by Samuel Johnson during his Tour of Wales. Coffee and biscuits 11-12.30pm. Lunches available Broadleys Farm Restaurant. TEAS. *Adm £1.50 OAPs £1 Chd 25p (Share to St James's Church, Nantglyn®). Sun June 25 (11-6)*

Hartsheath ✂ (Dr M C Jones-Mortimer) Pontblyddyn. ½m S of intersection with A5104. Red brick lodge on E side of A541. Large woodland garden; many varieties of flowering cherries and crab apples. Tidy picnic lunchers welcomed. Lunch & Tea at Bridge Inn, Pontblyddyn. *Adm £1 Chd £1 (Share to Pontblyddyn Church®). Sun April 23 (12-5) Wed April 26 (2-5) Sun April 30 (12-5). Also private visits welcome weekdays Feb-May, Sept-Oct, please* **Tel 01352 770 204**

Hawarden Castle ♿✂ (Sir William & Lady Gladstone) On B5125 just E of Hawarden village. Large garden and picturesque ruined castle. *Adm £1.50 Chd/OAPs 50p. Suns April 9, May 14 (2-6)*

Llanfair T H Village Gardens, Abergele. 5m from Abergele A548 to Llanfairtalhaiarn Village, then follow signs in village. TEA. *Combined adm £2 OAP's £1 Chd free. Sun Aug 6 (2-6)*

Bronydd ♿✂ (Mr & Mrs Vernon Davies) 2 Lon Elwy. Small front flower garden with tubs and hanging baskets. To the side of house, raised bed with shrubs and climbers; patio area with tubs and alpine plants. Rear garden prize winning dahlias, chrysanthemums and sweet peas

Bryn Ffynnon ✂ (Mr & Mrs Gwylym Williams) Landscape hillside garden; trees, hedgerows and shrubs. Beautiful views over the village and towards Snowdonia

15 Glan Elwy ♿✂❀ (Mr & Mrs T O Willliams) Flower borders at front containing a variety of bedding plants mainly annuals; tubs and hanging baskets. Rear of house has 2 greenhouses and 4 flower borders containing various flowers

16 Glan Elwy ♿✂❀ (Mr & Mrs D O Davies) Lge densely planted garden; mainly annuals; tubs and hanging baskets; greenhouses and tunnel at back of house. 1st prize winner

17 Glan Elwy ♿✂ (Peter & Nanna Davies) Small flower garden at front; annuals and perennials with tubs and hanging baskets. Greenhouses at back and tunnel containing chrysanthemums

¶18 Glan Elwy (Mr & Mrs G Owen) First-prize winner for local garden; annuals and herbaceous borders; tubs and hanging baskets

¶Llangedwyn Hall ♿✂❀ (Mr & Mrs T M Bell) Llangedwyn; on the B4396 road to Llanrhaedr about 5m W of the Llynclys Xrds. Approx 4 acres; formal terraced garden on 3 levels designed and laid out in late C17 and early C18. Sunken rose garden and small water garden. TEAS. *Adm £1.50 OAP's & Chd 50p (Share to Llangedwyn Church®). Sun June 25 (2-6)*

¶Lynton ✂ (Mr & Mrs K A Knowlson) Abergele. A55 take slip rd to Abergele. Turn L at roundabout then over traffic lights, 1st L signed Llanfair T H, 3rd rd on L. Entrance through **33 Bryn Twr**. There are 2 connected gardens of approx ¾ acre in total containing patio and pond areas; mixed herbaceous and shrub borders. TEAS. *Combined adm £2.50 OAPs £2 Chd free (Share to St Michael's Abergele Scout Group). Sun June 11 (2-6)*

Merlyn ✂❀ (Drs J E & B E J Riding) Moelfre, Abergele. Leave A55 (Conwy or Chester direction) at Bodelwyddan Castle, proceed uphill by castle wall 1m to Xrds. 0.1m to T-junction. (white bungalow) R B5381 towards Betws yn Rhos for 2m, then fork L (signed Llanfair TH) after telephone box garden 0.4m on R. 2-acre garden developed from a field since 1987. Long mixed border; damp and gravel garden; many shrubs and old roses; rhododendrons and azaleas; spring garden. Views of sea. *Adm £1 Chd 50p. Private parties welcome Feb to Nov incl, please* **Tel 01745 824435**

The Mount ♿✂ (Mr & Mrs J Major) Higher Kinnerton. 6m W of Chester, L off A5104 just after it crosses A55. Approx 2-acre garden with mature trees; shrubs and lawns; kitchen garden, variety of perennial plants some interesting and unusual. *Adm £1.50 Chd free. Private parties welcome, please* **Tel 01244 660 275**. *Best months June and July*

The Old Rectory ♿✂❀ (Mr & Mrs John Arbuthnott) Llangynhafal, SE of Denbigh. N of Ruthin and E of B5429, signed at Cyffion Xrds. Medium-sized terrace country garden, herbaceous borders, shrubs and wall plants. Newly planted woodland. TEAS. *Adm £1 Chd 50p (Share to St Cynhafal's Church, Llangynhafal®). Sun June 18 (2-6)*

Pen-y-Wern ♿✂ (Dr & Mrs Forbes) Pontblyddyn, 5m SE of Mold, 7m NW of Wrexham. On E side of A541, ½ way between Pontblyddyn and Caergwrle. 2½-acre terraced country-house garden incl interesting small gardens. Shrubs and herbaceous borders; rose garden spectacular in June/July. Magnificent copper beech with canopy circumference of 250ft and other splendid trees. *Adm £1 Chd 50p (Share to Hope Parish Church®). Private visits welcome, please* **Tel 01978 760531**

Plas Ffordd Ddwr ♿✂❀ (Mr & Mrs D J Thomas) Llandyrnog. 2m E of Denbigh. Follow signs to Llandyrnog from roundabout at Ruthin end of Denbigh by-pass A525, house 2m on R. 2½-acre country garden, elevated position in Vale of Clwyd. Established shrubs, lawns and mature trees. Small woodland and pond; bring wellies if wet. TEAS. *Adm £1 Chd 50p (Share to St Asaph Cathedral Organ Restoration Appeal®). Sun April 30 (2-5)*

Plas Nantglyn ♿✂❀ (Mr & Mrs R Welch) Nantglyn. From Denbigh follow signs for Nantglyn in SW direction; nr phone box in Nantglyn straight over Xrds and bear R at fork, house 300yds on L. [OS Ref 116 003 613]. Large old established gardens with azaleas, rhododendrons, topiary, roses and herbaceous borders; fine trees; good views. Light lunches and TEAS. *Adm £1.50 Chd free. Sun June 18 (12-6)*

Plas-Yn-Rhos ♿❀ (Miss M E Graham) Gellifor. 3m N of Ruthin A494. L at Llanbedr DC on B5429 2¼m house on R. ¾-acre garden with wide views of the Clwydian range, surrounds old Welsh Farmhouse part dated 1594. Herbaceous borders; lawns with croquet; young wood; new 'acid' bed. (Gift stall and cream TEAS in aid of Clwyd Special Riding Centre) Large car park. *Adm £1 Chd 50p. Sun June 11 (1-5)*

¶Rhyllon ♿✂❀ (Mr & Mrs M Dodd & Mrs D M Dodd) From St Asaph take A55 towards Chester then 1st L and 1st house on R. 1 acre garden with herbaceous borders, pond area with mature trees and shrubs. Dried flower section. TEA. *Adm £1 Chd free. Sun July 9 (2-6)*

Rug ♿❀ (Lord and Lady Newborough) Follow A5 from Corwen over R Dee Bridge to traffic lights. About ¼m turn R off A5 by Lodge. Mainly beautiful trees, shrubs, bulbs and woodland garden to walk through. Dogs cemetery. 7-acre lake with RNLI and other model boats being sailed on open day; replanting of small grass and shrubs. TEAS. *Adm £1 OAPs and Chd 50p (Share to RNLI® & Orthopaedic Hospital Gobowen®). Sun May 7 (2-6)*

River House ♿✂❀ (Mrs Gwydyr-Jones) Erbistock. 5m S of Wrexham. On A528 Wrexham-Shrewsbury rd, ¼m before Overton Bridge (opp turning A539 to Ruabon). Small garden with unusual shrubs and plants. *Adm £1 Chd free. Sun June 11 (2-6)*

Three Chimneys ✂❀ (Mr & Mrs Hollington) 3m SW of Wrexham via Rhostyllen. From Wrexham A5152 fork R at Black Lion onto B5097. From Ruabon B5605 turn L onto B5426 signed Minera. Turn R ½m over bridge, L at Water Tower. Garden ¼m on L opp post box. Forester's garden of 1 acre; maples, conifers, cornus and sorbus species and varieties. Many small trees used in the manner of a herbaceous border. Very unusual and interesting. *Adm £1.50 Chd 25p. Oct 15 (1-5). Private visits welcome, May, please* **Tel 01978 841499**

Trem-Ar-For ✂❀ (Mr & Mrs L Whittaker) 125 Cwm Rd, Dyserth. From Dyserth to Rhuddlan rd A5151. Turn L at Xrds signed Cwm, fork L and at traffic de-restriction sign house on L. ¾-acre limestone terraced hillside garden with dramatic views towards Snowdon and Anglesey. A highly specialised garden with many rare and interesting plants with special emphasis on alpines, daphnes and specie paeonies. TEA. *Adm £1 Chd 50p (Share to North Wales Wildlife Trust©). Private visits welcome April to Sept, please* **Tel 01745 570349**

Tyn-Y-Craig ✂ (Maj & Mrs Harry Robertson) Llandrillo. [Grid ref: SJ008377] 1½m from Llandrillo towards Bala off the B4401 Corwen to Bala Rd. Developed over 20 yrs, a hillside garden approx 1½ acres, incorporating 6 descending landscaped pools. *Adm £1 Chd 50p. Private visits welcome, mid April to mid June, please* **Tel 01490 440257**

Regular Openers. See head of county section.

Welsh College of Horticulture ♿❀ Northop. Village of Northop is 3m from Mold and close to the A55 expressway. Mature gardens incorporating many national award winning features. Commercial sections. Garden Centre and retail sections where produce and garden sundries can be purchased. A Golf Course is being constructed for the teaching of Greenkeeping Skills. Car parking. *Adm £2 OAP's & Chd 50p families £3.50. Sun Sept 17 (10-5)*

2 Woodside Cottages ✂❀ (Mrs J L Wilson) Halton. 7m N of Oswestry. Follow A5-A483. R off roundabout signed Halton. R at next roundabout ¼m under bridge and down hill. Garden on L. Alternatively N through Chirk (towards Llangollen) ¾m turn R (signed Black Park) ½m on R. A small but interesting cottage garden with a variety of different features incl alpine, heather, shrubbery, pond and bog areas. Over 100 hardy geraniums can be seen amongst the many unusual herbaceous plants and shrubs. TEAS. *Adm £1 Chd 50p (Share to Clwyd Special Riding Trust©). Sun May 28 (12-5). Private visits welcome, please* **Tel 01691 777824**

Dyfed

Hon County Organisers:

North (Ceredigion District) — Mrs Stewart Neal, Llwyncelyn, Glandyfi, Machynlleth, Powys, SY20 8SS

South (Carmarthen, Dinefwr, Pembroke & Preseli Districts) — Mrs Duncan Drew, Cwm-Pibau, New Moat, Clarbeston, Dyfed SA63 4RE

DATES OF OPENING

By appointment
For telephone numbers and other details see garden descriptions. Private visits welcomed

Blaengwrfach Isaf, nr Llandyssul
The Forge, Narberth
Great Griggs, Llanteg
Hean Castle, Saundersfoot
Living Garden, Bryn
Llanllyr, Talsarn
The Mill House, Machynlleth
Old Cilgwyn Gardens, Newcastle Emlyn
Penrallt Ffynnon, Newcastle Emlyn
Plas Llidiardau, Llanilar
Post House, nr Whitland
Winllan, nr Lampeter

Parties only
Bryngolau, Llannon
Maesyrynn, Nantycaws, Carmarthen

Regular openings
For details see garden descriptions

Cae Hir, Cribyn. Daily, see text
Hilton Court Nurseries, Roch. Daily March to Oct.
Saundersfoot Bay Leisure Park. Daily April 1 to Oct 2

April 4 Saturday
Colby Woodland Garden, Narberth

April 23 Sunday
Pant-yr-Holiad, Rhydlewis

May 7 Sunday
Post House, nr Whitland

May 14 Sunday
Pant-yr-Holiad, Rhydlewis
Post House, nr Whitland

May 21 Sunday
Cae Hir, Cribyn
Great Griggs, Llanteg
Llwyncelyn, Glandyfi ‡
The Mill House, Machynlleth ‡

May 28 Sunday
Ffynone, Boncath
Hean Castle, Saundersfoot

June 4 Sunday
Bryngoleu, Llannon
Danhiraeth, Drefach-Velindre
Living Garden, Bryn
Pant-yr-Holiad, Rhydlewis

June 11 Sunday
Cae Hir, Cribyn
Slebech Hall, Haverfordwest

June 18 Sunday
Llanllyr, Talsarn

July 2 Sunday
Living Garden, Bryn

July 8 Saturday
Maesyrynn, Nantycaws, Carmarthen

July 9 Sunday
Cae Hir, Cribyn
Danhiraeth, Drefach-Velindre
Maesyrynn, Nantycaws, Carmarthen

July 16 Sunday
Plas Llidiardau, Llanilar

July 22 Saturday
Millinford, nr Haverfordwest

July 23 Sunday
Great Griggs, Llanteg
Millinford, nr Haverfordwest

July 26 Wednesday
7 Maes yr Awel, Ponterwyd

July 29 Saturday
7 Maes yr Awel, Ponterwyd

August 27 Sunday
Llanerchaeron, Ciliau Aeron, Aberaeron

DESCRIPTIONS OF GARDENS

Blaengwrfach Isaf ✲❀ (Mrs Gail M Farmer) Bancyffordd, 2m W of Llandysul. Leaving Llandysul on Cardigan rd, by Half Moon pub fork left; continue on this road; approx 1½m, after village sign Bancyffordd farm track on right. ¾-acre garden incorporating woodland, wild and cottage garden aspects within a secluded and sheltered area. Created by present owners over the past 20 years. Many specie and shrub roses; old-fashioned and scented plants grown in variety of ways amongst unusual trees planted for all year interest. Areas specially created with bees, butterflies and birds in mind; new pathway bordered by wild-flower meadow. Included in 'English Private Gardens'. Adjacent craft workshops. Teas in village 1m. *Adm 75p Chd free. Private visits welcome April, May, June, Oct (10-4), please* **Tel 01559 362604**

Bryngoleu ♿✲❀ (Mr & Mrs Ivor Russell) Llannon. 13m from Swansea, 7m from Llanelli. From junction 49 (Pont Abraham) on M4 take A48(T) in the direction of Cross Hands. Turn L after approx 3kms towards Village of Llwyn Teg. At [map ref SN 56 E on OS 159.] ½-acre garden with converted stable block, leading to extensive choice of walks each about ½m long in mature and newly developing woodlands and alongside natural streams. 15 acres overall incl a lake; fine views of the surrounding countryside as shown on SC4 TV. Ample seating. TEA. *Adm £1.50 Chd 50p. Sun June 4 (11-5). Private parties welcome, please* **Tel 01269 842343**

Cae Hir ✲❀ (Mr Wil Akkermans) Cribyn. W on A482 from Lampeter. After 5m turn S on B4337. Cae Hir is 2m on L. Beautiful and peaceful 6-acre garden on exposed W facing slope. Entirely created and maintained by owner from 4 overgrown fields of rough grazing. Started in 1985. Many unusual features found unexpectedly around each corner including red, yellow and blue sub-gardens, bonsai 'room', stonework, ponds, lovely views; new water and bog garden and white garden. As featured on radio and TV. TEA. *Adm £1.50 Chd 50p. Open daily except Mons April to Oct (1-6). Also open Bank Hols. For NGS Suns May 21, June 11, July 9 (1-6)*

Colby Woodland Garden ❀ (The National Trust) ½m inland from Amroth and 2m E of Saundersfoot. Signposted by Brown Tourist Signs on the coast rd and the A477. 8-acre woodland garden in a secluded and tranquil valley with a fine collection of rhododendrons and azaleas. Tea rooms and gallery. Walled garden open by kind permission of Mr & Mrs A Scourfield Lewis. TEAS. *Adm £2.60 Chd £1.10. Sat April 8 (10-5). Large parties by appt, please* **Tel 01834 811885**

Danhiraeth ✲❀ (Mrs Hewitt) Velindre. Take A484 from Carmarthen (18m), or Newcastle Emlyn (4m). From Carmarthen follow sign-posts for Drefach-Felindre 2m N of Cwm-Duad. From Newcastle Emlyn follow sign-post for Drefach-Felindre, 2m E of Newcastle Emlyn. In Drefach-Felindre take turning up hill by church for approx ½m. Turn R down un-gated farm track for about ½m. Entrance via green door, ring bell, parking ltd. 1-acre woodland garden; informal terraces, ponds, statues, fountain and waterfall, ornamental trees and shrub roses. TEA. *Adm £1 No children due to water hazard. Suns June 4, July 9 (1-6)*

The Dingle ♿✲ (Mrs A J Jones) Crundale. On approaching Haverfordwest from Carmarthen on A40, take R turn at 1st roundabout signed Fishguard & Cardigan. At next roundabout take R turn on to B4329. ½m on fork R opp General Picton; then 1st right into Dingle Lane. 3-acres plantsman's garden; rose garden; formal beds; scree; herbaceous border; unusual shrubs; water garden; woodland walk. Picturesque and secluded; free roaming peacocks. Nursery adjoining. Tearoom. *Adm £1 Chd 50p (Share to Cancer Relief Macmillan Nurses Fund®). Daily (except Tues) March 13 to Oct 16 (10-6)*

Ffynone (Earl & Countess Lloyd George of Dwyfor) Boncath. From Newcastle Emlyn take A484 to Cenarth, turn left on B4332, turn left again at crossroads just before Newchapel. Large woodland garden in process of restoration. Lovely views, fine specimen trees, rhododendrons, azaleas. Ask for descriptive leaflet. House by John Nash (1793), not shown. Later additions and garden terraces by F. Inigo Thomas c1904. TEA. *Adm £1 Chd free. Sun May 28 (2-6)*

The Forge ♿ (I & S Mcleod-Baikie) Landshipping. Nearest town Narbeth. Landshipping well sign posted. Pass New Park with pillar box; 200yds further on, gate on R. Approx 9 acres recently planted woodland garden with many varieties of bulbs, trees and shrub roses. Small, pretty very charming. Featured in NGS video 2. *Private visits welcome mid-March to mid-April and also in June, please* **Tel 01834 891279**

Great Griggs ♿❀ (M A & W A Owen) Llanteg, nr Amroth. A477 from St Clears, past Red Roses, next village Llanteg. Signposted on LH-side Colby Woodland Garden, turn L immed, 2nd entrance on R. ½-acre garden made from part of field in the last 10yrs. Mainly shrub and alpines; stonework incl seating; fish and duck ponds with ornamental water fowl. Unusual pets. TEAS. *Adm £1 Chd 50p. Suns May 21, July 23 (2-6). Private visits also welcome, please* **Tel 0834 83414**

Hean Castle ♿✲❀ (Mr & Mrs T Lewis) Saundersfoot. 1m N of Saundersfoot. 1½m SE of Kilgetty. Take Amroth road from Saundersfoot or the Sardis road from Kilgetty. 2-acres; mixed borders with some unusual plants and shrubs; rose garden; walled garden and greenhouse; conifers; pot plants and troughs. Good view. TEAS. *Adm £1.50 Chd free. Suns May 28 (11-5). Also private visits welcome, please* **Tel 0834 812222**

Hilton Court Nurseries ♿✲❀ (Mrs Cheryl Lynch) Roch. From Haverfordwest take the A487 to St Davids. 6m from Haverfordwest signs L to Hilton Court Nurseries. 4 acres of garden with superb setting overlooking ponds and woodlands. Spectacular lily ponds in July and August; wild flower walks; unusual trees and shrubs giving colour throughout the year. Nursery adjoining. TEAS. *Collecting box. Daily March to October 1 (9.30-5.30), October (10.30-4)*

Living Garden ✻❀ (Alan C Clarke Esq) 4a Brynmorlais Bryn, Llanelli; 2½m NE of town on B4297. Parking 'Royal Oak' Bryn. Garden near by (signed). Long, slim plantsman's garden subdivided for interest. Wide range of plants; terracotta ware, pools and water features. TEAS in aid of Relate. *Adm £1 Chd 25p. Sun June 4, July 2 (2-5.30); also private visits welcome, please* **Tel 01554 821274** *April to Oct*

¶Llanerchaeron ♿✻❀ (P G James) The National Trust. Lampeter. 2m inland from Aberaeron, to the N of the A482 Lampeter to Aberaeron rd. Formerly the pleasure grounds and kitchen gardens to Llanerchaeron House, these 12-acre gardens are undergoing restoration by volunteers and others under the direction of The National Trust with very limited resources. The lake and surrounding woods and paths are yet to be restored. Visitors can see restoration at a very early stage. TEA. *Adm £1.80. Sun Aug 27 (10-4)*

Llanllyr ♿✻❀ (Mr & Mrs Robert Gee) Talsarn. 6m NW of Lampeter on B4337 to Llanrhystud. Garden of about 4 acres, originally laid out in 1830s, renovated, replanted and extended since 1986. Mixed borders; lawns; bulbs; large fish pond with bog and water plants. Formal water garden. Shrub rose borders; foliage, species and old-fashioned plants. TEAS *Adm £1.50 Chd 50p. Sun June 18 (2-6). Private visits welcome April to Oct. Please write*

¶Llwyncelyn ✻❀ (Mr & Mrs Stewart Neal). Glandyfi. On A487 from Aberystwyth (12m) to Machynlleth (6m). Coming from Aberystwyth pass through Eglwysfach. Turn R up drive with grey double-fronted garage, just before Glandyfi sign. Approx 8-acre woodland garden with small arboretum incl collection of specie and hybrid rhododendrons, azaleas, embothrium etc; herbaceous border and kitchen garden. A dingle fernery runs alongside a tributary to the Dyfi. Lovely view of Mill House waterfalls. TEA. *Adm £1.50 Acc chd 50p. Sun May 21 (2-6)*

7 Maes yr Awel ✻❀ (Mrs Beryl Birch) Ponterwyd. From Aberystwyth take A44 towards Llangurig. At Ponterwyd Village, turn R on to A4120 Devil's Bridge rd, then turn 1st L almost immed. Small hillside garden in mountainous surroundings. 16yrs challenging gardening on steep acid meadowland at an altitude of approx 800ft have resulted in sheltered 'hidden' gardens with pools and fountain, herbaceous plantings, flowering shrubs and specimen trees. Ample seating; large conservatory for refreshments in inclement weather. TEA. *Adm 70p Acc chd free. Wed, Sat July 26, 29 (12-5)*

¶Maesyrynn ♿❀ (Mr & Mrs Thomas) Nantycaws. From Carmarthen take A48 dual carriageway E towards Swansea. After approx 3m turn L for Nantycaws. From Swansea, sign reads Police HQ and Nantycaws. Drive 300yds BP garage on L. Turn R into lane opp; 2nd bungalow on L. Plantsman's cottage garden approx ½ acre. Mainly herbaceous beds and shrubs. Pond and water feature, pergolas and raised beds. Highly productive vegetable garden with greenhouses. Lovely views in rural setting. TEAS. *Adm £1 Chd free (Share to Coleshill Social Centre, Llanelli©). Sat, Sun July 8, 9 (10-6). Parties welcome June to Sept, please* **Tel 01267 234198**

The Mill House ✻ (Prof & Mrs J M Pollock) Glandyfi. On main A487 rd from Aberystwyth to Machynlleth, 5½m from Machynlleth. Coming from Aberystwyth direction, pass through Eglwysfach village; turn R up lane which is almost directly opposite roadside sign for Glandyfi (on L) Mill House is 2nd house up this lane (approx 150yds). [OS 691963] Approx 1-acre garden of a former water mill. Mainly woodland in character with azaleas, rhododendrons, mill pond, stream and waterfalls. *Collecting Box. Private visits welcome Suns, Weds May 3, 7, 10, 14, 17, 21, 24, 28, 31 (11-5.30) please* **Tel 01654 781342**

Millinford ✻❀ (Drs B W & A D Barton) Millin, The Rhos, 3m E of Haverfordwest; on A40 to Carmarthen turn R signed The Rhos, take turn to Millin, R at Millin Chapel then immediate L over river bridge. 4 acres on bank of Millin Creek. Plantsman's garden, large collection of trees and shrubs with alpine area, herbaceous borders and small lake. TEAS. *Adm £1.50 Chd 50p (Share to NSPCC®). Sat, Sun July 22, 23 (11-6)*

Old Cilgwyn Gardens ♿ (Mr & Mrs E Fitzwilliams) Newcastle Emlyn. Situated 1m N of Newcastle Emlyn on the B4571, turn R into entrance gates in dip in rd. 12-acre woodland garden set in parkland, 53 acres of which are Sites of Special Scientific Interest; some of the oldest oaks or remains that exist in UK, snowdrops, daffodils, bluebells, azaleas, rhododendrons etc; all planted since 1945 but many new rhododendrons planted in last few yrs, ponds and Chinese bridge. For those prepared to walk, a 100yr-old tulip tree can be seen on the S.S.S.I. land. *Adm £1.50. Private parties welcome all year, please* **Tel 01239 710244**

Pant-yr-Holiad ✻❀ (Mr & Mrs G H Taylor) Rhydlewis, 12m NW Llandysul. NE Cardigan. From coast rd take B4334 at Brynhoffnant S towards Rhydlewis; after 1m turn left; driveway 2nd L. 5-acres embracing walled garden housing tender plants, alpine beds, water features, rare trees and shrubs in woodland setting; extensive collection rhododendron species; fancy water-fowl. Recently completed area with collections of birch and unusual herbaceous plants. TEA. *Adm £1.50 Chd 50p (Share to Rhydlewis Village Hall®). Only open Suns April 23, May 14, June 4 (2-5)*

Penrallt Ffynnon ❀ (Mr R D Lord & Ms Jane Lord) Cwm-cou, 3m NW of Newcastle Emlyn. Follow Cwm-cou to Cardigan rd (B4570) up long hill for 1¼m; turn right for 150yds; ignore sharp left bend, bear right along narrow lane for 400yds. Maturing collection of trees and shrubs in 4½ acres; crammed with some stunning plantings; eucalyptus species, maples, cherries, shrub roses, conifers, camellia hedge; rhododendrons, flowering Christmas to June; many varieties of daffodil. All year interest but especially Feb to early summer & autumn colour. Seeds for sale. *Collecting box. Private visits welcome all year, please* **Tel 01239 710654**

Regular Openers. Too many days to include in diary. Usually there is a wide range of plants giving year-round interest. See head of county section for the name and garden description for times etc.

¶**Plas Llidiardau** ♿✂❀ (L A Stalbow & G Taylor) Llanilar. 7m SE of Aberystwyth. Take A487 Aberystwyth to Aberaeron rd. 3m S of Aberystwyth turn onto A485 to Tregaron and Llanilar. From Llanilar take B4575 to Trawsgoed. Plas Llidiardau is ¾m on R. 7-acre garden on old landscaped site continuously developed and planted since 1985. Wide selection of unusual plants in a variety of environments. Double herbaceous borders, formal pond, gravel garden, walled garden, organic raised beds, wooded areas, stream, meadow walk. TEAS in aid of Llanilar Community Development Association. *Adm £1.50 Chd 50p. Sun July 16 (1-6). Private visits welcome May to July, please* **Tel 01974 241434**

Post House ✂❀ (Mrs Jo Kenaghan) Cwmbach 6m N of St Clears. From Carmarthen W on A40. Take B4298 through Meidrim; leave by centre lane signed Llanboidy. Turn right at Xrds signed Blaenwaun; right at Xrds to Cwmbach; garden bottom of hill. From Whitland E on A40, left at Ivydean nurseries, right at 3rd Xrds signed Cwmbach. 4-acre valley garden; rhododendrons, azaleas, camellias, unusual trees and shrubs underplanted with hardy orchids, anemonies, trilliums, wild snowdrops, bluebells, etc. Large pool, bog garden. Old roses, herbaceous plants. Greenhouses and conservatory. Plants for sale. TEAS. *Adm £1.50 OAP's & Chd £1.* ▲*Suns May 7, 14 (2pm onwards). Private parties welcome, please* **Tel 01994 484213**

Saundersfoot Bay Leisure Park ♿❀ (Ian Shuttleworth Esq) Broadfield, Saundersfoot. On B4316, ¾m S from centre of Saundersfoot. Interesting layout of lawns, shrubs and herbaceous borders with many plants of botanical interest in 20-acre modern holiday leisure park. Large rock garden and water feature; laburnum walk; Japanese Garden. Holders of a National collection of Pontentilla fruticosa. Tea Saundersfoot. *Adm free. April 1 to Oct 28 daily (10-5)*

Slebech Hall ♿❀ (The Lady Jean Philipps) 6m E of Haverfordwest. From Carmarthen via A40, take 1st turn left after Canaston Bridge, signed The Rhos; drive on left, about ½m with 1 white lodge. Bus: Haverfordwest-Tenby or Haverfordwest-Carmarthen; bus stop 3m. Large garden; fine position on bank of the Cleddau; picturesque ruins of Church of St. John of Jerusalem in garden. TEAS. *Adm £1 Chd free (Share to Uzmaston Church Restoration Fund®). Sun June 11 (2-6.30)*

Winllan (Mr & Mrs Ian Callan) Talsarn. 8m NNW of Lampeter on B4342, Talsarn-Llangeitho rd. 6-acres wildlife garden with large pond, herb-rich meadow, small woodland and 600 yds of river bank walk. Over 200 species of wildflowers with attendant butterflies, dragonflies and birds. Limited suitability for wheelchairs. *Adm £1.50 Chd 50p (under 12 free). Open May & June daily (12-6). Also private visits welcome July & Aug, please* **Tel 01570-470612**

The Glamorgans

Hon County Organiser: Mrs Christopher Cory, Penllyn Castle, Cowbridge, South Glamorgan CF7 7RQ Tel 01446 772780

DATES OF OPENING

By appointment

For telephone numbers and other details see garden descriptions. Private visits welcomed

11 Arno Road, Little Coldbrook
Beech Croft, Moulton, nr Barry
Dumgoyne, Radyr
11 Eastcliff, Southgate, Swansea
Ffynnon Deilo, Pendoylan
Pontygwaith Farm, Edwardsville
Ty Gwyn Gardens, Penylan, Cardiff
19 Westfield Road, Glyncoch, Pontypridd
9 Willowbrook Gardens, Mayals, Swansea

Parties only

Cwmpennar Gardens
24 Elm Grove Place, Dinas Powis

April 30 Sunday
Merthyr Mawr House, Bridgend

May 7 Sunday
Penllyn Castle, Cowbridge

May 14 Sunday
9 Willowbrook Garden, Mayals, Swansea

May 21 Sunday
Coedarhydyglyn, Cardiff

May 28 Sunday
Dumgoyne, Radyr
Springside, Pen-y-Turnpike, Dinas Powys

June 4 Sunday
Dumgoyne, Radyr
Llanvithyn House, Llancarfan

June 18 Sunday
The Clock House, Llandaff
Gelly Farm, Cymmer

June 24 Saturday
Cwmpennar Gardens

June 25 Sunday
Cwmpennar Gardens
11 Eastcliff, Southgate, Swansea

July 2 Sunday
Pontygwaith Farm, Edwardsville
Ty Gwyn Gardens, Penylan, Cardiff

July 9 Sunday
Beech Croft, Moulton, nr Barry

July 16 Sunday
29 Min-y-Coed, Radyr
Pantygôg, Pont Lasse, Swansea

August 6 Sunday
29 Min-y-Coed, Radyr
Pontygwaith Farm, Edwardsville

DESCRIPTIONS OF GARDENS

11 Arno Road ✇❀ (Mrs D Palmer) Little Coldbrook. From A4050 Cardiff to Barry, take roundabout marked Barry Docks and Sully. Then 2nd R into Coldbrook Rd, 2nd L into Langlands Rd, then 6th R into Norwood Cresc; 1st L into Arno Rd. 40ft × 30ft informal plantsman's garden with ponds, herbaceous plants, gravelled area planted with low growing plants. Hardy geraniums; penstemons specialities. TEAS. *Adm £1. Private visits welcome weekends and Wednesdays May to Oct, please* **Tel 01446 743642**

¶Beech Croft ❀ (Mr & Mrs P J Heath) Moulton. 2m from Barry/3m from A48. Turning off A4266 (Five Mile Lane) to Moulton and Llancarfan opp The Three Horseshoes. ¾ acre; part Camping and Caravan Club Hideway Site. No special features; varied shrubs, bedding plants, fish pond, kitchen garden. Wheelchairs with care. TEA. *Adm £1 Chd 50p. Sun July 9 (2-6). Private visits welcome, please* **Tel 01446 735877**

The Clock House ♿✇❀ (Prof & Mrs Bryan Hibbard) Cathedral Close, Llandaff, 2m W of Cardiff. Follow signs to Cathedral via A4119. Bus: Cardiff alight Maltsters Arms. Small walled garden; fine old trees; wide variety of shrubs and plants; important collection of shrub, species and old roses. NT stall. TEA. *Adm £1.50 Acc chd free. Sun June 18 (2-6)*

Coedarhydyglyn ♿ (Sir Cennydd Traherne) 5m W of Cardiff. Bus: Western Welsh, Cardiff-Cowbridge, alight gates. Natural terrain, pleasant situation; lawns, flowering shrubs, good collection of conifers; Japanese garden, fine trees. TEA. *Adm £1 Chd 20p (Share to Cardiff and District Samaritans®). Sun May 21 (2.30-6)*

Cwmpennar Gardens ✇❀ Mountain Ash 1m. From A4059 turn R 100yds past the traffic lights; follow sign to Cefnpennar, follow rd uphill through woods for ¾m, bear R sharply uphill before bus shelter, gardens 200yds. Car park 100yds past bus shelter. Mixture of formal and informal gardens with some natural woodland in all 3 of conservation interest. Variety of shrubs, rhododendrons and azaleas, rockeries, shrub roses; new plantings of shrubs and roses; water features. Rich in bird life, with nest boxes usually occupied. Gardens high on mountain side in secluded rural surroundings of coal mining valley. Gardens filmed for television. TEAS. Glamorgan Wildlife Trust Sales stall. *Combined adm £1 Chd 50p (Share to St Margarets Church Restoration Fund®). Sat, Sun June 24, 25 (2-6)*

The Cottage (Judge & Mrs Hugh Jones)
Ivy Cottage (Mr & Mrs D H Phillips)
Woodview (Mrs V Bebb)

Dumgoyne ✇❀ (Mr & Mrs Hubert Jackson) 90 Heol Isaf, Radyr. A4119 Cardiff-Llantrisant rd; 2m W of Llandaff Rd turn R on to B4262 for Radyr. Rhondda buses: alight at Radyr turning. Cardiff bus service 33 stops near house. Small, immaculate, Chelsea-inspired garden; large glasshouse with superb collection of pelargoniums. *Adm £1 Acc chd free (Share to Radyr Chain Voluntary Orgn.©). For NGS, special plant sale days Suns May 28, June 4 (2.30-5). Private visits welcome Sats, Suns, plant sales always available, please* **Tel 01222 842550**

11 Eastcliff ♿✇❀ (Mrs Gill James) Southgate. Take the Swansea to Gower road and travel 6m to Pennard. Go through the village of Southgate and take the 2nd exit off the roundabout. Garden 200yds on the L. Seaside garden approx ⅓ acre and developed in a series of island and bordered beds for spring and summer interest. A large number of white and silver plants. Unusual plants and shrubs. TEA. *Adm £1 Chd free. Sun June 25 (2-5). Also private visits welcome, please* **Tel 01792 233310**

24 Elm Grove Place ♿✇❀ (Mr & Mrs J Brockhurst) Dinas Powis. Elm Grove Place is a cul-de-sac 200yds E of Dinas Powis Railway Station on the Cardiff to Barry rd (A4055) under railway bridge, 4m from Cardiff, 3m from Barry. Plantsman's garden 60m × 30m, herbaceous, shrubs, greenhouse and several alpine and scree beds; patio area with some unusual container plants; pergola with clematis, wisteria and jasmine. TEA. *Adm £1 Chd free. Private visits welcome anytime between May 1 to Sept 1, please* **Tel 01222 513681**

Ffynnon Deilo ✇ (Mr & Mrs John Lloyd) Pendoylan Cowbridge 4½m. A48 Cardiff to Cowbridge. From Cardiff turn R at Sycamore Cross (½-way between St Nicholas and Bonvilston) to Peterston-Super-Ely; take 2nd L garden ¾m on R. Cottage garden with fish pond & Holy Well; interesting plants. Difficult for wheelchairs. TEA. *Adm £1.50 Chd free (£1 each for parties over 10). Private visits welcome April to Aug, please* **Tel 01446 760292**

Gelly Farm ✇❀ (Mrs A Appleton, Mrs L Howells, Mrs S Howells) Cymmer. 10m N E of Port Talbot, on A4107, ½m beyond Cymmer, towards Treorchy, turning off rd on R. 4 small varied gardens and 1 vegetable garden grouped around the farmyard of a historically listed working hill farmstead on the slopes of a steep valley 'as much a cultural experience as a horticultural one'. TEAS £1. *Adm £1.50 Chd free (Share to The Royal Agricultural Benevolent Institution®). Sun June 18 (2-6)*

Llanvithyn House ✇❀ (Mr & Mrs L H W Williams) Llancarfan 1.8m S of A48 at Bonvilston, sign for Llancarfan 100yds W of Bonvilston Garage, 1m N of Llancarfan. Medium-size garden on site of C6 monastery. C17 gatehouse. Lawns, interesting trees, shrubs, borders. TEAS if fine. *Adm £1.50 Chd 25p. Sun June 4 (2-6)*

Merthyr Mawr House ♿✇❀ (Mr & Mrs Murray McLaggan) Merthyr Mawr. 2m SW of Bridgend. Large garden with flowering borders, shrubs, scree garden; wood garden with chapel ruin C14 on site of Iron Age fort. TEA. *Adm £1.50 Chd £1 (Share to Princess of Wales Hospital, Bridgend CRMF®). Sun April 30 (2-6)*

29 Min-y-Coed ✇❀ (Mr & Mrs J H Taylor) Radyr, 6m from Cardiff. On A4119 2m W of Llandaff turn R on B4262 towards Morganstown. From M4 junction 32 on A470 to Taffs Well turn L, then L to B4262 for Radyr. Hillside terraced informal garden with year round colour. TEAS. *Adm £1 Chd free. Suns July 16, Aug 6 (2-5.30)*

¶Pantygôg ♿✂ (Mr & Mrs R H David) Pont Lasse. 5m N of Swansea. Junction 46 M4. Turn L and follow signs for Morriston Hospital for 1m. Just before the hospital turn L. Drive 200yds. Pantygôg, 2nd bungalow on R. Just over 2 acres, half of which is a new garden currently being developed. Trees, shrubs, herbaceous and kitchen garden. TEA. *Adm £1 Chd 50p. Sun July 16 (2-6)*

Penllyn Castle ♿✂ (Mrs Christopher Cory) 3m NW of Cowbridge. From A48 turn N at Pentre Meyrick. Turn 1st R and at T-junction straight ahead through gate, leaving church on L. Large garden with fine views; old trees and some new planting; spring shrubs (rhododendrons and magnolias) and bulbs. TEA. *Adm £1.50 Chd 50p. Sun May 7 (2-6)*

Pontygwaith Farm ♿❀ (Mr & Mrs R J G Pearce) Edwardsville. Take A4054 Old Cardiff to Merthyr Rd. Travel N for approx 3m through Quaker's Yard and Edwardsville. 1m out of Edwardsville turn sharp L by old bus shelter. Garden at bottom of hill. Medium-sized garden; surrounding C17. farmhouse adjacent to Trevithick's Tramway; situated in picturesque wooded valley; fish pond, lawns, perennial borders. TEAS. *Adm £1 Chd 50p. Suns July 2 Aug 6 (2-6). Private visits welcome, please* **Tel 01443 411137**

Springside ✂❀ (Prof & Mrs Michael Laurence) Dinas Powys. From Cardiff take B4055 to Penarth and Dinas Powys as far as the Leckwith (Cardiff Distributor Rd) roundabout. Then take B4267 to Llandough, up Leckwith Hill past Leckwith Village, take R-hand fork in rd into Pen-y-Turnpike as far as the 30mph sign. Turn R immed. into Springside. Undulating 2-acre garden recently rescued after 30yrs of wilderness. Spacious, with views and newly planted trees: small ponds and old village water supply returned to nature, where children must be supervised; vegetable garden. Parking in the grounds only available in dry weather. TEA. *Adm £1.50 Chd 50p (Share to Dinas Powys Orchestra©). Sun May 28 (2-6)*

Ty Gwyn Gardens ✂❀ Penylan, Cardiff. N from city centre. Ty Gwyn Rd links Penylan Hill (nr Roath Park) with Cyncoed Road. Take Cardiff East (junction 29) off M4. Take Llanedeyrn interchange exit off Eastern Avenue. Take Cyncoed exit off small roundabout. TEAS at 10 Ty Gwyn Rd. *Combined adm £2 Chd free. Sun July 2 (2-6)*

The George Thomas Centre for Hospice Care ❀ (The George Thomas Memorial Trust) City garden on 2 levels divided by a lovely wisteria. 1st level has an interesting herbaceous bed; 2nd level has a reclaimed bank and some good camellia shrubs; also well established pond. Much new planting. *Private visits welcome, please* **Tel 01222 485345**

8 Ty Gwyn Rd (Mr & Mrs Colin Daniel) Next door to George Thomas Centre. Reorganised during 1993; several new trees planted; gazebo, patio; pond with koi carp and waterfall

19 Westfield Road ✂❀ (Mr & Mrs Brian Dockerill) Glyncoch Pontypridd. From Pontypridd travel 1.5m N along B4273. Take L turn by school. At top of hill follow rd to L. Take first R and R again into Westfield Rd. ½-acre organic garden divided by hedges and dry stone walls into smaller enclosures each with a separate character. Sunny borders near the house lead on to areas under large trees with the emphasis on shade loving and woodland species. The wide range of plants grown enables us to welcome visitors to see something of interest throughout the yr. TEAS. *Adm £1 Chd 50p. Private visits welcome, please* **Tel 01443 402999**

9 Willowbrook Gardens ✂ (Dr & Mrs Gallagher) Mayals, 4m W of Swansea on A4067 (Mumbles) rd to Blackpill; take B4436 (Mayals) rd; 1st R leads to Westport Ave along W boundary of Clyne Park; 1st L into cul-de-sac. ½-acre informal garden designed to give natural effect with balance of form and colour between various areas linked by lawns; unusual trees suited to small suburban garden, esp conifers and maples; rock and water garden. TEAS. *Adm £1.20 Chd 30p. Sun May 14 (2-6) also private visits welcome, please* **Tel 01792 403268**

Gwent

Hon County Organiser: Mrs Glynne Clay, Lower House Farm, Nantyderry, Abergavenny NP7 9DP Tel 01873 880257

Asst Hon County Organiser: Mrs R L Thompson, Llangwilym House, Llanfihangel Gobion, Abergavenny Tel 01873 840269

DATES OF OPENING

By appointment

For telephone numbers and other details see garden descriptions. Private visits welcomed

Castle House, Usk
The Chain Garden, Abergavenny
The Graig, nr Raglan
Great Campston, Llanfihangel Crucorney
Lower House Farm, Nantyderry
Orchard House, Coed Morgan, Abergavenny
Penpergwm Lodge, nr Abergavenny
Tredegar House & Park, Newport
Trostrey Lodge, Bettws Newydd, nr Usk
Veddw House, The Veddw, Devauden
Wern Farm, Glascoed

Regular openings
For details see garden description

Part-y-Seal, Grosmont, nr Abergavenny. 1st and 3rd Sun May 21 to Aug 20 and Aug 27
Penpergwm Lodge, nr Abergavenny. Thurs, Fris & Sats April 1 to Aug 31
Tredegar House & Park, Newport. Easter to end Oct

April 9 Sunday
Great Campston, Llanfihangel Crucorney
April 16 Sunday
Llanover, nr Abergavenny
May 7 Sunday
Lower House Farm, Nantyderry
May 8 Monday
Lower House Farm, Nantyderry
May 14 Sunday
Part-y-Seal, Grosmont, nr Abergavenny
May 21 Sunday
Bryngwyn Manor, Raglan
Chwarelau Farm, Llanfapley, nr Abergavenny
May 28 Sunday
Llan-y-Nant, Coed Morgan, nr Abergavenny
May 29 Monday
Traligael, Whitebrook
June 4 Sunday
The Graig & Box Tree Cottage, nr Raglan ‡
Trostrey Lodge, Bettws Newydd, nr Usk ‡
June 7 Wednesday
Trostrey Lodge, Bettws Newydd, nr Usk
June 11 Sunday
Oakgrove, St Arvans, Chepstow ‡
Veddw House, The Veddw, Devauden ‡
June 18 Sunday
Grace Dieu Court, Dingestow
Wern Farm, Glascoed
June 25 Sunday
Llanfair Court, nr Abergavenny ‡
Penpergwm Lodge, nr Abergavenny ‡
July 1 Saturday
Great Campston, Llanfihangel Crucorney
July 2 Sunday
Court St Lawrence, Llangovan, nr Usk
Great Campston, Llanfihangel Crucorney
July 9 Sunday
Great Killough, nr Abergavenny ‡
Orchard House, Coed Morgan, nr Abergavenny ‡
July 16 Sunday
Clytha Park, nr Abergavenny
Veddw House, The Veddw, Devauden
July 18 Tuesday
Veddw House, The Veddw, Devauden
July 23 Sunday
Brooklands, Mardy, Abergavenny
July 30 Sunday
Tredegar House & Park, Newport
August 13 Sunday
Veddw House, The Veddw, Devauden
August 27 Sunday
Lower House Farm, Nantyderry
August 28 Monday
Lower House Farm, Nantyderry
September 3 Sunday
Castle House, Usk
Great Campston, Llanfihangel Crucorney
September 10 Sunday
Tredegar House & Park, Newport
September 17 Sunday
Part-y-Seal, Grosmont, nr Abergavenny
Veddw House, The Veddw, Devauden

DESCRIPTIONS OF GARDENS

Brooklands ✲❀ (Mr & Mrs D G Gordon) Mardy. From Monmouth, Newport and Merthyr, take the A465 rd to Hereford at roundabout 1m S of Abergavenny. Take 1st turning L. Brooklands approx ½m from that junction. Approx 1½ acres; herbaceous, lge rockery garden, woodland walk. **Brooklands Bungalow** (Mr & Mrs G Smith) Small ornamental garden adjacent to the Gavenny R linked to adjoining 3-acre woodland walk by footbridge. TEAS. *Adm £1.50 Chd 75p, 5 and under free. Sun July 23 (2-6)*

Bryngwyn Manor ♿✲ (Mr S Inglefield) 2m W of Raglan. Turn S off old A40 (Abergavenny-Raglan rd) at Croes Bychan (Raglan Garden Centre); house ¼m up lane. 3 acres; good trees, mixed borders, spring bulbs. TEAS. *Adm £1.50 Chd under 10 free. Sun May 21 (2-6)*

Castle House (Mr & Mrs J H L Humphreys) Usk; 200yds from Usk centre; turn up lane by fire station. Medium-sized garden; a flower garden of orderly disorder around ruins of Usk Castle. TEAS. *Adm £1 Chd free. Sun Sept 3 (2-6). Private visits also welcome, please* **Tel 0129167 2563**

The Chain Garden ✲ (Mrs C F R Price) Chapel Rd; 1m N of Abergavenny. Turn off A40 (on Brecon side of town) into Chapel Rd, garden at top of rd. 2 acres with stream; lawns; rhododendrons; shrubs, fruit and vegetables. *Adm £1 Chd free. Private visits welcome April 1 to Sept 30, please* **Tel 01873 853825**

Chwarelau Farm ✲❀ (Mr & Mrs Maurice Trowbridge) On B4233 3½m E of Abergavenny. Medium-sized garden with magnificent views, approached down 200yd drive fringed by ornamental trees and shrubs. TEA. *Adm £1 Chd 50p. Sun May 21 (2-6)*

Clytha Park ♿ (R Hanbury-Tenison Esq) ½ way between Abergavenny and Raglan on old rd (not A40). 5 acres; C18 layout; trees, shrubs; lake. Teas in aid of Cafod. *Adm £1 Chd 50p. Sun July 16 (2-6)*

Court St Lawrence ♿❀ (Mrs G D Inkin) Llangovan, 6m SW of Monmouth, 5m NE of Usk, between Pen-y-Clawdd and Llangovan. 5 acres of garden and woodland with trees, shrubs, lake, roses etc. TEAS, plants and produce stalls. *Adm £1 Chd 25p. Sun July 2 (2-6)*

Grace Dieu Court ♿✲❀ (Mr & Mrs David McIntyre) Dingestow. 1½m NW of Dingestow Village which is 1m N of old Raglan-Monmouth rd (not dual carriageway). 3-acre open country garden in rolling countryside. Started from scratch in 1986. Mostly roses as shrubs, climbers and hedges; 2 lge ponds; herbaceous border, young specimen trees, shrubs and fine old oaks. TEAS. *Adm £1.50 Chd 50p. Sun June 18 (2-6)*

The Graig ♿✂❀ (Mrs Rainforth) Pen-y-Clawdd, SW of Monmouth. Turn S from Raglan-Monmouth rd (not motorway) at sign to Pen-y-Clawdd. Bus: Newport-Monmouth, alight Keen's shop, ½m. Mixed cottage garden with interesting shrubs & roses. TEAS. *Private visits welcome, please* **Tel 01600 83270.** Also open **Box Tree Cottage** ♿✂❀ (Mr & Mrs A Ward) Dingestow. On old A40 between Mitchel Troy & Raglan; ¾m from The Graig. 1-acre cottage garden; mixed borders, lawn, shrubs, conifers. *Combined adm £1.50 Chd free. Sun June 4 (2-6)*

Great Campston ✂❀ (Mr & Mrs A D Gill) 7m NE of Abergavenny; 2m towards Grosmont off A465 at Llanfihangel Crucorney. Drive on R just before brow of hill. Pretty 2-acre garden set in wonderful surroundings. Designed and planted from scratch by Mrs Gill, a garden designer; wide variety of interesting plants and trees enhanced by lovely stone walls, paving and summer house with fantastic views. The house stands 750ft above sea level on S facing hillside with spring fed stream feeding 2 ponds. TEAS. *Adm £2 Chd 50p (Share to 'Mind'®). Sun April 9; Sat, Sun July 1, 2; Sun Sept 3 (2-6). Private visits welcome, please* **Tel 01873 890633**

Great Killough ♿✂❀ (Mr & Mrs John F Ingledew) Llantilio Crossenny, 6m E of Abergavenny. S of B4233. 3-acre garden created in the 1960s to complement mediaeval house. TEAS. *Adm £1 Chd free (Share to Barnardo's®). Sun July 9 (2-6)*

Llanfair Court ♿ (Sir William Crawshay) 5m SE of Abergavenny. Route old A40 and B4598. Medium-sized garden, herbaceous border, flowering shrubs, roses, water garden; modern sculpture. TEAS. *Adm £1 Chd 50p. Sun June 25 (2-6)*

Llanover ♿ (R A E Herbert, Esq) S of Abergavenny. Bus: Abergavenny-Pontypool, alight drive gates. Large water garden; some rare plants, magnolias. TEAS. *Adm £1.50 Chd 50p. Sun April 16 (2-6)*

Llan-y-Nant ♿❀ (Mr & Mrs Charles Pitchford) Coed Morgan. 4m from Abergavenny, 5m from Raglan on old A40 (now B4598) Raglan to Abergavenny rd. Turn up lane opp 'Chart House' inn; pass Monmouthshire Hunt Kennels 500yds on R. 3 acres of garden and woodlands. Lawn, beds, shrubs, herbs, alpines and kitchen garden. Small lake with wild life. TEAS. *Adm £1.50 Chd 50p. Sun May 28 (2-6)*

Lower House Farm ✂❀ (Mr & Mrs Glynne Clay) Nantyderry, 7m SE of Abergavenny. From Usk-Abergavenny rd, B4598, turn off at Chain Bridge. Medium-sized garden designed for all year interest; mixed borders, fern island, bog garden, herb bed, paved area, unusual plants. Late flowering perennials. Featured in magazines and on T.V. and in NGS video 1. TEAS. *Adm £1.50 Chd 50p. Suns, Mons May 7, 8; Aug 27, 28 (2-6). Private visits also welcome, please* **Tel 01873 880257**

Oakgrove ♿✂❀ (Mr & Mrs C Hughes Davies) St Arvans. 1½m from Chepstow on A466 towards Monmouth, drive on L after racecourse. 2½ acres; fine beech trees, herbaceous borders, shrub roses; grey and silver border; recently established collection of fagus and nothofagus; wild garden. TEAS. *Adm £1.50 Chd 50p. Sun June 11 (2-6)*

Orchard House ♿✂❀ (Mr & Mrs B R Hood) Coed Morgan. 1½m N of old Raglan-Abergavenny rd. Approx 6m from Abergavenny. Turn opp King of Prussia or The Charthouse. A garden of approx 1 acre with mixed borders of unusual herbaceous plants and shrubs, rosebeds and lawn. TEAS in aid of St David's Church. *Adm £1 Chd 30p. Sun July 9 (2-6). Private visits welcome April to Sept, please* **Tel 01873 840289**

¶Part-y-Seal ✂ (Mr & Mrs F Ong) Grosmont. 12m NE of Abergavenny. Route A465 and B4347. 1m S of Grosmont Village/Castle. 3 acres of mixed gardens set in beautiful surroundings, fine mature trees, lawns, terraces, rhododendrons, azaleas, roses, herbaceous borders, walled garden, and large kitchen garden. (Cane and rattan furniture for sale at main house.) TEAS. *Adm £1 Chd 30p. 1st and 3rd Suns from May 21 to Aug 20, Aug 27 (2-6). For NGS Suns May 14, Sept 17 (2-6)*

Penpergwm Lodge ♿❀ (Mr & Mrs Simon Boyle) 3m SE of Abergavenny. From Abergavenny take B 4598 towards Usk, after 2½m turn L opp King of Prussia Inn. Entrance 300yds on L. A 3-acre formal garden with mature trees, hedges & lawns; interesting potager with arches of vines & roses, mixed unusual plants & vegetables; rose walk, apple & pear pergola and S-facing terraces with sun-loving plants & special colour themes. Nursery with rare plants, many from the garden, specialising in unusual hardy perennials. Home of Catriona Boyle's School of Gardening, now in its 9th yr. Featured on Welsh TV and in Hortus and featured on NGS video 3. TEAS Sats only (and Sun June 25 in aid of St Cadoc's Church). *Adm £1.50 Chd free. Thurs, Fris, Sats April 1 to Aug 31 (2-6). Sun June 25 (2-6). Private visits welcome, please* **Tel 01873 840208**

Traligael ❀ (Mr & Mrs E C Lysaght) 4m S of Monmouth via B4293 turn L for Whitebrook, or 3½m from A466 at Bigsweir Bridge past Whitebrook; garden alongside lane. 3-acre garden in woodland setting with water garden; rhododendrons and shrubs. *Adm £1 Chd free. Mon May 29 (2-6)*

Tredegar House & Park ♿✂❀ (Newport Borough Council) 2m SW of Newport Town Centre. Signposted from A48 (Cardiff rd) and M4 junction 28. Set in 90 acres of historic parkland surrounding a magnificent late C17 house (also open) are a series of C17 & C18 formal walled gardens. The early C18 Orangery Garden is currently being recreated following extensive archaeological and research work. The orangery is also open. The central Cedar Garden has wide recently revived herbaceous borders. On NGS days the private gardens around the Curator's Cottage and Home Farm Cottage are also open. Away from the house is an Edwardian sunken garden restored mid 1980s. Spectacular rhododendrons border the lake. TEAS. *Adm £1.50 Chd 50p (Share to The Friends of Tredegar House and Park®). For NGS Suns July 30, Sept 10 (11-6). House, Gardens etc open Easter to end of Oct, for details, please* **Tel 01633 815880**

Trostrey Lodge ✣❀ (Mr & Mrs R Pemberton) Bettws Newydd. Half way between Raglan and Abergavenny on old road (not A40). Turning to Bettws Newydd opposite Clytha gates, 1m on R. Pretty walled garden and small orchard in fine landscape; interesting plants; bring and buy plant sale; ice creams. *Adm £1 Chd free (Share to St David's Foundation®, Sun June 4 and Society for Welfare of Horses and Ponies® on Wed June 7). Sun, Wed June 4, 7 (2-6)*

¶Veddw House ✣❀ (Mr Charles Hawes & Mrs Anne Wareham) The Veddw. Devauden is midway on B4293 Monmouth to Chepstow rd. Veddw House is ¼m E of Devauden off rd running along N of Chepstow Park Wood. 1st house on R down lane at bottom of hill. 2½-acre garden still being developed with passionate enthusiasm. Divided into a variety of small gardens incl a formal vegetable garden. Also walks in 2-acre wood. *Adm £1.50 Chd 50p (Share to Gwent Branch CPRW®). Suns June 11, July 16, Aug 13, Sept 17, (2-6) Tues July 18 (6-8). Private visits welcome, please* **Tel 01291 650836**

Wern Farm ✣❀ (Mr & Mrs W A Harris) Between Usk and Little Mill on A472. Turn at signpost for Glascoed village, 1m from main rd (Beaufort Inn or Monkswood Garage). 1½-acres completely new garden created since 1984 following natural contours of ground; trees, shrubs, herbaceous plants, alpines, shrub roses; rockery; herbs; veg garden; small aviary; ¼ acre of flowers grown for drying. Demonstration of Bee-keeping by professional keeper and demonstration of wool spinning with organically dyed wool. Small nursery with many rare and unusual plants for sale. TEAS. *Adm £1.20 Chd 30p. Sun June 18 (2-6); Private visits also welcome, please* **Tel 01495 785363**

Gwynedd & Anglesey

Hon County Organisers:
(Anglesey & North Gwynedd) Mrs B S Osborne, Foxbrush, Port Dinorwic, Felinheli, Gwynedd LL56 4JZ Tel 01248 670463
(South Gwynedd) Mrs W N Jones, Waen Fechan, Islaw'r Dref, Dolgellau LL40 1TS Tel 01341 423479

DATES OF OPENING

By appointment

For telephone numbers and other details see garden descriptions. Private visits welcomed

Bont Fechan Farm, Llanystumdwy
Bryn Golygfa, Bontddu
Bryn Meifod, Glan Conwy
Bryniau, Boduan
Brynmelyn, Ffestiniog
Bryn-y-Bont, Nantmor
Foxbrush, Port Dinorwic, Felinheli
Glandderwen, Bontddu
Gwyndy Bach, Llandrygarn
Hafod Garregog, Nantmor
Hen Ysgoldy, Llanfrothen
Henllys Lodge, Beaumaris
Pencarreg, Glyn Garth, Menai Bridge
Penrhyn Castle, nr Bangor
Plas Muriau, Bettws-y-Coed
Plas Penhelig, Aberdovey

Parties only

Cefn Bere, Dolgellau
Crug Farm, nr Caernarfon
Maenan Hall, Llanrwst

Regular openings

For details see garden descriptions

Crug Farm, nr Caernarfon. Thurs to Suns & Bank Hol Mons Feb 26 to Sept 25.
Farchynys Cottage, Bontddu. Daily Sun to Fri.
Plas Muriau, Bettws-y-Coed. Thurs April to Sept incl
Plas Penhelig, Aberdovey. Wed to Sun April 1 to mid-Oct.

Sunday 19 March
Bryniau, Boduan

Sunday 16 April
Bont Fechan Farm, Llanystumdwy
Bryn Castell, Llanddona, Anglesey
Bryniau, Boduan
Crug Farm, nr Caernarfon ‡
Foxbrush, Port Dinorwic, Felinheli ‡

Monday 17 April
Crug Farm, nr Caernarfon ‡
Foxbrush, Port Dinorwic, Felinheli ‡

Sunday 30 April
Gilfach, Rowen, nr Conwy

Sunday 7 May
Bryniau, Boduan

Thursday 11 May
Plas Newydd, Llanfair Pwll

Sunday 14 May
Bont Fechan Farm, Llanystumdwy
Hafod Garregog, Nantmor

Wednesday 17 May
Farchynys Cottage, Bontddu

Sunday 21 May
Farchynys Cottage, Bontddu
Maenan Hall, Llanrwst

Sunday 28 May
Bryn Eisteddfod, Glan Conwy
Bryn Golygfa, Bontddu
Bryniau, Boduan
Crug Farm, nr Caernarfon ‡
Foxbrush, Port Dinorwic, Felinheli ‡
Glandderwen, Bontddu
Penrhyn Castle, nr Bangor
Pen-y-Parc, Beaumaris

Monday 29 May
Bryn Golygfa, Bontddu
Crug Farm, nr Caernarfon
Glandderwen, Bontddu

Saturday 17 June
Henllys Lodge, Beaumaris

Sunday 18 June
Bryniau, Boduan
Henllys Lodge, Beaumaris

Sunday 25 June
Foxbrush, Port Dinorwic, Felinheli
Sunday 2 July
Bont Fechan Farm, Llanystumdwy
Bryn Castell, Llanddona, Anglesey
Gilfach, Rowen, nr Conwy
The Herb Garden, Pentre Berw
Sunday 9 July
Bryniau, Boduan
Gwyndy Bach, Llandrygarn
Henllys Lodge, Beaumaris
Sunday 16 July
Crug Farm, nr Caernarfon
Sunday 30 July
Bryniau, Boduan
Sunday 20 August
Bont Fechan Farm, Llanystumdwy
Bryniau, Boduan
Gilfach, Rowen, nr Conwy
Maenan Hall, Llanrwst
Sunday 27 August
Crug Farm, nr Caernarfon
Monday 28 August
Crug Farm, nr Caernarfon
Sunday 10 September
Bryniau, Boduan
Sunday 1 October
Bryniau, Boduan
Sunday 22 October
Bryniau, Boduan

DESCRIPTIONS OF GARDENS

Bont Fechan Farm ♿❀ (Mr & Mrs J D Bean) Llanystumdwy. 2 m from Criccieth on the A487 to Pwllheli on the L-hand side of the main rd. Small garden with rockery, pond, herbaceous border, steps to river, large variety of plants. Nicely planted tubs. TEAS. *Adm 75p Chd 25p. Suns April 16, May 14, July 2, Aug 20 (11-5). Private visits welcome, please* **Tel 01766 522604**

¶Bryn Castell ✿❀ (Lady Grace Gibson) Wern. 3m NW of Beaumaris. First L opp telephone box before entering village. 1m down single track rd towards Wern-y-Wylan. 2 acres semi-wild gardens surrounding remote farmhouse with beautiful views. Pond and bog garden, wildflower lawns with bulbs and orchids; cottage garden with old roses and herbaceous plants; conservatory with vine. TEAS. *Adm £1 Chd free. Suns April 16, July 2 (11-5)*

Bryn Eisteddfod ♿ (Dr Michael Senior) Glan Conwy. 3½m SE Llandudno 3m W Colwyn Bay; up the hill (Bryn-y-Maen direction) from Glan Conwy Corner where A470 joins A55. 8 acres of landscaped grounds incl mature shrubbery, arboretum, old walled 'Dutch' garden, large lawn with ha-ha. Extensive views over Conwy Valley, Snowdonia National Park, Conwy Castle, town and estuary. TEA. *Adm £1 Chd 50p. Sun May 28 (2-5)*

Bryn Golygfa ✿❀ (Mrs K & Mr R Alexander) Dolgellau. 5m W of Dolgellau. Take A496 to Bontddu; garden is N 100yds past Bontddu Hall Hotel. Small garden on steep hillside; mixed planting incl rhododendrons and alpines. *Adm 50p Chd 25p. Sun, Mon May 28, 29 (11-5). Private visits welcome mid-May to mid-Aug, please* **Tel 01341 430260**

Bryn Meifod ✿❀ (Dr & Mrs K Lever) Graig Glan Conwy. Just off A470 1½m S of Glan Conwy. Follow signs for Aberconwy Nursery. ¾-acre garden developed over 25yrs but extensively replanted in the last 6yrs. Unusual trees and shrubs, scree and peat beds. Good autumn colours. Wide ranging collection of alpines especially autumn gentians and saxifrages. Extensive views towards Snowdonia and the Carneddau. *Collection Box. Private visits welcome, June to Sept, please* **Tel 01492 580875/580836**

Bryniau ❀ (P W Wright & J E Humphreys) Boduan. ½m down lane opp. St Buan's Church, Boduan, which is halfway between Nefyn and Pwllheli on the A497. New garden created since 1988 on almost pure sand. Over 80 types of trees; hundreds of shrubs, many unusual, showing that with a little effort, one can grow virtually anything anywhere. Plants & woodcraft for sale. TEAS. *Adm £1 Chd free. Suns March 19, April 16, May 7, 28, June 18, July 9, 30, Aug 20, Sept 10, Oct 1, 22 (11-6) and private visits welcome, please* **Tel 01758 7213 38**

Brynmelyn ✿ (Mr & Mrs A S Taylor) Cymerau Isaf. About 2m SW of Blaenau Ffestiniog, on A496 Maentwrog-Blaenau Ffestiniog Rd. Enter by lower gate in layby opp junction to Manod, by footpath sign. After 100yds leave car at garage and follow small footpath to R of garage, descending to stone bridge and Cymerau Falls. Continue over bridge and up hill, follow footpath L; garden about ¼m from garage. Upland garden surrounded by National Nature Reserve containing wide variety of plants providing interest throughout the season. *Adm £1 Chd 50p (Share to The National Osteoporosis Society®). Private visits welcome April 1 to Sept 15* **Tel Ffestiniog 01766 762684**. *Please telephone before 9.30 am or after dusk*

Bryn-y-Bont ❀ (Miss J Entwisle) Nantmor. 2½m S of Beddgelert, turn L over Aberglaslyn Bridge into A4085, 500yds turn L up hill, 2nd house on R. Small garden created since 1978 on S facing wooded hillside over looking Glaslyn Vale (As featured on Radio Wales 'Get Gardening' in 1990). *Adm £1 Chd free. Private visits welcome mid April to mid Sept (11-5pm). Parties welcome, please* **Tel 01766 890448**

Cefn Bere ✿ (Mr & Mrs Maldwyn Thomas) Cae Deintur, Dolgellau. Turn L at top of main bridge on Bala-Barmouth Rd (not the by-pass); turn R within 20yds; 2nd R behind school and first L half way up short hill. Small garden; extensive collection of alpines, bulbs and rare plants. Tea Dolgellau. *Collecting box. Private parties welcome, spring, summer and autumn months, please* **Tel Dolgellau 01341 422768**

Crug Farm ✿❀ (Mr & Mrs B Wynn-Jones) Griffiths Crossing. 2m NE of Caernarfon ¼m off main A487 Caernarfon to Bangor Road. Follow signs from roundabout to 'Crug Farm Plants'. Plantsman's garden; ideally situated; 2 to 3 acres grounds to old country house. Gardens filled with choice, unusual collections of climbers, and herbaceous plants; over 300 species of hardy geraniums. Featured in 'The Garden' and on BBC TV. Only partly suitable wheelchairs. TEAS in aid of local charities. *Collecting box for walled display garden open Thurs, Fri, Sat, Suns & Bank Hols Feb 26 to Sept 25 (10-6). See calendar for openings of private gardens. Adm £1 Chd free. Natural Rock garden only open Suns & Mons April 16, 17, May 28, 29, Sun July 16, Sun, Mon Aug 27, 28 (10-6). Private parties welcome please,* **Tel 01248 670232**

Farchynys Cottage ✂❀ (Mrs G Townshend) Bontddu. On A496 Dolgellau-Barmouth rd; well signed W of Bontddu village. 4 acres; partly well-established garden, with attractive, unusual shrubs and trees; partly natural woodland first extensive planting in 1982, new plantings each year. Silver Cup winner 'Wales in Bloom' 1987 Committee Award 1985, 1986 and 1989. Car park. TEAS. *Adm £1 Chd free. Open daily Sun to Fri (2-5).* ▲*For NGS Wed, Sun May 17, 21 (11-5).* **Tel 01341 430245**

Foxbrush ♿❀ (Mr & Mrs B S Osborne) Aber Pwll, Port Dinorwic, Felinheli. On Bangor to Caernarfon Road, entering village opp. layby with Felinheli sign post. Fascinating 3-acre country garden on site of old mill and created around winding river; rare and interesting plants; ponds and small wooded area. Extensive plant collections incl rhododendrons, ferns, primula, alpines, clematis and roses; 45ft long pergola; fan-shaped knot garden with traditional and unusual herbs; coaches welcome. Craft studio with jewellery, gifts. TEA. *Adm £1 Chd free. Suns April 16, 17, May 28, June 25 (10-5). Also private visits welcome, please* **Tel 01248 670463**

Gilfach ✂ (James & Isoline Greenhalgh) Rowen. At Xrds 100yds E of Rowen (4m S of Conwy) S towards Llanrwst, past Rowen School on L; turn up 2nd drive on L, signposted. 1-acre country garden on S facing slope overlooking Conwy Valley; set in 35 acres farm and woodland; mature shrubs; herbaceous border; small pool. Partly suitable wheelchairs which are welcome. Magnificent views of River Conwy and mountains. TEAS. *Adm £1 Chd 10p. Suns April 30, July 2, Aug 20 (11-5)*

Glandderwen ✂ (A M Reynolds Esq) 5m W of Dolgellau. Take A496 to Bontddu. Garden is on S 100yds past Bontddu Hall Hotel; large white wooden gates. ½-acre on N bank of Mawddach Estuary facing Cader Idris; set amid large oaks; shrubs, trees; steep and rocky nature. *Adm 50p Chd 25p. Sun, Mon, May 28, 29 (11-5). Private visits welcome May 1 to Sept 30* **Tel 01341 430229**

Gwyndy Bach ♿✂❀ (Keith & Rosa Andrew) Llandrygarn. From Llangefni take the B5109 towards Bodedern, the cottage is exactly 5m out on the L. A ¾-acre artist's garden set amidst rugged Anglesey landscape. Romantically planted in intimate 'rooms' with interesting plants and shrubs, old roses and secluded lily pond. Studio attached. TEAS. *Adm £1 Chd free. Sun July 9 (11-5.30). Also private visits welcome, please* **Tel 01407 720651**

Hafod Garregog ❀ (Mr & Mrs Hugh Mason) Nantmor, 5m N of Penrhyndeudraeth on A4085 towards Aberglaslyn. Garden in woodland setting with fine mountain views; trees, shrubs, flowers and vegetables; woodland bluebell walk. Shown on BBC's 'Gardener's World'. Now one of 'The Great Little Gardens of North Wales' Home of Rhys Goch Eryri AD 1430. Situated above R Hafod. Parties welcome. New garden being made. TEAS. *Adm £1 Chd free. Sun May 14 (11-5). Private visits welcome April to Oct* **Tel 01766 890282**

Hen Ysgoldy ✂ (Mr & Mrs Michael Jenkins) Llanfrothen. From Garreg via B4410, after ½m L; garden 200yds on R. Natural garden with streams and established trees, incl magnolias, eucalyptus and embothrium. Shrubs incl a variety of azaleas and rhododendrons, mixed borders planted for colour and interest most of the year round. *Collecting box. Private visits welcome April 1 to Aug 31* **Tel 01766 771231**

Henllys Lodge ♿✂❀ (Mr & Mrs K H Lane) Beaumaris. Past Beaumaris Castle, ½m turn L, 1st L again. Lodge at entrance to Henllys Hall Hotel drive. Approx 1-acre country garden, planted in traditional cottage style using perennials, shrubs, old roses and featuring extensive collection of hardy geraniums. Small woodland area. Stunning views across Menai Straits. TEAS. *Adm £1 Chd free. Sat, Sun June 17, 18, July 9 (2-5.30). Private visits welcome, please* **Tel 01248 810106**

The Herb Garden, Plant Hunter's Nursery ✂❀ (Mr & Mrs Tremaine-Stevenson) Pentre Berw. Follow A5 towards Holyhead Herb Garden is 1st R after Holland Arms Hotel. 1m from Gaerwen. Park in Holland Arms Garden Centre, secondary car park. Small pretty cottage garden, planted with many unusual and old-fashioned plants. A mixture of herbs, wild flowers, old roses and perennials mixed with gay abandon. Also stream, moisture plants and camomile lawn. Just under 2 acres in all the most part being plant nursery. Sensible shoes recommended. Teas at the 'Holland Arms' Garden Centre opp. *Adm £1. Sun July 2 (10-6)*

Maenan Hall ❀ (The Hon Christopher McLaren) Exactly 2m N of Llanrwst on E side of A470, ¼m S of Priory Hotel. Gardens created since 1956 by the late Christabel, Lady Aberconway and then present owner; 10 acres; lawns, shrub, rose and walled gardens; rhododendron dell; many species of beautiful and interesting plants, shrubs and trees set amongst mature oaks and other hardwoods; fine views of mountains across Conway valley. Home-made TEAS. *Adm £1.50 Chd 50p (Share to Hope House Childrens Respite Hospice© Sun May 21 & Margaret Mee Amazon Trust Aug 20©). Suns May 21, Aug 20 (10-5) Last entry 4pm*

Pencarreg ♿❀ (Miss G Jones) Glyn Garth. 1½m NE of A545 Menai Bridge towards Beaumaris, Glan Y Menai Drive is turning on R, Pencarreg is 100yds on R. Parking in lay-by on main rd, ltd parking on courtyard for small cars & disabled. This beautiful garden, with a wealth of species planted for all-yr interest, has colour, achieved by the use of common & unusual shrubs. A small stream creates another delightful and sympathetically-exploited feature. The garden terminates at the cliff edge & this too has been skilfully planted. The views to the Menai Straits & the Carneddi Mountains in the distance make it obvious why this garden has been featured in two television programmes. *Collecting Box (Share to Snowdonia National Park Society©). Private visits welcome all year, please* **Tel 01248 713545**

Penrhyn Castle ♿❀ (The National Trust) 3m E of Bangor on A5122. Buses from Llandudno, Caernarvon. Betws-y-Coed; alight: Grand Lodge Gate. Large gardens; fine trees, shrubs, wild garden, good views. Castle was rebuilt in 1830 for 1st Lord Penrhyn, incorporating part of C15 building on C8 site of home of Welsh Princes. Museum of dolls; museum of locomotives and quarry rolling stock. NT Shop. TEAS and light lunches. Guide dogs admitted into Castle. *Adm £2 Chd £1. For NGS Sun May 28 (12-6). Last adm ½ hr prior to closing. Private visits welcome, please* **Tel 01248 353084**

Pen-y-Parc (Mrs E E Marsh) Beaumaris. A545 Menai Bridge-Beaumaris rd; after Anglesey Boatyard 1st left; after Golf Club 1st drive on left. NOT very easy for wheelchairs. 6 acres; beautiful grounds, magnificent views over Menai Strait; azaleas, rhododendrons and heathers; interesting terrain with rock outcrops used to advantage for recently planted conifer and rock gardens; small lake in natural setting; 2 further enclosed gardens. We would like to share the pleasure of this garden. TEA. *Adm £1 Chd 25p. Sun May 28 (11-5)*

Plas Muriau ✿❀ (Lorna & Tony Scharer) Betws-y-Coed. On A470 approx ¼m N of Waterloo Bridge, Betws-y-Coed; entrance by minor junction to Capel Garmon. A large garden dating from the 1870s recently restored. About 1 acre open to visitors. A structured garden within a woodland setting, with maginificent views. Unusual perennials and herbs, wild flowers, bulbs and roses. Many unusual plants for sale at adjacent nursery, Gwydir Plants. *Adm £1 Thurs April to Sept incl (11-5) or by arrangement at nursery or by appt. Please,* **Tel 01690 710201**

Plas Newydd ♿✿ (The Marquess of Anglesey; The National Trust) Isle of Anglesey. 1m SW of Llanfairpwll and A5, on A4080. Gardens with massed shrubs, fine trees, and lawns sloping down to Menai Strait. Magnificent views to Snowdonia. C18 house by James Wyatt contains Rex Whistler's largest wall painting; also Military Museum. TEAS and light lunches. *Adm house & garden £3.80 Group £3 Chd £1.90, garden only £1.90, Chd £1, Family Adm £9.50. Every day except Sats March 31 to Sept 29. Fris and Suns only Oct 1 to 29. For NGS Thurs May 11 (12-5) last entry 4.30pm. Garden open from 11am*

Plas Penhelig (Mr & Mrs A C Richardson) Aberdovey, between 2 railway bridges. Driveway to hotel by island and car park. 14 acres overlooking estuary, exceptional views. Particularly lovely in spring: bulbs, daffodils, rhododendrons, azaleas; rock and water gardens, mature tree heathers, magnolias, euphorbias; herbaceous borders, rose garden; wild and woodland flowers encouraged in large orchard; formal walled garden, large range of greenhouses, peaches, herbs. TEAS. *Adm £1 Chd 50p. Wed to Sun incl: April 1 to mid-Oct (2.30-5.30). Collecting box*

By Appointment Gardens. See head of county section

Powys

Hon County Organisers:

(North – Montgomeryshire) Captain R Watson, Westwinds, Kerry, Newtown, Powys Tel 01686 670605

(South – Brecknock & Radnor) Miss Shan Egerton, Pen-y-Maes, Hay on Wye, Via Hereford HR3 5PP Tel 01497 820423

Assistant County Organiser:

S. Powys Lady Milford, Llanstephan House, Llanstephan, Brecon. Powys LD3 OYR Tel 01982 560693

Hon County Treasurer: North Elwyn Pugh Esq, Post Office, Kerry, Newtown Tel 01686 670221

DATES OF OPENING

By appointment

For telephone numbers and other details see garden descriptions. Private visits welcomed

Ashford House, Talybont-on-Usk
The Bushes, Berriew
Cedar House, Trelydan
Diamond Cottage, Buttington
Hill Crest, Brooks, Welshpool
The Old Vicarage, Llangorse Gardens
Point Farm, Newtown
Tiled House, The Rhos, Knighton
Treholford, Cathedine, Brecon
Upper Dolley, Dolley Green, Presteigne

Parties only

Fraithwen, Tregynon, Newtown
Llysdinam, Newbridge-on-Wye
Maenllwyd Isaf, Abermule
Treberfydd, nr Bwlch
The Walled Garden, Knill, nr Kington

Regular openings

For details see garden descriptions

Ashford House, Talybont on Usk. Tues April 1 to Oct 1

Diamond Cottage, Buttington. Every Tues from April 18 to July 25.

Mill Cottage, Abbeycwmhir. For dates see text.

April 23 Sunday

Gliffaes Country House Hotel, Crickhowell

April 30 Sunday

Maesllwch Castle, Glasbury-on-Wye

May 13 Saturday

Cae Hywel, Llansantffraid-ym-Mechain

May 14 Sunday
Cae Hywel, Llansantffraid-ym-Mechain
Glanwye, Builth Wells
Trawscoed Hall, Welshpool

May 21 Sunday
Bronhyddon, Llansantffraid-ym-Mechain
Garth House, Garth

May 29 Monday
Llysdinam, Newbridge-on-Wye

May 30 Tuesday
Powis Castle Gardens, Welshpool

June 4 Sunday
Bodynfoel Hall, Llanfechain
Gregynog, Tregynon ‡
Llanstephan House, Llanstephan
Lower Cefn Perfa, Kerry, nr Newtown
Point Farm, Newtown ‡

June 11 Sunday
Ashford House, Talybont on Usk
The Bushes, Berriew

June 14 Wednesday
Ashford House, Talybont on Usk

June 18 Sunday
Cedar House, Trelydan
Llangorse Gardens
The Millers House, Welshpool
Tiled House, The Rhos, Knighton

June 21 Wednesday
Llangorse Gardens

June 25 Sunday
Carrog, Llanfrynach, Brecon
Manascin, Pencelli, Brecon

July 1 Saturday
Upper Dolley, Dolley Green, Presteigne

July 2 Sunday
Treberfydd, nr Bwlch
Upper Dolley, Dolley Green, Presteigne

July 9 Sunday
Parc Gwynne, Glasbury on Wye
Tiled House, The Rhos, Knighton

July 16 Sunday
Moor Park, nr Crickhowell

July 23 Sunday
Fraithwen, Tregynon, Newtown

July 30 Sunday
Tiled House, The Rhos, Knighton
Treholford, Cathedine, Brecon

August 6 Sunday
Talybont Gardens
Point Farm, Newtown

August 13 Sunday
Kerry Gardens, Kerry, nr Newtown

August 20 Sunday
Llysdinam, Newbridge-on-Wye

August 27 Sunday
Tiled House, The Rhos, Knighton

September 3 Sunday
The Bushes, Berriew

October 8 Sunday
Gliffaes Country House Hotel, Crickhowell

DESCRIPTIONS OF GARDENS

Ashford House ❀ (Mr & Mrs D A Anderson) Brecon. ¾m E of Talybont on Usk on B4558 signed from A40 through village. Walled garden of about 1 acre surrounded by woodland and wild garden approx 4 acres altogether. Mixed shrub and herbaceous borders; new small formal garden; meadow garden and pond; alpine house and beds; vegetables. The whole garden has gradually been restored and developed since 1979. Bring and buy plant stall. Suitable in parts for wheelchairs. TEAS. *Adm £1.50 Chd free (Share to Save the Children®). Open Tues April 1 to Oct 1 (2-6). For NGS Sun, Wed June 11, 14 (2-6)*

Bodynfoel Hall ♿❀ (Maj & Mrs Bonnor-Maurice) Llanfechain, 10m N of Welshpool. Via A490 to Llanfyllin. Take B4393 to Llanfechain, follow signs to Bodynfoel. 3½ acres; gardens and woodland; lakes; young and mature trees; shrub roses and heather bank. TEAS. *Adm £1 OAPs 50p Chd free. Sun June 4 (2-6)* **Tel 01691 648486**

Bronhyddon ❀ (Mr & Mrs R Jones-Perrott) Llansantffraid-ym-Mechain. 10m N Welshpool on A495 on E side in centre of village. Long drive; parking in fields below house. Wood having been almost clear felled now planted with choice young trees & shrubs on acid soil on S facing slope. Grass rides have been made and in spring is a mass of bluebells and foxgloves; a mature stand has anemones, snowdrops & primroses. Both areas lead out of small garden in front of house with elegant Regency verandahs & balconies. TEAS. *Adm £1 Chd free. Sun May 21 (2-6)*

The Bushes ✲❀ (Mr & Mrs Hywel Williams) Berriew. 8m Welshpool on B4390 midway Berriew and Manafon. Set in the picturesque Rhiew Valley, this pretty ⅔-acre garden surrounds the old stone cottage on a S-facing site. Designed into terraced 'rooms' and planted with interesting variety of perennials, shrub and climbers and use of groundcover plants; pools, cobbled and paved areas. TEAS in aid of Cystic Fibrosis Trust. *Adm £1 Chd free. Suns June 11, Sept 3 (2-6). Private visits also welcome May to Oct, please* **Tel 01686 650338**

Cae Hywel ❀ (Miss Judith M Jones) Llansantffraid-ym-Mechain, 10m N of Welshpool. On A495; on E (Oswestry) side of village. Car park in village. 1 acre; S facing slope on different levels; rock garden; herb garden; interesting shrubs, trees and plants. Partly suitable for wheelchairs. TEAS. *Adm £1 Chd free. Sat, Sun May 13, 14 (2-6)*

Carrog ♿❀ (Lt Col & Mrs R J M Sinnett) Llanfrynach. 3m SE of Brecon. LLanfrynach is signed from A40 flyover, just E of Brecon. The village is just off B4558. ⅔-acre of mixed borders of shrubs, herbaceous plants and roses. TEAS. *Adm £1 Chd free. Sun June 25 (2-6)*

¶**Cedar House** ✲❀ (Mrs Joan Orr) Trelydan. 2½m from Welshpool, going N on A490. Turn R up Windmill Lane past The Millers House and follow directions. L at end of Windmill Lane to 2nd house, Trelydan Hall Drive. 1¾ acres of garden and woodland. Bridge over stream leads to woodland walk. Noted for roses growing up trees. *Combined adm with* **The Millers House** *£1 Chd free. Sun June 18 (2-6). Private visits welcome, please* **Tel 01938 552720**

Diamond Cottage ✲❀ (Mr & Mrs D T Dorril) Buttington. 4½m NE of Welshpool. From Welshpool take A458 Shrewsbury Rd. Turn R into Heldre Lane, R at next junction, R at Xrds up the hill. From Shrewsbury, turn L 100yds past 'Little Chef' into Sale Lane, L at next junction, R at Xrds. Parking in lane above cottage. 1.7-acre garden created since 1988 on N facing slope of Long Mountain at 700ft. Unusual herbaceous plants and shrubs; natural wooded dingle with small stream; large vegetable garden, patio and pools. Extensive views to Berwyn Mountains. TEAS. *Adm £1 Chd free. Every Tues April 18 to July 25 (2-6). Private visits welcome, please* **Tel 01938 570570**

Fraithwen ✿❀ (Mr & Mrs David Thomas) Tregynon. 6m N of Newtown on B4389 midway between villages of Bettws, Cedewain and Tregynon. 1-acre garden created in the last 10yrs; herbaceous borders, rockeries and ponds packed with interesting, unusual and rare plants and shrubs for colour throughout the year. Also on display antique horse-drawn machinery and implements. TEAS. *Adm £1 Chd free (Share to Bettws Community Hall®). Sun July 23 (2-6). Private parties welcome, please* **Tel 01686 650307**

Garth House ♿❀ (Mr & Mrs F A Wilson) Garth on A483 6m W of Builth Wells. Drive gates in village of Garth by Garth Inn. Large wood with azaleas and rhododendrons; water and shrub garden; herbaceous garden; fine views. Historic connection with Charles Wesley & the Gwynne family. TEAS. *Adm £1 Chd free. Sun May 21 (2-6)*

Glanwye ♿❀ (Mr & Mrs David Vaughan, G & H Kidston) 2m SE Builth Wells on A470. Large garden, rhododendrons, azaleas; herbaceous borders, extensive hedges, newly sown wild flower meadow; long woodland walk with bluebells and other woodland flowers. Good views of R Wye. Cream TEAS. *Adm £1.50 Chd free (Share to Llanddewi Cwm and Alltmawr Church®). Sun May 14 (2-5.30)*

Gliffaes Country House Hotel ♿❀ (Mr & Mrs Brabner) 3m W of Crickhowell on A40. Large garden; spring bulbs; azaleas & rhododendrons, new ornamental pond; heathers; shrubs; ornamental trees; fine maples; autumn colour; fine position high above R. Usk. Cream Teas available at hotel. *April to Dec. For NGS Adm £1 Chd 50p (collecting box). Suns April 23, Oct 8 (2-5)*

Gregynog ♿❀ (University of Wales) Tregynon, 7m N of Newtown. A483 Welshpool to Newtown Rd, turn W at B4389 for Bettws Cedewain, 1m through village gates on left. Large garden; fine banks, rhododendrons and azaleas; dell with specimen shrubs; formal garden; colour-coded walks starting from car park. Descriptive leaflet available. Early C19 black and white house; site inhabited since C12. TEAS. *Adm £1 Chd 10p. Sun June 4 (2-6)*

¶Hill Crest ❀ (Mr J D & Mrs P Horton) Brooks. 9m W of Welshpool. Turn R to Berriew Village, then L by the Lion Hotel, through village towards Bettws Cedewain. Turn R after 3m to Brooks then 1m up hill past telephone kiosk on L. 8m E from Newtown. Through Bettws Cedewain. Take Brooks Rd, after 3m turn L. House at top of hill on L. Approx 1 acre of mixed shrub borders, heathers, alpines and bog area; hillside arboretum with rhododendron walk, pine, spruce mixed conifers and deciduous wooded area planted with daffodils. *Adm £1 Chd 10p. Private visits welcome, please* **Tel 01686 640541**

Kerry Gardens ♿✿ 3m S of Newtown. Take A489 to Craven Arms. Some gardens featured on BBC TV Wales. Start from Kerry Lamb car park. TEAS in aid of village hall. *Combined adm £1.50 Chd 10p. Sun Aug 13 (2-6)*

Mar-Jon Dolforgan View (Mrs O Hughes) Interesting garden; wide variety of annuals, plants and shrubs

Post Office (Mr & Mrs E Pugh) Leeks, spray chrysanthemums and fuchsias grown for exhibition also small colourful garden

Westwinds (Captain & Mrs R Watson) Colourful garden; rockery, pools, shrubs, flower beds. TEAS

Llangorse Gardens ❀ Llangorse is on B4560 4m off A40 at Bwlch, 6½m from Brecon and 4½m from Talgarth. Park in village. Teas in village. *Combined adm £1.50 Acc chd free. Sun, Wed June 18, 21 (2-6)*

The Neuadd (Mr & Mrs P Johnson) Informal garden of approx 1 acre with mixed borders of interesting trees, shrubs and herbaceous plants, emphasis on good foliage and unusual forms of cottage garden and native plants; small vegetable and fruit garden, meadow gardens and copse. Maintained by owners on organic lines to encourage wild life

The Old Vicarage ♿✿ (Major & Mrs J B Anderson) Small family garden maintained by owners with interesting herbaceous and shrub borders; lawns, trees and vegetables. Plants usually for sale in aid of NGS. *Private visits welcome Spring to Oct*, please **Tel 01874 658639**

Llanstephan House ♿✿❀ (Lord & Lady Milford) Llanstephan. Off small rd between Boughrood and Erwood Bridge on opp side of R Wye to A470 (Brecon-Builth Wells rd). Large garden with rhododendrons, azaleas, shrubs, old-fashioned roses, walled kitchen garden. Beautiful views of Wye Valley and Black Mountains. TEAS. *Adm £1.50 Chd free. Sun June 4 (2-5)*

Llysdinam ♿❀ (Lady Delia Venables-Llewelyn & Llysdinam Charitable Trust) Newbridge-on-Wye, SW of Llandrindod Wells. Turn W off A479 at Newbridge-on-Wye; right immediately after crossing R Wye; entrance up hill. Large garden. Azaleas; rhododendrons, water garden and herbaceous borders; shrubs; woodland garden; kitchen garden; fine view of Wye Valley. TEAS. *Adm £1.50 Chd free (Share to NSPCC®). Mon May 29, Sun Aug 20 (2-6). Private parties welcome, please* **Tel 0159 789200**

Lower Cefn Perfa ✿❀ (Mr & Mrs J Dugdale) Kerry, Newtown. Follow signs off A489. 2-acre garden planned with low maintenance and all-yr interest in mind. Various rhododendrons and perennials in riverside setting of natural beauty. Woodland walk. Cream TEAS in aid of Powys Branch British Red Cross Soc Holiday for the disabled. *Adm £1 Chd free. Sun June 4 (2-6)*

Maenllwyd Isaf ♿✿ (Mrs Denise Hatchard) Abermule, 5m NE of Newtown & 10m S of Welshpool. On B4368 Abermule to Craven Arms, 1½m from Abermule. 3 acres; unusual shrubs and plants; goldfish pool; 'wild' pool; R Mule. C16 listed house. *Adm £1 Chd free (Share to Winged Fellowship Trust®). Private visits welcome all year. Gardening clubs etc welcome, please* **Tel 01686 630204**

Maesllwch Castle (Walter de Winton Esq) Glasbury-on-Wye. Turn off A438 immediately N of Glasbury bridge. Through Glasbury ½m turn R at Church. Medium-sized, garden owner maintained. Exceptional views from terrace across R. Wye to Black Mountains. Old walled garden, woodland walk, fine trees, C18 gingko tree. TEA. *Adm £1.50 Chd free (Share to All Saints Church, Glasbury®). Sun April 30 (2-5)*

Manascin ❀ (Lady Watson) Pencelli. 3m SE of Brecon on B4558 pink house in Pencelli Village. Small garden, many features; small pond with water lilies and fountain; shrubs; roses, lilies and vegetable patch. TEAS at **Carrog**. *Adm £1 Chd free. Sun June 25 (2-6)*

Mill Cottage ✂❀ (Mr & Mrs B D Parfitt) Abbeycwmhir. 8m N of Llandrindod Wells. Turning L off A483, 1m N of Crossgates Roundabout, then 3½m on L, signposted Abbeycwmhir. ⅓-acre garden of unusual and rare shrubs, small trees and climbers. Numerous ericaceae. Narrow paths and steps; limited parking. Many rare plants for sale. TEAS. *Adm £1 Chd 50p. Sun to Sat incl, May 6-14, June 3-11, July 8-16, August 5-13, Sept 23-Oct 8 (midday to dusk)*

The Millers House ♿✂❀ (Mr & Mrs Mark Kneale) Welshpool. About 1¼m NW of Welshpool on rd to Guilsfield A490; turn R into Windmill Lane; 4th cottage on L. 1½-acre country garden begun in 1988. Superb views. Mixed shrub and herbaceous borders, roses, climbers; pool. Ornamental and fruit trees incl a planting of 12 hardy eucalyptus. TEAS. *Combined adm with* **Cedar House** *£1 Chd free. Sun June 18 (2-6)*

Moor Park ♿✂ (Mr & the Hon Mrs L Price) Llanbedr. Turn off A40 at Fire Station in Crickhowell; continue 2m, signed Llanbedr. 5 acres; roses, borders, trees and walled kitchen garden. Lake, water garden under construction; woodland walk. TEAS. *Adm £1.50 Chd free. Sun July 16 (2-6)*

Parc Gwynne ♿❀ (Mr & Mrs W Windham) Glasbury on Wye. From Brecon towards Hereford on A438 cross Glasbury Bridge, 1st L signposted Boughrood and 1st L at War Memorial. Entrance across green. Small riverside garden, mainly herbaceous, incl white border. TEAS & bring & buy plant stall. *Adm £1.50 Chd free (Share to Queen Mary's Clothing Guild® & All Saints Church Glasbury®). Sun July 9 (2-5)*

¶Point Farm ♿✂❀ (Mr & Mrs F Podmore) Bryn Lane, Newtown. From town centre head N across river to roundabout. Take R-hand rd off roundabout into Commercial St. L at fork into Llanfair Rd towards hospital. Bryn Lane is on L-hand side of the hospital. Point Farm is 1½m along Bryn Lane from the hospital, on R-hand side. The ½-acre garden is 750′ above sea level with magnificent views of unspoilt countryside. Suitable herbaceous plants and shrubs have been planted to accommodate dry shade, sunny borders and boggy conditions. TEAS in aid of Montgomery Multiple Sclerosis Society. *Adm £1 Acc chd free. Suns June 4, Aug 6 (2-6). Private visits welcome, please* **Tel 01686 625709**

Powis Castle Gardens ✂❀ (The National Trust) Welshpool. Turn off A483 ¾m out of Welshpool, up Red Lane for ¼m. Gardens laid out in 1720 with most famous hanging terraces in the world; enormous yew hedges; lead statuary, large wild garden. Part of garden suitable for wheelchairs, top terrace only. TEA. The date shown below is a *Special opening* for NGS; garden only. *Adm gardens only (Castle closed) £3.50 Chd £1.50 N.T. members also pay.* ▲*Tues May 30 (12-6)*

Talybont Gardens ♿✂ Talybont-on-Usk. ½m from turning off A40. 6m E of Brecon, signposted Talybont. Teas in village. *Combined adm £1.50 Chd free. Sun August 6 (2-6)*

Cartrefle (Mrs J F Fox) Small compact garden with variety of trees, shrubs, vegetables and an abundance of flowers in pots and tubs as well as the normal flower beds. Also a water garden feature

Lonicera (Mr & Mrs G Davies) A garden of varied interest incorporating several small feature gardens extending to approx. ¼ acre. These include a modern rose garden with dwarf conifers: herbaceous and woody perennials; colourful summer bedding displays; window boxes, hanging baskets and patio tubs forming extensive house frontage display; greenhouses. *(Share to Arthritis & Rheumatism Council®)*

¶Tiled House ✂❀ (Mr & Mrs J L Holmes) Rhos-y-Meirch, Knighton. From Presteigne take the B355 R to Knighton. Follow this rd uphill through Norton and over the top. ½m downhill take the B4357 signposted Whitton. 1st R 100yds just past telephone box then 1st R again (200yds). Tiled House is 3rd on the R. From Knighton follow B355 to Presteigne and take 1st R ¾ way up hill B4357 to Whitton. ¾ acre of developing garden carved from hillside at 1000′ on Offas Dyke, overlooking a high valley with views to Radnor Forest. Owner maintained. Sheltered courtyard, terraced beds, mixed and shrub borders; enclosed pastel garden, herb garden and small new woodland area. TEAS. *Adm £1 Chd free (Share to Full House, Hereford®). Suns June 18, July 9, 30, Aug 27 (11-6). Private visits welcome June to Oct, please* **Tel 01547 528602**

Trawscoed Hall ✂❀ (Mr & Mrs J T K Trevor) 3m N of Welshpool on Llanfyllin Road. Long drive through woodlands, lovely panoramic views from S facing sloping gardens with interesting plants. 2 acres. Magnificent wisteria covering front of fine Georgian house (not open) built 1777. Granary dating from 1772. Nature trails through prize-winning woodlands. TEAS in aid of Asthma Research. *Adm £1 Chd free. Sun May 14 (2-6)*

Treberfydd ✂ (Lt Col & Mrs D Garnons Williams) Bwlch. 2¼m W of Bwlch. From A40 at Bwlch turning marked Llangorse then L for Pennorth. From Brecon, leave A40 at Llanhamlach. 2¼m to sign Llangasty Church but go over cattle grid to house. Large garden; lawns, roses, trees, rock garden. Plants for sale at commercial nursery. TEAS. *Adm £1.50 Chd free (Share to Llangasty Church®). Sun July 2 (2-6)*

¶Treholford ❀ (Mr & Mrs J A V Blackham) Cathedine. Turn off A40 between Crickhowell and Brecon at Bwlch for Llangorse. 2m on R. 5-acre garden overlooking Llangorse Lake; lawns with specimen trees, rock garden, pools and greenhouses incl a cacti house; walled kitchen garden with box hedges and rose arches. TEAS. *Adm £1.50 Chd free (Share to St Michael's Church, Cathedine®). Sun July 30 (2-6). Private visits welcome, please* **Tel 01874 730278**

Upper Dolley ♿✗❀ (Mrs B P Muggleton) Dolley Green. Take B4356 W out of Presteigne towards Whitton. At Dolley Green, 2m from Presteigne, turn L down 'No Through Road' by red brick church; Upper Dolley is 100yds on L. From Knighton take B4355 to turning for Whitton, B4357. Turn L at Whitton B4356 to brick church; turn R. 2-acre country garden with open views of Lugg Valley; variety of borders with many shrub roses and large natural pond; C16 Grade 2 listed house (not open). Cream TEAS weather permitting. *Adm £1 Chd 50p (Share to The Bible Society®). Sat, Sun July 1, 2 (2-6). Private visits welcome June, July, Aug, please* **Tel 01547 560273**

The Walled Garden ♿ (Miss C M Mills) Knill, 3m from Kington and Presteigne. Off B4362 Walton-Presteigne rd to Knill village; right over cattle grid; keep right down drive. 3 acres; walled garden; stream; bog garden; primulas; shrub roses. Nr C13 Church in lovely valley. *Adm £1 Chd 50p. Private visits welcome any day (10-7), please* **Tel 01544 267411**

STOP PRESS

Devon

¶**Winkfield** ♿✂❀ (Mr & Mrs R W Ramsdale) Colyford. On A3052 at Colyford. Next to St Michael's Chapel of Ease. Ample parking at Memorial Hall opp. Seaton 1½m. Garden approx 1 acre. Wide variety of hardy herbaceous plants, with iris, grasses and agapanthus a feature. Victorian soak-away pond. National Reference Collections of Heuchara and Sidalcea. TEAS. *Adm £1 Chd free (Share to Friends of Seaton Hospital®). Wed June 21, Sun July 9 (2-5.30)*

The Counties of England and Wales

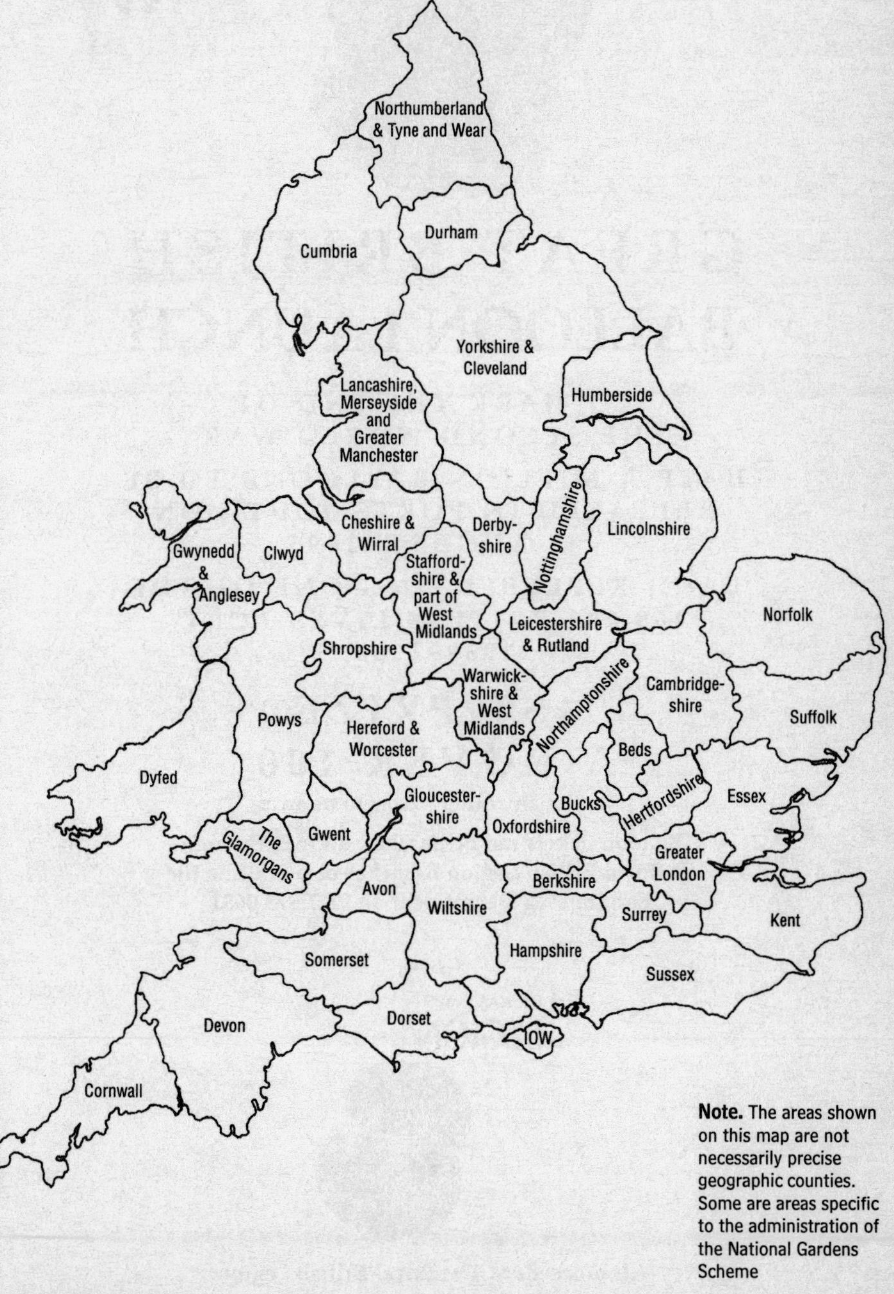

Note. The areas shown on this map are not necessarily precise geographic counties. Some are areas specific to the administration of the National Gardens Scheme

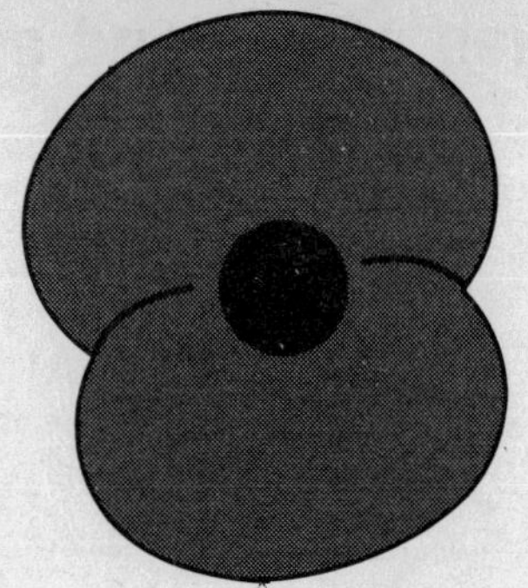

GREAT BRITISH BALLOON LAUNCH

TO MARK THE END OF
THE SECOND WORLD WAR

HALF A MILLION BALLOONS TO BE
RELEASED IN PORTSMOUTH ON
15 AUGUST, 1995

EACH REPRESENTING ONE OF THE
468,000 BRITISH LIVES LOST
1939–1945

1ST PRIZE
A ROVER 100

and many other prizes to be won

Balloon tickets can be purchased for £1 through all Royal British Legion Branches or by calling the Fundraising Department on 0171 973 0633

All proceeds to The Royal British Legion

Registered Charity No. 219279

Index to Gardens

This index lists all gardens alphabetically and gives the counties in which they are to be found. Refer to the relevant county pages where the garden and its details will be found, again in alphabetical order. The following unorthodox county abbreviations are used: C & W—Cheshire and Wirral; L & R—Leicestershire and Rutland; G & A—Gwynedd and Anglesey. An * denotes a garden which will not be in its normal alphabetical order as it is a group garden and will be found under the Group Garden name but still within the county indicated.

A

B

C

D

E

F

G

H

M

N

O

P

Q

R

S

W

Y

Index to Advertisers

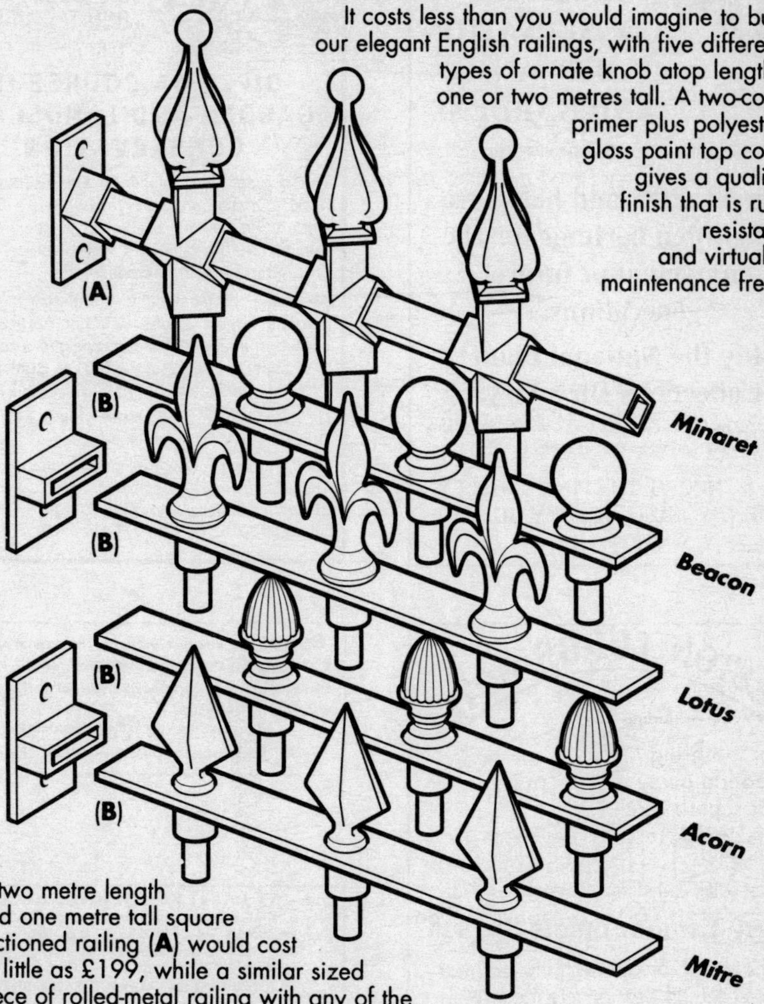

inchbald
school of design

'An excellent design school, intelligently and professionally run'

Stephan Lacey MA (Oxon)
Garden writer and journalist

The school offers a wide variety of courses in garden design
For further information contact
Andrew Wilson
Inchbald School of Design (C.GE)
32 Eccleston Square
London SW1V 1PB
Telephone 071 630 9011

SNOWDONIA

Peaceful part 16thC guest house with young garden up in the mountains. Open views. Bodnant and "Naturally Gwynedd" nearby. Walks direct from house.
Short or long breaks brochure 0766 830847.

ANN & ROGER BOWDEN
specialise in HOSTA PLANTS

National Collection of 300 plants in 1 acre ornamental garden, open for viewing. Send 3x1st class stamps for illustrated catalogue of 90 varieties. Mail order.
Visitors by arrangement only
Tel: 0183 784 0481
Sticklepath, Okehampton, Devon
Collecting box

Above Lake Windermere

In magnificent private gardens, with brilliant views across Lake Windermere, Lindeth Fell is a classical Lakeland Country House in an idyllic setting, quietly removed from the busy village below.

Here you can wander through tranquil grounds, relax in stylish surroundings and enjoy superb English cooking in a warm and friendly atmosphere – at highly competitive prices.

ETB ♛♛♛♛ – Highly Commended
AA ★★ + Red Rosette
RAC ★★ H C & R Merits
And in Most Selective Guides

See listing under Cumbria

LINDETH FELL COUNTRY HOUSE HOTEL
WINDERMERE, CUMBRIA LA23 3JP
Telephone: WINDERMERE (015394) 43286

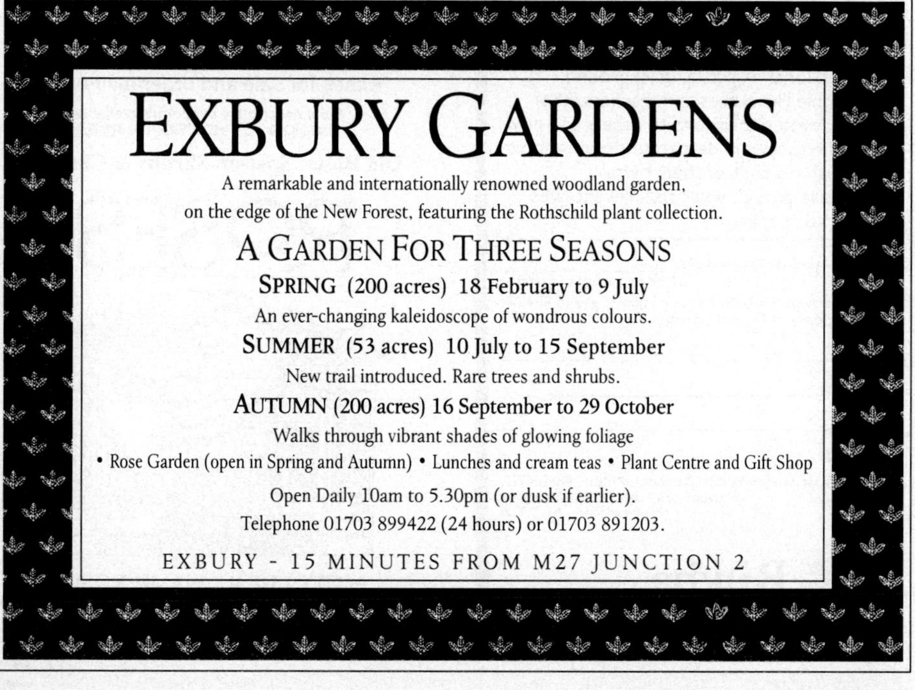

EXBURY GARDENS
A remarkable and internationally renowned woodland garden,
on the edge of the New Forest, featuring the Rothschild plant collection.
A GARDEN FOR THREE SEASONS
SPRING (200 acres) 18 February to 9 July
An ever-changing kaleidoscope of wondrous colours.
SUMMER (53 acres) 10 July to 15 September
New trail introduced. Rare trees and shrubs.
AUTUMN (200 acres) 16 September to 29 October
Walks through vibrant shades of glowing foliage
• Rose Garden (open in Spring and Autumn) • Lunches and cream teas • Plant Centre and Gift Shop
Open Daily 10am to 5.30pm (or dusk if earlier).
Telephone 01703 899422 (24 hours) or 01703 891203.
EXBURY - 15 MINUTES FROM M27 JUNCTION 2